Physically Based Rendering is a terrific book. It covers all the marvelous math, fascinating physics, practical software engineering, and clever tricks that are necessary to write a state-of-the-art photorealistic renderer. All of these topics are dealt with in a clear and pedagogical manner without omitting the all-important practical details.

pbrt is not just a "toy" implementation of a ray tracer but a general and robust full-scale global illumination renderer. It contains many important optimizations to reduce execution time and memory consumption for complex scenes. Furthermore, pbrt is easy to extend to experiment with other rendering algorithm variations.

This book is not only a textbook for students but also a useful reference book for practitioners in the field. The third edition has been extended with new sections on bidirectional path tracing, realistic camera models, and a state-of-the-art explanation of subsurface scattering.

Per Christensen
Senior Software Developer, RenderMan Products, Pixar Animation Studios

Looking for a job in research or high end rendering? Get your kick-start education and create your own project with this book that comes along with both theory and real examples, meaning real code and real content for your renderer.

With their third edition, Matt Pharr, Greg Humphreys, and Wenzel Jakob provide easy access to even the most advanced rendering techniques like multiplexed Metropolis light transport and quasi-Monte Carlo methods. Most importantly, the framework lets you skip the bootstrap pain of getting data into and out of your renderer.

The holistic approach of literate programming results in a clear logic of an easy-to-study text. If you are serious about graphics, there is no way around this unique and extremely valuable book that is closest to the state of the art.

Alexander Keller
Director of Research, NVIDIA

Physically Based Rendering

FROM THEORY TO IMPLEMENTATION

THIRD EDITION

MATT PHARR

WENZEL JAKOB

GREG HUMPHREYS

AMSTERDAM · BOSTON · HEIDELBERG · LONDON
NEW YORK · OXFORD · PARIS · SAN DIEGO
SAN FRANCISCO · SINGAPORE · SYDNEY · TOKYO

Morgan Kaufmann is an imprint of Elsevier

Morgan Kaufmann is an imprint of Elsevier
50 Hampshire Street, 5th Floor, Cambridge, MA 02139, USA

Notices
Knowledge and best practice in this field are constantly changing. As new research and experience broaden our understanding, changes in research methods, professional practices, or medical treatment may become necessary.

Practitioners and researchers must always rely on their own experience and knowledge in evaluating and using any information, methods, compounds, or experiments described herein. In using such information or methods they should be mindful of their own safety and the safety of others, including parties for whom they have a professional responsibility.

To the fullest extent of the law, neither the Publisher nor the authors, contributors, or editors, assume any liability for any injury and/or damage to persons or property as a matter of products liability, negligence or otherwise, or from any use or operation of any methods, products, instructions, or ideas contained in the material herein.

Library of Congress Cataloging-in-Publication Data
A catalog record for this book is available from the Library of Congress

British Library Cataloguing-in-Publication Data
A catalogue record for this book is available from the British Library

ISBN: 978-0-12-800645-0

For information on all Morgan Kaufmann publications
visit our website at https://www.elsevier.com/

Printed in the United States of America
Last digit is print number: 11 10 9 8 7 6

Publisher: Todd Green
Editorial Project Manager: Jennifer Pierce
Production Project Manager: Mohana Natarajan
Cover Designer: Victoria Pearson

Typeset by: Windfall Software and SPi global

To **Deirdre**, who even let me bring the manuscript on our honeymoon.

M. P.

To **Olesya**, who thought it was cute that my favorite book is a computer program.

W. J.

To **Isabel and Leila**, the two most extraordinary people I've ever met. May your pixels never be little squares.

G. H.

ABOUT THE AUTHORS

Matt Pharr is a Software Engineer at Google. He previously co-founded Neoptica, which was acquired by Intel, and co-founded Exluna, which was acquired by NVIDIA. He has a B.S. degree from Yale and a Ph.D. from the Stanford Graphics Lab, where he worked under the supervision of Pat Hanrahan.

Wenzel Jakob is an assistant professor in the School of Computer and Communication Sciences at École Polytechnique Fédérale de Lausanne (EPFL). His research interests revolve around material appearance modeling, rendering algorithms, and the high-dimensional geometry of light paths. Wenzel obtained his Ph.D. at Cornell University under the supervision of Steve Marschner, after which he joined ETH Zürich for post-doctoral studies under the supervision of Olga Sorkine Hornung. Wenzel is also the lead developer of the Mitsuba renderer, a research-oriented rendering system.

Greg Humphreys is Director of Engineering at FanDuel, having previously worked on the Chrome graphics team at Google and the OptiX GPU ray-tracing engine at NVIDIA. Before that, he was a professor of Computer Science at the University of Virginia, where he conducted research in both high-performance and physically based computer graphics, as well as computer architecture and visualization. Greg has a B.S.E. degree from Princeton and a Ph.D. in Computer Science from Stanford under the supervision of Pat Hanrahan. When he's not tracing rays, Greg can usually be found playing tournament bridge.

Contents

---

* An asterisk denotes a section with advanced content that can be skipped on a first reading.

Preface

[Just as] other information should be available to those who want to learn and understand, program source code is the only means for programmers to learn the art from their predecessors. It would be unthinkable for playwrights not to allow other playwrights to read their plays [or to allow them] at theater performances where they would be barred even from taking notes. Likewise, any good author is well read, as every child who learns to write will read hundreds of times more than it writes. Programmers, however, are expected to invent the alphabet and learn to write long novels all on their own. Programming cannot grow and learn unless the next generation of programmers has access to the knowledge and information gathered by other programmers before them. —Erik Naggum

Rendering is a fundamental component of computer graphics. At the highest level of abstraction, rendering is the process of converting a description of a three-dimensional scene into an image. Algorithms for animation, geometric modeling, texturing, and other areas of computer graphics all must pass their results through some sort of rendering process so that they can be made visible in an image. Rendering has become ubiquitous; from movies to games and beyond, it has opened new frontiers for creative expression, entertainment, and visualization.

In the early years of the field, research in rendering focused on solving fundamental problems such as determining which objects are visible from a given viewpoint. As effective solutions to these problems have been found and as richer and more realistic scene descriptions have become available thanks to continued progress in other areas of graphics, modern rendering has grown to include ideas from a broad range of disciplines, including physics and astrophysics, astronomy, biology, psychology and the study of perception, and pure and applied mathematics. The interdisciplinary nature of rendering is one of the reasons that it is such a fascinating area of study.

This book presents a selection of modern rendering algorithms through the documented source code for a complete rendering system. Nearly all of the images in this book, including the one on the front cover, were rendered by this software. All of the algorithms that came together to generate these images are described in these pages. The system, pbrt, is written using a programming methodology called *literate programming* that mixes prose describing the system with the source code that implements it. We believe that the literate programming approach is a valuable way to introduce ideas in computer graphics and computer science in general. Often, some of the subtleties of an algorithm can be unclear or hidden until it is implemented, so seeing an actual implementation is a good way to acquire a solid understanding of that algorithm's details. Indeed, we believe that deep understanding of a small number of algorithms in this manner provides a stronger base for further study of computer graphics than does superficial understanding of many.

In addition to clarifying how an algorithm is implemented in practice, presenting these algorithms in the context of a complete and nontrivial software system also allows us to address issues in the design and implementation of medium-sized rendering systems. The design of a rendering system's basic abstractions and interfaces has substantial implications for both the elegance of the implementation and the ability to extend it later, yet the trade-offs in this design space are rarely discussed.

pbrt and the contents of this book focus exclusively on *photorealistic rendering*, which can be defined variously as the task of generating images that are indistinguishable from those that a camera would capture in a photograph or as the task of generating images that evoke the same response from a human observer as looking at the actual scene. There are many reasons to focus on photorealism. Photorealistic images are crucial for the movie special-effects industry because computer-generated imagery must often be mixed seamlessly with footage of the real world. In entertainment applications where all of the imagery is synthetic, photorealism is an effective tool for making the observer forget that he or she is looking at an environment that does not actually exist. Finally, photorealism gives a reasonably well-defined metric for evaluating the quality of the rendering system's output.

AUDIENCE

There are three main audiences that this book is intended for. The first is students in graduate or upper-level undergraduate computer graphics classes. This book assumes existing knowledge of computer graphics at the level of an introductory college-level course, although certain key concepts such as basic vector geometry and transformations will be reviewed here. For students who do not have experience with programs that have tens of thousands of lines of source code, the literate programming style gives a gentle introduction to this complexity. We pay special attention to explaining the reasoning behind some of the key interfaces and abstractions in the system in order to give these readers a sense of why the system is structured in the way that it is.

The second audience is advanced graduate students and researchers in computer graphics. For those doing research in rendering, the book provides a broad introduction to the area, and the pbrt source code provides a foundation that can be useful to build upon (or at least to use bits of source code from). For those working in other areas, we believe that having a thorough understanding of rendering can be helpful context to carry along.

Our final audience is software developers in industry. Although many of the ideas in this book will likely be familiar to this audience, seeing explanations of the algorithms presented in the literate style may provide new perspectives. pbrt includes implementations of a number of advanced and/or difficult-to-implement algorithms and techniques, such as subdivision surfaces, Monte Carlo sampling algorithms, bidirectional path tracing, Metropolis sampling, and subsurface scattering; these should be of particular interest to experienced practitioners in rendering. We hope that delving into one particular organization of a complete and nontrivial rendering system will also be thought provoking to this audience.

OVERVIEW AND GOALS

pbrt is based on the *ray-tracing* algorithm. Ray tracing is an elegant technique that has its origins in lens making; Carl Friedrich Gauß traced rays through lenses by hand in the 19th century. Ray-tracing algorithms on computers follow the path of infinitesimal rays of light through the scene until they intersect a surface. This approach gives a simple method for finding the first visible object as seen from any particular position and direction and is the basis for many rendering algorithms.

pbrt was designed and implemented with three main goals in mind: it should be *complete*, it should be *illustrative*, and it should be *physically based*.

Completeness implies that the system should not lack key features found in high-quality commercial rendering systems. In particular, it means that important practical issues, such as antialiasing, robustness, numerical precision, and the ability to efficiently render complex scenes, should all be addressed thoroughly. It is important to consider these issues from the start of the system's design, since these features can have subtle implications for all components of the system and can be quite difficult to retrofit into the system at a later stage of implementation.

Our second goal means that we tried to choose algorithms, data structures, and rendering techniques with care and with an eye toward readability and clarity. Since their implementations will be examined by more readers than is the case for many other rendering systems, we tried to select the most elegant algorithms that we were aware of and implement them as well as possible. This goal also required that the system be small enough for a single person to understand completely. We have implemented pbrt using an extensible architecture, with the core of the system implemented in terms of a set of carefully designed abstract base classes, and as much of the specific functionality as possible in implementations of these base classes. The result is that one doesn't need to understand all of the specific implementations in order to understand the basic structure of the system. This makes it easier to delve deeply into parts of interest and skip others, without losing sight of how the overall system fits together.

There is a tension between the two goals of being complete and being illustrative. Implementing and describing every possible useful technique would not only make this book unacceptably long, but also would make the system prohibitively complex for most readers. In cases where pbrt lacks a particularly useful feature, we have attempted to design the architecture so that the feature could be added without altering the overall system design.

The basic foundations for physically based rendering are the laws of physics and their mathematical expression. pbrt was designed to use the correct physical units and concepts for the quantities it computes and the algorithms it implements. When configured to do so, pbrt can compute images that are *physically correct*; they accurately reflect the lighting as it would be in a real-world version of the scene. One advantage of the decision to use a physical basis is that it gives a concrete standard of program correctness: for simple scenes, where the expected result can be computed in closed form, if pbrt doesn't compute the same result, we know there must be a bug in the implementation.

Similarly, if different physically based lighting algorithms in pbrt give different results for the same scene, or if pbrt doesn't give the same results as another physically based renderer, there is certainly an error in one of them. Finally, we believe that this physically based approach to rendering is valuable because it is rigorous. When it is not clear how a particular computation should be performed, physics gives an answer that guarantees a consistent result.

Efficiency was given lower priority than these three goals. Since rendering systems often run for many minutes or hours in the course of generating an image, efficiency is clearly important. However, we have mostly confined ourselves to *algorithmic* efficiency rather than low-level code optimization. In some cases, obvious micro-optimizations take a backseat to clear, well-organized code, although we did make some effort to optimize the parts of the system where most of the computation occurs.

In the course of presenting pbrt and discussing its implementation, we hope to convey some hard-learned lessons from years of rendering research and development. There is more to writing a good renderer than stringing together a set of fast algorithms; making the system both flexible and robust is a difficult task. The system's performance must degrade gracefully as more geometry or light sources are added to it or as any other axis of complexity is pushed. Numerical stability must be handled carefully, and algorithms that don't waste floating-point precision are critical.

The rewards for developing a system that addresses all these issues are enormous—it is a great pleasure to write a new renderer or add a new feature to an existing renderer and use it to create an image that couldn't be generated before. Our most fundamental goal in writing this book was to bring this opportunity to a wider audience. Readers are encouraged to use the system to render the example scenes in the pbrt software distribution as they progress through the book. Exercises at the end of each chapter suggest modifications to the system that will help clarify its inner workings and more complex projects to extend the system by adding new features.

The Web site for this book is located at *www.pbrt.org*. The latest version of the pbrt source code is available from this site, and we will also post errata and bug fixes, additional scenes to render, and supplemental utilities. Any bugs in pbrt or errors in this text that are not listed at the Web site can be reported to the email address *bugs@pbrt.org*. We greatly value your feedback!

CHANGES BETWEEN THE FIRST AND SECOND EDITIONS

Six years passed between the publication of the first edition of this book in 2004 and the second edition in 2010. In that time, thousands of copies of the book were sold, and the pbrt software was downloaded thousands of times from the book's Web site. The pbrt user base gave us a significant amount of feedback and encouragement, and our experience with the system guided many of the decisions we made in making changes between the version of pbrt presented in the first edition and the version in the second edition. In addition to a number of bug fixes, we also made several significant design changes and enhancements:

- Removal of the plugin architecture. The first version of pbrt used a run-time plugin architecture to dynamically load code for implementations of objects like shapes, lights, integrators, cameras, and other objects that were used in the scene currently being rendered. This approach allowed users to extend pbrt with new object types (e.g., new shape primitives) without recompiling the entire rendering system. This approach initially seemed elegant, but it complicated the task of supporting pbrt on multiple platforms and it made debugging more difficult. The only new usage scenario that it truly enabled (binary-only distributions of pbrt or binary plugins) was actually contrary to our pedagogical and open-source goals. Therefore, the plugin architecture was dropped in this edition.
- Removal of the image-processing pipeline. The first version of pbrt provided a tone-mapping interface that converted high-dynamic-range (HDR) floating-point output images directly into low-dynamic-range TIFFs for display. This functionality made sense in 2004, as support for HDR images was still sparse. In 2010, however, advances in digital photography had made HDR images commonplace. Although the theory and practice of tone mapping are elegant and worth learning, we decided to focus the new book exclusively on the process of image formation and skip the topic of image display. Interested readers should read the book written by Reinhard et al. (2010) for a thorough and modern treatment of the HDR image display process.
- Task parallelism. Multicore architectures became ubiquitous, and we felt that pbrt would not remain relevant without the ability to scale to the number of locally available cores. We also hoped that the parallel programming implementation details documented in this book would help graphics programmers understand some of the subtleties and complexities in writing scalable parallel code (e.g., choosing appropriate task granularities), which is still a difficult and too infrequently taught topic.
- Appropriateness for "production" rendering. The first version of pbrt was intended exclusively as a pedagogical tool and a stepping-stone for rendering research. Indeed, we made a number of decisions in preparing the first edition that were contrary to use in a production environment, such as limited support for image-based lighting, no support for motion blur, and a photon mapping implementation that wasn't robust in the presence of complex lighting. With much improved support for these features as well as support for subsurface scattering and Metropolis light transport, we feel that with the second edition, pbrt became much more suitable for rendering very high-quality images of complex environments.

CHANGES BETWEEN THE SECOND AND THIRD EDITIONS

With the passage of another six years, it was time to update and extend the book and the pbrt system. We continued to learn from readers' and users' experiences to better understand which topics were most useful to cover. Further, rendering research continued apace; many parts of the book were due for an update to reflect current best practices. We made significant improvements on a number of fronts:

- Bidirectional light transport. The third version of pbrt now includes a full-featured bidirectional path tracer, including full support for volumetric light transport and multiple importance sampling to weight paths. An all-new Metropolis light transport integrator uses components of the bidirectional path tracer, allowing for a particularly succinct implementation of that algorithm. The foundations of these algorithms were established approximately fifteen years ago; it's overdue to have solid support for them in pbrt.
- Subsurface scattering. The appearance of many objects—notably, skin and translucent objects—is a result of subsurface light transport. Our implementation of subsurface scattering in the second edition reflected the state of the art in the early 2000s; we have thoroughly updated both our BSSRDF models and our subsurface light transport algorithms to reflect the progress made in ten subsequent years of research. We now use a considerably more accurate diffusion solution together with a ray-tracing-based sampling technique, removing the need for the costly preprocessing step used in the second edition.
- Numerically robust intersections. The effects of floating-point round-off error in geometric ray intersection calculations have been a long-standing challenge in ray tracing: they can cause small errors to be present throughout the image. We have focused on this issue and derived conservative (but tight) bounds of this error, which makes our implementation more robust to this issue than previous rendering systems.
- Participating media representation. We have significantly improved the way that scattering media are described and represented in the system; this allows for more accurate results with nested scattering media. A new sampling technique enables unbiased rendering of heterogeneous media in a way that cleanly integrates with all of the other parts of the system.
- Measured materials. This edition includes a new technique to represent and evaluate measured materials using a sparse frequency-space basis. This approach is convenient because it allows for exact importance sampling, which was not possible with the representation used in the previous edition.
- Photon mapping. A significant step forward for photon mapping algorithms has been the development of variants that don't require storing all of the photons in memory. We have replaced pbrt's photon mapping algorithm with an implementation based on stochastic progressive photon mapping, which efficiently renders many difficult light transport effects.
- Sample generation algorithms. The distribution of sample values used for numerical integration in rendering algorithms can have a surprisingly large effect on the quality of the final results. We have thoroughly updated our treatment of this topic, covering new approaches and efficient implementation techniques in more depth than before.

Many other parts of the system have been improved and updated to reflect progress in the field: microfacet reflection models are treated in more depth, with much better sampling techniques; a new "curve" shape has been added for modeling hair and other fine geometry; and a new camera model that simulates realistic lens systems is now available. Throughout the book, we have made numerous smaller changes to more clearly explain and illustrate the key concepts in physically based rendering systems like pbrt.

ACKNOWLEDGMENTS

Pat Hanrahan has contributed to this book in more ways than we could hope to acknowledge; we owe a profound debt to him. He tirelessly argued for clean interfaces and finding the right abstractions to use throughout the system, and his understanding of and approach to rendering deeply influenced its design. His willingness to use pbrt and this manuscript in his rendering course at Stanford was enormously helpful, particularly in the early years of its life when it was still in very rough form; his feedback throughout this process has been crucial for bringing the text to its current state. Finally, the group of people that Pat helped assemble at the Stanford Graphics Lab, and the open environment that he fostered, made for an exciting, stimulating, and fertile environment. Matt and Greg both feel extremely privileged to have been there.

We owe a debt of gratitude to the many students who used early drafts of this book in courses at Stanford and the University of Virginia between 1999 and 2004. These students provided an enormous amount of feedback about the book and pbrt. The teaching assistants for these courses deserve special mention: Tim Purcell, Mike Cammarano, Ian Buck, and Ren Ng at Stanford, and Nolan Goodnight at Virginia. A number of students in those classes gave particularly valuable feedback and sent bug reports and bug fixes; we would especially like to thank Evan Parker and Phil Beatty. A draft of the manuscript of this book was used in classes taught by Bill Mark and Don Fussell at the University of Texas, Austin, and Raghu Machiraju at Ohio State University; their feedback was invaluable, and we are grateful for their adventurousness in incorporating this system into their courses, even while it was still being edited and revised.

Matt Pharr would like to acknowledge colleagues and co-workers in rendering-related endeavors who have been a great source of education and who have substantially influenced his approach to writing renderers and his understanding of the field. Particular thanks go to Craig Kolb, who provided a cornerstone of Matt's early computer graphics education through the freely available source code to the rayshade ray-tracing system, and Eric Veach, who has also been generous with his time and expertise. Thanks also to Doug Shult and Stan Eisenstat for formative lessons in mathematics and computer science during high school and college, respectively, and most important to Matt's parents, for the education they've provided and continued encouragement along the way. Finally, thanks also to Nick Triantos, Jayant Kolhe, and NVIDIA for their understanding and support through the final stages of the preparation of the first edition of the book.

Greg Humphreys is very grateful to all the professors and TAs who tolerated him when he was an undergraduate at Princeton. Many people encouraged his interest in graphics, specifically Michael Cohen, David Dobkin, Adam Finkelstein, Michael Cox, Gordon Stoll, Patrick Min, and Dan Wallach. Doug Clark, Steve Lyon, and Andy Wolfe also supervised various independent research boondoggles without even laughing once. Once, in a group meeting about a year-long robotics project, Steve Lyon became exasperated and yelled, "Stop telling me why it can't be done, and figure out how to do it!"—an impromptu lesson that will never be forgotten. Eric Ristad fired Greg as a summer research assistant after his freshman year (before the summer even began), pawning him off on an unsuspecting Pat Hanrahan and beginning an advising relationship that would span 10 years and both coasts. Finally, Dave Hanson taught Greg that literate programming was a great way to work and that computer programming can be a beautiful and subtle art form.

Wenzel Jakob was excited when the first edition of pbrt arrived in his mail during his undergraduate studies in 2004. Needless to say, this had a lasting effect on his career—thus Wenzel would like to begin by thanking his co-authors for inviting him to become a part of third edition of this book. Wenzel is extremely indebted to Steve Marschner, who was his PhD advisor during a fulfilling five years at Cornell University. Steve brought him into the world of research and remains a continuous source of inspiration. Wenzel is also thankful for the guidance and stimulating research environment created by the other members of the graphics group, including Kavita Bala, Doug James, and Bruce Walter. Wenzel spent a wonderful postdoc with Olga Sorkine Hornung who introduced him to geometry processing. Olga's support for Wenzel's involvement in this book is deeply appreciated.

For the first edition, we are also grateful to Don Mitchell, for his help with understanding some of the details of sampling and reconstruction; Thomas Kollig and Alexander Keller, for explaining the finer points of low-discrepancy sampling; and Christer Ericson, who had a number of suggestions for improving our kd-tree implementation. For the second edition, we're thankful to Christophe Hery and Eugene d'Eon for helping us with the nuances of subsurface scattering.

For the third edition, we'd especially like to thank Leo Grünschloß for reviewing our sampling chapter; Alexander Keller for suggestions about topics for that chapter; Eric Heitz for extensive help with microfacets (and reviewing our text on that topic); Thiago Ize for thoroughly reviewing the text on floating-point error; Tom van Bussel for reporting a number of errors in our BSSRDF code; Ralf Habel for reviewing our BSSRDF text; and Toshiya Hachisuka and Anton Kaplanyan for extensive review and comments about our light transport chapters. Discussions with Eric Veach about floating-point round-off error and ray tracing were extremely helpful to our development of our approach to that topic. We'd also like to thank Per Christensen, Doug Epps, Luca Fascione, Marcos Fajardo, Christiphe Hery, John "Spike" Hughes, Andrew Kensler, Alan King, Chris Kulla, Morgan McGuire, Andy Selle, and Ingo Wald for helpful discussions, suggestions, and pointers to research.

We would also like to thank the book's reviewers, all of whom had insightful and constructive feedback about the manuscript at various stages of its progress. We'd particularly like to thank the reviewers who provided feedback on both the first and second editions of the book: Ian Ashdown, Per Christensen, Doug Epps, Dan Goldman, Eric Haines, Erik Reinhard, Pete Shirley, Peter-Pike Sloan, Greg Ward, and a host of anonymous reviewers. For the second edition, Janne Kontkanen, Nelson Max, Bill Mark, and Eric Tabellion also contributed numerous helpful suggestions.

Many people have contributed to not only pbrt but to our own better understanding of rendering through bug reports, patches, and suggestions about better implementation approaches. A few have made particularly substantial contributions over the years—we would especially like to thank Solomon Boulos, Stephen Chenney, John Danks, Kevin Egan, Volodymyr Kachurovskyi, and Ke Xu.

In addition, we would like to thank Rachit Agrawal, Frederick Akalin, Mark Bolstad, Thomas de Bodt, Brian Budge, Mark Colbert, Yunjian Ding, Tao Du, Shaohua Fan, Etienne Ferrier, Nigel Fisher, Jeppe Revall Frisvad, Robert G. Graf, Asbjørn Heid, Keith Jeffery, Greg Johnson, Aaron Karp, Donald Knuth, Martin Kraus, Murat Kurt, Larry Lai, Craig McNaughton, Swaminathan Narayanan, Anders Nilsson, Jens Olsson, Vincent Pegoraro, Srinath Ravichandiran, Sébastien Speierer, Nils Thuerey, Xiong Wei, Wei-Wei Xu, Arek Zimny, and Matthias Zwicker for their suggestions and bug reports. Finally, we would like to thank the *LuxRender* developers and the *LuxRender* community, particularly Terrence Vergauwen, Jean-Philippe Grimaldi, and Asbjørn Heid; it has been a delight to see the rendering system they have built from pbrt's foundation, and we have learned from reading their source code and implementations of new rendering algorithms.

Special thanks to Martin Preston and Steph Bruning from Framestore for their help with our being able to use a frame from *Gravity* (image courtesy of Warner Bros. and Framestore), and to Joe Letteri, Dave Gouge, and Luca Fascione from Weta Digital for their help with the frame from *The Hobbit: The Battle of the Five Armies* (© 2014 Warner Bros. Entertainment Inc. and Metro-Goldwyn-Mayer Pictures Inc. (US, Canada & New Line Foreign Territories), © 2014 Metro-Goldwyn-Mayer Pictures Inc. and Warner Bros. Entertainment Inc. (all other territories). All Rights Reserved.

PRODUCTION

For the production of the first edition, we would also like to thank Tim Cox (senior editor), for his willingness to take on this slightly unorthodox project and for both his direction and patience throughout the process. We are very grateful to Elisabeth Beller (project manager), who has gone well beyond the call of duty for this book; her ability to keep this complex project in control and on schedule has been remarkable, and we particularly thank her for the measurable impact she has had on the quality of the final result. Thanks also to Rick Camp (editorial assistant) for his many contributions along the way. Paul Anagnostopoulos and Jacqui Scarlott at Windfall Software did the book's composition; their ability to take the authors' homebrew literate programming file format and turn it into high-quality final output while also juggling the multiple unusual types of indexing we asked for is greatly appreciated. Thanks also to Ken DellaPenta (copyeditor) and Jennifer McClain (proofreader) as well as to Max Spector at Chen Design (text and cover designer), and Steve Rath (indexer).

For the second edition, we'd like to thank Greg Chalson who talked us into expanding and updating the book; Greg also ensured that Paul Anagnostopoulos at Windfall Software would again do the book's composition. We'd like to thank Paul again for his efforts in working with this book's production complexity. Finally, we'd also like to thank Todd Green, Paul Gottehrer, and Heather Scherer at Elsevier.

For the third edition, we'd like to thank Todd Green from Elsevier, who oversaw this go-round, and Amy Invernizzi, who kept the train on the rails throughout the process. We were delighted to have Paul Anagnostopoulos at Windfall Software part of this process for a third time; his efforts have been critical to the book's high production value, which is so important to us.

SCENES AND MODELS

Many people and organizations have generously supplied us with scenes and models for use in this book and the pbrt distribution. Their generosity has been invaluable in helping us create interesting example images throughout the text.

The bunny, Buddha, and dragon models are courtesy of the Stanford Computer Graphics Laboratory's scanning repository. The "killeroo" model is included with permission of Phil Dench and Martin Rezard (3D scan and digital representations by headus, design and clay sculpt by Rezard). The dragon model scan used in Chapters 8 and 9 is courtesy of Christian Schüller, and thanks to Yasutoshi Mori for the sports car used in Chapters 7 and 12. The glass used to illustrate caustics in Figures 16.9 and 16.11 is thanks to Simon Wendsche, and the physically accurate smoke data sets were created by Duc Nguyen and Ron Fedkiw.

The head model used to illustrate subsurface scattering was made available by Infinite Realities, Inc. under a Creative Commons Attribution 3.0 license. Thanks to "Wig42" for the breakfast table scene used in Figure 16.8 and "guismo" for the coffee splash scene used in Figure 15.5; both were was posted to *blendswap.com* also under a Creative Commons Attribution 3.0 license.

Nolan Goodnight created environment maps with a realistic skylight model, and Paul Debevec provided numerous high dynamic-range environment maps. Thanks also to Bernhard Vogl (*dativ.at/lightprobes/*) for environment maps that we used in numerous figures. Marc Ellens provided spectral data for a variety of light sources, and the spectral RGB measurement data for a variety of displays is courtesy of Tom Lianza at X-Rite.

We are most particularly grateful to Guillermo M. Leal Llaguno of Evolución Visual, *www.evvisual.com*, who modeled and rendered the San Miguel scene that was featured on the cover of the second edition and is still used in numerous figures in the book. We would also especially like to thank Marko Dabrovic (*www.3lhd.com*) and Mihovil Odak at RNA Studios (*www.rna.hr*), who supplied a bounty of excellent models and scenes, including the Sponza atrium, the Sibenik cathedral, and the Audi TT car model. Many thanks are also due to Florent Boyer (*www.florentboyer.com*), who provided the contemporary house scene used in some of the images in Chapter 16.

ABOUT THE COVER

The "Countryside" scene on the cover of the book was created by Jan-Walter Schliep, Burak Kahraman, and Timm Dapper of Laubwerk (*www.laubwerk.com*). The scene features 23,241 individual plants, with a total of 3.1 billion triangles. (Thanks to object instancing, only 24 million triangles need to be stored in memory.) The pbrt files that describe the scene geometry require 1.1 GB of on-disk storage. There are a total of 192 texture maps, representing 528 MB of texture data. The scene is one of the example scenes that are available from the pbrt Web site.

ADDITIONAL READING

Donald Knuth's article *Literate Programming* (Knuth 1984) describes the main ideas behind literate programming as well as his web programming environment. The seminal TEX typesetting system was written with web and has been published as a series of books (Knuth 1986; Knuth 1993a). More recently, Knuth has published a collection of graph algorithms in literate format in *The Stanford GraphBase* (Knuth 1993b). These programs are enjoyable to read and are excellent presentations of their respective algorithms. The Web site *www.literateprogramming.com* has pointers to many articles about literate programming, literate programs to download, and a variety of literate programming systems; many refinements have been made since Knuth's original development of the idea.

The only other literate programs we know of that have been published as books are the implementation of the lcc compiler, which was written by Christopher Fraser and David Hanson and published as *A Retargetable C Compiler: Design and Implementation* (Fraser and Hanson 1995), and Martin Ruckert's book on the *mp3* audio format, *Understanding MP3* (Ruckert 2005).

CHAPTER ONE

01 INTRODUCTION

Rendering is the process of producing an image from the description of a 3D scene. Obviously, this is a very broad task, and there are many ways to approach it. *Physically based* techniques attempt to simulate reality; that is, they use principles of physics to model the interaction of light and matter. While a physically based approach may seem to be the most obvious way to approach rendering, it has only been widely adopted in practice over the past 10 or so years. Section 1.7 at the end of this chapter gives a brief history of physically based rendering and its recent adoption for offline rendering for movies and for interactive rendering for games.

This book describes pbrt, a physically based rendering system based on the ray-tracing algorithm. Most computer graphics books present algorithms and theory, sometimes combined with snippets of code. In contrast, this book couples the theory with a complete implementation of a fully functional rendering system. The source code to the system (as well as example scenes and a collection of data for rendering) can be found on the pbrt Web site, *pbrt.org*.

1.1 LITERATE PROGRAMMING

While writing the TEX typesetting system, Donald Knuth developed a new programming methodology based on the simple but revolutionary idea that *programs should be written more for people's consumption than for computers' consumption*. He named this methodology *literate programming*. This book (including the chapter you're reading now) is a long literate program. This means that in the course of reading this book, you will read the *full* implementation of the pbrt rendering system, not just a high-level description of it.

Literate programs are written in a metalanguage that mixes a document formatting language (e.g., TEX or HTML) and a programming language (e.g., C++). Two separate systems process the program: a "weaver" that transforms the literate program into a

Physically Based Rendering: From Theory To Implementation.
http://dx.doi.org/10.1016/B978-0-12-800645-0.50001-4

document suitable for typesetting and a "tangler" that produces source code suitable for compilation. Our literate programming system is homegrown, but it was heavily influenced by Norman Ramsey's noweb system.

The literate programming metalanguage provides two important features. The first is the ability to mix prose with source code. This feature makes the description of the program just as important as its actual source code, encouraging careful design and documentation. Second, the language provides mechanisms for presenting the program code to the reader in an order that is entirely different from the compiler input. Thus, the program can be described in a logical manner. Each named block of code is called a *fragment*, and each fragment can refer to other fragments by name.

As a simple example, consider a function InitGlobals() that is responsible for initializing all of a program's global variables:[1]

```
void InitGlobals() {
    nMarbles = 25.7;
    shoeSize = 13;
    dielectric = true;
}
```

Despite its brevity, this function is hard to understand without any context. Why, for example, can the variable nMarbles take on floating-point values? Just looking at the code, one would need to search through the entire program to see where each variable is declared and how it is used in order to understand its purpose and the meanings of its legal values. Although this structuring of the system is fine for a compiler, a human reader would much rather see the initialization code for each variable presented separately, near the code that actually declares and uses the variable.

In a literate program, one can instead write InitGlobals() like this:

```
⟨Function Definitions⟩ ≡
    void InitGlobals() {
        ⟨Initialize Global Variables 2⟩
    }
```

This defines a fragment, called ⟨*Function Definitions*⟩, that contains the definition of the InitGlobals() function. The InitGlobals() function itself refers to another fragment, ⟨*Initialize Global Variables*⟩. Because the initialization fragment has not yet been defined, we don't know anything about this function except that it will probably contain assignments to global variables. This is just the right level of abstraction for now, since no variables have been declared yet. When we introduce the global variable shoeSize somewhere later in the program, we can then write

```
⟨Initialize Global Variables⟩ ≡                                        2
    shoeSize = 13;
```

---

1   The example code in this section is merely illustrative and is not part of pbrt itself.

Here we have started to define the contents of ⟨*Initialize Global Variables*⟩. When the literate program is tangled into source code for compilation, the literate programming system will substitute the code `shoeSize = 13;` inside the definition of the `InitGlobals()` function. Later in the text, we may define another global variable, `dielectric`, and we can append its initialization to the fragment:

⟨*Initialize Global Variables*⟩ +≡   2
```
    dielectric = true;
```

The +≡ symbol after the fragment name shows that we have added to a previously defined fragment. When tangled, the result of these three fragments is the code

```
void InitGlobals() {
    shoeSize = 13;
    dielectric = true;
}
```

In this way, we can decompose complex functions into logically distinct parts, making them much easier to understand. For example, we can write a complicated function as a series of fragments:

⟨*Function Definitions*⟩ +≡
```
    void complexFunc(int x, int y, double *values) {
        ⟨Check validity of arguments⟩
        if (x < y) {
            ⟨Swap parameter values⟩
        }
        ⟨Do precomputation before loop⟩
        ⟨Loop through and update values array⟩
    }
```

Again, the contents of each fragment are expanded inline in `complexFunc()` for compilation. In the document, we can introduce each fragment and its implementation in turn. This decomposition lets us present code a few lines at a time, making it easier to understand. Another advantage of this style of programming is that by separating the function into logical fragments, each with a single and well-delineated purpose, each one can then be written, verified, or read independently. In general, we will try to make each fragment less than 10 lines long.

In some sense, the literate programming system is just an enhanced macro substitution package tuned to the task of rearranging program source code. This may seem like a trivial change, but in fact literate programming is quite different from other ways of structuring software systems.

1.1.1 INDEXING AND CROSS-REFERENCING

The following features are designed to make the text easier to navigate. Indices in the page margins give page numbers where the functions, variables, and methods used on that page are defined. Indices at the end of the book collect all of these identifiers so that it's possible to find definitions by name. Appendix C, "Index of Fragments," lists the pages where each fragment is defined and the pages where it is used. Within the text, a defined fragment name is followed by a list of page numbers on which that fragment is used. For example, a hypothetical fragment definition such as

⟨*A fascinating fragment*⟩ ≡   **184, 690**
    nMarbles += .001;

indicates that this fragment is used on pages 184 and 690. Occasionally we elide fragments from the printed book that are either boilerplate code or substantially the same as other fragments; when these fragments are used, no page numbers will be listed.

When a fragment is used inside another fragment, the page number on which it is first defined appears after the fragment name. For example,

⟨*Do something interesting*⟩+≡   **500**
    InitializeSomethingInteresting();
    ⟨*Do something else interesting* **486**⟩
    CleanUp();

indicates that the ⟨*Do something else interesting*⟩ fragment is defined on page 486. If the definition of the fragment is not included in the book, no page number will be listed.

1.2 PHOTOREALISTIC RENDERING AND THE RAY-TRACING ALGORITHM

The goal of photorealistic rendering is to create an image of a 3D scene that is indistinguishable from a photograph of the same scene. Before we describe the rendering process, it is important to understand that in this context the word *indistinguishable* is imprecise because it involves a human observer, and different observers may perceive the same image differently. Although we will cover a few perceptual issues in this book, accounting for the precise characteristics of a given observer is a very difficult and largely unsolved problem. For the most part, we will be satisfied with an accurate simulation of the physics of light and its interaction with matter, relying on our understanding of display technology to present the best possible image to the viewer.

Almost all photorealistic rendering systems are based on the ray-tracing algorithm. Ray tracing is actually a very simple algorithm; it is based on following the path of a ray of light through a scene as it interacts with and bounces off objects in an environment. Although there are many ways to write a ray tracer, all such systems simulate at least the following objects and phenomena:

- *Cameras:* A camera model determines how and from where the scene is being viewed, including how an image of the scene is recorded on a sensor. Many rendering systems generate viewing rays starting at the camera that are then traced into the scene.
- *Ray–object intersections:* We must be able to tell precisely where a given ray intersects a given geometric object. In addition, we need to determine certain properties of the object at the intersection point, such as a surface normal or its material. Most ray tracers also have some facility for testing the intersection of a ray with multiple objects, typically returning the closest intersection along the ray.

- *Light sources:* Without lighting, there would be little point in rendering a scene. A ray tracer must model the distribution of light throughout the scene, including not only the locations of the lights themselves but also the way in which they distribute their energy throughout space.
- *Visibility:* In order to know whether a given light deposits energy at a point on a surface, we must know whether there is an uninterrupted path from the point to the light source. Fortunately, this question is easy to answer in a ray tracer, since we can just construct the ray from the surface to the light, find the closest ray–object intersection, and compare the intersection distance to the light distance.
- *Surface scattering:* Each object must provide a description of its appearance, including information about how light interacts with the object's surface, as well as the nature of the reradiated (or *scattered*) light. Models for surface scattering are typically parameterized so that they can simulate a variety of appearances.
- *Indirect light transport:* Because light can arrive at a surface after bouncing off or passing through other surfaces, it is usually necessary to trace additional rays originating at the surface to fully capture this effect.
- *Ray propagation:* We need to know what happens to the light traveling along a ray as it passes through space. If we are rendering a scene in a vacuum, light energy remains constant along a ray. Although true vacuums are unusual on Earth, they are a reasonable approximation for many environments. More sophisticated models are available for tracing rays through fog, smoke, the Earth's atmosphere, and so on.

We will briefly discuss each of these simulation tasks in this section. In the next section, we will show pbrt's high-level interface to the underlying simulation components and follow the progress of a single ray through the main rendering loop. We will also present the implementation of a surface scattering model based on Turner Whitted's original ray-tracing algorithm.

1.2.1 CAMERAS

Nearly everyone has used a camera and is familiar with its basic functionality: you indicate your desire to record an image of the world (usually by pressing a button or tapping a screen), and the image is recorded onto a piece of film or an electronic sensor. One of the simplest devices for taking photographs is called the *pinhole camera*. Pinhole cameras consist of a light-tight box with a tiny hole at one end (Figure 1.1). When the hole is uncovered, light enters this hole and falls on a piece of photographic paper that is affixed to the other end of the box. Despite its simplicity, this kind of camera is still used today, frequently for artistic purposes. Very long exposure times are necessary to get enough light on the film to form an image.

Although most cameras are substantially more complex than the pinhole camera, it is a convenient starting point for simulation. The most important function of the camera is to define the portion of the scene that will be recorded onto the film. In Figure 1.1, we can see how connecting the pinhole to the edges of the film creates a double pyramid that extends into the scene. Objects that are not inside this pyramid cannot be imaged onto the film. Because actual cameras image a more complex shape than a pyramid, we will refer to the region of space that can potentially be imaged onto the film as the *viewing volume*.

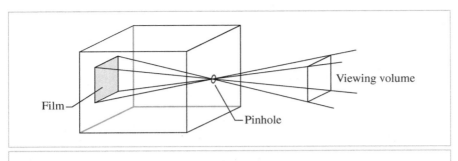

Figure 1.1: A Pinhole Camera.

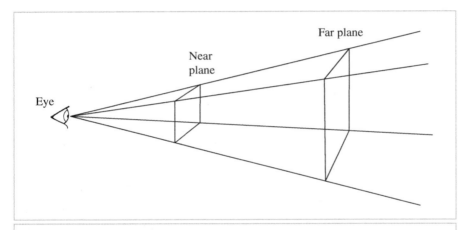

Figure 1.2: When we simulate a pinhole camera, we place the film in front of the hole at the near plane, and the hole is renamed the *eye*.

Another way to think about the pinhole camera is to place the film plane in *front* of the pinhole but at the same distance (Figure 1.2). Note that connecting the hole to the film defines exactly the same viewing volume as before. Of course, this is not a practical way to build a real camera, but for simulation purposes it is a convenient abstraction. When the film (or image) plane is in front of the pinhole, the pinhole is frequently referred to as the *eye*.

Now we come to the crucial issue in rendering: at each point in the image, what color value does the camera record? If we recall the original pinhole camera, it is clear that only light rays that travel along the vector between the pinhole and a point on the film can contribute to that film location. In our simulated camera with the film plane in front of the eye, we are interested in the amount of light traveling from the image point to the eye.

Therefore, an important task of the camera simulator is to take a point on the image and generate *rays* along which incident light will contribute to that image location. Because a ray consists of an origin point and a direction vector, this task is particularly simple for the pinhole camera model of Figure 1.2: it uses the pinhole for the origin and the vector from the pinhole to the near plane as the ray's direction. For more complex camera models involving multiple lenses, the calculation of the ray that corresponds to a given point on the image may be more involved. (Section 6.4 describes the implementation of such a model.)

With the process of converting image locations to rays completely encapsulated in the camera module, the rest of the rendering system can focus on evaluating the lighting along those rays, and a variety of camera models can be supported. pbrt's camera abstraction is described in detail in Chapter 6.

1.2.2 RAY–OBJECT INTERSECTIONS

Each time the camera generates a ray, the first task of the renderer is to determine which object, if any, that ray intersects first and where the intersection occurs. This intersection point is the visible point along the ray, and we will want to simulate the interaction of light with the object at this point. To find the intersection, we must test the ray for intersection against all objects in the scene and select the one that the ray intersects first. Given a ray r, we first start by writing it in *parametric form*:

$$r(t) = o + t\mathbf{d},$$

where o is the ray's origin, $\mathbf{d}$ is its direction vector, and t is a parameter whose legal range is $(0, \infty)$. We can obtain a point along the ray by specifying its parametric t value and evaluating the above equation.

It is often easy to find the intersection between the ray r and a surface defined by an implicit function $F(x, y, z) = 0$. We first substitute the ray equation into the implicit equation, producing a new function whose only parameter is t. We then solve this function for t and substitute the smallest positive root into the ray equation to find the desired point. For example, the implicit equation of a sphere centered at the origin with radius r is

$$x^2 + y^2 + z^2 - r^2 = 0.$$

Substituting the ray equation, we have

$$\left(o_x + t\mathbf{d}_x\right)^2 + \left(o_y + t\mathbf{d}_y\right)^2 + \left(o_z + t\mathbf{d}_z\right)^2 - r^2 = 0.$$

All of the values besides t are known, giving us an easily solved quadratic equation in t. If there are no real roots, the ray misses the sphere; if there are roots, the smallest positive one gives the intersection point.

The intersection point alone is not enough information for the rest of the ray tracer; it needs to know certain properties of the surface at the point. First, a representation of the material at the point must be determined and passed along to later stages of the ray-tracing algorithm. Second, additional geometric information about the intersection point will also be required in order to shade the point. For example, the surface normal $\mathbf{n}$ is always required. Although many ray tracers operate with only $\mathbf{n}$, more sophisticated rendering systems like pbrt require even more information, such as various partial derivatives of position and surface normal with respect to the local parameterization of the surface.

Of course, most scenes are made up of multiple objects. The brute-force approach would be to test the ray against each object in turn, choosing the minimum positive t value of all intersections to find the closest intersection. This approach, while correct, is very slow, even for scenes of modest complexity. A better approach is to incorporate an *acceleration structure* that quickly rejects whole groups of objects during the ray intersection process. This ability to quickly cull irrelevant geometry means that ray tracing frequently runs in $O(I \log N)$ time, where I is the number of pixels in the image and N is the number of objects in the scene.[2] (Building the acceleration structure itself is necessarily at least $O(N)$ time, however.)

pbrt's geometric interface and implementations of it for a variety of shapes is described in Chapter 3, and the acceleration interface and implementations are shown in Chapter 4.

1.2.3 LIGHT DISTRIBUTION

The ray–object intersection stage gives us a point to be shaded and some information about the local geometry at that point. Recall that our eventual goal is to find the amount of light leaving this point in the direction of the camera. In order to do this, we need to know how much light is *arriving* at this point. This involves both the *geometric* and *radiometric* distribution of light in the scene. For very simple light sources (e.g., point lights), the geometric distribution of lighting is a simple matter of knowing the position of the lights. However, point lights do not exist in the real world, and so physically based lighting is often based on *area* light sources. This means that the light source is associated with a geometric object that emits illumination from its surface. However, we will use point lights in this section to illustrate the components of light distribution; rigorous discussion of light measurement and distribution is the topic of Chapters 5 and 12.

We frequently would like to know the amount of light power being deposited on the differential area surrounding the intersection point (Figure 1.3). We will assume that the point light source has some power Φ associated with it and that it radiates light equally in all directions. This means that the power per area on a unit sphere surrounding the light is $\Phi/(4\pi)$. (These measurements will be explained and formalized in Section 5.4.)

If we consider two such spheres (Figure 1.4), it is clear that the power per area at a point on the larger sphere must be less than the power at a point on the smaller sphere because the same total power is distributed over a larger area. Specifically, the power per area arriving at a point on a sphere of radius r is proportional to $1/r^2$. Furthermore, it can be shown that if the tiny surface patch dA is tilted by an angle θ away from the vector from the surface point to the light, the amount of power deposited on dA is proportional

---

2   Although ray tracing's logarithmic complexity is often heralded as one of its key strengths, this complexity is typically only true on average. A number of ray-tracing algorithms that have guaranteed logarithmic running time have been published in the computational geometry literature, but these algorithms only work for certain types of scenes and have very expensive preprocessing and storage requirements. Szirmay-Kalos and Márton provide pointers to the relevant literature (Szirmay-Kalos and Márton 1998). One consolation is that scenes representing realistic environments generally don't exhibit this worst-case behavior. In practice, the ray intersection algorithms presented in this book are sublinear, but without expensive preprocessing and huge memory usage it is always possible to construct worst-case scenes where ray tracing runs in $O(IN)$ time.

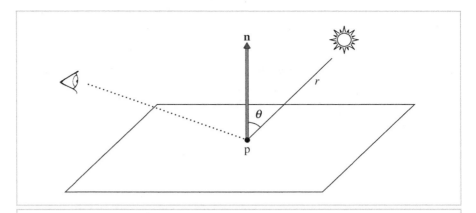

Figure 1.3: Geometric construction for determining the power per area arriving at a point due to a point light source. The distance from the point to the light source is denoted by r.

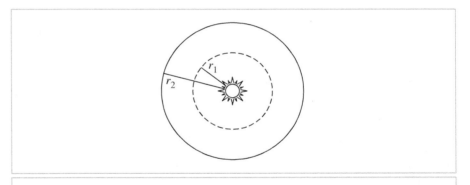

Figure 1.4: Since the point light radiates light equally in all directions, the same total power is deposited on all spheres centered at the light.

to $\cos \theta$. Putting this all together, the differential power per area dE (the *differential irradiance*) is

$$dE = \frac{\Phi \cos \theta}{4\pi r^2}.$$

Readers already familiar with basic lighting in computer graphics will notice two familiar laws encoded in this equation: the cosine falloff of light for tilted surfaces mentioned above, and the one-over-r-squared falloff of light with distance.

Scenes with multiple lights are easily handled because illumination is *linear:* the contribution of each light can be computed separately and summed to obtain the overall contribution.

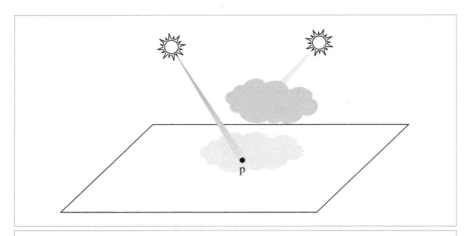

Figure 1.5: A light source only deposits energy on a surface if the source is not obscured as seen from the receiving point. The light source on the left illuminates the point p, but the light source on the right does not.

1.2.4 VISIBILITY

The lighting distribution described in the previous section ignores one very important component: *shadows*. Each light contributes illumination to the point being shaded only if the path from the point to the light's position is unobstructed (Figure 1.5).

Fortunately, in a ray tracer it is easy to determine if the light is visible from the point being shaded. We simply construct a new ray whose origin is at the surface point and whose direction points toward the light. These special rays are called *shadow rays*. If we trace this ray through the environment, we can check to see whether any intersections are found between the ray's origin and the light source by comparing the parametric *t* value of any intersections found to the parametric *t* value along the ray of the light source position. If there is no blocking object between the light and the surface, the light's contribution is included.

1.2.5 SURFACE SCATTERING

We now are able to compute two pieces of information that are vital for proper shading of a point: its location and the incident lighting.[3] Now we need to determine how the incident lighting is *scattered* at the surface. Specifically, we are interested in the amount of light energy scattered back along the ray that we originally traced to find the intersection point, since that ray leads to the camera (Figure 1.6).

Each object in the scene provides a *material*, which is a description of its appearance properties at each point on the surface. This description is given by the *bidirectional reflectance distribution function* (BRDF). This function tells us how much energy is reflected

---

3   Readers already familiar with rendering might object that the discussion in this section considers only direct lighting. Rest assured that pbrt does support global illumination.

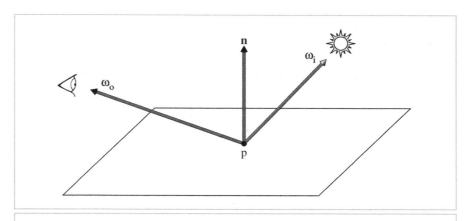

Figure 1.6: The Geometry of Surface Scattering. Incident light arriving along direction ω_i interacts with the surface at point p and is scattered back toward the camera along direction ω_o. The amount of light scattered toward the camera is given by the product of the incident light energy and the BRDF.

from an incoming direction ω_i to an outgoing direction ω_o. We will write the BRDF at p as $f_r(p, \omega_o, \omega_i)$. Now, computing the amount of light L scattered back toward the camera is straightforward:

```
for each light:
    if light is not blocked:
        incident_light = light.L(point)
        amount_reflected =
            surface.BRDF(hit_point, camera_vector, light_vector)
        L += amount_reflected * incident_light
```

Here we are using the symbol L to represent the light; this represents a slightly different unit for light measurement than dE, which was used before. L represents *radiance*, a unit for measuring light that we will see much of in the following.

It is easy to generalize the notion of a BRDF to transmitted light (obtaining a BTDF) or to general scattering of light arriving from either side of the surface. A function that describes general scattering is called a *bidirectional scattering distribution function* (BSDF). pbrt supports a variety of BSDF models; they are described in Chapter 8. More complex yet is the *bidirectional subsurface scattering reflectance distribution function* (BSSRDF), which models light that exits a surface at a different point than it enters. The BSSRDF is described in Sections 5.6.2, 11.4, and 15.5.

1.2.6 INDIRECT LIGHT TRANSPORT

Turner Whitted's original paper on ray tracing (1980) emphasized its *recursive* nature, which was the key that made it possible to include indirect specular reflection and transmission in rendered images. For example, if a ray from the camera hits a shiny object like a mirror, we can reflect the ray about the surface normal at the intersection point and recursively invoke the ray-tracing routine to find the light arriving at the point on the

Figure 1.7: A Prototypical Example of Early Ray Tracing. Note the use of mirrored and glass objects, which emphasizes the algorithm's ability to handle these kinds of surfaces.

mirror, adding its contribution to the original camera ray. This same technique can be used to trace transmitted rays that intersect transparent objects. For a long time, most early ray-tracing examples showcased mirrors and glass balls (Figure 1.7) because these types of effects were difficult to capture with other rendering techniques.

In general, the amount of light that reaches the camera from a point on an object is given by the sum of light emitted by the object (if it is itself a light source) and the amount of reflected light. This idea is formalized by the *light transport equation* (also often known as the *rendering equation*), which says that the outgoing radiance $L_o(p, \omega_o)$ from a point p in direction ω_o is the emitted radiance at that point in that direction, $L_e(p, \omega_o)$, plus the incident radiance from all directions on the sphere S^2 around p scaled by the BSDF $f(p, \omega_o, \omega_i)$ and a cosine term:

$$L_o(p, \omega_o) = L_e(p, \omega_o) + \int_{S^2} f(p, \omega_o, \omega_i)\, L_i(p, \omega_i)\, |\cos \theta_i|\, d\omega_i. \qquad [1.1]$$

We will show a more complete derivation of this equation in Sections 5.6.1 and 14.4. Solving this integral analytically is not possible except for the simplest of scenes, so we must either make simplifying assumptions or use numerical integration techniques.

Whitted's algorithm simplifies this integral by ignoring incoming light from most directions and only evaluating $L_i(p, \omega_i)$ for directions to light sources and for the directions of perfect reflection and refraction. In other words, it turns the integral into a sum over a small number of directions.

Whitted's method can be extended to capture more effects than just perfect mirrors and glass. For example, by tracing many recursive rays near the mirror-reflection direction and averaging their contributions, we obtain an approximation of glossy reflection. In

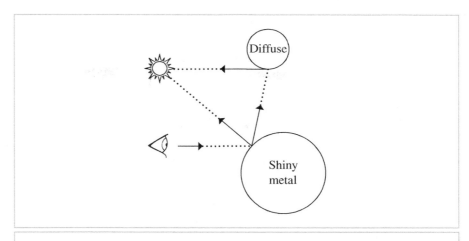

Figure 1.8: Recursive ray tracing associates an entire tree of rays with each image location.

fact, we can *always* recursively trace a ray whenever we hit an object. For example, we can randomly choose a reflection direction ω_i and weight the contribution of this newly spawned ray by evaluating the BRDF $f_r(p, \omega_o, \omega_i)$. This simple but powerful idea can lead to very realistic images because it captures all of the interreflection of light between objects. Of course, we need to know when to terminate the recursion, and choosing directions completely at random may make the rendering algorithm slow to converge to a reasonable result. These problems can be addressed, however; these issues are the topics of Chapters 13 through 16.

When we trace rays recursively in this manner, we are really associating a *tree* of rays with each image location (Figure 1.8), with the ray from the camera at the root of this tree. Each ray in this tree can have a *weight* associated with it; this allows us to model, for example, shiny surfaces that do not reflect 100% of the incoming light.

1.2.7 RAY PROPAGATION

The discussion so far has assumed that rays are traveling through a vacuum. For example, when describing the distribution of light from a point source, we assumed that the light's power was distributed equally on the surface of a sphere centered at the light without decreasing along the way. The presence of *participating media* such as smoke, fog, or dust can invalidate this assumption. These effects are important to simulate: even if we are not making a rendering of a smoke-filled room, almost all outdoor scenes are affected substantially by participating media. For example, Earth's atmosphere causes objects that are farther away to appear less saturated (Figure 1.9).

There are two ways in which a participating medium can affect the light propagating along a ray. First, the medium can *extinguish* (or *attenuate*) light, either by absorbing it or by scattering it in a different direction. We can capture this effect by computing the *transmittance* T between the ray origin and the intersection point. The transmittance

Figure 1.9: Earth's Atmosphere Decreases Saturation with Distance. The scene on the top is rendered without simulating this phenomenon, while the scene on the bottom includes an atmospheric model. This sort of atmospheric attenuation is an important depth cue when viewing real scenes and adds a sense of scale to the rendering on the bottom.

Figure 1.10: A Spotlight Shining on a Sphere through Fog. Notice that the shape of the spotlight's lighting distribution and the sphere's shadow are clearly visible due to the additional scattering in the participating medium.

tells us how much of the light scattered at the intersection point makes it back to the ray origin.

A participating medium can also add to the light along a ray. This can happen either if the medium emits light (as with a flame) or if the medium scatters light from other directions back along the ray (Figure 1.10). We can find this quantity by numerically evaluating the *volume light transport equation,* in the same way we evaluated the light transport equation to find the amount of light reflected from a surface. We will leave the description of participating media and volume rendering until Chapters 11 and 15. For now, it will suffice to say that we can compute the effect of participating media and incorporate its effect into the amount of light carried by the ray.

1.3 pbrt: SYSTEM OVERVIEW

pbrt is structured using standard object-oriented techniques: abstract base classes are defined for important entities (e.g., a Shape abstract base class defines the interface that all geometric shapes must implement, the Light abstract base class acts similarly for lights, etc.). The majority of the system is implemented purely in terms of the interfaces provided by these abstract base classes; for example, the code that checks for occluding objects between a light source and a point being shaded calls the Shape intersection

Table 1.1: Main Interface Types. Most of pbrt is implemented in terms of 10 key abstract base classes, listed here. Implementations of each of these can easily be added to the system to extend its functionality.

Base class	Directory	Section
Shape	shapes/	3.1
Aggregate	accelerators/	4.2
Camera	cameras/	6.1
Sampler	samplers/	7.2
Filter	filters/	7.8
Material	materials/	9.2
Texture	textures/	10.3
Medium	media/	11.3
Light	lights/	12.2
Integrator	integrators/	1.3.3

methods and doesn't need to consider the particular types of shapes that are present in the scene. This approach makes it easy to extend the system, as adding a new shape only requires implementing a class that implements the Shape interface and linking it into the system.

pbrt is written using a total of 10 key abstract base classes, summarized in Table 1.1. Adding a new implementation of one of these types to the system is straightforward; the implementation must inherit from the appropriate base class, be compiled and linked into the executable, and the object creation routines in Appendix B must be modified to create instances of the object as needed as the scene description file is parsed. Section B.4 discusses extending the system in this manner in more detail.

The pbrt source code distribution is available from *pbrt.org*. (A large collection of example scenes is also available as a separate download.) All of the code for the pbrt core is in the src/core directory, and the main() function is contained in the short file src/main/pbrt.cpp. Various implementations of instances of the abstract base classes are in separate directories: src/shapes has implementations of the Shape base class, src/materials has implementations of Material, and so forth.

Throughout this section are a number of images rendered with extended versions of pbrt. Of them, Figures 1.11 through 1.14 are notable: not only are they visually impressive but also each of them was created by a student in a rendering course where the final class project was to extend pbrt with new functionality in order to render an interesting image. These images are among the best from those courses. Figures 1.15 and 1.16 were rendered with *LuxRender*, a GPL-licensed rendering system originally based on the pbrt source code from the first edition of the book. (See *www.luxrender.net* for more information about *LuxRender*.)

Figure 1.11: Guillaume Poncin and Pramod Sharma extended pbrt in numerous ways, implementing a number of complex rendering algorithms, to make this prize-winning image for Stanford's cs348b rendering competition. The trees are modeled procedurally with L-systems, a glow image processing filter increases the apparent realism of the lights on the tree, snow was modeled procedurally with metaballs, and a subsurface scattering algorithm gave the snow its realistic appearance by accounting for the effect of light that travels beneath the snow for some distance before leaving it.

1.3.1 PHASES OF EXECUTION

pbrt can be conceptually divided into two phases of execution. First, it parses the scene description file provided by the user. The scene description is a text file that specifies the geometric shapes that make up the scene, their material properties, the lights that illuminate them, where the virtual camera is positioned in the scene, and parameters to all of the individual algorithms used throughout the system. Each statement in the input file has a direct mapping to one of the routines in Appendix B; these routines comprise the procedural interface for describing a scene. The scene file format is documented on the pbrt Web site, *pbrt.org*.

The end results of the parsing phase are an instance of the Scene class and an instance of the Integrator class. The Scene contains a representation of the contents of the scene (geometric objects, lights, etc.), and the Integrator implements an algorithm to render it. The integrator is so-named because its main task is to evaluate the integral from Equation (1.1).

Integrator 25

Scene 23

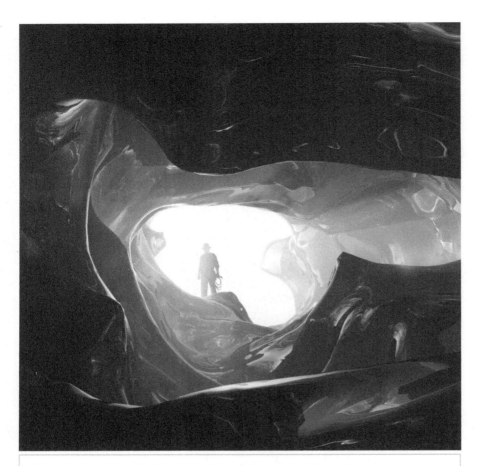

Figure 1.12: Abe Davis, David Jacobs, and Jongmin Baek rendered this amazing image of an ice cave to take the grand prize in the 2009 Stanford CS348b rendering competition. They first implemented a simulation of the physical process of glaciation, the process where snow falls, melts, and refreezes over the course of many years, forming stratified layers of ice. They then simulated erosion of the ice due to melted water runoff before generating a geometric model of the ice. Scattering of light inside the volume was simulated with volumetric photon mapping; the blue color of the ice is entirely due to modeling the wavelength-dependent absorption of light in the ice volume.

Once the scene has been specified, the second phase of execution begins, and the main rendering loop executes. This phase is where pbrt usually spends the majority of its running time, and most of this book describes code that executes during this phase. The rendering loop is performed by executing an implementation of the Integrator::Render() method, which is the focus of Section 1.3.4.

This chapter will describe a particular Integrator subclass named SamplerIntegrator, whose Render() method determines the light arriving at a virtual film plane for a large number of rays that model the process of image formation. After the contributions of all of these film samples have been computed, the final image is written to a file. The scene

Integrator 25
Integrator::Render() 25
SamplerIntegrator 25

Figure 1.13: Lingfeng Yang implemented a bidirectional texture function to simulate the appearance of cloth, adding an analytic self-shadowing model, to render this image that took first prize in the 2009 Stanford CS348b rendering competition.

description data in memory are deallocated, and the system then resumes processing statements from the scene description file until no more remain, allowing the user to specify another scene to be rendered, if desired.

1.3.2 SCENE REPRESENTATION

pbrt's main() function can be found in the file main/pbrt.cpp. This function is quite simple; it first loops over the provided command-line arguments in argv, initializing values in the Options structure and storing the filenames provided in the arguments. Running pbrt with --help as a command-line argument prints all of the options that can be specified on the command line. The fragment that parses the command-line argu-

main() 21

Figure 1.14: Jared Jacobs and Michael Turitzin added an implementation of Kajiya and Kay's texel-based fur rendering algorithm (Kajiya and Kay 1989) to pbrt and rendered this image, where both the fur on the dog and the shag carpet are rendered with the texel fur algorithm.

ments, ⟨*Process command-line arguments*⟩, is straightforward and therefore not included in the book here.

The options structure is then passed to the pbrtInit() function, which does systemwide initialization. The main() function then parses the given scene description(s), leading to the creation of a Scene and an Integrator. After all rendering is done, pbrtCleanup() does final cleanup before the system exits.

The pbrtInit() and pbrtCleanup() functions appear in a *mini-index* in the page margin, along with the number of the page where they are actually defined. The mini-indices have pointers to the definitions of almost all of the functions, classes, methods, and member variables used or referred to on each page.

Figure 1.15: This contemporary indoor scene was modeled and rendered by Florent Boyer (*www.florentboyer.com*). The image was rendered using *LuxRender*, a GPL-licensed physically-based rendering system originally based on pbrt's source code. Modeling and texturing were done using Blender.

⟨*Main program*⟩ ≡
```
int main(int argc, char *argv[]) {
    Options options;
    std::vector<std::string> filenames;
    ⟨Process command-line arguments⟩
    pbrtInit(options);
    ⟨Process scene description 21⟩
    pbrtCleanup();
    return 0;
}
```

If pbrt is run with no input filenames provided, then the scene description is read from standard input. Otherwise it loops through the provided filenames, processing each file in turn.

⟨*Process scene description*⟩ ≡   21
```
if (filenames.size() == 0) {
    ⟨Parse scene from standard input 22⟩
} else {
    ⟨Parse scene from input files 22⟩
}
```

The ParseFile() function parses a scene description file, either from standard input or from a file on disk; it returns false if it was unable to open the file. The mechanics of parsing scene description files will not be described in this book; the parser implementation can be found in the lex and yacc files core/pbrtlex.ll and core/pbrtparse.y,

Figure 1.16: Martin Lubich modeled this scene of the Austrian Imperial Crown and rendered it using *LuxRender*, an open source fork of the pbrt codebase. The scene was modeled in Blender and consists of approximately 1.8 million vertices. It is illuminated by six area light sources with emission spectra based on measured data from a real-world light source and was rendered with 1280 samples per pixel in 73 hours of computation on a quad-core CPU. See Martin's Web site, *www.loramel.net*, for more information, including downloadable Blender scene files.

respectively. Readers who want to understand the parsing subsystem but are not familiar with these tools may wish to consult Levine, Mason, and Brown (1992).

We use the common UNIX idiom that a file named "-" represents standard input:

⟨*Parse scene from standard input*⟩ ≡   21
```
ParseFile("-");
```

If a particular input file can't be opened, the Error() routine reports this information to the user. Error() uses the same format string semantics as printf().

⟨*Parse scene from input files*⟩ ≡   21
```
for (const std::string &f : filenames)
    if (!ParseFile(f))
        Error("Couldn't open scene file \"%s\"", f.c_str());
```

Error() 1068
ParseFile() 21
Scene 23

As the scene file is parsed, objects are created that represent the lights and geometric primitives in the scene. These are all stored in the Scene object, which is created by the

RenderOptions::MakeScene() method in Section B.3.7 in Appendix B. The Scene class is declared in core/scene.h and defined in core/scene.cpp.

⟨*Scene Declarations*⟩ ≡
```
class Scene {
public:
    ⟨Scene Public Methods 23⟩
    ⟨Scene Public Data 23⟩
private:
    ⟨Scene Private Data 23⟩
};
```

⟨*Scene Public Methods*⟩ ≡   **23**
```
Scene(std::shared_ptr<Primitive> aggregate,
    const std::vector<std::shared_ptr<Light>> &lights)
    : lights(lights), aggregate(aggregate) {
    ⟨Scene Constructor Implementation 24⟩
}
```

Each light source in the scene is represented by a Light object, which specifies the shape of a light and the distribution of energy that it emits. The Scene stores all of the lights using a vector of shared_ptr instances from the C++ standard library. pbrt uses shared pointers to track how many times objects are referenced by other instances. When the last instance holding a reference (the Scene in this case) is destroyed, the reference count reaches zero and the Light can be safely freed, which happens automatically at that point.

While some renderers support separate light lists per geometric object, allowing a light to illuminate only some of the objects in the scene, this idea does not map well to the physically based rendering approach taken in pbrt, so pbrt only supports a single global per-scene list. Many parts of the system need access to the lights, so the Scene makes them available as a public member variable.

⟨*Scene Public Data*⟩ ≡   **23**
```
std::vector<std::shared_ptr<Light>> lights;
```

Each geometric object in the scene is represented by a Primitive, which combines two objects: a Shape that specifies its geometry, and a Material that describes its appearance (e.g., the object's color, whether it has a dull or glossy finish). All of the geometric primitives are collected into a single aggregate Primitive in the Scene member variable Scene::aggregate. This aggregate is a special kind of primitive that itself holds references to many other primitives. Because it implements the Primitive interface it appears no different from a single primitive to the rest of the system. The aggregate implementation stores all the scene's primitives in an acceleration data structure that reduces the number of unnecessary ray intersection tests with primitives that are far away from a given ray.

⟨*Scene Private Data*⟩ ≡   **23**
```
std::shared_ptr<Primitive> aggregate;
```

The constructor caches the bounding box of the scene geometry in the worldBound member variable.

⟨*Scene Constructor Implementation*⟩ ≡   **23**
```
    worldBound = aggregate->WorldBound();
```

⟨*Scene Private Data*⟩ +≡   **23**
```
    Bounds3f worldBound;
```

The bound is made available via the WorldBound() method.

⟨*Scene Public Methods*⟩ +≡   **23**
```
    const Bounds3f &WorldBound() const { return worldBound; }
```

Some Light implementations find it useful to do some additional initialization after the scene has been defined but before rendering begins. The Scene constructor calls their Preprocess() methods to allow them to do so.

⟨*Scene Constructor Implementation*⟩ +≡   **23**
```
    for (const auto &light : lights)
        light->Preprocess(*this);
```

The Scene class provides two methods related to ray–primitive intersection. Its Intersect() method traces the given ray into the scene and returns a Boolean value indicating whether the ray intersected any of the primitives. If so, it fills in the provided SurfaceInteraction structure with information about the closest intersection point along the ray. The SurfaceInteraction structure is defined in Section 4.1.

⟨*Scene Method Definitions*⟩ ≡
```
    bool Scene::Intersect(const Ray &ray, SurfaceInteraction *isect) const {
        return aggregate->Intersect(ray, isect);
    }
```

A closely related method is Scene::IntersectP(), which checks for the existence of intersections along the ray but does not return any information about those intersections. Because this routine doesn't need to search for the closest intersection or compute any additional information about intersections, it is generally more efficient than Scene::Intersect(). This routine is used for shadow rays.

⟨*Scene Method Definitions*⟩ +≡
```
    bool Scene::IntersectP(const Ray &ray) const {
        return aggregate->IntersectP(ray);
    }
```

1.3.3 INTEGRATOR INTERFACE AND SamplerIntegrator

Rendering an image of the scene is handled by an instance of a class that implements the Integrator interface. Integrator is an abstract base class that defines the Render() method that must be provided by all integrators. In this section, we will define one Integrator implementation, the SamplerIntegrator. The basic integrator interfaces are defined in core/integrator.h, and some utility functions used by integrators are in core/integrator.cpp. The implementations of the various integrators are in the integrators directory.

⟨*Integrator Declarations*⟩ ≡
```
class Integrator {
public:
    ⟨Integrator Interface 25⟩
};
```

The method that Integrators must provide is Render(); it is passed a reference to the Scene to use to compute an image of the scene or more generally, a set of measurements of the scene lighting. This interface is intentionally kept very general to permit a wide range of implementations—for example, one could implement an Integrator that takes measurements only at a sparse set of positions distributed through the scene rather than generating a regular 2D image.

⟨*Integrator Interface*⟩ ≡   25
```
virtual void Render(const Scene &scene) = 0;
```

In this chapter, we'll focus on SamplerIntegrator, which is an Integrator subclass, and the WhittedIntegrator, which implements the SamplerIntegrator interface. (Implementations of other SamplerIntegrators will be introduced in Chapters 14 and 15; the integrators in Chapter 16 inherit directly from Integrator.) The name of the Sampler Integrator derives from the fact that its rendering process is driven by a stream of *sample*s from a Sampler; each such sample identifies a point on the image at which the integrator should compute the arriving light to form the image.

⟨*SamplerIntegrator Declarations*⟩ ≡
```
class SamplerIntegrator : public Integrator {
public:
    ⟨SamplerIntegrator Public Methods 26⟩
protected:
    ⟨SamplerIntegrator Protected Data 26⟩
private:
    ⟨SamplerIntegrator Private Data 25⟩
};
```

The SamplerIntegrator stores a pointer to a Sampler. The role of the sampler is subtle, but its implementation can substantially affect the quality of the images that the system generates. First, the sampler is responsible for choosing the points on the image plane from which rays are traced. Second, it is responsible for supplying the sample positions used by integrators for estimating the value of the light transport integral, Equation (1.1). For example, some integrators need to choose random points on light sources to compute illumination from area lights. Generating a good distribution of these samples is an important part of the rendering process that can substantially affect overall efficiency; this topic is the main focus of Chapter 7.

⟨*SamplerIntegrator Private Data*⟩ ≡   25
```
std::shared_ptr<Sampler> sampler;
```

The Camera object controls the viewing and lens parameters such as position, orientation, focus, and field of view. A Film member variable inside the Camera class handles image storage. The Camera classes are described in Chapter 6, and Film is described in

Section 7.9. The Film is responsible for writing the final image to a file and possibly displaying it on the screen as it is being computed.

⟨*SamplerIntegrator Protected Data*⟩ ≡   25
```
std::shared_ptr<const Camera> camera;
```

The SamplerIntegrator constructor stores pointers to these objects in member variables. The SamplerIntegrator is created in the RenderOptions::MakeIntegrator() method, which is in turn called by pbrtWorldEnd(), which is called by the input file parser when it is done parsing a scene description from an input file and is ready to render the scene.

⟨*SamplerIntegrator Public Methods*⟩ ≡   25
```
SamplerIntegrator(std::shared_ptr<const Camera> camera,
        std::shared_ptr<Sampler> sampler)
    : camera(camera), sampler(sampler) { }
```

SamplerIntegrator implementations may optionally implement the Preprocess() method. It is called after the Scene has been fully initialized and gives the integrator a chance to do scene-dependent computation, such as allocating additional data structures that are dependent on the number of lights in the scene, or precomputing a rough representation of the distribution of radiance in the scene. Implementations that don't need to do anything along these lines can leave this method unimplemented.

⟨*SamplerIntegrator Public Methods*⟩ +≡   25
```
virtual void Preprocess(const Scene &scene, Sampler &sampler) { }
```

1.3.4 THE MAIN RENDERING LOOP

After the Scene and the Integrator have been allocated and initialized, the Integrator:: Render() method is invoked, starting the second phase of pbrt's execution: the main rendering loop. In the SamplerIntegrator's implementation of this method, at each of a series of positions on the image plane, the method uses the Camera and the Sampler to generate a ray into the scene and then uses the Li() method to determine the amount of light arriving at the image plane along that ray. This value is passed to the Film, which records the light's contribution. Figure 1.17 summarizes the main classes used in this method and the flow of data among them.

⟨*SamplerIntegrator Method Definitions*⟩ ≡
```
void SamplerIntegrator::Render(const Scene &scene) {
    Preprocess(scene, *sampler);
    ⟨Render image tiles in parallel 27⟩
    ⟨Save final image after rendering 32⟩
}
```

So that rendering can proceed in parallel on systems with multiple processing cores, the image is decomposed into small tiles of pixels. Each tile can be processed independently and in parallel. The ParallelFor() function, which is described in more detail in Section A.6, implements a parallel for loop, where multiple iterations may run in parallel. A C++ lambda expression provides the loop body. Here, a variant of ParallelFor() that loops over a 2D domain is used to iterate over the image tiles.

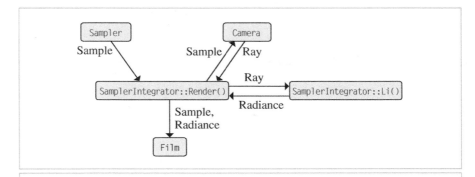

Figure 1.17: Class Relationships for the Main Rendering Loop in the SamplerIntegrator:: Render() Method in core/integrator.cpp. The Sampler provides a sequence of sample values, one for each image sample to be taken. The Camera turns a sample into a corresponding ray from the film plane, and the Li() method implementation computes the radiance along that ray arriving at the film. The sample and its radiance are given to the Film, which stores their contribution in an image. This process repeats until the Sampler has provided as many samples as are necessary to generate the final image.

⟨Render image tiles in parallel⟩ ≡   26
    ⟨Compute number of tiles, nTiles, to use for parallel rendering 28⟩
    ParallelFor2D(
        [&](Point2i tile) {
            ⟨Render section of image corresponding to tile 28⟩
        }, nTiles);

There are two factors to trade off in deciding how large to make the image tiles: load-balancing and per-tile overhead. On one hand, we'd like to have significantly more tiles than there are processors in the system: consider a four-core computer with only four tiles. In general, it's likely that some of the tiles will take less processing time than others; the ones that are responsible for parts of the image where the scene is relatively simple will usually take less processing time than parts of the image where the scene is relatively complex. Therefore, if the number of tiles was equal to the number of processors, some processors would finish before others and sit idle while waiting for the processor that had the longest running tile. Figure 1.18 illustrates this issue; it shows the distribution of execution time for the tiles used to render the shiny sphere scene in Figure 1.7. The longest running one took 151 times longer than the shortest one.

On the other hand, having tiles that are too small is also inefficient. There is a small fixed overhead for a processing core to determine which loop iteration it should run next; the more tiles there are, the more times this overhead must be paid.

For simplicity, pbrt always uses 16 × 16 tiles; this granularity works well for almost all images, except for very low-resolution ones. We implicitly assume that the small image case isn't particularly important to render at maximum efficiency. The Film's GetSampleBounds() method returns the extent of pixels over which samples must be generated for the image being rendered. The addition of tileSize - 1 in the computation of nTiles results in a number of tiles that is rounded to the next higher integer when the

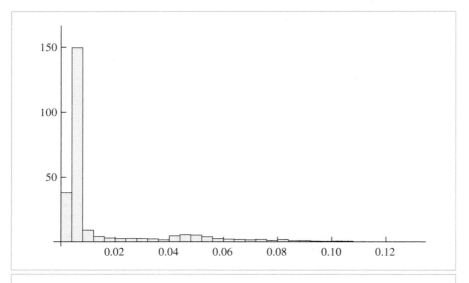

Figure 1.18: Histogram of Time Spent Rendering Each Tile for the Scene in Figure 1.7. The horizontal axis measures time in seconds. Note the wide variation in execution time, illustrating that different parts of the image required substantially different amounts of computation.

sample bounds along an axis are not exactly divisible by 16. This means that the lambda function invoked by ParallelFor() must be able to deal with partial tiles containing some unused pixels.

⟨*Compute number of tiles,* nTiles, *to use for parallel rendering*⟩ ≡   **27**
```
    Bounds2i sampleBounds = camera->film->GetSampleBounds();
    Vector2i sampleExtent = sampleBounds.Diagonal();
    const int tileSize = 16;
    Point2i nTiles((sampleExtent.x + tileSize - 1) / tileSize,
                   (sampleExtent.y + tileSize - 1) / tileSize);
```

When the parallel for loop implementation that is defined in Appendix A.6.4 decides to run a loop iteration on a particular processor, the lambda will be called with the tile's coordinates. It starts by doing a little bit of setup work, determining which part of the film plane it is responsible for and allocating space for some temporary data before using the Sampler to generate image samples, the Camera to determine corresponding rays leaving the film plane, and the Li() method to compute radiance along those rays arriving at the film.

⟨*Render section of image corresponding to* tile⟩ ≡   **27**
    ⟨*Allocate* MemoryArena *for tile* **29**⟩
    ⟨*Get sampler instance for tile* **29**⟩
    ⟨*Compute sample bounds for tile* **29**⟩
    ⟨*Get* FilmTile *for tile* **30**⟩
    ⟨*Loop over pixels in tile to render them* **30**⟩
    ⟨*Merge image tile into* Film **32**⟩

Implementations of the Li() method will generally need to temporarily allocate small amounts of memory for each radiance computation. The large number of resulting allocations can easily overwhelm the system's regular memory allocation routines (e.g., malloc() or new), which must maintain and synchronize elaborate internal data structures to track sets of free memory regions among processors. A naive implementation could potentially spend a fairly large fraction of its computation time in the memory allocator.

To address this issue, we will pass an instance of the MemoryArena class to the Li() method. MemoryArena instances manage pools of memory to enable higher performance allocation than what is possible with the standard library routines.

The arena's memory pool is always released in its entirety, which removes the need for complex internal data structures. Instances of this class can only be used by a single thread—concurrent access without additional synchronization is not permitted. We create a unique MemoryArena for each loop iteration that can be used directly, which also ensures that the arena is only accessed by a single thread.

⟨*Allocate* MemoryArena *for tile*⟩ ≡   28
    MemoryArena arena;

Most Sampler implementations find it useful to maintain some state, such as the coordinates of the current pixel being sampled. This means that multiple processing threads cannot use a single Sampler concurrently. Therefore, Samplers provide a Clone() method to create a new instance of a given Sampler; it takes a seed that is used by some implementations to seed a pseudo-random number generator so that the same sequence of pseudo-random numbers isn't generated in every tile. (Note that not all Samplers use pseudo-random numbers; those that don't just ignore the seed.)

⟨*Get sampler instance for tile*⟩ ≡   28
    int seed = tile.y * nTiles.x + tile.x;
    std::unique_ptr<Sampler> tileSampler = sampler->Clone(seed);

Next, the extent of pixels to be sampled in this loop iteration is computed based on the tile indices. Two issues must be accounted for in this computation: first, the overall pixel bounds to be sampled may not be equal to the full image resolution. For example, the user may have specified a "crop window" of just a subset of pixels to sample. Second, if the image resolution isn't an exact multiple of 16, then the tiles on the right and bottom images won't be a full 16 × 16.

⟨*Compute sample bounds for tile*⟩ ≡   28
    int x0 = sampleBounds.pMin.x + tile.x * tileSize;
    int x1 = std::min(x0 + tileSize, sampleBounds.pMax.x);
    int y0 = sampleBounds.pMin.y + tile.y * tileSize;
    int y1 = std::min(y0 + tileSize, sampleBounds.pMax.y);
    Bounds2i tileBounds(Point2i(x0, y0), Point2i(x1, y1));

Finally, a FilmTile is acquired from the Film. This class provides a small buffer of memory to store pixel values for the current tile. Its storage is private to the loop iteration, so pixel values can be updated without worrying about other threads concurrently modifying the same pixels. The tile is merged into the film's storage once the work for rendering it is done; serializing concurrent updates to the image is handled then.

⟨*Get* FilmTile *for tile*⟩ ≡   28
```
std::unique_ptr<FilmTile> filmTile =
    camera->film->GetFilmTile(tileBounds);
```

Rendering can now proceed. The implementation loops over all of the pixels in the tile using a range-based for loop that automatically uses iterators provided by the Bounds2 class. The cloned Sampler is notified that it should start generating samples for the current pixel, and samples are processed in turn until StartNextSample() returns false. (As we'll see in Chapter 7, taking multiple samples per pixel can greatly improve final image quality.)

⟨*Loop over pixels in tile to render them*⟩ ≡   28
```
for (Point2i pixel : tileBounds) {
    tileSampler->StartPixel(pixel);
    do {
        ⟨Initialize CameraSample for current sample  30⟩
        ⟨Generate camera ray for current sample  31⟩
        ⟨Evaluate radiance along camera ray  31⟩
        ⟨Add camera ray's contribution to image  32⟩
        ⟨Free MemoryArena memory from computing image sample value  32⟩
    } while (tileSampler->StartNextSample());
}
```

The CameraSample structure records the position on the film for which the camera should generate the corresponding ray. It also stores time and lens position sample values, which are used when rendering scenes with moving objects and for camera models that simulate non-pinhole apertures, respectively.

⟨*Initialize* CameraSample *for current sample*⟩ ≡   30
```
CameraSample cameraSample = tileSampler->GetCameraSample(pixel);
```

The Camera interface provides two methods to generate rays: Camera::GenerateRay(), which returns the ray for a given image sample position, and Camera::GenerateRay Differential(), which returns a *ray differential*, which incorporates information about the rays that the Camera would generate for samples that are one pixel away on the image plane in both the *x* and *y* directions. Ray differentials are used to get better results from some of the texture functions defined in Chapter 10, making it possible to compute how quickly a texture varies with respect to the pixel spacing, a key component of texture antialiasing.

After the ray differential has been returned, the ScaleDifferentials() method scales the differential rays to account for the actual spacing between samples on the film plane for the case where multiple samples are taken per pixel.

The camera also returns a floating-point weight associated with the ray. For simple camera models, each ray is weighted equally, but camera models that more accurately model the process of image formation by lens systems may generate some rays that contribute more than others. Such a camera model might simulate the effect of less light arriving at the edges of the film plane than at the center, an effect called *vignetting*. The returned weight will be used later to scale the ray's contribution to the image.

⟨*Generate camera ray for current sample*⟩ ≡   30
```
RayDifferential ray;
Float rayWeight = camera->GenerateRayDifferential(cameraSample, &ray);
ray.ScaleDifferentials(1 / std::sqrt(tileSampler->samplesPerPixel));
```

Note the capitalized floating-point type Float: depending on the compilation flags of pbrt, this is an alias for either float or double. More detail on this design choice is provided in Section A.1.

Given a ray, the next task is to determine the radiance arriving at the image plane along that ray. The Li() method takes care of this task.

⟨*Evaluate radiance along camera ray*⟩ ≡   30
```
Spectrum L(0.f);
if (rayWeight > 0)
    L = Li(ray, scene, *tileSampler, arena);
```
⟨*Issue warning if unexpected radiance value is returned*⟩

Li() is a pure virtual method that returns the incident radiance at the origin of a given ray; each subclass of SamplerIntegrator must provide an implementation of this method. The parameters to Li() are the following:

- ray: the ray along which the incident radiance should be evaluated.
- scene: the Scene being rendered. The implementation will query the scene for information about the lights and geometry, and so on.
- sampler: a sample generator used to solve the light transport equation via Monte Carlo integration.
- arena: a MemoryArena for efficient temporary memory allocation by the integrator. The integrator should assume that any memory it allocates with the arena will be freed shortly after the Li() method returns and thus should not use the arena to allocate any memory that must persist for longer than is needed for the current ray.
- depth: the number of ray bounces from the camera that have occurred up until the current call to Li().

The method returns a Spectrum that represents the incident radiance at the origin of the ray:

⟨*SamplerIntegrator Public Methods*⟩ +≡   25
```
virtual Spectrum Li(const RayDifferential &ray, const Scene &scene,
        Sampler &sampler, MemoryArena &arena, int depth = 0) const = 0;
```

A common side effect of bugs in the rendering process is that impossible radiance values are computed. For example, division by zero results in radiance values equal either to the IEEE floating-point infinity or "not a number" value. The renderer looks for this possibility, as well as for spectra with negative contributions, and prints an error message when it encounters them. Here we won't include the fragment that does this, ⟨*Issue warning if unexpected radiance value is returned*⟩. See the implementation in core/integrator.cpp if you're interested in its details.

After the radiance arriving at the ray's origin is known, the image can be updated: the FilmTile::AddSample() method updates the pixels in the tile's image given the results from a sample. The details of how sample values are recorded in the film are explained in Sections 7.8 and 7.9.

⟨*Add camera ray's contribution to image*⟩ ≡   30
```
filmTile->AddSample(cameraSample.pFilm, L, rayWeight);
```

After processing a sample, all of the allocated memory in the MemoryArena is freed together when MemoryArena::Reset() is called. (See Section 9.1.1 for an explanation of how the MemoryArena is used to allocate memory to represent BSDFs at intersection points.)

⟨*Free* MemoryArena *memory from computing image sample value*⟩ ≡   30
```
arena.Reset();
```

Once radiance values for all of the samples in a tile have been computed, the FilmTile is handed off to the Film's MergeFilmTile() method, which handles adding the tile's pixel contributions to the final image. Note that the std::move() function is used to transfer ownership of the unique_ptr to MergeFilmTile().

⟨*Merge image tile into* Film⟩ ≡   28
```
camera->film->MergeFilmTile(std::move(filmTile));
```

After all of the loop iterations have finished, the SamplerIntegrator's Render() method calls the Film's WriteImage() method to write the image out to a file.

⟨*Save final image after rendering*⟩ ≡   26
```
camera->film->WriteImage();
```

1.3.5 AN INTEGRATOR FOR WHITTED RAY TRACING

Chapters 14 and 15 include the implementations of many different integrators, based on a variety of algorithms with differing levels of accuracy. Here we will present an integrator based on Whitted's ray-tracing algorithm. This integrator accurately computes reflected and transmitted light from specular surfaces like glass, mirrors, and water, although it doesn't account for other types of indirect lighting effects like light bouncing off a wall and illuminating a room. The WhittedIntegrator class can be found in the integrators/whitted.h and integrators/whitted.cpp files in the pbrt distribution.

⟨*WhittedIntegrator Declarations*⟩ ≡
```
class WhittedIntegrator : public SamplerIntegrator {
public:
    ⟨WhittedIntegrator Public Methods 33⟩
private:
    ⟨WhittedIntegrator Private Data 33⟩
};
```

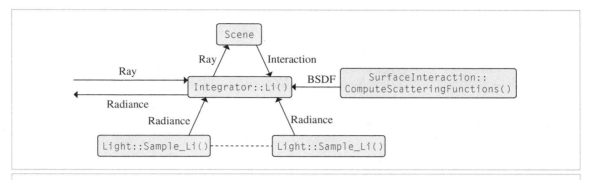

Figure 1.19: Class Relationships for Surface Integration. The main rendering loop in the `SamplerIntegrator` computes a camera ray and passes it to the `Li()` method, which returns the radiance along that ray arriving at the ray's origin. After finding the closest intersection, it computes the material properties at the intersection point, representing them in the form of a BSDF. It then uses the Lights in the Scene to determine the illumination there. Together, these give the information needed to compute the radiance reflected back along the ray at the intersection point.

⟨*WhittedIntegrator Public Methods*⟩ ≡   **32**
```
WhittedIntegrator(int maxDepth, std::shared_ptr<const Camera> camera,
        std::shared_ptr<Sampler> sampler)
    : SamplerIntegrator(camera, sampler), maxDepth(maxDepth) { }
```

The Whitted integrator works by recursively evaluating radiance along reflected and refracted ray directions. It stops the recursion at a predetermined maximum depth, `WhittedIntegrator::maxDepth`. By default, the maximum recursion depth is five. Without this termination criterion, the recursion might never terminate (imagine, e.g., a hall-of-mirrors scene). This member variable is initialized in the `WhittedIntegrator` constructor (not included here), based on parameters set in the scene description file.

⟨*WhittedIntegrator Private Data*⟩ ≡   **32**
```
const int maxDepth;
```

As a `SamplerIntegrator` implementation, the `WhittedIntegrator` must provide an implementation of the `Li()` method, which returns the radiance arriving at the origin of the given ray. Figure 1.19 summarizes the data flow among the main classes used during integration at surfaces.

⟨*WhittedIntegrator Method Definitions*⟩ ≡
```
Spectrum WhittedIntegrator::Li(const RayDifferential &ray,
        const Scene &scene, Sampler &sampler, MemoryArena &arena,
        int depth) const {
    Spectrum L(0.);
```
    ⟨*Find closest ray intersection or return background radiance* **34**⟩
    ⟨*Compute emitted and reflected light at ray intersection point* **34**⟩
```
    return L;
}
```

The first step is to find the first intersection of the ray with the shapes in the scene. The `Scene::Intersect()` method takes a ray and returns a Boolean value indicating whether it intersected a shape. For rays where an intersection was found, it initializes the provided SurfaceInteraction with geometric information about the intersection.

If no intersection was found, radiance may be carried along the ray due to light sources that don't have associated geometry. One example of such a light is the InfiniteArea Light, which can represent illumination from the sky. The Light::Le() method allows such lights to return their radiance along a given ray.

⟨*Find closest ray intersection or return background radiance*⟩ ≡   33
```
SurfaceInteraction isect;
if (!scene.Intersect(ray, &isect)) {
    for (const auto &light : scene.lights)
        L += light->Le(ray);
    return L;
}
```

Otherwise a valid intersection has been found. The integrator must determine how light is scattered by the surface of the shape at the intersection point, determine how much illumination is arriving from light sources at the point, and apply an approximation to Equation (1.1) to compute how much light is leaving the surface in the viewing direction. Because this integrator ignores the effect of participating media like smoke or fog, the radiance leaving the intersection point is the same as the radiance arriving at the ray's origin.

⟨*Compute emitted and reflected light at ray intersection point*⟩ ≡   33
```
⟨Initialize common variables for Whitted integrator 34⟩
⟨Compute scattering functions for surface interaction 35⟩
⟨Compute emitted light if ray hit an area light source 35⟩
⟨Add contribution of each light source 36⟩
if (depth + 1 < maxDepth) {
    ⟨Trace rays for specular reflection and refraction 37⟩
}
```

Figure 1.20 shows a few quantities that will be used frequently in the fragments to come. n is the surface normal at the intersection point and the normalized direction from the hit point back to the ray origin is stored in wo; Cameras are responsible for normalizing the direction component of generated rays, so there's no need to renormalize it here. Normalized directions are denoted by the ω symbol in this book, and in pbrt's code we will use wo to represent ω_o, the outgoing direction of scattered light.

⟨*Initialize common variables for Whitted integrator*⟩ ≡   34
```
Normal3f n = isect.shading.n;
Vector3f wo = isect.wo;
```

If an intersection was found, it's necessary to determine how the surface's material scatters light. The ComputeScatteringFunctions() method handles this task, evaluating texture functions to determine surface properties and then initializing a representation of the BSDF (and possibly BSSRDF) at the point. This method generally needs to allocate memory for the objects that constitute this representation; because this memory only

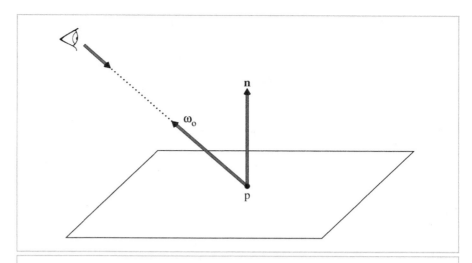

Figure 1.20: Geometric Setting for the Whitted Integrator. p is the ray intersection point and **n** is its surface normal. The direction in which we'd like to compute reflected radiance is ω_o; it is the vector pointing in the opposite direction of the incident ray.

needs to be available for the current ray, the MemoryArena is provided for it to use for its allocations.

⟨*Compute scattering functions for surface interaction*⟩ ≡   **34**
    isect.ComputeScatteringFunctions(ray, arena);

In case the ray happened to hit geometry that is emissive (such as an area light source), the integrator accounts for any emitted radiance by calling the SurfaceInteraction::Le() method. This gives the first term of the light transport equation, Equation (1.1) on page 12. If the object is not emissive, this method returns a black spectrum.

⟨*Compute emitted light if ray hit an area light source*⟩ ≡   **34**
    L += isect.Le(wo);

For each light, the integrator calls the Light::Sample_Li() method to compute the radiance from that light falling on the surface at the point being shaded. This method also returns the direction vector from the point being shaded to the light source, which is stored in the variable wi (denoting an incident direction ω_i).[4]

The spectrum returned by this method does not account for the possibility that some other shape may block light from the light and prevent it from reaching the point being shaded. Instead, it returns a VisibilityTester object that can be used to determine if any primitives block the surface point from the light source. This test is done by tracing a shadow ray between the point being shaded and the light to verify that the path is

---

4   When considering light scattering at a surface location, pbrt uses the convention that ω_i always refers to the direction from which the quantity of interest (radiance in this case) arrives, rather than the direction from which the Integrator reached the surface.

clear. pbrt's code is organized in this way so that it can avoid tracing the shadow ray unless necessary: this way it can first make sure that the light falling on the surface *would* be scattered in the direction ω_o if the light isn't blocked. For example, if the surface is not transmissive, then light arriving at the back side of the surface doesn't contribute to reflection.

The Sample_Li() method also returns the probability density for the light to have sampled the direction wi in the pdf variable. This value is used for Monte Carlo integration with complex area light sources where light is arriving at the point from many directions even though just one direction is sampled here; for simple lights like point lights, the value of pdf is one. The details of how this probability density is computed and used in rendering are the topics of Chapters 13 and 14; in the end, the light's contribution must be divided by pdf, so this is done by the implementation here.

If the arriving radiance is nonzero and the BSDF indicates that some of the incident light from the direction ω_i is in fact scattered to the outgoing direction ω_o, then the integrator multiplies the radiance value L_i by the value of the BSDF f and the cosine term. The cosine term is computed using the AbsDot() function, which returns the absolute value of the dot product between two vectors. If the vectors are normalized, as both wi and n are here, this is equal to the absolute value of the cosine of the angle between them (Section 2.2.1).

This product represents the light's contribution to the light transport equation integral, Equation (1.1), and it is added to the total reflected radiance L. After all lights have been considered, the integrator has computed the total contribution of *direct lighting*—light that arrives at the surface directly from emissive objects (as opposed to light that has reflected off other objects in the scene before arriving at the point).

⟨*Add contribution of each light source*⟩ ≡   34
```
for (const auto &light : scene.lights) {
    Vector3f wi;
    Float pdf;
    VisibilityTester visibility;
    Spectrum Li = light->Sample_Li(isect, sampler.Get2D(), &wi,
                                   &pdf, &visibility);
    if (Li.IsBlack() || pdf == 0) continue;
    Spectrum f = isect.bsdf->f(wo, wi);
    if (!f.IsBlack() && visibility.Unoccluded(scene))
        L += f * Li * AbsDot(wi, n) / pdf;
}
```

This integrator also handles light scattered by perfectly specular surfaces like mirrors or glass. It is fairly simple to use properties of mirrors to find the reflected directions (Figure 1.21) and to use Snell's law to find the transmitted directions (Section 8.2). The integrator can then recursively follow the appropriate ray in the new direction and add its contribution to the reflected radiance at the point originally seen from the camera. The computation of the effect of specular reflection and transmission is handled in separate utility methods so these functions can easily be reused by other SamplerIntegrator implementations.

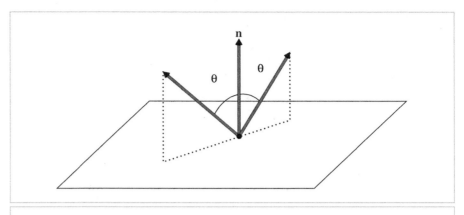

Figure 1.21: Reflected rays due to perfect specular reflection make the same angle with the surface normal as the incident ray.

⟨*Trace rays for specular reflection and refraction*⟩ ≡   34
```
L += SpecularReflect(ray, isect, scene, sampler, arena, depth);
L += SpecularTransmit(ray, isect, scene, sampler, arena, depth);
```

⟨*SamplerIntegrator Method Definitions*⟩ +≡
```
Spectrum SamplerIntegrator::SpecularReflect(const RayDifferential &ray,
        const SurfaceInteraction &isect, const Scene &scene,
        Sampler &sampler, MemoryArena &arena, int depth) const {
    ⟨Compute specular reflection direction wi and BSDF value 38⟩
    ⟨Return contribution of specular reflection 38⟩
}
```

In the `SpecularReflect()` and `SpecularTransmit()` methods, the `BSDF::Sample_f()` method returns an incident ray direction for a given outgoing direction and a given mode of light scattering. This method is one of the foundations of the Monte Carlo light transport algorithms that will be the subject of the last few chapters of this book. Here, we will use it to find only outgoing directions corresponding to perfect specular reflection or refraction, using flags to indicate to `BSDF::Sample_f()` that other types of reflection should be ignored. Although `BSDF::Sample_f()` can sample random directions leaving the surface for probabilistic integration algorithms, the randomness is constrained to be consistent with the BSDF's scattering properties. In the case of perfect specular reflection or refraction, only one direction is possible, so there is no randomness at all.

The calls to `BSDF::Sample_f()` in these functions initialize wi with the chosen direction and return the BSDF's value for the directions (ω_o, ω_i). If the value of the BSDF is nonzero, the integrator uses the `SamplerIntegrator::Li()` method to get the incoming radiance along ω_i, which in this case will in turn resolve to the `WhittedIntegrator::Li()` method.

⟨*Compute specular reflection direction* wi *and BSDF value*⟩ ≡   37
```
Vector3f wo = isect.wo, wi;
Float pdf;
BxDFType type = BxDFType(BSDF_REFLECTION | BSDF_SPECULAR);
Spectrum f = isect.bsdf->Sample_f(wo, &wi, sampler.Get2D(), &pdf, type);
```

In order to use ray differentials to antialias textures that are seen in reflections or refractions, it is necessary to know how reflection and transmission affect the screen-space footprint of rays. The fragments that compute the ray differentials for these rays are defined later, in Section 10.1.3. Given the fully initialized ray differential, a recursive call to Li() provides incident radiance, which is scaled by the value of the BSDF, the cosine term, and divided by the PDF, as per Equation (1.1).

⟨*Return contribution of specular reflection*⟩ ≡   37
```
const Normal3f &ns = isect.shading.n;
if (pdf > 0 && !f.IsBlack() && AbsDot(wi, ns) != 0) {
    ⟨Compute ray differential rd for specular reflection 607⟩
    return f * Li(rd, scene, sampler, arena, depth + 1) * AbsDot(wi, ns) /
        pdf;
}
else
    return Spectrum(0.f);
```

The SpecularTransmit() method is essentially the same as SpecularReflect() but just requests the BSDF_TRANSMISSION specular component of the BSDF, if any, rather than the BSDF_REFLECTION component used by SpecularReflect(). We therefore won't include its implementation in the text of the book here.

1.4 PARALLELIZATION OF pbrt

It's now nearly impossible to buy a new laptop or desktop computer with only one processing core. (The same even holds for mobile phones, for that matter.) The computer systems of today and of the future will increasingly feature multiple processing cores, both on CPUs and on highly parallel throughput processors like GPUs. At the same time, the computational capabilities of their cores are only improving slowly; as such, significant increases in performance over time are now only available to programs that can run in parallel, with many separate threads of execution performing computation simultaneously on multiple cores.

Writing a parallel program is more difficult than writing a serial program. When two computations that the programmer believes are independent are executing simultaneously but then interact unexpectedly, the program may crash or generate unexpected results. However, such a bug may not manifest itself again if the program is run again, perhaps due to those particular computations not running simultaneously during the next run. Fortunately, increasingly good tools to help developers find these sorts of interactions are increasingly available.[5]

For a parallel program to scale well to many processors, it needs to be able to provide a substantial amount of independent computation: any computation dependent on results of prior computation can't be run concurrently with the computation it depends on. Fortunately, most rendering algorithms based on ray tracing have abundant parallelism; for the SamplerIntegrator, each image sample is independent of all of the other ones, and many millions of samples may be used for high-quality images.

One of the biggest challenges with parallel ray tracing is the impact of non-parallel phases of computation. For example, it's not as easy to effectively parallelize the construction of many acceleration structures while the scene is being constructed than it is to parallelize rendering. While this may seem like a minor issue, *Amdahl's law*, which describes the speedup of a workload that has both serial and parallel phases, points to the challenge. Given n cores performing computation and a workload where the fraction s of its overall computation is inherently serial, then the maximum speedup possible is

$$\frac{1}{s + \frac{1}{n}(1 - s)}.$$

Thus, even with an infinite number of cores, the maximum speedup is $1/s$. If, for example, a seemingly innocuous 5% of the run time is spent in a serial phase of parsing the scene file and building acceleration structures, the maximum speedup possible is $1/0.05 = 20\times$, no matter how quickly the parallel phase executes.

1.4.1 DATA RACES AND COORDINATION

In pbrt, we assume that the computation is running on processors that provide *coherent shared memory*. The main idea of coherent shared memory is that all threads can read and write to a common set of memory locations and that changes to memory made by one thread will eventually be seen by other threads. These properties greatly simplify the implementation of the system as there's no need to explicitly communicate data between cores. (Coherent shared memory is generally available on today's CPUs and is likely to continue to be on future CPUs. On the other hand, if one is running a computation across multiple computers in a cluster, coherent shared memory is generally not available.)

Although coherent shared memory relieves the need for separate threads to explicitly communicate data with each other, they still need to *coordinate* their access to shared data; a danger of coherent shared memory is *data races*. If two threads modify the same memory location without coordination between the two of them, the program will almost certainly compute incorrect results or even crash. Consider the example of two processors simultaneously running the following innocuous-looking code, where globalCounter starts with a value of two:

---

5   We found the open-source tool helgrind, part of the valgrind suite of tools, instrumental for helping to find bugs in pbrt's parallel code as we were developing it. "Thread sanitizer" is also well regarded.

```
extern int globalCounter;
if (--globalCounter == 0)
    printf("done!\n");
```

Because the two threads don't coordinate their reading and writing of globalCounter, it is possible that "done" will be printed zero, one, or even two times! The assembly instructions generated by the compiler are likely to correspond to steps something like the following:

```
extern int globalCounter;
int temp = globalCounter;
temp = temp - 1;
globalCounter = temp;
if (globalCounter == 0)
    printf("done!\n");
```

Now, consider different ways this code could be executed on two processors. For example, the second processor could start executing slightly after the first one, but the first one could go idle for a few cycles after executing the first few instructions:

```
Thread A                          Thread B
int temp = globalCounter;
temp = temp - 1;                  (idle)
globalCounter = temp;

                                  int temp = globalCounter;
// (idle)                         temp = temp - 1;
                                  globalCounter = temp;
if (globalCounter == 0)           if (globalCounter == 0)
    printf("done!\n");                printf("done!\n");
```

(Many unpredictable events can cause these sorts of execution bubbles, ranging from the OS interrupting the thread to cache misses.) In this ordering, both threads read the value of zero from globalCounter, and both execute the printf() call. In this case, the error is not fatal, but if instead the system was freeing resources in the if block, then it would attempt to free the same resources twice, which would very likely cause a crash. Consider now this potential execution order:

```
Thread A                          Thread B
int temp = globalCounter;         int temp = globalCounter;
temp = temp - 1;                  temp = temp - 1;
globalCounter = temp;             // (idle)
// (idle)                         globalCounter = temp;
if (globalCounter == 0)           if (globalCounter == 0)
    printf("done!\n");                printf("done!\n");
```

In this case, globalCounter ends up with a value of one, and neither thread executes the if block. These examples illustrate the principle that when multiple threads of execution are accessing shared modified data, they must somehow synchronize their access.

Two main mechanisms are available today for doing this type of synchronization: mutual exclusion and atomic operations. Mutual exclusion is implemented with std::mutex objects in pbrt. A std::mutex can be used to protect access to some resource, ensuring that only one thread can access it at a time. Consider the following updated version of the previous computation; here a std::lock_guard object acquires a lock on the mutex and releases it when it goes out of scope at the final brace.

```
extern int globalCounter;
extern std::mutex globalCounterMutex;
{ std::lock_guard<std::mutex> lock(globalCounterMutex);
  int temp = globalCounter;
  temp = temp - 1;
  globalCounter = temp;
  if (globalCounter == 0)
      printf("done!\n");
}
```

If two threads are executing this code and try to acquire the mutex at the same time, then the mutex will allow only one of them to proceed, stalling the other one in the std::lock_guard constructor. Only when the first thread has finished the computation and its std::lock_guard goes out of scope, releasing the lock on the mutex, is the second thread able to acquire the mutex itself and continue the computation.

```
Thread A                                Thread B
{ std::lock_guard<std::mutex> lock(     { std::lock_guard<std::mutex> lock(
      globalCounterMutex);                    globalCounterMutex);
  int temp = globalCounter;             // (stalled by mutex)
  .
  .
  .
} // (mutex released)
                                        // (mutex acquired)
                                        int temp = globalCounter;
                                        .
                                        .
                                        .
                                        } // (mutex released)
```

With correct mutual exclusion here, the printf() will only be executed once, no matter what the ordering of execution between the two threads is.

Atomic memory operations (or *atomics*) are the other option for correctly performing this type of memory update with multiple threads. Atomics are machine instructions that guarantee that their respective memory updates will be performed in a single transaction. (*Atomic* in this case refers to the notion that the memory updates are indivisible.) The implementations of atomic operations in pbrt are from the C++11 standard library and are further discussed in Appendix A.6.2. Using atomics, the computation above could be written to use the std::atomic<int> type, which has overloaded add, subtract, increment, and decrement operations, as below:

```
extern std::atomic<int> globalCounter;
if (--globalCounter == 0)
    printf("done!\n");
```

The std::atomic -- operator subtracts 1 from the given variable, globalCounter, and returns the previous value of the variable. Using an atomic operation ensures that if two threads simultaneously try to update the variable then not only will the final value of the variable be the expected value but each thread will be returned the value of the variable after its update alone. In this example, then, globalCounter will end up with a value of zero, as expected, with one thread guaranteed to have the value one returned from the atomic subtraction and the other thread guaranteed to have zero returned.

An additional option, *transactional memory*, is just starting to become available in CPUs as of this writing. With transactional memory, a set of memory writes are bundled as a transaction; if no other threads access those memory locations while the transaction is executing, then all of the writes are committed in a single atomic operation. Otherwise, it is rolled back and none of the writes reach memory, and thus the computation has had no effect; the transaction must then be tried again. Transactional memory helps bridge the fine-grained operation of atomics and the higher overhead of mutexes. However, because it isn't yet widely available, transactional memory isn't currently used in pbrt.

Section A.6 in Appendix A has more information about parallel programming, with additional details on performance issues and pitfalls, as well as the various routines used in the parallel implementation of pbrt.

1.4.2 CONVENTIONS IN pbrt

In pbrt (as is the case for most ray tracers) the vast majority of data at render time is read only (e.g., the scene description and texture maps). Almost all of the parsing of the scene file and creation of the scene representation in memory is done with a single thread of execution, so there are no synchronization issues during that phase of execution.[6] During rendering, concurrent read access to all of the read-only data by multiple threads works with no problems; we only need to be concerned with situations where data in memory is being modified.

When adding new code to pbrt, it's important to make sure to not inadvertently add code that modifies shared data without proper synchronization. This is usually straight-forward; for example, when adding a new Shape implementation, the Shape will normally only perform read accesses to its member variables after it has been created. Some-times, however, shared data may be inadvertently introduced. Consider the following code idiom, often seen in single-threaded code:

```
static bool firstCall = true;
if (firstCall) {
    .
    .   additional initialization
    .
    firstCall = false;
}
```

BVHAccel 256

Shape 123

---

6   The two exceptions are some image resampling performed on image texture maps, and construction of one variant of the
     BVHAccel, though both of these are highly localized.

This code is unsafe with multiple threads of execution, as multiple threads may see the value of firstCall as true and all execute the initialization code. Writing this safely requires either atomic operations or mutexes. (This particular idiom can also be implemented safely using the std::call_once() function.)

1.4.3 THREAD SAFETY EXPECTATIONS IN pbrt

Many class methods in pbrt are required to be safe for multiple concurrent threads of execution. Particular instances of these methods must either be safe naturally due to not updating shared global data or due to using mutexes or atomic operations to safely perform any updates that are needed.

As a general rule, the low-level classes and structures in the system are not thread-safe. For example, the Point3f class, which stores three float values to represent a point in 3D space, is not safe for multiple threads to call methods that modify it at the same time. (Multiple threads can use Point3fs as read-only data simultaneously, of course.) The run-time overhead to make Point3f thread-safe would have a substantial effect on performance with little benefit in return.

The same is true for classes like Vector3f, Normal3f, Spectrum, Transform, Quaternion, and SurfaceInteraction. These classes are usually either created at scene construction time and then used as read-only data or allocated on the stack during rendering and used only by a single thread.

The utility classes MemoryArena (used for high-performance temporary memory allocation) and RNG (pseudo-random number generation) are also not safe for use by multiple threads; these classes store state that is modified when their methods are called, and the overhead from protecting modification to their state with mutual exclusion would be excessive relative to the amount of computation they perform. Consequently, in code like the SamplerIntegrator::Render() method above, the implementation allocates per-thread instances of these classes on the stack.

With two exceptions, implementations of the higher level abstract base classes listed in Table 1.1 are all expected to be safe for multiple threads to use simultaneously. With a little care, it is usually straightforward to implement specific instances of these base classes so they don't modify any shared state in their methods.

The first exceptions are the SamplerIntegrator and Light Preprocess() methods. These are called by the system during scene construction, and implementations of them generally modify shared state in their implementations—for example, by building data structures that represent the distribution of illumination in the scene. Therefore, it's helpful to allow the implementer to assume that only a single thread will call into these methods. (This is a separate issue from the consideration that implementations of these methods that are computationally intensive may use ParallelFor() to parallelize their computation.)

The second exception is the Sampler; its methods are also not expected to be thread safe. This is another instance where this requirement would impose an excessive performance and scalability impact; many threads simultaneously trying to get samples from a single

Sampler would limit the system's overall performance. Therefore, as described in Section 1.3.4, a unique Sampler is created for each image tile using Sampler::Clone(); this sampler can then be used for just the one tile, without any mutual exclusion overhead.

All stand-alone functions in pbrt are thread-safe (as long as multiple threads don't pass pointers to the same data to them).

1.5 HOW TO PROCEED THROUGH THIS BOOK

We wrote this book assuming it will be read in roughly front-to-back order. Generally, we tried to minimize the number of forward references to ideas and interfaces that haven't yet been introduced, but we do assume that the reader is acquainted with the previous content at any particular point in the text. However, some sections go into depth about advanced topics that some readers may wish to skip over (particularly on first reading); each advanced section is identified by an asterisk in its title.

Because of the modular nature of the system, the main requirement is that the reader be familiar with the low-level classes like Point3f, Ray, and Spectrum; the interfaces defined by the abstract base classes listed in Table 1.1; and the rendering loop in Sampler Integrator::Render(). Given that knowledge, for example, the reader who doesn't care about precisely how a camera model based on a perspective projection matrix maps CameraSamples to rays can skip over the implementation of that camera and can just remember that the Camera::GenerateRayDifferential() method somehow turns a CameraSample into a RayDifferential.

The rest of this book is divided into four main parts of a few chapters each. First, Chapters 2 through 4 define the main geometric functionality in the system. Chapter 2 has the low-level classes like Point3f, Ray, and Bounds3f. Chapter 3 defines the Shape interface, gives implementations of a number of shapes, and shows how to perform ray-shape intersection tests. Chapter 4 has the implementations of the acceleration structures for speeding up ray tracing by skipping tests with primitives that a ray can be shown to definitely not intersect.

The second part covers the image formation process. First, Chapter 5 introduces the physical units used to measure light and the Spectrum class that represents wavelength-varying distributions (i.e., color). Chapter 6 defines the Camera interface and has a few different camera implementations. The Sampler classes that place samples on the image plane are the topic of Chapter 7, and the overall process of turning radiance values on the film into images suitable for display is explained in Section 7.9.

The third part of the book is about light and how it scatters from surfaces and participating media. Chapter 8 includes a set of building-block classes that define a variety of types of reflection from surfaces. Materials, described in Chapter 9, use these reflection functions to implement a number of different surface materials, such as plastic, glass, and metal. Chapter 10 introduces texture, which describes variation in material properties (color, roughness, etc.) over surfaces, and Chapter 11 has the abstractions that describe how light is scattered and absorbed in participating media. Finally, Chapter 12 has the interface for light sources and a number of light source implementations.

The last part brings all of the ideas from the rest of the book together to implement a number of interesting light transport algorithms. Chapter 13 introduces the theory of Monte Carlo integration, a statistical technique for estimating the value of complex integrals, and describes low-level routines for applying Monte Carlo to illumination and light scattering. The integrators in Chapters 14, 15, and 16 use Monte Carlo integration to compute more accurate approximations of the light transport equation than the WhittedIntegrator, using techniques like path tracing, bidirectional path tracing, Metropolis light transport, and photon mapping.

Chapter 17, the last chapter of the book, provides a brief retrospective and discussion of system design decisions along with a number of suggestions for more far-reaching projects than those in the exercises. Appendices describe utility functions and details of how the scene description is created as the input file is parsed.

1.5.1 THE EXERCISES

At the end of each chapter you will find exercises related to the material covered in that chapter. Each exercise is marked as one of three levels of difficulty:

- ➊ An exercise that should take only an hour or two
- ➋ A reading and/or implementation task that would be suitable for a course assignment and should take between 10 and 20 hours of work
- ➌ A suggested final project for a course that will likely take 40 hours or more to complete

1.6 USING AND UNDERSTANDING THE CODE

We wrote pbrt in C++ but focused on readability for non-C++ experts by limiting usage of esoteric features of the language. Staying close to the core language features also helps with the system's portability. In particular, we avoid multiple inheritance, run-time exception handling, and excessive use of C++11 and C++14 features. We also use only a small subset of C++'s extensive standard library.

We will occasionally omit short sections of pbrt's source code from the book. For example, when there are a number of cases to be handled, all with nearly identical code, we will present one case and note that the code for the remaining cases has been omitted from the text. Of course, all the omitted code can be found in the pbrt source code distribution.

1.6.1 POINTER OR REFERENCE?

C++ provides two different mechanisms for passing the address of a data structure to a function or method: pointers and references. If a function argument is not intended as an output variable, either can be used to save the expense of passing the entire structure on the stack. By convention, pbrt uses pointers when the argument will be completely changed by the function or method, references when some of its internal state will be changed but it won't be fully re-initialized, and const references when it won't be changed at all. One important exception to this rule is that we will always use a pointer when we

WhittedIntegrator 32

want to be able to pass `nullptr` to indicate that a parameter is not available or should not be used.

1.6.2 ABSTRACTION VERSUS EFFICIENCY

One of the primary tensions when designing interfaces for software systems is making a reasonable trade-off between abstraction and efficiency. For example, many programmers religiously make all data in all classes `private` and provide methods to obtain or modify the values of the data items. For simple classes (e.g., `Vector3f`), we believe that approach needlessly hides a basic property of the implementation—that the class holds three floating-point coordinates—that we can reasonably expect to never change. Of course, using no information hiding and exposing all details of all classes' internals leads to a code maintenance nightmare. Yet, we believe that there is nothing wrong with judiciously exposing basic design decisions throughout the system. For example, the fact that a `Ray` is represented with a point, a vector, and values that give its extent, time, and recursion depth is a decision that doesn't need to be hidden behind a layer of abstraction. Code elsewhere is shorter and easier to understand when details like these are exposed.

An important thing to keep in mind when writing a software system and making these sorts of trade-offs is the expected final size of the system. The core of pbrt (excluding the implementations of specific shapes, lights, and so forth), where all of the basic interfaces, abstractions, and policy decisions are defined, is under 20,000 lines of code. Adding additional functionality to the system will generally only increase the amount of code in the implementations of the various abstract base classes. pbrt is never going to grow to be a million lines of code; this fact can and should be reflected in the amount of information hiding used in the system. It would be a waste of programmer time (and likely a source of run-time inefficiency) to design the interfaces to accommodate a system of that level of complexity.

1.6.3 CODE OPTIMIZATION

We tried to make pbrt efficient through the use of well-chosen algorithms rather than through local micro-optimizations, so that the system can be more easily understood. However, we applied some local optimizations to the parts of pbrt that account for the most execution time, as long as doing so didn't make the code too hard to understand. There are two main local optimization principles used throughout the code:

- On current CPU architectures, the slowest mathematical operations are divides, square roots, and trigonometric functions. Addition, subtraction, and multiplication are generally 10 to 50 times faster than those operations. Reducing the number of slow mathematical operations can help performance substantially; for example, instead of repeatedly dividing by some value v, we will often precompute the reciprocal $1/v$ and multiply by that instead.
- The speed of CPUs continues to grow more quickly than the speed at which data can be loaded from main memory into the CPU. This means that waiting for values to be fetched from memory can be a major performance limitation. Organizing algorithms and data structures in ways that give good performance from memory caches can speed up program execution much more than reducing the total number of instructions executed. Section A.4 in Appendix A discusses general principles

Ray 73
Vector3f 60

for memory-efficient programming; these ideas are mostly applied in the ray intersection acceleration structures of Chapter 4 and the image map representation in Section 10.4.3, although they influence many of the design decisions throughout the system.

1.6.4 THE BOOK WEB SITE

We created a companion Web site for this book, located at *pbrt.org*. The Web site includes the system's source code, documentation, images rendered with pbrt, example scenes, errata, and links to a bug reporting system. We encourage you to visit the Web site and subscribe to the pbrt mailing list.

1.6.5 EXTENDING THE SYSTEM

One of our goals in writing this book and building the pbrt system was to make it easier for developers and researchers to experiment with new (or old!) ideas in rendering. One of the great joys in computer graphics is writing new software that makes a new image; even small changes to the system can be fun to experiment with. The exercises throughout the book suggest many changes to make to the system, ranging from small tweaks to major open-ended research projects. Section B.4 in Appendix B has more information about the mechanics of adding new implementations of the abstract base classes listed in Table 1.1.

1.6.6 BUGS

Although we made every effort to make pbrt as correct as possible through extensive testing, it is inevitable that some bugs are still present.

If you believe you have found a bug in the system, please do the following:

1. Reproduce the bug with an unmodified copy of the latest version of pbrt.
2. Check the online discussion forum and the bug-tracking system at *pbrt.org*. Your issue may be a known bug, or it may be a commonly misunderstood feature.
3. Try to find the simplest possible test case that demonstrates the bug. Many bugs can be demonstrated by scene description files that are just a few lines long, and debugging is much easier with a simple scene than a complex one.
4. Submit a detailed bug report using our online bug-tracking system. Make sure that you include the scene file that demonstrates the bug and a detailed description of why you think pbrt is not behaving correctly with the scene. If you can provide a patch to the code that fixes the bug, all the better!

We will periodically release updated versions of pbrt with bug fixes and minor enhancements. (Be aware that we often let bug reports accumulate for a few months before going through them; don't take this as an indication that we don't value them!) However, we will not make major changes to the pbrt source code so that it doesn't diverge from the system described here in the book.

1.7 A BRIEF HISTORY OF PHYSICALLY BASED RENDERING

Through the early years of computer graphics in the 1970s, the most important problems to solve were fundamental issues like visibility algorithms and geometric representations. When a megabyte of RAM was a rare and expensive luxury and when a computer capable of a million floating-point operations per second cost hundreds of thousands of dollars, the complexity of what was possible in computer graphics was correspondingly limited, and any attempt to accurately simulate physics for rendering was infeasible.

As computers have become more capable and less expensive, it became possible to consider more computationally demanding approaches to rendering, which in turn has made physically based approaches viable. This progression is neatly explained by *Blinn's law*: "as technology advances, rendering time remains constant."

Jim Blinn's simple statement captures an important constraint: given a certain number of images that must be rendered (be it a handful for a research paper or over a hundred thousand for a feature film), it's only possible to take so much processing time for each one. One has a certain amount of computation available and one has some amount of time available before rendering must be finished, so the maximum computation per image is necessarily limited.

Blinn's law also expresses the observation that there remains a gap between the images people would like to be able to render and the images that they can render: as computers have become faster, content creators have continued to be use increased computational capability to render more complex scenes with more sophisticated rendering algorithms, rather than rendering the same scenes as before, just more quickly. Rendering continues to consume all of the computational capabilities made available to it.

1.7.1 RESEARCH

Physically based approaches to rendering started to be seriously considered by graphics researchers in the 1980s. Whitted's paper (1980) introduced the idea of using ray tracing for global lighting effects, opening the door to accurately simulating the distribution of light in scenes. The rendered images his approach produced were markedly different from any that had been seen before, which spurred excitement about this approach.

Another notable early advancement in physically based rendering was Cook and Torrance's reflection model (1981, 1982), which introduced microfacet reflection models to graphics. Among other contributions, they showed that accurately modeling microfacet reflection made it possible to render metal surfaces accurately; metal was not well rendered by earlier approaches.

Shortly afterward, Goral et al. (1984) made connections between the thermal transfer literature and rendering, showing how to incorporate global diffuse lighting effects using a physically based approximation of light transport. This method was based on finite-element methods, where areas of surfaces in the scene exchanged energy with each other. This approach came to be referred to as "radiosity," after a related physical unit. Following work by Cohen and Greenberg (1985) and Nishita and Nakamae (1985) introduced important improvements. Once again, a physically based approach led to images with lighting effects that hadn't previously been seen in rendered images, which led to many researchers pursuing improvements in this area.

While the radiosity approach was strongly based on physical units and conservation of energy, in time it became clear that it didn't lead to viable rendering algorithms: the asymptotic computational complexity was a difficult-to-manage $O(n^2)$, and it was necessary to be able to re-tessellate geometric models along shadow boundaries for good results; researchers had difficulty developing robust and efficient tessellation algorithms for this purpose and radiosity's adoption in practice was limited.

During the radiosity years, a small group of researchers pursued physically based approaches to rendering that were based on ray tracing and Monte Carlo integration. At the time, many looked at their work with skepticism; objectionable noise in images due to variance from Monte Carlo integration seemed unavoidable, while radiosity-based methods quickly gave visually pleasing results, at least on relatively simple scenes.

In 1984, Cook, Porter, and Carpenter introduced distributed ray tracing, which generalized Whitted's algorithm to compute motion blur and defocus blur from cameras, blurry reflection from glossy surfaces, and illumination from area light sources (Cook et al. 1984), showing that ray tracing was capable of generating a host of important lighting effects.

Shortly afterward, Kajiya (1986) introduced path tracing; he set out a rigorous formulation of the rendering problem (the light transport integral equation) and showed how to apply Monte Carlo integration to solve it. This work required immense amounts of computation: to render a 256×256 pixel image of two spheres with path tracing required 7 hours of computation on an IBM 4341 computer, which cost roughly \$280,000 when it was first released (Farmer 1981). With von Herzen, Kajiya also introduced the volume-rendering equation to graphics (Kajiya and von Herzen 1984); this equation rigorously describes the scattering of light in participating media.

Both Cook et al.'s and Kajiya's work once again led to images unlike any that had been seen before, demonstrating the value of physically based methods. In subsequent years, important work on Monte Carlo for realistic image synthesis was described in papers by Arvo and Kirk (1990) and Kirk and Arvo (1991). Shirley's Ph.D. dissertation (1990) and follow-on work by Shirley et al. (1996) were important contributions to Monte Carlo–based efforts. Hall's book, *Illumination and Color in Computer Generated Imagery*, (1989) is one of the first books to present rendering in a physically based framework, and Andrew Glassner's *Principles of Digital Image Synthesis* rigorously laid out foundations of the field (1995). Ward's *Radiance* rendering system was an early open source physically based rendering system, focused on lighting design (Ward 1994), and Slusallek's *Vision* renderer was deisgned to bridge the gap between physically based approaches and the then widely used RenderMan interface, which wasn't physically based (Slusallek 1996).

Following Torrance and Cook's work, much of the research in the Program of Computer Graphics at Cornell University investigated physically based approaches. The motivations for this work were summarized by Greenberg et al. (1997), who made a strong argument for a physically accurate rendering based on measurements of the material properties of real-world objects and on deep understanding of the human visual system.

A crucial step forward for physically based rendering was Veach's work, described in detail in his dissertation (Veach 1997). Veach advanced key theoretical foundations of Monte Carlo rendering while also developing new algorithms like multiple importance sampling, bidirectional path tracing, and Metropolis light transport that greatly improved its efficiency. Using Blinn's law as a guide, we believe that these significant improvements in efficiency were critical to practical adoption of these approaches.

Around this time, as computers became faster and more parallel, a number of researchers started pursuing real-time ray tracing; Wald, Slusallek, and Benthin wrote an influential paper that described a highly optimized ray tracer that was much more efficient than previous ray tracers (Wald et al. 2001b). Many subsequent papers introduced increasingly more efficient ray-tracing algorithms. Though most of this work wasn't physically based, the results led to great progress in ray-tracing acceleration structures and performance of the geometric components of ray tracing. Because physically based rendering generally makes substantial use of ray tracing, this work has in turn had the same helpful effect as faster computers have, making it possible to render more complex scenes with physical approaches.

At this point, we'll end our summary of the key steps in the research progress of physically based rendering; much more has been done. The "Further Reading" sections in all of the subsequent chapters of this book cover this work in detail.

1.7.2 PRODUCTION

With more capable computers in the 1980s, computer graphics could start to be used for animation and film production. Early examples include Jim Blinn's rendering of the Voyager 2 Flyby of Saturn in 1981 and visual effects in the movies *Star Trek II: The Wrath of Khan* (1982), *Tron* (1982), and *The Last Starfighter* (1984).

In early production use of computer-generated imagery, rasterization-based rendering (notably, the Reyes algorithm (Cook et al. 1987)) was the only viable option. One reason was that not enough computation was available for complex reflection models or for the global lighting effects that physically based ray tracing could provide. More significantly, rasterization had the important advantage that it didn't require that the entire scene representation fit into main memory.

When RAM was much less plentiful, almost any interesting scene was too large to fit into main memory. Rasterization-based algorithms made it possible to render scenes while having only a small subset of the full scene representation in memory at any time. Global lighting effects are difficult to achieve if the whole scene can't fit into main memory; for many years, with limited computer systems, content creators effectively decided that geometric and texture complexity was more important to visual realism than lighting complexity (and in turn physical accuracy).

Many practitioners at this time also believed that physically based approaches were undesirable for production: one of the great things about computer graphics is that one can cheat reality with impunity to achieve a desired artistic effect. For example, lighting designers on regular movies often struggle to place light sources so that they aren't visible to the camera or spend a lot of effort placing a light to illuminate an actor without shining too much light on the background. Computer graphics offers the opportunity to, for example, implement a light source model that shines twice as much light on a character as on a background object, in a fairly straightforward manner. For many years, this capability seemed much more useful than physical accuracy.

Visual effects practitioners who had the specific need to match rendered imagery to filmed real-world environments pioneered capturing real-world lighting and shading effects and were early adopters of physically based approaches in the late 1990s and early 2000s. (See Snow (2010) for a history of ILM's early work in this area, for example.)

During this time, the Blue Sky studio adopted a physically based pipeline early in their history (Ohmer 1997). The photorealism of an advertisement they made for a Braun shaver in 1992 caught the attenation of many, and their short film, *Bunny*, shown in 1998, was an early example of Monte Carlo global illumination used in production. Its visual look was substantially different from those of films and shorts rendered with Reyes and was widely noted. Subsequent feature films from Blue Sky also followed this approach. Unfortunately, Blue Sky never published significant technical details of their approach, limiting their wider influence.

During the early 2000s, the *mental ray* ray-tracing system was used by a number of studios, mostly for visual effects. It was a very efficient ray tracer with sophisticated global illumination algorithm implementations. The main focus of its developers was computer-aided design and product design applications, so it lacked features like the ability to handle extremely complex scenes and the enormous numbers of texture maps that film production demanded.

After *Bunny*, another watershed moment came in 2001, when Marcos Fajardo came to the SIGGRAPH with an early version of his *Arnold* renderer. He showed images in the Monte Carlo image synthesis course that not only had complex geometry, textures, and global illumination but also were rendered in tens of minutes. While these scenes weren't of the complexity of those used in film production at the time, his results showed many the creative opportunities from global illumination in complex scenes.

Fajardo brought *Arnold* to Sony Pictures Imageworks, where work started to transform it to a production-capable physically based rendering system. Work on efficient motion blur, programmable shading, support for massively complex scenes and deferred loading of scene geometry, and support for texture caching, where only a small subset of the texture in the scene is kept in memory, were all important areas to be addressed. *Arnold* was first used on the movie *Monster House* and is now generally available as a product.

In the mid-2000s, Pixar's RenderMan renderer started to support hybrid rasterization and ray-tracing algorithms and included a number of innovative algorithms for computing global illumination solutions in complex scenes. RenderMan was recently rewritten to be a physically based ray tracer, following the general system architecture of pbrt (Christensen 2015).

One of the main reasons that physically based Monte Carlo approaches to rendering have been successful in production is that they end up improving the productivity of artists. Some of the important factors have been:

Figure 1.22: *Gravity* (2013) featured spectacular computer-generated imagery of a realistic space environment with volumetric scattering and large numbers of anisotropic metal surfaces. The image was generated using Arnold, a physically based rendering system that accounts for global illumination. Image courtesy of Warner Bros. and Framestore.

- The algorithms involved have essentially just a single quality knob: how many samples to take per pixel; this is extremely helpful for artists. Ray-tracing algorithms are also suited to both progressive refinement and quickly computing rough previews by taking just a few samples per pixel; rasterization-based renderers don't have equivalent capabilities.
- Adopting physically based reflection models has made it easier to design surface materials. Earlier, when reflection models that didn't necessarily conserve energy were used, an object might be placed in a single lighting environment while its surface reflection parameters were adjusted. The object might look great in that environment, but it would often appear completely wrong when moved to another lighting environment because surfaces were actually reflecting too little or too much energy: surface properties had been set to unreasonable values.
- The quality of shadows computed with ray tracing is much better than it is with rasterization. Eliminating the need to tweak shadow map resolutions, biases, and other parameters has eliminated an unpleasant task of lighting artists. Further, physically based methods bring with them bounce lighting and other soft-lighting effects from the method itself, rather than as an artistically tuned manual process.

As of this writing, physically based rendering is used widely for producing computer-generated imagery for movies; Figures 1.22 and 1.23 show images from two recent movies that used physically based approaches.

Figure 1.23: This image from *The Hobbit: The Battle of the Five Armies* (2014) was also rendered using a physically based rendering system; the characters feature heterogeneous subsurface scattering and vast amounts of geometric detail. Image by Weta Digital, courtesy of Warner Bros. and Metro-Goldwyn-Mayer.

FURTHER READING

In a seminal early paper, Arthur Appel (1968) first described the basic idea of ray tracing to solve the hidden surface problem and to compute shadows in polygonal scenes. Goldstein and Nagel (1971) later showed how ray tracing could be used to render scenes with quadric surfaces. Kay and Greenberg (1979) described a ray-tracing approach to rendering transparency, and Whitted's seminal *CACM* article described the general recursive ray-tracing algorithm that is implemented in this chapter, accurately simulating reflection and refraction from specular surfaces and shadows from point light sources (Whitted 1980). Heckbert (1987) was the first to explore realistic rendering of dessert.

Notable early books on physically based rendering and image synthesis include Cohen and Wallace's *Radiosity and Realistic Image Synthesis* (1993), Sillion and Puech's *Radiosity and Global Illumination* (1994), and Ashdown's *Radiosity: A Programmer's Perspective* (1994), all of which primarily describe the finite-element radiosity method.

In a paper on ray-tracing system design, Kirk and Arvo (1988) suggested many principles that have now become classic in renderer design. Their renderer was implemented as a core kernel that encapsulated the basic rendering algorithms and interacted with primitives and shading routines via a carefully constructed object-oriented interface. This approach made it easy to extend the system with new primitives and acceleration methods. pbrt's design is based on these ideas.

Another good reference on ray-tracer design is *Introduction to Ray Tracing* (Glassner 1989a), which describes the state of the art in ray tracing at that time and has a chapter by Heckbert that sketches the design of a basic ray tracer. More recently, Shirley and Morley's *Realistic Ray Tracing* (2003) gives an easy-to-understand introduction to ray tracing and includes the complete source code to a basic ray tracer. Suffern's book (2007) also provides a gentle introduction to ray tracing.

Researchers at Cornell University have developed a rendering testbed over many years; its design and overall structure were described by Trumbore, Lytle, and Greenberg (1993). Its predecessor was described by Hall and Greenberg (1983). This system is a loosely coupled set of modules and libraries, each designed to handle a single task (ray–object intersection acceleration, image storage, etc.) and written in a way that makes it easy to combine appropriate modules to investigate and develop new rendering algorithms. This testbed has been quite successful, serving as the foundation for much of the rendering research done at Cornell.

Radiance was the first widely available open source renderer based fundamentally on physical quantities. It was designed to perform accurate lighting simulation for architectural design. Ward described its design and history in a paper and a book (Ward 1994; Larson and Shakespeare 1998). *Radiance* is designed in the UNIX style, as a set of interacting programs, each handling a different part of the rendering process. This general type of rendering architecture was first described by Duff (1985).

Glassner's (1993) *Spectrum* rendering architecture also focuses on physically based rendering, approached through a signal-processing-based formulation of the problem. It is an extensible system built with a plug-in architecture; pbrt's approach of using parameter/value lists for initializing implementations of the main abstract interfaces is similar to *Spectrum*'s. One notable feature of *Spectrum* is that all parameters that describe the scene can be functions of time.

Slusallek and Seidel (1995, 1996; Slusallek 1996) described the *Vision* rendering system, which is also physically based and designed to support a wide variety of light transport algorithms. In particular, it had the ambitious goal of supporting both Monte Carlo and finite-element-based light transport algorithms.

Many papers have been written that describe the design and implementation of other rendering systems, including renderers for entertainment and artistic applications. The Reyes architecture, which forms the basis for Pixar's RenderMan renderer, was first described by Cook et al. (1987), and a number of improvements to the original algorithm have been summarized by Apodaca and Gritz (2000). Gritz and Hahn (1996) described the *BMRT* ray tracer. The renderer in the Maya modeling and animation system was described by Sung et al. (1998), and some of the internal structure of the *mental ray* renderer is described in Driemeyer and Herken's book on its API (Driemeyer and Herken 2002). The design of the high-performance *Manta* interactive ray tracer is described by Bigler et al. (2006).

The source code to pbrt is licensed under the BSD License; this has made it possible for other developers to use pbrt code as a basis for their efforts. *LuxRender*, available from *www.luxrender.net*, is a physically based renderer built using pbrt as a starting point; it offers a number of additional features and has a rich set of scene export plugins for modeling systems.

Ray Tracing News, an electronic newsletter compiled by Eric Haines dates to 1987 and is occasionally still published. It's a very good resource for general ray-tracing information and has particularly useful discussions about intersection acceleration approaches, implementation issues, and tricks of the trade. More recently, the forums at *ompf2.com* have been frequented by many experienced ray-tracer developers.

The object-oriented approach used to structure pbrt makes the system easy to understand but is not the only way to structure rendering systems. An important counterpoint to the object-oriented approach is *data-oriented design* (DoD), a way of programming that has notably been advocated by a number of game developers (for whom performance is critical). The key tenet behind DoD is that many principles of traditional object-oriented design are incompatible with high-performance software systems as they lead to cache-inefficient layout of data in memory. Instead, its proponents argue for driving system design first from considerations of the layout of data in memory and how those data are transformed by the program. See, for example, Mike Acton's keynote at the C++ Conference (Acton 2014).

EXERCISE

⓿ **1.1** A good way to gain an understanding of pbrt is to follow the process of computing the radiance value for a single ray in a debugger. Build a version of pbrt with debugging symbols and set up your debugger to run pbrt with the killeroo-simple.pbrt scene from the scenes directory. Set breakpoints in the SamplerIntegrator::Render() method and trace through the process of how a ray is generated, how its radiance value is computed, and how its contribution is added to the image. The first time you do this, you may want to specify that only a single thread of execution should be used by providing --nthreads 1 as command-line arguments to pbrt; doing so ensures that all computation is done in the main processing thread, which may make it easier to understand what is going on, depending on how easy your debugger makes it to step through the program when it is running multiple threads.

As you gain more understanding about the details of the system later in the book, repeat this process and trace through particular parts of the system more carefully.

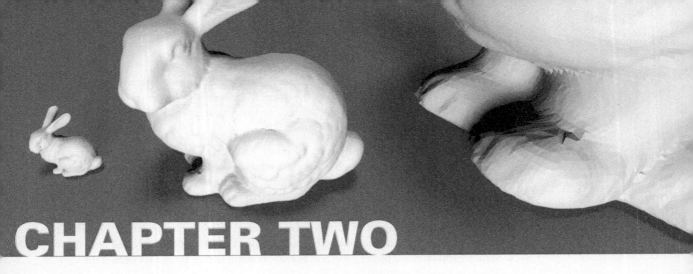

CHAPTER TWO

02 GEOMETRY AND TRANSFORMATIONS

Almost all nontrivial graphics programs are built on a foundation of geometric classes. These classes represent mathematical constructs like points, vectors, and rays. Because these classes are ubiquitous throughout the system, good abstractions and efficient implementations are critical. This chapter presents the interface to and implementation of pbrt's geometric foundation. Note that these are not the classes that represent the actual scene geometry (triangles, spheres, etc.); those classes are the topic of Chapter 3.

The geometric classes in this chapter are defined in the files core/geometry.h and core/geometry.cpp in the pbrt distribution, and the implementations of transformation matrices (Section 2.7) are in the files core/transform.h and core/transform.cpp.

2.1 COORDINATE SYSTEMS

As is typical in computer graphics, pbrt represents three-dimensional points, vectors, and normal vectors with three coordinate values: x, y, and z. These values are meaningless without a *coordinate system* that defines the origin of the space and gives three linearly independent vectors that define the x, y, and z axes of the space. Together, the origin and three vectors are called the *frame* that defines the coordinate system. Given an arbitrary point or direction in 3D, its (x, y, z) coordinate values depend on its relationship to the frame. Figure 2.1 shows an example that illustrates this idea in 2D.

In the general n-dimensional case, a frame's origin p_o and its n linearly independent basis vectors define an n-dimensional *affine space*. All vectors $\mathbf{v}$ in the space can be expressed as a linear combination of the basis vectors. Given a vector $\mathbf{v}$ and the basis vectors $\mathbf{v}_i$, there is a unique set of scalar values s_i such that

$$\mathbf{v} = s_1 \mathbf{v}_1 + \cdots + s_n \mathbf{v}_n.$$

Physically Based Rendering: From Theory To Implementation.
http://dx.doi.org/10.1016/B978-0-12-800645-0.50002-6

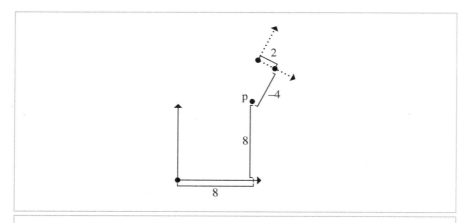

Figure 2.1: In 2D, the (x, y) coordinates of a point p are defined by the relationship of the point to a particular 2D coordinate system. Here, two coordinate systems are shown; the point might have coordinates (8, 8) with respect to the coordinate system with its coordinate axes drawn in solid lines but have coordinates (2, −4) with respect to the coordinate system with dashed axes. In either case, the 2D point p is at the same absolute position in space.

The scalars s_i are the *representation* of $\mathbf{v}$ with respect to the basis $\{\mathbf{v}_1, \mathbf{v}_2, \ldots, \mathbf{v}_n\}$ and are the coordinate values that we store with the vector. Similarly, for all points p, there are unique scalars s_i such that the point can be expressed in terms of the origin p_o and the basis vectors

$$p = p_o + s_1 \mathbf{v}_1 + \cdots + s_n \mathbf{v}_n.$$

Thus, although points and vectors are both represented by x, y, and z coordinates in 3D, they are distinct mathematical entities and are not freely interchangeable.

This definition of points and vectors in terms of coordinate systems reveals a paradox: to define a frame we need a point and a set of vectors, but we can only meaningfully talk about points and vectors with respect to a particular frame. Therefore, in three dimensions we need a *standard frame* with origin (0, 0, 0) and basis vectors (1, 0, 0), (0, 1, 0), and (0, 0, 1). All other frames will be defined with respect to this canonical coordinate system, which we call *world space*.

2.1.1 COORDINATE SYSTEM HANDEDNESS

There are two different ways that the three coordinate axes can be arranged, as shown in Figure 2.2. Given perpendicular x and y coordinate axes, the z axis can point in one of two directions. These two choices are called *left-handed* and *right-handed*. The choice between the two is arbitrary but has a number of implications for how some of the geometric operations throughout the system are implemented. pbrt uses a left-handed coordinate system.

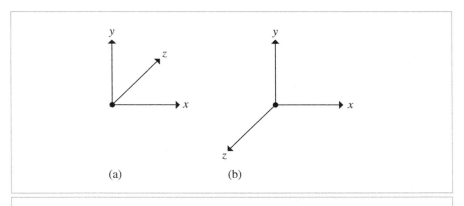

Figure 2.2: (a) In a left-handed coordinate system, the z axis points into the page when the x and y axes are oriented with x pointing to the right and y pointing up. (b) In a right-handed system, the z axis points out of the page.

2.2 VECTORS

pbrt provides both 2D and 3D vector classes. Both are parameterized by the type of the underlying vector element, thus making it easy to instantiate vectors of both integer and floating-point types.

⟨*Vector Declarations*⟩ ≡
```
    template <typename T> class Vector2 {
    public:
        ⟨Vector2 Public Methods⟩
        ⟨Vector2 Public Data 59⟩
    };
```

⟨*Vector Declarations*⟩ +≡
```
    template <typename T> class Vector3 {
    public:
        ⟨Vector3 Public Methods 60⟩
        ⟨Vector3 Public Data 59⟩
    };
```

In the following, we will generally only include implementations of Vector3 methods; all have Vector2 parallels that have straightforward implementation differences.

A vectors is represented with a tuple of components that gives its representation in terms of the x, y, z (in 3D) axes of the space it is defined in. The individual components of a 3D vector **v** will be written $\mathbf{v}_x$, $\mathbf{v}_y$, and $\mathbf{v}_z$.

⟨*Vector2 Public Data*⟩ ≡   59
```
    T x, y;
```

⟨*Vector3 Public Data*⟩ ≡   59
```
    T x, y, z;
```

An alternate implementation would be to have a single template class that is also parameterized with an integer number of dimensions and to represent the coordinates with an
array of that many T values. While this approach would reduce the total amount of code,
individual components of the vector couldn't be accessed as v.x and so forth. We believe
that in this case, a bit more code in the vector implementations is worthwhile in return
for more transparent access to elements.

However, some routines do find it useful to be able to easily loop over the components
of vectors; the vector classes also provide a C++ operator to index into the components
so that, given a vector v, v[0] == v.x and so forth.

⟨*Vector3 Public Methods*⟩ ≡   59
```
T operator[](int i) const {
    Assert(i >= 0 && i <= 2);
    if (i == 0) return x;
    if (i == 1) return y;
    return z;
}
T &operator[](int i) {
    Assert(i >= 0 && i <= 2);
    if (i == 0) return x;
    if (i == 1) return y;
    return z;
}
```

For convenience, a number of widely used types of vectors are given a typedef, so that
they have more concise names in code elsewhere.

⟨*Vector Declarations*⟩ +≡
```
typedef Vector2<Float> Vector2f;
typedef Vector2<int>   Vector2i;
typedef Vector3<Float> Vector3f;
typedef Vector3<int>   Vector3i;
```

Readers who have been exposed to object-oriented design may question our decision to
make the vector element data publicly accessible. Typically, data members are only accessible inside their class, and external code that wishes to access or modify the contents of a
class must do so through a well-defined API of selector and mutator functions. Although
we generally agree with this design principle (though see the discussion of data-oriented
design in the "Further Reading" section of Chapter 1), it is not appropriate here. The
purpose of selector and mutator functions is to hide the class's internal implementation
details. In the case of vectors, hiding this basic part of their design gains nothing and adds
bulk to code that uses them.

By default, the (x, y, z) values are set to zero, although the user of the class can optionally
supply values for each of the components. If the user does supply values, we check that
none of them has the floating-point "not a number" (NaN) value using the Assert()
macro. When compiled in optimized mode, this macro disappears from the compiled
code, saving the expense of verifying this case. NaNs almost certainly indicate a bug in
the system; if a NaN is generated by some computation, we'd like to catch it as soon as

possible in order to make isolating its source easier. (See Section 3.9.1 for more discussion of NaN values.)

⟨*Vector3 Public Methods*⟩ +≡   59
```
Vector3() { x = y = z = 0; }
Vector3(T x, T y, T z)
    : x(x), y(y), z(z) {
    Assert(!HasNaNs());
}
```

The code to check for NaNs just calls the `std::isnan()` function on each of the *x*, *y*, and *z* components.

⟨*Vector3 Public Methods*⟩ +≡   59
```
bool HasNaNs() const {
    return std::isnan(x) || std::isnan(y) || std::isnan(z);
}
```

Addition and subtraction of vectors are done component-wise. The usual geometric interpretation of vector addition and subtraction is shown in Figures 2.3 and 2.4.

⟨*Vector3 Public Methods*⟩ +≡   59
```
Vector3<T> operator+(const Vector3<T> &v) const {
    return Vector3(x + v.x, y + v.y, z + v.z);
}
Vector3<T>& operator+=(const Vector3<T> &v) {
    x += v.x; y += v.y; z += v.z;
    return *this;
}
```

The code for subtracting two vectors is similar and therefore not shown here.

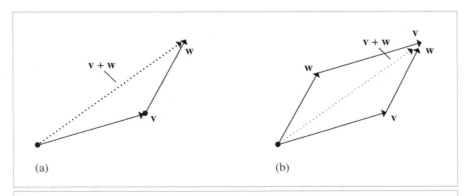

(a)   (b)

Figure 2.3: (a) Vector addition: $\mathbf{v} + \mathbf{w}$. (b) Notice that the sum $\mathbf{v} + \mathbf{w}$ forms the diagonal of the parallelogram formed by $\mathbf{v}$ and $\mathbf{w}$, which shows the commutativity of vector addition: $\mathbf{v} + \mathbf{w} = \mathbf{w} + \mathbf{v}$.

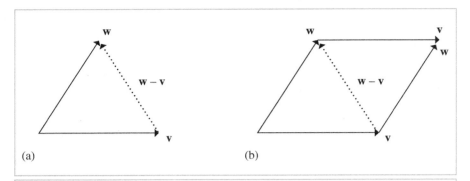

Figure 2.4: (a) Vector subtraction. (b) The difference $-\mathbf{v} - \mathbf{w}$ is the other diagonal of the parallelogram formed by $\mathbf{v}$ and $\mathbf{w}$.

A vector can be multiplied component-wise by a scalar, thereby changing its length. Three functions are needed in order to cover all of the different ways that this operation may be written in source code (i.e., v*s, s*v, and v *= s):

⟨*Vector3 Public Methods*⟩ +≡   **59**
```
Vector3<T> operator*(T s) const { return Vector3<T>(s*x, s*y, s*z); }
Vector3<T> &operator*=(T s) {
    x *= s; y *= s; z *= s;
    return *this;
}
```

⟨*Geometry Inline Functions*⟩ ≡
```
template <typename T> inline Vector3<T>
operator*(T s, const Vector3<T> &v) { return v * s; }
```

Similarly, a vector can be divided component-wise by a scalar. The code for scalar division is similar to scalar multiplication, although division of a scalar by a vector is not well defined and so is not permitted.

In the implementation of these methods, we use a single division to compute the scalar's reciprocal and then perform three component-wise multiplications. This is a useful trick for avoiding division operations, which are generally much slower than multiplies on modern CPUs.[1]

We use the Assert() macro to make sure that the provided divisor is not zero; this should never happen and would indicate a bug elsewhere in the system.

---

1   It is a common misconception that these sorts of optimizations are unnecessary because the compiler will perform the necessary analysis. Compilers are generally restricted from performing many transformations of this type. For division, the IEEE floating-point standard requires that $x/x = 1$ for all x, but if we compute $1/x$ and store it in a variable and then multiply x by that value, it is not guaranteed that 1 will be the result. In this case, we are willing to lose that guarantee in exchange for higher performance. See Section 3.9 for more discussion of these issues.

⟨*Vector3 Public Methods*⟩ +≡   59
```
    Vector3<T> operator/(T f) const {
        Assert(f != 0);
        Float inv = (Float)1 / f;
        return Vector3<T>(x * inv, y * inv, z * inv);
    }

    Vector3<T> &operator/=(T f) {
        Assert(f != 0);
        Float inv = (Float)1 / f;
        x *= inv; y *= inv; z *= inv;
        return *this;
    }
```

The Vector3 class also provides a unary negation operator that returns a new vector pointing in the opposite direction of the original one:

⟨*Vector3 Public Methods*⟩ +≡   59
```
    Vector3<T> operator-() const { return Vector3<T>(-x, -y, -z); }
```

Finally, Abs() returns a vector with the absolute value operation applied to its components.

⟨*Geometry Inline Functions*⟩ +≡
```
    template <typename T> Vector3<T> Abs(const Vector3<T> &v) {
        return Vector3<T>(std::abs(v.x), std::abs(v.y), std::abs(v.z));
    }
```

2.2.1 DOT AND CROSS PRODUCT

Two useful operations on vectors are the dot product (also known as the scalar or inner product) and the cross product. For two vectors $\mathbf{v}$ and $\mathbf{w}$, their *dot product* $(\mathbf{v} \cdot \mathbf{w})$ is defined as:

$$\mathbf{v}_x\mathbf{w}_x + \mathbf{v}_y\mathbf{w}_y + \mathbf{v}_z\mathbf{w}_z.$$

⟨*Geometry Inline Functions*⟩ +≡
```
    template <typename T> inline T
    Dot(const Vector3<T> &v1, const Vector3<T> &v2) {
        return v1.x * v2.x + v1.y * v2.y + v1.z * v2.z;
    }
```

The dot product has a simple relationship to the angle between the two vectors:

$$(\mathbf{v} \cdot \mathbf{w}) = \|\mathbf{v}\| \, \|\mathbf{w}\| \cos \theta, \qquad\qquad [2.1]$$

Assert() 1069
Float 1062
Vector3 59

where θ is the angle between $\mathbf{v}$ and $\mathbf{w}$, and $\|\mathbf{v}\|$ denotes the length of the vector $\mathbf{v}$. It follows from this that $(\mathbf{v} \cdot \mathbf{w})$ is zero if and only if $\mathbf{v}$ and $\mathbf{w}$ are perpendicular, provided that neither $\mathbf{v}$ nor $\mathbf{w}$ is *degenerate*—equal to $(0, 0, 0)$. A set of two or more mutually perpendicular vectors is said to be *orthogonal*. An orthogonal set of unit vectors is called *orthonormal*.

It immediately follows from Equation (2.1) that if **v** and **w** are unit vectors, their dot product is the cosine of the angle between them. As the cosine of the angle between two vectors often needs to be computed for rendering, we will frequently make use of this property.

A few basic properties directly follow from the definition. For example, if **u**, **v**, and **w** are vectors and s is a scalar value, then:

$$(\mathbf{u} \cdot \mathbf{v}) = (\mathbf{v} \cdot \mathbf{u})$$
$$(s\mathbf{u} \cdot \mathbf{v}) = s(\mathbf{v} \cdot \mathbf{u})$$
$$(\mathbf{u} \cdot (\mathbf{v} + \mathbf{w})) = (\mathbf{u} \cdot \mathbf{v}) + (\mathbf{u} \cdot \mathbf{w}).$$

We will frequently need to compute the absolute value of the dot product as well. The AbsDot() function does this for us so that a separate call to std::abs() isn't necessary.

⟨*Geometry Inline Functions*⟩ +≡
```
template <typename T>
inline T AbsDot(const Vector3<T> &v1, const Vector3<T> &v2) {
    return std::abs(Dot(v1, v2));
}
```

The *cross product* is another useful operation for 3D vectors. Given two vectors in 3D, the cross product $\mathbf{v} \times \mathbf{w}$ is a vector that is perpendicular to both of them. Given orthogonal vectors **v** and **w**, then $\mathbf{v} \times \mathbf{w}$ is defined to be a vector such that $(\mathbf{v}, \mathbf{w}, \mathbf{v} \times \mathbf{w})$ form a coordinate system.

The cross product is defined as:

$$(\mathbf{v} \times \mathbf{w})_x = \mathbf{v}_y \mathbf{w}_z - \mathbf{v}_z \mathbf{w}_y$$
$$(\mathbf{v} \times \mathbf{w})_y = \mathbf{v}_z \mathbf{w}_x - \mathbf{v}_x \mathbf{w}_z$$
$$(\mathbf{v} \times \mathbf{w})_z = \mathbf{v}_x \mathbf{w}_y - \mathbf{v}_y \mathbf{w}_x.$$

A way to remember this is to compute the determinant of the matrix:

$$\mathbf{v} \times \mathbf{w} = \begin{vmatrix} i & j & k \\ \mathbf{v}_x & \mathbf{v}_y & \mathbf{v}_z \\ \mathbf{w}_x & \mathbf{w}_y & \mathbf{w}_z \end{vmatrix},$$

where i, j, and k represent the axes $(1, 0, 0)$, $(0, 1, 0)$, and $(0, 0, 1)$, respectively. Note that this equation is merely a memory aid and not a rigorous mathematical construction, since the matrix entries are a mix of scalars and vectors.

In the implementation here, the vector elements are converted to double-precision (regardless of the type of Float) before the subtractions in the Cross() function. Using extra precision for 32-bit floating-point values here protects against error from catastrophic cancellation, a type of floating-point error that can happen when subtracting two values that are very close together. This isn't a theoretical concern: this change was necessary to fix bugs that came up from this issue previously. See Section 3.9 for more information on floating-point rounding error.

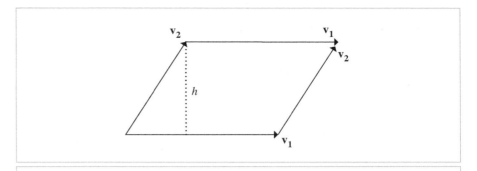

Figure 2.5: The area of a parallelogram with edges given by vectors $\mathbf{v}_1$ and $\mathbf{v}_2$ is equal to $\mathbf{v}_1 h$. From Equation (2.2), the length of the cross product of $\mathbf{v}_1$ and $\mathbf{v}_2$ is equal to the product of the two vector lengths times the sine of the angle between them—the parallelogram area.

⟨*Geometry Inline Functions*⟩ +≡
```
template <typename T> inline Vector3<T>
Cross(const Vector3<T> &v1, const Vector3<T> &v2) {
    double v1x = v1.x, v1y = v1.y, v1z = v1.z;
    double v2x = v2.x, v2y = v2.y, v2z = v2.z;
    return Vector3<T>((v1y * v2z) - (v1z * v2y),
                      (v1z * v2x) - (v1x * v2z),
                      (v1x * v2y) - (v1y * v2x));
}
```

From the definition of the cross product, we can derive

$$\|\mathbf{v} \times \mathbf{w}\| = \|\mathbf{v}\|\,\|\mathbf{w}\| \sin\theta, \qquad\qquad\qquad [2.2]$$

where θ is the angle between $\mathbf{v}$ and $\mathbf{w}$. An important implication of this is that the cross product of two perpendicular unit vectors is itself a unit vector. Note also that the result of the cross product is a degenerate vector if $\mathbf{v}$ and $\mathbf{w}$ are parallel.

This definition also shows a convenient way to compute the area of a parallelogram (Figure 2.5). If the two edges of the parallelogram are given by vectors $\mathbf{v}_1$ and $\mathbf{v}_2$, and it has height h, the area is given by $\|\mathbf{v}_1\|h$. Since $h = \sin\theta\,\|\mathbf{v}_2\|$, we can use Equation (2.2) to see that the area is $\|\mathbf{v}_1 \times \mathbf{v}_2\|$.

2.2.2 NORMALIZATION

It is often necessary to *normalize* a vector—that is, to compute a new vector pointing in the same direction but with unit length. A normalized vector is often called a *unit vector*. The notation used in this book for normalized vectors is that $\hat{\mathbf{v}}$ is the normalized version of $\mathbf{v}$. To normalize a vector, it's first useful to be able to compute its length.

Float 1062
Vector3 59

⟨*Vector3 Public Methods*⟩ +≡   59
```
Float LengthSquared() const { return x * x + y * y + z * z; }
Float Length() const { return std::sqrt(LengthSquared()); }
```

Normalize() normalizes a vector. It divides each component by the length of the vector, $\|v\|$. It returns a new vector; it does *not* normalize the vector in place:

⟨*Geometry Inline Functions*⟩ +≡
```
template <typename T> inline Vector3<T>
Normalize(const Vector3<T> &v) { return v / v.Length(); }
```

2.2.3 MISCELLANEOUS OPERATIONS

A few additional operations are useful when working with vectors. The MinComponent() and MaxComponent() methods return the smallest and largest coordinate value, respectively.

⟨*Geometry Inline Functions*⟩ +≡
```
template <typename T> T
MinComponent(const Vector3<T> &v) {
    return std::min(v.x, std::min(v.y, v.z));
}
template <typename T> T
MaxComponent(const Vector3<T> &v) {
    return std::max(v.x, std::max(v.y, v.z));
}
```

Related, MaxDimension() returns the index of the component with the largest value.

⟨*Geometry Inline Functions*⟩ +≡
```
template <typename T> int
MaxDimension(const Vector3<T> &v) {
    return (v.x > v.y) ? ((v.x > v.z) ? 0 : 2) :
           ((v.y > v.z) ? 1 : 2);
}
```

Component-wise minimum and maximum operations are also available.

⟨*Geometry Inline Functions*⟩ +≡
```
template <typename T> Vector3<T>
Min(const Vector3<T> &p1, const Vector3<T> &p2) {
    return Vector3<T>(std::min(p1.x, p2.x), std::min(p1.y, p2.y),
                      std::min(p1.z, p2.z));
}
template <typename T> Vector3<T>
Max(const Vector3<T> &p1, const Vector3<T> &p2) {
    return Vector3<T>(std::max(p1.x, p2.x), std::max(p1.y, p2.y),
                      std::max(p1.z, p2.z));
}
```

Vector3 59

Finally, Permute() permutes the coordinate values according to the index values provided.

⟨*Geometry Inline Functions*⟩ +≡
```
template <typename T> Vector3<T>
Permute(const Vector3<T> &v, int x, int y, int z) {
    return Vector3<T>(v[x], v[y], v[z]);
}
```

2.2.4 COORDINATE SYSTEM FROM A VECTOR

We will frequently want to construct a local coordinate system given only a single 3D vector. Because the cross product of two vectors is orthogonal to both, we can apply the cross product two times to get a set of three orthogonal vectors for the coordinate system. Note that the two vectors generated by this technique are unique only up to a rotation about the given vector.

The implementation of this function assumes that the vector passed in, v1, has already been normalized. It first constructs a perpendicular vector by zeroing one of the components of the original vector, swapping the remaining two, and negating one of them. Inspection of the two cases should make clear that v2 will be normalized and that the dot product $(\mathbf{v}_1 \cdot \mathbf{v}_2)$ must be equal to zero. Given these two perpendicular vectors, a single cross product gives the third, which by definition will be perpendicular to the first two.

⟨*Geometry Inline Functions*⟩ +≡
```
template <typename T> inline void
CoordinateSystem(const Vector3<T> &v1, Vector3<T> *v2, Vector3<T> *v3) {
    if (std::abs(v1.x) > std::abs(v1.y))
        *v2 = Vector3<T>(-v1.z, 0, v1.x) /
                std::sqrt(v1.x * v1.x + v1.z * v1.z);
    else
        *v2 = Vector3<T>(0, v1.z, -v1.y) /
                std::sqrt(v1.y * v1.y + v1.z * v1.z);
    *v3 = Cross(v1, *v2);
}
```

2.3 POINTS

A point is a zero-dimensional location in 2D or 3D space. The Point2 and Point3 classes in pbrt represent points in the obvious way: using x, y, z (in 3D) coordinates with respect to a coordinate system. Although the same representation is used for vectors, the fact that a point represents a position whereas a vector represents a direction leads to a number of important differences in how they are treated. Points are denoted in text by p.

In this section, we'll continue the approach of only including implementations of the 3D point methods in the Point3 class here.

⟨*Point Declarations*⟩ ≡
```
template <typename T> class Point2 {
public:
    ⟨Point2 Public Methods 68⟩
    ⟨Point2 Public Data 68⟩
};
```

⟨*Point Declarations*⟩ +≡
```
template <typename T> class Point3 {
public:
    ⟨Point3 Public Methods 68⟩
    ⟨Point3 Public Data 68⟩
};
```

As with vectors, it's helpful to have shorter type names for commonly used point types.

⟨*Point Declarations*⟩ +≡
```
typedef Point2<Float> Point2f;
typedef Point2<int>   Point2i;
typedef Point3<Float> Point3f;
typedef Point3<int>   Point3i;
```

⟨*Point2 Public Data*⟩ ≡   67
```
T x, y;
```

⟨*Point3 Public Data*⟩ ≡   68
```
T x, y, z;
```

Also like vectors, a Point3 constructor takes parameters to set the x, y, and z coordinate values.

⟨*Point3 Public Methods*⟩ ≡   68
```
Point3() { x = y = z = 0; }
Point3(T x, T y, T z) : x(x), y(y), z(z) {
    Assert(!HasNaNs());
}
```

It can be useful to convert a Point3 to a Point2 by dropping the *z* coordinate. The constructor that does this conversion has the explicit qualifier so that this conversion can't happen without an explicit cast, lest it happen unintentionally.

⟨*Point2 Public Methods*⟩ ≡   67
```
explicit Point2(const Point3<T> &p) : x(p.x), y(p.y) {
    Assert(!HasNaNs());
}
```

It's also useful to be able to convert a point with one element type (e.g., a Point3f) to a point of another one (e.g., Point3i) as well as to be able to convert a point to a vector with a different underlying element type. The following constructor and conversion operator provide these conversions. Both also require an explicit cast, to make it clear in source code when they are being used.

Float 1062
Point2 67
Point3 68

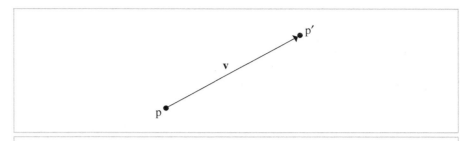

Figure 2.6: Obtaining the Vector between Two Points. The vector $p' - p$ is given by the component-wise subtraction of the points p' and p.

⟨*Point3 Public Methods*⟩ +≡   **68**
```
template <typename U> explicit Point3(const Point3<U> &p)
    : x((T)p.x), y((T)p.y), z((T)p.z) {
    Assert(!HasNaNs());
}
template <typename U> explicit operator Vector3<U>() const {
    return Vector3<U>(x, y, z);
}
```

There are certain Point3 methods that either return or take a Vector3. For instance, one can add a vector to a point, offsetting it in the given direction to obtain a new point.

⟨*Point3 Public Methods*⟩ +≡   **68**
```
Point3<T> operator+(const Vector3<T> &v) const {
    return Point3<T>(x + v.x, y + v.y, z + v.z);
}
Point3<T> &operator+=(const Vector3<T> &v) {
    x += v.x; y += v.y; z += v.z;
    return *this;
}
```

Alternately, one can subtract one point from another, obtaining the vector between them, as shown in Figure 2.6.

⟨*Point3 Public Methods*⟩ +≡   **68**
```
Vector3<T> operator-(const Point3<T> &p) const {
    return Vector3<T>(x - p.x, y - p.y, z - p.z);
}
Point3<T> operator-(const Vector3<T> &v) const {
    return Point3<T>(x - v.x, y - v.y, z - v.z);
}
```

Point3 68
Vector3 59

Subtracting a vector from a point gives a new point.

⟨*Point3 Public Methods*⟩ +≡   68

```
    Point3<T> &operator-=(const Vector3<T> &v) {
        x -= v.x; y -= v.y; z -= v.z;
        return *this;
    }
```

The distance between two points can be computed by subtracting them to compute the vector between them and then finding the length of that vector:

⟨*Geometry Inline Functions*⟩ +≡

```
    template <typename T> inline Float
    Distance(const Point3<T> &p1, const Point3<T> &p2) {
        return (p1 - p2).Length();
    }
    template <typename T> inline Float
    DistanceSquared(const Point3<T> &p1, const Point3<T> &p2) {
        return (p1 - p2).LengthSquared();
    }
```

Although in general it doesn't make sense mathematically to weight points by a scalar or add two points together, the point classes still allow these operations in order to be able to compute weighted sums of points, which is mathematically meaningful as long as the weights used all sum to one. The code for scalar multiplication and addition with points is identical to the corresponding code for vectors, so it is not shown here.

On a related note, it's useful to be able to linearly interpolate between two points. Lerp() returns p0 at t==0, p1 at t==1, and linearly interpolates between them at other values of t. For t<0 or t>1, Lerp() extrapolates.

⟨*Geometry Inline Functions*⟩ +≡

```
    template <typename T> Point3<T>
    Lerp(Float t, const Point3<T> &p0, const Point3<T> &p1) {
        return (1 - t) * p0 + t * p1;
    }
```

The Min() and Max() functions return points representing the component-wise minimums and maximums of the two given points.

⟨*Geometry Inline Functions*⟩ +≡

```
    template <typename T> Point3<T>
    Min(const Point3<T> &p1, const Point3<T> &p2) {
        return Point3<T>(std::min(p1.x, p2.x), std::min(p1.y, p2.y),
                         std::min(p1.z, p2.z));
    }
    template <typename T> Point3<T>
    Max(const Point3<T> &p1, const Point3<T> &p2) {
        return Point3<T>(std::max(p1.x, p2.x), std::max(p1.y, p2.y),
                         std::max(p1.z, p2.z));
    }
```

Float 1062
Point3 68
Vector3 59

Floor(), Ceil(), and Abs() apply the corresponding operation component-wise to the given point.

⟨*Geometry Inline Functions*⟩ +≡
```
template <typename T> Point3<T> Floor(const Point3<T> &p) {
    return Point3<T>(std::floor(p.x), std::floor(p.y), std::floor(p.z));
}
template <typename T> Point3<T> Ceil(const Point3<T> &p) {
    return Point3<T>(std::ceil(p.x), std::ceil(p.y), std::ceil(p.z));
}
template <typename T> Point3<T> Abs(const Point3<T> &p) {
    return Point3<T>(std::abs(p.x), std::abs(p.y), std::abs(p.z));
}
```

And finally, Permute() permutes the coordinate values according to the provided permutation.

⟨*Geometry Inline Functions*⟩ +≡
```
template <typename T> Point3<T>
Permute(const Point3<T> &p, int x, int y, int z) {
    return Point3<T>(p[x], p[y], p[z]);
}
```

2.4 NORMALS

A *surface normal* (or just *normal*) is a vector that is perpendicular to a surface at a particular position. It can be defined as the cross product of any two nonparallel vectors that are tangent to the surface at a point. Although normals are superficially similar to vectors, it is important to distinguish between the two of them: because normals are defined in terms of their relationship to a particular surface, they behave differently than vectors in some situations, particularly when applying transformations. This difference is discussed in Section 2.8.

⟨*Normal Declarations*⟩ ≡
```
template <typename T> class Normal3 {
public:
    ⟨Normal3 Public Methods 72⟩
    ⟨Normal3 Public Data⟩
};
```

⟨*Normal Declarations*⟩ +≡
```
typedef Normal3<Float> Normal3f;
```

Float 1062
Normal3 71
Point3 68
Vector3 59

The implementations of Normal3s and Vector3s are very similar. Like vectors, normals are represented by three components x, y, and z; they can be added and subtracted to compute new normals; and they can be scaled and normalized. However, a normal cannot be added to a point, and one cannot take the cross product of two normals. Note that, in an unfortunate turn of terminology, normals are *not* necessarily normalized.

Normal3 provides an extra constructor that initializes a Normal3 from a Vector3. Because
Normal3s and Vector3s are different in subtle ways, we want to make sure that this conversion doesn't happen when we don't intend it to, so the C++ explicit keyword is again
used here. Vector3 also provides a constructor that converts the other way. Thus, given
the declarations Vector3f v; and Normal3f n;, then the assignment n = v is illegal, so it is
necessary to explicitly convert the vector, as in n = Normal3f(v).

⟨*Normal3 Public Methods*⟩ ≡   71
```
    explicit Normal3<T>(const Vector3<T> &v) : x(v.x), y(v.y), z(v.z) {
        Assert(!v.HasNaNs());
    }
```

⟨*Geometry Inline Functions*⟩ +≡
```
    template <typename T> inline
    Vector3<T>::Vector3(const Normal3<T> &n) : x(n.x), y(n.y), z(n.z) {
        Assert(!n.HasNaNs());
    }
```

The Dot() and AbsDot() functions are also overloaded to compute dot products between
the various possible combinations of normals and vectors. This code won't be included in
the text here. We also won't include implementations of all of the various other Normal3
methods here, since they are similar to those for vectors.

One new operation to implement comes from the fact it's often necessary to flip a surface
normal so that it lies in the same hemisphere as a given vector—for example, the surface
normal that lies in the same hemisphere as an outgoing ray is frequently needed. The
Faceforward() utility function encapsulates this small computation. (pbrt also provides
variants of this function for the other three combinations of Vector3s and Normal3s as
parameters.) Be careful when using the other instances, though: when using the version
that takes two Vector3s, for example, ensure that the first parameter is the one that should
be returned (possibly flipped) and the second is the one to test against. Reversing the two
parameters will give unexpected results.

⟨*Geometry Inline Functions*⟩ +≡
```
    template <typename T> inline Normal3<T>
    Faceforward(const Normal3<T> &n, const Vector3<T> &v) {
        return (Dot(n, v) < 0.f) ? -n : n;
    }
```

2.5 RAYS

A *ray* is a semi-infinite line specified by its origin and direction. pbrt represents a Ray
with a Point3f for the origin and a Vector3f for the direction. We only need rays with
floating-point origins and directions, so Ray isn't a template class parameterized by an
arbitrary type, as points, vectors, and normals were. A ray is denoted by r; it has origin o
and direction **d**, as shown in Figure 2.7.

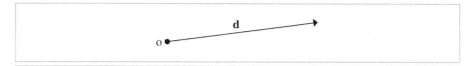

Figure 2.7: A ray is a semi-infinite line defined by its origin o and its direction vector **d**.

⟨*Ray Declarations*⟩ ≡
```
class Ray {
public:
    ⟨Ray Public Methods 74⟩
    ⟨Ray Public Data 73⟩
};
```

Because we will be referring to these variables often throughout the code, the origin and direction members of a Ray are succinctly named o and d. Note that we again make the data publicly available for convenience.

⟨*Ray Public Data*⟩ ≡   73
```
Point3f o;
Vector3f d;
```

The *parametric form* of a ray expresses it as a function of a scalar value t, giving the set of points that the ray passes through:

$$\mathrm{r}(t) = \mathrm{o} + t\mathbf{d} \quad 0 < t < \infty. \tag{2.3}$$

The Ray also includes a member variable that limits the ray to a segment along its infinite extent. This field, tMax, allows us to restrict the ray to a segment of points $[\mathrm{o}, \mathrm{r}(t_{max})]$.

Notice that this field is declared as mutable, meaning that it can be changed even if the Ray that contains it is const—thus, when a ray is passed to a method that takes a const Ray &, that method is not allowed to modify its origin or direction but can modify its extent. This convention fits one of the most common uses of rays in the system, as parameters to ray–object intersection testing routines, which will record the offsets to the closest intersection in tMax.

⟨*Ray Public Data*⟩ +≡   73
```
mutable Float tMax;
```

Each ray has a time value associated with it. In scenes with animated objects, the rendering system constructs a representation of the scene at the appropriate time for each ray.

⟨*Ray Public Data*⟩ +≡   73
```
Float time;
```

Finally, each ray records the medium containing its origin. The Medium class, introduced in Section 11.3, encapsulates the (potentially spatially varying) properties of media such as a foggy atmosphere, smoke, or scattering liquids like milk or shampoo. Associating this information with rays makes it possible for other parts of the system to account correctly for the effect of rays passing from one medium to another.

⟨*Ray Public Data*⟩ +≡   73
```
const Medium *medium;
```

Constructing Rays is straightforward. The default constructor relies on the Point3f and Vector3f constructors to set the origin and direction to (0, 0, 0). Alternately, a particular point and direction can be provided. If an origin and direction are provided, the constructor allows a value to be given for tMax, the ray's time and medium.

⟨*Ray Public Methods*⟩ ≡   73
```
Ray() : tMax(Infinity), time(0.f), medium(nullptr) { }
Ray(const Point3f &o, const Vector3f &d, Float tMax = Infinity,
    Float time = 0.f, const Medium *medium = nullptr)
    : o(o), d(d), tMax(tMax), time(time), medium(medium) { }
```

Because position along a ray can be thought of as a function of a single parameter t, the Ray class overloads the function application operator for rays. This way, when we need to find the point at a particular position along a ray, we can write code like:

```
Ray r(Point3f(0, 0, 0), Vector3f(1, 2, 3));
Point3f p = r(1.7);
```

⟨*Ray Public Methods*⟩ +≡   73
```
Point3f operator()(Float t) const { return o + d * t; }
```

2.5.1 RAY DIFFERENTIALS

In order to be able to perform better antialiasing with the texture functions defined in Chapter 10, pbrt can keep track of some additional information with rays. In Section 10.1, this information will be used to compute values that are used by the Texture class to estimate the projected area on the image plane of a small part of the scene. From this, the Texture can compute the texture's average value over that area, leading to a higher-quality final image.

RayDifferential is a subclass of Ray that contains additional information about two auxiliary rays. These extra rays represent camera rays offset by one sample in the x and y direction from the main ray on the film plane. By determining the area that these three rays project to on an object being shaded, the Texture can estimate an area to average over for proper antialiasing.

Because the RayDifferential class inherits from Ray, geometric interfaces in the system can be written to take const Ray & parameters, so that either a Ray or RayDifferential can be passed to them. Only the routines that need to account for antialiasing and texturing require RayDifferential parameters.

⟨*Ray Declarations*⟩ +≡

```
class RayDifferential : public Ray {
public:
    ⟨RayDifferential Public Methods 75⟩
    ⟨RayDifferential Public Data 75⟩
};
```

The RayDifferential constructors mirror the Ray's constructors.

⟨*RayDifferential Public Methods*⟩ ≡   75

```
RayDifferential() { hasDifferentials = false; }
RayDifferential(const Point3f &o, const Vector3f &d,
        Float tMax = Infinity, Float time = 0.f,
        const Medium *medium = nullptr)
    : Ray(o, d, tMax, time, medium) {
    hasDifferentials = false;
}
```

⟨*RayDifferential Public Data*⟩ ≡   75

```
bool hasDifferentials;
Point3f rxOrigin, ryOrigin;
Vector3f rxDirection, ryDirection;
```

There is a constructor to create RayDifferentials from Rays. The constructor sets hasDifferentials to false initially because the neighboring rays, if any, are not known.

⟨*RayDifferential Public Methods*⟩ +≡   75

```
RayDifferential(const Ray &ray) : Ray(ray) {
    hasDifferentials = false;
}
```

Camera implementations in pbrt compute differentials for rays leaving the camera under the assumption that camera rays are spaced one pixel apart. Integrators such as the SamplerIntegrator can generate multiple camera rays per pixel, in which case the actual distance between samples is lower. The fragment ⟨*Generate camera ray for current sample*⟩ encountered in Chapter 1 called the ScaleDifferentials() method defined below to update differential rays for an estimated sample spacing of s.

⟨*RayDifferential Public Methods*⟩ +≡   75

```
void ScaleDifferentials(Float s) {
    rxOrigin = o + (rxOrigin - o) * s;
    ryOrigin = o + (ryOrigin - o) * s;
    rxDirection = d + (rxDirection - d) * s;
    ryDirection = d + (ryDirection - d) * s;
}
```

2.6 BOUNDING BOXES

Many parts of the system operate on axis-aligned regions of space. For example, multi-threading in pbrt is implemented by subdividing the image into rectangular tiles that

can be processed independently, and the bounding volume hierarchy in Section 4.3 uses
3D boxes to bound geometric primitives in the scene. The Bounds2 and Bounds3 template
classes are used to represent the extent of these sorts of regions. Both are parameterized
by a type T that is used to represent the coordinates of its extents.

⟨*Bounds Declarations*⟩ ≡
```
template <typename T> class Bounds2 {
public:
    ⟨Bounds2 Public Methods⟩
    ⟨Bounds2 Public Data⟩
};
```

⟨*Bounds Declarations*⟩ +≡
```
template <typename T> class Bounds3 {
public:
    ⟨Bounds3 Public Methods 76⟩
    ⟨Bounds3 Public Data 77⟩
};
```

⟨*Bounds Declarations*⟩ +≡
```
typedef Bounds2<Float> Bounds2f;
typedef Bounds2<int>   Bounds2i;
typedef Bounds3<Float> Bounds3f;
typedef Bounds3<int>   Bounds3i;
```

There are a few possible representations for these sorts of bounding boxes; pbrt uses *axis-aligned bounding boxes* (AABBs), where the box edges are mutually perpendicular and aligned with the coordinate system axes. Another possible choice is *oriented bounding boxes* (OBBs), where the box edges on different sides are still perpendicular to each other but not necessarily coordinate-system aligned. A 3D AABB can be described by one of its vertices and three lengths, each representing the distance spanned along the x, y, and z coordinate axes. Alternatively, two opposite vertices of the box can describe it. We chose the two-point representation for pbrt's Bounds2 and Bounds3 classes; they store the positions of the vertex with minimum coordinate values and of the one with maximum coordinate values. A 2D illustration of a bounding box and its representation is shown in Figure 2.8.

The default constructors create an empty box by setting the extent to an invalid configuration, which violates the invariant that pMin.x <= pMax.x (and similarly for the other dimensions). By initializing two corner points with the largest and smallest representable number, any operations involving an empty box (e.g., Union()) will yield the correct result.

⟨*Bounds3 Public Methods*⟩ ≡   76
```
Bounds3() {
    T minNum = std::numeric_limits<T>::lowest();
    T maxNum = std::numeric_limits<T>::max();
    pMin = Point3<T>(maxNum, maxNum, maxNum);
    pMax = Point3<T>(minNum, minNum, minNum);
}
```

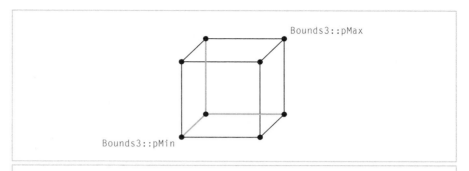

Figure 2.8: An Axis-Aligned Bounding Box. The Bounds2 and Bounds3 classes store only the coordinates of the minimum and maximum points of the box; the other box corners are implicit in this representation.

⟨*Bounds3 Public Data*⟩ ≡   76
```
Point3<T> pMin, pMax;
```

It is also useful to be able to initialize a Bounds3 to enclose a single point:

⟨*Bounds3 Public Methods*⟩ +≡   76
```
Bounds3(const Point3<T> &p) : pMin(p), pMax(p) { }
```

If the caller passes two corner points (p1 and p2) to define the box, the constructor needs to find their component-wise minimum and maximum values since p1 and p2 are not necessarily chosen so that p1.x <= p2.x, and so on.

⟨*Bounds3 Public Methods*⟩ +≡   76
```
Bounds3(const Point3<T> &p1, const Point3<T> &p2)
    : pMin(std::min(p1.x, p2.x), std::min(p1.y, p2.y),
           std::min(p1.z, p2.z)),
      pMax(std::max(p1.x, p2.x), std::max(p1.y, p2.y),
           std::max(p1.z, p2.z)) {
}
```

In some cases, it's also useful to use array indexing to select between the two points at the corners of the box. The implementations of these methods select between pMin and pMax based on the value of i.

⟨*Bounds3 Public Methods*⟩ +≡   76
```
const Point3<T> &operator[](int i) const;
Point3<T> &operator[](int i);
```

The Corner() method returns the coordinates of one of the eight corners of the bounding box.

⟨*Bounds3 Public Methods*⟩ +≡   76
```
Point3<T> Corner(int corner) const {
    return Point3<T>((*this)[(corner & 1)].x,
                     (*this)[(corner & 2) ? 1 : 0].y,
                     (*this)[(corner & 4) ? 1 : 0].z);
}
```

Given a bounding box and a point, the Union() function returns a new bounding box
that encompasses that point as well as the original box.

⟨*Geometry Inline Functions*⟩ +≡
```
template <typename T> Bounds3 <T>
Union(const Bounds3<T> &b, const Point3<T> &p) {
    return Bounds3<T>(Point3<T>(std::min(b.pMin.x, p.x),
                                std::min(b.pMin.y, p.y),
                                std::min(b.pMin.z, p.z)),
                      Point3<T>(std::max(b.pMax.x, p.x),
                                std::max(b.pMax.y, p.y),
                                std::max(b.pMax.z, p.z)));
}
```

It is similarly possible to construct a new box that bounds the space encompassed by two
other bounding boxes. The definition of this function is similar to the earlier Union()
method that takes a Point3f; the difference is that the pMin and pMax of the second box
are used for the std::min() and std::max() tests, respectively.

⟨*Geometry Inline Functions*⟩ +≡
```
template <typename T> Bounds3<T>
Union(const Bounds3<T> &b1, const Bounds3<T> &b2) {
    return Bounds3<T>(Point3<T>(std::min(b1.pMin.x, b2.pMin.x),
                                std::min(b1.pMin.y, b2.pMin.y),
                                std::min(b1.pMin.z, b2.pMin.z)),
                      Point3<T>(std::max(b1.pMax.x, b2.pMax.x),
                                std::max(b1.pMax.y, b2.pMax.y),
                                std::max(b1.pMax.z, b2.pMax.z)));
}
```

The intersection of two bounding boxes can be found by computing the maximum
of their two respective minimum coordinates and the minimum of their maximum
coordinates. (See Figure 2.9.)

⟨*Geometry Inline Functions*⟩ +≡
```
template <typename T> Bounds3<T>
Intersect(const Bounds3<T> &b1, const Bounds3<T> &b2) {
    return Bounds3<T>(Point3<T>(std::max(b1.pMin.x, b2.pMin.x),
                                std::max(b1.pMin.y, b2.pMin.y),
                                std::max(b1.pMin.z, b2.pMin.z)),
                      Point3<T>(std::min(b1.pMax.x, b2.pMax.x),
                                std::min(b1.pMax.y, b2.pMax.y),
                                std::min(b1.pMax.z, b2.pMax.z)));
}
```

Bounds3 76
Point3 68
Point3f 68

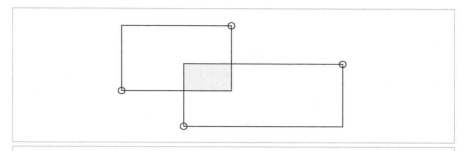

Figure 2.9: Intersection of Two Bounding Boxes. Given two bounding boxes with pMin and pMax points denoted by open circles, the bounding box of their area of intersection (shaded region) has a minimum point with coordinates given by the maximum of the coordinates of the minimum points of the two boxes in each dimension. Similarly, its maximum point is given by the minimums of the boxes' maximum coordinates.

We are able to determine if two bounding boxes overlap by seeing if their extents overlap in all of x, y, and z:

⟨*Geometry Inline Functions*⟩ +≡
```
template <typename T>
bool Overlaps(const Bounds3<T> &b1, const Bounds3<T> &b2) {
    bool x = (b1.pMax.x >= b2.pMin.x) && (b1.pMin.x <= b2.pMax.x);
    bool y = (b1.pMax.y >= b2.pMin.y) && (b1.pMin.y <= b2.pMax.y);
    bool z = (b1.pMax.z >= b2.pMin.z) && (b1.pMin.z <= b2.pMax.z);
    return (x && y && z);
}
```

Three 1D containment tests determine if a given point is inside the bounding box:

⟨*Geometry Inline Functions*⟩ +≡
```
template <typename T>
bool Inside(const Point3<T> &p, const Bounds3<T> &b) {
    return (p.x >= b.pMin.x && p.x <= b.pMax.x &&
            p.y >= b.pMin.y && p.y <= b.pMax.y &&
            p.z >= b.pMin.z && p.z <= b.pMax.z);
}
```

The InsideExclusive() variant of Inside() doesn't consider points on the upper boundary to be inside the bounds. It is mostly useful with integer-typed bounds.

⟨*Geometry Inline Functions*⟩ +≡
```
template <typename T>
bool InsideExclusive(const Point3<T> &p, const Bounds3<T> &b) {
    return (p.x >= b.pMin.x && p.x < b.pMax.x &&
            p.y >= b.pMin.y && p.y < b.pMax.y &&
            p.z >= b.pMin.z && p.z < b.pMax.z);
}
```

The Expand() function pads the bounding box by a constant factor in both dimensions.

Bounds3 76
Bounds3::pMax 77
Bounds3::pMin 77
Point3 68

⟨*Geometry Inline Functions*⟩ +≡
```
template <typename T, typename U> inline Bounds3<T>
Expand(const Bounds3<T> &b, U delta) {
    return Bounds3<T>(b.pMin - Vector3<T>(delta, delta, delta),
                      b.pMax + Vector3<T>(delta, delta, delta));
}
```

`Diagonal()` returns the vector along the box diagonal from the minimum point to the maximum point.

⟨*Bounds3 Public Methods*⟩ +≡   76
```
Vector3<T> Diagonal() const { return pMax - pMin; }
```

Methods for computing the surface area of the six faces of the box and the volume inside of it are also frequently useful.

⟨*Bounds3 Public Methods*⟩ +≡   76
```
T SurfaceArea() const {
    Vector3<T> d = Diagonal();
    return 2 * (d.x * d.y + d.x * d.z + d.y * d.z);
}
```

⟨*Bounds3 Public Methods*⟩ +≡   76
```
T Volume() const {
    Vector3<T> d = Diagonal();
    return d.x * d.y * d.z;
}
```

The `Bounds3::MaximumExtent()` method returns the index of which of the three axes is longest. This is useful, for example, when deciding which axis to subdivide when building some of the ray-intersection acceleration structures.

⟨*Bounds3 Public Methods*⟩ +≡   76
```
int MaximumExtent() const {
    Vector3<T> d = Diagonal();
    if (d.x > d.y && d.x > d.z)
        return 0;
    else if (d.y > d.z)
        return 1;
    else
        return 2;
}
```

The `Lerp()` method linearly interpolates between the corners of the box by the given amount in each dimension.

⟨*Bounds3 Public Methods*⟩ +≡   76
```
Point3<T> Lerp(const Point3f &t) const {
    return Point3<T>(::Lerp(t.x, pMin.x, pMax.x),
                     ::Lerp(t.y, pMin.y, pMax.y),
                     ::Lerp(t.z, pMin.z, pMax.z));
}
```

Offset() returns the continuous position of a point relative to the corners of the box, where a point at the minimum corner has offset $(0, 0, 0)$, a point at the maximum corner has offset $(1, 1, 1)$, and so forth.

⟨*Bounds3 Public Methods*⟩ +≡   76
```
Vector3<T> Offset(const Point3<T> &p) const {
    Vector3<T> o = p - pMin;
    if (pMax.x > pMin.x) o.x /= pMax.x - pMin.x;
    if (pMax.y > pMin.y) o.y /= pMax.y - pMin.y;
    if (pMax.z > pMin.z) o.z /= pMax.z - pMin.z;
    return o;
}
```

Bounds3 also provides a method that returns the center and radius of a sphere that bounds the bounding box. In general, this may give a far looser fit than a sphere that bounded the original contents of the Bounds3 directly, although it is a useful method to have available.

⟨*Bounds3 Public Methods*⟩ +≡   76
```
void BoundingSphere(Point3<T> *center, Float *radius) const {
    *center = (pMin + pMax) / 2;
    *radius = Inside(*center, *this) ? Distance(*center, pMax) : 0;
}
```

Finally, for integer bounds, there is an iterator class that fulfills the requirements of a C++ forward iterator (i.e., it can only be advanced). The details are slightly tedious and not particularly interesting, so the code isn't included in the book. Having this definition makes it possible to write code using range-based for loops to iterate over integer coordinates in a bounding box:

```
Bounds2i b = ...;
for (Point2i p : b) {
    .
    .
    .
}
```

As implemented, the iteration goes up to but doesn't visit points equal to the maximum extent in each dimension.

2.7 TRANSFORMATIONS

In general, a *transformation* $\mathbf{T}$ is a mapping from points to points and from vectors to vectors:

$$\mathrm{p}' = \mathbf{T}(\mathrm{p}) \qquad \mathbf{v}' = \mathbf{T}(\mathbf{v}).$$

The transformation $\mathbf{T}$ may be an arbitrary procedure. However, we will consider a subset of all possible transformations in this chapter. In particular, they will be

- *Linear:* If $\mathbf{T}$ is an arbitrary linear transformation and s is an arbitrary scalar, then $\mathbf{T}(s\mathbf{v}) = s\mathbf{T}(\mathbf{v})$ and $\mathbf{T}(\mathbf{v}_1 + \mathbf{v}_2) = \mathbf{T}(\mathbf{v}_1) + \mathbf{T}(\mathbf{v}_2)$. These two properties can greatly simplify reasoning about transformations.

- *Continuous:* Roughly speaking, T maps the neighborhoods around p and v to neighborhoods around p′ and v′.
- *One-to-one and invertible:* For each p, T maps p to a single unique p′. Furthermore, there exists an inverse transform $\mathbf{T}^{-1}$ that maps p′ back to p.

We will often want to take a point, vector, or normal defined with respect to one coordinate frame and find its coordinate values with respect to another frame. Using basic properties of linear algebra, a 4 × 4 matrix can be shown to express the linear transformation of a point or vector from one frame to another. Furthermore, such a 4 × 4 matrix suffices to express all linear transformations of points and vectors within a fixed frame, such as translation in space or rotation around a point. Therefore, there are two different (and incompatible!) ways that a matrix can be interpreted:

- *Transformation of the frame:* Given a point, the matrix could express how to compute a *new* point in the same frame that represents the transformation of the original point (e.g., by translating it in some direction).
- *Transformation from one frame to another:* A matrix can express the coordinates of a point or vector in a new frame in terms of the coordinates in the original frame.

Most uses of transformations in pbrt are for transforming points from one frame to another.

In general, transformations make it possible to work in the most convenient coordinate space. For example, we can write routines that define a virtual camera, assuming that the camera is located at the origin, looks down the z axis, and has the y axis pointing up and the x axis pointing right. These assumptions greatly simplify the camera implementation. Then, to place the camera at any point in the scene looking in any direction, we just construct a transformation that maps points in the scene's coordinate system to the camera's coordinate system. (See Section 6.1.1 for more information about camera coordinate spaces in pbrt.)

2.7.1 HOMOGENEOUS COORDINATES

Given a frame defined by $(p, \mathbf{v}_1, \mathbf{v}_2, \mathbf{v}_3)$, there is ambiguity between the representation of a point (p_x, p_y, p_z) and a vector (v_x, v_y, v_z) with the same (x, y, z) coordinates. Using the representations of points and vectors introduced at the start of the chapter, we can write the point as the inner product $[s_1\, s_2\, s_3\, 1][\mathbf{v}_1\, \mathbf{v}_2\, \mathbf{v}_3\, p_o]^T$ and the vector as the inner product $[s_1'\, s_2'\, s_3'\, 0][\mathbf{v}_1\, \mathbf{v}_2\, \mathbf{v}_3\, p_o]^T$. These four vectors of three s_i values and a zero or one are called the *homogeneous* representations of the point and the vector. The fourth coordinate of the homogeneous representation is sometimes called the *weight*. For a point, its value can be any scalar other than zero: the homogeneous points $[1, 3, -2, 1]$ and $[-2, -6, 4, -2]$ describe the same Cartesian point $(1, 3, -2)$. Converting homogeneous points into ordinary points entails dividing the first three components by the weight:

$$(x, y, z, w) = \left(\frac{x}{w}, \frac{y}{w}, \frac{z}{w} \right).$$

We will use these facts to see how a transformation matrix can describe how points and vectors in one frame can be mapped to another frame. Consider a matrix **M** that describes the transformation from one coordinate system to another:

$$\mathbf{M} = \begin{pmatrix} m_{0,0} & m_{0,1} & m_{0,2} & m_{0,3} \\ m_{1,0} & m_{1,1} & m_{1,2} & m_{1,3} \\ m_{2,0} & m_{2,1} & m_{2,2} & m_{2,3} \\ m_{3,0} & m_{3,1} & m_{3,2} & m_{3,3} \end{pmatrix}.$$

(In this book, we define matrix element indices starting from zero, so that equations and source code correspond more directly.) Then if the transformation represented by $\mathbf{M}$ is applied to the x axis vector $(1, 0, 0)$, we have

$$\mathbf{Mx} = \mathbf{M}[1\,0\,0\,0]^T = [m_{0,0}\,m_{1,0}\,m_{2,0}\,m_{3,0}]^T.$$

Thus, directly reading the columns of the matrix shows how the basis vectors and the origin of the current coordinate system are transformed by the matrix:

$$\mathbf{My} = [m_{0,1}\,m_{1,1}\,m_{2,1}\,m_{3,1}]^T$$
$$\mathbf{Mz} = [m_{0,2}\,m_{1,2}\,m_{2,2}\,m_{3,2}]^T$$
$$\mathbf{Mp} = [m_{0,3}\,m_{1,3}\,m_{2,3}\,m_{3,3}]^T.$$

In general, by characterizing how the basis is transformed, we know how any point or vector specified in terms of that basis is transformed. Because points and vectors in the current coordinate system are expressed in terms of the current coordinate system's frame, applying the transformation to them directly is equivalent to applying the transformation to the current coordinate system's basis and finding their coordinates in terms of the transformed basis.

We will not use homogeneous coordinates explicitly in our code; there is no Homogeneous class in pbrt. However, the various transformation routines in the next section will implicitly convert points, vectors, and normals to homogeneous form, transform the homogeneous points, and then convert them back before returning the result. This isolates the details of homogeneous coordinates in one place (namely, the implementation of transformations).

⟨*Transform Declarations*⟩ ≡
```
class Transform {
public:
    ⟨Transform Public Methods 84⟩
private:
    ⟨Transform Private Data 84⟩
};
```

A transformation is represented by the elements of the matrix m, a Matrix4x4 object. The low-level Matrix4x4 class is defined in Section A.5.3. The matrix m is stored in *row-major* form, so element m[i][j] corresponds to $m_{i,j}$, where i is the row number and j is the column number. For convenience, the Transform also stores the inverse of the matrix m in the Transform::mInv member; for pbrt's needs, it is better to have the inverse easily available than to repeatedly compute it as needed.

Matrix4x4 1081
Transform 83
Transform::mInv 84

This representation of transformations is relatively memory hungry: assuming 4 bytes of storage for a Float value, a Transform requires 128 bytes of storage. Used naïvely, this approach can be wasteful; if a scene has millions of shapes but only a few thousand unique transformations, there's no reason to redundantly store the same transform many times in memory. Therefore, Shapes in pbrt store a pointer to a Transform, and the scene specification code defined in Section B.3.5 uses a TransformCache to ensure that all shapes that share the same transformation point to a single instance of that transformation in memory.

This decision to share transformations implies a loss of flexibility, however: the elements of a Transform shouldn't be modified after it is created if the Transform is shared by multiple objects in the scene (and those objects don't expect it to be changing.) This limitation isn't a problem in practice, since the transformations in a scene are typically created when pbrt parses the scene description file and don't need to change later at rendering time.

⟨*Transform Private Data*⟩ ≡   83
    Matrix4x4 m, mInv;

2.7.2 BASIC OPERATIONS

When a new Transform is created, it defaults to the *identity transformation*—the transformation that maps each point and each vector to itself. This transformation is represented by the *identity matrix*:

$$
I = \begin{pmatrix} 1 & 0 & 0 & 0 \\ 0 & 1 & 0 & 0 \\ 0 & 0 & 1 & 0 \\ 0 & 0 & 0 & 1 \end{pmatrix}.
$$

The implementation here relies on the default Matrix4x4 constructor to fill in the identity matrix for m and mInv.

⟨*Transform Public Methods*⟩ ≡   83
    Transform() { }

A Transform can also be created from a given matrix. In this case, the given matrix must be explicitly inverted.

⟨*Transform Public Methods*⟩ +≡   83
    Transform(const Float mat[4][4]) {
        m = Matrix4x4(mat[0][0], mat[0][1], mat[0][2], mat[0][3],
                      mat[1][0], mat[1][1], mat[1][2], mat[1][3],
                      mat[2][0], mat[2][1], mat[2][2], mat[2][3],
                      mat[3][0], mat[3][1], mat[3][2], mat[3][3]);
        mInv = Inverse(m);
    }

⟨*Transform Public Methods*⟩ +≡   83
    Transform(const Matrix4x4 &m) : m(m), mInv(Inverse(m)) { }

The most commonly used constructor takes a reference to the transformation matrix along with an explicitly provided inverse. This is a superior approach to computing the inverse in the constructor because many geometric transformations have very simple inverses and we can avoid the expense and potential loss of numeric precision from computing a general 4×4 matrix inverse. Of course, this places the burden on the caller to make sure that the supplied inverse is correct.

⟨*Transform Public Methods*⟩ +≡   83
```
Transform(const Matrix4x4 &m, const Matrix4x4 &mInv)
    : m(m), mInv(mInv) {
}
```

The Transform representing the inverse of a Transform can be returned by just swapping the roles of mInv and m.

⟨*Transform Public Methods*⟩ +≡   83
```
friend Transform Inverse(const Transform &t) {
    return Transform(t.mInv, t.m);
}
```

Transposing the two matrices in the transform to compute a new transform can also be useful.

⟨*Transform Public Methods*⟩ +≡   83
```
friend Transform Transpose(const Transform &t) {
    return Transform(Transpose(t.m), Transpose(t.mInv));
}
```

We provide Transform equality (and inequality) testing methods; their implementation is straightforward and not included here. Transform also provides an IsIdentity() method that checks to see if the transformation is the identity.

2.7.3 TRANSLATIONS

One of the simplest transformations is the *translation transformation*, $\mathbf{T}(\Delta x, \Delta y, \Delta z)$. When applied to a point p, it translates p's coordinates by Δx, Δy, and Δz, as shown in Figure 2.10. As an example, $\mathbf{T}(2, 2, 1)(x, y, z) = (x + 2, y + 2, z + 1)$.

Translation has some simple properties:

$$\mathbf{T}(0, 0, 0) = \mathbf{I}$$
$$\mathbf{T}(x_1, y_1, z_1)\mathbf{T}(x_2, y_2, z_2) = \mathbf{T}(x_1 + x_2, y_1 + y_2, z_1 + z_2)$$
$$\mathbf{T}(x_1, y_1, z_1)\mathbf{T}(x_2, y_2, z_2) = \mathbf{T}(x_2, y_2, z_2)\mathbf{T}(x_1, y_1, z_1)$$
$$\mathbf{T}^{-1}(x, y, z) = \mathbf{T}(-x, -y, -z).$$

Translation only affects points, leaving vectors unchanged. In matrix form, the translation transformation is

$$\mathbf{T}(\Delta x, \Delta y, \Delta z) = \begin{pmatrix} 1 & 0 & 0 & \Delta x \\ 0 & 1 & 0 & \Delta y \\ 0 & 0 & 1 & \Delta z \\ 0 & 0 & 0 & 1 \end{pmatrix}.$$

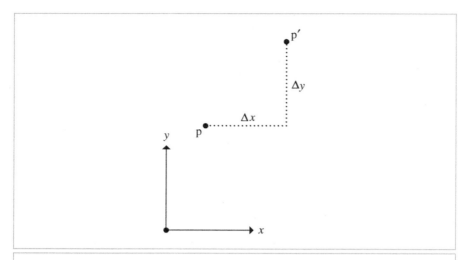

Figure 2.10: Translation in 2D. Adding offsets Δx and Δy to a point's coordinates correspondingly changes its position in space.

When we consider the operation of a translation matrix on a point, we see the value of homogeneous coordinates. Consider the product of the matrix for $\mathbf{T}(\Delta x, \Delta y, \Delta z)$ with a point p in homogeneous coordinates $[x \ y \ z \ 1]$:

$$
\begin{pmatrix}
1 & 0 & 0 & \Delta x \\
0 & 1 & 0 & \Delta y \\
0 & 0 & 1 & \Delta z \\
0 & 0 & 0 & 1
\end{pmatrix}
\begin{pmatrix}
x \\ y \\ z \\ 1
\end{pmatrix}
=
\begin{pmatrix}
x + \Delta x \\
y + \Delta y \\
z + \Delta z \\
1
\end{pmatrix}.
$$

As expected, we have computed a new point with its coordinates offset by $(\Delta x, \Delta y, \Delta z)$. However, if we apply $\mathbf{T}$ to a vector $\mathbf{v}$, we have

$$
\begin{pmatrix}
1 & 0 & 0 & \Delta x \\
0 & 1 & 0 & \Delta y \\
0 & 0 & 1 & \Delta z \\
0 & 0 & 0 & 1
\end{pmatrix}
\begin{pmatrix}
x \\ y \\ z \\ 0
\end{pmatrix}
=
\begin{pmatrix}
x \\ y \\ z \\ 0
\end{pmatrix}.
$$

The result is the same vector $\mathbf{v}$. This makes sense because vectors represent directions, so translation leaves them unchanged.

We will define a routine that creates a new Transform matrix to represent a given translation—it is a straightforward application of the translation matrix equation. This routine fully initializes the Transform that is returned, also initializing the matrix that represents the inverse of the translation.

Transform 83

⟨*Transform Method Definitions*⟩ ≡
```
Transform Translate(const Vector3f &delta) {
    Matrix4x4 m(1, 0, 0, delta.x,
                0, 1, 0, delta.y,
                0, 0, 1, delta.z,
                0, 0, 0,       1);
    Matrix4x4 minv(1, 0, 0, -delta.x,
                   0, 1, 0, -delta.y,
                   0, 0, 1, -delta.z,
                   0, 0, 0,        1);
    return Transform(m, minv);
}
```

2.7.4 SCALING

Another basic transformation is the *scale transformation*, $\mathbf{S}(s_x, s_y, s_z)$. It has the effect of taking a point or vector and multiplying its components by scale factors in x, y, and z: $\mathbf{S}(2, 2, 1)(x, y, z) = (2x, 2y, z)$. It has the following basic properties:

$$\mathbf{S}(1, 1, 1) = \mathbf{I}$$
$$\mathbf{S}(x_1, y_1, z_1)\mathbf{S}(x_2, y_2, z_2) = \mathbf{S}(x_1 x_2, y_1 y_2, z_1 z_2)$$
$$\mathbf{S}^{-1}(x, y, z) = \mathbf{S}\left(\frac{1}{x}, \frac{1}{y}, \frac{1}{z}\right).$$

We can differentiate between *uniform scaling*, where all three scale factors have the same value, and *nonuniform scaling*, where they may have different values. The general scale matrix is

$$\mathbf{S}(x, y, z) = \begin{pmatrix} x & 0 & 0 & 0 \\ 0 & y & 0 & 0 \\ 0 & 0 & z & 0 \\ 0 & 0 & 0 & 1 \end{pmatrix}.$$

⟨*Transform Method Definitions*⟩ +≡
```
Transform Scale(Float x, Float y, Float z) {
    Matrix4x4 m(x, 0, 0, 0,
                0, y, 0, 0,
                0, 0, z, 0,
                0, 0, 0, 1);
    Matrix4x4 minv(1/x,   0,   0, 0,
                     0, 1/y,   0, 0,
                     0,   0, 1/z, 0,
                     0,   0,   0, 1);
    return Transform(m, minv);
}
```

Float 1062
Matrix4x4 1081
Transform 83
Vector3f 60

It's useful to be able to test if a transformation has a scaling term in it; an easy way to do this is to transform the three coordinate axes and see if any of their lengths are appreciably different from one.

⟨*Transform Public Methods*⟩ +≡   83
```
    bool HasScale() const {
        Float la2 = (*this)(Vector3f(1, 0, 0)).LengthSquared();
        Float lb2 = (*this)(Vector3f(0, 1, 0)).LengthSquared();
        Float lc2 = (*this)(Vector3f(0, 0, 1)).LengthSquared();
#define NOT_ONE(x) ((x) < .999f || (x) > 1.001f)
        return (NOT_ONE(la2) || NOT_ONE(lb2) || NOT_ONE(lc2));
#undef NOT_ONE
    }
```

2.7.5 x, y, AND z AXIS ROTATIONS

Another useful type of transformation is the *rotation transformation*, **R**. In general, we can define an arbitrary axis from the origin in any direction and then rotate around that axis by a given angle. The most common rotations of this type are around the x, y, and z coordinate axes. We will write these rotations as $\mathbf{R}_x(\theta)$, $\mathbf{R}_y(\theta)$, and so on. The rotation around an arbitrary axis (x, y, z) is denoted by $\mathbf{R}_{(x,y,z)}(\theta)$.

Rotations also have some basic properties:

$$\mathbf{R}_a(0) = \mathbf{I}$$
$$\mathbf{R}_a(\theta_1)\mathbf{R}_a(\theta_2) = \mathbf{R}_a(\theta_1 + \theta_2)$$
$$\mathbf{R}_a(\theta_1)\mathbf{R}_a(\theta_2) = \mathbf{R}_a(\theta_2)\mathbf{R}_a(\theta_1)$$
$$\mathbf{R}_a^{-1}(\theta) = \mathbf{R}_a(-\theta) = \mathbf{R}_a^T(\theta),$$

where $\mathbf{R}^T$ is the matrix transpose of **R**. This last property, that the inverse of **R** is equal to its transpose, stems from the fact that **R** is an *orthogonal matrix*; its upper 3×3 components are all orthogonal to each other. Fortunately, the transpose is much easier to compute than a full matrix inverse.

For a left-handed coordinate system, the matrix for rotation around the x axis is

$$\mathbf{R}_x(\theta) = \begin{pmatrix} 1 & 0 & 0 & 0 \\ 0 & \cos\theta & -\sin\theta & 0 \\ 0 & \sin\theta & \cos\theta & 0 \\ 0 & 0 & 0 & 1 \end{pmatrix}.$$

Figure 2.11 gives an intuition for how this matrix works. It's easy to see that it leaves the x axis unchanged:

$$\mathbf{R}_x(\theta)[1\,0\,0\,0]^T = [1\,0\,0\,0]^T.$$

It maps the y axis (0, 1, 0) to (0, $\cos\theta$, $\sin\theta$) and the z axis to (0, $-\sin\theta$, $\cos\theta$). The y and z axes remain in the same plane, perpendicular to the x axis, but are rotated by the given angle. An arbitrary point in space is similarly rotated about the x axis by this transformation while staying in the same yz plane as it was originally.

The implementation of the RotateX() function is straightforward.

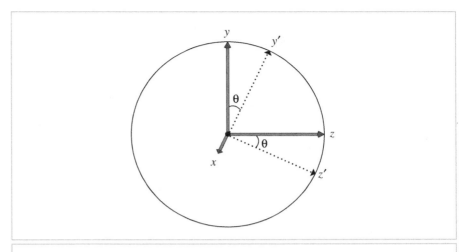

Figure 2.11: Rotation by an angle θ about the x axis leaves the x coordinate unchanged. The y and z axes are mapped to the vectors given by the dashed lines; y and z coordinates move accordingly.

⟨*Transform Method Definitions*⟩ +≡
```
Transform RotateX(Float theta) {
    Float sinTheta = std::sin(Radians(theta));
    Float cosTheta = std::cos(Radians(theta));
    Matrix4x4 m(1,        0,          0, 0,
                0, cosTheta, -sinTheta, 0,
                0, sinTheta,  cosTheta, 0,
                0,        0,          0, 1);
    return Transform(m, Transpose(m));
}
```

Similarly, for rotation around y and z, we have

$$\mathbf{R}_y(\theta) = \begin{pmatrix} \cos\theta & 0 & \sin\theta & 0 \\ 0 & 1 & 0 & 0 \\ -\sin\theta & 0 & \cos\theta & 0 \\ 0 & 0 & 0 & 1 \end{pmatrix} \qquad \mathbf{R}_z(\theta) = \begin{pmatrix} \cos\theta & -\sin\theta & 0 & 0 \\ \sin\theta & \cos\theta & 0 & 0 \\ 0 & 0 & 1 & 0 \\ 0 & 0 & 0 & 1 \end{pmatrix}.$$

The implementations of RotateY() and RotateZ() follow directly and are not included here.

2.7.6 ROTATION AROUND AN ARBITRARY AXIS

We also provide a routine to compute the transformation that represents rotation around an arbitrary axis. The usual derivation of this matrix is based on computing rotations that map the given axis to a fixed axis (e.g., z), performing the rotation there, and then rotating the fixed axis back to the original axis. A more elegant derivation can be constructed with vector algebra.

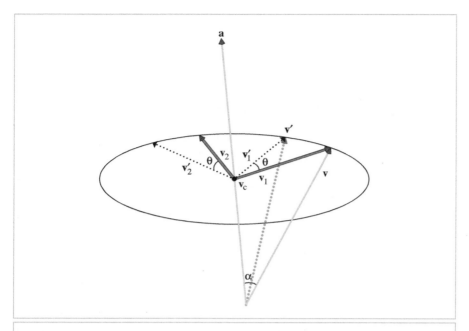

Figure 2.12: A vector **v** can be rotated around an arbitrary axis **a** by constructing a coordinate system $(\mathbf{p}, \mathbf{v}_1, \mathbf{v}_2)$ in the plane perpendicular to the axis that passes through **v**'s end point and rotating the vectors $\mathbf{v}_1$ and $\mathbf{v}_2$ about **p**. Applying this rotation to the axes of the coordinate system $(1, 0, 0)$, $(0, 1, 0)$, and $(0, 0, 1)$ gives the general rotation matrix for this rotation.

Consider a normalized direction vector **a** that gives the axis to rotate around by angle θ, and a vector **v** to be rotated (Figure 2.12). First, we can compute the vector $\mathbf{v}_c$ along the axis **a** that is in the plane through the end point of **v** and is parallel to **a**. Assuming **v** and **a** form an angle α, we have

$$\mathbf{v}_c = \mathbf{a}\,\|\mathbf{v}\| \cos\alpha = \mathbf{a}(\mathbf{v} \cdot \mathbf{a}).$$

We now compute a pair of basis vectors $\mathbf{v}_1$ and $\mathbf{v}_2$ in this plane. Trivially, one of them is

$$\mathbf{v}_1 = \mathbf{v} - \mathbf{v}_c,$$

and the other can be computed with a cross product

$$\mathbf{v}_2 = (\mathbf{v}_1 \times \mathbf{a}).$$

Because **a** is normalized, $\mathbf{v}_1$ and $\mathbf{v}_2$ have the same length, equal to the length of the vector between **v** and $\mathbf{v}_c$. To now compute the rotation by an angle θ about $\mathbf{v}_c$ in the plane of rotation, the rotation formulas earlier give us

$$\mathbf{v}' = \mathbf{v}_c + \mathbf{v}_1 \cos\theta + \mathbf{v}_2 \sin\theta.$$

To convert this to a rotation matrix, we apply this formula to the basis vectors $(1, 0, 0)$, $(0, 1, 0)$, and $(0, 0, 1)$ to get the values of the rows of the matrix. The result of all this is encapsulated in the following function. As with the other rotation matrices, the inverse is equal to the transpose.

⟨*Transform Method Definitions*⟩ +≡
```
Transform Rotate(Float theta, const Vector3f &axis) {
    Vector3f a = Normalize(axis);
    Float sinTheta = std::sin(Radians(theta));
    Float cosTheta = std::cos(Radians(theta));
    Matrix4x4 m;
    ⟨Compute rotation of first basis vector 91⟩
    ⟨Compute rotations of second and third basis vectors⟩
    return Transform(m, Transpose(m));
}
```

⟨*Compute rotation of first basis vector*⟩ ≡   91
```
m.m[0][0] = a.x * a.x + (1 - a.x * a.x) * cosTheta;
m.m[0][1] = a.x * a.y * (1 - cosTheta) - a.z * sinTheta;
m.m[0][2] = a.x * a.z * (1 - cosTheta) + a.y * sinTheta;
m.m[0][3] = 0;
```

The code for the other two basis vectors follows similarly and isn't included here.

2.7.7 THE LOOK-AT TRANSFORMATION

The *look-at transformation* is particularly useful for placing a camera in the scene. The caller specifies the desired position of the camera, a point the camera is looking at, and an "up" vector that orients the camera along the viewing direction implied by the first two parameters. All of these values are given in world space coordinates. The look-at construction then gives a transformation between camera space and world space (Figure 2.13).

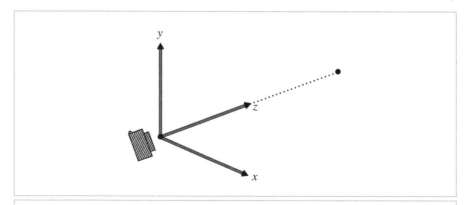

Float 1062
Matrix4x4 1081
Transform 83
Transform::Transpose() 85
Vector3::Normalize() 66
Vector3f 60

Figure 2.13: Given a camera position, the position being looked at from the camera, and an "up" direction, the look-at transformation describes a transformation from a left-handed viewing coordinate system where the camera is at the origin looking down the +z axis, and the +y axis is along the up direction.

In order to find the entries of the look-at transformation matrix, we use principles described earlier in this section: the columns of a transformation matrix give the effect of the transformation on the basis of a coordinate system.

⟨*Transform Method Definitions*⟩ +≡
```
    Transform LookAt(const Point3f &pos, const Point3f &look,
            const Vector3f &up) {
        Matrix4x4 cameraToWorld;
        ⟨Initialize fourth column of viewing matrix 92⟩
        ⟨Initialize first three columns of viewing matrix 92⟩
        return Transform(Inverse(cameraToWorld), cameraToWorld);
    }
```

The easiest column is the fourth one, which gives the point that the camera space origin, $[0 \ 0 \ 0 \ 1]^T$, maps to in world space. This is clearly just the camera position, supplied by the user.

⟨*Initialize fourth column of viewing matrix*⟩ ≡   92
```
    cameraToWorld.m[0][3] = pos.x;
    cameraToWorld.m[1][3] = pos.y;
    cameraToWorld.m[2][3] = pos.z;
    cameraToWorld.m[3][3] = 1;
```

The other three columns aren't much more difficult. First, LookAt() computes the normalized direction vector from the camera location to the look-at point; this gives the vector coordinates that the z axis should map to and, thus, the third column of the matrix. (In a left-handed coordinate system, camera space is defined with the viewing direction down the $+z$ axis.) The first column, giving the world space direction that the $+x$ axis in camera space maps to, is found by taking the cross product of the user-supplied "up" vector with the recently computed viewing direction vector. Finally, the "up" vector is recomputed by taking the cross product of the viewing direction vector with the transformed x axis vector, thus ensuring that the y and z axes are perpendicular and we have an orthonormal viewing coordinate system.

⟨*Initialize first three columns of viewing matrix*⟩ ≡   92
```
    Vector3f dir = Normalize(look - pos);
    Vector3f left = Normalize(Cross(Normalize(up), dir));
    Vector3f newUp = Cross(dir, left);
    cameraToWorld.m[0][0] = left.x;
    cameraToWorld.m[1][0] = left.y;
    cameraToWorld.m[2][0] = left.z;
    cameraToWorld.m[3][0] = 0.;
    cameraToWorld.m[0][1] = newUp.x;
    cameraToWorld.m[1][1] = newUp.y;
    cameraToWorld.m[2][1] = newUp.z;
    cameraToWorld.m[3][1] = 0.;
    cameraToWorld.m[0][2] = dir.x;
    cameraToWorld.m[1][2] = dir.y;
    cameraToWorld.m[2][2] = dir.z;
    cameraToWorld.m[3][2] = 0.;
```

Cross() 65
Inverse() 1081
LookAt() 92
Matrix4x4 1081
Point3f 68
Transform 83
Vector3::Normalize() 66
Vector3f 60

2.8 APPLYING TRANSFORMATIONS

We can now define routines that perform the appropriate matrix multiplications to transform points and vectors. We will overload the function application operator to describe these transformations; this lets us write code like:

```
Point3f p = ...;
Transform T = ...;
Point3f pNew = T(p);
```

2.8.1 POINTS

The point transformation routine takes a point (x, y, z) and implicitly represents it as the homogeneous column vector $[x \ y \ z \ 1]^T$. It then transforms the point by premultiplying this vector with the transformation matrix. Finally, it divides by w to convert back to a nonhomogeneous point representation. For efficiency, this method skips the division by the homogeneous weight, w, when $w = 1$, which is common for most of the transformations that will be used in pbrt—only the projective transformations defined in Chapter 6 will require this division.

⟨*Transform Inline Functions*⟩ ≡
```
template <typename T> inline Point3<T>
Transform::operator()(const Point3<T> &p) const {
    T x = p.x, y = p.y, z = p.z;
    T xp = m.m[0][0]*x + m.m[0][1]*y + m.m[0][2]*z + m.m[0][3];
    T yp = m.m[1][0]*x + m.m[1][1]*y + m.m[1][2]*z + m.m[1][3];
    T zp = m.m[2][0]*x + m.m[2][1]*y + m.m[2][2]*z + m.m[2][3];
    T wp = m.m[3][0]*x + m.m[3][1]*y + m.m[3][2]*z + m.m[3][3];
    if (wp == 1) return Point3<T>(xp, yp, zp);
    else         return Point3<T>(xp, yp, zp) / wp;
}
```

2.8.2 VECTORS

The transformations of vectors can be computed in a similar fashion. However, the multiplication of the matrix and the row vector is simplified since the implicit homogeneous w coordinate is zero.

⟨*Transform Inline Functions*⟩ +≡
```
template <typename T> inline Vector3<T>
Transform::operator()(const Vector3<T> &v) const {
    T x = v.x, y = v.y, z = v.z;
    return Vector3<T>(m.m[0][0]*x + m.m[0][1]*y + m.m[0][2]*z,
                      m.m[1][0]*x + m.m[1][1]*y + m.m[1][2]*z,
                      m.m[2][0]*x + m.m[2][1]*y + m.m[2][2]*z);
}
```

2.8.3 NORMALS

Normals do not transform in the same way that vectors do, as shown in Figure 2.14. Although tangent vectors transform in the straightforward way, normals require special

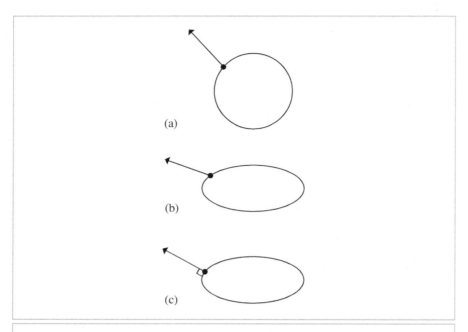

Figure 2.14: Transforming Surface Normals. (a) Original circle. (b) When scaling the circle to be half as tall in the y direction, simply treating the normal as a direction and scaling it in the same manner gives a normal that is no longer perpendicular to the surface. (c) A properly transformed normal.

treatment. Because the normal vector $\mathbf{n}$ and any tangent vector $\mathbf{t}$ on the surface are orthogonal by construction, we know that

$$\mathbf{n} \cdot \mathbf{t} = \mathbf{n}^T \mathbf{t} = 0.$$

When we transform a point on the surface by some matrix $\mathbf{M}$, the new tangent vector $\mathbf{t}'$ at the transformed point is $\mathbf{Mt}$. The transformed normal $\mathbf{n}'$ should be equal to $\mathbf{Sn}$ for some 4×4 matrix $\mathbf{S}$. To maintain the orthogonality requirement, we must have

$$
\begin{aligned}
0 &= (\mathbf{n}')^T \mathbf{t}' \\
&= (\mathbf{Sn})^T \mathbf{Mt} \\
&= (\mathbf{n})^T \mathbf{S}^T \mathbf{Mt}.
\end{aligned}
$$

This condition holds if $\mathbf{S}^T \mathbf{M} = \mathbf{I}$, the identity matrix. Therefore, $\mathbf{S}^T = \mathbf{M}^{-1}$, and so $\mathbf{S} = (\mathbf{M}^{-1})^T$, and we see that normals must be transformed by the inverse transpose of the transformation matrix. This detail is one of the main reasons why Transforms maintain their inverses.

Note that this method does not explicitly compute the transpose of the inverse when transforming normals. It just indexes into the inverse matrix in a different order (compare to the code for transforming Vector3fs).

Transform 83

Vector3f 60

⟨Transform Inline Functions⟩ +≡
```
template <typename T> inline Normal3<T>
Transform::operator()(const Normal3<T> &n) const {
    T x = n.x, y = n.y, z = n.z;
    return Normal3<T>(mInv.m[0][0]*x + mInv.m[1][0]*y + mInv.m[2][0]*z,
                      mInv.m[0][1]*x + mInv.m[1][1]*y + mInv.m[2][1]*z,
                      mInv.m[0][2]*x + mInv.m[1][2]*y + mInv.m[2][2]*z);
}
```

2.8.4 RAYS

Transforming rays is conceptually straightforward: it's a matter of transforming the constituent origin and direction and copying the other data members. (pbrt also provides a similar method for transforming RayDifferentials.)

The approach used in pbrt to manage floating-point round-off error introduces some subtleties that require a small adjustment to the transformed ray origin. The ⟨*Offset ray origin to edge of error bounds*⟩ fragment handles these details; it is defined in Section 3.9.4, where round-off error and pbrt's mechanisms for dealing with it are discussed.

⟨Transform Inline Functions⟩ +≡
```
inline Ray Transform::operator()(const Ray &r) const {
    Vector3f oError;
    Point3f o = (*this)(r.o, &oError);
    Vector3f d = (*this)(r.d);
    ⟨Offset ray origin to edge of error bounds and compute tMax 233⟩
    return Ray(o, d, tMax, r.time, r.medium);
}
```

2.8.5 BOUNDING BOXES

The easiest way to transform an axis-aligned bounding box is to transform all eight of its corner vertices and then compute a new bounding box that encompasses those points. The implementation of this approach is shown below; one of the exercises for this chapter is to implement a technique to do this computation more efficiently.

⟨Transform Method Definitions⟩ +≡
```
Bounds3f Transform::operator()(const Bounds3f &b) const {
    const Transform &M = *this;
    Bounds3f ret(M(Point3f(b.pMin.x, b.pMin.y, b.pMin.z)));
    ret = Union(ret, M(Point3f(b.pMax.x, b.pMin.y, b.pMin.z)));
    ret = Union(ret, M(Point3f(b.pMin.x, b.pMax.y, b.pMin.z)));
    ret = Union(ret, M(Point3f(b.pMin.x, b.pMin.y, b.pMax.z)));
    ret = Union(ret, M(Point3f(b.pMin.x, b.pMax.y, b.pMax.z)));
    ret = Union(ret, M(Point3f(b.pMax.x, b.pMax.y, b.pMin.z)));
    ret = Union(ret, M(Point3f(b.pMax.x, b.pMin.y, b.pMax.z)));
    ret = Union(ret, M(Point3f(b.pMax.x, b.pMax.y, b.pMax.z)));
    return ret;
}
```

2.8.6 COMPOSITION OF TRANSFORMATIONS

Having defined how the matrices representing individual types of transformations are constructed, we can now consider an aggregate transformation resulting from a series of individual transformations. Finally, we will see the real value of representing transformations with matrices.

Consider a series of transformations **ABC**. We'd like to compute a new transformation **T** such that applying **T** gives the same result as applying each of **A**, **B**, and **C** in reverse order; that is, $A(B(C(p))) = T(p)$. Such a transformation **T** can be computed by multiplying the matrices of the transformations **A**, **B**, and **C** together. In pbrt, we can write:

```
Transform T = A * B * C;
```

Then we can apply T to Point3fs p as usual, Point3f pp = T(p), instead of applying each transformation in turn: Point3f pp = A(B(C(p))).

We use the C++ * operator to compute the new transformation that results from post-multiplying a transformation with another transformation t2. In matrix multiplication, the (i, j)th element of the resulting matrix is the inner product of the ith row of the first matrix with the jth column of the second.

The inverse of the resulting transformation is equal to the product of t2.mInv * mInv. This is a result of the matrix identity

$$(AB)^{-1} = B^{-1}A^{-1}.$$

⟨*Transform Method Definitions*⟩ +≡
```
    Transform Transform::operator*(const Transform &t2) const {
        return Transform(Matrix4x4::Mul(m, t2.m),
                         Matrix4x4::Mul(t2.mInv, mInv));
    }
```

2.8.7 TRANSFORMATIONS AND COORDINATE SYSTEM HANDEDNESS

Certain types of transformations change a left-handed coordinate system into a right-handed one, or vice versa. Some routines will need to know if the handedness of the source coordinate system is different from that of the destination. In particular, routines that want to ensure that a surface normal always points "outside" of a surface might need to flip the normal's direction after transformation if the handedness changes.

Fortunately, it is easy to tell if handedness is changed by a transformation: it happens only when the determinant of the transformation's upper-left 3×3 submatrix is negative.

⟨*Transform Method Definitions*⟩ +≡
```
    bool Transform::SwapsHandedness() const {
        Float det =
            m.m[0][0] * (m.m[1][1] * m.m[2][2] - m.m[1][2] * m.m[2][1]) -
            m.m[0][1] * (m.m[1][0] * m.m[2][2] - m.m[1][2] * m.m[2][0]) +
            m.m[0][2] * (m.m[1][0] * m.m[2][1] - m.m[1][1] * m.m[2][0]);
        return det < 0;
    }
```

Figure 2.15: Spinning Spheres. Three spheres, spinning at different rates using the transformation animation code implemented in this section. Note that the reflections of the spheres are blurry as well as the spheres themselves.

*2.9 ANIMATING TRANSFORMATIONS

pbrt supports keyframe matrix animation for cameras and geometric primitives in the scene. Rather than just supplying a single transformation to place the corresponding object in the scene, the user may supply a number of *keyframe* transformations, each one associated with a particular point in time. This makes it possible for the camera to move and for objects in the scene to be moving during the time the simulated camera's shutter is open. Figure 2.15 shows three spheres animated using keyframe matrix animation in pbrt.

In general, the problem of interpolating between keyframe matrices is under-defined. As one example, if we have a rotation about the *x* axis of 179 degrees followed by another of 181 degrees, does this represent a small rotation of 2 degrees or a large rotation of −358 degrees? For another example, consider two matrices where one is the identity and the other is a 180-degree rotation about the *z* axis. There are an infinite number of ways to go from one orientation to the other.

Keyframe matrix interpolation is an important problem in computer animation, where a number of different approaches have been developed. Fortunately, the problem of matrix interpolation in a renderer is generally less challenging than it is for animation systems for two reasons.

First, in a renderer like pbrt, we generally have a keyframe matrix at the camera shutter open time and another at the shutter close time; we only need to interpolate between the two of them across the time of a single image. In animation systems, the matrices are generally available at a lower time frequency, so that there are many frames between

---

*   This section covers advanced topics and may be skipped on a first reading.

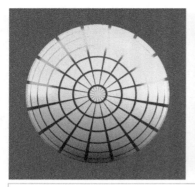  

Figure 2.16: (left) Sphere with a grid of lines as a texture, not rotating. (middle) Sphere rotating 90 degrees during the course of the frame, using the technique for interpolating transformations implemented in this section. (right) Sphere rotating 90 degrees using direct interpolation of matrix components to interpolate transformations. In this case, the animated sphere incorrectly grows larger. Furthermore, the lines toward the outside of the sphere, which should remain sharp, incorrectly become blurry.

pairs of keyframe matrices; as such, there's more opportunity to notice shortcomings in the interpolation.

Second, in a physically based renderer, the longer the period of time over which we need to interpolate the pair of matrices, the longer the virtual camera shutter is open and the more motion blur there will be in the final image; the increased amount of motion blur often hides sins of the interpolation.

The most straightforward approach to interpolate transformations defined by keyframe matrices—directly interpolating the individual components of the matrices—is not a good one, as it will generally lead to unexpected and undesirable results. For example, if the transformations apply different rotations, then even if we have a rigid-body motion, the intermediate matrices may scale the object, which is clearly undesirable. (If the matrices have a full 180-degree rotation between them, the object may be scaled down to nothing at the middle of the interpolation!)

Figure 2.16 shows a sphere that rotates 90 degrees over the course of the frame; direct interpolation of matrix elements (on the right) gives a less accurate result than the approach implemented in this section (in the middle).

The approach used for transformation interpolation in pbrt is based on *matrix decomposition*—given an arbitrary transformation matrix M, we decompose it into a concatentation of scale (S), rotation (R), and translation (T) transformations,

$$M = SRT,$$

where each of those components is independently interpolated and then the composite interpolated matrix is found by multiplying the three interpolated matrices together.

Interpolation of translation and scale can be performed easily and accurately with linear interpolation of the components of their matrices; interpolating rotations is more difficult. Before describing the matrix decomposition implementation in pbrt, we will first introduce *quaternions*, an elegant representation of rotations that leads to effective methods for interpolating them.

2.9.1 QUATERNIONS

Quaternions were originally invented by Sir William Rowan Hamilton in 1843 as a generalization of complex numbers. He determined that just as in two dimensions (x, y), where complex numbers could be defined as a sum of a real and an imaginary part $x + yi$, with $i^2 = -1$, a generalization could be made to four dimensions, giving quaternions.

A quaternion is a four-tuple,

$$q = (x, y, z, w) = w + xi + yj + zk, \qquad [2.4]$$

where i, j, and k are defined[2] so that $i^2 = j^2 = k^2 = ijk = -1$. Other important relationships between the components are that $ij = k$ and $ji = -k$. This implies that quaternion multiplication is generally not commutative.

A quaternion can be represented as a quadruple $\mathbf{q} = (\mathbf{q}_x, \mathbf{q}_y, \mathbf{q}_z, \mathbf{q}_w)$ or as $\mathbf{q} = (\mathbf{q}_{xyz}, \mathbf{q}_w)$, where $\mathbf{q}_{xyz}$ is an imaginary 3-vector and $\mathbf{q}_w$ is the real part. We will use both representations interchangeably in this section.

An expression for the product of two arbitrary quaternions can be found by expanding their definition in terms of real and imaginary components:

$$\mathbf{qq}' = (\mathbf{q}_w + \mathbf{q}_x i + \mathbf{q}_y j + \mathbf{q}_z k)(\mathbf{q}'_w + \mathbf{q}'_x i + \mathbf{q}'_y j + \mathbf{q}'_z k).$$

Collecting terms and using identities among the components like those listed above (e.g., $i^2 = -1$), the result can be expressed concisely using vector cross and dot products:

$$(\mathbf{qq}')_{xyz} = \mathbf{q}_{xyz} \times \mathbf{q}'_{xyz} + \mathbf{q}_w \mathbf{q}'_{xyz} + \mathbf{q}'_w \mathbf{q}_{xyz}$$

$$(\mathbf{qq}')_w = \mathbf{q}_w \mathbf{q}'_w - (\mathbf{q}_{xyz} \cdot \mathbf{q}'_{xyz}). \qquad [2.5]$$

There is a useful relationship between unit quaternions (quaternions whose components satisfy $x^2 + y^2 + z^2 + w^2 = 1$) and the space of rotations in $\mathbb{R}^3$: specifically, a rotation of angle 2θ about a unit axis $\hat{v}$ can be mapped to a unit quaternion $(\hat{v} \sin \theta, \cos \theta)$, in which case the following quaternion product is equivalent to applying the rotation to a point p expressed in homogeneous coordinate form:

$$p' = qpq^{-1}.$$

Furthermore, the product of several rotation quaternions produces another quaternion that is equivalent to applying the rotations in sequence.

The implementation of the `Quaternion` class in pbrt is in the files `core/quaternion.h` and `core/quaternion.cpp`. The default constructor initializes a unit quaternion.

⟨*Quaternion Public Methods*⟩ ≡

```
Quaternion() : v(0, 0, 0), w(1) { }
```

---

2   Hamilton found the discovery of this relationship among the components compelling enough that he used a knife to carve the formula on the bridge he was crossing when it came to him.

We use a `Vector3f` to represent the xyz components of the quaternion; doing so lets us make use of various methods of `Vector3f` in the implementation of some of the methods below.

⟨*Quaternion Public Data*⟩ ≡
```
Vector3f v;
Float w;
```

Addition and subtraction of quaternions is performed component-wise. This follows directly from the definition in Equation (2.4). For example,

$$q + q' = w + xi + yj + zk + w' + x'i + y'j + z'k$$
$$= (w + w') + (x + x')i + (y + y')j + (z + z')k.$$

Other arithmetic methods (subtraction, multiplication, and division by a scalar) are defined and implemented similarly and won't be included here.

⟨*Quaternion Public Methods*⟩ +≡
```
Quaternion &operator+=(const Quaternion &q) {
    v += q.v;
    w += q.w;
    return *this;
}
```

The inner product of two quaternions is implemented by its `Dot()` method, and a quaternion can be normalized by dividing by its length.

⟨*Quaternion Inline Functions*⟩ ≡
```
inline Float Dot(const Quaternion &q1, const Quaternion &q2) {
    return Dot(q1.v, q2.v) + q1.w * q2.w;
}
```

⟨*Quaternion Inline Functions*⟩ +≡
```
inline Quaternion Normalize(const Quaternion &q) {
    return q / std::sqrt(Dot(q, q));
}
```

It's useful to be able to compute the transformation matrix that represents the same rotation as a quaternion. In particular, after interpolating rotations with quaternions in the `AnimatedTransform` class, we'll need to convert the interpolated rotation back to a transformation matrix to compute the final composite interpolated transformation.

To derive the rotation matrix for a quaternion, recall that the transformation of a point by a quaternion is given by $p' = qpq^{-1}$. We want a matrix M that performs the same transformation, so that $p' = Mp$. If we expand out the quaternion multiplication qpq^{-1} using Equation (2.5), simplify with the quaternion basis identities, collect terms, and represent the result in a matrix, we can determine that the following 3×3 matrix represents the same transformation:

$$M = \begin{pmatrix} 1 - 2(q_y^2 + q_z^2) & 2(q_x q_y + q_z q_w) & 2q_x q_z - q_y q_w) \\ 2(q_x q_y - q_z q_w) & 1 - 2(q_x^2 + q_z^2) & 2(q_y q_z + q_x q_w) \\ 2(q_x q_z + q_y q_w) & 2(q_y q_z - q_x q_w) & 1 - 2(q_x^2 + q_y^2) \end{pmatrix}. \qquad \text{(2.6)}$$

This computation is implemented in the method `Quaternion::ToTransform()`. We won't include its implementation here since it's a direct implementation of Equation (2.6).

⟨*Quaternion Public Methods*⟩ +≡
```
    Transform ToTransform() const;
```

Note that we could alternatively use the fact that a unit quaternion represents a rotation $(q_{xyz} \sin \theta, \cos \theta)$ of angle 2θ around the unit axis $\hat{q}_{xyz}$ to compute a rotation matrix. First we would compute the angle of rotation θ as $\theta = 2 \arccos q_w$, and then we'd use the previously defined `Rotate()` function, passing it the axis $\hat{q}_{xyz}$ and the rotation angle θ. However, this alternative would be substantially less efficient, requiring multiple calls to trigonometric functions, while the approach implemented here only uses floating-point addition, subtraction, and multiplication.

It is also useful to be able to create a quaternion from a rotation matrix. For this purpose, `Quaternion` provides a constructor that takes a `Transform`. The appropriate quaternion can be computed by making use of relationships between elements of the rotation matrix in Equation (2.6) and quaternion components. For example, if we subtract the transpose of this matrix from itself, then the (0, 1) component of the resulting matrix has the value $-4q_w q_z$. Thus, given a particular instance of a rotation matrix with known values, it's possible to use a number of relationships like this between the matrix values and the quaternion components to generate a system of equations that can be solved for the quaternion components.

We won't include the details of the derivation or the actual implementation here in the text; for more information about how to derive this technique, including handling numerical robustness, see Shoemake (1991).

⟨*Quaternion Public Methods*⟩ +≡
```
    Quaternion(const Transform &t);
```

2.9.2 QUATERNION INTERPOLATION

The last quaternion function we will define, `Slerp()`, interpolates between two quaternions using spherical linear interpolation. Spherical linear interpolation gives constant speed motion along great circle arcs on the surface of a sphere and consequently has two desirable properties for interpolating rotations:

- The interpolated rotation path exhibits *torque minimization*: the path to get between two rotations is the shortest possible path in rotation space.
- The interpolation has *constant angular velocity*: the relationship between change in the animation parameter t and the change in the resulting rotation is constant over the course of interpolation (in other words, the speed of interpolation is constant across the interpolation range).

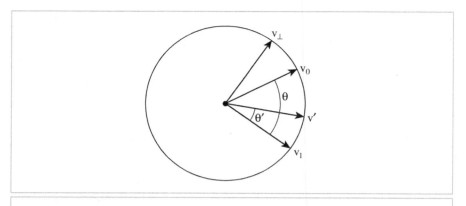

Figure 2.17: To understand quaternion spherical linear interpolation, consider in 2D two vectors on the unit sphere, v_0 and v_1, with angle θ between them. We'd like to be able to compute the interpolated vector at some angle θ' between the two of them. To do so, we can find a vector that's orthogonal to v_1, $v_\perp$ and then apply the trigonometric identity $v' = v_1 \cos \theta' + v_\perp \sin \theta'$.

See the "Further Reading" section at the end of the chapter for references that discuss more thoroughly what characteristics a good interpolated rotation should have.

Spherical linear interpolation for quaternions was originally presented by Shoemake (1985) as follows, where two quaternions q_1 and q_2 are given and $t \in [0, 1]$ is the parameter value to interpolate between them:

$$slerp(\mathbf{q}_1, \mathbf{q}_2, t) = \frac{\mathbf{q}_1 \sin((1-t)\theta) + \mathbf{q}_2 \sin(t\theta)}{\sin \theta}.$$

An intuitive way to understand Slerp() was presented by Blow (2004). As context, given the quaternions to interpolate between, q_1 and q_2, denote by θ the angle between them. Then, given a parameter value $t \in [0, 1]$, we'd like to find the intermediate quaternion q' that makes angle $\theta' = \theta t$ between it and q_1, along the path from q_1 to q_2.

An easy way to compute q' is to first compute an orthogonal coordinate system in the space of quaternions where one axis is q_1 and the other is a quaternion orthogonal to q_1 such that the two axes form a basis that spans q_1 and q_2. Given such a coordinate system, we can compute rotations with respect to q_1. (See Figure 2.17, which illustrates the concept in the 2D setting.) An orthogonal vector $q_\perp$ can be found by projecting q_1 onto q_2 and then subtracting the orthogonal projection from q_2; the remainder is guaranteed to be orthogonal to q_1:

$$\mathbf{q}_\perp = \mathbf{q}_2 - (\mathbf{q}_1 \cdot \mathbf{q}_2)\mathbf{q}_1. \tag{2.7}$$

Given the coordinate system, quaternions along the animation path are given by

$$\mathbf{q}' = \mathbf{q}_1 \cos(\theta t) + \mathbf{q}_\perp \sin(\theta t). \tag{2.8}$$

The implementation of the Slerp() function checks to see if the two quaternions are nearly parallel, in which case it uses regular linear interpolation of quaternion components in order to avoid numerical instability. Otherwise, it computes an orthogonal

Slerp() 103

quaternion qperp using Equation (2.7) and then computes the interpolated quaternion with Equation (2.8).

⟨*Quaternion Method Definitions*⟩ ≡
```
Quaternion Slerp(Float t, const Quaternion &q1,
                 const Quaternion &q2) {
    Float cosTheta = Dot(q1, q2);
    if (cosTheta > .9995f)
        return Normalize((1 - t) * q1 + t * q2);
    else {
        Float theta = std::acos(Clamp(cosTheta, -1, 1));
        Float thetap = theta * t;
        Quaternion qperp = Normalize(q2 - q1 * cosTheta);
        return q1 * std::cos(thetap) + qperp * std::sin(thetap);
    }
}
```

2.9.3 AnimatedTransform IMPLEMENTATION

Given the foundations of the quaternion infrastructure, we can now implement the AnimatedTransform class, which implements keyframe transformation interpolation in pbrt. Its constructor takes two transformations and the time values they are associated with.

As mentioned earlier, AnimatedTransform decomposes the given composite transformation matrices into scaling, rotation, and translation components. The decomposition is performed by the AnimatedTransform::Decompose() method.

⟨*AnimatedTransform Method Definitions*⟩ ≡
```
AnimatedTransform::AnimatedTransform(const Transform *startTransform,
        Float startTime, const Transform *endTransform, Float endTime)
    : startTransform(startTransform), endTransform(endTransform),
      startTime(startTime), endTime(endTime),
      actuallyAnimated(*startTransform != *endTransform) {
    Decompose(startTransform->m, &T[0], &R[0], &S[0]);
    Decompose(endTransform->m, &T[1], &R[1], &S[1]);
    ⟨Flip R[1] if needed to select shortest path 106⟩
    hasRotation = Dot(R[0], R[1]) < 0.9995f;
    ⟨Compute terms of motion derivative function⟩
}
```

⟨*AnimatedTransform Private Data*⟩ ≡
```
const Transform *startTransform, *endTransform;
const Float startTime, endTime;
const bool actuallyAnimated;
Vector3f T[2];
Quaternion R[2];
Matrix4x4 S[2];
bool hasRotation;
```

Given the composite matrix for a transformation, information has been lost about any individual transformations that were composed to compute it. For example, given the matrix for the product of a translation and then a scale, an equal matrix could also be computed by first scaling and then translating (by different amounts). Thus, we need to choose a canonical sequence of transformations for the decomposition. For our needs here, the specific choice made isn't significant. (It would be more important in an animation system that was decomposing composite transformations in order to make them editable by changing individual components, for example.)

We will handle only affine transformations here, which is what is needed for animating cameras and geometric primitives in a rendering system; perspective transformations aren't generally relevant to animation of objects like these.

The transformation decomposition we will use is the following:

$$\mathbf{M} = \mathbf{TRS}, \qquad [2.9]$$

where $\mathbf{M}$ is the given transformation, $\mathbf{T}$ is a translation, $\mathbf{R}$ is a rotation, and $\mathbf{S}$ is a scale. $\mathbf{S}$ is actually a generalized scale (Shoemake and Duff call it *stretch*) that represents a scale in *some* coordinate system, just not necessarily the current one. In any case, it can still be correctly interpolated with linear interpolation of its components. The Decompose() method computes the decomposition given a Matrix4x4.

⟨*AnimatedTransform Method Definitions*⟩ +≡
```
void AnimatedTransform::Decompose(const Matrix4x4 &m, Vector3f *T,
        Quaternion *Rquat, Matrix4x4 *S) {
    ⟨Extract translation T from transformation matrix 104⟩
    ⟨Compute new transformation matrix M without translation 104⟩
    ⟨Extract rotation R from transformation matrix 105⟩
    ⟨Compute scale S using rotation and original matrix 105⟩
}
```

Extracting the translation $\mathbf{T}$ is easy; it can be found directly from the appropriate elements of the 4×4 transformation matrix.

⟨*Extract translation* T *from transformation matrix*⟩ ≡   104
```
T->x = m.m[0][3];
T->y = m.m[1][3];
T->z = m.m[2][3];
```

Since we are assuming an affine transformation (no projective components), after we remove the translation, what is left is the upper 3×3 matrix that represents scaling and rotation together. This matrix is copied into a new matrix M for further processing.

⟨*Compute new transformation matrix* M *without translation*⟩ ≡   104
```
Matrix4x4 M = m;
for (int i = 0; i < 3; ++i)
    M.m[i][3] = M.m[3][i] = 0.f;
M.m[3][3] = 1.f;
```

Matrix4x4 1081
Matrix4x4::m 1081
Quaternion 99
Vector3f 60

Next we'd like to extract the pure rotation component of M. We'll use a technique called *polar decomposition* to do this. It can be shown that the polar decomposition of a matrix

M into rotation **R** and scale **S** can be computed by successively averaging **M** with its inverse transpose

$$\mathbf{M}_{i+1} = \frac{1}{2}\left(\mathbf{M}_i + (\mathbf{M}_i^T)^{-1}\right) \qquad\qquad [2.10]$$

until convergence, at which point $\mathbf{M}_i = \mathbf{R}$. (It's easy to see that if **M** is a pure rotation, then averaging it with its inverse transpose will leave it unchanged, since its inverse is equal to its transpose. The "Further Reading" section has more references that discuss why this series converges to the rotation component of the original transformation.) Shoemake and Duff (1992) proved that the resulting matrix is the closest orthogonal matrix to **M**—a desirable property.

To compute this series, we iteratively apply Equation (2.10) until either the difference between successive terms is small or a fixed number of iterations have been performed. In practice, this series generally converges quickly.

⟨*Extract rotation* R *from transformation matrix*⟩ ≡   **104**
```
Float norm;
int count = 0;
Matrix4x4 R = M;
do {
    ⟨Compute next matrix Rnext in series 105⟩
    ⟨Compute norm of difference between R and Rnext 105⟩
    R = Rnext;
} while (++count < 100 && norm > .0001);
*Rquat = Quaternion(R);
```

⟨*Compute next matrix* Rnext *in series*⟩ ≡   **105**
```
Matrix4x4 Rnext;
Matrix4x4 Rit = Inverse(Transpose(R));
for (int i = 0; i < 4; ++i)
    for (int j = 0; j < 4; ++j)
        Rnext.m[i][j] = 0.5f * (R.m[i][j] + Rit.m[i][j]);
```

⟨*Compute norm of difference between* R *and* Rnext⟩ ≡   **105**
```
norm = 0;
for (int i = 0; i < 3; ++i) {
    Float n = std::abs(R.m[i][0] - Rnext.m[i][0]) +
              std::abs(R.m[i][1] - Rnext.m[i][1]) +
              std::abs(R.m[i][2] - Rnext.m[i][2]);
    norm = std::max(norm, n);
}
```

Once we've extracted the rotation from **M**, the scale is all that's left. We would like to find the matrix **S** that satisfies $\mathbf{M} = \mathbf{RS}$. Now that we know both **R** and **M**, we just solve for $\mathbf{S} = \mathbf{R}^{-1}\mathbf{M}$.

⟨*Compute scale* S *using rotation and original matrix*⟩ ≡   **104**
```
*S = Matrix4x4::Mul(Inverse(R), M);
```

For every rotation matrix, there are two unit quaternions that correspond to the matrix that only differ in sign. If the dot product of the two rotations that we have extracted is negative, then a slerp between them won't take the shortest path between the two corresponding rotations. Negating one of them (here the second was chosen arbitrarily) causes the shorter path to be taken instead.

⟨*Flip* R[1] *if needed to select shortest path*⟩ ≡   **103**
```
if (Dot(R[0], R[1]) < 0)
    R[1] = -R[1];
```

The Interpolate() method computes the interpolated transformation matrix at a given time. The matrix is found by interpolating the previously extracted translation, rotation, and scale and then multiplying them together to get a composite matrix that represents the effect of the three transformations together.

⟨*AnimatedTransform Method Definitions*⟩ +≡
```
void AnimatedTransform::Interpolate(Float time, Transform *t) const {
    ⟨Handle boundary conditions for matrix interpolation 106⟩
    Float dt = (time - startTime) / (endTime - startTime);
    ⟨Interpolate translation at dt 106⟩
    ⟨Interpolate rotation at dt 107⟩
    ⟨Interpolate scale at dt 107⟩
    ⟨Compute interpolated matrix as product of interpolated components 107⟩
}
```

If the given time value is outside the time range of the two transformations stored in the AnimatedTransform, then the transformation at the start time or end time is returned, as appropriate. The AnimatedTransform constructor also checks whether the two Transforms stored are the same; if so, then no interpolation is necessary either. All of the classes in pbrt that support animation always store an AnimatedTransform for their transformation, rather than storing either a Transform or AnimatedTransform as appropriate. This simplifies their implementations, though it does make it worthwhile to check for this case here and not unnecessarily do the work to interpolate between two equal transformations.

⟨*Handle boundary conditions for matrix interpolation*⟩ ≡   **106**
```
if (!actuallyAnimated || time <= startTime) {
    *t = *startTransform;
    return;
}
if (time >= endTime) {
    *t = *endTransform;
    return;
}
```

The dt variable stores the offset in the range from startTime to endTime; it is zero at startTime and one at endTime. Given dt, interpolation of the translation is trivial.

⟨*Interpolate translation at* dt⟩ ≡   **106**
```
Vector3f trans = (1 - dt) * T[0] + dt * T[1];
```

The rotation is interpolated between the start and end rotations using the Slerp() routine (Section 2.9.2).

⟨*Interpolate rotation at* dt⟩ ≡   **106**
```
Quaternion rotate = Slerp(dt, R[0], R[1]);
```

Finally, the interpolated scale matrix is computed by interpolating the individual elements of the start and end scale matrices. Because the Matrix4x4 constructor sets the matrix to the identity matrix, we don't need to initialize any of the other elements of scale.

⟨*Interpolate scale at* dt⟩ ≡   **106**
```
Matrix4x4 scale;
for (int i = 0; i < 3; ++i)
    for (int j = 0; j < 3; ++j)
        scale.m[i][j] = Lerp(dt, S[0].m[i][j], S[1].m[i][j]);
```

Given the three interpolated parts, the product of their three transformation matrices gives us the final result.

⟨*Compute interpolated matrix as product of interpolated components*⟩ ≡   **106**
```
*t = Translate(trans) * rotate.ToTransform() * Transform(scale);
```

AnimatedTransform also provides a number of methods that apply interpolated transformations directly, using the provided time for Point3fs and Vector3fs and Ray::time for Rays. These methods are more efficient than calling AnimatedTransform::Interpolate() and then using the returned matrix when there is no actual animation since a copy of the transformation matrix doesn't need to be made in that case.

⟨*AnimatedTransform Public Methods*⟩ ≡
```
Ray operator()(const Ray &r) const;
RayDifferential operator()(const RayDifferential &r) const;
Point3f operator()(Float time, const Point3f &p) const;
Vector3f operator()(Float time, const Vector3f &v) const;
```

2.9.4 BOUNDING MOVING BOUNDING BOXES

Given a Bounds3f that is transformed by an animated transformation, it's useful to be able to compute a bounding box that encompasses all of its motion over the animation time period. For example, if we can bound the motion of an animated geometric primitive, then we can intersect rays with this bound to determine if the ray might intersect the object before incurring the cost of interpolating the primitive's bound to the ray's time to check that intersection. The AnimatedTransform::MotionBounds() method performs this computation, taking a bounding box and returning the bounding box of its motion over the AnimatedTransform's time range.

There are two easy cases: first, if the keyframe matrices are equal, then we can arbitrarily apply only the starting transformation to compute the full bounds. Second, if the transformation only includes scaling and/or translation, then the bounding box that encompasses the bounding box's transformed positions at both the start time and the end time bounds all of its motion. To see why this is so, consider the position of a transformed point p as a function of time; we'll denote this function of two matrices, a point, and a time by $a(\mathbf{M}_0, \mathbf{M}_1, \mathrm{p}, t)$.

Since in this case the rotation component of the decomposition is the identity, then with our matrix decomposition we have

$$a(\mathbf{M}_0, \mathbf{M}_1, \mathrm{p}, t) = \mathbf{T}(t)\mathbf{S}(t)\mathrm{p},$$

where the translation and scale are both written as functions of time. Assuming for simplicity that $\mathbf{S}(t)$ is a regular scale, we can find expressions for the components of $a(\mathbf{M}_0, \mathbf{M}_1, \mathrm{p}, t)$. For example, for the x component, we have:

$$
\begin{aligned}
a(\mathbf{M}_0, \mathbf{M}_1, \mathrm{p}, t)_x &= [(1-t)s_{0,0} + ts'_{0,0}]\mathrm{p}_x + (1-t)d_{0,3} + td'_{0,3} \\
&= [s_{0,0}\mathrm{p}_x + d_{0,3}] + [-s_{0,0}\mathrm{p}_x + s'_{0,0}\mathrm{p}_x - d_{0,3} + d'_{0,3}]t,
\end{aligned}
$$

where $s_{0,0}$ is the corresponding element of the scale matrix for $\mathbf{M}_0$, $s'_{0,0}$ is the same scale matrix element for $\mathbf{M}_1$, and the translation matrix elements are similarly denoted by d. (We chose d for "delta" here since t is already claimed for time.) As a linear function of t, the extrema of this function are at the start and end times. The other coordinates and the case for a generalized scale follow similarly.

⟨*AnimatedTransform Method Definitions*⟩ +≡
```
Bounds3f AnimatedTransform::MotionBounds(const Bounds3f &b) const {
    if (!actuallyAnimated)
        return (*startTransform)(b);
    if (hasRotation == false)
        return Union((*startTransform)(b), (*endTransform)(b));
    ⟨Return motion bounds accounting for animated rotation 108⟩
}
```

For the general case with animated rotations, the motion function may have extrema at points in the middle of the time range. We know of no simple way to find these points. Many renderers address this issue by sampling a large number of times in the time range, computing the interpolated transformation at each one, and taking the union of all of the corresponding transformed bounding boxes. Here, we will develop a more well-grounded method that lets us robustly compute these motion bounds.

We use a slightly simpler conservative bound that entails computing the motion of the eight corners of the bounding box individually and finding the union of those bounds.

⟨*Return motion bounds accounting for animated rotation*⟩ ≡   **108**
```
Bounds3f bounds;
for (int corner = 0; corner < 8; ++corner)
    bounds = Union(bounds, BoundPointMotion(b.Corner(corner)));
return bounds;
```

For each bounding box corner p, we need to find the extrema of a over the animation time range. Recall from calculus that the extrema of a continuous function over some domain are either at the boundary points of the domain or at points where the function's first derivative is zero. Thus, the overall bound is given by the union of the positions at the start and end of motion as well as the position at any extrema.

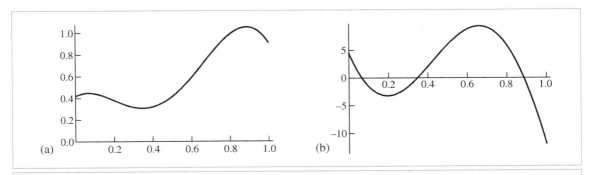

Figure 2.18: (a) Motion of the x coordinate of a point p as a function of time, as determined by two keyframe matrices. (b) The derivative of the motion function, Equation (2.12). Note that extrema of the motion function in the given time range correspond to zeros of the derivative.

Figure 2.18 shows a plot of one coordinate of the motion function and its derivative for an interesting motion path of a point. Note that the maximum value of the function over the time range is reached at a point where the derivative has a zero.

To bound the motion of a single point, we start our derivation by following the approach used for the no-rotation case, expanding out the three **T**, **R**, and **S** components of Equation (2.9) as functions of time and finding their product. We have:

$$a(\mathbf{M_0}, \mathbf{M_1}, \mathrm{p}, t) = \mathbf{T}(t)\mathbf{R}(t)\mathbf{S}(t)\mathrm{p}. \qquad [2.11]$$

The result is quite complex when expanded out, mostly due to the slerp and the conversion of the resulting quaternion to a matrix; a computer algebra system is a requirement for working with this function.

The derivative $\partial a(\mathbf{M_0}, \mathbf{M_1}, \mathrm{p}, t)/\partial t$ is also quite complex—in its full algebraic glory, over 2,000 operations are required to evaluate its value for a given pair of decomposed matrices, point and time. However, given specific transformation matrices and a specific point, a is simplified substantially; we'll denote the specialized function of t alone as $a_{\mathbf{M},\mathrm{p}}(t)$. Evaluating its derivative requires roughly 10 floating-point operations, a sine, and a cosine to evaluate for each coordinate:

$$\frac{da_{\mathbf{M},\mathrm{p}}(t)}{dt} = c_1 + (c_2 + c_3\, t)\, \cos(2\theta\, t) + (c_4 + c_5\, t)\, \sin(2\theta\, t), \qquad [2.12]$$

where θ is the arc cosine of the dot product of the two quaternions and where the five coefficients c_i are 3-vectors that depend on the two matrices and the position p. This specialization works out well, since we will need to evaluate the function at many time values for a given point.

We now have two tasks: first, given a pair of keyframe matrices and a point p, we first need to be able to efficiently compute the values of the coefficients c_i. Then, given the relatively simple function defined by c_i and θ, we need to find the zeros of Equation (2.12), which may represent the times at which motion extrema occur.

For the first task, we will first factor out the contributions to the coefficients that depend on the keyframe matrices from those that depend on the point p, under the assumption that bounding boxes for multiple points' motion will be computed for each pair of keyframe matrices (as is the case here). The result is fortunately quite simple—the c_i vectors are are linear functions of the point's x, y, and z components.

$$c_i(\mathrm{p}) = k_{i,c} + k_{i,x}\mathrm{p}_x + k_{i,y}\mathrm{p}_y + k_{i,z}\mathrm{p}_z.$$

Thus, given the k_i coefficients and a particular point p we want to bound the motion of, we can efficiently compute the coefficients c_i of the derivative function in Equation (2.12). The DerivativeTerm structure encapsulates these coefficients and this computation.

⟨*AnimatedTransform Private Data*⟩ +≡
```
struct DerivativeTerm {
    DerivativeTerm(Float c, Float x, Float y, Float z)
        : kc(c), kx(x), ky(y), kz(z) { }
    Float kc, kx, ky, kz;
    Float Eval(const Point3f &p) const {
        return kc + kx * p.x + ky * p.y + kz * p.z;
    }
};
```

The attributes c1-c5 store derivative information corresponding to the five terms in Equation (2.12). The three array elements correspond to the three dimensions of space.

⟨*AnimatedTransform Private Data*⟩ +≡
```
DerivativeTerm c1[3], c2[3], c3[3], c4[3], c5[3];
```

The fragment ⟨*Compute terms of motion derivative function*⟩ in the AnimatedTransform constructor, not included here, initializes these terms, via automatically generated code. Given that it requires a few thousand floating-point operations, doing this work once and amortizing over the multiple bounding box corners is helpful. The k_i coefficients are more easily computed if we assume a canonical time range $[0, 1]$; later, we'll have to remap the t values of zeros of the motion function to the actual shutter time range.

Given the coefficients k_i based on the keyframe matrices, BoundPointMotion() computes a robust bound of the motion of p.

⟨*AnimatedTransform Method Definitions*⟩ +≡
```
Bounds3f AnimatedTransform::BoundPointMotion(const Point3f &p) const {
    Bounds3f bounds((*startTransform)(p), (*endTransform)(p));
    Float cosTheta = Dot(R[0], R[1]);
    Float theta = std::acos(Clamp(cosTheta, -1, 1));
    for (int c = 0; c < 3; ++c) {
        ⟨Find any motion derivative zeros for the component c 111⟩
        ⟨Expand bounding box for any motion derivative zeros found 111⟩
    }
    return bounds;
}
```

The IntervalFindZeros() function, to be introduced shortly, numerically finds zeros of Equation (2.12). Up to four are possible.

⟨*Find any motion derivative zeros for the component* c⟩ ≡   **110**
```
Float zeros[4];
int nZeros = 0;
IntervalFindZeros(c1[c].Eval(p), c2[c].Eval(p), c3[c].Eval(p),
                  c4[c].Eval(p), c5[c].Eval(p), theta,
                  Interval(0., 1.), zeros, &nZeros);
```

The zeros are found over $t \in [0, 1]$, so we need to interpolate within the time range before calling the method to transform the point at the corresponding time. Note also that the extremum is only at one of the x, y, and z dimensions, and so the bounds only need to be updated in that one dimension. For convenience, here we just use the Union() function, which considers all dimensions, even though two could be ignored.

⟨*Expand bounding box for any motion derivative zeros found*⟩ ≡   **110**
```
for (int i = 0; i < nZeros; ++i) {
    Point3f pz = (*this)(Lerp(zeros[i], startTime, endTime), p);
    bounds = Union(bounds, pz);
}
```

Finding zeros of the motion derivative function, Equation (2.12), can't be done algebraically; numerical methods are necessary. Fortunately, the function is well behaved—it's fairly smooth and has a limited number of zeros. (Recall the plot in Figure 2.18, which was an unusually complex representative.)

While we could use a bisection-based search or Newton's method, we'd risk missing zeros when the function only briefly crosses the axis. Therefore, we'll use *interval arithmetic*, an extension of arithmetic that gives insight about the behavior of functions over ranges of values, which makes it possible to robustly find zeros of functions.

To understand the basic idea of interval arithmetic, consider, for example, the function $f(x) = 2x$. If we have an interval of values $[a, b] \in \mathbb{R}$, then we can see that over the interval, the range of f is the interval $[2a, 2b]$. In other words $f([a, b]) \subset [2a, 2b]$.

More generally, all of the basic operations of arithmetic have *interval extensions* that describe how they operate on intervals. For example, given two intervals $[a, b]$ and $[c, d]$,

$$[a, b] + [c, d] \subset [a + c, b + d].$$

In other words, if we add together two values where one is in the range $[a, b]$ and the second is in $[c, d]$, then the result must be in the range $[a + c, b + d]$.

Interval arithmetic has the important property that the intervals that it gives are conservative. In particular, if $f([a, b]) \subset [c, d]$ and if $c > 0$, then we know for sure that no value in $[a, b]$ causes f to be negative. In the following, we will show how to compute Equation (2.12) over intervals and will take advantage of the conservative bounds of computed intervals to efficiently find small intervals with zero crossings where regular root finding methods can be reliably used.

First we will define an Interval class that represents intervals of real numbers.

⟨*Interval Definitions*⟩ ≡
```
class Interval {
public:
   ⟨Interval Public Methods 112⟩
   Float low, high;
};
```

An interval can be initialized with a single value, representing a single point on the real
number line, or with two values that specify an interval with non-zero width.

⟨*Interval Public Methods*⟩ ≡   112
```
Interval(Float v) : low(v), high(v) { }
Interval(Float v0, Float v1)
   : low(std::min(v0, v1)), high(std::max(v0, v1)) { }
```

The class also provides overloads for the basic arithmetic operations. Note that for subtraction, the high value of the second interval is subtracted from the low value of the
first.[3]

⟨*Interval Public Methods*⟩ +≡   112
```
Interval operator+(const Interval &i) const {
    return Interval(low + i.low, high + i.high);
}
Interval operator-(const Interval &i) const {
    return Interval(low - i.high, high - i.low);
}
```

For multiplication, which sides of each interval determine the minimum and maximum
values of the result interval depend on the signs of the respective values. Multiplying
the various possibilities and taking the overall minimum and maximum is easier than
working through which ones to use and multiplying these.

⟨*Interval Public Methods*⟩ +≡   112
```
Interval operator*(const Interval &i) const {
    return Interval(std::min(std::min(low * i.low,  high * i.low),
                             std::min(low * i.high, high * i.high)),
                    std::max(std::max(low * i.low,  high * i.low),
                             std::max(low * i.high, high * i.high)));
}
```

We have also implemented Sin() and Cos() functions for Intervals. The implementations assume that the given interval is in $[0, 2\pi]$, which is the case for our use of these
functions. Here we only include the implementation of Sin(); Cos() is quite similar in
basic structure.

---

3   Readers who have already read Section 3.9 or who are already familiar with floating-point round-off error may note a crack
    in our claims of robustness: when the floating-point value of one of the interval bounds is computed, the result is rounded to
    the nearest floating-point value, which may be larger or smaller than the fully precise result. To be fully robust, the floating-
    point rounding mode must be set to round down for the lower value of the extent and to round up for the upper. Changing
    the rounding mode is generally fairly expensive on modern CPUs, and this issue is a very minor one for this application;
    therefore our implementation leaves the rounding mode unchanged.

⟨*Interval Definitions*⟩ +≡
```
inline Interval Sin(const Interval &i) {
    Float sinLow = std::sin(i.low), sinHigh = std::sin(i.high);
    if (sinLow > sinHigh)
        std::swap(sinLow, sinHigh);
    if (i.low < Pi / 2 && i.high > Pi / 2)
        sinHigh = 1.;
    if (i.low < (3.f / 2.f) * Pi && i.high > (3.f / 2.f) * Pi)
        sinLow = -1.;
    return Interval(sinLow, sinHigh);
}
```

Given the interval machinery, we can now implement the IntervalFindZeros() function, which finds the t values of any zero crossings of Equation (2.12) over the given interval tInterval.

⟨*Interval Definitions*⟩ +≡
```
void IntervalFindZeros(Float c1, Float c2, Float c3, Float c4,
        Float c5, Float theta, Interval tInterval, Float *zeros,
        int *zeroCount, int depth = 8) {
    ⟨Evaluate motion derivative in interval form, return if no zeros 113⟩
    if (depth > 0) {
        ⟨Split tInterval and check both resulting intervals 114⟩
    } else {
        ⟨Use Newton's method to refine zero 114⟩
    }
}
```

The function starts by computing the interval range over tInterval. If the range doesn't span zero, then there are no zeros of the function over tInterval and the function can return.

⟨*Evaluate motion derivative in interval form, return if no zeros*⟩ ≡   113
```
Interval range = Interval(c1) +
    (Interval(c2) + Interval(c3) * tInterval) *
        Cos(Interval(2 * theta) * tInterval) +
    (Interval(c4) + Interval(c5) * tInterval) *
        Sin(Interval(2 * theta) * tInterval);
if (range.low > 0. || range.high < 0. || range.low == range.high)
    return;
```

Float 1062
Interval 112
Interval::high 112
Interval::low 112
Pi 1063

If the interval range does span zero, then there may be one or more zeros in the interval tInterval, but it's also possible that there actually aren't any, since the interval bounds are conservative but not as tight as possible. The function splits tInterval into two parts and recursively checks the two sub-intervals. Reducing the size of the interval domain generally reduces the extent of the interval range, which may allow us to determine that there are no zeros in one or both of the new intervals.

⟨*Split* tInterval *and check both resulting intervals*⟩ ≡   113
```
Float mid = (tInterval.low + tInterval.high) * 0.5f;
IntervalFindZeros(c1, c2, c3, c4, c5, theta,
    Interval(tInterval.low, mid), zeros, zeroCount, depth - 1);
IntervalFindZeros(c1, c2, c3, c4, c5, theta,
    Interval(mid, tInterval.high), zeros, zeroCount, depth - 1);
```

Once we have a narrow interval where the interval value of the motion derivative function spans zero, the implementation switches to a few iterations of Newton's method to find the zero, starting at the midpoint of the interval. Newton's method requires the derivative of the function; since we're finding zeros of the motion derivative function, this is the second derivative of Equation (2.11):

$$\frac{d^2 a_{\mathrm{M,p}}(t)_x}{dt^2} = c_{3,x} + 2\theta(c_{4,x} + c_{5,x}t)\cos(2\theta\,t) + c_{5,x} - 2\theta(c_{2,x} + c_{3,x}t)\sin(2\theta\,t).$$

⟨*Use Newton's method to refine zero*⟩ ≡   113
```
Float tNewton = (tInterval.low + tInterval.high) * 0.5f;
for (int i = 0; i < 4; ++i) {
    Float fNewton = c1 +
        (c2 + c3 * tNewton) * std::cos(2.f * theta * tNewton) +
        (c4 + c5 * tNewton) * std::sin(2.f * theta * tNewton);
    Float fPrimeNewton =
        (c3 + 2 * (c4 + c5 * tNewton) * theta) *
            std::cos(2.f * tNewton * theta) +
        (c5 - 2 * (c2 + c3 * tNewton) * theta) *
            std::sin(2.f * tNewton * theta);
    if (fNewton == 0 || fPrimeNewton == 0)
        break;
    tNewton = tNewton - fNewton / fPrimeNewton;
}
zeros[*zeroCount] = tNewton;
(*zeroCount)++;
```

Note that if there were multiple zeros of the function in tInterval when Newton's method is used, then we will only find one of them here. However, because the interval is quite small at this point, the impact of this error should be minimal. In any case, we haven't found this issue to be a problem in practice.

2.10 INTERACTIONS

The last abstraction in this chapter, SurfaceInteraction, represents local information at a point on a 2D surface. For example, the ray–shape intersection routines in Chapter 3 return information about the local differential geometry at intersection points in a SurfaceInteraction. Later, the texturing code in Chapter 10 computes material properties given a point on a surface represented by a SurfaceInteraction. The closely related MediumInteraction class is used to represent points where light scatters in participating media like smoke or clouds; it will be defined in Section 11.3 after additional preliminaries have been introduced. The implementations of these classes are in the files core/interaction.h and core/interaction.cpp.

Both SurfaceInteraction and MediumInteraction inherit from a generic Interaction class, which provides some common member variables and methods. Some parts of the system (notably the light source implementations) operate with respect to Interactions, as the differences between surface and medium interactions don't matter to them.

⟨*Interaction Declarations*⟩ ≡
```
struct Interaction {
    ⟨Interaction Public Methods 115⟩
    ⟨Interaction Public Data 115⟩
};
```

A number of Interaction constructors are available; depending on what sort of interaction is being constructed and what sort of information about it is relevant, corresponding sets of parameters are accepted. This one is the most general of them.

⟨*Interaction Public Methods*⟩ ≡   **115**
```
Interaction(const Point3f &p, const Normal3f &n, const Vector3f &pError,
        const Vector3f &wo, Float time,
        const MediumInterface &mediumInterface)
    : p(p), time(time), pError(pError), wo(wo), n(n),
        mediumInterface(mediumInterface) { }
```

All interactions must have a point p and time associated with them.

⟨*Interaction Public Data*⟩ ≡   **115**
```
Point3f p;
Float time;
```

For interactions where the point p was computed by ray intersection, some floating-point error is generally present in the p value. pError gives a conservative bound on this error; it's (0, 0, 0) for points in participating media. See Section 3.9 for more on pbrt's approach to managing floating-point error and in particular Section 3.9.4 for how this bound is computed for various shapes.

⟨*Interaction Public Data*⟩ +≡   **115**
```
Vector3f pError;
```

For interactions that lie along a ray (either from a ray–shape intersection or from a ray passing through participating media), the negative ray direction is stored in wo, which corresponds to ω_o, the notation we use for the outgoing direction when computing lighting at points. For other types of interaction points where the notion of an outgoing direction doesn't apply (e.g., those found by randomly sampling points on the surface of shapes), wo has the value (0, 0, 0).

⟨*Interaction Public Data*⟩ +≡   **115**
```
Vector3f wo;
```

For interactions on surfaces, n stores the surface normal at the point.

⟨*Interaction Public Data*⟩ +≡   **115**
   Normal3f n;

⟨*Interaction Public Methods*⟩ +≡   **115**
```
    bool IsSurfaceInteraction() const {
        return n != Normal3f();
    }
```

Interactions also need to record the scattering media at their point (if any); this is handled by an instance of the MediumInterface class, which is defined in Section 11.3.1.

⟨*Interaction Public Data*⟩ +≡   **115**
   MediumInterface mediumInterface;

2.10.1 SURFACE INTERACTION

The geometry of particular point on a surface (often a position found by intersecting a ray against the surface) is represented by a SurfaceInteraction. Having this abstraction lets most of the system work with points on surfaces without needing to consider the particular type of geometric shape the points lie on; the SurfaceInteraction abstraction supplies enough information about the surface point to allow the shading and geometric operations in the rest of pbrt to be implemented generically.

⟨*SurfaceInteraction Declarations*⟩ ≡
```
    class SurfaceInteraction : public Interaction {
    public:
        ⟨SurfaceInteraction Public Methods⟩
        ⟨SurfaceInteraction Public Data 116⟩
    };
```

In addition to the point p and surface normal n from the Interaction base class, the SurfaceInteraction also stores (u, v) coordinates from the parameterization of the surface and the parametric partial derivatives of the point $\partial p/\partial u$ and $\partial p/\partial v$. See Figure 2.19 for a depiction of these values. It's also useful to have a pointer to the Shape that the point lies on (the Shape class will be introduced in the next chapter) as well as the partial derivatives of the surface normal.

⟨*SurfaceInteraction Public Data*⟩ ≡   **116**
```
    Point2f uv;
    Vector3f dpdu, dpdv;
    Normal3f dndu, dndv;
    const Shape *shape = nullptr;
```

This representation implicitly assumes that shapes have a parametric description—that for some range of (u, v) values, points on the surface are given by some function f such that $p = f(u, v)$. Although this isn't true for all shapes, all of the shapes that pbrt supports do have at least a local parametric description, so we will stick with the parametric representation since this assumption is helpful elsewhere (e.g., for antialiasing of textures in Chapter 10).

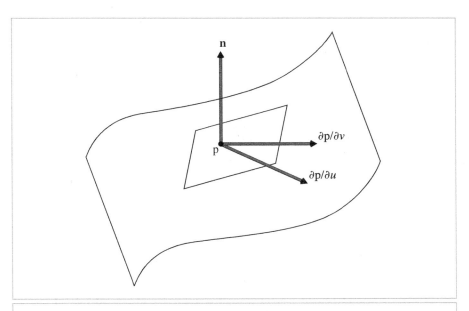

Figure 2.19: The Local Differential Geometry around a Point p. The parametric partial derivatives of the surface, $\partial p/\partial u$ and $\partial p/\partial v$, lie in the tangent plane but are not necessarily orthogonal. The surface normal $\mathbf{n}$ is given by the cross product of $\partial p/\partial u$ and $\partial p/\partial v$. The vectors $\partial \mathbf{n}/\partial u$ and $\partial \mathbf{n}/\partial v$ (not shown here) record the differential change in surface normal as we move u and v along the surface.

The SurfaceInteraction constructor takes parameters that set all of these values. It computes the normal as the cross product of the partial derivatives.

⟨*SurfaceInteraction Method Definitions*⟩ ≡
```
SurfaceInteraction::SurfaceInteraction(const Point3f &p,
        const Vector3f &pError, const Point2f &uv, const Vector3f &wo,
        const Vector3f &dpdu, const Vector3f &dpdv,
        const Normal3f &dndu, const Normal3f &dndv,
        Float time, const Shape *shape)
    : Interaction(p, Normal3f(Normalize(Cross(dpdu, dpdv))), pError, wo,
                      time, nullptr),
      uv(uv), dpdu(dpdu), dpdv(dpdv), dndu(dndu), dndv(dndv),
      shape(shape) {
    ⟨Initialize shading geometry from true geometry 118⟩
    ⟨Adjust normal based on orientation and handedness 119⟩
}
```

SurfaceInteraction stores a second instance of a surface normal and the various partial derivatives to represent possibly perturbed values of these quantities as can be generated by bump mapping or interpolated per-vertex normals with triangles. Some parts of the system use this shading geometry, while others need to work with the original quantities.

⟨*SurfaceInteraction Public Data*⟩ +≡   116
```
struct {
    Normal3f n;
    Vector3f dpdu, dpdv;
    Normal3f dndu, dndv;
} shading;
```

The shading geometry values are initialized in the constructor to match the original surface geometry. If shading geometry is present, it generally isn't computed until some time after the SurfaceInteraction constructor runs. The SetShadingGeometry() method, to be defined shortly, updates the shading geometry.

⟨*Initialize shading geometry from true geometry*⟩ ≡   117
```
shading.n = n;
shading.dpdu = dpdu;
shading.dpdv = dpdv;
shading.dndu = dndu;
shading.dndv = dndv;
```

The surface normal has special meaning to pbrt, which assumes that, for closed shapes, the normal is oriented such that it points to the outside of the shape. For geometry used as an area light source, light is emitted from only the side of the surface that the normal points toward; the other side is black. Because normals have this special meaning, pbrt provides a mechanism for the user to reverse the orientation of the normal, flipping it to point in the opposite direction. The ReverseOrientation directive in pbrt's input file flips the normal to point in the opposite, non-default direction. Therefore, it is necessary to check if the given Shape has the corresponding flag set and, if so, switch the normal's direction here.

However, one other factor plays into the orientation of the normal and must be accounted for here as well. If the Shape's transformation matrix has switched the handedness of the object coordinate system from pbrt's default left-handed coordinate system to a right-handed one, we need to switch the orientation of the normal as well. To see why this is so, consider a scale matrix $S(1, 1, -1)$. We would naturally expect this scale to switch the direction of the normal, although because we have computed the normal by $\mathbf{n} = \partial\mathbf{p}/\partial u \times \partial\mathbf{p}/\partial v$,

$$S(1, 1, -1)\frac{\partial\mathbf{p}}{\partial u} \times S(1, 1, -1)\frac{\partial\mathbf{p}}{\partial v} = S(-1, -1, 1)\frac{\partial\mathbf{p}}{\partial u} \times \frac{\partial\mathbf{p}}{\partial v}$$
$$= S(-1, -1, 1)\mathbf{n}$$
$$\neq S(1, 1, -1)\mathbf{n}.$$

Therefore, it is also necessary to flip the normal's direction if the transformation switches the handedness of the coordinate system, since the flip won't be accounted for by the computation of the normal's direction using the cross product.

The normal's direction is swapped if one but not both of these two conditions is met; if both were met, their effect would cancel out. The exclusive-OR operation tests this condition.

⟨*Adjust normal based on orientation and handedness*⟩ ≡   **117**
```
if (shape && (shape->reverseOrientation ^
                shape->transformSwapsHandedness)) {
    n *= -1;
    shading.n *= -1;
}
```

When a shading coordinate frame is computed, the `SurfaceInteraction` is updated via
its `SetShadingGeometry()` method.

⟨*SurfaceInteraction Method Definitions*⟩ +≡
```
void SurfaceInteraction::SetShadingGeometry(const Vector3f &dpdus,
        const Vector3f &dpdvs, const Normal3f &dndus,
        const Normal3f &dndvs, bool orientationIsAuthoritative) {
    ⟨Compute shading.n for SurfaceInteraction 119⟩
    ⟨Initialize shading partial derivative values 119⟩
}
```

After performing the same cross product (and possibly flipping the orientation of the
normal) as before to compute an initial shading normal, the implementation then flips
either the shading normal or the true geometric normal if needed so that the two normals
lie in the hemisphere. Since the shading normal generally represents a relatively small
perturbation of the geometric normal, the two of them should always be in the same
hemisphere. Depending on the context, either the geometric normal or the shading
normal may more authoritatively point toward the correct "outside" of the surface, so
the caller passes a Boolean value that determines which should be flipped if needed.

⟨*Compute* shading.n *for* SurfaceInteraction⟩ ≡   **119**
```
shading.n = Normalize((Normal3f)Cross(dpdus, dpdvs));
if (shape && (shape->reverseOrientation ^
                shape->transformSwapsHandedness))
    shading.n = -shading.n;
if (orientationIsAuthoritative)
    n = Faceforward(n, shading.n);
else
    shading.n = Faceforward(shading.n, n);
```

⟨*Initialize* shading *partial derivative values*⟩ ≡   **119**
```
shading.dpdu = dpdus;
shading.dpdv = dpdvs;
shading.dndu = dndus;
shading.dndv = dndvs;
```

We'll add a method to `Transform` to transform `SurfaceInteraction`s. Most members are
either transformed directly or copied, as appropriate, but given the approach that pbrt
uses for bounding floating-point error in computed intersection points, transforming
the p and pError member variables requires special care. The fragment that handles this,
⟨*Transform* p *and* pError *in* SurfaceInteraction⟩ is defined in Section 3.9, when floating-
point rounding error is discussed.

⟨*Transform Method Definitions*⟩ +≡
```
  SurfaceInteraction
  Transform::operator()(const SurfaceInteraction &si) const {
      SurfaceInteraction ret;
      ⟨Transform p and pError in SurfaceInteraction 229⟩
      ⟨Transform remaining members of SurfaceInteraction⟩
      return ret;
  }
```

FURTHER READING

DeRose, Goldman, and their collaborators have argued for an elegant "coordinate-free" approach to describing vector geometry for graphics, where the fact that positions and directions happen to be represented by (x, y, z) coordinates with respect to a particular coordinate system is deemphasized and where points and vectors themselves record which coordinate system they are expressed in terms of (Goldman 1985; DeRose 1989; Mann, Litke, and DeRose 1997). This makes it possible for a software layer to ensure that common errors like adding a vector in one coordinate system to a point in another coordinate system are transparently handled by transforming them to a common coordinate system first. We have not followed this approach in pbrt, although the principles behind this approach are well worth understanding and keeping in mind when working with coordinate systems in computer graphics.

Schneider and Eberly's *Geometric Tools for Computer Graphics* is influenced by the coordinate-free approach and covers the topics of this chapter in much greater depth (Schneider and Eberly 2003). It is also full of useful geometric algorithms for graphics. A classic and more traditional introduction to the topics of this chapter is *Mathematical Elements for Computer Graphics* by Rogers and Adams (1990). Note that their book uses a row-vector representation of points and vectors, however, which means that our matrices would be transposed when expressed in their framework, and that they multiply points and vectors by matrices to transform them (p**M**), rather than multiplying matrices by points as we do (**M**p). Homogeneous coordinates were only briefly mentioned in this chapter, although they are the basis of projective geometry, where they are the foundation of many elegant algorithms. Stolfi's book is an excellent introduction to this topic (Stolfi 1991).

There are many good books on linear algebra and vector geometry. We have found Lang (1986) and Buck (1978) to be good references on these respective topics. See also Akenine-Möller et al.'s *Real-Time Rendering* book (2008) for a solid graphics-based introduction to linear algebra.

The subtleties of how normal vectors are transformed were first widely understood in the graphics community after articles by Wallis (1990) and Turkowski (1990b).

Shoemake (1985) introduced quaternions to graphics and showed their utility for animating rotations. Using polar matrix decomposition for animating transformations was described by Shoemake and Duff (1992); Higham (1986) developed the algorithm for extracting the rotation from a composite rotation and scale matrix by successively adding the matrix to its inverse transpose. Shoemake's chapters in *Graphics Gems* (1991, 1994,

SurfaceInteraction 116
Transform 83

1994) respectively give more details on the derivation of the conversion from matrices to quaternions and the implementation of polar matrix decomposition.

We followed Blow's derivation of spherical linear interpolation (2004) in our exposition in this chapter. Bloom et al. (2004) discuss desirable properties of interpolation of rotations for animation in computer graphics and which approaches deliver which of these properties. See Eberly (2011) for a more efficient implementation of a Slerp() function, based on approximating the trigonometric functions involved with polynomials. For more sophisticated approaches to rotation interpolation, see Ramamoorthi and Barr (1997) and Buss and Fillmore (2001). A technique to efficiently compute a matrix to rotate one vector to another was presented by Akenine-Möller and Hughes (1999).

Interval arithmetic is a tool that's often useful in rendering; see Moore's book (1966) for a well-written introduction.

EXERCISES

● **2.1** Find a more efficient way to transform axis-aligned bounding boxes by taking advantage of the symmetries of the problem: because the eight corner points are linear combinations of three axis-aligned basis vectors and a single corner point, their transformed bounding box can be found much more efficiently than by the method we presented (Arvo 1990).

● **2.2** Instead of boxes, tighter bounds around objects could be computed by using the intersections of many nonorthogonal slabs. Extend the bounding box representation in pbrt to allow the user to specify a bound comprised of arbitrary slabs.

  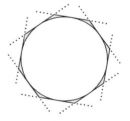

| Axis-aligned | Non-axis-aligned | Arbitrary |
| bounding box | bounding box | bounding slabs |

● **2.3** Change pbrt so that it transforms Normal3fs just like Vector3fs, and create a scene that gives a clearly incorrect image due to this bug. (Don't forget to eliminate this change from your copy of the source code when you're done!)

● **2.4** If only the translation components of a transformation are time varying, for example, then the AnimatedTransform implementation does unnecessary computation in interpolating between two rotations that are the same. Modify the AnimatedTransform impemention so that it avoids this work in cases where the full generality of its current implementation isn't necessary. How much of a performance difference do you observe for scenes where your optimizations are applicable?

CHAPTER THREE

0３ SHAPES

In this chapter, we will present pbrt's abstraction for geometric primitives such as spheres and triangles. Careful abstraction of geometric shapes in a ray tracer is a key component of a clean system design, and shapes are the ideal candidate for an object-oriented approach. All geometric primitives implement a common interface, and the rest of the renderer can use this interface without needing any details about the underlying shape. This makes it possible to separate the geometric and shading subsystems of pbrt.

pbrt hides details about primitives behind a two-level abstraction. The Shape class provides access to the raw geometric properties of the primitive, such as its surface area and bounding box, and provides a ray intersection routine. The Primitive class encapsulates additional nongeometric information about the primitive, such as its material properties. The rest of the renderer then deals only with the abstract Primitive interface. This chapter will focus on the geometry-only Shape class; the Primitive interface is a key topic of Chapter 4.

3.1 BASIC SHAPE INTERFACE

The interface for Shapes is defined in the source file core/shape.h, and definitions of common Shape methods can be found in core/shape.cpp. The Shape base class defines the general Shape interface. It also exposes a few public data members that are useful for all Shape implementations.

⟨*Shape Declarations*⟩ ≡
```
class Shape {
public:
    ⟨Shape Interface 125⟩
    ⟨Shape Public Data 124⟩
};
```

Physically Based Rendering: From Theory To Implementation.
http://dx.doi.org/10.1016/B978-0-12-800645-0.50003-8

All shapes are defined in object coordinate space; for example, all spheres are defined in a coordinate system where the center of the sphere is at the origin. In order to place a sphere at another position in the scene, a transformation that describes the mapping from object space to world space must be provided. The Shape class stores both this transformation and its inverse.

Shapes also take a Boolean parameter, reverseOrientation, that indicates whether their surface normal directions should be reversed from the default. This capability is useful because the orientation of the surface normal is used to determine which side of a shape is "outside." For example, shapes that emit illumination are emissive only on the side the surface normal lies on. The value of this parameter is managed via the ReverseOrientation statement in pbrt input files.

Shapes also store the return value of the Transform::SwapsHandedness() call for their object-to-world transformation. This value is needed by the SurfaceInteraction constructor that is called each time a ray intersection is found, so the Shape constructor computes it once and stores it.

⟨*Shape Method Definitions*⟩ ≡
```
Shape::Shape(const Transform *ObjectToWorld,
        const Transform *WorldToObject, bool reverseOrientation)
    : ObjectToWorld(ObjectToWorld), WorldToObject(WorldToObject),
      reverseOrientation(reverseOrientation),
      transformSwapsHandedness(ObjectToWorld->SwapsHandedness()) {
}
```

An important detail is that shapes store pointers to their transformations rather than Transform objects directly. Recall from Section 2.7 that Transform objects are represented by a total of 32 floats, requiring 128 bytes of memory; because multiple shapes in the scene will frequently have the same transformation applied to them, pbrt keeps a pool of Transforms so that they can be re-used and passes pointers to the shared Transforms to the shapes. As such, the Shape destructor does not delete its Transform pointers, leaving the Transform management code to manage that memory instead.

⟨*Shape Public Data*⟩ ≡   123
```
const Transform *ObjectToWorld, *WorldToObject;
const bool reverseOrientation;
const bool transformSwapsHandedness;
```

3.1.1 BOUNDING

The scenes that pbrt will render will often contain objects that are computationally expensive to process. For many operations, it is often useful to have a 3D *bounding volume* that encloses an object. For example, if a ray does not pass through a particular bounding volume, pbrt can avoid processing all of the objects inside of it for that ray.

Axis-aligned bounding boxes are a convenient bounding volume, as they require only six floating-point values to store and fit many shapes well. Furthermore, it's fairly inexpensive to test for the intersection of a ray with an axis-aligned bounding box. Each Shape implementation must therefore be capable of bounding itself with an axis-aligned

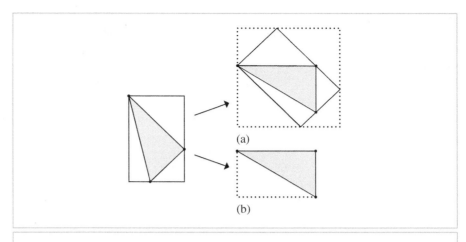

Figure 3.1: (a) A world space bounding box of a triangle is computed by transforming its object space bounding box to world space and then finding the bounding box that encloses the resulting bounding box; a sloppy bound may result. (b) However, if the triangle's vertices are first transformed from object space to world space and then bounded, the fit of the bounding box can be much better.

bounding box represented by a Bounds3f. There are two different bounding methods. The first, ObjectBound(), returns a bounding box in the shape's object space.

⟨*Shape Interface*⟩ ≡   123
```
virtual Bounds3f ObjectBound() const = 0;
```

The second bounding method, WorldBound(), returns a bounding box in world space. pbrt provides a default implementation of this method that transforms the object space bound to world space. Shapes that can easily compute a tighter world space bound should override this method, however. An example of such a shape is a triangle (Figure 3.1).

⟨*Shape Method Definitions*⟩ +≡
```
Bounds3f Shape::WorldBound() const {
    return (*ObjectToWorld)(ObjectBound());
}
```

3.1.2 RAY–BOUNDS INTERSECTIONS

Given the use of Bounds3f instances to bound shapes, we will add a Bounds3 method, Bounds3::IntersectP(), that checks for a ray–box intersection and returns the two parametric *t* values of the intersection, if any.

One way to think of bounding boxes is as the intersection of three slabs, where a slab is the region of space between two parallel planes. To intersect a ray against a box, we intersect the ray against each of the box's three slabs in turn. Because the slabs are aligned with the three coordinate axes, a number of optimizations can be made in the ray–slab tests.

The basic ray-bounding box intersection algorithm works as follows: we start with a parametric interval that covers that range of positions *t* along the ray where we're interested in finding intersections; typically, this is (0, ∞). We will then successively compute the two

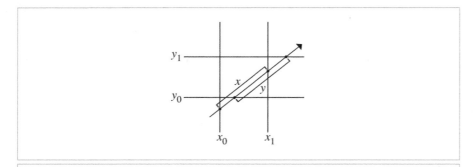

Figure 3.2: Intersecting a Ray with an Axis-Aligned Bounding Box. We compute intersection points with each slab in turn, progressively narrowing the parametric interval. Here, in 2D, the intersection of the x and y extents along the ray gives the extent where the ray is inside the box.

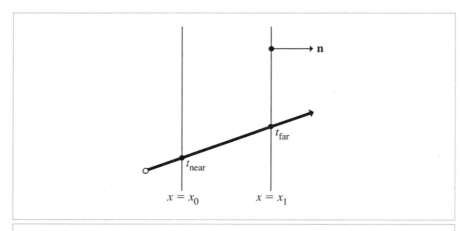

Figure 3.3: Intersecting a Ray with an Axis-Aligned Slab. The two planes shown here are described by $x = c$ for constant values c. The normal of each plane is $(1, 0, 0)$. Unless the ray is parallel to the planes, it will intersect the slab twice, at parametric positions t_{near} and t_{far}.

parametric t positions where the ray intersects each axis-aligned slab. We compute the set intersection of the per-slab intersection interval with the current intersection interval, returning failure if we find that the resulting interval is degenerate. If, after checking all three slabs, the interval is nondegenerate, we have the parametric range of the ray that is inside the box. Figure 3.2 illustrates this process, and Figure 3.3 shows the basic geometry of a ray and a slab.

If the Bounds3::IntersectP() method returns true, the intersection's parametric range is returned in the optional arguments hitt0 and hitt1. Intersections outside of the (0, Ray::tMax) range of the ray are ignored. If the ray's origin is inside the box, 0 is returned for hitt0.

Bounds3::IntersectP() 127

⟨*Geometry Inline Functions*⟩ +≡
```
    template <typename T>
    inline bool Bounds3<T>::IntersectP(const Ray &ray, Float *hitt0,
            Float *hitt1) const {
        Float t0 = 0, t1 = ray.tMax;
        for (int i = 0; i < 3; ++i) {
            ⟨Update interval for ith bounding box slab 128⟩
        }
        if (hitt0) *hitt0 = t0;
        if (hitt1) *hitt1 = t1;
        return true;
    }
```

For each pair of planes, this routine needs to compute two ray–plane intersections. For example, the slab described by two planes perpendicular to the x axis can be described by planes through points $(x_1, 0, 0)$ and $(x_2, 0, 0)$, each with normal $(1, 0, 0)$. Consider the first t value for a plane intersection, t_1. The parametric t value for the intersection between a ray with origin o and direction $\mathbf{d}$ and a plane $ax + by + cz + d = 0$ can be found by substituting the ray equation into the plane equation:

$$0 = a(o_x + t\mathbf{d}_x) + b(o_y + t\mathbf{d}_y) + c(o_z + t\mathbf{d}_z) + d$$
$$= (a, b, c) \cdot o + t(a, b, c) \cdot \mathbf{d} + d.$$

Solving for t gives

$$t = \frac{-d - ((a, b, c) \cdot o)}{((a, b, c) \cdot \mathbf{d})}.$$

Because the y and z components of the plane's normal are zero, b and c are zero, and a is one. The plane's d coefficient is $-x_1$. We can use this information and the definition of the dot product to simplify the calculation substantially:

$$t_1 = \frac{x_1 - o_x}{\mathbf{d}_x}.$$

The code to compute the t values of the slab intersections starts by computing the reciprocal of the corresponding component of the ray direction so that it can multiply by this factor instead of performing multiple divisions. Note that, although it divides by this component, it is not necessary to verify that it is nonzero. If it is zero, then invRayDir will hold an infinite value, either $-\infty$ or ∞, and the rest of the algorithm still works correctly.[1]

Float 1062
Ray 73
Ray::tMax 73

1   This assumes that the architecture being used supports IEEE floating-point arithmetic (Institute of Electrical and Electronic Engineers 1985), which is universal on modern systems. The relevant properties of IEEE floating-point arithmetic are that for all $v > 0$, $v/0 = \infty$ and for all $w < 0$, $w/0 = -\infty$, where ∞ is a special value such that any positive number multiplied by ∞ gives ∞ and any negative number multiplied by ∞ gives $-\infty$, and so on. See Section 3.9.1 for more information about floating-point arithmetic.

⟨*Update interval for* i*th bounding box slab*⟩ ≡   127
```
Float invRayDir = 1 / ray.d[i];
Float tNear = (pMin[i] - ray.o[i]) * invRayDir;
Float tFar  = (pMax[i] - ray.o[i]) * invRayDir;
```
⟨*Update parametric interval from slab intersection t values* **128**⟩

The two distances are reordered so that tNear holds the closer intersection and tFar the farther one. This gives a parametric range [tNear, tFar], which is used to compute the set intersection with the current range [t0, t1] to compute a new range. If this new range is empty (i.e., t0 > t1), then the code can immediately return failure.

There is another floating-point-related subtlety here: in the case where the ray origin is in the plane of one of the bounding box slabs and the ray lies in the plane of the slab, it is possible that tNear or tFar will be computed by an expression of the form 0/0, which results in an IEEE floating-point "not a number" (NaN) value. Like infinity values, NaNs have well-specified semantics: for example, any logical comparison involving a NaN always evaluates to false. Therefore, the code that updates the values of t0 and t1 is carefully written so that if tNear or tFar is NaN, then t0 or t1 won't ever take on a NaN value but will always remain unchanged.

⟨*Update parametric interval from slab intersection t values*⟩ ≡   128
```
if (tNear > tFar) std::swap(tNear, tFar);
```
⟨*Update* tFar *to ensure robust ray–bounds intersection* **221**⟩
```
t0 = tNear > t0 ? tNear : t0;
t1 = tFar  < t1 ? tFar  : t1;
if (t0 > t1) return false;
```

Bounds3 also provides a specialized IntersectP() method that takes the reciprocal of the ray's direction as an additional parameter, so that the three reciprocals don't need to be computed each time IntersectP() is called.

This version also takes precomputed values that indicate whether each direction component is negative, which makes it possible to eliminate the comparisons of the computed tNear and tFar values in the original routine and just directly compute the respective near and far values. Because the comparisons that order these values from low to high in the original code are dependent on computed values, they can be inefficient for processors to execute, since the computation of their values must be completely finished before the comparison can be made.

This routine returns true if the ray segment is entirely inside the bounding box, even if the intersections are not within the ray's (0, tMax) range.

⟨*Geometry Inline Functions*⟩ +≡
```
template <typename T>
inline bool Bounds3<T>::IntersectP(const Ray &ray, const Vector3f &invDir,
        const int dirIsNeg[3]) const {
```

```
    const Bounds3f &bounds = *this;
    ⟨Check for ray intersection against x and y slabs 129⟩
    ⟨Check for ray intersection against z slab⟩
    return (tMin < ray.tMax) && (tMax > 0);
}
```

If the ray direction vector is negative, the "near" parametric intersection will be found with the slab with the larger of the two bounding values, and the far intersection will be found with the slab with the smaller of them. The implementation can use this observation to compute the near and far parametric values in each direction directly.

⟨*Check for ray intersection against x and y slabs*⟩ ≡   **128**
```
    Float tMin =  (bounds[  dirIsNeg[0]].x - ray.o.x) * invDir.x;
    Float tMax =  (bounds[1-dirIsNeg[0]].x - ray.o.x) * invDir.x;
    Float tyMin = (bounds[  dirIsNeg[1]].y - ray.o.y) * invDir.y;
    Float tyMax = (bounds[1-dirIsNeg[1]].y - ray.o.y) * invDir.y;
    ⟨Update tMax and tyMax to ensure robust bounds intersection⟩
    if (tMin > tyMax || tyMin > tMax)
        return false;
    if (tyMin > tMin) tMin = tyMin;
    if (tyMax < tMax) tMax = tyMax;
```

The fragment ⟨*Check for ray intersection against z slab*⟩ is analogous and isn't included here.

This intersection test is at the heart of traversing the BVHAccel acceleration structure, which is introduced in Section 4.3. Because so many ray–bounding box intersection tests are performed while traversing the BVH tree, we found that this optimized method provided approximately a 15% performance improvement in overall rendering time compared to using the Bounds3::IntersectP() variant that didn't take the precomputed direction reciprocals and signs.

3.1.3 INTERSECTION TESTS

Shape implementations must provide an implementation of one (and possibly two) methods that test for ray intersections with their shape. The first, Shape::Intersect(), returns geometric information about a single ray–shape intersection corresponding to the first intersection, if any, in the (0, tMax) parametric range along the ray.

⟨*Shape Interface*⟩ +≡   **123**
```
    virtual bool Intersect(const Ray &ray, Float *tHit,
        SurfaceInteraction *isect, bool testAlphaTexture = true) const = 0;
```

There are a few important things to keep in mind when reading (and writing) intersection routines:

- The Ray structure contains a Ray::tMax member that defines the endpoint of the ray. Intersection routines must ignore any intersections that occur after this point.
- If an intersection is found, its parametric distance along the ray should be stored in the tHit pointer that is passed into the intersection routine. If there are multiple intersections along the ray, the closest one should be reported.
- Information about an intersection is stored in the SurfaceInteraction structure, which completely captures the local geometric properties of a surface. This class is used heavily throughout pbrt, and it serves to cleanly isolate the geometric portion of the ray tracer from the shading and illumination portions. The Surface Interaction class was defined in Section 2.10.[2]
- The rays passed into intersection routines are in world space, so shapes are responsible for transforming them to object space if needed for intersection tests. The intersection information returned should be in world space.

Some shape implementations support cutting away some of their surfaces using a texture; the testAlphaTexture parameter indicates whether those that do should perform this operation for the current intersection test.

The second intersection test method, Shape::IntersectP(), is a predicate function that determines whether or not an intersection occurs, without returning any details about the intersection itself. The Shape class provides a default implementation of the IntersectP() method that calls the Shape::Intersect() method and just ignores the additional information computed about intersection points. As this can be fairly wasteful, almost all shape implementations in pbrt provide a more efficient implementation for IntersectP() that determines whether an intersection exists without computing all of its details.

⟨Shape Interface⟩ +≡   123
```
virtual bool IntersectP(const Ray &ray,
        bool testAlphaTexture = true) const {
    Float tHit = ray.tMax;
    SurfaceInteraction isect;
    return Intersect(ray, &tHit, &isect, testAlphaTexture);
}
```

3.1.4 SURFACE AREA

In order to properly use Shapes as area lights, it is necessary to be able to compute the surface area of a shape in object space.

---

2 Almost all ray tracers use this general idiom for returning geometric information about intersections with shapes. As an optimization, many will only partially initialize the intersection information when an intersection is found, storing just enough information so that the rest of the values can be computed later if actually needed. This approach saves work in the case where a closer intersection is later found with another shape. In our experience, the extra work to compute all the information isn't substantial, and for renderers that have complex scene data management algorithms (e.g., discarding geometry from main memory when too much memory is being used and writing it to disk), the deferred approach may fail because the shape is no longer in memory.

⟨*Shape Interface*⟩ +≡   123
```
virtual Float Area() const = 0;
```

3.1.5 SIDEDNESS

Many rendering systems, particularly those based on scan line or z-buffer algorithms, support the concept of shapes being "one-sided"—the shape is visible if seen from the front but disappears when viewed from behind. In particular, if a geometric object is closed and always viewed from the outside, then the back-facing parts of it can be discarded without changing the resulting image. This optimization can substantially improve the speed of these types of hidden surface removal algorithms. The potential for improved performance is reduced when using this technique with ray tracing, however, since it is often necessary to perform the ray–object intersection before determining the surface normal to do the back-facing test. Furthermore, this feature can lead to a physically inconsistent scene description if one-sided objects are not in fact closed. For example, a surface might block light when a shadow ray is traced from a light source to a point on another surface, but not if the shadow ray is traced in the other direction. For all of these reasons, pbrt doesn't support this feature.

3.2 SPHERES

Spheres are a special case of a general type of surface called *quadrics*—surfaces described by quadratic polynomials in x, y, and z. They are the simplest type of curved surface that is useful to a ray tracer and are a good starting point for general ray intersection routines. pbrt supports six types of quadrics: spheres, cones, disks (a special case of a cone), cylinders, hyperboloids, and paraboloids.

Many surfaces can be described in one of two main ways: in *implicit form* and in *parametric form*. An implicit function describes a 3D surface as

$$f(x, y, z) = 0.$$

The set of all points (x, y, z) that fulfill this condition defines the surface. For a unit sphere at the origin, the familiar implicit equation is $x^2 + y^2 + z^2 - 1 = 0$. Only the set of points one unit from the origin satisfies this constraint, giving the unit sphere's surface.

Many surfaces can also be described parametrically using a function to map 2D points to 3D points on the surface. For example, a sphere of radius r can be described as a function of 2D spherical coordinates (θ, ϕ), where θ ranges from 0 to π and ϕ ranges from 0 to 2π (Figure 3.4):

$$x = r \, \sin \theta \, \cos \phi$$
$$y = r \, \sin \theta \, \sin \phi$$
$$z = r \, \cos \theta.$$

We can transform this function $f(\theta, \phi)$ into a function $f(u, v)$ over $[0, 1]^2$ and also generalize it slightly to allow partial spheres that only sweep out $\theta \in [\theta_{min}, \theta_{max}]$ and $\phi \in [0, \phi_{max}]$ with the substitution

Float 1062

$$\phi = u \, \phi_{max}$$
$$\theta = \theta_{min} + v(\theta_{max} - \theta_{min}).$$

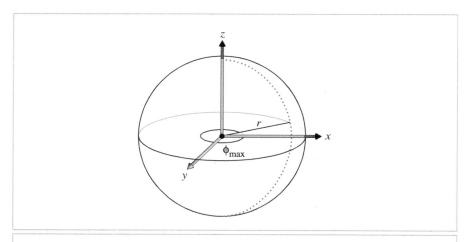

Figure 3.4: Basic Setting for the Sphere Shape. It has a radius of r and is centered at the object space origin. A partial sphere may be described by specifying a maximum ϕ value.

Figure 3.5: Two Spheres. On the left is a complete sphere, and on the right is a partial sphere (with $z_{max} < r$ and $\phi_{max} < 2\pi$). Note that the texture map used shows the (u, v) parameterization of the shape; the singularity at one of the poles is visible in the complete sphere.

This form is particularly useful for texture mapping, where it can be directly used to map a texture defined over $[0, 1]^2$ to the sphere. Figure 3.5 shows an image of two spheres; a grid image map has been used to show the (u, v) parameterization.

As we describe the implementation of the sphere shape, we will make use of both the implicit and parametric descriptions of the shape, depending on which is a more natural way to approach the particular problem we're facing.

The Sphere class represents a sphere that is centered at the origin in object space. Its implementation is in the files shapes/sphere.h and shapes/sphere.cpp.

⟨*Sphere Declarations*⟩ ≡
```
class Sphere : public Shape {
public:
    ⟨Sphere Public Methods 133⟩
private:
    ⟨Sphere Private Data 133⟩
};
```

To place a sphere elsewhere in the scene, the user must apply an appropriate transformation when specifying the sphere in the input file. It takes both the object-to-world and world-to-object transformations as parameters to the constructor, passing them along to the parent Shape constructor.

The radius of the sphere can have an arbitrary positive value, and the sphere's extent can be truncated in two different ways. First, minimum and maximum z values may be set; the parts of the sphere below and above these planes, respectively, are cut off. Second, considering the parameterization of the sphere in spherical coordinates, a maximum ϕ value can be set. The sphere sweeps out ϕ values from 0 to the given ϕ_{max} such that the section of the sphere with spherical ϕ values above ϕ_{max} is also removed.

⟨*Sphere Public Methods*⟩ ≡   133
```
Sphere(const Transform *ObjectToWorld, const Transform *WorldToObject,
        bool reverseOrientation, Float radius, Float zMin, Float zMax,
        Float phiMax)
    : Shape(ObjectToWorld, WorldToObject, reverseOrientation),
      radius(radius), zMin(Clamp(std::min(zMin, zMax), -radius, radius)),
      zMax(Clamp(std::max(zMin, zMax), -radius, radius)),
      thetaMin(std::acos(Clamp(zMin / radius, -1, 1))),
      thetaMax(std::acos(Clamp(zMax / radius, -1, 1))),
      phiMax(Radians(Clamp(phiMax, 0, 360))) { }
```

⟨*Sphere Private Data*⟩ ≡   133
```
const Float radius;
const Float zMin, zMax;
const Float thetaMin, thetaMax, phiMax;
```

3.2.1 BOUNDING

Computing an object space bounding box for a sphere is straightforward. The implementation here uses the values of z_{min} and z_{max} provided by the user to tighten up the bound when less than an entire sphere is being rendered. However, it doesn't do the extra work to compute a tighter bounding box when ϕ_{max} is less than $3\pi/2$. This improvement is left as an exercise.

⟨*Sphere Method Definitions*⟩ ≡
```
Bounds3f Sphere::ObjectBound() const {
    return Bounds3f(Point3f(-radius, -radius, zMin),
                    Point3f( radius,  radius, zMax));
}
```

3.2.2 INTERSECTION TESTS

The task of deriving a ray–sphere intersection test is simplified by the fact that the sphere is centered at the origin. However, if the sphere has been transformed to another position in world space, then it is necessary to transform rays to object space before intersecting them with the sphere, using the world-to-object transformation. Given a ray in object space, the intersection computation can be performed in object space instead.[3]

The following fragment shows the entire intersection method:

⟨*Sphere Method Definitions*⟩ +≡
```
bool Sphere::Intersect(const Ray &r, Float *tHit,
        SurfaceInteraction *isect, bool testAlphaTexture) const {
    Float phi;
    Point3f pHit;
    ⟨Transform Ray to object space 134⟩
    ⟨Compute quadratic sphere coefficients 135⟩
    ⟨Solve quadratic equation for t values 136⟩
    ⟨Compute sphere hit position and φ 137⟩
    ⟨Test sphere intersection against clipping parameters 137⟩
    ⟨Find parametric representation of sphere hit 137⟩
    ⟨Compute error bounds for sphere intersection 225⟩
    ⟨Initialize SurfaceInteraction from parametric information 140⟩
    ⟨Update tHit for quadric intersection 140⟩
    return true;
}
```

First, the given world space ray is transformed to the sphere's object space. The remainder of the intersection test will take place in that coordinate system. The oErr and dErr variables respectively bound the floating-point round-off error in the transformed ray's origin and direction that was introduced by applying the transformation. (See Section 3.9 for more information about floating-point arithmetic and its implications for accurate ray intersection calculations.)

⟨*Transform* Ray *to object space*⟩ ≡   **134, 141, 144, 148, 173**
```
Vector3f oErr, dErr;
Ray ray = (*WorldToObject)(r, &oErr, &dErr);
```

---

3   This is something of a classic theme in computer graphics. By transforming the problem to a particular restricted case, it is possible to more easily and efficiently do an intersection test: that is, many terms of the equations cancel out since the sphere is always at (0, 0, 0). No overall generality is lost, since an appropriate translation can be applied to the ray for spheres at other positions.

If a sphere is centered at the origin with radius r, its implicit representation is

$$x^2 + y^2 + z^2 - r^2 = 0.$$

By substituting the parametric representation of the ray from Equation (2.3) into the implicit sphere equation, we have

$$\left(o_x + t\mathbf{d}_x\right)^2 + \left(o_y + t\mathbf{d}_y\right)^2 + \left(o_z + t\mathbf{d}_z\right)^2 = r^2.$$

Note that all elements of this equation besides t are known values. The t values where the equation holds give the parametric positions along the ray where the implicit sphere equation holds and thus the points along the ray where it intersects the sphere. We can expand this equation and gather the coefficients for a general quadratic equation in t,

$$at^2 + bt + c = 0,$$

where[4]

$$a = \mathbf{d}_x^2 + \mathbf{d}_y^2 + \mathbf{d}_z^2$$
$$b = 2(\mathbf{d}_x o_x + \mathbf{d}_y o_y + \mathbf{d}_z o_z)$$
$$c = o_x^2 + o_y^2 + o_z^2 - r^2.$$

This result directly translates to this fragment of source code. Note that in this code, instances of the EFloat class, not Floats, are used to represent floating-point values. EFloat tracks accumulated floating-point rounding error; its use is discussed in Section 3.9. For now, it can just be read as being equivalent to Float.

⟨*Compute quadratic sphere coefficients*⟩ ≡   134, 141
    ⟨*Initialize* EFloat *ray coordinate values* **135**⟩
```
EFloat a = dx * dx + dy * dy + dz * dz;
EFloat b = 2 * (dx * ox + dy * oy + dz * oz);
EFloat c = ox * ox + oy * oy + oz * oz - EFloat(radius) * EFloat(radius);
```

The ray origin and direction values used in the intersection test are initialized with the floating-point error bounds from transforming the ray to object space.

⟨*Initialize* EFloat *ray coordinate values*⟩ ≡   135, 144
```
EFloat ox(ray.o.x, oErr.x), oy(ray.o.y, oErr.y), oz(ray.o.z, oErr.z);
EFloat dx(ray.d.x, dErr.x), dy(ray.d.y, dErr.y), dz(ray.d.z, dErr.z);
```

There are two possible solutions to the quadratic equation, giving zero, one, or two nonimaginary t values where the ray intersects the sphere.

EFloat 218

Sphere::radius 133

4   Some ray tracers require that the direction vector of a ray be normalized, meaning $a = 1$. This can lead to subtle errors, however, if the caller forgets to normalize the ray direction. Of course, these errors can be avoided by normalizing the direction in the ray constructor, but this wastes effort when the provided direction is *already* normalized. To avoid this needless complexity, pbrt never insists on vector normalization in intersection routines. This is particularly helpful since it reduces the amount of computation needed to transform rays to object space, because no normalization is necessary there.

⟨*Solve quadratic equation for* t *values*⟩ ≡   **134, 141, 144**
    EFloat t0, t1;
    if (!Quadratic(a, b, c, &t0, &t1))
       return false;
    ⟨*Check quadric shape* t0 *and* t1 *for nearest intersection* **136**⟩

The Quadratic() utility function solves a quadratic equation, returning false if there
are no real solutions and returning true and setting t0 and t1 appropriately if there
are solutions. It is defined later in Section 3.9.4, where we discuss how to implement
it robustly using floating-point arithmetic.

The computed parametric distances t0 and t1 track uncertainty due to errors in the
original ray parameters and errors accrued in Quadratic(); the lower and upper range
of the uncertainty interval can be queried using the methods EFloat::LowerBound() and
EFloat::UpperBound().

The fragment ⟨*Check quadric shape* t0 *and* t1 *for nearest intersection*⟩ takes the two
intersection *t* values and determines which, if any, is the closest valid intersection. For
an intersection to be valid, its *t* value must be greater than zero and less than ray.tMax.
The following code uses the error intervals provided by the EFloat class and only accepts
intersections that are unequivocally in the range (0, tMax).

Since t_0 is guaranteed to be less than or equal to t_1 (and 0 is less than tMax), then if t_0
is greater than tMax or t_1 is less than 0, it is certain that both intersections are out of
the range of interest. Otherwise, t_0 is the tentative hit *t* value. It may be less than 0,
however, in which case we ignore it and try t_1. If that is also out of range, we have no
valid intersection. If there is an intersection, then tShapeHit is initialized to hold the
parametric *t* value for the intersection.

⟨*Check quadric shape* t0 *and* t1 *for nearest intersection*⟩ ≡   **136**
    if (t0.UpperBound() > ray.tMax || t1.LowerBound() <= 0)
       return false;
    EFloat tShapeHit = t0;
    if (tShapeHit.LowerBound() <= 0) {
       tShapeHit = t1;
       if (tShapeHit.UpperBound() > ray.tMax)
          return false;
    }

Given the parametric distance along the ray to the intersection with a full sphere, the
intersection point pHit can be computed as that offset along the ray.

It is next necessary to handle partial spheres with clipped *z* or *φ* ranges—intersections
that are in clipped areas must be ignored. The implementation starts by computing the
φ value for the hit point. Using the parametric representation of the sphere,

$$\frac{y}{x} = \frac{r \sin \theta \, \sin \phi}{r \sin \theta \, \cos \phi} = \tan \phi,$$

so $\phi = \arctan y/x$. It is necessary to remap the result of the standard library's std::atan()
function to a value between 0 and 2π, to match the sphere's original definition.

EFloat 218
EFloat::LowerBound() 220
EFloat::UpperBound() 220
Quadratic() 1079
Ray::tMax 73

⟨*Compute sphere hit position and* ϕ⟩ ≡   **134, 137, 141**
```
pHit = ray((Float)tShapeHit);
```
⟨*Refine sphere intersection point* **225**⟩
```
if (pHit.x == 0 && pHit.y == 0) pHit.x = 1e-5f * radius;
phi = std::atan2(pHit.y, pHit.x);
if (phi < 0) phi += 2 * Pi;
```

Due to floating-point precision limitations, this computed intersection point pHit may lie a bit to one side of the actual sphere surface; the ⟨*Refine sphere intersection point*⟩ fragment, which is defined in Section 3.9.4, improves the precision of this value.

The hit point can now be tested against the specified minima and maxima for z and ϕ. One subtlety is that it's important to skip the z tests if the z range includes the entire sphere; the computed pHit.z value may be slightly out of the z range due to floating-point round-off, so we should only perform this test when the user expects the sphere to be partially incomplete. If the t_0 intersection wasn't actually valid, the routine tries again with t_1.

⟨*Test sphere intersection against clipping parameters*⟩ ≡   **134, 141**
```
if ((zMin > -radius && pHit.z < zMin) ||
    (zMax <  radius && pHit.z > zMax) || phi > phiMax) {
    if (tShapeHit == t1) return false;
    if (t1.UpperBound() > ray.tMax) return false;
    tShapeHit = t1;
```
    ⟨*Compute sphere hit position and* ϕ **137**⟩
```
    if ((zMin > -radius && pHit.z < zMin) ||
        (zMax <  radius && pHit.z > zMax) || phi > phiMax)
        return false;
}
```

At this point in the routine, it is certain that the ray hits the sphere. The method next computes u and v values by scaling the previously computed ϕ value for the hit to lie between 0 and 1 and by computing a θ value between 0 and 1 for the hit point, based on the range of θ values for the given sphere. Then it finds the parametric partial derivatives of position $\partial\mathrm{p}/\partial u$ and $\partial\mathrm{p}/\partial v$ and surface normal $\partial\mathrm{n}/\partial u$ and $\partial\mathrm{n}/\partial v$.

⟨*Find parametric representation of sphere hit*⟩ ≡   **134**
```
Float u = phi / phiMax;
Float theta = std::acos(Clamp(pHit.z / radius, -1, 1));
Float v = (theta - thetaMin) / (thetaMax - thetaMin);
```
⟨*Compute sphere* $\partial\mathrm{p}/\partial u$ *and* $\partial\mathrm{p}/\partial v$ **138**⟩
⟨*Compute sphere* $\partial\mathrm{n}/\partial u$ *and* $\partial\mathrm{n}/\partial v$ **139**⟩

Computing the partial derivatives of a point on the sphere is a short exercise in algebra. Here we will show how the x component of $\partial\mathrm{p}/\partial u$, $\partial\mathrm{p}_x/\partial u$, is calculated; the other components are found similarly. Using the parametric definition of the sphere, we have

$$x = r \sin \theta \cos \phi$$

$$\frac{\partial \mathrm{p}_x}{\partial u} = \frac{\partial}{\partial u} (r \sin \theta \cos \phi)$$

$$= r \sin \theta \frac{\partial}{\partial u} (\cos \phi)$$

$$= r \sin \theta (-\phi_{\max} \sin \phi).$$

Using a substitution based on the parametric definition of the sphere's y coordinate, this simplifies to

$$\frac{\partial \mathrm{p}_x}{\partial u} = -\phi_{\max} y.$$

Similarly,

$$\frac{\partial \mathrm{p}_y}{\partial u} = \phi_{\max} x,$$

and

$$\frac{\partial \mathrm{p}_z}{\partial u} = 0.$$

A similar process gives $\partial \mathrm{p}/\partial v$. The complete result is

$$\frac{\partial \mathrm{p}}{\partial u} = (-\phi_{\max} y, \phi_{\max} x, 0)$$

$$\frac{\partial \mathrm{p}}{\partial v} = (\theta_{\max} - \theta_{\min})(z \cos \phi, z \sin \phi, -r \sin \theta).$$

⟨*Compute sphere* $\partial \mathrm{p}/\partial u$ *and* $\partial \mathrm{p}/\partial v$⟩ ≡   137
```
Float zRadius = std::sqrt(pHit.x * pHit.x + pHit.y * pHit.y);
Float invZRadius = 1 / zRadius;
Float cosPhi = pHit.x * invZRadius;
Float sinPhi = pHit.y * invZRadius;
Vector3f dpdu(-phiMax * pHit.y, phiMax * pHit.x, 0);
Vector3f dpdv = (thetaMax - thetaMin) *
    Vector3f(pHit.z * cosPhi, pHit.z * sinPhi,
            -radius * std::sin(theta));
```

⋆ 3.2.3 PARTIAL DERIVATIVES OF NORMAL VECTORS

It is also useful to determine how the normal changes as we move along the surface in the u and v directions. For example, the antialiasing techniques in Chapter 10 are dependent on this information to antialias textures on objects that are seen reflected in curved surfaces. The differential changes in normal $\partial \mathbf{n}/\partial u$ and $\partial \mathbf{n}/\partial v$ are given by the *Weingarten equations* from differential geometry:

$$\frac{\partial \mathbf{n}}{\partial u} = \frac{fF - eG}{EG - F^2} \frac{\partial \mathrm{p}}{\partial u} + \frac{eF - fE}{EG - F^2} \frac{\partial \mathrm{p}}{\partial v}$$

$$\frac{\partial \mathbf{n}}{\partial v} = \frac{gF - fG}{EG - F^2} \frac{\partial \mathrm{p}}{\partial u} + \frac{fF - gE}{EG - F^2} \frac{\partial \mathrm{p}}{\partial v},$$

where E, F, and G are coefficients of the *first fundamental form* and are given by

$$E = \left| \frac{\partial \mathbf{p}}{\partial u} \right|^2$$

$$F = \left(\frac{\partial \mathbf{p}}{\partial u} \cdot \frac{\partial \mathbf{p}}{\partial v} \right)$$

$$G = \left| \frac{\partial \mathbf{p}}{\partial v} \right|^2 .$$

These are easily computed with the $\partial \mathbf{p}/\partial u$ and $\partial \mathbf{p}/\partial v$ values found earlier. The e, f, and g are coefficients of the *second fundamental form*,

$$e = \left(\mathbf{n} \cdot \frac{\partial^2 \mathbf{p}}{\partial u^2} \right)$$

$$f = \left(\mathbf{n} \cdot \frac{\partial^2 \mathbf{p}}{\partial u \partial v} \right)$$

$$g = \left(\mathbf{n} \cdot \frac{\partial^2 \mathbf{p}}{\partial v^2} \right) .$$

The two fundamental forms capture elementary metric properties of a surface, including notions of distance, angle, and curvature; see a differential geometry textbook such as Gray (1993) for details. To find e, f, and g, it is necessary to compute the second-order partial derivatives $\partial^2 \mathbf{p}/\partial u^2$ and so on.

For spheres, a little more algebra gives the second derivatives:

$$\frac{\partial^2 \mathbf{p}}{\partial u^2} = -\phi_{\max}^2 (x, y, 0)$$

$$\frac{\partial^2 \mathbf{p}}{\partial u \partial v} = (\theta_{\max} - \theta_{\min}) \, z \, \phi_{\max} (- \sin \phi, \cos \phi, 0)$$

$$\frac{\partial^2 \mathbf{p}}{\partial v^2} = -(\theta_{\max} - \theta_{\min})^2 (x, y, z).$$

⟨*Compute sphere* $\partial \mathbf{n}/\partial u$ *and* $\partial \mathbf{n}/\partial v$⟩ ≡   **137**

```
Vector3f d2Pduu = -phiMax * phiMax * Vector3f(pHit.x, pHit.y, 0);
Vector3f d2Pduv = (thetaMax - thetaMin) * pHit.z * phiMax *
                  Vector3f(-sinPhi, cosPhi, 0.);
Vector3f d2Pdvv = -(thetaMax - thetaMin) * (thetaMax - thetaMin) *
                  Vector3f(pHit.x, pHit.y, pHit.z);
```
⟨*Compute coefficients for fundamental forms* **140**⟩
⟨*Compute* $\partial \mathbf{n}/\partial u$ *and* $\partial \mathbf{n}/\partial v$ *from fundamental form coefficients* **140**⟩

⟨*Compute coefficients for fundamental forms*⟩ ≡   **139, 146**
```
Float E = Dot(dpdu, dpdu);
Float F = Dot(dpdu, dpdv);
Float G = Dot(dpdv, dpdv);
Vector3f N = Normalize(Cross(dpdu, dpdv));
Float e = Dot(N, d2Pduu);
Float f = Dot(N, d2Pduv);
Float g = Dot(N, d2Pdvv);
```

⟨*Compute* ∂n/∂u *and* ∂n/∂v *from fundamental form coefficients*⟩ ≡   **139, 146**
```
Float invEGF2 = 1 / (E * G - F * F);
Normal3f dndu = Normal3f((f * F - e * G) * invEGF2 * dpdu +
                         (e * F - f * E) * invEGF2 * dpdv);
Normal3f dndv = Normal3f((g * F - f * G) * invEGF2 * dpdu +
                         (f * F - g * E) * invEGF2 * dpdv);
```

3.2.4 SurfaceInteraction INITIALIZATION

Having computed the surface parameterization and all the relevant partial derivatives, the SurfaceInteraction structure can be initialized with the geometric information for this intersection. The pError value passed to the SurfaceInteraction constructor bounds the rounding error in the computed pHit point. It is initialized in the fragment ⟨*Compute error bounds for sphere intersection*⟩, which is defined later, in Section 3.9.4.

⟨*Initialize* SurfaceInteraction *from parametric information*⟩ ≡   **134, 144, 148**
```
*isect = (*ObjectToWorld)(
    SurfaceInteraction(pHit, pError, Point2f(u, v), -ray.d, dpdu, dpdv,
                       dndu, dndv, ray.time, this));
```

Since there is an intersection, the tHit parameter to the Intersect() method is updated with the parametric hit distance along the ray, which was stored in tShapeHit. Updating *tHit allows subsequent intersection tests to terminate early if the potential hit would be farther away than the existing intersection.

⟨*Update* tHit *for quadric intersection*⟩ ≡   **134, 144, 148**
```
*tHit = (Float)tShapeHit;
```

A natural question to ask at this point is, "What effect does the world-to-object transformation have on the correct parametric distance to return?" Indeed, the intersection method has found a parametric distance to the intersection for the object space ray, which may have been translated, rotated, scaled, or worse when it was transformed from world space. However, it can be shown that the parametric distance to an intersection in object space is exactly the same as it would have been if the ray was left in world space and the intersection had been done there and, thus, tHit can be set directly. Note that if the object space ray's direction had been normalized after the transformation, then this would no longer be the case and a correction factor related to the unnormalized ray's length would be needed. This is another motivation for not normalizing the object space ray's direction vector after transformation.

The Sphere::IntersectP() routine is almost identical to Sphere::Intersect(), but it does not initialize the SurfaceInteraction structure. Because the Intersect() and

IntersectP() methods are always so closely related, in the following we will not show implementations of IntersectP() for the remaining shapes.

⟨*Sphere Method Definitions*⟩ +≡
```
bool Sphere::IntersectP(const Ray &r, bool testAlphaTexture) const {
    Float phi;
    Point3f pHit;
    ⟨Transform Ray to object space 134⟩
    ⟨Compute quadratic sphere coefficients 135⟩
    ⟨Solve quadratic equation for t values 136⟩
    ⟨Compute sphere hit position and φ 137⟩
    ⟨Test sphere intersection against clipping parameters 137⟩
    return true;
}
```

3.2.5 SURFACE AREA

To compute the surface area of quadrics, we use a standard formula from integral calculus. If a curve $y = f(x)$ from $x = a$ to $x = b$ is revolved around the x axis, the surface area of the resulting swept surface is

$$2\pi \int_a^b f(x)\sqrt{1 + \left(f'(x)\right)^2}\, dx,$$

where $f'(x)$ denotes the derivative df/dx.[5] Since most of our surfaces of revolution are only partially swept around the axis, we will instead use the formula

$$\phi_{max} \int_a^b f(x)\sqrt{1 + \left(f'(x)\right)^2}\, dx.$$

The sphere is a surface of revolution of a circular arc. The function that defines the profile curve along the z axis of the sphere is

$$f(z) = \sqrt{r^2 - z^2},$$

and its derivative is

$$f'(z) = -\frac{z}{\sqrt{r^2 - z^2}}.$$

Recall that the sphere is clipped at z_{min} and z_{max}. The surface area is therefore

$$A = \phi_{max} \int_{z_{min}}^{z_{max}} \sqrt{r^2 - z^2}\sqrt{1 + \frac{z^2}{r^2 - z^2}}\, dz$$

$$= \phi_{max} \int_{z_{min}}^{z_{max}} \sqrt{r^2 - z^2 + z^2}\, dz$$

$$= \phi_{max} \int_{z_{min}}^{z_{max}} r\, dz$$

$$= \phi_{max}\, r\, (z_{max} - z_{min}).$$

Float 1062
Point3f 68
Ray 73
Sphere 133

---

5   See Anton, Bivens, and Davis (2001) for a derivation.

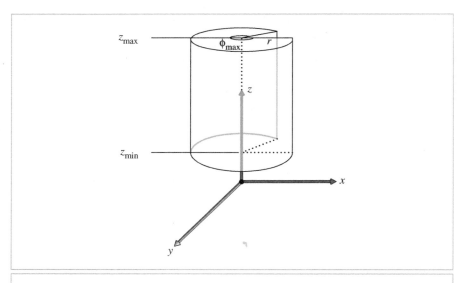

Figure 3.6: Basic Setting for the Cylinder Shape. It has a radius of r and covers a range along the z axis. A partial cylinder may be swept by specifying a maximum ϕ value.

For the full sphere $\phi_{max} = 2\pi$, $z_{min} = -r$, and $z_{max} = r$, so we have the standard formula $A = 4\pi r^2$, confirming that the formula makes sense.

⟨*Sphere Method Definitions*⟩ $+\equiv$
```
Float Sphere::Area() const {
    return phiMax * radius * (zMax - zMin);
}
```

3.3 CYLINDERS

⟨*Cylinder Declarations*⟩ $\equiv$
```
class Cylinder : public Shape {
public:
    ⟨Cylinder Public Methods 143⟩
protected:
    ⟨Cylinder Private Data 143⟩
};
```

Another useful quadric is the cylinder; pbrt provides cylinder Shapes that are centered around the z axis. The implementation is in the files shapes/cylinder.h and shapes/cylinder.cpp. The user supplies a minimum and maximum z value for the cylinder, as well as a radius and maximum ϕ sweep value (Figure 3.6).

In parametric form, a cylinder is described by the following equations:

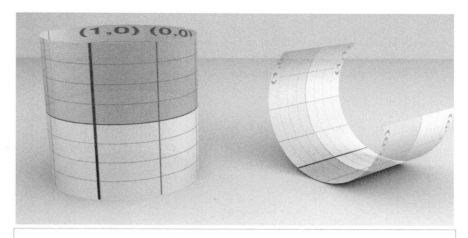

Figure 3.7: Two Cylinders. A complete cylinder is on the left, and a partial cylinder is on the right.

$$\phi = u \, \phi_{\max}$$
$$x = r \cos \phi$$
$$y = r \sin \phi$$
$$z = z_{\min} + v(z_{\max} - z_{\min}).$$

Figure 3.7 shows a rendered image of two cylinders. Like the sphere image, the left cylinder is a complete cylinder, while the right one is a partial cylinder because it has a $\phi_{\max}$ value less than 2π.

⟨*Cylinder Public Methods*⟩ ≡   142

```
Cylinder(const Transform *ObjectToWorld, const Transform *WorldToObject,
        bool reverseOrientation, Float radius, Float zMin, Float zMax,
        Float phiMax)
    : Shape(ObjectToWorld, WorldToObject, reverseOrientation),
      radius(radius), zMin(std::min(zMin, zMax)),
      zMax(std::max(zMin, zMax)),
      phiMax(Radians(Clamp(phiMax, 0, 360))) { }
```

⟨*Cylinder Private Data*⟩ ≡   142

```
const Float radius, zMin, zMax, phiMax;
```

3.3.1 BOUNDING

As was done with the sphere, the cylinder bounding method computes a conservative bounding box using the z range but without taking into account the maximum ϕ.

⟨*Cylinder Method Definitions*⟩ ≡

```
Bounds3f Cylinder::ObjectBound() const {
    return Bounds3f(Point3f(-radius, -radius, zMin),
                    Point3f( radius,  radius, zMax));
}
```

3.3.2 INTERSECTION TESTS

The ray–cylinder intersection formula can be found by substituting the ray equation into the cylinder's implicit equation, similarly to the sphere case. The implicit equation for an infinitely long cylinder centered on the z axis with radius r is

$$x^2 + y^2 - r^2 = 0.$$

Substituting the ray equation, Equation (2.3), we have

$$\left(o_x + t\mathbf{d}_x\right)^2 + \left(o_y + t\mathbf{d}_y\right)^2 = r^2.$$

When we expand this and find the coefficients of the quadratic equation $at^2 + bt + c$, we have

$$a = \mathbf{d}_x^2 + \mathbf{d}_y^2$$
$$b = 2(\mathbf{d}_x o_x + \mathbf{d}_y o_y)$$
$$c = o_x^2 + o_y^2 - r^2.$$

⟨*Compute quadratic cylinder coefficients*⟩ ≡   **144**
    ⟨*Initialize* EFloat *ray coordinate values* 135⟩
    EFloat a = dx * dx + dy * dy;
    EFloat b = 2 * (dx * ox + dy * oy);
    EFloat c = ox * ox + oy * oy - EFloat(radius) * EFloat(radius);

The solution process for the quadratic equation is similar for all quadric shapes, so some fragments from the Sphere intersection method will be reused in the following.

⟨*Cylinder Method Definitions*⟩ +≡
    bool Cylinder::Intersect(const Ray &r, Float *tHit,
        SurfaceInteraction *isect, bool testAlphaTexture) const {
        Float phi;
        Point3f pHit;
        ⟨*Transform* Ray *to object space* 134⟩
        ⟨*Compute quadratic cylinder coefficients* 144⟩
        ⟨*Solve quadratic equation for* t *values* 136⟩
        ⟨*Compute cylinder hit point and* ϕ 145⟩
        ⟨*Test cylinder intersection against clipping parameters* 145⟩
        ⟨*Find parametric representation of cylinder hit* 145⟩
        ⟨*Compute error bounds for cylinder intersection* 225⟩
        ⟨*Initialize* SurfaceInteraction *from parametric information* 140⟩
        ⟨*Update* tHit *for quadric intersection* 140⟩
        return true;
    }

Cylinder 142
EFloat 218
Float 1062
Point3f 68
Ray 73
Sphere 133
SurfaceInteraction 116

As with spheres, the implementation here refines the computed intersection point to ameliorate the effect of accumulated rounding error in the point computed by evaluating the ray equation; see Section 3.9.4. We can then invert the parametric description of the cylinder to compute ϕ from x and y; it turns out that the result is the same as for the sphere.

⟨*Compute cylinder hit point and* ϕ⟩ ≡   144, 145
```
pHit = ray((Float)tShapeHit);
```
⟨*Refine cylinder intersection point* 225⟩
```
phi = std::atan2(pHit.y, pHit.x);
if (phi < 0) phi += 2 * Pi;
```

The next part of the intersection method makes sure that the hit is in the specified z range and that the angle ϕ is acceptable. If not, it rejects the hit and checks t_1 if it has not already been tried—this resembles the conditional logic in Sphere::Intersect().

⟨*Test cylinder intersection against clipping parameters*⟩ ≡   144
```
if (pHit.z < zMin || pHit.z > zMax || phi > phiMax) {
    if (tShapeHit == t1) return false;
    tShapeHit = t1;
    if (t1.UpperBound() > ray.tMax) return false;
    ⟨Compute cylinder hit point and φ 145⟩
    if (pHit.z < zMin || pHit.z > zMax || phi > phiMax)
        return false;
}
```

Again the u value is computed by scaling ϕ to lie between 0 and 1. Straightforward inversion of the parametric equation for the cylinder's z value gives the v parametric coordinate.

⟨*Find parametric representation of cylinder hit*⟩ ≡   144
```
Float u = phi / phiMax;
Float v = (pHit.z - zMin) / (zMax - zMin);
```
⟨*Compute cylinder* $\partial p/\partial u$ *and* $\partial p/\partial v$ 145⟩
⟨*Compute cylinder* $\partial n/\partial u$ *and* $\partial n/\partial v$ 146⟩

The partial derivatives for a cylinder are quite easy to derive:

$$\frac{\partial \mathrm{p}}{\partial u} = (-\phi_{\max} y, \ \phi_{\max} x, \ 0)$$

$$\frac{\partial \mathrm{p}}{\partial v} = (0, \ 0, \ z_{\max} - z_{\min}).$$

⟨*Compute cylinder* $\partial p/\partial u$ *and* $\partial p/\partial v$⟩ ≡   145
```
Vector3f dpdu(-phiMax * pHit.y, phiMax * pHit.x, 0);
Vector3f dpdv(0, 0, zMax - zMin);
```

We again use the Weingarten equations to compute the parametric partial derivatives of the cylinder normal. The relevant partial derivatives are

$$\frac{\partial^2 \mathrm{p}}{\partial u^2} = -\phi_{\max}^2 (x, \ y, \ 0)$$

$$\frac{\partial^2 \mathrm{p}}{\partial u \partial v} = (0, 0, 0)$$

$$\frac{\partial^2 \mathrm{p}}{\partial v^2} = (0, 0, 0).$$

⟨*Compute cylinder* ∂n/∂u *and* ∂n/∂v⟩ ≡   **145**
```
Vector3f d2Pduu = -phiMax * phiMax * Vector3f(pHit.x, pHit.y, 0);
Vector3f d2Pduv(0, 0, 0), d2Pdvv(0, 0, 0);
```
⟨*Compute coefficients for fundamental forms* **140**⟩
⟨*Compute* ∂n/∂u *and* ∂n/∂v *from fundamental form coefficients* **140**⟩

3.3.3 SURFACE AREA

A cylinder is just a rolled-up rectangle. If you unroll the rectangle, its height is $z_{max} - z_{min}$, and its width is $r\phi_{max}$:

⟨*Cylinder Method Definitions*⟩ +≡
```
Float Cylinder::Area() const {
    return (zMax - zMin) * radius * phiMax;
}
```

3.4 DISKS

⟨*Disk Declarations*⟩ ≡
```
class Disk : public Shape {
public:
    ⟨Disk Public Methods 146⟩
private:
    ⟨Disk Private Data 147⟩
};
```

The disk is an interesting quadric since it has a particularly straightforward intersection routine that avoids solving the quadratic equation. In pbrt, a Disk is a circular disk of radius r at height h along the z axis. It is implemented in the files shapes/disk.h and shapes/disk.cpp.

In order to describe partial disks, the user may specify a maximum ϕ value beyond which the disk is cut off (Figure 3.8). The disk can also be generalized to an annulus by specifying an inner radius, r_i. In parametric form, it is described by

$$\phi = u\,\phi_{max}$$
$$x = ((1-v)r_i + vr)\cos\phi$$
$$y = ((1-v)r_i + vr)\sin\phi$$
$$z = h.$$

Figure 3.9 is a rendered image of two disks.

⟨*Disk Public Methods*⟩ ≡   **146**
```
Disk(const Transform *ObjectToWorld, const Transform *WorldToObject,
     bool reverseOrientation, Float height, Float radius,
     Float innerRadius, Float phiMax)
    : Shape(ObjectToWorld, WorldToObject, reverseOrientation),
      height(height), radius(radius), innerRadius(innerRadius),
      phiMax(Radians(Clamp(phiMax, 0, 360))) { }
```

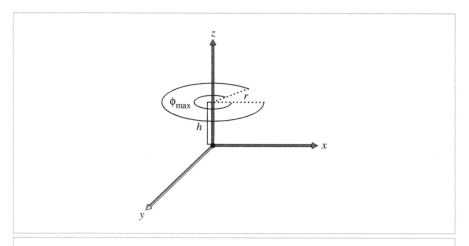

Figure 3.8: Basic Setting for the Disk Shape. The disk has radius r and is located at height h along the z axis. A partial disk may be swept by specifying a maximum ϕ value and an inner radius r_i.

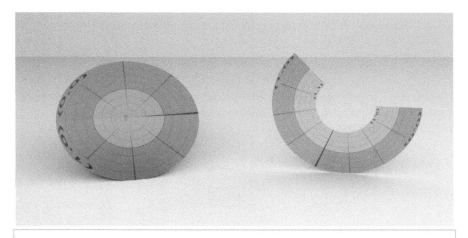

Figure 3.9: Two Disks. A complete disk is on the left, and a partial disk is on the right.

⟨*Disk Private Data*⟩ ≡   **146**
```
const Float height, radius, innerRadius, phiMax;
```

3.4.1 BOUNDING

Float 1062

The bounding method is quite straightforward; it computes a bounding box centered at the height of the disk along z, with extent of radius in both the x and y directions.

⟨*Disk Method Definitions*⟩ ≡
```
Bounds3f Disk::ObjectBound() const {
    return Bounds3f(Point3f(-radius, -radius, height),
                    Point3f( radius,  radius, height));
}
```

3.4.2 INTERSECTION TESTS

Intersecting a ray with a disk is also easy. The intersection of the ray with the $z = h$ plane that the disk lies in is found and the intersection point is checked to see if it lies inside the disk.

⟨*Disk Method Definitions*⟩ +≡
```
bool Disk::Intersect(const Ray &r, Float *tHit,
        SurfaceInteraction *isect, bool testAlphaTexture) const {
    ⟨Transform Ray to object space  134⟩
    ⟨Compute plane intersection for disk  148⟩
    ⟨See if hit point is inside disk radii and φmax  149⟩
    ⟨Find parametric representation of disk hit  149⟩
    ⟨Refine disk intersection point  225⟩
    ⟨Compute error bounds for disk intersection  225⟩
    ⟨Initialize SurfaceInteraction from parametric information  140⟩
    ⟨Update tHit for quadric intersection  140⟩
    return true;
}
```

The first step is to compute the parametric t value where the ray intersects the plane that the disk lies in. We want to find t such that the z component of the ray's position is equal to the height of the disk. Thus,

$$h = o_z + t\mathbf{d}_z$$

and

$$t = \frac{h - o_z}{\mathbf{d}_z}.$$

The intersection method computes a t value checks to see if it is inside the legal range of values $(0, tMax)$. If not, the routine can return false.

⟨*Compute plane intersection for disk*⟩ ≡   148
```
    ⟨Reject disk intersections for rays parallel to the disk's plane  149⟩
    Float tShapeHit = (height - ray.o.z) / ray.d.z;
    if (tShapeHit <= 0 || tShapeHit >= ray.tMax)
        return false;
```

If the ray is parallel to the disk's plane (i.e., the z component of its direction is zero), no intersection is reported. The case where a ray is both parallel to the disk's plane and lies within the plane is somewhat ambiguous, but it's most reasonable to define intersecting

Bounds3f 76
Disk 146
Disk::height 147
Disk::radius 147
Float 1062
Point3f 68
Ray 73
SurfaceInteraction 116

a disk edge-on as "no intersection." This case must be handled explicitly so that NaN floating-point values aren't generated by the following code.

⟨*Reject disk intersections for rays parallel to the disk's plane*⟩ ≡   148
```
if (ray.d.z == 0)
    return false;
```

Now the intersection method can compute the point pHit where the ray intersects the plane. Once the plane intersection is known, false is returned if the distance from the hit to the center of the disk is more than Disk::radius or less than Disk::innerRadius. This process can be optimized by actually computing the squared distance to the center, taking advantage of the fact that the x and y coordinates of the center point $(0, 0, \text{height})$ are zero, and the z coordinate of pHit is equal to height.

⟨*See if hit point is inside disk radii and* ϕ_{max}⟩ ≡   148
```
Point3f pHit = ray(tShapeHit);
Float dist2 = pHit.x * pHit.x + pHit.y * pHit.y;
if (dist2 > radius * radius || dist2 < innerRadius * innerRadius)
    return false;
```
⟨*Test disk ϕ value against* ϕ_{max} **149**⟩

If the distance check passes, a final test makes sure that the ϕ value of the hit point is between zero and ϕ_{max}, specified by the caller. Inverting the disk's parameterization gives the same expression for ϕ as the other quadric shapes.

⟨*Test disk ϕ value against* ϕ_{max}⟩ ≡   149
```
Float phi = std::atan2(pHit.y, pHit.x);
if (phi < 0) phi += 2 * Pi;
if (phi > phiMax)
    return false;
```

If we've gotten this far, there is an intersection with the disk. The parameter u is scaled to reflect the partial disk specified by ϕ_{max}, and v is computed by inverting the parametric equation. The equations for the partial derivatives at the hit point can be derived with a process similar to that used for the previous quadrics. Because the normal of a disk is the same everywhere, the partial derivatives $\partial\mathbf{n}/\partial u$ and $\partial\mathbf{n}/\partial v$ are both trivially $(0, 0, 0)$.

⟨*Find parametric representation of disk hit*⟩ ≡   148
```
Float u = phi / phiMax;
Float rHit = std::sqrt(dist2);
Float oneMinusV = ((rHit - innerRadius) /
                   (radius - innerRadius));
Float v = 1 - oneMinusV;
Vector3f dpdu(-phiMax * pHit.y, phiMax * pHit.x, 0);
Vector3f dpdv = Vector3f(pHit.x, pHit.y, 0.) * (innerRadius - radius) /
                        rHit;
Normal3f dndu(0, 0, 0), dndv(0, 0, 0);
```

3.4.3 SURFACE AREA

Disks have trivially computed surface area, since they're just portions of an annulus:

$$A = \frac{\phi_{max}}{2}(r^2 - r_i^2).$$

⟨*Disk Method Definitions*⟩ +≡

```
Float Disk::Area() const {
    return phiMax * 0.5 * (radius * radius - innerRadius * innerRadius);
}
```

3.5 OTHER QUADRICS

pbrt supports three more quadrics: cones, paraboloids, and hyperboloids. They are implemented in the source files shapes/cone.h, shapes/cone.cpp, shapes/paraboloid.h, shapes/paraboloid.cpp, shapes/hyperboloid.h, and shapes/hyperboloid.cpp. We won't include their full implementations here, since the techniques used to derive their quadratic intersection coefficients, parametric coordinates, and partial derivatives should now be familiar. However, we will briefly summarize the implicit and parametric forms of these shapes. A rendered image of the three of them is in Figure 3.10.

3.5.1 CONES

The implicit equation of a cone centered on the z axis with radius r and height h is

$$\left(\frac{hx}{r}\right)^2 + \left(\frac{hy}{r}\right)^2 - (z - h)^2 = 0.$$

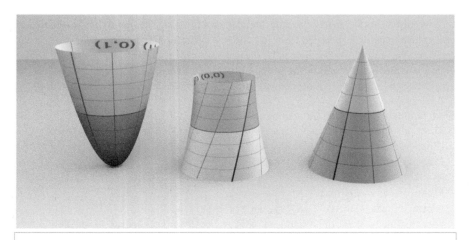

Figure 3.10: The Remaining Quadric Shapes. From left to right: the paraboloid, the hyperboloid, and the cone.

Cones are also described parametrically:

$$\phi = u\, \phi_{max}$$
$$x = r(1-v)\cos\phi$$
$$y = r(1-v)\sin\phi$$
$$z = vh.$$

The partial derivatives at a point on a cone are

$$\frac{\partial p}{\partial u} = (-\phi_{max}y,\, \phi_{max}x,\, 0)$$

$$\frac{\partial p}{\partial v} = \left(-\frac{x}{1-v},\, -\frac{y}{1-v},\, h\right),$$

and the second partial derivatives are

$$\frac{\partial^2 p}{\partial u^2} = -\phi_{max}^2(x,\, y,\, 0)$$

$$\frac{\partial^2 p}{\partial u \partial v} = \frac{\phi_{max}}{1-v}(y,\, -x,\, 0)$$

$$\frac{\partial^2 p}{\partial v^2} = (0,\, 0,\, 0).$$

3.5.2 PARABOLOIDS

The implicit equation of a paraboloid centered on the z axis with radius r and height h is

$$\frac{hx^2}{r^2} + \frac{hy^2}{r^2} - z = 0,$$

and its parametric form is

$$\phi = u\, \phi_{max}$$
$$z = v(z_{max} - z_{min})$$
$$r = r_{max}\sqrt{\frac{z}{z_{max}}}$$
$$x = r\cos\phi$$
$$y = r\sin\phi.$$

The partial derivatives are

$$\frac{\partial p}{\partial u} = (-\phi_{max}y,\, \phi_{max}x,\, 0)$$

$$\frac{\partial p}{\partial v} = (z_{max} - z_{min})\left(\frac{x}{2z},\, \frac{y}{2z},\, 1\right),$$

and

$$\frac{\partial^2 \mathrm{p}}{\partial u^2} = -\phi_{\max}^2 (x, y, 0)$$

$$\frac{\partial^2 \mathrm{p}}{\partial u \partial v} = \phi_{\max}(z_{\max} - z_{\min}) \left(-\frac{y}{2z}, \frac{x}{2z}, 0 \right)$$

$$\frac{\partial^2 \mathrm{p}}{\partial v^2} = -(z_{\max} - z_{\min})^2 \left(\frac{x}{4z^2}, \frac{y}{4z^2}, 0 \right).$$

3.5.3 HYPERBOLOIDS

Finally, the implicit form of the hyperboloid is

$$x^2 + y^2 - z^2 = -1,$$

and the parametric form is

$$\phi = u\,\phi_{\max}$$
$$x_r = (1 - v)x_1 + v\,x_2$$
$$y_r = (1 - v)y_1 + v\,y_2$$
$$x = x_r \cos\phi - y_r \sin\phi$$
$$y = x_r \sin\phi + y_r \cos\phi$$
$$z = (1 - v)z_1 + v\,z_2.$$

The partial derivatives are

$$\frac{\partial \mathrm{p}}{\partial u} = (-\phi_{\max}y, \phi_{\max}x, 0)$$

$$\frac{\partial \mathrm{p}}{\partial v} = ((x_2 - x_1) \cos\phi - (y_2 - y_1) \sin\phi, (x_2 - x_1) \sin\phi + (y_2 - y_1) \cos\phi, z_2 - z_1),$$

and

$$\frac{\partial^2 \mathrm{p}}{\partial u^2} = -\phi_{\max}^2 (x, y, 0)$$

$$\frac{\partial^2 \mathrm{p}}{\partial u \partial v} = \phi_{\max} \left(-\frac{\partial \mathrm{p}_y}{\partial v}, \frac{\partial \mathrm{p}_x}{\partial v}, 0 \right)$$

$$\frac{\partial^2 \mathrm{p}}{\partial v^2} = (0, 0, 0).$$

3.6 TRIANGLE MESHES

The triangle is one of the most commonly used shapes in computer graphics; complex scenes may be modeled using millions of triangles to achieve great detail. (Figure 3.11 shows an image of a complex triangle mesh of over four million triangles.) While a natural representation would be to have a `Triangle` shape implementation where each triangle stored the positions of its three vertices, a more memory-efficient representation is to separately store entire triangle meshes with an array of vertex positions where each individual triangle just stores three offsets into this array for its three vertices.

Figure 3.11: Ganesha Model. This triangle mesh contains over four million individual triangles. It was created from a real statue using a 3D scanner that uses structured light to determine shapes of objects.

To see why this is the case, consider the celebrated Euler-Poincaré formula, which relates the number of vertices V, edges E, and faces F on closed discrete meshes as

$$V - E + F = 2(1 - g),$$

where $g \in \mathbb{N}$ is the *genus* of the mesh. The genus is usually a small number and can be interpreted as the number of "handles" in the mesh (analogous to a handle of a teacup). On a triangle mesh, the number of edges and vertices is furthermore related by the identity

$$E = \frac{3}{2}F.$$

This can be seen by dividing each edge into two parts associated with the two adjacent triangles. There are $3F$ such half-edges, and all co-located pairs constitute the E mesh edges. For large closed triangle meshes, the overall effect of the genus usually becomes negligible and we can combine the previous two equations (with $g = 0$) to obtain

$$V \approx 2F.$$

In other words, there are approximately twice as many vertices as faces. Since each face references three vertices, every vertex is (on average) referenced a total of six times. Thus, when vertices are shared, the total amortized storage required per triangle will be 12 bytes of memory for the offsets (at 4 bytes for three 32-bit integer offsets) plus half of the storage for one vertex—6 bytes, assuming three 4-byte floats are used to store the vertex position—for a total of 18 bytes per triangle. This is much better than the 36 bytes per triangle that storing the three positions directly would require. The relative storage savings are even better when there are per-vertex surface normals or texture coordinates in a mesh.

pbrt uses the `TriangleMesh` structure to store the shared information about a triangle mesh.

⟨*Triangle Declarations*⟩ ≡
```
struct TriangleMesh {
    ⟨TriangleMesh Public Methods⟩
    ⟨TriangleMesh Data 155⟩
};
```

The arguments to the `TriangleMesh` constructor are as follows:

- `ObjectToWorld`: The object-to-world transformation for the mesh.
- `nTriangles`: The total number of triangles in the mesh.
- `vertexIndices`: A pointer to an array of vertex indices. For the ith triangle, its three vertex positions are P[vertexIndices[3*i]], P[vertexIndices[3*i+1]], and P[vertexIndices[3*i+2]].
- `nVertices`: The total number of vertices in the mesh.
- `P`: An array of `nVertices` vertex positions.
- `S`: An optional array of tangent vectors, one per vertex in the mesh. These are used to compute shading tangents.
- `N`: An optional array of normal vectors, one per vertex in the mesh. If present, these are interpolated across triangle faces to compute shading normals.
- `UV`: An optional array of parametric (u, v) values, one for each vertex.
- `alphaMask`: An optional *alpha mask* texture, which can be used to cut away parts of triangle surfaces.

Triangles have a dual role among the shapes in pbrt: not only are they frequently directly specified in scene description files, but other shapes often tessellate themselves into triangle meshes. For example, subdivision surfaces end up creating a mesh of triangles to approximate the smooth limit surface. Ray intersections are performed against these triangles, rather than directly against the subdivision surface (Section 3.8.2).

Due to this second role, it's important that code that creates triangle meshes be able to specify the parameterization of the triangles. If a triangle was created by evaluating the position of a parametric surface at three particular (u, v) coordinate values, for example, those (u, v) values should be interpolated to compute the (u, v) value at ray intersection points inside the triangle. Explicitly specified (u, v) values are also useful for texture mapping, where an external program that created a triangle mesh may want to assign (u, v) coordinates to the mesh so that a texture map assigns color to the mesh surface in the desired way.

TriangleMesh 154

The `TriangleMesh` constructor copies the relevant information and stores it in member variables. In particular, it makes its own copies of `vertexIndices`, P, N, S, and UV, allowing the caller to retain ownership of the data being passed in.

⟨*Triangle Method Definitions*⟩ ≡
```
TriangleMesh::TriangleMesh(const Transform &ObjectToWorld,
        int nTriangles, const int *vertexIndices, int nVertices,
        const Point3f *P, const Vector3f *S, const Normal3f *N,
        const Point2f *UV,
        const std::shared_ptr<Texture<Float>> &alphaMask)
    : nTriangles(nTriangles), nVertices(nVertices),
      vertexIndices(vertexIndices, vertexIndices + 3 * nTriangles),
      alphaMask(alphaMask) {
    ⟨Transform mesh vertices to world space 155⟩
    ⟨Copy UV, N, and S vertex data, if present⟩
}
```

⟨*TriangleMesh Data*⟩ ≡   154
```
const int nTriangles, nVertices;
std::vector<int> vertexIndices;
std::unique_ptr<Point3f[]> p;
std::unique_ptr<Normal3f[]> n;
std::unique_ptr<Vector3f[]> s;
std::unique_ptr<Point2f[]> uv;
std::shared_ptr<Texture<Float>> alphaMask;
```

Unlike the other shapes that leave the shape description in object space and then transform incoming rays from world space to object space, triangle meshes transform the shape into world space and thus save the work of transforming incoming rays into object space and the work of transforming the intersection's geometric representation out to world space. This is a good idea because this operation can be performed once at startup, avoiding transforming rays many times during rendering. Using this approach with quadrics is more complicated, although possible—see Exercise 3.1 at the end of the chapter for more information.

⟨*Transform mesh vertices to world space*⟩ ≡   155
```
p.reset(new Point3f[nVertices]);
for (int i = 0; i < nVertices; ++i)
    p[i] = ObjectToWorld(P[i]);
```

The fragment ⟨*Copy uv, N, and S vertex data, if present*⟩ just allocates the appropriate amount of space and copies the appropriate values. Normals and tangent vectors, if present, are also transformed to object space. This fragment's implementation isn't included here.

3.6.1 TRIANGLE

The `Triangle` class actually implements the `Shape` interface. It represents a single triangle.

⟨*Triangle Declarations*⟩ +≡
```
class Triangle : public Shape {
public:
    ⟨Triangle Public Methods 156⟩
private:
    ⟨Triangle Private Methods 164⟩
    ⟨Triangle Private Data 156⟩
};
```

`Triangle` doesn't store much data—just a pointer to the parent `TriangleMesh` that it came from and a pointer to its three vertex indices in the mesh.

⟨*Triangle Public Methods*⟩ ≡   156
```
Triangle(const Transform *ObjectToWorld, const Transform *WorldToObject,
        bool reverseOrientation,
        const std::shared_ptr<TriangleMesh> &mesh, int triNumber)
    : Shape(ObjectToWorld, WorldToObject, reverseOrientation),
      mesh(mesh) {
    v = &mesh->vertexIndices[3 * triNumber];
}
```

Note that the implementation stores a pointer to the first vertex *index*, instead of storing three pointers to the vertices themselves. This reduces the amount of storage required for each `Triangle` at a cost of another level of indirection.

⟨*Triangle Private Data*⟩ ≡   156
```
std::shared_ptr<TriangleMesh> mesh;
const int *v;
```

Because a number of other shape representations in pbrt convert themselves into triangle meshes, the utility function `CreateTriangleMesh()` takes care of creating an underlying `TriangleMesh` as well as a `Triangle` for each triangle in the mesh. It returns a vector of triangle shapes.

⟨*Triangle Method Definitions*⟩ +≡
```
std::vector<std::shared_ptr<Shape>> CreateTriangleMesh(
        const Transform *ObjectToWorld, const Transform *WorldToObject,
        bool reverseOrientation, int nTriangles,
        const int *vertexIndices, int nVertices, const Point3f *p,
        const Vector3f *s, const Normal3f *n, const Point2f *uv,
        const std::shared_ptr<Texture<Float>> &alphaMask) {
    std::shared_ptr<TriangleMesh> mesh = std::make_shared<TriangleMesh>(
        *ObjectToWorld, nTriangles, vertexIndices, nVertices, p, s, n, uv,
        alphaMask);
    std::vector<std::shared_ptr<Shape>> tris;
    for (int i = 0; i < nTriangles; ++i)
        tris.push_back(std::make_shared<Triangle>(ObjectToWorld,
            WorldToObject, reverseOrientation, mesh, i));
    return tris;
}
```

The object space bound of a triangle is easily found by computing a bounding box that encompasses its three vertices. Because the vertex positions p are transformed to world space in the constructor, the implementation here has to transform them back to object space before computing their bound.

⟨*Triangle Method Definitions*⟩ +≡
```
Bounds3f Triangle::ObjectBound() const {
    ⟨Get triangle vertices in p0, p1, and p2 157⟩
    return Union(Bounds3f((*WorldToObject)(p0), (*WorldToObject)(p1)),
            (*WorldToObject)(p2));
}
```

⟨*Get triangle vertices in* p0, p1, *and* p2⟩ ≡   157, 167, 839
```
const Point3f &p0 = mesh->p[v[0]];
const Point3f &p1 = mesh->p[v[1]];
const Point3f &p2 = mesh->p[v[2]];
```

The Triangle shape is one of the shapes that can compute a better world space bound than can be found by transforming its object space bounding box to world space. Its world space bound can be directly computed from the world space vertices.

⟨*Triangle Method Definitions*⟩ +≡
```
Bounds3f Triangle::WorldBound() const {
    ⟨Get triangle vertices in p0, p1, and p2 157⟩
    return Union(Bounds3f(p0, p1), p2);
}
```

3.6.2 TRIANGLE INTERSECTION

The structure of the triangle shape's Intersect() method follows the form of earlier intersection test methods: a geometric test is applied to determine if there is an intersection and, if so, further information is computed about the intersection to return in the given SurfaceInteraction.

⟨*Triangle Method Definitions*⟩ +≡
```
bool Triangle::Intersect(const Ray &ray, Float *tHit,
        SurfaceInteraction *isect, bool testAlphaTexture) const {
    ⟨Get triangle vertices in p0, p1, and p2 157⟩
    ⟨Perform ray–triangle intersection test 158⟩
    ⟨Compute triangle partial derivatives 164⟩
    ⟨Compute error bounds for triangle intersection 227⟩
    ⟨Interpolate (u, v) parametric coordinates and hit point 164⟩
    ⟨Test intersection against alpha texture, if present 165⟩
    ⟨Fill in SurfaceInteraction from triangle hit 165⟩
    *tHit = t;
    return true;
}
```

pbrt's ray–triangle intersection test is based on first computing an affine transformation that transforms the ray such that its origin is at $(0, 0, 0)$ in the transformed coordinate system and such that its direction is along the $+z$ axis. Triangle vertices are also transformed into this coordinate system before the intersection test is performed. In the following, we'll see that applying this coordinate system transformation simplifies the intersection test logic since, for example, the x and y coordinates of any intersection point must be zero. Later, in Section 3.9.3, we'll see that this transformation makes it possible to have a *watertight* ray–triangle intersection algorithm, such that intersections with tricky rays like those that hit the triangle right on the edge are never incorrectly reported as misses.

⟨*Perform ray–triangle intersection test*⟩ ≡   157
    ⟨*Transform triangle vertices to ray coordinate space* 158⟩
    ⟨*Compute edge function coefficients* e0, e1, *and* e2 161⟩
    ⟨*Fall back to double-precision test at triangle edges*⟩
    ⟨*Perform triangle edge and determinant tests* 162⟩
    ⟨*Compute scaled hit distance to triangle and test against ray t range* 162⟩
    ⟨*Compute barycentric coordinates and t value for triangle intersection* 163⟩
    ⟨*Ensure that computed triangle t is conservatively greater than zero* 234⟩

There are three steps to computing the transformation from world space to the ray–triangle intersection coordinate space: a translation $\mathbf{T}$, a coordinate permutation $\mathbf{P}$, and a shear $\mathbf{S}$. Rather than computing explicit transformation matrices for each of these and then computing an aggregate transformation matrix $\mathbf{M} = \mathbf{SPT}$ to transform vertices to the coordinate space, the following implementation applies each step of the transformation directly, which ends up being a more efficient approach.

⟨*Transform triangle vertices to ray coordinate space*⟩ ≡   158
    ⟨*Translate vertices based on ray origin* 158⟩
    ⟨*Permute components of triangle vertices and ray direction* 159⟩
    ⟨*Apply shear transformation to translated vertex positions* 159⟩

The translation that places the ray origin at the origin of the coordinate system is:

$$\mathbf{T} = \begin{pmatrix} 1 & 0 & 0 & -o_x \\ 0 & 1 & 0 & -o_y \\ 0 & 0 & 1 & -o_z \\ 0 & 0 & 0 & 1 \end{pmatrix}.$$

This transformation doesn't need to be explicitly applied to the ray origin, but we will apply it to the three triangle vertices.

⟨*Translate vertices based on ray origin*⟩ ≡   158
```
Point3f p0t = p0 - Vector3f(ray.o);
Point3f p1t = p1 - Vector3f(ray.o);
Point3f p2t = p2 - Vector3f(ray.o);
```

Point3f 68
Vector3f 60

Next, the three dimensions of the space are permuted so that the z dimension is the one where the absolute value of the ray's direction is largest. The x and y dimensions are arbitrarily assigned to the other two dimensions. This step ensures that if, for example, the original ray's z direction is zero, then a dimension with non-zero magnitude is mapped to $+z$.

For example, if the ray's direction had the largest magnitude in x, the permutation would be:

$$\mathbf{T} = \begin{pmatrix} 0 & 1 & 0 & 0 \\ 0 & 0 & 1 & 0 \\ 1 & 0 & 0 & 0 \\ 0 & 0 & 0 & 1 \end{pmatrix}.$$

As before, it's easiest to just permute the dimensions of the ray direction and the translated triangle vertices directly.

⟨*Permute components of triangle vertices and ray direction*⟩ ≡   158
```
int kz = MaxDimension(Abs(ray.d));
int kx = kz + 1; if (kx == 3) kx = 0;
int ky = kx + 1; if (ky == 3) ky = 0;
Vector3f d = Permute(ray.d, kx, ky, kz);
p0t = Permute(p0t, kx, ky, kz);
p1t = Permute(p1t, kx, ky, kz);
p2t = Permute(p2t, kx, ky, kz);
```

Finally, a shear transformation aligns the ray direction with the $+z$ axis:

$$\mathbf{S} = \begin{pmatrix} 1 & 0 & -\mathbf{d}_x/\mathbf{d}_z & 0 \\ 0 & 1 & -\mathbf{d}_y/\mathbf{d}_z & 0 \\ 0 & 0 & 1/\mathbf{d}_z & 0 \\ 0 & 0 & 0 & 1 \end{pmatrix}.$$

To see how this transformation works, consider its operation on the ray direction vector $[\mathbf{d}_x \ \mathbf{d}_y \ \mathbf{d}_z \ 0]^T$.

For now, only the x and y dimensions are sheared; we can wait and shear the z dimension only if the ray actually intersects the triangle.

⟨*Apply shear transformation to translated vertex positions*⟩ ≡   158
```
Float Sx = -d.x / d.z;
Float Sy = -d.y / d.z;
Float Sz = 1.f / d.z;
p0t.x += Sx * p0t.z;
p0t.y += Sy * p0t.z;
p1t.x += Sx * p1t.z;
p1t.y += Sy * p1t.z;
p2t.x += Sx * p2t.z;
p2t.y += Sy * p2t.z;
```

Float 1062
Point3::Permute() 71
Vector3::Abs() 63
Vector3::MaxDimension() 66
Vector3::Permute() 66
Vector3f 60

Note that the calculations for the coordinate permutation and the shear coefficients only depend on the given ray; they are independent of the triangle. In a high-performance ray tracer, we might want to compute these values once and store them in the Ray class, rather than recomputing them for each triangle the ray is intersected with.

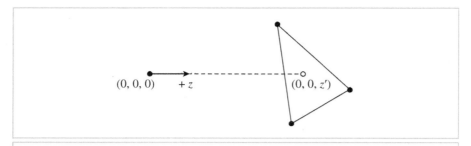

Figure 3.12: In the ray–triangle intersection coordinate system, the ray starts at the origin and goes along the $+z$ axis. The intersection test can be performed by considering only the xy projection of the ray and the triangle vertices, which in turn reduces to determining if the 2D point $(0, 0)$ is within the triangle.

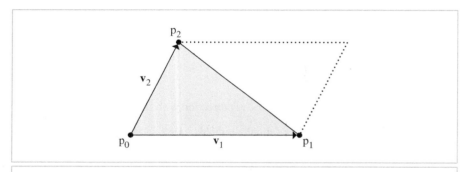

Figure 3.13: The area of a triangle with two edges given by vectors v_1 and v_2 is one-half of the area of the parallelogram shown here. The parallelogram area is given by the length of the cross product of $\mathbf{v}_1$ and $\mathbf{v}_2$.

With the triangle vertices transformed to this coordinate system, our task now is to find if the ray starting from the origin and traveling along the $+z$ axis intersects the transformed triangle. Because of the way the coordinate system was constructed, this problem is equivalent to the 2D problem of determining if the x, y coordinates $(0, 0)$ are inside the xy projection of the triangle (Figure 3.12).

To understand how the intersection algorithm works, first recall from Figure 2.5 that the cross product of two vectors gives the area of the parallelogram that they define. In 2D, with vectors $\mathbf{a}$ and $\mathbf{b}$, the area is

$$\mathbf{a}_x\mathbf{b}_y - \mathbf{b}_x\mathbf{a}_y.$$

Half of this area is the area of the triangle that they define. Thus, we can see that in 2D, the area of a triangle with vertices p_0, p_1, and p_2 is

$$\frac{1}{2}(p_{1x} - p_{0x})(p_{2y} - p_{0y}) - (p_{2x} - p_{0x})(p_{1y} - p_{0y}).$$

Figure 3.13 visualizes this geometrically.

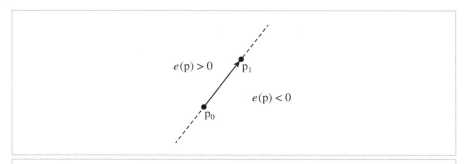

Figure 3.14: The edge function $e(\mathrm{p})$ characterizes points with respect to an oriented line between two points p_0 and p_1. The value of the edge function is positive for points p to the left of the line, zero for points on the line, and negative for points to the right of the line. The ray–triangle intersection algorithm uses an edge function that is twice the signed area of the triangle formed by the three points.

We'll use this expression of triangle area to define a signed *edge function*: given two triangle vertices p_0 and p_1, then we can define the directed edge function e as the function that gives the area of the triangle given by p_0, p_1, and a given third point p:

$$e(\mathrm{p}) = (\mathrm{p}_{1x} - \mathrm{p}_{0x})(\mathrm{p}_y - \mathrm{p}_{0y}) - (\mathrm{p}_x - \mathrm{p}_{0x})(\mathrm{p}_{1y} - \mathrm{p}_{0y}). \qquad [3.1]$$

(See Figure 3.14.) The edge function gives a positive value for points to the left of the line, and negative value for points to the right. Thus, if a point has edge function values of the same sign for all three edges of a triangle, it must be on the same side of all three edges and thus must be inside the triangle.

Thanks to the coordinate system transformation, the point we're testing p is $(0, 0)$. This simplifies the edge function expressions. For example, for the edge e_0 from p_1 to p_2, we have:

$$\begin{aligned}
e_0(\mathrm{p}) &= (\mathrm{p}_{2x} - \mathrm{p}_{1x})(\mathrm{p}_y - \mathrm{p}_{1y}) - (\mathrm{p}_x - \mathrm{p}_{1x})(\mathrm{p}_{2y} - \mathrm{p}_{1y}) \\
&= (\mathrm{p}_{2x} - \mathrm{p}_{1x})(-\mathrm{p}_{1y}) - (-\mathrm{p}_{1x})(\mathrm{p}_{2y} - \mathrm{p}_{1y}) \\
&= \mathrm{p}_{1x}\,\mathrm{p}_{2y} - \mathrm{p}_{2x}\,\mathrm{p}_{1y}.
\end{aligned} \qquad [3.2]$$

In the following, we'll use the indexing scheme that the edge function e_i corresponds to the directed edge from vertex p_i to $\mathrm{p}_{(i+1) \bmod 3}$.

⟨*Compute edge function coefficients* e0, e1, *and* e2⟩ ≡   158
```
    Float e0 = p1t.x * p2t.y - p1t.y * p2t.x;
    Float e1 = p2t.x * p0t.y - p2t.y * p0t.x;
    Float e2 = p0t.x * p1t.y - p0t.y * p1t.x;
```

In the rare case that any of the edge function values is exactly zero, it's not possible to be sure if the ray hits the triangle or not, and the edge equations are reevaluated using double-precision floating-point arithmetic. (Section 3.9.3 discusses the need for this step in more detail.) The fragment that implements this computation, ⟨*Fall back to double-precision test at triangle edges*⟩, is just a reimplementation of ⟨*Compute edge function coefficients* e0, e1, *and* e2⟩ using doubles and so isn't included here.

Float 1062

Given the values of the three edge functions, we have our first two opportunities to determine that there is no intersection. First, if the signs of the edge function values differ, then the point $(0, 0)$ is not on the same side of all three edges and therefore is outside the triangle. Second, if the sum of the three edge function values is zero, then the ray is approaching the triangle edge-on, and we report no intersection. (For a closed triangle mesh, the ray will hit a neighboring triangle instead.)

⟨*Perform triangle edge and determinant tests*⟩ ≡   158
```
if ((e0 < 0 || e1 < 0 || e2 < 0) && (e0 > 0 || e1 > 0 || e2 > 0))
    return false;
Float det = e0 + e1 + e2;
if (det == 0)
    return false;
```

Because the ray starts at the origin, has unit length, and is along the $+z$ axis, the z coordinate value of the intersection point is equal to the intersection's parametric t value. To compute this z value, we first need to go ahead and apply the shear transformation to the z coordinates of the triangle vertices. Given these z values, the *barycentric coordinates* of the intersection point in the triangle can be used to interpolate them across the triangle. They are given by dividing each edge function value by the sum of edge function values:

$$b_i = \frac{e_i}{e_0 + e_1 + e_2}.$$

Thus, the b_i sum to one.

The interpolated z value is given by

$$z = b_0 z_0 + b_1 z_1 + b_2 z_2,$$

where z_i are the coordinates of the three vertices in the ray–triangle intersection coordinate system.

In order to save the cost of the floating-point division to compute b_i in cases where the final t value is out of the range of valid t values, the implementation here first computes t by interpolating z_i with e_i (in other words, not yet performing the division by $d = e_0 + e_1 + e_2$). If the sign of d and the sign of the interpolated t value are different, then the final t value will certainly be negative and thus not a valid intersection.

Along similar lines,

$$t < t_{max} = \begin{cases} \sum_i e_i z_i < t_{max}(e_0 + e_1 + e_2) & \text{If } e_0 + e_1 + e_2 > 0 \\ \sum_i e_i z_i > t_{max}(e_0 + e_1 + e_2) & \text{otherwise.} \end{cases}$$

⟨*Compute scaled hit distance to triangle and test against ray t range*⟩ ≡   158
```
p0t.z *= Sz;
p1t.z *= Sz;
p2t.z *= Sz;
Float tScaled = e0 * p0t.z + e1 * p1t.z + e2 * p2t.z;
if (det < 0 && (tScaled >= 0 || tScaled < ray.tMax * det))
    return false;
else if (det > 0 && (tScaled <= 0 || tScaled > ray.tMax * det))
    return false;
```

Float 1062

We now know that there is a valid intersection and will go ahead and pay the cost of the floating-point division to compute actual barycentric coordinates as well as the actual t value for the intersection.

⟨*Compute barycentric coordinates and t value for triangle intersection*⟩ ≡   158
```
Float invDet = 1 / det;
Float b0 = e0 * invDet;
Float b1 = e1 * invDet;
Float b2 = e2 * invDet;
Float t = tScaled * invDet;
```

In order to generate consistent tangent vectors over triangle meshes, it is necessary to compute the partial derivatives $\partial p/\partial u$ and $\partial p/\partial v$ using the parametric (u, v) values at the triangle vertices, if provided. Although the partial derivatives are the same at all points on the triangle, the implementation here recomputes them each time an intersection is found. Although this results in redundant computation, the storage savings for large triangle meshes can be significant.

A triangle can be described by the set of points

$$p_0 + u\frac{\partial p}{\partial u} + v\frac{\partial p}{\partial v},$$

for some p_0, where u and v range over the parametric coordinates of the triangle. We also know the three vertex positions p_i, $i = 0$, 1, 2, and the texture coordinates (u_i, v_i) at each vertex. From this it follows that the partial derivatives of p must satisfy

$$p_i = p_0 + u_i\frac{\partial p}{\partial u} + v_i\frac{\partial p}{\partial v}.$$

In other words, there is a unique affine mapping from the 2D (u, v) space to points on the triangle (such a mapping exists even though the triangle is specified in 3D space because the triangle is planar). To compute expressions for $\partial p/\partial u$ and $\partial p/\partial v$, we start by computing the differences $p_0 - p_2$ and $p_1 - p_2$, giving the matrix equation

$$\begin{pmatrix} u_0 - u_2 & v_0 - v_2 \\ u_1 - u_2 & v_1 - v_2 \end{pmatrix} \begin{pmatrix} \partial p/\partial u \\ \partial p/\partial v \end{pmatrix} = \begin{pmatrix} p_0 - p_2 \\ p_1 - p_2 \end{pmatrix}.$$

Thus,

$$\begin{pmatrix} \partial p/\partial u \\ \partial p/\partial v \end{pmatrix} = \begin{pmatrix} u_0 - u_2 & v_0 - v_2 \\ u_1 - u_2 & v_1 - v_2 \end{pmatrix}^{-1} \begin{pmatrix} p_0 - p_2 \\ p_1 - p_2 \end{pmatrix}.$$

Inverting a 2×2 matrix is straightforward. The inverse of the (u, v) differences matrix is

Float 1062

$$\frac{1}{(u_0 - u_2)(v_1 - v_2) - (v_0 - v_2)(u_1 - u_2)} \begin{pmatrix} v_1 - v_2 & -(v_0 - v_2) \\ -(u_1 - u_2) & u_0 - u_2 \end{pmatrix}.$$

⟨*Compute triangle partial derivatives*⟩ ≡   **157**
```
Vector3f dpdu, dpdv;
Point2f uv[3];
GetUVs(uv);
```
⟨*Compute deltas for triangle partial derivatives* **164**⟩
```
Float determinant = duv02[0] * duv12[1] - duv02[1] * duv12[0];
if (determinant == 0) {
```
⟨*Handle zero determinant for triangle partial derivative matrix* **164**⟩
```
} else {
    Float invdet = 1 / determinant;
    dpdu = ( duv12[1] * dp02 - duv02[1] * dp12) * invdet;
    dpdv = (-duv12[0] * dp02 + duv02[0] * dp12) * invdet;
}
```

⟨*Compute deltas for triangle partial derivatives*⟩ ≡   **164**
```
Vector2f duv02 = uv[0] - uv[2], duv12 = uv[1] - uv[2];
Vector3f dp02 = p0 - p2, dp12 = p1 - p2;
```

Finally, it is necessary to handle the case when the matrix is singular and therefore cannot be inverted. Note that this only happens when the user-supplied per-vertex parameterization values are degenerate. In this case, the Triangle just chooses an arbitrary coordinate system about the triangle's surface normal, making sure that it is orthonormal:

⟨*Handle zero determinant for triangle partial derivative matrix*⟩ ≡   **164**
```
CoordinateSystem(Normalize(Cross(p2 - p0, p1 - p0)), &dpdu, &dpdv);
```

To compute the intersection point and the (u, v) parametric coordinates at the hit point, the barycentric interpolation formula is applied to the vertex positions and the (u, v) coordinates at the vertices. As we'll see in Section 3.9.4, this gives a more precise result for the intersection point than evaluating the parametric ray equation using t.

⟨*Interpolate* (u, v) *parametric coordinates and hit point*⟩ ≡   **157**
```
Point3f pHit = b0 * p0 + b1 * p1 + b2 * p2;
Point2f uvHit = b0 * uv[0] + b1 * uv[1] + b2 * uv[2];
```

The utility routine GetUVs() returns the (u, v) coordinates for the three vertices of the triangle, either from the Triangle, if it has them, or returning default values if explicit (u, v) coordinates were not specified with the mesh.

⟨*Triangle Private Methods*⟩ ≡   **156**
```
void GetUVs(Point2f uv[3]) const {
    if (mesh->uv) {
        uv[0] = mesh->uv[v[0]];
        uv[1] = mesh->uv[v[1]];
        uv[2] = mesh->uv[v[2]];
    } else {
        uv[0] = Point2f(0, 0);
        uv[1] = Point2f(1, 0);
        uv[2] = Point2f(1, 1);
    }
}
```

Before a successful intersection is reported, the intersection point is tested against an alpha mask texture, if one has been assigned to the shape. This texture can be thought of as a 1D function over the triangle's surface, where at any point where its value is zero, the intersection is ignored, effectively treating that point on the triangle as not being present. (Chapter 10 defines the texture interface and implementations in more detail.) Alpha masks can be helpful for representing objects like leaves: a leaf can be modeled as a single triangle, with an alpha mask "cutting out" the edges so that a leaf shape remains. This functionality is less often useful for other shapes, so pbrt only supports it for triangles.

⟨*Test intersection against alpha texture, if present*⟩ ≡   157
```
if (testAlphaTexture && mesh->alphaMask) {
    SurfaceInteraction isectLocal(pHit, Vector3f(0,0,0), uvHit,
        Vector3f(0,0,0), dpdu, dpdv, Normal3f(0,0,0), Normal3f(0,0,0),
        ray.time, this);
    if (mesh->alphaMask->Evaluate(isectLocal) == 0)
        return false;
}
```

Now we certainly have a valid intersection and can update the values pointed to by the pointers passed to the intersection routine. Unlike other shapes' implementations, the code that initializes the SurfaceInteraction structure here doesn't need to transform the partial derivatives to world space, since the triangle's vertices were already transformed to world space. Like the disk, the partial derivatives of the triangle's normal are also both (0, 0, 0), since it is flat.

⟨*Fill in* SurfaceInteraction *from triangle hit*⟩ ≡   157
```
*isect = SurfaceInteraction(pHit, pError, uvHit, -ray.d, dpdu, dpdv,
    Normal3f(0, 0, 0), Normal3f(0, 0, 0), ray.time, this);
```
⟨*Override surface normal in* isect *for triangle* **165**⟩
```
if (mesh->n || mesh->s) {
```
⟨*Initialize* Triangle *shading geometry* **166**⟩
```
}
```
⟨*Ensure correct orientation of the geometric normal* **166**⟩

The SurfaceInteraction constructor initializes the geometric normal n as the normalized cross product of dpdu and dpdv. This works well for most shapes, but in the case of triangle meshes it is preferable to rely on an initialization that does not depend on the underlying texture coordinates: it is fairly common to encounter meshes with bad parameterizations that do not preserve the orientation of the mesh, in which case the geometric normal would have an incorrect orientation.

We therefore initialize the geometric normal using the normalized cross product of the edge vectors dp02 and dp12, which results in the same normal up to a potential sign difference that depends on the exact order of triangle vertices (also known as the triangle's *winding order*). 3D modeling packages generally try to ensure that triangles in a mesh have consisting winding orders, which makes this approach more robust.

⟨*Override surface normal in* isect *for triangle*⟩ ≡   165
```
isect->n = isect->shading.n = Normal3f(Normalize(Cross(dp02, dp12)));
```

When interpolated normals are available, then we consider those to be the most authoritative source of orientation information. In this case, we flip the orientation of isect->n if the angle between it and the interpolated normal is greater than 180 degrees.

⟨*Ensure correct orientation of the geometric normal*⟩ ≡   165
```
if (mesh->n)
    isect->n = Faceforward(isect->n, isect->shading.n);
else if (reverseOrientation ^ transformSwapsHandedness)
    isect->n = isect->shading.n = -isect->n;
```

3.6.3 SHADING GEOMETRY

With Triangles, the user can provide normal vectors and tangent vectors at the vertices of the mesh that are interpolated to give normals and tangents at points on the faces of triangles. Shading geometry with interpolated normals can make otherwise faceted triangle meshes appear to be smoother than they geometrically are. If either shading normals or shading tangents have been provided, they are used to initialize the shading geometry in the SurfaceInteraction.

⟨*Initialize* Triangle *shading geometry*⟩ ≡   165
```
    ⟨Compute shading normal ns for triangle 166⟩
    ⟨Compute shading tangent ss for triangle 166⟩
    ⟨Compute shading bitangent ts for triangle and adjust ss 167⟩
    ⟨Compute ∂n/∂u and ∂n/∂v for triangle shading geometry⟩
    isect->SetShadingGeometry(ss, ts, dndu, dndv, true);
```

Given the barycentric coordinates of the intersection point, it's straightforward to compute the shading normal by interpolating among the appropriate vertex normals, if present.

⟨*Compute shading normal* ns *for triangle*⟩ ≡   166
```
    Normal3f ns;
    if (mesh->n) ns = Normalize(b0 * mesh->n[v[0]] +
                                b1 * mesh->n[v[1]] +
                                b2 * mesh->n[v[2]]);
    else
        ns = isect->n;
```

The shading tangent is computed similarly.

⟨*Compute shading tangent* ss *for triangle*⟩ ≡   166
```
    Vector3f ss;
    if (mesh->s) ss = Normalize(b0 * mesh->s[v[0]] +
                                b1 * mesh->s[v[1]] +
                                b2 * mesh->s[v[2]]);
    else
        ss = Normalize(isect->dpdu);
```

The bitangent vector ts is found using the cross product of ss and ns, giving a vector orthogonal to the two of them. Next, ss is overwritten with the cross product of ns and ts; this ensures that the cross product of ss and ts gives ns. Thus, if per-vertex n and s values are provided and if the interpolated **n** and **s** values aren't perfectly orthogonal, **n** will be preserved and **s** will be modified so that the coordinate system is orthogonal.

⟨*Compute shading bitangent* ts *for triangle and adjust* ss⟩ ≡   **166**
```
Vector3f ts = Cross(ss, ns);
if (ts.LengthSquared() > 0.f) {
    ts = Normalize(ts);
    ss = Cross(ts, ns);
}
else
    CoordinateSystem((Vector3f)ns, &ss, &ts);
```

The code to compute the partial derivatives $\partial n/\partial u$ and $\partial n/\partial v$ of the shading normal is almost identical to the code to compute the partial derivatives $\partial p/\partial u$ and $\partial p/\partial v$. Therefore, it has been elided from the text here.

3.6.4 SURFACE AREA

Using the fact that the area of a parallelogram is given by the length of the cross product of the two vectors along its sides, the Area() method computes the triangle area as half the area of the parallelogram formed by two of its edge vectors (Figure 3.13).

⟨*Triangle Method Definitions*⟩ +≡
```
Float Triangle::Area() const {
    ⟨Get triangle vertices in p0, p1, and p2 157⟩
    return 0.5 * Cross(p1 - p0, p2 - p0).Length();
}
```

*3.7 CURVES

While triangles can be used to represent thin shapes for modeling fine geometry like hair, fur, or fields of grass, it's worthwhile to have a specialized Shape in order to more efficiently render these sorts of objects, since many individual instances of them are often present. The Curve shape, introduced in this section, represents thin geometry modeled with cubic Bézier splines, which are defined by four control points, p_0, p_1, p_2, and p_3. The Bézier spline passes through the first and last control points; intermediate points are given by the polynomial

$$p(u) = (1-u)^3 p_0 + 3(1-u)^2 u p_1 + 3(1-u)u^2 p_2 + u^3 p_3. \qquad \text{[3.3]}$$

(See Figure 3.15.) Given a curve specified in another cubic basis, such as a Hermite spline, it's easy enough to convert to Bézier basis, so the implementation here leaves that burden on the user. This functionality could be easily added if it was frequently needed.

The Curve shape is defined by a 1D Bézier curve along with a width that is linearly interpolated from starting and ending widths along its extent. Together, these define a flat

CoordinateSystem() 67
Cross() 65
Curve 168
Float 1062
Triangle 156
Vector3::Length() 65
Vector3::LengthSquared() 65
Vector3f 60

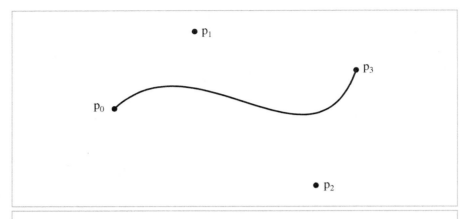

Figure 3.15: A cubic Bézier curve is defined by four control points, p_i. The curve $p(u)$, defined in Equation (3.3), passes through the first and last control points at $u = 0$ and $u = 1$, respectively.

Figure 3.16: Basic Geometry of the Curve Shape. A 1D Bézier curve is offset by half of the specified width in both the directions orthogonal to the curve at each point along it. The resulting area represents the curve's surface.

2D surface (Figure 3.16).[6] It's possible to directly intersect rays with this representation without tessellating it, which in turn makes it possible to efficiently render smooth curves without using too much storage. Figure 3.17 shows a bunny model with fur modeled with over one million Curves.

⟨*Curve Declarations*⟩ ≡
```
class Curve : public Shape {
public:
    ⟨Curve Public Methods 170⟩
private:
    ⟨Curve Private Methods⟩
    ⟨Curve Private Data 170⟩
};
```

---

6   Note the abuse of terminology: while a curve is a 1D mathematical entity, a Curve shape represents a 2D surface. In the following, we'll generally refer to the Shape as a curve. The 1D entity will be distinguished by the name "Bézier curve" when the distinction wouldn't otherwise be clear.

Figure 3.17: Furry Bunny. Bunny model with over one million Curve shapes used to model fur. Here, we've used unrealistically long curves to better show off the Curve's capabilities.

There are three types of curves that the Curve shape can represent, shown in Figure 3.18.

- Flat: Curves with this representation are always oriented to face the ray being intersected with them; they are useful for modeling fine swept cylindrical shapes like hair or fur.
- Cylinder: For curves that span a few pixels on the screen (like spaghetti seen from not too far away), the Curve shape can compute a shading normal that makes the curve appear to actually be a cylinder.
- Ribbon: This variant is useful for modeling shapes that don't actually have a cylindrical cross section (such as a blade of grass).

The CurveType enumerant records which of them a given Curve instance models.

The flat and cylinder curve variants are intended to be used as convenient approximations of deformed cylinders. It should be noted that intersections found with respect to them do not correspond to a physically realizable 3D shape, which can potentially lead to minor inconsistencies when taking a scene with true cylinders as a reference.

⟨*CurveType Declarations*⟩ ≡
```
enum class CurveType { Flat, Cylinder, Ribbon };
```

Curve 168

Given a curve specified in a pbrt scene description file, it can be worthwhile to split it into a few segments, each covering part of the *u* parametric range of the curve. (One reason

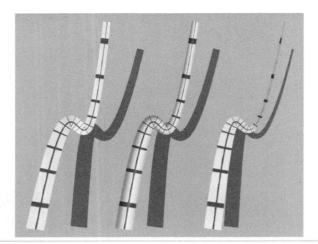

Figure 3.18: The Three Types of Curves That the Curve Shape Can Represent. On the left is a flat curve that is always oriented to be perpendicular to a ray approaching it. The middle is a variant of this curve where the shading normal is set so that the curve appears to be cylindrical. On the right is a ribbon, which has a fixed orientation at its starting and ending points; intermediate orientations are smoothly interpolated between them.

for doing so is that axis-aligned bounding boxes don't tightly bound wiggly curves, but subdividing Bézier splines makes them less wiggly—the *variation diminishing property* of polynomial splines.) Therefore, the Curve constructor takes both a parametric range of u values, $[u_{\min}, u_{\max}]$, as well as a pointer to a CurveCommon structure, which stores the control points and other information about the curve that is shared across curve segments. In this way, the memory footprint for individual curve segments is minimized, which makes it easier to keep many of them in memory.

⟨*Curve Public Methods*⟩ ≡   168
```
Curve(const Transform *ObjectToWorld, const Transform *WorldToObject,
        bool reverseOrientation, const std::shared_ptr<CurveCommon> &common,
        Float uMin, Float uMax)
    : Shape(ObjectToWorld, WorldToObject, reverseOrientation),
        common(common), uMin(uMin), uMax(uMax) { }
```

⟨*Curve Private Data*⟩ ≡   168
```
const std::shared_ptr<CurveCommon> common;
const Float uMin, uMax;
```

The CurveCommon constructor mostly just initializes member variables with values passed into it for the control points, the curve width, etc. The control points provided to it should be in the curve's object space.

For Ribbon curves, CurveCommon stores a surface normal to orient the curve at each endpoint. The constructor precomputes the angle between the two normal vectors and one over the sine of this angle; these values will be useful when computing the orientation of the curve at arbitrary points along its extent.

⟨*Curve Method Definitions*⟩ ≡
```
CurveCommon::CurveCommon(const Point3f c[4], Float width0, Float width1,
        CurveType type, const Normal3f *norm)
    : type(type), cpObj{c[0], c[1], c[2], c[3]},
      width{width0, width1} {
    if (norm) {
        n[0] = Normalize(norm[0]);
        n[1] = Normalize(norm[1]);
        normalAngle = std::acos(Clamp(Dot(n[0], n[1]), 0, 1));
        invSinNormalAngle = 1 / std::sin(normalAngle);
    }
}
```

⟨*CurveCommon Declarations*⟩ ≡
```
struct CurveCommon {
    const CurveType type;
    const Point3f cpObj[4];
    const Float width[2];
    Normal3f n[2];
    Float normalAngle, invSinNormalAngle;
};
```

Bounding boxes of Curves can be computed by taking advantage of the *convex hull property*, a property of Bézier curves that says that they must lie within the convex hull of their control points. Therefore, the bounding box of the control points gives a conservative bound of the underlying curve. The ObjectBound() method first computes a bounding box of the control points of the 1D Bézier segment to bound the spline along the center of the curve. These bounds are then expanded by half the maximum width the curve takes on over its parametric extent to get the 3D bounds of the Shape that the Curve represents.

⟨*Curve Method Definitions*⟩ +≡
```
Bounds3f Curve::ObjectBound() const {
    ⟨Compute object-space control points for curve segment, cpObj 172⟩
    Bounds3f b = Union(Bounds3f(cpObj[0], cpObj[1]),
                       Bounds3f(cpObj[2], cpObj[3]));
    Float width[2] = { Lerp(uMin, common->width[0], common->width[1]),
                       Lerp(uMax, common->width[0], common->width[1]) };
    return Expand(b, std::max(width[0], width[1]) * 0.5f);
}
```

The CurveCommon class stores the control points for the full curve, but Curve instances generally need the four control points that represent the Bézier curve for its u extent. These control points are computed using a technique called *blossoming*. The blossom $p(u_0, u_1, u_2)$ of a cubic Bézier spline is defined by three stages of linear interpolation, starting with the original control points:

$$
\begin{aligned}
a_i &= (1 - u_0)p_i + u_0\, p_{i+1} \quad i \in [0, 1, 2] \\
b_j &= (1 - u_1)a_j + u_1\, a_{j+1} \quad j \in [0, 1] \\
c &= (1 - u_2)b_0 + u_2\, b_1
\end{aligned}
$$

[3.4]

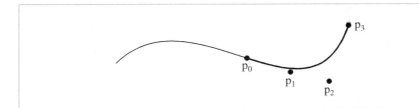

Figure 3.19: Blossoming to Find Control Points for a Segment of a Bézier Curve. The four blossoms in Equation (3.5) give the control points for the curve from u_{min} to u_{max}. Blossoming provides an elegant method to compute the Bézier control points of the curve that represent a subset of the overall curve.

The blossom $p(u, u, u)$ gives the curve's value at position u. (To verify this for yourself, expand Equation (3.4) using $u_i = u$, simplify, and compare to Equation (3.3).)

BlossomBezier() implements this computation.

⟨*Curve Utility Functions*⟩ ≡
```
    static Point3f BlossomBezier(const Point3f p[4], Float u0, Float u1,
            Float u2) {
        Point3f a[3] = { Lerp(u0, p[0], p[1]),
                         Lerp(u0, p[1], p[2]),
                         Lerp(u0, p[2], p[3]) };
        Point3f b[2] = { Lerp(u1, a[0], a[1]), Lerp(u1, a[1], a[2]) };
        return Lerp(u2, b[0], b[1]);
    }
```

The four control points for the curve segment over the range u_{min} to u_{max} are given by the blossoms:

$$\begin{aligned}
p_0 &= p(u_{min}, u_{min}, u_{min}) \\
p_1 &= p(u_{min}, u_{min}, u_{max}) \\
p_2 &= p(u_{min}, u_{max}, u_{max}) \\
p_3 &= p(u_{max}, u_{max}, u_{max})
\end{aligned}$$

[3.5]

(Figure 3.19).

Given this machinery, it's straightforward to compute the four control points for the curve segment that a Curve is responsible for.

⟨*Compute object-space control points for curve segment,* cpObj⟩ ≡   171, 173
```
    Point3f cpObj[4];
    cpObj[0] = BlossomBezier(common->cpObj, uMin, uMin, uMin);
    cpObj[1] = BlossomBezier(common->cpObj, uMin, uMin, uMax);
    cpObj[2] = BlossomBezier(common->cpObj, uMin, uMax, uMax);
    cpObj[3] = BlossomBezier(common->cpObj, uMax, uMax, uMax);
```

The Curve intersection algorithm is based on discarding curve segments as soon as it can be determined that the ray definitely doesn't intersect them and otherwise recursively splitting the curve in half to create two smaller segments that are then tested. Eventually, the curve is linearly approximated for an efficient intersection test. After some preparation, the recursiveIntersect() call starts this process with the full segment that the Curve represents.

⟨*Curve Method Definitions*⟩ +≡
```
bool Curve::Intersect(const Ray &r, Float *tHit,
        SurfaceInteraction *isect, bool testAlphaTexture) const {
    ⟨Transform Ray to object space 134⟩
    ⟨Compute object-space control points for curve segment, cpObj 172⟩
    ⟨Project curve control points to plane perpendicular to ray 173⟩
    ⟨Compute refinement depth for curve, maxDepth⟩
    return recursiveIntersect(ray, tHit, isect, cp, Inverse(objectToRay),
                              uMin, uMax, maxDepth);
}
```

Like the ray–triangle intersection algorithm from Section 3.6.2, the ray–curve intersection test is based on transforming the curve to a coordinate system with the ray's origin at the origin of the coordinate system and the ray's direction aligned to be along the +z axis. Performing this transformation at the start greatly reduces the number of operations that must be performed for intersection tests.

For the Curve shape, we'll need an explicit representation of the transformation, so the LookAt() function is used to generate it here. The origin is the ray's origin, the "look at" point is a point offset from the origin along the ray's direction, and the "up" direction is an arbitrary direction orthogonal to the ray direction.

⟨*Project curve control points to plane perpendicular to ray*⟩ ≡   173
```
Vector3f dx, dy;
CoordinateSystem(ray.d, &dx, &dy);
Transform objectToRay = LookAt(ray.o, ray.o + ray.d, dx);
Point3f cp[4] = { objectToRay(cpObj[0]), objectToRay(cpObj[1]),
                  objectToRay(cpObj[2]), objectToRay(cpObj[3]) };
```

The maximum number of times to subdivide the curve is computed so that the maximum distance from the eventual linearized curve at the finest refinement level is bounded to be less than a small fixed distance. We won't go into the details of this computation, which is implemented in the fragment ⟨*Compute refinement depth for curve,* maxDepth⟩.

The recursiveIntersect() method then tests whether the given ray intersects the given curve segment over the given parametric range [u0, u1].

⟨*Curve Method Definitions*⟩ +≡
```
bool Curve::recursiveIntersect(const Ray &ray, Float *tHit,
        SurfaceInteraction *isect, const Point3f cp[4],
        const Transform &rayToObject, Float u0, Float u1,
        int depth) const {
    ⟨Try to cull curve segment versus ray 174⟩
    if (depth > 0) {
        ⟨Split curve segment into sub-segments and test for intersection 175⟩
    } else {
        ⟨Intersect ray with curve segment 176⟩
    }
}
```

The method starts by checking to see if the ray intersects the curve segment's bounding box; if it doesn't, no intersection is possible and it can return immediately.

⟨*Try to cull curve segment versus ray*⟩ ≡   174
```
    ⟨Compute bounding box of curve segment, curveBounds 174⟩
    ⟨Compute bounding box of ray, rayBounds 174⟩
    if (Overlaps(curveBounds, rayBounds) == false)
        return false;
```

Along the lines of the implementation in Curve::ObjectBound(), a conservative bounding box for the segment can be found by taking the bounds of the curve's control points and expanding by half of the maximum width of the curve over the u range being considered.

⟨*Compute bounding box of curve segment, curveBounds*⟩ ≡   174
```
    Bounds3f curveBounds =
        Union(Bounds3f(cp[0], cp[1]), Bounds3f(cp[2], cp[3]));
    Float maxWidth = std::max(Lerp(u0, common->width[0], common->width[1]),
                              Lerp(u1, common->width[0], common->width[1]));
    curveBounds = Expand(curveBounds, 0.5 * maxWidth);
```

Because the ray's origin is at $(0, 0, 0)$ and its direction is aligned with the $+z$ axis in the intersection space, its bounding box only includes the origin in x and y (Figure 3.20); its z extent is given by the z range that its parametric extent covers.

⟨*Compute bounding box of ray, rayBounds*⟩ ≡   174
```
    Float rayLength = ray.d.Length();
    Float zMax = rayLength * ray.tMax;
    Bounds3f rayBounds(Point3f(0, 0, 0), Point3f(0, 0, zMax));
```

If the ray does intersect the curve's bounding box and the recursive splitting hasn't bottomed out, then the curve is split in half along the parametric u range. SubdivideBezier() computes seven control points: the first four correspond to the control points for the first half of the split curve, and the last four (starting with the last control point of the first half) correspond to the control points for the second half. Two calls to recursiveIntersect() test the two sub-segments.

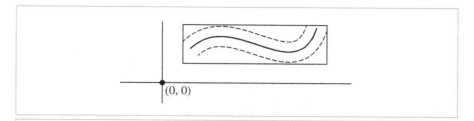

Figure 3.20: Ray–Curve Bounds Test. In the ray coordinate system, the ray's origin is at $(0, 0, 0)$ and its direction is aligned with the $+z$ axis. Therefore, if the 2D point $(x, y) = (0, 0)$ is outside the xy bounding box of the curve segment, then it's impossible that the ray intersects the curve.

⟨*Split curve segment into sub-segments and test for intersection*⟩ ≡   174

```
Float uMid = 0.5f * (u0 + u1);
Point3f cpSplit[7];
SubdivideBezier(cp, cpSplit);
return (recursiveIntersect(ray, tHit, isect, &cpSplit[0], rayToObject,
                           u0, uMid, depth - 1) ||
        recursiveIntersect(ray, tHit, isect, &cpSplit[3], rayToObject,
                           uMid, u1, depth - 1));
```

While we could use the BlossomBezier() function to compute the control points of the subdivided curves, they can be more efficiently computed by taking advantage of the fact that we're always splitting the curve exactly in the middle of its parametric extent. This computation is implemented in the SubdivideBezier() function; the seven control points it computes correspond to using $(0, 0, 0)$, $(0, 0, 1/2)$, $(0, 1/2, 1/2)$, $(1/2, 1/2, 1/2)$, $(1/2, 1/2, 1)$, $(1/2, 1, 1)$, and $(1, 1, 1)$ as blossoms in Equation (3.4).

⟨*Curve Utility Functions*⟩ +≡

```
inline void SubdivideBezier(const Point3f cp[4], Point3f cpSplit[7]) {
    cpSplit[0] = cp[0];
    cpSplit[1] = (cp[0] + cp[1]) / 2;
    cpSplit[2] = (cp[0] + 2 * cp[1] + cp[2]) / 4;
    cpSplit[3] = (cp[0] + 3 * cp[1] + 3 * cp[2] + cp[3]) / 8;
    cpSplit[4] = (cp[1] + 2 * cp[2] + cp[3]) / 4;
    cpSplit[5] = (cp[2] + cp[3]) / 2;
    cpSplit[6] = cp[3];
}
```

After a number of subdivisions, an intersection test is performed. Parts of this test are made more efficient by using a linear approximation of the curve; the variation diminishing property allows us to make this approximation without introducing too much error.

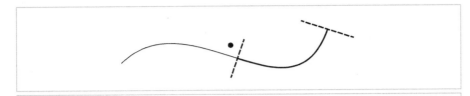

Figure 3.21: Curve Segment Boundaries. The intersection test for a segment of a larger curve computes edge functions for the lines that are perpendicular to the segment endpoints (dashed lines). If a potential intersection point (solid dot) is on the other side of edge than the segment, it is rejected; another curve segment (if present on that side) should account for this intersection instead.

⟨*Intersect ray with curve segment*⟩ ≡   174
    ⟨*Test ray against segment endpoint boundaries* 176⟩
    ⟨*Compute line w that gives minimum distance to sample point* 178⟩
    ⟨*Compute u coordinate of curve intersection point and* hitWidth 179⟩
    ⟨*Test intersection point against curve width* 179⟩
    ⟨*Compute v coordinate of curve intersection point* 180⟩
    ⟨*Compute hit* t *and partial derivatives for curve intersection* 180⟩
    return true;

It's important that the intersection test only accept intersections that are on the Curve's surface for the u segment currently under consideration. Therefore, the first step of the intersection test is to compute edge functions for lines perpendicular to the curve starting point and ending point and to classify the potential intersection point against them (Figure 3.21).

⟨*Test ray against segment endpoint boundaries*⟩ ≡   176
    ⟨*Test sample point against tangent perpendicular at curve start* 177⟩
    ⟨*Test sample point against tangent perpendicular at curve end*⟩

Projecting the curve control points into the ray coordinate system makes this test more efficient for two reasons. First, because the ray's direction is oriented with the $+z$ axis, the problem is reduced to a 2D test in x and y. Second, because the ray origin is at the origin of the coordinate system, the point we need to classify is $(0, 0)$, which simplifies evaluating the edge function, just like the ray–triangle intersection test.

Edge functions were introduced for ray–triangle intersection tests in Equation (3.1); see also Figure 3.14. To define the edge function, we need any two points on the line perpendicular to the curve going through starting point. The first control point, p_0, is a fine choice for the first point. For the second one, we'll compute the vector perpendicular to the curve's tangent and add that offset to the control point.

Differentiation of Equation (3.3) shows that the tangent to the curve at the first control point p_0 is $3(p_1 - p_0)$. The scaling factor doesn't matter here, so we'll use $t = p_1 - p_0$ here. Computing the vector perpendicular to the tangent is easy in 2D: it's just necessary to swap the x and y coordinates and negate one of them. (To see why this works, consider the dot product $(x, y) \cdot (y, -x) = xy + -yx = 0$. Because the cosine of the angle between the two vectors is zero, they must be perpendicular.) Thus, the second point on the edge is

$$p_0 + (p_{1y} - p_{0y}, -(p_{1x} - p_{0x})) = p_0 + (p_{1y} - p_{0y}, p_{0x} - p_{1x}).$$

Substituting these two points into the definition of the edge function, Equation (3.1), and simplifying gives

$$e(p) = (p_{1y} - p_{0y})(p_y - p_{0y}) - (p_x - p_{0x})(p_{0x} - p_{1x}).$$

Finally, substituting $p = (0, 0)$ gives the final expression to test:

$$e((0, 0)) = (p_{1y} - p_{0y})(-p_{0y}) + p_{0x}(p_{0x} - p_{1x}).$$

⟨*Test sample point against tangent perpendicular at curve start*⟩ ≡   176
```
  Float edge = (cp[1].y - cp[0].y) * -cp[0].y +
               cp[0].x * (cp[0].x - cp[1].x);
  if (edge < 0)
      return false;
```

The ⟨*Test sample point against tangent perpendicular at curve end*⟩ fragment, not included here, does the corresponding test at the end of the curve.

The next part of the test is to determine the u value along the curve segment where the point $(0, 0)$ is closest to the curve. This will be the intersection point, if it's no farther than the curve's width away from the center at that point. Determining this distance for a cubic Bézier curve is not efficient, so instead this intersection approach approximates the curve with a linear segment to compute this u value.

We'll linearly approximate the Bézier curve with a line segment from its starting point p_0 to its end point p_3 that is parameterized by w. In this case, the position is p_0 at $w = 0$ and p_3 at $w = 1$ (Figure 3.22). Our task now is to compute the value of w along the line corresponding to the point on the line p' that is closest to the point p. The key insight to apply is that at p', the vector from the corresponding point on the line to p will be perpendicular to the line (Figure 3.23 (a)).

Equation (2.1) gives us a relationship between the dot product of two vectors, their lengths, and the cosine of the angle between them. In particular, it shows us how to

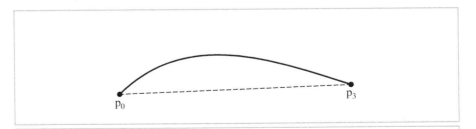

Figure 3.22: Approximation of a Cubic Bézier Curve with a Linear Segment. For part of the ray–curve intersection test, we approximate the Bézier with a linear segment (dashed line) passing through its starting and ending points. (In practice, after being subdivided, the curve will be already nearly linear, so the error is less than this figure suggests.)

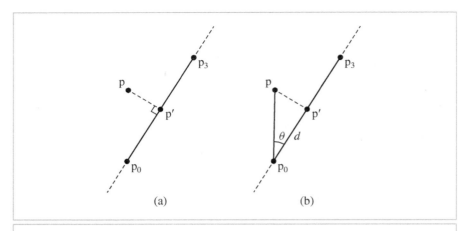

Figure 3.23: (a) Given an infinite line and a point p, then the vector from the point to the closest point on the line, p′, is perpendicular to the line. (b) Because this vector is perpendicular, we can compute the distance from the first point of the line to the point of closest approach, p′ as $d = \|p - p_0\| \cos \theta$.

compute the cosine of the angle between the vector from p_0 to p and the vector from p_0 to p_3:

$$\cos \theta = \frac{(p - p_0) \cdot (p_3 - p_0)}{\|p - p_0\| \|p_3 - p_0\|}.$$

Because the vector from p′ to p is perpendicular to the line (Figure 3.23(b)), then we can compute the distance along the line from p_0 to p′ as

$$d = \|p - p_0\| \cos \theta = \frac{(p - p_0) \cdot (p_3 - p_0)}{\|p_3 - p_0\|}.$$

Finally, the parametric offset w along the line is the ratio of d to the line's length,

$$w = \frac{d}{\|p_3 - p_0\|} = \frac{(p - p_0) \cdot (p_3 - p_0)}{\|p_3 - p_0\|^2}.$$

The computation of the value of w is in turn slightly simplified from the fact that $p = (0, 0)$ in the intersection coordinate system.

⟨*Compute line w that gives minimum distance to sample point*⟩ ≡   176
```
Vector2f segmentDirection = Point2f(cp[3]) - Point2f(cp[0]);
Float denom = segmentDirection.LengthSquared();
if (denom == 0)
    return false;
Float w = Dot(-Vector2f(cp[0]), segmentDirection) / denom;
```

Dot() 63
Float 1062
Point2f 68
Vector2f 60

The parametric u coordinate of the (presumed) closest point on the Bézier curve to the candidate intersection point is computed by linearly interpolating along the u range of the segment. Given this u value, the width of the curve at that point can be computed.

⟨*Compute u coordinate of curve intersection point and* hitWidth⟩ ≡   **176**
```
Float u = Clamp(Lerp(w, u0, u1), u0, u1);
Float hitWidth = Lerp(u, common->width[0], common->width[1]);
Normal3f nHit;
if (common->type == CurveType::Ribbon) {
    ⟨Scale hitWidth based on ribbon orientation 179⟩
}
```

For Ribbon curves, the curve is not always oriented to face the ray. Rather, its orientation is interpolated between two surface normals given at each endpoint. Here, spherical linear interpolation is used to interpolate the normal at *u* (recall Section 2.9.2). The curve's width is then scaled by the cosine of the angle between the normalized ray direction and the ribbon's orientation so that it reflects the visible width of the curve from the given direction.

⟨*Scale* hitWidth *based on ribbon orientation*⟩ ≡   **179**
```
Float sin0 = std::sin((1 - u) * common->normalAngle) *
    common->invSinNormalAngle;
Float sin1 = std::sin(u * common->normalAngle) *
    common->invSinNormalAngle;
nHit = sin0 * common->n[0] + sin1 * common->n[1];
hitWidth *= AbsDot(nHit, ray.d) / rayLength;
```

To finally classify the potential intersection as a hit or miss, the Bézier curve must still be evaluated at *u* using the EvalBezier() function. (Because the control points cp represent the curve segment currently under consideration, it's important to use *w* rather than *u* in the function call, however, since *w* is in the range [0, 1].) The derivative of the curve at this point will be useful shortly, so it's recorded now.

We'd like to test whether the distance from p to this point on the curve pc is less than half the curve's width. Because p = (0, 0), we can equivalently test whether the distance from pc to the origin is less than half the width or, equivalently, whether the squared distance is less than one quarter the width squared. If this test passes, the last thing to check is if the intersection point is in the ray's parametric *t* range.

⟨*Test intersection point against curve width*⟩ ≡   **176**
```
Vector3f dpcdw;
Point3f pc = EvalBezier(cp, Clamp(w, 0, 1), &dpcdw);
Float ptCurveDist2 = pc.x * pc.x + pc.y * pc.y;
if (ptCurveDist2 > hitWidth * hitWidth * .25)
    return false;
if (pc.z < 0 || pc.z > zMax)
    return false;
```

EvalBezier() computes the blossom $p(u, u, u)$ to evaluate a point on a Bézier spline. It optionally also returns the derivative of the curve at the point.

⟨*Curve Utility Functions*⟩ +≡
```
static Point3f EvalBezier(const Point3f cp[4], Float u,
        Vector3f *deriv = nullptr) {
    Point3f cp1[3] = { Lerp(u, cp[0], cp[1]), Lerp(u, cp[1], cp[2]),
                       Lerp(u, cp[2], cp[3]) };
    Point3f cp2[2] = { Lerp(u, cp1[0], cp1[1]), Lerp(u, cp1[1], cp1[2]) };
    if (deriv)
        *deriv = (Float)3 * (cp2[1] - cp2[0]);
    return Lerp(u, cp2[0], cp2[1]);
}
```

If the earlier tests have all passed, we have found a valid intersection, and the v coordinate of the intersection point can now be computed. The curve's v coordinate ranges from 0 to 1, taking on the value 0.5 at the center of the curve; here, we classify the intersection point, (0, 0), with respect to an edge function going through the point on the curve pc and a point along its derivative to determine which side of the center the intersection point is on and in turn how to compute v.

⟨*Compute v coordinate of curve intersection point*⟩ ≡   176
```
Float ptCurveDist = std::sqrt(ptCurveDist2);
Float edgeFunc = dpcdw.x * -pc.y + pc.x * dpcdw.y;
Float v = (edgeFunc > 0) ? 0.5f + ptCurveDist / hitWidth :
                           0.5f - ptCurveDist / hitWidth;
```

Finally, the partial derivatives are computed, and the SurfaceInteraction for the intersection can be initialized.

⟨*Compute hit* t *and partial derivatives for curve intersection*⟩ ≡   176
```
if (tHit != nullptr) {
    *tHit = pc.z / rayLength;
    ⟨Compute error bounds for curve intersection 227⟩
    ⟨Compute ∂p/∂u and ∂p/∂v for curve intersection 180⟩
    *isect = (*ObjectToWorld)(SurfaceInteraction(
        ray(pc.z), pError, Point2f(u, v), -ray.d, dpdu, dpdv,
        Normal3f(0, 0, 0), Normal3f(0, 0, 0), ray.time, this));
}
```

The partial derivative $\partial p / \partial u$ comes directly from the derivative of the underlying Bézier curve. The second partial derivative, $\partial p / \partial v$, is computed in different ways based on the type of the curve. For ribbons, we have $\partial p / \partial u$ and the surface normal, and so $\partial p / \partial v$ must be the vector such that $\partial p / \partial u \times \partial p / \partial v = \mathbf{n}$ and has length equal to the curve's width.

⟨*Compute $\partial p / \partial u$ and $\partial p / \partial v$ for curve intersection*⟩ ≡   180
```
Vector3f dpdu, dpdv;
EvalBezier(common->cpObj, u, &dpdu);
```

```
if (common->type == CurveType::Ribbon)
    dpdv = Normalize(Cross(nHit, dpdu)) * hitWidth;
else {
    ⟨Compute curve ∂p/∂v for flat and cylinder curves 181⟩
}
```

For flat and cylinder curves, we transform $\partial p/\partial u$ to the intersection coordinate system. For flat curves, we know that $\partial p/\partial v$ lies in the xy plane, is perpendicular to $\partial p/\partial u$, and has length equal to hitWidth. We can find the 2D perpendicular vector using the same approach as was used earlier for the perpendicular curve segment boundary edges.

⟨*Compute curve* $\partial p/\partial v$ *for flat and cylinder curves*⟩ ≡   180
```
Vector3f dpduPlane = (Inverse(rayToObject))(dpdu);
Vector3f dpdvPlane = Normalize(Vector3f(-dpduPlane.y, dpduPlane.x, 0)) *
                     hitWidth;
if (common->type == CurveType::Cylinder) {
    ⟨Rotate dpdvPlane to give cylindrical appearance 181⟩
}
dpdv = rayToObject(dpdvPlane);
```

The $\partial p/\partial v$ vector for cylinder curves is rotated around the dpduPlane axis so that its appearance resembles a cylindrical cross-section.

⟨*Rotate* dpdvPlane *to give cylindrical appearance*⟩ ≡   181
```
Float theta = Lerp(v, -90., 90.);
Transform rot = Rotate(-theta, dpduPlane);
dpdvPlane = rot(dpdvPlane);
```

The Curve::Area() method, not included here, first approximates the curve length by the length of its control hull. It then multiplies this length by the average curve width over its extent to approximate the overall surface area.

*3.8 SUBDIVISION SURFACES

The last shape representation that we'll define in this chapter implements *subdivision surfaces*, a representation that is particularly well suited to describing complex smooth shapes. The subdivision surface for a particular mesh is defined by repeatedly subdividing the faces of the mesh into smaller faces and then finding the new vertex locations using weighted combinations of the old vertex positions.

For appropriately chosen subdivision rules, this process converges to give a smooth *limit surface* as the number of subdivision steps goes to infinity. In practice, just a few levels of subdivision typically suffice to give a good approximation of the limit surface. Figure 3.24 shows a simple example of a subdivision, where a tetrahedron has been subdivided zero, one, two, and six times. Figure 3.25 shows the effect of applying subdivision to the Killeroo model; on the top is the original control mesh, and below is the subdivision surface that the control mesh represents.

Figure 3.24: Subdivision of a Tetrahedron. From left to right, zero, one, two, and six subdivision steps have been used. (At zero levels, the vertices are just moved to lie on the limit surface.) As more subdivision is done, the mesh approaches the limit surface, the smooth surface described by the original mesh. Notice how the specular highlights become progressively more accurate and the silhouette edges appear smoother as more levels of subdivision are performed.

Although originally developed in the 1970s, subdivision surfaces have seen widespread use in recent years thanks to some important advantages over polygonal and spline-based representations of surfaces. The advantages of subdivision include the following:

- Subdivision surfaces are smooth, as opposed to polygon meshes, which appear faceted when viewed close up, regardless of how finely they are modeled.
- Much of the existing infrastructure in modeling systems can be retargeted to subdivision. The classic toolbox of techniques for modeling polygon meshes can be applied to modeling subdivision control meshes.
- Subdivision surfaces are well suited to describing objects with complex topology, since they start with a control mesh of arbitrary (manifold) topology. Parametric surface models generally don't handle complex topology well.
- Subdivision methods are often generalizations of spline-based surface representations, so spline surfaces can often just be run through general subdivision surface renderers.
- It is easy to add detail to a localized region of a subdivision surface simply by adding faces to appropriate parts of the control mesh. This is much harder with spline representations.

Here, we will describe an implementation of *Loop subdivision surfaces.*[7] The Loop subdivision rules are based on triangular faces in the control mesh; faces with more than three vertices are triangulated at the start. At each subdivision step, all faces split into four child faces (Figure 3.26). New vertices are added along all of the edges of the original mesh, with positions computed using weighted averages of nearby vertices. Furthermore, the position of each original vertex is updated with a weighted average of its position and its new neighbors' positions. The implementation here uses weights based on improvements to Loop's method developed by Hoppe et al. (1994). We will not include discussion here about how these weights are derived. They must be chosen carefully to ensure that the limit surface actually has particular desirable smoothness properties, although subtle mathematics is necessary to prove that they indeed do this.

---

7   Named after the inventor of the subdivision rules used, Charles Loop.

Figure 3.25: Subdivision Applied to the Killeroo Model. The control mesh (top) describes the subdivision surface shown below it. Subdivision is well suited to modeling shapes like this one, since it's easy to add detail locally by refining the control mesh, and there are no limitations on the topology of the final surface. *(Model courtesy of headus/Rezard.)*

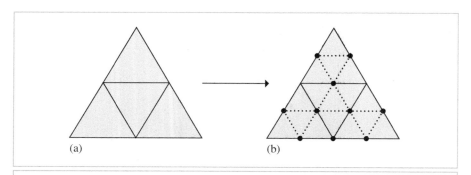

(a)   (b)

Figure 3.26: Basic Refinement Process for Loop Subdivision. (a) The control mesh before subdivision. (b) The new mesh after one subdivision step. Each triangular face of the mesh has been subdivided into four new faces by splitting each of the edges and connecting the new vertices with new edges.

Rather than being implemented as a Shape in pbrt, subdivision surfaces are generated by a function, LoopSubdivide(), that applies the subdivision rules to a mesh represented by a collection of vertices and vertex indices and returns a vector of Triangles that represent the final subdivided mesh.

⟨*LoopSubdiv Function Definitions*⟩ ≡
```
    std::vector<std::shared_ptr<Shape>> LoopSubdivide(
            const Transform *ObjectToWorld, const Transform *WorldToObject,
            bool reverseOrientation, int nLevels, int nIndices,
            const int *vertexIndices, int nVertices, const Point3f *p) {
        std::vector<SDVertex *> vertices;
        std::vector<SDFace *> faces;
        ⟨Allocate LoopSubdiv vertices and faces 185⟩
        ⟨Set face to vertex pointers 187⟩
        ⟨Set neighbor pointers in faces 188⟩
        ⟨Finish vertex initialization 190⟩
        ⟨Refine subdivision mesh into triangles 193⟩
    }
```

3.8.1 MESH REPRESENTATION

The parameters to LoopSubdivide() specify a triangle mesh in exactly the same format used in the TriangleMesh constructor (Section 3.6): each face is described by three integer vertex indices, giving offsets into the vertex array p for the face's three vertices. We will need to process this data to determine which faces are adjacent to each other, which faces are adjacent to which vertices, and so on, in order to implement the subdivision algorithm.

We will shortly define SDVertex and SDFace structures, which hold data for vertices and faces in the subdivision mesh. LoopSubdivide() starts by allocating one instance of the SDVertex class for each vertex in the mesh and an SDFace for each face. For now, these are mostly uninitialized.

⟨*Allocate* LoopSubdiv *vertices and faces*⟩ ≡   184
```
    std::unique_ptr<SDVertex[]> verts(new SDVertex[nVertices]);
    for (int i = 0; i < nVertices; ++i) {
        verts[i] = SDVertex(p[i]);
        vertices.push_back(&verts[i]);
    }
    int nFaces = nIndices / 3;
    std::unique_ptr<SDFace[]> fs(new SDFace[nFaces]);
    for (int i = 0; i < nFaces; ++i)
        faces.push_back(&fs[i]);
```

The Loop subdivision scheme, like most other subdivision schemes, assumes that the control mesh is *manifold*—no more than two faces share any given edge. Such a mesh may be closed or open: a *closed mesh* has no boundary, and all faces have adjacent faces across each of their edges. An *open mesh* has some faces that do not have all three neighbors. The implementation here supports both closed and open meshes.

In the interior of a triangle mesh, most vertices are adjacent to six faces and have six neighbor vertices directly connected to them with edges. On the boundaries of an open mesh, most vertices are adjacent to three faces and four vertices. The number of vertices directly adjacent to a vertex is called the vertex's *valence*. Interior vertices with valence other than six, or boundary vertices with valence other than four, are called *extraordinary vertices*; otherwise, they are called *regular*.[8] Loop subdivision surfaces are smooth everywhere except at their extraordinary vertices.

Each SDVertex stores its position p, a Boolean that indicates whether it is a regular or extraordinary vertex, and a Boolean that records if it lies on the boundary of the mesh. It also holds a pointer to an arbitrary face adjacent to it; this pointer gives a starting point for finding all of the adjacent faces. Finally, there is a pointer to store the corresponding SDVertex for the next level of subdivision, if any.

⟨*LoopSubdiv Local Structures*⟩ ≡
```
    struct SDVertex {
        ⟨SDVertex Constructor 185⟩
        ⟨SDVertex Methods⟩
        Point3f p;
        SDFace *startFace = nullptr;
        SDVertex *child = nullptr;
        bool regular = false, boundary = false;
    };
```

⟨*SDVertex Constructor*⟩ ≡   185
```
    SDVertex(const Point3f &p = Point3f(0, 0, 0)) : p(p) { }
```

The SDFace structure is where most of the topological information about the mesh is maintained. Because all faces are triangular, faces always store pointers to their three

---

8 These terms are commonly used in the modeling literature, although *irregular* versus *regular* or *extraordinary* versus *ordinary* might be more intuitive.

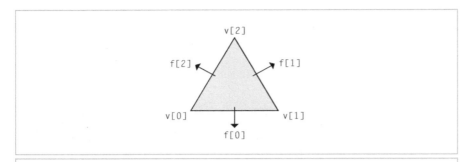

Figure 3.27: Each triangular face stores three pointers to `SDVertex` objects `v[i]` and three pointers to neighboring faces `f[i]`. Neighboring faces are indexed using the convention that the `i`th edge is the edge from `v[i]` to `v[(i+1)%3]`, and the neighbor across the `i`th edge is in `f[i]`.

vertices and pointers to the adjacent faces across its three edges. The corresponding face neighbor pointers will be `nullptr` if the face is on the boundary of an open mesh.

The face neighbor pointers are indexed such that if we label the edge from `v[i]` to `v[(i+1)%3]` as the `i`th edge, then the neighbor face across that edge is stored in `f[i]` (Figure 3.27). This labeling convention is important to keep in mind. Later when we are updating the topology of a newly subdivided mesh, we will make extensive use of it to navigate around the mesh. Similarly to the `SDVertex` class, the `SDFace` also stores pointers to child faces at the next level of subdivision.

⟨*LoopSubdiv Local Structures*⟩ +≡
```
struct SDFace {
    ⟨SDFace Constructor⟩
    ⟨SDFace Methods 191⟩
    SDVertex *v[3];
    SDFace *f[3];
    SDFace *children[4];
};
```

The `SDFace` constructor is straightforward—it simply sets these various pointers to `nullptr`—so it is not shown here.

In order to simplify navigation of the `SDFace` data structure, we'll provide macros that make it easy to determine the vertex and face indices before or after a particular index. These macros add appropriate offsets and compute the result modulus three to handle cycling around.

⟨*LoopSubdiv Macros*⟩ ≡
```
#define NEXT(i) (((i) + 1) % 3)
#define PREV(i) (((i) + 2) % 3)
```

In addition to requiring a manifold mesh, the subdivision code expects that the control mesh specified by the user will be *consistently ordered*—each *directed edge* in the mesh can be present only once. An edge that is shared by two faces should be specified in a different direction by each face. Consider two vertices, v_0 and v_1, with an edge between them. We

SDFace 186
SDVertex 185

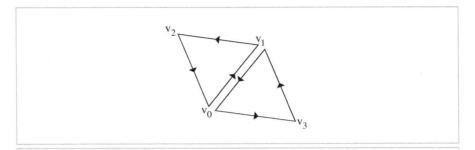

Figure 3.28: All of the faces in the input mesh must be specified so that each shared edge is given no more than once in each direction. Here, the edge from v_0 to v_1 is traversed from v_0 to v_1 by one face and from v_1 to v_0 by the other. Another way to think of this is in terms of face orientation: all faces' vertices should be given consistently in either clockwise or counterclockwise order, as seen from outside the mesh.

expect that one of the triangular faces that has this edge will specify its three vertices so that v_0 is before v_1, and that the other face will specify its vertices so that v_1 is before v_0 (Figure 3.28). A Möbius strip is one example of a surface that cannot be consistently ordered, but such surfaces come up rarely in rendering so in practice this restriction is not a problem. Poorly formed mesh data from other programs that don't create consistently ordered meshes can be troublesome, however.

Given this assumption about the input data, the `LoopSubdivide()` can now initialize the mesh's topological data structures. It first loops over all of the faces and sets their `v` pointers to point to their three vertices. It also sets each vertex's `SDVertex::startFace` pointer to point to one of the vertex's neighboring faces. It doesn't matter which of its adjacent faces is used, so the implementation just keeps resetting it each time it comes across another face that the vertex is incident to, thus ensuring that all vertices have a non-`nullptr` face pointer by the time the loop is complete.

⟨*Set face to vertex pointers*⟩ ≡   184
```
const int *vp = vertexIndices;
for (int i = 0; i < nFaces; ++i, vp += 3) {
    SDFace *f = faces[i];
    for (int j = 0; j < 3; ++j) {
        SDVertex *v = vertices[vp[j]];
        f->v[j] = v;
        v->startFace = f;
    }
}
```

Now it is necessary to set each face's `f` pointer to point to its neighboring faces. This is a bit trickier, since face adjacency information isn't directly specified in the data passed to `LoopSubdivide()`. The implementation here loops over the faces and creates an `SDEdge` object for each of their three edges. When it comes to another face that shares the same edge, it can update both faces' neighbor pointers.

⟨*LoopSubdiv Local Structures*⟩ +≡
```
struct SDEdge {
    ⟨SDEdge Constructor 188⟩
    ⟨SDEdge Comparison Function 188⟩
    SDVertex *v[2];
    SDFace *f[2];
    int f0edgeNum;
};
```

The SDEdge constructor takes pointers to the two vertices at each end of the edge. It orders them so that v[0] holds the one that is first in memory. This code may seem strange, but it is simply relying on the fact that pointers in C++ are effectively numbers that can be manipulated like integers[9] and that the ordering of vertices on an edge is arbitrary. Sorting the two vertices based on the addresses of their pointers guarantees that the edge (v_a, v_b) is correctly recognized as the same as the edge (v_b, v_a), regardless of what order the vertices are provided in.

⟨*SDEdge Constructor*⟩ ≡   188
```
SDEdge(SDVertex *v0 = nullptr, SDVertex *v1 = nullptr) {
    v[0] = std::min(v0, v1);
    v[1] = std::max(v0, v1);
    f[0] = f[1] = nullptr;
    f0edgeNum = -1;
}
```

The class also defines an ordering operation for SDEdge objects so that they can be stored in other data structures that rely on ordering being well defined.

⟨*SDEdge Comparison Function*⟩ ≡   188
```
bool operator<(const SDEdge &e2) const {
    if (v[0] == e2.v[0]) return v[1] < e2.v[1];
    return v[0] < e2.v[0];
}
```

Now the LoopSubdivide() function can get to work, looping over the edges in all of the faces and updating the neighbor pointers as it goes. It uses a set to store the edges that have only one adjacent face so far. The set makes it possible to search for a particular edge in $O(\log n)$ time.

⟨*Set neighbor pointers in* faces⟩ ≡   184
```
std::set<SDEdge> edges;
for (int i = 0; i < nFaces; ++i) {
    SDFace *f = faces[i];
    for (int edgeNum = 0; edgeNum < 3; ++edgeNum) {
        ⟨Update neighbor pointer for edgeNum 189⟩
    }
}
```

---

9   Segmented architectures notwithstanding.

For each edge in each face, the loop body creates an edge object and sees if the same edge has been seen previously. If so, it initializes both faces' neighbor pointers across the edge. If not, it adds the edge to the set of edges. The indices of the two vertices at the ends of the edge, v0 and v1, are equal to the edge index and the edge index plus one.

⟨*Update neighbor pointer for* edgeNum⟩ ≡   **188**
```
int v0 = edgeNum, v1 = NEXT(edgeNum);
SDEdge e(f->v[v0], f->v[v1]);
if (edges.find(e) == edges.end()) {
    ⟨Handle new edge 189⟩
} else {
    ⟨Handle previously seen edge 189⟩
}
```

Given an edge that hasn't been encountered before, the current face's pointer is stored in the edge object's f[0] member. Because the input mesh is assumed to be manifold, there can be at most one other face that shares this edge. When such a face is discovered, it can be used to initialize the neighboring face field. Storing the edge number of this edge in the current face allows the neighboring face to initialize its corresponding edge neighbor pointer.

⟨*Handle new edge*⟩ ≡   **189**
```
e.f[0] = f;
e.f0edgeNum = edgeNum;
edges.insert(e);
```

When the second face on an edge is found, the neighbor pointers for each of the two faces are set. The edge is then removed from the edge set, since no edge can be shared by more than two faces.

⟨*Handle previously seen edge*⟩ ≡   **189**
```
e = *edges.find(e);
e.f[0]->f[e.f0edgeNum] = f;
f->f[edgeNum] = e.f[0];
edges.erase(e);
```

Now that all faces have proper neighbor pointers, the boundary and regular flags in each of the vertices can be set. In order to determine if a vertex is a boundary vertex, we'll define an ordering of faces around a vertex (Figure 3.29). For a vertex v[i] on a face f, we define the vertex's *next face* as the face across the edge from v[i] to v[NEXT(i)] and the *previous face* as the face across the edge from v[PREV(i)] to v[i].

By successively going to the next face around v, we can iterate over the faces adjacent to it. If we eventually return to the face we started at, then we are at an interior vertex; if we come to an edge with a nullptr neighbor pointer, then we're at a boundary vertex (Figure 3.30). Once the initialization routine has determined if this is a boundary vertex, it computes the valence of the vertex and sets the regular flag if the valence is 6 for an interior vertex or 4 for a boundary vertex; otherwise, it is an extraordinary vertex.

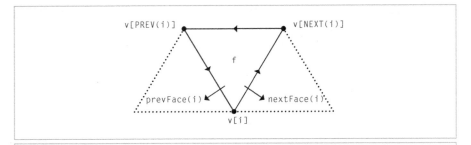

Figure 3.29: Given a vertex `v[i]` and a face that it is incident to, `f`, we define the *next face* as the face adjacent to `f` across the edge from `v[i]` to `v[NEXT(i)]`. The previous face is defined analogously.

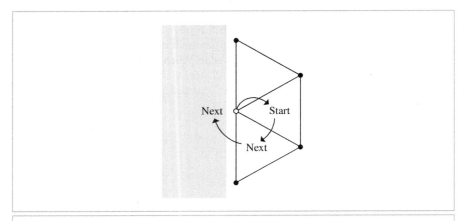

Figure 3.30: We can determine if a vertex is a boundary vertex by starting from the adjacent face `startFace` and following next face pointers around the vertex. If we come to a face that has no next neighbor face, then the vertex is on a boundary. If we return to `startFace`, it's an interior vertex.

⟨*Finish vertex initialization*⟩ ≡   184

```
for (int i = 0; i < nVertices; ++i) {
    SDVertex *v = vertices[i];
    SDFace *f = v->startFace;
    do {
        f = f->nextFace(v);
    } while (f && f != v->startFace);
    v->boundary = (f == nullptr);
    if (!v->boundary && v->valence() == 6)
        v->regular = true;
    else if (v->boundary && v->valence() == 4)
        v->regular = true;
    else
        v->regular = false;
}
```

Because the valence of a vertex is frequently needed, we provide the method SDVertex::valence().

⟨*LoopSubdiv Inline Functions*⟩ ≡
```
inline int SDVertex::valence() {
    SDFace *f = startFace;
    if (!boundary) {
        ⟨Compute valence of interior vertex 191⟩
    } else {
        ⟨Compute valence of boundary vertex 191⟩
    }
}
```

To compute the valence of a nonboundary vertex, this method counts the number of the adjacent faces starting by following each face's neighbor pointers around the vertex until it reaches the starting face. The valence is equal to the number of faces visited.

⟨*Compute valence of interior vertex*⟩ ≡   191
```
int nf = 1;
while ((f = f->nextFace(this)) != startFace)
    ++nf;
return nf;
```

For boundary vertices we can use the same approach, although in this case, the valence is one more than the number of adjacent faces. The loop over adjacent faces is slightly more complicated here: it follows pointers to the next face around the vertex until it reaches the boundary, counting the number of faces seen. It then starts again at startFace and follows previous face pointers until it encounters the boundary in the other direction.

⟨*Compute valence of boundary vertex*⟩ ≡   191
```
int nf = 1;
while ((f = f->nextFace(this)) != nullptr)
    ++nf;
f = startFace;
while ((f = f->prevFace(this)) != nullptr)
    ++nf;
return nf + 1;
```

SDFace::vnum() is a utility function that finds the index of a given vertex pointer. It is a fatal error to pass a pointer to a vertex that isn't part of the current face—this case would represent a bug elsewhere in the subdivision code.

⟨*SDFace Methods*⟩ ≡   186
```
int vnum(SDVertex *vert) const {
    for (int i = 0; i < 3; ++i)
        if (v[i] == vert) return i;
    Severe("Basic logic error in SDFace::vnum()");
    return -1;
}
```

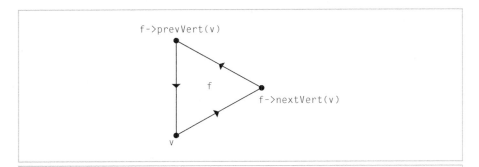

Figure 3.31: Given a vertex v on a face f, the method `f->prevVert(v)` returns the previous vertex around the face from v, and `f->nextVert(v)` returns the next vertex, where "next" and "previous" are defined by the original ordering of vertices when this face was defined.

Since the next face for a vertex v[i] on a face f is over the ith edge (recall the mapping of edge neighbor pointers from Figure 3.27), we can find the appropriate face neighbor pointer easily given the index i for the vertex, which the vnum() utility function provides. The previous face is across the edge from PREV(i) to i, so the method returns f[PREV(i)] for the previous face.

⟨*SDFace Methods*⟩ +≡   186
```
SDFace *nextFace(SDVertex *vert) {
    return f[vnum(vert)];
}
```

⟨*SDFace Methods*⟩ +≡   186
```
SDFace *prevFace(SDVertex *vert) {
    return f[PREV(vnum(vert))];
}
```

It is also useful to be able to get the next and previous vertices around a face starting at any vertex. The `SDFace::nextVert()` and `SDFace::prevVert()` methods do just that (Figure 3.31).

⟨*SDFace Methods*⟩ +≡   186
```
SDVertex *nextVert(SDVertex *vert) {
    return v[NEXT(vnum(vert))];
}
```

⟨*SDFace Methods*⟩ +≡   186
```
SDVertex *prevVert(SDVertex *vert) {
    return v[PREV(vnum(vert))];
}
```

3.8.2 SUBDIVISON

Now we can show how subdivision proceeds with the modified Loop rules. The implementation here applies subdivision a fixed number of times to generate a triangle mesh for rendering; Exercise 3.11 at the end of the chapter discusses adaptive subdivision, where each original face is subdivided enough times so that the result looks smooth from a particular viewpoint rather than just using a fixed number of levels of subdivision, which may over-subdivide some areas while simultaneously under-subdividing others.

The ⟨*Refine subdivision mesh into triangles*⟩ fragment repeatedly applies the subdivision rules to the mesh, each time generating a new mesh to be used as the input to the next step. After each subdivision step, the f and v arrays are updated to point to the faces and vertices from the level of subdivision just computed. When it's done subdividing, a triangle mesh representation of the surface is returned.

An instance of the MemoryArena class is used to allocate temporary storage through this process. This class, defined in Section A.4.3, provides a custom memory allocation method that quickly allocates memory, automatically freeing the memory when it goes out of scope.

⟨*Refine subdivision mesh into triangles*⟩ ≡   184
```
std::vector<SDFace *> f = faces;
std::vector<SDVertex *> v = vertices;
MemoryArena arena;
for (int i = 0; i < nLevels; ++i) {
    ⟨Update f and v for next level of subdivision 194⟩
}
⟨Push vertices to limit surface 203⟩
⟨Compute vertex tangents on limit surface 203⟩
⟨Create triangle mesh from subdivision mesh⟩
```

The main loop of a subdivision step proceeds as follows: it creates vectors to store the vertices and faces at the current level of subdivision and then proceeds to compute new vertex positions and update the topological representation for the refined mesh. Figure 3.32 shows the basic refinement rules for faces in the mesh. Each face is split into

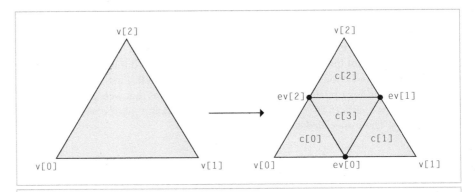

Figure 3.32: Basic Subdivision of a Single Triangular Face. Four child faces are created, ordered such that the ith child face is adjacent to the ith vertex of the original face and the fourth child face is in the center of the subdivided face. Three edge vertices need to be computed; they are numbered so that the ith edge vertex is along the ith edge of the original face.

four child faces, such that the ith child face is next to the ith vertex of the input face and the final face is in the center. Three new vertices are then computed along the split edges of the original face.

⟨*Update* f *and* v *for next level of subdivision*⟩ ≡   193
```
std::vector<SDFace *> newFaces;
std::vector<SDVertex *> newVertices;
```
⟨*Allocate next level of children in mesh tree* 194⟩
⟨*Update vertex positions and create new edge vertices* 194⟩
⟨*Update new mesh topology* 201⟩
⟨*Prepare for next level of subdivision* 203⟩

First, storage is allocated for the updated values of the vertices already present in the input mesh. The method also allocates storage for the child faces. It doesn't yet do any initialization of the new vertices and faces other than setting the regular and boundary flags for the vertices since subdivision leaves boundary vertices on the boundary and interior vertices in the interior and it doesn't change the valence of vertices in the mesh.

⟨*Allocate next level of children in mesh tree*⟩ ≡   194
```
for (SDVertex *vertex : v) {
    vertex->child = arena.Alloc<SDVertex>();
    vertex->child->regular = vertex->regular;
    vertex->child->boundary = vertex->boundary;
    newVertices.push_back(vertex->child);
}
for (SDFace *face : f) {
    for (int k = 0; k < 4; ++k) {
        face->children[k] = arena.Alloc<SDFace>();
        newFaces.push_back(face->children[k]);
    }
}
```

Computing New Vertex Positions

Before worrying about initializing the topology of the subdivided mesh, the refinement method computes positions for all of the vertices in the mesh. First, it considers the problem of computing updated positions for all of the vertices that were already present in the mesh; these vertices are called *even vertices*. It then computes the new vertices on the split edges. These are called *odd vertices*.

⟨*Update vertex positions and create new edge vertices*⟩ ≡   194
⟨*Update vertex positions for even vertices* 195⟩
⟨*Compute new odd edge vertices* 198⟩

Different techniques are used to compute the updated positions for each of the different types of even vertices—regular and extraordinary, boundary and interior. This gives four cases to handle.

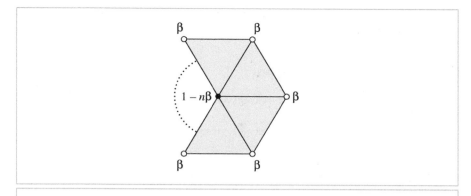

Figure 3.33: The new position v′ for a vertex v is computed by weighting the adjacent vertices v_i by a weight β and weighting v by $(1 - n\beta)$, where n is the valence of v. The adjacent vertices v_i are collectively referred to as the *one-ring* around v.

⟨*Update vertex positions for even vertices*⟩ ≡   **194**
```
for (SDVertex *vertex : v) {
    if (!vertex->boundary) {
        ⟨Apply one-ring rule for even vertex 196⟩
    } else {
        ⟨Apply boundary rule for even vertex 197⟩
    }
}
```

For both types of interior vertices, we take the set of vertices adjacent to each vertex (called the *one-ring* around it, reflecting the fact that it's a ring of neighbors) and weight each of the neighbor vertices by a weight β (Figure 3.33). The vertex we are updating, in the center, is weighted by $1 - n\beta$, where n is the valence of the vertex. Thus, the new position v′ for a vertex v is

$$v' = (1 - n\beta)v + \sum_{i=1}^{N} \beta v_i.$$

This formulation ensures that the sum of weights is one, which guarantees the convex hull property of Loop subdivision surfaces, which ensures that the final mesh is in the convex hull of the control mesh. The position of the vertex being updated is only affected by vertices that are nearby; this is known as *local support*. Loop subdivision is particularly efficient because its subdivision rules all have this property.

The specific weight β used for this step is a key component of the subdivision method and must be chosen carefully in order to ensure smoothness of the limit surface, among other desirable properties.[10] The beta() function that follows computes a β value based

---

10 Again, see the papers cited at the start of this section and in the "Further Reading" section for information about how values like β are derived.

on the vertex's valence that ensures smoothness. For regular interior vertices, beta()
returns 1/16. Since this is a common case, the implementation uses 1/16 directly instead
of calling beta() every time.

⟨*Apply one-ring rule for even vertex*⟩ ≡   195
```
if (vertex->regular)
    vertex->child->p = weightOneRing(vertex, 1.f / 16.f);
else
    vertex->child->p = weightOneRing(vertex, beta(vertex->valence()));
```

⟨*LoopSubdiv Inline Functions*⟩ +≡
```
inline Float beta(int valence) {
    if (valence == 3) return 3.f / 16.f;
    else return 3.f / (8.f * valence);
}
```

The weightOneRing() function loops over the one-ring of adjacent vertices and applies
the given weight to compute a new vertex position. It uses the SDVertex::oneRing()
method, defined in the following, which returns the positions of the vertices around the
vertex vert.

⟨*LoopSubdiv Function Definitions*⟩ +≡
```
static Point3f weightOneRing(SDVertex *vert, Float beta) {
    ⟨Put vert one-ring in pRing 196⟩
    Point3f p = (1 - valence * beta) * vert->p;
    for (int i = 0; i < valence; ++i)
        p += beta * pRing[i];
    return p;
}
```

Because a variable number of vertices are in the one-rings, we use the ALLOCA() macro to
efficiently allocate space to store their positions.

⟨*Put vert one-ring in pRing*⟩ ≡   196, 198
```
int valence = vert->valence();
Point3f *pRing = ALLOCA(Point3f, valence);
vert->oneRing(pRing);
```

The oneRing() method assumes that the pointer passed in points to an area of memory
large enough to hold the one-ring around the vertex.

⟨*LoopSubdiv Function Definitions*⟩ +≡
```
void SDVertex::oneRing(Point3f *p) {
    if (!boundary) {
        ⟨Get one-ring vertices for interior vertex 197⟩
    } else {
        ⟨Get one-ring vertices for boundary vertex 197⟩
    }
}
```

It's relatively easy to get the one-ring around an interior vertex by looping over the faces adjacent to the vertex and for each face retaining the vertex after the center vertex. (Brief sketching with pencil and paper should convince you that this process returns all of the vertices in the one-ring.)

⟨*Get one-ring vertices for interior vertex*⟩ ≡   196
```
SDFace *face = startFace;
do {
    *p++ = face->nextVert(this)->p;
    face = face->nextFace(this);
} while (face != startFace);
```

The one-ring around a boundary vertex is a bit trickier. The implementation here carefully stores the one-ring in the given Point3f array so that the first and last entries in the array are the two adjacent vertices along the boundary. This ordering is important because the adjacent boundary vertices will often be weighted differently from the adjacent vertices that are in the interior of the mesh. Doing so requires that we first loop around neighbor faces until we reach a face on the boundary and then loop around the other way, storing vertices one by one.

⟨*Get one-ring vertices for boundary vertex*⟩ ≡   196
```
SDFace *face = startFace, *f2;
while ((f2 = face->nextFace(this)) != nullptr)
    face = f2;
*p++ = face->nextVert(this)->p;
do {
    *p++ = face->prevVert(this)->p;
    face = face->prevFace(this);
} while (face != nullptr);
```

For vertices on the boundary, the new vertex's position is based only on the two neighboring boundary vertices (Figure 3.34). Not depending on interior vertices ensures that two abutting surfaces that share the same vertices on the boundary will have abutting limit surfaces. The weightBoundary() utility function applies the given weighting on the two neighbor vertices v_1 and v_2 to compute the new position v' as

$$v' = (1 - 2\beta)v + \beta v_1 + \beta v_2.$$

The same weight of 1/8 is used for both regular and extraordinary vertices.

⟨*Apply boundary rule for even vertex*⟩ ≡   195
```
vertex->child->p = weightBoundary(vertex, 1.f / 8.f);
```

The weightBoundary() utility function applies the given weights at a boundary vertex. Because the SDVertex::oneRing() function orders the boundary vertex's one-ring such that the first and last entries are the boundary neighbors, the implementation here is particularly straightforward.

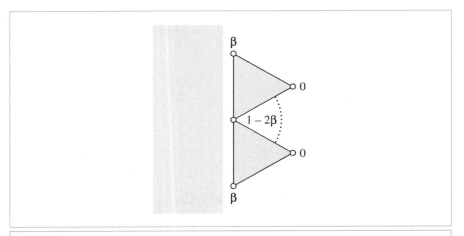

Figure 3.34: Subdivision on a Boundary Edge. The new position for the vertex in the center is computed by weighting it and its two neighbor vertices by the weights shown.

⟨*LoopSubdiv Function Definitions*⟩ +≡
```
static Point3f weightBoundary(SDVertex *vert, Float beta) {
    ⟨Put vert one-ring in pRing 196⟩
    Point3f p = (1 - 2 * beta) * vert->p;
    p += beta * pRing[0];
    p += beta * pRing[valence - 1];
    return p;
}
```

Now the refinement method computes the positions of the odd vertices—the new vertices along the split edges of the mesh. It loops over each edge of each face in the mesh, computing the new vertex that splits the edge (Figure 3.35). For interior edges, the new vertex is found by weighting the two vertices at the ends of the edge and the two vertices across from the edge on the adjacent faces. It loops through all three edges of each face, and each time it comes to an edge that hasn't been seen before it computes and stores the new odd vertex for the edge in the edgeVerts associative array.

⟨*Compute new odd edge vertices*⟩ ≡   194
```
std::map<SDEdge, SDVertex *> edgeVerts;
for (SDFace *face : f) {
    for (int k = 0; k < 3; ++k) {
        ⟨Compute odd vertex on kth edge 199⟩
    }
}
```

As was done when setting the face neighbor pointers in the original mesh, an SDEdge object is created for the edge and checked to see if it is in the set of edges that have already been visited. If it isn't, the new vertex on this edge is computed and added to the map, which is an associative array structure that performs efficient lookups.

Float 1062
Point3f 68
SDEdge 188
SDFace 186
SDVertex 185
SDVertex::p 185

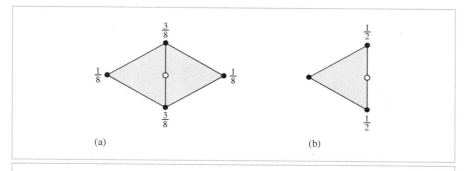

Figure 3.35: Subdivision Rule for Edge Split. The position of the new odd vertex, marked with an open circle, is found by weighting the two vertices at the ends of the edge and the two vertices opposite it on the adjacent triangles. (a) The weights for an interior vertex; (b) the weights for a boundary vertex.

⟨*Compute odd vertex on kth edge*⟩ ≡   198
```
    SDEdge edge(face->v[k], face->v[NEXT(k)]);
    SDVertex *vert = edgeVerts[edge];
    if (!vert) {
        ⟨Create and initialize new odd vertex 199⟩
        ⟨Apply edge rules to compute new vertex position 200⟩
        edgeVerts[edge] = vert;
    }
```

In Loop subdivision, the new vertices added by subdivision are always regular. (This means that the proportion of extraordinary vertices with respect to regular vertices will decrease with each level of subdivision.) Therefore, the `regular` member of the new vertex can immediately be set to `true`. The `boundary` member can also be easily initialized, by checking to see if there is a neighbor face across the edge that is being split. Finally, the new vertex's `startFace` pointer can also be set here. For all odd vertices on the edges of a face, the center child (child face number three) is guaranteed to be adjacent to the new vertex.

⟨*Create and initialize new odd vertex*⟩ ≡   199
```
    vert = arena.Alloc<SDVertex>();
    newVertices.push_back(vert);
    vert->regular = true;
    vert->boundary = (face->f[k] == nullptr);
    vert->startFace = face->children[3];
```

For odd boundary vertices, the new vertex is just the average of the two adjacent vertices. For odd interior vertices, the two vertices at the ends of the edge are given weight 3/8, and the two vertices opposite the edge are given weight 1/8 (Figure 3.35). These last two vertices can be found using the `SDFace::otherVert()` utility function, which returns the vertex opposite a given edge of a face.

⟨*Apply edge rules to compute new vertex position*⟩ ≡   199

```
if (vert->boundary) {
    vert->p =  0.5f * edge.v[0]->p;
    vert->p += 0.5f * edge.v[1]->p;
} else {
    vert->p =  3.f/8.f * edge.v[0]->p;
    vert->p += 3.f/8.f * edge.v[1]->p;
    vert->p += 1.f/8.f * face->otherVert(edge.v[0], edge.v[1])->p;
    vert->p += 1.f/8.f *
        face->f[k]->otherVert(edge.v[0], edge.v[1])->p;
}
```

The `SDFace::otherVert()` method is self-explanatory:

⟨*SDFace Methods*⟩ +≡   186

```
SDVertex *otherVert(SDVertex *v0, SDVertex *v1) {
    for (int i = 0; i < 3; ++i)
        if (v[i] != v0 && v[i] != v1)
            return v[i];
    Severe("Basic logic error in SDVertex::otherVert()");
    return nullptr;
}
```

Updating Mesh Topology

In order to keep the details of the topology update as straightforward as possible, the numbering scheme for the subdivided faces and their vertices has been chosen carefully (Figure 3.36). Review the figure carefully; the conventions shown are key to the next few pages.

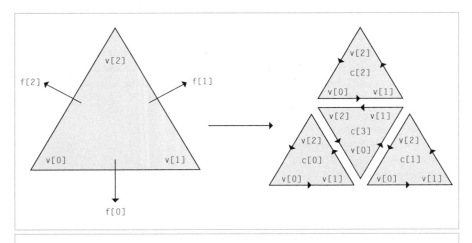

Figure 3.36: Each face is split into four child faces, such that the ith child is adjacent to the ith vertex of the original face, and such that the ith child face's ith vertex is the child of the ith vertex of the original face. The vertices of the center child are oriented such that the ith vertex is the odd vertex along the ith edge of the parent face.

There are four main tasks required to update the topological pointers of the refined mesh:

1. The odd vertices' SDVertex::startFace pointers need to store a pointer to one of their adjacent faces.
2. Similarly, the even vertices' SDVertex::startFace pointers must be set.
3. The new faces' f[i] pointers need to be set to point to the neighboring faces.
4. The new faces' v[i] pointers need to point to the appropriate vertices.

The startFace pointers of the odd vertices were already initialized when they were first created. We'll handle the other three tasks in order here.

⟨*Update new mesh topology*⟩ ≡   194
    ⟨*Update even vertex face pointers* **201**⟩
    ⟨*Update face neighbor pointers* **201**⟩
    ⟨*Update face vertex pointers* **202**⟩

If a vertex is the ith vertex of its startFace, then it is guaranteed that it will be adjacent to the ith child face of startFace. Therefore, it is just necessary to loop through all the parent vertices in the mesh, and for each one find its vertex index in its startFace. This index can then be used to find the child face adjacent to the new even vertex.

⟨*Update even vertex face pointers*⟩ ≡   201
```
for (SDVertex *vertex : v) {
    int vertNum = vertex->startFace->vnum(vertex);
    vertex->child->startFace =
        vertex->startFace->children[vertNum];
}
```

Next, the face neighbor pointers for the newly created faces are updated. We break this into two steps: one to update neighbors among children of the same parent, and one to do neighbors across children of different parents. This involves some tricky pointer manipulation.

⟨*Update face neighbor pointers*⟩ ≡   201
```
for (SDFace *face : f) {
    for (int j = 0; j < 3; ++j) {
        ⟨Update children f pointers for siblings 201⟩
        ⟨Update children f pointers for neighbor children 202⟩
    }
}
```

For the first step, recall that the interior child face is always stored in children[3]. Furthermore, the k + 1st child face (for k = 0, 1, 2) is across the kth edge of the interior face, and the interior face is across the k + 1st edge of the kth face.

⟨*Update children f pointers for siblings*⟩ ≡   201
```
face->children[3]->f[j] = face->children[NEXT(j)];
face->children[j]->f[NEXT(j)] = face->children[3];
```

We'll now update the children's face neighbor pointers that point to children of other parents. Only the first three children need to be addressed here; the interior child's neighbor pointers have already been fully initialized. Inspection of Figure 3.36 reveals that the kth and PREV(k)th edges of the ith child need to be set. To set the kth edge of the kth child, we first find the kth edge of the parent face, then the neighbor parent f2 across that edge. If f2 exists (meaning we aren't on a boundary), the neighbor parent index for the vertex v[k] is found. That index is equal to the index of the neighbor child we are searching for. This process is then repeated to find the child across the PREV(k)th edge.

⟨*Update children f pointers for neighbor children*⟩ ≡   **201**
```
SDFace *f2 = face->f[j];
face->children[j]->f[j] =
    f2 ? f2->children[f2->vnum(face->v[j])] : nullptr;
f2 = face->f[PREV(j)];
face->children[j]->f[PREV(j)] =
    f2 ? f2->children[f2->vnum(face->v[j])] : nullptr;
```

Finally, we handle the fourth step in the topological updates: setting the children faces' vertex pointers.

⟨*Update face vertex pointers*⟩ ≡   **201**
```
for (SDFace *face : f) {
    for (int j = 0; j < 3; ++j) {
        ⟨Update child vertex pointer to new even vertex 202⟩
        ⟨Update child vertex pointer to new odd vertex 202⟩
    }
}
```

For the kth child face (for k = 0, 1, 2), the kth vertex corresponds to the even vertex that is adjacent to the child face. For the noninterior child faces, there is one even vertex and two odd vertices; for the interior child face, there are three odd vertices. This vertex can be found by following the child pointer of the parent vertex, available from the parent face.

⟨*Update child vertex pointer to new even vertex*⟩ ≡   **202**
```
face->children[j]->v[j] = face->v[j]->child;
```

To update the rest of the vertex pointers, the edgeVerts associative array is reused to find the odd vertex for each split edge of the parent face. Three child faces have that vertex as an incident vertex. The vertex indices for the three faces are easily found, again based on the numbering scheme established in Figure 3.36.

⟨*Update child vertex pointer to new odd vertex*⟩ ≡   **202**
```
SDVertex *vert = edgeVerts[SDEdge(face->v[j], face->v[NEXT(j)])];
face->children[j]->v[NEXT(j)] = vert;
face->children[NEXT(j)]->v[j] = vert;
face->children[3]->v[j] = vert;
```

After the geometric and topological work has been done for a subdivision step, the newly created vertices and faces are moved into the v and f arrays:

⟨*Prepare for next level of subdivision*⟩ ≡   194
```
f = newFaces;
v = newVertices;
```

To the Limit Surface and Output

One of the remarkable properties of subdivision surfaces is that there are special subdivision rules that give the positions that the vertices of the mesh would have if we continued subdividing forever. We apply these rules here to initialize an array of limit surface positions, pLimit. Note that it's important to temporarily store the limit surface positions somewhere other than in the vertices while the computation is taking place. Because the limit surface position of each vertex depends on the original positions of its surrounding vertices, the original positions of all vertices must remain unchanged until the computation is complete.

The limit rule for a boundary vertex weights the two neighbor vertices by 1/5 and the center vertex by 3/5. The rule for interior vertices is based on a function loopGamma(), which computes appropriate vertex weights based on the valence of the vertex.

⟨*Push vertices to limit surface*⟩ ≡   193
```
std::unique_ptr<Point3f[]> pLimit(new Point3f[v.size()]);
for (size_t i = 0; i < v.size(); ++i) {
    if (v[i]->boundary)
        pLimit[i] = weightBoundary(v[i], 1.f / 5.f);
    else
        pLimit[i] = weightOneRing(v[i], loopGamma(v[i]->valence()));
}
for (size_t i = 0; i < v.size(); ++i)
    v[i]->p = pLimit[i];
```

⟨*LoopSubdiv Inline Functions*⟩ +≡
```
inline Float loopGamma(int valence) {
    return 1.f / (valence + 3.f / (8.f * beta(valence)));
}
```

In order to generate a smooth-looking triangle mesh with per-vertex surface normals, a pair of nonparallel tangent vectors to the limit surface is computed at each vertex. As with the limit rule for positions, this is an analytic computation that gives the precise tangents on the actual limit surface.

⟨*Compute vertex tangents on limit surface*⟩ ≡   193
```
std::vector<Normal3f> Ns;
Ns.reserve(v.size());
std::vector<Point3f> pRing(16, Point3f());
```

```
for (SDVertex *vertex : v) {
    Vector3f S(0,0,0), T(0,0,0);
    int valence = vertex->valence();
    if (valence > (int)pRing.size())
        pRing.resize(valence);
    vertex->oneRing(&pRing[0]);
    if (!vertex->boundary) {
        ⟨Compute tangents of interior face  204⟩
    } else {
        ⟨Compute tangents of boundary face  206⟩
    }
    Ns.push_back(Normal3f(Cross(S, T)));
}
```

Figure 3.37 shows the setting for computing tangents in the mesh interior. The center vertex is given a weight of zero, and the neighbors are given weights w_i. To compute the first tangent vector **s**, the weights are

$$w_i = \cos\left(\frac{2\pi i}{n}\right),$$

where n is the valence of the vertex. The second tangent **t** is computed with weights

$$w_i = \sin\left(\frac{2\pi i}{n}\right).$$

⟨*Compute tangents of interior face*⟩ ≡   203
```
for (int j = 0; j < valence; ++j) {
    S += std::cos(2 * Pi * j / valence) * Vector3f(pRing[j]);
    T += std::sin(2 * Pi * j / valence) * Vector3f(pRing[j]);
}
```

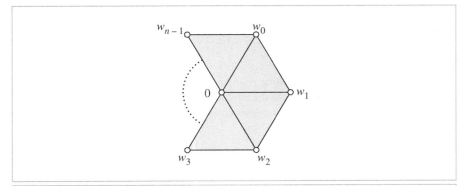

Pi 1063

Vector3f 60

Figure 3.37: To compute tangents for interior vertices, the one-ring vertices are weighted with weights w_i. The center vertex, where the tangent is being computed, always has a weight of 0.

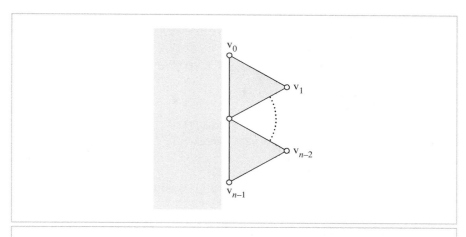

Figure 3.38: Tangents at boundary vertices are also computed as weighted averages of the adjacent vertices. However, some of the boundary tangent rules incorporate the value of the center vertex.

Tangents on boundary vertices are a bit trickier. Figure 3.38 shows the ordering of vertices in the one-ring expected in the following discussion.

The first tangent, known as the *across tangent*, is given by the vector between the two neighboring boundary vertices:

$$\mathbf{s} = \mathbf{v}_{n-1} - \mathbf{v}_0.$$

The second tangent, known as the *transverse tangent*, is computed based on the vertex's valence. The center vertex is given a weight w_c and the one-ring vertices are given weights specified by a vector $(w_0, w_1, \ldots, w_{n-1})$. The transverse tangent rules we will use are

Valence	w_c	w_i
2	-2	$(1, 1)$
3	-1	$(0, 1, 0)$
4 (regular)	-2	$(-1, 2, 2, -1)$

For valences of 5 and higher, $w_c = 0$ and

$$w_0 = w_{n-1} = \sin \theta$$
$$w_i = (2 \cos \theta - 2) \ \sin(\theta i),$$

where

$$\theta = \frac{\pi}{n - 1}.$$

Although we will not prove it here, these weights sum to zero for all values of i. This guarantees that the weighted sum is in fact a tangent vector.

⟨*Compute tangents of boundary face*⟩ ≡   203

```
    S = pRing[valence - 1] - pRing[0];
    if (valence == 2)
        T = Vector3f(pRing[0] + pRing[1] - 2 * vertex->p);
    else if (valence == 3)
        T = pRing[1] - vertex->p;
    else if (valence == 4) // regular
        T = Vector3f(-1 * pRing[0] +  2 * pRing[1] + 2 * pRing[2] +
                     -1 * pRing[3] + -2 * vertex->p);
    else {
        Float theta = Pi / float(valence - 1);
        T = Vector3f(std::sin(theta) * (pRing[0] + pRing[valence - 1]));
        for (int k = 1; k < valence - 1; ++k) {
            Float wt = (2 * std::cos(theta) - 2) * std::sin((k) * theta);
            T += Vector3f(wt * pRing[k]);
        }
        T = -T;
    }
```

Finally, the fragment ⟨*Create triangle mesh from subdivision mesh*⟩ initializes a vector of Triangles corresponding to the triangulation of the limit surface. We won't include it here, since it's just a straightforward transformation of the subdivided mesh into an indexed triangle mesh.

*3.9 MANAGING ROUNDING ERROR

Thus far, we've been discussing ray–shape intersection algorithms purely with respect to idealized arithmetic operations based on the real numbers. This approach has gotten us far, although the fact that computers can only represent finite quantities and therefore can't actually represent all of the real numbers is important. In place of real numbers, computers use floating-point numbers, which have fixed storage requirements. However, error may be introduced each time a floating-point operation is performed, since the result may not be representable in the designated amount of memory.

The accumulation of this error has a few implications for the accuracy of intersection tests. First, it's possible that it will cause valid intersections to be missed completely—for example, if a computed intersection's t value is negative even though the precise value is positive. Furthermore, computed ray–shape intersection points may be above or below the actual surface of the shape. This leads to a problem: when new rays are traced starting from computed intersection points for shadow rays and reflection rays, if the ray origin is below the actual surface, we may find an incorrect re-intersection with the surface. Conversely, if the origin is too far above the surface, shadows and reflections may appear detached. (See Figure 3.39.)

Typical practice to address this issue in ray tracing is to offset spawned rays by a fixed "ray epsilon" value, ignoring any intersections along the ray $p + t d$ closer than some t_{min} value. Figure 3.40 shows why this approach requires fairly high t_{min} values to work

Float 1062
Pi 1063
Vector3f 60

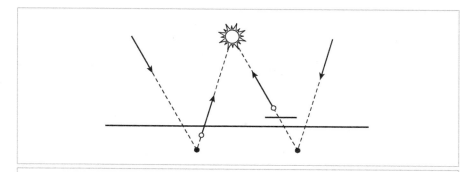

Figure 3.39: Geometric Settings for Rounding-Error Issues That Can Cause Visible Errors in Images. The incident ray on the left intersects the surface. On the left, the computed intersection point (black circle) is slightly below the surface and a too-low "epsilon" offsetting the origin of the shadow ray leads to an incorrect self-intersection, as the shadow ray origin (white circle) is still below the surface; thus the light is incorrectly determined to be occluded. On the right a too-high "epsilon" causes a valid intersection to be missed as the ray's origin is past the occluding surface.

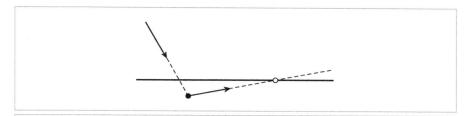

Figure 3.40: If the computed intersection point (filled circle) is below the surface and the spawned ray is oblique, incorrect re-intersections may occur some distance from the ray origin (open circle). If a minimum t value along the ray is used to discard nearby intersections, a relatively large t_{min} is needed to handle oblique rays well.

effectively: if the spawned ray is fairly oblique to the surface, incorrect ray intersections may occur quite some distance from the ray origin. Unfortunately, large t_{min} values cause ray origins to be relatively far from the original intersection points, which in turn can cause valid nearby intersections to be missed, leading to loss of fine detail in shadows and reflections.

In this section, we'll introduce the ideas underlying floating-point arithmetic and describe techniques for analyzing the error in floating-point computations. We'll then apply these methods to the ray–shape algorithms introduced earlier in this chapter and show how to compute ray intersection points with bounded error. This will allow us to conservatively position ray origins so that incorrect self-intersections are never found, while keeping ray origins extremely close to the actual intersection point so that incorrect misses are minimized. In turn, no additional "ray epsilon" values are needed.

3.9.1 FLOATING-POINT ARITHMETIC

Computation must be performed on a finite representation of numbers that fits in a finite amount of memory; the infinite set of real numbers just can't be represented on a computer. One such finite representation is fixed point, where given a 16-bit integer, for example, one might map it to positive real numbers by dividing by 256. This would allow us to represent the range $[0, 65535/256] = [0, 255 + 255/256]$ with equal spacing of $1/256$ between values. Fixed-point numbers can be implemented efficiently using integer arithmetic operations (a property that made them popular on early PCs that didn't support floating-point computation), but they suffer from a number of shortcomings; among them, the maximum number they can represent is limited, and they aren't able to accurately represent very small numbers near zero.

An alternative representation for real numbers on computers is floating-point numbers. These are based on representing numbers with a sign, a significand,[11] and an exponent: essentially, the same representation as scientific notation but with a fixed number of digits devoted to significand and exponent. (In the following, we will assume base-2 digits exclusively.) This representation makes it possible to represent and perform computations on numbers with a wide range of magnitudes while using a fixed amount of storage.

Programmers using floating-point arithmetic are generally aware that floating point is imprecise; this understanding sometimes leads to a belief that floating-point arithmetic is unpredictable. In this section we'll see that floating-point arithmetic has a carefully designed foundation that in turn makes it possible to compute conservative bounds on the error introduced in a particular computation. For ray-tracing calculations, this error is often surprisingly small.

Modern CPUs and GPUs nearly ubiquitously implement a model of floating-point arithmetic based on a standard promulgated by the Institute of Electrical and Electronics Engineers (1985, 2008). (Henceforth when we refer to floats, we will specifically be referring to 32-bit floating-point numbers as specified by IEEE 754.) The IEEE 754 technical standard specifies the format of floating-point numbers in memory as well as specific rules for precision and rounding of floating-point computations; it is these rules that make it possible to reason rigorously about the error present in a given floating-point value.

Floating-Point Representation

The IEEE standard specifies that 32-bit floats are represented with a sign bit, 8 bits for the exponent, and 23 bits for the significand. With 8 bits, the exponent e_b ranges from 0 to 255; the actual exponent used, e_b, is computed by biasing e:

$$e_b = e - 127.$$

The significand actually has 24 bits of precision when a *normalized* floating-point value is stored. When a number expressed with significand and exponent is normalized, there

---

11 The word *mantissa* is often used in place of *significand*, though floating-point purists note that *mantissa* has a different meaning in the context of logarithms and thus prefer *significand*. We follow this usage here.

are no leading zeros in the significand. In binary, this means that the leading digit of the significand must be one; in turn, there's no need to store this value explicitly. Thus, the implicit leading one digit with the 23 digits encoding the fractional part of the significand gives a total of 24 bits of precision.

Given a sign $s = \pm1$, significand m, and exponent e, the corresponding floating-point value is

$$s \times 1.m \times 2^{e-127}.$$

For example, with a normalized significand, the floating-point number 6.5 is written as $1.101_2 \times 2^2$, where the 2 subscript denotes a base-2 value. (If binary decimals aren't immediately intuitive, note that the first number to the right of the decimal contributes $2^{-1} = 1/2$, and so forth.) Thus, we have

$$(1 \times 2^0 + 1 \times 2^{-1} + 0 \times 2^{-2} + 1 \times 2^{-3}) \times 2^2 = 1.625 \times 2^2 = 6.5.$$

$e_b = 2$, so $e = 129 = 1000001_2$ and $m = 10100000000000000000000_2$.

Floats are laid out in memory with the sign bit at the most significant bit of the 32-bit value (with negative signs encoded with a one bit), then the exponent, and the significand. Thus, for the value 6.5 the binary in-memory representation of the value is

$$0\ 10000001\ 10100000000000000000000 = 40d00000_{16}.$$

Similarly the floating-point value 1.0 has $m = 0 \ldots 0_2$ and $e_b = 0$, so $e = 127 = 01111111_2$ and its binary representation is:

$$0\ 01111111\ 00000000000000000000000 = 3f800000_{16}.$$

This hexadecimal number is a value worth remembering, as it often comes up in memory dumps when debugging.

An implication of this representation is that the spacing between representable floats between two adjacent powers of two is uniform throughout the range. (It corresponds to increments of the significand bits by one.) In a range $[2^e, 2^{e+1})$, the spacing is

$$2^{e-23}. \tag{3.6}$$

Thus, for floating-point numbers between 1 and 2, $e = 0$, and the spacing between floating-point values is $2^{-23} \approx 1.19209\ldots \times 10^{-7}$. This spacing is also referred to as the magnitude of a *unit in last place* ("ulp"); note that the magnitude of an ulp is determined by the floating-point value that it is with respect to—ulps are relatively larger at numbers with bigger magnitudes than they are at numbers with smaller magnitudes.

As we've described the representation so far, it's impossible to exactly represent zero as a floating-point number. This is obviously an unacceptable state of affairs, so the minimum exponent $e = 0$, or $e_b = -127$, is set aside for special treatment. With this exponent, the floating-point value is interpreted as not having the implicit leading one bit in the significand, which means that a significand of all zero bits results in

$$s \times 0.0 \cdots 0_2 \times 2^{-127} = 0.$$

Eliminating the leading one significand bit also makes it possible to represent *denormalized* numbers: if the leading one was always present, then the smallest 32-bit float would be

$$1.0 \cdots 0_2 \times 2^{-127} \approx 5.8774718 \times 10^{-39}.$$

Without the leading one bit, the minimum value is

$$0.00 \cdots 1_2 \times 2^{-126} = 2^{-126} \times 2^{-23} \approx 1.4012985 \times 10^{-45}.$$

Providing some capability to represent these small values can make it possible to avoid needing to round very small values to zero.

Note that there is both a "positive" and "negative" zero value with this representation. This detail is mostly transparent to the programmer. For example, the standard guarantees that the comparison -0.0 == 0.0 evaluates to true, even though the in-memory representations of these two values are different.

The maximum exponent, $e = 255$, is also reserved for special treatment. Therefore, the largest regular floating-point value that can be represented has $e = 254$ (or $e_b = 127$) and is approximately

$$3.402823 \ldots \times 10^{38}.$$

With $e_b = 255$, if the significand bits are all zero, the value corresponds to positive or negative infinity, according to the sign bit. Infinite values result when performing computations like 1/0 in floating point, for example. Arithmetic operations with infinity result in infinity. For comparisons, positive infinity is larger than any non-infinite value and similarly for negative infinity.

The MaxFloat and Infinity constants are initialized to be the largest representable and "infinity" floating-point values, respectively. We make them available in separate constants so that code that uses these values doesn't need to use the wordy C++ standard library calls to get their values.

⟨*Global Constants*⟩ ≡
```
    static constexpr Float MaxFloat = std::numeric_limits<Float>::max();
    static constexpr Float Infinity = std::numeric_limits<Float>::infinity();
```

With $e_b = 255$, non-zero significand bits correspond to special NaN values, which result from operations like taking the square root of a negative number or trying to compute 0/0. NaNs propagate through computations: any arithmetic operation where one of the operands is a NaN itself always returns NaN. Thus, if a NaN emerges from a long chain of computations, we know that something went awry somewhere along the way. In debug builds, pbrt has many Assert() statements that check for NaN values, as we almost never expect them to come up in the regular course of events. Any comparison with a NaN value returns false; thus, checking for !(x == x) serves to check if a value is not a

Assert() 1069
Float 1062

number.[12] For clarity, we use the C++ standard library function std::isnan() to check for not-a-number values.

Utility Routines

For certain low-level operations, it can be useful to be able to interpret a floating-point value in terms of its constituent bits and to convert the bits representing a floating-point value to an actual float or double.

One natural approach to this would be to take a pointer to a value to be converted and cast it to a pointer to the other type:

```
float f = ...;
uint32_t bits = *((uint32_t *)&f);
```

However, modern versions of C++ specify that it's illegal to cast a pointer of one type, float, to a different type, uint32_t. (This restriction allows the compiler to optimize more aggressively in its analysis of whether two pointers may point to the same memory location, which can inhibit storing values in registers.)

Another common approach is to use a union with elements of both types, assigning to one type and reading from the other:

```
union FloatBits {
    float f;
    uint32_t ui;
};
FloatBits fb;
fb.f = ...;
uint32_t bits = fb.ui;
```

This, too, is illegal: the C++ standard says that reading an element of a union different from the one last one assigned to is undefined behavior.

These conversions can be properly made using memcpy() to copy from a pointer to the source type to a pointer to the destination type:

⟨*Global Inline Functions*⟩ ≡
```
inline uint32_t FloatToBits(float f) {
    uint32_t ui;
    memcpy(&ui, &f, sizeof(float));
    return ui;
}
```

---

12 This is one of a few places where compilers must not perform seemingly obvious and safe algebraic simplifications with expressions that include floating-point values—this particular comparison must not be simplified to false. Enabling compiler "fast math" or "perform unsafe math optimizations" flags may allow these optimizations to be performed. In turn, buggy behavior may be introduced in pbrt.

⟨*Global Inline Functions*⟩ +≡
```
inline float BitsToFloat(uint32_t ui) {
    float f;
    memcpy(&f, &ui, sizeof(uint32_t));
    return f;
}
```

While a call to the memcpy() function may seem gratuitously expensive to avoid these issues, in practice good compilers turn this into a no-op and just reinterpret the contents of the register or memory as the other type. (Versions of these functions that convert between double and uint64_t are also available in pbrt but are similar and are therefore not included here.)

These conversions can be used to implement functions that bump a floating-point value up or down to the next greater or next smaller representable floating-point value.[13] They are useful for some conservative rounding operations that we'll need in code to follow. Thanks to the specifics of the in-memory representation of floats, these operations are quite efficient.

⟨*Global Inline Functions*⟩ +≡
```
inline float NextFloatUp(float v) {
    ⟨Handle infinity and negative zero for NextFloatUp() 212⟩
    ⟨Advance v to next higher float 213⟩
}
```

There are two important special cases: if v is positive infinity, then this function just returns v unchanged. Negative zero is skipped forward to positive zero before continuing on to the code that advances the significand. This step must be handled explicitly, since the bit patterns for −0.0 and 0.0 aren't adjacent.

⟨*Handle infinity and negative zero for* NextFloatUp()⟩ ≡   212
```
if (std::isinf(v) && v > 0.)
    return v;
if (v == -0.f)
    v = 0.f;
```

Conceptually, given a floating-point value, we would like to increase the significand by one, where if the result overflows, the significand is reset to zero and the exponent is increased by one. Fortuitously, adding one to the in-memory integer representation of a float achieves this: because the exponent lies at the high bits above the significand, adding one to the low bit of the significand will cause a one to be carried all the way up into the exponent if the significand is all ones and otherwise will advance to the next higher significand for the current exponent. Note also that when the highest representable finite floating-point value's bit representation is incremented, the bit pattern for positive floating-point infinity is the result.

---

13 These functions are equivalent to std::nextafter(v, Infinity) and std::nextafter(v, -Infinity), but are more efficient since they don't try to handle NaN values or deal with signaling floating-point exceptions.

For negative values, subtracting one from the bit representation similarly advances to the next value.

⟨*Advance* v *to next higher float*⟩ ≡   212
```
    uint32_t ui = FloatToBits(v);
    if (v >= 0) ++ui;
    else        --ui;
    return BitsToFloat(ui);
```

The NextFloatDown() function, not included here, follows the same logic but effectively in reverse. pbrt also provides versions of these functions for doubles.

Arithmetic Operations

IEEE 754 provides important guarantees about the properties of floating-point arithmetic: specifically, it guarantees that addition, subtraction, multiplication, division, and square root give the same results given the same inputs and that these results are the floating-point number that is closest to the result of the underlying computation if it had been performed in infinite-precision arithmetic.[14] It is remarkable that this is possible on finite-precision digital computers at all; one of the achievements in IEEE 754 was the demonstration that this level of accuracy is possible and can be implemented fairly efficiently in hardware.

Using circled operators to denote floating-point arithmetic operations and sqrt for floating-point square root, these precision guarantees can be written as:

$$
\begin{aligned}
a \oplus b &= \text{round}(a + b) \\
a \ominus b &= \text{round}(a - b) \\
a \otimes b &= \text{round}(a * b) \\
a \oslash b &= \text{round}(a/b) \\
\text{sqrt}(a) &= \text{round}(\sqrt{a})
\end{aligned}
$$ [3.7]

where round(x) indicates the result of rounding a real number to the closest floating-point value.

This bound on the rounding error can also be represented with an interval of real numbers: for example, for addition, we can say that the rounded result is within an interval

$$
\begin{aligned}
a \oplus b &= \text{round}(a + b) \subset (a + b)(1 \pm \epsilon) \\
&= [(a + b)(1 - \epsilon), (a + b)(1 + \epsilon)]
\end{aligned}
$$ [3.8]

for some ϵ. The amount of error introduced from this rounding can be no more than half the floating-point spacing at $a + b$—if it was more than half the floating-point spacing, then it would be possible to round to a different floating-point number with less error (Figure 3.41).

For 32-bit floats, we can bound the floating-point spacing at $a + b$ from above using Equation (3.6) (i.e., an ulp at that value) by $(a + b)2^{-23}$, so half the spacing is bounded

BitsToFloat() 212
FloatToBits() 211

---

14   IEEE float allows the user to select one of a number of rounding modes, but we will assume the default—round to nearest even—here.

Figure 3.41: The IEEE standard specifies that floating-point calculations must be implemented as if the calculation was performed with infinite-precision real numbers and then rounded to the nearest representable float. Here, an infinite precision result in the real numbers is denoted by a filled dot, with the representable floats around it denoted by ticks in a number line. We can see that the error introduced by rounding to the nearest float, δ, can be no more than half the spacing between floats.

from above by $(a + b)2^{-24}$ and so $|\epsilon| \leq 2^{-24}$. This bound is the *machine epsilon*.[15] For 32-bit floats, $\epsilon_m = 2^{-24} \approx 5.960464 \ldots \times 10^{-8}$.

⟨*Global Constants*⟩ +≡
```
static constexpr Float MachineEpsilon =
        std::numeric_limits<Float>::epsilon() * 0.5;
```

Thus, we have

$$a \oplus b = \text{round}(a + b) \subset (a + b)(1 \pm \epsilon_m)$$
$$= [(a + b)(1 - \epsilon_m), (a + b)(1 + \epsilon_m)].$$

Analogous relations hold for the other arithmetic operators and the square root operator.[16]

A number of useful properties follow directly from Equation (3.7). For a floating-point number x,

- $1 \otimes x = x$.
- $x \oslash x = 1$.
- $x \oplus 0 = x$.
- $x \ominus x = 0$.
- $2 \otimes x$ and $x \oslash 2$ are exact; no rounding is performed to compute the final result. More generally, any multiplication by or division by a power of two gives an exact result (assuming there's no overflow or underflow).
- $x \oslash 2^i = x \otimes 2^{-i}$ for all integer i, assuming 2^i doesn't overflow.

All of these properties follow from the principle that the result must be the nearest floating-point value to the actual result; when the result can be represented exactly, the exact result must be computed.

Error Propagation

Using the guarantees of IEEE floating-point arithmetic, it is possible to develop methods to analyze and bound the error in a given floating-point computation. For more details

---

15   The C and C++ standards unfortunately define the machine epsilon in their own special way, which is that it is the magnitude of one ulp above the number 1. For a 32-bit float, this value is 2^{-23}, which is twice as large as the machine epsilon as the term   Float 1062
     is used in numerical analysis.
16   This bound assumes that there's no overflow or underflow in the computation; these possibilities can be easily handled (Higham 2002, p. 56) but aren't generally important for our application here.

on this topic, see the excellent book by Higham (2002), as well as Wilkinson's earlier classic (1963).

Two measurements of error are useful in this effort: absolute and relative. If we perform some floating-point computation and get a rounded result $\tilde{a}$, we say that the magnitude of the difference between $\tilde{a}$ and the result of doing that computation in the real numbers is the *absolute error*, δ_a:

$$\delta_a = |\tilde{a} - a|.$$

Relative error, δ_r, is the ratio of the absolute error to the precise result:

$$\delta_r = \left| \frac{\tilde{a} - a}{a} \right| = \left| \frac{\delta_a}{a} \right|, \tag{3.9}$$

as long as $a \neq 0$. Using the definition of relative error, we can thus write the computed value $\tilde{a}$ as a perturbation of the exact result a:

$$\tilde{a} = a \pm \delta_a = a(1 \pm \delta_r).$$

As a first application of these ideas, consider computing the sum of four numbers, a, b, c, and d, represented as floats. If we compute this sum as r = (((a + b) + c) + d), Equation (3.8) gives us

$$(((a \oplus b) \oplus c) \oplus d) \subset ((((a + b)(1 \pm \epsilon_m)) + c)(1 \pm \epsilon_m) + d)(1 \pm \epsilon_m)$$
$$= (a + b)(1 \pm \epsilon_m)^3 + c(1 \pm \epsilon_m)^2 + d(1 \pm \epsilon_m).$$

Because ϵ_m is small, higher order powers of ϵ_m can be bounded by an additional ϵ_m term, and so we can bound the $(1 \pm \epsilon_m)^n$ terms with

$$(1 \pm \epsilon_m)^n \leq (1 \pm (n + 1)\epsilon_m).$$

(As a practical matter, $(1 \pm n\epsilon_m)$ almost bounds these terms, since higher powers of ϵ_m get very small very quickly, but the above is a fully conservative bound.)

This bound lets us simplify the result of the addition to:

$$(a + b)(1 \pm 4\epsilon_m) + c(1 \pm 3\epsilon_m) + d(1 \pm 2\epsilon_m) =$$
$$a + b + c + d + [\pm 4\epsilon_m(a + b) \pm 3\epsilon_m c \pm 2\epsilon_m d].$$

The term in square brackets gives the absolute error: its magnitude is bounded by

$$4\epsilon_m|a + b| + 3\epsilon_m|c| + 2\epsilon_m|d|. \tag{3.10}$$

Thus, if we add four floating-point numbers together with the above parenthesization, we can be certain that the difference between the final rounded result and the result we would get if we added them with infinite-precision real numbers is bounded by Equation (3.10); this error bound is easily computed given specific values of a, b, c, and d.

This is a fairly interesting result; we see that the magnitude of $a + b$ makes a relatively large contribution to the error bound, especially compared to d. (This result gives a sense for why, if adding a large number of floating-point numbers together, sorting them from small to large magnitudes generally gives a result with a lower final error than an arbitrary ordering.)

Our analysis here has implicitly assumed that the compiler would generate instructions according to the expression used to define the sum. Compilers are required to follow the form of the given floating-point expressions in order to not break carefully crafted computations that may have been designed to minimize round-off error. Here again is a case where certain transformations that would be valid on expressions with integers can not be safely applied when floats are involved.

What happens if we change the expression to the algebraically equivalent float r = (a + b) + (c + d)? This corresponds to the floating-point computation

$$((a \oplus b) \oplus (c \oplus d)).$$

If we apply the same process of applying Equation (3.8), expanding out terms, converting higher-order $(1 \pm \epsilon_m)^n$ terms to $(1 \pm (n + 1)\epsilon_m)$, we get absolute error bounds of

$$3\epsilon_m|a + b| + 3\epsilon_m|c + d|,$$

which are lower than the first formulation if $|a + b|$ is relatively large, but possibly higher if $|d|$ is relatively large.

This approach to computing error is known as *forward error analysis*; given inputs to a computation, we can apply a fairly mechanical process that provides conservative bounds on the error in the result. The derived bounds in the result may overstate the actual error—in practice, the signs of the error terms are often mixed, so that there is cancellation when they are added.[17] An alternative approach is *backward error analysis*, which treats the computed result as exact and provides bounds on perturbations on the inputs that give the same result. This approach can be more useful when analyzing the stability of a numerical algorithm but is less applicable to deriving conservative error bounds on the geometric computations we're interested in here.

The conservative bounding of $(1 \pm \epsilon_m)^n$ by $(1 \pm (n + 1)\epsilon_m)$ is somewhat unsatisfying since it adds a whole ϵ_m term purely to conservatively bound the sum of various higher powers of ϵ_m. Higham (2002, Section 3.1) gives an approach to more tightly bound products of $(1 \pm \epsilon_m)$ error terms. If we have $(1 \pm \epsilon_m)^n$, it can be shown that this value is bounded by $1 + \theta_n$, where

$$|\theta_n| \le \frac{n\,\epsilon_m}{1 - n\,\epsilon_m}, \qquad\qquad [3.11]$$

as long as $n\,\epsilon_m < 1$ (which will certainly be the case for the calculations we're considering). Note that the denominator of this expression will be just less than one for reasonable n values, so it just barely increases $n\epsilon_m$ to achieve a conservative bound.

We will denote this bound by γ_n:

$$\gamma_n = \frac{n\,\epsilon_m}{1 - n\,\epsilon_m}.$$

---

17 Some numerical analysts use a rule of thumb that the number of ulps of error in practice is often close to the square root of the bound's number of ulps, thanks to the cancellation of error in intermediate results.

The function that computes its value is declared as constexpr so that any invocations with compile-time constants will generally be replaced with the corresponding floating-point return value.

⟨*Global Inline Functions*⟩ +≡
```
inline constexpr Float gamma(int n) {
    return (n * MachineEpsilon) / (1 - n * MachineEpsilon);
}
```

Using the γ notation, our bound on the error of the sum of the four values is

$$|a + b|\gamma_3 + |c|\gamma_2 + |d|\gamma_1.$$

An advantage of this approach is that quotients of $(1 \pm \epsilon_m)^n$ terms can also be bounded with the γ function. Given

$$\frac{(1 \pm \epsilon_m)^m}{(1 \pm \epsilon_m)^n},$$

the interval is bounded by $(1 \pm \gamma_{m+n})$. Thus, γ can be used to collect ϵ_m terms from both sides of an equality over to one side by dividing them through; this will be useful in some of the following derivations. (Note that because $(1 \pm \epsilon_m)$ terms represent intervals, canceling them would be incorrect:

$$\frac{(1 \pm \epsilon_m)^m}{(1 \pm \epsilon_m)^n} \neq (1 \pm \epsilon_m)^{m-n};$$

the γ_{m+n} bounds must be used instead.)

Given inputs to some computation that themselves carry some amount of error, it's instructive to see how this error is carried through various elementary arithmetic operations. Given two values, $a(1 \pm \gamma_i)$ and $b(1 \pm \gamma_j)$ that each carry accumulated error from earlier operations, consider their product. Using the definition of $\otimes$, the result is in the interval:

$$a(1 \pm \gamma_i) \otimes b(1 \pm \gamma_j) \subset ab(1 \pm \gamma_{i+j+1}),$$

where we've used the relationship $(1 \pm \gamma_i)(1 \pm \gamma_j) \subset (1 \pm \gamma_{i+j})$, which follows directly from Equation (3.11).

The relative error in this result is bounded by:

$$\left| \frac{ab\,\gamma_{i+j+1}}{ab} \right| = \gamma_{i+j+1},$$

and so the final error is thus just roughly $(i + j + 1)/2$ ulps at the value of the product—about as good as we might hope for given the error going into the multiplication. (The situation for division is similarly good.)

Unfortunately, with addition and subtraction, it's possible for the relative error to increase substantially. Using the same definitions of the values being operated on, consider

$$a(1 \pm \gamma_i) \oplus b(1 \pm \gamma_j),$$

which is in the interval $a(1 \pm \gamma_{i+1}) + b(1 \pm \gamma_{j+1})$, and so the absolute error is bounded by $|a|\gamma_{i+1} + |b|\gamma_{j+1}$.

Float 1062
MachineEpsilon 214

If the signs of a and b are the same, then the absolute error is bounded by $|a + b|\gamma_{i+j+1}$ and the relative error is around $(i + j + 1)/2$ ulps around the computed value.

However, if the signs of a and b differ (or, equivalently, they are the same but subtraction is performed), then the relative error can be quite high. Consider the case where $a \approx -b$: the relative error is

$$\frac{|a|\gamma_{i+1} + |b|\gamma_{j+1}}{a + b} \approx \frac{2|a|\gamma_{i+j+1}}{a + b}.$$

The numerator's magnitude is proportional to the original value $|a|$ yet is divided by a very small number, and thus the relative error is quite high. This substantial increase in relative error is called *catastrophic cancellation*. Equivalently, we can have a sense of the issue from the fact that the absolute error is in terms of the magnitude of $|a|$, though it's now in relation to a value much smaller than a.

Running Error Analysis

In addition to working out error bounds algebraically, we can also have the computer do this work for us as some computation is being performed. This approach is known as *running error analysis*. The idea behind it is simple: each time a floating-point operation is performed, we also compute terms that compute intervals based on Equation (3.7) to compute a running bound on the error that has been accumulated so far. While this approach can have higher run-time overhead than deriving expressions that give an error bound directly, it can be convenient when derivations become unwieldy.

pbrt provides a simple EFloat class, which mostly acts like a regular float but uses operator overloading to provide all of the regular arithmetic operations on floats while computing these error bounds.

Similar to the Interval class from Chapter 2, EFloat keeps track of an interval that describes the uncertainty of a value of interest. In contrast to Interval, EFloat's intervals arise due to errors in intermediate floating-point arithmetic rather than uncertainty of the input parameters.

⟨*EFloat Public Methods*⟩ ≡
```
    EFloat() { }
    EFloat(float v, float err = 0.f) : v(v), err(err) {
        ⟨Store high-precision reference value in EFloat 219⟩
    }
```

EFloat maintains a computed value v and the absolute error bound, err.

⟨*EFloat Private Data*⟩ ≡
```
    float v;
    float err;
```

In debug builds, EFloat also maintains a highly precise version of v that can be used as a reference value to compute an accurate approximation of the relative error. In optimized builds, we'd generally rather not pay the overhead for computing this additional value.

⟨*Store high-precision reference value in* EFloat⟩ ≡   218
```
#ifndef NDEBUG
ld = v;
#endif // NDEBUG
```

⟨*EFloat Private Data*⟩ +≡
```
#ifndef NDEBUG
long double ld;
#endif // NDEBUG
```

The implementation of the addition operation for this class is essentially an implementation of the relevant definitions. We have:

$$(a \pm \delta_a) \oplus (b \pm \delta_b) = ((a \pm \delta_a) + (b \pm \delta_b))(1 \pm \gamma_1)$$
$$= a + b + [\pm\delta_a \pm \delta_b \pm (a + b)\gamma_1 \pm \gamma_1\delta_a \pm \gamma_1\delta_b].$$

And so the absolute error (in brackets) is bounded by

$$\delta_a + \delta_b + \gamma_1(|a + b| + \delta_a + \delta_b).$$

⟨*EFloat Public Methods*⟩ +≡
```
EFloat operator+(EFloat f) const {
    EFloat r;
    r.v = v + f.v;
#ifndef NDEBUG
    r.ld = ld + f.ld;
#endif  // DEBUG
    r.err = err + f.err +
        gamma(1) * (std::abs(v + f.v) + err + f.err);
    return r;
}
```

The implementations for the other arithmetic operations for EFloat are analogous.

Note that this implementation neglects the issue that the computation of errors will itself be affected by rounding error. If this was a concern, we could switch the floating-point rounding mode so that it always rounded the error bounds up to positive infinity, but this tends to be a fairly expensive operation since it causes a full pipeline flush on current processors. Here, we use the default rounding mode; in the following, the error bounds are expanded by one ulp when they are used to account for this issue.

The float value in an EFloat is available via a type conversion operator; it has an explicit qualifier to require the caller to have an explicit (float) cast to extract the floating-point value. The requirement to use an explicit cast reduces the risk of an unintended round trip from EFloat to Float and back, thus losing the accumulated error bounds.

⟨*EFloat Public Methods*⟩ +≡
```
explicit operator float() const { return v; }
```

If a series of computations is performed using EFloat rather than float-typed variables, then at any point in the computation, the GetAbsoluteError() method can be called to find a bound on the absolute error of the computed value.

⟨*EFloat Public Methods*⟩ +≡
```
float GetAbsoluteError() const { return err; }
```

The bounds of the error interval are available via the UpperBound() and LowerBound() methods. Their implementations use NextFloatUp() and NextFloatDown() to expand the returned values by one ulp, respectively, ensuring that the interval is conservative.

⟨*EFloat Public Methods*⟩ +≡
```
float UpperBound() const { return NextFloatUp(v + err); }
float LowerBound() const { return NextFloatDown(v - err); }
```

In debug builds, methods are available to get both the relative error as well as the precise value maintained in ld.

⟨*EFloat Public Methods*⟩ +≡
```
#ifndef NDEBUG
float GetRelativeError() const { return std::abs((ld - v)/ld); }
long double PreciseValue() const { return ld; }
#endif
```

pbrt also provides a variant of the Quadratic() function that operates on coefficients that may have error and returns error bounds with the t0 and t1 values. The implementation is the same as the regular Quadratic() function, just using EFloat.

⟨*EFloat Inline Functions*⟩ ≡
```
inline bool Quadratic(EFloat A, EFloat B, EFloat C,
                      EFloat *t0, EFloat *t1);
```

With the floating-point error fundamentals in place, we'll now focus on using these tools to provide robust intersection operations.

3.9.2 CONSERVATIVE RAY–BOUNDS INTERSECTIONS

Floating-point round-off error can cause the ray–bounding box intersection test to miss cases where a ray actually does intersect the box. While it's acceptable to have occasional false positives from ray–box intersection tests, we'd like to never miss an actual intersection—getting this right is important for the correctness of the BVHAccel acceleration data structure in Section 4.3 so that valid ray–shape intersections aren't missed.

The ray–bounding box test introduced in Section 3.1.2 is based on computing a series of ray–slab intersections to find the parametric t_{min} along the ray where the ray enters the bounding box and the t_{max} where it exits. If $t_{min} < t_{max}$, the ray passes through the box; otherwise it misses it. With floating-point arithmetic, there may be error in the computed t values—if the computed t_{min} value is greater than t_{max} purely due to round-off error, the intersection test will incorrectly return a false result.

Recall that the computation to find the t value for a ray intersection with a plane perpendicular to the x axis at a point x is $t = (x - o_x)/d_x$. Expressed as a floating-point computation and applying Equation (3.7), we have

$$t = (x \ominus o_x) \otimes (1 \oslash \mathbf{d}_x) \subset \frac{x - o_x}{\mathbf{d}_x}(1 \pm \epsilon)^3,$$

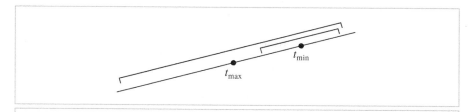

Figure 3.42: If the error bounds of the computed t_{min} and t_{max} values overlap, the comparison $t_{min} < t_{max}$ may not actually indicate if a ray hit a bounding box. It's better to conservatively return true in this case than to miss an actual intersection. Extending t_{max} by twice its error bound ensures that the comparison is conservative.

and so

$$t(1 \pm \gamma_3) = \frac{x - o_x}{d_x}.$$

The difference between the computed result t and the precise result is bounded by $\gamma_3|t|$.

If we consider the intervals around the computed t values that bound the fully precise value of t, then the case we're concerned with is when the intervals overlap; if they don't, then the comparison of computed values will give the correct result (Figure 3.42). If the intervals do overlap, it's impossible to know the actual ordering of the t values. In this case, increasing t_{max} by twice the error bound, $2\gamma_3 t_{max}$, before performing the comparison ensures that we conservatively return true in this case.

We can now define the fragment for the ray–bounding box test in Section 3.1.2 that makes this adjustment.

⟨*Update* tFar *to ensure robust ray–bounds intersection*⟩ ≡   **128**
    tFar *= 1 + 2 * gamma(3);

The fragments for the Bounds3::IntersectP() method, ⟨*Update* tMax *and* tyMax *to ensure robust bounds intersection*⟩ and ⟨*Update* tzMax *to ensure robust bounds intersection*⟩, are similar and therefore not included here.

3.9.3 ROBUST TRIANGLE INTERSECTIONS

The details of the ray–triangle intersection algorithm in Section 3.6.2 were carefully designed to avoid cases where rays could incorrectly pass through an edge or vertex shared by two adjacent triangles without generating an intersection. Fittingly, an intersection algorithm with this guarantee is referred to as being *watertight*.

Recall that the algorithm is based on transforming triangle vertices into a coordinate system with the ray's origin at its origin and the ray's direction aligned along the $+z$ axis. Although round-off error may be introduced by transforming the vertex positions to this coordinate system, this error doesn't affect the watertightness of the intersection test, since the same transformation is applied to all triangles. (Further, this error is quite small, so it doesn't significantly impact the accuracy of the computed intersection points.)

gamma() 217

Given vertices in this coordinate system, the three edge functions defined in Equation (3.1) are evaluated at the point $(0, 0)$; the corresponding expressions, Equation (3.2), are quite straightforward. The key to the robustness of the algorithm is that with floating-point arithmetic, the edge function evaluations are guaranteed to have the correct sign. In general, we have

$$(a \otimes b) \ominus (c \otimes d). \qquad\qquad [3.12]$$

First, note that if $ab = cd$, then Equation (3.12) evaluates to exactly zero, even in floating point. We therefore just need to show that if $ab > cd$, then $(a \otimes b) \ominus (c \otimes d)$ is never negative. If $ab > cd$, then $(a \otimes b)$ must be greater than or equal to $(c \otimes d)$. In turn, their difference must be greater than or equal to zero. (These properties both follow from the fact that floating-point arithmetic operations are all rounded to the nearest representable floating-point value.)

If the value of the edge function is zero, then it's impossible to tell whether it is exactly zero or whether a small positive or negative value has rounded to zero. In this case, the fragment ⟨*Fall back to double-precision test at triangle edges*⟩ reevaluates the edge function with double precision; it can be shown that doubling the precision suffices to accurately distinguish these cases, given 32-bit floats as input.

The overhead caused by this additional precaution is minimal: in a benchmark with 88 million ray intersection tests, the double-precision fallback had to be used in less than 0.0000023% of the cases.

3.9.4 BOUNDING INTERSECTION POINT ERROR

We'll now apply this machinery for analyzing rounding error to derive conservative bounds on the absolute error in computed ray-shape intersection points, which allows us to construct bounding boxes that are guaranteed to include an intersection point on the actual surface (Figure 3.43). These bounding boxes provide the basis of the algorithm for generating spawned ray origins that will be introduced in Section 3.9.5.

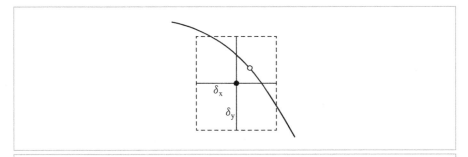

Figure 3.43: Shape intersection algorithms in pbrt compute an intersection point, shown here in the 2D setting with a filled circle. The absolute error in this point is bounded by δ_x and δ_y, giving a small box around the point. Because these bounds are conservative, we know that the actual intersection point on the surface (open circle) must lie somewhere within the box.

It's useful to start by looking at the sources of error in conventional approaches to computing intersection points. It is common practice in ray tracing to compute 3D intersection points by first solving the parametric ray equation $o + td$ for a value t_{hit} where a ray intersects a surface and then computing the hit point p with $p = o + t_{hit}d$. If t_{hit} carries some error δ_t, then we can bound the error in the computed intersection point. Considering the x coordinate, for example, we have

$$x = o_x \oplus (t_{hit} \pm \delta_t) \otimes d_x$$
$$\subset o_x \oplus (t_{hit} \pm \delta_t)d_x(1 \pm \gamma_1)$$
$$\subset o_x(1 \pm \gamma_1) + (t_{hit} \pm \delta_t)d_x(1 \pm \gamma_2)$$
$$= o_x + t_{hit}d_x + [\pm o_x\gamma_1 \pm \delta_t d_x \pm t_{hit}d_x\gamma_2 \pm \delta_t d_x\gamma_2].$$

The error term (in square brackets) is bounded by

$$\gamma_1|o_x| + \delta_t(1 \pm \gamma_2)|d_x| + \gamma_2|t_{hit}d_x|. \tag{3.13}$$

There are two things to see from Equation (3.13): first, the magnitudes of the terms that contribute to the error in the computed intersection point (o_x, d_x, and $t_{hit}d_x$) may be quite different from the magnitude of the intersection point. Thus, there is a danger of catastrophic cancellation in the intersection point's computed value. Second, ray intersection algorithms generally perform tens of floating-point operations to compute t values, which in turn means that we can expect δ_t to be at least of magnitude $\gamma_n t$, with n in the tens (and possibly much more, due to catastrophic cancellation). Each of these terms may be significant with respect to the magnitude of the computed point x.

Together, these factors can lead to relatively large error in the computed intersection point. We'll develop better approaches shortly.

Reprojection: Quadrics

We'd like to reliably compute intersection points on surfaces with just a few ulps of error rather than the hundreds of ulps of error that intersection points computed with the parametric ray equation may have. Previously, Woo et al. (1996) suggested using the first intersection point computed as a starting point for a second ray–plane intersection, for ray–polygon intersections. From the bounds in Equation (3.13), we can see why the second intersection point will be much closer to the surface than the first: the t_{hit} value along the second ray will be quite close to zero, so that the magnitude of the absolute error in t_{hit} will be quite small, and thus using this value in the parametric ray equation will give a point quite close to the surface (Figure 3.44). Further, the ray origin will have similar magnitude to the intersection point, so the $\gamma_1|o_x|$ term won't introduce much additional error.

Although the second intersection point computed with this approach is much closer to the plane of the surface, it still suffers from error by being offset due to error in the first computed intersection. The farther away the ray origin from the intersection point (and thus, the larger the absolute error in t_{hit}), the larger this error will be. In spite of this error, the approach has merit: we're generally better off with a computed intersection point that is quite close to the actual surface, even if offset from the most accurate possible intersection point, than we are with a point that is some distance above or below the surface (and likely also far from the most accurate intersection point).

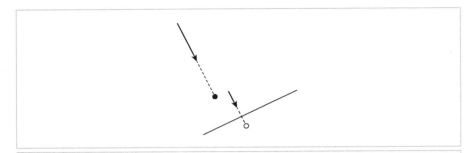

Figure 3.44: Re-intersection to Improve the Accuracy of the Computed Intersection Point.
Given a ray and a surface, an initial intersection point has been computed with the ray equation (filled circle). This point may be fairly inaccurate due to rounding error but can be used as the origin for a second ray–shape intersection. The intersection point computed from this second intersection (open circle) is much closer to the surface, though it may be shifted from the true intersection point due to error in the first computed intersection.

Rather than doing a full re-intersection computation, which may not only be computationally costly but also will still have error in the computed t value, an effective approach is to refine computed intersection points by reprojecting them to the surface. The error bounds for these reprojected points are often remarkably small.

It should be noted that these reprojection error bounds don't capture tangential errors that were present in the original intersection p—the main focus here is to detect errors that might cause the reprojected point p' to fall below the surface.

Consider a ray–sphere intersection: given a computed intersection point (e.g., from the ray equation) p with a sphere at the origin with radius r, we can reproject the point onto the surface of the sphere by scaling it with the ratio of the sphere's radius to the computed point's distance to the origin, computing a new point $p' = (x', y', z')$ with

$$x' = x \frac{r}{\sqrt{x^2 + y^2 + z^2}},$$

and so forth. The floating-point computation is

$$x' = x \otimes r \oslash \mathsf{sqrt}((x \otimes x) \oplus (y \otimes y) \oplus (z \otimes z))$$

$$\subset \frac{xr(1 \pm \epsilon_m)^2}{\sqrt{x^2(1 \pm \epsilon_m)^3 + y^2(1 \pm \epsilon_m)^3 + z^2(1 \pm \epsilon_m)^2}(1 \pm \epsilon_m)}$$

$$\subset \frac{xr(1 \pm \gamma_2)}{\sqrt{x^2(1 \pm \gamma_3) + y^2(1 \pm \gamma_3) + z^2(1 \pm \gamma_2)}(1 \pm \gamma_1)}$$

Because x^2, y^2, and z^2 are all positive, the terms in the square root can share the same γ term, and we have

$$x' \subset \frac{xr(1 \pm \gamma_2)}{\sqrt{(x^2 + y^2 + z^2)(1 \pm \gamma_4)}(1 \pm \gamma_1)}$$

$$= \frac{xr(1 \pm \gamma_2)}{\sqrt{(x^2 + y^2 + z^2)}\sqrt{(1 \pm \gamma_4)}(1 \pm \gamma_1)}$$

$$\subset \frac{xr}{\sqrt{(x^2 + y^2 + z^2)}}(1 \pm \gamma_5)$$ [3.14]

$$= x'(1 \pm \gamma_5).$$

Thus, the absolute error of the reprojected x coordinate is bounded by $\gamma_5|x'|$ (and similarly for y' and z') and is thus no more than 2.5 ulps in each dimension from a point on the surface of the sphere.

Here is the fragment that reprojects the intersection point for the Sphere shape.

⟨*Refine sphere intersection point*⟩ ≡   137
```
pHit *= radius / Distance(pHit, Point3f(0, 0, 0));
```

The error bounds follow from Equation (3.14).

⟨*Compute error bounds for sphere intersection*⟩ ≡   134
```
Vector3f pError = gamma(5) * Abs((Vector3f)pHit);
```

Reprojection algorithms and error bounds for other quadrics can be defined similarly: for example, for a cylinder along the z axis, only the x and y coordinates need to be reprojected, and the error bounds in x and y turn out to be only γ_3 times their magnitudes.

⟨*Refine cylinder intersection point*⟩ ≡   145
```
Float hitRad = std::sqrt(pHit.x * pHit.x + pHit.y * pHit.y);
pHit.x *= radius / hitRad;
pHit.y *= radius / hitRad;
```

⟨*Compute error bounds for cylinder intersection*⟩ ≡   144
```
Vector3f pError = gamma(3) * Abs(Vector3f(pHit.x, pHit.y, 0));
```

The disk shape is particularly easy; we just need to set the z coordinate of the point to lie on the plane of the disk.

⟨*Refine disk intersection point*⟩ ≡   148
```
pHit.z = height;
```

In turn, we have a point with zero error; it lies exactly on the surface on the disk.

⟨*Compute error bounds for disk intersection*⟩ ≡   148
```
Vector3f pError(0, 0, 0);
```

Parametric Evaluation: Triangles

Another effective approach to computing precise intersection points is to use the parametric representation of a shape to compute accurate intersection points. For example, the triangle intersection algorithm in Section 3.6.2 computes three edge function values e_0, e_1, and e_2 and reports an intersection if all three have the same sign. Their values can be used to find the barycentric coordinates

$$b_i = \frac{e_i}{e_0 + e_1 + e_2}.$$

Attributes v_i at the triangle vertices (including the vertex positions) can be interpolated across the face of the triangle by

$$v' = b_0 v_0 + b_1 v_1 + b_2 v_2.$$

We can show that interpolating the positions of the vertices in this manner gives a point very close to the surface of the triangle. First consider precomputing the inverse sum of e_i:

$$d = 1 \oslash (e_0 \oplus e_1 \oplus e_2)$$

$$\subset \frac{1}{(e_0 + e_1)(1 \pm \epsilon_m)^2 + e_2(1 \pm \epsilon_m)}(1 \pm \epsilon_m).$$

Because all e_i have the same sign if there is an intersection, we can collect the e_i terms and conservatively bound d:

$$d \subset \frac{1}{(e_0 + e_1 + e_2)(1 \pm \epsilon_m)^2}(1 \pm \epsilon_m)$$

$$\subset \frac{1}{e_0 + e_1 + e_2}(1 \pm \gamma_3).$$

If we now consider interpolation of the x coordinate of the position in the triangle corresponding to the edge function values, we have

$$x' = ((e_0 \otimes x_0) \oplus (e_1 \otimes x_1) \oplus (e_2 \otimes x_2)) \otimes d$$

$$\subset (e_0 x_0 (1 \pm \epsilon_m)^3 + e_1 x_1 (1 \pm \epsilon_m)^3 + e_2 x_2 (1 \pm \epsilon_m)^2) d (1 \pm \epsilon_m)$$

$$\subset (e_0 x_0 (1 \pm \gamma_4) + e_1 x_1 (1 \pm \gamma_4) + e_2 x_2 (1 \pm \gamma_3)) d.$$

Using the bounds on d,

$$x \subset \frac{e_0 x_0 (1 \pm \gamma_7) + e_1 x_1 (1 \pm \gamma_7) + e_2 x_2 (1 \pm \gamma_6)}{e_0 + e_1 + e_2}$$

$$= b_0 x_0 (1 \pm \gamma_7) + b_1 x_1 (1 \pm \gamma_7) + b_2 x_2 (1 \pm \gamma_6).$$

Thus, we can finally see that the absolute error in the computed x' value is in the interval

$$\pm b_0 x_0 \gamma_7 \pm b_1 x_1 \gamma_7 \pm b_2 x_2 \gamma_7,$$

which is bounded by

$$\gamma_7(|b_0 x_0| + |b_1 x_1| + |b_2 x_2|). \tag{3.15}$$

(Note that the $b_2 x_2$ term could have a γ_6 factor instead of γ_7, but the difference between the two is very small so we choose a slightly simpler final expression.) Equivalent bounds hold for y' and z'.

Triangle::Intersect() 157

Equation (3.15) lets us bound the error in the interpolated point computed in Triangle::Intersect().

⟨*Compute error bounds for triangle intersection*⟩ ≡   157
```
Float xAbsSum = (std::abs(b0 * p0.x) + std::abs(b1 * p1.x) +
                 std::abs(b2 * p2.x));
Float yAbsSum = (std::abs(b0 * p0.y) + std::abs(b1 * p1.y) +
                 std::abs(b2 * p2.y));
Float zAbsSum = (std::abs(b0 * p0.z) + std::abs(b1 * p1.z) +
                 std::abs(b2 * p2.z));
Vector3f pError = gamma(7) * Vector3f(xAbsSum, yAbsSum, zAbsSum);
```

Other Shapes

For shapes where we may not want to derive reprojection methods and tight error bounds, running error analysis can be quite useful: we implement all of the intersection calculations using EFloat instead of Float, compute a t_{hit} value, and use the parametric ray equation to compute a hit point. We can then find conservative bounds on the error in the computed intersection point via the EFloat GetAbsoluteError() method.

⟨*Compute error bounds for intersection computed with ray equation*⟩ ≡   227
```
EFloat px = ox + tShapeHit * dx;
EFloat py = oy + tShapeHit * dy;
EFloat pz = oz + tShapeHit * dz;
Vector3f pError = Vector3f(px.GetAbsoluteError(), py.GetAbsoluteError(),
                           pz.GetAbsoluteError());
```

This approach is used for cones, paraboloids, and hyperboloids in pbrt.

⟨*Compute error bounds for cone intersection*⟩ ≡
    ⟨*Compute error bounds for intersection computed with ray equation* 227⟩

Because the Curve shape orients itself to face incident rays, rays leaving it must be offset by twice the curve's width in order to not incorrectly re-intersect it when it's reoriented to face them.

⟨*Compute error bounds for curve intersection*⟩ ≡   180
```
Vector3f pError(2 * hitWidth, 2 * hitWidth, 2 * hitWidth);
```

Effect of Transformations

The last detail to attend to in order to bound the error in computed intersection points is the effect of transformations, which introduce additional rounding error when they are applied to computed intersection points.

The quadric Shapes in pbrt transform world space rays into object space before performing ray–shape intersections and then transform computed intersection points back to world space. Both of these transformation steps introduce rounding error that needs to be accounted for in order to maintain robust world space bounds around intersection points.

If possible, it's best to try to avoid coordinate-system transformations of rays and intersection points. For example, it's better to transform triangle vertices to world space and intersect world space rays with them than to transform rays to object space and then transform intersection points to world space.[18] Transformations are still useful—for example, for the quadrics and for object instancing, so we'll show how to bound the error that they introduce.

We'll start by considering the error introduced by transforming a point (x, y, z) that is exact—i.e., without any accumulated error. Given a 4×4 non-projective transformation matrix with elements denoted by $m_{i,j}$, the transformed point x' is

$$
\begin{aligned}
x' &= ((m_{0,0} \otimes x) \oplus (m_{0,1} \otimes y)) \oplus ((m_{0,2} \otimes z) \oplus m_{0,3}) \\
&\subset m_{0,0}x(1 \pm \epsilon_{\mathrm{m}})^3 + m_{0,1}y(1 \pm \epsilon_{\mathrm{m}})^3 + m_{0,2}z(1 \pm \epsilon_{\mathrm{m}})^3 + m_{0,3}(1 \pm \epsilon_{\mathrm{m}})^2 \\
&\subset (m_{0,0}x + m_{0,1}y + m_{0,2}z + m_{0,3}) + \gamma_3(\pm m_{0,0}x \pm m_{0,1}y \pm m_{0,2}z \pm m_{0,3}) \\
&\subset (m_{0,0}x + m_{0,1}y + m_{0,2}z + m_{0,3}) \pm \gamma_3(|m_{0,0}x| + |m_{0,1}y| + |m_{0,2}z| + |m_{0,3}|).
\end{aligned}
$$

Thus, the absolute error in the result is bounded by

$$
\gamma_3(|m_{0,0}x| + |m_{0,1}y| + |m_{0,2}z| + |m_{0,3}|). \tag{3.16}
$$

Similar bounds follow for the transformed y' and z' coordinates.

We'll use this result to add a method to the Transform class that also returns the absolute error in the transformed point due to applying the transformation.

⟨Transform Inline Functions⟩ +≡
```
template <typename T> inline Point3<T>
Transform::operator()(const Point3<T> &p, Vector3<T> *pError) const {
    T x = p.x, y = p.y, z = p.z;
    ⟨Compute transformed coordinates from point pt⟩
    ⟨Compute absolute error for transformed point  229⟩
    if (wp == 1) return Point3<T>(xp, yp, zp);
    else         return Point3<T>(xp, yp, zp) / wp;

}
```

The fragment ⟨Compute transformed coordinates from point pt⟩ isn't included here; it implements the same matrix/point multiplication as in Section 2.8.

Note that the code that computes error bounds is buggy if the matrix is projective and the homogeneous w coordinate of the projected point is not one; this nit currently isn't a problem for pbrt's usage of this method.

---

18 Although rounding error is introduced when transforming triangle vertices to world space (for example), this error doesn't
    add error that needs to be handled in computing intersection points. In other words, the transformed vertices may represent
    a perturbed representation of the scene, but they are the most precise representation available given the transformation.

⟨*Compute absolute error for transformed point*⟩ ≡   228
```
T xAbsSum = (std::abs(m.m[0][0] * x) + std::abs(m.m[0][1] * y) +
             std::abs(m.m[0][2] * z) + std::abs(m.m[0][3]));
T yAbsSum = (std::abs(m.m[1][0] * x) + std::abs(m.m[1][1] * y) +
             std::abs(m.m[1][2] * z) + std::abs(m.m[1][3]));
T zAbsSum = (std::abs(m.m[2][0] * x) + std::abs(m.m[2][1] * y) +
             std::abs(m.m[2][2] * z) + std::abs(m.m[2][3]));
*pError = gamma(3) * Vector3<T>(xAbsSum, yAbsSum, zAbsSum);
```

The result in Equation (3.16) assumes that the point being transformed is exact. If the point itself has error bounded by δ_x, δ_y, and δ_z, then the transformed x coordinate is given by:

$$x' = (m_{0,0} \otimes (x \pm \delta_x) \oplus m_{0,1} \otimes (y \pm \delta_y)) \oplus (m_{0,2} \otimes (z \pm \delta_z) \oplus m_{0,3}).$$

Applying the definition of floating-point addition and multiplication's error bounds, we have:

$$x' = m_{0,0}(x \pm \delta_x)(1 \pm \epsilon_m)^3 + m_{0,1}(y \pm \delta_y)(1 \pm \epsilon_m)^3 +$$
$$m_{0,2}(z \pm \delta_z)(1 \pm \epsilon_m)^3 + m_{0,3}(1 \pm \epsilon_m)^2.$$

Transforming to use γ, we can find the absolute error term to be bounded by

$$(\gamma_3 + 1)(|m_{0,0}|\delta_x + |m_{0,1}|\delta_y + |m_{0,2}|\delta_z) +$$
$$\gamma_3(|m_{0,0}x| + |m_{0,1}y| + |m_{0,2}z| + |m_{0,3}|). \tag{3.17}$$

The Transform class also provides an operator() that takes a point and its own absolute error and returns the absolute error in the result, applying Equation (3.17). The definition is straightforward, so isn't included in the text here.

⟨*Transform Public Methods*⟩ +≡   83
```
template <typename T> inline Point3<T>
operator()(const Point3<T> &p, const Vector3<T> &pError,
        Vector3<T> *pTransError) const;
```

The Transform class also provides methods to transform vectors and rays, returning the resulting error. The vector error bound derivations (and thence, implementations) are very similar to those for points, and so also aren't included here.

⟨*Transform Public Methods*⟩ +≡   83
```
template <typename T> inline Vector3<T>
operator()(const Vector3<T> &v, Vector3<T> *vTransError) const;
template <typename T> inline Vector3<T>
operator()(const Vector3<T> &v, const Vector3<T> &vError,
        Vector3<T> *vTransError) const;
```

This method is used to transform the intersection point and its error bounds in the Transform::operator() method for SurfaceInteractions.

⟨*Transform* p *and* pError *in* SurfaceInteraction⟩ ≡   120
```
ret.p = (*this)(si.p, si.pError, &ret.pError);
```

3.9.5 ROBUST SPAWNED RAY ORIGINS

Computed intersection points and their error bounds give us a small 3D box that bounds a region of space. We know that the precise intersection point must be somewhere inside this box and that thus the surface must pass through the box (at least enough to present the point where the intersection is). (Recall Figure 3.43.) Having these boxes makes it possible to position the origins of rays leaving the surface so that they are always on the right side of the surface so that they don't incorrectly reintersect it. When tracing spawned rays leaving the intersection point p, we offset their origins enough to ensure that they are past the boundary of the error box and thus won't incorrectly re-intersect the surface.

In order to ensure that the spawned ray origin is definitely on the right side of the surface, we move far enough along the normal so that the plane perpendicular to the normal is outside the error bounding box. To see how to do this, consider a computed intersection point at the origin, where the plane equation for the plane going through the intersection point is just

$$f(x, y, z) = \mathbf{n}_x x + \mathbf{n}_y y + \mathbf{n}_z z,$$

the plane is implicitly defined by $f(x, y, z) = 0$, and the normal is $(\mathbf{n}_x, \mathbf{n}_y, \mathbf{n}_z)$.

For a point not on the plane, the value of the plane equation $f(x, y, z)$ gives the offset along the normal that gives a plane that goes through the point. We'd like to find the maximum value of $f(x, y, z)$ for the eight corners of the error bounding box; if we offset the plane plus and minus this offset, we have two planes that don't intersect the error box that should be (locally) on opposite sides of the surface, at least at the computed intersection point offset along the normal (Figure 3.45).

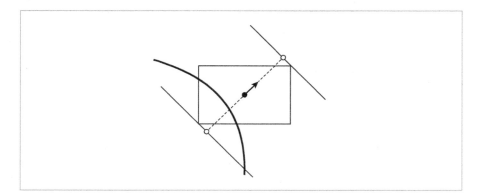

Figure 3.45: Given a computed intersection point (filled circle) with surface normal (arrow) and error bounds (rectangle), we compute two planes offset along the normal that are offset just far enough so that they don't intersect the error bounds. The points on these planes along the normal from the computed intersection point give us the origins for spawned rays (open circles); one of the two is selected based on the ray direction so that the spawned ray won't pass through the error bounding box. By construction, such rays can't incorrectly re-intersect the actual surface (thick line).

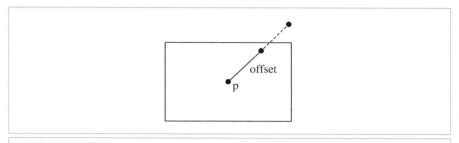

Figure 3.46: The rounded value of the offset point p+offset computed in `OffsetRayOrigin()` may end up in the interior of the error box rather than on its boundary, which in turn introduces the risk of incorrect self-intersections if the rounded point is on the wrong side of the surface. Advancing each coordinate of the computed point one floating-point value away from p ensures that it is outside of the error box.

If the eight corners of the error bounding box are given by $(\pm\delta_x, \pm\delta_y, \pm\delta_z)$, then the maximum value of $f(x, y, z)$ is easily computed:

$$d = |\mathbf{n}_x|\delta_x + |\mathbf{n}_y|\delta_y + |\mathbf{n}_z|\delta_z.$$

Computing spawned ray origins by offsetting along the surface normal in this way has a few advantages: assuming that the surface is locally planar (a reasonable assumption, especially at the very small scale of the intersection point error bounds), moving along the normal allows us to get from one side of the surface to the other while moving the shortest distance. In general, minimizing the distance that ray origins are offset is desirable for maintaining shadow and reflection detail.

⟨*Geometry Inline Functions*⟩ +≡

```
inline Point3f OffsetRayOrigin(const Point3f &p, const Vector3f &pError,
                               const Normal3f &n, const Vector3f &w) {
    Float d = Dot(Abs(n), pError);
    Vector3f offset = d * Vector3f(n);
    if (Dot(w, n) < 0)
        offset = -offset;
    Point3f po = p + offset;
    ⟨Round offset point po away from p 232⟩
    return po;
}
```

We also must handle round-off error when computing the offset point: when offset is added to p, the result will in general need to be rounded to the nearest floating-point value. In turn, it may be rounded down toward p such that the resulting point is in the interior of the error box rather than in its boundary (Figure 3.46). Therefore, the offset point is rounded away from p here to ensure that it's not inside the box.[19]

---

19 The observant reader may now wonder about the effect of rounding error when computing the error bounds that are passed into this function. Indeed, these bounds should also be computed with rounding toward positive infinity. We ignore that issue under the expectation that the additional offset of one ulp here will be enough to cover that error.

Alternatively, the floating-point rounding mode could have been set to round toward plus or minus infinity (based on the sign of the value). Changing the rounding mode is generally fairly expensive, so we just shift the floating-point value by one ulp here. This will sometimes cause a value already outside of the error box to go slightly farther outside it, but because the floating-point spacing is so small, this isn't a problem in practice.

⟨*Round offset point* po *away from* p⟩ ≡   **231**
```
for (int i = 0; i < 3; ++i) {
    if (offset[i] > 0)      po[i] = NextFloatUp(po[i]);
    else if (offset[i] < 0) po[i] = NextFloatDown(po[i]);
}
```

Given the OffsetRayOrigin() function, we can now implement the Interaction methods that generate rays leaving intersection points.

⟨*Interaction Public Methods*⟩ +≡   **115**
```
Ray SpawnRay(const Vector3f &d) const {
    Point3f o = OffsetRayOrigin(p, pError, n, d);
    return Ray(o, d, Infinity, time, GetMedium(d));
}
```

The approach we've developed so far addresses the effect of floating-point error at the origins of rays leaving surfaces; there is a related issue for shadow rays to area light sources: we'd like to find any intersections with shapes that are very close to the light source and actually occlude it, while avoiding reporting incorrect intersections with the surface of the light source. Unfortunately, our implementation doesn't address this issue, so we set the tMax value of shadow rays to be just under one so that they stop before the surface of light sources.

⟨*Interaction Public Methods*⟩ +≡   **115**
```
Ray SpawnRayTo(const Point3f &p2) const {
    Point3f origin = OffsetRayOrigin(p, pError, n, p2 - p);
    Vector3f d = p2 - origin;
    return Ray(origin, d, 1 - ShadowEpsilon, time, GetMedium(d));
}
```

⟨*Global Constants*⟩ +≡
```
const Float ShadowEpsilon = 0.0001f;
```

The other variant of SpawnRayTo(), which takes an Interaction, is analogous.

One last issue must be dealt with in order to maintain robust spawned ray origins: error introduced when performing transformations. Given a ray in one coordinate system where its origin was carefully computed to be on the appropriate side of some surface, transforming that ray to another coordinate system may introduce error in the transformed origin such that the origin is no longer on the correct side of the surface it was spawned from.

Therefore, whenever a ray is transformed by the Ray variant of Transform::operator() (which was implemented in Section 2.8.4), its origin is advanced to the edge of the bounds on the error that was introduced by the transformation. This ensures that the origin conservatively remains on the correct side of the surface it was spawned from, if any.

⟨*Offset ray origin to edge of error bounds and compute* tMax⟩ ≡   **95**
```
    Float lengthSquared = d.LengthSquared();
    Float tMax = r.tMax;
    if (lengthSquared > 0) {
        Float dt = Dot(Abs(d), oError) / lengthSquared;
        o += d * dt;
        tMax -= dt;
    }
```

3.9.6 AVOIDING INTERSECTIONS BEHIND RAY ORIGINS

Bounding the error in computed intersection points allows us to compute ray origins that are guaranteed to be on the right side of the surface so that a ray with infinite precision wouldn't incorrectly intersect the surface it's leaving. However, a second source of rounding error must also be addressed: the error in parametric t values computed for ray–shape intersections. Rounding error can lead to an intersection algorithm computing a value $t > 0$ for the intersection point even though the t value for the actual intersection is negative (and thus should be ignored).

It's possible to show that some intersection test algorithms always return a t value with the correct sign; this is the best case, as no further computation is needed to bound the actual error in the computed t value. For example, consider the ray–axis-aligned slab computation: $t = (x \ominus o_x) \oslash \mathbf{d}_x$. IEEE guarantees that if $a > b$, then $a \ominus b \geq 0$ (and if $a < b$, then $a \ominus b \leq 0$). To see why this is so, note that if $a > b$, then the real number $a - b$ must be greater than zero. When rounded to a floating-point number, the result must be either zero or a positive float; there's no a way a negative floating-point number could be the closest floating-point number. Second, floating-point division returns the correct sign; these together guarantee that the sign of the computed t value is correct. (Or that $t = 0$, but this case is fine, since our test for an intersection is carefully chosen to be $t > 0$.)

For shape intersection routines that use EFloat, the computed t value in the end has an error bound associated with it, and no further computation is necessary to perform this test. See the definition of the fragment ⟨*Check quadric shape* t0 *and* t1 *for nearest intersection*⟩ in Section 3.2.2.

Triangles

EFloat introduces computational overhead that we'd prefer to avoid for more commonly used shapes where efficient intersection code is more important. For these shapes, we can derive efficient-to-evaluate conservative bounds on the error in computed t values. The ray–triangle intersection algorithm in Section 3.6.2 computes a final t value by computing three edge function values e_i and using them to compute a barycentric-weighted sum of transformed vertex z coordinates, z_i:

$$t = \frac{e_0 z_0 + e_1 z_1 + e_2 z_2}{e_0 + e_1 + e_2}$$ [3.18]

By successively bounding the error in these terms and then in the final t value, we can conservatively check that it is positive.

Dot() 63
Float 1062
Vector3::Abs() 63
Vector3::LengthSquared() 65

⟨*Ensure that computed triangle t is conservatively greater than zero*⟩ ≡   **158**
    ⟨*Compute δ_z term for triangle t error bounds* **234**⟩
    ⟨*Compute δ_x and δ_y terms for triangle t error bounds* **234**⟩
    ⟨*Compute δ_e term for triangle t error bounds* **235**⟩
    ⟨*Compute δ_t term for triangle t error bounds and check* t **235**⟩

Given a ray r with origin o, direction **d**, and a triangle vertex p, the projected z coordinate is

$$z = (1 \oslash \mathbf{d}_z) \otimes (\mathrm{p}_z \ominus \mathrm{o}_z)$$

Applying the usual approach, we can find that the maximum error in z_i for each of three vertices of the triangle p_i is bounded by $\gamma_3|z_i|$, and we can thus find a conservative upper bound for the error in *any* of the z positions by taking the maximum of these errors:

$$\delta_z = \gamma_3 \max_i |z_i|.$$

⟨*Compute δ_z term for triangle t error bounds*⟩ ≡   **234**
    Float maxZt = MaxComponent(Abs(Vector3f(p0t.z, p1t.z, p2t.z)));
    Float deltaZ = gamma(3) * maxZt;

The edge function values are computed as the difference of two products of transformed x and y vertex positions:

$$e_0 = (x_1 \otimes y_2) \ominus (y_1 \otimes x_2)$$
$$e_1 = (x_2 \otimes y_0) \ominus (y_2 \otimes x_0)$$
$$e_2 = (x_0 \otimes y_1) \ominus (y_0 \otimes x_1).$$

Bounds for the error in the transformed positions x_i and y_i are

$$\delta_x = \gamma_5(\max_i |x_i| + \max_i |z_i|)$$
$$\delta_y = \gamma_5(\max_i |y_i| + \max_i |z_i|).$$

⟨*Compute δ_x and δ_y terms for triangle t error bounds*⟩ ≡   **234**
    Float maxXt = MaxComponent(Abs(Vector3f(p0t.x, p1t.x, p2t.x)));
    Float maxYt = MaxComponent(Abs(Vector3f(p0t.y, p1t.y, p2t.y)));
    Float deltaX = gamma(5) * (maxXt + maxZt);
    Float deltaY = gamma(5) * (maxYt + maxZt);

Taking the maximum error over all three of the vertices, the $x_i \otimes y_j$ products in the edge functions are bounded by

$$(\max_i |x_i| + \delta_x)(\max_i |y_i| + \delta_y)(1 \pm \epsilon_\mathrm{m}),$$

which have an absolute error bound of

$$\delta_{xy} = \gamma_2 \max_i |x_i| \max_i |y_i| + \delta_y \max_i |x_i| + \delta_x \max_i |y_i| + \cdots.$$

Dropping the (negligible) higher order terms of products of γ and δ terms, the error bound on the difference of two x and y terms for the edge function is

Float 1062
Vector3f 60

$$\delta_e = 2(\gamma_2 \max_i |x_i| \max_i |y_i| + \delta_y \max_i |x_i| + \delta_x \max_i |y_i|).$$

⟨*Compute δ_e term for triangle t error bounds*⟩ ≡   234
```
Float deltaE = 2 * (gamma(2) * maxXt * maxYt + deltaY * maxXt +
                    deltaX * maxYt);
```

Again bounding error by taking the maximum of error over all of the e_i terms, the error bound for the computed value of the numerator of t in Equation (3.18) is

$$\delta_t = 3(\gamma_3 \max_i |e_i| \max_i |z_i| + \delta_e \max_i |z_i| + \delta_z \max_i |e_i|).$$

A computed t value (before normalization by the sum of e_i) must be greater than this value for it to be accepted as a valid intersection that definitely has a positive t value.

⟨*Compute δ_t term for triangle t error bounds and check t*⟩ ≡   234
```
Float maxE = MaxComponent(Abs(Vector3f(e0, e1, e2)));
Float deltaT = 3 * (gamma(3) * maxE * maxZt + deltaE * maxZt +
                    deltaZ * maxE) * std::abs(invDet);
if (t <= deltaT)
    return false;
```

Although it may seem that we have made a number of choices to compute looser bounds than we could, in the interests of efficiency, in practice the bounds on error in t are extremely small. For a regular scene that fills a bounding box roughly ±10 in each dimension, our t error bounds near ray origins are generally around 10^{-7}.

3.9.7 DISCUSSION

Minimizing and bounding numerical error in other geometric computations (e.g., partial derivatives of surface positions, interpolated texture coordinates, etc.) are much less important than they are for the positions of ray intersections. In a similar vein, the computations involving color and light in physically based rendering generally don't present trouble with respect to round-off error; they involve sums of products of positive numbers (usually with reasonably close magnitudes); hence catastrophic cancellation is not a commonly encountered issue. Furthermore, these sums are of few enough terms that accumulated error is small: the variance that is inherent in the Monte Carlo algorithms used for them dwarfs any floating-point error in computing them.

Interestingly enough, we saw an increase of roughly 20% in overall ray-tracing execution time after replacing the previous version of pbrt's old ad hoc method to avoid incorrect self-intersections with the method described in this section. (In comparison, rendering with double-precision floating point causes an increase in rendering time of roughly 30%.) Profiling showed that very little of the additional time was due to the additional computation to find error bounds; this is not surprising, as the incremental computation our method requires is limited—most of the error bounds are just scaled sums of absolute values of terms that have already been computed.

The majority of this slowdown is actually due to an increase in ray–object intersection tests. The reason for this increase in intersection tests was first identified by Wächter (2008, p. 30); when ray origins are very close to shape surfaces, more nodes of intersection acceleration hierarchies must be visited when tracing spawned rays than if overly loose offsets are used. Thus, more intersection tests are performed near the ray origin.

Float 1062
Vector3f 60

While this reduction in performance is unfortunate, it is actually a direct result of the greater accuracy of the method; it is the price to be paid for more accurate resolution of valid nearby intersections.

FURTHER READING

An Introduction to Ray Tracing has an extensive survey of algorithms for ray–shape intersection (Glassner 1989a). Goldstein and Nagel (1971) discussed ray–quadric intersections, and Heckbert (1984) discussed the mathematics of quadrics for graphics applications in detail, with many citations to literature in mathematics and other fields. Hanrahan (1983) described a system that automates the process of deriving a ray intersection routine for surfaces defined by implicit polynomials; his system emits C source code to perform the intersection test and normal computation for a surface described by a given equation. Mitchell (1990) showed that interval arithmetic could be applied to develop algorithms for robustly computing intersections with implicit surfaces that cannot be described by polynomials and are thus more difficult to accurately compute intersections for; more recent work in this area was done by Knoll et al. (2009). See Moore's book (1966) for an introduction to interval arithmetic.

Other notable early papers related to ray–shape intersection include Kajiya's (1983) work on computing intersections with surfaces of revolution and procedurally generated fractal terrains. Fournier et al.'s (1982) paper on rendering procedural stochastic models and Hart et al.'s (1989) paper on finding intersections with fractals illustrate the broad range of shape representations that can be used with ray-tracing algorithms.

Kajiya (1982) developed the first algorithm for computing intersections with parametric patches. Subsequent work on more efficient techniques for direct ray intersection with patches includes papers by Stürzlinger (1998), Martin et al. (2000), and Roth et al. (2001). Benthin et al. (2004) presented more recent results and include additional references to previous work. Ramsey et al. (2004) describe an efficient algorithm for computing intersections with bilinear patches, and Ogaki and Tokuyoshi (2011) introduce a technique for directly intersecting smooth surfaces generated from triangle meshes with per-vertex normals.

An excellent introduction to differential geometry was written by Gray (1993); Section 14.3 of his book presents the Weingarten equations.

The ray–triangle intersection test in Section 3.6 was developed by Woop et al. (2013). See Möller and Trumbore (1997) for another widely used ray–triangle intersection algorithm. A ray–quadrilateral intersection routine was developed by Lagae and Dutré (2005). Shevtsov et al. (2007a) described a highly optimized ray–triangle intersection routine for modern CPU architectures and included a number of references to other recent approaches. An interesting approach for developing a fast ray–triangle intersection routine was introduced by Kensler and Shirley (2006): they implemented a program that performed a search across the space of mathematically equivalent ray–triangle tests, automatically generating software implementations of variations and then benchmarking them. In the end, they found a more efficient ray–triangle routine than had been in use previously.

Phong and Crow (1975) first introduced the idea of interpolating per-vertex shading normals to give the appearance of smooth surfaces from polygonal meshes.

The layout of triangle meshes in memory can have a measurable impact on performance in many situations. In general, if triangles that are close together in 3D space are close together in memory, cache hit rates will be higher, and overall system performance will benefit. See Yoon et al. (2005) and Yoon and Lindstrom (2006) for algorithms for creating cache-friendly mesh layouts in memory.

The curve intersection algorithm in Section 3.7 is based on the approach developed by Nakamaru and Ohno (2002). Earlier methods for computing ray intersections with generalized cylinders are also applicable to rendering curves, though they are much less efficient (Bronsvoort and Klok 1985; de Voogt, van der Helm, and Bronsvoort 2000). The book by Farin (2001) provides an excellent general introduction to splines, and the blossoming approach used in Section 3.7 was introduced by Ramshaw (1987).

One challenge with rendering thin geometry like hair and fur is that thin geometry may require many pixel samples to be accurately resolved, which in turn increases rendering time. van Swaaij (2006) described a system that precomputed voxel grids to represent hair and fur, storing aggregate information about multiple hairs in a small region of space for more efficient rendering. More recently, Qin et al. (2014) described an approach based on cone tracing for rendering fur, where narrow cones are traced instead of rays. In turn, all of the curves that intersect a cone can be considered in computing the cone's contribution, allowing high-quality rendering with a small number of cones per pixel.

Subdivision surfaces were invented by Doo and Sabin (1978) and Catmull and Clark (1978). The Loop subdivision method was originally developed by Charles Loop (1987), although the implementation in pbrt uses the improved rules for subdivision and tangents along boundary edges developed by Hoppe et al. (1994). There has been extensive subsequent work in subdivision surfaces. The SIGGRAPH course notes give a good summary of the state of the art in the year 2000 and also have extensive references (Zorin et al. 2000). See also Warren's book on the topic (Warren 2002). Müller et al. (2003) described an approach that refines a subdivision surface on demand for the rays to be tested for intersection with it. (See also Benthin et al. (2007) for a related approach.)

An exciting development in subdivision surfaces is the ability to evaluate them at arbitrary points on the surface (Stam 1998). Subdivision surface implementations like the one in this chapter are often relatively inefficient, spending as much time dereferencing pointers as they do applying subdivision rules. Stam's approach avoids these inefficiencies. Bolz and Schröder (2002) suggest an improved implementation approach that precomputes a number of quantities that make it possible to compute the final mesh much more efficiently. More recently, Patney et al. (2009) have demonstrated a very efficient approach for tessellating subdivision surfaces on data-parallel throughput processors.

Higham's (2002) book on floating-point computation is excellent; it also develops the γ_n notation that we have used in Section 3.9. Other good references to this topic are Wilkinson (1994) and Goldberg (1991). While we have derived floating-point error bounds manually, see the *Gappa* system by Daumas and Melquiond (2010) for a tool that automatically derives forward error bounds of floating-point computations.

The incorrect self-intersection problem has been a known problem for ray-tracing practitioners for quite some time (Haines 1989; Amanatides and Mitchell 1990). In addition to offsetting rays by an "epsilon" at their origin, approaches that have been suggested include ignoring intersections with the object that was previously intersected, "root polishing" (Haines 1989; Woo et al. 1996), where the computed intersection point is refined to become more numerically accurate; and using higher precision floating-point representations (e.g., `double` instead of `float`).

Kalra and Barr (1989) and Dammertz and Keller (2006) developed algorithms for numerically robust intersections based on recursively subdividing object bounding boxes, discarding boxes that don't encompass the object's surface, and discarding boxes missed by the ray. Both of these approaches are much less efficient than traditional ray–object intersection algorithms as well as the techniques introduced in Section 3.9.

Salesin et al. (1989) introduced techniques to derive robust primitive operations for computational geometry that accounted for floating-point round-off error, and Ize showed how to perform numerically robust ray–bounding box intersections (Ize 2013); his approach is implemented in Section 3.9.2. (With a more careful derivation, he shows that a scale factor of $2\gamma_2$ can actually be used to increase tMax, rather than the $2\gamma_3$ we have derived here.) Wächter (2008) discussed self-intersection issues in his thesis; he suggested recomputing the intersection point starting from the initial intersection (root polishing) and offsetting spawned rays along the normal by a fixed small fraction of the intersection point's magnitude. The approach implemented in this chapter uses his approach of offsetting ray origins along the normal but is based on conservative bounds on the offsets based on the numerical error present in computed intersection points. (As it turns out, our bounds are generally tighter than Wächter's offsets while also being provably conservative.)

EXERCISES

⊘ **3.1**   One nice property of mesh-based shapes like triangle meshes and subdivision surfaces is that the shape's vertices can be transformed into world space, so that it isn't necessary to transform rays into object space before performing ray intersection tests. Interestingly enough, it is possible to do the same thing for ray–quadric intersections.

The implicit forms of the quadrics in this chapter were all of the form

$$Ax^2 + Bxy + Cxz + Dy^2 + Eyz + Fz^2 + G = 0,$$

where some of the constants $A \ldots G$ were zero. More generally, we can define quadric surfaces by the equation

$$Ax^2 + By^2 + Cz^2 + 2Dxy + 2Eyz + 2Fxz + 2Gx + 2Hy + 2Iz + J = 0,$$

where most of the parameters $A \ldots J$ don't directly correspond to the earlier $A \ldots G$. In this form, the quadric can be represented by a 4×4 symmetric matrix **Q**:

$$[x \quad y \quad z \quad 1] \begin{pmatrix} A & D & F & G \\ D & B & E & H \\ F & E & C & I \\ G & H & I & J \end{pmatrix} \begin{bmatrix} x \\ y \\ z \\ 1 \end{bmatrix} = \mathbf{p}^T \mathbf{Q} \mathbf{p} = 0.$$

Given this representation, first show that the matrix $\mathbf{Q}'$ representing a quadric transformed by the matrix $\mathbf{M}$ is

$$\mathbf{Q}' = (\mathbf{M}^T)^{-1} \mathbf{Q} \mathbf{M}^{-1}.$$

To do so, show that for any point $\mathbf{p}$ where $\mathbf{p}^T \mathbf{Q} \mathbf{p} = 0$, if we apply a transformation $\mathbf{M}$ to $\mathbf{p}$ and compute $\mathbf{p}' = \mathbf{M}\mathbf{p}$, we'd like to find $\mathbf{Q}'$ so that $(\mathbf{p}')^T \mathbf{Q}' \mathbf{p}' = 0$.

Next, substitute the ray equation into the earlier more general quadric equation to compute coefficients for the quadratic equation $at^2 + bt + c = 0$ in terms of entries of the matrix $\mathbf{Q}$ to pass to the Quadratic() function.

Now implement this approach in pbrt and use it instead of the original quadric intersection routines. Note that you will still need to transform the resulting world space hit points into object space to test against θ_{max}, if it is not 2π, and so on. How does performance compare to the original scheme?

❶ **3.2**   Improve the object space bounding box routines for the quadrics to properly account for $\phi_{max} < 3\pi/2$, and compute tighter bounding boxes when possible. How much does this improve performance when rendering scenes with partial quadric shapes?

❷ **3.3**   There is room to optimize the implementations of the various quadric primitives in pbrt in a number of ways. For example, for complete spheres some of the tests in the intersection routine related to partial spheres are unnecessary. Furthermore, some of the quadrics have calls to trigonometric functions that could be turned into simpler expressions using insight about the geometry of the particular primitives. Investigate ways to speed up these methods. How much does doing so improve the overall run time of pbrt when rendering scenes with quadrics?

❶ **3.4**   Currently pbrt recomputes the partial derivatives $\partial p/\partial u$ and $\partial p/\partial v$ for triangles every time they are needed, even though they are constant for each triangle. Precompute these vectors and analyze the speed/storage trade-off, especially for large triangle meshes. How do the depth complexity of the scene and the size of triangles in the image affect this trade-off?

❷ **3.5**   Implement a general polygon primitive that supports an arbitrary number of vertices and convex or concave polygons as a new Shape in pbrt. You can assume that a valid polygon has been provided and that all of the vertices of the polygon lie on the same plane, although you might want to issue a warning when this is not the case.

Quadratic() 1079
Shape 123

An efficient technique for computing ray–polygon intersections is to find the plane equation for the polygon from its normal and a point on the plane. Then compute the intersection of the ray with that plane and project the intersection point and the polygon vertices to 2D. Then apply a 2D point-in-polygon test

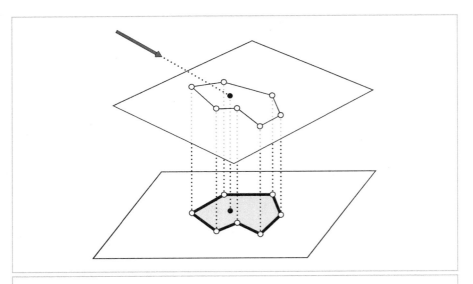

Figure 3.47: A ray–polygon intersection test can be performed by finding the point where the ray intersects the polygon's plane, projecting the hit point and polygon vertices onto an axis-aligned plane, and doing a 2D point-in-polygon test there.

to determine if the point is inside the polygon. An easy way to do this is to effectively do a 2D ray-tracing computation, intersect the ray with each of the edge segments, and count how many it goes through. If it goes through an odd number of them, the point is inside the polygon and there is an intersection. See Figure 3.47 for an illustration of this idea.

You may find it helpful to read the article by Haines (1994) that surveys a number of approaches for efficient point-in-polygon tests. Some of the techniques described there may be helpful for optimizing this test. Furthermore, Section 13.3.3 of Schneider and Eberly (2003) discusses strategies for getting all the corner cases right: for example, when the 2D ray is aligned precisely with an edge or passes through a vertex of the polygon.

● 3.6   Constructive solid geometry (CSG) is a classic solid modeling technique, where complex shapes are built up by considering the union, intersection, and differences of more primitive shapes. For example, a sphere could be used to create pits in a cylinder if a shape was modeled as the difference of a cylinder and set of spheres that partially overlapped it. See Hoffmann (1989) for further information about CSG.

Add support for CSG to pbrt and render images that demonstrate interesting shapes that can be rendered using CSG. You may want to read Roth (1982), which first described how ray tracing could be used to render models described by CSG, as well as Amanatides and Mitchell (1990), which discusses precision-related issues for CSG ray tracing.

3.7   Procedurally described parametric surfaces: Write a Shape that takes a general
mathematical expression of the form $f(u, v) \rightarrow (x, y, z)$ that describes a parametric surface as a function of (u, v). Evaluate the given function at a grid of
(u, v) positions, and create a triangle mesh that approximates the given surface.

3.8   Adaptive curve refinement: adjust the number of levels of recursive refinement
used for intersection with Curve shapes based on the on-screen area that they
cover. One approach is to take advantage of the RayDifferential class, which
represents the image space area that a given ray represents. (However, currently,
only Rays—not RayDifferentials—are passed to the Shape::Intersect()
method, so you'd need to modify other parts of the system to make ray differentials available.) Alternatively, you could modify the Camera to provide
information about the projected length of vectors between points in world
space on the image plane and make the camera available during Curve creation.

3.9   Almost all methods for subdivision surfaces are based on either refining a mesh
of triangles or a mesh of quadrilaterals. If a rendering system only supports
one type of mesh, meshes of the other type are typically tessellated to make
faces of the expected type in a preprocessing step. However, doing this can
introduce artifacts in the final subdivision surface. Read Stam and Loop's paper
on a hybrid subdivision scheme that supports meshes with both quadrilateral
and triangular faces (Stam and Loop 2003), and implement their method.
Demonstrate cases where the subdivision surface that your implementation
creates does not have artifacts that are present in the output from pbrt's current
subdivision implementation.

3.10   The smoothness of subdivision surfaces isn't always desirable. Sometimes it is
useful to be able to flag some edges of a subdivision control mesh as "creases"
and apply different subdivision rules there to preserve a sharp edge. Extend
the subdivision surface implementation in this chapter so that some edges can
be denoted as creases, and use the boundary subdivision rules to compute the
positions of vertices along those edges. Render images showing the difference
this makes.

3.11   Adaptive subdivision: a weakness of the subdivision surface implementation
in Section 3.8 is that each face is always refined a fixed number of times: this
may mean that some faces are underrefined, leading to visible faceting in the
triangle mesh, and some faces are overrefined, leading to excessive memory use
and rendering time. With adaptive subdivision, individual faces are no longer
subdivided once a particular error threshold has been reached.

An easy error threshold to implement computes the face normals of each face
and its directly adjacent faces. If they are sufficiently close to each other (e.g., as
tested via dot products), then the limit surface for that face will be reasonably
flat and further refinement will likely make little difference to the final surface.
Alternatively, you might want to approximate the area that a subdivided face
covers on the image plane and continue subdividing until this area becomes
sufficiently small. This approximation could be done using ray differentials;

see Section 10.1.1 for an explanation of how to relate the ray differential to the screen space footprint.

The trickiest part of this exercise is that some faces that don't need subdivision due to the flatness test will still need to be subdivided in order to provide vertices so that neighboring faces that do need to subdivide can get their vertex one-rings. In particular, adjacent faces can differ by no more than one level of subdivision. You may find it useful to read recent papers by Patney et al. (2009) and Fisher et al. (2009) for discussion of how to avoid cracks in adaptively subdivided meshes.

⊚ 3.12   Ray-tracing point-sampled geometry: extending methods for rendering complex models represented as a collection of point samples (Levoy and Whitted 1985; Pfister et al. 2000; Rusinkiewicz and Levoy 2000), Schaufler and Jensen (2000) have described a method for intersecting rays with collections of oriented point samples in space. They probabilistically determined that an intersection has occurred when a ray approaches a sufficient local density of point samples and computes a surface normal with a weighted average of the nearby samples. Read their paper and extend pbrt to support a point-sampled geometry shape. Do any of pbrt's basic interfaces need to be extended or generalized to support a shape like this?

⊚ 3.13   Deformation motion blur: the TransformedPrimitive in Section 4.1.2 of Chapter 4 supports animated shapes via transformations of primitives that vary over time. However, this type of animation isn't general enough to represent a triangle mesh where each vertex has a position given at the start time and another one at the end time. (For example, this type of animation description can be used to describe a running character model where different parts of the body are moving in different ways.) Implement a more general Triangle shape that supports specifying vertex positions at the start and end of frame and interpolates between them based on the ray time passed to the intersection methods. Be sure to update the bounding routines appropriately.

Triangle meshes with very large amounts of motion may exhibit poor performance due to triangles sweeping out very large bounding boxes and thus many ray–triangle intersections being performed that don't hit the triangle. Can you come up with approaches that could be used to reduce the impact of this problem?

⊚ 3.14   Implicit functions: just as implicit definitions of the quadric shapes are a useful starting point for deriving ray-intersection algorithms, more complex implicit functions can also be used to define interesting shapes. In particular, difficult-to-model organic shapes, water drops, and so on can be well represented by implicit surfaces. Blinn (1982a) introduced the idea of directly rendering implicit surfaces, and Wyvill and Wyvill (1989) gave a basis function for implicit surfaces with a number of advantages compared to Blinn's.

Implement a method for finding ray intersections with general implicit surfaces and add it to pbrt. You may wish to read papers by Kalra and Barr (1989) and Hart (1996) for methods for ray tracing them. Mitchell's algorithm for

TransformedPrimitive 252

robust ray intersections with implicit surfaces using interval arithmetic gives another effective method for finding these intersections (Mitchell 1990), and more recently Knoll et al. (2009) described refinements to this idea. You may find an approach along these lines easier to implement than the others. See Moore's book on interval arithmetic as needed for reference (Moore 1966).

● 3.15 L-systems: a very successful technique for procedurally modeling plants was introduced to graphics by Alvy Ray Smith (1984), who applied *Lindenmayer systems* (L-systems) to model branching plant structures. Prusinkiewicz and collaborators have generalized this approach to encompass a much wider variety of types of plants and effects that determine their appearance (Prusinkiewicz 1986; Prusinkiewicz, James, and Mech 1994; Deussen et al. 1998; Prusinkiewicz et al. 2001). L-systems describe the branching structure of these types of shapes via a grammar. The grammar can be evaluated to form expressions that describe a topological representation of a plant, which can then be translated into a geometric representation. Add an L-system primitive to pbrt that takes a grammar as input and evaluates it to create the shape it describes.

● 3.16 Given an arbitrary point (x, y, z), what bound on the error from applying a scale transformation of $(2, 1, 4)$ is given by Equation (3.16)? How much error is actually introduced?

● 3.17 The quadric shapes all use the EFloat class for their intersection tests in order to be able to bound the error in the computed t value so that intersections behind the ray origin aren't incorrectly reported as actual intersections. First, measure the performance difference when using regular Floats for one or more quadrics when rendering a scene that includes those shapes. Next, manually derive conservative error bounds for t values computed by those shapes as was done for triangles in Section 3.9.6. Implement your method. You may find it useful to use the EFloat class to empirically test your derivation's correctness. Measure the performance difference with your implementation.

● 3.18 One detail thwarts the watertightness of the current Triangle shape implementation: the translation and shearing of triangle vertices introduces round-off error, which must be accounted for in the extent of triangles' bounding boxes; see Section 3.3 of Woop et al. (2013) for discussion (and a solution). Modify pbrt to incorporate a solution to this shortcoming. Can you find scenes where small image errors are eliminated thanks to your fix?

● 3.19 Rendering in camera space: because floating-point arithmetic provides more precision near the origin than farther away from it, transforming the scene to a coordinate system with the camera at the origin can reduce the impact of error due to insufficient floating-point precision. (For example, consider the difference between rendering a scene in world space with the camera at (100000, 100000, 100000), looking at a unit sphere two units away versus a scene with the camera at the origin, also looking at a sphere two units away: many more bits of precision are available to represent intersection points in the latter case.)

EFloat 218
Triangle 156

Modify pbrt to primarily perform rendering computations in camera space, rather than world space, as it does currently. You'll need to modify the Camera implementations to return camera-space rays and modify shapes to transform incoming rays from camera space to object space. You'll want to transform the vertices of TriangleMeshes all the way to camera space. Measure the performance of your implementation versus an unmodified version of pbrt and render a variety of scenes with both systems. (In particular, make sure you test some scenes that have the camera far from the world space origin.) What sort of image differences do you see?

CHAPTER FOUR

04 PRIMITIVES AND INTERSECTION ACCELERATION

The classes described in the last chapter focus exclusively on representing geometric properties of 3D objects. Although the Shape class provides a convenient abstraction for geometric operations such as intersection and bounding, it doesn't contain enough information to fully describe an object in a scene. For example, it is necessary to bind material properties to each shape in order to specify its appearance. To accomplish these goals, this chapter introduces the Primitive abstract base class and provides a number of implementations.

Shapes to be rendered directly are represented by the GeometricPrimitive class. This class combines a Shape with a description of its appearance properties. So that the geometric and shading portions of pbrt can be cleanly separated, these appearance properties are encapsulated in the Material class, which is described in Chapter 9.

The TransformedPrimitive class handles two more general uses of Shapes in the scene: shapes with animated transformation matrices and object instancing, which can greatly reduce the memory requirements for scenes that contain many instances of the same geometry at different locations (such as the one in Figure 4.1). Implementing each of these features essentially requires injecting an additional transformation matrix between the Shape's notion of world space and the actual scene world space. Therefore, both are handled by a single class.

This chapter also introduces the Aggregate class, which represents a container that can hold many Primitives. pbrt uses this class as a base for *acceleration structures*—data structures that help reduce the otherwise $O(n)$ complexity of testing a ray for intersection with all n objects in a scene. Most rays will intersect only a few primitives and miss

Physically Based Rendering: From Theory To Implementation.
http://dx.doi.org/10.1016/B978-0-12-800645-0.50004-X

Figure 4.1: This outdoor scene makes heavy use of instancing as a mechanism for compressing the scene's description. There are only 24 million unique triangles in the scene, although, thanks to object reuse through instancing, the total geometric complexity is 3.1 billion triangles. (*Scene courtesy of Laubwerk.*)

the others by a large distance. If an intersection acceleration algorithm can reject whole groups of primitives at once, there will be a substantial performance improvement compared to simply testing each ray against each primitive in turn. One benefit from reusing the Primitive interface for these acceleration structures is that it makes it easy to support hybrid approaches where an accelerator of one type holds accelerators of other types.

This chapter describes the implementation of two accelerators, one, BVHAccel, based on building a hierarchy of bounding boxes around objects in the scene, and the second, KdTreeAccel, based on adaptive recursive spatial subdivision. While many other acceleration structures have been proposed, almost all ray tracers today use one of these two. The "Further Reading" section at the end of this chapter has extensive references to other possibilities.

4.1 PRIMITIVE INTERFACE AND GEOMETRIC PRIMITIVES

The abstract Primitive base class is the bridge between the geometry processing and shading subsystems of pbrt.

⟨*Primitive Declarations*⟩ ≡
```
class Primitive {
public:
    ⟨Primitive Interface 249⟩
};
```

BVHAccel 256
KdTreeAccel 285
Primitive 248

There are a number of geometric routines in the `Primitive` interface, all of which are similar to a corresponding `Shape` method. The first, `Primitive::WorldBound()`, returns a box that encloses the primitive's geometry in world space. There are many uses for such a bound; one of the most important is to place the `Primitive` in the acceleration data structures.

⟨*Primitive Interface*⟩ ≡   **248**
```
virtual Bounds3f WorldBound() const = 0;
```

The next two methods provide ray intersection tests. One difference between the two base classes is that `Shape::Intersect()` returns the parametric distance along the ray to the intersection in a `Float *` output variable, while `Primitive::Intersect()` is responsible for updating `Ray::tMax` with this value if an intersection is found.

⟨*Primitive Interface*⟩ +≡   **248**
```
virtual bool Intersect(const Ray &r, SurfaceInteraction *) const = 0;
virtual bool IntersectP(const Ray &r) const = 0;
```

Upon finding an intersection, the `Primitive`'s `Intersect()` method is also responsible for initializing additional `SurfaceInteraction` member variables, including a pointer to the `Primitive` that the ray hit.

⟨*SurfaceInteraction Public Data*⟩ +≡   **116**
```
const Primitive *primitive = nullptr;
```

`Primitive` objects have a few methods related to non-geometric properties as well. The first, `Primitive::GetAreaLight()`, returns a pointer to the `AreaLight` that describes the primitive's emission distribution, if the primitive is itself a light source. If the primitive is not emissive, this method should return `nullptr`.

⟨*Primitive Interface*⟩ +≡   **248**
```
virtual const AreaLight *GetAreaLight() const = 0;
```

`GetMaterial()` returns a pointer to the material instance assigned to the primitive. If `nullptr` is returned, ray intersections with the primitive should be ignored; the primitive only serves to delineate a volume of space for participating media. This method is also used to check if two rays have intersected the same object by comparing their `Material` pointers.

⟨*Primitive Interface*⟩ +≡   **248**
```
virtual const Material *GetMaterial() const = 0;
```

The third material-related method, `ComputeScatteringFunctions()`, initializes representations of the light-scattering properties of the material at the intersection point on the surface. The BSDF object (introduced in Section 9.1) describes local light-scattering properties at the intersection point. If applicable, this method also initializes a BSSRDF, which describes subsurface scattering inside the primitive—light that enters the surface at points far from where it exits. While subsurface light transport has little effect on the appearance of objects like metal, cloth, or plastic, it is the dominant light-scattering mechanism for biological materials like skin, thick liquids like milk, etc. The BSSRDF is supported by an extension of the path tracing algorithm discussed in Section 15.

In addition to a MemoryArena to allocate memory for the BSDF and/or BSSRDF, this method takes a TransportMode enumerant that indicates whether the ray path that found this intersection point started from the camera or from a light source; as will be discussed further in Section 16.1, this detail has important implications for how some parts of material models are evaluated. The allowMultipleLobes parameter controls a detail of how some types of BRDFs are represented; it is discussed further in Section 9.2. Section 9.1.1 discusses the use of the MemoryArena for BSDF memory allocation in more detail.

⟨*Primitive Interface*⟩ +≡   248
```
    virtual void ComputeScatteringFunctions(SurfaceInteraction *isect,
        MemoryArena &arena, TransportMode mode,
        bool allowMultipleLobes) const = 0;
```

The BSDF and BSSRDF pointers for the point are stored in the SurfaceInteraction passed to ComputeScatteringFunctions().

⟨*SurfaceInteraction Public Data*⟩ +≡   116
```
    BSDF *bsdf = nullptr;
    BSSRDF *bssrdf = nullptr;
```

4.1.1 GEOMETRIC PRIMITIVES

The GeometricPrimitive class represents a single shape (e.g., a sphere) in the scene. One GeometricPrimitive is allocated for each shape in the scene description provided by the user. This class is implemented in the files core/primitive.h and core/primitive.cpp.

⟨*GeometricPrimitive Declarations*⟩ ≡
```
    class GeometricPrimitive : public Primitive {
    public:
        ⟨GeometricPrimitive Public Methods⟩
    private:
        ⟨GeometricPrimitive Private Data 250⟩
    };
```

Each GeometricPrimitive holds a reference to a Shape and its Material. In addition, because primitives in pbrt may be area light sources, it stores a pointer to an AreaLight object that describes its emission characteristics (this pointer is set to nullptr if the primitive does not emit light). Finally, the MediumInterface attribute encodes information about the participating media on the inside and outside of the primitive.

⟨*GeometricPrimitive Private Data*⟩ ≡   250
```
    std::shared_ptr<Shape> shape;
    std::shared_ptr<Material> material;
    std::shared_ptr<AreaLight> areaLight;
    MediumInterface mediumInterface;
```

The GeometricPrimitive constructor just initializes these variables from the parameters passed to it. It's straightforward, so we don't include it here.

Most of the methods of the Primitive interface related to geometric processing are simply forwarded to the corresponding Shape method. For example, GeometricPrimitive::

Intersect() calls the Shape::Intersect() method of its enclosed Shape to do the actual intersection test and initialize a SurfaceInteraction to describe the intersection, if any. It also uses the returned parametric hit distance to update the Ray::tMax member. The advantage of storing the distance to the closest hit in Ray::tMax is that this makes it easy to avoid performing intersection tests with any primitives that lie farther along the ray than any already-found intersections.

⟨*GeometricPrimitive Method Definitions*⟩ ≡

```
bool GeometricPrimitive::Intersect(const Ray &r,
        SurfaceInteraction *isect) const {
    Float tHit;
    if (!shape->Intersect(r, &tHit, isect))
        return false;
    r.tMax = tHit;
    isect->primitive = this;
    ⟨Initialize SurfaceInteraction::mediumInterface after Shape intersection 685⟩
    return true;
}
```

We won't include the implementations of the GeometricPrimitive's WorldBound() or IntersectP() methods here; they just forward these requests on to the Shape in a similar manner. Similarly, GetAreaLight() just returns the GeometricPrimitive::areaLight member.

Finally, the ComputeScatteringFunctions() method just forwards the request on to the Material.

⟨*GeometricPrimitive Method Definitions*⟩ +≡

```
void GeometricPrimitive::ComputeScatteringFunctions(
        SurfaceInteraction *isect, MemoryArena &arena, TransportMode mode,
        bool allowMultipleLobes) const {
    if (material)
        material->ComputeScatteringFunctions(isect, arena, mode,
            allowMultipleLobes);
}
```

4.1.2 TransformedPrimitive: OBJECT INSTANCING AND ANIMATED PRIMITIVES

TransformedPrimitive holds a single Primitive and also includes an AnimatedTransform that is injected in between the underlying primitive and its representation in the scene. This extra transformation enables two useful features: object instancing and primitives with animated transformations.

Object instancing is a classic technique in rendering that reuses transformed copies of a single collection of geometry at multiple positions in a scene. For example, in a model of a concert hall with thousands of identical seats, the scene description can be compressed substantially if all of the seats refer to a shared geometric representation of a single seat. The ecosystem scene in Figure 4.1 has 23,241 individual plants of various types, although only 31 unique plant models. Because each plant model is instanced multiple times with a different transformation for each instance, the complete scene has a total of 3.1 billion triangles, although only 24 million triangles are stored in memory, thanks to primitive reuse through object instancing. pbrt uses just over 7 GB of memory when rendering this scene with object instancing (1.7 GB for BVHs, 2.3 GB for triangle meshes, and 3 GB for texture maps), but would need upward of 516 GB to render it without instancing.

Animated transformations enable rigid-body animation of primitives in the scene via the AnimatedTransform class. See Figure 2.15 for an image that exhibits motion blur due to animated transformations.

Recall that the Shapes of Chapter 3 themselves had object-to-world transformations applied to them to place them in the scene. If a shape is held by a TransformedPrimitive, then the shape's notion of world space isn't the actual scene world space—only after the TransformedPrimitive's transformation is also applied is the shape actually in world space. For the applications here, it makes sense for the shape to not be at all aware of the additional transformations being applied. For animated shapes, it's simpler to isolate all of the handling of animated transformations to a single class here, rather than require all Shapes to support AnimatedTransforms. Similarly, for instanced primitives, letting Shapes know all of the instance transforms is of limited utility: we wouldn't want the TriangleMesh to make a copy of its vertex positions for each instance transformation and transform them all the way to world space, since this would negate the memory savings of object instancing.

⟨*TransformedPrimitive Declarations*⟩ ≡
```
class TransformedPrimitive : public Primitive {
public:
    ⟨TransformedPrimitive Public Methods 252⟩
private:
    ⟨TransformedPrimitive Private Data 252⟩
};
```

The TransformedPrimitive constructor takes a reference to the Primitive that represents the model, and the transformation that places it in the scene. If the geometry is described by multiple Primitives, the calling code is responsible for placing them in an Aggregate implementation so that only a single Primitive needs to be stored here. For the code that creates aggregates as needed, see the pbrtObjectInstance() function in Section B.3.6 of Appendix B for the case of primitive instances, and see the pbrtShape() function in Section B.3.5 for animated shapes.

⟨*TransformedPrimitive Public Methods*⟩ ≡   252
```
TransformedPrimitive(std::shared_ptr<Primitive> &primitive,
        const AnimatedTransform &PrimitiveToWorld)
    : primitive(primitive), PrimitiveToWorld(PrimitiveToWorld) { }
```

⟨*TransformedPrimitive Private Data*⟩ ≡   252
```
std::shared_ptr<Primitive> primitive;
const AnimatedTransform PrimitiveToWorld;
```

The key task of the TransformedPrimitive is to bridge the Primitive interface that it implements and the Primitive that it holds a pointer to, accounting for the effects of the additional transformation that it holds. The TransformedPrimitive's PrimitiveToWorld transformation defines the transformation from the coordinate system of this particular instance of the geometry to world space. If the `primitive` member has its own transformation, that should be interpreted as the transformation from object space to the `TransformedPrimitive`'s coordinate system. The complete transformation to world space requires both of these transformations together.

As such, the `TransformedPrimitive::Intersect()` method transforms the given ray to the primitive's coordinate system and passes the transformed ray to its `Intersect()` routine. If a hit is found, the `tMax` value from the transformed ray needs to be copied into the ray r originally passed to the `Intersect()` routine.

⟨*TransformedPrimitive Method Definitions*⟩ ≡
```
bool TransformedPrimitive::Intersect(const Ray &r,
        SurfaceInteraction *isect) const {
    ⟨Compute ray after transformation by PrimitiveToWorld 253⟩
    if (!primitive->Intersect(ray, isect))
        return false;
    r.tMax = ray.tMax;
    ⟨Transform instance's intersection data to world space 253⟩
    return true;
}
```

To transform the ray, we need to interpolate the transformation based on the ray's time. Although we want to transform the ray r from world space to primitive space, here we actually interpolate `PrimitiveToWorld` and then invert the resulting `Transform` to get the transformation. This surprising approach is necessary because of how the polar decomposition-based transformation interpolation algorithm in Section 2.9.3 works: interpolating `PrimitiveToWorld` to some time and inverting it doesn't necessarily give the same result as interpolating its inverse, the animated world to primitive transformation, directly. Because `Primitive::WorldBound()` uses `PrimitiveToWorld` to compute the primitive's bounding box, we must also interpolate `PrimitiveToWorld` here for consistency.

⟨*Compute* ray *after transformation by* PrimitiveToWorld⟩ ≡   253
```
Transform InterpolatedPrimToWorld;
PrimitiveToWorld.Interpolate(r.time, &InterpolatedPrimToWorld);
Ray ray = Inverse(InterpolatedPrimToWorld)(r);
```

Finally, the `SurfaceInteraction` at the intersection point needs to be transformed to world space; the primitive's intersection member will already have transformed the `SurfaceInteraction` to its notion of world space, so here we only need to apply the effect of the additional transformation held here.

⟨*Transform instance's intersection data to world space*⟩ ≡   253
```
if (!InterpolatedPrimToWorld.IsIdentity())
    *isect = InterpolatedPrimToWorld(*isect);
```

The rest of the geometric `Primitive` methods are forwarded on to the shared instance, with the results similarly transformed as needed by the `TransformedPrimitive`'s transformation.

⟨*TransformedPrimitive Public Methods*⟩ +≡   252
```
Bounds3f WorldBound() const {
    return PrimitiveToWorld.MotionBounds(primitive->WorldBound());
}
```

The `TransformedPrimitive` `GetAreaLight()`, `GetMaterial()`, and `ComputeScattering` `Functions()` methods should never be called. The corresponding methods of the primitive that the ray actually hit should always be called instead. Therefore, any attempt to call the `TransformedPrimitive` implementations of these methods (not shown here) results in a run-time error.

4.2 AGGREGATES

Acceleration structures are one of the components at the heart of any ray tracer. Without algorithms to reduce the number of unnecessary ray intersection tests, tracing a single ray through a scene would take time linear in the number of primitives in the scene, since the ray would need to be tested against each primitive in turn to find the closest intersection. However, doing so is extremely wasteful in most scenes, since the ray passes nowhere near the vast majority of primitives. The goals of acceleration structures are to allow the quick, simultaneous rejection of *groups* of primitives and to order the search process so that nearby intersections are likely to be found first so that farther away ones can potentially be ignored.

Because ray–object intersections can account for the bulk of execution time in ray tracers, there has been a substantial amount of research into algorithms for ray intersection acceleration. We will not try to explore all of this work here but refer the interested reader to references in the "Further Reading" section at the end of this chapter and in particular Arvo and Kirk's chapter in *An Introduction to Ray Tracing* (Glassner 1989a), which has a useful taxonomy for classifying different approaches to ray-tracing acceleration.

Broadly speaking, there are two main approaches to this problem: spatial subdivision and object subdivision. Spatial subdivision algorithms decompose 3D space into regions (e.g., by superimposing a grid of axis-aligned boxes on the scene) and record which primitives overlap which regions. In some algorithms, the regions may also be adaptively subdivided based on the number of primitives that overlap them. When a ray intersection needs to be found, the sequence of these regions that the ray passes through is computed and only the primitives in the overlapping regions are tested for intersection.

In contrast, object subdivision is based on progressively breaking the objects in the scene down into smaller sets of constituent objects. For example, a model of a room might be broken down into four walls, a ceiling, and a chair. If a ray doesn't intersect the room's bounding volume, then all of its primitives can be culled. Otherwise, the ray is tested against each of them. If it hits the chair's bounding volume, for example, then it might be tested against each of its legs, the seat, and the back. Otherwise, the chair is culled.

Both of these approaches have been quite successful at solving the general problem of ray intersection computational requirements; there's no fundamental reason to prefer one over the other. The `KdTreeAccel` in this chapter is based on the spatial subdivision approach, and the `BVHAccel` is based on object subdivision.

The Aggregate class provides an interface for grouping multiple Primitive objects together. Because Aggregates themselves implement the Primitive interface, no special support is required elsewhere in pbrt for intersection acceleration. Integrators can be written as if there was just a single Primitive in the scene, checking for intersections without needing to be concerned about how they're actually found. Furthermore, by implementing acceleration in this way, it is easy to experiment with new acceleration techniques by simply adding a new Aggregate primitive to pbrt.

⟨*Aggregate Declarations*⟩ ≡
```
class Aggregate : public Primitive {
public:
    ⟨Aggregate Public Methods⟩
};
```

Like TransformedPrimitives do, the implementation of the Aggregate intersection methods leave the SurfaceInteraction::primitive pointer set to the primitive that the ray actually hit, not the aggregate that holds the primitive. Because pbrt uses this pointer to obtain information about the primitive being hit (its reflection and emission properties), the GetAreaLight(), GetMaterial(), and ComputeScatteringFunctions() methods of Aggregates should never be called, so the implementations of those methods (not shown here) issue a run-time error.

4.3 BOUNDING VOLUME HIERARCHIES

Bounding volume hierarchies (BVHs) are an approach for ray intersection acceleration based on primitive subdivision, where the primitives are partitioned into a hierarchy of disjoint sets. (In contrast, spatial subdivision generally partitions space into a hierarchy of disjoint sets.) Figure 4.2 shows a bounding volume hierarchy for a simple scene. Primitives are stored in the leaves, and each node stores a bounding box of the primitives in the nodes beneath it. Thus, as a ray traverses through the tree, any time it doesn't intersect a node's bounds, the subtree beneath that node can be skipped.

One property of primitive subdivision is that each primitive appears in the hierarchy only once. In contrast, a primitive may overlap multiple spatial regions with spatial subdivision and thus may be tested for intersection multiple times as the ray passes through them.[1] Another implication of this property is that the amount of memory needed to represent the primitive subdivision hierarchy is bounded. For a binary BVH that stores a single primitive in each leaf, the total number of nodes is $2n - 1$, where n is the number of primitives. There will be n leaf nodes and $n - 1$ interior nodes. If leaves store multiple primitives, fewer nodes are needed.

BVHs are more efficient to build than kd-trees, which generally deliver slightly faster ray intersection tests than BVHs but take substantially longer to build. On the other hand,

---

1   The *mailboxing* technique can be used to avoid these multiple intersections for accelerators that use spatial subdivision, though its implementation can be tricky in the presence of multi-threading. More information on mailboxing is available in the "Further Reading" section.

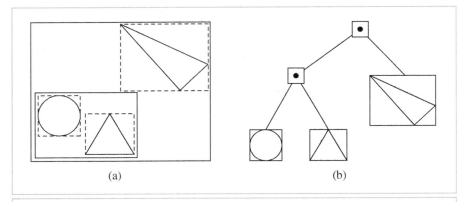

Figure 4.2: Bounding Volume Hierarchy for a Simple Scene. (a) A small collection of primitives, with bounding boxes shown by dashed lines. The primitives are aggregated based on proximity; here, the sphere and the equilateral triangle are bounded by another bounding box before being bounded by a bounding box that encompasses the entire scene (both shown in solid lines). (b) The corresponding bounding volume hierarchy. The root node holds the bounds of the entire scene. Here, it has two children, one storing a bounding box that encompasses the sphere and equilateral triangle (that in turn has those primitives as its children) and the other storing the bounding box that holds the skinny triangle.

BVHs are generally more numerically robust and less prone to missed intersections due to round-off errors than kd-trees are.

The BVH accelerator, BVHAccel, is defined in accelerators/bvh.h and accelerators/ bvh.cpp. In addition to the primitives to be stored and the maximum number of primitives that can be in any leaf node, its constructor takes an enumerant value that describes which of four algorithms to use when partitioning primitives to build the tree. The default, SAH, indicates that an algorithm based on the "surface area heuristic," discussed in Section 4.3.2, should be used. An alternative, HLBVH, which is discussed in Section 4.3.3, can be constructed more efficiently (and more easily parallelized), but it doesn't build trees that are as effective as SAH. The remaining two approaches use even less computation to build the tree but create fairly low-quality trees.

⟨*BVHAccel Public Types*⟩ ≡
```
enum class SplitMethod { SAH, HLBVH, Middle, EqualCounts };
```

⟨*BVHAccel Method Definitions*⟩ ≡
```
BVHAccel::BVHAccel(const std::vector<std::shared_ptr<Primitive>> &p,
        int maxPrimsInNode, SplitMethod splitMethod)
    : maxPrimsInNode(std::min(255, maxPrimsInNode)), primitives(p),
      splitMethod(splitMethod) {
    if (primitives.size() == 0)
        return;
    ⟨Build BVH from primitives 257⟩
}
```

BVHAccel 256
Primitive 248
SplitMethod 256

⟨*BVHAccel Private Data*⟩ ≡
```
const int maxPrimsInNode;
const SplitMethod splitMethod;
std::vector<std::shared_ptr<Primitive>> primitives;
```

4.3.1 BVH CONSTRUCTION

There are three stages to BVH construction in the implementation here. First, bounding information about each primitive is computed and stored in an array that will be used during tree construction. Next, the tree is built using the algorithm choice encoded in splitMethod. The result is a binary tree where each interior node holds pointers to its children and each leaf node holds references to one or more primitives. Finally, this tree is converted to a more compact (and thus more efficient) pointerless representation for use during rendering. (The implementation is more straightforward with this approach, versus computing the pointerless representation directly during tree construction, which is also possible.)

⟨*Build BVH from* primitives⟩ ≡   **256**
    ⟨*Initialize* primitiveInfo *array for primitives* **257**⟩
    ⟨*Build BVH tree for primitives using* primitiveInfo **258**⟩
    ⟨*Compute representation of depth-first traversal of BVH tree* **281**⟩

For each primitive to be stored in the BVH, we store the centroid of its bounding box, its complete bounding box, and its index in the primitives array in an instance of the BVHPrimitiveInfo structure.

⟨*Initialize* primitiveInfo *array for primitives*⟩ ≡   **257**
```
std::vector<BVHPrimitiveInfo> primitiveInfo(primitives.size());
for (size_t i = 0; i < primitives.size(); ++i)
    primitiveInfo[i] = { i, primitives[i]->WorldBound() };
```

⟨*BVHAccel Local Declarations*⟩ ≡
```
struct BVHPrimitiveInfo {
    BVHPrimitiveInfo(size_t primitiveNumber, const Bounds3f &bounds)
        : primitiveNumber(primitiveNumber), bounds(bounds),
          centroid(.5f * bounds.pMin + .5f * bounds.pMax) { }
    size_t primitiveNumber;
    Bounds3f bounds;
    Point3f centroid;
};
```

Hierarchy construction can now begin. If the HLBVH construction algorithm has been selected, HLBVHBuild() is called to build the tree. The other three construction algorithms are all handled by recursiveBuild(). The initial calls to these functions are passed all of the primitives to be stored in the tree. They return a pointer to the root of the tree, which is represented with the BVHBuildNode structure. Tree nodes should be allocated with the provided MemoryArena, and the total number created should be stored in *totalNodes.

One important side effect of the tree construction process is that a new array of pointers to primitives is returned via the orderedPrims parameter; this array stores the primitives ordered so that the primitives in leaf nodes occupy contiguous ranges in the array. It is swapped with the original primitives array after tree construction.

⟨*Build BVH tree for primitives using* primitiveInfo⟩ ≡   257
```
MemoryArena arena(1024 * 1024);
int totalNodes = 0;
std::vector<std::shared_ptr<Primitive>> orderedPrims;
BVHBuildNode *root;
if (splitMethod == SplitMethod::HLBVH)
    root = HLBVHBuild(arena, primitiveInfo, &totalNodes, orderedPrims);
else
    root = recursiveBuild(arena, primitiveInfo, 0, primitives.size(),
                          &totalNodes, orderedPrims);
primitives.swap(orderedPrims);
```

Each BVHBuildNode represents a node of the BVH. All nodes store a Bounds3f, which represents the bounds of all of the children beneath the node. Each interior node stores pointers to its two children in children. Interior nodes also record the coordinate axis along which primitives were partitioned for distribution to their two children; this information is used to improve the performance of the traversal algorithm. Leaf nodes need to record which primitive or primitives are stored in them; the elements of the BVHAccel::primitives array from the offset firstPrimOffset up to but not including firstPrimOffset + nPrimitives are the primitives in the leaf. (Hence the need for reordering the primitives array, so that this representation can be used, rather than, for example, storing a variable-sized array of primitive indices at each leaf node.)

⟨*BVHAccel Local Declarations*⟩ +≡
```
struct BVHBuildNode {
    ⟨BVHBuildNode Public Methods 258⟩
    Bounds3f bounds;
    BVHBuildNode *children[2];
    int splitAxis, firstPrimOffset, nPrimitives;
};
```

We'll distinguish between leaf and interior nodes by whether their children pointers have the value nullptr or not, respectively.

⟨*BVHBuildNode Public Methods*⟩ ≡   258
```
void InitLeaf(int first, int n, const Bounds3f &b) {
    firstPrimOffset = first;
    nPrimitives = n;
    bounds = b;
    children[0] = children[1] = nullptr;
}
```

The InitInterior() method requires that the two children nodes already have been created, so that their pointers can be passed in. This requirement makes it easy to compute the bounds of the interior node, since the children bounds are immediately available.

⟨*BVHBuildNode Public Methods*⟩ +≡   **258**
```
void InitInterior(int axis, BVHBuildNode *c0, BVHBuildNode *c1) {
    children[0] = c0;
    children[1] = c1;
    bounds = Union(c0->bounds, c1->bounds);
    splitAxis = axis;
    nPrimitives = 0;
}
```

In addition to a MemoryArena used for allocating nodes and the array of BVHPrimitiveInfo
structures, recursiveBuild() takes as parameters the range [start, end). It is responsible for returning a BVH for the subset of primitives represented by the range from
primitiveInfo[start] up to and including primitiveInfo[end-1]. If this range covers
only a single primitive, then the recursion has bottomed out and a leaf node is created.
Otherwise, this method partitions the elements of the array in that range using one of
the partitioning algorithms and reorders the array elements in the range accordingly, so
that the ranges from [start, mid) and [mid, end) represent the partitioned subsets. If the
partitioning is successful, these two primitive sets are in turn passed to recursive calls that
will themselves return pointers to nodes for the two children of the current node.

totalNodes tracks the total number of BVH nodes that have been created; this number
is used so that exactly the right number of the more compact LinearBVHNodes can be
allocated later. Finally, the orderedPrims array is used to store primitive references as
primitives are stored in leaf nodes of the tree. This array is initially empty; when a
leaf node is created, recursiveBuild() adds the primitives that overlap it to the end of
the array, making it possible for leaf nodes to just store an offset into this array and a
primitive count to represent the set of primitives that overlap it. Recall that when tree
construction is finished, BVHAccel::primitives is replaced with the ordered primitives
array created here.

⟨*BVHAccel Method Definitions*⟩ +≡
```
BVHBuildNode *BVHAccel::recursiveBuild(MemoryArena &arena,
        std::vector<BVHPrimitiveInfo> &primitiveInfo, int start,
        int end, int *totalNodes,
        std::vector<std::shared_ptr<Primitive>> &orderedPrims) {
    BVHBuildNode *node = arena.Alloc<BVHBuildNode>();
    (*totalNodes)++;
    ⟨Compute bounds of all primitives in BVH node 260⟩
    int nPrimitives = end - start;
    if (nPrimitives == 1) {
        ⟨Create leaf BVHBuildNode 260⟩
    } else {
        ⟨Compute bound of primitive centroids, choose split dimension dim 261⟩
        ⟨Partition primitives into two sets and build children 261⟩
    }
    return node;
}
```

⟨*Compute bounds of all primitives in BVH node*⟩ ≡   259

```
Bounds3f bounds;
for (int i = start; i < end; ++i)
    bounds = Union(bounds, primitiveInfo[i].bounds);
```

At leaf nodes, the primitives overlapping the leaf are appended to the orderedPrims array and a leaf node object is initialized.

⟨*Create leaf* BVHBuildNode⟩ ≡   259, 261, 268

```
int firstPrimOffset = orderedPrims.size();
for (int i = start; i < end; ++i) {
    int primNum = primitiveInfo[i].primitiveNumber;
    orderedPrims.push_back(primitives[primNum]);
}
node->InitLeaf(firstPrimOffset, nPrimitives, bounds);
return node;
```

For interior nodes, the collection of primitives must be partitioned between the two children subtrees. Given *n* primitives, there are in general $2^n - 2$ possible ways to partition them into two nonempty groups. In practice when building BVHs, one generally considers partitions along a coordinate axis, meaning that there are about $6n$ candidate partitions. (Along each axis, each primitive may be put into the first partition or the second partition.)

Here, we choose just one of the three coordinate axes to use in partitioning the primitives. We select the axis associated with the largest extent when projecting the bounding box centroid for the current set of primitives. (An alternative would be to try all three axes and select the one that gave the best result, but in practice this approach works well.) This approach gives good partitions in many scenes; Figure 4.3 illustrates the strategy.

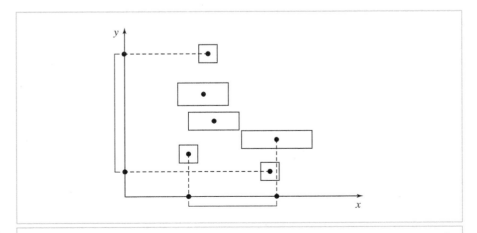

Figure 4.3: Choosing the Axis along Which to Partition Primitives. The BVHAccel chooses an axis along which to partition the primitives based on which axis has the largest range of the centroids of the primitives' bounding boxes. Here, in two dimensions, their extent is largest along the *y* axis (filled points on the axes), so the primitives will be partitioned in *y*.

The general goal in partitioning here is to select a partition of primitives that doesn't have too much overlap of the bounding boxes of the two resulting primitive sets—if there is substantial overlap then it will more frequently be necessary to traverse both children subtrees when traversing the tree, requiring more computation than if it had been possible to more effectively prune away collections of primitives. This idea of finding effective primitive partitions will be made more rigorous shortly, in the discussion of the surface area heuristic.

⟨*Compute bound of primitive centroids, choose split dimension* dim⟩ ≡   259
```
    Bounds3f centroidBounds;
    for (int i = start; i < end; ++i)
        centroidBounds = Union(centroidBounds, primitiveInfo[i].centroid);
    int dim = centroidBounds.MaximumExtent();
```

If all of the centroid points are at the same position (i.e., the centroid bounds have zero volume), then recursion stops and a leaf node is created with the primitives; none of the splitting methods here is effective in that (unusual) case. The primitives are otherwise partitioned using the chosen method and passed to two recursive calls to recursiveBuild().

⟨*Partition primitives into two sets and build children*⟩ ≡   259
```
    int mid = (start + end) / 2;
    if (centroidBounds.pMax[dim] == centroidBounds.pMin[dim]) {
        ⟨Create leaf BVHBuildNode 260⟩
    } else {
        ⟨Partition primitives based on splitMethod⟩
        node->InitInterior(dim,
                           recursiveBuild(arena, primitiveInfo, start, mid,
                                          totalNodes, orderedPrims),
                           recursiveBuild(arena, primitiveInfo, mid, end,
                                          totalNodes, orderedPrims));
    }
```

We won't include the code fragment ⟨*Partition primitives based on* splitMethod⟩ here; it just uses the value of BVHAccel::splitMethod to determine which primitive partitioning scheme to use. These three schemes will be described in the following few pages.

A simple splitMethod is Middle, which first computes the midpoint of the primitives' centroids along the splitting axis. This method is implemented in the fragment ⟨*Partition primitives through node's midpoint*⟩. The primitives are classified into the two sets, depending on whether their centroids are above or below the midpoint. This partitioning is easily done with the std::partition() C++ standard library function, which takes a range of elements in an array and a comparison function and orders the elements in the array so that all of the elements that return true for the given predicate function appear

in the range before those that return false for it.[2] std::partition() returns a pointer
to the first element that had a false value for the predicate, which is converted into an
offset into the primitiveInfo array so that we can pass it to the recursive call. Figure 4.4
illustrates this approach, including cases where it does and does not work well.

If the primitives all have large overlapping bounding boxes, this splitting method may
fail to separate the primitives into two groups. In that case, execution falls through to the
SplitMethod::EqualCounts approach to try again.

⟨*Partition primitives through node's midpoint*⟩ ≡
```
Float pmid = (centroidBounds.pMin[dim] + centroidBounds.pMax[dim]) / 2;
BVHPrimitiveInfo *midPtr =
    std::partition(&primitiveInfo[start], &primitiveInfo[end-1]+1,
        [dim, pmid](const BVHPrimitiveInfo &pi) {
            return pi.centroid[dim] < pmid;
        });
mid = midPtr - &primitiveInfo[0];
if (mid != start && mid != end)
    break;
```

When splitMethod is SplitMethod::EqualCounts, the ⟨*Partition primitives into equally
sized subsets*⟩ fragment runs. It partitions the primitives into two equal-sized subsets such
that the first half of the n of them are the $n/2$ with smallest centroid coordinate values
along the chosen axis, and the second half are the ones with the largest centroid coordinate values. While this approach can sometimes work well, the case in Figure 4.4(b) is
one where this method also fares poorly.

This scheme is also easily implemented with a standard library call, std::nth_element().
It takes a start, middle, and ending pointer as well as a comparison function. It orders
the array so that the element at the middle pointer is the one that would be there if the
array was fully sorted, and such that all of the elements before the middle one compare
to less than the middle element and all of the elements after it compare to greater than it.
This ordering can be done in $O(n)$ time, with n the number of elements, which is more
efficient than the $O(n \log n)$ of completely sorting the array.

⟨*Partition primitives into equally sized subsets*⟩ ≡   **265**
```
mid = (start + end) / 2;
std::nth_element(&primitiveInfo[start], &primitiveInfo[mid],
                &primitiveInfo[end-1]+1,
    [dim](const BVHPrimitiveInfo &a, const BVHPrimitiveInfo &b) {
        return a.centroid[dim] < b.centroid[dim];
    });
```

---

2   In the call to std::partition(), note the unusual expression of the indexing of the primitiveInfo array, &primitive
     Info[end-1]+1. The code is written in this way for somewhat obscure reasons. In the C and C++ programming languages, it
     is legal to compute the pointer one element past the end of an array so that iteration over array elements can continue until
     the current pointer is equal to the endpoint. To that end, we would like to just write the expression &primitiveInfo[end] here.
     However, primitiveInfo was allocated as a C++ vector; some vector implementations issue a run-time error if the offset
     passed to their [] operator is past the end of the array. Because we're not trying to reference the value of the element one
     past the end of the array but just compute its address, this operation is in fact safe. Therefore, we compute the same address
     in the end with the expression used here, while also satisfying any vector error checking.

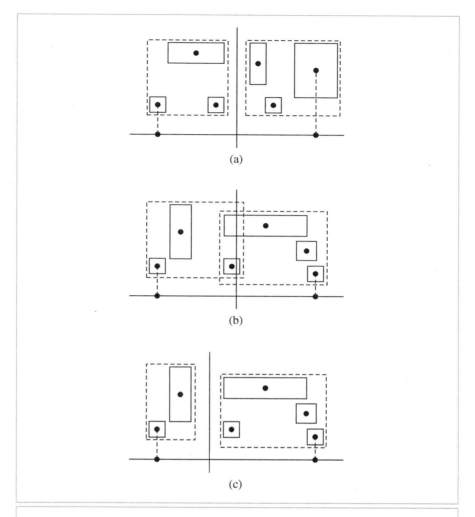

(a)

(b)

(c)

Figure 4.4: Splitting Primitives Based on the Midpoint of Centroids on an Axis. (a) For some distributions of primitives, such as the one shown here, splitting based on the midpoint of the centroids along the chosen axis works well. (The bounding boxes of the two resulting primitive groups are shown with dashed lines.) (b) For distributions like this one, the midpoint is a suboptimal choice; the two resulting bounding boxes overlap substantially. (c) If the same group of primitives from (b) is instead split along the line shown here, the resulting bounding boxes are smaller and don't overlap at all, leading to better performance when rendering.

4.3.2 THE SURFACE AREA HEURISTIC

The two primitive partitioning approaches above can work well for some distributions of primitives, but they often choose partitions that perform poorly in practice, leading to more nodes of the tree being visited by rays and hence unnecessarily inefficient ray–primitive intersection computations at rendering time. Most of the best current algorithms for building acceleration structures for ray-tracing are based on the "surface area heuristic" (SAH), which provides a well-grounded cost model for answering questions like "which of a number of partitions of primitives will lead to a better BVH for ray–primitive intersection tests?," or "which of a number of possible positions to split space in a spatial subdivision scheme will lead to a better acceleration structure?"

The SAH model estimates the computational expense of performing ray intersection tests, including the time spent traversing nodes of the tree and the time spent on ray–primitive intersection tests for a particular partitioning of primitives. Algorithms for building acceleration structures can then follow the goal of minimizing total cost. Typically, a greedy algorithm is used that minimizes the cost for each single node of the hierarchy being built individually.

The ideas behind the SAH cost model are straightforward: at any point in building an adaptive acceleration structure (primitive subdivision or spatial subdivision), we could just create a leaf node for the current region and geometry. In that case, any ray that passes through this region will be tested against all of the overlapping primitives and will incur a cost of

$$\sum_{i=1}^{N} t_{\text{isect}}(i),$$

where N is the number of primitives and $t_{\text{isect}}(i)$ is the time to compute a ray–object intersection with the ith primitive.

The other option is to split the region. In that case, rays will incur the cost

$$c(A, B) = t_{\text{trav}} + p_A \sum_{i=1}^{N_A} t_{\text{isect}}(a_i) + p_B \sum_{i=1}^{N_B} t_{\text{isect}}(b_i), \qquad [4.1]$$

where t_{trav} is the time it takes to traverse the interior node and determine which of the children the ray passes through, p_A and p_B are the probabilities that the ray passes through each of the child nodes (assuming binary subdivision), a_i and b_i are the indices of primitives in the two children nodes, and N_A and N_B are the number of primitives that overlap the regions of the two child nodes, respectively. The choice of how primitives are partitioned affects both the values of the two probabilities as well as the set of primitives on each side of the split.

In pbrt, we will make the simplifying assumption that $t_{\text{isect}}(i)$ is the same for all of the primitives; this assumption is probably not too far from reality, and any error that it introduces doesn't seem to affect the performance of accelerators very much. Another possibility would be to add a method to Primitive that returned an estimate of the number of CPU cycles its intersection test requires.

The probabilities p_A and p_B can be computed using ideas from geometric probability. It can be shown that for a convex volume A contained in another convex volume B, the conditional probability that a uniformly distributed random ray passing through B will also pass through A is the ratio of their surface areas, s_A and s_B:

$$p(A|B) = \frac{s_A}{s_B}.$$

Primitive 248

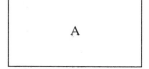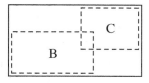

Figure 4.5: If a node of the bounding hierarchy with surface area s_A is split into two children with surface areas s_B and s_C, the probabilities that a ray passing through A also passes through B and C are given by s_B/s_A and s_C/s_A, respectively.

Because we are interested in the cost for rays passing through the node, we can use this result directly. Thus, if we are considering refining a region of space A such that there are two new subregions with bounds B and C (Figure 4.5), the probability that a ray passing through A will also pass through either of the subregions is easily computed.

When splitMethod has the value SplitMethod::SAH, the SAH is used for building the BVH; a partition of the primitives along the chosen axis that gives a minimal SAH cost estimate is found by considering a number of candidate partitions. (This is the default SplitMethod, and it creates the most efficient trees for rendering.) However, once it has refined down to a small handful of primitives, the implementation switches over to partitioning into equally sized subsets. The incremental computational cost for applying the SAH at this point isn't worthwhile.

⟨*Partition primitives using approximate SAH*⟩ ≡
    if (nPrimitives <= 4) {
        ⟨*Partition primitives into equally sized subsets* **262**⟩
    } else {
        ⟨*Allocate BucketInfo for SAH partition buckets* **266**⟩
        ⟨*Initialize BucketInfo for SAH partition buckets* **266**⟩
        ⟨*Compute costs for splitting after each bucket* **267**⟩
        ⟨*Find bucket to split at that minimizes SAH metric* **267**⟩
        ⟨*Either create leaf or split primitives at selected SAH bucket* **268**⟩
    }

Rather than exhaustively considering all $2n$ possible partitions along the axis, computing the SAH for each to select the best, the implementation here instead divides the range along the axis into a small number of buckets of equal extent. It then only considers partitions at bucket boundaries. This approach is more efficient than considering all partitions while usually still producing partitions that are nearly as effective. This idea is illustrated in Figure 4.6.

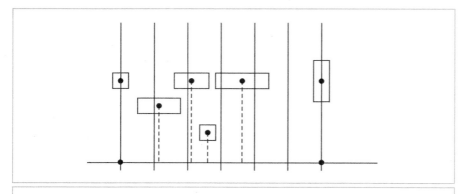

Figure 4.6: Choosing a Splitting Plane with the Surface Area Heuristic for BVHs. The projected extent of primitive bounds centroids is projected onto the chosen split axis. Each primitive is placed in a bucket along the axis based on the centroid of its bounds. The implementation then estimates the cost for splitting the primitives along the planes along each of the bucket boundaries (solid lines); whichever one gives the minimum cost per the surface area heuristic is selected.

⟨*Allocate* BucketInfo *for SAH partition buckets*⟩ ≡   **265**
```
constexpr int nBuckets = 12;
struct BucketInfo {
    int count = 0;
    Bounds3f bounds;
};
BucketInfo buckets[nBuckets];
```

For each primitive in the range, we determine the bucket that its centroid lies in and update the bucket's bounds to include the primitive's bounds.

⟨*Initialize* BucketInfo *for SAH partition buckets*⟩ ≡   **265**
```
for (int i = start; i < end; ++i) {
    int b = nBuckets *
        centroidBounds.Offset(primitiveInfo[i].centroid)[dim];
    if (b == nBuckets) b = nBuckets - 1;
    buckets[b].count++;
    buckets[b].bounds = Union(buckets[b].bounds, primitiveInfo[i].bounds);
}
```

For each bucket, we now have a count of the number of primitives and the bounds of all of their respective bounding boxes. We want to use the SAH to estimate the cost of splitting at each of the bucket boundaries. The fragment below loops over all of the buckets and initializes the cost[i] array to store the estimated SAH cost for splitting after the ith bucket. (It doesn't consider a split after the last bucket, which by definition wouldn't split the primitives.)

We arbitrarily set the estimated intersection cost to 1, and then set the estimated traversal cost to 1/8. (One of the two of them can always be set to 1 since it is the relative, rather than absolute, magnitudes of the estimated traversal and intersection costs that

determine their effect.) While the absolute amount of computation for node traversal—
a ray–bounding box intersection—is only slightly less than the amount of computation
needed to intersect a ray with a shape, ray–primitive intersection tests in pbrt go through
two virtual function calls, which add significant overhead, so we estimate their cost here
as eight times more than the ray–box intersection.

This computation has $O(n^2)$ complexity in the number of buckets, though a linear-time
implementation based on a forward scan over the buckets and a backward scan over the
buckets that incrementally compute and store bounds and counts is possible. For the
small n here, the performance impact is generally acceptable, though for a more highly
optimized renderer addressing this inefficiency may be worthwhile.

⟨*Compute costs for splitting after each bucket*⟩ ≡   265

```
Float cost[nBuckets - 1];
for (int i = 0; i < nBuckets - 1; ++i) {
    Bounds3f b0, b1;
    int count0 = 0, count1 = 0;
    for (int j = 0; j <= i; ++j) {
        b0 = Union(b0, buckets[j].bounds);
        count0 += buckets[j].count;
    }
    for (int j = i+1; j < nBuckets; ++j) {
        b1 = Union(b1, buckets[j].bounds);
        count1 += buckets[j].count;
    }
    cost[i] = .125f + (count0 * b0.SurfaceArea() +
                       count1 * b1.SurfaceArea()) / bounds.SurfaceArea();
}
```

Given all of the costs, a linear scan through the cost array finds the partition with
minimum cost.

⟨*Find bucket to split at that minimizes SAH metric*⟩ ≡   265

```
Float minCost = cost[0];
int minCostSplitBucket = 0;
for (int i = 1; i < nBuckets - 1; ++i) {
    if (cost[i] < minCost) {
        minCost = cost[i];
        minCostSplitBucket = i;
    }
}
```

If the chosen bucket boundary for partitioning has a lower estimated cost than building
a node with the existing primitives or if more than the maximum number of primitives
allowed in a node is present, the std::partition() function is used to do the work
of reordering nodes in the primitiveInfo array. Recall from its usage earlier that this
function ensures that all elements of the array that return true from the given predicate
appear before those that return false and that it returns a pointer to the first element
where the predicate returns false. Because we arbitrarily set the estimated intersection

cost to 1 previously, the estimated cost for just creating a leaf node is equal to the number of primitives, nPrimitives.

⟨*Either create leaf or split primitives at selected SAH bucket*⟩ ≡   **265**
```
      Float leafCost = nPrimitives;
      if (nPrimitives > maxPrimsInNode || minCost < leafCost) {
          BVHPrimitiveInfo *pmid = std::partition(&primitiveInfo[start],
              &primitiveInfo[end-1]+1,
              [=](const BVHPrimitiveInfo &pi) {
                  int b = nBuckets * centroidBounds.Offset(pi.centroid)[dim];
                  if (b == nBuckets) b = nBuckets - 1;
                  return b <= minCostSplitBucket;
              });
          mid = pmid - &primitiveInfo[0];
      } else {
          ⟨Create leaf BVHBuildNode 260⟩
      }
```

4.3.3 LINEAR BOUNDING VOLUME HIERARCHIES

While building bounding volume hierarchies using the surface area heuristic gives very good results, that approach does have two disadvantages: first, many passes are taken over the scene primitives to compute the SAH costs at all of the levels of the tree. Second, top-down BVH construction is difficult to parallelize well: the most obvious parallelization approach—performing parallel construction of independent subtrees—suffers from limited independent work until the top few levels of the tree have been built, which in turn inhibits parallel scalability. (This second issue is particularly an issue on GPUs, which perform poorly if massive parallelism isn't available.)

Linear bounding volume hierarchies (LBVHs) were developed to address these issues. With LBVHs, the tree is built with a small number of lightweight passes over the primitives; tree construction time is linear in the number of primitives. Further, the algorithm quickly partitions the primitives into clusters that can be processed independently. This processing can be fairly easily parallelized and is well suited to GPU implementation.

The key idea behind LBVHs is to turn BVH construction into a sorting problem. Because there's no single ordering function for sorting multi-dimensional data, LBVHs are based on *Morton codes*, which map nearby points in n dimensions to nearby points along the 1D line, where there is an obvious ordering function. After the primitives have been sorted, spatially nearby clusters of primitives are in contiguous segments of the sorted array.

Morton codes are based on a simple transformation: given n-dimensional integer coordinate values, their Morton-coded representation is found by interleaving the bits of the coordinates in base 2. For example, consider a 2D coordinate (x, y) where the bits of x and y are denoted by x_i and y_i. The corresponding Morton-coded value is

$$\cdots y_3\,x_3\,y_2\,x_2\,y_1\,x_1\,y_0\,x_0.$$

Bounds3::Offset() 81
BVHAccel::maxPrimsInNode 257
BVHPrimitiveInfo 257
Float 1062

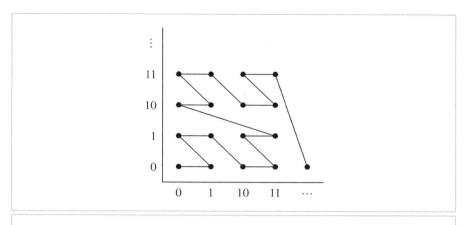

Figure 4.7: The Order That Points Are Visited along the Morton Curve. Coordinate values along the x and y axes are shown in binary. If we connect the integer coordinate points in the order of their Morton indices, we see that the Morton curve visits the points along a hierarchical "z"-shaped path.

Figure 4.7 shows a plot of the 2D points in Morton order—note that they are visited along a path that follows a reversed "z" shape. (The Morton path is sometimes called "z-order" for this reason.) We can see that points with coordinates that are close together in 2D are generally close together along the Morton curve.[3]

A Morton-encoded value also encodes useful information about the position of the point that it represents. Consider the case of 4-bit coordinate values in 2D: the x and y coordinates are integers in $[0, 15]$ and the Morton code has 8 bits: $y_3\,x_3\,y_2\,x_2\,y_1\,x_1\,y_0\,x_0$. Many interesting properties follow from the encoding; a few examples include:

- For a Morton-encoded 8-bit value where the high bit y_3 is set, then we know that the high bit of its underlying y coordinate is set and thus $y \geq 8$ (Figure 4.8(a)).
- The next bit value, x_3, splits the x axis in the middle (Figure 4.8(b)). If y_3 is set and x_3 is off, for example, then the corresponding point must lie in the shaded area of Figure 4.8(c). In general, points with a number of matching high bits lie in a power-of-two sized and aligned region of space determined by the matching bit values.
- The value of y_2 splits the y axis into four regions (Figure 4.8(d)).

Another way to interpret these bit-based properties is in terms of Morton-coded values. For example, Figure 4.8(a) corresponds to the index being in the range $[128, 255]$, and Figure 4.8(c) corresponds to $[128, 191]$. Thus, given a set of sorted Morton indices, we could find the range of points corresponding to an area like Figure 4.8(c) by performing a binary search to find each endpoint in the array.

LBVHs are BVHs built by partitioning primitives using splitting planes that are at the midpoint of each region of space (i.e., equivalent to the `SplitMethod::Middle` path

---

3   Many GPUs store texture maps in memory using a Morton layout. One advantage of doing so is that when performing bilinear interpolation between four texel values, the values are much more likely to be close together in memory than if the texture is laid out in scanline order. In turn, texture cache performance benefits.

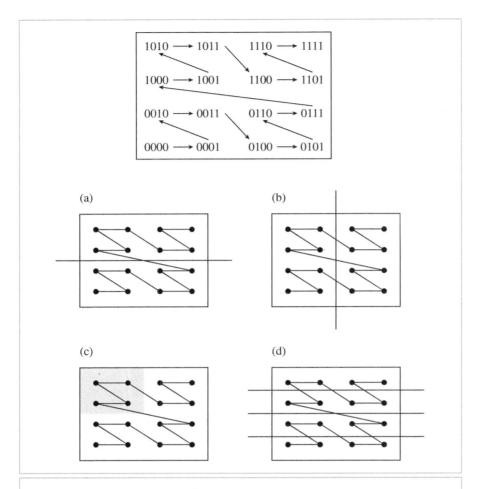

Figure 4.8: Implications of the Morton Encoding. The values of various bits in the Morton value indicate the region of space that the corresponding coordinate lies in. (a) In 2D, the high bit of the Morton-coded value of a point's coordinates define a splitting plane along the middle of the y axis. If the high bit is set, the point is above the plane. (b) Similarly, the second-highest bit of the Morton value splits the x axis in the middle. (c) If the high y bit is 1 and the high x bit is 0, then the point must lie in the shaded region. (d) The second-from-highest y bit splits the y axis into four regions.

defined earlier). Partitioning is extremely efficient, as it's based on properties of the Morton encoding described above.

Just reimplementing Middle in a different manner isn't particularly interesting, so in the implementation here, we'll build a *hierarchical linear bounding volume hierarchy* (HLBVH). With this approach, Morton-curve-based clustering is used to first build trees for the lower levels of the hierarchy (referred to as "treelets" in the following) and the top levels of the tree are then created using the surface area heuristic. The HLBVHBuild() method implements this approach and returns the root node of the resulting tree.

⟨*BVHAccel Method Definitions*⟩ +≡
```
BVHBuildNode *BVHAccel::HLBVHBuild(MemoryArena &arena,
        const std::vector<BVHPrimitiveInfo> &primitiveInfo,
        int *totalNodes,
        std::vector<std::shared_ptr<Primitive>> &orderedPrims) const {
    ⟨Compute bounding box of all primitive centroids 271⟩
    ⟨Compute Morton indices of primitives 271⟩
    ⟨Radix sort primitive Morton indices 273⟩
    ⟨Create LBVH treelets at bottom of BVH 275⟩
    ⟨Create and return SAH BVH from LBVH treelets 280⟩
}
```

The BVH is built using only the centroids of primitive bounding boxes to sort them—
it doesn't account for the actual spatial extent of each primitive. This simplification is
critical to the performance that HLBVHs offer, but it also means that for scenes with
primitives that span a wide range of sizes, the tree that is built won't account for this
variation as an SAH-based tree would.

Because the Morton encoding operates on integer coordinates, we first need to bound the
centroids of all of the primitives so that we can quantize centroid positions with respect
to the overall bounds.

⟨*Compute bounding box of all primitive centroids*⟩ ≡   271
```
Bounds3f bounds;
for (const BVHPrimitiveInfo &pi : primitiveInfo)
    bounds = Union(bounds, pi.centroid);
```

Given the overall bounds, we can now compute the Morton code for each primitive. This
is a fairly lightweight calculation, but given that there may be millions of primitives, it's
worth parallelizing. Note that a loop chunk size of 512 is passed to ParallelFor() below;
this causes worker threads to be given groups of 512 primitives to process rather than
one at a time as would otherwise be the default. Because the amount of work performed
per primitive to compute the Morton code is relatively small, this granularity better
amortizes the overhead of distributing tasks to the worker threads.

⟨*Compute Morton indices of primitives*⟩ ≡   271
```
std::vector<MortonPrimitive> mortonPrims(primitiveInfo.size());
ParallelFor(
    [&](int i) {
        ⟨Initialize mortonPrims[i] for ith primitive 272⟩
    }, primitiveInfo.size(), 512);
```

A MortonPrimitive instance is created for each primitive; it stores the index of the primitive in the primitiveInfo array as well as its Morton code.

⟨*BVHAccel Local Declarations*⟩ +≡
```
struct MortonPrimitive {
    int primitiveIndex;
    uint32_t mortonCode;
};
```

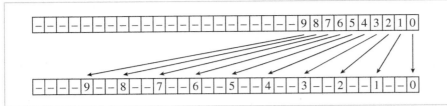

Figure 4.9: Bit Shifts to Compute 3D Morton Codes. The LeftShift3() function takes a 32-bit integer value and for the bottom 10 bits, shifts the ith bit to be in position $3i$—in other words, shifts it $2i$ places to the left. All other bits are set to zero.

We use 10 bits for each of the x, y, and z dimensions, giving a total of 30 bits for the Morton code. This granularity allows the values to fit into a single 32-bit variable. Floating-point centroid offsets inside the bounding box are in $[0, 1]$, so we scale them by 2^{10} to get integer coordinates that fit in 10 bits. (For the edge case of offsets exactly equal to 1, an out-of-range quantized value of 1024 may result; this case is handled in the forthcoming EncodeMorton3() function.)

⟨*Initialize* mortonPrims[i] *for* ith *primitive*⟩ ≡   271
```
constexpr int mortonBits = 10;
constexpr int mortonScale = 1 << mortonBits;
mortonPrims[i].primitiveIndex = primitiveInfo[i].primitiveNumber;
Vector3f centroidOffset = bounds.Offset(primitiveInfo[i].centroid);
mortonPrims[i].mortonCode = EncodeMorton3(centroidOffset * mortonScale);
```

To compute 3D Morton codes, first we'll define a helper function: LeftShift3() takes a 32-bit value and returns the result of shifting the ith bit to be at the $3i$th bit, leaving zeros in other bits. Figure 4.9 illustrates this operation.

The most obvious approach to implement this operation, shifting each bit value individually, isn't the most efficient. (It would require a total of 9 shifts, along with logical ORs to compute the final value.) Instead, we can decompose each bit's shift into multiple shifts of power-of-two size that together shift the bit's value to its final position. Then, all of the bits that need to be shifted a given power-of-two number of places can be shifted together. The LeftShift3() function implements this computation, and Figure 4.10 shows how it works.

⟨*BVHAccel Utility Functions*⟩ ≡
```
inline uint32_t LeftShift3(uint32_t x) {
    if (x == (1 << 10)) --x;
    x = (x | (x << 16)) & 0b00000011000000000000000011111111;
    x = (x | (x <<  8)) & 0b00000011000000001111000000001111;
    x = (x | (x <<  4)) & 0b00000011000011000011000011000011;
    x = (x | (x <<  2)) & 0b00001001001001001001001001001001;
    return x;
}
```

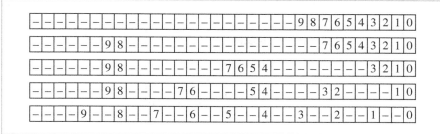

Figure 4.10: Power-of-Two Decomposition of Morton Bit Shifts. The bit shifts to compute the Morton code for each 3D coordinate are performed in a series of shifts of power-of-two size. First, bits 8 and 9 are shifted 16 places to the left. This places bit 8 in its final position. Next bits 4 through 7 are shifted 8 places. After shifts of 4 and 2 places (with appropriate masking so that each bit is shifted the right number of places in the end), all bits are in the proper position. This computation is implemented by the `LeftShift3()` function.

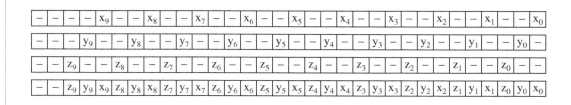

Figure 4.11: Final Interleaving of Coordinate Values. Given interleaved values for x, y, and z computed by `LeftShift3()`, the final Morton-encoded value is computed by shifting y and z one and two places, respectively, and then ORing together the results.

`EncodeMorton3()` takes a 3D coordinate value where each component is a floating-point value between 0 and 2^{10}. It converts these values to integers and then computes the Morton code by expanding the three 10-bit quantized values so that their ith bits are at position $3i$, then shifting the y bits over one more, the z bits over two more, and ORing together the result (Figure 4.11).

⟨*BVHAccel Utility Functions*⟩ +≡
```
inline uint32_t EncodeMorton3(const Vector3f &v) {
    return (LeftShift3(v.z) << 2) | (LeftShift3(v.y) << 1) |
        LeftShift3(v.x);
}
```

Once the Morton indices have been computed, we'll sort the `mortonPrims` by Morton index value using a radix sort. We have found that for BVH construction, our radix sort implementation is noticeably faster than using `std::sort()` from our system's standard library (which is a mixture of a quicksort and an insertion sort).

⟨*Radix sort primitive Morton indices*⟩ ≡   271
```
RadixSort(&mortonPrims);
```

Recall that a radix sort differs from most sorting algorithms in that it isn't based on comparing pairs of values but rather is based on bucketing items based on some key. Radix sort can be used to sort integer values by sorting them one digit at a time, going from the rightmost digit to the leftmost. Especially with binary values, it's worth sorting multiple digits at a time; doing so reduces the total number of passes taken over the data. In the implementation here, bitsPerPass sets the number of bits processed per pass; with the value 6, we have 5 passes to sort the 30 bits.

⟨*BVHAccel Utility Functions*⟩ +≡
```
static void RadixSort(std::vector<MortonPrimitive> *v) {
    std::vector<MortonPrimitive> tempVector(v->size());
    constexpr int bitsPerPass = 6;
    constexpr int nBits = 30;
    constexpr int nPasses = nBits / bitsPerPass;
    for (int pass = 0; pass < nPasses; ++pass) {
        ⟨Perform one pass of radix sort, sorting bitsPerPass bits 274⟩
    }
    ⟨Copy final result from tempVector, if needed 275⟩
}
```

The current pass will sort bitsPerPass bits, starting at lowBit.

⟨*Perform one pass of radix sort, sorting* bitsPerPass *bits*⟩ ≡   **274**
```
int lowBit = pass * bitsPerPass;
⟨Set in and out vector pointers for radix sort pass 274⟩
⟨Count number of zero bits in array for current radix sort bit 274⟩
⟨Compute starting index in output array for each bucket 275⟩
⟨Store sorted values in output array 275⟩
```

The in and out references correspond to the vector to be sorted and the vector to store the sorted values in, respectively. Each pass through the loop alternates between the input vector *v and the temporary vector for each of them.

⟨*Set in and out vector pointers for radix sort pass*⟩ ≡   **274**
```
std::vector<MortonPrimitive> &in  = (pass & 1) ? tempVector : *v;
std::vector<MortonPrimitive> &out = (pass & 1) ? *v : tempVector;
```

If we're sorting n bits per pass, then there are 2^n buckets that each value may land in. We first count how many values will land in each bucket; this will let us determine where to store sorted values in the output array. To compute the bucket index for the current value, the implementation shifts the index so that the bit at index lowBit is at bit 0 and then masks off the low bitsPerPass bits.

⟨*Count number of zero bits in array for current radix sort bit*⟩ ≡   **274**
```
constexpr int nBuckets = 1 << bitsPerPass;
int bucketCount[nBuckets] = { 0 };
constexpr int bitMask = (1 << bitsPerPass) - 1;
for (const MortonPrimitive &mp : in) {
    int bucket = (mp.mortonCode >> lowBit) & bitMask;
    ++bucketCount[bucket];
}
```

Given the count of how many values land in each bucket, we can compute the offset in the output array where each bucket's values start; this is just the sum of how many values land in the preceding buckets.

⟨*Compute starting index in output array for each bucket*⟩ ≡   274
```
int outIndex[nBuckets];
outIndex[0] = 0;
for (int i = 1; i < nBuckets; ++i)
    outIndex[i] = outIndex[i - 1] + bucketCount[i - 1];
```

Now that we know where to start storing values for each bucket, we can take another pass over the primitives to recompute the bucket that each one lands in and to store their MortonPrimitives in the output array. This completes the sorting pass for the current group of bits.

⟨*Store sorted values in output array*⟩ ≡   274
```
for (const MortonPrimitive &mp : in) {
    int bucket = (mp.mortonCode >> lowBit) & bitMask;
    out[outIndex[bucket]++] = mp;
}
```

When sorting is done, if an odd number of radix sort passes were performed, then the final sorted values need to be copied from the temporary vector to the output vector that was originally passed to RadixSort().

⟨*Copy final result from* tempVector, *if needed*⟩ ≡   274
```
if (nPasses & 1)
    std::swap(*v, tempVector);
```

Given the sorted array of primitives, we'll find clusters of primitives with nearby centroids and then create an LBVH over the primitives in each cluster. This step is a good one to parallelize as there are generally many clusters and each cluster can be processed independently.

⟨*Create LBVH treelets at bottom of BVH*⟩ ≡   271
    ⟨*Find intervals of primitives for each treelet* 276⟩
    ⟨*Create LBVHs for treelets in parallel* 277⟩

Each primitive cluster is represented by an LBVHTreelet. It encodes the index in the mortonPrims array of the first primitive in the cluster as well as the number of following primitives. (See Figure 4.12.)

⟨*BVHAccel Local Declarations*⟩ +≡
```
struct LBVHTreelet {
    int startIndex, nPrimitives;
    BVHBuildNode *buildNodes;
};
```

Recall from Figure 4.8 that a set of points with Morton codes that match in their high bit values lie in a power-of-two aligned and sized subset of the original volume. Because we have already sorted the mortonPrims array by Morton-coded value, primitives with matching high bit values are already together in contiguous sections of the array.

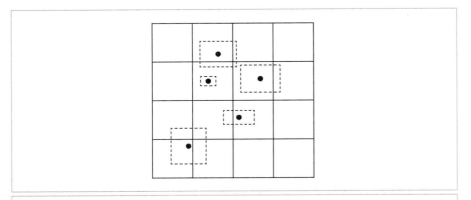

Figure 4.12: Primitive Clusters for LBVH Treelets. Primitive centroids are clustered in a uniform grid over their bounds. An LBVH is created for each cluster of primitives within a cell that are in contiguous sections of the sorted Morton index values.

Here we'll find sets of primitives that have the same values for the high 12 bits of their 30-bit Morton codes. Clusters are found by taking a linear pass through the mortonPrims array and finding the offsets where any of the high 12 bits changes. This corresponds to clustering primitives in a regular grid of $2^{12} = 4096$ total grid cells with $2^4 = 16$ cells in each dimension. In practice, many of the grid cells will be empty, though we'll still expect to find many independent clusters here.

⟨*Find intervals of primitives for each treelet*⟩ ≡   275
```
std::vector<LBVHTreelet> treeletsToBuild;
for (int start = 0, end = 1; end <= (int)mortonPrims.size(); ++end) {
    uint32_t mask = 0b00111111111111000000000000000000;
    if (end == (int)mortonPrims.size() ||
        ((mortonPrims[start].mortonCode & mask) !=
         (mortonPrims[end].mortonCode & mask))) {
        ⟨Add entry to treeletsToBuild for this treelet 277⟩
        start = end;
    }
}
```

When a cluster of primitives has been found for a treelet, BVHBuildNodes are immediately allocated for it. (Recall that the number of nodes in a BVH is bounded by twice the number of leaf nodes, which in turn is bounded by the number of primitives). It's simpler to pre-allocate this memory now in a serial phase of execution than during parallel construction of LBVHs.

One important detail here is the false value passed to MemoryArena::Alloc(); it indicates that the constructors of the underlying objects being allocated should not be executed. To our surprise, running the BVHBuildNode constructors introduced significant overhead and meaningfully reduced overall HLBVH construction performance. Because all of the members of BVHBuildNode will be initialized in code to follow, the initialization performed by the constructor is unnecessary here in any case.

⟨*Add entry to* `treeletsToBuild` *for this treelet*⟩ ≡   276
```
int nPrimitives = end - start;
int maxBVHNodes = 2 * nPrimitives;
BVHBuildNode *nodes = arena.Alloc<BVHBuildNode>(maxBVHNodes, false);
treeletsToBuild.push_back({start, nPrimitives, nodes});
```

Once the primitives for each treelet have been identified, we can create LBVHs for them in parallel. When construction is finished, the `buildNodes` pointer for each `LBVHTreelet` will point to the root of the corresponding LBVH.

There are two places where the worker threads building LBVHs must coordinate with each other. First, the total number of nodes in all of the LVBHs needs to be computed and returned via the `totalNodes` pointer passed to `HLBVHBuild()`. Second, when leaf nodes are created for the LBVHs, a contiguous segment of the `orderedPrims` array is needed to record the indices of the primitives in the leaf node. Our implementation uses atomic variables for both—`atomicTotal` to track the number of nodes and `orderedPrimsOffset` for the index of the next available entry in `orderedPrims`.

⟨*Create LBVHs for treelets in parallel*⟩ ≡   275
```
std::atomic<int> atomicTotal(0), orderedPrimsOffset(0);
orderedPrims.resize(primitives.size());
ParallelFor(
    [&](int i) {
        ⟨Generate ith LBVH treelet 277⟩
    }, treeletsToBuild.size());
*totalNodes = atomicTotal;
```

The work of building the treelet is performed by `emitLBVH()`, which takes primitives with centroids in some region of space and successively partitions them with splitting planes that divide the current region of space into two halves along the center of the region along one of the three axes.

Note that instead of taking a pointer to the atomic variable `atomicTotal` to count the number of nodes created, `emitLBVH()` updates a non-atomic local variable. The fragment here then only updates `atomicTotal` once per treelet when each treelet is done. This approach gives measurably better performance than the alternative—having the worker threads frequently modify `atomicTotal` over the course of their execution. (See the discussion of the overhead of multi-core memory coherence models in Appendix A.6.1.)

⟨*Generate ith LBVH treelet*⟩ ≡   277
```
int nodesCreated = 0;
const int firstBitIndex = 29 - 12;
LBVHTreelet &tr = treeletsToBuild[i];
tr.buildNodes =
    emitLBVH(tr.buildNodes, primitiveInfo, &mortonPrims[tr.startIndex],
             tr.nPrimitives, &nodesCreated, orderedPrims,
             &orderedPrimsOffset, firstBitIndex);
atomicTotal += nodesCreated;
```

Thanks to the Morton encoding, the current region of space doesn't need to be explicitly represented in emitLBVH(): the sorted MortonPrims passed in have some number of matching high bits, which in turn corresponds to a spatial bound. For each of the remaining bits in the Morton codes, this function tries to split the primitives along the plane corresponding to the bit bitIndex (recall Figure 4.8(d)) and then calls itself recursively. The index of the next bit to try splitting with is passed as the last argument to the function: initially it's $29 - 12$, since 29 is the index of the 30th bit with zero-based indexing, and we previously used the high 12 bits of the Morton-coded value to cluster the primitives; thus, we know that those bits must all match for the cluster.

⟨*BVHAccel Method Definitions*⟩ +≡
```
BVHBuildNode *BVHAccel::emitLBVH(BVHBuildNode *&buildNodes,
        const std::vector<BVHPrimitiveInfo> &primitiveInfo,
        MortonPrimitive *mortonPrims, int nPrimitives, int *totalNodes,
        std::vector<std::shared_ptr<Primitive>> &orderedPrims,
        std::atomic<int> *orderedPrimsOffset, int bitIndex) const {
    if (bitIndex == -1 || nPrimitives < maxPrimsInNode) {
        ⟨Create and return leaf node of LBVH treelet 278⟩
    } else {
        int mask = 1 << bitIndex;
        ⟨Advance to next subtree level if there's no LBVH split for this bit 279⟩
        ⟨Find LBVH split point for this dimension 279⟩
        ⟨Create and return interior LBVH node 279⟩
    }
}
```

After emitLBVH() has partitioned the primitives with the final low bit, no more splitting is possible and a leaf node is created. Alternatively, it also stops and makes a leaf node if it's down to a small number of primitives.

Recall that orderedPrimsOffset is the offset to the next available element in the ordered Prims array. Here, the call to fetch_add() atomically adds the value of nPrimitives to orderedPrimsOffset and returns its old value before the addition. Because these operations are atomic, multiple LBVH construction threads can concurrently carve out space in the orderedPrims array without data races. Given space in the array, leaf construction is similar to the approach implemented earlier in ⟨*Create leaf* BVHBuildNode⟩.

⟨*Create and return leaf node of LBVH treelet*⟩ ≡   **278**
```
(*totalNodes)++;
BVHBuildNode *node = buildNodes++;
Bounds3f bounds;
int firstPrimOffset = orderedPrimsOffset->fetch_add(nPrimitives);
for (int i = 0; i < nPrimitives; ++i) {
    int primitiveIndex = mortonPrims[i].primitiveIndex;
    orderedPrims[firstPrimOffset + i] = primitives[primitiveIndex];
    bounds = Union(bounds, primitiveInfo[primitiveIndex].bounds);
}
node->InitLeaf(firstPrimOffset, nPrimitives, bounds);
return node;
```

It may be the case that all of the primitives lie on the same side of the splitting plane; since the primitives are sorted by their Morton index, this case can be efficiently checked by seeing if the first and last primitive in the range both have the same bit value for this plane. In this case, emitLBVH() proceeds to the next bit without unnecessarily creating a node.

⟨*Advance to next subtree level if there's no LBVH split for this bit*⟩ ≡   278
```
if ((mortonPrims[0].mortonCode & mask) ==
    (mortonPrims[nPrimitives - 1].mortonCode & mask))
    return emitLBVH(buildNodes, primitiveInfo, mortonPrims, nPrimitives,
                    totalNodes, orderedPrims, orderedPrimsOffset,
                    bitIndex - 1);
```

If there are primitives on both sides of the splitting plane, then a binary search efficiently finds the dividing point where the bitIndexth bit goes from 0 to 1 in the current set of primitives.

⟨*Find LBVH split point for this dimension*⟩ ≡   278
```
int searchStart = 0, searchEnd = nPrimitives - 1;
while (searchStart + 1 != searchEnd) {
    int mid = (searchStart + searchEnd) / 2;
    if ((mortonPrims[searchStart].mortonCode & mask) ==
        (mortonPrims[mid].mortonCode & mask))
        searchStart = mid;
    else
        searchEnd = mid;
}
int splitOffset = searchEnd;
```

Given the split offset, the method can now claim a node to use as an interior node and recursively build LBVHs for both partitioned sets of primitives. Note a further efficiency benefit from Morton encoding: entries in the mortonPrims array don't need to be copied or reordered for the partition: because they are all sorted by their Morton code value and because it is processing bits from high to low, the two spans of primitives are already on the correct sides of the partition plane.

⟨*Create and return interior LBVH node*⟩ ≡   278
```
(*totalNodes)++;
BVHBuildNode *node = buildNodes++;
BVHBuildNode *lbvh[2] = {
    emitLBVH(buildNodes, primitiveInfo, mortonPrims, splitOffset,
             totalNodes, orderedPrims, orderedPrimsOffset, bitIndex - 1),
    emitLBVH(buildNodes, primitiveInfo, &mortonPrims[splitOffset],
             nPrimitives - splitOffset, totalNodes, orderedPrims,
             orderedPrimsOffset, bitIndex - 1)
};
int axis = bitIndex % 3;
node->InitInterior(axis, lbvh[0], lbvh[1]);
return node;
```

Once all of the LBVH treelets have been created, buildUpperSAH() creates a BVH of all the treelets. Since there are generally tens or hundreds of them (and in any case, no more than 4096), this step takes very little time.

⟨*Create and return SAH BVH from LBVH treelets*⟩ ≡   **271**
```
std::vector<BVHBuildNode *> finishedTreelets;
for (LBVHTreelet &treelet : treeletsToBuild)
    finishedTreelets.push_back(treelet.buildNodes);
return buildUpperSAH(arena, finishedTreelets, 0,
                     finishedTreelets.size(), totalNodes);
```

The implementation of this method isn't included here, as it follows the same approach as fully SAH-based BVH construction, just over treelet root nodes rather than scene primitives.

⟨*BVHAccel Private Methods*⟩ ≡
```
BVHBuildNode *buildUpperSAH(MemoryArena &arena,
    std::vector<BVHBuildNode *> &treeletRoots, int start, int end,
    int *totalNodes) const;
```

4.3.4 COMPACT BVH FOR TRAVERSAL

Once the BVH tree is built, the last step is to convert it into a compact representation—doing so improves cache, memory, and thus overall system performance. The final BVH is stored in a linear array in memory. The nodes of the original tree are laid out in depth-first order, which means that the first child of each interior node is immediately after the node in memory. In this case, only the offset to the second child of each interior node must be stored explicitly. See Figure 4.13 for an illustration of the relationship between tree topology and node order in memory.

The LinearBVHNode structure stores the information needed to traverse the BVH. In addition to the bounding box for each node, for leaf nodes it stores the offset and

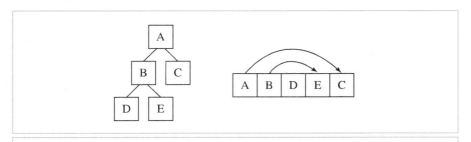

Figure 4.13: Linear Layout of a BVH in Memory. The nodes of the BVH (left) are stored in memory in depth-first order (right). Therefore, for any interior node of the tree (A and B in this example), the first child is found immediately after the parent node in memory. The second child is found via an offset pointer, represented here with lines with arrows. Leaf nodes of the tree (D, E, and C) have no children.

primitive count for the primitives in the node. For interior nodes, it stores the offset to the second child as well as which of the coordinate axes the primitives were partitioned along when the hierarchy was built; this information is used in the traversal routine below to try to visit nodes in front-to-back order along the ray.

⟨*BVHAccel Local Declarations*⟩ +≡
```
struct LinearBVHNode {
    Bounds3f bounds;
    union {
        int primitivesOffset;    // leaf
        int secondChildOffset;   // interior
    };
    uint16_t nPrimitives;   // 0 -> interior node
    uint8_t axis;           // interior node: xyz
    uint8_t pad[1];         // ensure 32 byte total size
};
```

This structure is padded to ensure that it's 32 bytes large. Doing so ensures that, if the nodes are allocated such that the first node is cache-line aligned, then none of the subsequent nodes will straddle cache lines (as long as the cache line size is at least 32 bytes, which is the case on modern CPU architectures).

The built tree is transformed to the `LinearBVHNode` representation by the `flattenBVH Tree()` method, which performs a depth-first traversal and stores the nodes in memory in linear order.

⟨*Compute representation of depth-first traversal of BVH tree*⟩ ≡   257
```
nodes = AllocAligned<LinearBVHNode>(totalNodes);
int offset = 0;
flattenBVHTree(root, &offset);
```

The pointer to the array of `LinearBVHNodes` is stored as a `BVHAccel` member variable so that it can be freed in the `BVHAccel` destructor.

⟨*BVHAccel Private Data*⟩ +≡
```
LinearBVHNode *nodes = nullptr;
```

Flattening the tree to the linear representation is straightforward; the `*offset` parameter tracks the current offset into the `BVHAccel::nodes` array. Note that the current node is added to the array before the recursive calls to process its children (if the node is an interior node).

⟨*BVHAccel Method Definitions*⟩ +≡
```
int BVHAccel::flattenBVHTree(BVHBuildNode *node, int *offset) {
    LinearBVHNode *linearNode = &nodes[*offset];
    linearNode->bounds = node->bounds;
    int myOffset = (*offset)++;
    if (node->nPrimitives > 0) {
        linearNode->primitivesOffset = node->firstPrimOffset;
        linearNode->nPrimitives = node->nPrimitives;
    } else {
        ⟨Create interior flattened BVH node 282⟩
    }
    return myOffset;
}
```

At interior nodes, recursive calls are made to flatten the two subtrees. The first one ends up immediately after the current node in the array, as desired, and the offset of the second one, returned by its recursive flattenBVHTree() call, is stored in this node's secondChildOffset member.

⟨*Create interior flattened BVH node*⟩ ≡   **282**
```
linearNode->axis = node->splitAxis;
linearNode->nPrimitives = 0;
flattenBVHTree(node->children[0], offset);
linearNode->secondChildOffset =
    flattenBVHTree(node->children[1], offset);
```

4.3.5 TRAVERSAL

The BVH traversal code is quite simple—there are no recursive function calls and only a tiny amount of data to maintain about the current state of the traversal. The Intersect() method starts by precomputing a few values related to the ray that will be used repeatedly.

⟨*BVHAccel Method Definitions*⟩ +≡
```
bool BVHAccel::Intersect(const Ray &ray,
        SurfaceInteraction *isect) const {
    bool hit = false;
    Vector3f invDir(1 / ray.d.x, 1 / ray.d.y, 1 / ray.d.z);
    int dirIsNeg[3] = { invDir.x < 0, invDir.y < 0, invDir.z < 0 };
    ⟨Follow ray through BVH nodes to find primitive intersections 283⟩
    return hit;
}
```

Each time the while loop in Intersect() starts an iteration, currentNodeIndex holds the offset into the nodes array of the node to be visited. It starts with a value of 0, representing the root of the tree. The nodes that still need to be visited are stored in the nodesToVisit[] array, which acts as a stack; toVisitOffset holds the offset to the next free element in the stack.

⟨*Follow ray through BVH nodes to find primitive intersections*⟩ ≡   282
```
    int toVisitOffset = 0, currentNodeIndex = 0;
    int nodesToVisit[64];
    while (true) {
        const LinearBVHNode *node = &nodes[currentNodeIndex];
        ⟨Check ray against BVH node 283⟩
    }
```

At each node, we check to see if the ray intersects the node's bounding box (or starts inside of it). We visit the node if so, testing for intersection with its primitives if it's a leaf node or processing its children if it's an interior node. If no intersection is found, then the offset of the next node to be visited is retrieved from nodesToVisit[] (or traversal is complete if the stack is empty).

⟨*Check ray against BVH node*⟩ ≡   283
```
    if (node->bounds.IntersectP(ray, invDir, dirIsNeg)) {
        if (node->nPrimitives > 0) {
            ⟨Intersect ray with primitives in leaf BVH node 283⟩
        } else {
            ⟨Put far BVH node on nodesToVisit stack, advance to near node 284⟩
        }
    } else {
        if (toVisitOffset == 0) break;
        currentNodeIndex = nodesToVisit[--toVisitOffset];
    }
```

If the current node is a leaf, then the ray must be tested for intersection with the primitives inside it. The next node to visit is then found from the nodesToVisit stack; even if an intersection is found in the current node, the remaining nodes must be visited, in case one of them yields a closer intersection. However, if an intersection is found, the ray's tMax value will be updated to the intersection distance; this makes it possible to efficiently discard any remaining nodes that are farther away than the intersection.

⟨*Intersect ray with primitives in leaf BVH node*⟩ ≡   283
```
    for (int i = 0; i < node->nPrimitives; ++i)
        if (primitives[node->primitivesOffset + i]->Intersect(ray, isect))
            hit = true;
    if (toVisitOffset == 0) break;
    currentNodeIndex = nodesToVisit[--toVisitOffset];
```

For an interior node that the ray hits, it is necessary to visit both of its children. As described above, it's desirable to visit the first child that the ray passes through before visiting the second one, in case there is a primitive that the ray intersects in the first one, so that the ray's tMax value can be updated, thus reducing the ray's extent and thus the number of node bounding boxes it intersects.

An efficient way to perform a front-to-back traversal without incurring the expense of intersecting the ray with both child nodes and comparing the distances is to use the sign of the ray's direction vector for the coordinate axis along which primitives were partitioned for the current node: if the sign is negative, we should visit the second child before the first child, since the primitives that went into the second child's subtree were on the upper side of the partition point. (And conversely for a positive-signed direction.) Doing this is straightforward: the offset for the node to be visited first is copied to currentNodeIndex, and the offset for the other node is added to the nodesToVisit stack. (Recall that the first child is immediately after the current node due to the depth-first layout of nodes in memory.)

⟨*Put far BVH node on* nodesToVisit *stack, advance to near node*⟩ ≡   283
```
if (dirIsNeg[node->axis]) {
    nodesToVisit[toVisitOffset++] = currentNodeIndex + 1;
    currentNodeIndex = node->secondChildOffset;
} else {
    nodesToVisit[toVisitOffset++] = node->secondChildOffset;
    currentNodeIndex = currentNodeIndex + 1;
}
```

The BVHAccel::IntersectP() method is essentially the same as the regular intersection method, with the two differences that Primitive's IntersectP() methods are called rather than Intersect(), and traversal stops immediately when any intersection is found.

4.4 KD-TREE ACCELERATOR

Binary space partitioning (BSP) trees adaptively subdivide space with planes. A BSP tree starts with a bounding box that encompasses the entire scene. If the number of primitives in the box is greater than some threshold, the box is split in half by a plane. Primitives are then associated with whichever half they overlap, and primitives that lie in both halves are associated with both of them. (This is in contrast to BVHs, where each primitive is assigned to only one of the two subgroups after a split.)

The splitting process continues recursively either until each leaf region in the resulting tree contains a sufficiently small number of primitives or until a maximum depth is reached. Because the splitting planes can be placed at arbitrary positions inside the overall bound and because different parts of 3D space can be refined to different degrees, BSP trees can easily handle uneven distributions of geometry.

Two variations of BSP trees are *kd-trees* and *octrees*. A kd-tree simply restricts the splitting plane to be perpendicular to one of the coordinate axes; this makes both traversal and construction of the tree more efficient, at the cost of some flexibility in how space is subdivided. The octree uses three axis-perpendicular planes to simultaneously split the box into eight regions at each step (typically by splitting down the center of the extent in each direction). In this section, we will implement a kd-tree for ray intersection acceleration in the KdTreeAccel class. Source code for this class can be found in the files accelerators/kdtreeaccel.h and accelerators/kdtreeaccel.cpp.

KdTreeAccel 285

LinearBVHNode::
    secondChildOffset
    281

Primitive 248

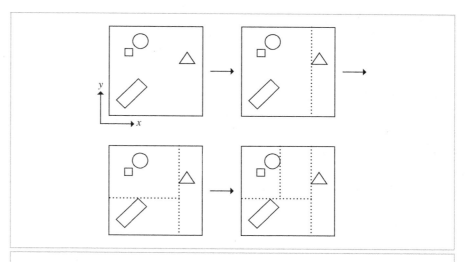

Figure 4.14: The kd-tree is built by recursively splitting the bounding box of the scene geometry along one of the coordinate axes. Here, the first split is along the *x* axis; it is placed so that the triangle is precisely alone in the right region and the rest of the primitives end up on the left. The left region is then refined a few more times with axis-aligned splitting planes. The details of the refinement criteria—which axis is used to split space at each step, at which position along the axis the plane is placed, and at what point refinement terminates—can all substantially affect the performance of the tree in practice.

⟨*KdTreeAccel Declarations*⟩ ≡
```
class KdTreeAccel : public Aggregate {
public:
    ⟨KdTreeAccel Public Methods 302⟩
private:
    ⟨KdTreeAccel Private Methods⟩
    ⟨KdTreeAccel Private Data 286⟩
};
```

In addition to the primitives to be stored, the KdTreeAccel constructor takes a few parameters that are used to guide the decisions that will be made as the tree is built; these parameters are stored in member variables (isectCost, traversalCost, maxPrims, maxDepth, and emptyBonus) for later use. See Figure 4.14 for an overview of how the tree is built.

⟨*KdTreeAccel Method Definitions*⟩ ≡
```
KdTreeAccel::KdTreeAccel(
        const std::vector<std::shared_ptr<Primitive>> &p,
        int isectCost, int traversalCost, Float emptyBonus,
        int maxPrims, int maxDepth)
    : isectCost(isectCost), traversalCost(traversalCost),
      maxPrims(maxPrims), emptyBonus(emptyBonus), primitives(p) {
    ⟨Build kd-tree for accelerator 289⟩
}
```

⟨*KdTreeAccel Private Data*⟩ ≡   285

```
const int isectCost, traversalCost, maxPrims;
const Float emptyBonus;
std::vector<std::shared_ptr<Primitive>> primitives;
```

4.4.1 TREE REPRESENTATION

The kd-tree is a binary tree, where each interior node always has both children and where leaves of the tree store the primitives that overlap them. Each interior node must provide access to three pieces of information:

- Split axis: which of the x, y, or z axes was split at this node
- Split position: the position of the splitting plane along the axis
- Children: information about how to reach the two child nodes beneath it

Each leaf node needs to record only which primitives overlap it.

It is worth going through a bit of trouble to ensure that all interior nodes and many leaf nodes use just 8 bytes of memory (assuming 4-byte Floats) because doing so ensures that eight nodes will fit into a 64-byte cache line. Because there are often many nodes in the tree and because many nodes are generally accessed for each ray, minimizing the size of the node representation substantially improves cache performance. Our initial implementation used a 16-byte node representation; when we reduced the size to 8 bytes we obtained nearly a 20% speed increase.

Both leaves and interior nodes are represented by the following KdAccelNode structure. The comments after each union member indicate whether a particular field is used for interior nodes, leaf nodes, or both.

⟨*KdTreeAccel Local Declarations*⟩ ≡
```
struct KdAccelNode {
    ⟨KdAccelNode Methods 288⟩
    union {
        Float split;                // Interior
        int onePrimitive;           // Leaf
        int primitiveIndicesOffset; // Leaf
    };
    union {
        int flags;      // Both
        int nPrims;     // Leaf
        int aboveChild; // Interior
    };
};
```

The two low-order bits of the KdAccelNode::flags variable are used to differentiate between interior nodes with x, y, and z splits (where these bits hold the values 0, 1, and 2, respectively) and leaf nodes (where these bits hold the value 3). It is relatively easy to store leaf nodes in 8 bytes: since the low 2 bits of KdAccelNode::flags are used to indicate that this is a leaf, the upper 30 bits of KdAccelNode::nPrims are available to record how many primitives overlap it. Then, if just a single primitive overlaps a

KdAccelNode leaf, an integer index into the KdTreeAccel::primitives array identifies the Primitive. If more than one primitive overlaps, then their indices are stored in a segment of KdTreeAccel::primitiveIndices. The offset to the first index for the leaf is stored in KdAccelNode::primitiveIndicesOffset and the indices for the rest directly follow.

⟨*KdTreeAccel Private Data*⟩ +≡   285
```
std::vector<int> primitiveIndices;
```

Leaf nodes are easy to initialize, though we have to be careful with the details since both flags and nPrims share the same storage; we need to be careful to not clobber data for one of them while initializing the other. Furthermore, the number of primitives must be shifted two bits to the left before being stored so that the low two bits of KdAccelNode::flags can both be set to 1 to indicate that this is a leaf node.

⟨*KdTreeAccel Method Definitions*⟩ +≡
```
void KdAccelNode::InitLeaf(int *primNums, int np,
        std::vector<int> *primitiveIndices) {
    flags = 3;
    nPrims |= (np << 2);
    ⟨Store primitive ids for leaf node 287⟩
}
```

For leaf nodes with zero or one overlapping primitives, no additional memory allocation is necessary thanks to the KdAccelNode::onePrimitive field. For the case where multiple primitives overlap, storage is allocated in the primitiveIndices array.

⟨*Store primitive ids for leaf node*⟩ ≡   287
```
if (np == 0)
    onePrimitive = 0;
else if (np == 1)
    onePrimitive = primNums[0];
else {
    primitiveIndicesOffset = primitiveIndices->size();
    for (int i = 0; i < np; ++i)
        primitiveIndices->push_back(primNums[i]);
}
```

Getting interior nodes down to 8 bytes is also reasonably straightforward. A Float (which is 32 bits in size when Floats are defined to be floats) stores the position along the chosen split axis where the node splits space, and, as explained earlier, the lowest 2 bits of KdAccelNode::flags are used to record which axis the node was split along. All that is left is to store enough information to find the two children of the node as we're traversing the tree.

Rather than storing two pointers or offsets, we lay the nodes out in a way that lets us only store one child pointer: all of the nodes are allocated in a single contiguous block of memory, and the child of an interior node that is responsible for space below the splitting plane is always stored in the array position immediately after its parent (this layout also improves cache performance, by keeping at least one child close to its parent in memory). The other child, representing space above the splitting plane, will end up somewhere else in the array; a single integer offset, KdAccelNode::aboveChild, stores its position in the nodes array. This representation is similar to the one used for BVH nodes in Section 4.4.3.

Given all those conventions, the code to initialize an interior node is straightforward. As in the InitLeaf() method, it's important to assign the value to flags before setting aboveChild and to compute the logical OR of the shifted above child value so as not to clobber the bits stored in flags.

⟨KdAccelNode Methods⟩ ≡   286
```
void InitInterior(int axis, int ac, Float s) {
    split = s;
    flags = axis;
    aboveChild |= (ac << 2);
}
```

Finally, we'll provide a few methods to extract various values from the node, so that callers don't have to be aware of the details of its representation in memory.

⟨KdAccelNode Methods⟩ +≡   286
```
Float SplitPos() const { return split; }
int nPrimitives() const { return nPrims >> 2; }
int SplitAxis() const { return flags & 3; }
bool IsLeaf() const { return (flags & 3) == 3; }
int AboveChild() const { return aboveChild >> 2; }
```

4.4.2 TREE CONSTRUCTION

The kd-tree is built with a recursive top-down algorithm. At each step, we have an axis-aligned region of space and a set of primitives that overlap that region. Either the region is split into two subregions and turned into an interior node or a leaf node is created with the overlapping primitives, terminating the recursion.

As mentioned in the discussion of KdAccelNodes, all tree nodes are stored in a contiguous array. KdTreeAccel::nextFreeNode records the next node in this array that is available, and KdTreeAccel::nAllocedNodes records the total number that have been allocated. By setting both of them to 0 and not allocating any nodes at start-up, the implementation here ensures that an allocation will be done immediately when the first node of the tree is initialized.

It is also necessary to determine a maximum tree depth if one wasn't given to the constructor. Although the tree construction process will normally terminate naturally at a reasonable depth, it is important to cap the maximum depth so that the amount of memory used for the tree cannot grow without bound in pathological cases. We have found that the value $8 + 1.3 \log(N)$ gives a reasonable maximum depth for a variety of scenes.

⟨*Build kd-tree for accelerator*⟩ ≡   285
```
nextFreeNode = nAllocedNodes = 0;
if (maxDepth <= 0)
    maxDepth = std::round(8 + 1.3f * Log2Int(primitives.size()));
```
⟨*Compute bounds for kd-tree construction* **289**⟩
⟨*Allocate working memory for kd-tree construction* **292**⟩
⟨*Initialize* primNums *for kd-tree construction* **289**⟩
⟨*Start recursive construction of kd-tree* **289**⟩

⟨*KdTreeAccel Private Data*⟩ +≡   285
```
KdAccelNode *nodes;
int nAllocedNodes, nextFreeNode;
```

Because the construction routine will be repeatedly using the bounding boxes of the primitives along the way, they are stored in a vector before tree construction starts so that the potentially slow Primitive::WorldBound() methods don't need to be called repeatedly.

⟨*Compute bounds for kd-tree construction*⟩ ≡   289
```
std::vector<Bounds3f> primBounds;
for (const std::shared_ptr<Primitive> &prim : primitives) {
    Bounds3f b = prim->WorldBound();
    bounds = Union(bounds, b);
    primBounds.push_back(b);
}
```

⟨*KdTreeAccel Private Data*⟩ +≡   285
```
Bounds3f bounds;
```

One of the parameters to the tree construction routine is an array of primitive indices indicating which primitives overlap the current node. Because all primitives overlap the root node (when the recursion begins) we start with an array initialized with values from zero through primitives.size()-1.

⟨*Initialize* primNums *for kd-tree construction*⟩ ≡   289
```
std::unique_ptr<int[]> primNums(new int[primitives.size()]);
for (size_t i = 0; i < primitives.size(); ++i)
    primNums[i] = i;
```

KdTreeAccel::buildTree() is called for each tree node. It is responsible for deciding if the node should be an interior node or leaf and updating the data structures appropriately. The last three parameters, edges, prims0, and prims1, are pointers to data that is allocated in the ⟨*Allocate working memory for kd-tree construction*⟩ fragment, which will be defined and documented in a few pages.

⟨*Start recursive construction of kd-tree*⟩ ≡   289
```
buildTree(0, bounds, primBounds, primNums.get(), primitives.size(),
          maxDepth, edges, prims0.get(), prims1.get());
```

The main parameters to KdTreeAccel::buildTree() are the offset into the array of KdAccelNodes to use for the node that it creates, nodeNum; the bounding box that gives the region of space that the node covers, nodeBounds; and the indices of primitives that overlap it, primNums. The remainder of the parameters will be described later, closer to where they are used.

⟨*KdTreeAccel Method Definitions*⟩ +≡
```
void KdTreeAccel::buildTree(int nodeNum, const Bounds3f &nodeBounds,
        const std::vector<Bounds3f> &allPrimBounds, int *primNums,
        int nPrimitives, int depth,
        const std::unique_ptr<BoundEdge[]> edges[3],
        int *prims0, int *prims1, int badRefines) {
    ⟨Get next free node from nodes array 290⟩
    ⟨Initialize leaf node if termination criteria met 290⟩
    ⟨Initialize interior node and continue recursion 290⟩
}
```

If all of the allocated nodes have been used up, node memory is reallocated with twice as many entries and the old values are copied. The first time KdTreeAccel::buildTree() is called, KdTreeAccel::nAllocedNodes is 0 and an initial block of tree nodes is allocated.

⟨*Get next free node from* nodes *array*⟩ ≡   **290**
```
if (nextFreeNode == nAllocedNodes) {
    int nNewAllocNodes = std::max(2 * nAllocedNodes, 512);
    KdAccelNode *n = AllocAligned<KdAccelNode>(nNewAllocNodes);
    if (nAllocedNodes > 0) {
        memcpy(n, nodes, nAllocedNodes * sizeof(KdAccelNode));
        FreeAligned(nodes);
    }
    nodes = n;
    nAllocedNodes = nNewAllocNodes;
}
++nextFreeNode;
```

A leaf node is created (stopping the recursion) either if there are a sufficiently small number of primitives in the region or if the maximum depth has been reached. The depth parameter starts out as the tree's maximum depth and is decremented at each level.

⟨*Initialize leaf node if termination criteria met*⟩ ≡   **290**
```
if (nPrimitives <= maxPrims || depth == 0) {
    nodes[nodeNum].InitLeaf(primNums, nPrimitives, &primitiveIndices);
    return;
}
```

If this is an internal node, it is necessary to choose a splitting plane, classify the primitives with respect to that plane, and recurse.

⟨*Initialize interior node and continue recursion*⟩ ≡   **290**
  ⟨*Choose split axis position for interior node* **293**⟩
  ⟨*Create leaf if no good splits were found* **296**⟩
  ⟨*Classify primitives with respect to split* **296**⟩
  ⟨*Recursively initialize children nodes* **297**⟩

Our implementation chooses a split using the SAH introduced in Section 4.3.2. The SAH is applicable to kd-trees as well as BVHs; here, the estimated cost is computed for a series of candidate splitting planes in the node, and the split that gives the lowest cost is chosen.

In the implementation here, the intersection cost t_{isect} and the traversal cost t_{trav} can be set by the user; their default values are 80 and 1, respectively. Ultimately, it is the ratio of these two values that determines the behavior of the tree-building algorithm.[4] The greater ratio between these values compared to the values used for BVH construction reflects the fact that visiting a kd-tree node is less expensive than visiting a BVH node.

One modification to the SAH used for BVH trees is that for kd-trees it is worth giving a slight preference to choosing splits where one of the children has no primitives overlapping it, since rays passing through these regions can immediately advance to the next kd-tree node without any ray–primitive intersection tests. Thus, the revised costs for unsplit and split regions are, respectively,

$$t_{\text{isect}}N \quad \text{and} \quad t_{\text{trav}} + (1 - b_{\text{e}})(p_B N_B t_{\text{isect}} + p_A N_A t_{\text{isect}}),$$

where b_{e} is a "bonus" value that is zero unless one of the two regions is completely empty, in which case it takes on a value between 0 and 1.

Given a way to compute the probabilities for the cost model, the only problem to address is how to generate candidate splitting positions and how to efficiently compute the cost for each candidate. It can be shown that the minimum cost with this model will be attained at a split that is coincident with one of the faces of one of the primitive's bounding boxes—there's no need to consider splits at intermediate positions. (To convince yourself of this, consider the behavior of the cost function between the edges of the faces.) Here, we will consider all bounding box faces inside the region for one or more of the three coordinate axes.

The cost for checking all of these candidates thus can be kept relatively low with a carefully structured algorithm. To compute these costs, we will sweep across the projections of the bounding boxes onto each axis and keep track of which gives the lowest cost (Figure 4.15). Each bounding box has two edges on each axis, each of which is represented by an instance of the BoundEdge structure. This structure records the position of the edge along the axis, whether it represents the start or end of a bounding box (going from low to high along the axis), and which primitive it is associated with.

⟨*KdTreeAccel Local Declarations*⟩ +≡
```
enum class EdgeType { Start, End };
```

---

4   Many other implementations of this approach seem to use values for these costs that are much closer together, sometimes even approaching equal values (for example, see Hurley et al. 2002). The values used here gave the best performance for a number of test scenes in pbrt. We suspect that this discrepancy is due to the fact that ray–primitive intersection tests in pbrt require two virtual function calls and a ray world-to-object-space transformation, in addition to the cost of performing the actual intersection test. Highly optimized ray tracers that only support triangle primitives don't pay any of that additional cost. See Section 17.1.1 for further discussion of this design trade-off.

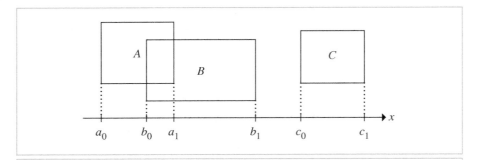

Figure 4.15: Given an axis along which we'd like to consider possible splits, the primitives' bounding boxes are projected onto the axis, which leads to an efficient algorithm to track how many primitives would be on each side of a particular splitting plane. Here, for example, a split at a_1 would leave A completely below the splitting plane, B straddling it, and C completely above it. Each point on the axis, a_0, a_1, b_0, b_1, c_0, and c_1, is represented by an instance of the BoundEdge structure.

⟨*KdTreeAccel Local Declarations*⟩ +≡
```
struct BoundEdge {
    ⟨BoundEdge Public Methods 292⟩
    Float t;
    int primNum;
    EdgeType type;
};
```

⟨*BoundEdge Public Methods*⟩ ≡   292
```
BoundEdge(Float t, int primNum, bool starting)
    : t(t), primNum(primNum) {
    type = starting ? EdgeType::Start : EdgeType::End;
}
```

At most, 2 * primitives.size() BoundEdges are needed for computing costs for any tree node, so the memory for the edges for all three axes is allocated once and then reused for each node that is created.

⟨*Allocate working memory for kd-tree construction*⟩ ≡   289
```
std::unique_ptr<BoundEdge[]> edges[3];
for (int i = 0; i < 3; ++i)
    edges[i].reset(new BoundEdge[2 * primitives.size()]);
```

After determining the estimated cost for creating a leaf, KdTreeAccel::buildTree() chooses an axis to try to split along and computes the cost function for each candidate split. bestAxis and bestOffset record the axis and bounding box edge index that have given the lowest cost so far, bestCost. invTotalSA is initialized to the reciprocal of the node's surface area; its value will be used when computing the probabilities of rays passing through each of the candidate children nodes.

290

⟨*Choose split axis position for interior node*⟩ ≡

```
int bestAxis = -1, bestOffset = -1;
Float bestCost = Infinity;
Float oldCost = isectCost * Float(nPrimitives);
Float totalSA = nodeBounds.SurfaceArea();
Float invTotalSA = 1 / totalSA;
Vector3f d = nodeBounds.pMax - nodeBounds.pMin;
```
⟨*Choose which axis to split along* **293**⟩
```
int retries = 0;
retrySplit:
```
⟨*Initialize edges for* axis **293**⟩
⟨*Compute cost of all splits for* axis *to find best* **294**⟩

This method first tries to find a split along the axis with the largest spatial extent; if successful, this choice helps to give regions of space that tend toward being square in shape. This is an intuitively sensible approach. Later, if it was unsuccessful in finding a good split along this axis, it will go back and try the others in turn.

⟨*Choose which axis to split along*⟩ ≡   293
```
int axis = nodeBounds.MaximumExtent();
```

First the edges array for the axis is initialized using the bounding boxes of the overlapping primitives. The array is then sorted from low to high along the axis so that it can sweep over the box edges from first to last.

⟨*Initialize edges for* axis⟩ ≡   293
```
for (int i = 0; i < nPrimitives; ++i) {
    int pn = primNums[i];
    const Bounds3f &bounds = allPrimBounds[pn];
    edges[axis][2 * i] =     BoundEdge(bounds.pMin[axis], pn, true);
    edges[axis][2 * i + 1] = BoundEdge(bounds.pMax[axis], pn, false);
}
```
⟨*Sort* edges *for* axis **293**⟩

The C++ standard library routine sort() requires that the structure being sorted define an ordering; this is done using the BoundEdge::t values. However, one subtlety is that if the BoundEdge::t values match, it is necessary to try to break the tie by comparing the node's types; this is necessary since sort() depends on the fact that the only time a < b and b < a are both false is when a == b.

⟨*Sort* edges *for* axis⟩ ≡   293
```
std::sort(&edges[axis][0], &edges[axis][2*nPrimitives],
    [](const BoundEdge &e0, const BoundEdge &e1) -> bool {
        if (e0.t == e1.t)
            return (int)e0.type < (int)e1.type;
        else return e0.t < e1.t;
});
```

Given the sorted array of edges, we'd like to quickly compute the cost function for a split at each one of them. The probabilities for a ray passing through each child node are easily computed using their surface areas, and the number of primitives on each side of the split is tracked by the variables nBelow and nAbove. We would like to keep their values updated such that if we chose to split at edgeT for a particular pass through the loop, nBelow will give the number of primitives that would end up below the splitting plane and nAbove would give the number above it.[5]

At the first edge, all primitives must be above that edge by definition, so nAbove is initialized to nPrimitives and nBelow is set to 0. When the loop is considering a split at the end of a bounding box's extent, nAbove needs to be decremented, since that box, which must have previously been above the splitting plane, will no longer be above it if splitting is done at the point. Similarly, after calculating the split cost, if the split candidate was at the start of a bounding box's extent, then the box will be on the below side for all subsequent splits. The tests at the start and end of the loop body update the primitive counts for these two cases.

⟨*Compute cost of all splits for* axis *to find best*⟩ ≡   293
```
    int nBelow = 0, nAbove = nPrimitives;
    for (int i = 0; i < 2 * nPrimitives; ++i) {
        if (edges[axis][i].type == EdgeType::End) --nAbove;
        Float edgeT = edges[axis][i].t;
        if (edgeT > nodeBounds.pMin[axis] &&
            edgeT < nodeBounds.pMax[axis]) {
            ⟨Compute cost for split at ith edge 295⟩
        }
        if (edges[axis][i].type == EdgeType::Start) ++nBelow;
    }
```

belowSA and aboveSA hold the surface areas of the two candidate child bounds; they are easily computed by adding up the areas of the six faces.

⟨*Compute child surface areas for split at* edgeT⟩ ≡   295
```
    int otherAxis0 = (axis + 1) % 3, otherAxis1 = (axis + 2) % 3;
    Float belowSA = 2 * (d[otherAxis0] * d[otherAxis1] +
                        (edgeT - nodeBounds.pMin[axis]) *
                        (d[otherAxis0] + d[otherAxis1]));
    Float aboveSA = 2 * (d[otherAxis0] * d[otherAxis1] +
                        (nodeBounds.pMax[axis] - edgeT) *
                        (d[otherAxis0] + d[otherAxis1]));
```

Given all of this information, the cost for a particular split can be computed.

---

5   When multiple bounding box faces project to the same point on the axis, this invariant may not be true at those points. However, as implemented here it will only overestimate the counts and, more importantly, will have the correct value for one of the multiple times through the loop at each of those points, so the algorithm functions correctly in the end anyway.

⟨*Compute cost for split at* i*th edge*⟩ ≡   294
    ⟨*Compute child surface areas for split at* edgeT **294**⟩
    Float pBelow = belowSA * invTotalSA;
    Float pAbove = aboveSA * invTotalSA;
    Float eb = (nAbove == 0 || nBelow == 0) ? emptyBonus : 0;
    Float cost = traversalCost +
                    isectCost * (1 - eb) * (pBelow * nBelow + pAbove * nAbove);
    ⟨*Update best split if this is lowest cost so far* **295**⟩

If the cost computed for this candidate split is the best one so far, the details of the split
are recorded.

⟨*Update best split if this is lowest cost so far*⟩ ≡   295
    if (cost < bestCost) {
        bestCost = cost;
        bestAxis = axis;
        bestOffset = i;
    }

It may happen that there are no possible splits found in the previous tests (Figure 4.16
illustrates a case where this may happen). In this case, there isn't a single candidate
position at which to split the node along the current axis. At this point, splitting is tried
for the other two axes in turn. If neither of them can find a split (when retries is equal
to 2), then there is no useful way to refine the node, since both children will still have
the same number of overlapping primitives. When this condition occurs, all that can be
done is to give up and make a leaf node.

It is also possible that the best split will have a cost that is still higher than the cost for not
splitting the node at all. If it is substantially worse and there aren't too many primitives,
a leaf node is made immediately. Otherwise, badRefines keeps track of how many bad

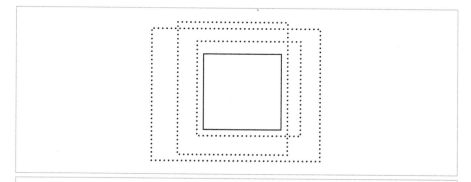

Figure 4.16: If multiple bounding boxes (dotted lines) overlap a kd-tree node (solid lines) as shown
here, there is no possible split position that can result in fewer than all of the primitives being on both
sides of it.

Float 1062

splits have been made so far above the current node of the tree. It's worth allowing a few slightly poor refinements since later splits may be able to find better ones given a smaller subset of primitives to consider.

⟨*Create leaf if no good splits were found*⟩ ≡   290
```
if (bestAxis == -1 && retries < 2) {
    ++retries;
    axis = (axis + 1) % 3;
    goto retrySplit;
}
if (bestCost > oldCost) ++badRefines;
if ((bestCost > 4 * oldCost && nPrimitives < 16) ||
    bestAxis == -1 || badRefines == 3) {
    nodes[nodeNum].InitLeaf(primNums, nPrimitives, &primitiveIndices);
    return;
}
```

Having chosen a split position, the bounding box edges can be used to classify the primitives as being above, below, or on both sides of the split in the same way as was done to keep track of nBelow and nAbove in the earlier code. Note that the bestOffset entry in the arrays is skipped in the loops below; this is necessary so that the primitive whose bounding box edge was used for the split isn't incorrectly categorized as being on both sides of the split.

⟨*Classify primitives with respect to split*⟩ ≡   290
```
int n0 = 0, n1 = 0;
for (int i = 0; i < bestOffset; ++i)
    if (edges[bestAxis][i].type == EdgeType::Start)
        prims0[n0++] = edges[bestAxis][i].primNum;
for (int i = bestOffset + 1; i < 2 * nPrimitives; ++i)
    if (edges[bestAxis][i].type == EdgeType::End)
        prims1[n1++] = edges[bestAxis][i].primNum;
```

Recall that the node number of the "below" child of this node in the kd-tree nodes array is the current node number plus one. After the recursion has returned from that side of the tree, the nextFreeNode offset is used for the "above" child. The only other important detail here is that the prims0 memory is passed directly for reuse by both children, while the prims1 pointer is advanced forward first. This is necessary since the current invocation of KdTreeAccel::buildTree() depends on its prims1 values being preserved over the first recursive call to KdTreeAccel::buildTree() in the following, since it must be passed as a parameter to the second call. However, there is no corresponding need to preserve the edges values or to preserve prims0 beyond its immediate use in the first recursive call.

⟨*Recursively initialize children nodes*⟩ ≡   290
```
Float tSplit = edges[bestAxis][bestOffset].t;
Bounds3f bounds0 = nodeBounds, bounds1 = nodeBounds;
bounds0.pMax[bestAxis] = bounds1.pMin[bestAxis] = tSplit;
buildTree(nodeNum + 1, bounds0, allPrimBounds, prims0, n0,
        depth - 1, edges, prims0, prims1 + nPrimitives, badRefines);
int aboveChild = nextFreeNode;
nodes[nodeNum].InitInterior(bestAxis, aboveChild, tSplit);
buildTree(aboveChild, bounds1, allPrimBounds, prims1, n1,
        depth - 1, edges, prims0, prims1 + nPrimitives, badRefines);
```

Thus, much more space is needed for the prims1 array of integers for storing the worst-case possible number of overlapping primitive numbers than for the prims0 array, which only needs to handle the primitives at a single level at a time.

⟨*Allocate working memory for kd-tree construction*⟩ +≡   289
```
std::unique_ptr<int[]> prims0(new int[primitives.size()]);
std::unique_ptr<int[]> prims1(new int[(maxDepth+1) * primitives.size()]);
```

4.4.3 TRAVERSAL

Figure 4.17 shows the basic process of ray traversal through the tree. Intersecting the ray with the tree's overall bounds gives initial tMin and tMax values, marked with points in the figure. As with the BVHAccel in this chapter, if the ray misses the overall primitive bounds, this method can immediately return false. Otherwise, it starts to descend into the tree, starting at the root. At each interior node, it determines which of the two children the ray enters first and processes both children in order. Traversal ends either when the ray exits the tree or when the closest intersection is found.

⟨*KdTreeAccel Method Definitions*⟩ +≡
```
bool KdTreeAccel::Intersect(const Ray &ray,
        SurfaceInteraction *isect) const {
    ⟨Compute initial parametric range of ray inside kd-tree extent 297⟩
    ⟨Prepare to traverse kd-tree for ray 298⟩
    ⟨Traverse kd-tree nodes in order for ray 299⟩
}
```

The algorithm starts by finding the overall parametric range $[t_{min}, t_{max}]$ of the ray's overlap with the tree, exiting immediately if there is no overlap.

⟨*Compute initial parametric range of ray inside kd-tree extent*⟩ ≡   297
```
Float tMin, tMax;
if (!bounds.IntersectP(ray, &tMin, &tMax))
    return false;
```

The array of KdToDo structures is used to record the nodes yet to be processed for the ray; it is ordered so that the last active entry in the array is the next node that should be considered. The maximum number of entries needed in this array is the maximum

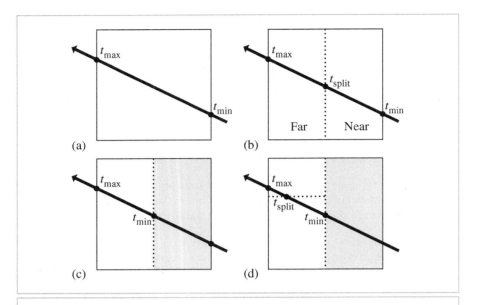

Figure 4.17: Traversal of a Ray through the kd-Tree. (a) The ray is intersected with the bounds of the tree, giving an initial parametric $[t_{min}, t_{max}]$ range to consider. (b) Because this range is nonempty, it is necessary to consider the two children of the root node here. The ray first enters the child on the right, labeled "near," where it has a parametric range $[t_{min}, t_{split}]$. If the near node is a leaf with primitives in it, ray–primitive intersection tests are performed; otherwise, its children nodes are processed. (c) If no hit is found in the node, or if a hit is found beyond $[t_{min}, t_{split}]$, then the far node, on the left, is processed. (d) This sequence continues—processing tree nodes in a depth-first, front-to-back traversal—until the closest intersection is found or the ray exits the tree.

depth of the kd-tree; the array size used in the following should be more than enough in practice.

⟨*Prepare to traverse kd-tree for ray*⟩ ≡   297
```
Vector3f invDir(1 / ray.d.x, 1 / ray.d.y, 1 / ray.d.z);
constexpr int maxTodo = 64;
KdToDo todo[maxTodo];
int todoPos = 0;
```

⟨*KdTreeAccel Declarations*⟩ +≡
```
struct KdToDo {
    const KdAccelNode *node;
    Float tMin, tMax;
};
```

The traversal continues through the nodes, processing a single leaf or interior node each time through the loop. The values tMin and tMax will always hold the parametric range for the ray's overlap with the current node.

⟨*Traverse kd-tree nodes in order for ray*⟩ ≡   297
```
    bool hit = false;
    const KdAccelNode *node = &nodes[0];
    while (node != nullptr) {
```
     ⟨*Bail out if we found a hit closer than the current node* **299**⟩
```
        if (!node->IsLeaf()) {
```
      ⟨*Process kd-tree interior node* **299**⟩
```
        } else {
```
      ⟨*Check for intersections inside leaf node* **301**⟩
      ⟨*Grab next node to process from todo list* **302**⟩
```
        }
    }
    return hit;
```

An intersection may have been previously found in a primitive that overlaps multiple nodes. If the intersection was outside the current node when first detected, it is necessary to keep traversing the tree until we come to a node where tMin is beyond the intersection. Only then is it certain that there is no closer intersection with some other primitive.

⟨*Bail out if we found a hit closer than the current node*⟩ ≡   299
```
    if (ray.tMax < tMin) break;
```

For interior tree nodes the first thing to do is to intersect the ray with the node's splitting plane; given the intersection point, we can determine if one or both of the children nodes need to be processed and in what order the ray passes through them.

⟨*Process kd-tree interior node*⟩ ≡   299
  ⟨*Compute parametric distance along ray to split plane* **299**⟩
  ⟨*Get node children pointers for ray* **300**⟩
  ⟨*Advance to next child node, possibly enqueue other child* **301**⟩

The parametric distance to the split plane is computed in the same manner as was done in computing the intersection of a ray and an axis-aligned plane for the ray–bounding box test. We use the precomputed invDir value to save a divide each time through the loop.

⟨*Compute parametric distance along ray to split plane*⟩ ≡   299
```
    int axis = node->SplitAxis();
    Float tPlane = (node->SplitPos() - ray.o[axis]) * invDir[axis];
```

Float 1062

KdAccelNode 286

KdAccelNode::IsLeaf() 288

KdAccelNode::SplitAxis() 288

KdAccelNode::SplitPos() 288

KdTreeAccel::nodes 289

Ray::o 73

Ray::tMax 73

Now it is necessary to determine the order in which the ray encounters the children nodes so that the tree is traversed in front-to-back order along the ray. Figure 4.18 shows the geometry of this computation. The position of the ray's origin with respect to the splitting plane is enough to distinguish between the two cases, ignoring for now the case where the ray doesn't actually pass through one of the two nodes. The rare case when the ray's origin lies on the splitting plane requires careful handling in this case, as its direction needs to be used instead to discriminate between the two cases.

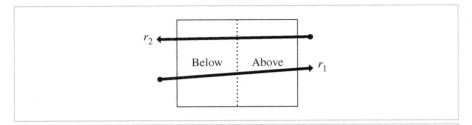

Figure 4.18: The position of the origin of the ray with respect to the splitting plane can be used to determine which of the node's children should be processed first. If the origin of a ray like r_1 is on the "below" side of the splitting plane, we should process the below child before the above child, and vice versa.

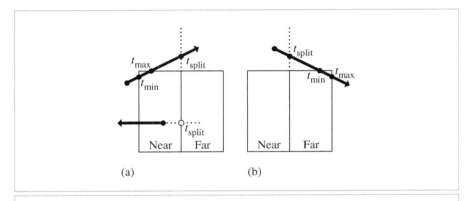

Figure 4.19: Two cases where both children of a node don't need to be processed because the ray doesn't overlap them. (a) The top ray intersects the splitting plane beyond the ray's t_{max} position and thus doesn't enter the far child. The bottom ray is facing away from the splitting plane, indicated by a negative t_{split} value. (b) The ray intersects the plane before the ray's t_{min} value, indicating that the near child doesn't need processing.

⟨*Get node children pointers for ray*⟩ ≡   299
```
const KdAccelNode *firstChild, *secondChild;
int belowFirst = (ray.o[axis] <  node->SplitPos()) ||
                 (ray.o[axis] == node->SplitPos() && ray.d[axis] <= 0);
if (belowFirst) {
    firstChild = node + 1;
    secondChild = &nodes[node->AboveChild()];
} else {
    firstChild = &nodes[node->AboveChild()];
    secondChild = node + 1;
}
```

KdAccelNode 286
KdAccelNode::SplitPos() 288
Ray::o 73

It may not be necessary to process both children of this node. Figure 4.19 shows some configurations where the ray only passes through one of the children. The ray will never miss both children, since otherwise the current interior node should never have been visited.

The first if test in the following code corresponds to Figure 4.19(a): only the near node needs to be processed if it can be shown that the ray doesn't overlap the far node because it faces away from it or doesn't overlap it because $t_{\mathrm{split}} > t_{\mathrm{max}}$. Figure 4.19(b) shows the similar case tested in the second if test: the near node may not need processing if the ray doesn't overlap it. Otherwise, the else clause handles the case of both children needing processing; the near node will be processed next, and the far node goes on the todo list.

⟨*Advance to next child node, possibly enqueue other child*⟩ ≡   299
```
if (tPlane > tMax || tPlane <= 0)
    node = firstChild;
else if (tPlane < tMin)
    node = secondChild;
else {
    ⟨Enqueue secondChild in todo list 301⟩
    node = firstChild;
    tMax = tPlane;
}
```

⟨*Enqueue* secondChild *in todo list*⟩ ≡   301
```
todo[todoPos].node = secondChild;
todo[todoPos].tMin = tPlane;
todo[todoPos].tMax = tMax;
++todoPos;
```

If the current node is a leaf, intersection tests are performed against the primitives in the leaf.

⟨*Check for intersections inside leaf node*⟩ ≡   299
```
int nPrimitives = node->nPrimitives();
if (nPrimitives == 1) {
    const std::shared_ptr<Primitive> &p = primitives[node->onePrimitive];
    ⟨Check one primitive inside leaf node 301⟩
} else {
    for (int i = 0; i < nPrimitives; ++i) {
        int index = primitiveIndices[node->primitiveIndicesOffset + i];
        const std::shared_ptr<Primitive> &p = primitives[index];
        ⟨Check one primitive inside leaf node 301⟩
    }
}
```

Processing an individual primitive is just a matter of passing the intersection request on to the primitive.

⟨*Check one primitive inside leaf node*⟩ ≡   301
```
if (p->Intersect(ray, isect))
    hit = true;
```

After doing the intersection tests at the leaf node, the next node to process is loaded from the todo array. If no more nodes remain, then the ray has passed through the tree without hitting anything.

⟨*Grab next node to process from todo list*⟩ ≡   299
```
if (todoPos > 0) {
    --todoPos;
    node = todo[todoPos].node;
    tMin = todo[todoPos].tMin;
    tMax = todo[todoPos].tMax;
}
else
    break;
```

Like the BVHAccel, the KdTreeAccel has a specialized intersection method for shadow rays that is not shown here. It is similar to the Intersect() method but calls the Primitive:: IntersectP() method and returns true as soon as it finds any intersection without worrying about finding the closest one.

⟨*KdTreeAccel Public Methods*⟩ ≡   285
```
bool IntersectP(const Ray &ray) const;
```

FURTHER READING

After the introduction of the ray-tracing algorithm, an enormous amount of research was done to try to find effective ways to speed it up, primarily by developing improved ray-tracing acceleration structures. Arvo and Kirk's chapter in *An Introduction to Ray Tracing* (Glassner 1989a) summarizes the state of the art as of 1989 and still provides an excellent taxonomy for categorizing different approaches to ray intersection acceleration.

Kirk and Arvo (1988) introduced the unifying principle of *meta-hierarchies*. They showed that by implementing acceleration data structures to conform to the same interface as is used for primitives in the scene, it's easy to mix and match different intersection acceleration schemes. pbrt follows this model since the Aggregate inherits from the Primitive base class.

Grids

Fujimoto, Tanaka, and Iwata (1986) introduced uniform grids, a spatial subdivision approach where the scene bounds are decomposed into equally sized grid cells. More efficient grid traversal methods were described by Amanatides and Woo (1987) and Cleary and Wyvill (1988). Snyder and Barr (1987) described a number of key improvements to this approach and showed the use of grids for rendering extremely complex scenes. Hierarchical grids, where grid cells with many primitives in them are themselves refined into grids, were introduced by Jevans and Wyvill (1989). More complex techniques for hierarchical grids were developed by Cazals, Drettakis, and Puech (1995) and Klimaszewski and Sederberg (1997).

Ize et al. (2006) developed an efficient algorithm for parallel construction of grids. One of their interesting findings was that grid construction performance quickly became limited by available memory bandwidth as the number of processing cores used increased.

Choosing an optimal grid resolution is important for getting good performance from grids. A good paper on this topic is by Ize et al. (2007), who provided a solid foundation for fully automatically selecting the resolution and for deciding when to refine into subgrids when using hierarchical grids. They derived theoretical results using a number of simplifying assumptions and then showed the applicability of the results to rendering real-world scenes. Their paper also includes a good selection of pointers to previous work in this area.

Lagae and Dutré (2008a) described an innovative representation for uniform grids based on hashing that has the desirable properties that not only does each primitive have a single index into a grid cell but also each cell has only a single primitive index. They show that this representation has very low memory usage and is still quite efficient.

Hunt and Mark (2008a) showed that building grids in perspective space, where the center of projection is the camera or a light source, can make tracing rays from the camera or light substantially more efficient. Although this approach requires multiple acceleration structures, the performance benefits from multiple specialized structures for different classes of rays can be substantial. Their approach is also notable in that it is in some ways a middle ground between rasterization and ray tracing.

Bounding Volume Hierarchies

Clark (1976) first suggested using bounding volumes to cull collections of objects for standard visible-surface determination algorithms. Building on this work, Rubin and Whitted (1980) developed the first hierarchical data structures for scene representation for fast ray tracing, although their method depended on the user to define the hierarchy. Kay and Kajiya (1986) implemented one of the first practical object subdivision approaches based on bounding objects with collections of slabs. Goldsmith and Salmon (1987) described the first algorithm for automatically computing bounding volume hierarchies. Although their algorithm was based on estimating the probability of a ray intersecting a bounding volume based on the volume's surface area, it was much less effective than modern SAH BVH approaches.

The BVHAccel implementation in this chapter is based on the construction algorithm described by Wald (2007) and Günther et al. (2007). The bounding box test is the one introduced by Williams et al. (2005). An even more efficient bounding box test that does additional precomputation in exchange for higher performance when the same ray is tested for intersection against many bounding boxes was developed by Eisemann et al. (2007); we leave implementing their method for an exercise.

The BVH traversal algorithm used in pbrt was concurrently developed by a number of researchers; see the notes by Boulos and Haines (2006) for more details and background. Another option for tree traversal is that of Kay and Kajiya (1986); they maintained a heap of nodes ordered by ray distance. On GPUs, which have relatively limited amounts of on-chip memory, maintaining a stack of to-be-visited nodes for each ray may have a prohibitive memory cost. Foley and Sugerman (2005) introduced a "stackless" kd-tree traversal algorithm that periodically backtracks and searches starting from the tree

BVHAccel 256

root to find the next node to visit rather than storing all nodes to visit explicitly. Laine (2010) made a number of improvements to this approach, reducing the frequency of retraversals from the tree root and applying the approach to BVHs.

A number of researchers have developed techniques for improving the quality of BVHs after construction. Yoon et al. (2007) and Kensler (2008) presented algorithms that make local adjustments to the BVH, and Kopta et al. (2012) reused BVHs over multiple frames of an animation, maintaining their quality by updating the parts that bound moving objects. See also Bittner et al. (2013), Karras and Aila (2013), and Bittner et al. (2014) for recent work in this area.

Most current methods for building BVHs are based on top-down construction of the tree, first creating the root node and then partitioning the primitives into children and continuing recursively. An alternative approach was demonstrated by Walter et al. (2008), who showed that bottom-up construction, where the leaves are created first and then agglomerated into parent nodes, is a viable option. Gu et al. (2013b) developed a much more efficient implementation of this approach and showed its suitability for parallel implementation.

One shortcoming of BVHs is that even a small number of relatively large primitives that have overlapping bounding boxes can substantially reduce the efficiency of the BVH: many of the nodes of the tree will be overlapping, solely due to the overlapping bounding boxes of geometry down at the leaves. Ernst and Greiner (2007) proposed "split clipping" as a solution; the restriction that each primitive only appears once in the tree is lifted, and the bounding boxes of large input primitives are subdivided into a set of tighter sub-bounds that are then used for tree construction. Dammertz and Keller (2008a) observed that the problematic primitives are the ones with a large amount of empty space in their bounding box relative to their surface area, so they subdivided the most egregious triangles and reported substantial performance improvements. Stich et al. (2009) developed an approach that splits primitives during BVH construction, making it possible to only split primitives when an SAH cost reduction was found. See also Popov et al.'s paper (2009) on a theoretically optimum BVH partitioning algorithm and its relationship to previous approaches, and Karras and Aila (2013) for improved criteria for deciding when to split triangles. Woop et al. (2014) developed an approach to building BVHs for long, thin geometry like hair and fur; because this sort of geometry is quite thin with respect to the volume of its bounding boxes, it normally has poor performance with most acceleration structures.

The memory requirements for BVHs can be significant. In our implementation, each node is 32 bytes. With up to 2 BVH tree nodes needed per primitive in the scene, the total overhead may be as high as 64 bytes per primitive. Cline et al. (2006) suggested a more compact representation for BVH nodes, at some expense of efficiency. First, they quantized the bounding box stored in each node using 8 or 16 bytes to encode its position with respect to the node's parent's bounding box. Second, they used *implicit indexing*, where the node i's children are at positions $2i$ and $2i + 1$ in the node array (assuming a 2× branching factor). They showed substantial memory savings, with moderate performance impact. Bauszat et al. (2010) developed another space-efficient BVH representation. See also Segovia and Ernst (2010), who developed compact representations of both BVH nodes and triangle meshes.

Yoon and Manocha (2006) described algorithms for cache-efficient layout of BVHs and kd-trees and demonstrated performance improvements from using them. See also Ericson's book (2004) for extensive discussion of this topic.

The linear BVH was introduced by Lauterbach et al. (2009). Pantaleoni and Luebke (2010) developed the HLBVH generalization, using the SAH at the upper levels of the tree. They also noted that the upper bits of the Morton coded values can be used to efficiently find clusters of primitives—both of these ideas are used in our HLBVH implementation. Garanzha et al. (2011) introduced further improvements to the HLBVH, most of them targeting GPU implementations.

Other than the HLBVH path, the BVH construction implementations in the BVHAccel here haven't been parallelized. See Wald (2012) for an approach for high-performance parallel BVH construction using the SAH throughout.

kd-trees

Glassner (1984) introduced the use of octrees for ray intersection acceleration. Use of the kd-tree for ray tracing was first described by Kaplan (1985). Kaplan's tree construction algorithm always split nodes down their middle; MacDonald and Booth (1990) introduced the SAH approach, estimating ray–node traversal probabilities using relative surface areas. Naylor (1993) has also written on general issues of constructing good kd-trees. Havran and Bittner (2002) revisited many of these issues and introduced useful improvements. Adding a bonus factor to the SAH for tree nodes that are completely empty, as is done in our implementation, was suggested by Hurley et al. (2002). See Havran's Ph.D. thesis (2000) for an excellent overview of high-performance kd-construction and traversal algorithms.

Jansen (1986) first developed the efficient ray traversal algorithm for kd-trees. Arvo (1988) also investigated this problem and discussed it in a note in *Ray Tracing News*. Sung and Shirley (1992) described a ray traversal algorithm's implementation for a BSP-tree accelerator; our KdTreeAccel traversal code is loosely based on theirs.

The asymptotic complexity of the kd-tree construction algorithm in pbrt is $O(n \log^2 n)$. Wald and Havran (2006) showed that it's possible to build kd-trees in $(n \log n)$ time with some additional implementation complexity; they reported a 2 to 3× speedup in construction time for typical scenes.

The best kd-trees for ray tracing are built using "perfect splits," where the primitive being inserted into the tree is clipped to the bounds of the current node at each step. This eliminates the issue that, for example, an object's bounding box may intersect a node's bounding box and thus be stored in it, even though the object itself doesn't intersect the node's bounding box. This approach was introduced by Havran and Bittner (2002) and discussed further by Hurley et al. (2002) and Wald and Havran (2006). See also Soupikov et al. (2008). Even with perfect splits, large primitives may still be stored in many kd-tree leaves; Choi et al. (2013) suggest storing some primitives in interior nodes to address this issue.

BVHAccel 256
KdTreeAccel 285

kd-tree construction tends to be much slower than BVH construction (especially if "perfect splits" are used), so parallel construction algorithms are of particular interest. Recent work in this area includes that of Shevtsov et al. (2007b) and Choi et al. (2010), who presented efficient parallel kd-tree construction algorithms with good scalability to multiple processors.

The Surface Area Heuristic

A number of researchers have investigated improvements to the SAH since its introduction to ray tracing by MacDonald and Booth (1990). Fabianowski et al. (2009) derived a version that replaces the assumption that rays are uniformly distributed throughout space with the assumption that ray origins are uniformly distributed inside the scene's bounding box. Hunt and Mark (2008b) introduced a new SAH that accounts for the fact that rays generally aren't uniformly distributed but rather that many of them originate from a single point or a set of nearby points (cameras and light sources, respectively). Hunt (2008) showed how the SAH should be modified when the "mailboxing" optimization is being used, and Vinkler et al. (2012) used assumptions about the visibility of primitives to adjust their SAH cost. Ize and Hansen (2011) derived a "ray termination surface area heuristic" (RTSAH), which they use to adjust BVH traversal order for shadow rays in order to more quickly find intersections with occluders. See also Moulin et al. (2015), who adapted the SAH to account for shadow rays being occluded during kd-tree traversal.

Evaluating the SAH can be costly, particularly when many different splits or primitive partitions are being considered. One solution to this problem is to only compute it at a subset of the candidate points—for example, along the lines of the bucketing approach used in the BVHAccel in pbrt. Hurley et al. (2002) suggested this approach for building kd-trees, and Popov et al. (2006) discusses it in detail. Shevtsov et al. (2007b) introduced the improvement of binning the full extents of triangles, not just their centroids.

Hunt et al. (2006) noted that if you only have to evaluate the SAH at one point, for example, you don't need to sort the primitives but only need to do a linear scan over them to compute primitive counts and bounding boxes at the point. They showed that approximating the SAH with a piecewise quadratic based on evaluating it at a number of individual positions and using that to choose a good split leads to effective trees. A similar approximation was used by Popov et al. (2006).

While the SAH has led to very effective kd-trees and BVHs, it has become clear that it isn't perfect: a number of researchers have noted that it's not unusual to encounter cases where a kd-tree or BVH with a higher SAH-estimated cost gives better performance than one with lower estimated cost. Aila et al. (2013) survey some of these results and propose two additional heuristics that help address them; one accounts for the fact that most rays start on surfaces—ray origins aren't actually randomly distributed throughout the scene, and another accounts for SIMD divergence when multiple rays traverse the hierarchy together. While these new heuristics are effective at explaining why a given tree delivers the performance that it does, it's not yet clear how to incorporate them into tree construction algorithms.

Other Topics in Acceleration Structures

Weghorst, Hooper, and Greenberg (1984) discussed the trade-offs of using various shapes for bounding volumes and suggested projecting objects to the screen and using a z-buffer rendering to accelerate finding intersections for camera rays.

BVHAccel 256

A number of researchers have investigated the applicability of general BSP trees, where the splitting planes aren't necessarily axis aligned, as they are with kd-trees. Kammaje and Mora (2007) built BSP trees using a preselected set of candidate splitting planes. Budge et al. (2008) developed a number of improvements to their approach, though their results only approached kd-tree performance in practice due to a slower construction stage and slower traversal than kd-trees. Ize et al. (2008) showed a BSP implementation that renders scenes faster than modern kd-trees but at the cost of extremely long construction times.

There are many techniques for traversing a collection of rays through the acceleration structure together, rather than just one at a time. This approach ("packet tracing") is an important component of high-performance ray tracing; it's discussed in more depth in Section 17.2.2.

Animated primitives present two challenges to ray tracers: first, renderers that try to reuse acceleration structures over multiple frames of an animation must update the acceleration structures if objects are moving. Wald et al. (2007a) showed how to incrementally update BVHs in this case, and Garanzha (2009) suggested creating clusters of nearby primitives and then building BVHs of those clusters (thus lightening the load on the BVH construction algorithm). A second problem is that for primitives that are moving quickly, the bounding boxes of their full motion over the frame time may be quite large, leading to many unnecessary ray–primitive intersection tests. Notable work on this issue includes Glassner (1988), who generalized ray tracing (and an octree for acceleration) to four dimensions, adding time. More recently, Grünschloß et al. (2011) developed improvements to BVHs for moving primitives. See also Wald et al.'s (2007b) survey paper on ray tracing animated scenes.

An innovative approach to acceleration structures was suggested by Arvo and Kirk (1987), who introduced a 5D data structure that subdivided based on both 3D spatial and 2D ray directions. Another interesting approach for scenes described with triangle meshes was developed by Lagae and Dutré (2008b): they computed a constrained tetrahedralization, where all triangle faces of the model are represented in the tetrahedralization. Rays are then stepped through tetrahedra until they intersect a triangle from the scene description. This approach is still a few times slower than the state-of-the-art in kd-trees and BVHs but is an interesting new way to think about the problem.

There is an interesting middle ground between kd-trees and BVHs, where the tree node holds a splitting plane for each child rather than just a single splitting plane. For example, this refinement makes it possible to do object subdivision in a kd-tree-like acceleration structure, putting each primitive in just one subtree and allowing the subtrees to overlap, while still preserving many of the benefits of efficient kd-tree traversal. Ooi et al. (1987) first introduced this refinement to kd-trees for storing spatial data, naming it the "spatial kd-tree" (skd-tree). Skd-trees have recently been applied to ray tracing by a number of researchers, including Zachmann (2002), Woop et al. (2006), Wächter and Keller (2006), Havran et al. (2006), and Zuniga and Uhlmann (2006).

When spatial subdivision approaches like grids or kd-trees are used, primitives may overlap multiple nodes of the structure and a ray may be tested for intersection with the same primitive multiple times as it passes through the structure. Arnaldi, Priol, and Bouatouch (1987) and Amanatides and Woo (1987) developed the "mailboxing" technique to address this issue: each ray is given a unique integer identifier, and each primitive records the id of the last ray that was tested against it. If the ids match, then the intersection test is unnecessary and can be skipped.

While effective, this approach doesn't work well with a multi-threaded ray tracer. To address this issue, Benthin (2006) suggested storing a small per-ray hash table to record ids of recently intersected primitives. Shevtsov et al. (2007a) maintained a small array of the last *n* intersected primitive ids and searched it linearly before performing intersection tests. Although some primitives may still be checked multiple times with both of these approaches, they usually eliminate most redundant tests.

EXERCISES

● 4.1 What kinds of scenes are worst-case scenarios for the two acceleration structures in pbrt? (Consider specific geometric configurations that the approaches will respectively be unable to handle well.) Construct scenes with these characteristics, and measure the performance of pbrt as you add more primitives. How does the worst case for one behave when rendered with the other?

● 4.2 Implement a hierarchical grid accelerator where you refine cells that have an excessive number of primitives overlapping them to instead hold a finer subgrid to store its geometry. (See, for example, Jevans and Wyvill (1989) for one approach to this problem and Ize et al. (2007) for effective methods for deciding when refinement is worthwhile.) Compare both accelerator construction performance and rendering performance to a non-hierarchical grid as well as to the accelerators in this chapter.

● 4.3 Implement smarter overlap tests for building accelerators. Using objects' bounding boxes to determine which sides of a kd-tree split they overlap can hurt performance by causing unnecessary intersection tests. Therefore, add a `bool Shape::Overlaps(const Bounds3f &) const` method to the shape interface that takes a world space bounding box and determines if the shape truly overlaps the given bound.

A default implementation could get the world bound from the shape and use that for the test, and specialized versions could be written for frequently used shapes. Implement this method for `Spheres` and `Triangles`, and modify `KdTreeAccel` to call it. You may find it helpful to read Akenine-Möller's paper (2001) on fast triangle-box overlap testing. Measure the change in pbrt's overall performance caused by this change, separately accounting for increased time spent building the acceleration structure and reduction in ray–object intersection time due to fewer intersections. For a variety of scenes, determine how many fewer intersection tests are performed thanks to this improvement.

● 4.4 Implement "split clipping" in pbrt's BVH implementation. Read the papers by Ernst and Greiner (2007), Dammertz and Keller (2008a), Stich et al. (2009), and Karras and Aila (2013), and implement one of their approaches to subdivide primitives with large bounding boxes relative to their surface area into multiple subprimitives for tree construction. (Doing so will probably require

KdTreeAccel 285

modification to the Shape interface; you will probably want to design a new interface that allows some shapes to indicate that they are unable to subdivide themselves, so that you only need to implement this method for triangles, for example.) Measure the improvement for rendering actual scenes; a compelling way to gather this data is to do the experiment that Dammertz and Keller did, where a scene is rotated around an axis over progressive frames of an animation. Typically, many triangles that are originally axis aligned will have very loose bounding boxes as they rotate more, leading to a substantial performance degradation if split clipping isn't used.

● 4.5   The 30-bit Morton codes used for the HLBVH construction algorithm in the BVHAccel may be insufficient for large scenes (note that they can only represent $2^{10} = 1024$ steps in each dimension.) Modify the BVHAccel to use 64-bit integers with 63-bit Morton codes for HLBVHs. Compare the performance of your approach to the original one with a variety of scenes. Are there scenes where performance is substantially improved? Are there any where there is a loss of performance?

● 4.6   Investigate alternative SAH cost functions for building BVHs or kd-trees. How much can a poor cost function hurt its performance? How much improvement can be had compared to the current one? (See the discussion in the "Further Reading" section for ideas about how the SAH may be improved.)

● 4.7   Construction time for the BVHAccel and particularly the KdTreeAccel can be a meaningful portion of overall rendering time yet, other than HLBVHs, the implementations in this chapter do not parallelize building the acceleration structures. Investigate techniques for parallel construction of accelerators such as described by Wald (2007) and Shevtsov et al. (2007b), and implement one of them in pbrt. How much of a speedup do you achieve in accelerator construction? How does the speedup scale with additional processors? Measure how much of a speedup your changes translate to for overall rendering. For what types of scenes does your implementation have the greatest impact?

● 4.8   The idea of using spatial data structures for ray intersection acceleration can be generalized to include spatial data structures that themselves hold other spatial data structures rather than just primitives. Not only could we have a grid that has subgrids inside the grid cells that have many primitives in them, but we could also have the scene organized into a hierarchical bounding volume where the leaf nodes are grids that hold smaller collections of spatially nearby primitives. Such hybrid techniques can bring the best of a variety of spatial data structure-based ray intersection acceleration methods. In pbrt, because both geometric primitives and intersection accelerators inherit from the Primitive base class and thus provide the same interface, it's easy to mix and match in this way.

Modify pbrt to build hybrid acceleration structures—for example, using a BVH to coarsely sort the scene geometry and then uniform grids at the leaves of the tree to manage dense, spatially local collections of geometry. Measure the running time and memory use for rendering schemes with this method compared to the current accelerators.

4.9   Eisemann et al. (2007) described an even more efficient ray–box intersection test than is used in the BVHAccel. It does more computation at the start for each ray but makes up for this work with fewer computations to do tests for individual bounding boxes. Implement their method in pbrt, and measure the change in rendering time for a variety of scenes. Are there simple scenes where the additional upfront work doesn't pay off? How does the improvement for highly complex scenes compare to the improvement for simpler scenes?

4.10 Read the paper by Segovia and Ernst (2010) on memory-efficient BVHs, and implement their approach in pbrt. How does memory usage with their approach compare to that for the BVHAccel? Compare rendering performance with your approach to pbrt's current performance. Discuss how your results compare to the results reported in their paper.

4.11 Modify pbrt to use the "mailboxing" optimization in the KdTreeAccel to avoid repeated intersections with primitives that overlap multiple kd-tree nodes. Given that pbrt is multi-threaded, you will probably do best to consider either the hashed mailboxing approach suggested by Benthin (2006) or the inverse mailboxing algorithm of Shevtsov et al. (2007a). Measure the performance change compared to the current implementation for a variety of scenes. How does the change in running time relates to changes in reported statistics about the number of ray–primitive intersection tests?

4.12 It is often possible to introduce some approximation into the computation of shadows from very complex geometry (consider, e.g., the branches and leaves of a tree casting a shadow). Lacewell et al. (2008) suggested augmenting the acceleration structure with a prefiltered directionally varying representation of occlusion for regions of space. As shadow rays pass through these regions, an approximate visibility probability can be returned rather than a binary result, and the cost of tree traversal and object intersection tests is reduced. Implement such an approach in pbrt, and compare its performance to the current implementation. Do you see any changes in rendered images?

CHAPTER FIVE

05 COLOR AND RADIOMETRY

In order to precisely describe how light is represented and sampled to compute images, we must first establish some background in *radiometry*—the study of the propagation of electromagnetic radiation in an environment. Of particular interest in rendering are the wavelengths (λ) of electromagnetic radiation between approximately 380 nm and 780 nm, which account for light visible to humans.[1] The lower wavelengths ($\lambda \approx 400$ nm) are the bluish colors, the middle wavelengths ($\lambda \approx 550$ nm) are the greens, and the upper wavelengths ($\lambda \approx 650$ nm) are the reds.

In this chapter, we will introduce four key quantities that describe electromagnetic radiation: flux, intensity, irradiance, and radiance. These radiometric quantities are each described by their *spectral power distribution* (SPD)—a distribution function of wavelength that describes the amount of light at each wavelength. The Spectrum class, which is defined in Section 5.1, is used to represent SPDs in pbrt.

5.1 SPECTRAL REPRESENTATION

The SPDs of real-world objects can be quite complicated; Figure 5.1 shows graphs of the spectral distribution of emission from a fluorescent light and the spectral distribution of the reflectance of lemon skin. A renderer doing computations with SPDs needs a compact, efficient, and accurate way to represent functions like these. In practice, some trade-off needs to be made between these qualities.

A general framework for investigating these issues can be developed based on the problem of finding good *basis functions* to represent SPDs. The idea behind basis functions

---

1   The full range of perceptible wavelengths slightly extends beyond this interval, though the eye's sensitivity at these wavelengths is lower by many orders of magnitude. The range 360–830 nm is often used as a conservative bound when tabulating spectral curves.

Physically Based Rendering: From Theory To Implementation.
http://dx.doi.org/10.1016/B978-0-12-800645-0.50005-1

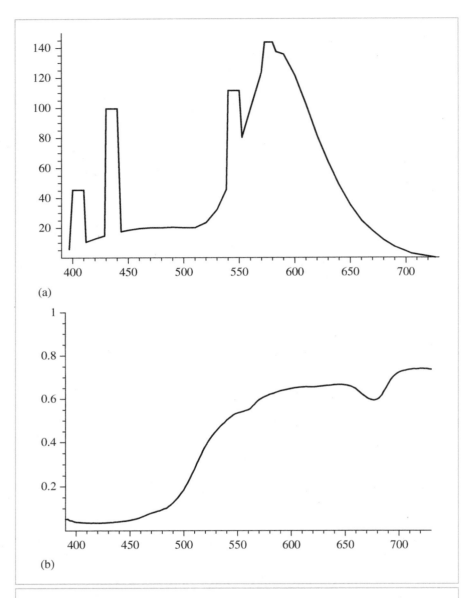

(a)

(b)

Figure 5.1: (a) Spectral power distributions of a fluorescent light and (b) the reflectance of lemon skin. Wavelengths around 400 nm are bluish colors, greens and yellows are in the middle range of wavelengths, and reds have wavelengths around 700 nm. The fluorescent light's SPD is even spikier than shown here, where the SPDs have been binned into 10-nm ranges; it actually emits much of its illumination at single discrete frequencies.

is to map the infinite-dimensional space of possible SPD functions to a low-dimensional space of coefficients $c_i \in \mathbb{R}$. For example, a trivial basis function is the constant function $B(\lambda) = 1$. An arbitrary SPD would be represented in this basis by a single coefficient c equal to its average value, so that its approximation would be $cB(\lambda) = c$. This is obviously a poor approximation, since most SPDs are much more complex than this single basis function is capable of representing accurately.

Many different basis functions have been investigated for spectral representation in computer graphics; the "Further Reading" section cites a number of papers and further resources on this topic. Different sets of basis functions can offset substantially different trade-offs in the complexity of the key operations like converting an arbitrary SPD into a set of coefficients (projecting it into the basis), computing the coefficients for the SPD given by the product of two SPDs expressed in the basis, and so on. In this chapter, we'll introduce two representations that can be used for spectra in pbrt: RGBSpectrum, which follows the typical computer graphics practice of representing SPDs with coefficients representing a mixture of red, green, and blue colors, and SampledSpectrum, which represents the SPD as a set of point samples over a range of wavelengths.

5.1.1 THE Spectrum TYPE

Throughout pbrt, we have been careful to implement all computations involving SPDs in terms of the Spectrum type, using a specific set of built-in operators (addition, multiplication, etc.). The Spectrum type hides the details of the particular spectral representation used, so that changing this detail of the system only requires changing the Spectrum implementation; other code can remain unchanged. The implementations of the Spectrum type are in the files core/spectrum.h and core/spectrum.cpp.

The selection of which spectrum representation is used for the Spectrum type in pbrt is done with a typedef in the file core/pbrt.h. By default, pbrt uses the more efficient but less accurate RGB representation.

⟨*Global Forward Declarations*⟩ ≡
```
typedef RGBSpectrum Spectrum;
// typedef SampledSpectrum Spectrum;
```

We have not written the system such that the selection of which Spectrum implementation to use could be resolved at run time; to switch to a different representation, the entire system must be recompiled. One advantage to this design is that many of the various Spectrum methods can be implemented as short functions that can be inlined by the compiler, rather than being left as stand-alone functions that have to be invoked through the relatively slow virtual method call mechanism. Inlining frequently used short functions like these can give a substantial improvement in performance. A second advantage is that structures in the system that hold instances of the Spectrum type can hold them directly rather than needing to allocate them dynamically based on the spectral representation chosen at run time.

5.1.2 CoefficientSpectrum IMPLEMENTATION

Both of the representations implemented in this chapter are based on storing a fixed number of samples of the SPD. Therefore, we'll start by defining the CoefficientSpectrum template class, which represents a spectrum as a particular number of samples given as the nSpectrumSamples template parameter. Both RGBSpectrum and SampledSpectrum are partially implemented by inheriting from CoefficientSpectrum.

⟨*Spectrum Declarations*⟩ ≡
```
template <int nSpectrumSamples> class CoefficientSpectrum {
public:
    ⟨CoefficientSpectrum Public Methods 316⟩
    ⟨CoefficientSpectrum Public Data 318⟩
protected:
    ⟨CoefficientSpectrum Protected Data 316⟩
};
```

One CoefficientSpectrum constructor is provided; it initializes a spectrum with a constant value across all wavelengths.

⟨*CoefficientSpectrum Public Methods*⟩ ≡   316
```
CoefficientSpectrum(Float v = 0.f) {
    for (int i = 0; i < nSpectrumSamples; ++i)
        c[i] = v;
}
```

⟨*CoefficientSpectrum Protected Data*⟩ ≡   316
```
Float c[nSpectrumSamples];
```

A variety of arithmetic operations on Spectrum objects are needed; the implementations in CoefficientSpectrum are all straightforward. First, we define operations to add pairs of spectral distributions. For the sampled representation, it's easy to show that each sample value for the sum of two SPDs is equal to the sum of the corresponding sample values.

⟨*CoefficientSpectrum Public Methods*⟩ +≡   316
```
CoefficientSpectrum &operator+=(const CoefficientSpectrum &s2) {
    for (int i = 0; i < nSpectrumSamples; ++i)
        c[i] += s2.c[i];
    return *this;
}
```

⟨*CoefficientSpectrum Public Methods*⟩ +≡   316
```
CoefficientSpectrum operator+(const CoefficientSpectrum &s2) const {
    CoefficientSpectrum ret = *this;
    for (int i = 0; i < nSpectrumSamples; ++i)
        ret.c[i] += s2.c[i];
    return ret;
}
```

Similarly, subtraction, multiplication, division, and unary negation are defined component-wise. These methods are very similar to the ones already shown, so we won't include them here. pbrt also provides equality and inequality tests, also not included here.

It is often useful to know if a spectrum represents an SPD with value zero everywhere. If, for example, a surface has zero reflectance, the light transport routines can avoid the computational cost of casting reflection rays that have contributions that would eventually be multiplied by zeros and thus do not need to be traced.

⟨*CoefficientSpectrum Public Methods*⟩ +≡   316
```
    bool IsBlack() const {
        for (int i = 0; i < nSpectrumSamples; ++i)
            if (c[i] != 0.) return false;
        return true;
    }
```

The Spectrum implementation (and thus the CoefficientSpectrum implementation) must also provide implementations of a number of slightly more esoteric methods, including those that take the square root of an SPD or raise the function it represents to a given power. These are needed for some of the computations performed by the Fresnel classes in Chapter 8, for example. The implementation of Sqrt() takes the square root of each component to give the square root of the SPD. The implementations of Pow() and Exp() are analogous and won't be included here.

⟨*CoefficientSpectrum Public Methods*⟩ +≡   316
```
    friend CoefficientSpectrum Sqrt(const CoefficientSpectrum &s) {
        CoefficientSpectrum ret;
        for (int i = 0; i < nSpectrumSamples; ++i)
            ret.c[i] = std::sqrt(s.c[i]);
        return ret;
    }
```

It's frequently useful to be able to linearly interpolate between two SPDs with a parameter t.

⟨*Spectrum Inline Functions*⟩ ≡
```
    inline Spectrum Lerp(Float t, const Spectrum &s1, const Spectrum &s2) {
        return (1 - t) * s1 + t * s2;
    }
```

Some portions of the image processing pipeline will want to clamp a spectrum to ensure that the function it represents is within some allowable range.

⟨*CoefficientSpectrum Public Methods*⟩ +≡   316
```
    CoefficientSpectrum Clamp(Float low = 0, Float high = Infinity) const {
        CoefficientSpectrum ret;
        for (int i = 0; i < nSpectrumSamples; ++i)
            ret.c[i] = ::Clamp(c[i], low, high);
        return ret;
    }
```

Finally, we provide a debugging routine to check if any of the sample values of the SPD is the not-a-number (NaN floating-point value). This situation can happen due to an accidental division by 0; Assert()s throughout the system use this method to catch this case close to where it happens.

⟨*CoefficientSpectrum Public Methods*⟩ +≡   **316**
```
    bool HasNaNs() const {
        for (int i = 0; i < nSpectrumSamples; ++i)
            if (std::isnan(c[i])) return true;
        return false;
    }
```

Most of the spectral computations in pbrt can be implemented using the basic operations we have defined so far. However, in some cases it's necessary to be able to iterate over a set of spectral samples that represent an SPD—for example to perform a spectral sample-based table lookup or to evaluate a piecewise function over wavelengths. Classes that need this functionality in pbrt include the TabulatedBSSRDF class, which is used for subsurface scattering, and the HomogeneousMedium and GridDensityMedium classes.

For these uses, CoefficientSpectrum provides a public constant, nSamples, that gives the number of samples used to represent the SPD and an operator[] method to access individual sample values.

⟨*CoefficientSpectrum Public Data*⟩ ≡   **316**
```
    static const int nSamples = nSpectrumSamples;
```

⟨*CoefficientSpectrum Public Methods*⟩ +≡   **316**
```
    Float &operator[](int i) {
        return c[i];
    }
```

Note that the presence of this sample accessor imposes the implicit assumption that the spectral representation is a set of coefficients that linearly scale a fixed set of basis functions. If, for example, a Spectrum implementation instead represented SPDs as a sum of Gaussians where the coefficients c_i alternatingly scaled the Gaussians and set their width,

$$S(\lambda) = \sum_i^N c_{2i} \, e^{-c_{2i+1}},$$

then the code that currently uses this accessor would need to be modified, perhaps to instead operate on a version of the SPD that had been converted to a set of linear coefficients. While this crack in the Spectrum abstraction is not ideal, it simplifies other parts of the current system and isn't too hard to clean up if one adds spectral representations, where this assumption isn't correct.

5.2 THE SampledSpectrum CLASS

SampledSpectrum uses the CoefficientSpectrum infrastructure to represent an SPD with uniformly spaced samples between a starting and an ending wavelength. The wavelength range covers from 400 nm to 700 nm—the range of the visual spectrum where the human visual system is most sensitive. The number of samples, 60, is generally more than enough to accurately represent complex SPDs for rendering. (See the "Further Reading" section for background on sampling rate requirements for SPDs.) Thus, the first sample represents the wavelength range [400, 405), the second represents [405, 410), and so forth. These values can easily be changed here as needed.

⟨*Spectrum Utility Declarations*⟩ ≡
```
static const int sampledLambdaStart = 400;
static const int sampledLambdaEnd = 700;
static const int nSpectralSamples = 60;
```

⟨*Spectrum Declarations*⟩ +≡
```
class SampledSpectrum : public CoefficientSpectrum<nSpectralSamples> {
public:
    ⟨SampledSpectrum Public Methods 319⟩
private:
    ⟨SampledSpectrum Private Data 324⟩
};
```

By inheriting from the CoefficientSpectrum class, SampledSpectrum automatically has all of the basic spectrum arithmetic operations defined earlier. The main methods left to define for it are those that initialize it from spectral data and convert the SPD it represents to other spectral representations (such as RGB). The constructor for initializing it with a constant SPD is straightforward.

⟨*SampledSpectrum Public Methods*⟩ ≡   319
```
SampledSpectrum(Float v = 0.f) : CoefficientSpectrum(v) { }
```

We will often be provided spectral data as a set of (λ_i, v_i) samples, where the ith sample has some value v_i at wavelength λ_i. In general, the samples may have an irregular spacing and there may be more or fewer of them than the SampledSpectrum stores. (See the directory scenes/spds in the pbrt distribution for a variety of SPDs for use with pbrt, many of them with irregular sample spacing.)

The FromSampled() method takes arrays of SPD sample values v at given wavelengths lambda and uses them to define a piecewise linear function to represent the SPD. For each SPD sample in the SampledSpectrum, it uses the AverageSpectrumSamples() utility function, defined below, to compute the average of the piecewise linear function over the range of wavelengths that each SPD sample is responsible for.

⟨*SampledSpectrum Public Methods*⟩ +≡   319
```
static SampledSpectrum FromSampled(const Float *lambda,
                                   const Float *v, int n) {
    ⟨Sort samples if unordered, use sorted for returned spectrum 320⟩
    SampledSpectrum r;
    for (int i = 0; i < nSpectralSamples; ++i) {
        ⟨Compute average value of given SPD over ith sample's range 320⟩
    }
    return r;
}
```

The AverageSpectrumSamples() function requires that the (λ_i, v_i) values be sorted by wavelength. The SpectrumSamplesSorted() function checks that they are; if not,

SortSpectrumSamples() sorts them. Note that we allocate new storage for the sorted samples and do not modify the values passed in by the caller; in general, doing so would likely be unexpected behavior for a user of this function (who shouldn't need to worry about these requirements of its specific implementation). We won't include the implementations of either of these two functions here, as they are straightforward.

⟨*Sort samples if unordered, use sorted for returned spectrum*⟩ ≡   319, 333
```
    if (!SpectrumSamplesSorted(lambda, v, n)) {
        std::vector<Float> slambda(&lambda[0], &lambda[n]);
        std::vector<Float> sv(&v[0], &v[n]);
        SortSpectrumSamples(&slambda[0], &sv[0], n);
        return FromSampled(&slambda[0], &sv[0], n);
    }
```

In order to compute the value for the ith spectral sample, we compute the range of wavelengths that it's responsible for—lambda0 to lambda1—and use the AverageSpectrumSamples() function to compute the average value of the given piecewise linear SPD over that range. This is a 1D instance of sampling and reconstruction, a topic that will be discussed in more detail in Chapter 7.

⟨*Compute average value of given SPD over ith sample's range*⟩ ≡   319
```
    Float lambda0 = Lerp(Float(i) / Float(nSpectralSamples),
                         sampledLambdaStart, sampledLambdaEnd);
    Float lambda1 = Lerp(Float(i + 1) / Float(nSpectralSamples),
                         sampledLambdaStart, sampledLambdaEnd);
    r.c[i] = AverageSpectrumSamples(lambda, v, n, lambda0, lambda1);
```

Figure 5.2 shows the basic approach taken by AverageSpectrumSamples(): it iterates over each of the linear segments between samples that are partially or fully within the range of

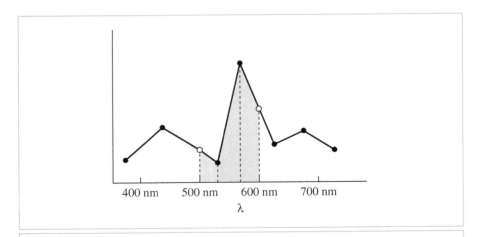

Figure 5.2: When resampling an irregularly defined SPD, we need to compute the average value of the piecewise linear function defined by the SPD samples. Here, we want to average the value from 500 nm to 600 nm—the shaded region under the plot. The FromSampled() function does this by computing the areas of each of the regions denoted by dashed lines in this figure.

wavelengths, lambdaStart to lambdaEnd. For each such segment, it computes the average value over its range, scales the average by the wavelength range the segment covers, and accumulates a sum of these values. The final average value is this sum divided by the total wavelength range.

⟨*Spectrum Method Definitions*⟩ ≡
```
Float AverageSpectrumSamples(const Float *lambda, const Float *vals,
        int n, Float lambdaStart, Float lambdaEnd) {
    ⟨Handle cases with out-of-bounds range or single sample only  321⟩
    Float sum = 0;
    ⟨Add contributions of constant segments before/after samples  321⟩
    ⟨Advance to first relevant wavelength segment  322⟩
    ⟨Loop over wavelength sample segments and add contributions  322⟩
    return sum / (lambdaEnd - lambdaStart);
}
```

The function starts by checking for and handling the edge cases where the range of wavelengths to average over is outside the range of provided wavelengths or the case where there is only a single sample, in which case the average value is trivially computed. We assume that the SPD has a constant value (the values at the two respective endpoints) outside of the provided sample range; if this isn't a reasonable assumption for a particular set of data, the data provided should have explicit values of (for example) 0 at the endpoints.

⟨*Handle cases with out-of-bounds range or single sample only*⟩ ≡   321
```
if (lambdaEnd  <= lambda[0])     return vals[0];
if (lambdaStart >= lambda[n - 1]) return vals[n - 1];
if (n == 1) return vals[0];
```

Having handled these cases, the next step is to check to see if part of the range to average over goes beyond the first and/or last sample value. If so, we accumulate the contribution of the constant segment(s), scaled by the out-of-bounds wavelength range.

⟨*Add contributions of constant segments before/after samples*⟩ ≡   321
```
if (lambdaStart < lambda[0])
    sum += vals[0] * (lambda[0] - lambdaStart);
if (lambdaEnd > lambda[n-1])
    sum += vals[n - 1] * (lambdaEnd - lambda[n - 1]);
```

And now we advance to the first index i where the starting wavelength of the interpolation range overlaps the segment from λ_i to λ_{i+1}. A more efficient implementation would use a binary search rather than a linear search here.[2] However, this code is currently only called at scene initialization time, so the lack of these optimizations doesn't currently impact rendering performance.

Float 1062

---

[2]   An even more efficient implementation would take advantage of the fact that the calling code will generally ask for interpolated values over a series of adjacent wavelength ranges, and possibly take all of the ranges in a single call. It could then incrementally find the starting index for the next interpolation starting from the end of the previous one.

⟨*Advance to first relevant wavelength segment*⟩ ≡   321
```
int i = 0;
while (lambdaStart > lambda[i + 1]) ++i;
```

The loop below iterates over each of the linear segments that the averaging range overlaps. For each one, it computes the average value over the wavelength range segLambda
Start to segLambdaEnd by averaging the values of the function at those two points. The values in turn are computed by interp(), a lambda function that linearly interpolates between the two endpoints at the given wavelength.

The std::min() and std::max() calls below compute the wavelength range to average over within the segment; note that they naturally handle the cases where lambdaStart, lambdaEnd, or both of them are within the current segment.

⟨*Loop over wavelength sample segments and add contributions*⟩ ≡   321
```
auto interp = [lambda, vals](Float w, int i) {
    return Lerp((w - lambda[i]) / (lambda[i + 1] - lambda[i]),
                vals[i], vals[i + 1]);
};
for (; i+1 < n && lambdaEnd >= lambda[i]; ++i) {
    Float segLambdaStart = std::max(lambdaStart, lambda[i]);
    Float segLambdaEnd =   std::min(lambdaEnd,   lambda[i + 1]);
    sum += 0.5 * (interp(segLambdaStart, i) + interp(segLambdaEnd, i)) *
        (segLambdaEnd - segLambdaStart);
}
```

5.2.1 XYZ COLOR

A remarkable property of the human visual system makes it possible to represent colors for human perception with just three floating-point numbers. The *tristimulus theory* of color perception says that all visible SPDs can be accurately represented for human observers with three values, x_λ, y_λ, and z_λ. Given an SPD $S(\lambda)$, these values are computed by integrating its product with the *spectral matching curves* $X(\lambda)$, $Y(\lambda)$, and $Z(\lambda)$:

$$x_\lambda = \frac{1}{\int Y(\lambda)d\lambda} \int_\lambda S(\lambda)\, X(\lambda)\, d\lambda$$

$$y_\lambda = \frac{1}{\int Y(\lambda)d\lambda} \int_\lambda S(\lambda)\, Y(\lambda)\, d\lambda \qquad [5.1]$$

$$z_\lambda = \frac{1}{\int Y(\lambda)d\lambda} \int_\lambda S(\lambda)\, Z(\lambda)\, d\lambda.$$

These curves were determined by the Commission Internationale de l'Éclairage (CIE) standards body after a series of experiments with human test subjects and are graphed in Figure 5.3. It is believed that these matching curves are generally similar to the responses of the three types of color-sensitive cones in the human retina. Remarkably, SPDs with substantially different distributions may have very similar x_λ, y_λ, and z_λ values. To the human observer, such SPDs actually appear the same visually. Pairs of such spectra are called *metamers*.

Float 1062

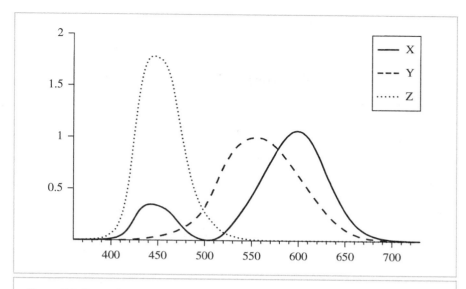

Figure 5.3: Computing the XYZ Values for an Arbitrary SPD. The SPD is convolved with each of the three matching curves to compute the values x_λ, y_λ, and z_λ, using Equation (5.1).

This brings us to a subtle point about representations of spectral power distributions. Most color spaces attempt to model colors that are visible to humans and therefore use only three coefficients, exploiting the tristimulus theory of color perception. Although XYZ works well to represent a given SPD to be displayed for a human observer, it is *not* a particularly good set of basis functions for spectral computation. For example, although XYZ values would work well to describe the perceived color of lemon skin or a fluorescent light individually (recall Figure 5.1), the product of their respective XYZ values is likely to give a noticeably different XYZ color than the XYZ value computed by multiplying more accurate representations of their SPDs and *then* computing the XYZ value.

pbrt provides the values of the standard $X(\lambda)$, $Y(\lambda)$, and $Z(\lambda)$ response curves sampled at 1-nm increments from 360 nm to 830 nm. The wavelengths of the ith sample in the arrays below are given by the ith element of CIE_lambda; having the wavelengths of the samples explicitly represented in this way makes it easy to pass the XYZ samples into functions like AverageSpectrumSamples() that take such an array of wavelengths as a parameter.

⟨*Spectral Data Declarations*⟩ ≡

```
static const int nCIESamples = 471;
extern const Float CIE_X[nCIESamples];
extern const Float CIE_Y[nCIESamples];
extern const Float CIE_Z[nCIESamples];
extern const Float CIE_lambda[nCIESamples];
```

SampledSpectrum uses these samples to compute the XYZ matching curves in its spectral representation (i.e., themselves as SampledSpectrums).

⟨*SampledSpectrum Private Data*⟩ ≡   319
```
static SampledSpectrum X, Y, Z;
```

The `SampledSpectrum` XYZ matching curves are computed in the `SampledSpectrum::Init()` method, which is called at system startup time by the `pbrtInit()` function defined in Section B.2.

⟨*SampledSpectrum Public Methods*⟩ +≡   319
```
static void Init() {
    ⟨Compute XYZ matching functions for SampledSpectrum 324⟩
    ⟨Compute RGB to spectrum functions for SampledSpectrum⟩
}
```

⟨*General* pbrt *Initialization*⟩ ≡   1109
```
SampledSpectrum::Init();
```

Given the wavelength range and number of samples for `SampledSpectrum`, computing the values of the matching functions for each sample is just a matter of computing the sample's wavelength range and using the `AverageSpectrumSamples()` routine.

⟨*Compute XYZ matching functions for* SampledSpectrum⟩ ≡   324
```
for (int i = 0; i < nSpectralSamples; ++i) {
    Float wl0 = Lerp(Float(i) / Float(nSpectralSamples),
                     sampledLambdaStart, sampledLambdaEnd);
    Float wl1 = Lerp(Float(i + 1) / Float(nSpectralSamples),
                     sampledLambdaStart, sampledLambdaEnd);
    X.c[i] = AverageSpectrumSamples(CIE_lambda, CIE_X, nCIESamples,
                                    wl0, wl1);
    Y.c[i] = AverageSpectrumSamples(CIE_lambda, CIE_Y, nCIESamples,
                                    wl0, wl1);
    Z.c[i] = AverageSpectrumSamples(CIE_lambda, CIE_Z, nCIESamples,
                                    wl0, wl1);
}
```

All `Spectrum` implementations in pbrt must provide a method that converts their SPD to $(x_\lambda, y_\lambda, z_\lambda)$ coefficients. This method is called, for example, in the process of updating pixels in the image. When a `Spectrum` representing the light carried along a ray from the camera is provided to the `Film`, the `Film` converts the SPD into XYZ coefficients as a first step in the process of finally turning them into RGB values used for storage and/or display.

To compute XYZ coefficients, `SampledSpectrum` computes the integrals from Equation (5.1) with a Riemann sum:

$$x_\lambda \approx \frac{1}{\int Y(\lambda)\mathrm{d}\lambda} \frac{\lambda_{\text{end}} - \lambda_{\text{start}}}{N} \sum_{i=0}^{N-1} X_i c_i,$$

and so forth.

⟨*SampledSpectrum Public Methods*⟩ +≡   319
```
void ToXYZ(Float xyz[3]) const {
    xyz[0] = xyz[1] = xyz[2] = 0.f;
    for (int i = 0; i < nSpectralSamples; ++i) {
        xyz[0] += X.c[i] * c[i];
        xyz[1] += Y.c[i] * c[i];
        xyz[2] += Z.c[i] * c[i];
    }
    Float scale = Float(sampledLambdaEnd - sampledLambdaStart) /
        Float(CIE_Y_integral * nSpectralSamples);
    xyz[0] *= scale;
    xyz[1] *= scale;
    xyz[2] *= scale;
}
```

The value of the integral $\int Y(\lambda)d\lambda$ is used in a number of calculations like these; it's therefore useful to have its value available directly via the CIE_Y_integral constant.

⟨*Spectral Data Declarations*⟩ +≡
```
static const Float CIE_Y_integral = 106.856895;
```

The y coefficient of XYZ color is closely related to *luminance*, which measures the perceived brightness of a color. Luminance is described in more detail in Section 5.4.3. We provide a method to compute y alone in a separate method as often only the luminance of a spectrum is desired. (For example, some of the light transport algorithms in Chapters 14–16 use luminance as a measure of the relative importance of light-carrying paths through the scene.)

⟨*SampledSpectrum Public Methods*⟩ +≡   319
```
Float y() const {
    Float yy = 0.f;
    for (int i = 0; i < nSpectralSamples; ++i)
        yy += Y.c[i] * c[i];
    return yy * Float(sampledLambdaEnd - sampledLambdaStart) /
        Float(CIE_Y_integral * nSpectralSamples);
}
```

5.2.2 RGB COLOR

When we display an RGB color on a display, the spectrum that is actually displayed is basically determined by the weighted sum of three spectral response curves, one for each of red, green, and blue, as emitted by the display's phosphors, LED or LCD elements, or plasma cells.[3] Figure 5.4 plots the red, green, and blue distributions emitted by a LED display and a LCD display; note that they are remarkably different. Figure 5.5 in turn shows the SPDs that result from displaying the RGB color (0.6, 0.3, 0.2) on those displays. Not surprisingly, the resulting SPDs are quite different as well. This example

---

3   This model is admittedly a simplification in that it neglects any additional processing the display does; in particular, many displays perform nonlinear remappings of the displayed values.

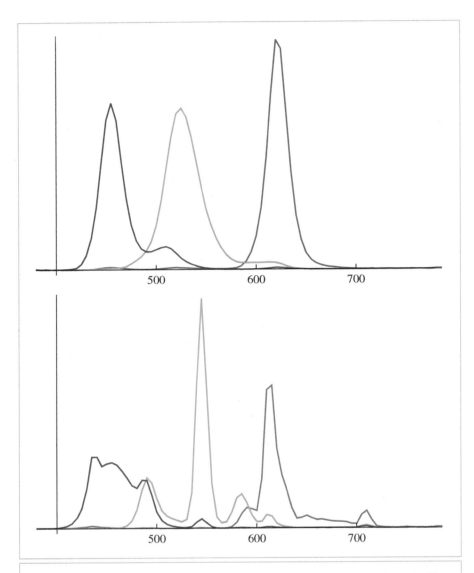

Figure 5.4: Red, Green, and Blue Emission Curves for an LCD Display and an LED Display. The top plot shows the curves for an LCD display, and the bottom shows them for an LED. These two displays have quite different emission profiles. *(Data courtesy of X-Rite, Inc.)*

illustrates that using RGB values provided by the user to describe a particular color is actually only meaningful given knowledge of the characteristics of the display they were using when they selected the RGB values.

Given an $(x_\lambda, y_\lambda, z_\lambda)$ representation of an SPD, we can convert it to corresponding RGB coefficients, given the choice of a particular set of SPDs that define red, green, and blue for a display of interest. Given the spectral response curves $R(\lambda)$, $G(\lambda)$, and $B(\lambda)$, for a

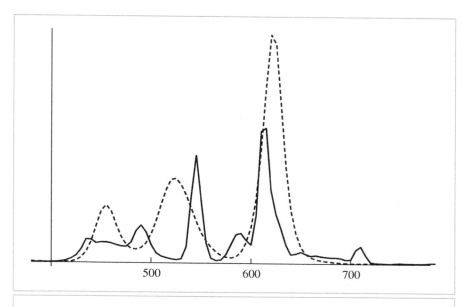

Figure 5.5: SPDs from Displaying the RGB Color $(0.6, 0.3, 0.2)$ **on LED and LCD Displays.** The resulting emitted SPDs are remarkably different, even given the same RGB values, due to the different emission curves illustrated in Figure 5.4.

particular display, RGB coefficients can be computed by integrating the response curves with the SPD $S(\lambda)$:

$$r = \int R(\lambda)S(\lambda)d\lambda = \int R(\lambda)(x_\lambda X(\lambda) + y_\lambda Y(\lambda) + z_\lambda Z(\lambda))\, d\lambda$$

$$= x_\lambda \int R(\lambda)X(\lambda)\, d\lambda + y_\lambda \int R(\lambda)Y(\lambda)\, d\lambda + z_\lambda \int R(\lambda)Z(\lambda)\, d\lambda.$$

The integrals of the products of $R(\lambda)X(\lambda)$ and so forth can be precomputed for given response curves, making it possible to express the full conversion as a matrix:

$$\begin{bmatrix} r \\ g \\ b \end{bmatrix} = \begin{pmatrix} \int R(\lambda)X(\lambda)d\lambda & \int R(\lambda)Y(\lambda)d\lambda & \int R(\lambda)Z(\lambda)d\lambda \\ \int G(\lambda)X(\lambda)d\lambda & \int G(\lambda)Y(\lambda)d\lambda & \int G(\lambda)Z(\lambda)d\lambda \\ \int B(\lambda)X(\lambda)d\lambda & \int B(\lambda)Y(\lambda)d\lambda & \int B(\lambda)Z(\lambda)d\lambda \end{pmatrix} \begin{bmatrix} x_\lambda \\ y_\lambda \\ z_\lambda \end{bmatrix}.$$

The conversion routines implemented in pbrt are based on a standard set of these RGB spectra that has been defined for high-definition television.

⟨*Spectrum Utility Declarations*⟩ $+\equiv$
```
inline void XYZToRGB(const Float xyz[3], Float rgb[3]) {
    rgb[0] =  3.240479f*xyz[0] - 1.537150f*xyz[1] - 0.498535f*xyz[2];
    rgb[1] = -0.969256f*xyz[0] + 1.875991f*xyz[1] + 0.041556f*xyz[2];
    rgb[2] =  0.055648f*xyz[0] - 0.204043f*xyz[1] + 1.057311f*xyz[2];
}
```

Float 1062

The inverse of this matrix gives coefficients to convert given RGB values expressed with respect to a particular set of RGB response curves to $(x_\lambda, y_\lambda, z_\lambda)$ coefficients.

⟨*Spectrum Utility Declarations*⟩ +≡
```
inline void RGBToXYZ(const Float rgb[3], Float xyz[3]) {
    xyz[0] = 0.412453f*rgb[0] + 0.357580f*rgb[1] + 0.180423f*rgb[2];
    xyz[1] = 0.212671f*rgb[0] + 0.715160f*rgb[1] + 0.072169f*rgb[2];
    xyz[2] = 0.019334f*rgb[0] + 0.119193f*rgb[1] + 0.950227f*rgb[2];
}
```

Given these functions, a SampledSpectrum can convert to RGB coefficients by first converting to XYZ and then using the XYZToRGB() utility function.

⟨*SampledSpectrum Public Methods*⟩ +≡   319
```
void ToRGB(Float rgb[3]) const {
    Float xyz[3];
    ToXYZ(xyz);
    XYZToRGB(xyz, rgb);
}
```

An RGBSpectrum can also be created easily, using the ToRGB() method.

⟨*SampledSpectrum Public Methods*⟩ +≡   319
```
RGBSpectrum ToRGBSpectrum() const;
```

Going the other way and converting from RGB or XYZ values to a SPD isn't as easy: the problem is highly under-constrained. Recall that an infinite number of different SPDs have the same $(x_\lambda, y_\lambda, z_\lambda)$ (and thus RGB) coefficients. Thus, given an RGB or $(x_\lambda, y_\lambda, z_\lambda)$ value, there are an infinite number of possible SPDs that could be chosen for it. There are a number of desirable criteria that we'd like a conversion function to have:

- If all of the RGB coefficients have the same value, the resulting SPD should be constant.
- In general, it's desirable that the computed SPD be smooth. Most real-world objects have relatively smooth spectra. (The main source of spiky spectra is light sources, especially fluorescents. Fortunately, actual spectral data are more commonly available for illuminants than they are for reflectances.)

The smoothness goal is one of the reasons why constructing an SPD as a weighted sum of a display's $R(\lambda)$, $G(\lambda)$, and $B(\lambda)$ SPDs is not a good solution: as shown in Figure 5.4, those functions are generally irregular and spiky, and a weighted sum of them will thus not be a very smooth SPD. Although the result will be a metamer of the given RGB values, it's likely not an accurate representation of the SPD of the actual object.

Here we implement a method for converting RGBs to SPDs suggested by Smits (1999) that tries to achieve the goals above. This approach is based on the observation that a good start is to compute individual SPDs for red, green, and blue that are smooth and such that computing the weighted sum of them with the given RGB coefficients and then converting back to RGB give a result that is close to the original RGB coefficients. He found such spectra through a numerical optimization procedure.

Smits observed that two additional improvements could be made to this basic approach. First, rather than representing constant spectra by the sums of the computed red, green, and blue SPDs, the sum of which isn't exactly constant, it's better to represent constant spectra with constant SPDs. Second, mixtures of colors like yellow (a mixture of red and green) that are a mixture of two of the primaries are better represented by their own precomputed smooth SPDs rather than the sum of SPDs for the two corresponding primaries.

The following arrays store SPDs that meet these criteria, with their samples' wavelengths in RGB2SpectLambda[] (these data were generated by Karl vom Berge).

⟨*Spectral Data Declarations*⟩ +≡
```
static const int nRGB2SpectSamples = 32;
extern const Float RGB2SpectLambda[nRGB2SpectSamples];
extern const Float RGBRefl2SpectWhite[nRGB2SpectSamples];
extern const Float RGBRefl2SpectCyan[nRGB2SpectSamples];
extern const Float RGBRefl2SpectMagenta[nRGB2SpectSamples];
extern const Float RGBRefl2SpectYellow[nRGB2SpectSamples];
extern const Float RGBRefl2SpectRed[nRGB2SpectSamples];
extern const Float RGBRefl2SpectGreen[nRGB2SpectSamples];
extern const Float RGBRefl2SpectBlue[nRGB2SpectSamples];
```

If a given RGB color describes illumination from a light source, better results are achieved if the conversion tables are computed using the spectral power distribution of a representative illumination source to define "white" rather than using a constant spectrum as they are for the tables above that are used for reflectances. The RGBIllum2Spect arrays use the D65 spectral power distribution, which has been standardized by the CIE to represent midday sunlight. (The D65 illuminant will be discussed more in Section 12.1.2.)

⟨*Spectral Data Declarations*⟩ +≡
```
extern const Float RGBIllum2SpectWhite[nRGB2SpectSamples];
extern const Float RGBIllum2SpectCyan[nRGB2SpectSamples];
extern const Float RGBIllum2SpectMagenta[nRGB2SpectSamples];
extern const Float RGBIllum2SpectYellow[nRGB2SpectSamples];
extern const Float RGBIllum2SpectRed[nRGB2SpectSamples];
extern const Float RGBIllum2SpectGreen[nRGB2SpectSamples];
extern const Float RGBIllum2SpectBlue[nRGB2SpectSamples];
```

The fragment ⟨*Compute RGB to spectrum functions for* SampledSpectrum⟩, which is called from SampledSpectrum::Init(), isn't included here; it initializes the following SampledSpectrum values by resampling the RGBRefl2Spect and RGBIllum2Spect distributions using the AverageSpectrumSamples() function.

⟨*SampledSpectrum Private Data*⟩ +≡   **319**
```
static SampledSpectrum rgbRefl2SpectWhite, rgbRefl2SpectCyan;
static SampledSpectrum rgbRefl2SpectMagenta, rgbRefl2SpectYellow;
static SampledSpectrum rgbRefl2SpectRed, rgbRefl2SpectGreen;
static SampledSpectrum rgbRefl2SpectBlue;
```

⟨*SampledSpectrum Private Data*⟩ +≡　　　　　　　　　　　　　　　319

```
static SampledSpectrum rgbIllum2SpectWhite, rgbIllum2SpectCyan;
static SampledSpectrum rgbIllum2SpectMagenta, rgbIllum2SpectYellow;
static SampledSpectrum rgbIllum2SpectRed, rgbIllum2SpectGreen;
static SampledSpectrum rgbIllum2SpectBlue;
```

The `SampledSpectrum::FromRGB()` method converts from the given RGB values to a full SPD. In addition to the RGB values, it takes an enumeration value that denotes whether the RGB value represents surface reflectance or an illuminant; the corresponding `rgbIllum2Spect` or `rgbRefl2Spect` values are used for the conversion.

⟨*Spectrum Utility Declarations*⟩ +≡

```
enum class SpectrumType { Reflectance, Illuminant };
```

⟨*Spectrum Method Definitions*⟩ +≡

```
SampledSpectrum SampledSpectrum::FromRGB(const Float rgb[3],
                                         SpectrumType type) {
    SampledSpectrum r;
    if (type == SpectrumType::Reflectance) {
        ⟨Convert reflectance spectrum to RGB 330⟩
    } else {
        ⟨Convert illuminant spectrum to RGB⟩
    }
    return r.Clamp();
}
```

Here we'll show the conversion process for reflectances. The computation for illuminants is the same, just using the different conversion values. First, the implementation determines whether the red, green, or blue channel is the smallest.

⟨*Convert reflectance spectrum to RGB*⟩ ≡　　　　　　　　　　　　330

```
if (rgb[0] <= rgb[1] && rgb[0] <= rgb[2]) {
    ⟨Compute reflectance SampledSpectrum with rgb[0] as minimum 331⟩
} else if (rgb[1] <= rgb[0] && rgb[1] <= rgb[2]) {
    ⟨Compute reflectance SampledSpectrum with rgb[1] as minimum⟩
} else {
    ⟨Compute reflectance SampledSpectrum with rgb[2] as minimum⟩
}
```

Here is the code for the case of a red component being the smallest. (The cases for green and blue are analogous and not included in the book here.) If red is the smallest, we know that green and blue have greater values than red. As such, we can start to convert the final SPD to return by assigning to it the value of the red component times the white spectrum in `rgbRefl2SpectWhite`. Having done this, the remaining RGB value left to process is $(0, g - r, b - r)$. The code in turn determines which of the remaining two components is the smallest. This value, times the cyan (green and blue) spectrum, is added to the result and we're left with either $(0, g - b, 0)$ or $(0, 0, b - g)$. Based on whether the green or blue channel is non-zero, the green or blue SPD is scaled by the remainder and the conversion is complete.

⟨*Compute reflectance* SampledSpectrum *with* rgb[0] *as minimum*⟩ ≡   330
```
    r += rgb[0] * rgbRefl2SpectWhite;
    if (rgb[1] <= rgb[2]) {
        r += (rgb[1] - rgb[0]) * rgbRefl2SpectCyan;
        r += (rgb[2] - rgb[1]) * rgbRefl2SpectBlue;
    } else {
        r += (rgb[2] - rgb[0]) * rgbRefl2SpectCyan;
        r += (rgb[1] - rgb[2]) * rgbRefl2SpectGreen;
    }
```

Given the method to convert from RGB, converting from XYZ color is easy. We first convert from XYZ to RGB and then use the FromRGB() method.

⟨*SampledSpectrum Public Methods*⟩ +≡   319
```
    static SampledSpectrum FromXYZ(const Float xyz[3],
            SpectrumType type = SpectrumType::Reflectance) {
        Float rgb[3];
        XYZToRGB(xyz, rgb);
        return FromRGB(rgb, type);
    }
```

Finally, we provide a constructor that converts from an instance of the RGBSpectrum class, again using the infrastructure above.

⟨*Spectrum Method Definitions*⟩ +≡
```
    SampledSpectrum::SampledSpectrum(const RGBSpectrum &r, SpectrumType t) {
        Float rgb[3];
        r.ToRGB(rgb);
        *this = SampledSpectrum::FromRGB(rgb, t);
    }
```

5.3 RGBSpectrum IMPLEMENTATION

The RGBSpectrum implementation here represents SPDs with a weighted sum of red, green, and blue components. Recall that this representation is ill defined: given two different computer displays, having them display the same RGB value won't cause them to emit the same SPD. Thus, in order for a set of RGB values to specify an actual SPD, we must know the monitor primaries that they are defined in terms of; this information is generally not provided along with RGB values.

The RGB representation is nevertheless convenient: almost all 3D modeling and design tools use RGB colors, and most 3D content is specified in terms of RGB. Furthermore, it's computationally and storage efficient, requiring just three floating-point values to represent. Our implementation of RGBSpectrum inherits from CoefficientSpectrum, specifying three components to store. Thus, all of the arithmetic operations defined earlier are automatically available for the RGBSpectrum.

⟨*Spectrum Declarations*⟩ +≡
```
class RGBSpectrum : public CoefficientSpectrum<3> {
public:
    ⟨RGBSpectrum Public Methods 332⟩
};
```

⟨*RGBSpectrum Public Methods*⟩ ≡   **332**
```
RGBSpectrum(Float v = 0.f) : CoefficientSpectrum<3>(v) { }
RGBSpectrum(const CoefficientSpectrum<3> &v)
    : CoefficientSpectrum<3>(v) { }
```

Beyond the basic arithmetic operators, the RGBSpectrum needs to provide methods to convert to and from XYZ and RGB representations. For the RGBSpectrum these are trivial. Note that FromRGB() takes a SpectrumType parameter like the SampledSpectrum instance of this method. Although it's unused here, the FromRGB() methods of these two classes must have matching signatures so that the rest of the system can call them consistently regardless of which spectral representation is being used.

⟨*RGBSpectrum Public Methods*⟩ +≡   **332**
```
static RGBSpectrum FromRGB(const Float rgb[3],
        SpectrumType type = SpectrumType::Reflectance) {
    RGBSpectrum s;
    s.c[0] = rgb[0];
    s.c[1] = rgb[1];
    s.c[2] = rgb[2];
    return s;
}
```

Similarly, spectrum representations must be able to convert themselves to RGB values. For the RGBSpectrum, the implementation can sidestep the question of what particular RGB primaries are used to represent the spectral distribution and just return the RGB coefficients directly, assuming that the primaries are the same as the ones already being used to represent the color.

⟨*RGBSpectrum Public Methods*⟩ +≡   **332**
```
void ToRGB(Float *rgb) const {
    rgb[0] = c[0];
    rgb[1] = c[1];
    rgb[2] = c[2];
}
```

All spectrum representations must also be able to convert themselves to an RGBSpectrum object. This is again trivial here.

⟨*RGBSpectrum Public Methods*⟩ +≡   **332**
```
const RGBSpectrum &ToRGBSpectrum() const {
    return *this;
}
```

The implementations of the RGBSpectrum::ToXYZ(), RGBSpectrum::FromXYZ(), and RGBSpectrum::y() methods are based on the RGBToXYZ() and XYZToRGB() functions defined above and are not included here.

To create an RGB spectrum from an arbitrary sampled SPD, FromSampled() converts the spectrum to XYZ and then to RGB. It evaluates the piecewise linear sampled spectrum at 1-nm steps, using the InterpolateSpectrumSamples() utility function, at each of the wavelengths where there is a value for the CIE matching functions. It then uses this value to compute the Riemann sum to approximate the XYZ integrals.

⟨*RGBSpectrum Public Methods*⟩ +≡   332
```
    static RGBSpectrum FromSampled(const Float *lambda, const Float *v,
                                   int n) {
        ⟨Sort samples if unordered, use sorted for returned spectrum 320⟩
        Float xyz[3] = { 0, 0, 0 };
        for (int i = 0; i < nCIESamples; ++i) {
            Float val = InterpolateSpectrumSamples(lambda, v, n,
                                                   CIE_lambda[i]);
            xyz[0] += val * CIE_X[i];
            xyz[1] += val * CIE_Y[i];
            xyz[2] += val * CIE_Z[i];
        }
        Float scale = Float(CIE_lambda[nCIESamples-1] - CIE_lambda[0]) /
            Float(CIE_Y_integral * nCIESamples);
        xyz[0] *= scale;
        xyz[1] *= scale;
        xyz[2] *= scale;
        return FromXYZ(xyz);
    }
```

InterpolateSpectrumSamples() takes a possibly irregularly sampled set of wavelengths and SPD values (λ_i, v_i) and returns the value of the SPD at the given wavelength λ, linearly interpolating between the two sample values that bracket λ. The FindInterval() function defined in Appendix A performs a binary search through the sorted wavelength array lambda to find the interval containing 1.

⟨*Spectrum Method Definitions*⟩ +≡
```
    Float InterpolateSpectrumSamples(const Float *lambda, const Float *vals,
                                     int n, Float l) {
        if (l <= lambda[0])      return vals[0];
        if (l >= lambda[n - 1])  return vals[n - 1];
        int offset = FindInterval(n,
            [&](int index) { return lambda[index] <= l; });
        Float t = (l - lambda[offset]) / (lambda[offset+1] - lambda[offset]);
        return Lerp(t, vals[offset], vals[offset + 1]);
    }
```

5.4 RADIOMETRY

Radiometry provides a set of ideas and mathematical tools to describe light propagation and reflection. It forms the basis of the derivation of the rendering algorithms that will be used throughout the rest of this book. Interestingly enough, radiometry wasn't originally derived from first principles using the physics of light but was built on an abstraction of light based on particles flowing through space. As such, effects like polarization of light do not naturally fit into this framework, although connections have since been made between radiometry and Maxwell's equations, giving radiometry a solid basis in physics.

Radiative transfer is the phenomenological study of the transfer of radiant energy. It is based on radiometric principles and operates at the *geometric optics* level, where macroscopic properties of light suffice to describe how light interacts with objects much larger than the light's wavelength. It is not uncommon to incorporate phenomena from wave optics models of light, but these results need to be expressed in the language of radiative transfer's basic abstractions.[4] In this manner, it is possible to describe interactions of light with objects of approximately the same size as the wavelength of the light, and thereby model effects like dispersion and interference. At an even finer level of detail, quantum mechanics is needed to describe light's interaction with atoms. Fortunately, direct simulation of quantum mechanical principles is unnecessary for solving rendering problems in computer graphics, so the intractability of such an approach is avoided.

In pbrt, we will assume that geometric optics is an adequate model for the description of light and light scattering. This leads to a few basic assumptions about the behavior of light that will be used implicitly throughout the system:

- *Linearity:* The combined effect of two inputs to an optical system is always equal to the sum of the effects of each of the inputs individually.
- *Energy conservation:* When light scatters from a surface or from participating media, the scattering events can never produce more energy than they started with.
- *No polarization:* We will ignore polarization of the electromagnetic field; therefore, the only relevant property of light is its distribution by wavelength (or, equivalently, frequency).
- *No fluorescence or phosphorescence:* The behavior of light at one wavelength is completely independent of light's behavior at other wavelengths or times. As with polarization, it is not too difficult to include these effects, but they would add relatively little practical value to the system.
- *Steady state:* Light in the environment is assumed to have reached equilibrium, so its radiance distribution isn't changing over time. This happens nearly instantaneously with light in realistic scenes, so it is not a limitation in practice. Note that phosphorescence also violates the steady-state assumption.

The most significant loss from adopting a geometric optics model is that diffraction and interference effects cannot easily be accounted for. As noted by Preisendorfer (1965), this

---

4   Preisendorfer (1965) has connected radiative transfer theory to Maxwell's classical equations describing electromagnetic fields. His framework both demonstrates their equivalence and makes it easier to apply results from one worldview to the other. More recent work was done in this area by Fante (1981).

is a hard problem to fix because, for example, the total flux over two areas isn't necessarily equal to the sum of the power received over each individual area in the presence of those effects (p. 24).

5.4.1 BASIC QUANTITIES

There are four radiometric quantities that are central to rendering: flux, irradiance/ radiant exitance, intensity, and radiance. They can each be derived from energy (measured in joules) by successively taking limits over time, area, and directions. All of these radiometric quantities are in general wavelength dependent. For the remainder of this chapter, we will not make this dependence explicit, but this property is important to keep in mind.

Energy

Our starting point is energy, which is measured in joules (J). Sources of illumination emit photons, each of which is at a particular wavelength and carries a particular amount of energy. All of the basic radiometric quantities are effectively different ways of measuring photons. A photon at wavelength λ carries energy

$$Q = \frac{hc}{\lambda},$$

where c is the speed of light, 299,472,458 m/s, and h is Planck's constant, $h \approx 6.626 \times 10^{-34}$ m^2 kg/s.

Flux

Energy measures work over some period of time, though under the steady-state assumption generally used in rendering, we're mostly interested in measuring light at an instant. *Radiant flux*, also known as *power*, is the total amount of energy passing through a surface or region of space per unit time. Radiant flux can be found by taking the limit of differential energy per differential time:

$$\Phi = \lim_{\Delta t \to 0} \frac{\Delta Q}{\Delta t} = \frac{dQ}{dt}.$$

Its units are joules/second (J/s), or more commonly, watts (W).

For example, given a light that emitted $Q = 200,000$ J over the course of an hour, if the same amount of energy was emitted at all times over the hour, we can find that the light source's flux was

$$\Phi = 200,000 \text{ J}/3600 \text{ s} \approx 55.6 \text{ W}.$$

Conversely, given flux as a function of time, we can integrate over a range of times to compute the total energy:

$$Q = \int_{t_0}^{t_1} \Phi(t) \, dt.$$

Note that our notation here is slightly informal: among other issues, because photons are actually discrete quanta means that it's not really meaningful to take limits that go to zero for differential time. For the purposes of rendering, where the number of

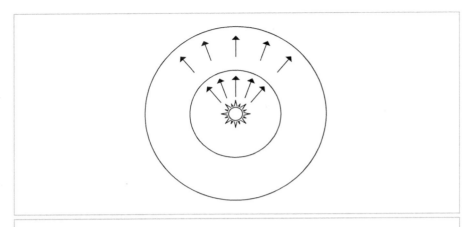

photons is enormous with respect to the measurements we're interested in, this detail isn't problematic in practice.

Total emission from light sources is generally described in terms of flux. Figure 5.6 shows flux from a point light source measured by the total amount of energy passing through imaginary spheres around the light. Note that the total amount of flux measured on either of the two spheres in Figure 5.6 is the same—although less energy is passing through any local part of the large sphere than the small sphere, the greater area of the large sphere means that the total flux is the same.

Irradiance and Radiant Exitance

Any measurement of flux requires an area over which photons per time is being measured. Given a finite area A, we can define the average density of power over the area by $E = \Phi/A$. This quantity is either *irradiance* (E), the area density of flux arriving at a surface, or *radiant exitance* (M), the area density of flux leaving a surface. These measurements have units of W/m². (The term *irradiance* is sometimes also used to refer to flux leaving a surface, but for clarity we'll use different terms for the two cases.)

For the point light source example in Figure 5.6, irradiance at a point on the outer sphere is less than the irradiance at a point on the inner sphere, since the surface area of the outer sphere is larger. In particular, if the point source is illuminating the same amount of illumination in all directions, then for a sphere in this configuration that has radius r,

$$E = \frac{\Phi}{4\pi r^2}.$$

This fact explains why the amount of energy received from a light at a point falls off with the squared distance from the light.

More generally, we can define irradiance and radiant exitance by taking the limit of differential power per differential area at a point p:

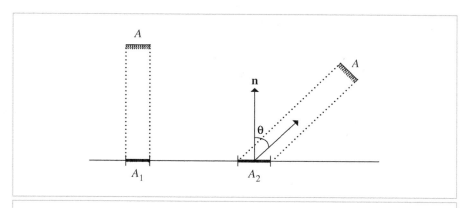

Figure 5.7: Lambert's Law. Irradiance arriving at a surface varies according to the cosine of the angle of incidence of illumination, since illumination is over a larger area at larger incident angles.

$$E(p) = \lim_{\Delta A \to 0} \frac{\Delta \Phi(p)}{\Delta A} = \frac{d\Phi(p)}{dA}.$$

We can also integrate irradiance over an area to find power:

$$\Phi = \int_A E(p)\, dA.$$

The irradiance equation can also help us understand the origin of *Lambert's law*, which says that the amount of light energy arriving at a surface is proportional to the cosine of the angle between the light direction and the surface normal (Figure 5.7). Consider a light source with area A and flux Φ that is illuminating a surface. If the light is shining directly down on the surface (as on the left side of the figure), then the area on the surface receiving light A_1 is equal to A. Irradiance at any point inside A_1 is then

$$E_1 = \frac{\Phi}{A}.$$

However, if the light is at an angle to the surface, the area on the surface receiving light is larger. If A is small, then the area receiving flux, A_2, is roughly $A/\cos \theta$. For points inside A_2, the irradiance is therefore

$$E_2 = \frac{\Phi \cos \theta}{A}.$$

Solid Angle and Intensity

In order to define intensity, we first need to define the notion of a *solid angle*. Solid angles are just the extension of 2D angles in a plane to an angle on a sphere. The *planar angle* is the total angle subtended by some object with respect to some position (Figure 5.8). Consider the unit circle around the point p; if we project the shaded object onto that circle, some length of the circle s will be covered by its projection. The arc length of s (which is the same as the angle θ) is the angle subtended by the object. Planar angles are measured in *radians*.

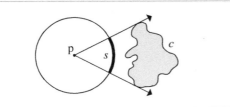

Figure 5.8: Planar Angle. The planar angle of an object c as seen from a point p is equal to the angle it subtends as seen from p or, equivalently, as the length of the arc s on the unit sphere.

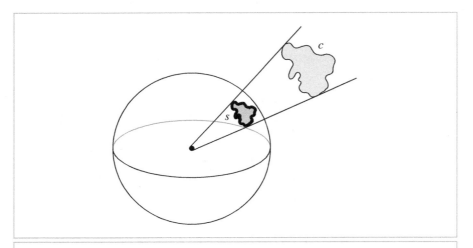

Figure 5.9: Solid Angle. The solid angle s subtended by an object c in three dimensions is computed by projecting c onto the unit sphere and measuring the area of its projection.

The solid angle extends the 2D unit circle to a 3D unit sphere (Figure 5.9). The total area s is the solid angle subtended by the object. Solid angles are measured in *steradians* (sr). The entire sphere subtends a solid angle of 4π sr, and a hemisphere subtends 2π sr.

The set of points on the unit sphere centered at a point p can be used to describe the vectors anchored at p. We will usually use the symbol ω to indicate these directions, and we will use the convention that ω is a normalized vector.

Consider now an infinitesimal light source emitting photons. If we center this light source within the unit sphere, we can compute the angular density of emitted power. *Intensity*, denoted by I, is this quantity; it has units W/sr. Over the entire sphere of directions, we have

$$I = \frac{\Phi}{4\pi},$$

but more generally we're interested in taking the limit of a differential cone of directions:

$$I = \lim_{\Delta\omega \to 0} \frac{\Delta\Phi}{\Delta\omega} = \frac{d\Phi}{d\omega}.$$

As usual, we can go back to power by integrating intensity: given intensity as a function of direction $I(\omega)$, we can integrate over a finite set of directions Ω to recover the intensity:

$$\Phi = \int_\Omega I(\omega)\, d\omega.$$

Intensity describes the directional distribution of light, but it is only meaningful for point light sources.

Radiance

The final, and most important, radiometric quantity is *radiance*, L. Irradiance and radiant exitance give us differential power per differential area at a point p, but they don't distinguish the directional distribution of power. Radiance takes this last step and measures irradiance or radiant exitance with respect to solid angles. It is defined by

$$L(p, \omega) = \lim_{\Delta\omega \to 0} \frac{\Delta E_\omega(p)}{\Delta\omega} = \frac{dE_\omega(p)}{d\omega},$$

where we have used E_ω to denote irradiance at the surface that is perpendicular to the direction ω. In other words, radiance is not measured with respect to the irradiance incident at the surface p lies on. In effect, this change of measurement area serves to eliminate the $\cos\theta$ term from Lambert's law in the definition of radiance.

Radiance is the flux density per unit area, per unit solid angle. In terms of flux, it is defined by

$$L = \frac{d\Phi}{d\omega\, dA^\perp}, \tag{5.2}$$

where $dA^\perp$ is the projected area of dA on a hypothetical surface perpendicular to ω (Figure 5.10). Thus, it is the limit of the measurement of incident light at the surface as a cone of incident directions of interest $d\omega$ becomes very small and as the local area of interest on the surface dA also becomes very small.

Of all of these radiometric quantities, radiance will be the one used most frequently throughout the rest of the book. An intuitive reason for this is that in some sense it's the most fundamental of all the radiometric quantities; if radiance is given, then all of the other values can be computed in terms of integrals of radiance over areas and directions. Another nice property of radiance is that it remains constant along rays through empty space. It is thus a natural quantity to compute with ray tracing.

5.4.2 INCIDENT AND EXITANT RADIANCE FUNCTIONS

When light interacts with surfaces in the scene, the radiance function L is generally not continuous across the surface boundaries. In the most extreme case of a fully opaque surface (e.g., a mirror), the radiance function slightly above and slightly below a surface could be completely unrelated.

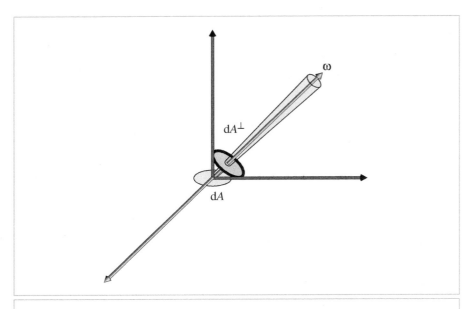

Figure 5.10: Radiance L is defined as flux per unit solid angle $d\omega$ per unit projected area $dA^{\perp}$.

It therefore makes sense to take one-sided limits at the discontinuity to distinguish between the radiance function just above and below

$$L^{+}(p, \omega) = \lim_{t \to 0^{+}} L(p + t\mathbf{n}_{p}, \omega),$$
$$L^{-}(p, \omega) = \lim_{t \to 0^{-}} L(p + t\mathbf{n}_{p}, \omega),$$

[5.3]

where $\mathbf{n}_{p}$ is the surface normal at p. However, keeping track of one-sided limits throughout the text is unnecessarily cumbersome.

We prefer to solve this ambiguity by making a distinction between radiance arriving at the point (e.g., due to illumination from a light source) and radiance leaving that point (e.g., due to reflection from a surface).

Consider a point p on the surface of an object. There is some distribution of radiance arriving at the point that can be described mathematically by a function of position and direction. This function is denoted by $L_{i}(p, \omega)$ (Figure 5.11). The function that describes the outgoing reflected radiance from the surface at that point is denoted by $L_{o}(p, \omega)$. Note that in both cases the direction vector ω is oriented to point away from p, but be aware that some authors use a notation where ω is reversed for L_{i} terms so that it points toward p.

There is a simple relation between these more intuitive incident and exitant radiance functions and the one-sided limits from Equation (5.3):

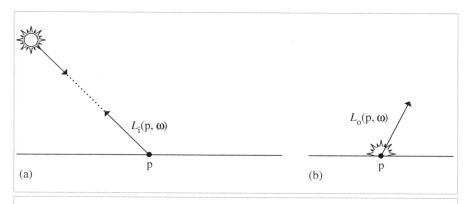

Figure 5.11: (a) The incident radiance function $L_i(p, \omega)$ describes the distribution of radiance arriving at a point as a function of position and direction. (b) The exitant radiance function $L_o(p, \omega)$ gives the distribution of radiance leaving the point. Note that for both functions, ω is oriented to point away from the surface, and, thus, for example, $L_i(p, -\omega)$ gives the radiance arriving on the other side of the surface than the one where ω lies.

$$L_i(p, \omega) = \begin{cases} L^+(p, -\omega), & \omega \cdot \mathbf{n}_p > 0 \\ L^-(p, -\omega), & \omega \cdot \mathbf{n}_p < 0 \end{cases}$$

$$L_o(p, \omega) = \begin{cases} L^+(p, \omega), & \omega \cdot \mathbf{n}_p > 0 \\ L^-(p, \omega), & \omega \cdot \mathbf{n}_p < 0 \end{cases}$$

Throughout the book, we will use the idea of incident and exitant radiance functions to resolve ambiguity in the radiance function at boundaries.

Another property to keep in mind is that at a point in space where there is no surface (i.e. in free space), L is continuous, so $L^+ = L^-$, which means

$$L_o(p, \omega) = L_i(p, -\omega) = L(p, \omega).$$

In other words, L_i and L_o only differ by a direction reversal.

5.4.3 LUMINANCE AND PHOTOMETRY

All of the radiometric measurements like flux, radiance, and so forth have corresponding photometric measurements. *Photometry* is the study of visible electromagnetic radiation in terms of its perception by the human visual system. Each spectral radiometric quantity can be converted to its corresponding photometric quantity by integrating against the spectral response curve $V(\lambda)$, which describes the relative sensitivity of the human eye to various wavelengths.[5]

Luminance measures how bright a spectral power distribution appears to a human observer. For example, luminance accounts for the fact that an SPD with a particular

---

5   The spectral response curve model is based on experiments done in a normally illuminated indoor environment. Because sensitivity to color decreases in dark environments, it doesn't model the human visual system's response well under all lighting situations. Nonetheless, it forms the basis for the definition of luminance and other related photometric properties.

Table 5.1: Representative Luminance Values for a Number of Lighting Conditions.

Condition	Luminance (cd/m^2, or nits)
Sun at horizon	600,000
60-watt lightbulb	120,000
Clear sky	8,000
Typical office	100–1,000
Typical computer display	1–100
Street lighting	1–10
Cloudy moonlight	0.25

Table 5.2: Radiometric Measurements and Their Photometric Analogs.

Radiometric	Unit	Photometric	Unit
Radiant energy	joule (Q)	Luminous energy	talbot (T)
Radiant flux	watt (W)	Luminous flux	lumen (lm)
Intensity	W/sr	Luminous intensity	lm/sr = candela (cd)
Irradiance	W/m^2	Illuminance	lm/m^2 = lux (lx)
Radiance	W/(m^{2}sr)	Luminance	lm/(m^{2}sr) = cd/m^2 = nit

amount of energy in the green wavelengths will appear brighter to a human than an SPD with the same amount of energy in blue.

We will denote luminance by Y; it related to spectral radiance $L(\lambda)$ by

$$Y = \int_\lambda L(\lambda)\, V(\lambda)\, \mathrm{d}\lambda.$$

Luminance and the spectral response curve $V(\lambda)$ are closely related to the XYZ representation of color (Section 5.2.1). The CIE $Y(\lambda)$ tristimulus curve was chosen to be proportional to $V(\lambda)$ so that

$$Y = 683 \int_\lambda L(\lambda)\, Y(\lambda)\, \mathrm{d}\lambda.$$

The units of luminance are candelas per meter squared (cd/m^2), where the candela is the photometric equivalent of radiant intensity. Some representative luminance values are given in Table 5.1.

All of the other radiometric quantities that we have introduced in this chapter have photometric equivalents; they are summarized in Table 5.2.[6]

---

6   The various photometric quantities have fairly unusual names; the somewhat confusing state of affairs was nicely summarized by Jim Kajiya: "Thus one nit is one lux per steradian is one candela per square meter is one lumen per square meter per steradian. Got it?"

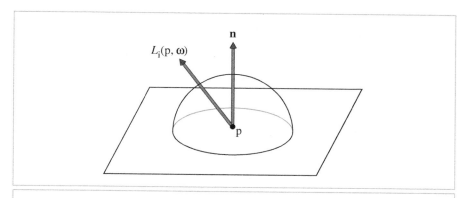

Figure 5.12: Irradiance at a point p is given by the integral of radiance times the cosine of the incident direction over the entire upper hemisphere above the point.

5.5 WORKING WITH RADIOMETRIC INTEGRALS

One of the most frequent tasks in rendering is the evaluation of integrals of radiometric quantities. In this section, we will present some tricks that can make this task easier. To illustrate the use of these techniques, we will use the computation of irradiance at a point as an example. Irradiance at a point p with surface normal **n** due to radiance over a set of directions Ω is

$$E(\mathrm{p}, \mathbf{n}) = \int_{\Omega} L_i(\mathrm{p}, \omega) \, |\cos \theta| \, d\omega, \qquad [5.4]$$

where $L_i(\mathrm{p}, \omega)$ is the incident radiance function (Figure 5.12) and the $\cos \theta$ term in this integral is due to the $dA^{\perp}$ term in the definition of radiance. θ is measured as the angle between ω and the surface normal **n**. Irradiance is usually computed over the hemisphere $\mathcal{H}^2(\mathbf{n})$ of directions about a given surface normal **n**.

5.5.1 INTEGRALS OVER PROJECTED SOLID ANGLE

The various cosine terms in the integrals for radiometric quantities can often distract from what is being expressed in the integral. This problem can be avoided using *projected solid angle* rather than solid angle to measure areas subtended by objects being integrated over. The projected solid angle subtended by an object is determined by projecting the object onto the unit sphere, as was done for the solid angle, but then projecting the resulting shape down onto the unit disk that is perpendicular to the surface normal (Figure 5.13). Integrals over hemispheres of directions with respect to cosine-weighted solid angle can be rewritten as integrals over projected solid angle.

The projected solid angle measure is related to the solid angle measure by

$$d\omega^{\perp} = |\cos \theta| \, d\omega,$$

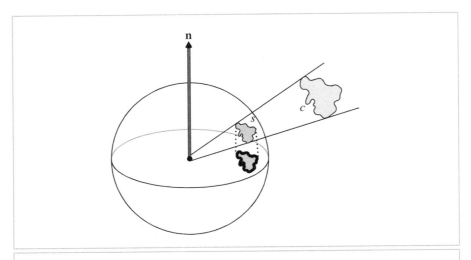

Figure 5.13: The projected solid angle subtended by an object c is the cosine-weighted solid angle that it subtends. It can be computed by finding the object's solid angle s, projecting it down to the plane perpendicular to the surface normal, and measuring its area there. Thus, the projected solid angle depends on the surface normal where it is being measured, since the normal orients the plane of projection.

so the irradiance-from-radiance integral over the hemisphere can be written more simply as

$$E(\mathrm{p}, \mathbf{n}) = \int_{\mathcal{H}^2(\mathbf{n})} L_\mathrm{i}(\mathrm{p}, \omega) \, \mathrm{d}\omega^\perp.$$

For the rest of this book, we will write integrals over directions in terms of solid angle, rather than projected solid angle. In other sources, however, projected solid angle may be used, and so it is always important to be aware of the integrand's actual measure.

Just as we found irradiance in terms of incident radiance, we can also compute the total flux emitted from some object over the hemisphere surrounding the normal by integrating over the object's surface area A:

$$\Phi = \int_A \int_{\mathcal{H}^2(\mathbf{n})} L_\mathrm{o}(\mathrm{p}, \omega) \, \cos\theta \, \mathrm{d}\omega \, \mathrm{d}A$$

$$= \int_A \int_{\mathcal{H}^2(\mathbf{n})} L_\mathrm{o}(\mathrm{p}, \omega) \, \mathrm{d}\omega^\perp \, \mathrm{d}A.$$

5.5.2 INTEGRALS OVER SPHERICAL COORDINATES

It is often convenient to transform integrals over solid angle into integrals over spherical coordinates (θ, ϕ). Recall that an (x, y, z) direction vector can also be written in terms of spherical angles (Figure 5.14):

$$x = \sin\theta \, \cos\phi$$
$$y = \sin\theta \, \sin\phi$$
$$z = \cos\theta.$$

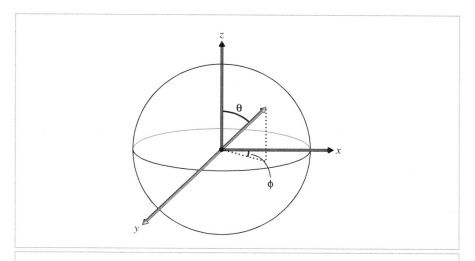

Figure 5.14: A direction vector can be written in terms of spherical coordinates (θ, ϕ) if the x, y, and z basis vectors are given as well. The spherical angle formulae make it easy to convert between the two representations.

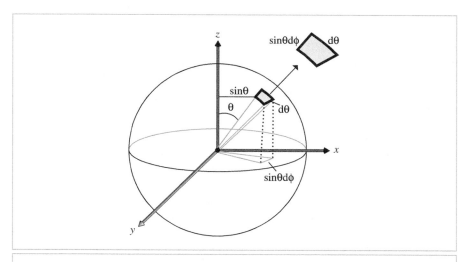

Figure 5.15: The differential area dA subtended by a differential solid angle is the product of the differential lengths of the two edges $\sin\theta d\phi$ and $d\theta$. The resulting relationship, $d\omega = \sin\theta d\theta d\phi$, is the key to converting between integrals over solid angles and integrals over spherical angles.

In order to convert an integral over a solid angle to an integral over (θ, ϕ), we need to be able to express the relationship between the differential area of a set of directions $d\omega$ and the differential area of a (θ, ϕ) pair (Figure 5.15). The differential area $d\omega$ is the product of the differential lengths of its sides, $\sin\theta \, d\phi$ and $d\theta$. Therefore,

$$d\omega = \sin\theta \, d\theta \, d\phi. \tag{5.5}$$

We can thus see that the irradiance integral over the hemisphere, Equation (5.4) with $\Omega = \mathcal{H}^2(\mathbf{n})$, can equivalently be written as

$$E(\mathrm{p}, \mathbf{n}) = \int_0^{2\pi} \int_0^{\pi/2} L_\mathrm{i}(\mathrm{p}, \theta, \phi) \cos\theta \, \sin\theta \, \mathrm{d}\theta \, \mathrm{d}\phi.$$

If the radiance is the same from all directions, the equation simplifies to $E = \pi L_\mathrm{i}$.

For convenience, we'll define two functions that convert θ and ϕ values into (x, y, z) direction vectors. The first function applies the earlier equations directly. Notice that these functions are passed the sine and cosine of θ, rather than θ itself. This is because the sine and cosine of θ are often already available to the caller. This is not normally the case for ϕ, however, so ϕ is passed in as is.

⟨*Geometry Inline Functions*⟩ +≡
```
inline Vector3f SphericalDirection(Float sinTheta,
        Float cosTheta, Float phi) {
    return Vector3f(sinTheta * std::cos(phi),
                    sinTheta * std::sin(phi),
                    cosTheta);
}
```

The second function takes three basis vectors representing the x, y, and z axes and returns the appropriate direction vector with respect to the coordinate frame defined by them:

⟨*Geometry Inline Functions*⟩ +≡
```
inline Vector3f SphericalDirection(Float sinTheta, Float cosTheta,
        Float phi, const Vector3f &x, const Vector3f &y,
        const Vector3f &z) {
    return sinTheta * std::cos(phi) * x +
        sinTheta * std::sin(phi) * y + cosTheta * z;
}
```

The conversion of a direction (x, y, z) to spherical angles can be found by

$$\theta = \arccos z$$
$$\phi = \arctan \frac{y}{x}.$$

The corresponding functions follow. Note that SphericalTheta() assumes that the vector v has been normalized before being passed in; the clamp is purely to avoid errors from std::acos() if |v.z| is slightly greater than 1 due to floating-point round-off error.

⟨*Geometry Inline Functions*⟩ +≡
```
inline Float SphericalTheta(const Vector3f &v) {
    return std::acos(Clamp(v.z, -1, 1));
}
```

⟨*Geometry Inline Functions*⟩ +≡
```
inline Float SphericalPhi(const Vector3f &v) {
    Float p = std::atan2(v.y, v.x);
    return (p < 0) ? (p + 2 * Pi) : p;
}
```

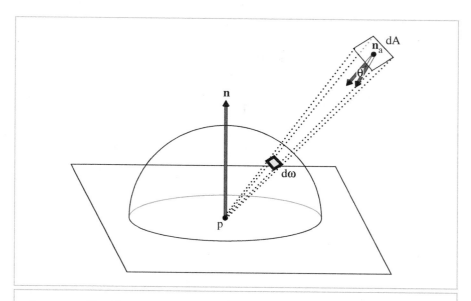

Figure 5.16: The differential solid angle subtended by a differential area dA is equal to $dA \cos \theta / r^2$, where θ is the angle between dA's surface normal and the vector to the point p and r is the distance from p to dA.

5.5.3 INTEGRALS OVER AREA

One last transformation of integrals that can simplify computation is to turn integrals over directions into integrals over area. Consider the irradiance integral in Equation (5.4) again, and imagine there is a quadrilateral with constant outgoing radiance and we'd like to compute the resulting irradiance at a point p. Computing this value as an integral over directions is not straightforward, since given a particular direction it is nontrivial to determine if the quadrilateral is visible in that direction. It's much easier to compute the irradiance as an integral over the area of the quadrilateral.

Differential area is related to differential solid angle (as viewed from a point p) by

$$d\omega = \frac{dA \cos \theta}{r^2},$$ (5.6)

where θ is the angle between the surface normal of dA and the vector to p, and r is the distance from p to dA (Figure 5.16). We will not derive this result here, but it can be understood intuitively: if dA is at distance 1 from p and is aligned exactly so that it is perpendicular to $d\omega$, then $d\omega = dA$, $\theta = 0$, and Equation (5.6) holds. As dA moves farther away from p, or as it rotates so that it's not aligned with the direction of $d\omega$, the r^2 and $\cos \theta$ terms compensate accordingly to reduce $d\omega$.

Therefore, we can write the irradiance integral for the quadrilateral source as

$$E(\mathrm{p}, \mathbf{n}) = \int_A L \cos \theta_i \, \frac{\cos \theta_o \, dA}{r^2},$$

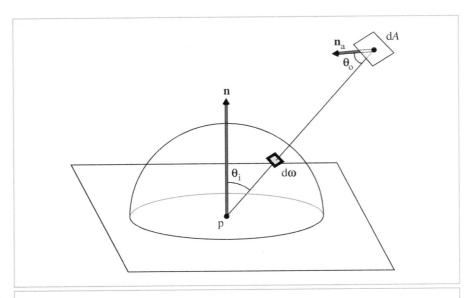

Figure 5.17: To compute irradiance at a point p from a quadrilateral source, it's easier to integrate over the surface area of the source than to integrate over the irregular set of directions that it subtends. The relationship between solid angles and areas given by Equation (5.6) lets us go back and forth between the two approaches.

where L is the emitted radiance from the surface of the quadrilateral, θ_i is the angle between the surface normal at p and the direction from p to the point p′ on the light, and θ_o is the angle between the surface normal at p′ on the light and the direction from p′ to p (Figure 5.17).

5.6 SURFACE REFLECTION

When light is incident on a surface, the surface scatters the light, reflecting some of it back into the environment. There are two main effects that need to be described to model this reflection: the spectral distribution of the reflected light and its directional distribution. For example, the skin of a lemon mostly absorbs light in the blue wavelengths but reflects most of the light in the red and green wavelengths (recall the lemon skin reflectance SPD in Figure 5.1). Therefore, when it is illuminated with white light, its color is yellow. The skin has pretty much the same color no matter what direction it's being observed from, although for some directions a highlight—a brighter area that is more white than yellow—is visible. In contrast, the light reflected from a point in a mirror depends almost entirely on the viewing direction. At a fixed point on the mirror, as the viewing angle changes, the object that is reflected in the mirror changes accordingly.

Reflection from translucent surfaces is more complex; a variety of materials ranging from skin and leaves to wax and liquids exhibit *subsurface light transport*, where light that enters the surface at one point exits it some distance away. (Consider, for example, how shining a flashlight in one's mouth makes one's cheeks light up, as light that enters the inside of the cheeks passes through the skin and exits the face.)

There are two abstractions for describing these mechanisms for light reflection: the BRDF and the BSSRDF, described in Sections 5.6.1 and 5.6.2, respectively. The BRDF describes surface reflection at a point neglecting the effect of subsurface light transport; for materials where this transport mechanism doesn't have a significant effect, this simplification introduces little error and makes the implementation of rendering algorithms much more efficient. The BSSRDF generalizes the BRDF and describes the more general setting of light reflection from translucent materials.

5.6.1 THE BRDF

The *bidirectional reflectance distribution function* (BRDF) gives a formalism for describing reflection from a surface. Consider the setting in Figure 5.18: we'd like to know how much radiance is leaving the surface in the direction ω_o toward the viewer, $L_o(p, \omega_o)$, as a result of incident radiance along the direction ω_i, $L_i(p, \omega_i)$.

If the direction ω_i is considered as a differential cone of directions, the differential irradiance at p is

$$dE(p, \omega_i) = L_i(p, \omega_i) \; \cos \theta_i \; d\omega_i. \tag{5.7}$$

A differential amount of radiance will be reflected in the direction ω_o due to this irradiance. Because of the linearity assumption from geometric optics, the reflected differential radiance is proportional to the irradiance

$$dL_o(p, \omega_o) \propto dE(p, \omega_i).$$

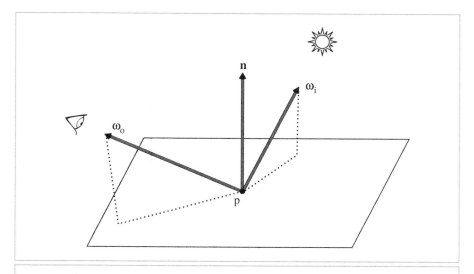

Figure 5.18: The BRDF. The bidirectional reflectance distribution function is a 4D function over pairs of directions ω_i and ω_o that describes how much incident light along ω_i is scattered from the surface in the direction ω_o.

The constant of proportionality defines the surface's BRDF for the particular pair of directions ω_i and ω_o:

$$f_r(p, \omega_o, \omega_i) = \frac{dL_o(p, \omega_o)}{dE(p, \omega_i)} = \frac{dL_o(p, \omega_o)}{L_i(p, \omega_i) \cos \theta_i \, d\omega_i}. \qquad [5.8]$$

Physically based BRDFs have two important qualities:

1. *Reciprocity:* For all pairs of directions ω_i and ω_o, $f_r(p, \omega_i, \omega_o) = f_r(p, \omega_o, \omega_i)$.
2. *Energy conservation:* The total energy of light reflected is less than or equal to the energy of incident light. For all directions ω_o,

$$\int_{\mathcal{H}^2(n)} f_r(p, \omega_o, \omega') \, \cos \theta' \, d\omega' \leq 1.$$

The surface's *bidirectional transmittance distribution function* (BTDF), which describes the distribution of transmitted light, can be defined in a manner similar to that for the BRDF. The BTDF is generally denoted by $f_t(p, \omega_o, \omega_i)$, where ω_i and ω_o are in opposite hemispheres around p. Remarkably, the BTDF does not obey reciprocity as defined above; we will discuss this issue in detail in Sections 8.2 and 16.1.3.

For convenience in equations, we will denote the BRDF and BTDF when considered together as $f(p, \omega_o, \omega_i)$; we will call this the *bidirectional scattering distribution function* (BSDF). Chapter 8 is entirely devoted to describing a variety of BSDFs that are useful for rendering.

Using the definition of the BSDF, we have

$$dL_o(p, \omega_o) = f(p, \omega_o, \omega_i) \, L_i(p, \omega_i) \, |\cos \theta_i| \, d\omega_i.$$

Here an absolute value has been added to the $\cos \theta_i$ term. This is done because surface normals in pbrt are not reoriented to lie on the same side of the surface as ω_i (many other rendering systems do this, although we find it more useful to leave them in their natural orientation as given by the Shape). Doing so makes it easier to consistently apply conventions like "the surface normal is assumed to point outside the surface" elsewhere in the system. Thus, applying the absolute value to $\cos \theta$ terms like these ensures that the desired quantity is actually calculated.

We can integrate this equation over the sphere of incident directions around p to compute the outgoing radiance in direction ω_o due to the incident illumination at p from all directions:

$$L_o(p, \omega_o) = \int_{\mathcal{S}^2} f(p, \omega_o, \omega_i) \, L_i(p, \omega_i) \, |\cos \theta_i| \, d\omega_i. \qquad [5.9]$$

This is a fundamental equation in rendering; it describes how an incident distribution of light at a point is transformed into an outgoing distribution, based on the scattering properties of the surface. It is often called the *scattering equation* when the sphere $\mathcal{S}^2$ is the domain (as it is here), or the *reflection equation* when just the upper hemisphere $\mathcal{H}^2(n)$ is being integrated over. One of the key tasks of the integration routines in Chapters 14 and 16 is to evaluate this integral at points on surfaces in the scene.

Shape 123

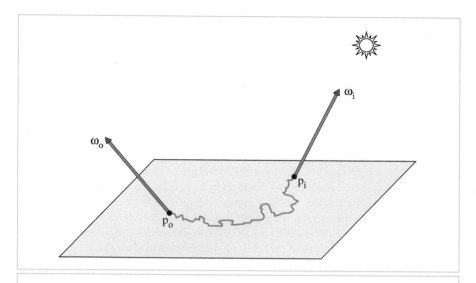

Figure 5.19: The bidirectional scattering surface reflectance distribution function generalizes the BSDF to account for light that exits the surface at a point other than where it enters. It is often more difficult to evaluate than the BSDF, although subsurface light transport makes a substantial contribution to the appearance of many real-world objects.

5.6.2 THE BSSRDF

The *bidirectional scattering surface reflectance distribution function* (BSSRDF) is the formalism that describes scattering from materials that exhibit a significant amount of subsurface light transport. It is a distribution function $S(p_o, \omega_o, p_i, \omega_i)$ that describes the ratio of exitant differential radiance at point p_o in direction ω_o to the incident differential flux at p_i from direction ω_i (Figure 5.19):

$$S(p_o, \omega_o, p_i, \omega_i) = \frac{dL_o(p_o, \omega_o)}{d\Phi(p_i, \omega_i)}. \qquad [5.10]$$

The generalization of the scattering equation for the BSSRDF requires integration over surface area *and* incoming direction, turning the 2D scattering Equation (5.9) into a 4D integral. With two more dimensions to integrate over, it is substantially more complex to use in rendering algorithms.

$$L_o(p_o, \omega_o) = \int_A \int_{\mathcal{H}^2(n)} S(p_o, \omega_o, p_i, \omega_i)\, L_i(p_i, \omega_i)\, |\cos\theta_i|\, d\omega_i\, dA. \qquad [5.11]$$

As the distance between points p_i and p_o increases, the value of S generally diminishes. This fact can be a substantial help in implementations of subsurface scattering algorithms.

Light transport beneath a surface is described by the same principles as volume light transport in participating media and is described by the equation of transfer, which is introduced in Section 15.1. Subsurface scattering is thus based on the same effects as light scattering in clouds and smoke, just at a smaller scale.

FURTHER READING

Meyer was one of the first researchers to closely investigate spectral representations in graphics (Meyer and Greenberg 1980; Meyer et al. 1986). Hall (1989) summarized the state of the art in spectral representations through 1989, and Glassner's *Principles of Digital Image Synthesis* (1995) covers the topic through the mid-1990s. Survey articles by Hall (1999), Johnson and Fairchild (1999), and Devlin et al. (2002) are good resources on this topic.

Borges (1991) analyzed the error introduced from the tristimulus representation when used for spectral computation. Peercy (1993) developed a technique based on choosing basis functions in a scene-dependent manner: by looking at the SPDs of the lights and reflecting objects in the scene, a small number of spectral basis functions that could accurately represent the scene's SPDs were found using characteristic vector analysis. Rougeron and Péroche (1997) projected all SPDs in the scene onto a hierarchical basis (the Haar wavelets), and showed that this adaptive representation can be used to stay within a desired error bound. Ward and Eydelberg-Vileshin (2002) developed a method for improving the spectral results from a regular RGB-only rendering system by carefully adjusting the color values provided to the system before rendering.

Another approach to spectral representation was investigated by Sun et al. (2001), who partitioned SPDs into a smooth base SPD and a set of spikes. Each part was represented differently, using basis functions that worked well for each of these parts of the distribution. Drew and Finlayson (2003) applied a "sharp" basis, which is adaptive but has the property that computing the product of two functions in the basis doesn't require a full matrix multiplication as many other basis representations do.

When using a point-sampled representation (like SampledSpectrum), it can be difficult to know how many samples are necessary for accurate results. Lehtonen et al. (2006) studied this issue and determined that a 5-nm sample spacing was sufficient for real-world SPDs.

Evans and McCool (1999) introduced stratified wavelength clusters for representing SPDs: the idea is that each spectral computation uses a small fixed number of samples at representative wavelengths, chosen according to the spectral distribution of the light source. Subsequent computations use different wavelengths, such that individual computations are relatively efficient (being based on a small number of samples), but, in the aggregate over a large number of computations, the overall range of wavelengths is well covered. Related to this approach is the idea of computing the result for just a single wavelength in each computation and averaging the results together: this was the method used by Walter et al. (1997) and Morley et al. (2006).

Radziszewski et al. (2009) proposed a technique that generates light-carrying paths according to a single wavelength, while tracking their contribution at several additional wavelengths using efficient SIMD instructions. Combining these contributions using multiple importance sampling led to reduced variance when simulating dispersion through rough refractive boundaries. Wilkie et al. (2014) used equally spaced point samples in the wavelength domain and showed how this approach can also be used for photon mapping and rendering of participating media.

SampledSpectrum 319

Glassner (1989b) has written an article on the underconstrained problem of converting RGB values (e.g., as selected by the user from a display) to an SPD. Smits (1999) developed an improved method that is the one we have implemented in Section 5.2.2. See Meng et al. (2015) for recent work in this area, including thorough discussion of the complexities involved in doing these conversions accurately.

McCluney's book on radiometry is an excellent introduction to the topic (McCluney 1994). Preisendorfer (1965) also covered radiometry in an accessible manner and delved into the relationship between radiometry and the physics of light. Nicodemus et al. (1977) carefully defined the BRDF, BSSRDF, and various quantities that can be derived from them. See Moon and Spencer (1936, 1948) and Gershun (1939) for classic early introductions to radiometry. Finally, Lambert's seminal early writings about photometry from the mid-18th century have been translated into English by DiLaura (Lambert 1760).

Correctly implementing radiometric computations can be tricky: one missed cosine term and one is computing a completely different quantity than expected. Debugging these sorts of issues can be quite time-consuming. Ou and Pellacini (2010) showed how to use C++'s type system to associate units with each term of these sorts of computations so that, for example, trying to add a radiance value to another value that represents irradiance would trigger a compile time error.

EXERCISES

● **5.1** How many photons would a 50-W lightbulb that emits light at the single wavelength $\lambda = 600$ nm emit in 1 second?

❷ **5.2** Implement a new representation for spectral basis functions in `pbrt`. Compare both image quality and rendering time to the `RGBSpectrum` and `SampledSpectrum` representations implemented in this chapter. Be sure to include tricky situations like fluorescent lighting.

● **5.3** Compute the irradiance at a point due to a unit-radius disk h units directly above its normal with constant outgoing radiance of 10 W/m^2 sr. Do the computation twice, once as an integral over solid angle and once as an integral over area. (Hint: If the results don't match at first, see Section 13.6.2.)

● **5.4** Similarly, compute the irradiance at a point due to a square quadrilateral with outgoing radiance of 10 W/m^2 sr that has sides of length 1 and is 1 unit directly above the point in the direction of its surface normal.

CHAPTER SIX

06 CAMERA MODELS

In Chapter 1, we described the pinhole camera model that is commonly used in computer graphics. This model is easy to describe and simulate, but it neglects important effects that lenses have on light passing through them that occur with real cameras. For example, everything rendered with a pinhole camera is in sharp focus—a state of affairs not possible with real lens systems. Such images often look computer generated. More generally, the distribution of radiance leaving a lens system is quite different from the distribution entering it; modeling this effect of lenses is important for accurately simulating the radiometry of image formation.

Camera lens systems also introduce various aberrations that affect the images that they form; for example, *vignetting* causes a darkening toward the edges of images due to less light making it through to the edges of the film or sensor than to the center. Lenses can also cause *pincushion* or *barrel* distortion, which causes straight lines to be imaged as curves. Although lens designers work to minimize aberrations in their designs, they can still have a meaningful effect on images.

Like the Shapes from Chapter 3, cameras in pbrt are represented by an abstract base class. This chapter describes the Camera class and two of its key methods: Camera::GenerateRay() and Camera::GenerateRayDifferential(). The first method computes the world space ray corresponding to a sample position on the film plane. By generating these rays in different ways based on different models of image formation, the cameras in pbrt can create many types of images of the same 3D scene. The second method not only generates this ray but also computes information about the image area that the ray is sampling; this information is used for anti-aliasing computations in Chapter 10, for example. In Section 16.1.1, a few additional Camera methods will be introduced to support bidirectional light transport algorithms.

In this chapter, we will show a few implementations of the Camera interface, starting by implementing the ideal pinhole model with some generalizations and finishing with

Physically Based Rendering: From Theory To Implementation.
http://dx.doi.org/10.1016/B978-0-12-800645-0.50006-3

a fairly realistic model that simulates light passing through a collection of glass lens elements to form an image, similar to real-world cameras.

6.1 CAMERA MODEL

The abstract Camera base class holds generic camera options and defines the interface that all camera implementations must provide. It is defined in the files core/camera.h and core/camera.cpp.

⟨*Camera Declarations*⟩ ≡
 class Camera {
 public:
  ⟨*Camera Interface* 356⟩
  ⟨*Camera Public Data* 356⟩
 };

The base Camera constructor takes several parameters that are appropriate for all camera types. One of the most important is the transformation that places the camera in the scene, which is stored in the CameraToWorld member variable. The Camera stores an AnimatedTransform (rather than just a regular Transform) so that the camera itself can be moving over time.

Real-world cameras have a shutter that opens for a short period of time to expose the film to light. One result of this nonzero exposure time is *motion blur*: objects that are in motion relative to the camera during the exposure are blurred. All Cameras therefore store a shutter open and shutter close time and are responsible for generating rays with associated times at which to sample the scene. Given an appropriate distribution of ray times between the shutter open time and the shutter close time, it is possible to compute images that exhibit motion blur.

Cameras also contain an pointer to an instance of the Film class to represent the final image (Film is described in Section 7.9), and a pointer to a Medium instance to represent the scattering medium that the camera lies in (Medium is described in Section 11.3).

Camera implementations must pass along parameters that set these values to the Camera constructor. We will only show the constructor's prototype here because its implementation just copies the parameters to the corresponding member variables.

⟨*Camera Interface*⟩ ≡   356
 Camera(const AnimatedTransform &CameraToWorld, Float shutterOpen,
   Float shutterClose, Film *film, const Medium *medium);

⟨*Camera Public Data*⟩ ≡   356
 AnimatedTransform CameraToWorld;
 const Float shutterOpen, shutterClose;
 Film *film;
 const Medium *medium;

The first method that camera subclasses need to implement is Camera::GenerateRay(), which should compute the ray corresponding to a given sample. It is important that the direction component of the returned ray be normalized—many other parts of the system will depend on this behavior.

⟨*Camera Interface*⟩ +≡   356

```
virtual Float GenerateRay(const CameraSample &sample,
                          Ray *ray) const = 0;
```

The CameraSample structure holds all of the sample values needed to specify a camera ray. Its pFilm member gives the point on the film to which the generated ray carries radiance. The point on the lens the ray passes through is in pLens (for cameras that include the notion of lenses), and CameraSample::time gives the time at which the ray should sample the scene; implementations should use this value to linearly interpolate within the shutterOpen–shutterClose time range. (Choosing these various sample values carefully can greatly increase the quality of final images; this is the topic of much of Chapter 7.)

GenerateRay() also returns a floating-point value that affects how much the radiance arriving at the film plane along the generated ray will contribute to the final image. Simple camera models can just return a value of 1, but cameras that simulate real physical lens systems like the one in Section 6.4 to set this value to indicate how much light the ray carries through the lenses based on their optical properties. (See Sections 6.4.7 and 13.6.6 for more information about how exactly this weight is computed and used.)

⟨*Camera Declarations*⟩ +≡

```
struct CameraSample {
    Point2f pFilm;
    Point2f pLens;
    Float time;
};
```

The GenerateRayDifferential() method computes a main ray like GenerateRay() but also computes the corresponding rays for pixels shifted one pixel in the x and y directions on the film plane. This information about how camera rays change as a function of position on the film helps give other parts of the system a notion of how much of the film area a particular camera ray's sample represents, which is particularly useful for anti-aliasing texture map lookups.

⟨*Camera Method Definitions*⟩ ≡

```
Float Camera::GenerateRayDifferential(const CameraSample &sample,
    RayDifferential *rd) const {
    Float wt = GenerateRay(sample, rd);
    ⟨Find camera ray after shifting one pixel in the x direction 358⟩
    ⟨Find camera ray after shifting one pixel in the y direction⟩
    rd->hasDifferentials = true;
    return wt;
}
```

Finding the ray for one pixel over in x is just a matter of initializing a new CameraSample and copying the appropriate values returned by calling GenerateRay() into the Ray Differential structure. The implementation of the fragment ⟨*Find ray after shifting one pixel in the y direction*⟩ follows similarly and isn't included here.

⟨*Find camera ray after shifting one pixel in the x direction*⟩ ≡   **357**
```
CameraSample sshift = sample;
sshift.pFilm.x++;
Ray rx;
Float wtx = GenerateRay(sshift, &rx);
if (wtx == 0) return 0;
rd->rxOrigin = rx.o;
rd->rxDirection = rx.d;
```

6.1.1 CAMERA COORDINATE SPACES

We have already made use of two important modeling coordinate spaces, object space and world space. We will now introduce an additional coordinate space, *camera space*, which has the camera at its origin. We have:

- *Object space:* This is the coordinate system in which geometric primitives are defined. For example, spheres in pbrt are defined to be centered at the origin of their object space.
- *World space:* While each primitive may have its own object space, all objects in the scene are placed in relation to a single world space. Each primitive has an object-to-world transformation that determines where it is located in world space. World space is the standard frame that all other spaces are defined in terms of.
- *Camera space:* A camera is placed in the scene at some world space point with a particular viewing direction and orientation. This camera defines a new coordinate system with its origin at the camera's location. The z axis of this coordinate system is mapped to the viewing direction, and the y axis is mapped to the up direction. This is a handy space for reasoning about which objects are potentially visible to the camera. For example, if an object's camera space bounding box is entirely behind the $z = 0$ plane (and the camera doesn't have a field of view wider than 180 degrees), the object will not be visible to the camera.

6.2 PROJECTIVE CAMERA MODELS

One of the fundamental issues in 3D computer graphics is the *3D viewing problem:* how to project a 3D scene onto a 2D image for display. Most of the classic approaches can be expressed by a 4×4 projective transformation matrix. Therefore, we will introduce a projection matrix camera class, ProjectiveCamera, and then define two camera models based on it. The first implements an orthographic projection, and the other implements a perspective projection—two classic and widely used projections.

⟨*Camera Declarations*⟩ +≡
```
class ProjectiveCamera : public Camera {
public:
    ⟨ProjectiveCamera Public Methods 360⟩
protected:
    ⟨ProjectiveCamera Protected Data 360⟩
};
```

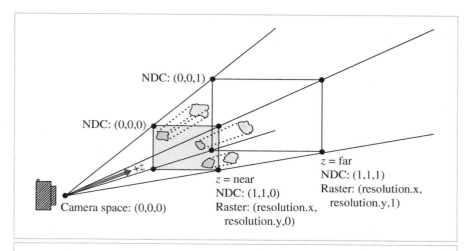

Figure 6.1: Several camera-related coordinate spaces are commonly used to simplify the implementation of Cameras. The camera class holds transformations between them. Scene objects in world space are viewed by the camera, which sits at the origin of camera space and points along the $+z$ axis. Objects between the near and far planes are projected onto the film plane at $z =$ near in camera space. The film plane is at $z = 0$ in raster space, where x and y range from $(0, 0)$ to (resolution.x, resolution.y). Normalized device coordinate (NDC) space normalizes raster space so that x and y range from $(0, 0)$ to $(1, 1)$.

Three more coordinate systems (summarized in Figure 6.1) are useful for defining and discussing projective cameras:

- *Screen space:* Screen space is defined on the film plane. The camera projects objects in camera space onto the film plane; the parts inside the *screen window* are visible in the image that is generated. Depth z values in screen space range from 0 to 1, corresponding to points at the near and far clipping planes, respectively. Note that, although this is called "screen" space, it is still a 3D coordinate system, since z values are meaningful.
- *Normalized device coordinate (NDC) space:* This is the coordinate system for the actual image being rendered. In x and y, this space ranges from $(0, 0)$ to $(1, 1)$, with $(0, 0)$ being the upper-left corner of the image. Depth values are the same as in screen space, and a linear transformation converts from screen to NDC space.
- *Raster space:* This is almost the same as NDC space, except the x and y coordinates range from $(0, 0)$ to (resolution.x, resolution.y).

Projective cameras use 4×4 matrices to transform among all of these spaces, but cameras with unusual imaging characteristics can't necessarily represent all of these transformations with matrices.

Camera 356

ProjectiveCamera 358

In addition to the parameters required by the Camera base class, the ProjectiveCamera takes the projective transformation matrix, the screen space extent of the image, and additional parameters related to depth of field. Depth of field, which will be described and implemented at the end of this section, simulates the blurriness of out-of-focus objects that occurs in real lens systems.

⟨*ProjectiveCamera Public Methods*⟩ ≡   358
```
    ProjectiveCamera(const AnimatedTransform &CameraToWorld,
            const Transform &CameraToScreen, const Bounds2f &screenWindow,
            Float shutterOpen, Float shutterClose, Float lensr, Float focald,
            Film *film, const Medium *medium)
        : Camera(CameraToWorld, shutterOpen, shutterClose, film, medium),
          CameraToScreen(CameraToScreen) {
        ⟨Initialize depth of field parameters 374⟩
        ⟨Compute projective camera transformations 360⟩
    }
```

ProjectiveCamera implementations pass the projective transformation up to the base class constructor shown here. This transformation gives the camera-to-screen projection; from that, the constructor can easily compute the other transformation that will be needed, to go all the way from raster space to camera space.

⟨*Compute projective camera transformations*⟩ ≡   360
```
    ⟨Compute projective camera screen transformations 360⟩
    RasterToCamera = Inverse(CameraToScreen) * RasterToScreen;
```

⟨*ProjectiveCamera Protected Data*⟩ ≡   358
```
    Transform CameraToScreen, RasterToCamera;
```

The only nontrivial transformation to compute in the constructor is the screen-to-raster projection. In the following code, note the composition of transformations where (reading from bottom to top), we start with a point in screen space, translate so that the upper-left corner of the screen is at the origin, and then scale by the reciprocal of the screen width and height, giving us a point with x and y coordinates between 0 and 1 (these are NDC coordinates). Finally, we scale by the raster resolution, so that we end up covering the entire raster range from $(0, 0)$ up to the overall raster resolution. An important detail here is that the y coordinate is inverted by this transformation; this is necessary because increasing y values move up the image in screen coordinates but down in raster coordinates.

⟨*Compute projective camera screen transformations*⟩ ≡   360
```
    ScreenToRaster = Scale(film->fullResolution.x,
                           film->fullResolution.y, 1) *
        Scale(1 / (screenWindow.pMax.x - screenWindow.pMin.x),
              1 / (screenWindow.pMin.y - screenWindow.pMax.y), 1) *
        Translate(Vector3f(-screenWindow.pMin.x, -screenWindow.pMax.y, 0));
    RasterToScreen = Inverse(ScreenToRaster);
```

⟨*ProjectiveCamera Protected Data*⟩ +≡   358
```
    Transform ScreenToRaster, RasterToScreen;
```

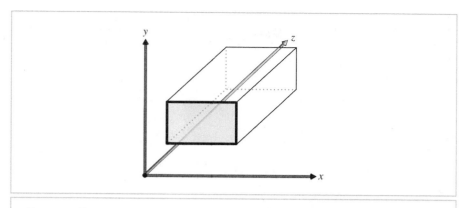

Figure 6.2: The orthographic view volume is an axis-aligned box in camera space, defined such that objects inside the region are projected onto the $z =$ near face of the box.

6.2.1 ORTHOGRAPHIC CAMERA

⟨*OrthographicCamera Declarations*⟩ ≡
```
class OrthographicCamera : public ProjectiveCamera {
public:
    ⟨OrthographicCamera Public Methods 361⟩
private:
    ⟨OrthographicCamera Private Data 363⟩
};
```

The orthographic camera, defined in the files cameras/orthographic.h and cameras/orthographic.cpp, is based on the orthographic projection transformation. The orthographic transformation takes a rectangular region of the scene and projects it onto the front face of the box that defines the region. It doesn't give the effect of *foreshortening*—objects becoming smaller on the image plane as they get farther away—but it does leave parallel lines parallel, and it preserves relative distance between objects. Figure 6.2 shows how this rectangular volume defines the visible region of the scene. Figure 6.3 compares the result of using the orthographic projection for rendering to the perspective projection defined in the next section.

The orthographic camera constructor generates the orthographic transformation matrix with the Orthographic() function, which will be defined shortly.

⟨*OrthographicCamera Public Methods*⟩ ≡   361
```
OrthographicCamera(const AnimatedTransform &CameraToWorld,
        const Bounds2f &screenWindow, Float shutterOpen,
        Float shutterClose, Float lensRadius, Float focalDistance,
        Film *film, const Medium *medium)
    : ProjectiveCamera(CameraToWorld, Orthographic(0, 1),
                    screenWindow, shutterOpen, shutterClose,
                    lensRadius, focalDistance, film, medium) {
    ⟨Compute differential changes in origin for orthographic camera rays 363⟩
}
```

Figure 6.3: Images of the Church Model. Rendered with (left) orthographic and (right) perspective cameras. Note that features like the stairs, checks on the floor, and back windows are rendered quite differently with the two models. The lack of foreshortening makes the orthographic view feel like it has less depth, although it does preserve parallel lines, which can be a useful property.

The orthographic viewing transformation leaves x and y coordinates unchanged but maps z values at the near plane to 0 and z values at the far plane to 1. To do this, the scene is first translated along the z axis so that the near plane is aligned with $z = 0$. Then, the scene is scaled in z so that the far plane maps to $z = 1$. The composition of these two transformations gives the overall transformation. (For a ray tracer like pbrt, we'd like the near plane to be at 0 so that rays start at the plane that goes through the camera's position; the far plane offset doesn't particularly matter.)

⟨*Transform Method Definitions*⟩ +≡
```
Transform Orthographic(Float zNear, Float zFar) {
    return Scale(1, 1, 1 / (zFar - zNear)) *
           Translate(Vector3f(0, 0, -zNear));
}
```

Thanks to the simplicity of the orthographic projection, it's easy to directly compute the differential rays in the x and y directions in the GenerateRayDifferential() method. The directions of the differential rays will be the same as the main ray (as they are for all rays generated by an orthographic camera), and the difference in origins will be the same for all rays. Therefore, the constructor here precomputes how much the ray origins shift in camera space coordinates due to a single pixel shift in the x and y directions on the film plane.

⟨*Compute differential changes in origin for orthographic camera rays*⟩ ≡   361
```
dxCamera = RasterToCamera(Vector3f(1, 0, 0));
dyCamera = RasterToCamera(Vector3f(0, 1, 0));
```

⟨*OrthographicCamera Private Data*⟩ ≡   361
```
Vector3f dxCamera, dyCamera;
```

We can now go through the code to take a sample point in raster space and turn it into a camera ray. The process is summarized in Figure 6.4. First, the raster space sample position is transformed into a point in camera space, giving a point located on the near plane, which is the origin of the camera ray. Because the camera space viewing direction points down the z axis, the camera space ray direction is $(0, 0, 1)$.

If depth of field has been enabled for this scene, the ray's origin and direction are modified so that depth of field is simulated. Depth of field will be explained later in this section. The ray's time value is set by linearly interpolating between the shutter open and shutter

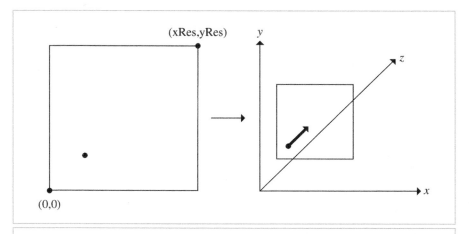

Figure 6.4: To create a ray with the orthographic camera, a raster space position on the film plane is transformed to camera space, giving the ray's origin on the near plane. The ray's direction in camera space is $(0, 0, 1)$, down the z axis.

close times by the CameraSample::time offset (which is in the range [0, 1)). Finally, the ray is transformed into world space before being returned.

⟨*OrthographicCamera Definitions*⟩ ≡
```
Float OrthographicCamera::GenerateRay(const CameraSample &sample,
        Ray *ray) const {
    ⟨Compute raster and camera sample positions 364⟩
    *ray = Ray(pCamera, Vector3f(0, 0, 1));
    ⟨Modify ray for depth of field 374⟩
    ray->time = Lerp(sample.time, shutterOpen, shutterClose);
    ray->medium = medium;
    *ray = CameraToWorld(*ray);
    return 1;
}
```

Once all of the transformation matrices have been set up, it's easy to transform the raster space sample point to camera space.

⟨*Compute raster and camera sample positions*⟩ ≡   364, 367
```
Point3f pFilm = Point3f(sample.pFilm.x, sample.pFilm.y, 0);
Point3f pCamera = RasterToCamera(pFilm);
```

The implementation of GenerateRayDifferential() performs the same computation to generate the main camera ray. The differential ray origins are found using the offsets computed in the OrthographicCamera constructor, and then the full ray differential is transformed to world space.

⟨*OrthographicCamera Definitions*⟩ +≡
```
Float OrthographicCamera::GenerateRayDifferential(
        const CameraSample &sample, RayDifferential *ray) const {
    ⟨Compute main orthographic viewing ray⟩
    ⟨Compute ray differentials for OrthographicCamera 364⟩
    ray->time = Lerp(sample.time, shutterOpen, shutterClose);
    ray->hasDifferentials = true;
    ray->medium = medium;
    *ray = CameraToWorld(*ray);
    return 1;
}
```

⟨*Compute ray differentials for* OrthographicCamera⟩ ≡   364
```
if (lensRadius > 0) {
    ⟨Compute OrthographicCamera ray differentials accounting for lens⟩
} else {
    ray->rxOrigin = ray->o + dxCamera;
    ray->ryOrigin = ray->o + dyCamera;
    ray->rxDirection = ray->ryDirection = ray->d;
}
```

6.2.2 PERSPECTIVE CAMERA

The perspective projection is similar to the orthographic projection in that it projects a volume of space onto a 2D film plane. However, it includes the effect of foreshortening: objects that are far away are projected to be smaller than objects of the same size that are closer. Unlike the orthographic projection, the perspective projection doesn't preserve distances or angles, and parallel lines no longer remain parallel. The perspective projection is a reasonably close match to how an eye or camera lens generates images of the 3D world. The perspective camera is implemented in the files `cameras/perspective.h` and `cameras/perspective.cpp`.

⟨*PerspectiveCamera Declarations*⟩ ≡
```
class PerspectiveCamera : public ProjectiveCamera {
public:
    ⟨PerspectiveCamera Public Methods 367⟩
private:
    ⟨PerspectiveCamera Private Data 367⟩
};
```

⟨*PerspectiveCamera Method Definitions*⟩ ≡
```
PerspectiveCamera::PerspectiveCamera(
        const AnimatedTransform &CameraToWorld,
        const Bounds2f &screenWindow, Float shutterOpen,
        Float shutterClose, Float lensRadius, Float focalDistance,
        Float fov, Film *film, const Medium *medium)
    : ProjectiveCamera(CameraToWorld, Perspective(fov, 1e-2f, 1000.f),
                    screenWindow, shutterOpen, shutterClose,
                    lensRadius, focalDistance, film, medium) {
    ⟨Compute differential changes in origin for perspective camera rays 367⟩
    ⟨Compute image plane bounds at z = 1 for PerspectiveCamera 951⟩
}
```

The perspective projection describes perspective viewing of the scene. Points in the scene are projected onto a viewing plane perpendicular to the z axis. The `Perspective()` function computes this transformation; it takes a field-of-view angle in `fov` and the distances to a near z plane and a far z plane. After the perspective projection, points at the near z plane are mapped to have $z = 0$, and points at the far plane have $z = 1$ (Figure 6.5). For rendering systems based on rasterization, it's important to set the positions of these planes carefully; they determine the z range of the scene that is rendered, but setting them with too many orders of magnitude variation between their values can lead to numerical precision errors. For a ray tracers like pbrt, they can be set arbitrarily as they are here.

⟨*Transform Method Definitions*⟩ +≡
```
Transform Perspective(Float fov, Float n, Float f) {
    ⟨Perform projective divide for perspective projection 366⟩
    ⟨Scale canonical perspective view to specified field of view 367⟩
}
```

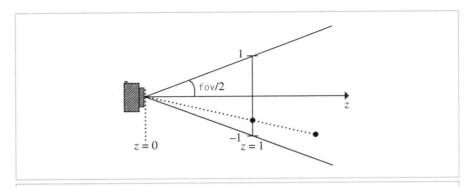

Figure 6.5: The perspective transformation matrix projects points in camera space onto the film plane. The x' and y' coordinates of the projected points are equal to the unprojected x and y coordinates divided by the z coordinate. The projected z' coordinate is computed so that points on the near plane map to $z' = 0$ and points on the far plane map to $z' = 1$.

The transformation is most easily understood in two steps:

1. Points p in camera space are projected onto the viewing plane. A bit of algebra shows that the projected x' and y' coordinates on the viewing plane can be computed by dividing x and y by the point's z coordinate value. The projected z depth is remapped so that z values at the near plane are 0 and z values at the far plane are 1. The computation we'd like to do is

$$x' = x/z$$
$$y' = y/z$$
$$z' = \frac{f(z-n)}{z(f-n)}.$$

All of this computation can be encoded in a 4×4 matrix using homogeneous coordinates:

$$\begin{bmatrix} 1 & 0 & 0 & 0 \\ 0 & 1 & 0 & 0 \\ 0 & 0 & \frac{f}{f-n} & -\frac{fn}{f-n} \\ 0 & 0 & 1 & 0 \end{bmatrix}$$

⟨*Perform projective divide for perspective projection*⟩ ≡   **365**
```
Matrix4x4 persp(1, 0,              0,              0,
                0, 1,              0,              0,
                0, 0, f / (f - n), -f*n / (f - n),
                0, 0,              1,              0);
```

2. The angular field of view (fov) specified by the user is accounted for by scaling the (x, y) values on the projection plane so that points inside the field of view project to coordinates between $[-1, 1]$ on the view plane. For square images, both x and y lie between $[-1, 1]$ in screen space. Otherwise, the direction in which the image is narrower maps to $[-1, 1]$, and the wider direction maps to a proportionally larger   Matrix4x4 1081

range of screen space values. Recall that the tangent is equal to the ratio of the opposite side of a right triangle to the adjacent side. Here the adjacent side has length 1, so the opposite side has the length tan(fov/2). Scaling by the reciprocal of this length maps the field of view to range from $[-1, 1]$.

⟨*Scale canonical perspective view to specified field of view*⟩ ≡   **365**
```
Float invTanAng = 1 / std::tan(Radians(fov) / 2);
return Scale(invTanAng, invTanAng, 1) * Transform(persp);
```

Similar to the OrthographicCamera, information about how the camera rays generated by the PerspectiveCamera change as we shift pixels on the film plane can be precomputed in the constructor. Here, we compute the change in position on the near perspective plane in camera space with respect to shifts in pixel location.

⟨*Compute differential changes in origin for perspective camera rays*⟩ ≡   **365**
```
dxCamera = (RasterToCamera(Point3f(1, 0, 0)) -
                  RasterToCamera(Point3f(0, 0, 0)));
dyCamera = (RasterToCamera(Point3f(0, 1, 0)) -
                  RasterToCamera(Point3f(0, 0, 0)));
```

⟨*PerspectiveCamera Private Data*⟩ ≡   **365**
```
Vector3f dxCamera, dyCamera;
```

With the perspective projection, all rays originate from the origin, $(0, 0, 0)$, in camera space. A ray's direction is given by the vector from the origin to the point on the near plane, pCamera, that corresponds to the provided CameraSample's pFilm location. In other words, the ray's vector direction is component-wise equal to this point's position, so rather than doing a useless subtraction to compute the direction, we just initialize the direction directly from the point pCamera.

⟨*PerspectiveCamera Method Definitions*⟩ +≡
```
Float PerspectiveCamera::GenerateRay(const CameraSample &sample,
        Ray *ray) const {
    ⟨Compute raster and camera sample positions 364⟩
    *ray = Ray(Point3f(0, 0, 0), Normalize(Vector3f(pCamera)));
    ⟨Modify ray for depth of field 374⟩
    ray->time = Lerp(sample.time, shutterOpen, shutterClose);
    ray->medium = medium;
    *ray = CameraToWorld(*ray);
    return 1;
}
```

The GenerateRayDifferential() method follows the implementation of GenerateRay(), except for an additional fragment that computes the differential rays.

⟨*PerspectiveCamera Public Methods*⟩ ≡   **365**
```
Float GenerateRayDifferential(const CameraSample &sample,
                              RayDifferential *ray) const;
```

⟨*Compute offset rays for* `PerspectiveCamera` *ray differentials*⟩ ≡

```
if (lensRadius > 0) {
    ⟨Compute PerspectiveCamera ray differentials accounting for lens⟩
} else {
    ray->rxOrigin = ray->ryOrigin = ray->o;
    ray->rxDirection = Normalize(Vector3f(pCamera) + dxCamera);
    ray->ryDirection = Normalize(Vector3f(pCamera) + dyCamera);
}
```

6.2.3 THE THIN LENS MODEL AND DEPTH OF FIELD

An ideal pinhole camera that only allows rays passing through a single point to reach the film isn't physically realizable; while it's possible to make cameras with extremely small apertures that approach this behavior, small apertures allow relatively little light to reach the film sensor. With a small aperture, long exposure times are required to capture enough photons to accurately capture the image, which in turn can lead to blur from objects in the scene moving while the camera shutter is open.

Real cameras have lens systems that focus light through a finite-sized aperture onto the film plane. Camera designers (and photographers using cameras with adjustable apertures) face a trade-off: the larger the aperture, the more light reaches the film and the shorter the exposures that are needed. However, lenses can only focus on a single plane (the *focal plane*), and the farther objects in the scene are from this plane, the blurrier they are. The larger the aperture, the more pronounced this effect is: objects at depths different from the one the lens system has in focus become increasingly blurry.

The camera model in Section 6.4 implements a fairly accurate simulation of lens systems in realistic cameras. For the simple camera models introduced so far, we can apply a classic approximation from optics, the *thin lens approximation*, to model the effect of finite apertures with traditional computer graphics projection models. The thin lens approximation models an optical system as a single lens with spherical profiles, where the thickness of the lens is small relative to the radius of curvature of the lens. (The more general thick lens approximation, which doesn't assume that the lens's thickness is negligible, is introduced in Section 6.4.3.)

Under the thin lens approximation, parallel incident rays passing through the lens focus at a point called behind the lens called the *focal point*. The distance the focal point is behind the lens, f, is the lens's *focal length*. If the film plane is placed at a distance equal to the focal length behind the lens, then objects infinitely far away will be in focus, as they image to a single point on the film.

Figure 6.6 illustrates the basic setting. Here we've followed the typical lens coordinate system convention of placing the lens perpendicular to the z axis, with the lens at $z = 0$ and the scene along $-z$. (Note that this is a different coordinate system from the one we used for camera space, where the viewing direction is $+z$.) Distances on the scene side of the lens are denoted with unprimed variables z, and distances on the film side of the lens (positive z) are primed, z'.

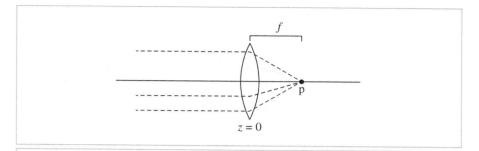

Figure 6.6: A thin lens, located along the z axis at $z = 0$. Parallel incident rays (dashed lines) passing through a thin lens all pass through a point p, the focal point. The distance between the lens and the focal point, f, is the lens's focal length.

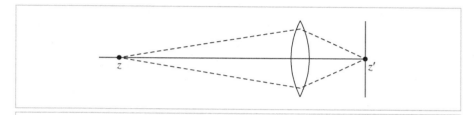

Figure 6.7: To focus a thin lens at a depth z in the scene, Equation (6.2) can be used to compute the distance z' on the film side of the lens that points at z focus to. Focusing is performed by adjusting the distance between the lens and the film plane.

For points in the scene at a depth z from a thin lens with focal length f, the *Gaussian lens equation* relates the distances from the object to the lens and from lens to the image of the point:

$$\frac{1}{z'} - \frac{1}{z} = \frac{1}{f}. \tag{6.1}$$

Note that for $z = -\infty$, we have $z' = f$, as expected.

We can use the Gaussian lens equation to solve for the distance between the lens and the film that sets the plane of focus at some z, the *focal distance* (Figure 6.7):

$$z' = \frac{fz}{f + z}. \tag{6.2}$$

A point that doesn't lie on the plane of focus is imaged to a disk on the film plane, rather than to a single point. This boundary of this disk is called the *circle of confusion*. The size of the circle of confusion is affected by the diameter of the aperture that light rays pass through, the focal distance, and the distance between the object and the lens. Figures 6.8 and 6.9 show this effect, depth of field, in a scene with a series of copies of the dragon model. Figure 6.8(a) is rendered with an infinitesimal aperture and thus without any

(a)

(b)

Figure 6.8: (a) Scene rendered with no depth of field and (b) depth of field due to a relatively small lens aperture, which gives only a small amount of blurriness in the out-of-focus regions.

depth of field effects. Figures 6.8(b) and 6.9 show the increase in blurriness as the size of the lens aperture is increased. Note that the second dragon from the right remains in focus throughout all of the images, as the plane of focus has been placed at its depth. Figure 6.10 shows depth of field used to render the landscape scene. Note how the effect draws the viewer's eye to the in-focus grass in the center of the image.

In practice, objects do not have to be exactly on the plane of focus to appear in sharp focus; as long as the circle of confusion is roughly smaller than a pixel on the film sensor, objects appear to be in focus. The range of distances from the lens at which objects appear in focus is called the lens's *depth of field*.

The Gaussian lens equation also lets us compute the size of the circle of confusion; given a lens with focal length f that is focused at a distance z_f, the film plane is at z'_f. Given another point at depth z, the Gaussian lens equation gives the distance z' that the lens focuses the point to. This point is either in front of or behind the film plane; Figure 6.11(a) shows the case where it is behind.

The diameter of the circle of confusion is given by the intersection of the cone between z' and the lens with the film plane. If we know the diameter of the lens d_l, then we can use

Figure 6.9: As the size of the lens aperture increases, the size of the circle of confusion in the out-of-focus areas increases, giving a greater amount of blur on the film plane.

Figure 6.10: Depth of field gives a greater sense of depth and scale to this part of the landscape scene. (*Scene courtesy of Laubwerk.*)

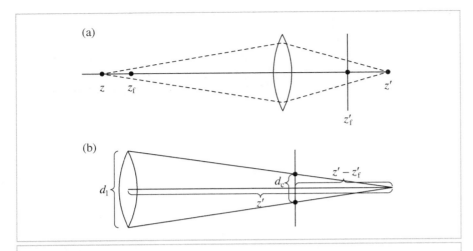

Figure 6.11: (a) If a thin lens with focal length f is focused at some depth z_f, then the distance from the lens to the film plane is z'_f, given by the Gaussian lens equation. A point in the scene at depth $z \neq z_f$ will be imaged as a circle on the film plane; here z focuses at z', which is behind the film plane. (b) To compute the diameter of the circle of confusion, we can apply similar triangles: the ratio of d_l, the diameter of the lens, to z' must be the same as the ratio of d_c the diameter of the circle of confusion, to $z' - z'_f$.

similar triangles to solve for the diameter of the circle of confusion d_c (Figure 6.11(b)):

$$\frac{d_l}{z'} = \frac{d_c}{|z' - z'_f|}.$$

Solving for d_c, we have

$$d_c = \left| \frac{d_l\,(z' - z'_f)}{z'} \right|.$$

Applying the Gaussian lens equation to express the result in terms of scene depths, we can find that

$$d_c = \left| \frac{d_l\,f\,(z - z_f)}{z(f + z_f)} \right|.$$

Note that the diameter of the circle of confusion is proportional to the diameter of the lens. The lens diameter is often expressed as the lens's *f-number* n, which expresses diameter as a fraction of focal length, $d_l = f/n$.

Figure 6.12 shows a graph of this function for a 50-mm focal length lens with a 25-mm aperture, focused at $z_f = 1\,\text{m}$. Note that the blur is asymmetric with depth around the focal plane and grows much more quickly for objects in front of the plane of focus than for objects behind it.

Modeling a thin lens in a ray tracer is remarkably straightforward: all that is necessary is to choose a point on the lens and find the appropriate ray that starts on the lens at that point such that objects in the plane of focus are in focus on the film (Figure 6.13).

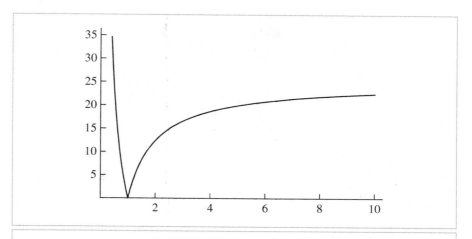

Figure 6.12: The diameter of the circle of confusion as a function of depth for a 50-mm focal length lens with 25-mm aperture, focused at 1 meter.

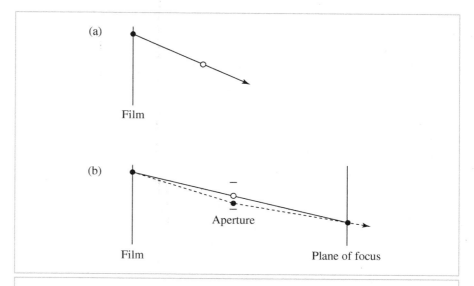

Figure 6.13: (a) For a pinhole camera model, a single camera ray is associated with each point on the film plane (filled circle), given by the ray that passes through the single point of the pinhole lens (empty circle). (b) For a camera model with a finite aperture, we sample a point (filled circle) on the disk-shaped lens for each ray. We then compute the ray that passes through the center of the lens (corresponding to the pinhole model) and the point where it intersects the plane of focus (solid line). We know that all objects in the plane of focus must be in focus, regardless of the lens sample position. Therefore, the ray corresponding to the lens position sample (dashed line) is given by the ray starting on the lens sample point and passing through the computed intersection point on the plane of focus.

Figure 6.14: Landscape scene with depth of field and only four samples per pixel: the depth of field is undersampled and the image is grainy. (*Scene courtesy of Laubwerk.*)

Therefore, projective cameras take two extra parameters for depth of field: one sets the size of the lens aperture, and the other sets the focal distance.

⟨*ProjectiveCamera Protected Data*⟩ +≡   358
```
Float lensRadius, focalDistance;
```

⟨*Initialize depth of field parameters*⟩ ≡   360
```
lensRadius = lensr;
focalDistance = focald;
```

It is generally necessary to trace many rays for each image pixel in order to adequately sample the lens for smooth depth of field. Figure 6.14 shows the landscape scene from Figure 6.10 with only four samples per pixel (Figure 6.10 had 128 samples per pixel).

⟨*Modify ray for depth of field*⟩ ≡   364, 367
```
if (lensRadius > 0) {
    ⟨Sample point on lens 374⟩
    ⟨Compute point on plane of focus 375⟩
    ⟨Update ray for effect of lens 375⟩
}
```

The ConcentricSampleDisk() function, defined in Chapter 13, takes a (u, v) sample position in $[0, 1)^2$ and maps it to a 2D unit disk centered at the origin $(0, 0)$. To turn this into a point on the lens, these coordinates are scaled by the lens radius. The CameraSample class provides the (u, v) lens-sampling parameters in the pLens member variable.

⟨*Sample point on lens*⟩ ≡   374
```
Point2f pLens = lensRadius * ConcentricSampleDisk(sample.pLens);
```

The ray's origin is this point on the lens. Now it is necessary to determine the proper direction for the new ray. We know that *all* rays from the given image sample through the lens must converge at the same point on the plane of focus. Furthermore, we know that rays pass through the center of the lens without a change in direction, so finding the appropriate point of convergence is a matter of intersecting the unperturbed ray from the pinhole model with the plane of focus and then setting the new ray's direction to be the vector from the point on the lens to the intersection point.

For this simple model, the plane of focus is perpendicular to the z axis and the ray starts at the origin, so intersecting the ray through the lens center with the plane of focus is straightforward. The t value of the intersection is given by

$$t = \frac{focalDistance}{\mathbf{d}_z}.$$

⟨*Compute point on plane of focus*⟩ ≡   374
```
Float ft = focalDistance / ray->d.z;
Point3f pFocus = (*ray)(ft);
```

Now the ray can be initialized. The origin is set to the sampled point on the lens, and the direction is set so that the ray passes through the point on the plane of focus, pFocus.

⟨*Update ray for effect of lens*⟩ ≡   374
```
ray->o = Point3f(pLens.x, pLens.y, 0);
ray->d = Normalize(pFocus - ray->o);
```

To compute ray differentials with the thin lens, the approach used in the fragment ⟨*Update ray for effect of lens*⟩ is applied to rays offset one pixel in the x and y directions on the film plane. The fragments that implement this, ⟨*Compute* OrthographicCamera *ray differentials accounting for lens*⟩ and ⟨*Compute* PerspectiveCamera *ray differentials accounting for lens*⟩, aren't included here.

6.3 ENVIRONMENT CAMERA

One advantage of ray tracing compared to scan line or rasterization-based rendering methods is that it's easy to employ unusual image projections. We have great freedom in how the image sample positions are mapped into ray directions, since the rendering algorithm doesn't depend on properties such as straight lines in the scene always projecting to straight lines in the image.

In this section, we will describe a camera model that traces rays in all directions around a point in the scene, giving a 2D view of everything that is visible from that point. Consider a sphere around the camera position in the scene; choosing points on that sphere gives directions to trace rays in. If we parameterize the sphere with spherical coordinates, each point on the sphere is associated with a (θ, ϕ) pair, where $\theta \in [0, \pi]$ and $\phi \in [0, 2\pi]$. (See Section 5.5.2 for more details on spherical coordinates.) This type of image is particularly useful because it represents all of the incident light at a point on the scene. (One important use of this image representation is environment lighting—a rendering technique that uses image-based representations of light in a scene.) Figure 6.15 shows

Figure 6.15: The San Miguel model rendered with the `EnvironmentCamera`, which traces rays in all directions from the camera position. The resulting image gives a representation of all light arriving at that point in the scene and can be used for the image-based lighting techniques described in Chapters 12 and 14.

this camera in action with the San Miguel model. θ values range from 0 at the top of the image to π at the bottom of the image, and ϕ values range from 0 to 2π, moving from left to right across the image.[1]

⟨*EnvironmentCamera Declarations*⟩ ≡
```
class EnvironmentCamera : public Camera {
public:
    ⟨EnvironmentCamera Public Methods 376⟩
};
```

The `EnvironmentCamera` derives directly from the `Camera` class, not the `ProjectiveCamera` class. This is because the environmental projection is nonlinear and cannot be captured by a single 4×4 matrix. This camera is defined in the files `cameras/environment.h` and `cameras/environment.cpp`.

⟨*EnvironmentCamera Public Methods*⟩ ≡   376
```
EnvironmentCamera(const AnimatedTransform &CameraToWorld,
        Float shutterOpen, Float shutterClose, Film *film,
        const Medium *medium)
    : Camera(CameraToWorld, shutterOpen, shutterClose, film, medium) {
}
```

---

1   Readers familiar with cartography will recognize this as an equirectangular projection.

⟨*EnvironmentCamera Method Definitions*⟩ ≡
```
Float EnvironmentCamera::GenerateRay(const CameraSample &sample,
        Ray *ray) const {
    ⟨Compute environment camera ray direction 377⟩
    *ray = Ray(Point3f(0, 0, 0), dir, Infinity,
            Lerp(sample.time, shutterOpen, shutterClose));
    ray->medium = medium;
    *ray = CameraToWorld(*ray);
    return 1;
}
```

To compute the (θ, ϕ) coordinates for this ray, NDC coordinates are computed from the raster image sample position and then scaled to cover the (θ, ϕ) range. Next, the spherical coordinate formula is used to compute the ray direction, and finally the direction is converted to world space. (Note that because the y direction is "up" in camera space, here the y and z coordinates in the spherical coordinate formula are exchanged in comparison to usage elsewhere in the system.)

⟨*Compute environment camera ray direction*⟩ ≡   377
```
Float theta = Pi * sample.pFilm.y / film->fullResolution.y;
Float phi = 2 * Pi * sample.pFilm.x / film->fullResolution.x;
Vector3f dir(std::sin(theta) * std::cos(phi), std::cos(theta),
            std::sin(theta) * std::sin(phi));
```

*6.4 REALISTIC CAMERAS

The thin lens model makes it possible to render images with blur due to depth of field, but it is a fairly rough approximation of actual camera lens systems, which are comprised of a series of multiple *lens elements,* each of which modifies the distribution of radiance passing through it. (Figure 6.16 shows a cross section of a 22-mm focal length wide-angle lens with eight elements.) Even basic cell phone cameras tend to have on the order of five individual lens elements, while DSLR lenses may have ten or more. In general, more complex lens systems with larger numbers of lens elements can create higher quality images than simpler lens systems.

This section discusses the implementation of RealisticCamera, which simulates the focusing of light through lens systems like the one in Figure 6.16 to render images like Figure 6.17. Its implementation is based on ray tracing, where the camera follows ray paths through the lens elements, accounting for refraction at the interfaces between media (air, different types of glass) with different indices of refraction, until the ray path either exits the optical system or until it is absorbed by the aperture stop or lens housing. Rays leaving the front lens element represent samples of the camera's response profile and can be used with integrators that estimate the incident radiance along arbitrary rays, such as the SamplerIntegrator. The RealisticCamera implementation is in the files cameras/realistic.h and cameras/realistic.cpp.

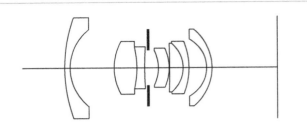

Figure 6.16: Cross section of a wide-angle lens system (scenes/lenses/wide.22.dat in the pbrt distribution). The lens coordinate system has the film plane perpendicular to the z axis and located at $z = 0$. The lenses are to the left, along negative z, and then the scene is to the left of the lenses. The aperture stop, indicated by the thick black lines in the middle of the lens system, blocks rays that hit it. In many lens systems, the size of the aperture stop can be adjusted to trade off between shorter exposure times (with larger apertures) and more depth of field (with smaller apertures).

Figure 6.17: Image rendered using a fish-eye lens with a very wide field of view. Note the darkening at the edges, which is due to accurate simulation of the radiometry of image formation (Section 6.4.7) and the distortion of straight lines to curves, which is characteristic of many wide-angle lenses but isn't accounted for when using projection matrices to represent the lens projection model.

⟨*RealisticCamera Declarations*⟩ ≡
```
class RealisticCamera : public Camera {
public:
      ⟨RealisticCamera Public Methods⟩
private:
      ⟨RealisticCamera Private Declarations 381⟩
      ⟨RealisticCamera Private Data 379⟩
      ⟨RealisticCamera Private Methods 381⟩
};
```

Camera 356

In addition to the usual transformation to place the camera in the scene, the Film, and the shutter open and close times, the RealisticCamera constructor takes a filename for a lens system description file, the distance to the desired plane of focus, and a diameter for the aperture stop. The effect of the simpleWeighting parameter is described later, in Section 13.6.6, after preliminaries related to Monte Carlo integration in Chapter 13 and the radiometry of image formation in Section 6.4.7.

⟨*RealisticCamera Method Definitions*⟩ ≡
```
RealisticCamera::RealisticCamera(const AnimatedTransform &CameraToWorld,
        Float shutterOpen, Float shutterClose, Float apertureDiameter,
        Float focusDistance, bool simpleWeighting, const char *lensFile,
        Film *film, const Medium *medium)
    : Camera(CameraToWorld, shutterOpen, shutterClose, film, medium),
      simpleWeighting(simpleWeighting) {
    ⟨Load element data from lens description file⟩
    ⟨Compute lens–film distance for given focus distance 389⟩
    ⟨Compute exit pupil bounds at sampled points on the film 390⟩
}
```

⟨*RealisticCamera Private Data*⟩ ≡   378
```
const bool simpleWeighting;
```

After loading the lens description file from disk, the constructor adjusts the spacing between the lenses and the film so that the plane of focus is at the desired depth, focusDistance, and then precomputes some information about which areas of the lens element closest to the film carry light from the scene to the film, as seen from various points on the film plane. After background material has been introduced, the fragments ⟨*Compute lens–film distance for given focus distance*⟩ and ⟨*Compute exit pupil bounds at sampled points on the film*⟩ will be defined in Sections 6.4.4 and 6.4.5, respectively.

6.4.1 LENS SYSTEM REPRESENTATION

A lens system is made from a series of lens elements, where each element is generally some form of glass. A lens system designer's challenge is to design a series of elements that form high-quality images on a film or sensor subject to limitations of space (e.g., the thickness of mobile phone cameras is very limited in order to keep phones thin), cost, and ease of manufacture.

It's easiest to manufacture lenses with cross sections that are spherical, and lens systems are generally symmetric around the *optical axis*, which is conventionally denoted by z. We will assume both of these properties in the remainder of this section. As in Section 6.2.3, lens systems are defined using a coordinate system where the film is aligned with the $z = 0$ plane and lenses are to the left of the film, along the $-z$ axis.

Lens systems are commonly represented in terms of the series of interfaces between the individual lens elements (or air) rather than having an explicit representation of each element. Table 6.1 shows the quantities that define each interface. The last entry in the table defines the rightmost interface, which is shown in Figure 6.18: it's a section of a sphere with radius equal to the curvature radius. The thickness of an element is the

Table 6.1: Tabular description of the lens system in Figure 6.16. Each line describes the interface between two lens elements, the interface between an element and air, or the aperture stop. The first line describes the leftmost interface. The element with radius 0 corresponds to the aperture stop. Distances are measured in mm.

Curvature Radius	Thickness	Index of Refraction	Aperture Diameter
35.98738	1.21638	1.54	23.716
11.69718	9.9957	1	17.996
13.08714	5.12622	1.772	12.364
−22.63294	1.76924	1.617	9.812
71.05802	0.8184	1	9.152
0	2.27766	0	8.756
−9.58584	2.43254	1.617	8.184
−11.28864	0.11506	1	9.152
−166.7765	3.09606	1.713·	10.648
−7.5911	1.32682	1.805	11.44
−16.7662	3.98068	1	12.276
−7.70286	1.21638	1.617	13.42
−11.97328	(depends on focus)	1	17.996

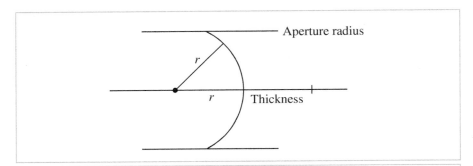

Figure 6.18: A lens interface (solid curved line) intersecting the optical axis at a position z. The interface geometry is described by the interface's aperture radius, which describes its extent above and below the optical axis, and the element's curvature radius r. If the element has a spherical cross section, then its profile is given by a sphere with center a distance r away on the optical axis, where the sphere also passes through z. If r is negative, the element interface is concave as seen from the scene (as is shown here); otherwise it is convex. The thickness of the lens gives the distance to the next interface to the right, or the distance to the film plane for the rearmost interface.

distance along *z* to the next element to the right (or to the film plane), and the index of refraction is for the medium to the right of the interface. The element's extent above and below the *z* axis is set by the aperture diameter.

The LensElementInterface structure represents a single lens element interface.

⟨*RealisticCamera Private Declarations*⟩ ≡   378
```
struct LensElementInterface {
    Float curvatureRadius;
    Float thickness;
    Float eta;
    Float apertureRadius;
};
```

The fragment ⟨*Load element data from lens description file*⟩, not included here, reads the lens elements and initializes the RealisticCamera::elementInterfaces array. See comments in the source code for details of the file format, which parallels the structure of Table 6.1, and see the directory scenes/lenses in the pbrt distribution for a number of example lens descriptions.

Two adjustments are made to the values read from the file: first, lens systems are traditionally described in units of millimeters, but pbrt assumes a scene measured in meters. Therefore, the fields other than the index of refraction are scaled by 1/1000. Second, the element's diameter is divided by two; the radius is a more convenient quantity to have at hand in the code to follow.

⟨*RealisticCamera Private Data*⟩ +≡   378
```
std::vector<LensElementInterface> elementInterfaces;
```

Once the element interface descriptions have been loaded, it's useful to have a few values related to the lens system easily at hand. LensRearZ() and LensFrontZ() return the *z* depths of the rear and front elements of the lens system, respectively. Note that the returned *z* depths are in camera space, not lens space, and thus have positive values.

⟨*RealisticCamera Private Methods*⟩ ≡   378
```
Float LensRearZ() const {
    return elementInterfaces.back().thickness;
}
```

Finding the front element's *z* position requires summing all of the element thicknesses (see Figure 6.19). This value isn't needed in any code that is in a performance-sensitive part of the system, so recomputing it when needed is fine. If performance of this method was a concern, it would be better to cache this value in the RealisticCamera.

⟨*RealisticCamera Private Methods*⟩ +≡   378
```
Float LensFrontZ() const {
    Float zSum = 0;
    for (const LensElementInterface &element : elementInterfaces)
        zSum += element.thickness;
    return zSum;
}
```

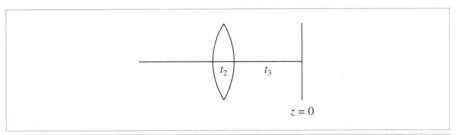

Figure 6.19: The Relationship between Element Thickness and Position on the Optical Axis. The film plane is at $z = 0$, and the rear element's thickness, t_3, gives the distance to its interface from the film; the rear interface intersects the axis here at $z = -t_3$. The next element has a thickness t_2 and is positioned at $z = -t_3 - t_2$, and so forth. The front element intersects the z axis at $\sum_i -t_i$.

RearElementRadius() returns the aperture radius of the rear element in meters.

⟨*RealisticCamera Private Methods*⟩ +≡   378

```
Float RearElementRadius() const {
    return elementInterfaces.back().apertureRadius;
}
```

6.4.2 TRACING RAYS THROUGH LENSES

Given a ray starting from the film side of the lens system, TraceLensesFromFilm() computes intersections with each element in turn, terminating the ray and returning false if its path is blocked along the way through the lens system. Otherwise it returns true and initializes *rOut with the exiting ray in camera space. During traversal, elementZ tracks the z intercept of the current lens element. Because the ray is starting from the film, the lenses are traversed in reverse order compared to how they are stored in elementInterfaces.

⟨*RealisticCamera Method Definitions*⟩ +≡

```
bool RealisticCamera::TraceLensesFromFilm(const Ray &rCamera,
        Ray *rOut) const {
    Float elementZ = 0;
    ⟨Transform rCamera from camera to lens system space 383⟩
    for (int i = elementInterfaces.size() - 1; i >= 0; --i) {
        const LensElementInterface &element = elementInterfaces[i];
        ⟨Update ray from film accounting for interaction with element 383⟩
    }
    ⟨Transform rLens from lens system space back to camera space 385⟩
    return true;
}
```

Because the camera points down the $+z$ axis in pbrt's camera space but lenses are along $-z$, the z components of the origin and direction of the ray need to be negated. While this is a simple enough transformation that it could be applied directly, we prefer an explicit Transform to make the intent clear.

⟨*Transform* rCamera *from camera to lens system space*⟩ ≡   382
```
static const Transform CameraToLens = Scale(1, 1, -1);
Ray rLens = CameraToLens(rCamera);
```

Recall from Figure 6.19 how the z intercept of elements is computed: because we are visiting the elements from back-to-front, the element's thickness must be subtracted from elementZ to compute its z intercept before the element interaction is accounted for.

⟨*Update ray from film accounting for interaction with* element⟩ ≡   382
```
elementZ -= element.thickness;
```
   ⟨*Compute intersection of ray with lens element* **383**⟩
   ⟨*Test intersection point against element aperture* **384**⟩
   ⟨*Update ray path for element interface interaction* **385**⟩

Given the element's z axis intercept, the next step is to compute the parametric t value along the ray where it intersects the element interface (or the plane of the aperture stop). For the aperture stop, a ray–plane test (following Section 3.1.2) is used. For spherical interfaces, IntersectSphericalElement() performs this test and also returns the surface normal if an intersection is found; the normal will be needed for computing the refracted ray direction.

⟨*Compute intersection of ray with lens element*⟩ ≡   383
```
Float t;
Normal3f n;
bool isStop = (element.curvatureRadius == 0);
if (isStop)
    t = (elementZ - rLens.o.z) / rLens.d.z;
else {
    Float radius = element.curvatureRadius;
    Float zCenter = elementZ + element.curvatureRadius;
    if (!IntersectSphericalElement(radius, zCenter, rLens, &t, &n))
        return false;
}
```

The IntersectSphericalElement() method is generally similar to Sphere::Intersect(), though it's specialized for the fact that the element's center is along the z axis (and thus, the center's x and y components are zero). The fragments ⟨*Compute* t0 *and* t1 *for ray–element intersection*⟩ and ⟨*Compute surface normal of element at ray intersection point*⟩ aren't included in the text here due to their similarity with the Sphere::Intersect() implementation.

⟨*RealisticCamera Method Definitions*⟩ +≡
```
bool RealisticCamera::IntersectSphericalElement(Float radius,
        Float zCenter, const Ray &ray, Float *t, Normal3f *n) {
```
    ⟨*Compute* t0 *and* t1 *for ray–element intersection*⟩
    ⟨*Select intersection* t *based on ray direction and element curvature* **384**⟩
    ⟨*Compute surface normal of element at ray intersection point*⟩
```
    return true;
}
```

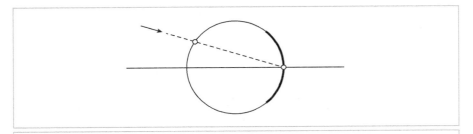

Figure 6.20: When computing the intersection of a ray with a spherical lens element, the first intersection of the ray with the full sphere isn't necessarily the desired one. Here, the second intersection is the one on the actual element interface (thick line) and the first should be ignored.

There is, however, a subtlety in choosing which intersection point to return: the closest intersection with $t > 0$ isn't necessarily on the element interface; see Figure 6.20.[2] For example, for a ray approaching from the scene and intersecting a concave lens (with negative curvature radius), the farther of the two intersections should be returned regardless of whether the closer one has $t > 0$. Fortunately, simple logic based on the ray direction and the curvature radius indicates which t value to use.

⟨*Select intersection t based on ray direction and element curvature*⟩ ≡   383
```
bool useCloserT = (ray.d.z > 0) ^ (radius < 0);
*t = useCloserT ? std::min(t0, t1) : std::max(t0, t1);
if (*t < 0)
    return false;
```

Each lens element extends for some radius around the optical axis; if the intersection point with the element is outside this radius, then the ray will actually intersect the lens housing and terminate. In a similar fashion, if a ray intersects the aperture stop, it also terminates. Therefore, here we test the intersection point against the appropriate limit for the current element, either terminating the ray or updating its origin to the current intersection point if it survives.

⟨*Test intersection point against element aperture*⟩ ≡   383
```
Point3f pHit = rLens(t);
Float r2 = pHit.x * pHit.x + pHit.y * pHit.y;
if (r2 > element.apertureRadius * element.apertureRadius)
    return false;
rLens.o = pHit;
```

If the current element is the aperture, the ray's path isn't affected by traveling through the element's interface. For glass (or, forbid, plastic) lens elements, the ray's direction changes at the interface as it goes from a medium with one index of refraction to one with another. (The ray may be passing from air to glass, from glass to air, or from glass with one index of refraction to a different type of glass with a different index of refraction.)

Float 1062

LensElementInterface::
     apertureRadius
     381

Point3f 68

Ray::o 73

---

2   As usual, "subtlety" means "the authors spent a number of hours debugging this."

Section 8.2 discusses how a change in index of refraction at the boundary between two media changes the direction of a ray and the amount of radiance carried by the ray. (In this case, we can ignore the change of radiance, as it cancels out if the ray is in the same medium going into the lens system as it is when it exits—here, both are air.) The Refract() function is defined in Section 8.2.3; note that it expects that the incident direction will point away from the surface, so the ray direction is negated before being passed to it. This function returns false in the presence of total internal reflection, in which case the ray path terminates. Otherwise, the refracted direction is returned in w.

In general, some light passing through an interface like this is transmitted and some is reflected. Here we ignore reflection and assume perfect transmission. Though an approximation, it is a reasonable one: lenses are generally manufactured with coatings designed to reduce the reflection to around 0.25% of the radiance carried by the ray. (However, modeling this small amount of reflection can be important for capturing effects like lens flare.)

⟨*Update ray path for element interface interaction*⟩ ≡   383
```
if (!isStop) {
    Vector3f w;
    Float etaI = element.eta;
    Float etaT = (i > 0 && elementInterfaces[i - 1].eta != 0) ?
        elementInterfaces[i - 1].eta : 1;
    if (!Refract(Normalize(-rLens.d), n, etaI / etaT, &w))
        return false;
    rLens.d = w;
}
```

If the ray has successfully made it out of the front lens element, it just needs to be transformed from lens space to camera space.

⟨*Transform* rLens *from lens system space back to camera space*⟩ ≡   382
```
if (rOut != nullptr) {
    static const Transform LensToCamera = Scale(1, 1, -1);
    *rOut = LensToCamera(rLens);
}
```

The TraceLensesFromScene() method is quite similar to TraceLensesFromFilm() and isn't included here. The main differences are that it traverses the elements from front-to-back rather than back-to-front. Note that it assumes that the ray passed to it is already in camera space; the caller is responsible for performing the transformation if the ray is starting from world space. The returned ray is in camera space, leaving the rear lens element toward the film.

⟨*RealisticCamera Private Methods*⟩ +≡   378
```
bool TraceLensesFromScene(const Ray &rCamera, Ray *rOut) const;
```

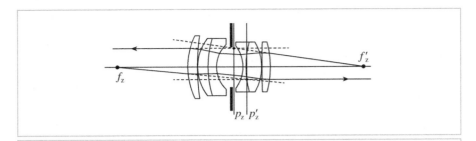

Figure 6.21: Computing the Cardinal Points of a Lens System. The lens system described in the file `lenses/dgauss.dat` with an incident ray from the scene parallel to the optical axis (above the axis), and a ray from the film parallel to the optical axis (below). The intersections with the optical axis of the rays leaving the lens system due to these incident rays give the two focal points, f_z' (on the film side) and f_z (on the scene side). The principal planes $z = p_z$ and $z = p_z'$ are given by the intersection of the extension of each pair of incident and exiting rays with the original rays and are shown here as planes perpendicular to the axis.

6.4.3 THE THICK LENS APPROXIMATION

The thin lens approximation used in Section 6.2.3 was based on the simplifying assumption that the lens system had 0 thickness along the optical axis. The thick lens approximation of a lens system is slightly more accurate in that it accounts for the lens system's z extent. After introducing the basic concepts of the thick lenses here, we'll use the thick lens approximation to determine how far to place the lens system from the film in order to focus at the desired focal depth in Section 6.4.4.

The thick lens approximation represents a lens system by two pairs of distances along the optical axis—the *focal points* and the depths of the *principal planes*; these are two of the *cardinal points* of a lens system. If rays parallel to the optical axis are traced through an ideal lens system, all of the rays will intersect the optical axis at the same point—this is the focal point. (In practice, real lens systems aren't perfectly ideal and incident rays at different heights will intersect the optical axis along a small range of z values—this is the *spherical aberration*.) Given a specific lens system, we can trace rays parallel to the optical axis through it from each side and compute their intersections with the z axis to find the focal points. (See Figure 6.21.)

Each principal plane is found by extending the incident ray parallel to the optical axis and the ray leaving the lens until they intersect; the z depth of the intersection gives the depth of the corresponding principal plane. Figure 6.21 shows a lens system with its focal points f_z and f_z' and principal planes at z values p_z and p_z'. (As in Section 6.2.3, primed variables represent points on the film side of the lens system, and unprimed variables represent points in the scene being imaged.)

Given the ray leaving the lens, finding the focal point requires first computing the t_f value where the ray's x and y components are zero. If the entering ray was offset from the optical axis only along x, then we'd like to find t_f such that $o_x + t_f \mathbf{d}_x = 0$. Thus,

$$t_f = -o_x/\mathbf{d}_x.$$

In a similar manner, to find the t_p for the principal plane where the ray leaving the lens has the same x height as the original ray, we have $o_x + t_p \mathbf{d}_x = x$, and so

$$t_{\mathrm{p}} = (x - \mathrm{o}_x)/\mathbf{d}_x.$$

Once these two t values have been computed, the ray equation can be used to find the z coordinates of the corresponding points.

The ComputeCardinalPoints() method computes the z depths of the focal point and the principal plane for the given rays. Note that it assumes that the rays are in camera space but returns z values along the optical axis in lens space.

⟨*RealisticCamera Method Definitions*⟩ +≡
```
void RealisticCamera::ComputeCardinalPoints(const Ray &rIn,
        const Ray &rOut, Float *pz, Float *fz) {
    Float tf = -rOut.o.x / rOut.d.x;
    *fz = -rOut(tf).z;
    Float tp = (rIn.o.x - rOut.o.x) / rOut.d.x;
    *pz = -rOut(tp).z;
}
```

The ComputeThickLensApproximation() method computes both pairs of cardinal points for the lens system.

⟨*RealisticCamera Method Definitions*⟩ +≡
```
void RealisticCamera::ComputeThickLensApproximation(Float pz[2],
        Float fz[2]) const {
    ⟨Find height x from optical axis for parallel rays 387⟩
    ⟨Compute cardinal points for film side of lens system 387⟩
    ⟨Compute cardinal points for scene side of lens system 388⟩
}
```

First, we must choose a height along the x axis for the rays to be traced. It should be far enough from $x = 0$ so that there is sufficient numeric precision to accurately compute where rays leaving the lens system intersect the z axis, but not so high up the x axis that it hits the aperture stop on the ray through the lens system. Here, we use a small fraction of the film's diagonal extent; this works well unless the aperture stop is extremely small.

⟨*Find height x from optical axis for parallel rays*⟩ ≡   387
```
    Float x = .001 * film->diagonal;
```

To construct the ray from the scene entering the lens system rScene, we offset a bit from the front of the lens. (Recall that the ray passed to TraceLensesFromScene() should be in camera space.)

⟨*Compute cardinal points for film side of lens system*⟩ ≡   387
```
    Ray rScene(Point3f(x, 0, LensFrontZ() + 1), Vector3f(0, 0, -1));
    Ray rFilm;
    TraceLensesFromScene(rScene, &rFilm);
    ComputeCardinalPoints(rScene, rFilm, &pz[0], &fz[0]);
```

An equivalent process starting from the film side of the lens system gives us the other two cardinal points.

⟨*Compute cardinal points for scene side of lens system*⟩ ≡   387
```
rFilm = Ray(Point3f(x, 0, LensRearZ() - 1), Vector3f(0, 0, 1));
TraceLensesFromFilm(rFilm, &rScene);
ComputeCardinalPoints(rFilm, rScene, &pz[1], &fz[1]);
```

6.4.4 FOCUSING

Lens systems can be focused at a given depth in the scene by moving the system in relation to the film so that a point at the desired focus depth images to a point on the film plane. The Gaussian lens equation, (6.3), gives us a relation that we can solve to focus a thick lens.

For thick lenses, the Gaussian lens equation relates distances from a point in the scene at z and the point it focuses to z' by

$$\frac{1}{z' - p_z'} - \frac{1}{z - p_z} = \frac{1}{f}.$$ [6.3]

For thin lenses, $p_z = p_z' = 0$, and Equation (6.1) follows.

If we know the positions p_z and p_z' of the principal planes and the focal length of the lens f and would like to focus at some depth z along the optical axis, then we need to determine how far to translate the system δ so that

$$\frac{1}{z' - p_z' + \delta} - \frac{1}{z - p_z + \delta} = \frac{1}{f}.$$

The focal point on the film side should be at the film, so $z' = 0$, and $z = z_f$, the given focus depth. The only unknown is δ, and some algebraic manipulation gives us

$$\delta = \frac{1}{2}\left(p_z - z_f + p_z' - \sqrt{(p_z - z_f - z')(z - z_f - 4f - p_z')}\right).$$ [6.4]

(There are actually two solutions, but this one, which is the closer of the two, gives a small adjustment to the lens position and is thus the appropriate one.)

FocusThickLens() focuses the lens system using this approximation. After computing δ, it returns the offset along the z axis from the film where the lens system should be placed.

⟨*RealisticCamera Method Definitions*⟩ +≡
```
Float RealisticCamera::FocusThickLens(Float focusDistance) {
    Float pz[2], fz[2];
    ComputeThickLensApproximation(pz, fz);
    ⟨Compute translation of lens, delta, to focus at focusDistance 389⟩
    return elementInterfaces.back().thickness + delta;
}
```

Equation (6.4) gives the offset δ. The focal length of the lens f is the distance between the cardinal points f_z' and p_z'. Note also that the negation of the focus distance is used for z, since the optical axis points along negative z.

⟨*Compute translation of lens,* delta, *to focus at* focusDistance⟩ ≡   388
```
Float f = fz[0] - pz[0];
Float z = -focusDistance;
Float delta = 0.5f * (pz[1] - z + pz[0] -
    std::sqrt((pz[1] - z - pz[0]) * (pz[1] - z - 4 * f - pz[0])));
```

We can now finally implement the fragment in the RealisticCamera constructor that focuses the lens system. (Recall that the thickness of the rearmost element interface is the distance from the interface to the film.)

⟨*Compute lens–film distance for given focus distance*⟩ ≡   379
```
elementInterfaces.back().thickness = FocusThickLens(focusDistance);
```

6.4.5 THE EXIT PUPIL

From a given point on the film plane, not all rays toward the rear lens element will successfully exit the lens system; some will be blocked by the aperture stop or will intersect the lens system enclosure. In turn, not all points on the rear lens element transmit radiance to the point on the film. The set of points on the rear element that do carry light through the lens system is called the *exit pupil*; its size and position vary across viewpoints on the film plane. (Analogously, the entrance pupil is the area over the front lens element where rays from a given point in the scene will reach the film.)

Figure 6.22 shows the exit pupil as seen from two points on the film plane with a wide angle lens. The exit pupil gets smaller for points toward the edges of the film. An implication of this shrinkage is vignetting.

When tracing rays starting from the film, we'd like to avoid tracing too many rays that don't make it through the lens system; therefore, it's worth limiting sampling to the exit pupil itself and a small area around it rather than, for example, wastefully sampling the entire area of the rear lens element.

Computing the exit pupil at each point on the film plane before tracing a ray would be prohibitively expensive; instead the RealisticCamera implementation precomputes exit pupil bounds along segments of a line on the film plane. Since we assumed that the lens system is radially symmetric around the optical axis, exit pupil bounds will also be radially symmetric, and bounds for arbitrary points on the film plane can be found by rotating these segment bounds appropriately (Figure 6.23). These bounds are then used to efficiently find exit pupil bounds for specific film sample positions.

One important subtlety to be aware of is that because the lens system is focused by translating it along the optical axis, the shape and position of the exit pupil change when the focus of the lens system is adjusted. Therefore, it's critical that these bounds be computed after focusing.[3]

Float 1062

LensElementInterface::
  thickness
  381

RealisticCamera::
  elementInterfaces
  381

RealisticCamera::
  FocusThickLens()
  388

---

3   See footnote 2.

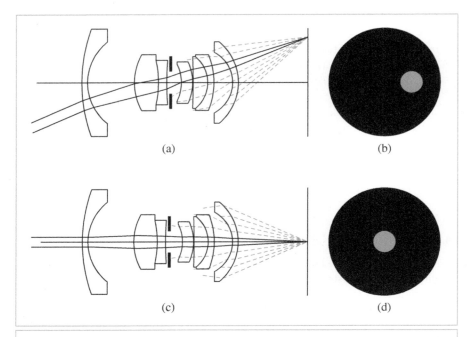

(a)   (b)

(c)   (d)

Figure 6.22: The Exit Pupil for a 22-mm-Wide Angle Lens with a 5.5-mm Aperture (f/4). (a) Rays from a point at the edge of the film plane entering the rear lens element at various points. Dashed lines indicate rays that are blocked and don't exit the lens system. (b) Image of the exit pupil as seen from the vantage point in (a). The rear lens element is black, while the exit pupil is shown in gray. (c) At the center of the film, a different region of the exit pupil allows rays out into the scene. (d) Image of the exit pupil as seen from the center of the film.

⟨*Compute exit pupil bounds at sampled points on the film*⟩ ≡   379
```
int nSamples = 64;
exitPupilBounds.resize(nSamples);
ParallelFor(
    [&](int i) {
        Float r0 = (Float)i / nSamples * film->diagonal / 2;
        Float r1 = (Float)(i + 1) / nSamples * film->diagonal / 2;
        exitPupilBounds[i] = BoundExitPupil(r0, r1);
    }, nSamples);
```

⟨*RealisticCamera Private Data*⟩ +≡   378
```
std::vector<Bounds2f> exitPupilBounds;
```

The BoundExitPupil() method computes a 2D bounding box of the exit pupil as seen from a point along a segment on the film plane. The bounding box is computed by attempting to trace rays through the lens system at a set of points on a plane tangent to the rear lens element. The bounding box of the rays that make it through the lens system gives an approximate bound on the exit pupil—see Figure 6.24.

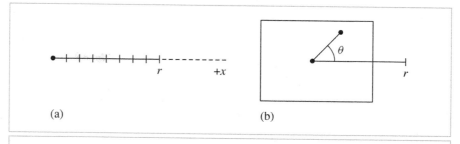

Figure 6.23: Precomputing Exit Pupil Bounds. (a) The `RealisticCamera` computes bounds of the exit pupil at a series of segments along the x axis of the film plane, up to the distance r from the center of the film to a corner. (b) Due to the assumption of radial symmetry, we can find exit pupil bounds for an arbitrary point on the film (solid dot) by computing the angle θ between the point and the x axis. If a point is sampled in the original exit pupil bounds and is then rotated by $-\theta$, we have a point in the exit pupil bounds at the original point.

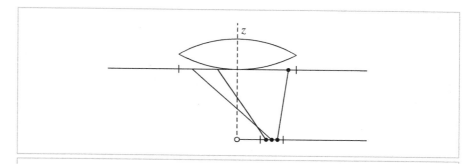

Figure 6.24: 2D Illustration of How Exit Pupil Bounds Are Computed. `BoundExitPupil()` takes an interval along the x axis on the film. It samples a series of points along the interval (bottom of the figure). For each point, it also samples a point on the bounding box of the rear lens element's extent on the plane tangent to its rear. It computes the bounding box on the tangent plane of all of the rays that make it through the lens system from points along the interval.

⟨*RealisticCamera Method Definitions*⟩ +≡
```
Bounds2f RealisticCamera::BoundExitPupil(Float pFilmX0,
        Float pFilmX1) const {
    Bounds2f pupilBounds;
    ⟨Sample a collection of points on the rear lens to find exit pupil 392⟩
    ⟨Return entire element bounds if no rays made it through the lens system 393⟩
    ⟨Expand bounds to account for sample spacing 393⟩
    return pupilBounds;
}
```

Bounds2f 76

Float 1062

The implementation samples the exit pupil fairly densely—at a total of 1024^2 points for each segment. We've found this sampling rate to provide good exit pupil bounds in practice.

⟨*Sample a collection of points on the rear lens to find exit pupil*⟩ ≡   391
```
const int nSamples = 1024 * 1024;
int nExitingRays = 0;
```
⟨*Compute bounding box of projection of rear element on sampling plane* 392⟩
```
for (int i = 0; i < nSamples; ++i) {
```
    ⟨*Find location of sample points on x segment and rear lens element* 392⟩
    ⟨*Expand pupil bounds if ray makes it through the lens system* 392⟩
```
}
```

The bounding box of the rear element in the plane perpendicular to it is not enough to be a conservative bound of the projection of the exit pupil on that plane; because the element is generally curved, rays that pass through the plane outside of that bound may themselves intersect the valid extent of the rear lens element. Rather than compute a precise bound, we'll increase the bounds substantially. The result is that many of the samples taken to compute the exit pupil bound will be wasted; in practice, this is a minor price to pay, as these samples are generally quickly terminated during the lens ray-tracing phase.

⟨*Compute bounding box of projection of rear element on sampling plane*⟩ ≡   392
```
Float rearRadius = RearElementRadius();
Bounds2f projRearBounds(Point2f(-1.5f * rearRadius, -1.5f * rearRadius),
                        Point2f( 1.5f * rearRadius,  1.5f * rearRadius));
```

The x sample point on the film is found by linearly interpolating between the x interval endpoints. The RadicalInverse() function that is used to compute the interpolation offsets for the sample point inside the exit pupil bounding box will be defined later, in Section 7.4.1. There, we will see that the sampling strategy implemented here corresponds to using Hammersley points in 3D; the resulting point set minimizes gaps in the coverage of the overall 3D domain, which in turn ensures an accurate exit pupil bound estimate.

⟨*Find location of sample points on x segment and rear lens element*⟩ ≡   392
```
Point3f pFilm(Lerp((i + 0.5f) / nSamples, pFilmX0, pFilmX1), 0, 0);
Float u[2] = { RadicalInverse(0, i), RadicalInverse(1, i) };
Point3f pRear(Lerp(u[0], projRearBounds.pMin.x, projRearBounds.pMax.x),
              Lerp(u[1], projRearBounds.pMin.y, projRearBounds.pMax.y),
              LensRearZ());
```

Now we can construct a ray from pFilm to pRear and determine if it is within the exit pupil by seeing if it makes it out of the front of the lens system. If so, the exit pupil bounds are expanded to include this point. If the sampled point is already inside the exit pupil's bounding box as computed so far, then we can skip the lens ray tracing step to save a bit of unnecessary work.

⟨*Expand pupil bounds if ray makes it through the lens system*⟩ ≡   392
```
if (Inside(Point2f(pRear.x, pRear.y), pupilBounds) ||
    TraceLensesFromFilm(Ray(pFilm, pRear - pFilm), nullptr)) {
    pupilBounds = Union(pupilBounds, Point2f(pRear.x, pRear.y));
    ++nExitingRays;
}
```

It may be that none of the sample rays makes it through the lens system; this case can legitimately happen with some very wide-angle lenses where the exit pupil vanishes at the edges of the film extent, for example. In this case, the bound doesn't matter and BoundExitPupil() returns the bound that encompasses the entire rear lens element.

⟨*Return entire element bounds if no rays made it through the lens system*⟩ ≡   391
```
if (nExitingRays == 0)
    return projRearBounds;
```

While one sample may have made it through the lens system and one of its neighboring samples didn't, it may well be that another sample very close to the neighbor actually would have made it out. Therefore, the final bound is expanded by roughly the spacing between samples in each direction in order to account for this uncertainty.

⟨*Expand bounds to account for sample spacing*⟩ ≡   391
```
pupilBounds = Expand(pupilBounds,
                2 * projRearBounds.Diagonal().Length() /
                std::sqrt(nSamples));
```

Given the precomputed bounds stored in RealisticCamera::exitPupilBounds, the SampleExitPupil() method can fairly efficiently find the bounds on the exit pupil for a given point on the film plane. It then samples a point inside this bounding box for the ray from the film to pass through. In order to accurately model the radiometry of image formation, the following code will need to know the area of this bounding box, so it is returned via sampleBoundsArea.

⟨*RealisticCamera Method Definitions*⟩ +≡
```
Point3f RealisticCamera::SampleExitPupil(const Point2f &pFilm,
        const Point2f &lensSample, Float *sampleBoundsArea) const {
    ⟨Find exit pupil bound for sample distance from film center 393⟩
    ⟨Generate sample point inside exit pupil bound 393⟩
    ⟨Return sample point rotated by angle of pFilm with +x axis 394⟩
}
```

⟨*Find exit pupil bound for sample distance from film center*⟩ ≡   393
```
Float rFilm = std::sqrt(pFilm.x * pFilm.x + pFilm.y * pFilm.y);
int rIndex = rFilm / (film->diagonal / 2) * exitPupilBounds.size();
rIndex = std::min((int)exitPupilBounds.size() - 1, rIndex);
Bounds2f pupilBounds = exitPupilBounds[rIndex];
if (sampleBoundsArea) *sampleBoundsArea = pupilBounds.Area();
```

Given the pupil's bounding box, a point inside it is sampled via linear interpolation with the provided lensSample value, which is in $[0, 1)^2$.

⟨*Generate sample point inside exit pupil bound*⟩ ≡   393
```
Point2f pLens = pupilBounds.Lerp(lensSample);
```

Because the exit pupil bound was computed from a point on the film along the $+x$ axis but the point pFilm is an arbitrary point on the film, the sample point in the exit pupil bound must be rotated by the same angle as pFilm makes with the $+x$ axis.

⟨*Return sample point rotated by angle of* pFilm *with* +*x axis*⟩ ≡   394
```
    Float sinTheta = (rFilm != 0) ? pFilm.y / rFilm : 0;
    Float cosTheta = (rFilm != 0) ? pFilm.x / rFilm : 1;
    return Point3f(cosTheta * pLens.x - sinTheta * pLens.y,
                   sinTheta * pLens.x + cosTheta * pLens.y,
                   LensRearZ());
```

6.4.6 GENERATING RAYS

Now that we have the machinery to trace rays through lens systems and to sample points in the exit pupil bound from points on the film plane, transforming a CameraSample into a ray leaving the camera is fairly straightforward: we need to compute the sample's position on the film plane and generate a ray from this point to the rear lens element, which is then traced through the lens system.

⟨*RealisticCamera Method Definitions*⟩ +≡
```
    Float RealisticCamera::GenerateRay(const CameraSample &sample,
            Ray *ray) const {
        ⟨Find point on film, pFilm, corresponding to sample.pFilm 394⟩
        ⟨Trace ray from pFilm through lens system 394⟩
        ⟨Finish initialization of RealisticCamera ray 395⟩
        ⟨Return weighting for RealisticCamera ray 783⟩
    }
```

The CameraSample::pFilm value is with respect to the overall resolution of the image in pixels. Here, we're operating with a physical model of a sensor, so we start by converting back to a sample in $[0, 1)^2$. Next, the corresponding point on the film is found by linearly interpolating with this sample value over its area.

⟨*Find point on film,* pFilm, *corresponding to* sample.pFilm⟩ ≡   394
```
    Point2f s(sample.pFilm.x / film->fullResolution.x,
              sample.pFilm.y / film->fullResolution.y);
    Point2f pFilm2 = film->GetPhysicalExtent().Lerp(s);
    Point3f pFilm(-pFilm2.x, pFilm2.y, 0);
```

SampleExitPupil() then gives us a point on the plane tangent to the rear lens element, which in turn lets us determine the ray's direction. In turn, we can trace this ray through the lens system. If the ray is blocked by the aperture stop or otherwise doesn't make it through the lens system, GenerateRay() returns a 0 weight. (Callers should be sure to check for this case.)

⟨*Trace ray from* pFilm *through lens system*⟩ ≡   394
```
    Float exitPupilBoundsArea;
    Point3f pRear = SampleExitPupil(Point2f(pFilm.x, pFilm.y), sample.pLens,
                                    &exitPupilBoundsArea);
    Ray rFilm(pFilm, pRear - pFilm, Infinity,
              Lerp(sample.time, shutterOpen, shutterClose));
    if (!TraceLensesFromFilm(rFilm, ray))
        return 0;
```

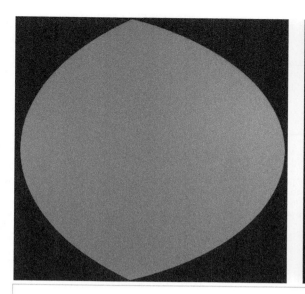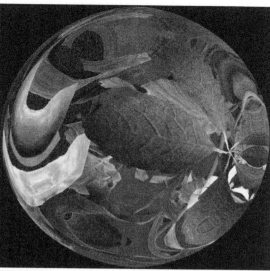

Figure 6.25: The Exit Pupil, as Seen from Two Points on the Film Plane in Figure 6.17. (a) The exit pupil as seen from a point where the scene is in sharp focus; the incident radiance is effectively constant over its area. (b) As seen from a pixel in an out-of-focus area, the exit pupil is a small image of part of the scene, with potentially rapidly varying radiance.

If the ray does successfully exit the lens system, then the usual details have to be handled to finish its initialization.

⟨*Finish initialization of* RealisticCamera *ray*⟩ ≡   394
```
*ray = CameraToWorld(*ray);
ray->d = Normalize(ray->d);
ray->medium = medium;
```

The fragment ⟨*Return weighting for* RealisticCamera *ray*⟩ will be defined later, in Section 13.6.6, after some necessary background from Monte Carlo integration has been introduced.

6.4.7 THE CAMERA MEASUREMENT EQUATION

Given this more accurate simulation of the process of real image formation, it's also worthwhile to more carefully define the radiometry of the measurement made by a film or a camera sensor. Rays from the exit pupil to the film carry radiance from the scene; as considered from a point on the film plane, there is thus a set of directions from which radiance is incident. The distribution of radiance leaving the exit pupil is affected by the amount of defocus blur seen by the point on the film—Figure 6.25 shows two renderings of the exit pupil's radiance as seen from two points on the film.

Given the incident radiance function, we can define the irradiance at a point on the film plane. If we start with the definition of irradiance in terms of radiance, Equation (5.4), we can then convert from an integral over solid angle to an integral over area (in this case, an area of the plane tangent to the rear lens element that bounds the exit pupil, A_e) using

Camera::CameraToWorld 356
Camera::medium 356
Ray::d 73
Ray::medium 74
Vector3::Normalize() 66

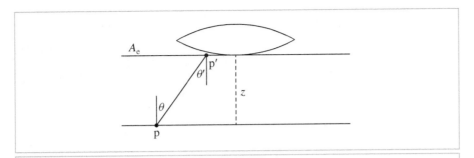

Figure 6.26: Geometric setting for the irradiance measurement equation, (6.5). Radiance can be measured as it passes through points p′ on the plane tangent to the rear lens element to a point on the film plane p. z is the axial distance from the film plane to the rear element tangent plane, `RealisticCamera::LensRearZ()`, and θ is the angle between the vector from p′ to p and the optical axis.

Equation (5.6). This gives us the irradiance for a point p on the film plane:

$$E(\mathrm{p}) = \int_{A_e} L_i(\mathrm{p}, \mathrm{p}') \frac{|\cos\theta \cos\theta'|}{||\mathrm{p}' - \mathrm{p}||^2}\, dA_e.$$

Figure 6.26 shows the geometry of the situation. Because the film plane is perpendicular to the exit pupil plane, $\theta = \theta'$. We can further take advantage of the fact that the distance between p and p′ is equal to the axial distance from the film plane to the exit pupil (which we'll denote here by z) times $\cos\theta$. Putting this all together, we have

$$E(\mathrm{p}) = \frac{1}{z^2} \int_{A_e} L_i(\mathrm{p}, \mathrm{p}') |\cos^4\theta|\, dA_e. \tag{6.5}$$

For cameras where the extent of the film is relatively large with respect to the distance z, the $\cos^4\theta$ term can meaningfully reduce the incident irradiance—this factor also contributes to vignetting. Most modern digital cameras correct for this effect with preset correction factors that increase pixel values toward the edges of the sensor.

Integrating irradiance at a point on the film over the time that the shutter is open gives *fluence*, which is the radiometric unit for energy per area, J/m^2.

$$H(\mathrm{p}) = \frac{1}{z^2} \int_{t_0}^{t_1} \int_{A_e} L_i(\mathrm{p}, \mathrm{p}', t') |\cos^4\theta|\, dA_e\, dt'. \tag{6.6}$$

Measuring fluence at a point captures the effect that the amount of energy received on the film plane is partially related to the length of time the camera shutter is open.

Photographic film (or CCD or CMOS sensors in digital cameras) actually measure radiant energy over a small area.[4] Taking Equation (6.6) and also integrating over sensor pixel area, A_p, we have

RealisticCamera::LensRearZ()
381

---

4   A typical size for pixels in digital cameras in 2015-era mobile phones is 1.5 microns per side.

$$J = \frac{1}{z^2} \int_{A_p} \int_{t_0}^{t_1} \int_{A_e} L_i(p, p', t') \, |\cos^4 \theta| \, dA_e \, dt' \, dA_p, \tag{6.7}$$

the Joules arriving at a pixel.

In Section 13.2, we'll see how Monte Carlo can be applied to estimate the values of these various integrals. Then in Section 13.6.6 we will define the fragment ⟨*Return weighting for* RealisticCamera *ray*⟩ in RealisticCamera::GenerateRay(); various approaches to computing the weight allow us to compute each of these quantities. Section 16.1.1 defines the *importance function* of a camera model, which characterizes its sensitivity to incident illumination arriving along different rays.

FURTHER READING

In his seminal Sketchpad system, Sutherland (1963) was the first to use projection matrices for computer graphics. Akenine-Möller, Haines, and Hoffman (2008) have provided a particularly well-written derivation of the orthographic and perspective projection matrices. Other good references for projections are Rogers and Adams's *Mathematical Elements for Computer Graphics* (1990), and Eberly's book (2001) on game engine design.

An unusual projection method was used by Greene and Heckbert (1986) for generating images for Omnimax® theaters. The EnvironmentCamera in this chapter is similar to the camera model described by Musgrave (1992).

Potmesil and Chakravarty (1981, 1982, 1983) did early work on depth of field and motion blur in computer graphics. Cook and collaborators developed a more accurate model for these effects based on the thin lens model; this is the approach used for the depth of field calculations in Section 6.2.3 (Cook, Porter, and Carpenter 1984; Cook 1986). See Adams and Levoy (2007) for a broad analysis of the types of radiance measurements that can be taken with cameras that have non-pinhole apertures.

Kolb, Mitchell, and Hanrahan (1995) showed how to simulate complex camera lens systems with ray tracing in order to model the imaging effects of real cameras; the RealisticCamera in Section 6.4 is based on their approach. Steinert et al. (2011) improve a number of details of this simulation, incorporating wavelength-dependent effects and accounting for both diffraction and glare. Our approach for approximating the exit pupil in Section 6.4.5 is similar to theirs. See the books by Hecht (2002) and Smith (2007) for excellent introductions to optics and lens systems.

Hullin et al. (2012) use polynomials to model the effect of lenses on rays passing through them; they are able to construct polynomials that approximate entire lens systems from polynomial approximations of individual lenses. This approach saves the computational expense of tracing rays through lenses, though for complex scenes, this cost is generally negligible in relation to the rest of rendering computations. Hanika and Dachsbacher (2014) improved the accuracy of this approach and showed how to combine the method with bidirectional path tracing.

RealisticCamera::
GenerateRay()
394

Chen et al. (2009) describe the implementation a fairly complete simulation of a digital camera, including the analog-to-digital conversion and noise in the measured pixel values inherent in this process.

EXERCISES

⊘ **6.1** Some types of cameras expose the film by sliding a rectangular slit across the film. This leads to interesting effects when objects are moving in a different direction from the exposure slit (Glassner 1999; Stephenson 2006). Furthermore, most digital cameras read out pixel values from scanlines in succession over a period of a few milliseconds; this leads to *rolling shutter* artifacts, which have similar visual characteristics. Modify the way that time samples are generated in one or more of the camera implementations in this chapter to model such effects. Render images with moving objects that clearly show the effect of accounting for this issue.

⊘ **6.2** Write an application that loads images rendered by the EnvironmentCamera, and uses texture mapping to apply them to a sphere centered at the eyepoint such that they can be viewed interactively. The user should be able to freely change the viewing direction. If the correct texture-mapping function is used for generating texture coordinates on the sphere, the image generated by the application will appear as if the viewer was at the camera's location in the scene when it was rendered, thus giving the user the ability to interactively look around the scene.

⊘ **6.3** The aperture stop in the RealisticCamera is modeled as a perfect circle; for cameras with adjustable apertures, the aperture is generally formed by movable blades with straight edges and is thus an n-gon. Modify the RealisticCamera to model a more realistic aperture shape and render images showing the differences from your model. You may find it useful to render a scene with small, bright, out-of-focus objects (e.g., specular highlights), to show off the differences.

⊘ **6.4** The standard model for depth of field in computer graphics models the circle of confusion as imaging a point in the scene to a disk with uniform intensity, although many real lenses produce circles of confusion with nonlinear variation such as a Gaussian distribution. This effect is known as "Bokeh" (Buhler and Wexler 2002). For example, catadioptric (mirror) lenses produce doughnut-shaped highlights when small points of light are viewed out of focus. Modify the implementation of depth of field in the RealisticCamera to produce images with this effect (e.g., by biasing the distribution of lens sample positions). Render images showing the difference between this and the standard model.

⊘ **6.5** *Focal stack rendering:* a focal stack is a series of images of a fixed scene where the camera is focused at a different distance for each image. Hasinoff and Kutulakos (2011) and Jacobs et al. (2012) introduce a number of applications of focal stacks, including freeform depth of field, where the user can specify arbitrary depths that are in focus, achieving effects not possible with traditional optics. Render focal stacks with pbrt and write an interactive tool to control focus effects with them.

⊙ **6.6** *Light field camera:* Ng et al. (2005) discuss the physical design and applications of a camera that captures small images of the exit pupil across the film, rather than averaging the radiance over the entire exit pupil at each pixel, as conventional cameras do. Such a camera captures a representation of the light field—the spatially and directionally varying distribution of radiance arriving at the camera sensor. By capturing the light field, a number of interesting operations are possible, including refocusing photographs after they have been taken. Read Ng et al.'s paper and implement a Camera in pbrt that captures the light field of a scene. Write a tool to allow users to interactively refocus these light fields.

⊛ 6.7 The RealisticCamera implementation places the film at the center of and perpendicular to the optical axis. While this is the most common configuration of actual cameras, interesting effects can be achieved by adjusting the film's placement with respect to the lens system.

For example, the plane of focus in the current implementation is always perpendicular to the optical axis; if the film plane (or the lens system) is tilted so that the film isn't perpendicular to the optical axis, then the plane of focus is no longer perpendicular to the optical axis. (This can be useful for landscape photography, for example, where aligning the plane of focus with the ground plane allows greater depth of field even with larger apertures.) Alternatively, the film plane can be shifted so that it's not centered on the optical axis; this shift can be used to keep the plane of focus aligned with a very tall object, for example.

Modify RealisticCamera to allow one or both of these adjustments and render images showing the result. Note that a number of places in the current implementation (e.g., the exit pupil computation) have assumptions that will be violated by these changes that you will need to address.

CHAPTER SEVEN

Although the final output of a renderer like pbrt is a 2D grid of colored pixels, incident radiance is actually a continuous function defined over the film plane. The manner in which the discrete pixel values are computed from this continuous function can noticeably affect the quality of the final image generated by the renderer; if this process is not performed carefully, artifacts will be present. Conversely, if it is performed well, a relatively small amount of additional computation to this end can substantially improve the quality of the rendered images.

This chapter starts by introducing *sampling theory*—the theory of taking discrete sample values from functions defined over continuous domains and then using those samples to reconstruct new functions that are similar to the original. Building on principles of sampling theory as well as ideas from low-discrepancy point sets, which are a particular type of well-distributed sample points, the Samplers defined in this chapter generate *n*-dimensional sample vectors in various ways.[1] Five Sampler implementations are described in this chapter, spanning a variety of approaches to the sampling problem.

This chapter concludes with the Filter class and the Film class. The Filter is used to determine how multiple samples near each pixel are blended together to compute the final pixel value, and the Film class accumulates image sample contributions into pixels of images.

---

1   Recall that in the previous chapter Cameras used CameraSamples to place points on the film plane, on the lens, and in time—the CameraSample values are set by taking the first few dimensions of these sample vectors.

Physically Based Rendering: From Theory To Implementation.
http://dx.doi.org/10.1016/B978-0-12-800645-0.50007-5

7.1 SAMPLING THEORY

A digital image is represented as a set of pixel values, typically aligned on a rectangular grid. When a digital image is displayed on a physical device, these values are used to determine the spectral power emitted by pixels on the display. When thinking about digital images, it is important to differentiate between image pixels, which represent the value of a function at a particular sample location, and display pixels, which are physical objects that emit light with some distribution. (For example, in an LCD display, the color and brightness may change substantially when the display is viewed at oblique angles.) Displays use the image pixel values to construct a new image function over the display surface. This function is defined at all points on the display, not just the infinitesimal points of the digital image's pixels. This process of taking a collection of sample values and converting them back to a continuous function is called *reconstruction*.

In order to compute the discrete pixel values in the digital image, it is necessary to sample the original continuously defined image function. In pbrt, like most other ray-tracing renderers, the only way to get information about the image function is to sample it by tracing rays. For example, there is no general method that can compute bounds on the variation of the image function between two points on the film plane. While an image could be generated by just sampling the function precisely at the pixel positions, a better result can be obtained by taking more samples at different positions and incorporating this additional information about the image function into the final pixel values. Indeed, for the best quality result, the pixel values should be computed such that the reconstructed image on the display device is as close as possible to the original image of the scene on the virtual camera's film plane. Note that this is a subtly different goal from expecting the display's pixels to take on the image function's actual value at their positions. Handling this difference is the main goal of the algorithms implemented in this chapter.[2]

Because the sampling and reconstruction process involves approximation, it introduces error known as *aliasing*, which can manifest itself in many ways, including jagged edges or flickering in animations. These errors occur because the sampling process is not able to capture all of the information from the continuously defined image function.

As an example of these ideas, consider a 1D function (which we will interchangeably refer to as a signal), given by $f(x)$, where we can evaluate $f(x')$ at any desired location x' in the function's domain. Each such x' is called a *sample position*, and the value of $f(x')$ is the *sample value*. Figure 7.1 shows a set of samples of a smooth 1D function, along with a reconstructed signal $\tilde{f}$ that approximates the original function f. In this example, $\tilde{f}$ is a piecewise linear function that approximates f by linearly interpolating neighboring sample values (readers already familiar with sampling theory will recognize this as reconstruction with a hat function). Because the only information available about

---

2   In this book, we will ignore issues related to the characteristics of physical display pixels and will work under the assumption that the display performs the ideal reconstruction process described later in this section. This assumption is patently at odds with how actual displays work, but it avoids unnecessary complication of the analysis here. Chapter 3 of Glassner (1995) has a good treatment of nonidealized display devices and their impact on the image sampling and reconstruction process.

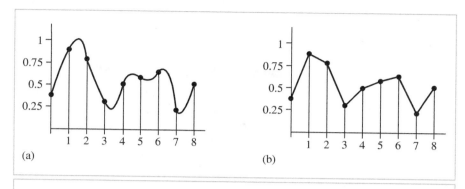

Figure 7.1: (a) By taking a set of *point samples* of $f(x)$ (indicated by black dots), we determine the value of the function at those positions. (b) The sample values can be used to *reconstruct* a function $\tilde{f}(x)$ that is an approximation to $f(x)$. The sampling theorem, introduced in Section 7.1.3, makes a precise statement about the conditions on $f(x)$, the number of samples taken, and the reconstruction technique used under which $\tilde{f}(x)$ is exactly the same as $f(x)$. The fact that the original function can sometimes be reconstructed exactly from point samples alone is remarkable.

f comes from the sample values at the positions x', $\tilde{f}$ is unlikely to match f perfectly since there is no information about f's behavior between the samples.

Fourier analysis can be used to evaluate the quality of the match between the reconstructed function and the original. This section will introduce the main ideas of Fourier analysis with enough detail to work through some parts of the sampling and reconstruction processes but will omit proofs of many properties and skip details that aren't directly relevant to the sampling algorithms used in pbrt. The "Further Reading" section of this chapter has pointers to more detailed information about these topics.

7.1.1 THE FREQUENCY DOMAIN AND THE FOURIER TRANSFORM

One of the foundations of Fourier analysis is the Fourier transform, which represents a function in the *frequency domain*. (We will say that functions are normally expressed in the *spatial domain*.) Consider the two functions graphed in Figure 7.2. The function in Figure 7.2(a) varies relatively slowly as a function of x, while the function in Figure 7.2(b) varies much more rapidly. The more slowly varying function is said to have lower frequency content. Figure 7.3 shows the frequency space representations of these two functions; the lower frequency function's representation goes to 0 more quickly than does the higher frequency function.

Most functions can be decomposed into a weighted sum of shifted sinusoids. This remarkable fact was first described by Joseph Fourier, and the Fourier transform converts a function into this representation. This frequency space representation of a function gives insight into some of its characteristics—the distribution of frequencies in the sine functions corresponds to the distribution of frequencies in the original function. Using this form, it is possible to use Fourier analysis to gain insight into the error that is introduced by the sampling and reconstruction process and how to reduce the perceptual impact of this error.

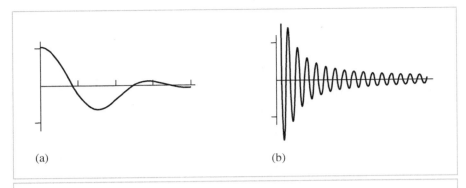

(a)   (b)

Figure 7.2: (a) Low-frequency function and (b) high-frequency function. Roughly speaking, the higher frequency a function is, the more quickly it varies over a given region.

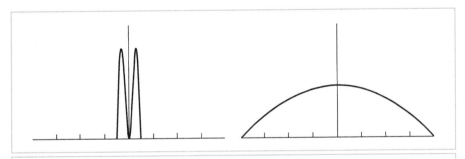

Figure 7.3: **Frequency Space Representations of the Functions in Figure 7.2.** The graphs show the contribution of each frequency ω to each of the functions in the spatial domain.

The Fourier transform of a 1D function $f(x)$ is[3]

$$F(\omega) = \int_{-\infty}^{\infty} f(x)\, e^{-i2\pi\omega x} dx. \qquad [7.1]$$

(Recall that $e^{ix} = \cos x + i \sin x$, where $i = \sqrt{-1}$.) For simplicity, here we will consider only *even* functions where $f(-x) = f(x)$, in which case the Fourier transform of f has no imaginary terms. The new function F is a function of *frequency*, ω.[4] We will denote the Fourier transform operator by $\mathcal{F}$, such that $\mathcal{F}\{f(x)\} = F(\omega)$. $\mathcal{F}$ is clearly a linear operator—that is, $\mathcal{F}\{af(x)\} = a\mathcal{F}\{f(x)\}$ for any scalar a, and $\mathcal{F}\{f(x) + g(x)\} = \mathcal{F}\{f(x)\} + \mathcal{F}\{g(x)\}$.

---

3   The reader should be warned that the constants in front of these integrals are not always the same in different fields. For example, some authors (including many in the physics community) prefer to multiply both integrals by $1/\sqrt{2\pi}$.

4   In this chapter, we will use the ω symbol to denote frequency. Throughout the rest of the book, ω denotes normalized direction vectors. This overloading of notation should never be confusing, given the contexts where these symbols are used. Similarly, when we refer to a function's "spectrum," we are referring to its distribution of frequencies in its frequency space representation, rather than anything related to color.

Table 7.1: Fourier Pairs. Functions in the spatial domain and their frequency space representations. Because of the symmetry properties of the Fourier transform, if the left column is instead considered to be frequency space, then the right column is the spatial equivalent of those functions as well.

Spatial Domain	Frequency Space Representation
Box: $f(x) = 1$ if $|x| < 1/2$, 0 otherwise	Sinc: $f(\omega) = \text{sinc}(\omega) = \sin(\pi\omega)/(\pi\omega)$
Gaussian: $f(x) = e^{-\pi x^2}$	Gaussian: $f(\omega) = e^{-\pi\omega^2}$
Constant: $f(x) = 1$	Delta: $f(\omega) = \delta(\omega)$
Sinusoid: $f(x) = \cos x$	Translated delta: $f(\omega) = \pi(\delta(1 - 2\pi\omega) + \delta(1 + 2\pi\omega))$
Shah: $f(x) = \text{Ш}_T(x) = T \sum_i \delta(x - Ti)$	Shah: $f(\omega) = \text{Ш}_{1/T}(\omega) = (1/T) \sum_i \delta(\omega - i/T)$

Equation (7.1) is called the *Fourier analysis* equation, or sometimes just the *Fourier transform*. We can also transform from the frequency domain back to the spatial domain using the *Fourier synthesis* equation, or the *inverse Fourier transform*:

$$f(x) = \int_{-\infty}^{\infty} F(\omega) \, e^{i2\pi\omega x} \, d\omega. \qquad (7.2)$$

Table 7.1 shows a number of important functions and their frequency space representations. A number of these functions are based on the Dirac delta distribution, a special function that is defined such that $\int \delta(x) dx = 1$, and for all $x \neq 0$, $\delta(x) = 0$. An important consequence of these properties is that

$$\int f(x) \, \delta(x) \, dx = f(0).$$

The delta distribution cannot be expressed as a standard mathematical function, but instead is generally thought of as the limit of a unit area box function centered at the origin with width approaching 0.

7.1.2 IDEAL SAMPLING AND RECONSTRUCTION

Using frequency space analysis, we can now formally investigate the properties of sampling. Recall that the sampling process requires us to choose a set of equally spaced sample positions and compute the function's value at those positions. Formally, this corresponds to multiplying the function by a "shah," or "impulse train," function, an infinite sum of equally spaced delta functions. The shah $\text{Ш}_T(x)$ is defined as

$$\text{Ш}_T(x) = T \sum_{i=-\infty}^{\infty} \delta(x - iT),$$

where T defines the period, or *sampling rate*. This formal definition of sampling is illustrated in Figure 7.4. The multiplication yields an infinite sequence of values of the function at equally spaced points:

$$\text{Ш}_T(x)f(x) = T \sum_i \delta(x - iT)f(iT).$$

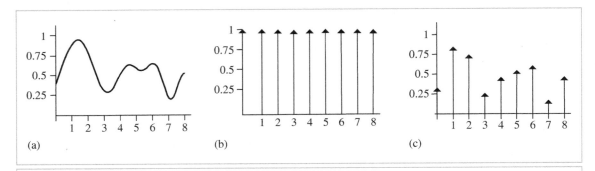

(a)   (b)   (c)

Figure 7.4: Formalizing the Sampling Process. (a) The function $f(x)$ is multiplied by (b) the shah function $\mathrm{III}_T(x)$, giving (c) an infinite sequence of scaled delta functions that represent its value at each sample point.

These sample values can be used to define a reconstructed function $\tilde{f}$ by choosing a reconstruction filter function $r(x)$ and computing the *convolution*

$$\big(\mathrm{III}_T(x)f(x)\big) \otimes r(x),$$

where the convolution operation $\otimes$ is defined as

$$f(x) \otimes g(x) = \int_{-\infty}^{\infty} f(x')\, g(x - x')\, \mathrm{d}x'.$$

For reconstruction, convolution gives a weighted sum of scaled instances of the reconstruction filter centered at the sample points:

$$\tilde{f}(x) = T \sum_{i=-\infty}^{\infty} f(iT)\, r(x - iT).$$

For example, in Figure 7.1, the triangle reconstruction filter, $r(x) = \max(0,\, 1 - |x|)$, was used. Figure 7.5 shows the scaled triangle functions used for that example.

We have gone through a process that may seem gratuitously complex in order to end up at an intuitive result: the reconstructed function $\tilde{f}(x)$ can be obtained by interpolating among the samples in some manner. By setting up this background carefully, however, Fourier analysis can now be applied to the process more easily.

We can gain a deeper understanding of the sampling process by analyzing the sampled function in the frequency domain. In particular, we will be able to determine the conditions under which the original function can be exactly recovered from its values at the sample locations—a very powerful result. For the discussion here, we will assume for now that the function $f(x)$ is *band limited*—there exists some frequency ω_0 such that $f(x)$ contains no frequencies greater than ω_0. By definition, band-limited functions have frequency space representations with compact support, such that $F(\omega) = 0$ for all $|\omega| > \omega_0$. Both of the spectra in Figure 7.3 are band limited.

An important idea used in Fourier analysis is the fact that the Fourier transform of the product of two functions $\mathcal{F}\{f(x)g(x)\}$ can be shown to be the convolution of their individual Fourier transforms $F(\omega)$ and $G(\omega)$:

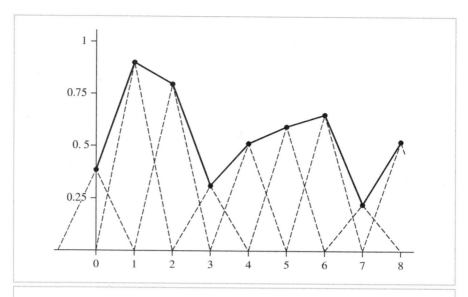

Figure 7.5: The sum of instances of the triangle reconstruction filter, shown with dashed lines, gives the reconstructed approximation to the original function, shown with a solid line.

$$\mathcal{F}\{f(x)g(x)\} = F(\omega) \otimes G(\omega).$$

It is similarly the case that convolution in the spatial domain is equivalent to multiplication in the frequency domain:

$$\mathcal{F}\{f(x) \otimes g(x)\} = F(\omega)G(\omega). \qquad \qquad [7.3]$$

These properties are derived in the standard references on Fourier analysis. Using these ideas, the original sampling step in the spatial domain, where the product of the shah function and the original function $f(x)$ is found, can be equivalently described by the convolution of $F(\omega)$ with another shah function in frequency space.

We also know the spectrum of the shah function $\text{Ш}_T(x)$ from Table 7.1; the Fourier transform of a shah function with period T is another shah function with period $1/T$. This reciprocal relationship between periods is important to keep in mind: it means that if the samples are farther apart in the spatial domain, they are closer together in the frequency domain.

Thus, the frequency domain representation of the sampled signal is given by the convolution of $F(\omega)$ and this new shah function. Convolving a function with a delta function just yields a copy of the function, so convolving with a shah function yields an infinite sequence of copies of the original function, with spacing equal to the period of the shah (Figure 7.6). This is the frequency space representation of the series of samples.

Now that we have this infinite set of copies of the function's spectrum, how do we reconstruct the original function? Looking at Figure 7.6, the answer is obvious: just discard all of the spectrum copies except the one centered at the origin, giving the original

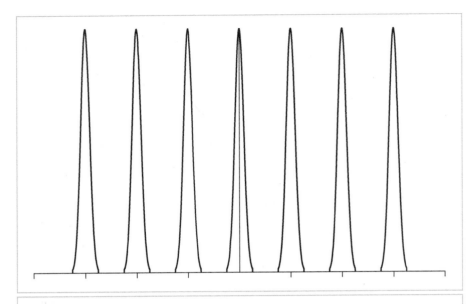

Figure 7.6: The Convolution of $F(\omega)$ **and the Shah Function.** The result is infinitely many copies of F.

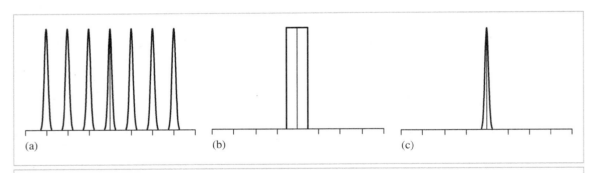

(a)   (b)   (c)

Figure 7.7: Multiplying (a) a series of copies of $F(\omega)$ by (b) the appropriate box function yields (c) the original spectrum.

$F(\omega)$. In order to throw away all but the center copy of the spectrum, we multiply by a box function of the appropriate width (Figure 7.7). The box function $\Pi_T(x)$ of width T is defined as

$$\Pi_T(x) = \begin{cases} 1/(2T) & |x| < T \\ 0 & \text{otherwise.} \end{cases}$$

This multiplication step corresponds to convolution with the reconstruction filter in the spatial domain. This is the ideal sampling and reconstruction process. To summarize:

$$\tilde{F} = \left(F(\omega) \otimes \text{Ш}_{1/T}(\omega)\right) \Pi_T(\omega).$$

This is a remarkable result: we have been able to determine the exact frequency space representation of $f(x)$, purely by sampling it at a set of regularly spaced points. Other than knowing that the function was band limited, no additional information about the composition of the function was used.

Applying the equivalent process in the spatial domain will likewise recover $f(x)$ exactly. Because the inverse Fourier transform of the box function is the sinc function, ideal reconstruction in the spatial domain is

$$\tilde{f} = \big(f(x)\text{Ш}_T(x)\big) \otimes \text{sinc}(x),$$

or

$$\tilde{f}(x) = \sum_{i=-\infty}^{\infty} \text{sinc}(x - i)f(i).$$

Unfortunately, because the sinc function has infinite extent, it is necessary to use all of the sample values $f(i)$ to compute any particular value of $\tilde{f}(x)$ in the spatial domain. Filters with finite spatial extent are preferable for practical implementations even though they don't reconstruct the original function perfectly.

A commonly used alternative in graphics is to use the box function for reconstruction, effectively averaging all of the sample values within some region around x. This is a very poor choice, as can be seen by considering the box filter's behavior in the frequency domain: This technique attempts to isolate the central copy of the function's spectrum by *multiplying by a sinc*, which not only does a bad job of selecting the central copy of the function's spectrum but includes high-frequency contributions from the infinite series of other copies of it as well.

7.1.3 ALIASING

Beyond the issue of the sinc function's infinite extent, one of the most serious practical problems with the ideal sampling and reconstruction approach is the assumption that the signal is band limited. For signals that are not band limited, or signals that aren't sampled at a sufficiently high sampling rate for their frequency content, the process described earlier will reconstruct a function that is different from the original signal.

The key to successful reconstruction is the ability to exactly recover the original spectrum $F(\omega)$ by multiplying the sampled spectrum with a box function of the appropriate width. Notice that in Figure 7.6, the copies of the signal's spectrum are separated by empty space, so perfect reconstruction is possible. Consider what happens, however, if the original function was sampled with a lower sampling rate. Recall that the Fourier transform of a shah function Ш_T with period T is a new shah function with period $1/T$. This means that if the spacing between samples increases in the spatial domain, the sample spacing decreases in the frequency domain, pushing the copies of the spectrum $F(\omega)$ closer together. If the copies get too close together, they start to overlap.

Because the copies are added together, the resulting spectrum no longer looks like many copies of the original (Figure 7.8). When this new spectrum is multiplied by a box function, the result is a spectrum that is similar but not equal to the original $F(\omega)$: high-frequency details in the original signal leak into lower frequency regions of the spectrum

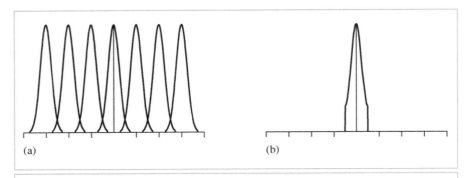

(a)   (b)

Figure 7.8: (a) When the sampling rate is too low, the copies of the function's spectrum overlap, resulting in (b) aliasing when reconstruction is performed.

of the reconstructed signal. These new low-frequency artifacts are called *aliases* (because high frequencies are "masquerading" as low frequencies), and the resulting signal is said to be *aliased*. Figure 7.9 shows the effects of aliasing from undersampling and then reconstructing the 1D function $f(x) = 1 + \cos(4x^2)$.

A possible solution to the problem of overlapping spectra is to simply increase the sampling rate until the copies of the spectrum are sufficiently far apart to not overlap, thereby eliminating aliasing completely. In fact, the *sampling theorem* tells us exactly what rate is required. This theorem says that as long as the frequency of uniform sample points ω_s is greater than twice the maximum frequency present in the signal ω_0, it is possible to reconstruct the original signal perfectly from the samples. This minimum sampling frequency is called the *Nyquist frequency*.

For signals that are not band limited ($\omega_0 = \infty$), it is impossible to sample at a high enough rate to perform perfect reconstruction. Non-band-limited signals have spectra with infinite support, so no matter how far apart the copies of their spectra are (i.e., how high a sampling rate we use), there will always be overlap. Unfortunately, few of the interesting functions in computer graphics are band limited. In particular, any function containing a discontinuity cannot be band limited, and therefore we cannot perfectly sample and reconstruct it. This makes sense because the function's discontinuity will always fall between two samples and the samples provide no information about the location of the discontinuity. Thus, it is necessary to apply different methods besides just increasing the sampling rate in order to counteract the error that aliasing can introduce to the renderer's results.

7.1.4 ANTIALIASING TECHNIQUES

If one is not careful about sampling and reconstruction, myriad artifacts can appear in the final image. It is sometimes useful to distinguish between artifacts due to sampling and those due to reconstruction; when we wish to be precise we will call sampling artifacts *prealiasing* and reconstruction artifacts *postaliasing*. Any attempt to fix these errors is broadly classified as *antialiasing*. This section reviews a number of antialiasing techniques beyond just increasing the sampling rate everywhere.

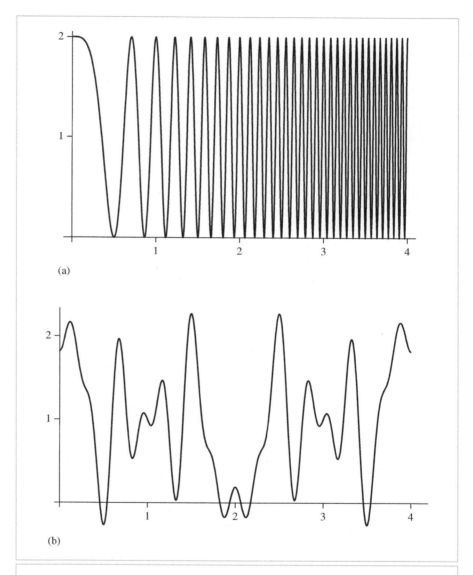

(a)

(b)

Figure 7.9: Aliasing from Point Sampling the Function $1 + \cos(4x^2)$. (a) The function. (b) The reconstructed function from sampling it with samples spaced 0.125 units apart and performing perfect reconstruction with the sinc filter. Aliasing causes the high-frequency information in the original function to be lost and to reappear as lower frequency error.

Nonuniform Sampling

Although the image functions that we will be sampling are known to have infinite-frequency components and thus can't be perfectly reconstructed from point samples, it is possible to reduce the visual impact of aliasing by varying the spacing between samples in a nonuniform way. If ξ denotes a random number between 0 and 1, a nonuniform set of samples based on the impulse train is

$$\sum_{i=-\infty}^{\infty} \delta\left(x - \left(i + \frac{1}{2} - \xi\right)T\right).$$

For a fixed sampling rate that isn't sufficient to capture the function, both uniform and nonuniform sampling produce incorrect reconstructed signals. However, nonuniform sampling tends to turn the regular aliasing artifacts into noise, which is less distracting to the human visual system. In frequency space, the copies of the sampled signal end up being randomly shifted as well, so that when reconstruction is performed the result is random error rather than coherent aliasing.

Adaptive Sampling

Another approach that has been suggested to combat aliasing is *adaptive supersampling*: if we can identify the regions of the signal with frequencies higher than the Nyquist limit, we can take additional samples in those regions without needing to incur the computational expense of increasing the sampling frequency everywhere. It can be difficult to get this approach to work well in practice, because finding all of the places where supersampling is needed is difficult. Most techniques for doing so are based on examining adjacent sample values and finding places where there is a significant change in value between the two; the assumption is that the signal has high frequencies in that region.

In general, adjacent sample values cannot tell us with certainty what is really happening between them: even if the values are the same, the functions may have huge variation between them. Alternatively, adjacent samples may have substantially different values without any aliasing actually being present. For example, the texture-filtering algorithms in Chapter 10 work hard to eliminate aliasing due to image maps and procedural textures on surfaces in the scene; we would not want an adaptive sampling routine to needlessly take extra samples in an area where texture values are changing quickly but no excessively high frequencies are actually present.

Prefiltering

Another approach to eliminating aliasing that sampling theory offers is to filter (i.e., blur) the original function so that no high frequencies remain that can't be captured accurately at the sampling rate being used. This approach is applied in the texture functions of Chapter 10. While this technique changes the character of the function being sampled by removing information from it, blurring is generally less objectionable than aliasing.

Recall that we would like to multiply the original function's spectrum with a box filter with width chosen so that frequencies above the Nyquist limit are removed. In the spatial domain, this corresponds to convolving the original function with a sinc filter,

$$f(x) \otimes \text{sinc}(2\omega_s x).$$

In practice, we can use a filter with finite extent that works well. The frequency space representation of this filter can help clarify how well it approximates the behavior of the ideal sinc filter.

Figure 7.10 shows the function $1 + \cos(4x^2)$ convolved with a variant of the sinc with finite extent that will be introduced in Section 7.8. Note that the high-frequency details

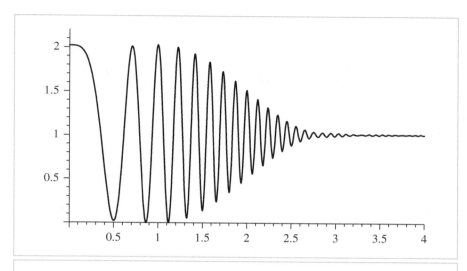

Figure 7.10: Graph of the function $1 + \cos(4x^2)$ convolved with a filter that removes frequencies beyond the Nyquist limit for a sampling rate of $T = 0.125$. High-frequency detail has been removed from the function, so that the new function can at least be sampled and reconstructed without aliasing.

have been eliminated; this function can be sampled and reconstructed at the sampling rate used in Figure 7.9 without aliasing.

7.1.5 APPLICATION TO IMAGE SYNTHESIS

The application of these ideas to the 2D case of sampling and reconstructing images of rendered scenes is straightforward: we have an image, which we can think of as a function of 2D (x, y) image locations to radiance values L:

$$f(x, y) \rightarrow L.$$

The good news is that, with our ray tracer, we can evaluate this function at any (x, y) point that we choose. The bad news is that it's not generally possible to prefilter f to remove the high frequencies from it before sampling. Therefore, the samplers in this chapter will use both strategies of increasing the sampling rate beyond the basic pixel spacing in the final image as well as nonuniformly distributing the samples to turn aliasing into noise.

It is useful to generalize the definition of the scene function to a higher dimensional function that also depends on the time t and (u, v) lens position at which it is sampled. Because the rays from the camera are based on these five quantities, varying any of them gives a different ray and thus a potentially different value of f. For a particular image position, the radiance at that point will generally vary across both time (if there are moving objects in the scene) and position on the lens (if the camera has a finite-aperture lens).

Even more generally, because many of the integrators defined in Chapters 14 through 16 use statistical techniques to estimate the radiance along a given ray, they may return a different radiance value when repeatedly given the same ray. If we further extend the scene radiance function to include sample values used by the integrator (e.g., values used to choose points on area light sources for illumination computations), we have an even higher dimensional image function

$$f(x, y, t, u, v, i_1, i_2, \ldots) \rightarrow L.$$

Sampling all of these dimensions well is an important part of generating high-quality imagery efficiently. For example, if we ensure that nearby (x, y) positions on the image tend to have dissimilar (u, v) positions on the lens, the resulting rendered images will have less error because each sample is more likely to account for information about the scene that its neighboring samples do not. The Sampler classes in the next few sections will address the issue of sampling all of these dimensions effectively.

7.1.6 SOURCES OF ALIASING IN RENDERING

Geometry is one of the most common causes of aliasing in rendered images. When projected onto the image plane, an object's boundary introduces a step function—the image function's value instantaneously jumps from one value to another. Not only do step functions have infinite frequency content as mentioned earlier, but, even worse, the perfect reconstruction filter causes artifacts when applied to aliased samples: ringing artifacts appear in the reconstructed function, an effect known as the *Gibbs phenomenon*. Figure 7.11 shows an example of this effect for a 1D function. Choosing an effective

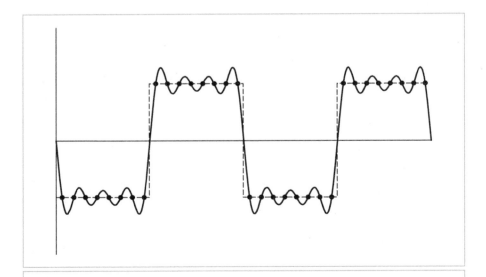

Figure 7.11: Illustration of the Gibbs Phenomenon. When a function hasn't been sampled at the Nyquist rate and the set of aliased samples is reconstructed with the sinc filter, the reconstructed function will have "ringing" artifacts, where it oscillates around the true function. Here a 1D step function (dashed line) has been sampled with a sample spacing of 0.125. When reconstructed with the sinc, the ringing appears (solid line).

Sampler 421

reconstruction filter in the face of aliasing requires a mix of science, artistry, and personal taste, as we will see later in this chapter.

Very small objects in the scene can also cause geometric aliasing. If the geometry is small enough that it falls between samples on the image plane, it can unpredictably disappear and reappear over multiple frames of an animation.

Another source of aliasing can come from the texture and materials on an object. *Shading aliasing* can be caused by texture maps that haven't been filtered correctly (addressing this problem is the topic of much of Chapter 10) or from small highlights on shiny surfaces. If the sampling rate is not high enough to sample these features adequately, aliasing will result. Furthermore, a sharp shadow cast by an object introduces another step function in the final image. While it is possible to identify the position of step functions from geometric edges on the image plane, detecting step functions from shadow boundaries is more difficult.

The key insight about aliasing in rendered images is that we can never remove all of its sources, so we must develop techniques to mitigate its impact on the quality of the final image.

7.1.7 UNDERSTANDING PIXELS

There are two ideas about pixels that are important to keep in mind throughout the remainder of this chapter. First, it is crucial to remember that the pixels that constitute an image are point samples of the image function at discrete points on the image plane; there is no "area" associated with a pixel. As Alvy Ray Smith (1995) has emphatically pointed out, thinking of pixels as small squares with finite area is an incorrect mental model that leads to a series of errors. By introducing the topics of this chapter with a signal processing approach, we have tried to lay the groundwork for a more accurate mental model.

The second issue is that the pixels in the final image are naturally defined at discrete integer (x, y) coordinates on a pixel grid, but the Samplers in this chapter generate image samples at continuous floating-point (x, y) positions. The natural way to map between these two domains is to round continuous coordinates to the nearest discrete coordinate; this is appealing since it maps continuous coordinates that happen to have the same value as discrete coordinates to that discrete coordinate. However, the result is that given a set of discrete coordinates spanning a range $[x_0, x_1]$, the set of continuous coordinates that covers that range is $[x_0 - 1/2, x_1 + 1/2)$. Thus, any code that generates continuous sample positions for a given discrete pixel range is littered with 1/2 offsets. It is easy to forget some of these, leading to subtle errors.

If we instead truncate continuous coordinates c to discrete coordinates d by

$$d = \lfloor c \rfloor,$$

Sampler 421

and convert from discrete to continuous by

$$c = d + 1/2,$$

Figure 7.12: Pixels in an image can be addressed with either *discrete* or *continuous* coordinates. A discrete image five pixels wide covers the continuous pixel range $[0, 5)$. A particular discrete pixel d's coordinate in the continuous representation is $d + 1/2$.

then the range of continuous coordinates for the discrete range $[x_0, x_1]$ is naturally $[x_0, x_1 + 1)$ and the resulting code is much simpler (Heckbert 1990a). This convention, which we will adopt in pbrt, is shown graphically in Figure 7.12.

7.2 SAMPLING INTERFACE

As first introduced in Section 7.1.5, the rendering approach implemented in pbrt involves choosing sample points in additional dimensions beyond 2D points on the image plane. Various algorithms will be used to generate these points, but all of their implementations inherit from an abstract Sampler class that defines their interface. The core sampling declarations and functions are in the files core/sampler.h and core/sampler.cpp. Each of the sample generation implementations is in its own source files in the samplers/ directory.

The task of a Sampler is to generate a sequence of n-dimensional samples in $[0, 1)^n$, where one such sample vector is generated for each image sample and where the number of dimensions n in each sample may vary, depending on the calculations performed by the light transport algorithms. (See Figure 7.13.)

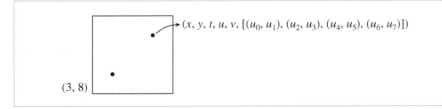

Figure 7.13: Samplers generate an n-dimensional sample vector for each of the image samples taken to generate the final image. Here, the pixel $(3, 8)$ is being sampled, and there are two image samples in the pixel area. The first two dimensions of the sample vector give the (x, y) offset of the sample within the pixel, and the next three dimensions determine the time and lens position of the corresponding camera ray. Subsequent dimensions are used by the Monte Carlo light transport algorithms in Chapters 14, 15, and 16. Here, the light transport algorithm has requested a 2D array of four samples in the sample vector; these values might be used to select four points on an area light source to compute the radiance for the image sample, for example.

Sampler 421

Because sample values must be strictly less than 1, it's useful to define a constant, OneMinusEpsilon, that represents the largest representable floating-point constant that is less than 1. Later, we will clamp sample vector values to be no larger than this value.

⟨*Random Number Declarations*⟩ ≡
```
#ifdef PBRT_FLOAT_IS_DOUBLE
    static const Float OneMinusEpsilon = 0x1.fffffffffffffp-1;
#else
    static const Float OneMinusEpsilon = 0x1.fffffep-1;
#endif
```

The simplest possible implementation of a Sampler would just return uniform random values in [0, 1) each time an additional component of the sample vector was needed. Such a sampler would produce correct images but would require many more samples (and thus, many more rays traced and much more time) to create images of the same quality achievable with more sophisticated samplers. The run-time expense for using better sampling patterns is approximately the same as that for lower-quality patterns like uniform random numbers; because evaluating the radiance for each image sample is much more expensive than computing the sample's component values, doing this work pays dividends (Figure 7.14).

A few characteristics of these sample vectors are assumed in the following:

- The first five dimensions generated by Samplers are generally used by the Camera. In this case, the first two are specifically used to choose a point on the image inside the current pixel area; the third is used to compute the time at which the sample should be taken; and the fourth and fifth dimensions give a (u, v) lens position for depth of field.
- Some sampling algorithms generate better samples in some dimensions of the sample vector than in others. Elsewhere in the system, we assume that in general, the earlier dimensions have the most well-placed sample values.

Note also that the n-dimensional samples generated by the Sampler are generally not represented explicitly or stored in their entirety but are often generated incrementally as needed by the light transport algorithm. (However, storing the entire sample vector and making incremental changes to its components is the basis of the MLTSampler in Section 16.4.4, which is used by the MLTIntegrator in Section 16.4.5.)

⋆ 7.2.1 EVALUATING SAMPLE PATTERNS: DISCREPANCY

Fourier analysis gave us one way of evaluating the quality of a 2D sampling pattern, but it took us only as far as being able to quantify the improvement from adding more evenly spaced samples in terms of the band-limited frequencies that could be represented. Given the presence of infinite frequency content from edges in images and given the need for $(n > 2)$-dimensional sample vectors for Monte Carlo light transport algorithms, Fourier analysis alone isn't enough for our needs.

Given a renderer and a candidate algorithm for placing samples, one way to evaluate the algorithm's effectiveness is to use that sampling pattern to render an image and to compute the error in the image compared to a reference image rendered with a large

(a)

(b)

Figure 7.14: Scene rendered with (a) a relatively ineffective sampler and (b) a carefully designed sampler, using the same number of samples for each. The improvement in image quality, ranging from the edges of the highlights to the quality of the glossy reflections, is noticeable.

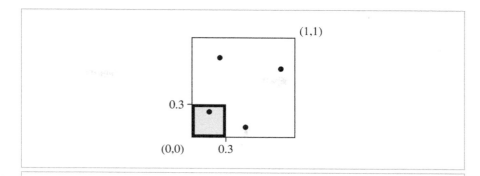

Figure 7.15: The discrepancy of a box (shaded) given a set of 2D sample points in $[0, 1)^2$. One of the four sample points is inside the box, so this set of points would estimate the box's area to be $1/4$. The true area of the box is $0.3 \times 0.3 = .09$, so the discrepancy for this particular box is $.25 - .09 = .16$. In general, we're interested in finding the maximum discrepancy of all possible boxes (or some other shape).

number of samples. We will use this approach to compare sampling algorithms later in this chapter, though it only tells us how well the algorithm did for one specific scene, and it doesn't give us a sense of the quality of the sample points without going through the rendering process.

Outside of Fourier analysis, mathematicians have developed a concept called *discrepancy* that can be used to evaluate the quality of a pattern of n-dimensional sample positions. Patterns that are well distributed (in a manner to be formalized shortly) have low discrepancy values, and thus the sample pattern generation problem can be considered to be one of finding a suitable *low-discrepancy* pattern of points.[5] A number of deterministic techniques have been developed that generate low-discrepancy point sets, even in high-dimensional spaces. (Most of the sampling algorithms used later in this chapter use these techniques.)

The basic idea of discrepancy is that the quality of a set of points in an n-dimensional space $[0, 1)^n$ can be evaluated by looking at regions of the domain $[0, 1)^n$, counting the number of points inside each region, and comparing the volume of each region to the number of sample points inside. In general, a given fraction of the volume should have roughly the same fraction of the total number of sample points inside of it. While it's not possible for this always to be the case, we can still try to use patterns that minimize the maximum difference between the actual volume and the volume estimated by the points (the *discrepancy*). Figure 7.15 shows an example of the idea in two dimensions.

To compute the discrepancy of a set of points, we first pick a family of shapes B that are subsets of $[0, 1)^n$. For example, boxes with one corner at the origin are often used. This

---

5   Of course, using discrepancy in this way implicitly assumes that the metric used to compute discrepancy is one that has good correlation with the quality of a pattern for image sampling, which may be a slightly different thing, particularly given the involvement of the human visual system in the process.

corresponds to

$$B = \{[0, v_1] \times [0, v_2] \times \cdots \times [0, v_n]\},$$

where $0 \leq v_i < 1$. Given a sequence of sample points $P = x_1, \ldots, x_N$, the discrepancy of P with respect to B is[6]

$$D_N(B, P) = \sup_{b \in B} \left| \frac{\sharp\{x_i \in b\}}{N} - V(b) \right|, \qquad [7.4]$$

where $\sharp\{x_i \in b\}$ is the number of points in b and $V(b)$ is the volume of b.

The intuition for why Equation (7.4) is a reasonable measure of quality is that the value $\sharp\{x_i \in b\}/N$ is an approximation of the volume of the box b given by the particular points P. Therefore, the discrepancy is the worst error over all possible boxes from this way of approximating volume. When the set of shapes B is the set of boxes with a corner at the origin, this value is called the *star discrepancy*, $D_N^*(P)$. Another popular option for B is the set of all axis-aligned boxes, where the restriction that one corner be at the origin has been removed.

For a few particular point sets, the discrepancy can be computed analytically. For example, consider the set of points in one dimension

$$x_i = \frac{i}{N}.$$

We can see that the star discrepancy of x_i is

$$D_N^*(x_1, \ldots, x_n) = \frac{1}{N}.$$

For example, take the interval $b = [0, 1/N)$. Then $V(b) = 1/N$, but $\sharp\{x_i \in b\} = 0$. This interval (and the intervals $[0, 2/N)$, etc.) is the interval where the largest differences between volume and fraction of points inside the volume are seen.

The star discrepancy of this sequence can be improved by modifying it slightly:

$$x_i = \frac{i - \frac{1}{2}}{N}. \qquad [7.5]$$

Then

$$D_N^*(x_i) = \frac{1}{2N}.$$

The bounds for the star discrepancy of a sequence of points in one dimension have been shown to be

$$D_N^*(x_i) = \frac{1}{2N} + \max_{1 \leq i \leq N} \left| x_i - \frac{2i - 1}{2N} \right|.$$

Thus, the earlier sequence from Equation (7.5) has the lowest possible discrepancy for a sequence in 1D. In general, it is much easier to analyze and compute bounds for the

---

6   The sup operator is the continuous analog of the discrete max operator. That is, sup $f(x)$ is a constant-valued function of x that passes through the maximum value taken on by $f(x)$.

discrepancy of sequences in 1D than for those in higher dimensions. For less simply constructed point sequences and for sequences in higher dimensions and for more irregular shapes than boxes, the discrepancy often must be estimated numerically by constructing a large number of shapes b, computing their discrepancy, and reporting the maximum value found.

The astute reader will notice that according to the low-discrepancy measure, this uniform sequence in 1D is optimal, but earlier in this chapter we claimed that irregular jittered patterns were perceptually superior to uniform patterns for image sampling in 2D since they replaced aliasing error with noise. In that framework, uniform samples are clearly not optimal. Fortunately, low-discrepancy patterns in higher dimensions are much less uniform than they are in one dimension and thus usually work reasonably well as sample patterns in practice. Nevertheless, their underlying uniformity means that low-discrepancy patterns can be more prone to visually objectionable aliasing than patterns with pseudo-random variation.

Discrepancy alone isn't necessarily a good metric: some low-discrepancy point sets exhibit some clumping of samples, where two or more samples may be quite close together. The Sobol$'$ sampler in Section 7.7 particularly suffers from this issue—see Figure 7.36, which shows a plot of its first two dimensions. Intuitively, samples that are too close together aren't a good use of sampling resources: the closer one sample is to another, the less likely it is to give useful new information about the function being sampled. Therefore, computing the minimum distance between any two samples in a set of points has also proved to be a useful metric of sample pattern quality; the higher the minimum distance, the better.

There are a variety of algorithms for generating *Poisson disk* sampling patterns that score well by this metric. By construction, no two points in a Poisson disk pattern are closer than some distance d. Studies have shown that the rods and cones in the eye are distributed in a similar way, which further validates the idea that this distribution is a good one for imaging. In practice, we have found that Poisson disk patterns work very well for sampling 2D images but are less effective than the better low discrepancy patterns for the higher-dimensional sampling done in more complex rendering situations; see the "Further Reading" section for more information.

7.2.2 BASIC SAMPLER INTERFACE

The Sampler base class not only defines the interface to samplers but also provides some common functionality for use by Sampler implementations.

```
⟨Sampler Declarations⟩ ≡
    class Sampler {
    public:
        ⟨Sampler Interface 422⟩
        ⟨Sampler Public Data 422⟩
    protected:
        ⟨Sampler Protected Data 425⟩
    private:
        ⟨Sampler Private Data 426⟩
    };
```

All `Sampler` implementations must supply the constructor with the number of samples that will be generated for each pixel in the final image. In rare cases, it may be useful for the system to model the film as having only a single "pixel" that covers the entire viewing region. (This overloading of the definition of pixel is something of a stretch, but we allow it to simplify certain implementation aspects.) Since this "pixel" could potentially have billions of samples, we store the sample count using a variable with 64 bits of precision.

⟨*Sampler Method Definitions*⟩ ≡
```
Sampler::Sampler(int64_t samplesPerPixel)
    : samplesPerPixel(samplesPerPixel) { }
```

⟨*Sampler Public Data*⟩ ≡   421
```
const int64_t samplesPerPixel;
```

When the rendering algorithm is ready to start work on a given pixel, it starts by calling `StartPixel()`, providing the coordinates of the pixel in the image. Some `Sampler` implementations use the knowledge of which pixel is being sampled to improve the overall distribution of the samples that they generate for the pixel, while others ignore this information.

⟨*Sampler Interface*⟩ ≡   421
```
virtual void StartPixel(const Point2i &p);
```

The `Get1D()` method returns the sample value for the next dimension of the current sample vector, and `Get2D()` returns the sample values for the next two dimensions. While a 2D sample value could be constructed by using values returned by a pair of calls to `Get1D()`, some samplers can generate better point distributions if they know that two dimensions will be used together.

⟨*Sampler Interface*⟩ +≡   421
```
virtual Float Get1D() = 0;
virtual Point2f Get2D() = 0;
```

In pbrt, we don't support requests for 3D or higher dimensional sample values from samplers because these are generally not needed for the types of rendering algorithms implemented here. If necessary, multiple values from lower dimensional components can be used to construct higher dimensional sample points.

A sharp edge of these interfaces is that code that uses sample values must be carefully written so that it always requests sample dimensions in the same order. Consider the following code:

```
sampler->StartPixel(p);
do {
  Float v = a(sampler->Get1D());
  if (v > 0)
      v += b(sampler->Get1D());
  v += c(sampler->Get1D());
} while (sampler->StartNextSample());
```

In this case, the first dimension of the sample vector will always be passed to the function `a()`; when the code path that calls `b()` is executed, `b()` will receive the second dimension.

However, if the `if` test isn't always true or false, then `c()` will sometimes receive a sample from the second dimension of the sample vector and otherwise receive a sample from the third dimension. Thus, efforts by the sampler to provide well-distributed sample points in each dimension being evaluated have been thwarted. Code that uses `Samplers` should therefore be carefully written so that it consistently consumes sample vector dimensions to avoid this issue.

For convenience, the `Sampler` base class provides a method that initializes a `CameraSample` for a given pixel.

⟨*Sampler Method Definitions*⟩ +≡
```
CameraSample Sampler::GetCameraSample(const Point2i &pRaster) {
    CameraSample cs;
    cs.pFilm = (Point2f)pRaster + Get2D();
    cs.time = Get1D();
    cs.pLens = Get2D();
    return cs;
}
```

Some rendering algorithms make use of arrays of sample values for some of the dimensions they sample; most sample-generation algorithms can generate higher quality arrays of samples than series of individual samples by accounting for the distribution of sample values across all elements of the array and across the samples in a pixel.

If arrays of samples are needed, they must be requested before rendering begins. The `Request[12]DArray()` methods should be called for each such dimension's array before rendering begins—for example, in methods that override the `SamplerIntegrator::Preprocess()` method. For example, in a scene with two area light sources, where the integrator traces four shadow rays to the first source and eight to the second, the integrator would ask for two 2D sample arrays for each image sample, with four and eight samples each. (A 2D array is required because two dimensions are needed to parameterize the surface of a light.) In Section 13.7, we will see how using arrays of samples corresponds to more densely sampling some of the dimensions of the light transport integral using the Monte Carlo technique of "splitting."

⟨*Sampler Interface*⟩ +≡   **421**
```
void Request1DArray(int n);
void Request2DArray(int n);
```

Most `Samplers` can do a better job of generating some particular sizes of these arrays than others. For example, samples from the `ZeroTwoSequenceSampler` are much better distributed in quantities that are in powers of 2. The `Sampler::RoundCount()` method helps communicate this information. Code that needs arrays of samples should call this method with the desired number of samples to be taken, giving the `Sampler` an opportunity to adjust the number of samples to a better number. The returned value should then be used as the number of samples to actually request from the `Sampler`. The default implementation returns the given count unchanged.

⟨*Sampler Interface*⟩ +≡   421
```
virtual int RoundCount(int n) const {
    return n;
}
```

During rendering, the Get[12]DArray() methods can be called to get a pointer to the start of a previously requested array of samples for the current dimension. Along the lines of Get1D() and Get2D(), these return a pointer to an array of samples whose size is given by the parameter n to the corresponding call to Request[12]DArray() during initialization. The caller must also provide the array size to the "get" method, which is used to verify that the returned buffer has the expected size.

⟨*Sampler Interface*⟩ +≡   421
```
const Float *Get1DArray(int n);
const Point2f *Get2DArray(int n);
```

When the work for one sample is complete, the integrator calls StartNextSample(). This call notifies the Sampler that subsequent requests for sample components should return values starting at the first dimension of the next sample for the current pixel. This method returns true until the number of the originally requested samples per pixel have been generated (at which point the caller should either start work on another pixel or stop trying to use more samples.)

⟨*Sampler Interface*⟩ +≡   421
```
virtual bool StartNextSample();
```

Sampler implementations store a variety of state about the current sample: which pixel is being sampled, how many dimensions of the sample have been used, and so forth. It is therefore natural for it to be unsafe for a single Sampler to be used concurrently by multiple threads. The Clone() method generates a new instance of an initial Sampler for use by a rendering thread; it takes a seed value for the sampler's random number generator (if any), so that different threads see different sequences of random numbers. Reusing the same pseudo-random number sequence across multiple image tiles can lead to subtle image artifacts, such as repeating noise patterns.

Implementations of the various Clone() methods aren't generally interesting, so they won't be included in the text here.

⟨*Sampler Interface*⟩ +≡   421
```
virtual std::unique_ptr<Sampler> Clone(int seed) = 0;
```

Some light transport algorithms (notably stochastic progressive photon mapping in Section 16.2) don't use all of the samples in a pixel before going to the next pixel, but instead jump around pixels, taking one sample at a time in each one. The SetSampleNumber() method allows integrators to set the index of the sample in the current pixel to generate next. This method returns false once sampleNum is greater than or equal to the number of originally requested samples per pixel.

⟨*Sampler Interface*⟩ +≡   421
```
virtual bool SetSampleNumber(int64_t sampleNum);
```

7.2.3 SAMPLER IMPLEMENTATION

The Sampler base class provides implementations of some of the methods in its interface. First, the StartPixel() method implementation records the coordinates of the current pixel being sampled and resets currentPixelSampleIndex, the sample number in the pixel currently being generated, to zero. Note that this is a virtual method with an implementation; subclasses that override this method are required to explicitly call Sampler::StartPixel().

⟨*Sampler Method Definitions*⟩ +≡
```
void Sampler::StartPixel(const Point2i &p) {
    currentPixel = p;
    currentPixelSampleIndex = 0;
    ⟨Reset array offsets for next pixel sample 426⟩
}
```

The current pixel coordinates and sample number within the pixel are made available to Sampler subclasses, though they should treat these as read-only values.

⟨*Sampler Protected Data*⟩ ≡   **421**
```
    Point2i currentPixel;
    int64_t currentPixelSampleIndex;
```

When the pixel sample is advanced or explicitly set, currentPixelSampleIndex is updated accordingly. As with StartPixel(), the methods StartNextSample() and SetSampleNumber() are both virtual implementations; these implementations also must be explicitly called by overridden implementations of them in Sampler subclasses.

⟨*Sampler Method Definitions*⟩ +≡
```
bool Sampler::StartNextSample() {
    ⟨Reset array offsets for next pixel sample 426⟩
    return ++currentPixelSampleIndex < samplesPerPixel;
}
```

⟨*Sampler Method Definitions*⟩ +≡
```
bool Sampler::SetSampleNumber(int64_t sampleNum) {
    ⟨Reset array offsets for next pixel sample 426⟩
    currentPixelSampleIndex = sampleNum;
    return currentPixelSampleIndex < samplesPerPixel;
}
```

The base Sampler implementation also takes care of recording requests for arrays of sample components and allocating storage for their values. The sizes of the requested sample arrays are stored in samples1DArraySizes and samples2DArraySizes, and memory for an entire pixel's worth of array samples is allocated in sampleArray1D and sampleArray2D. The first n values in each allocation are used for the corresponding array for the first sample in the pixel, and so forth.

⟨*Sampler Method Definitions*⟩ +≡
```
void Sampler::Request1DArray(int n) {
    samples1DArraySizes.push_back(n);
    sampleArray1D.push_back(std::vector<Float>(n * samplesPerPixel));
}
```

⟨*Sampler Method Definitions*⟩ +≡
```
void Sampler::Request2DArray(int n) {
    samples2DArraySizes.push_back(n);
    sampleArray2D.push_back(std::vector<Point2f>(n * samplesPerPixel));
}
```

⟨*Sampler Protected Data*⟩ +≡   421
```
std::vector<int> samples1DArraySizes, samples2DArraySizes;
std::vector<std::vector<Float>> sampleArray1D;
std::vector<std::vector<Point2f>> sampleArray2D;
```

As arrays in the current sample are accessed by the Get[12]DArray() methods, array1D Offset and array2DOffset are updated to hold the index of the next array to return for the sample vector.

⟨*Sampler Private Data*⟩ ≡   421
```
size_t array1DOffset, array2DOffset;
```

When a new pixel is started or when the sample number in the current pixel changes, these array offsets must be reset to 0.

⟨*Reset array offsets for next pixel sample*⟩ ≡   425
```
array1DOffset = array2DOffset = 0;
```

Returning the appropriate array pointer is a matter of first choosing the appropriate array based on how many have been consumed in the current sample vector and then returning the appropriate instance of it based on the current pixel sample index.

⟨*Sampler Method Definitions*⟩ +≡
```
const Float *Sampler::Get1DArray(int n) {
    if (array1DOffset == sampleArray1D.size())
        return nullptr;
    return &sampleArray1D[array1DOffset++][currentPixelSampleIndex * n];
}
```

⟨*Sampler Method Definitions*⟩ +≡
```
const Point2f *Sampler::Get2DArray(int n) {
    if (array2DOffset == sampleArray2D.size())
        return nullptr;
    return &sampleArray2D[array2DOffset++][currentPixelSampleIndex * n];
}
```

7.2.4 PIXEL SAMPLER

While some sampling algorithms can easily incrementally generate elements of each sample vector, others more naturally generate all of the dimensions' sample values for all of the sample vectors for a pixel at the same time. The PixelSampler class implements some functionality that is useful for the implementation of these types of samplers.

⟨*Sampler Declarations*⟩ +≡
```
class PixelSampler : public Sampler {
public:
    ⟨PixelSampler Public Methods⟩
protected:
    ⟨PixelSampler Protected Data 427⟩
};
```

The number of dimensions of the sample vectors that will be used by the rendering algorithm isn't known ahead of time. (Indeed, it's only determined implicitly by the number of Get1D() and Get2D() calls and the requested arrays.) Therefore, the PixelSampler constructor takes a maximum number of dimensions for which non-array sample values will be computed by the Sampler. If all of these dimensions of components are consumed, then the PixelSampler just returns uniform random values for additional dimensions.

For each precomputed dimension, the constructor allocates a vector to store sample values, with one value for each sample in the pixel. These vectors are indexed as sample1D[dim][pixelSample]; while interchanging the order of these indices might seem more sensible, this memory layout—where all of the sample component values for all of the samples for a given dimension are contiguous in memory—turns out to be more convenient for code that generates these values.

⟨*Sampler Method Definitions*⟩ +≡
```
PixelSampler::PixelSampler(int64_t samplesPerPixel,
        int nSampledDimensions)
    : Sampler(samplesPerPixel) {
    for (int i = 0; i < nSampledDimensions; ++i) {
        samples1D.push_back(std::vector<Float>(samplesPerPixel));
        samples2D.push_back(std::vector<Point2f>(samplesPerPixel));
    }
}
```

The key responsibility of Sampler implementations that inherit from PixelSampler then is to fill in the samples1D and samples2D arrays (in addition to sampleArray1D and sampleArray2D) in their StartPixel() methods.

current1DDimension and current2DDimension store the offsets into the respective arrays for the current pixel sample. They must be reset to 0 at the start of each new sample.

⟨*PixelSampler Protected Data*⟩ ≡   427
```
std::vector<std::vector<Float>> samples1D;
std::vector<std::vector<Point2f>> samples2D;
int current1DDimension = 0, current2DDimension = 0;
```

⟨*Sampler Method Definitions*⟩ +≡
```
bool PixelSampler::StartNextSample() {
    current1DDimension = current2DDimension = 0;
    return Sampler::StartNextSample();
}
```

⟨*Sampler Method Definitions*⟩ +≡
```
bool PixelSampler::SetSampleNumber(int64_t sampleNum) {
    current1DDimension = current2DDimension = 0;
    return Sampler::SetSampleNumber(sampleNum);
}
```

Given sample values in the arrays computed by the PixelSampler subclass, the implementation of Get1D() is just a matter of returning values for successive dimensions until all of the computed dimensions have been consumed, at which point uniform random values are returned.

⟨*Sampler Method Definitions*⟩ +≡
```
Float PixelSampler::Get1D() {
    if (current1DDimension < samples1D.size())
        return samples1D[current1DDimension++][currentPixelSampleIndex];
    else
        return rng.UniformFloat();
}
```

The PixelSampler::Get2D() follows similarly, so it won't be included here.

The random number generator used by the PixelSampler is protected rather than private; this is a convenience for some of its subclasses that also need random numbers when they initialize samples1D and samples2D.

⟨*PixelSampler Protected Data*⟩ +≡   427
```
RNG rng;
```

7.2.5 GLOBAL SAMPLER

Other algorithms for generating samples are very much not pixel-based but naturally generate consecutive samples that are spread across the entire image, visiting completely different pixels in succession. (Many such samplers are effectively placing each additional sample such that it fills the biggest hole in the n-dimensional sample space, which naturally leads to subsequent samples being inside different pixels.) These sampling algorithms are somewhat problematic with the Sampler interface as described so far: consider, for example, a sampler that generates the series of sample values shown in the middle column of Table 7.2 for the first two dimensions. These sample values are multiplied by the image resolution in each dimension to get sample positions in the image plane (here we're considering a 2 × 3 image for simplicity.) Note that for the sampler here (actually the HaltonSampler), each pixel is visited by each sixth sample. If we are rendering an image with three samples per pixel, then to generate all of the samples for the pixel (0, 0), we need to generate the samples with indices 0, 6, and 12, and so forth.

Table 7.2: The HaltonSampler generates the coordinates in the middle column for the first two dimensions. Because it is a GlobalSampler, it must define an inverse mapping from the pixel coordinates to sample indices; here, it places samples across a 2 × 3 pixel image, by scaling the first coordinate by 2 and the second coordinate by three, giving the pixel sample coordinates in the right column.

Sample index	$[0, 1)^2$ sample coordinates	Pixel sample coordinates
0	(0.000000, 0.000000)	(0.000000, 0.000000)
1	(0.500000, 0.333333)	(1.000000, 1.000000)
2	(0.250000, 0.666667)	(0.500000, 2.000000)
3	(0.750000, 0.111111)	(1.500000, 0.333333)
4	(0.125000, 0.444444)	(0.250000, 1.333333)
5	(0.625000, 0.777778)	(1.250000, 2.333333)
6	(0.375000, 0.222222)	(0.750000, 0.666667)
7	(0.875000, 0.555556)	(1.750000, 1.666667)
8	(0.062500, 0.888889)	(0.125000, 2.666667)
9	(0.562500, 0.037037)	(1.125000, 0.111111)
10	(0.312500, 0.370370)	(0.625000, 1.111111)
11	(0.812500, 0.703704)	(1.625000, 2.111111)
12	(0.187500, 0.148148)	(0.375000, 0.444444)
$\vdots$		

Given the existence of such samplers, we could have defined the Sampler interface so that it specifies the pixel being rendered for each sample rather than the other way around (i.e., the Sampler being told which pixel to render).

However, there were good reasons to adopt the current design: this approach makes it easy to decompose the film into small image tiles for multi-threaded rendering, where each thread computes pixels in a local region that can be efficiently merged into the final image. Thus, we must require that such samplers generate samples out of order, so that all samples for each pixel are generated in succession.

The GlobalSampler helps bridge between the expectations of the Sampler interface and the natural operation of these types of samplers. It provides implementations of all of the pure virtual Sampler methods, implementing them in terms of three new pure virtual methods that its subclasses must implement instead.

⟨*Sampler Declarations*⟩ +≡
```
class GlobalSampler : public Sampler {
public:
    ⟨GlobalSampler Public Methods 429⟩
private:
    ⟨GlobalSampler Private Data 430⟩
};
```

⟨*GlobalSampler Public Methods*⟩ ≡   **429**
```
GlobalSampler(int64_t samplesPerPixel) : Sampler(samplesPerPixel) { }
```

There are two methods that implementations must provide. The first one, GetIndexFor
Sample(), performs the inverse mapping from the current pixel and given sample index
to a global index into the overall set of sample vectors. For example, for the Sampler that
generated the values in Table 7.2, if currentPixel was (0, 2), then GetIndexForSample(0)
would return 2, since the corresponding pixel sample coordinates for sample index 2,
(0.25, 0.666667) correspond to the first sample that lands in that pixel's area.

⟨*GlobalSampler Public Methods*⟩ +≡   429
```
virtual int64_t GetIndexForSample(int64_t sampleNum) const = 0;
```

Closely related, SampleDimension() returns the sample value for the given dimension of
the indexth sample vector in the sequence. Because the first two dimensions are used to
offset into the current pixel, they are handled specially: the value returned by implementations of this method should be the sample offset within the current pixel, rather than
the original $[0, 1)^2$ sample value. For the example in Table 7.2, SampleDimension(4,1)
would return 0.333333, since the second dimension of the sample with index 4 is that
offset into the pixel (0, 1).

⟨*GlobalSampler Public Methods*⟩ +≡   429
```
virtual Float SampleDimension(int64_t index, int dimension) const = 0;
```

When it's time to start to generate samples for a pixel, it's necessary to reset the dimension
of the sample and find the index of the first sample in the pixel. As with all samplers,
values for sample arrays are all generated next.

⟨*Sampler Method Definitions*⟩ +≡
```
void GlobalSampler::StartPixel(const Point2i &p) {
    Sampler::StartPixel(p);
    dimension = 0;
    intervalSampleIndex = GetIndexForSample(0);
    ⟨Compute arrayEndDim for dimensions used for array samples 431⟩
    ⟨Compute 1D array samples for GlobalSampler 431⟩
    ⟨Compute 2D array samples for GlobalSampler⟩
}
```

The dimension member variable tracks the next dimension that the sampler implementation will be asked to generate a sample value for; it's incremented as Get1D() and Get2D()
are called. intervalSampleIndex records the index of the sample that corresponds to the
current sample s_i in the current pixel.

⟨*GlobalSampler Private Data*⟩ ≡   429
```
int dimension;
int64_t intervalSampleIndex;
```

It's necessary to decide which dimensions of the sample vector to use for array samples.
Under the assumption that the earlier dimensions will be better quality than later dimensions, it's important to set aside the first few dimensions for the CameraSample, since the
quality of those sample values often has a large impact on final image quality.

Therefore, the first dimensions up to arrayStartDim are devoted to regular 1D and
2D samples, and then the subsequent dimensions are devoted to first 1D and then

2D array samples. Finally, higher dimensions starting at arrayEndDim are used for further non-array 1D and 2D samples. It isn't possible to compute arrayEndDim when the GlobalSampler constructor runs, since array samples haven't been requested yet by the integrators. Therefore, this value is computed (repeatedly and redundantly) in the StartPixel() method.

⟨*GlobalSampler Private Data*⟩ +≡   **429**
```
static const int arrayStartDim = 5;
int arrayEndDim;
```

The total number of array samples for all pixel samples is given by the product of the number of pixel samples and the requested sample array size.

⟨*Compute* arrayEndDim *for dimensions used for array samples*⟩ ≡   **430**
```
arrayEndDim = arrayStartDim +
                 sampleArray1D.size() + 2 * sampleArray2D.size();
```

Actually generating the array samples is just a matter of computing the number of needed values in the current sample dimension.

⟨*Compute 1D array samples for* GlobalSampler⟩ ≡   **430**
```
for (size_t i = 0; i < samples1DArraySizes.size(); ++i) {
    int nSamples = samples1DArraySizes[i] * samplesPerPixel;
    for (int j = 0; j < nSamples; ++j) {
        int64_t index = GetIndexForSample(j);
        sampleArray1D[i][j] =
            SampleDimension(index, arrayStartDim + i);
    }
}
```

The 2D sample arrays are generated analogously; the ⟨*Compute 2D array samples for* GlobalSampler⟩ fragment isn't included here.

When the pixel sample changes, it's necessary to reset the current sample dimension counter and to compute the sample index for the next sample inside the pixel.

⟨*Sampler Method Definitions*⟩ +≡
```
bool GlobalSampler::StartNextSample() {
    dimension = 0;
    intervalSampleIndex = GetIndexForSample(currentPixelSampleIndex + 1);
    return Sampler::StartNextSample();
}
```

⟨*Sampler Method Definitions*⟩ +≡
```
bool GlobalSampler::SetSampleNumber(int64_t sampleNum) {
    dimension = 0;
    intervalSampleIndex = GetIndexForSample(sampleNum);
    return Sampler::SetSampleNumber(sampleNum);
}
```

Given this machinery, getting regular 1D sample values is just a matter of skipping over the dimensions allocated to array samples and passing the current sample index and dimension to the implementation's SampleDimension() method.

⟨*Sampler Method Definitions*⟩ +≡
```
Float GlobalSampler::Get1D() {
    if (dimension >= arrayStartDim && dimension < arrayEndDim)
        dimension = arrayEndDim;
    return SampleDimension(intervalSampleIndex, dimension++);
}
```

2D samples follow analogously.

⟨*Sampler Method Definitions*⟩ +≡
```
Point2f GlobalSampler::Get2D() {
    if (dimension + 1 >= arrayStartDim && dimension < arrayEndDim)
        dimension = arrayEndDim;
    Point2f p(SampleDimension(intervalSampleIndex, dimension),
              SampleDimension(intervalSampleIndex, dimension + 1));
    dimension += 2;
    return p;
}
```

7.3 STRATIFIED SAMPLING

The first Sampler implementation that we will introduce subdivides pixel areas into rectangular regions and generates a single sample inside each region. These regions are commonly called *strata*, and this sampler is called the StratifiedSampler. The key idea behind stratification is that by subdividing the sampling domain into nonoverlapping regions and taking a single sample from each one, we are less likely to miss important features of the image entirely, since the samples are guaranteed not to all be close together. Put another way, it does us no good if many samples are taken from nearby points in the sample space, since each new sample doesn't add much new information about the behavior of the image function. From a signal processing viewpoint, we are implicitly defining an overall sampling rate such that the smaller the strata are, the more of them we have, and thus the higher the sampling rate.

The stratified sampler places each sample at a random point inside each stratum by *jittering* the center point of the stratum by a random amount up to half the stratum's width and height. The nonuniformity that results from this jittering helps turn aliasing into noise, as discussed in Section 7.1. The sampler also offers an unjittered mode, which gives uniform sampling in the strata; this mode is mostly useful for comparisons between different sampling techniques rather than for rendering high quality images.

Direct application of stratification to high-dimensional sampling quickly leads to an intractable number of samples. For example, if we divided the 5D image, lens, and time sample space into four strata in each dimension, the total number of samples per pixel would be $4^5 = 1024$. We could reduce this impact by taking fewer samples in some dimensions (or not stratifying some dimensions, effectively using a single stratum), but

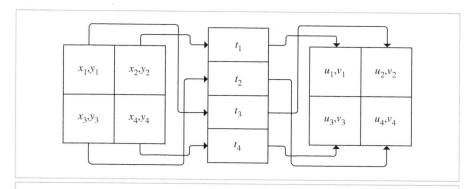

Figure 7.16: We can generate a good sample pattern that reaps the benefits of stratification without requiring that all of the sampling dimensions be stratified simultaneously. Here, we have split (x, y) image position, time t, and (u, v) lens position into independent strata with four regions each. Each is sampled independently, then a time sample and a lens sample are randomly associated with each image sample. We retain the benefits of stratification in each of the individual dimensions without having to exponentially increase the total number of samples.

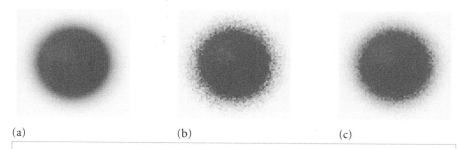

(a)   (b)   (c)

Figure 7.17: **Effect of Sampling Patterns in Rendering a Purple Sphere with Depth of Field.** (a) A high-quality reference image of a blurry sphere. (b) An image generated with random sampling in each pixel without stratification. (c) An image generated with the same number of samples, but with the `StratifiedSampler`, which stratified both the image and, more importantly for this image, the lens samples. Stratification makes a substantial improvement for this situation.

we would then lose the benefit of having well-stratified samples in those dimensions. This problem with stratification is known as the *curse of dimensionality*.

We can reap most of the benefits of stratification without paying the price in excessive total sampling by computing lower dimensional stratified patterns for subsets of the domain's dimensions and then randomly associating samples from each set of dimensions. (This process is sometimes called *padding*.) Figure 7.16 shows the basic idea: we might want to take just four samples per pixel but still have the samples be stratified over all dimensions. We independently generate four 2D stratified image samples, four 1D stratified time samples, and four 2D stratified lens samples. Then we randomly associate a time and lens sample value with each image sample. The result is that each pixel has samples that together have good coverage of the sample space. Figure 7.17 shows the improvement in image quality from using stratified lens samples versus using unstratified random samples when rendering depth of field.

StratifiedSampler 434

Figure 7.18 shows a comparison of a few sampling patterns. The first is a completely random pattern: we generated a number of samples without using the strata at all. The result is terrible; some regions have few samples and other areas have clumps of many samples. The second is a uniform stratified pattern. In the last, the uniform pattern has been jittered, with a random offset added to each sample's location, keeping it inside its cell. This gives a better overall distribution than the purely random pattern while preserving the benefits of stratification, though there are still some clumps of samples and some regions that are undersampled. Figure 7.19 shows images rendered using the StratifiedSampler and shows how jittered sample positions turn aliasing artifacts into less objectionable noise.

⟨*StratifiedSampler Declarations*⟩ ≡
```
    class StratifiedSampler : public PixelSampler {
    public:
        ⟨StratifiedSampler Public Methods 434⟩
    private:
        ⟨StratifiedSampler Private Data 434⟩
    };
```

⟨*StratifiedSampler Public Methods*⟩ ≡   434
```
    StratifiedSampler(int xPixelSamples, int yPixelSamples,
            bool jitterSamples, int nSampledDimensions)
        : PixelSampler(xPixelSamples * yPixelSamples, nSampledDimensions),
          xPixelSamples(xPixelSamples), yPixelSamples(yPixelSamples),
          jitterSamples(jitterSamples) { }
```

⟨*StratifiedSampler Private Data*⟩ ≡   434
```
    const int xPixelSamples, yPixelSamples;
    const bool jitterSamples;
```

As a PixelSampler subclass, the implementation of StartPixel() must both generate 1D and 2D samples for the number of dimensions nSampledDimensions passed to the PixelSampler constructor as well as samples for the requested arrays.

⟨*StratifiedSampler Method Definitions*⟩ ≡
```
    void StratifiedSampler::StartPixel(const Point2i &p) {
        ⟨Generate single stratified samples for the pixel 437⟩
        ⟨Generate arrays of stratified samples for the pixel 440⟩
        PixelSampler::StartPixel(p);
    }
```

After the initial stratified samples are generated, they are randomly shuffled; this is the padding approach described at the start of the section. If this shuffling wasn't done, then the sample dimensions' values would be correlated in a way that would lead to errors in images—for example, both the first 2D sample used to choose the film location as well as the first 2D lens sample would always both be in the lower left stratum adjacent to the origin.

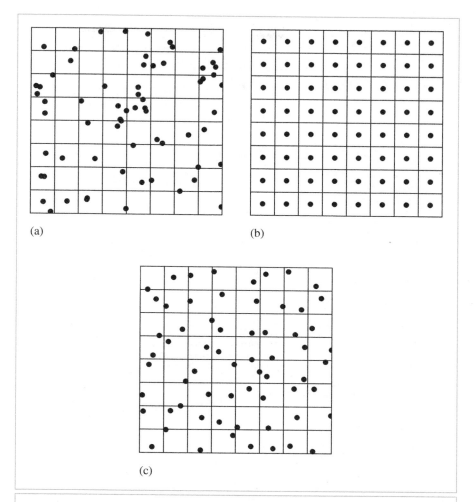

(a)

(b)

(c)

Figure 7.18: Three 2D Sampling Patterns. (a) The random pattern is an ineffective pattern, with many clumps of samples that leave large sections of the image poorly sampled. (b) A uniform stratified pattern is better distributed but can exacerbate aliasing artifacts. (c) A stratified jittered pattern turns aliasing from the uniform pattern into high-frequency noise while still maintaining the benefits of stratification.

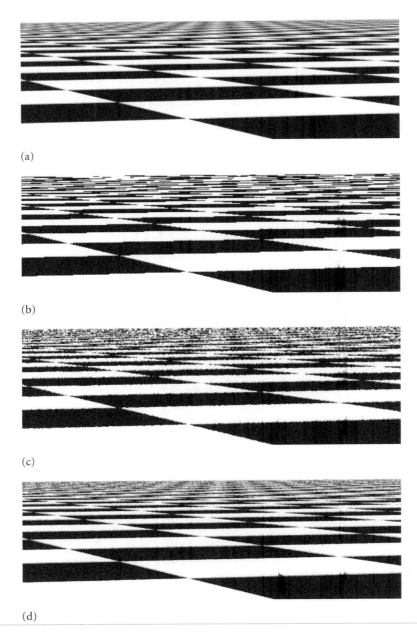

(a)

(b)

(c)

(d)

Figure 7.19: Comparison of Image Sampling Methods with a Checkerboard Texture. This is a difficult image to render well, since the checkerboard's frequency with respect to the pixel spacing tends toward infinity as we approach the horizon. (a) A reference image, rendered with 256 samples per pixel, showing something close to an ideal result. (b) An image rendered with one sample per pixel, with no jittering. Note the jaggy artifacts at the edges of checks in the foreground. Notice also the artifacts in the distance where the checker function goes through many cycles between samples; as expected from the signal processing theory presented earlier, that detail reappears incorrectly as lower frequency aliasing. (c) The result of jittering the image samples, still with just one sample per pixel. The regular aliasing of the second image has been replaced by less objectionable noise artifacts. (d) The result of four jittered samples per pixel is still inferior to the reference image but is substantially better than the previous result.

⟨*Generate single stratified samples for the pixel*⟩ ≡   **434**

```
for (size_t i = 0; i < samples1D.size(); ++i) {
    StratifiedSample1D(&samples1D[i][0], xPixelSamples * yPixelSamples,
                       rng, jitterSamples);
    Shuffle(&samples1D[i][0], xPixelSamples * yPixelSamples, 1, rng);
}
for (size_t i = 0; i < samples2D.size(); ++i) {
    StratifiedSample2D(&samples2D[i][0], xPixelSamples, yPixelSamples,
                       rng, jitterSamples);
    Shuffle(&samples2D[i][0], xPixelSamples * yPixelSamples, 1, rng);
}
```

The 1D and 2D stratified sampling routines are implemented as utility functions. Both loop over the given number of strata in the domain and place a sample point in each one.

⟨*Sampling Function Definitions*⟩ ≡

```
void StratifiedSample1D(Float *samp, int nSamples, RNG &rng,
        bool jitter) {
    Float invNSamples = (Float)1 / nSamples;
    for (int i = 0; i < nSamples; ++i) {
        Float delta = jitter ? rng.UniformFloat() : 0.5f;
        samp[i] = std::min((i + delta) * invNSamples, OneMinusEpsilon);
    }
}
```

StratifiedSample2D() similarly generates samples in the range $[0, 1)^2$.

⟨*Sampling Function Definitions*⟩ +≡

```
void StratifiedSample2D(Point2f *samp, int nx, int ny, RNG &rng,
        bool jitter) {
    Float dx = (Float)1 / nx, dy = (Float)1 / ny;
    for (int y = 0; y < ny; ++y)
        for (int x = 0; x < nx; ++x) {
            Float jx = jitter ? rng.UniformFloat() : 0.5f;
            Float jy = jitter ? rng.UniformFloat() : 0.5f;
            samp->x = std::min((x + jx) * dx, OneMinusEpsilon);
            samp->y = std::min((y + jy) * dy, OneMinusEpsilon);
            ++samp;
        }
}
```

The Shuffle() function randomly permutes an array of count sample values, each of which has nDimensions dimensions. (In other words, blocks of values of size nDimensions are permuted.)

⟨*Sampling Inline Functions*⟩ ≡
```
template <typename T>
void Shuffle(T *samp, int count, int nDimensions, RNG &rng) {
    for (int i = 0; i < count; ++i) {
        int other = i + rng.UniformUInt32(count - i);
        for (int j = 0; j < nDimensions; ++j)
            std::swap(samp[nDimensions * i + j],
                      samp[nDimensions * other + j]);
    }
}
```

Arrays of samples present us with a quandary: for example, if an integrator asks for an array of 64 2D sample values in the sample vector for each sample in a pixel, the sampler has two different goals to try to fulfill:

1. It's desirable that the samples in the array themselves be well distributed in 2D (e.g., by using an 8 × 8 stratified grid). Stratification here will improve the quality of the computed results for each individual sample vector.
2. It's desirable to ensure that each the samples in the array for one image sample isn't too similar to any of the sample values for samples nearby in the image. Rather, we'd like the points to be well distributed with respect to their neighbors, so that over the region around a single pixel, there is good coverage of the entire sample space.

Rather than trying to solve both of these problems simultaneously here, the Stratified Sampler only addresses the first one. The other samplers later in this chapter will revisit this issue with more sophisticated techniques and solve both of them simultaneously to various degrees.

A second complication comes from the fact that the caller may have asked for an arbitrary number of samples per image sample, so stratification may not be easily applied. (For example, how do we generate a stratified 2D pattern of seven samples?) We could just generate an $n \times 1$ or $1 \times n$ stratified pattern, but this only gives us the benefit of stratification in one dimension and no guarantee of a good pattern in the other dimension. A StratifiedSampler::RoundSize() method could round requests up to the next number that's the square of integers, but instead we will use an approach called *Latin hypercube sampling* (LHS), which can generate any number of samples in any number of dimensions with a reasonably good distribution.

LHS uniformly divides each dimension's axis into n regions and generates a jittered sample in each of the n regions along the diagonal, as shown on the left in Figure 7.20. These samples are then randomly shuffled in each dimension, creating a pattern with good distribution. An advantage of LHS is that it minimizes clumping of the samples when they are projected onto any of the axes of the sampling dimensions. This property is in contrast to stratified sampling, where $2n$ of the $n \times n$ samples in a 2D pattern may project to essentially the same point on each of the axes. Figure 7.21 shows this worst-case situation for a stratified sampling pattern.

In spite of addressing the clumping problem, LHS isn't necessarily an improvement to stratified sampling; it's easy to construct cases where the sample positions are essentially

RNG 1065
RNG::UniformUInt32() 1066
StratifiedSampler 434

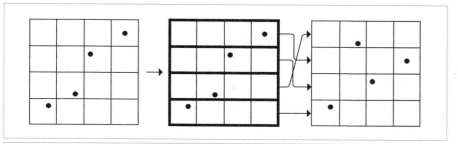

Figure 7.20: Latin hypercube sampling (sometimes called *n*-rooks sampling) chooses samples such that only a single sample is present in each row and each column of a grid. This can be done by generating random samples in the cells along the diagonal and then randomly permuting their coordinates. One advantage of LHS is that it can generate any number of samples with a good distribution, not just *m* × *n* samples, as with stratified patterns.

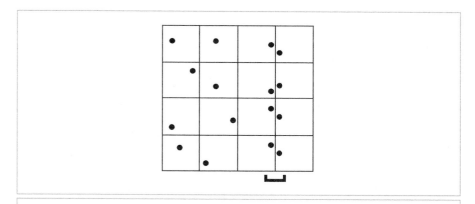

Figure 7.21: A Worst-Case Situation for Stratified Sampling. In an *n* × *n* 2D pattern, up to 2*n* of the points may project to essentially the same point on one of the axes. When "unlucky" patterns like this are generated, the quality of the results computed with them usually suffers.

colinear and large areas of the sampling domain have no samples near them (e.g., when the permutation of the original samples is the identity, leaving them all where they started). In particular, as *n* increases, Latin hypercube patterns are less and less effective compared to stratified patterns.[7]

The general-purpose `LatinHypercube()` function generates an arbitrary number of LHS samples in an arbitrary dimension. The number of elements in the `samples` array should thus be `nSamples*nDim`.

LatinHypercube() 440

---

7   We will revisit this issue in the following sections, where we will discuss sample patterns that are simultaneously stratified and distributed in a Latin hypercube pattern.

⟨*Sampling Function Definitions*⟩ +≡
```
void LatinHypercube(Float *samples, int nSamples, int nDim, RNG &rng) {
    ⟨Generate LHS samples along diagonal  440⟩
    ⟨Permute LHS samples in each dimension  440⟩
}
```

⟨*Generate LHS samples along diagonal*⟩ ≡   440
```
Float invNSamples = (Float)1 / nSamples;
for (int i = 0; i < nSamples; ++i)
    for (int j = 0; j < nDim; ++j) {
        Float sj = (i + (rng.UniformFloat())) * invNSamples;
        samples[nDim * i + j] = std::min(sj, OneMinusEpsilon);
    }
```

To do the permutation, this function loops over the samples, randomly permuting the
sample points in one dimension at a time. Note that this is a different permutation
than the earlier Shuffle() routine: that routine does one permutation, keeping all nDim
sample points in each sample together, while here nDim separate permutations of a single
dimension at a time are done (Figure 7.22).[8]

⟨*Permute LHS samples in each dimension*⟩ ≡   440
```
for (int i = 0; i < nDim; ++i) {
    for (int j = 0; j < nSamples; ++j) {
        int other = j + rng.UniformUInt32(nSamples - j);
        std::swap(samples[nDim * j + i], samples[nDim * other + i]);
    }
}
```

Given the LatinHypercube() function, we can now write the code to compute sample
arrays for the current pixel. 1D samples are stratified and then randomly shuffled, while
2D samples are generated using Latin hypercube sampling.

⟨*Generate arrays of stratified samples for the pixel*⟩ ≡   434
```
for (size_t i = 0; i < samples1DArraySizes.size(); ++i)
    for (int64_t j = 0; j < samplesPerPixel; ++j) {
        int count = samples1DArraySizes[i];
        StratifiedSample1D(&sampleArray1D[i][j * count], count, rng,
                           jitterSamples);
        Shuffle(&sampleArray1D[i][j * count], count, 1, rng);
    }
for (size_t i = 0; i < samples2DArraySizes.size(); ++i)
    for (int64_t j = 0; j < samplesPerPixel; ++j) {
        int count = samples2DArraySizes[i];
        LatinHypercube(&sampleArray2D[i][j * count].x, count, 2, rng);
    }
```

---

8   While it's not necessary to permute the first dimension of the LHS pattern, the implementation here does so anyway, since
    making the elements of the first dimension be randomly ordered means that LHS patterns can be used in conjunction with
    sampling patterns from other sources without danger of correlation between their sample points.

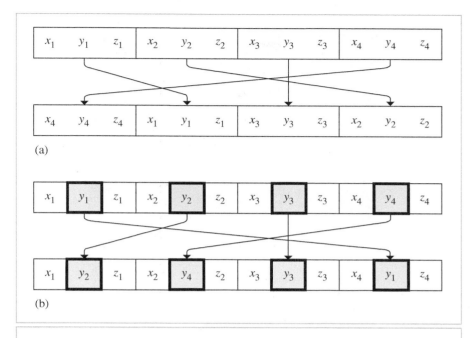

Figure 7.22: (a) The permutation done by the `Shuffle()` routine moves entire blocks of nDims elements around. (b) The permutation for Latin hypercube sampling permutes each dimension's samples independently. Here, the shuffling of the second dimension's samples from a four-element pattern of three dimensions is shown.

Starting with the scene in Figure 7.23, Figure 7.24 shows the improvement from good samples for the `DirectLightingIntegrator`. Image (a) was computed with 1 image sample per pixel, each with 16 shadow samples, and image (b) was computed with 16 image samples per pixel, each with 1 shadow sample. Because the `StratifiedSampler` could generate a good LHS pattern for the first case, the quality of the shadow is much better, even with the same total number of shadow samples taken.

*7.4 THE HALTON SAMPLER

The underlying goal of the `StratifiedSampler` is to generate a well-distributed but nonuniform set of sample points, with no two sample points too close together and no excessively large regions of the sample space that have no samples. As Figure 7.18 showed, a jittered pattern does this much better than a random pattern does, although its quality can suffer when samples in adjacent strata happen to be close to the shared boundary of their two strata.

This section introduces the `HaltonSampler`, which is based on algorithms that directly generate low-discrepancy point sets. Unlike the points generated by the `Stratified Sampler`, the `HaltonSampler` not only generates points that are guaranteed to not clump too closely together, but it also generates points that are simultaneously well distributed

Figure 7.23: Area Light Sampling Example Scene.

(a)

(b)

Figure 7.24: Sampling an Area Light with Samples from the Stratified Sampler. (a) shows the result of using 1 image sample per pixel and 16 shadow samples, and (b) shows the result of 16 image samples, each with just 1 shadow sample. The total number of shadow samples is the same in both cases, but because the version with 16 shadow samples per image sample is able to use an LHS pattern, all of the shadow samples in a pixel's area are well distributed, while in the second image the implementation here has no way to prevent them from being poorly distributed. The difference is striking.

over all of the dimensions of the sample vector—not just one or two dimensions at a time, as the StratifiedSampler did.

7.4.1 HAMMERSLEY AND HALTON SEQUENCES

The Halton and Hammersley sequences are two closely related low-discrepancy point sets. Both are based on a construction called the *radical inverse*, which is based on the fact that a positive integer value a can be expressed in a base b with a sequence of digits $d_m(a) \ldots d_2(a)d_1(a)$ uniquely determined by

$$a = \sum_{i=1}^{m} d_i(a)b^{i-1}, \tag{7.6}$$

where all digits $d_i(a)$ are between 0 and $b - 1$.

The radical inverse function Φ_b in base b converts a nonnegative integer a to a fractional value in $[0, 1)$ by reflecting these digits about the radix point:

$$\Phi_b(a) = 0.d_1(a)d_2(a) \ldots d_m(a). \tag{7.7}$$

Thus, the contribution of the digit $d_i(a)$ to the radical inverse is $d_i(a)/b^i$.

One of the simplest low-discrepancy sequences is the *van der Corput sequence*, which is a 1D sequence given by the radical inverse function in base 2:

$$x_a = \Phi_2(a).$$

Table 7.3 shows the first few values of the van der Corput sequence. Notice how it recursively splits the intervals of the 1D line in half, generating a sample point at the center of each interval. The discrepancy of this sequence is

$$D_N^*(P) = O\left(\frac{\log N}{N}\right),$$

which matches the best discrepancy that has been attained for infinite sequences in

Table 7.3: The radical inverse $\Phi_2(a)$ of the first few non-negative integers, computed in base 2. Notice how successive values of $\Phi_2(a)$ are not close to any of the previous values of $\Phi_2(a)$. As more and more values of the sequence are generated, samples are necessarily closer to previous samples, although with a minimum distance that is guaranteed to be reasonably good.

a	Base 2	$\Phi_2(a)$
0	0	0
1	1	$0.1 = 1/2$
2	10	$0.01 = 1/4$
3	11	$0.11 = 3/4$
4	100	$0.001 = 1/8$
5	101	$0.101 = 5/8$
⋮		

n dimensions,

$$D_N^*(P) = O\left(\frac{(\log N)^n}{N}\right).$$

To generate points in an n-dimensional Halton sequence, we use the radical inverse base b, with a different base for each dimension of the pattern. The bases used must all be relatively prime to each other, so a natural choice is to use the first n prime numbers $(p_1, \ldots, p_n)$:

$$x_a = (\Phi_2(a), \Phi_3(a), \Phi_5(a), \ldots, \Phi_{p_n}(a)).$$

One of the most useful characteristics of the Halton sequence is that it can be used even if the total number of samples needed isn't known in advance; all prefixes of the sequence are well distributed, so as additional samples are added to the sequence low discrepancy will be maintained. (However, its distribution is best when the total number of samples is the product of powers of the bases $\Pi(p_i)^{k_i}$ for exponents k_i.)

The discrepancy of an n-dimensional Halton sequence is

$$D_N^*(x_a) = O\left(\frac{(\log N)^n}{N}\right),$$

which is asymptotically optimal.

If the number of samples N is fixed, the Hammersley point set can be used, giving slightly lower discrepancy. Hammersley point sets are defined by

$$x_a = \left(\frac{a}{N}, \Phi_{b_1}(a), \Phi_{b_2}(a), \ldots, \Phi_{b_n}(a)\right),$$

where N is the total number of samples to be taken and as before all of the bases b_i are relatively prime. Figure 7.25(a) shows a plot of the first 216 points of the 2D Halton sequence. Figure 7.25(b) shows the first 256 points of the Hammersley sequence.

The function RadicalInverse() computes the radical inverse for a given number a using the baseIndexth prime number as the base. The function is implemented using an enormous switch statement, where baseIndex is mapped to the appropriate prime number and then a separate RadicalInverseSpecialized() template function actually computes the radical inverse. (The reason for the curious switch-based structure will be explained in a few pages.)

⟨*Low Discrepancy Function Definitions*⟩ ≡
```
Float RadicalInverse(int baseIndex, uint64_t a) {
    switch (baseIndex) {
        case 0:
            ⟨Compute base-2 radical inverse 446⟩
        case 1: return RadicalInverseSpecialized<3>(a);
        case 2: return RadicalInverseSpecialized<5>(a);
        case 3: return RadicalInverseSpecialized<7>(a);
        ⟨Remainder of cases for RadicalInverse()⟩
    }
}
```

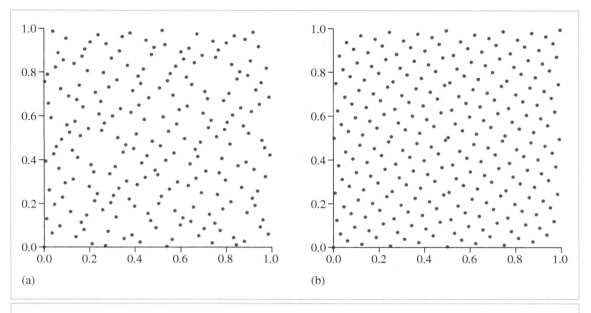

Figure 7.25: The First Points of Two Low-Discrepancy Sequences in 2D. (a) Halton (216 points), (b) Hammersley (256 points).

For the base-2 radical inverse, we can take advantage of the fact that numbers in digital computers are already represented in base 2 to compute the radical inverse more efficiently. For a 64-bit value a, we have from Equation (7.6)

$$a = \sum_{i=1}^{64} d_i(a) 2^{i-1}.$$

First consider the result of reversing the bits of a, still considering it as an integer value, which gives

$$\sum_{i=1}^{64} d_i(a) 2^{64-i}.$$

If we then divide this value by 2^{64}, we have

$$\sum_{i=1}^{64} d_i(a) 2^{-i},$$

which is $\Phi_2(a)$. Thus, the base-2 radical inverse can equivalently be computed with a bit reverse and a power-of-two division.

The bits of an integer quantity can be efficiently reversed with a series of logical bit operations. The first line of the ReverseBits32() function, which reverses the bits of a 32-bit integer, swaps the lower 16 bits with the upper 16 bits of the value. The next line simultaneously swaps the first 8 bits of the result with the second 8 bits and the third 8 bits with the fourth. This process continues until the last line, which swaps adjacent bits.

To understand this code, it's helpful to write out the binary values of the various hexadecimal constants. For example, 0xff00ff00 is 11111111000000001111111100000000 in binary; it's easy to see that a bitwise OR with this value masks off the first and third 8-bit quantities.

⟨*Low Discrepancy Inline Functions*⟩ ≡
```
inline uint32_t ReverseBits32(uint32_t n) {
    n = (n << 16) | (n >> 16);
    n = ((n & 0x00ff00ff) << 8) | ((n & 0xff00ff00) >> 8);
    n = ((n & 0x0f0f0f0f) << 4) | ((n & 0xf0f0f0f0) >> 4);
    n = ((n & 0x33333333) << 2) | ((n & 0xcccccccc) >> 2);
    n = ((n & 0x55555555) << 1) | ((n & 0xaaaaaaaa) >> 1);
    return n;
}
```

The bits of a 64-bit value can then be reversed by reversing the two 32-bit components individually and then interchanging them.

⟨*Low Discrepancy Inline Functions*⟩ +≡
```
inline uint64_t ReverseBits64(uint64_t n) {
    uint64_t n0 = ReverseBits32((uint32_t)n);
    uint64_t n1 = ReverseBits32((uint32_t)(n >> 32));
    return (n0 << 32) | n1;
}
```

To compute the base-2 radical inverse, then, we reverse the bits and multiply by $1/2^{64}$, where the hexadecimal floating-point constant 0x1p-64 is used for the value 2^{-64}. As explained in Section 3.9.1, implementing a power-of-two division via the corresponding power-of-two multiplication gives the same result with IEEE floating point. (And floating-point multiplication is generally more efficient than floating-point division.)

⟨*Compute base-2 radical inverse*⟩ ≡   **444**
```
return ReverseBits64(a) * 0x1p-64;
```

For other bases, the RadicalInverseSpecialized() template function computes the radical inverse by computing the digits d_i starting with d_1 and computing a series v_i where $v_1 = d_1$, $v_2 = bd_1 + d_2$ such that

$$v_n = b^{n-1}d_1 + b^{n-2}d_2 + \cdots + d_n.$$

(For example, in base 10, it would convert the value 1234 to 4321.) This value can be found entirely using integer arithmetic, without accumulating any round-off error.

The final value of the radical inverse is then found by converting to floating-point and multiplying by $1/b^n$, where n is the number of digits in the value, to get the value in Equation (7.7). The term for this multiplication is built up in invBaseN as the digits are processed.

⟨*Low Discrepancy Static Functions*⟩ ≡

```
template <int base>
static Float RadicalInverseSpecialized(uint64_t a) {
    const Float invBase = (Float)1 / (Float)base;
    uint64_t reversedDigits = 0;
    Float invBaseN = 1;
    while (a) {
        uint64_t next  = a / base;
        uint64_t digit = a - next * base;
        reversedDigits = reversedDigits * base + digit;
        invBaseN *= invBase;
        a = next;
    }
    return std::min(reversedDigits * invBaseN, OneMinusEpsilon);
}
```

A natural question to ask would be why a template function parameterized on the base is used here (rather than, say, a regular function call that took the base as a parameter, which would avoid the generation of a separate code path for each base). The motivation is that integer division is shockingly slow on modern CPUs, and much more efficient approaches are possible for division by a compile-time constant.

For example, integer division of a 32-bit value by 3 can be computed exactly by multiplying this value by 2863311531 to get a 64-bit intermediate and then shifting the result right by 33 bits; these are both fairly efficient operations. (A similar approach can be used for dividing 64-bit values by 3, but the magic constant is much larger; see Warren (2006) for more about these techniques.) Thus, using a template function here allows the compiler to see that the division to compute the value of next in the while loop is actually a division by a constant and gives it a chance to apply this optimization. The code with this optimization runs 5.9 times faster on a 2015-era laptop than an implementation based on integer division instructions.

Another optimization is that we avoid computing a running sum over reversed digits multiplied by the reciprocal base; instead, this multiplication is postponed all the way until the end when the loop terminates. The main issue here is that floating-point and integer units on current processors operate fairly independently from each other. Referencing an integer variable within a floating computation in a tight loop would introduce pipeline bubbles related to the amount of time that is needed to convert and move the values from one unit to the other.

It will be useful to be able to compute the inverse of the radical inverse function; the InverseRadicalInverse() function takes the reversed integer digits in some base, corresponding to value in the RadicalInverseSpecialized() template function immediately before being multiplied by the $1/b^n$ factor to convert to a floating-point value in $[0, 1)$. Note that in order to be able to compute the inverse correctly, the total number of digits in the original value must be known: for example, both 1234 and 123400 are converted to 4321 after the integer-only part of the radical inverse algorithm; trailing zeros become leading zeros, which are lost.

Float 1062
OneMinusEpsilon 417
RadicalInverseSpecialized()
   447

⟨*Low Discrepancy Inline Functions*⟩ +≡
```
template <int base> inline uint64_t
InverseRadicalInverse(uint64_t inverse, int nDigits) {
    uint64_t index = 0;
    for (int i = 0; i < nDigits; ++i) {
        uint64_t digit = inverse % base;
        inverse /= base;
        index = index * base + digit;
    }
    return index;
}
```

The Hammersley and Halton sequences have the shortcoming that as the base b increases, sample values can exhibit surprisingly regular patterns. This issue can be addressed with *scrambled* Halton and Hammersley sequences, where a permutation is applied to the digits when computing the radical inverse:

$$\Psi_b(a) = 0.p(d_1(a))p(d_2(a)) \ldots p(d_m(a)),\qquad\qquad [7.8]$$

where p is a permutation of the digits $(0, 1, \ldots, b - 1)$. Note that the same permutation is used for each digit, and the same permutation is used for generating all of the sample points in a given base b. Figure 7.26 shows the effect of scrambling with the Halton sequence. In the following, we will use random permutations, though specific construc-

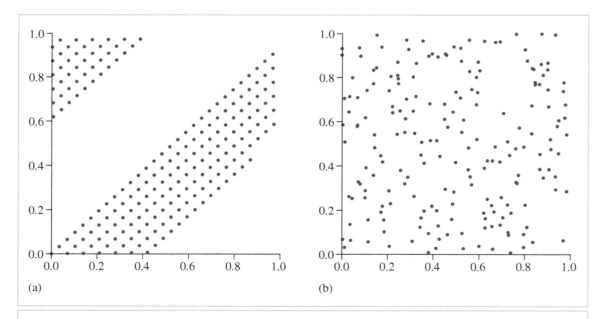

(a)   (b)

Figure 7.26: Plot of Halton Sample Values with and without Scrambling. (a) In higher dimensions of the sample vector, projections of sample values start to exhibit regular structure. Here, points from the dimensions $(\Phi_{29}(a), \Phi_{31}(a))$ are shown. (b) Scrambled sequences, Equation (7.8), break up this structure by randomly permuting the digits of sample indices.

tions of permutations can give slightly better results; see the "Further Reading" section for more details.

The ComputeRadicalInversePermutations() function computes these random permutation tables. It initializes a single contiguous array for all of the permutations, where the first two values are a permutation of the integers zero and one for $b = 2$, the next three values are a permutation of 0, 1, 2 for $b = 3$, and so forth for successive prime bases. At entry to the for loop below, p points to the start of the permutation array to initialize for the current prime base.

⟨*Low Discrepancy Function Definitions*⟩ +≡
```
std::vector<uint16_t> ComputeRadicalInversePermutations(RNG &rng) {
    std::vector<uint16_t> perms;
    ⟨Allocate space in perms for radical inverse permutations 449⟩
    uint16_t *p = &perms[0];
    for (int i = 0; i < PrimeTableSize; ++i) {
        ⟨Generate random permutation for ith prime base 449⟩
        p += Primes[i];
    }
    return perms;
}
```

The total size of the permutation array is given by the sum of the prime numbers up to the end of a precomputed table of prime numbers.

⟨*Allocate space in* perms *for radical inverse permutations*⟩ ≡   **449**
```
int permArraySize = 0;
for (int i = 0; i < PrimeTableSize; ++i)
    permArraySize += Primes[i];
perms.resize(permArraySize);
```

⟨*Low Discrepancy Declarations*⟩ ≡
```
static constexpr int PrimeTableSize = 1000;
extern const int Primes[PrimeTableSize];
```

⟨*Low Discrepancy Data Definitions*⟩ ≡
```
const int Primes[PrimeTableSize] = {
    2, 3, 5, 7, 11,
    ⟨Subsequent prime numbers⟩
};
```

Generating each permutation is easy: we just initialize p to the identity permutation for the current prime length and then randomly shuffle its values.

Primes 449
PrimeTableSize 449
RNG 1065
Shuffle() 438

⟨*Generate random permutation for* i*th prime base*⟩ ≡   **449**
```
for (int j = 0; j < Primes[i]; ++j)
    p[j] = j;
Shuffle(p, Primes[i], 1, rng);
```

The ScrambledRadicalInverse() function is essentially the same as RadicalInverse() except that it puts each digit through the permutation table for the given base. See

Exercise 7.1 for discussion of a more efficient implementation for the base-2 case, following RadicalInverse().

⟨*Low Discrepancy Function Definitions*⟩ +≡
```
Float ScrambledRadicalInverse(int baseIndex, uint64_t a,
        const uint16_t *perm) {
    switch (baseIndex) {
        case 0: return ScrambledRadicalInverseSpecialized<2>(perm, a);
        case 1: return ScrambledRadicalInverseSpecialized<3>(perm, a);
        case 2: return ScrambledRadicalInverseSpecialized<5>(perm, a);
        case 3: return ScrambledRadicalInverseSpecialized<7>(perm, a);
        ⟨Remainder of cases for ScrambledRadicalInverse()⟩
    }
}
```

The implementation below also accounts for a special case that can arise when perm maps the digit 0 to a nonzero value. In this case, the iteration stops prematurely once a reaches 0, incorrectly missing an infinitely long suffix of digits with value perm[0]. Fortunately, this is a geometric series with a simple analytic solution whose value is added in the last line.

⟨*Low Discrepancy Static Functions*⟩ +≡
```
template <int base>
static Float ScrambledRadicalInverseSpecialized(const uint16_t *perm,
        uint64_t a) {
    const Float invBase = (Float)1 / (Float)base;
    uint64_t reversedDigits = 0;
    Float invBaseN = 1;
    while (a) {
        uint64_t next  = a / base;
        uint64_t digit = a - next * base;
        reversedDigits = reversedDigits * base + perm[digit];
        invBaseN *= invBase;
        a = next;
    }
    return std::min(invBaseN * (reversedDigits +
                    invBase * perm[0] / (1 - invBase)), OneMinusEpsilon);
}
```

7.4.2 HALTON SAMPLER IMPLEMENTATION

The HaltonSampler generates sample vectors using the Halton sequence. Unlike the StratifiedSampler, it is fully deterministic; it uses no pseudo-random numbers in its operation. However, Halton samples can be lead to aliasing if the image isn't sufficiently well sampled. Figure 7.27 compares the results of sampling a checkerboard texture using a Halton-based sampler to using the stratified sampler from the previous section. Note the unpleasant pattern along edges in the foreground and toward the horizon.

⟨*HaltonSampler Declarations*⟩ ≡
```
class HaltonSampler : public GlobalSampler {
public:
    ⟨HaltonSampler Public Methods⟩
```

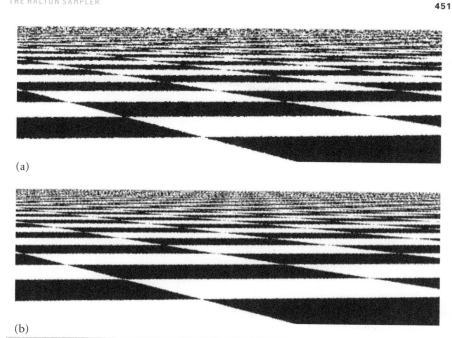

(a)

(b)

Figure 7.27: Comparison of the Stratified Sampler to a Low-Discrepancy Sampler Based on Halton Points on the Image Plane. (a) The jittered stratified sampler with a single sample per pixel and (b) the `HaltonSampler` sampler with a single sample per pixel. Note that although the Halton pattern is able to reproduce the checker pattern farther toward the horizon than the stratified pattern, there is a regular structure to the error in the low-discrepancy pattern that is visually distracting; it doesn't turn aliasing into less objectionable noise as well as the jittered approach.

```
private:
    〈HaltonSampler Private Data 452〉
    〈HaltonSampler Private Methods 452〉
};

〈HaltonSampler Method Definitions〉 ≡
    HaltonSampler::HaltonSampler(int samplesPerPixel,
            const Bounds2i &sampleBounds)
        : GlobalSampler(samplesPerPixel) {
        〈Generate random digit permutations for Halton sampler 452〉
        〈Find radical inverse base scales and exponents that cover sampling area 452〉
        〈Compute stride in samples for visiting each pixel area 453〉
        〈Compute multiplicative inverses for baseScales〉
    }
```

The permutation tables for the scrambled radical inverses are shared across all `Halton Sampler` instances and are computed the first time the constructor runs. For pbrt's requirements, this approach is fine: the current implementation only uses different sampler instances for different tiles of the image, where we'd like to always use the same permutations anyway. For other uses, it could be worthwhile to have more control over when different permutations are used.

⟨*Generate random digit permutations for Halton sampler*⟩ ≡   451
```
if (radicalInversePermutations.size() == 0) {
    RNG rng;
    radicalInversePermutations = ComputeRadicalInversePermutations(rng);
}
```

⟨*HaltonSampler Private Data*⟩ ≡   450
```
static std::vector<uint16_t> radicalInversePermutations;
```

The utility method `PermutationForDimension()` returns a pointer to the start of the permutation array for the given dimension.

⟨*HaltonSampler Private Methods*⟩ ≡   450
```
const uint16_t *PermutationForDimension(int dim) const {
    if (dim >= PrimeTableSize)
        Severe("HaltonSampler can only sample %d dimensions.",
               PrimeTableSize);
    return &radicalInversePermutations[PrimeSums[dim]];
}
```

To be able to quickly find the offset for a given dimension, it's helpful to have the sums of the prime numbers preceding each prime.

⟨*Low Discrepancy Data Definitions*⟩ +≡
```
const int PrimeSums[PrimeTableSize] = {
    0, 2, 5, 10, 17,
    ⟨Subsequent prime sums⟩
};
```

To map the first two dimensions of samples from $[0, 1)^2$ to pixel coordinates, the `HaltonSampler` finds the smallest scale factor $(2^j, 3^k)$ that is larger than the lower of either the image resolution or `kMaxResolution` in each dimension. (We will see shortly how this specific choice of scales makes it easy to see which pixel a sample lands in.) After scaling, any samples outside the image extent will be simply ignored.

For images with resolution greater than `kMaxResolution` in one or both dimensions, a tile of Halton points is repeated across the image. This resolution limit helps maintain sufficient floating-point precision in the computed sample values.

⟨*Find radical inverse base scales and exponents that cover sampling area*⟩ ≡   451
```
Vector2i res = sampleBounds.pMax - sampleBounds.pMin;
for (int i = 0; i < 2; ++i) {
    int base = (i == 0) ? 2 : 3;
    int scale = 1, exp = 0;
    while (scale < std::min(res[i], kMaxResolution)) {
        scale *= base;
        ++exp;
    }
    baseScales[i] = scale;
    baseExponents[i] = exp;
}
```

For each dimension, baseScales holds the scale factor, 2^j or 3^k, and baseExponents holds the exponents j and k.

⟨*HaltonSampler Private Data*⟩ +≡   450
```
Point2i baseScales, baseExponents;
```

⟨*HaltonSampler Local Constants*⟩ ≡
```
static constexpr int kMaxResolution = 128;
```

To see why the HaltonSampler uses this scheme to map samples to pixel coordinates, consider the effect of scaling a value computed with the radical inverse base b by a factor b^n. If the digits of a expressed in base b are $d_i(a)$, then recall that the radical inverse is the value $0.d_1(a)d_2(a) \ldots$, base b. If we multiply this value by b^2, for example, we have $d_1(a)d_2(a).d_3(a) \ldots$; the first two digits have moved to the left of the radix point, and the fractional component of the value starts with $d_3(a)$.

This operation—scaling by b^n—forms the core of being able to determine which sample indices land in which pixels. Considering the first two digits in the above example, we can see that the integer component of the scaled value ranges from 0 to $b^2 - 1$ and that as a increases, its last two digits in base b take on any particular value once in every b^2 values in this range.

Given a value x, $0 \le x \le b^2 - 1$, we can find the first value a that gives the value x in the integer components. By definition, the digits of x in base b are $d_2(x)d_1(x)$. Thus, if $d_1(a) = d_2(x)$ and $d_2(a) = d_1(x)$, then the scaled value of a's radical inverse will have an integer component equal to x.

Because the bases $b = 2$ and $b = 3$ used in the HaltonSampler for pixel samples are relatively prime, it follows that if the sample values are scaled by some $(2^j, 3^k)$, then any particular pixel in the range $(0, 0) \rightarrow (2^j - 1, 3^k - 1)$ will be visited once every $2^j 3^k$ samples. This product is stored in sampleStride.

⟨*Compute stride in samples for visiting each pixel area*⟩ ≡   451
```
sampleStride = baseScales[0] * baseScales[1];
```

⟨*HaltonSampler Private Data*⟩ +≡   450
```
int sampleStride;
```

The sample index for the first Halton sample that lands in currentPixel is stored in offsetForCurrentPixel. After this offset has first been computed for the first sample in the current pixel, subsequent samples in the pixel are found at increments of sampleStride samples in the Halton sequence.

⟨*HaltonSampler Method Definitions*⟩ +≡
```
int64_t HaltonSampler::GetIndexForSample(int64_t sampleNum) const {
    if (currentPixel != pixelForOffset) {
        ⟨Compute Halton sample offset for currentPixel⟩
        pixelForOffset = currentPixel;
    }
    return offsetForCurrentPixel + sampleNum * sampleStride;
}
```

⟨*HaltonSampler Private Data*⟩ +≡   **450**
```
mutable Point2i pixelForOffset = Point2i(std::numeric_limits<int>::max(),
                                 std::numeric_limits<int>::max());
mutable int64_t offsetForCurrentPixel;
```

Computing the index of the first sample in a given pixel (x, y) where the samples have been scaled by $(2^j, 3^k)$ involves computing the inverse radical inverse of the last j digits of x in base 2, which we'll denote by x_r, and of the last k digits of y in base 3, y_r. This gives us a system of equations

$$x_r \equiv (i \bmod 2^j)$$

$$y_r \equiv (i \bmod 3^k),$$

where the index i that satisfies these equations is the index of a sample that lies within the given pixel, after scaling. We don't include the code that solves for i ⟨*Compute Halton sample offset for* currentPixel⟩ here in the book; see Grünschloß et al. (2012) for details of the algorithm used to find i.

The computation of sample offsets doesn't account for random digit permutations, so those aren't included in the sample values computed here. Also, because the low baseExponents[i] digits of the first two dimensions are used to select which pixel is sampled, these digits must be discarded before computing the radical inverse for the first two dimensions of the sample vector, since the SampleDimension() method is supposed to return the fractional offset within the pixel being sampled. Higher dimensions are just sampled directly, including the random permutations.

⟨*HaltonSampler Method Definitions*⟩ +≡
```
Float HaltonSampler::SampleDimension(int64_t index, int dim) const {
    if (dim == 0)
        return RadicalInverse(dim, index >> baseExponents[0]);
    else if (dim == 1)
        return RadicalInverse(dim, index / baseScales[1]);
    else
        return ScrambledRadicalInverse(dim, index,
            PermutationForDimension(dim));
}
```

*★*7.5 (0, 2)-SEQUENCE SAMPLER

Another approach for generating high-quality samples takes advantage of a remarkable property of certain low-discrepancy sequences that allows us to satisfy two desirable properties of samples (only one of which was satisfied with the StratifiedSampler): they generate sample vectors for a pixel's worth of image samples such that the sample values for each pixel sample are well distributed with respect to each other, and simultaneously such that the aggregate collection of sample values for all of the pixel samples in the pixel are collectively well distributed.

This sequence uses the first two dimensions of a low-discrepancy sequence derived by Sobol'.[9] This sequence is a special type of low-discrepancy sequence known as a (0, 2)-sequence. (0, 2)-sequences are stratified in a very general way. For example, the first 16 samples in a (0, 2)-sequence satisfy the stratification constraint from stratified sampling in Section 7.3, meaning there is just one sample in each of the boxes of extent $(\frac{1}{4}, \frac{1}{4})$. However, they also satisfy the Latin hypercube constraint, as only one of them is in each of the boxes of extent $(\frac{1}{16}, 1)$ and $(1, \frac{1}{16})$. Furthermore, there is only one sample in each of the boxes of extent $(\frac{1}{2}, \frac{1}{8})$ and $(\frac{1}{8}, \frac{1}{2})$. Figure 7.28 shows all of the possibilities for dividing the domain into regions where the first 16 samples of a (0, 2)-sequence satisfy the stratification properties. Each succeeding sequence of 16 samples from this pattern also satisfies these distribution properties.

In general, any sequence of length $2^{l_1+l_2}$ (where l_i is a nonnegative integer) from a (0, 2)-sequence satisfies this general stratification constraint. The set of *elementary intervals* in two dimensions, base 2, is defined as

$$E = \left\{ \left[\frac{a_1}{2^{l_1}}, \frac{a_1 + 1}{2^{l_1}} \right) \times \left[\frac{a_2}{2^{l_2}}, \frac{a_2 + 1}{2^{l_2}} \right) \right\},$$

where the integer $a_i = 0, 1, 2, 4, \ldots, 2^{l_i} - 1$. One sample from each of the first $2^{l_1+l_2}$ values in the sequence will be in each of the elementary intervals. Furthermore, the same property is true for each subsequent set of $2^{l_1+l_2}$ values.

To understand now how (0, 2)-sequences can be applied to generating 2D samples, consider a pixel with 2×2 image samples, each with an array of 4×4 2D samples. The first $(2 \times 2) \times (4 \times 4) = 2^6$ values of a (0, 2)-sequence are well distributed with respect to each other according to the corresponding set of elementary intervals. Furthermore, the first $4 \times 4 = 2^4$ samples are themselves well distributed according to their corresponding elementary intervals, as are the next 2^4 of them, and the subsequent ones, and so on. Therefore, we can use the first 16 (0, 2)-sequence samples for the samples for the 4×4 array for the first image sample for a pixel, then the next 16 for the next image sample, and so forth. The result is an extremely well-distributed set of sample points.

7.5.1 SAMPLING WITH GENERATOR MATRICES

The Sobol' sequence is based on a different mechanism for generating sample points than the HaltonSampler, which used the radical inverse in various dimensions. Even with the integer divides in the radical inverse function converted to multiplies and shifts, the amount of computation needed to compute the billions of samples that can be needed for high-quality, high-resolution renderings can still be significant. Most of the computational expense comes from the cost of performing non-base-2 computation on computers that natively operate in base 2. (Consider the contrast between the ⟨*Compute base-2 radical inverse*⟩ fragment and the RadicalInverseSpecialized() template function.)

Given the high cost of non-base-2 operations, it's natural to try to develop sample generation algorithms that operate entirely in base 2. One such approach that has been effective

---

9   The SobolSampler in Section 7.7 uses all of the dimensions of the Sobol' sequence.

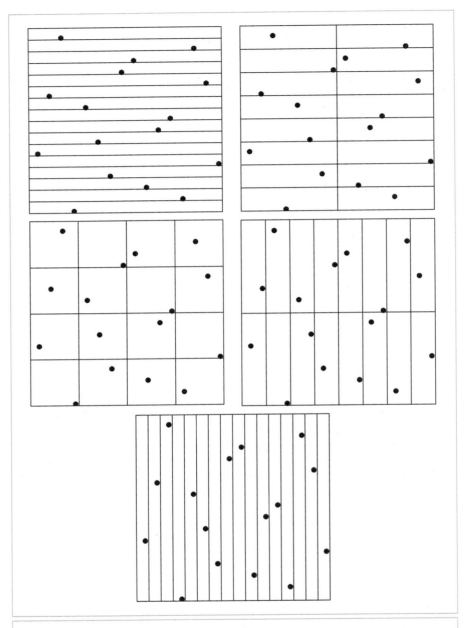

Figure 7.28: A sampling pattern that has a single sample in all of the base 2 elementary intervals. It satisfies both the 4 × 4 stratification and Latin hypercube constraints as well as the other two stratification constraints shown.

has been to use *generator matrices* that allow all computation to be done in the same base. Instead of using a different base in each dimension, as the Halton sampler did, a different generator matrix is used in each dimension. With well-chosen matrices for each sampled dimension, it's possible to generate very good low-discrepancy distributions of points. For example, (0, 2)-sequences can be defined using two specific generator matrices in base 2.

To see how generator matrices are used, consider an n-digit number a in base b, where the ith digit of a is $d_i(a)$ and where we have an $n \times n$ generator matrix $\mathbf{C}$. Then the corresponding sample point $x_a \in [0, 1)$ is defined by

$$x_a = [b^{-1} \, b^{-2} \, \cdots \, b^n] \begin{bmatrix} c_{1,1} & c_{1,2} & \cdots & c_{1,n} \\ c_{2,1} & \ddots & & c_{2,n} \\ \vdots & & \ddots & \vdots \\ c_{n,1} & \cdots & \cdots & c_{n,n} \end{bmatrix} \begin{bmatrix} d_1(a) \\ d_2(a) \\ \vdots \\ d_n(a) \end{bmatrix}, \qquad [7.9]$$

where all arithmetic is performed in the ring $\mathbb{Z}_b$ (in other words, when all operations are performed modulo b). This construction gives a total of b^n points as a ranges from 0 to $b^n - 1$. If the generator matrix is the identity matrix, then this definition corresponds to the regular radical inverse, base b. (It's worth pausing to make sure you see this connection between Equations (7.7) and (7.9) before continuing.)

In this section, we will exclusively use $b = 2$ and $n = 32$. While introducing a 32×32 matrix to the sample generation algorithm may not seem like a step toward better performance, we'll see that in the end the sampling code can be mapped to an implementation that uses a small number of bit operations to perform this computation in an extremely efficient manner.

The first step toward high performance comes from the fact that we're working in base 2; as such, all entries of $\mathbf{C}$ are either 0 or 1 and thus we can represent either each row or each column of the matrix with a single unsigned 32-bit integer. We'll choose to represent columns of the matrix as uint32t_ts; this choice leads to a very efficient algorithm for multiplying the d_i column vector by $\mathbf{C}$.

Now consider the task of computing the $\mathbf{C}[d_i(a)]^T$ matrix-vector product; using the definition of matrix-vector multiplication, we have:

$$\begin{bmatrix} c_{1,1} & c_{1,2} & \cdots & c_{1,n} \\ c_{2,1} & \ddots & & c_{2,n} \\ \vdots & & \ddots & \vdots \\ c_{n,1} & \cdots & \cdots & c_{n,n} \end{bmatrix} \begin{bmatrix} d_1(a) \\ d_2(a) \\ \vdots \\ d_n(a) \end{bmatrix} = d_1 \begin{bmatrix} c_{1,1} \\ c_{2,1} \\ \vdots \\ c_{n,1} \end{bmatrix} + \cdots + d_n \begin{bmatrix} c_{1,n} \\ c_{2,n} \\ \vdots \\ c_{n,n} \end{bmatrix}. \qquad [7.10]$$

In other words, for each digit of d_i that has a value of 1, the corresponding column of $\mathbf{C}$ should be summed. This addition can in turn be performed very efficiently in $\mathbb{Z}_2$: in that setting, addition corresponds to the exclusive OR operation. (Consider the combinations of the two possible operand values—0 and 1—and the result of adding them mod 2, and compare to the values computed by exclusive OR with the same operand values.) Thus, the multiplication $\mathbf{C}[d_i(a)]^T$ is just a matter of exclusive ORing together the columns i of $\mathbf{C}$ where $d_i(a)$'s bit is 1. This computation is implemented in the MultiplyGenerator() function.

⟨*Low Discrepancy Inline Functions*⟩ +≡
```
inline uint32_t MultiplyGenerator(const uint32_t *C, uint32_t a) {
    uint32_t v = 0;
    for (int i = 0; a != 0; ++i, a >>= 1)
        if (a & 1)
            v ^= C[i];
    return v;
}
```

Going back to Equation (7.9) now, if we denote the column vector from the product $v = C[d_i(a)]^T$, then consider now the vector product

$$x_a = \begin{bmatrix} 2^{-1} & 2^{-2} & \cdots & 2^{-n} \end{bmatrix} \begin{bmatrix} v_1 \\ v_2 \\ \vdots \\ v_n \end{bmatrix} = \sum_{i=1}^{32} 2^{-i} v_i. \qquad [7.11]$$

Because the entries of v are stored in a single uint32_t, their value interpreted as a uint32_t is

$$v = v_1 + 2v_2 + \cdots = \sum_{i=1}^{32} 2^{i-1} v_i.$$

If we were to reverse the order of the bits in the uint32_t, then we would have the value

$$v' = \sum_{i=1}^{32} 2^{32-i} v_i.$$

This is a more useful value: if we divide this value by 2^{32}, we get Equation (7.11), which is x_a, the value we're trying to compute.

Thus, if we take the result of the MultiplyGenerator() function, reverse the order of the bits in the returned value (e.g., by using ReverseBits32()), and then divide that integer value by 2^{32} to compute a floating-point value in $[0, 1)$, we've computed our sample value.

To save the small cost of reversing the bits, we can equivalently reverse the bits in all of the columns of the generator matrix C before passing it to MultiplyGenerator(). We will use that convention in the following.

To make (0, 2)-sequences useful in practice, we also need to be able to generate multiple different sets of 2D sample values for each image sample, and we would like to generate different sample values for each pixel. One approach to this problem would be to use carefully chosen nonoverlapping subsequences of the (0, 2)-sequence for each pixel.[10] Another approach is to randomly scramble the (0, 2)-sequence, giving a new (0, 2)-

---

10   This approach is taken by the Sobol′ sampler in Section 7.7.

sequence built by applying a random permutation to the base-b digits of the values in the original sequence.

The scrambling approach we will use is due to Kollig and Keller (2002). It repeatedly partitions and shuffles the unit square $[0, 1)^2$. In each of the two dimensions, it first divides the square in half and then swaps the two halves with 50% probability. Then it splits each of the intervals $[0, 0.5)$ and $[0.5, 1)$ in half and randomly exchanges each of those two halves. This process continues recursively all of the bits of the base-2 representation have been processed. This process was carefully designed so that it preserves the low-discrepancy properties of the set of points; otherwise, the advantages of the $(0, 2)$-sequence would be lost from the scrambling. Figure 7.29 shows an unscrambled $(0, 2)$-sequence and two randomly scrambled variations of it.

Two things make the scrambling process efficient: first, because we are scrambling two sequences that are computed in base 2, the digits d_i of the sequences are all 0 or 1, and scrambling a particular digit is equivalent to exclusive-ORing it with 0 or 1. Second, the simplification is made such that at each level l of the recursive scrambling, the same decision will be made as to whether to swap each of the 2^{l-1} pairs of subintervals or not. The result of these two design choices is that the scrambling can be encoded as a set of bits stored in a uint32_t and can be applied to the original digits via exclusive-OR operations.

The SampleGeneratorMatrix() function pulls these pieces together to generate sample values.

⟨*Low Discrepancy Inline Functions*⟩ +≡
```
inline Float SampleGeneratorMatrix(const uint32_t *C, uint32_t a,
        uint32_t scramble = 0) {
    return (MultiplyGenerator(C, a) ^ scramble) * 0x1p-32f;
}
```

The SampleGeneratorMatrix() function is already fairly efficient, performing a handful of arithmetic operations each time through the loop in MultiplyGenerator() that runs for a number of iterations equal to the base-2 logarithm of the value a. Remarkably, it's possible to do even better by changing the order in which samples are generated, enumerating them in *Gray code* order.

With Gray codes, successive binary values differ in only a single bit; the third column of Table 7.4 shows the first eight integers in Gray code order. Note that not only does only a single bit change between any pair of values but also that in any power-of-two-sized number of values n starting from 0, the Gray code enumerates all of the values from 0 to $n - 1$, just in a different order than usual.

Computing the nth Gray code value can be done very efficiently.

⟨*Low Discrepancy Inline Functions*⟩ +≡
```
inline uint32_t GrayCode(uint32_t n) {
    return (n >> 1) ^ n;
}
```

Float 1062
MultiplyGenerator() 458

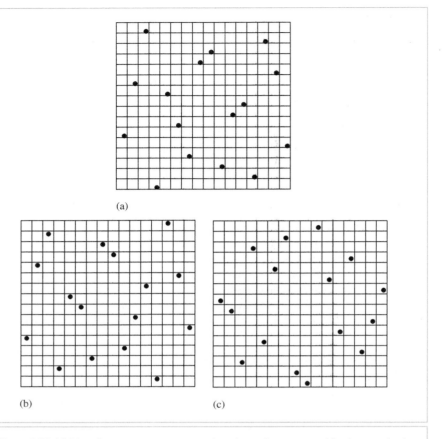

(a)

(b)   (c)

Figure 7.29: (a) A low-discrepancy (0, 2)-sequence-based sampling pattern and (b, c) two randomly scrambled instances of it. Random scrambling of low-discrepancy patterns is an effective way to eliminate the artifacts that would be present in images if we used the same sampling pattern in every pixel, while still preserving the low-discrepancy properties of the point set being used.

Table 7.4: The First Eight Integers, in Gray Code Order. Each Gray code value $g(n)$ differs by just a single bit from the previous one, $g(n-1)$. The index of the bit that changes is given by the number of trailing zeros in the binary value n. Note that with within any power-of-two-sized set of n values starting from 0, all of the integers between 0 and $n-1$ are represented, just in a different order than usual.

n (base 10)	n (binary)	$g(n)$	Changed Bit Index
0	000	000	n/a
1	001	001	0
2	010	011	1
3	011	010	0
4	100	110	2
5	101	111	0
6	110	101	1
7	111	100	0

By enumerating samples in Gray code order, we can take great advantage of the fact that only a single bit of $g(n)$ changes between subsequent samples. Assume that we have computed the product $\mathbf{C}[d_i(a)]^T = v$ for some index a: if another value a' differs by just one bit from a, then we only need to add or subtract one column of $\mathbf{C}$ from v to find $v' = \mathbf{C}[d_I(a')]^T$ (recall Equation (7.10)). Even better, *both* addition and subtraction mod 2 can be performed with exclusive OR, so it doesn't matter which operation is needed; we only need to know which bit changed. As can be seen from Table 7.4, the index of the bit that changes going from $g(i)$ to $g(i+1)$ is given by the number of trailing 0s in the binary representation of $i + 1$. Most CPU instruction sets can count trailing 0 bits in a single instruction.

Putting this all together, we can very efficiently generate a series of samples using a generator matrix in Gray code order. GrayCodeSample() takes a generator matrix C, a number of samples to generate n, and stores the corresponding samples in memory at the location pointed to by p.

⟨*Low Discrepancy Inline Functions*⟩ +≡

```
inline void GrayCodeSample(const uint32_t *C, uint32_t n,
        uint32_t scramble, Float *p) {
    uint32_t v = scramble;
    for (uint32_t i = 0; i < n; ++i) {
        p[i] = v * 0x1p-32f;  /* 1/2^32 */
        v ^= C[CountTrailingZeros(i + 1)];
    }
}
```

The x86 assembly code for heart of the inner loop (with the loop control logic elided) is wonderfully brief:

```
xorps      %xmm1, %xmm1
cvtsi2ssq  %rax, %xmm1
mulss      %xmm0, %xmm1
movss      %xmm1, (%rcx,%rdx,4)
incq       %rdx
bsfl       %edx, %eax
xorl       $31, %eax
xorl       (%rdi,%rax,4), %esi
```

Even if one isn't an x86 assembly language aficionado, one can appreciate that it's an incredibly short sequence of instructions to generate each sample value.

There is a second version of GrayCodeSample() (not included here) for generating 2D samples; it takes a generator matrix for each dimension and fills in an array of Point2f values with the samples.

CountTrailingZeros() 1064
Float 1062

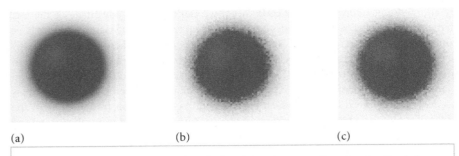

(a)   (b)   (c)

> **Figure 7.30: Comparisons of the Stratified and** $(0, 2)$**-Sequence Samplers for Rendering Depth of Field.** (a) A reference image of the blurred edge of an out-of-focus sphere, (b) an image rendered using the StratifiedSampler, and (c) an image using the ZeroTwoSequenceSampler. The ZeroTwoSequenceSampler's results are better than the stratified image, although the difference is smaller than the difference between stratified and random sampling.

7.5.2 SAMPLER IMPLEMENTATION

The ZeroTwoSequenceSampler generates samples for positions on the film plane, lens, and other 2D samples using scrambled $(0, 2)$-sequences, and generates 1D samples with scrambled van der Corput sequences. Figure 7.30 compares the result of using a $(0, 2)$-sequence for sampling the lens for the depth of field to using a stratified pattern.

⟨*ZeroTwoSequenceSampler Declarations*⟩ ≡
```
class ZeroTwoSequenceSampler : public PixelSampler {
public:
    ⟨ZeroTwoSequenceSampler Public Methods 462⟩
};
```

The constructor rounds the number of samples per pixel up to a power of 2 if necessary, since subsets of $(0, 2)$-sequences that are not a power of 2 in size are much less well distributed over $[0, 1)^2$ than those that are.

⟨*ZeroTwoSequenceSampler Method Definitions*⟩ ≡
```
ZeroTwoSequenceSampler::ZeroTwoSequenceSampler(int64_t samplesPerPixel,
        int nSampledDimensions)
    : PixelSampler(RoundUpPow2(samplesPerPixel), nSampledDimensions) {
}
```

⟨*ZeroTwoSequenceSampler Public Methods*⟩ ≡   462
```
int RoundCount(int count) const { return RoundUpPow2(count); }
```

Since the ZeroTwoSequenceSampler is a PixelSampler, its StartPixel() method must not only generate array sample values for the samples in the pixel but must also generate samples for a number of dimensions of non-array samples.

⟨*ZeroTwoSequenceSampler Method Definitions*⟩ +≡
```
void ZeroTwoSequenceSampler::StartPixel(const Point2i &p) {
    ⟨Generate 1D and 2D pixel sample components using (0, 2)-sequence 463⟩
    ⟨Generate 1D and 2D array samples using (0, 2)-sequence 463⟩
    PixelSampler::StartPixel(p);
}
```

Generating the samples for the non-array dimensions expected by the PixelSampler is a matter of filling in the appropriate vectors with the appropriate number of sample values.

⟨*Generate 1D and 2D pixel sample components using (0, 2)-sequence*⟩ ≡   463
```
for (size_t i = 0; i < samples1D.size(); ++i)
    VanDerCorput(1, samplesPerPixel, &samples1D[i][0], rng);
for (size_t i = 0; i < samples2D.size(); ++i)
    Sobol2D(1, samplesPerPixel, &samples2D[i][0], rng);
```

The sample vector dimensions with array samples are similar, though with multiple sample values in each dimension.

⟨*Generate 1D and 2D array samples using (0, 2)-sequence*⟩ ≡   463
```
for (size_t i = 0; i < samples1DArraySizes.size(); ++i)
    VanDerCorput(samples1DArraySizes[i], samplesPerPixel,
                &sampleArray1D[i][0], rng);
for (size_t i = 0; i < samples2DArraySizes.size(); ++i)
    Sobol2D(samples2DArraySizes[i], samplesPerPixel,
            &sampleArray2D[i][0], rng);
```

The VanDerCorput() function generates a number of scrambled 1D sample values using the Gray code-based sampling machinery. Although a specialized implementation of this function that took advantage of the structure of the identity matrix could be written, here we use the existing Gray code implementation, which is more than sufficiently efficient.

⟨*Low Discrepancy Inline Functions*⟩ +≡
```
inline void VanDerCorput(int nSamplesPerPixelSample, int nPixelSamples,
        Float *samples, RNG &rng) {
    uint32_t scramble = rng.UniformUInt32();
    ⟨Define CVanDerCorput Generator Matrix 464⟩
    int totalSamples = nSamplesPerPixelSample * nPixelSamples;
    GrayCodeSample(CVanDerCorput, totalSamples, scramble, samples);
    ⟨Randomly shuffle 1D sample points 464⟩
}
```

The generator matrix for the 1D van der Corput sequence is just the identity matrix but with each column's bits reversed, as per the earlier convention.

⟨*Define* CVanDerCorput *Generator Matrix*⟩ ≡   **463**

```
const uint32_t CVanDerCorput[] = {
    0b10000000000000000000000000000000,
    0b1000000000000000000000000000000,
    0b100000000000000000000000000000,
    0b10000000000000000000000000000,
    ⟨Remainder of Van Der Corput generator matrix entries⟩
};
```

There is a subtle implementation detail that must be accounted for when using scrambled (0, 2)-sequences.[11] Often, integrators will use samples from more than one of the sampling patterns that the sampler creates in the process of computing the values of particular integrals. For example, they might use a sample from a 1D pattern to select one of the N light sources in the scene to sample illumination from and then might use a sample from a 2D pattern to select a sample point on that light source, if it is an area light.

Even if these two patterns are computed with random scrambling with different random scramble values for each one, some correlation can still remain between elements of these patterns, such that the ith element of the 1D pattern and the ith element of the 2D pattern are related. As such, in the earlier area lighting example, the distribution of sample points on each light source would not in general cover the entire light due to this correlation, leading to unusual rendering errors.

This problem can be solved easily enough by randomly shuffling the various dimensions individually after they are generated. After generating a scrambled 1D low-discrepancy sampling pattern, giving a well-distributed set of samples across all of the image samples for this pixel, this function shuffles these samples in two ways. Consider, for example, a pixel with 8 image samples, each of which has 4 1D samples for the integrator (giving a total of 32 integrator samples). First, it shuffles samples within each of the 8 groups of 4 samples, putting each set of 4 into a random order. Next, it shuffles each of the 8 groups of 4 samples as a block, with respect to the other blocks of 4 samples.

⟨*Randomly shuffle 1D sample points*⟩ ≡   **463**

```
for (int i = 0; i < nPixelSamples; ++i)
    Shuffle(samples + i * nSamplesPerPixelSample,
            nSamplesPerPixelSample, 1, rng);
Shuffle(samples, nPixelSamples, nSamplesPerPixelSample, rng);
```

The Sobol2D() function follows a similar structure to VanDerCorput() but uses two generator matrices to generate the first two dimensions of Sobol′ points. Its implementation isn't included here.

⟨*Low Discrepancy Declarations*⟩ +≡

```
inline void Sobol2D(int nSamplesPerPixelSample, int nPixelSamples,
        Point2f *samples, RNG &rng);
```

---

11   Indeed, the importance of this issue wasn't fully appreciated by the authors until after going through the process of debugging some unexpected noise patterns in rendered images when this sampler was being used.

(a)

(b)

Figure 7.31: When the ZeroTwoSequenceSampler is used for the area light sampling example, similar results are generated (a) with both 1 image sample and 16 light samples as well as (b) with 16 image samples and 1 light sample, thanks to the (0, 2)-sequence sampling pattern that ensures good distribution of samples over the pixel area in both cases. Compare these images to Figure 7.24, where the stratified pattern generates a much worse set of light samples when only 1 light sample is taken for each of the 16 image samples.

Figure 7.31 shows the result of using the (0, 2)-sequence for the area lighting example scene. Note that not only does it give a visibly better image than stratified patterns, but it also does well with one light sample per image sample, unlike the stratified sampler.

*7.6 MAXIMIZED MINIMAL DISTANCE SAMPLER

The (0, 2)-sequence sampler is more effective than the stratified sampler, thanks to being stratified over all elementary intervals. However, it still sometimes generates sample points that are close together. An alternative is to use a different pair of generator matrices that not only generate (0, 2)-sequences but that are also specially designed to maximize the distance between samples; this approach is implemented by the MaxMinDistSampler. (See the "Further Reading" section for more details about the origin of these generator matrices.)

⟨*MaxMinDistSampler Declarations*⟩ ≡

```
class MaxMinDistSampler : public PixelSampler {
public:
    ⟨MaxMinDistSampler Public Methods 466⟩
private:
    ⟨MaxMinDistSampler Private Data 466⟩
};
```

PixelSampler 427

ZeroTwoSequenceSampler 462

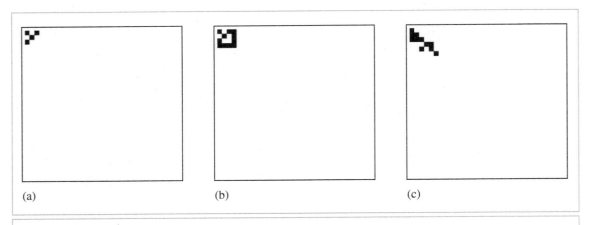

(a)   (b)   (c)

Figure 7.32: Generator matrices for $n = 8$, 16, and 64 sample patterns for the MaxMinDistSampler. As before, all matrix elements are either 0 or 1, and 1 elements are shown as filled squares here.

There are 17 of these specialized matrices, one for each power-of-two number of samples up to 2^{17} samples; a pointer to the appropriate one is stored in CPixel in the constructor.

⟨*MaxMinDistSampler Public Methods*⟩ ≡   465
```
MaxMinDistSampler(int64_t samplesPerPixel, int nSampledDimensions)
    : PixelSampler(RoundUpPow2(samplesPerPixel), nSampledDimensions) {
    CPixel = CMaxMinDist[Log2Int(samplesPerPixel)];
}
```

⟨*MaxMinDistSampler Private Data*⟩ ≡   465
```
const uint32_t *CPixel;
```

Figure 7.32 shows a few of these matrices and Figure 7.33 shows the points that one of them generates. Note that the same sampling pattern is used in each of the 2×2 pixels shown there; when the matrices were found, distance between sample points was evaluated using *toroidal topology*—as if the unit square was rolled into a torus—to allow for high-quality sample tiling.

⟨*Low Discrepancy Declarations*⟩ +≡
```
extern uint32_t CMaxMinDist[17][32];
```

The MaxMinDistSampler uses the generator matrix to compute the pixel samples. The first 2D sample dimension's value is set by uniformly stepping in the first dimension and the second comes from the generator matrix.

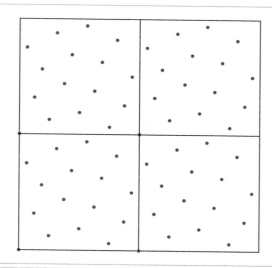

Figure 7.33: A grid of 2 × 2 pixels, each sampled with 16 samples from the `MaxMinDistSampler`. Though the same sample points are used in each pixel, their placement has been optimized so that not only are they well distributed within each pixel, but when they are tiled across pixels, sample points also aren't too close to those in neighboring pixels.

⟨*MaxMinDistSampler Method Definitions*⟩ ≡

```
void MaxMinDistSampler::StartPixel(const Point2i &p) {
    Float invSPP = (Float)1 / samplesPerPixel;
    for (int i = 0; i < samplesPerPixel; ++i)
        samples2D[0][i] = Point2f(i * invSPP,
                                  SampleGeneratorMatrix(CPixel, i));
    Shuffle(&samples2D[0][0], samplesPerPixel, 1, rng);
    ⟨Generate remaining samples for MaxMinDistSampler⟩
    PixelSampler::StartPixel(p);
}
```

The remaining dimensions are sampled using the first two Sobol' matrices, like the `ZeroTwoSequenceSampler`. We have found slightly better results with this approach (versus using the `CMaxMinDist` matrices) for samples in non-image dimensions of the sample vector. Therefore, the corresponding fragment ⟨*Generate remaining samples for* `MaxMinDistSampler`⟩ isn't included here.

*7.7 SOBOL' SAMPLER

The last `Sampler` in this chapter is based on a series of generator matrices due to Sobol'. The samples from the sequence that these matrices generate are distinguished by both being very efficient to implement—thanks to being entirely based on base-2

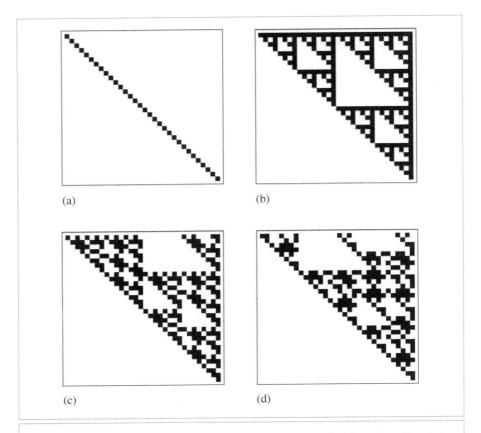

(a)   (b)

(c)   (d)

Figure 7.34: Generator matrices for the first four dimensions of the Sobol′ sequence. Note their regular structure.

computations—while also being extremely well distributed over all n dimensions of the sample vector. Figure 7.34 shows the first few Sobol′ generator matrices, and Figure 7.35 compares it to stratified and Halton points with the depth of field scene.

The weakness of the Sobol′ points is that they are prone to structural grid artifacts before convergence; a sense of this issue can be seen in the image sample points shown in Figure 7.36 and in the images in Figure 7.37. In exchange for this weakness, Sobol′ sequences are extremely well distributed over all n dimensions of the sample vector.

⟨*SobolSampler Declarations*⟩ ≡
```
class SobolSampler : public GlobalSampler {
public:
    ⟨SobolSampler Public Methods 470⟩
private:
    ⟨SobolSampler Private Data 470⟩
};
```

GlobalSampler 429

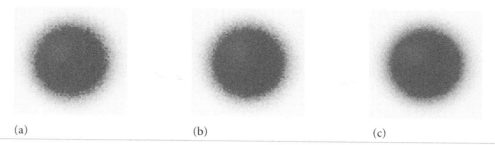

(a)   (b)   (c)

Figure 7.35: Comparisons of the Stratified, Halton, and Sobol´ Samplers for Rendering Depth of Field. (a) An image rendered using the `StratifiedSampler`, (b) an image rendered using the `HaltonSampler`, and (c) an image using the `SobolSampler`. Both low-discrepancy samplers are better than the stratified sampler. In spite of the structured grid artifacts visible with this undersampled image with the `SobolSampler`, the Sobol´ sequence often provides a faster rate of convergence than the Halton sequence.

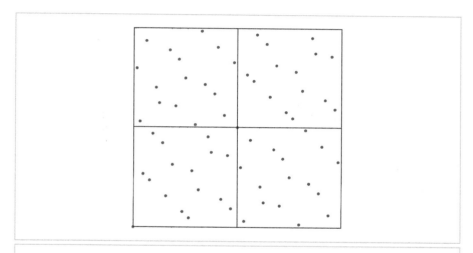

Figure 7.36: A grid of 2 × 2 pixels, sampled with 16 Sobol´ samples each. Note that there is a fair amount of structure as well as many samples close to others. The very good distribution properties of the sequence over all n dimensions of the sample vector generally make up for these shortcomings.

Figure 7.37: Undersampled images rendered with (a) the Halton sampler and (b) the Sobol´ sampler. Both exhibit visible structure, though with different visual characteristics. The Sobol´ sequence in particular exhibits a clearly visible checkerboard structure.

The SobolSampler uniformly scales the first two dimensions by the smallest power of 2 that causes the $[0, 1)^2$ sample domain to cover the image area to be sampled. As with the HaltonSampler, this specific scaling scheme is chosen in order to make it easier to compute the reverse mapping from pixel coordinates to the sample indices that land in each pixel.

⟨*SobolSampler Public Methods*⟩ ≡   468
```
SobolSampler(int64_t samplesPerPixel, const Bounds2i &sampleBounds)
    : GlobalSampler(RoundUpPow2(samplesPerPixel)),
      sampleBounds(sampleBounds) {
    resolution = RoundUpPow2(std::max(sampleBounds.Diagonal().x,
                                      sampleBounds.Diagonal().y));
    log2Resolution = Log2Int(resolution);
}
```

⟨*SobolSampler Private Data*⟩ ≡   468
```
const Bounds2i sampleBounds;
int resolution, log2Resolution;
```

The SobolIntervalToIndex() function returns the index of the sampleNumth sample in the pixel p, if the $[0, 1)^2$ sampling domain has been scaled by $2^{\text{log2Resolution}}$ to cover the pixel sampling area.

⟨*Low Discrepancy Declarations*⟩ +≡
```
inline uint64_t SobolIntervalToIndex(const uint32_t log2Resolution,
    uint64_t sampleNum, const Point2i &p);
```

The general approach used to derive the algorithm it implements is similar to that used by the Halton sampler in its GetIndexForSample() method. Here, scaling by a power of two means that the base-2 logarithm of the scale gives the number of digits of the $\mathbf{C}[d_i(a)]^T$ product that form the scaled sample's integer component. To find the values of a that give a particular integer value after scaling, we can compute the inverse of $\mathbf{C}$: given

$$v = \mathbf{C}[d_i(a)]^T,$$

then equivalently

$$\mathbf{C}^{-1}v = [d_i(a)]^T.$$

We won't include the implementation of this method here.

⟨*SobolSampler Method Definitions*⟩ ≡
```
int64_t SobolSampler::GetIndexForSample(int64_t sampleNum) const {
    return SobolIntervalToIndex(log2Resolution, sampleNum,
        Point2i(currentPixel - sampleBounds.pMin));
}
```

Computing the sample value for a given sample index and dimension is straightforward given the SobolSample() function.

⟨*SobolSampler Method Definitions*⟩ +≡
```
Float SobolSampler::SampleDimension(int64_t index, int dim) const {
    Float s = SobolSample(index, dim);
    ⟨Remap Sobol' dimensions used for pixel samples 472⟩
    return s;
}
```

The code for computing Sobol' sample values takes different paths for 32- and 64-bit floating-point values. Different generator matrices are used for these two cases, giving more bits of precision for 64-bit doubles.

⟨*Low Discrepancy Inline Functions*⟩ +≡
```
inline Float SobolSample(int64_t index, int dimension,
                         uint64_t scramble = 0) {
#ifdef PBRT_FLOAT_AS_DOUBLE
    return SobolSampleDouble(index, dimension, scramble);
#else
    return SobolSampleFloat(index, dimension, scramble);
#endif
}
```

The implementation of the SobolSampleFloat() function is quite similar to that of MultiplyGenerator(), with the differences that it takes a 64-bit index and that the matrices it uses have size 32×52. These larger matrices allow it to generate distinct sample values up to $a = 2^{52} - 1$, rather than $2^{32} - 1$, as with the 32×32 matrices used previously.

⟨*Low Discrepancy Inline Functions*⟩ +≡
```
inline float SobolSampleFloat(int64_t a, int dimension,
                              uint32_t scramble) {
    uint32_t v = scramble;
    for (int i = dimension * SobolMatrixSize; a != 0; a >>= 1, ++i)
        if (a & 1)
            v ^= SobolMatrices32[i];
    return v * 0x1p-32f; /* 1/2^32 */
}
```

⟨*Sobol Matrix Declarations*⟩ ≡
```
static constexpr int NumSobolDimensions = 1024;
static constexpr int SobolMatrixSize = 52;
extern const uint32_t SobolMatrices32[NumSobolDimensions *
                                      SobolMatrixSize];
```

The SobolSampleDouble() function is similar, except that it uses 64-bit Sobol' matrices. It is not included in the text here.

Because the SobolSampler is a GlobalSampler, the values returned for the first two dimensions need to be adjusted so that they are offsets from the current pixel. Here, the sample value is scaled up by the power-of-two scale computed in the constructor and then off-set by the lower corner of the sample bounds to find the corresponding raster sample location. The current integer pixel coordinate is subtracted to get a result in $[0, 1)$.

⟨*Remap Sobol′ dimensions used for pixel samples*⟩ ≡   471
```
if (dim == 0 || dim == 1)  {
    s = s * resolution + sampleBounds.pMin[dim];
    s = Clamp(s - currentPixel[dim], (Float)0, OneMinusEpsilon);
}
```

7.8 IMAGE RECONSTRUCTION

Given carefully chosen image samples, we need to convert the samples and their computed radiance values into pixel values for display or storage. According to signal processing theory, we need to do three things to compute final values for each of the pixels in the output image:

1. Reconstruct a continuous image function $\tilde{L}$ from the set of image samples.
2. Prefilter the function $\tilde{L}$ to remove any frequencies past the Nyquist limit for the pixel spacing.
3. Sample $\tilde{L}$ at the pixel locations to compute the final pixel values.

Because we know that we will be resampling the function $\tilde{L}$ at only the pixel locations, it's not necessary to construct an explicit representation of the function. Instead, we can combine the first two steps using a single filter function.

Recall that if the original function had been uniformly sampled at a frequency greater than the Nyquist frequency and reconstructed with the sinc filter, then the reconstructed function in the first step would match the original image function perfectly—quite a feat since we only have point samples. But because the image function almost always will have higher frequencies than could be accounted for by the sampling rate (due to edges, etc.), we chose to sample it nonuniformly, trading off noise for aliasing.

The theory behind ideal reconstruction depends on the samples being uniformly spaced. While a number of attempts have been made to extend the theory to nonuniform sampling, there is not yet an accepted approach to this problem. Furthermore, because the sampling rate is known to be insufficient to capture the function, perfect reconstruction isn't possible. Recent research in the field of sampling theory has revisited the issue of reconstruction with the explicit acknowledgment that perfect reconstruction is not generally attainable in practice. This slight shift in perspective has led to powerful new reconstruction techniques. See, for example, Unser (2000) for a survey of these developments. In particular, the goal of research in reconstruction theory has shifted from perfect reconstruction to developing reconstruction techniques that can be shown to minimize error between the reconstructed function and the original function, *regardless of whether the original was band limited*.

While the reconstruction techniques used in pbrt are not directly built on these new approaches, they serve to explain the experience of practitioners that applying perfect

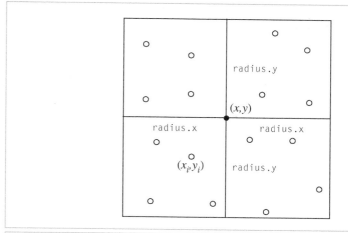

Figure 7.38: 2D Image Filtering. To compute a filtered pixel value for the pixel marked with a filled circle located at (x, y), all of the image samples inside the box around (x, y) with extent `radius.x` and `radius.y` need to be considered. Each of the image samples (x_i, y_i), denoted by open circles, is weighted by a 2D filter function, $f(x - x_i, y - y_i)$. The weighted average of all samples is the final pixel value.

reconstruction techniques to samples taken for image synthesis generally does not result in the highest quality images.

To reconstruct pixel values, we will consider the problem of interpolating the samples near a particular pixel. To compute a final value for a pixel $I(x, y)$, interpolation results in computing a weighted average

$$I(x, y) = \frac{\sum_i f(x - x_i, y - y_i)\, w(x_i, y_i)\, L(x_i, y_i)}{\sum_i f(x - x_i, y - y_i)}, \tag{7.12}$$

where

- $L(x_i, y_i)$ is the radiance value of the ith sample located at (x_i, y_i)
- $w(x_i, y_i)$ is the sample contribution weight returned by the Camera. As described in Sections 6.4.7 and 13.6.6, the manner in which these weights are computed determines which radiometric quantity the film measures.
- f is the filter function.

Figure 7.38 shows a pixel at location (x, y) that has a pixel filter with extent `radius.x` in the x direction and `radius.y` in the y direction. All of the samples inside the box given by the filter extent may contribute to the pixel's value, depending on the filter function's value for $f(x - x_i, y - y_i)$.

The sinc filter is not an appropriate choice here: recall that the ideal sinc filter is prone to ringing when the underlying function has frequencies beyond the Nyquist limit (Gibbs phenomenon), meaning edges in the image have faint replicated copies of the edge in nearby pixels. Furthermore, the sinc filter has *infinite support*: it doesn't fall off to zero at a finite distance from its center, so all of the image samples would need to be filtered for each output pixel. In practice, there is no single best filter function. Choosing the best one for a particular scene takes a mixture of quantitative evaluation and qualitative judgment.

7.8.1 FILTER FUNCTIONS

All filter implementations in pbrt are derived from an abstract Filter class, which provides the interface for the $f(x, y)$ functions used in filtering; see Equation (7.12). The Film class (described in the Section 7.9) stores a pointer to a Filter and uses it to filter image sample contributions when accumulating them into the final image. (Figure 7.39 shows comparisons of zoomed-in regions of images rendered using a variety of the filters from this section to reconstruct pixel values.) The Filter base class is defined in the files core/filter.h and core/filter.cpp.

⟨*Filter Declarations*⟩ ≡
```
class Filter {
public:
    ⟨Filter Interface 474⟩
    ⟨Filter Public Data 475⟩
};
```

All filters are centered at the origin (0, 0) and define a radius beyond which they have a value of 0; this width may be different in the x and y directions. The constructor takes the radius values and stores them along with their reciprocals, for use by the filter implementations. The filter's overall extent in each direction (its *support*) is twice the value of its corresponding radius (Figure 7.40).

⟨*Filter Interface*⟩ ≡   474
```
Filter(const Vector2f &radius)
    : radius(radius),
      invRadius(Vector2f(1 / radius.x, 1 / radius.y)) { }
```

 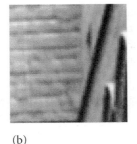 

(a)   (b)   (c)

Figure 7.39: The pixel reconstruction filter used to convert the image samples into pixel values can have a noticeable effect on the character of the final image. Here, we see blowups of a region of the brick wall in the Sponza atrium scene, filtered with (a) the box filter, (b) Gaussian, and (c) Mitchell–Netravali filter. Note that the Mitchell filter gives the sharpest image, while the Gaussian blurs it. The box is the least desirable, since it allows high-frequency aliasing to leak into the final image. (Note artifacts on the top edges of arches, for example.)

Film 484
Filter 474
Vector2f 60

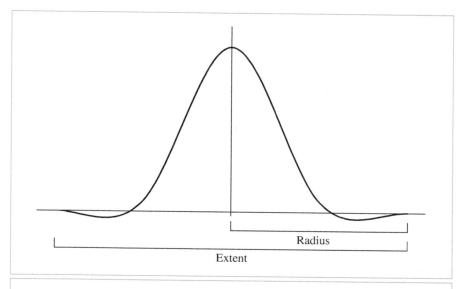

Figure 7.40: The extent of filters in pbrt is specified in terms of their radius from the origin to its cutoff point. The support of a filter is its total non-zero extent, here equal to twice its radius.

⟨*Filter Public Data*⟩ ≡   474
    const Vector2f radius, invRadius;

The sole method that Filter implementations need to provide is Evaluate(). It takes as a parameter a 2D point that gives the position of the sample point relative to the center of the filter. The filter's value at that point is returned. Code elsewhere in the system will never call the filter function with points outside of the filter's extent, so filter implementations don't need to check for this case.

⟨*Filter Interface*⟩ +≡   474
    virtual Float Evaluate(const Point2f &p) const = 0;

Box Filter

One of the most commonly used filters in graphics is the *box filter* (and, in fact, when filtering and reconstruction aren't addressed explicitly, the box filter is the *de facto* result). The box filter equally weights all samples within a square region of the image. Although computationally efficient, it's just about the worst filter possible. Recall from the discussion in Section 7.1 that the box filter allows high-frequency sample data to leak into the reconstructed values. This causes postaliasing—even if the original sample values were at a high enough frequency to avoid aliasing, errors are introduced by poor filtering.

Figure 7.41(a) shows a graph of the box filter, and Figure 7.42 shows the result of using the box filter to reconstruct two 1D functions. For the step function we used previously to illustrate the Gibbs phenomenon, the box does reasonably well. However, the results are much worse for a sinusoidal function that has increasing frequency along the x axis. Not only does the box filter do a poor job of reconstructing the function when the frequency is low, giving a discontinuous result even though the original function was smooth, but it

Filter 474
Float 1062
Point2f 68
Vector2f 60

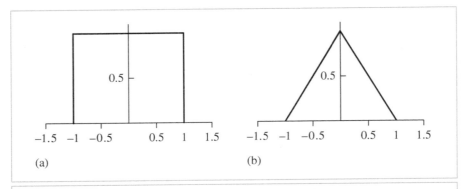

Figure 7.41: Graphs of the (a) box filter and (b) triangle filter. Although neither of these is a particularly good filter, they are both computationally efficient, easy to implement, and good baselines for evaluating other filters.

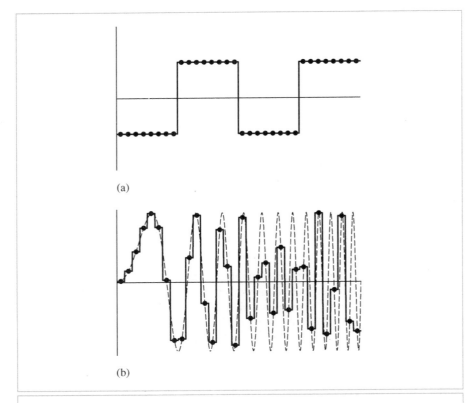

Figure 7.42: The box filter reconstructing (a) a step function and (b) a sinusoidal function with increasing frequency as x increases. This filter does well with the step function, as expected, but does an extremely poor job with the sinusoidal function.

also does an extremely poor job of reconstruction as the function's frequency approaches and passes the Nyquist limit.

⟨*BoxFilter Declarations*⟩ ≡
```
class BoxFilter : public Filter {
public:
    BoxFilter(const Vector2f &radius) : Filter(radius) { }
    Float Evaluate(const Point2f &p) const;
};
```

Because the evaluation function won't be called with (x, y) values outside of the filter's extent, it can always return 1 for the filter function's value.

⟨*BoxFilter Method Definitions*⟩ ≡
```
Float BoxFilter::Evaluate(const Point2f &p) const {
    return 1.;
}
```

Triangle Filter
The triangle filter gives slightly better results than the box: samples at the filter center have a weight of 1, and the weight falls off linearly to the square extent of the filter. See Figure 7.41(b) for a graph of the triangle filter.

⟨*TriangleFilter Declarations*⟩ ≡
```
class TriangleFilter : public Filter {
public:
    TriangleFilter(const Vector2f &radius) : Filter(radius) { }
    Float Evaluate(const Point2f &p) const;
};
```

Evaluating the triangle filter is simple: the implementation just computes a linear function based on the width of the filter in both the x and y directions.

⟨*TriangleFilter Method Definitions*⟩ ≡
```
Float TriangleFilter::Evaluate(const Point2f &p) const {
    return std::max((Float)0, radius.x - std::abs(p.x)) *
           std::max((Float)0, radius.y - std::abs(p.y));
}
```

Gaussian Filter
Unlike the box and triangle filters, the Gaussian filter gives a reasonably good result in practice. This filter applies a Gaussian bump that is centered at the pixel and radially symmetric around it. The Gaussian's value at the end of its extent is subtracted from the filter value, in order to make the filter go to 0 at its limit (Figure 7.43). The Gaussian does tend to cause slight blurring of the final image compared to some of the other filters, but this blurring can actually help mask any remaining aliasing in the image.

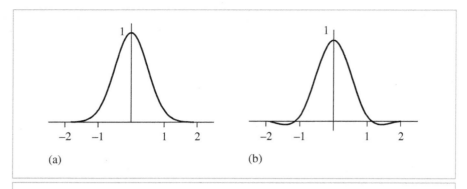

Figure 7.43: Graphs of (a) the Gaussian filter and (b) the Mitchell filter with $B = \frac{1}{3}$ and $C = \frac{1}{3}$, each with a width of 2. The Gaussian gives images that tend to be a bit blurry, while the negative lobes of the Mitchell filter help to accentuate and sharpen edges in final images.

⟨*GaussianFilter Declarations*⟩ ≡
```
class GaussianFilter : public Filter {
public:
    ⟨GaussianFilter Public Methods 478⟩
private:
    ⟨GaussianFilter Private Data 478⟩
    ⟨GaussianFilter Utility Functions 479⟩
};
```

The 1D Gaussian filter function of radius r is

$$f(x) = e^{-\alpha x^2} - e^{-\alpha r^2},$$

where α controls the rate of falloff of the filter. Smaller values cause a slower falloff, giving a blurrier image. The second term here ensures that the Gaussian goes to 0 at the end of its extent rather than having an abrupt cliff. For efficiency, the constructor precomputes the constant term for $e^{-\alpha r^2}$ in each direction.

⟨*GaussianFilter Public Methods*⟩ ≡   478
```
GaussianFilter(const Vector2f &radius, Float alpha)
    : Filter(radius), alpha(alpha),
      expX(std::exp(-alpha * radius.x * radius.x)),
      expY(std::exp(-alpha * radius.y * radius.y)) { }
```

Filter 474
Filter::radius 475
Float 1062
GaussianFilter 478
GaussianFilter::alpha 478
GaussianFilter::expX 478
GaussianFilter::expY 478
Vector2f 60

⟨*GaussianFilter Private Data*⟩ ≡   478
```
const Float alpha;
const Float expX, expY;
```

Since a 2D Gaussian function is separable into the product of two 1D Gaussians, the implementation calls the Gaussian() function twice and multiplies the results.

⟨*GaussianFilter Method Definitions*⟩ ≡
```
Float GaussianFilter::Evaluate(const Point2f &p) const {
    return Gaussian(p.x, expX) * Gaussian(p.y, expY);
}
```

⟨*GaussianFilter Utility Functions*⟩ ≡   **478**
```
Float Gaussian(Float d, Float expv) const {
    return std::max((Float)0, Float(std::exp(-alpha * d * d) - expv));
}
```

Mitchell Filter

Filter design is notoriously difficult, mixing mathematical analysis and perceptual experiments. Mitchell and Netravali (1988) have developed a family of parameterized filter functions in order to be able to explore this space in a systematic manner. After analyzing test subjects' subjective responses to images filtered with a variety of parameter values, they developed a filter that tends to do a good job of trading off between *ringing* (phantom edges next to actual edges in the image) and *blurring* (excessively blurred results)—two common artifacts from poor reconstruction filters.

Note from the graph in Figure 7.43(b) that this filter function takes on negative values out by its edges; it has *negative lobes*. In practice these negative regions improve the sharpness of edges, giving crisper images (reduced blurring). If they become too large, however, ringing tends to start to enter the image. Also, because the final pixel values can therefore become negative, they will eventually need to be clamped to a legal output range.

Figure 7.44 shows this filter reconstructing the two test functions. It does extremely well with both of them: there is minimal ringing with the step function, and it does a very good job with the sinusoidal function, up until the point where the sampling rate isn't sufficient to capture the function's detail.

⟨*MitchellFilter Declarations*⟩ ≡
```
class MitchellFilter : public Filter {
public:
    ⟨MitchellFilter Public Methods 479⟩
private:
    const Float B, C;
};
```

The Mitchell filter has two parameters called B and C. Although any values can be used for these parameters, Mitchell and Netravali recommend that they lie along the line $B + 2C = 1$.

⟨*MitchellFilter Public Methods*⟩ ≡   **479**
```
MitchellFilter(const Vector2f &radius, Float B, Float C)
    : Filter(radius), B(B), C(C) {
}
```

The Mitchell-Netravali filter is the product of 1D filter functions in the x and y directions and is therefore separable, like the Gaussian filter. (In fact, all of the provided filters in pbrt are separable.) Nevertheless, the Filter::Evaluate() interface does not enforce this requirement, giving more flexibility in implementing new filters in the future.

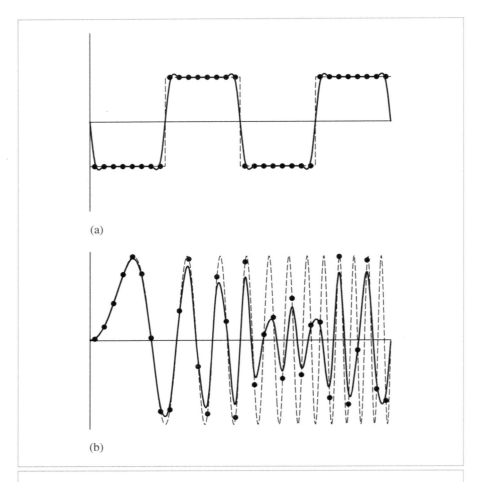

(a)

(b)

Figure 7.44: The Mitchell–Netravali Filter Used to Reconstruct the Example Functions. It does a good job with both of these functions, (a) introducing minimal ringing with the step function and (b) accurately representing the sinusoid until aliasing from undersampling starts to dominate.

⟨*MitchellFilter Method Definitions*⟩ ≡

```
Float MitchellFilter::Evaluate(const Point2f &p) const {
    return Mitchell1D(p.x * invRadius.x) * Mitchell1D(p.y * invRadius.y);
}
```

The 1D function used in the Mitchell filter is an even function defined over the range $[-2, 2]$. This function is made by joining a cubic polynomial defined over $[0, 1]$ with another cubic polynomial defined over $[1, 2]$. This combined polynomial is also reflected around the $x = 0$ plane to give the complete function. These polynomials are controlled by the B and C parameters and are chosen carefully to guarantee C^0 and C^1 continuity at $x = 0$, $x = 1$, and $x = 2$. The polynomials are

$f(x)$

$$= \frac{1}{6} \begin{cases} (12 - 9B - 6C)|x|^3 + (-18 + 12B + 6C)|x|^2 + (6 - 2B) & |x| < 1 \\ (-B - 6C)|x|^3 + (6B + 30C)|x|^2 + (-12B - 48C)|x| & 1 \le |x| < 2 \\ \quad + (8B + 24C) & \\ 0 & \text{otherwise.} \end{cases}$$

⟨*MitchellFilter Public Methods*⟩ +≡   479
```
Float Mitchell1D(Float x) const {
    x = std::abs(2 * x);
    if (x > 1)
        return ((-B - 6*C) * x*x*x + (6*B + 30*C) * x*x +
                (-12*B - 48*C) * x + (8*B + 24*C)) * (1.f/6.f);
    else
        return ((12 - 9*B - 6*C) * x*x*x +
                (-18 + 12*B + 6*C) * x*x +
                (6 - 2*B)) * (1.f/6.f);
}
```

Windowed Sinc Filter

Finally, the LanczosSincFilter class implements a filter based on the sinc function. In practice, the sinc filter is often multiplied by another function that goes to 0 after some distance. This gives a filter function with finite extent, which is necessary for an implementation with reasonable performance. An additional parameter τ controls how many cycles the sinc function passes through before it is clamped to a value of 0. Figure 7.45 shows a graph of three cycles of the sinc function, along with a graph of the windowing function we use, which was developed by Lanczos. The Lanczos window is just the central lobe of the sinc function, scaled to cover the τ cycles:

$$w(x) = \frac{\sin \pi x / \tau}{\pi x / \tau}.$$

Figure 7.45 also shows the filter that we will implement here, which is the product of the sinc function and the windowing function.

Figure 7.46 shows the windowed sinc's reconstruction results for uniform 1D samples. Thanks to the windowing, the reconstructed step function exhibits far less ringing than the reconstruction using the infinite-extent sinc function (compare to Figure 7.11). The windowed sinc filter also does extremely well at reconstructing the sinusoidal function until prealiasing begins.

⟨*Sinc Filter Declarations*⟩ ≡
```
class LanczosSincFilter : public Filter {
public:
    ⟨LanczosSincFilter Public Methods 483⟩
private:
    const Float tau;
};
```

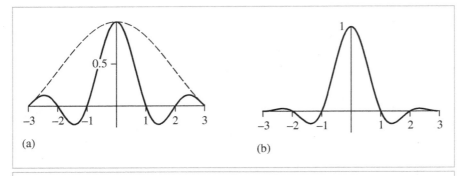

(a)   (b)

Figure 7.45: Graphs of the Sinc Filter. (a) The sinc function, truncated after three cycles (solid line) and the Lanczos windowing function (dashed line). (b) The product of these two functions, as implemented in the `LanczosSincFilter`.

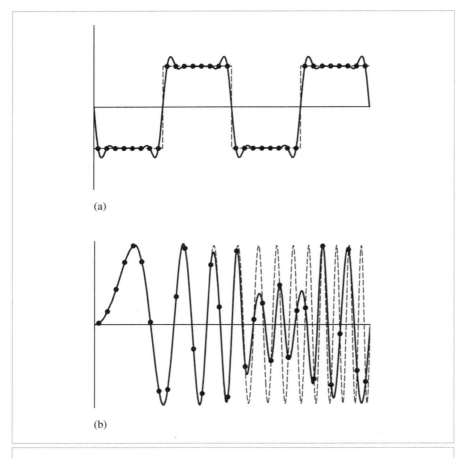

(a)

(b)

Figure 7.46: Results of Using the Windowed Sinc Filter to Reconstruct the Example Functions. Here, $\tau = 3$. (a) Like the infinite sinc, it suffers from ringing with the step function, although there is much less ringing in the windowed version. (b) The filter does quite well with the sinusoid, however.

⟨*LanczosSincFilter Public Methods*⟩ ≡   481
```
LanczosSincFilter(const Vector2f &radius, Float tau)
    : Filter(radius), tau(tau) { }
```

⟨*Sinc Filter Method Definitions*⟩ ≡
```
Float LanczosSincFilter::Evaluate(const Point2f &p) const {
    return WindowedSinc(p.x, radius.x) * WindowedSinc(p.y, radius.y);
}
```

The implementation computes the value of the sinc function and then multiplies it by the value of the Lanczos windowing function.

⟨*LanczosSincFilter Public Methods*⟩ +≡   481
```
Float Sinc(Float x) const {
    x = std::abs(x);
    if (x < 1e-5)  return 1;
    return std::sin(Pi * x) / (Pi * x);
}
```

⟨*LanczosSincFilter Public Methods*⟩ +≡   481
```
Float WindowedSinc(Float x, Float radius) const {
    x = std::abs(x);
    if (x > radius) return 0;
    Float lanczos = Sinc(x / tau);
    return Sinc(x) * lanczos;
}
```

7.9 FILM AND THE IMAGING PIPELINE

The type of film or sensor in a camera has a dramatic effect on the way that incident light is transformed into colors in an image. In pbrt, the Film class models the sensing device in the simulated camera. After the radiance is found for each camera ray, the Film implementation determines the sample's contribution to the pixels around the point on the film plane where the camera ray began and updates its representation of the image. When the main rendering loop exits, the Film writes the final image to a file.

For realistic camera models, Section 6.4.7 introduced the measurement equation, which describes how a sensor in a camera measures the amount of energy arriving over the sensor area over a period of time. For simpler camera models, we can consider the sensor to be measuring the average radiance over a small area over some period of time. The effect of the choice of which measurement to take is encapsulated in the weight for the ray returned by Camera::GenerateRayDifferential(). Therefore, the Film implementation can proceed without having to account for these variations, as long as it scales the provided radiance values by these weights.

This section introduces a single Film implementation that applies the pixel reconstruction equation to compute final pixel values. For a physically based renderer, it's generally best for the resulting images to be stored in a floating-point image format. Doing so provides more flexibility in how the output can be used than if a traditional image format with 8-bit unsigned integer values is used; floating-point formats avoid the substantial loss of information that comes from quantizing images to 8 bits.

In order to display such images on modern display devices, it is necessary to map these floating-point pixel values to discrete values for display. For example, computer monitors generally expect the color of each pixel to be described by an RGB color triple, not an arbitrary spectral power distribution. Spectra described by general basis function coefficients must therefore be converted to an RGB representation before they can be displayed. A related problem is that displays have a substantially smaller range of displayable radiance values than the range present in many real-world scenes. Therefore, pixel values must be mapped to the displayable range in a way that causes the final displayed image to appear as close as possible to the way it would appear on an ideal display device without this limitation. These issues are addressed by research into *tone mapping*; the "Further Reading" section has more information about this topic.

7.9.1 THE FILM CLASS

Film is defined in the files core/film.h and core/film.cpp.

⟨*Film Declarations*⟩ ≡
```
    class Film {
    public:
        ⟨Film Public Methods⟩
        ⟨Film Public Data  485⟩
    private:
        ⟨Film Private Data  486⟩
        ⟨Film Private Methods  493⟩
    };
```

A number of values are passed to the constructor: the overall resolution of the image in pixels; a crop window that may specify a subset of the image to render; the length of the diagonal of the film's physical area, which is specified to the constructor in millimeters but is converted to meters here; a filter function; the filename for the output image and parameters that control how the image pixel values are stored in files.

⟨*Film Method Definitions*⟩ ≡
```
    Film::Film(const Point2i &resolution, const Bounds2f &cropWindow,
            std::unique_ptr<Filter> filt, Float diagonal,
            const std::string &filename, Float scale)
        : fullResolution(resolution), diagonal(diagonal * .001),
          filter(std::move(filt)), filename(filename), scale(scale) {
        ⟨Compute film image bounds  485⟩
        ⟨Allocate film image storage  486⟩
        ⟨Precompute filter weight table  487⟩
    }
```

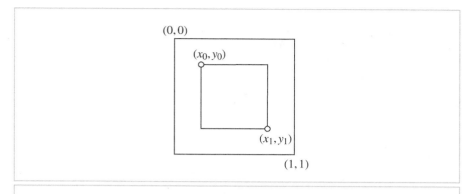

Figure 7.47: The image crop window specifies a subset of the image to be rendered. It is given in NDC space, with coordinates ranging from (0, 0) to (1, 1). The Film class only allocates space for and stores pixel values in the region inside the crop window.

⟨*Film Public Data*⟩ ≡   **484**
```
const Point2i fullResolution;
const Float diagonal;
std::unique_ptr<Filter> filter;
const std::string filename;
```

In conjunction with the overall image resolution, the crop window gives the bounds of pixels that need to be actually stored and written out. Crop windows are useful for debugging or for breaking a large image into small pieces that can be rendered on different computers and reassembled later. The crop window is specified in NDC space, with each coordinate ranging from 0 to 1 (Figure 7.47). Film::croppedPixelBounds stores the pixel bounds from the upper-left to the lower-right corners of the crop window. Fractional pixel coordinates are rounded up; this ensures that if an image is rendered in pieces with abutting crop windows, each final pixel will be present in only one of the subimages.

⟨*Compute film image bounds*⟩ ≡   **484**
```
croppedPixelBounds =
    Bounds2i(Point2i(std::ceil(fullResolution.x * cropWindow.pMin.x),
                     std::ceil(fullResolution.y * cropWindow.pMin.y)),
             Point2i(std::ceil(fullResolution.x * cropWindow.pMax.x),
                     std::ceil(fullResolution.y * cropWindow.pMax.y)));
```

⟨*Film Public Data*⟩ +≡   **484**
```
Bounds2i croppedPixelBounds;
```

Given the pixel resolution of the (possibly cropped) image, the constructor allocates an array of Pixel structures, one for each pixel. The running weighted sums of spectral pixel contributions are represented using XYZ colors (Section 5.2.1) and are stored in the xyz member variable. filterWeightSum holds the sum of filter weight values for the sample contributions to the pixel. splatXYZ holds an (unweighted) sum of sample splats. The pad member is unused; its sole purpose is to ensure that the Pixel structure is 32 bytes in size, rather than 28 as it would be otherwise (assuming 4-byte Floats; otherwise, it ensures a 64-byte structure). This padding ensures that a Pixel won't straddle a cache line, so that no more than one cache miss will be incurred when a Pixel is accessed (as long as the first Pixel in the array is allocated at the start of a cache line).

⟨*Film Private Data*⟩ ≡   484
```
struct Pixel {
    Float xyz[3] = { 0, 0, 0 };
    Float filterWeightSum = 0;
    AtomicFloat splatXYZ[3];
    Float pad;
};
std::unique_ptr<Pixel[]> pixels;
```

⟨*Allocate film image storage*⟩ ≡   484
```
pixels = std::unique_ptr<Pixel[]>(new Pixel[croppedPixelBounds.Area()]);
```

Two natural alternatives to using XYZ colors to store pixel values would be to use Spectrum values or to store RGB color. Here, it isn't worthwhile to store complete Spectrum values, even when doing full spectral rendering. Because the final colors written to the output file don't include the full set of Spectrum samples, converting to a tristimulus value here doesn't represent a loss of information versus storing Spectrums and converting to a tristimulus value on image output. Not storing complete Spectrum values in this case can save a substantial amount of memory if the Spectrum has a large number of samples. (If pbrt supported saving SampledSpectrum values to files, then this design choice would need to be revisited.)

We have chosen to use XYZ color rather than RGB to emphasize that XYZ is a display-independent representation of color, while RGB requires assuming a particular set of display response curves (Section 5.2.2). (In the end, we will, however, have to convert to RGB, since few image file formats store XYZ color.)

With typical filter settings, every image sample may contribute to 16 or more pixels in the final image. Particularly for simple scenes, where relatively little time is spent on ray intersection testing and shading computations, the time spent updating the image for each sample can be significant. Therefore, the Film precomputes a table of filter values so that we can avoid the expense of virtual function calls to the Filter::Evaluate() method as well as the expense of evaluating the filter and can instead use values from the table for filtering. The error introduced by not evaluating the filter at each sample's precise location isn't noticeable in practice.

The implementation here makes the reasonable assumption that the filter is defined such that $f(x, y) = f(|x|, |y|)$, so the table needs to hold values for only the positive quadrant of filter offsets. This assumption is true for all of the Filters currently available in pbrt and is true for most filters used in practice. This makes the table one-fourth the size and improves the coherence of memory accesses, leading to better cache performance.[12]

---

12 The implementation here could further take advantage of the fact that all filters currently in pbrt are separable, only allocating two 1D tables. However, to more easily allow different filter functions to be added, we don't assume separability here.

⟨*Precompute filter weight table*⟩ ≡   484

```
int offset = 0;
for (int y = 0; y < filterTableWidth; ++y) {
    for (int x = 0; x < filterTableWidth; ++x, ++offset) {
        Point2f p;
        p.x = (x + 0.5f) * filter->radius.x / filterTableWidth;
        p.y = (y + 0.5f) * filter->radius.y / filterTableWidth;
        filterTable[offset] = filter->Evaluate(p);
    }
}
```

⟨*Film Private Data*⟩ +≡   484

```
static constexpr int filterTableWidth = 16;
Float filterTable[filterTableWidth * filterTableWidth];
```

The Film implementation is responsible for determining the range of integer pixel values that the Sampler is responsible for generating samples for. The area to be sampled is returned by the GetSampleBounds() method. Because the pixel reconstruction filter generally spans a number of pixels, the Sampler must generate image samples a bit outside of the range of pixels that will actually be output. This way, even pixels at the boundary of the image will have an equal density of samples around them in all directions and won't be biased with only values from toward the interior of the image. This detail is also important when rendering images in pieces with crop windows, since it eliminates artifacts at the edges of the subimages.

Computing the sample bounds involves accounting for the half-pixel offsets when converting from discrete to continuous pixel coordinates, expanding by the filter radius, and then rounding outward.

⟨*Film Method Definitions*⟩ +≡

```
Bounds2i Film::GetSampleBounds() const {
    Bounds2f floatBounds(
        Floor(Point2f(croppedPixelBounds.pMin) + Vector2f(0.5f, 0.5f) -
                filter->radius),
        Ceil( Point2f(croppedPixelBounds.pMax) - Vector2f(0.5f, 0.5f) +
                filter->radius));
    return (Bounds2i)floatBounds;
}
```

GetPhysicalExtent() returns the actual extent of the film in the scene. This information is specifically needed by the RealisticCamera. Given the length of the film diagonal and the aspect ratio of the image, we can compute the size of the sensor in the x and y directions. If we denote the diagonal length by d and the width and height of the film sensor by x and y, then we know that $x^2 + y^2 = d^2$. We can define the aspect ratio a of the image by $a = y/x$, so $y = ax$, which gives $x^2 + (a^2x^2) = d^2$. Solving for x gives

$$x = \sqrt{\frac{d^2}{1 + a^2}}.$$

The implementation of GetPhysicalExtent() follows directly. The returned extent is centered around (0, 0).

⟨*Film Method Definitions*⟩ +≡
```
    Bounds2f Film::GetPhysicalExtent() const {
        Float aspect = (Float)fullResolution.y / (Float)fullResolution.x;
        Float x = std::sqrt(diagonal * diagonal / (1 + aspect * aspect));
        Float y = aspect * x;
        return Bounds2f(Point2f(-x / 2, -y / 2), Point2f(x / 2, y / 2));
    }
```

7.9.2 SUPPLYING PIXEL VALUES TO THE FILM

There are three ways that the sample contributions can be provided to the film. The first is driven by samples generated by the Sampler over tiles of the image. While the most straightforward interface would be to allow renderers to provide a film pixel location and a Spectrum with the contribution of the corresponding ray directly to the Film, it's not easy to provide a high-performance implementation of such a method in the presence of multi-threading, where multiple threads may end up trying to update the same portion of the image concurrently.

Therefore, Film defines an interface where threads can specify that they're generating samples in some extent of pixels with respect to the overall image. Given the sample bounds, GetFilmTile() in turn returns a pointer to a FilmTile object that stores contributions for the pixels in the corresponding region of the image. Ownership of the FilmTile and the data it stores is exclusive to the caller, so that thread can provide sample values to the FilmTile without worrying about contention with other threads. When it has finished work on the tile, the thread passes the completed tile back to the Film, which safely merges it into the final image.

⟨*Film Method Definitions*⟩ +≡
```
    std::unique_ptr<FilmTile> Film::GetFilmTile(
            const Bounds2i &sampleBounds) {
        ⟨Bound image pixels that samples in sampleBounds contribute to 489⟩
        return std::unique_ptr<FilmTile>(new FilmTile(tilePixelBounds,
            filter->radius, filterTable, filterTableWidth));
    }
```

Given a bounding box of the pixel area that samples will be generated in, there are two steps to compute the bounding box of image pixels that the sample values will contribute to. First, the effects of the discrete-to-continuous pixel coordinate transformation and the radius of the filter must be accounted for. Second, the resulting bound must be clipped to the overall image pixel bounds; pixels outside the image by definition don't need to be accounted for.

⟨*Bound image pixels that samples in* sampleBounds *contribute to*⟩ ≡   **488**
```
    Vector2f halfPixel = Vector2f(0.5f, 0.5f);
    Bounds2f floatBounds = (Bounds2f)sampleBounds;
    Point2i p0 = (Point2i)Ceil(floatBounds.pMin - halfPixel -
                               filter->radius);
    Point2i p1 = (Point2i)Floor(floatBounds.pMax - halfPixel +
                                filter->radius) + Point2i(1, 1);
    Bounds2i tilePixelBounds =
        Intersect(Bounds2i(p0, p1), croppedPixelBounds);
```

⟨*Film Declarations*⟩ +≡
```
    class FilmTile {
    public:
        ⟨FilmTile Public Methods 489⟩
    private:
        ⟨FilmTile Private Data 489⟩
    };
```

The FilmTile constructor takes a 2D bounding box that gives the bounds of the pixels in the final image that it must provide storage for as well as additional information about the reconstruction filter being used, including a pointer to the filter function values tabulated in ⟨*Precompute filter weight table*⟩.

⟨*FilmTile Public Methods*⟩ ≡   **489**
```
    FilmTile(const Bounds2i &pixelBounds, const Vector2f &filterRadius,
             const Float *filterTable, int filterTableSize)
        : pixelBounds(pixelBounds), filterRadius(filterRadius),
          invFilterRadius(1 / filterRadius.x, 1 / filterRadius.y),
          filterTable(filterTable), filterTableSize(filterTableSize) {
        pixels = std::vector<FilmTilePixel>(std::max(0, pixelBounds.Area()));
    }
```

⟨*FilmTile Private Data*⟩ ≡   **489**
```
    const Bounds2i pixelBounds;
    const Vector2f filterRadius, invFilterRadius;
    const Float *filterTable;
    const int filterTableSize;
    std::vector<FilmTilePixel> pixels;
```

For each pixel, both a sum of the weighted contributions from the pixel samples (according to the reconstruction filter weights) and a sum of the filter weights is maintained.

⟨*FilmTilePixel Declarations*⟩ ≡
```
    struct FilmTilePixel {
        Spectrum contribSum = 0.f;
        Float filterWeightSum = 0.f;
    };
```

Once the radiance carried by a ray for a sample has been computed, the Integrator calls FilmTile::AddSample(). It takes a sample and corresponding radiance value as well as the weight for the sample's contribution originally returned by Camera::GenerateRay Differential(). It updates the stored image using the reconstruction filter with the pixel filtering equation.

⟨*FilmTile Public Methods*⟩ +≡   **489**
```
    void AddSample(const Point2f &pFilm, const Spectrum &L,
            Float sampleWeight = 1.) {
        ⟨Compute sample's raster bounds 490⟩
        ⟨Loop over filter support and add sample to pixel arrays 491⟩
    }
```

To understand the operation of FilmTile::AddSample(), first recall the pixel filtering equation:

$$I(x, y) = \frac{\sum_i f(x - x_i, y - y_i)\, w(x_i, y_i)\, L(x_i, y_i)}{\sum_i f(x - x_i, y - y_i)}.$$

It computes each pixel's value $I(x, y)$ as the weighted sum of nearby samples' radiance values, using both a filter function f and the sample weight returned by the Camera $w(x_i, y_i)$ to compute the contribution of the radiance value to the final pixel value. Because all of the Filters in pbrt have finite extent, this method starts by computing which pixels will be affected by the current sample. Then, turning the pixel filtering equation inside out, it updates two running sums for each pixel (x, y) that is affected by the sample. One sum accumulates the numerator of the pixel filtering equation, and the other accumulates the denominator. At the end of rendering, the final pixel values are computed by performing the division.

To find which pixels a sample potentially contributes to, FilmTile::AddSample() converts the continuous sample coordinates to discrete coordinates by subtracting 0.5 from x and y. It then offsets this value by the filter radius in each direction (Figure 7.48), transforms it to the tile coordinate space, and takes the ceiling of the minimum coordinates and the floor of the maximum, since pixels outside the bound of the extent are unaffected by the sample. Finally, the pixel bounds are clipped to the bounds of the pixels in the tile. While the sample may theoretically contribute to pixels outside the tile, any such pixels must be outside the image extent.

⟨*Compute sample's raster bounds*⟩ ≡   **490**
```
    Point2f pFilmDiscrete = pFilm - Vector2f(0.5f, 0.5f);
    Point2i p0 = (Point2i)Ceil(pFilmDiscrete - filterRadius);
    Point2i p1 = (Point2i)Floor(pFilmDiscrete + filterRadius) + Point2i(1, 1);
    p0 = Max(p0, pixelBounds.pMin);
    p1 = Min(p1, pixelBounds.pMax);
```

Given the bounds of pixels that are affected by this sample, it's now possible to loop over all of those pixels and accumulate the filtered sample weights at each of them.

Camera::
GenerateRayDifferential()
357
FilmTile::AddSample() 490
Filter 474
Float 1062
Integrator 25
Point2::Ceil() 71
Point2::Floor() 71
Point2::Max() 70
Point2::Min() 70
Point2f 68
Point2i 68
Spectrum 315
Vector2f 60

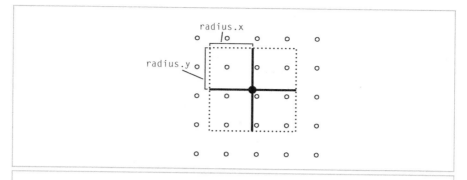

Figure 7.48: Given an image sample at some position on the image plane (solid dot), it is necessary to determine which pixel values (empty dots) are affected by the sample's contribution. This is done by taking the offsets in the x and y directions according to the pixel reconstruction filter's radius (solid lines) and finding the pixels inside this region.

⟨*Loop over filter support and add sample to pixel arrays*⟩ ≡   **490**
   ⟨*Precompute x and y filter table offsets* **492**⟩
   for (int y = p0.y; y < p1.y; ++y) {
      for (int x = p0.x; x < p1.x; ++x) {
         ⟨*Evaluate filter value at* (x, y) *pixel* **492**⟩
         ⟨*Update pixel values with filtered sample contribution* **492**⟩
      }
   }

Each discrete integer pixel (x, y) has an instance of the filter function centered around it. To compute the filter weight for a particular sample, it's necessary to find the offset from the pixel to the sample's position in discrete coordinates and evaluate the filter function. If we were evaluating the filter explicitly, the appropriate computation would be

```
filterWeight = filter->Evaluate(Point2i(x - pFilmDiscrete.x,
                                         y - pFilmDiscrete.y));
```

Instead, the implementation retrieves the appropriate filter weight from the table.

To find the filter weight for a pixel (x', y') given the sample position (x, y), this routine computes the offset $(x' - x, y' - y)$ and converts it into coordinates for the filter weights lookup table. This can be done directly by dividing each component of the sample offset by the filter radius in that direction, giving a value between 0 and 1, and then multiplying by the table size. This process can be further optimized by noting that along each row of pixels in the x direction, the difference in y, and thus the y offset into the filter table, is constant. Analogously, for each column of pixels, the x offset is constant. Therefore, before looping over the pixels here it's possible to precompute these indices and store them in two 1D arrays, saving repeated work in the loop.

⟨*Precompute x and y filter table offsets*⟩ ≡   491
```
int *ifx = ALLOCA(int, p1.x - p0.x);
for (int x = p0.x; x < p1.x; ++x) {
    Float fx = std::abs((x - pFilmDiscrete.x) *
                        invFilterRadius.x * filterTableSize);
    ifx[x - p0.x] = std::min((int)std::floor(fx), filterTableSize - 1);
}
int *ify = ALLOCA(int, p1.y - p0.y);
for (int y = p0.y; y < p1.y; ++y) {
    Float fy = std::abs((y - pFilmDiscrete.y) *
                        invFilterRadius.y * filterTableSize);
    ify[y - p0.y] = std::min((int)std::floor(fy), filterTableSize - 1);
}
```

Now at each pixel, the *x* and *y* offsets into the filter table can be found for the pixel, leading to the offset into the array and thus the filter value.

⟨*Evaluate filter value at* (*x*, *y*) *pixel*⟩ ≡   491
```
int offset = ify[y - p0.y] * filterTableSize + ifx[x - p0.x];
Float filterWeight = filterTable[offset];
```

For each affected pixel, we can now add its weighted spectral contribution and the filter weight to the appropriate value in the pixels array.

⟨*Update pixel values with filtered sample contribution*⟩ ≡   491
```
FilmTilePixel &pixel = GetPixel(Point2i(x, y));
pixel.contribSum += L * sampleWeight * filterWeight;
pixel.filterWeightSum += filterWeight;
```

The GetPixel() method takes pixel coordinates with respect to the overall image and converts them to coordinates in the film tile before indexing into the pixels array. In addition to the version here, there is also a const variant of the method that returns a const FilmTilePixel &.

⟨*FilmTile Public Methods*⟩ +≡   489
```
FilmTilePixel &GetPixel(const Point2i &p) {
    int width = pixelBounds.pMax.x - pixelBounds.pMin.x;
    int offset = (p.x - pixelBounds.pMin.x) +
                 (p.y - pixelBounds.pMin.y) * width;
    return pixels[offset];
}
```

Rendering threads present FilmTiles to be merged into the image stored by Film using the MergeFilmTile() method. Its implementation starts by acquiring a lock to a mutex in order to ensure that multiple threads aren't simultaneously modifying image pixel values. Note that because MergeFilmTile() takes a std::unique_ptr to the tile, ownership of the tile's memory is transferred when this method is called. Calling code should therefore no longer attempt to add contributions to a tile after calling this method. Storage for the

FilmTile is freed automatically at the end of the execution of MergeFilmTile() when the tile parameter goes out of scope.

⟨*Film Method Definitions*⟩ +≡
```
void Film::MergeFilmTile(std::unique_ptr<FilmTile> tile) {
    std::lock_guard<std::mutex> lock(mutex);
    for (Point2i pixel : tile->GetPixelBounds()) {
        ⟨Merge pixel into Film::pixels 493⟩
    }
}
```

⟨*Film Private Data*⟩ +≡   484
```
std::mutex mutex;
```

When merging a tile's contributions in the final image, it's necessary for calling code to be able to find the bound of pixels that the tile has contributions for.

⟨*FilmTile Public Methods*⟩ +≡   489
```
Bounds2i GetPixelBounds() const { return pixelBounds; }
```

For each pixel in the tile, it's just necessary to merge its contribution into the values stored in Film::pixels.

⟨*Merge* pixel *into* Film::pixels⟩ ≡   493
```
const FilmTilePixel &tilePixel = tile->GetPixel(pixel);
Pixel &mergePixel = GetPixel(pixel);
Float xyz[3];
tilePixel.contribSum.ToXYZ(xyz);
for (int i = 0; i < 3; ++i)
    mergePixel.xyz[i] += xyz[i];
mergePixel.filterWeightSum += tilePixel.filterWeightSum;
```

⟨*Film Private Methods*⟩ ≡   484
```
Pixel &GetPixel(const Point2i &p) {
    int width = croppedPixelBounds.pMax.x - croppedPixelBounds.pMin.x;
    int offset = (p.x - croppedPixelBounds.pMin.x) +
        (p.y - croppedPixelBounds.pMin.y) * width;
    return pixels[offset];
}
```

It's also useful for some Integrator implementations to be able to just provide values for all of the pixels in the entire image all at once. The SetImage() method allows this mode of operation. Note that number of elements in the array pointed to by the image parameter should be equal to croppedPixelBounds.Area(). The implementation of SetImage() is a straightforward matter of copying the given values after converting them to XYZ color.

⟨*Film Method Definitions*⟩ +≡
```
void Film::SetImage(const Spectrum *img) const {
    int nPixels = croppedPixelBounds.Area();
    for (int i = 0; i < nPixels; ++i) {
        Pixel &p = pixels[i];
        img[i].ToXYZ(p.xyz);
        p.filterWeightSum = 1;
        p.splatXYZ[0] = p.splatXYZ[1] = p.splatXYZ[2] = 0;
    }
}
```

Some light transport algorithms (notably bidirectional path tracing, which is introduced in Section 16.3) require the ability to "splat" contributions to arbitrary pixels. Rather than computing the final pixel value as a weighted average of contributing splats, splats are simply summed. Generally, the more splats that are around a given pixel, the brighter the pixel will be. The Pixel::splatXYZ member variable is declared to be of AtomicFloat type, which allows multiple threads to concurrently update pixel values via the AddSplat() method without additional synchronization.

⟨*Film Method Definitions*⟩ +≡
```
void Film::AddSplat(const Point2f &p, const Spectrum &v) {
    if (!InsideExclusive((Point2i)p, croppedPixelBounds))
        return;
    Float xyz[3];
    v.ToXYZ(xyz);
    Pixel &pixel = GetPixel((Point2i)p);
    for (int i = 0; i < 3; ++i)
        pixel.splatXYZ[i].Add(xyz[i]);
}
```

7.9.3 IMAGE OUTPUT

After the main rendering loop exits, the Integrator's Render() method generally calls the Film::WriteImage() method, which directs the film to do the processing necessary to generate the final image and store it in a file. This method takes a scale factor that is applied to the samples provided to the AddSplat() method. (See the end of Section 16.4.5 for further discussion of this scale factor's use with the MLTIntegrator.)

⟨*Film Method Definitions*⟩ +≡
```
void Film::WriteImage(Float splatScale) {
    ⟨Convert image to RGB and compute final pixel values 495⟩
    ⟨Write RGB image 496⟩
}
```

This method starts by allocating an array to store the final RGB pixel values. It then loops over all of the pixels in the image to fill in this array.

⟨*Convert image to RGB and compute final pixel values*⟩ ≡   **494**
```
std::unique_ptr<Float[]> rgb(new Float[3 * croppedPixelBounds.Area()]);
int offset = 0;
for (Point2i p : croppedPixelBounds) {
    ⟨Convert pixel XYZ color to RGB 495⟩
    ⟨Normalize pixel with weight sum 495⟩
    ⟨Add splat value at pixel 496⟩
    ⟨Scale pixel value by scale 496⟩
    ++offset;
}
```

Given information about the response characteristics of the display device being used, the pixel values can be converted to device-dependent RGB values from the device-independent XYZ tristimulus values. This conversion is another change of spectral basis, where the new basis is determined by the spectral response curves of the red, green, and blue elements of the display device. Here, weights to convert from XYZ to the device RGB based on the sRGB primaries are used; sRGB is a standardized color space that is supported by virtually all 2015-era displays and printers.

⟨*Convert pixel XYZ color to RGB*⟩ ≡   **495**
```
Pixel &pixel = GetPixel(p);
XYZToRGB(pixel.xyz, &rgb[3 * offset]);
```

As the RGB output values are being initialized, their final values from the pixel filtering equation are computed by dividing each pixel sample value by Pixel::filterWeightSum. This conversion can lead to RGB values where some components are negative; these are *out-of-gamut* colors that can't be represented with the chosen display primaries. Various approaches have been suggested to deal with this issue, ranging from clamping to 0, offsetting all components to lie within the gamut, or even performing a global optimization based on all of the pixels in the image. Reconstructed pixels may also end up with negative values due to negative lobes in the reconstruction filter function. Color components are clamped to 0 here to handle both of these cases.

⟨*Normalize pixel with weight sum*⟩ ≡   **495**
```
Float filterWeightSum = pixel.filterWeightSum;
if (filterWeightSum != 0) {
    Float invWt = (Float)1 / filterWeightSum;
    rgb[3 * offset  ] = std::max((Float)0, rgb[3 * offset    ] * invWt);
    rgb[3 * offset+1] = std::max((Float)0, rgb[3 * offset + 1] * invWt);
    rgb[3 * offset+2] = std::max((Float)0, rgb[3 * offset + 2] * invWt);
}
```

It's also necessary to add in the contributions of splatted values for this pixel to the final value.

⟨*Add splat value at pixel*⟩ ≡   495
```
Float splatRGB[3];
Float splatXYZ[3] = { pixel.splatXYZ[0], pixel.splatXYZ[1],
                      pixel.splatXYZ[2] };
XYZToRGB(splatXYZ, splatRGB);
rgb[3 * offset     ] += splatScale * splatRGB[0];
rgb[3 * offset + 1] += splatScale * splatRGB[1];
rgb[3 * offset + 2] += splatScale * splatRGB[2];
```

The final pixel value is scaled by a user-supplied factor (or by 1, if none was specified); this can be useful when writing images to 8-bit integer image formats to make the most of the limited dynamic range.

⟨*Scale pixel value by* scale⟩ ≡   495
```
rgb[3 * offset     ] *= scale;
rgb[3 * offset + 1] *= scale;
rgb[3 * offset + 2] *= scale;
```

⟨*Film Private Data*⟩ +≡   484
```
const Float scale;
```

The WriteImage() function, defined in Section A.2, handles the details of writing the image to a file. If writing to an 8-bit integer format, it applies gamma correction to the floating-point pixel values according to the sRGB standard before converting them to integers. (See the "Further Reading" section at the end of Chapter 10 for more information about gamma correction.)

⟨*Write RGB image*⟩ ≡   494
```
::WriteImage(filename, &rgb[0], croppedPixelBounds, fullResolution);
```

FURTHER READING

Sampling Theory and Aliasing

One of the best books on signal processing, sampling, reconstruction, and the Fourier transform is Bracewell's *The Fourier Transform and Its Applications* (2000). Glassner's *Principles of Digital Image Synthesis* (1995) has a series of chapters on the theory and application of uniform and nonuniform sampling and reconstruction to computer graphics. For an extensive survey of the history of and techniques for interpolation of sampled data, including the sampling theorem, see Meijering (2002). Unser (2000) also surveyed recent developments in sampling and reconstruction theory including the recent move away from focusing purely on band-limited functions. For more recent work in this area, see Eldar and Michaeli (2009).

Crow (1977) first identified aliasing as a major source of artifacts in computer-generated images. Using nonuniform sampling to turn aliasing into noise was introduced by Cook (1986) and Dippé and Wold (1985); their work was based on experiments by Yellot (1983), who investigated the distribution of photoreceptors in the eyes of monkeys. Dippé and Wold also first introduced the pixel filtering equation to graphics and developed a Poisson sample pattern with a minimum distance between samples. Lee, Redner, and Uselton (1985) developed a technique for adaptive sampling based on statistical tests that computed images to a given error tolerance. Mitchell investigated sampling patterns for ray tracing extensively. His 1987 and 1991 SIGGRAPH papers on this topic have many key insights.

Heckbert (1990a) wrote an article that explains possible pitfalls when using floating-point coordinates for pixels and develops the conventions used here.

Mitchell (1996b) investigated how much better stratified sampling patterns are than random patterns in practice. In general, the smoother the function being sampled, the more effective they are. For very quickly changing functions (e.g., pixel regions overlapped by complex geometry), sophisticated stratified patterns perform no better than unstratified random patterns. Therefore, for scenes with complex variation in the high-dimensional image function, the advantages of fancy sampling schemes compared to a simple stratified pattern are reduced.

Chiu, Shirley, and Wang (1994) suggested a *multijittered* 2D sampling technique based on randomly shuffling the x and y coordinates of a canonical jittered pattern that combines the properties of stratified and Latin hypercube approaches. More recently, Kensler (2013) showed that using the same permutation for both dimensions with their method gives much better results than independent permutations; he showed that this approach gives lower discrepancy than the Sobol' pattern while also maintaining the perceptual advantages of turning aliasing into noise due to using jittered samples.

Lagae and Dutré (2008c) surveyed the state of the art in generating Poisson disk sample patterns and compared the quality of the point sets that various algorithms generated. Of recent work in this area, see in particular the papers by Jones (2005), Dunbar and Humphreys (2006), Wei (2008), Li et al. (2010), and Ebeida et al. (2011, 2012). We note, however, the importance of Mitchell's (1991) observations that an n-dimensional Poisson disk distribution is not the ideal one for general integration problems in graphics; while it's useful for the projection of the first two dimensions on the image plane to have the Poisson-disk property, it's important that the other dimensions be more widely distributed than the Poisson-disk quality alone guarantees. Recently, Reinert et al. (2015) proposed a construction for n-dimensional Poisson disk samples that retain their characteristic sample separation under projection onto lower dimensional subsets.

pbrt doesn't include samplers that perform adaptive sampling—taking more samples in parts of the image with large variation. Though adaptive sampling has been an active area of research, our experience with the resulting algorithms has been that while most work well in some cases, few are robust across a wide range of scenes. Since initial work in adaptive sampling by Lee et al. (1985), Kajiya (1986), and Purgathofer (1987), a number of sophisticated and effective adaptive sampling methods have been developed in recent years. Notable work includes Hachisuka et al. (2008a), who adaptively sampled in the 5D domain of image location, time, and lens position, rather than just in image location, and introduced a novel multidimensional filtering method; Shinya (1993) and Egan et al. (2009), who developed adaptive sampling and reconstruction methods focused on rendering motion blur; and Overbeck et al. (2009), who developed adaptive sampling algorithms based on wavelets for image reconstruction. Recently, Belcour et al. (2013)

computed covariance of 5D imaging (image, time, and lens defocus) and applied adaptive sampling and high-quality reconstruction and Moon et al. (2014) have applied local regression theory to this problem.

Kirk and Arvo (1991) identified a subtle problem with adaptive sampling algorithms: in short, if a set of samples is both used to decide if more samples should be taken and is also added to the image, the end result is *biased* and doesn't converge to the correct result in the limit. Mitchell (1987) observed that standard image reconstruction techniques fail in the presence of adaptive sampling: the contribution of a dense clump of samples in part of the filter's extent may incorrectly have a large effect on the final value purely due to the number of samples taken in that region. He described a multi-stage box filter that addresses this issue.

Compressed sensing is a recent approach to sampling where the required sampling rate depends on the sparsity of the signal, not its frequency content. Sen and Darabi (2011) applied compressed sensing to rendering, allowing them to generate high-quality images at very low sampling rates.

Low-Discrepancy Sampling

Shirley (1991) first introduced the use of discrepancy to evaluate the quality of sample patterns in computer graphics. This work was built upon by Mitchell (1992), Dobkin and Mitchell (1993), and Dobkin, Eppstein, and Mitchell (1996). One important observation in Dobkin et al.'s paper is that the box discrepancy measure used in this chapter and in other work that applies discrepancy to pixel sampling patterns isn't particularly appropriate for measuring a sampling pattern's accuracy at randomly oriented edges through a pixel and that a discrepancy measure based on random edges should be used instead. This observation explains why some theoretically good low-discrepancy patterns do not perform as well as expected when used for image sampling.

Mitchell's first paper on discrepancy introduced the idea of using deterministic low-discrepancy sequences for sampling, removing all randomness in the interest of lower discrepancy (Mitchell 1992). Such *quasi-random* sequences are the basis of quasi–Monte Carlo methods, which will be described in Chapter 13. The seminal book on quasi-random sampling and algorithms for generating low-discrepancy patterns was written by Niederreiter (1992). For a more recent treatment, see Dick and Pillichshammer's excellent book (2010).

Faure (1992) described a deterministic approach for computing permutations for scrambled radical inverses. The implementation of the ComputeRadicalInversePermutations() function in this chapter uses random permutations, which are simpler to implement and work nearly as well in practice. The algorithms used for computing sample indices within given pixels in Sections 7.4 and 7.7 were introduced by Grünschloß et al. (2012).

Keller and collaborators have investigated quasi-random sampling patterns for a variety of applications in graphics (Keller 1996, 1997, 2001). The (0, 2)-sequence sampling techniques used in the ZeroTwoSequenceSampler are based on a paper by Kollig and Keller (2002). (0, 2)-sequences are one instance of a general type of low-discrepancy sequence known as (t, s)-sequences and (t, m, s)-nets. These are discussed further by Niederreiter (1992) and Dick and Pillichshammer (2010). Some of Kollig and Keller's techniques are based on algorithms developed by Friedel and Keller (2000). Keller (2001, 2006) argued that because low-discrepancy patterns tend to converge more quickly than others, they are the most efficient sampling approach for generating high-quality imagery.

The `MaxMinDistSampler` in Section 7.6 is based on generator matrices found by Grünschloß and collaborators (2008, 2009). Sobol' (1967) introduced the family of generator matrices used in Section 7.7; Wächter's Ph.D. dissertation discusses high-performance implementation of base-2 generator matrix operations (Wächter 2008). The Sobol' generator matrices our implementation uses are improved versions derived by Joe and Kuo (2008).

Filtering and Reconstruction

Cook (1986) first introduced the Gaussian filter to graphics. Mitchell and Netravali (1988) investigated a family of filters using experiments with human observers to find the most effective ones; the `MitchellFilter` in this chapter is the one they chose as the best. Kajiya and Ullner (1981) investigated image filtering methods that account for the effect of the reconstruction characteristics of Gaussian falloff from pixels in CRTs, and, more recently, Betrisey et al. (2000) described Microsoft's ClearType technology for display of text on LCDs. Alim (2013) has recently applied reconstruction techniques that attempt to minimize the error between the reconstructed image and the original continuous image, even in the presence of discontinuities.

There has been quite a bit of research into reconstruction filters for image resampling applications. Although this application is not the same as reconstructing nonuniform samples for image synthesis, much of this experience is applicable. Turkowski (1990a) reported that the Lanczos windowed sinc filter gives the best results of a number of filters for image resampling. Meijering et al. (1999) tested a variety of filters for image resampling by applying a series of transformations to images such that if perfect resampling had been done the final image would be the same as the original. They also found that the Lanczos window performed well (as did a few others) and that truncating the sinc without a window gave some of the worst results. Other work in this area includes papers by Möller et al. (1997) and Machiraju and Yagel (1996).

Even with a fixed sampling rate, clever reconstruction algorithms can be useful to improve image quality. See, for example, Reshetov (2009), who used image gradients to find edges across multiple pixels to estimate pixel coverage for antialiasing and Guertin et al. (2014), who developed a filtering approach for motion blur.

Lee and Redner (1990) first suggested using a median filter, where the median of a set of samples is used to find each pixel's value, as a noise reduction technique. More recently, Lehtinen et al. (2011, 2012), Kalantari and Sen (2013), Rousselle et al. (2012, 2013), Delbracio et al. (2014), Munkberg et al. (2014), and Bauszat et al. (2015) have developed filtering techniques to reduce noise in images rendered using Monte Carlo algorithms. Kalantari et al. (2015) applied machine learning to the problem of finding effective denoising filters and demonstrated impressive results.

Jensen and Christensen (1995) observed that it can be more effective to separate out the contributions to pixel values based on the type of illumination they represent; low-frequency indirect illumination can be filtered differently from high-frequency direct illumination, thus reducing noise in the final image. They developed an effective filtering technique based on this observation. An improvement to this approach was developed by

MaxMinDistSampler 465
MitchellFilter 479

Keller and collaborators with the *discontinuity buffer* (Keller 1998; Wald et al. 2002). In addition to filtering slowly varying quantities like indirect illumination separately from more quickly varying quantities like surface reflectance, the discontinuity buffer uses geometric quantities like the surface normal at nearby pixels to determine whether their corresponding values can be reasonably included at the current pixel. Kontkanen et al. (2004) built on these approaches to build a filtering approach for indirect illumination when using the irradiance caching algorithm.

Lessig et al. (2014) proposed a general framework for constructing quadrature rules tailored to specific integration problems such as stochastic ray tracing, spherical harmonics projection, and scattering by surfaces. When targeting band-limited functions, their approach subsumes the frequency-space approach presented in this chapter. An excellent tutorial about the underlying theory of *reproducing kernel bases* is provided in the article's supplemental material.

Perceptual Issues

A number of different approaches have been developed for mapping out-of-gamut colors to the displayable range; see Rougeron and Péroche's survey article for discussion of this issue and references to various approaches (Rougeron and Péroche 1998). This topic was also covered by Hall (1989).

Tone reproduction—algorithms for displaying high-dynamic-range images on low-dynamic-range display devices—became an active area of research starting with the work of Tumblin and Rushmeier (1993). The survey article of Devlin et al. (2002) summarizes most of the work in this area through 2002, giving pointers to the original papers. See Reinhard et al.'s book (2010) on high dynamic range imaging, which includes comprehensive coverage of this topic through 2010. More recently, Reinhard et al. (2012) have developed tone reproduction algorithms that consider both accurate brightness and color reproduction together, also accounting for the display and viewing environment.

The human visual system generally causes the brain to perceive that surfaces have the color of the underlying surface, regardless of the illumination spectrum—for example, white paper is perceived to be white, even under the yellow-ish illumination of an incandescent lightbulb. A number of methods have been developed to process photographs to perform *white balancing* to eliminate the tinge of light source colors; see Gijsenij et al. (2011) for a survey. White balancing is challenging, since the only information available to white balancing algorithms is the final pixel values. In a renderer, the problem is easier, as information is available directly about the light sources and the surface reflection properties; Wilkie and Weidlich (2009) developed an efficient method to perform accurate white balancing in a renderer with limited computational overhead.

For background information on properties of the human visual system, Wandell's book on vision is an excellent starting point (Wandell 1995). Ferwerda (2001) presented an overview of the human visual system for applications in graphics, and Malacara (2002) gave a concise overview of color theory and basic properties of how the human visual system processes color.

EXERCISES

⊘ 7.1 It's possible to implement a specialized version of ScrambledRadicalInverse() for base 2, along the lines of the implementation in RadicalInverse(). Determine how to map the random digit permutation to a single bitwise operation and implement this approach. Compare the values computed to those generated by the current implementation to ensure your method is correct and measure how much faster yours is by writing a small benchmark program.

⊘ 7.2 Currently, the third through fifth dimensions of each sample vector are consumed for time and lens samples, even though not all scenes need these sample values. Because lower dimensions in the sample vector are often better distributed than later ones, this can cause an unnecessary reduction in image quality.

Modify pbrt so that the camera can report its sample requirements and then use this information when samples are requested to initialize CameraSamples. Don't forget to update the value of GlobalSampler::arrayStartDim. Render images with the DirectLightingIntegrator and compare results to the current implementation. Do you see an improvement? How do results differ with different samplers? How do you explain any differences you see across samplers?

⊘ 7.3 Implement the improved multi-jittered sampling method introduced by Kensler (2013) as a new Sampler in pbrt. Compare image quality and rendering time to rendering with the StratifiedSampler, the HaltonSampler, and the SobolSampler.

⊘ 7.4 Keller (2004) and Dammertz and Keller (2008b) described the application of *rank-1 lattices* to image synthesis. Rank-1 lattices are another way of efficiently generating high-quality low-discrepancy sequences of sample points. Read their papers and implement a Sampler based on this approach. Compare results to the other samplers in pbrt.

⊘ 7.5 With pbrt's current FilmTile implementation, the pixel values in an image may change by small amounts if an image is rerendered, due to threads finishing tiles in different orders over subsequent runs. For example, a pixel that had a final value that came from samples from three different image sampling tiles, $v_1 + v_2 + v_3$, may sometimes have its value computed as $(v_1 + v_2) + v_3$ and sometimes as $v_1 + (v_2 + v_3)$. Due to floating-point round-off, these two values may be different. While these differences aren't normally a problem, they wreak havoc with automated testing scripts that might want to verify that a believed-to-be-innocuous change to the system didn't actually cause any differences in rendered images.

Modify Film::MergeFilmTile() so that it merges tiles in a consistent order so that final pixel values don't suffer from this inconsistency. (For example, your implementation might buffer up FilmTiles and only merge a tile when all neighboring tiles above and to its left have already been merged.) Ensure that your implementation doesn't introduce any meaningful performance regression. Measure the additional memory usage due to longer lived FilmTiles; how does it relate to total memory usage?

● 7.6   As mentioned in Section 7.9, the Film::AddSplat() method doesn't use a filter function but instead just splats the sample to the single pixel it's closest to, effectively using a box filter. In order to apply an arbitrary filter, the filter must be normalized so that it integrates to one over its domain; this constraint isn't currently required of Filters by pbrt. Modify the computation of filterTable in the Film constructor so that the tabulated function is normalized. (Don't forget that the table only stores one-quarter of the function's extent when computing the normalization factor.) Then modify the implementation of the AddSplat() method to use this filter. Investigate the execution time and image quality differences that result.

● 7.7   Modify pbrt to create images where the value stored in the Film for each camera ray is proportional to the time taken to compute the ray's radiance. (A 1-pixel-wide box filter is probably the most useful filter for this exercise.) Render images of a variety of scenes with this technique. What insight about the system's performance do the resulting images bring? You may need to scale pixel values or take their logarithm to see meaningful variation when you view them.

● 7.8   One of the advantages of the linearity assumption in radiometry is that the final image of a scene is the same as the sum of individual images that account for each light source's contribution (assuming a floating-point image file format is used that doesn't clip pixel radiance values). An implication of this property is that if a renderer creates a separate image for each light source, it is possible to write interactive lighting design tools that make it possible to quickly see the effects of scaling the contributions of individual lights in the scene without needing to rerender it from scratch. Instead, a light's individual image can be scaled and the final image regenerated by summing all of the light images again. (This technique was first applied for opera lighting design by Dorsey, Sillion, and Greenberg (1991).) Modify pbrt to output a separate image for each of the lights in the scene, and write an interactive lighting design tool that uses them in this manner.

● 7.9   Mitchell and Netravali (1988) noted that there is a family of reconstruction filters that use both the value of a function and its derivative at the point to do substantially better reconstruction than if just the value of the function is known. Furthermore, they report that they have derived closed-form expressions for the screen space derivatives of Lambertian and Phong reflection models, although they do not include these expressions in their paper. Investigate derivative-based reconstruction, and extend pbrt to support this technique. Because it will likely be difficult to derive expressions for the screen space derivatives for general shapes and BSDF models, investigate approximations based on finite differencing. Techniques built on the ideas behind the ray differentials of Section 10.1 may be fruitful for this effort.

⊕ **7.10** Image-based rendering is the general name for a set of techniques that use one or more images of a scene to synthesize new images from viewpoints different from the original ones. One such approach is light field rendering, where a set of images from a densely spaced set of positions is used (Levoy and Hanrahan 1996; Gortler et al. 1996). Read these two papers on light fields, and modify pbrt to directly generate light fields of scenes, without requiring that the renderer be run multiple times, once for each camera position. It will probably be necessary to write a specialized Camera, Sampler, and Film to do this. Also, write an interactive light field viewer that loads light fields generated by your implementation and generates new views of the scene.

⊕ **7.11** Rather than just storing spectral values in an image, it's often useful to store additional information about the objects in the scene that were visible at each pixel. See, for example, the SIGGRAPH papers by Perlin (1985a) and Saito and Takahashi (1990). For example, if the 3D position, surface normal, and BRDF of the object at each pixel are stored, then the scene can be efficiently rerendered after moving the light sources (Gershbein and Hanrahan 2000). Alternatively, if each sample stores information about all of the objects visible along its camera ray, rather than just the first one, new images from shifted viewpoints can be rerendered (Shade et al. 1998). Investigate representations for deep frame buffers and algorithms that use them; extend pbrt to support the creation of images like these, and develop tools that operate on them.

⊕ **7.12** Implement a median filter for image reconstruction: for each pixel, store the median of all of the samples within a filter extent around it. This task is complicated by the fact that filters in the current Film implementation must be *linear*—the value of the filter function is determined solely by the position of the sample with respect to the pixel position, and the value of the sample has no impact on the value of the filter function. Because the implementation assumes that filters are linear, and because it doesn't store sample values after adding their contribution to the image, implementing the median filter will require generalizing the Film or developing a new Film implementation.

Render images using integrators like the PathIntegrator that have objectionable image noise with regular image filters. How successful is the median filter at reducing noise? Are there visual shortcomings to using the median filter? Can you implement this approach without needing to store all of the image sample values before computing final pixel values?

⊕ **7.13** An alternative to the median filter is to discard the sample with the lowest contribution and the sample with the largest contribution in a pixel's filter region. This approach uses more of the information gathered during sampling. Implement this approach and compare the results to the median filter.

⊕ **7.14** Implement the discontinuity buffer, as described by Keller and collaborators (Keller 1998; Wald et al. 2002). You will probably need to modify the interface to the Integrators so that they can separately return direct and indirect illumination contributions and then pass these separately to the Film. Render images showing its effectiveness when rendering images with indirect illumination.

⊜ 7.15   Implement one of the recent adaptive sampling and reconstruction techniques
          such as the ones described by Hachisuka et al. (2008a), Egan et al. (2009),
          Overbeck et al. (2009), or Moon et al. (2014). How much more efficiently
          do they generate images of equal quality than just uniformly sampling at a
          high rate? How do they affect running time for simple scenes where adaptive
          sampling isn't needed?

⊜ 7.16   Investigate current research in tone reproduction algorithms (see, e.g., Rein-
          hard et al. 2010; 2012), and implement one or more of these algorithms. Use
          your implementation with a number of scenes rendered by pbrt, and discuss
          the improvements you see compared to viewing the images without tone re-
          production.

CHAPTER EIGHT

⊘⊠ REFLECTION MODELS

This chapter defines a set of classes for describing the way that light scatters at surfaces. Recall that in Section 5.6.1 we introduced the bidirectional reflectance distribution function (BRDF) abstraction to describe light reflection at a surface, the BTDF to describe transmission at a surface, and the BSDF to encompass both of these effects. In this chapter, we will start by defining a generic interface to these surface reflection and transmission functions.

Scattering from many surfaces is often best described as a spatially varying mixture of multiple BRDFs and BTDFs; in Chapter 9, we will introduce a BSDF object that combines multiple BRDFs and BTDFs to represent overall scattering from the surface. The current chapter sidesteps the issue of reflection and transmission properties that vary over the surface; the texture classes of Chapter 10 will address that problem. BRDFs and BTDFs explicitly only model scattering from light that enters and exits a surface at a single point. For surfaces that exhibit meaningful subsurface light transport, we will introduce the BSSRDF class, which models subsurface scattering, in Section 11.4 after some of the related theory is introduced in Chapter 11.

Surface reflection models come from a number of sources:

- *Measured data:* Reflection distribution properties of many real-world surfaces have been measured in laboratories. Such data may be used directly in tabular form or to compute coefficients for a set of basis functions.
- *Phenomenological models:* Equations that attempt to describe the qualitative properties of real-world surfaces can be remarkably effective at mimicking them. These types of BSDFs can be particularly easy to use, since they tend to have intuitive parameters that modify their behavior (e.g., "roughness").
- *Simulation:* Sometimes, low-level information is known about the composition of a surface. For example, we might know that a paint is comprised of colored particles of some average size suspended in a medium or that a particular fabric is comprised

Physically Based Rendering: From Theory To Implementation.
http://dx.doi.org/10.1016/B978-0-12-800645-0.50008-7

of two types of threads, each with known reflectance properties. In these cases, light scattering from the microgeometry can be simulated to generate reflection data. This simulation can be done either during rendering or as a preprocess, after which it may be fit to a set of basis functions for use during rendering.

- *Physical (wave) optics:* Some reflection models have been derived using a detailed model of light, treating it as a wave and computing the solution to Maxwell's equations to find how it scatters from a surface with known properties. These models tend to be computationally expensive, however, and usually aren't appreciably more accurate than models based on geometric optics are for rendering applications.

- *Geometric optics:* As with simulation approaches, if the surface's low-level scattering and geometric properties are known, then closed-form reflection models can sometimes be derived directly from these descriptions. Geometric optics makes modeling light's interaction with the surface more tractable, since complex wave effects like polarization can be ignored.

The "Further Reading" section at the end of this chapter gives pointers to a variety of such reflection models.

Before we define the relevant interfaces, a brief review of how they fit into the overall system is in order. If a SamplerIntegrator is used, the SamplerIntegrator::Li() method implementation is called for each ray. After finding the closest intersection with a geometric primitive, it calls the surface shader that is associated with the primitive. The surface shader is implemented as a method of Material subclasses and is responsible for deciding what the BSDF is at a particular point on the surface; it returns a BSDF object that holds BRDFs and BTDFs that it has allocated and initialized to represent scattering at that point. The integrator then uses the BSDF to compute the scattered light at the point, based on the incoming illumination at the point. (The process where a BDPTIntegrator, MLTIntegrator, or SPPMIntegrator is used rather than a SamplerIntegrator is broadly similar.)

Basic Terminology

In order to be able to compare the visual appearance of different reflection models, we will introduce some basic terminology for describing reflection from surfaces.

Reflection from surfaces can be split into four broad categories: *diffuse, glossy specular, perfect specular*, and *retro-reflective* (Figure 8.1). Most real surfaces exhibit reflection that is a mixture of these four types. Diffuse surfaces scatter light equally in all directions. Although a perfectly diffuse surface isn't physically realizable, examples of near-diffuse surfaces include dull chalkboards and matte paint. Glossy specular surfaces such as plastic or high-gloss paint scatter light preferentially in a set of reflected directions—they show blurry reflections of other objects. Perfect specular surfaces scatter incident light in a single outgoing direction. Mirrors and glass are examples of perfect specular surfaces. Finally, retro-reflective surfaces like velvet or the Earth's moon scatter light primarily back along the incident direction. Images throughout this chapter will show the differences between these various types of reflection when used in rendered scenes.

Given a particular category of reflection, the reflectance distribution function may be *isotropic* or *anisotropic*. Most objects are isotropic: if you choose a point on the surface

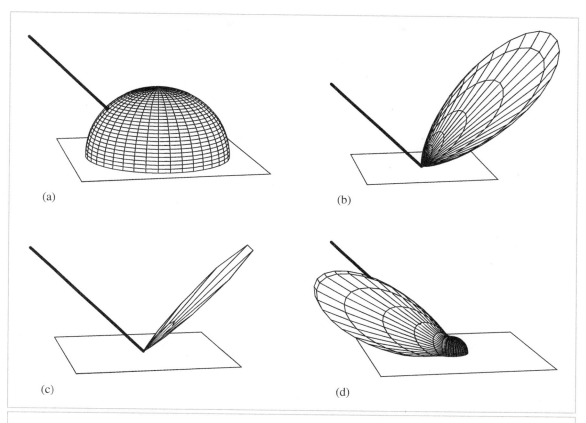

Figure 8.1: Reflection from a surface can be generally categorized by the distribution of reflected light from an incident direction (heavy lines): (a) diffuse, (b) glossy specular, (c) perfect specular, and (d) retro-reflective distributions.

and rotate it around its normal axis at that point, the distribution of light reflected doesn't change. In contrast, anisotropic materials reflect different amounts of light as you rotate them in this way. Examples of anisotropic surfaces include brushed metal, many types of cloth, and compact disks.

Geometric Setting

Reflection computations in pbrt are evaluated in a reflection coordinate system where the two tangent vectors and the normal vector at the point being shaded are aligned with the x, y, and z axes, respectively (Figure 8.2). All direction vectors passed to and returned from the BRDF and BTDF routines will be defined with respect to this coordinate system. It is important to understand this coordinate system in order to understand the BRDF and BTDF implementations in this chapter.

The shading coordinate system also gives a frame for expressing directions in spherical coordinates (θ, ϕ); the angle θ is measured from the given direction to the z axis, and ϕ is the angle formed with the x axis after projection of the direction onto the xy plane.

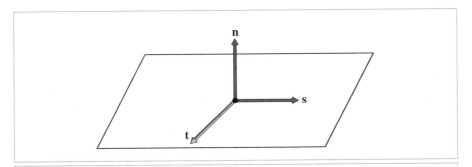

Figure 8.2: The Basic BSDF Interface Setting. The shading coordinate system is defined by the orthonormal basis vectors $(\mathbf{s}, \mathbf{t}, \mathbf{n})$. We will orient these vectors such that they lie along the x, y, and z axes in this coordinate system. Direction vectors ω in world space are transformed into the shading coordinate system before any of the BRDF or BTDF methods are called.

Given a direction vector ω in this coordinate system, it is easy to compute quantities like the cosine of the angle that it forms with the normal direction:

$$\cos\theta = (\mathbf{n} \cdot \omega) = ((0, 0, 1) \cdot \omega) = \omega_z.$$

We will provide utility functions to compute this value and some useful variations; their use helps clarify BRDF and BTDF implementations.

⟨*BSDF Inline Functions*⟩ ≡
```
inline Float CosTheta(const Vector3f &w) { return w.z; }
inline Float Cos2Theta(const Vector3f &w) { return w.z * w.z; }
inline Float AbsCosTheta(const Vector3f &w) { return std::abs(w.z); }
```

The value of $\sin^2\theta$ can be computed using the trigonometric identity $\sin^2\theta + \cos^2\theta = 1$, though we need to be careful to avoid taking the square root of a negative number in the rare case that 1 - Cos2Theta(w) is less than zero due to floating-point round-off error.

⟨*BSDF Inline Functions*⟩ +≡
```
inline Float Sin2Theta(const Vector3f &w) {
    return std::max((Float)0, (Float)1 - Cos2Theta(w));
}
inline Float SinTheta(const Vector3f &w) {
    return std::sqrt(Sin2Theta(w));
}
```

The tangent of the angle θ can be computed via the identity $\tan\theta = \sin\theta/\cos\theta$.

⟨*BSDF Inline Functions*⟩ +≡
```
inline Float TanTheta(const Vector3f &w) {
    return SinTheta(w) / CosTheta(w);
}
inline Float Tan2Theta(const Vector3f &w) {
    return Sin2Theta(w) / Cos2Theta(w);
}
```

Cos2Theta() 510
Float 1062
Vector3f 60

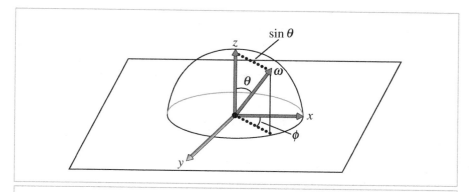

Figure 8.3: The values of $\sin \phi$ and $\cos \phi$ can be computed using the circular coordinate equations $x = r \cos \phi$ and $y = r \sin \phi$, where r, the length of the dashed line, is equal to $\sin \theta$.

We can similarly use the shading coordinate system to simplify the calculations for the sine and cosine of the ϕ angle (Figure 8.3). In the plane of the point being shaded, the vector ω has coordinates (x, y), which are given by $r \cos \phi$ and $r \sin \phi$, respectively. The radius r is $\sin \theta$, so

$$\cos \phi = \frac{x}{r} = \frac{x}{\sin \theta}$$
$$\sin \phi = \frac{y}{r} = \frac{y}{\sin \theta}.$$

⟨*BSDF Inline Functions*⟩ +≡
```
inline Float CosPhi(const Vector3f &w) {
    Float sinTheta = SinTheta(w);
    return (sinTheta == 0) ? 1 : Clamp(w.x / sinTheta, -1, 1);
}
inline Float SinPhi(const Vector3f &w) {
    Float sinTheta = SinTheta(w);
    return (sinTheta == 0) ? 0 : Clamp(w.y / sinTheta, -1, 1);
}
```

⟨*BSDF Inline Functions*⟩ +≡
```
inline Float Cos2Phi(const Vector3f &w) {
    return CosPhi(w) * CosPhi(w);
}
inline Float Sin2Phi(const Vector3f &w) {
    return SinPhi(w) * SinPhi(w);
}
```

The cosine of the angle $\Delta\phi$ between two vectors in the shading coordinate system can be found by zeroing the z coordinate of the two vectors to get 2D vectors and then normalizing them. The dot product of these two vectors gives the cosine of the angle between them. The implementation below rearranges the terms a bit for efficiency so that only a single square root operation needs to be performed.

⟨*BSDF Inline Functions*⟩ +≡
```
inline Float CosDPhi(const Vector3f &wa, const Vector3f &wb) {
    return Clamp((wa.x * wb.x + wa.y * wb.y) /
                 std::sqrt((wa.x * wa.x + wa.y * wa.y) *
                           (wb.x * wb.x + wb.y * wb.y)), -1, 1);
}
```

There are important conventions and implementation details to keep in mind when reading the code in this chapter and when adding BRDFs and BTDFs to pbrt:

- The incident light direction ω_i and the outgoing viewing direction ω_o will both be normalized and outward facing after being transformed into the local coordinate system at the surface.
- By convention in pbrt, the surface normal **n** always points to the "outside" of the object, which makes it easy to determine if light is entering or exiting transmissive objects: if the incident light direction ω_i is in the same hemisphere as **n**, then light is entering; otherwise, it is exiting. Therefore, one detail to keep in mind is that the normal may be on the opposite side of the surface than one or both of the ω_i and ω_o direction vectors. Unlike many other renderers, pbrt does not flip the normal to lie on the same side as ω_o.
- The local coordinate system used for shading may not be exactly the same as the coordinate system returned by the Shape::Intersect() routines from Chapter 3; they can be modified between intersection and shading to achieve effects like bump mapping. See Chapter 9 for examples of this kind of modification.
- Finally, BRDF and BTDF implementations should not concern themselves with whether ω_i and ω_o lie in the same hemisphere. For example, although a reflective BRDF should in principle detect if the incident direction is above the surface and the outgoing direction is below and always return no reflection in this case, here we will expect the reflection function to instead compute and return the amount of light reflected using the appropriate formulas for their reflection model, ignoring the detail that they are not in the same hemisphere. Higher level code in pbrt will ensure that only reflective or transmissive scattering routines are evaluated as appropriate. The value of this convention will be explained in Section 9.1.

8.1 BASIC INTERFACE

We will first define the interface for the individual BRDF and BTDF functions. BRDFs and BTDFs share a common base class, BxDF. Because both have the exact same interface, sharing the same base class reduces repeated code and allows some parts of the system to work with BxDFs generically without distinguishing between BRDFs and BTDFs.

BxDF 513
Clamp() 1062
Float 1062
Shape::Intersect() 129
Vector3f 60

⟨*BxDF Declarations*⟩ ≡
```
class BxDF {
public:
    ⟨BxDF Interface 513⟩
    ⟨BxDF Public Data 513⟩
};
```

The BSDF class, which will be introduced in Section 9.1, holds a collection of BxDF objects that together describe the scattering at a point on a surface. Although we are hiding the implementation details of the BxDF behind a common interface for reflective and transmissive materials, some of the light transport algorithms in Chapters 14 through 16 will need to distinguish between these two types. Therefore, all BxDFs have a BxDF::type member that holds flags from BxDFType. For each BxDF, the flags should have at least one of BSDF_REFLECTION or BSDF_TRANSMISSION set and exactly one of the diffuse, glossy, and specular flags. Note that there is no retro-reflective flag; retro-reflection is treated as glossy reflection in this categorization.

⟨*BSDF Declarations*⟩ ≡
```
enum BxDFType {
    BSDF_REFLECTION   = 1 << 0,
    BSDF_TRANSMISSION = 1 << 1,
    BSDF_DIFFUSE      = 1 << 2,
    BSDF_GLOSSY       = 1 << 3,
    BSDF_SPECULAR     = 1 << 4,
    BSDF_ALL          = BSDF_DIFFUSE | BSDF_GLOSSY | BSDF_SPECULAR |
                        BSDF_REFLECTION | BSDF_TRANSMISSION,
};
```

⟨*BxDF Interface*⟩ ≡   513
```
BxDF(BxDFType type) : type(type) { }
```

⟨*BxDF Public Data*⟩ ≡   513
```
const BxDFType type;
```

The MatchesFlags() utility method determines if the BxDF matches the user-supplied type flags:

⟨*BxDF Interface*⟩ +≡   513
```
bool MatchesFlags(BxDFType t) const {
    return (type & t) == type;
}
```

The key method that BxDFs provide is BxDF::f(). It returns the value of the distribution function for the given pair of directions. This interface implicitly assumes that light in different wavelengths is decoupled—energy at one wavelength will not be reflected at a different wavelength. By making this assumption, the effect of the reflection function can be represented directly with a Spectrum. Supporting fluorescent materials where this assumption is not true would require that this method return an $n \times n$ matrix that encoded the transfer of energy between spectral samples (where n is the number of samples in the Spectrum representation).

⟨*BxDF Interface*⟩ +≡   513
```
virtual Spectrum f(const Vector3f &wo, const Vector3f &wi) const = 0;
```

Not all BxDFs can be evaluated with the f() method. For example, perfectly specular objects like a mirror, glass, or water only scatter light from a single incident direction into a single outgoing direction. Such BxDFs are best described with delta distributions that are zero except for the single direction where light is scattered. These BxDFs need special handling in pbrt, so we will also provide the method BxDF::Sample_f(). This method is used both for handling scattering that is described by delta distributions as well as for randomly sampling directions from BxDFs that scatter light along multiple directions; this second application will be explained in the discussion of Monte Carlo BSDF sampling in Section 14.1.

BxDF::Sample_f() computes the direction of incident light ω_i given an outgoing direction ω_o and returns the value of the BxDF for the pair of directions. For delta distributions, it is necessary for the BxDF to choose the incident light direction in this way, since the caller has no chance of generating the appropriate ω_i direction.[1] The sample and pdf parameters aren't needed for delta distribution BxDFs, so they will be explained later, in Section 14.1, when we provide implementations of this method for nonspecular reflection functions.

⟨*BxDF Interface*⟩ +≡   513
```
virtual Spectrum Sample_f(const Vector3f &wo, Vector3f *wi,
    const Point2f &sample, Float *pdf,
    BxDFType *sampledType = nullptr) const;
```

8.1.1 REFLECTANCE

It can be useful to take the aggregate behavior of the 4D BRDF or BTDF, defined as a function over pairs of directions, and reduce it to a 2D function over a single direction, or even to a constant value that describes its overall scattering behavior.

The *hemispherical-directional reflectance* is a 2D function that gives the total reflection in a given direction due to constant illumination over the hemisphere, or, equivalently, total reflection over the hemisphere due to light from a given direction.[2] It is defined as

$$\rho_{hd}(\omega_o) = \int_{\mathcal{H}^2(n)} f_r(p, \omega_o, \omega_i) \, |\cos \theta_i| \, d\omega_i. \qquad [8.1]$$

The BxDF::rho() method computes the reflectance function ρ_{hd}. Some BxDFs can compute this value in closed form, although most use Monte Carlo integration to compute an approximation to it. For those BxDFs, the nSamples and samples parameters are used by the implementation of the Monte Carlo algorithm; they are explained in Section 14.1.5.

---

1   Delta distributions in reflection functions have some additional subtle implications for light transport algorithms. Sections 14.1.3 and 14.4.5 describe the issues in detail.

2   The fact that these two quantities are equal is due to the reciprocity of reflection functions. BTDFs are generally not reciprocal; see Section 16.1.3.

⟨*BxDF Interface*⟩ +≡   513
```
virtual Spectrum rho(const Vector3f &wo, int nSamples,
                     const Point2f *samples) const;
```

The *hemispherical-hemispherical reflectance* of a surface, denoted by ρ_{hh}, is a spectral value that gives the fraction of incident light reflected by a surface when the incident light is the same from all directions. It is

$$\rho_{hh} = \frac{1}{\pi} \int_{\mathcal{H}^2(n)} \int_{\mathcal{H}^2(n)} f_r(p, \omega_o, \omega_i) \, |\cos \theta_o \cos \theta_i| \, d\omega_o \, d\omega_i.$$

The BxDF::rho() method computes ρ_{hh} if no direction ω_o is provided. The remaining parameters are again used when computing a Monte Carlo estimate of the value of ρ_{hh}, if needed.

⟨*BxDF Interface*⟩ +≡   513
```
virtual Spectrum rho(int nSamples, const Point2f *samples1,
                     const Point2f *samples2) const;
```

8.1.2 BxDF SCALING ADAPTER

It is also useful to take a given BxDF and scale its contribution with a Spectrum value. The ScaledBxDF wrapper holds a BxDF * and a Spectrum and implements this functionality. This class is used by the MixMaterial (defined in Section 9.2.3), which creates BSDFs based on a weighted combination of two other materials.

⟨*BxDF Declarations*⟩ +≡
```
class ScaledBxDF : public BxDF {
public:
    ⟨ScaledBxDF Public Methods 515⟩
private:
    BxDF *bxdf;
    Spectrum scale;
};
```

⟨*ScaledBxDF Public Methods*⟩ ≡   515
```
ScaledBxDF(BxDF *bxdf, const Spectrum &scale)
    : BxDF(BxDFType(bxdf->type)), bxdf(bxdf), scale(scale) {
}
```

The implementations of the ScaledBxDF methods are straightforward; we'll only include f() here.

⟨*BxDF Method Definitions*⟩ ≡
```
Spectrum ScaledBxDF::f(const Vector3f &wo, const Vector3f &wi) const {
    return scale * bxdf->f(wo, wi);
}
```

8.2 SPECULAR REFLECTION AND TRANSMISSION

The behavior of light at perfectly smooth surfaces is relatively easy to characterize analytically using both the physical and geometric optics models. These surfaces exhibit perfect specular reflection and transmission of incident light; for a given ω_i direction, all light is scattered in a single outgoing direction ω_o. For specular reflection, this direction is the outgoing direction that makes the same angle with the normal as the incoming direction:

$$\theta_i = \theta_o,$$

and where $\phi_o = \phi_i + \pi$. For transmission, we again have $\phi_o = \phi_i + \pi$, and the outgoing direction θ_t is given by *Snell's law*, which relates the angle θ_t between the transmitted direction and the surface normal $\mathbf{n}$ to the angle θ_i between the incident ray and the surface normal $\mathbf{n}$. (One of the exercises at the end of this chapter is to derive Snell's law using Fermat's principle from optics.) Snell's law is based on the *index of refraction* for the medium that the incident ray is in and the index of refraction for the medium it is entering. The index of refraction describes how much more slowly light travels in a particular medium than in a vacuum. We will use the Greek letter η, pronounced "eta," to denote the index of refraction. Snell's law is

$$\eta_i \, \sin \theta_i = \eta_t \, \sin \theta_t. \qquad\qquad [8.2]$$

In general, the index of refraction varies with the wavelength of light. Thus, incident light generally scatters in multiple directions at the boundary between two different media, an effect known as *dispersion*. This effect can be seen when incident white light is split into spectral components by a prism. Common practice in graphics is to ignore this wavelength dependence, since this effect is generally not crucial for visual accuracy and ignoring it simplifies light transport calculations substantially. Alternatively, the paths of multiple beams of light (e.g., at a series of discrete wavelengths) can be tracked through the environment in which a dispersive object is found. The "Further Reading" section at the end of Chapter 14 has pointers to more information on this topic.

Figure 8.4 shows the effect of perfect specular reflection and transmission.

8.2.1 FRESNEL REFLECTANCE

In addition to the reflected and transmitted directions, it is also necessary to compute the fraction of incoming light that is reflected or transmitted. For physically accurate reflection or refraction, these terms are directionally dependent and cannot be captured by constant per-surface scaling amounts. The *Fresnel equations* describe the amount of light reflected from a surface; they are the solution to Maxwell's equations at smooth surfaces.

Given the index of refraction and the angle which the incident ray makes with the surface normal, the Fresnel equations specify the material's corresponding reflectance for two different polarization states of the incident illumination. Because the visual effect of polarization is limited in most environments, in pbrt we will make the common assumption that light is unpolarized; that is, it is randomly oriented with respect to the light wave. With this simplifying assumption, the Fresnel reflectance is the average of the squares of the parallel and perpendicular polarization terms.

(a)   (b)

Figure 8.4: Dragon model rendered with (a) perfect specular reflection and (b) perfect specular refraction. Image (b) excludes the effects of external and internal reflection; the resulting energy loss produces conspicuous dark regions. *(Model courtesy of Christian Schüller.)*

At this point, it is necessary to draw a distinction among several important classes of materials:

1. The first class is *dielectrics*, which are materials that don't conduct electricity. They have real-valued indices of refraction (usually in the range 1-3) and transmit[3] a portion of the incident illumination. Examples of dielectrics are glass, mineral oil, water, and air.

2. The second class consists of *conductors* such as metals. Valence electrons can freely move within the their atomic lattice, allowing electric currents to flow from one place to another. This fundamental atomic property translates into a profoundly different behavior when a conductor is subjected to electromagnetic radiation such as visible light: the material is opaque and reflects back a significant portion of the illumination.

   A portion of the light is also transmitted into the interior of the conductor, where it is rapidly absorbed: total absorption typically occurs within the top 0.1 μm of the material, hence only extremely thin metal films are capable of transmitting appreciable amounts of light. We ignore this effect in pbrt and only model the reflection component of conductors.

   In contrast to dielectrics, conductors have a complex-valued index of refraction $\bar{\eta} = \eta + ik$.

3. Semiconductors such as silicon or germanium are the third class though we will not consider them in this book.

---

3   Note that a dielectric can be filled with particles that absorb most or all of the transmitted light (e.g., petroleum). A dielectric such as water can also be turned into an electrolyte solution by adding ions that cause it to conduct electricity. Both of these aspects are unrelated to a material's intrinsic classification as a dielectric or conductor.

Table 8.1: Indices of refraction for a variety of objects, giving the ratio of the speed of light in a vacuum to the speed of light in the medium. These are generally wavelength-dependent quantities; these values are averages over the visible wavelengths.

Medium	Index of refraction η
Vacuum	1.0
Air at sea level	1.00029
Ice	1.31
Water (20°C)	1.333
Fused quartz	1.46
Glass	1.5–1.6
Sapphire	1.77
Diamond	2.42

Both conductors and dielectrics are governed by the same set of Fresnel equations. Despite this, we prefer to create a special evaluation function for dielectrics to benefit from the particularly simple form that these equations take on when the indices of refraction are guaranteed to be real-valued.

To compute the Fresnel reflectance at the interface of two dielectric media, we need to know the indices of refraction for the two media. Table 8.1 has the indices of refraction for a number of dielectric materials. The Fresnel reflectance formulae for dielectrics are

$$r_\parallel = \frac{\eta_t \cos \theta_i - \eta_i \cos \theta_t}{\eta_t \cos \theta_i + \eta_i \cos \theta_t},$$

$$r_\perp = \frac{\eta_i \cos \theta_i - \eta_t \cos \theta_t}{\eta_i \cos \theta_i + \eta_t \cos \theta_t},$$

where $r_\parallel$ is the Fresnel reflectance for parallel polarized light and $r_\perp$ is the reflectance for perpendicular polarized light, η_i and η_t are the indices of refraction for the incident and transmitted media, and ω_i and ω_t are the incident and transmitted directions. ω_t can be computed with Snell's law (see Section 8.2.3).

The cosine terms should all be greater than or equal to zero; for the purposes of computing these values, the geometric normal should be flipped to be on the same side as ω_i and ω_t when computing $\cos \theta_i$ and $\cos_t$, respectively.

For unpolarized light, the Fresnel reflectance is

$$F_r = \frac{1}{2}(r_\parallel^2 + r_\perp^2).$$

Due to conservation of energy, the energy transmitted by a dielectric is $1 - F_r$.

The function FrDielectric() computes the Fresnel reflection formula for dielectric materials and unpolarized light. The quantity $\cos \theta_i$ is passed in with the parameter cosThetaI.

FrDielectric() 519

⟨BxDF Utility Functions⟩ ≡

```
Float FrDielectric(Float cosThetaI, Float etaI, Float etaT) {
    cosThetaI = Clamp(cosThetaI, -1, 1);
    ⟨Potentially swap indices of refraction 519⟩
    ⟨Compute cosThetaT using Snell's law 520⟩
    Float Rparl = ((etaT * cosThetaI) - (etaI * cosThetaT)) /
                  ((etaT * cosThetaI) + (etaI * cosThetaT));
    Float Rperp = ((etaI * cosThetaI) - (etaT * cosThetaT)) /
                  ((etaI * cosThetaI) + (etaT * cosThetaT));
    return (Rparl * Rparl + Rperp * Rperp) / 2;
}
```

To find the cosine of the transmitted angle, cosThetaT, it is first necessary to determine if the incident direction is on the outside of the medium or inside it, so that the two indices of refraction can be interpreted appropriately.

The sign of the cosine of the incident angle indicates on which side of the medium the incident ray lies (Figure 8.5). If the cosine is between 0 and 1, the ray is on the outside, and if the cosine is between −1 and 0, the ray is on the inside. The parameters etaI and etaT are adjusted such that etaI has the index of refraction of the incident medium, and thus it is ensured that cosThetaI is nonnegative.

⟨Potentially swap indices of refraction⟩ ≡   **519**

```
bool entering = cosThetaI > 0.f;
if (!entering) {
    std::swap(etaI, etaT);
    cosThetaI = std::abs(cosThetaI);
}
```

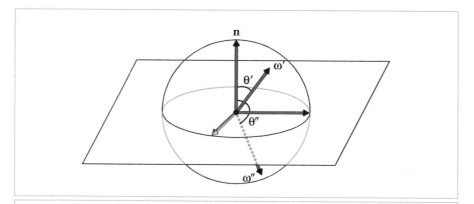

Figure 8.5: The cosine of the angle θ between a direction ω and the geometric surface normal indicates whether the direction is pointing outside the surface (in the same hemisphere as the normal) or inside the surface. In the standard reflection coordinate system, this test just requires checking the z component of the direction vector. Here, ω' is in the upper hemisphere, with a positive-valued cosine, while ω'' is in the lower hemisphere.

Once the indices of refraction are determined, we can compute the sine of the angle between the transmitted direction and the surface normal, $\sin \theta_t$, using Snell's law (Equation (8.2)). Finally, the cosine of this angle is found using the identity $\sin^2 \theta + \cos^2 \theta = 1$.

⟨*Compute* cosThetaT *using Snell's law*⟩ ≡   519
```
Float sinThetaI = std::sqrt(std::max((Float)0,
                             1 - cosThetaI * cosThetaI));
Float sinThetaT = etaI / etaT * sinThetaI;
⟨Handle total internal reflection 520⟩
Float cosThetaT = std::sqrt(std::max((Float)0,
                             1 - sinThetaT * sinThetaT));
```

When light is traveling from one medium to another medium with a lower index of refraction, none of the light at incident angles near grazing passes into the other medium. The largest angle at which this happens is called the *critical angle*; when θ_i is greater than the critical angle, *total internal reflection* occurs, and all of the light is reflected. That case is detected here by a value of $\sin \theta_t$ greater than one; in that case, the Fresnel equations are unnecessary.

⟨*Handle total internal reflection*⟩ ≡   520
```
if (sinThetaT >= 1)
    return 1;
```

We now focus on the general case of a complex index of refraction $\bar{\eta} = \eta + ik$, where some of the incident light is potentially absorbed by the material and turned into heat. In addition to the real part, the general Fresnel formula now also depends on the imaginary part k that is referred to as the *absorption coefficient*.

Figure 8.6 shows a plot of the index of refraction and absorption coefficient for gold; both of these are wavelength-dependent quantities. The directory scenes/spds/metals in the pbrt distribution has wavelength-dependent data for η and k for a variety of metals. Figure 9.4 in the next chapter shows a model rendered with a metal material.

The Fresnel reflectance at the boundary between a conductor and a dielectric medium is given by

$$r_\perp = \frac{a^2 + b^2 - 2a \cos \theta + \cos^2 \theta}{a^2 + b^2 + 2a \cos \theta + \cos^2 \theta}, \qquad (8.3)$$

$$r_\parallel = r_\perp \frac{\cos^2 \theta (a^2 + b^2) - 2a \cos \theta \sin^2 \theta + \sin^4 \theta}{\cos^2 \theta (a^2 + b^2) + 2a \cos \theta \sin^2 \theta + \sin^4 \theta}, \qquad (8.4)$$

where

$$a^2 + b^2 = \sqrt{(\eta^2 - k^2 - \sin^2 \theta)^2 + 4\eta^2 k^2},$$

and $\eta + ik = \bar{\eta}_t / \bar{\eta}_i$ is the relative index of refraction computed using a complex division operation. However, generally $\bar{\eta}_i$ will be a dielectric so that a normal real division can be used instead.

Float 1062

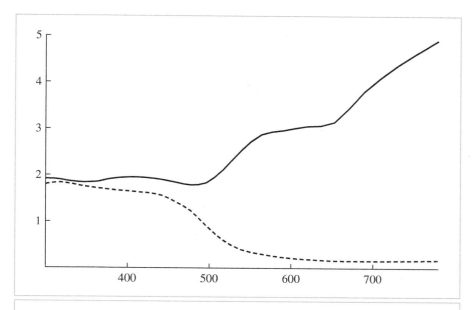

Figure 8.6: Absorption Coefficient and Index of Refraction of Gold. This plot shows the spectrally varying values of the absorption coefficient k (solid line) and the index of refraction η (dashed line) for gold, where the horizontal axis is wavelength in nm.

This computation is implemented by the FrConductor() function[4]; its implementation corresponds directly to Equations (8.3) and (8.4) and so isn't included here.

⟨*Reflection Declarations*⟩ ≡
```
Spectrum FrConductor(Float cosThetaI, const Spectrum &etaI,
    const Spectrum &etaT, const Spectrum &k);
```

For convenience, we will define an abstract Fresnel class that provides an interface for computing Fresnel reflection coefficients. Using implementations of this interface helps simplify the implementation of subsequent BRDFs that may need to support both forms.

⟨*BxDF Declarations*⟩ +≡
```
class Fresnel {
public:
    ⟨Fresnel Interface 522⟩
};
```

The only method provided by the Fresnel interface is Fresnel::Evaluate(). Given the cosine of the angle made by the incoming direction and the surface normal, it returns the amount of light reflected by the surface.

---

4   Note that this is a slight misnomer since the function technically subsumes the dielectric case when $k = 0$. That said, we chose this name to indicate that the function should only be used when dealing with conductors, since it is more expensive to evaluate than FrDielectric().

⟨*Fresnel Interface*⟩ ≡   **521**
```
virtual Spectrum Evaluate(Float cosI) const = 0;
```

Fresnel Conductors

FresnelConductor implements this interface for conductors.

⟨*BxDF Declarations*⟩ +≡
```
class FresnelConductor : public Fresnel {
public:
    ⟨FresnelConductor Public Methods 522⟩
private:
    Spectrum etaI, etaT, k;
};
```

Its constructor stores the given index of refraction η and absorption coefficient k.

⟨*FresnelConductor Public Methods*⟩ ≡   **522**
```
FresnelConductor(const Spectrum &etaI, const Spectrum &etaT,
    const Spectrum &k) : etaI(etaI), etaT(etaT), k(k) { }
```

The evaluation routine for FresnelConductor is also simple; it just calls the FrConductor() function defined earlier. Note that it takes the absolute value of cosThetaI before calling FrConductor(), since FrConductor() expects that the cosine will be measured with respect to the normal on the same side of the surface as ω_i, or, equivalently, that the absolute value of $\cos\theta_i$ should be used.

⟨*BxDF Method Definitions*⟩ +≡
```
Spectrum FresnelConductor::Evaluate(Float cosThetaI) const {
    return FrConductor(std::abs(cosThetaI), etaI, etaT, k);
}
```

Fresnel Dielectrics

FresnelDielectric similarly implements the Fresnel interface for dielectric materials.

⟨*BxDF Declarations*⟩ +≡
```
class FresnelDielectric : public Fresnel {
public:
    ⟨FresnelDielectric Public Methods 522⟩
private:
    Float etaI, etaT;
};
```

Its constructor stores the indices of refraction on the exterior and interior sides of the surface.

⟨*FresnelDielectric Public Methods*⟩ ≡   **522**
```
FresnelDielectric(Float etaI, Float etaT) : etaI(etaI), etaT(etaT) { }
```

The evaluation routine for FresnelDielectric analogously calls FrDielectric().

⟨*BxDF Method Definitions*⟩ +≡

```
Spectrum FresnelDielectric::Evaluate(Float cosThetaI) const {
    return FrDielectric(cosThetaI, etaI, etaT);
}
```

A Special Fresnel Interface

The FresnelNoOp implementation of the Fresnel interface returns 100% reflection for all incoming directions. Although this is physically implausible, it is a convenient capability to have available.

⟨*BxDF Declarations*⟩ +≡

```
class FresnelNoOp : public Fresnel {
public:
    Spectrum Evaluate(Float) const { return Spectrum(1.); }
};
```

8.2.2 SPECULAR REFLECTION

We can now implement the SpecularReflection class, which describes physically plausible specular reflection, using the Fresnel interface to compute the fraction of light that is reflected. First, we will derive the BRDF that describes specular reflection. Since the Fresnel equations give the fraction of light reflected, $F_r(\omega)$, then we need a BRDF such that

$$L_o(\omega_o) = \int f_r(\omega_o, \omega_i)\, L_i(\omega_i)\, |\cos\theta_i|\, d\omega_i = F_r(\omega_r)\, L_i(\omega_r),$$

where $\omega_r = R(\omega_o, \mathbf{n})$ is the specular reflection vector for ω_o reflected about the surface normal $\mathbf{n}$. (Recall that $\theta_r = \theta_o$ for specular reflection, and therefore $F_r(\omega_o) = F_r(\omega_r)$.)

Such a BRDF can be constructed using the Dirac delta distribution. Recall from Section 7.1 that the delta distribution has the useful property that

$$\int f(x)\, \delta(x - x_0)\, dx = f(x_0). \tag{8.5}$$

The delta distribution requires special handling compared to standard functions, however. In particular, numerical integration of integrals with delta distributions must explicitly account for the delta distribution. Consider the integral in Equation (8.5): if we tried to evaluate it using the trapezoid rule or some other numerical integration technique, by definition of the delta distribution there would be zero probability that any of the evaluation points x_i would have a nonzero value of $\delta(x_i)$. Rather, we must allow the delta distribution to determine the evaluation point itself. We will encounter delta distributions in light transport integrals both from specular BxDFs as well as from some of the light sources in Chapter 12.

Intuitively, we want the specular reflection BRDF to be zero everywhere except at the perfect reflection direction, which suggests the use of the delta distribution. A first guess might be to use delta functions to restrict the incident direction to the specular reflection direction ω_r. This would yield a BRDF of

$$f_r(\omega_o, \omega_i) = \delta(\omega_i - \omega_r) F_r(\omega_i).$$

Although this seems appealing, plugging it into the scattering equation, Equation (5.9), reveals a problem:

$$L_o(\omega_o) = \int \delta(\omega_i - \omega_r) F_r(\omega_i) L_i(\omega_i)|\cos\theta_i|\,d\omega_i$$

$$= F_r(\omega_r) L_i(\omega_r)|\cos\theta_r|.$$

This is not correct because it contains an extra factor of $\cos\theta_r$. However, we can divide out this factor to find the correct BRDF for perfect specular reflection:

$$f_r(p, \omega_o, \omega_i) = F_r(\omega_r)\frac{\delta(\omega_i - \omega_r)}{|\cos\theta_r|},$$

⟨*BxDF Declarations*⟩ +≡
```
class SpecularReflection : public BxDF {
public:
    ⟨SpecularReflection Public Methods 524⟩
private:
    ⟨SpecularReflection Private Data 524⟩
};
```

The SpecularReflection constructor takes a Spectrum that is used to scale the reflected color and a Fresnel object pointer that describes dielectric or conductor Fresnel properties.

⟨*SpecularReflection Public Methods*⟩ ≡   524
```
SpecularReflection(const Spectrum &R, Fresnel *fresnel)
    : BxDF(BxDFType(BSDF_REFLECTION | BSDF_SPECULAR)), R(R),
      fresnel(fresnel) { }
```

⟨*SpecularReflection Private Data*⟩ ≡   524
```
const Spectrum R;
const Fresnel *fresnel;
```

The rest of the implementation is straightforward. No scattering is returned from SpecularReflection::f(), since for an arbitrary pair of directions the delta function returns no scattering.[5]

⟨*SpecularReflection Public Methods*⟩ +≡   524
```
Spectrum f(const Vector3f &wo, const Vector3f &wi) const {
    return Spectrum(0.f);
}
```

However, we do implement the Sample_f() method, which selects an appropriate direction according to the delta distribution. It sets the output variable wi to be the reflection of the supplied direction wo about the surface normal. The *pdf value is set to be one;

---

5   If the caller happened to pass a vector and its perfect mirror direction, this function still returns zero. Although this might be a slightly confusing interface to these reflection functions, we still get the correct result in the end because reflection functions involving singularities with delta distributions receive special handling by the light transport routines (see Chapter 14).

Section 14.1.3 discusses some subtleties about the mathematical quantity that this value of one represents.

⟨*BxDF Method Definitions*⟩ +≡

```
Spectrum SpecularReflection::Sample_f(const Vector3f &wo,
        Vector3f *wi, const Point2f &sample, Float *pdf,
        BxDFType *sampledType) const {
    ⟨Compute perfect specular reflection direction 526⟩
    *pdf = 1;
    return fresnel->Evaluate(CosTheta(*wi)) * R / AbsCosTheta(*wi);
}
```

The desired incident direction is the reflection of ω_o around the surface normal, $R(\omega_o, \mathbf{n})$. This direction can be computed fairly easily using vector geometry. First, note that the incoming direction, the reflection direction, and the surface normal all lie in the same plane. We can decompose vectors ω that lie in a plane into a sum of two components: one parallel to $\mathbf{n}$, which we'll denote by $\omega_\parallel$, and one perpendicular, $\omega_\perp$.

These vectors are easily computed: if $\mathbf{n}$ and ω are normalized, then $\omega_\parallel$ is $(\cos\theta)\mathbf{n} = (\mathbf{n} \cdot \omega)\mathbf{n}$ (Figure 8.7). Because $\omega_\parallel + \omega_\perp = \omega$,

$$\omega_\perp = \omega - \omega_\parallel = \omega - (\mathbf{n} \cdot \omega)\mathbf{n}.$$

Figure 8.8 shows the setting for computing the reflected direction ω_r. We can see that both vectors have the same $\omega_\parallel$ component, and the value of $\omega_{r\perp}$ is the negation of $\omega_{o\perp}$. Therefore, we have

$$\begin{aligned}
\omega_r = \omega_{r\perp} + \omega_{r\parallel} &= -\omega_{o\perp} + \omega_{o\parallel} \\
&= -(\omega_o - (\mathbf{n} \cdot \omega_o)\mathbf{n}) + (\mathbf{n} \cdot \omega_o)\mathbf{n} \\
&= -\omega_o + 2(\mathbf{n} \cdot \omega_o)\mathbf{n}.
\end{aligned} \qquad [8.6]$$

The Reflect() function implements this computation.

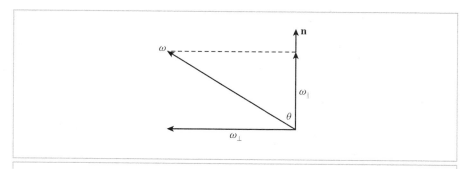

Figure 8.7: The parallel projection of a vector ω on to the normal $\mathbf{n}$ is given by $\omega_\parallel = (\cos\theta)\mathbf{n} = (\mathbf{n} \cdot \omega)\mathbf{n}$. The perpendicular component is given by $\omega_\perp = (\sin\theta)\mathbf{n}$ but is more easily computed by $\omega_\perp = \omega - \omega_\parallel$.

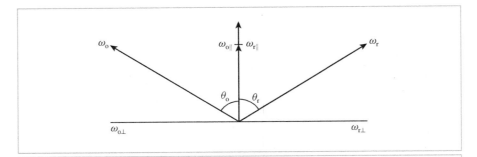

Figure 8.8: Because the angles θ_o and θ_r are equal, the parallel component of the perfect reflection direction $\omega_{r\parallel}$ is the same as the incident direction's: $\omega_{r\parallel} = \omega_{o\parallel}$. Its perpendicular component is just the incident direction's perpendicular component, negated.

⟨*BSDF Inline Functions*⟩ $+\equiv$
```
inline Vector3f Reflect(const Vector3f &wo, const Vector3f &n) {
    return -wo + 2 * Dot(wo, n) * n;
}
```

In the BRDF coordinate system, $\mathbf{n} = (0, 0, 1)$, and this expression is substantially simpler.

⟨*Compute perfect specular reflection direction*⟩ $\equiv$ 525, 817
```
*wi = Vector3f(-wo.x, -wo.y, wo.z);
```

8.2.3 SPECULAR TRANSMISSION

We will now derive the BTDF for specular transmission. Snell's law is the basis of the derivation. Not only does Snell's law give the direction for the transmitted ray, but it can also be used to show that radiance along a ray changes as the ray goes between media with different indices of refraction.

Consider incident radiance arriving at the boundary between two media, with indices of refraction η_i and η_o for the incoming and outgoing media, respectively (Figure 8.9). We use τ to denote the fraction of incident energy that is transmitted to the outgoing direction as given by the Fresnel equations, so $\tau = 1 - F_r(\omega_i)$. The amount of transmitted differential flux, then, is

$$d\Phi_o = \tau d\Phi_i.$$

If we use the definition of radiance, Equation (5.2), we have

$$L_o \cos\theta_o \, dA \, d\omega_o = \tau(L_i \cos\theta_i \, dA \, d\omega_i).$$

Expanding the solid angles to spherical angles, we have

$$L_o \cos\theta_o \, dA \sin\theta_o \, d\theta_o \, d\phi_o = \tau L_i \cos\theta_i \, dA \sin\theta_i \, d\theta_i \, d\phi_i. \tag{8.7}$$

We can now differentiate Snell's law with respect to θ, which gives the relation

$$\eta_o \cos\theta_o \, d\theta_o = \eta_i \cos\theta_i \, d\theta_i.$$

Dot() 63

Vector3f 60

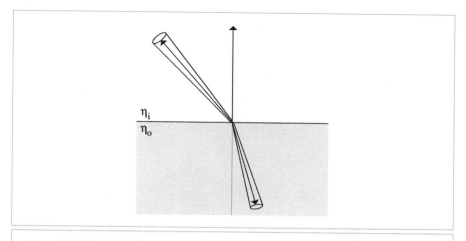

Figure 8.9: The amount of transmitted radiance at the boundary between media with different indices of refraction is scaled by the squared ratio of the two indices of refraction. Intuitively, this can be understood as the result of the radiance's differential solid angle being compressed or expanded as a result of transmission.

Rearranging terms, we have

$$\frac{\cos\theta_o \, d\theta_o}{\cos\theta_i \, d\theta_i} = \frac{\eta_i}{\eta_o}.$$

Substituting this relationship and Snell's law into Equation (8.7) and then simplifying, we have

$$L_o \, \eta_i^2 \, d\phi_o = \tau L_i \, \eta_o^2 \, d\phi_i.$$

Because $\phi_i = \phi_o + \pi$ and therefore $d\phi_i = d\phi_o$, we have the final relationship:

$$L_o = \tau L_i \frac{\eta_o^2}{\eta_i^2}. \tag{8.8}$$

As with the BRDF for specular reflection, we need to divide out a $\cos\theta_i$ term to get the right BTDF for specular transmission:

$$f_r(\omega_o, \omega_i) = \frac{\eta_o^2}{\eta_i^2}(1 - F_r(\omega_i))\frac{\delta(\omega_i - T(\omega_o, \mathbf{n}))}{|\cos\theta_i|},$$

where $T(\omega_o, \mathbf{n})$ is the specular transmission vector that results from specular transmission of ω_o through an interface with surface normal $\mathbf{n}$.

The $1 - F_r(\omega_i)$ term in this equation corresponds to an easily observed effect: transmission is stronger at near-perpendicular angles. For example, if you look straight down into a clear lake, you can see far into the water, but at grazing angles most of the light is reflected as if from a mirror.

The SpecularTransmission class is almost exactly the same as SpecularReflection except that the sampled direction is the direction for perfect specular transmission. Figure 8.10

Figure 8.10: When the BRDF for specular reflection and the BTDF for specular transmission are modulated with the Fresnel formula for dielectrics, the realistic angle-dependent variation of the amount of reflection and transmission gives a visually accurate representation of the glass. *(Model courtesy of Christian Schüller.)*

shows an image of the dragon model using specular reflection and transmission BRDF and BTDF to model glass.

⟨*BxDF Declarations*⟩ +≡
```
class SpecularTransmission : public BxDF {
public:
    ⟨SpecularTransmission Public Methods 528⟩
private:
    ⟨SpecularTransmission Private Data 529⟩
};
```

The SpecularTransmission constructor stores the indices of refraction on both sides of the surface, where etaA is the index of refraction above the surface (where the side the surface normal lies in is "above"), etaB is the index of refraction below the surface, and T gives a transmission scale factor. The TransportMode parameter indicates whether the incident ray that intersected the point where the BxDF was computed started from a light source or whether it was started from the camera. This distinction has implications for how the BxDF's contribution is computed.

⟨*SpecularTransmission Public Methods*⟩ ≡   528
```
SpecularTransmission(const Spectrum &T, Float etaA, Float etaB,
        TransportMode mode)
    : BxDF(BxDFType(BSDF_TRANSMISSION | BSDF_SPECULAR)), T(T), etaA(etaA),
        etaB(etaB), fresnel(etaA, etaB), mode(mode) {
}
```

Because conductors do not transmit light, a FresnelDielectric object is always used for the Fresnel computations.

⟨*SpecularTransmission Private Data*⟩ ≡   **528**
```
const Spectrum T;
const Float etaA, etaB;
const FresnelDielectric fresnel;
const TransportMode mode;
```

As with SpecularReflection, zero is always returned from SpecularTransmission::f(), since the BTDF is a scaled delta distribution.

⟨*SpecularTransmission Public Methods*⟩ +≡   **528**
```
Spectrum f(const Vector3f &wo, const Vector3f &wi) const {
    return Spectrum(0.f);
}
```

Equation (8.8) describes how radiance changes as a ray passes from one medium to another. However, it turns out that while this scaling should be applied for rays starting at light sources, it must *not* be applied for rays starting from the camera. This issue is discussed in more detail in Section 16.1, and the fragment that applies this scaling, ⟨*Account for non-symmetry with transmission to different medium*⟩, is defined there.

⟨*BxDF Method Definitions*⟩ +≡
```
Spectrum SpecularTransmission::Sample_f(const Vector3f &wo,
        Vector3f *wi, const Point2f &sample, Float *pdf,
        BxDFType *sampledType) const {
    ⟨Figure out which η is incident and which is transmitted 529⟩
    ⟨Compute ray direction for specular transmission 529⟩
    *pdf = 1;
    Spectrum ft = T * (Spectrum(1.) - fresnel.Evaluate(CosTheta(*wi)));
    ⟨Account for non-symmetry with transmission to different medium 961⟩
    return ft / AbsCosTheta(*wi);
}
```

The method first determines whether the incident ray is entering or exiting the refractive medium. pbrt uses the convention that the surface normal, and thus the $(0, 0, 1)$ direction in local reflection space, is oriented such that it points toward the outside of the object. Therefore, if the z component of the ω_o direction is greater than zero, the incident ray is coming from outside of the object.

⟨*Figure out which η is incident and which is transmitted*⟩ ≡   **529, 817**
```
bool entering = CosTheta(wo) > 0;
Float etaI = entering ? etaA : etaB;
Float etaT = entering ? etaB : etaA;
```

⟨*Compute ray direction for specular transmission*⟩ ≡   **529, 817**
```
if (!Refract(wo, Faceforward(Normal3f(0, 0, 1), wo), etaI / etaT, wi))
    return 0;
```

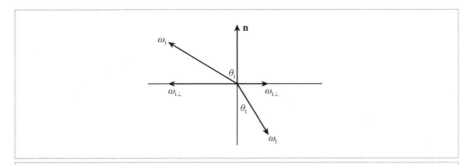

Figure 8.11: The Geometry of Specular Transmission. Given an incident direction ω and surface normal $\mathbf{n}$ with angle θ between them, the specularly transmitted direction makes an angle θ_t with the surface normal. This direction, ω_t, can be computed by using Snell's law to find its perpendicular component $\omega_{t\perp}$ and then computing the $\omega_{t\parallel}$ that gives a normalized result ω_t.

To derive the expression that gives the transmitted direction vector, we can follow a similar approach to the one we used earlier for specular reflection. Figure 8.11 shows the setting. This time, however, we'll start with the perpendicular component: if the incident vector is normalized and has perpendicular component $\omega_{i\perp}$, then we know from trigonometry and the definition of $\omega_\perp$ that the length of $\omega_{i\perp}$ is equal to $\sin\theta_i$. Snell's law tells us that $\sin\theta_t = \eta_i/\eta_t \sin\theta_i$. Negating the direction of $\omega_{i\perp}$ and adjusting the length accordingly, we have

$$\omega_{t\perp} = \frac{\eta_i}{\eta_t}(-\omega_{i\perp}).$$

Equivalently, because $\omega_\perp = \omega - \omega_\parallel$,

$$\omega_{t\perp} = \frac{\eta_i}{\eta_t}\left(-\omega_i + (\omega_i \cdot \mathbf{n})\mathbf{n}\right).$$

Now for $\omega_{t\parallel}$: we know that $\omega_{t\parallel}$ is parallel to $\mathbf{n}$ but facing in the opposite direction, and we also know that ω_t should be normalized. Putting these together,

$$\omega_{t\parallel} = -\left(\sqrt{1 - \|\omega_{t\perp}\|^2}\right)\mathbf{n}.$$

The full vector ω_t, then, is

$$\omega_t = \omega_{t\perp} + \omega_{t\parallel} = \frac{\eta_i}{\eta_t}(-\omega_i) + \left[\frac{\eta_i}{\eta_t}(\omega_i \cdot \mathbf{n}) - \sqrt{1 - \|\omega_{t\perp}\|^2}\right]\mathbf{n}.$$

Because $\|\omega_{t\perp}\| = \sin\theta_t$, the term under the square root is $1 - \sin^2\theta_t = \cos^2\theta_t$, which gives the final result:

$$\omega_t = \frac{\eta_i}{\eta_t}(-\omega_i) + \left[\frac{\eta_i}{\eta_t}(\omega_i \cdot \mathbf{n}) - \cos\theta_t\right]\mathbf{n}. \qquad [8.9]$$

The Refract() function computes the refracted direction wt given an incident direction wi, surface normal n in the same hemisphere was wi, and eta, the ratio of indices of refraction in the incident and transmitted media, respectively. The Boolean return value indicates whether a valid refracted ray was returned in *wt; it is false in the case of total internal refraction.

⟨*BSDF Inline Functions*⟩ +≡
```
inline bool Refract(const Vector3f &wi, const Normal3f &n, Float eta,
        Vector3f *wt) {
    ⟨Compute cos θt using Snell's law 531⟩
    *wt = eta * -wi + (eta * cosThetaI - cosThetaT) * Vector3f(n);
    return true;
}
```

Squaring both sides of Snell's law lets us compute $\cos \theta_t$:

$$\eta_i^2 \sin^2 \theta_i = \eta_t^2 \sin^2 \theta_t \qquad \sin^2 \theta_t = \frac{\eta_i^2}{\eta_t^2} \sin^2 \theta_i$$

$$1 - \cos^2 \theta_t = \frac{\eta_i^2}{\eta_t^2} \sin^2 \theta_i \qquad \cos \theta_t = \sqrt{1 - \frac{\eta_i^2}{\eta_t^2} \sin^2 \theta_i}$$

⟨*Compute* cos θt *using Snell's law*⟩ ≡   531
```
Float cosThetaI = Dot(n, wi);
Float sin2ThetaI = std::max(0.f, 1.f - cosThetaI * cosThetaI);
Float sin2ThetaT = eta * eta * sin2ThetaI;
⟨Handle total internal reflection for transmission 531⟩
Float cosThetaT = std::sqrt(1 - sin2ThetaT);
```

We need to handle the case of total internal reflection here as well. If the squared value of $\sin \theta_t$ is greater than or equal to one, total internal reflection has occurred, so false is returned.[6]

⟨*Handle total internal reflection for transmission*⟩ ≡   531
```
if (sin2ThetaT >= 1) return false;
```

8.2.4 FRESNEL-MODULATED SPECULAR REFLECTION AND TRANSMISSION

For better efficiency in some of the Monte Carlo light transport algorithms to come in Chapters 14 through 16, it's useful to have a single BxDF that represents both specular reflection and specular transmission together, where the relative weightings of the types of scattering are modulated by the dielectric Fresnel equations. Such a BxDF is provided in FresnelSpecular.

⟨*BxDF Declarations*⟩ +≡
```
class FresnelSpecular : public BxDF {
public:
    ⟨FresnelSpecular Public Methods 532⟩
private:
    ⟨FresnelSpecular Private Data 532⟩
};
```

BxDF 513
Dot() 63
Float 1062
Normal3f 71
Vector3f 60

---

[6]   The first version of pbrt had a test > 1 rather than ≥ 1 here. Though the difference between the two may seem innocuous, this discrepancy led to not-a-number values occasionally being computed due to the z component of ω_i being zero (in the tangent plane of the surface) and thus to the $1/\cos \theta$ term being infinite.

⟨*FresnelSpecular Public Methods*⟩ ≡   **531**
```
    FresnelSpecular(const Spectrum &R, const Spectrum &T, Float etaA,
            Float etaB, TransportMode mode)
        : BxDF(BxDFType(BSDF_REFLECTION | BSDF_TRANSMISSION | BSDF_SPECULAR)),
          R(R), T(T), etaA(etaA), etaB(etaB), fresnel(etaA, etaB),
          mode(mode) { }
```

Since we only focus on the dielectric case, a FresnelDielectric object is always used for the Fresnel computations.

⟨*FresnelSpecular Private Data*⟩ ≡   **531**
```
    const Spectrum R, T;
    const Float etaA, etaB;
    const FresnelDielectric fresnel;
    const TransportMode mode;
```

⟨*FresnelSpecular Public Methods*⟩ +≡   **531**
```
    Spectrum f(const Vector3f &wo, const Vector3f &wi) const {
        return Spectrum(0.f);
    }
```

Because some of the implementation details depend on principles of Monte Carlo integration that are introduced in Chapters 13 and 14, the implementation of the Sample_f() method is in Section 14.1.3.

8.3 LAMBERTIAN REFLECTION

One of the simplest BRDFs is the Lambertian model. It models a perfect diffuse surface that scatters incident illumination equally in all directions. Although this reflection model is not physically plausible, it is a reasonable approximation to many real-world surfaces such as matte paint.

⟨*BxDF Declarations*⟩ +≡
```
    class LambertianReflection : public BxDF {
    public:
        ⟨LambertianReflection Public Methods 532⟩
    private:
        ⟨LambertianReflection Private Data 532⟩
    };
```

The LambertianReflection constructor takes a reflectance spectrum R, which gives the fraction of incident light that is scattered.

⟨*LambertianReflection Public Methods*⟩ ≡   **532**
```
    LambertianReflection(const Spectrum &R)
        : BxDF(BxDFType(BSDF_REFLECTION | BSDF_DIFFUSE)), R(R) { }
```

⟨*LambertianReflection Private Data*⟩ ≡   **532**
```
    const Spectrum R;
```

The reflection distribution function for `LambertianReflection` is quite straightforward, since its value is constant. However, the value R/π must be returned, rather than the reflectance R supplied to the constructor. This can be seen by equating R to Equation (8.1), which defined ρ_{hd}, and solving for the BRDF's value.

⟨*BxDF Method Definitions*⟩ +≡
```
Spectrum LambertianReflection::f(const Vector3f &wo,
                                 const Vector3f &wi) const {
    return R * InvPi;
}
```

The directional-hemispherical and hemispherical-hemispherical reflectance values for a Lambertian BRDF are trivial to compute analytically, so the derivations are omitted in the text.

⟨*LambertianReflection Public Methods*⟩ +≡   532
```
Spectrum rho(const Vector3f &, int, const Point2f *) const { return R; }
Spectrum rho(int, const Point2f *, const Point2f *) const { return R; }
```

It's also useful to be able to represent perfect Lambertian transmission through a surface; this BTDF is implemented in `LambertianTransmission`. Its implementation closely follows `LambertianReflection` and thus isn't included here.

8.4 MICROFACET MODELS

Many geometric-optics-based approaches to modeling surface reflection and transmission are based on the idea that rough surfaces can be modeled as a collection of small *microfacets*. Surfaces comprised of microfacets are often modeled as heightfields, where the distribution of facet orientations is described statistically. Figure 8.12 shows cross sections of a relatively rough surface and a much smoother microfacet surface. When the

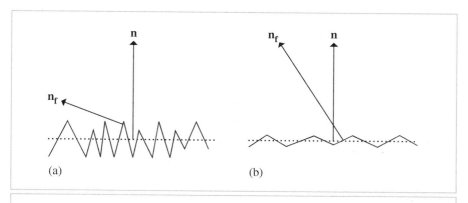

(a)   (b)

Figure 8.12: Microfacet surface models are often described by a function that gives the distribution of microfacet normals n_f with respect to the surface normal n. (a) The greater the variation of microfacet normals, the rougher the surface is. (b) Smooth surfaces have relatively little variation of microfacet normals.

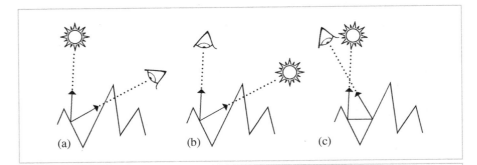

Figure 8.13: Three Important Geometric Effects to Consider with Microfacet Reflection Models. (a) *Masking*: the microfacet of interest isn't visible to the viewer due to occlusion by another microfacet. (b) *Shadowing*: analogously, light doesn't reach the microfacet. (c) *Interreflection*: light bounces among the microfacets before reaching the viewer.

distinction isn't clear, we'll use the term *microsurface* to describe microfacet surfaces and *macrosurface* to describe the underlying smooth surface (e.g., as represented by a Shape).

Microfacet-based BRDF models work by statistically modeling the scattering of light from a large collection of microfacets. If we assume that the differential area being illuminated, dA, is relatively large compared to the size of individual microfacets, then a large number of microfacets are illuminated and it's their aggregate behavior that determines the observed scattering.

The two main components of microfacet models are a representation of the distribution of facets and a BRDF that describes how light scatters from individual microfacets. Given these, the task is to derive a closed-form expression giving the BRDF that describes scattering from such a surface. Perfect mirror reflection is most commonly used for the microfacet BRDF, though specular transmission is useful for modeling many translucent materials, and the Oren–Nayar model (described in the next section) treats microfacets as Lambertian reflectors.

To compute reflection from such a model, local lighting effects at the microfacet level need to be considered (Figure 8.13). Microfacets may be occluded by another facet, may lie in the shadow of a neighboring microfacet, or interreflection may cause a microfacet to reflect more light than predicted by the amount of direct illumination and the low-level microfacet BRDF. Particular microfacet-based BRDF models consider each of these effects with varying degrees of accuracy. The general approach is to make the best approximations possible, while still obtaining an easily evaluated expression.

8.4.1 OREN–NAYAR DIFFUSE REFLECTION

Oren and Nayar (1994) observed that real-world objects do not exhibit perfect Lambertian reflection. Specifically, rough surfaces generally appear brighter as the illumination direction approaches the viewing direction. They developed a reflection model that describes rough surfaces by V-shaped microfacets described by a spherical Gaussian distri-

Shape 123

(a)   (b)

Figure 8.14: Dragon model rendered (a) with standard diffuse reflection from the LambertianReflection model and (b) with the OrenNayar model with a σ parameter of 20 degrees. Note the increase in reflection at the silhouette edges and the generally less-drawn-out transitions at light terminator edges with the Oren–Nayar model. (Model courtesy of Christian Schüller.)

bution with a single parameter σ, the standard deviation of the microfacet orientation angle.

Under the V-shape assumption, interreflection can be accounted for by only considering the neighboring microfacet; Oren and Nayar took advantage of this to derive a BRDF that models the aggregate reflection of the collection of grooves.

The resulting model, which accounts for shadowing, masking, and interreflection among the microfacets, does not have a closed-form solution, so they found the following approximation that fit it well:

$$f_r(\omega_i, \omega_o) = \frac{R}{\pi} \left(A + B \max(0, \cos(\phi_i - \phi_o)) \sin \alpha \tan \beta \right),$$

where if σ is in radians,

$$A = 1 - \frac{\sigma^2}{2(\sigma^2 + 0.33)}$$

$$B = \frac{0.45\sigma^2}{\sigma^2 + 0.09}$$

$$\alpha = \max(\theta_i, \theta_o)$$

$$\beta = \min(\theta_i, \theta_o).$$

LambertianReflection 532

OrenNayar 536

The implementation here precomputes and stores the values of the A and B parameters in the constructor to save work in evaluating the BRDF later. Figure 8.14 compares the difference between rendering with ideal diffuse reflection and with the Oren–Nayar model.

⟨*OrenNayar Public Methods*⟩ ≡
```
OrenNayar(const Spectrum &R, Float sigma)
    : BxDF(BxDFType(BSDF_REFLECTION | BSDF_DIFFUSE)), R(R) {
    sigma = Radians(sigma);
    Float sigma2 = sigma * sigma;
    A = 1.f - (sigma2 / (2.f * (sigma2 + 0.33f)));
    B = 0.45f * sigma2 / (sigma2 + 0.09f);
}
```

⟨*OrenNayar Private Data*⟩ ≡
```
const Spectrum R;
Float A, B;
```

Application of trigonometric identities can substantially improve the efficiency of the evaluation routine compared to a direct translation of the underlying equations. The implementation starts by computing the values of $\sin \theta_i$ and $\sin \theta_o$.

⟨*BxDF Method Definitions*⟩ +≡
```
Spectrum OrenNayar::f(const Vector3f &wo, const Vector3f &wi) const {
    Float sinThetaI = SinTheta(wi);
    Float sinThetaO = SinTheta(wo);
    ⟨Compute cosine term of Oren–Nayar model 536⟩
    ⟨Compute sine and tangent terms of Oren–Nayar model 537⟩
    return R * InvPi * (A + B * maxCos * sinAlpha * tanBeta);
}
```

To compute the $\max(0, \cos(\phi_i - \phi_o))$ term, we can apply the trigonometric identity

$$\cos(a - b) = \cos a \cos b + \sin a \sin b,$$

such that we just need to compute the sines and cosines of ϕ_i and ϕ_o.

⟨*Compute cosine term of Oren–Nayar model*⟩ ≡   536
```
Float maxCos = 0;
if (sinThetaI > 1e-4 && sinThetaO > 1e-4) {
    Float sinPhiI = SinPhi(wi), cosPhiI = CosPhi(wi);
    Float sinPhiO = SinPhi(wo), cosPhiO = CosPhi(wo);
    Float dCos = cosPhiI * cosPhiO + sinPhiI * sinPhiO;
    maxCos = std::max((Float)0, dCos);
}
```

Finally, the $\sin \alpha$ and $\tan \beta$ terms are found. Note that whichever of ω_i or ω_o has a larger value for $\cos \theta$ (i.e., a larger z component) has a smaller value for θ. We can set $\sin \alpha$ using the appropriate sine value computed at the beginning of the method. The tangent can then be computed using the identity $\tan \theta = \sin \theta / \cos \theta$.

⟨*Compute sine and tangent terms of Oren–Nayar model*⟩ ≡   536

```
Float sinAlpha, tanBeta;
if (AbsCosTheta(wi) > AbsCosTheta(wo)) {
    sinAlpha = sinThetaO;
    tanBeta = sinThetaI / AbsCosTheta(wi);
} else {
    sinAlpha = sinThetaI;
    tanBeta = sinThetaO / AbsCosTheta(wo);
}
```

8.4.2 MICROFACET DISTRIBUTION FUNCTIONS

Reflection models based on microfacets that exhibit perfect specular reflection and transmission have been effective at modeling light scattering from a variety of glossy materials, including metals, plastic, and frosted glass. Before we discuss the radiometric details of these models, we'll first introduce abstractions that encapsulate their geometric properties. The code here includes implementations of two widely used microfacet models. All of this code is in the files core/microfacet.h and core/microfacet.cpp.

MicrofacetDistribution defines the interface provided by microfacet implementations as well as some common functionality for them.

⟨*MicrofacetDistribution Declarations*⟩ ≡

```
class MicrofacetDistribution {
public:
    ⟨MicrofacetDistribution Public Methods 538⟩
protected:
    ⟨MicrofacetDistribution Protected Methods 808⟩
    ⟨MicrofacetDistribution Protected Data 808⟩
};
```

One important characteristic of a microfacet surface is represented by the distribution function $D(\omega_h)$, which gives the differential area of microfacets with the surface normal ω_h (recall Figure 8.12, which shows how surface roughness and the microfacet normal distribution function are related). In pbrt, microfacet distribution functions are defined in the same BSDF coordinate system as BxDFs; as such, a perfectly smooth surface could be described by a delta distribution that was non-zero only when ω_h was equal to the surface normal: $D(\omega_h) = \delta(\omega_h - (0, 0, 1))$.

Microfacet distribution functions must be *normalized* to ensure that they are physically plausible. Intuitively, if we consider incident rays on the microsurface along the normal direction **n**, then each ray must intersect the microfacet surface exactly once. More formally, given a differential area of the microsurface, dA, then the projected area of the microfacet faces above that area must be equal to dA (Figure 8.15). Mathematically, this

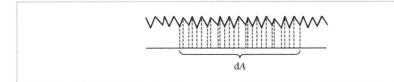

Figure 8.15: Given a differential area on a surface dA, then the microfacet normal distribution function $D(\omega_h)$ must be normalized such that the projected surface area of the microfacets above the area is equal to dA.

corresponds to the following requirement:[7]

$$\int_{\mathcal{H}^2(n)} D(\omega_h) \cos \theta_h \, d\omega_h = 1.$$

The method `MicrofacetDistribution::D()` corresponds to the function $D(\omega_h)$; implementations return the differential area of microfacets oriented with the given normal vector ω.

⟨*MicrofacetDistribution Public Methods*⟩ ≡   537
```
virtual Float D(const Vector3f &wh) const = 0;
```

A widely used microfacet distribution function based on a Gaussian distribution of microfacet slopes is due to Beckmann and Spizzichino (1963); our implementation is in the `BeckmannDistribution` class.

⟨*MicrofacetDistribution Declarations*⟩ +≡
```
class BeckmannDistribution : public MicrofacetDistribution {
public:
    ⟨BeckmannDistribution Public Methods⟩
private:
    ⟨BeckmannDistribution Private Methods⟩
    ⟨BeckmannDistribution Private Data 539⟩
};
```

The traditional definition of the Beckmann–Spizzichino model is

$$D(\omega_h) = \frac{e^{-\tan^2 \theta_h / \alpha^2}}{\pi \alpha^2 \cos^4 \theta_h}, \qquad [8.10]$$

where if σ is the RMS slope of the microfacets, then $\alpha = \sqrt{2}\sigma$.

It's useful to define an anisotropic distribution, where the normal distribution also varies depending on the azimuthal orientation of ω_h. For example, given a α_x for microfacets oriented perpendicular to the x axis and α_y for the y axis, then α values for intermediate orientations can be interpolated by constructing an ellipse through these values.

---

7   A common error in normalizing microfacet distributions is to perform this integral over solid angle instead of projected solid angle (i.e., to leave out the $\cos \theta_h$ term), which does not guarantee the existence of a heightfield with the right distribution.

The corresponding anisotropic microfacet distribution function is

$$D(\omega_h) = \frac{e^{-\tan^2\theta_h(\cos^2\phi_h/\alpha_x^2 + \sin^2\phi_h/\alpha_y^2)}}{\pi\alpha_x\alpha_y\cos^4\theta_h}.$$ [8.11]

Note that the original isotropic variant of the Beckmann–Spizzichino model falls out when $\alpha_x = \alpha_y$.

The alphax and alphay member variables are set in the BeckmannDistribution constructor, which is straightforward and therefore not included here.

⟨*BeckmannDistribution Private Data*⟩ ≡   538
```
const Float alphax, alphay;
```

The BeckmannDistribution::D() method is a direct translation of Equation (8.11). The only additional implementation detail is that infinite values of $\tan^2\theta$ must be handled specially. This case is actually valid—it happens at perfectly grazing directions. In this case, the code below ends up attempting to compute 0/0, which results in a "not a number" (NaN) value, which would eventually lead to a NaN value returned for the current pixel sample's radiance. Therefore, zero is explicitly returned for this case, as that is the value that $D(\omega_h)$ converges to as $\tan\theta_h$ goes to infinity.

⟨*MicrofacetDistribution Method Definitions*⟩ ≡
```
Float BeckmannDistribution::D(const Vector3f &wh) const {
    Float tan2Theta = Tan2Theta(wh);
    if (std::isinf(tan2Theta)) return 0.;
    Float cos4Theta = Cos2Theta(wh) * Cos2Theta(wh);
    return std::exp(-tan2Theta * (Cos2Phi(wh) / (alphax * alphax) +
                                  Sin2Phi(wh) / (alphay * alphay))) /
        (Pi * alphax * alphay * cos4Theta);
}
```

Another useful microfacet distribution function is due to Trowbridge and Reitz (1975).[8] Its anisotropic variant is given by

$$D(\omega_h) = \frac{1}{\pi\alpha_x\alpha_y\cos^4\theta_h\left(1 + \tan^2\theta_h(\cos^2\phi_h/\alpha_x^2 + \sin^2\phi_h/\alpha_y^2)\right)^2}.$$ [8.12]

In comparison to the Beckmann–Spizzichino model, Trowbridge–Reitz has higher tails—it falls off to zero more slowly for directions far from the surface normal. This characteristic matches the properties of many real-world surfaces well. See Figure 8.16 for a graph of these two microfacet distribution functions.

---

8   This model was independently derived by Walter et al. (2007), who dubbed it "GGX."

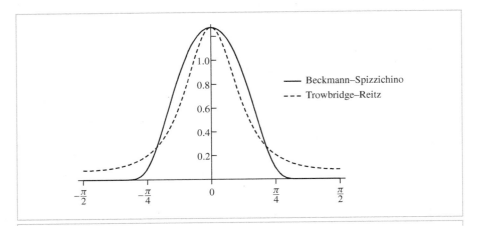

Figure 8.16: Graphs of isotropic Beckmann–Spizzichino and Trowbridge–Reitz microfacet distribution functions as a function of θ for $\alpha = 0.5$. Note that Trowbridge–Reitz has higher tails for values of θ with larger magnitudes.

⟨*MicrofacetDistribution Declarations*⟩ +≡
```
class TrowbridgeReitzDistribution : public MicrofacetDistribution {
public:
    ⟨TrowbridgeReitzDistribution Public Methods 540⟩
private:
    ⟨TrowbridgeReitzDistribution Private Methods⟩
    ⟨TrowbridgeReitzDistribution Private Data 540⟩
};
```

It can be convenient to specify the BRDF's roughness with a scalar parameter in $[0, 1]$, where values close to zero correspond to near-perfect specular reflection, rather than by specifying α values directly. The `RoughnessToAlpha()` method, not included here, performs a mapping from such roughness values to α values.

⟨*TrowbridgeReitzDistribution Public Methods*⟩ ≡   **540**
```
static inline Float RoughnessToAlpha(Float roughness);
```

⟨*TrowbridgeReitzDistribution Private Data*⟩ ≡   **540**
```
const Float alphax, alphay;
```

The `D()` method is a fairly direct transcription of Equation (8.12).

⟨*MicrofacetDistribution Method Definitions*⟩ +≡
```
Float TrowbridgeReitzDistribution::D(const Vector3f &wh) const {
    Float tan2Theta = Tan2Theta(wh);
    if (std::isinf(tan2Theta)) return 0.;
    const Float cos4Theta = Cos2Theta(wh) * Cos2Theta(wh);
    Float e = (Cos2Phi(wh) / (alphax * alphax) +
               Sin2Phi(wh) / (alphay * alphay)) * tan2Theta;
    return 1 / (Pi * alphax * alphay * cos4Theta * (1 + e) * (1 + e));
}
```

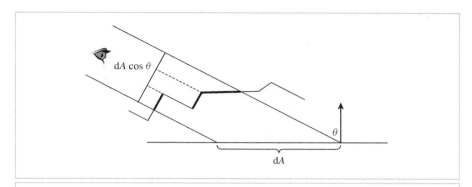

Figure 8.17: As seen from a viewer or a light source, a differential area on the surface has area $dA \cos \theta$, where $\cos \theta$ is the angle of the incident direction with the surface normal. The projected surface area of visible microfacets (thick lines) must be equal to $dA \cos \theta$ as well; the masking-shadowing function G_1 gives the fraction of the total microfacet area over dA that is visible in the given direction.

8.4.3 MASKING AND SHADOWING

The distribution of microfacet normals alone isn't enough to fully characterize the micro-surface for rendering. It's also important to account for the fact that some microfacets will be invisible from a given viewing or illumination direction because they are back-facing (and thus, other microfacets are in front of them) and also for the fact that some of the forward-facing microfacet area will be hidden since it's shadowed by back-facing micro-facets. These effects are accounted for by Smith's *masking-shadowing function* $G_1(\omega, \omega_h)$, which gives the fraction of microfacets with normal ω_h that are visible from direction ω. (Note that $0 \leq G_1(\omega, \omega_h) \leq 1$.) In the usual case where the probability a microfacet is visible is independent of its orientation ω_h, we can write this function as $G_1(\omega)$.

As shown in Figure 8.17, a differential area dA on the surface has area $dA \cos \theta$ when viewed from a direction ω that makes an angle θ with the surface normal. The area of visible microfacets seen from this direction must also be equal to $dA \cos \theta$, which leads to a normalization constraint for G_1:

$$\cos \theta = \int_{\mathcal{H}^2(\mathbf{n})} G_1(\omega, \omega_h) \max(0, \omega \cdot \omega_h)\, D(\omega_h)\, d\omega_h. \qquad [8.13]$$

In other words, the projected area of visible microfacets for a given direction ω must be equal to $(\omega \cdot \mathbf{n}) = \cos \theta$ times the differential area of the macrosurface dA.

Because the microfacets form a heightfield, every backfacing microfacet shadows a forward-facing microfacet of equal projected area in the direction ω. If $A^+(\omega)$ is the projected area of forward-facing microfacets as seen from the direction ω and $A^-(\omega)$ is the projected area of backward-facing microfacets from Equation (8.13), then $\cos \theta = A^+(\omega) - A^-(\omega)$. We can thus alternatively write the masking-shadowing function as the ratio of visible microfacet area to total forward-facing microfacet area:

$$G_1(\omega) = \frac{A^+(\omega) - A^-(\omega)}{A^+(\omega)}.$$

Shadowing-masking functions are traditionally expressed in terms of an auxiliary function $\Lambda(\omega)$, which measures invisible masked microfacet area per visible microfacet area.

$$\Lambda(\omega) = \frac{A^-(\omega)}{A^+(\omega) - A^-(\omega)} = \frac{A^-(\omega)}{\cos\theta}. \qquad [8.14]$$

The Lambda() method computes this function. Its implementation is specific to each microfacet distribution.

⟨*MicrofacetDistribution Public Methods*⟩ +≡   537
```
virtual Float Lambda(const Vector3f &w) const = 0;
```

Some algebra lets us express $G_1(\omega)$ in terms of $\Lambda(\omega)$:

$$G_1(\omega) = \frac{1}{1 + \Lambda(\omega)},$$

and therefore we can provide a G1() method in terms of Lambda().

⟨*MicrofacetDistribution Public Methods*⟩ +≡   537
```
Float G1(const Vector3f &w) const {
    return 1 / (1 + Lambda(w));
}
```

The microfacet distribution alone doesn't impose enough conditions to imply a specific $\Lambda(\omega)$ function; many functions can fulfill the constraint in Equation (8.13). If we assume that there is no correlation between the heights of nearby points on the microsurface, for example, then it's possible to find a unique $\Lambda(\omega)$ given $D(\omega_h)$. (For many microfacet models, a closed-form expression can be found.) Although the underlying assumption isn't true in reality—for actual microsurfaces, the height at a point is generally close to the heights of nearby points—the resulting $\Lambda(\omega)$ functions turn out to be fairly accurate when compared to measured reflection from actual surfaces.

Under the assumption of no correlation of the heights of nearby points, $\Lambda(\omega)$ for the isotropic Beckmann–Spizzichino distribution is

$$\Lambda(\omega) = \frac{1}{2} \left(\text{erf}(a) - 1 + \frac{e^{-a^2}}{a\sqrt{\pi}} \right), \qquad [8.15]$$

where $a = 1/(\alpha \tan\theta)$ and erf is the error function, $\text{erf}(x) = 2/\sqrt{\pi} \int_0^x e^{-x'^2} dx'$.

pbrt's computation of the Beckmann–Spizzichino $\Lambda(\omega)$ function is based on a rational polynomial approximation of Equation (8.15) that is much more efficient to evaluate because it avoids calling std::erf() and std::exp(), both of which are fairly expensive to evaluate.

Float 1062
MicrofacetDistribution::
    Lambda()
    542
Vector3f 60

⟨*MicrofacetDistribution Method Definitions*⟩ +≡
```
Float BeckmannDistribution::Lambda(const Vector3f &w) const {
    Float absTanTheta = std::abs(TanTheta(w));
    if (std::isinf(absTanTheta)) return 0.;
    ⟨Compute alpha for direction w 543⟩
    Float a = 1 / (alpha * absTanTheta);
    if (a >= 1.6f)
        return 0;
    return (1 - 1.259f * a + 0.396f * a * a) /
           (3.535f * a + 2.181f * a * a);
}
```

Masking-shadowing functions for anisotropic distributions are most easily computed by taking their corresponding isotropic function and stretching the underlying microsurface according to the α_x and α_y values. Equivalently, one can compute an interpolated α value for the direction of interest and use that with the isotropic function; see the "Further Reading" section at the end of this chapter for more details.

⟨*Compute* alpha *for direction* w⟩ ≡   543
```
Float alpha = std::sqrt(Cos2Phi(w) * alphax * alphax +
                        Sin2Phi(w) * alphay * alphay);
```

Under the uncorrelated height assumption, the form of $\Lambda(\omega)$ for the Trowbridge–Reitz distribution is quite simple:

$$\Lambda(\omega) = \frac{-1 + \sqrt{1 + \alpha^2 \tan^2 \theta}}{2}.$$

⟨*MicrofacetDistribution Method Definitions*⟩ +≡
```
Float TrowbridgeReitzDistribution::Lambda(const Vector3f &w) const {
    Float absTanTheta = std::abs(TanTheta(w));
    if (std::isinf(absTanTheta)) return 0.;
    ⟨Compute alpha for direction w 543⟩
    Float alpha2Tan2Theta = (alpha * absTanTheta) * (alpha * absTanTheta);
    return (-1 + std::sqrt(1.f + alpha2Tan2Theta)) / 2;
}
```

Figure 8.18 shows a plot of the Trowbridge–Reitz $G_1(\omega)$ function for a few values of α. Note that the function is close to one over much of the domain but falls to zero at grazing angles. Note also that increasing surface roughness (i.e., higher values of α) causes the function to fall off more quickly.

One last useful function related to the geometric properties of a microfacet distribution is $G(\omega_o, \omega_i)$, which gives the fraction of microfacets in a differential area that are visible from both directions ω_o and ω_i. Defining G requires some additional assumptions. For starters, we know that $G_1(\omega_o)$ gives the fraction of microfacets that are visible from the direction ω_o and $G_1(\omega_i)$ gives the fraction for ω_i. If we assume that the probability of a microfacet being visible from both directions is the probability that it is visible from each

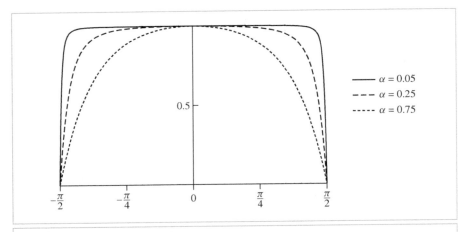

Figure 8.18: The Masking-Shadowing Function $G_1(\omega)$ **for the Trowbridge-Reitz Distribution.** Increasing surface roughness (higher α values) cause the function to fall off to zero more quickly.

direction independently, then we have

$$G(\omega_o, \omega_i) = G_1(\omega_o)\, G_1(\omega_i).$$

In practice, however, these probabilities aren't independent, and this formulation under-estimates G. To see why, consider the case where $\omega_o = \omega_i$; in this case any microfacet that is visible from ω_o is also visible from ω_i, and so $G(\omega_o, \omega_i) = G_1(\omega_o) = G_1(\omega_i)$. Because $G_1(\omega) \leq 1$, their product in this case will cause $G(\omega_o, \omega_i)$ to be too small (unless $G_1(\omega) = 1$, which is usually only true if $\omega = (0, 0, 1)$). More generally, the closer together the two directions are, the more correlation there is between $G_1(\omega_o)$ and $G_1(\omega_i)$.

A more accurate model can be derived assuming that microfacet visibility is more likely the higher up a given point on a microfacet is. This assumption leads to the model

$$G(\omega_o, \omega_i) = \frac{1}{1 + \Lambda(\omega_o) + \Lambda(\omega_i)}.$$

This approximation is fairly accurate in practice and is the one we'll use in pbrt. See the "Further Reading" section at the end of this chapter for pointers to information about this function's derivation as well as more sophisticated approaches to defining $G(\omega_o, \omega_i)$ functions.

⟨*MicrofacetDistribution Public Methods*⟩ +≡   **537**
```
Float G(const Vector3f &wo, const Vector3f &wi) const {
    return 1 / (1 + Lambda(wo) + Lambda(wi));
}
```

Float 1062

MicrofacetDistribution::
    Lambda()
    542

Vector3f 60

8.4.4 THE TORRANCE-SPARROW MODEL

An early microfacet model was developed by Torrance and Sparrow (1967) to model metallic surfaces. They modeled surfaces as collections of perfectly smooth mirrored microfacets. Because the microfacets are perfectly specular, only those with a normal

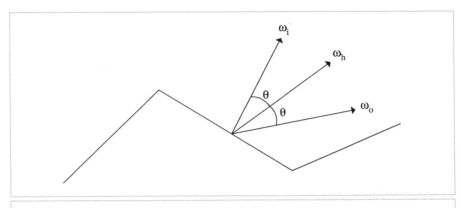

Figure 8.19: For perfectly specular microfacets and a given pair of directions ω_i and ω_o, only those microfacets with normal $\omega_h = \widehat{\omega_i + \omega_o}$ reflect light from ω_i to ω_o.

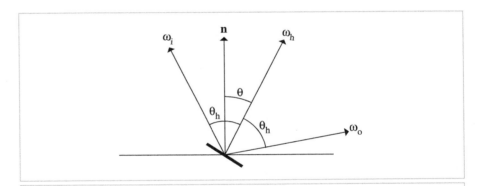

Figure 8.20: Setting for the Derivation of the Torrance–Sparrow Model. For directions ω_i and ω_o, only microfacets with normal ω_h reflect light. The angle between ω_h and $\mathbf{n}$ is denoted by θ, and the angle between ω_h and ω_o is denoted by θ_h. (The angle between ω_h and ω_i is also necessarily θ_h.)

equal to the *half-angle vector*,

$$\omega_h = \widehat{\omega_i + \omega_o},$$

cause perfect specular reflection from ω_i to ω_o (Figure 8.19).

The derivation of the Torrance–Sparrow model has a number of interesting steps; we'll go through it in detail here. First, consider the differential flux $d\Phi_h$ incident on the microfacets oriented with half-angle ω_h for directions ω_i and ω_o. From the definition of radiance, Equation (5.2), it is

$$d\Phi_h = L_i(\omega_i)\, d\omega\, dA^\perp(\omega_h) = L_i(\omega_i)\, d\omega\, \cos\theta_h\, dA(\omega_h),$$

where we have written $dA(\omega_h)$ for the area measure of the microfacets with orientation ω_h and $\cos\theta_h$ for the cosine of the angle between ω_i and ω_h (Figure 8.20).

The differential area of microfacets with orientation ω_h is

$$dA(\omega_h) = D(\omega_h)\, d\omega_h\, dA.$$

The first two terms of this product describe the differential area of facets per unit area that have the proper orientation, and the dA term converts this to differential area.

Therefore,

$$d\Phi_h = L_i(\omega_i)\, d\omega\ \cos\theta_h\, D(\omega_h)\, d\omega_h\, dA. \qquad [8.16]$$

If we assume that the microfacets individually reflect light according to Fresnel's law, the outgoing flux is

$$d\Phi_o = F_r(\omega_o)\, d\Phi_h. \qquad [8.17]$$

Again using the definition of radiance, the reflected outgoing radiance is

$$L(\omega_o) = \frac{d\Phi_o}{d\omega_o\ \cos\theta_o\, dA}.$$

If we substitute Equation (8.17) into this and then Equation (8.16) into the result, we have

$$L(\omega_o) = \frac{F_r(\omega_o)\, L_i(\omega_i)\, d\omega_i\, D(\omega_h)\, d\omega_h\, dA\ \cos\theta_h}{d\omega_o\, dA\ \cos\theta_o}.$$

In Section 14.1.1, we will derive an important relationship between $d\omega_h$ and $d\omega_o$ under specular reflection:

$$d\omega_h = \frac{d\omega_o}{4\cos\theta_h}. \qquad [8.18]$$

We can substitute this relationship into the previous equation and simplify, giving

$$L(\omega_o) = \frac{F_r(\omega_o)\, L_i(\omega_i)\, D(\omega_h)\, d\omega_i}{4\ \cos\theta_o}.$$

We can now apply the definition of the BRDF, Equation (5.8) and add the geometric attenuation term $G(\omega_o, \omega_i)$, which gives us the Torrance–Sparrow BRDF:

$$f_r(\omega_o, \omega_i) = \frac{D(\omega_h)\, G(\omega_o, \omega_i)\, F_r(\omega_o)}{4\ \cos\theta_o\ \cos\theta_i}. \qquad [8.19]$$

One of the nice things about the Torrance–Sparrow model is that the derivation doesn't depend on the particular microfacet distribution being used. Furthermore, it doesn't depend on a particular Fresnel function, so it can be used for both conductors and dielectrics. However, the relationship between $d\omega_h$ and $d\omega_o$ used in the derivation does depend on the assumption of specular reflection from microfacets.

MicrofacetReflection uses the Torrance–Sparrow model to implement a general microfacet-based BRDF.

⟨*BxDF Declarations*⟩ +≡
```
class MicrofacetReflection : public BxDF {
public:
    ⟨MicrofacetReflection Public Methods 547⟩
private:
    ⟨MicrofacetReflection Private Data 547⟩
};
```

Its constructor takes the reflectance, a pointer to a `MicrofacetDistribution` implementation, and a Fresnel function.

⟨*MicrofacetReflection Public Methods*⟩ ≡   547
```
MicrofacetReflection(const Spectrum &R,
        MicrofacetDistribution *distribution, Fresnel *fresnel)
    : BxDF(BxDFType(BSDF_REFLECTION | BSDF_GLOSSY)), R(R),
        distribution(distribution), fresnel(fresnel) { }
```

⟨*MicrofacetReflection Private Data*⟩ ≡   547
```
const Spectrum R;
const MicrofacetDistribution *distribution;
const Fresnel *fresnel;
```

Evaluating the terms of the Torrance–Sparrow BRDF is straightforward. For the Fresnel term, recall that given specular reflection, the angle θ_h is the same between ω_h and both ω_i and ω_o, so it doesn't matter which vector we use to compute the cosine of θ_h. We arbitrarily choose ω_i.

⟨*BxDF Method Definitions*⟩ +≡
```
Spectrum MicrofacetReflection::f(const Vector3f &wo,
        const Vector3f &wi) const {
    Float cosTheta0 = AbsCosTheta(wo), cosThetaI = AbsCosTheta(wi);
    Vector3f wh = wi + wo;
    ⟨Handle degenerate cases for microfacet reflection 547⟩
    wh = Normalize(wh);
    Spectrum F = fresnel->Evaluate(Dot(wi, wh));
    return R * distribution->D(wh) * distribution->G(wo, wi) * F /
            (4 * cosThetaI * cosTheta0);
}
```

Two edge cases that come up with incident and outgoing directions at glancing angles need to be handled explicitly to avoid NaN values being generated from the evaluation of the BRDF.

⟨*Handle degenerate cases for microfacet reflection*⟩ ≡   547
```
if (cosThetaI == 0 || cosTheta0 == 0) return Spectrum(0.);
if (wh.x == 0 && wh.y == 0 && wh.z == 0) return Spectrum(0.);
```

It's also possible to define a BTDF for transmission through microfacets that exhibit perfect specular transmission. In that setting, with transmission from a medium with index of refraction η_i to a medium with index of refraction η_t, then $d\omega_h$ and $d\omega_o$ are related by:

$$d\omega_h = \frac{\eta_o^2 \, |\omega_o \cdot \omega_h| \, d\omega_o}{(\eta_i(\omega_i \cdot \omega_h) + \eta_o(\omega_o \cdot \omega_h))^2}$$

This relationship can be used in place of Equation (8.18) in the derivation of the Torrance–Sparrow BRDF. The result is

$$f_r(\omega_o, \omega_i) = \frac{\eta^2 D(\omega_h) \, G(\omega_o, \omega_i) \, (1 - F_r(\omega_o))}{((\omega_o \cdot \omega_h) + \eta(\omega_i \cdot \omega_h))^2} \frac{|\omega_i \cdot \omega_h||\omega_o \cdot \omega_h|}{\cos \theta_o \, \cos \theta_i}, \qquad [8.20]$$

where $\eta = \eta_i/\eta_o$. For specular transmission, the half-angle vector is

$$\omega_h = \omega_o + \eta\omega_i.$$

(You may want to verify that this normal vector causes ω_o to be refracted in the direction ω_i, via Equation (8.9).)

The MicrofacetTransmission class implements this BTDF.

⟨*BxDF Declarations*⟩ +≡
```
    class MicrofacetTransmission : public BxDF {
    public:
        ⟨MicrofacetTransmission Public Methods 548⟩
    private:
        ⟨MicrofacetTransmission Private Data 548⟩
    };
```

⟨*MicrofacetTransmission Public Methods*⟩ ≡   548
```
    MicrofacetTransmission(const Spectrum &T,
            MicrofacetDistribution *distribution, Float etaA, Float etaB,
            TransportMode mode)
        : BxDF(BxDFType(BSDF_TRANSMISSION | BSDF_GLOSSY)),
          T(T), distribution(distribution), etaA(etaA), etaB(etaB),
          fresnel(etaA, etaB), mode(mode) { }
```

⟨*MicrofacetTransmission Private Data*⟩ ≡   548
```
    const Spectrum T;
    const MicrofacetDistribution *distribution;
    const Float etaA, etaB;
    const FresnelDielectric fresnel;
    const TransportMode mode;
```

Its f() method is a direct transcription of Equation (8.20). Its implementation is therefore not included here.

⟨*MicrofacetTransmission Public Methods*⟩ +≡   548
```
    Spectrum f(const Vector3f &wo, const Vector3f &wi) const;
```

Figure 8.21 shows the dragon rendered with the Torrance–Sparrow model and both reflection and transmission and Figure 8.22 compares the appearance of two spheres with an isotropic and anisotropic microfacet model lit by a light source simulating a distant environment.

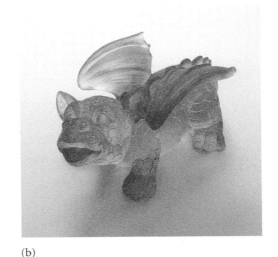

(a)   (b)

Figure 8.21: Dragon models rendered with the Torrance–Sparrow microfacet model featuring both reflection (a) and transmission (b). *(Model courtesy of Christian Schüller.)*

Figure 8.22: Spheres rendered with an isotropic microfacet distribution (left) and an anisotropic distribution (right). Note the different specular highlight shapes from the anisotropic model. We have used spheres here instead of the dragon, since anisotropic models like these depend on a globally consistent set of tangent vectors over the surface to orient the direction of anisotropy in a reasonable way.

8.5 FRESNEL INCIDENCE EFFECTS

Many BRDF models in graphics do not account for the fact that Fresnel reflection reduces the amount of light that reaches the bottom level of layered objects. Consider a polished wood table or a wall with glossy paint: if you look at their surfaces head-on, you primarily

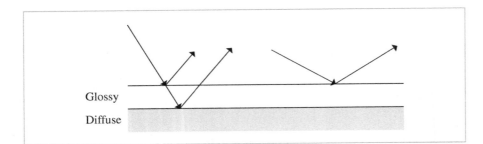

Figure 8.23: The FresnelBlend BRDF models the effect of a surface with a glossy layer on top of a diffuse substrate. As the angle of incidence of the vectors ω_i and ω_o heads toward glancing (right), the amount of light that reaches the diffuse substrate is reduced by Fresnel effects, and the diffuse layer becomes less visibly apparent.

see the wood or the paint pigment color. As you move your viewpoint toward a glancing angle, you see less of the underlying color as it is overwhelmed by increasing glossy reflection due to Fresnel effects.

In this section, we will implement a BRDF model developed by Ashikhmin and Shirley (2000, 2002) that models a diffuse underlying surface with a glossy specular surface above it. The effect of reflection from the diffuse surface is modulated by the amount of energy left after Fresnel effects have been considered. Figure 8.23 shows this idea: when the incident direction is close to the normal, most light is transmitted to the diffuse layer and the diffuse term dominates. When the incident direction is close to glancing, glossy reflection is the primary mode of reflection. The car model in Figures 12.19 and 12.20 uses this BRDF for its paint.

⟨*BxDF Declarations*⟩ +≡
```
class FresnelBlend : public BxDF {
public:
    ⟨FresnelBlend Public Methods 551⟩
private:
    ⟨FresnelBlend Private Data 550⟩
};
```

The model takes two spectra, representing diffuse and specular reflectance, and a microfacet distribution for the glossy layer.

⟨*BxDF Method Definitions*⟩ +≡
```
FresnelBlend::FresnelBlend(const Spectrum &Rd, const Spectrum &Rs,
                    MicrofacetDistribution *distribution)
    : BxDF(BxDFType(BSDF_REFLECTION | BSDF_GLOSSY)),
      Rd(Rd), Rs(Rs), distribution(distribution) { }
```

⟨*FresnelBlend Private Data*⟩ ≡
```
const Spectrum Rd, Rs;
MicrofacetDistribution *distribution;
```

This model is based on the weighted sum of a glossy specular term and a diffuse term. Accounting for reciprocity and energy conservation, the glossy specular term is derived as

$$f_r(p, \omega_o, \omega_i) = \frac{D(\omega_h) F(\omega_o)}{4(\omega_h \cdot \omega_i)(\max((n \cdot \omega_o), (n \cdot \omega_i)))},$$

where $D(\omega_h)$ is a microfacet distribution term and $F(\omega_o)$ represents Fresnel reflectance. Note that this is quite similar to the Torrance–Sparrow model.

The key to Ashikhmin and Shirley's model is the derivation of a diffuse term such that the model still obeys reciprocity and conserves energy. The derivation is dependent on an approximation to the Fresnel reflection equations due to Schlick (1993), who approximated Fresnel reflection as

$$F_r(\cos \theta) = R + (1 - R)(1 - \cos \theta)^5,$$

where R is the reflectance of the surface at normal incidence.

Given this Fresnel term, the diffuse term in the following equation successfully models Fresnel-based reduced diffuse reflection in a physically plausible manner:

$$f_r(p, \omega_i, \omega_o) = \frac{28 R_d}{23\pi} (1 - R_s) \left(1 - \left(1 - \frac{(n \cdot \omega_i)}{2}\right)^5\right) \left(1 - \left(1 - \frac{(n \cdot \omega_o)}{2}\right)^5\right).$$

We will not include the derivation of this result here.

⟨*FresnelBlend Public Methods*⟩ ≡   550

```
Spectrum SchlickFresnel(Float cosTheta) const {
    auto pow5 = [](Float v) { return (v * v) * (v * v) * v; };
    return Rs + pow5(1 - cosTheta) * (Spectrum(1.) - Rs);
}
```

⟨*BxDF Method Definitions*⟩ +≡

```
Spectrum FresnelBlend::f(const Vector3f &wo, const Vector3f &wi) const {
    auto pow5 = [](Float v) { return (v * v) * (v * v) * v; };
    Spectrum diffuse = (28.f/(23.f*Pi)) * Rd *
        (Spectrum(1.f) - Rs) *
        (1 - pow5(1 - .5f * AbsCosTheta(wi))) *
        (1 - pow5(1 - .5f * AbsCosTheta(wo)));
    Vector3f wh = wi + wo;
    if (wh.x == 0 && wh.y == 0 && wh.z == 0) return Spectrum(0);
    wh = Normalize(wh);
    Spectrum specular = distribution->D(wh) /
        (4 * AbsDot(wi, wh) *
            std::max(AbsCosTheta(wi), AbsCosTheta(wo))) *
            SchlickFresnel(Dot(wi, wh));
    return diffuse + specular;
}
```

Figure 8.24: Dragon models rendered using the `FourierBSDF` model. The surface of the dragon on the left has a BSDF that models the appeerence of rough gold; the one on the right is coated copper. *(Model courtesy of Christian Schüller.)*

8.6 FOURIER BASIS BSDFs

While reflection models like Torrance–Sparrow and Oren–Nayar can accurately represent many materials, some materials have BRDF shapes that don't match these models well. (Examples include layered materials like metals with smooth or rough coatings or fabrics, which are often partially retro-reflective.) One option for materials like these is to store their BSDF values in a large 3D or 4D lookup table, though this approach can require an unacceptable amount of storage—for example, if ω_i and ω_o are sampled in spherical angles with 1-degree spacing, then over one billion sample points are needed to represent the corresponding anisotropic BSDF in the form of a 4D lookup table.

Therefore, having a more compact representation that still represents the BSDF accurately is highly desirable. This section introduces the `FourierBSDF`, which represents BSDFs with sums of scaled cosine terms using the Fourier basis. This representation is accurate, space-efficient, and works well with Monte Carlo integration (see Section 14.1.4.) Figure 8.24 shows two instances of the dragon model rendered using this representation.

Here, we won't discuss how BSDFs are transformed into this representation, but we will focus on its use in rendering. See the "Further Reading" section at the end of this chapter for pointers to more details on those issues and the scenes/brdfs directory in the pbrt distribution for a variety of BSDFs represented in this format.

The `FourierBSDF` represents isotropic BSDFs by parameterizing the BSDF by a pair of spherical coordinates for the incident and outgoing directions, where μ_i and μ_o denote the cosines of the incident and outgoing zenith angles, respectively, and ϕ_i and ϕ_o are the azimuth angles:

FourierBSDF 555

$$f(\omega_i, \omega_o) = f(\mu_i, \phi_i, \mu_o, \phi_o).$$

The assumption of isotropy means that the function can be rewritten with a simpler dependence on the zenith angle cosines and the azimuth difference angle $\phi = \phi_i - \phi_o$:

$$f(\omega_i, \omega_o) = f(\mu_i, \mu_o, \phi_i - \phi_o) = f(\mu_i, \mu_o, \phi).$$

Isotropic BSDFs are generally also *even* functions of the azimuth difference, i.e.:

$$f(\mu_i, \mu_o, \phi) = f(\mu_i, \mu_o, -\phi). \tag{8.21}$$

Given these properties, the product of the BSDF with the cosine falloff is then represented as a Fourier series in the azimuth angle difference.

$$f(\mu_i, \mu_o, \phi_i - \phi_o)\, |\mu_i| = \sum_{k=0}^{m-1} a_k(\mu_i, \mu_o) \cos(k\,(\phi_i - \phi_o)) \tag{8.22}$$

Note how only cosine terms and no sine terms are needed due to Equation (8.21). The function evaluations $a_0(\mu_i, \mu_o), \ldots, a_{m-1}(\mu_i, \mu_o)$ denote the Fourier coefficients for a specific pair of zenith angle cosines.

Next, the functions a_k are discretized over their input arguments. We choose a set of zenith angle cosines $\bar{\mu} = \{\mu_0, \ldots, \mu_{n-1}\}$ and store the values of $a_k(\mu_i, \mu_j)$ for every pair $0 \le i, j < n$. Thus, we can think of each a_k as a $n \times n$ matrix, and the entire BRDF representation then consists of a set of m such matrices. Each describes a different azimuthal oscillation frequency in the material's response to incident illumination.

The maximum order m needed to evaluate Equation (8.22) to satisfactory accuracy varies: it depends on the particular zenith angles, so it's worth adapting the number of coefficients a_k to the complexity of the BSDF for a given pair of directions. Doing this is very important for the compactness of this representation.

To see the value of being able to vary the number of coefficients, consider nearly perfect specular reflection: when $\mu_i \approx \mu_o$, many coefficients are necessary to accurately represent the specular lobe, which is zero for almost all azimuth angle differences $\phi = \phi_i - \phi_o$ and then very large for a small set of directions around $\phi = \pi$, where the incident and outgoing directions are nearly opposite. However, when μ_i and μ_o aren't aligned, only a single term is needed to represent that the BSDF is zero (or has negligible value).[9]

For smoother BSDFs, most or all pairs of μ_i and μ_o angles require multiple coefficients a_k to represent their ϕ distribution accurately, but their smoothness means that not too many coefficients are generally needed for each a_k. The FourierBSDF representation exploits this property and only stores the sparse set of coefficients that is needed to achieve a desired accuracy. Thus, for most types of realistic BSDF data, the representation of Equation (8.22) is fairly compact; a few megabytes is typical.

FourierBSDFTable is a helper structure that holds all of the data for a BSDF represented in this manner. It's mostly a simple struct that collects data that's directly accessible to calling code, though it does provide a few utility methods.

---

9   Jakob et al. (2014a) showed that this adaptivity makes it possible to represent a shiny mirror with Beckmann roughness $\alpha = 0.01$ with 1% relative L^2 error using 51 MiB, while using the maximum order m needed for any pair of directions for all pairs of directions would require 28 GiB to achieve the same error.

⟨*BSDF Declarations*⟩ +≡
```
struct FourierBSDFTable {
    ⟨FourierBSDFTable Public Data 554⟩
    ⟨FourierBSDFTable Public Methods 554⟩
};
```

The Read() method initializes the structure for the BSDF stored in the given file. It returns true on success or false if an error was encountered while reading the file.

⟨*FourierBSDFTable Public Methods*⟩ ≡   554
```
static bool Read(const std::string &filename, FourierBSDFTable *table);
```

If the BSDF represents scattering at the boundary between two different media, then the FourierBSDFTable::eta member variable gives the relative index of refraction over the surface boundary (Section 8.2.3) mMax gives the maximum order m for any pair of μ_i, μ_o directions; this upper limit is useful when allocating temporary buffers to store a_k coefficients, for example.

⟨*FourierBSDFTable Public Data*⟩ ≡   554
```
Float eta;
int mMax;
```

nChannels gives the number of spectral channels available; in this implementation, it is either 1, representing a monochromatic BSDF, or 3, representing a BSDF with RGB colors. Here, the three-channel variant actually stores luminance, red, and blue, rather than red, green, and blue—representing luminance directly turns out to be useful for the Monte Carlo sampling routines defined in Section 14.1.4, since it provides aggregate information about the function over all color channels. The corresponding green color is easily computed from luminance, red, and blue, as we'll see shortly.

⟨*FourierBSDFTable Public Data*⟩ +≡   554
```
int nChannels;
```

The zenith angles are discretized into nMu directions, which are stored in the mu array. mu is sorted from low to high, so that binary search can be used to find the entry that's closest to a given μ_i or μ_o angle.

⟨*FourierBSDFTable Public Data*⟩ +≡   554
```
int nMu;
Float *mu;
```

To evaluate Equation (8.22), we need to know the target Fourier order m and all coefficients $a_0, \ldots, a_{m-1}$ corresponding to the directions ω_i and ω_o. For simplicity now, we'll present the basic ideas as if only the coefficients for the closest mu directions less than or equal to μ_i and μ_o are used, though the implementation to follow interpolates between coefficients from multiple mu values around the directions.

The order m of the Fourier representation is always bounded by mMax but varies with respect to the incident and outgoing zenith angle cosine μ_i and μ_o: how many orders are needed can be determined by querying an nMu × nMu integer matrix m.

Float 1062
FourierBSDFTable 554

⟨*FourierBSDFTable Public Data*⟩ +≡   554
    int *m;

To find *m* for a particular set of angles, we first perform two binary searches in the discretized directions mu to give the offsets oi and oo such that

$$\text{mu}[\text{oi}] \leq \mu_i < \text{mu}[\text{oi} + 1]$$
$$\text{mu}[\text{oo}] \leq \mu_o < \text{mu}[\text{oo} + 1]$$

Using these indices, the requisite order can be fetched from m[oo * nMu + oi].

All of the a_k coefficients for all of the pairs of discretized directions mu are packed into the a array. Because the maximum order (and thus, number of coefficients) varies and can even be zero depending on the characteristics of the BSDF for a given pair of directions, finding the offset into the a array is a two-step process:

1. First, the offsets oi and oo are used to index into the aOffset array to get an offset into a: offset = aOffset[oo * nMu + oi]. (The aOffset array thus has a total of nMu * nMu entries.)
2. Next, the *m* coefficients starting at a[offset] give the a_k values for the corresponding pair of directions. For the three color channel case, the first *m* coefficients after a[offset] encode coefficients for luminance, the next *m* correspond to the red channel, and then blue follows.

⟨*FourierBSDFTable Public Data*⟩ +≡   554
    int *aOffset;
    Float *a;

GetAk() is a small convenience method that, given offsets into the mu array for the incident and outgoing direction cosines, returns the order *m* of coefficients for the directions and a pointer to their coefficients.

⟨*FourierBSDFTable Public Methods*⟩ +≡   554
```
const Float *GetAk(int offsetI, int offsetO, int *mptr) const {
    *mptr = m[offsetO * nMu + offsetI];
    return a + aOffset[offsetO * nMu + offsetI];
}
```

The FourierBSDF class provides a bridge between the FourierBSDFTable representation and the BxDF interface. Instances of this class are created by the FourierMaterial class.

⟨*BxDF Declarations*⟩ +≡
```
class FourierBSDF : public BxDF {
public:
    ⟨FourierBSDF Public Methods 556⟩
private:
    ⟨FourierBSDF Private Data 556⟩
};
```

⟨*FourierBSDF Public Methods*⟩ ≡   555
```
FourierBSDF(const FourierBSDFTable &bsdfTable, TransportMode mode)
    : BxDF(BxDFType(BSDF_REFLECTION | BSDF_TRANSMISSION | BSDF_GLOSSY)),
      bsdfTable(bsdfTable), mode(mode) { }
```

The `FourierBSDF` class stores only a const reference to the table; the table is large enough that we definitely don't want to make a separate copy of it for each `FourierBSDF` instance. Only read-access is needed here, so this approach doesn't cause any problems. (`FourierMaterial` is responsible for the `FourierBSDFTable` storage.)

⟨*FourierBSDF Private Data*⟩ ≡   555
```
const FourierBSDFTable &bsdfTable;
const TransportMode mode;
```

Evaluating the BSDF is a matter of computing the cosines μ_i and μ_o, finding the corresponding coefficients a_k and maximum order, and then evaluating Equation (8.22).

⟨*BxDF Method Definitions*⟩ +≡
```
Spectrum FourierBSDF::f(const Vector3f &wo, const Vector3f &wi) const {
    ⟨Find the zenith angle cosines and azimuth difference angle 556⟩
    ⟨Compute Fourier coefficients aₖ for (μᵢ, μₒ) 557⟩
    ⟨Evaluate Fourier expansion for angle φ 558⟩
}
```

There is an important difference of convention in how directions are represented within the `FourierBSDF`: the incident direction ω_i is negated compared to the usual approach in pbrt. This difference is helpful when performing other computations such as computing BSDFs for layered materials using this representation.[10]

⟨*Find the zenith angle cosines and azimuth difference angle*⟩ ≡   556, 821
```
Float muI = CosTheta(-wi), muO = CosTheta(wo);
Float cosPhi = CosDPhi(-wi, wo);
```

So that the reconstructed BSDF is fairly smooth, the implementation here interpolates a_k coefficients over the product of the four quantized mu directions that surround μ_i and the four that surround μ_o. The interpolation is performed with a *tensor-product spline*, where weights for the sampled function values are computed separately for each parameter and then multiplied together. Each final Fourier coefficient a_k is thus computed by

$$a_k = \sum_{a=0}^{3} \sum_{b=0}^{3} a_k(o_i + a, o_o + b)\, w_i(a)\, w_o(b), \qquad [8.23]$$

where $a_k(i, j)$ gives the kth Fourier coefficient for the quantized directions μ_i, μ_j and w_i and w_o are the spline weights. This interpolation ensures sufficient smoothness even

---

10 For example, an implication of this convention is that for light passing unchanged through a medium, if we consider $a_k(\mu_i, \mu_o)$ as a matrix, then we have a diagonal matrix where the non-zero entries are the Fourier coefficients corresponding to a delta distribution that is zero for all $\phi \neq 0$. This property in turn makes the notation for these sorts of computations easier to work with.

when the discretization of directions μ_i is relatively coarse; the details of how these weights are computed will be explained in a few pages.

⟨*Compute Fourier coefficients a_k for (μ_i, μ_o)*⟩ ≡   556, 819
    ⟨*Determine offsets and weights for μ_i and μ_o* 557⟩
    ⟨*Allocate storage to accumulate* ak *coefficients* 557⟩
    ⟨*Accumulate weighted sums of nearby a_k coefficients* 557⟩

For each direction μ_i and μ_o, GetWeightsAndOffset() returns the offset of the first of the four mu values to be interpolated over and an array of four floating-point weights.

⟨*Determine offsets and weights for μ_i and μ_o*⟩ ≡   557
```
int offsetI, offsetO;
Float weightsI[4], weightsO[4];
if (!bsdfTable.GetWeightsAndOffset(muI, &offsetI, weightsI) ||
    !bsdfTable.GetWeightsAndOffset(muO, &offsetO, weightsO))
    return Spectrum(0.f);
```

The various a_k vectors in the 4×4 extent of the directions being interpolated over may have different orders m. Therefore, the implementation here allocates storage for the a_k values using the maximum possible order m times the number of channels for the size. For the multiple-channel case, the first bsdfTable.mMax entries of the ak array allocated here will be used for the first channel, the next mMax are for the second channel, and so forth. (Thus there is generally some unused space in the ak array for the usual case that the maximum order over the sixteen directions is less than mMax.) All of this storage is initialized to zero, so that subsequent code can add terms of Equation (8.23) to the corresponding entry in ak directly.

⟨*Allocate storage to accumulate* ak *coefficients*⟩ ≡   557
```
Float *ak = ALLOCA(Float, bsdfTable.mMax * bsdfTable.nChannels);
memset(ak, 0, bsdfTable.mMax * bsdfTable.nChannels * sizeof(Float));
```

Given weights, offsets, and storage for the result, the interpolation can now be performed.

⟨*Accumulate weighted sums of nearby a_k coefficients*⟩ ≡   557
```
int mMax = 0;
for (int b = 0; b < 4; ++b) {
    for (int a = 0; a < 4; ++a) {
        ⟨Add contribution of (a, b) to ak values 558⟩
    }
}
```

Given the weights and the starting offsets, adding each term of the sum in Equation (8.23) is a matter of getting the corresponding coefficients from the table for the offset and adding them to the running sum in ak.

⟨*Add contribution of* (a, b) *to* a_k *values*⟩ ≡   557
```
    Float weight = weightsI[a] * weightsO[b];
    if (weight != 0) {
        int m;
        const Float *ap = bsdfTable.GetAk(offsetI + a, offsetO + b, &m);
        mMax = std::max(mMax, m);
        for (int c = 0; c < bsdfTable.nChannels; ++c)
            for (int k = 0; k < m; ++k)
                ak[c * bsdfTable.mMax + k] += weight * ap[c * m + k];
    }
```

Given the final weighted coefficients in ak, a call to Fourier() computes the BSDF value for the first color channel. Error in Fourier reconstruction can manifest itself as negative values, so the returned value must be clamped to zero.

Recall from Equation (8.22) that the a_k coefficients represent the cosine-weighted BSDF. This cosine factor must be removed from the value returned from the f() method; the scale term encodes this factor.

⟨*Evaluate Fourier expansion for angle* ϕ⟩ ≡   556
```
    Float Y = std::max((Float)0, Fourier(ak, mMax, cosPhi));
    Float scale = muI != 0 ? (1 / std::abs(muI)) : (Float)0;
    ⟨Update scale to account for adjoint light transport 961⟩
    if (bsdfTable.nChannels == 1)
        return Spectrum(Y * scale);
    else {
        ⟨Compute and return RGB colors for tabulated BSDF 559⟩
    }
```

As with specular transmission, radiance is scaled as it passes from a medium with one index of refraction to another, but this scaling isn't applied to rays starting from the camera. A definition and discussion of the fragment ⟨*Update* scale *to account for adjoint light transport*⟩, which handles this adjustment, is provided in Section 16.1.

As mentioned earlier, when there are three color channels, the first channel encodes luminance and the next two are red and blue, respectively. To see how to compute a green channel value, consider the implementation of the function RGBToXYZ(), which uses the following equation to compute y_λ from red, green, and blue color components assuming the color primaries from the sRGB standard:

$$y_\lambda = 0.212671\,r + 0.715160\,g + 0.072169\,b.$$

In this case, we know y_λ, r, and b. Solving for g, we can find:

$$g = 1.39829\,y_\lambda - 0.100913\,b - 0.297375\,r.$$

As before, any color coefficients with negative values due to error in Fourier reconstruction must be clamped to zero.

⟨*Compute and return RGB colors for tabulated BSDF*⟩ ≡   558
```
Float R = Fourier(ak + 1 * bsdfTable.mMax, mMax, cosPhi);
Float B = Fourier(ak + 2 * bsdfTable.mMax, mMax, cosPhi);
Float G = 1.39829f * Y - 0.100913f * B - 0.297375f * R;
Float rgb[3] = { R * scale, G * scale, B * scale };
return Spectrum::FromRGB(rgb).Clamp();
```

We'll now define the Fourier() function, which takes an array of coefficients a_k, the maximum order m, and the cosine of the angle ϕ. It evaluates the weighted sum of cosines in Equation (8.22), which can be written in the simpler form with a_k now known:

$$f(\phi) = \sum_{k=0}^{m-1} a_k \cos(k\,\phi).\qquad\text{[8.24]}$$

The implementation of this function uses double precision for the sum of terms in order to minimize the impact of floating-point round-off error in computing the sum.

⟨*Fourier Interpolation Definitions*⟩ ≡
```
Float Fourier(const Float *a, int m, double cosPhi) {
    double value = 0.0;
    ⟨Initialize cosine iterates 559⟩
    for (int k = 0; k < m; ++k) {
        ⟨Add the current summand and update the cosine iterates 560⟩
    }
    return value;
}
```

As the number of coefficients increases, a naïve evaluation of Equation (8.24) involves a correspondingly large number of trigonometric function calls. This can lead to severe performance issues: current CPU architectures require a few hundred processor cycles for a single invocation of std::cos(). Therefore, it pays to use the *multiple angle formula* for cosines:

$$\cos(k\,\phi) = (2\cos\phi)\cos((k-1)\phi) - \cos((k-2)\phi)\qquad\text{[8.25]}$$

This expression expresses cosine of summand k in Equation (8.24) in terms of those used for the summands $k-1$ and $k-2$.

The implementation starts with the declaration of two variables for the current and preceding cosine variables, corresponding to values for the indices $k = -1$ and $k = 0$. Here, it's important to also use double precision to compute the $\cos(k\,\phi)$ values; once m has values in the thousands, accumulated floating-point rounding error with 32-bit floats can become noticeable when using the multiple angle formula.

⟨*Initialize cosine iterates*⟩ ≡   559
```
double cosKMinusOnePhi = cosPhi;
double cosKPhi = 1;
```

The body of the loop then adds the product of the current coefficient and cosine value to a running sum and computes the cosine values for the next iteration.

⟨*Add the current summand and update the cosine iterates*⟩ ≡   559
```
value += a[k] * cosKPhi;
double cosKPlusOnePhi = 2 * cosPhi * cosKPhi - cosKMinusOnePhi;
cosKMinusOnePhi = cosKPhi;
cosKPhi = cosKPlusOnePhi;
```

8.6.1 SPLINE INTERPOLATION

The last detail to explain is how the spline-based interpolation used to reconstruct the a_k coefficients works. The implementation here uses the Catmull–Rom spline, which can be expressed in 1D as a weighted sum over four control points, where the weight and the particular control points used depend on the parametric location along the curve's path where its value is being computed. The spline passes through the given control points and follows a fairly smooth curve along the way.

To understand how these weights are computed, first suppose we are given a set of values of a function f and its derivative f' at positions $x_0, x_1, \ldots, x_k$. For each interval $[x_i, x_{i+1}]$, we would like to approximate the function using a cubic polynomial

$$p_i(x) = ax^3 + bx^2 + cx + d, \hspace{2em} [8.26]$$

which is chosen so that it matches the function and its derivative at the sample locations, i.e., $p_i(x_i) = f(x_i)$, $p_i(x_{i+1}) = f(x_{i+1})$, $p_i'(x_i) = f'(x_i)$, and $p_i'(x_{i+1}) = f'(x_{i+1})$. For simplicity, let us just focus on the first interval and furthermore suppose that $[x_0, x_1] = [0, 1]$. Solving for the coefficients a, b, c, and d yields

$$a = f'(x_0) + f'(x_1) + 2f(x_0) - 2f(x_1),$$
$$b = 3f(x_1) - 3f(x_0) - 2f'(x_0) - f'(x_1),$$
$$c = f'(x_0),$$
$$d = f(x_0).$$

Note how all of the coefficients are linear in the function and derivative values, which lets us rewrite Equation (8.26) as

$$
\begin{aligned}
p(x) = {}& (2x^3 - 3x^2 + 1)f(x_0) \\
&+ (-2x^3 + 3x^2)f(x_1) \\
&+ (x^3 - 2x^2 + x)f'(x_0) \\
&+ (x^3 - x^2)f'(x_1).
\end{aligned}
\hspace{2em} [8.27]
$$

This kind of interpolant is convenient but unfortunately still too restrictive, since we cannot generally expect derivative information to be available: analytic derivatives of reflectance models are often cumbersome, and measured data does not provide them at all. We therefore estimate the derivatives at each $f(x_i)$ using central differences based on the two adjacent function values $f(x_{i-1})$ and $f(x_{i+1})$. The estimated derivative is then

$$f'(x_0) \approx \frac{f(x_1) - f(x_{-1})}{x_1 - x_{-1}} = \frac{f(x_1) - f(x_{-1})}{1 - x_{-1}}.$$

Similarly, the derivative at $f(x_1)$ can be estimated using the two adjacent function values:

$$f'(x_1) \approx \frac{f(x_2) - f(x_0)}{x_2 - x_0} = \frac{f(x_2) - f(x_0)}{x_2}.$$

If we substitute these two expressions into Equation (8.27) and again collect f terms, we have:

$$p(x) = \frac{x^3 - 2x^2 + x}{x_{-1} - 1} f(x_{-1})$$

$$+ \left(2x^3 - 3x^2 + 1 - \frac{x^3 - x^2}{x_2} \right) f(x_0)$$

$$+ \left(-2x^3 + 3x^2 + \frac{x^3 - 2x^2 + x}{1 - x_{-1}} \right) f(x_1)$$

$$+ \frac{x^3 - x^2}{x_2} f(x_2),$$

Note that the weights are independent of the function values: we can therefore also express this interpolation as

$$p(x) = w_0 f(x_{-1}) + w_1 f(x_0) + w_2 f(x_1) + w_3 f(x_2), \qquad \text{[8.28]}$$

with

$$w_0 = \frac{x^3 - 2x^2 + x}{x_{-1} - 1}$$

$$w_1 = 2x^3 - 3x^2 + 1 - \frac{x^3 - x^2}{x_2} = \left(2x^3 - 3x^2 + 1 \right) - w_3$$

$$w_2 = -2x^3 + 3x^2 + \frac{x^3 - 2x^2 + x}{1 - x_{-1}} = \left(-2x^3 + 3x^2 \right) + w_0$$

$$w_3 = \frac{x^3 - x^2}{x_2}. \qquad \text{[8.29]}$$

The `CatmullRomWeights()` function takes the variable x and the number of interpolation nodes and their positions as arguments. It does not use the function values in any way but instead computes the index offset and an array with four weights corresponding to the expressions in Equation (8.29).

CatmullRomWeights() 562

The code that computes these weights is useful beyond the task of BSDF reconstruction and is thus defined in the files core/interpolation.h and core/interpolation.cpp.

⟨*Spline Interpolation Definitions*⟩ ≡
```
    bool CatmullRomWeights(int size, const Float *nodes, Float x,
                           int *offset, Float *weights) {
        ⟨Return false if x is out of bounds 562⟩
        ⟨Search for the interval idx containing x 562⟩
        ⟨Compute the t parameter and powers 562⟩
        ⟨Compute initial node weights w₁ and w₂ 563⟩
        ⟨Compute first node weight w₀ 563⟩
        ⟨Compute last node weight w₃⟩
        return true;
    }
```

The first statement returns a failure when x is outside the domain of the function. Note the somewhat peculiar way of writing the conditional logic in negated form: this way, we can also catch NaN arguments, which by convention cause comparisons to evaluate to false.

⟨*Return* false *if* x *is out of bounds*⟩ ≡   562
```
    if (!(x >= nodes[0] && x <= nodes[size-1]))
        return false;
```

The FindInterval() helper function efficiently locates the index of the interval containing x via binary search. With its result, we can now set the *offset return value to the index of the node x_{i-1} and set variables x0 and x1 that delimit the extent of the domain of the corresponding spline segment.

Note that it's possible that this offset would cause an out-of-bounds array access when Equation (8.28) is evaluated. (Specifically, in the case where the offset is one element before the start of the nodes array, when idx == 0, or if idx equals the size of the array minus one.) In these cases, the corresponding interpolation weights will always be set to zero for any out-of-bounds entries. Code that uses these weights in pbrt is therefore carefully written to never access the function values array for any indices where the weight is zero.

⟨*Search for the interval* idx *containing* x⟩ ≡   562
```
    int idx = FindInterval(size, [&](int i) { return nodes[i] <= x; });
    *offset = idx - 1;
    Float x0 = nodes[idx], x1 = nodes[idx+1];
```

Because our derivation of the spline assumed the unit interval, we'll define a scaled variable t in [0, 1] in the code here. It's also useful to precompute some integer powers of t.

⟨*Compute the t parameter and powers*⟩ ≡   562
```
    Float t = (x - x0) / (x1 - x0), t2 = t * t, t3 = t2 * t;
```

The implementation starts by initializing the second and third weights w_1 and w_2 using the results from Equation (8.29). For starters, only the terms in parenthesis are included.

FindInterval() 1065
Float 1062

⟨*Compute initial node weights w_1 and w_2*⟩ ≡   562
```
weights[1] =  2 * t3 - 3 * t2 + 1;
weights[2] = -2 * t3 + 3 * t2;
```

There are two important details involved in computing the weights w_0 and w_3 from Equation (8.29). First, we need to introduce a scale factor of x1-x0, which corrects for the fact that the t values used in the code here incorporate a rescaling to the unit interval, while we actually want derivatives with respect to the original parameterization of the function.

Second, it's necessary to handle an edge condition: the usual case is that idx > 0 and a previous neighbor exists; in this case, weights[0] can be initialized directly and the w_0 term can be added to weights[2], completing its initialization. If there is no previous neighbor, then the derivative $f'(x_0)$ is instead approximated with the forward difference $f(x_1) - f(x_0)$. In this case, a similar algebraic process can be followed as was used to find the weights in Equation (8.29); the result is used here.

⟨*Compute first node weight w_0*⟩ ≡   562
```
if (idx > 0) {
    Float w0 = (t3 - 2 * t2 + t) * (x1 - x0) / (x1 - nodes[idx - 1]);
    weights[0]  = -w0;
    weights[2] +=  w0;
} else {
    Float w0 = t3 - 2 * t2 + t;
    weights[0]  = 0;
    weights[1] -= w0;
    weights[2] += w0;
}
```

The computation for the w_3 follows similarly and so the fragment that implements this part of the function, ⟨*Compute last node weight w_3*⟩, isn't included here.

Given this machinery, we can now define the implementation of the FourierBDFTable:: GetWeightsAndOffsets() method, which just calls into CatmullRomWeights(), passing it the sampled mu array.

⟨*BxDF Method Definitions*⟩ +≡
```
bool FourierBSDFTable::GetWeightsAndOffset(Float cosTheta, int *offset,
                                           Float weights[4]) const {
    return CatmullRomWeights(nMu, mu, cosTheta, offset, weights);
}
```

FURTHER READING

Phong (1975) developed an early empirical reflection model for glossy surfaces in computer graphics. Although neither reciprocal nor energy conserving, it was a cornerstone of the first synthetic images of non-Lambertian objects. The Torrance–Sparrow microfacet model is described in Torrance and Sparrow (1967); it was first introduced to graphics by Blinn (1977), and a variant of it was used by Cook and Torrance (1981,

1982). The Oren–Nayar Lambertian model is described in their 1994 paper (Oren and Nayar 1994).

Hall's (1989) book collected and described the state of the art in physically based surface reflection models for graphics; it remains a seminal reference. It discusses the physics of surface reflection in detail, with many pointers to the original literature and with many tables of useful measured data about reflection from real surfaces. Burley's (2012) more recent paper includes a thorough annotated bibliography of more recent work on reflection models for computer graphics.

Heitz's paper on microfacet shadowing-masking functions (2014a) provides a very well-written introduction to microfacet BSDF models in general, with many useful figures and explanations about details of the topic. See the papers by Beckmann and Spizzichino (1963) and Trowbridge and Reitz (1975) for the introduction of their respective microfacet distribution functions. Kurt et al. (2010) developed an anisotropic Beckmann–Spizzichino distribution function; see Heitz (2014a) for anisotropic variants of many other microfacet distribution functions. Early anisotropic BRDF models for computer graphics were developed by Kajiya (1985) and Poulin and Fournier (1990).

The microfacet masking-shadowing function in Equation (8.15) was introduced by Smith (1967), who used the assumption of no correlation between the height of the microsurface at nearby points to derive this result. Smith also first derived the normalization constraint in Equation (8.13). (This result was derived independently by Ashikhmin, Premoze, and Shirley (2000).) See Heitz (2014a) for further discussion of derivations of these functions. A more accurate $G(\omega_i, \omega_o)$ function for Gaussian microfacet surfaces that better accounts for the effects of correlation between the two directions was developed by Heitz et al. (2013), and the rational approximation to the Beckmann–Spizzichino $\Lambda(\omega)$ function used in this chapter is due to Heitz (2014a), which is derived from an approximation developed by Walter et al. (2007). Our derivation of the $\Lambda(\omega)$ function, Equation (8.14), is also due to Heitz (2015).

Stam (2001) developed a generalization of the Cook–Torrance model for transmission, and more recently Walter et al. (2007) revisited this problem. Weyrich et al. (2009) have developed methods to infer a microfacet distribution that matches a measured or desired reflection distribution. Remarkably, they show that it's possible to manufacture actual physical surfaces that match a desired reflection distribution fairly accurately. Simonot (2009) has developed a model that spans Oren–Nayar and Torrance–Sparrow: microfacets are modeled as Lambertian reflectors with a layer above them that ranges from perfectly transmissive to a perfect specular reflector. However, this model doesn't account for masking-shadowing effects and can't be evaluated in closed form.

The microfacet reflection models in this chapter are all based on the assumption that so many microfacets are visible in a pixel that they can be accurately described by their aggregate statistical behavior. This assumption isn't true for many real-world surfaces, where a relatively small number of microfacets may be visible in each pixel; examples of such surfaces include car paint and glittery plastics. Both Yan et al. (2014) and Jakob et al. (2014b) have developed techniques that model these cases well.

It can be useful to be able to find BSDFs for layered materials, such as a metal base surface tarnished with patina, or wood with a varnish coating. Hanrahan and Krueger (1993) modeled the layers of skin accounting for just a single scattering event in each layer, and Dorsey and Hanrahan (1996) rendered layered materials using the Kubelka–Munk theory, which accounts for multiple scattering within layers but assumes that radiance distribution doesn't vary as a function of direction.

Pharr and Hanrahan (2000) showed that Monte Carlo integration could be used to solve the *adding equations* to efficiently compute BSDFs for layered materials without needing either of these simplifications. The adding equations are integral equations that accurately describe the effect of multiple scattering in layered media that were derived by van De Hulst (1980) and Twomey et al. (1966). Weidlich and Wilkie (2007) rendered layered materials more efficiently by making a number of simplifying assumptions, and Jakob et al. (2014a) efficiently computed scattering in layered materials using the Fourier basis representation implemented here as the FourierBSDF.

A number of researchers have investigated BRDFs based on modeling the small-scale geometric features of a reflective surface. This work includes the computation of BRDFs from bump maps by Cabral, Max, and Springmeyer (1987), Fournier's normal distribution functions (Fournier 1992), and Westin, Arvo, and Torrance (1992), who applied Monte Carlo ray tracing to statistically model reflection from microgeometry and represented the resulting BRDFs with spherical harmonics. More recently, Wu et al. (2011) developed a system that made it possible to model microgeometry and specify its underlying BRDF while interactively previewing the resulting macro-scale BRDF.

Improvements in data-acquisition technology have led to increasing amounts of detailed real-world BRDF data, even including BRDFs that are spatially varying (sometimes called "bidirectional texture functions," BTFs) (Dana et al. 1999). Matusik et al. (2003a, 2003b) assembled an early database of measured isotropic BRDF data. See Müller et al. (2005) for a survey of work in BRDF measurement until the year 2005. Sun et al. (2007) measured BRDFs as they change over time—for example, due to paint drying, a wet surface becoming dry, or dust accumulating. While most BRDF measurement has been based on measuring reflected radiance due to a given amount of incident irradiance, Zhao et al. (2011) showed that CT imaging of the structure of fabrics led to very accurate reflection models.

Fitting measured BRDF data to parametric reflection models is a difficult problem. Rusinkiewicz (1998) made the influential observation that reparameterizing the measured data can make it substantially easier to compress or fit to models; this topic has been further investigated by Stark et al. (2005) and in Marscher's Ph.D. dissertation (1998). Ngan et al. (2005) analyzed the effectiveness of a variety of BRDF models for fitting measured data and showed that models based on the half-angle vector, rather than a reflection vector, tended to be more effective. See also the paper on this topic by Edwards et al. (2005).

Zickler et al. (2005) developed a method for representing BRDFs based on radial basis functions (RBFs)—they use them to interpolate irregularly sampled 5D spatially varying BRDFs. Weistroffer et al. (2007) have shown how to efficiently represent scattered reflectance data with RBFs without needing to resample them to have regular spacing. Wang et al. (2008a) demonstrated a successful approach for acquiring spatially varying anisotropic BRDFs. Pacanowski et al. (2012) developed a representation that could guarantee a given error bound between measured and fit data, and Bagher et al. (2012) introduced a parametric BRDF that accurately fit a wide variety of reflection function distributions using just six coefficients per color channel. More recently, Brady et al. (2014) found new analytic BRDF models that fit measured BRDFs well using genetic programming. Dupuy et al. (2015) developed an efficient and easily implemented approach for fitting measured BRDFs to microfacet distributions based on using power iterations to compute eigenvectors.

Kajiya and Kay (1989) developed an early reflection model for hair based on a model of individual hairs as cylinders with diffuse and glossy reflection properties. Their model determines the overall reflection from these cylinders, accounting for the effect of variation in surface normal over the hemisphere along the cylinder. For related work, see also the paper by Banks (1994), which discusses shading models for 1D primitives like hair. Goldman (1997) developed a probabilistic shading model that models reflection from collections of short hairs. Marschner et al. (2003) developed an accurate model of light scattering from human hair fibers that decomposes the reflected light into three components with distinct directional profiles based on the number of internal refraction events. Sadeghi et al. (2010) developed intuitive controls for physically based hair reflection models that made it easier to achieve a desired visual appearence. Further improvements to hair scattering models were introduced by d'Eon et al. (2011). Finally, see Ward et al.'s survey (2007) for extensive coverage of research in modeling, animating, and rendering hair.

Modeling reflection from a variety of specific types of surfaces has received attention from researchers, leading to specialized reflection models. Examples include Marschner et al.'s (2005) work on rendering wood, Günther et al.'s (2005) investigation of car paint, and Papas et al.'s (2014) model for paper.

Cloth remains particularly challenging material to render. Work in this area includes papers by Sattler et al. (2003), Irawan (2008), Schröder et al. (2011), Irawan and Marschner (2012), Zhao et al. (2012), and Sadeghi et al. (2013).

Nayar, Ikeuchi, and Kanade (1991) have shown that some reflection models based on physical (wave) optics have substantially similar characteristics to those based on geometric optics. The geometric optics approximations don't seem to cause too much error in practice, except on very smooth surfaces. This is a helpful result, giving experimental basis to the general belief that wave optics models aren't usually worth their computational expense for computer graphics applications.

The effect of the polarization of light is not modeled in pbrt, although for some scenes it can be an important effect; see, for example, the paper by Tannenbaum, Tannenbaum, and Wozny (1994) for information about how to extend a renderer to account for this effect. Similarly, the fact that indices of refraction of real-world objects usually vary as a function of wavelength is also not modeled here; see both Section 11.8 of Glassner's book (1995) and Devlin et al.'s survey article for information about these issues and references to previous work (Devlin et al. 2002). Fluorescence, where light is reflected at different wavelengths than the incident illumination, is also not modeled by pbrt; see Glassner (1994) and Wilkie et al. (2006) for more information on this topic.

Moravec (1981) was the first to apply a wave optics model to graphics. This area has also been investigated by Bahar and Chakrabarti (1987) and Stam (1999), who applied wave optics to model diffraction effects. For more recent work in this area, see the papers by Cuypers et al. (2012) and Musbach et al. (2013), who also provide extensive references to previous work on this topic.

EXERCISES

⓿ 8.1 A consequence of Fermat's principle from optics is that light traveling from a point p_1 in a medium with index of refraction η_1 to a point p_2 in a medium with index of refraction η_2 will follow a path that minimizes the time to get from the first point to the second point. Snell's law can be shown to follow from this fact directly.

Consider light traveling between two points p_1 and p_2 separated by a planar boundary. The light could potentially pass through the boundary while traveling from p_1 to p_2 at any point on the boundary (see Figure 8.25, which shows two such possible points p' and p''). Recall that the time it takes light to travel between two points in a medium with a constant index of refraction is proportional to the distance between them times the index of refraction in the medium. Using this fact, show that the point p' on the boundary that minimizes the total time to travel from p_1 to p_2 is the point where $\eta_1 \sin \theta_1 = \eta_2 \sin \theta_2$.

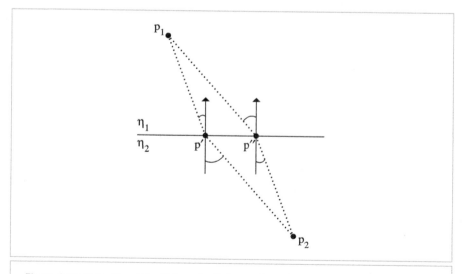

Figure 8.25: Derivation of Snell's Law. Snell's law can be derived using Fermat's principle, which says that light will follow the path that takes the least amount of time to pass between two points. The angle of refraction θ at the boundary between two media can thus be shown to be the one that minimizes the time spent going from p_1 to a point p on the boundary plus the time spent traveling the distance from that point to p_2.

● 8.2   Read the papers of Wolff and Kurlander (1990) and Tannenbaum, Tannenbaum, and Wozny (1994), and apply some of the techniques described to modify pbrt to model the effect of light polarization. Set up scenes and render images of them that demonstrate a significant difference when polarization is accurately modeled.

● 8.3   Construct a scene with an actual geometric model of a rough plane with a large number of mirrored microfacets, and illuminate it with an area light source.[11] Place the camera in the scene such that a very large number of microfacets are in each pixel's area, and render images of this scene using hundreds or thousands of pixel samples. Compare the result to using a flat surface with a microfacet-based BRDF model. How well can you get the two approaches to match if you try to tune the microfacet BRDF parameters? Can you construct examples where images rendered with the true microfacets are actually visibly more realistic due to better modeling the effects of masking, self-shadowing, and interreflection between microfacets?

● 8.4   Extend pbrt to be able to more accurately render interesting surfaces like wood (Marschner et al. 2005), cloth (Sattler et al. 2003), or car paint (Günther et al. 2005). Render images showing better visual results than when existing reflection functions in pbrt are used for these effects.

● 8.5   Implement a simulation-based approach to modeling reflection from complex microsurfaces, such as the one described by Westin, Arvo, and Torrance (1992). Modify pbrt so that you can provide a description of the microgeometry of a complex surface (like cloth, velvet, etc.), fire rays at the geometry from a variety of incident directions, and record the distribution and throughput for the rays that leave the surface. (You will likely need to modify the PathIntegrator from Chapter 14 to determine the distribution of outgoing light.) Record the distribution in a 3D table if the surface is isotropic or a 4D table if it is anisotropic, and use the table to compute BRDF values for rendering images. Demonstrate interesting reflection effects from complex surfaces using this approach. Investigate how the size of the table and the number of samples taken to compute entries in the table affect the accuracy of the final result.

● 8.6   Although pbrt features a Curve shape that provides fairly efficient intersection tests between rays and parametric curves (Section 3.7), it lacks a reflection model for hair. Choose one of the models described in the "Further Reading" section such as Marschner et al.'s (2003) or d'Eon et al.'s (2011), and implement it in pbrt. Either find a geometric model of hair or generate hair procedurally, and render images using your implementation.

Curve 168

PathIntegrator 875

---

11   An area light and not a point or directional light is necessary due to subtleties in how lights are seen in specular surfaces. With the light transport algorithms used in pbrt, infinitesimal point sources are never visible in mirrored surfaces. This is a typical limitation of ray-tracing renderers and usually not bothersome in practice.

CHAPTER NINE

09 MATERIALS

The BRDFs and BTDFs introduced in the previous chapter address only part of the problem of describing how a surface scatters light. Although they describe how light is scattered at a particular point on a surface, the renderer needs to determine *which* BRDFs and BTDFs are present at a point on a surface and what their parameters are. In this chapter, we describe a procedural shading mechanism that addresses this issue.

The basic idea behind pbrt's approach is that a *surface shader* is bound to each primitive in the scene. The surface shader is represented by an instance of the Material interface class, which has a method that takes a point on a surface and creates a BSDF object (and possibly a BSSRDF) that represents scattering at the point. The BSDF class holds a set of BxDFs whose contributions are summed to give the full scattering function. Materials, in turn, use instances of the Texture class (to be defined in the next chapter) to determine the material properties at particular points on surfaces. For example, an ImageTexture might be used to modulate the color of diffuse reflection across a surface. This is a somewhat different shading paradigm from the one that many rendering systems use; it is common practice to combine the function of the surface shader and the lighting integrator (see Chapter 14) into a single module and have the shader return the color of reflected light at the point. However, by separating these two components and having the Material return a BSDF, pbrt is better able to handle a variety of light transport algorithms.

9.1 BSDFs

The BSDF class represents a collection of BRDFs and BTDFs. Grouping them in this manner allows the rest of the system to work with composite BSDFs directly, rather than having to consider all of the components they may have been built from. Equally important, the

Physically Based Rendering: From Theory To Implementation.
http://dx.doi.org/10.1016/B978-0-12-800645-0.50009-9

BSDF class hides some of the details of shading normals from the rest of the system. Shading normals, either from per-vertex normals in triangle meshes or from bump mapping, can substantially improve the visual richness of rendered scenes, but because they are an *ad hoc* construct, they are tricky to incorporate into a physically based renderer. The issues that they introduce are handled in the BSDF implementation.

⟨*BSDF Declarations*⟩ +≡
```
    class BSDF {
    public:
        ⟨BSDF Public Methods 573⟩
        ⟨BSDF Public Data 573⟩
    private:
        ⟨BSDF Private Methods 576⟩
        ⟨BSDF Private Data 573⟩
    };
```

The BSDF constructor takes a SurfaceInteraction object that contains information about the differential geometry at the point on a surface as well as a parameter eta that gives the relative index of refraction over the boundary. For opaque surfaces, eta isn't used, and a value of one should be provided by the caller. (The default value of one for eta is for just this case.) The constructor computes an orthonormal coordinate system with the shading normal as one of the axes; this coordinate system will be useful for transforming directions to and from the BxDF coordinate system that is described in Figure 8.2. Throughout this section, we will use the convention that $\mathbf{n}_s$ denotes the shading normal and $\mathbf{n}_g$ the geometric normal (Figure 9.1).

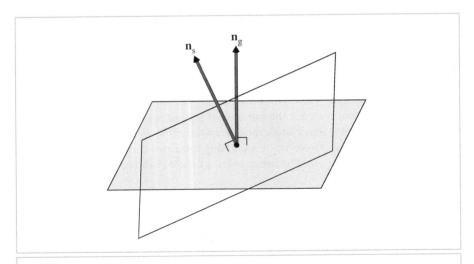

Figure 9.1: The geometric normal, $\mathbf{n}_g$, defined by the surface geometry, and the shading normal, $\mathbf{n}_s$, given by per-vertex normals and/or bump mapping, will generally define different hemispheres for integrating incident illumination to compute surface reflection. This inconsistency is important to handle carefully since it can otherwise lead to artifacts in images.

BSDF 572
BxDF 513
SurfaceInteraction 116

⟨*BSDF Public Methods*⟩ ≡   572
```
BSDF(const SurfaceInteraction &si, Float eta = 1)
    : eta(eta), ns(si.shading.n), ng(si.n),
      ss(Normalize(si.shading.dpdu)), ts(Cross(ns, ss)) { }
```

⟨*BSDF Public Data*⟩ ≡   572
```
const Float eta;
```

⟨*BSDF Private Data*⟩ ≡   572
```
const Normal3f ns, ng;
const Vector3f ss, ts;
```

The BSDF implementation stores only a limited number of individual BxDF components. It could easily be extended to allocate more space if more components were given to it, although this isn't necessary for any of the Material implementations in pbrt thus far, and the current limit of eight is plenty for almost all practical applications.

⟨*BSDF Public Methods*⟩ +≡   572
```
void Add(BxDF *b) {
    Assert(nBxDFs < MaxBxDFs);
    bxdfs[nBxDFs++] = b;
}
```

⟨*BSDF Private Data*⟩ +≡   572
```
int nBxDFs = 0;
static constexpr int MaxBxDFs = 8;
BxDF *bxdfs[MaxBxDFs];
```

For other parts of the system that need additional information about the particular BRDFs and BTDFs that are present, a method returns the number of BxDFs stored by the BSDF that match a particular set of BxDFType flags.

⟨*BSDF Public Methods*⟩ +≡   572
```
int NumComponents(BxDFType flags = BSDF_ALL) const;
```

The BSDF also has methods that perform transformations to and from the local coordinate system used by BxDFs. Recall that, in this coordinate system, the surface normal is along the z axis $(0, 0, 1)$, the primary tangent is $(1, 0, 0)$, and the secondary tangent is $(0, 1, 0)$. The transformation of directions into "shading space" simplifies many of the BxDF implementations in Chapter 8. Given three orthonormal vectors **s**, **t**, and **n** in world space, the matrix **M** that transforms vectors in world space to the local reflection space is

$$\mathbf{M} = \begin{pmatrix} s_x & s_y & s_z \\ t_x & t_y & t_z \\ n_x & n_y & n_z \end{pmatrix} = \begin{pmatrix} \mathbf{s} \\ \mathbf{t} \\ \mathbf{n} \end{pmatrix}.$$

To confirm this yourself, consider, for example, the value of **M** times the surface normal **n**, $\mathbf{Mn} = (\mathbf{s} \cdot \mathbf{n}, \mathbf{t} \cdot \mathbf{n}, \mathbf{n} \cdot \mathbf{n})$. Since **s**, **t**, and **n** are all orthonormal, the x and y components of **Mn** are zero. Since **n** is normalized, $\mathbf{n} \cdot \mathbf{n} = 1$. Thus, $\mathbf{Mn} = (0, 0, 1)$, as expected.

In this case, we don't need to compute the inverse transpose of **M** to transform normals (recall the discussion of transforming normals in Section 2.8.3). Because **M** is an orthogonal matrix (its rows and columns are mutually orthogonal), its inverse is equal to its transpose, so it is its own inverse transpose already.

⟨*BSDF Public Methods*⟩ +≡　　　　　　　　　　　　　　　　　　　　　　　572

```
Vector3f WorldToLocal(const Vector3f &v) const {
    return Vector3f(Dot(v, ss), Dot(v, ts), Dot(v, ns));
}
```

The method that takes vectors back from local space to world space transposes **M** to find its inverse before doing the appropriate dot products.

⟨*BSDF Public Methods*⟩ +≡　　　　　　　　　　　　　　　　　　　　　　　572

```
Vector3f LocalToWorld(const Vector3f &v) const {
    return Vector3f(ss.x * v.x + ts.x * v.y + ns.x * v.z,
                    ss.y * v.x + ts.y * v.y + ns.y * v.z,
                    ss.z * v.x + ts.z * v.y + ns.z * v.z);
}
```

Shading normals can cause a variety of undesirable artifacts in practice (Figure 9.2). Figure 9.2(a) shows a *light leak*: the geometric normal indicates that ω_i and ω_o lie on opposite sides of the surface, so if the surface is not transmissive, the light should have no contribution. However, if we directly evaluate the scattering equation, Equation (5.9), about the hemisphere centered around the shading normal, we will incorrectly incorporate the light from ω_i. This case demonstrates that $\mathbf{n_s}$ can't just be used as a direct replacement for $\mathbf{n_g}$ in rendering computations.

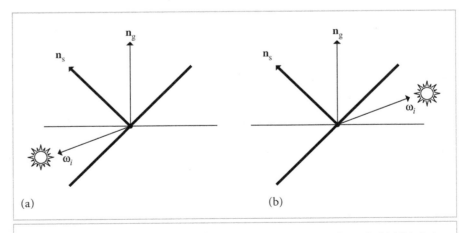

(a)　　　　　　　　　　　　　　　　　　　　(b)

BSDF::ns 573
BSDF::ss 573
BSDF::ts 573
Dot() 63
Vector3f 60

Figure 9.2: The Two Types of Errors That Result from Using Shading Normals. (a) A light leak: the geometric normal indicates that the light is on the back side of the surface, but the shading normal indicates the light is visible (assuming a reflective and not transmissive surface). (b) A dark spot: the geometric normal indicates that the surface is illuminated, but the shading normal indicates that the viewer is behind the lit side of the surface.

Figure 9.2(b) shows a similar tricky situation: the shading normal indicates that no light should be reflected to the viewer, since it is not in the same hemisphere as the illumination, while the geometric normal indicates that they are in the same hemisphere. Direct use of n_s would cause ugly black spots on the surface where this situation happens.

Fortunately, there is an elegant solution to these problems. When evaluating the BSDF, we can use the geometric normal to decide if we should be evaluating reflection or transmission: if ω_i and ω_o lie in the same hemisphere with respect to n_g, we evaluate the BRDFs, and otherwise we evaluate the BTDFs. In evaluating the scattering equation, however, the dot product of the normal and the incident direction is still taken with the shading normal rather than the geometric normal.

Now it should be clear why pbrt requires BxDFs to evaluate their values without regard to whether ω_i and ω_o are in the same or different hemispheres. This convention means that light leaks are avoided, since we will only evaluate the BTDFs for the situation in Figure 9.2(a), giving no reflection for a purely reflective surface. Similarly, black spots are avoided since we will evaluate the BRDFs for the situation in Figure 9.2(b), even though the shading normal would suggest that the directions are in different hemispheres.

Given these conventions, the method that evaluates the BSDF for a given pair of directions follows directly. It starts by transforming the world space direction vectors to local BSDF space and then determines whether it should use the BRDFs or the BTDFs. It then loops over the appropriate set and evaluates the sum of their contributions.

⟨BSDF Method Definitions⟩ ≡
```
Spectrum BSDF::f(const Vector3f &woW, const Vector3f &wiW,
                BxDFType flags) const {
    Vector3f wi = WorldToLocal(wiW), wo = WorldToLocal(woW);
    bool reflect = Dot(wiW, ng) * Dot(woW, ng) > 0;
    Spectrum f(0.f);
    for (int i = 0; i < nBxDFs; ++i)
        if (bxdfs[i]->MatchesFlags(flags) &&
            ((reflect && (bxdfs[i]->type & BSDF_REFLECTION)) ||
             (!reflect && (bxdfs[i]->type & BSDF_TRANSMISSION))))
            f += bxdfs[i]->f(wo, wi);
    return f;
}
```

pbrt also provides BSDF methods that return the BSDF's reflectances. (Recall the definition of reflectance in Section 8.1.1.) The two corresponding methods just loop over the BxDFs and sum the values returned by their BxDF::rho() methods; their straightforward implementations aren't included here. These methods take arrays of samples for BxDFs for use in Monte Carlo sampling algorithms if needed (recall the BxDF::rho() interface defined in Section 8.1.1, which takes such samples as well.)

⟨BSDF Public Methods⟩ +≡   572
```
Spectrum rho(int nSamples, const Point2f *samples1,
             const Point2f *samples2, BxDFType flags = BSDF_ALL) const;
Spectrum rho(const Vector3f &wo, int nSamples, const Point2f *samples,
             BxDFType flags = BSDF_ALL) const;
```

9.1.1 BSDF MEMORY MANAGEMENT

For each ray that intersects geometry in the scene, one or more BSDF objects will be created by the Integrator in the process of computing the radiance carried along the ray. (Integrators that account for multiple interreflections of light will generally create a number of BSDFs along the way.) Each of these BSDFs in turn has a number of BxDFs stored inside it, as created by the Materials at the intersection points.

A naïve implementation would use new and delete to dynamically allocate storage for both the BSDF as well as each of the BxDFs that it holds. Unfortunately, such an approach would be unacceptably inefficient—too much time would be spent in the dynamic memory management routines for a series of small memory allocations. Instead, the implementation here uses a specialized allocation scheme based on the MemoryArena class described in Section A.4.3.[1] A MemoryArena is passed into methods that allocate memory for BSDFs. For example, the SamplerIntegrator::Render() method creates a MemoryArena for each image tile and passes it to the integrators, which in turn pass it to the Material.

For the convenience of code that allocates BSDFs and BxDFs (e.g., the Materials in this chapter), there is a macro that hides some of the messiness of using the memory arena. Instead of using the new operator to allocate those objects like this:

```
BSDF *b = new BSDF;
BxDF *lam = new LambertianReflection(Spectrum(0.5f));
```

code should instead be written with the ARENA_ALLOC() macro, like this:

```
BSDF *b = ARENA_ALLOC(arena, BSDF);
BxDF *lam = ARENA_ALLOC(arena, LambertianReflection)(Spectrum(0.5f));
```

where arena is a MemoryArena.

The ARENA_ALLOC() macro uses the placement operator new to run the constructor for the object at the returned memory location.

⟨*Memory Declarations*⟩ ≡
```
#define ARENA_ALLOC(arena, Type) new (arena.Alloc(sizeof(Type))) Type
```

The BSDF destructor is a private method in order to ensure that it isn't inadvertently called (e.g., due to an attempt to delete a BSDF). Making the destructor private ensures a compile time error if it is called. Trying to delete memory allocated by the MemoryArena could lead to errors or crashes, since a pointer to the middle of memory managed by the MemoryArena would be passed to the system's dynamic memory freeing routine.

In turn, an implication of the allocation scheme here is that BSDF and BxDF destructors are never executed. This isn't a problem for the ones currently implemented in the system.

⟨*BSDF Private Methods*⟩ ≡   572
```
~BSDF() { }
```

---

1   MemoryArena allocates a large block of memory and responds to allocation requests via the MemoryArena::Alloc() call by returning successive sections of that block. It does not support freeing individual allocations but instead frees all of them simultaneously when the MemoryArena::Reset() method is called. The result of this approach is that both allocation and freeing of memory are extremely efficient.

9.2 MATERIAL INTERFACE AND IMPLEMENTATIONS

The abstract Material class defines the interface that material implementations must provide. The Material class is defined in the files core/material.h and core/material.cpp.

⟨*Material Declarations*⟩ ≡
```
class Material {
public:
    ⟨Material Interface 577⟩
};
```

A single method must be implemented by Materials: ComputeScatteringFunctions(). This method is given a SurfaceInteraction object that contains geometric properties at an intersection point on the surface of a shape. The method's implementation is responsible for determining the reflective properties at the point and initializing the SurfaceInteraction::bsdf member variable with a corresponding BSDF class instance. If the material includes subsurface scattering, then the SurfaceInteraction::bssrdf member should be initialized as well. (It should otherwise be left unchanged from its default nullptr value.) The BSSRDF class that represents subsurface scattering functions is defined later, in Section 11.4, after the foundations of volumetric scattering have been introduced.

Three additional parameters are passed to this method:

- A MemoryArena, which should be used to allocate memory for BSDFs and BSSRDFs.
- The TransportMode parameter, which indicates whether the surface intersection was found along a path starting from the camera or one starting from a light source; this detail has implications for how BSDFs and BSSRDFs are evaluated—see Section 16.1.
- Finally, the allowMultipleLobes parameter indicates whether the material should use BxDFs that aggregate multiple types of scattering into a single BxDF when such BxDFs are available. (An example of such a BxDF is FresnelSpecular, which includes both specular reflection and transmission.) These BxDFs can improve the quality of final results when used with Monte Carlo light transport algorithms but can introduce noise in images when used with the DirectLightingIntegrator and WhittedIntegrator. Therefore, the Integrator is allowed to control whether such BxDFs are used via this parameter.

⟨*Material Interface*⟩ ≡   577
```
virtual void ComputeScatteringFunctions(SurfaceInteraction *si,
    MemoryArena &arena, TransportMode mode,
    bool allowMultipleLobes) const = 0;
```

Since the usual interface to the intersection point used by Integrators is through an instance of the SurfaceInteraction class, we will add a convenience method ComputeScatteringFunctions() to that class. Its implementation first calls the Surface Interaction's ComputeDifferentials() method to compute information about the projected size of the surface area around the intersection on the image plane for use in texture antialiasing. Next, it forwards the request to the Primitive, which in turn will call the corresponding ComputeScatteringFunctions() method of its Material. (See, for example, the GeometricPrimitive::ComputeScatteringFunctions() implementation.)

⟨*SurfaceInteraction Method Definitions*⟩ +≡
```
void SurfaceInteraction::ComputeScatteringFunctions(
        const RayDifferential &ray, MemoryArena &arena,
        bool allowMultipleLobes, TransportMode mode) {
    ComputeDifferentials(ray);
    primitive->ComputeScatteringFunctions(this, arena, mode,
        allowMultipleLobes);
}
```

9.2.1 MATTE MATERIAL

The MatteMaterial material is defined in materials/matte.h and materials/matte.cpp. It is the simplest material in pbrt and describes a purely diffuse surface.

⟨*MatteMaterial Declarations*⟩ ≡
```
class MatteMaterial : public Material {
public:
    ⟨MatteMaterial Public Methods 578⟩
private:
    ⟨MatteMaterial Private Data 578⟩
};
```

This material is parameterized by a spectral diffuse reflection value, Kd, and a scalar roughness value, sigma. If sigma has the value zero at the point on a surface, Matte Material creates a LambertianReflection BRDF; otherwise, the OrenNayar model is used. Like all of the other Material implementations in this chapter, it also takes an optional scalar texture that defines an offset function over the surface. If its value is not nullptr, this texture is used to compute a shading normal at each point based on the function it defines. (Section 9.3 discusses the implementation of this computation.) Figure 8.14 in the previous chapter shows the MatteMaterial material with the dragon model.

⟨*MatteMaterial Public Methods*⟩ ≡   578
```
MatteMaterial(const std::shared_ptr<Texture<Spectrum>> &Kd,
              const std::shared_ptr<Texture<Float>> &sigma,
              const std::shared_ptr<Texture<Float>> &bumpMap)
    : Kd(Kd), sigma(sigma), bumpMap(bumpMap) { }
```

⟨*MatteMaterial Private Data*⟩ ≡   578
```
std::shared_ptr<Texture<Spectrum>> Kd;
std::shared_ptr<Texture<Float>> sigma, bumpMap;
```

The ComputeScatteringFunctions() method puts the pieces together, determining the bump map's effect on the shading geometry, evaluating the textures, and allocating and returning the appropriate BSDF.

⟨*MatteMaterial Method Definitions*⟩ ≡
```
void MatteMaterial::ComputeScatteringFunctions(SurfaceInteraction *si,
        MemoryArena &arena, TransportMode mode,
        bool allowMultipleLobes) const {
    ⟨Perform bump mapping with bumpMap, if present 579⟩
    ⟨Evaluate textures for MatteMaterial material and allocate BRDF 579⟩
}
```

If a bump map was provided to the MatteMaterial constructor, the Material::Bump()
method is called to calculate the shading normal at the point. This method will be defined
in the next section.

⟨*Perform bump mapping with* bumpMap, *if present*⟩ ≡   **579, 581, 584, 701**
```
if (bumpMap)
    Bump(bumpMap, si);
```

Next, the Textures that give the values of the diffuse reflection spectrum and the roughness are evaluated; texture implementations may return constant values, look up values
from image maps, or do complex procedural shading calculations to compute these values (the texture evaluation process is the subject of Chapter 10). Given these values, all
that needs to be done is to allocate a BSDF and then allocate the appropriate type of Lambertian BRDF and provide it to the BSDF. Because Textures may return negative values or
values otherwise outside of the expected range, these values are clamped to valid ranges
before they are passed to the BRDF constructor.

⟨*Evaluate textures for* MatteMaterial *material and allocate BRDF*⟩ ≡   **579**
```
si->bsdf = ARENA_ALLOC(arena, BSDF)(*si);
Spectrum r = Kd->Evaluate(*si).Clamp();
Float sig = Clamp(sigma->Evaluate(*si), 0, 90);
if (!r.IsBlack()) {
    if (sig == 0)
        si->bsdf->Add(ARENA_ALLOC(arena, LambertianReflection)(r));
    else
        si->bsdf->Add(ARENA_ALLOC(arena, OrenNayar)(r, sig));
}
```

9.2.2 PLASTIC MATERIAL

Plastic can be modeled as a mixture of a diffuse and glossy scattering function with
parameters controlling the particular colors and specular highlight size. The parameters to PlasticMaterial are two reflectivities, Kd and Ks, which respectively control the
amounts of diffuse reflection and glossy specular reflection.

Next is a roughness parameter that determines the size of the specular highlight. It can
be specified in two ways. First, if the remapRoughness parameter is true, then the given
roughness should vary from zero to one, where the higher the roughness value, the
larger the highlight. (This variant is intended to be fairly user-friendly.) Alternatively,
if the parameter is false, then the roughness is used to directly initialize the microfacet
distribution's α parameter (recall Section 8.4.2).

Figure 9.3: Dragon Rendered with a Plastic Material. Note the combination of diffuse and glossy specular reflection. *(Model courtesy of Christian Schüller.)*

Figure 9.3 shows a plastic dragon. `PlasticMaterial` is defined in `materials/plastic.h` and `materials/plastic.cpp`.

⟨*PlasticMaterial Declarations*⟩ ≡
```
class PlasticMaterial : public Material {
public:
    ⟨PlasticMaterial Public Methods 580⟩
private:
    ⟨PlasticMaterial Private Data 580⟩
};
```

⟨*PlasticMaterial Public Methods*⟩ ≡   580
```
PlasticMaterial(const std::shared_ptr<Texture<Spectrum>> &Kd,
                const std::shared_ptr<Texture<Spectrum>> &Ks,
                const std::shared_ptr<Texture<Float>> &roughness,
                const std::shared_ptr<Texture<Float>> &bumpMap,
                bool remapRoughness)
     : Kd(Kd), Ks(Ks), roughness(roughness), bumpMap(bumpMap),
       remapRoughness(remapRoughness) { }
```

⟨*PlasticMaterial Private Data*⟩ ≡   580
```
std::shared_ptr<Texture<Spectrum>> Kd, Ks;
std::shared_ptr<Texture<Float>> roughness, bumpMap;
const bool remapRoughness;
```

The PlasticMaterial::ComputeScatteringFunctions() method follows the same basic structure as MatteMaterial::ComputeScatteringFunctions(): it calls the bump-mapping function, evaluates textures, and then allocates BxDFs to use to initialize the BSDF.

⟨*PlasticMaterial Method Definitions*⟩ ≡
```
    void PlasticMaterial::ComputeScatteringFunctions(
            SurfaceInteraction *si, MemoryArena &arena, TransportMode mode,
            bool allowMultipleLobes) const {
        ⟨Perform bump mapping with bumpMap, if present 579⟩
        si->bsdf = ARENA_ALLOC(arena, BSDF)(*si);
        ⟨Initialize diffuse component of plastic material 581⟩
        ⟨Initialize specular component of plastic material 581⟩
    }
```

In Material implementations, it's worthwhile to skip creation of BxDF components that do not contribute to the scattering at a point. Doing so saves the renderer unnecessary work later when it's computing reflected radiance at the point. Therefore, the Lambertian component is only created if kd is non-zero.

⟨*Initialize diffuse component of plastic material*⟩ ≡   581
```
    Spectrum kd = Kd->Evaluate(*si).Clamp();
    if (!kd.IsBlack())
        si->bsdf->Add(ARENA_ALLOC(arena, LambertianReflection)(kd));
```

As with the diffuse component, the glossy specular component is skipped if it's not going to make a contribution to the overall BSDF.

⟨*Initialize specular component of plastic material*⟩ ≡   581
```
    Spectrum ks = Ks->Evaluate(*si).Clamp();
    if (!ks.IsBlack()) {
        Fresnel *fresnel = ARENA_ALLOC(arena, FresnelDielectric)(1.f, 1.5f);
        ⟨Create microfacet distribution distrib for plastic material 581⟩
        BxDF *spec =
            ARENA_ALLOC(arena, MicrofacetReflection)(ks, distrib, fresnel);
        si->bsdf->Add(spec);
    }
```

⟨*Create microfacet distribution distrib for plastic material*⟩ ≡   581
```
    Float rough = roughness->Evaluate(*si);
    if (remapRoughness)
        rough = TrowbridgeReitzDistribution::RoughnessToAlpha(rough);
    MicrofacetDistribution *distrib =
        ARENA_ALLOC(arena, TrowbridgeReitzDistribution)(rough, rough);
```

9.2.3 MIX MATERIAL

It's useful to be able to combine two Materials with varying weights. The MixMaterial takes two other Materials and a Spectrum-valued texture and uses the Spectrum returned by the texture to blend between the two materials at the point being shaded. It is defined in the files materials/mixmat.h and materials/mixmat.cpp.

⟨*MixMaterial Declarations*⟩ ≡
```
class MixMaterial : public Material {
public:
    ⟨MixMaterial Public Methods 582⟩
private:
    ⟨MixMaterial Private Data 582⟩
};
```

⟨*MixMaterial Public Methods*⟩ ≡   582
```
MixMaterial(const std::shared_ptr<Material> &m1,
            const std::shared_ptr<Material> &m2,
            const std::shared_ptr<Texture<Spectrum>> &scale)
    : m1(m1), m2(m2), scale(scale) { }
```

⟨*MixMaterial Private Data*⟩ ≡   582
```
std::shared_ptr<Material> m1, m2;
std::shared_ptr<Texture<Spectrum>> scale;
```

⟨*MixMaterial Method Definitions*⟩ ≡
```
void MixMaterial::ComputeScatteringFunctions(SurfaceInteraction *si,
        MemoryArena &arena, TransportMode mode,
        bool allowMultipleLobes) const {
    ⟨Compute weights and original BxDFs for mix material 582⟩
    ⟨Initialize si->bsdf with weighted mixture of BxDFs 583⟩
}
```

`MixMaterial::ComputeScatteringFunctions()` starts with its two constituent `Material`s initializing their respective BSDFs.

⟨*Compute weights and original* BxDFs *for mix material*⟩ ≡   582
```
Spectrum s1 = scale->Evaluate(*si).Clamp();
Spectrum s2 = (Spectrum(1.f) - s1).Clamp();
SurfaceInteraction si2 = *si;
m1->ComputeScatteringFunctions(si, arena, mode, allowMultipleLobes);
m2->ComputeScatteringFunctions(&si2, arena, mode, allowMultipleLobes);
```

It then scales BxDFs in the BSDF from the first material, b1, using the `ScaledBxDF` adapter class, and then scales the BxDFs from the second BSDF, adding all of these BxDF components to si->bsdf.

It may appear that there's a lurking memory leak in this code, in that the BxDF *s in si->bxdfs are clobbered by newly allocated ScaledBxDFs. However, recall that those BxDFs, like the new ones here, were allocated through a MemoryArena and thus their memory will be freed when the MemoryArena frees its entire block of memory.

⟨*Initialize* si->bsdf *with weighted mixture of* BxDF*s*⟩ ≡   582
```
int n1 = si->bsdf->NumComponents(), n2 = si2.bsdf->NumComponents();
for (int i = 0; i < n1; ++i)
    si->bsdf->bxdfs[i] =
        ARENA_ALLOC(arena, ScaledBxDF)(si->bsdf->bxdfs[i], s1);
for (int i = 0; i < n2; ++i)
    si->bsdf->Add(ARENA_ALLOC(arena, ScaledBxDF)(si2.bsdf->bxdfs[i], s2));
```

The implementation of MixMaterial::ComputeScatteringFunctions() needs direct access to the bxdfs member variables of the BSDF class. Because this is the only class that needs this access, we've just made MixMaterial a friend of BSDF rather than adding a number of accessor and setting methods.

⟨*BSDF Private Data*⟩ +≡   572
```
friend class MixMaterial;
```

9.2.4 FOURIER MATERIAL

The FourierMaterial class supports measured or synthetic BSDF data that has been tabulated into the directional basis that was introduced in Section 8.6. It is defined in the files materials/fourier.h and materials/fourier.cpp.

⟨*FourierMaterial Declarations*⟩ ≡
```
class FourierMaterial : public Material {
public:
    ⟨FourierMaterial Public Methods⟩
private:
    ⟨FourierMaterial Private Data 583⟩
};
```

The constructor is responsible for reading the BSDF from a file and initializing the FourierBSDFTable.

⟨*FourierMaterial Method Definitions*⟩ ≡
```
FourierMaterial::FourierMaterial(const std::string &filename,
        const std::shared_ptr<Texture<Float>> &bumpMap)
    : bumpMap(bumpMap) {
    FourierBSDFTable::Read(filename, &bsdfTable);
}
```

⟨*FourierMaterial Private Data*⟩ ≡   583
```
FourierBSDFTable bsdfTable;
std::shared_ptr<Texture<Float>> bumpMap;
```

Once the data is in memory, the ComputeScatteringFunctions() method's task is straightforward. After the usual bump-mapping computation, it just has to allocate a FourierBSDF and provide it access to the data in the table.

⟨*FourierMaterial Method Definitions*⟩ +≡

```
void FourierMaterial::ComputeScatteringFunctions(SurfaceInteraction *si,
        MemoryArena &arena, TransportMode mode,
        bool allowMultipleLobes) const {
    ⟨Perform bump mapping with bumpMap, if present 579⟩
    si->bsdf = ARENA_ALLOC(arena, BSDF)(*si);
    si->bsdf->Add(ARENA_ALLOC(arena, FourierBSDF)(bsdfTable, mode));
}
```

9.2.5 ADDITIONAL MATERIALS

Beyond these materials, there are eight more Material implementations available in pbrt, all in the materials/ directory. We will not show all of their implementations here, since they are all just variations on the basic themes introduced in the material implementations above. All take Textures that define scattering parameters, these textures are evaluated in the materials' respective ComputeScatteringFunctions() methods, and appropriate BxDFs are created and returned in a BSDF. See the documentation on pbrt's file format for a summary of the parameters that these materials take.

These materials include:

- GlassMaterial: Perfect or glossy specular reflection and transmission, weighted by Fresnel terms for accurate angular-dependent variation.
- MetalMaterial: Metal, based on the Fresnel equations for conductors and the Torrance–Sparrow model. Unlike plastic, metal includes no diffuse component. See the files in the directory scenes/spds/metals/ for measured spectral data for the indices of refraction η and absorption coefficients k for a variety of metals.
- MirrorMaterial: A simple mirror, modeled with perfect specular reflection.
- SubstrateMaterial: A layered model that varies between glossy specular and diffuse reflection depending on the viewing angle (based on the FresnelBlend BRDF).
- SubsurfaceMaterial and KdSubsurfaceMaterial: Materials that return BSSRDFs that describe materials that exhibit subsurface scattering.
- TranslucentMaterial: A material that describes diffuse and glossy specular reflection and transmission through the surface.
- UberMaterial: A "kitchen sink" material representing the union of many of the preceding materials. This is a highly parameterized material that is particularly useful when converting scenes from other file formats into pbrt's.

Figure 8.10 in the previous chapter shows the dragon model rendered with Glass Material, and Figure 9.4 shows it with the MetalMaterial. Figure 9.5 demonstrates the KdSubsurfaceMaterial.

9.3 BUMP MAPPING

All of the Materials defined in the previous section take an optional floating-point texture that defines a displacement at each point on the surface: each point p has a displaced point p′ associated with it, defined by $p' = p + d(p)n(p)$, where $d(p)$ is the offset returned by the displacement texture at p and $n(p)$ is the surface normal at p (Figure 9.6).

Figure 9.4: Dragon rendered with the `MetalMaterial`, based on realistic measured gold scattering data. *(Model courtesy of Christian Schüller.)*

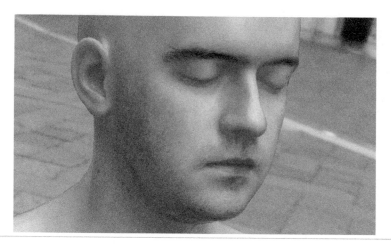

Figure 9.5: Head model rendered with the `KdSubsurfaceMaterial`, which models subsurface scattering (in conjunction with the subsurface scattering light transport techniques from Section 15.5). *(Model courtesy of Infinite Realities, Inc.)*

We would like to use this texture to compute shading normals so that the surface appears as if it actually had been offset by the displacement function, without modifying its geometry. This process is called *bump mapping*. For relatively small displacement functions, the visual effect of bump mapping can be quite convincing. This idea and

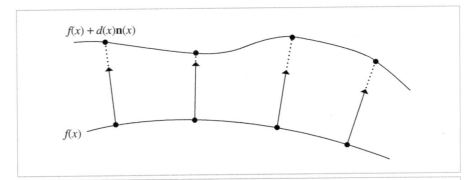

$f(x) + d(x)\mathbf{n}(x)$

$f(x)$

Figure 9.6: A displacement function associated with a material defines a new surface based on the old one, offset by the displacement amount along the normal at each point. pbrt doesn't compute a geometric representation of this displaced surface, but instead uses it to compute shading normals for bump mapping.

Figure 9.7: Using bump mapping to compute the shading normals for a sphere gives it the appearance of having much more geometric detail than is actually present.

the specific technique to compute these shading normals in a way that gives a plausible appearance of the actual displaced surface were developed by Blinn (1978).

Figure 9.7 shows the effect of applying bump mapping defined by an image map of a grid of lines to a sphere. A more complex example is shown in Figure 9.8, which shows a scene rendered with and without bump mapping. There, the bump map gives the appearance

(a)

(b)

Figure 9.8: The Sponza atrium model, rendered (a) without bump mapping and (b) with bump mapping. Bump mapping substantially increases the apparent geometric complexity of the model, without the increased rendering time and memory use that would result from a geometric representation with the equivalent amount of small-scale detail.

of a substantial amount of detail in the walls and floors that isn't actually present in the geometric model. Figure 9.9 shows one of the image maps used to define the bump function in Figure 9.8.

The Material::Bump() method is a utility routine for use by Material implementations. It is responsible for computing the effect of bump mapping at the point being shaded given a particular displacement Texture. So that future Material implementations aren't required to support bump mapping with this particular mechanism (or at all), we've placed this method outside of the hard-coded material evaluation pipeline and left it as a function that particular material implementations can call on their own.

Figure 9.9: One of the image maps used as a bump map for the Sponza atrium rendering in Figure 9.8.

The implementation of Material::Bump() is based on finding an approximation to the partial derivatives $\partial p/\partial u$ and $\partial p/\partial v$ of the displaced surface and using them in place of the surface's actual partial derivatives to compute the shading normal. (Recall that the surface normal is given by the cross product of these vectors, $\mathbf{n} = \partial p/\partial u \times \partial p/\partial v$.) Assume that the original surface is defined by a parametric function $p(u, v)$, and the bump offset function is a scalar function $d(u, v)$. Then the displaced surface is given by

$$p'(u, v) = p(u, v) + d(u, v)\mathbf{n}(u, v),$$

where $\mathbf{n}(u, v)$ is the surface normal at (u, v).

The partial derivatives of this function can be found using the chain rule. For example, the partial derivative in u is

$$\frac{\partial p'}{\partial u} = \frac{\partial p(u, v)}{\partial u} + \frac{\partial d(u, v)}{\partial u}\mathbf{n}(u, v) + d(u, v)\frac{\partial \mathbf{n}(u, v)}{\partial u}. \qquad [9.1]$$

We already have computed the value of $\partial p(u, v)/\partial u$; it's $\partial p/\partial u$ and is available in the SurfaceInteraction structure, which also stores the surface normal $\mathbf{n}(u, v)$ and the partial derivative $\partial \mathbf{n}(u, v)/\partial u = \partial \mathbf{n}/\partial u$. The displacement function $d(u, v)$ can be evaluated as needed, which leaves $\partial d(u, v)/\partial u$ as the only remaining term.

There are two possible approaches to finding the values of $\partial d(u, v)/\partial u$ and $\partial d(u, v)/\partial v$. One option would be to augment the Texture interface with a method to compute partial derivatives of the underlying texture function. For example, for image map textures mapped to the surface directly using its (u, v) parameterization, these partial derivatives can be computed by subtracting adjacent texels in the u and v directions. However, this approach is difficult to extend to complex procedural textures like some of the ones defined in Chapter 10. Therefore, pbrt directly computes these values with forward differencing in the Material::Bump() method, without modifying the Texture interface.

Recall the definition of the partial derivative:

$$\frac{\partial d(u, v)}{\partial u} = \lim_{\Delta_u \to 0} \frac{d(u + \Delta_u, v) - d(u, v)}{\Delta_u}.$$

Forward differencing approximates the value using a finite value of Δ_u and evaluating $d(u, v)$ at two positions. Thus, the final expression for $\partial p'/\partial u$ is the following (for simplicity, we have dropped the explicit dependence on (u, v) for some of the terms):

$$\frac{\partial p'}{\partial u} \approx \frac{\partial p}{\partial u} + \frac{d(u + \Delta_u, v) - d(u, v)}{\Delta_u}\mathbf{n} + d(u, v)\frac{\partial \mathbf{n}}{\partial u}.$$

Interestingly enough, most bump-mapping implementations ignore the final term under the assumption that $d(u, v)$ is expected to be relatively small. (Since bump mapping is mostly useful for approximating small perturbations, this is a reasonable assumption.) The fact that many renderers do not compute the values $\partial \mathbf{n}/\partial u$ and $\partial \mathbf{n}/\partial v$ may also have something to do with this simplification. An implication of ignoring the last term is that the magnitude of the displacement function then does not affect the bump-mapped partial derivatives; adding a constant value to it globally doesn't affect the final result, since only differences of the bump function affect it. pbrt computes all three terms since it has $\partial \mathbf{n}/\partial u$ and $\partial \mathbf{n}/\partial v$ readily available, although in practice this final term rarely makes a visually noticeable difference.

One important detail in the definition of Bump() is that the d parameter is declared to be of type const shared_ptr<Texture<Float>> &, rather than, for example, shared_ptr<Texture<Float>>. This difference is very important for performance, but the reason is subtle. If a C++ reference was not used here, then the shared_ptr implementation would need to increment the reference count for the temporary value passed to the method, and the reference count would need to be decremented when the method returned. This is an efficient operation with serial code, but with multiple threads of execution, it leads to a situation where multiple processing cores end up modifying the same memory location whenever different rendering tasks run this method with the same displacement texture. This state of affairs in turn leads to the expensive "read for ownership" operation described in Section A.6.1.[2]

⟨Material Method Definitions⟩ ≡

```
void Material::Bump(const std::shared_ptr<Texture<Float>> &d,
                    SurfaceInteraction *si) {
    ⟨Compute offset positions and evaluate displacement texture 590⟩
    ⟨Compute bump-mapped differential geometry 590⟩
}
```

---

2   As with many of the asides like this one, the underlying lesson was learned painfully by the authors: when we multi-threaded pbrt while working on the second edition of the book, we got this wrong. The issue was only discovered some months later in development when profiling the system revealed that calling Bump() was taking a surprising amount of time.

⟨Compute offset positions and evaluate displacement texture⟩ ≡   **589**
```
    SurfaceInteraction siEval = *si;
```
⟨Shift siEval du *in the u direction* **590**⟩
```
    Float uDisplace = d->Evaluate(siEval);
```
⟨Shift siEval dv *in the v direction⟩*
```
    Float vDisplace = d->Evaluate(siEval);
    Float displace = d->Evaluate(*si);
```

One remaining issue is how to choose the offsets Δ_u and Δ_v for the finite differencing computations. They should be small enough that fine changes in $d(u, v)$ are captured but large enough so that available floating-point precision is sufficient to give a good result. Here, we will choose Δ_u and Δ_v values that lead to an offset that is about half the image space pixel sample spacing and use them to update the appropriate member variables in the SurfaceInteraction to reflect a shift to the offset position. (See Section 10.1.1 for an explanation of how the image space distances are computed.)

Another detail to note in the following code: we recompute the surface normal **n** as the cross product of ∂p/∂u and ∂p/∂v rather than using si->shading.n directly. The reason for this is that the orientation of **n** may have been flipped (recall the fragment *⟨Adjust normal based on orientation and handedness⟩* in Section 2.10.1). However, we need the original normal here. Later, when the results of the computation are passed to SurfaceInteraction::SetShadingGeometry(), the normal we compute will itself be flipped if necessary.

⟨Shift siEval du *in the u direction⟩* ≡   **590**
```
    Float du = .5f * (std::abs(si->dudx) + std::abs(si->dudy));
    if (du == 0) du = .01f;
    siEval.p = si->p + du * si->shading.dpdu;
    siEval.uv = si->uv + Vector2f(du, 0.f);
    siEval.n = Normalize((Normal3f)Cross(si->shading.dpdu,
                                         si->shading.dpdv) +
                         du * si->dndu);
```

The *⟨Shift* siEval dv *in the v direction⟩* fragment is nearly the same as the fragment that shifts du, so it isn't included here.

Given the new positions and the displacement texture's values at them, the partial derivatives can be computed directly using Equation (9.1):

⟨Compute bump-mapped differential geometry⟩ ≡   **589**
```
    Vector3f dpdu = si->shading.dpdu +
        (uDisplace - displace) / du * Vector3f(si->shading.n) +
        displace * Vector3f(si->shading.dndu);
    Vector3f dpdv = si->shading.dpdv +
        (vDisplace - displace) / dv * Vector3f(si->shading.n) +
        displace * Vector3f(si->shading.dndv);
    si->SetShadingGeometry(dpdu, dpdv, si->shading.dndu, si->shading.dndv,
                           false);
```

FURTHER READING

Burley's article (2012) on a material model developed at Disney for feature films is an excellent read. It includes extensive discussion of features of real-world reflection functions that can be observed in Matusik et al.'s (2003b) measurements of one hundred BRDFs and analyzes the ways that existing BRDF models do and do not fit these features well. These insights are then used to develop an "artist-friendly" material model that can express a wide range of surface appearances. The model describes reflection with a single color and ten scalar parameters, all of which are in the range [0, 1] and have fairly predictable effects on the appearance of the resulting material.

Blinn (1978) invented the bump-mapping technique. Kajiya (1985) generalized the idea of bump mapping the normal to *frame mapping*, which also perturbs the surface's primary tangent vector and is useful for controlling the appearance of anisotropic reflection models. Mikkelsen's thesis (2008) carefully investigates a number of the assumptions underlying bump mapping, proposes generalizations, and addresses a number of subtleties with respect to its application to real-time rendering.

Snyder and Barr (1987) noted the light leak problem from per-vertex shading normals and proposed a number of work-arounds. The method we have used in this chapter is from Section 5.3 of Veach's thesis (1997); it is a more robust solution than those of Snyder and Barr.

Shading normals introduce a number of subtle problems for physically based light transport algorithms that we have not addressed in this chapter. For example, they can easily lead to surfaces that reflect more energy than was incident upon them, which can wreak havoc with light transport algorithms that are designed under the assumption of energy conservation. Veach (1996) investigated this issue in depth and developed a number of solutions. Section 16.1 of this book will return to this issue.

One visual shortcoming of bump mapping is that it doesn't naturally account for self-shadowing, where bumps cast shadows on the surface and prevent light from reaching nearby points. These shadows can have a significant impact on the appearance of rough surfaces. Max (1988) developed the *horizon mapping* technique, which performs a preprocess on bump maps stored in image maps to compute a term to account for this effect. This approach isn't directly applicable to procedural textures, however. Dana et al. (1999) measured spatially varying reflection properties from real-world surfaces, including these self-shadowing effects; they convincingly demonstrate this effect's importance for accurate image synthesis.

Another difficult issue related to bump mapping is that antialiasing bump maps that have higher frequency detail than can be represented in the image is quite difficult. In particular, it is not enough to remove high-frequency detail from the bump map function, but in general the BSDF needs to be modified to account for this detail. Fournier (1992) applied *normal distribution functions* to this problem, where the surface normal was generalized to represent a distribution of normal directions. Becker and Max (1993) developed algorithms for blending between bump maps and BRDFs that represented higher-frequency details. Schilling (1997, 2001) investigated this issue particularly for application to graphics hardware. More recently, effective approaches to filtering bump maps were developed by Han et al. (2007) and Olano and Baker (2010). Recent work by Dupuy et al. (2013) and Hery et al. (2014) addressed this issue by developing techniques that convert displacements into anisotropic distributions of Beckmann microfacets.

An alternative to bump mapping is displacement mapping, where the bump function is used to actually modify the surface geometry, rather than just perturbing the normal (Cook 1984; Cook, Carpenter, and Catmull 1987). Advantages of displacement mapping include geometric detail on object silhouettes and the possibility of accounting for self-shadowing. Patterson and collaborators described an innovative algorithm for displacement mapping with ray tracing where the geometry is unperturbed but the ray's direction is modified such that the intersections that are found are the same as would be found with the displaced geometry (Patterson, Hoggar, and Logie 1991; Logie and Patterson 1994). Heidrich and Seidel (1998) developed a technique for computing direct intersections with procedurally defined displacement functions.

As computers have become faster, another viable approach for displacement mapping has been to use an implicit function to define the displaced surface and to then take steps along rays until they find a zero crossing with the implicit function. At this point, an intersection has been found. This approach was first introduced by Hart (1996); see Donnelly (2005) for information about using this approach for displacement mapping on the GPU. This approach was recently popularized by Quilez on the *shadertoy* Web site (Quilez 2015).

With the advent of increased memory on computers and caching algorithms, the option of finely tessellating geometry and displacing its vertices for ray tracing has become feasible. Pharr and Hanrahan (1996) described an approach to this problem based on geometry caching, and Wang et al. (2000) described an adaptive tessellation algorithm that reduces memory requirements. Smits, Shirley, and Stark (2000) lazily tessellate individual triangles, saving a substantial amount of memory.

Measuring fine-scale surface geometry of real surfaces to acquire bump or displacement maps can be challenging. Johnson et al. (2011) developed a novel hand-held system that can measure detail down to a few microns, which more than suffices for these uses.

EXERCISES

⊘ 9.1 If the same Texture is bound to more than one component of a Material (e.g., to both PlasticMaterial::Kd and PlasticMaterial::Ks), the texture will be evaluated twice. This unnecessarily duplicated work may lead to a noticeable increase in rendering time if the Texture is itself computationally expensive. Modify the materials in pbrt to eliminate this problem. Measure the change in the system's performance, both for standard scenes as well as for contrived scenes that exhibit this redundancy.

⊘ 9.2 Implement the artist-friendly "Disney BRDF" described by Burley (2012). You will need both a new Material implementation as well as a few new BxDFs. Render a variety of scenes using your implementation. How easy do you find it to match the visual appearance of existing pbrt scenes when replacing Materials in them with this one? How quickly can you dial in the parameters of this material to achieve a given desired appearance?

⑨ 9.3 One form of aliasing that pbrt doesn't try to eliminate is specular highlight aliasing. Glossy specular surfaces with high specular exponents, particularly if they have high curvature, are susceptible to aliasing as small changes in incident direction or surface position (and thus surface normal) may cause the highlight's contribution to change substantially. Read Amanatides's paper on this topic (Amanatides 1992) and extend pbrt to reduce specular aliasing, either using his technique or by developing your own. Most of the quantities needed to do the appropriate computations are already available—$\partial \mathbf{n}/\partial x$ and $\partial \mathbf{n}/\partial y$ in the SurfaceInteraction, and so on—although it will probably be necessary to extend the BxDF interface to provide more information about the roughness of any MicrofacetDistributions they have.

② 9.4 Another approach to addressing specular highlight aliasing is to supersample the BSDF, evaluating it multiple times around the point being shaded. After reading the discussion of supersampling texture functions in Section 10.1, modify the BSDF::f() method to shift to a set of positions around the intersection point but within the pixel sampling rate around the intersection point and evaluate the BSDF at each one of them when the BSDF evaluation routines are called. (Be sure to account for the change in normal using its partial derivatives.) How well does this approach combat specular highlight aliasing?

③ 9.5 Read some of the papers on filtering bump maps referenced in the "Further Reading" section of this chapter, choose one of the techniques described there, and implement it in pbrt. Show both the visual artifacts from bump map aliasing without the technique you implement as well as examples of how well your implementation addresses them.

③ 9.6 Neyret (1996, 1998), Heitz and Neyret (2012), and Heitz et al. (2015) developed algorithms that take descriptions of complex shapes and their reflective properties and turn them into generalized reflection models at different resolutions, each with limited frequency content. The advantage of this representation is that it makes it easy to select an appropriate level of detail for an object based on its size on the screen, thus reducing aliasing. Read these papers and implement the algorithms described in them in pbrt. Show how they can be used to reduce geometric aliasing from detailed geometry, and extend them to address bump map aliasing.

③ 9.7 Use the triangular face refinement infrastructure from the Loop subdivision surface implementation in Section 3.8 to implement displacement mapping in pbrt. The usual approach to displacement mapping is to finely tessellate the geometric shape and then to evaluate the displacement function at its vertices, moving each vertex the given distance along its normal.

BSDF::f() 575

BxDF 513

SurfaceInteraction 116

Refine each face of the mesh until, when projected onto the image, it is roughly the size of the separation between pixels. To do this, you will need to be able to estimate the image pixel-based length of an edge in the scene when it is projected onto the screen. Use the texturing infrastructure in Chapter 10 to evaluate displacement functions. See Patney et al. (2009) and Fisher et al. (2009) for discussion of issues related to avoiding cracks in the mesh due to adaptive tessellation.

10 TEXTURE

We will now describe a set of interfaces and classes that allow us to incorporate texture into our material models. Recall that the materials in Chapter 9 are all based on various parameters that describe their characteristics (diffuse reflectance, glossiness, etc.). Because real-world material properties typically vary over surfaces, it is necessary to be able to represent this spatial variation. In pbrt, the texture abstractions serve this purpose. They are defined in a way that separates the pattern generation methods from the reflection model implementations, making it easy to combine them in arbitrary ways, thereby making it easier to create a wide variety of appearances.

In pbrt, a *texture* is a fairly general concept: it is a function that maps points in some domain (e.g., a surface's (u, v) parametric space or (x, y, z) object space) to values in some other domain (e.g., spectra or the real numbers). A variety of implementations of texture classes are available in the system. For example, pbrt has textures that represent zero-dimensional functions that return a constant in order to accommodate surfaces that have the same parameter value everywhere. Image map textures are two-dimensional functions of (s, t) parameter values that use a 2D array of pixel values to compute texture values at particular points (they are described in Section 10.4). There are even texture functions that compute values based on the values computed by other texture functions.

Textures may be a source of high-frequency variation in the final image. Figure 10.1 shows an image with severe aliasing due to a texture. Although the visual impact of this aliasing can be reduced with the nonuniform sampling techniques from Chapter 7, a better solution to this problem is to implement texture functions that adjust their frequency content based on the rate at which they are being sampled. For many texture functions, computing a reasonable approximation to the frequency content and antialiasing in this manner aren't too difficult and are substantially more efficient than reducing aliasing by increasing the image sampling rate.

Physically Based Rendering: From Theory To Implementation.
http://dx.doi.org/10.1016/B978-0-12-800645-0.50010-5

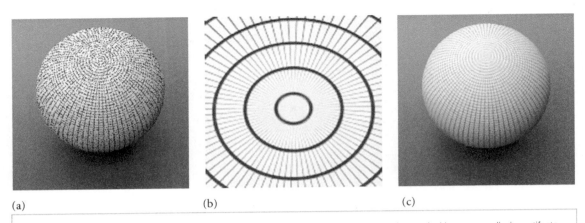

(a)   (b)   (c)

Figure 10.1: Texture Aliasing. (a) An image of a grid texture on a sphere with one sample per pixel has severe aliasing artifacts. (b) A zoomed-in area from near the top of the sphere gives a sense of how much high-frequency detail is present between adjacent pixel sample positions. (c) The texture function has taken into account the image sampling rate to prefilter its function and remove high-frequency detail, resulting in an antialiased image, even with a single sample per pixel.

The first section of this chapter will discuss the problem of texture aliasing and general approaches to solving it. We will then describe the basic texture interface and illustrate its use with a few simple texture functions. Throughout the remainder of the chapter, we will present a variety of more complex texture implementations, demonstrating the use of a number of different texture antialiasing techniques along the way.

10.1 SAMPLING AND ANTIALIASING

The sampling task from Chapter 7 was a frustrating one since the aliasing problem was known to be unsolvable from the start. The infinite frequency content of geometric edges and hard shadows *guarantees* aliasing in the final images, no matter how high the image sampling rate. (Our only consolation is that the visual impact of this remaining aliasing can be reduced to unobjectionable levels with a sufficient number of well-placed samples.)

Fortunately, for textures things are not this difficult from the start: either there is often a convenient analytic form of the texture function available, which makes it possible to remove excessively high frequencies before sampling it, or it is possible to be careful when evaluating the function so as not to introduce high frequencies in the first place. When this problem is carefully addressed in texture implementations, as is done through the rest of this chapter, there is usually no need for more than one sample per pixel in order to render an image without texture aliasing.

Two problems must be addressed in order to remove aliasing from texture functions:

1. The sampling rate in texture space must be computed. The screen space sampling rate is known from the image resolution and pixel sampling rate, but here we need to determine the resulting sampling rate on a surface in the scene in order to find the rate at which the texture function is being sampled.

2. Given the texture sampling rate, sampling theory must be applied to guide the computation of a texture value that doesn't have higher frequency variation than can be represented by the sampling rate (e.g., by removing excess frequencies beyond the Nyquist limit from the texture function).

These two issues will be addressed in turn throughout the rest of this section.

10.1.1 FINDING THE TEXTURE SAMPLING RATE

Consider an arbitrary texture function that is a function of position, $T(\mathrm{p})$, defined on a surface in the scene. If we ignore the complications introduced by visibility issues—the possibility that another object may occlude the surface at nearby image samples or that the surface may have a limited extent on the image plane—this texture function can also be expressed as a function over points (x, y) on the image plane, $T(f(x, y))$, where $f(x, y)$ is the function that maps image points to points on the surface. Thus, $T(f(x, y))$ gives the value of the texture function as seen at image position (x, y).

As a simple example of this idea, consider a 2D texture function $T(s, t)$ applied to a quadrilateral that is perpendicular to the z axis and has corners at the world space points $(0, 0, 0)$, $(1, 0, 0)$, $(1, 1, 0)$, and $(0, 1, 0)$. If an orthographic camera is placed looking down the z axis such that the quadrilateral precisely fills the image plane and if points p on the quadrilateral are mapped to 2D (s, t) texture coordinates by

$$s = \mathrm{p}_x \qquad t = \mathrm{p}_y,$$

then the relationship between (s, t) and screen (x, y) pixels is straightforward:

$$s = \frac{x}{x_\mathrm{r}} \qquad t = \frac{y}{y_\mathrm{r}},$$

where the overall image resolution is $(x_\mathrm{r}, y_\mathrm{r})$ (Figure 10.2). Thus, given a sample spacing of one pixel in the image plane, the sample spacing in (s, t) texture parameter space is $(1/x_\mathrm{r}, 1/y_\mathrm{r})$, and the texture function must remove any detail at a higher frequency than can be represented at that sampling rate.

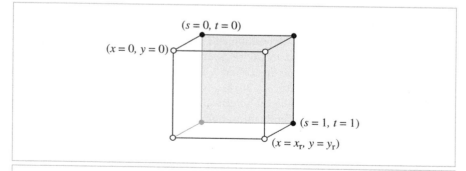

Figure 10.2: If a quadrilateral is viewed with an orthographic perspective such that the quadrilateral precisely fills the image plane, it's easy to compute the relationship between the sampling rate in (x, y) pixel coordinates and the texture sampling rate.

This relationship between pixel coordinates and texture coordinates, and thus the relationship between their sampling rates, is the key bit of information that determines the maximum frequency content allowable in the texture function. As a slightly more complex example, given a triangle with (s, t) texture coordinates at the vertices and viewed with a perspective projection, it's possible to analytically find the differences in s and t across the sample points on the image plane. This is the basis of basic texture map antialiasing in graphics processors.

For more complex scene geometry, camera projections, and mappings to texture coordinates, it is much more difficult to precisely determine the relationship between image positions and texture parameter values. Fortunately, for texture antialiasing, we don't need to be able to evaluate $f(x, y)$ for arbitrary (x, y) but just need to find the relationship between changes in pixel sample position and the resulting change in texture sample position at a particular point on the image. This relationship is given by the partial derivatives of this function, $\partial f/\partial x$ and $\partial f/\partial y$. For example, these can be used to find a first-order approximation to the value of f,

$$f(x', y') \approx f(x, y) + (x' - x)\frac{\partial f}{\partial x} + (y' - y)\frac{\partial f}{\partial y}.$$

If these partial derivatives are changing slowly with respect to the distances $x' - x$ and $y' - y$, this is a reasonable approximation. More importantly, the values of these partial derivatives give an approximation to the change in texture sample position for a shift of one pixel in the x and y directions, respectively, and thus directly yield the texture sampling rate. For example, in the previous quadrilateral example, $\partial s/\partial x = 1/x_r$, $\partial s/\partial y = 0$, $\partial t/\partial x = 0$, and $\partial t/\partial y = 1/y_r$.

The key to finding the values of these partial derivatives in the general case lies in the RayDifferential structure, which was defined in Section 2.5.1. This structure is initialized for each camera ray by the Camera::GenerateRayDifferential() method; it contains not only the ray actually being traced through the scene but also two additional rays, one offset horizontally one pixel sample from the camera ray and the other offset vertically by one pixel sample. All of the geometric ray intersection routines use only the main camera ray for their computations; the auxiliary rays are ignored (this is easy to do because RayDifferential is a subclass of Ray).

Here we will use the offset rays to estimate the partial derivatives of the mapping $p(x, y)$ from image position to world space position and the partial derivatives of the mappings $u(x, y)$ and $v(x, y)$ from (x, y) to (u, v) parametric coordinates, giving the partial derivatives of world space positions $\partial p/\partial x$ and $\partial p/\partial y$ and the partial derivatives of (u, v) parametric coordinates $\partial u/\partial x$, $\partial v/\partial x$, $\partial u/\partial y$, and $\partial v/\partial y$. In Section 10.2, we will see how these can be used to compute the screen space derivatives of arbitrary quantities based on p or (u, v) and consequently the sampling rates of these quantities. The values of these partial derivatives at the intersection point are stored in the SurfaceInteraction structure. They are declared as mutable, since they are set in a method that takes a const instance of that object.

⟨SurfaceInteraction Public Data⟩ +≡   116
    mutable Vector3f dpdx, dpdy;
    mutable Float dudx = 0, dvdx = 0, dudy = 0, dvdy = 0;

The SurfaceInteraction::ComputeDifferentials() method computes these values. It is called by SurfaceInteraction::ComputeScatteringFunctions() before the Material's ComputeScatteringFunctions() method is called so that these values will be available for any texture evaluation routines that are called by the material. Because ray differentials aren't available for all rays traced by the system (e.g., rays starting from light sources traced for photon mapping or bidirectional path tracing), the hasDifferentials field of the RayDifferential must be checked before these computations are performed. If the differentials are not present, then the derivatives are all set to zero (which will eventually lead to unfiltered point sampling of textures).

⟨*SurfaceInteraction Method Definitions*⟩ +≡
```
void SurfaceInteraction::ComputeDifferentials(
        const RayDifferential &ray) const {
    if (ray.hasDifferentials) {
        ⟨Estimate screen space change in p and (u, v) 601⟩
    } else {
        dudx = dvdx = 0;
        dudy = dvdy = 0;
        dpdx = dpdy = Vector3f(0, 0, 0);
    }
}
```

The key to computing these estimates is the assumption that the surface is locally flat with respect to the sampling rate at the point being shaded. This is a reasonable approximation in practice, and it is hard to do much better. Because ray tracing is a point-sampling technique, we have no additional information about the scene in between the rays we have traced. For highly curved surfaces or at silhouette edges, this approximation can break down, though this is rarely a source of noticeable error in practice.

For this approximation, we need the plane through the point p intersected by the main ray that is tangent to the surface. This plane is given by the implicit equation

$$ax + by + cz + d = 0,$$

where $a = \mathbf{n}_x$, $b = \mathbf{n}_y$, $c = \mathbf{n}_z$, and $d = -(\mathbf{n} \cdot \mathbf{p})$. We can then compute the intersection points $\mathbf{p}_x$ and $\mathbf{p}_y$ between the auxiliary rays r_x and r_y and this plane (Figure 10.3). These new points give an approximation to the partial derivatives of position on the surface $\partial \mathbf{p}/\partial x$ and $\partial \mathbf{p}/\partial y$, based on forward differences:

$$\frac{\partial \mathbf{p}}{\partial x} \approx \mathbf{p}_x - \mathbf{p}, \qquad \frac{\partial \mathbf{p}}{\partial y} \approx \mathbf{p}_y - \mathbf{p}.$$

Because the differential rays are offset one pixel sample in each direction, there's no need to divide these differences by a Δ value, since $\Delta = 1$.

⟨*Estimate screen space change in p and (u, v)*⟩ ≡   601
```
    ⟨Compute auxiliary intersection points with plane 602⟩
    dpdx = px - p;
    dpdy = py - p;
    ⟨Compute (u, v) offsets at auxiliary points 603⟩
```

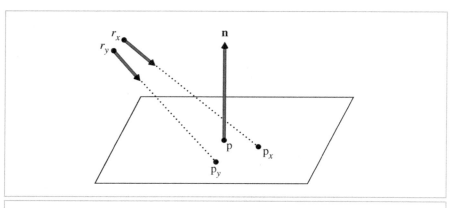

Figure 10.3: By approximating the local surface geometry at the intersection point with the tangent plane through p, approximations to the points at which the auxiliary rays r_x and r_y would intersect the surface can be found by finding their intersection points with the tangent plane p_x and p_y.

The ray–plane intersection algorithm described in Section 3.1.2 gives the t value where a ray described by origin o and direction **d** intersects a plane described by $ax + by + cz + d = 0$:

$$t = \frac{-((a, b, c) \cdot o) - d}{(a, b, c) \cdot \mathbf{d}}.$$

To compute this value for the two auxiliary rays, the plane's d coefficient is computed first. It isn't necessary to compute the a, b, and c coefficients, since they're available in n. We can then apply the formula directly.

⟨*Compute auxiliary intersection points with plane*⟩ ≡   601
```
Float d = Dot(n, Vector3f(p.x, p.y, p.z));
Float tx = -(Dot(n, Vector3f(ray.rxOrigin)) - d) /
    Dot(n, ray.rxDirection);
Point3f px = ray.rxOrigin + tx * ray.rxDirection;
Float ty = -(Dot(n, Vector3f(ray.ryOrigin)) - d) /
    Dot(n, ray.ryDirection);
Point3f py = ray.ryOrigin + ty * ray.ryDirection;
```

Using the positions p_x and p_y, an approximation to their respective (u, v) coordinates can be found by taking advantage of the fact that the surface's partial derivatives $\partial p/\partial u$ and $\partial p/\partial v$ form a (not necessarily orthogonal) coordinate system on the plane and that the coordinates of the auxiliary intersection points in terms of this coordinate system are their coordinates with respect to the (u, v) parameterization (Figure 10.4). Given a position p' on the plane, we can compute its position with respect to the coordinate system by

$$p' = p + \Delta_u \frac{\partial p}{\partial u} + \Delta_v \frac{\partial p}{\partial v},$$

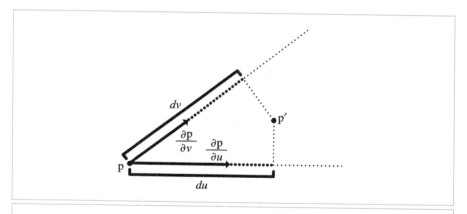

Figure 10.4: An estimate of the difference in (u, v) parametric coordinates from p to p' can be found by finding the coordinates of p' with respect to the coordinate system defined by p, $\partial p/\partial u$, and $\partial p/\partial v$.

or, equivalently,

$$
\begin{pmatrix} p'_x - p_x \\ p'_y - p_y \\ p'_z - p_z \end{pmatrix} = \begin{pmatrix} \partial p_x/\partial u & \partial p_x/\partial v \\ \partial p_y/\partial u & \partial p_y/\partial v \\ \partial p_z/\partial u & \partial p_z/\partial v \end{pmatrix} \begin{pmatrix} \Delta_u \\ \Delta_v \end{pmatrix}.
$$

A solution to this linear system of equations for one of the auxiliary points $p' = p_x$ or $p' = p_y$ gives the corresponding screen space partial derivatives $(\partial u/\partial x, \partial v/\partial x)$ or $(\partial u/\partial y, \partial v/\partial y)$, respectively.

This linear system has three equations with two unknowns—that is, it's overconstrained. We need to be careful since one of the equations may be degenerate—for example, if $\partial p/\partial u$ and $\partial p/\partial v$ are in the xy plane such that their z components are both zero, then the third equation will be degenerate. Therefore, we'd like to solve the system of equations using two equations that don't give a degenerate system. An easy way to do this is to take the cross product of $\partial p/\partial u$ and $\partial p/\partial v$, see which coordinate of the result has the largest magnitude, and use the other two. Their cross product is already available in n, so using this approach is straightforward. Even after all this, it may happen that the linear system has no solution (usually due to the partial derivatives not forming a coordinate system on the plane). In that case, all that can be done is to return arbitrary values.

⟨*Compute (u, v) offsets at auxiliary points*⟩ ≡   **601**
    ⟨*Choose two dimensions to use for ray offset computation* **604**⟩
    ⟨*Initialize A, Bx, and By matrices for offset computation* **604**⟩
    `if (!SolveLinearSystem2x2(A, Bx, &dudx, &dvdx))`
        `dudx = dvdx = 0;`
    `if (!SolveLinearSystem2x2(A, By, &dudy, &dvdy))`
        `dudy = dvdy = 0;`

⟨*Choose two dimensions to use for ray offset computation*⟩ ≡   603
```
int dim[2];
if (std::abs(n.x) > std::abs(n.y) && std::abs(n.x) > std::abs(n.z)) {
    dim[0] = 1; dim[1] = 2;
} else if (std::abs(n.y) > std::abs(n.z)) {
    dim[0] = 0; dim[1] = 2;
} else {
    dim[0] = 0; dim[1] = 1;
}
```

⟨*Initialize* A, Bx, *and* By *matrices for offset computation*⟩ ≡   603
```
Float A[2][2] = { { dpdu[dim[0]], dpdv[dim[0]] },
                  { dpdu[dim[1]], dpdv[dim[1]] } };
Float Bx[2] = { px[dim[0]] - p[dim[0]], px[dim[1]] - p[dim[1]] };
Float By[2] = { py[dim[0]] - p[dim[0]], py[dim[1]] - p[dim[1]] };
```

10.1.2 FILTERING TEXTURE FUNCTIONS

It is necessary to remove frequencies in texture functions that are past the Nyquist limit
for the texture sampling rate. The goal is to compute, with as few approximations as
possible, the result of the *ideal texture resampling* process, which says that in order to
evaluate $T(f(x, y))$ without aliasing, we must first band-limit it, removing frequencies
beyond the Nyquist limit by convolving it with the sinc filter:

$$T_b'(x, y) = \int_{-\infty}^{\infty} \int_{-\infty}^{\infty} \operatorname{sinc}(x') \operatorname{sinc}(y') \, T' \left(f(x + x', y + y') \right) \mathrm{d}x' \, \mathrm{d}y'.$$

The band-limited function in turn should then be convolved with the pixel filter $g(x, y)$
centered at the (x, y) point on the screen at which we want to evaluate the texture
function:

$$T_f'(x, y) = \int_{-y\text{Width}/2}^{y\text{Width}/2} \int_{-x\text{Width}/2}^{x\text{Width}/2} g(x', y') \, T_b'(x + x', y + y') \, \mathrm{d}x' \, \mathrm{d}y'.$$

This gives the theoretically perfect value for the texture as projected onto the screen.[1]

In practice, there are many simplifications that can be made to this process, with little
reduction in visual quality. For example, a box filter may be used for the band-limiting
step, and the second step is usually ignored completely, effectively acting as if the pixel
filter were a box filter, which makes it possible to do the antialiasing work completely
in texture space and simplifies the implementation significantly. The EWA filtering algorithm in Section 10.4.5 is a notable exception in that it assumes a Gaussian pixel filter.

---

1   One simplification that is present in this ideal filtering process is the implicit assumption that the texture function makes a
linear contribution to frequency content in the image, so that filtering out its high frequencies removes high frequencies from
the image. This is true for many uses of textures—for example, if an image map is used to modulate the diffuse term of a
MatteMaterial. However, if a texture is used to determine the roughness of a glossy specular object, for example, this linearity
assumption is incorrect, since a linear change in the roughness value has a non-linear effect on the reflected radiance from
the microfacet BRDF. We will ignore this issue here, since it isn't easily solved in general. The "Further Reading" section has
more discussion of this issue.

The box filter is easy to use, since it can be applied analytically by computing the average of the texture function over the appropriate region. Intuitively, this is a reasonable approach to the texture filtering problem, and it can be computed directly for many texture functions. Indeed, through the rest of this chapter, we will often use a box filter to average texture function values between samples and informally use the term *filter region* to describe the area being averaged over. This is the most common approach when filtering texture functions.

Even the box filter, with all of its shortcomings, gives acceptable results for texture filtering in many cases. One factor that helps is the fact that a number of samples are usually taken in each pixel. Thus, even if the filtered texture values used in each one are suboptimal, once they are filtered by the pixel reconstruction filter, the end result generally doesn't suffer too much.

An alternative to using the box filter to filter texture functions is to use the observation that the effect of the ideal sinc filter is to let frequency components below the Nyquist limit pass through unchanged but to remove frequencies past it. Therefore, if we know the frequency content of the texture function (e.g., if it is a sum of terms, each one with known frequency content), then if we replace the high-frequency terms with their average values, we are effectively doing the work of the sinc prefilter. This approach is known as *clamping* and is the basis for antialiasing in the textures based on the noise function in Section 10.6.

Finally, for texture functions where none of these techniques is easily applied, a final option is *supersampling*—the function is evaluated and filtered at multiple locations near the main evaluation point, thus increasing the sampling rate in texture space. If a box filter is used to filter these sample values, this is equivalent to averaging the value of the function. This approach can be expensive if the texture function is complex to evaluate, and as with image sampling a very large number of samples may be needed to remove aliasing. Although this is a brute-force solution, it is still more efficient than increasing the image sampling rate, since it doesn't incur the cost of tracing more rays through the scene.

★ 10.1.3 RAY DIFFERENTIALS FOR SPECULAR REFLECTION AND TRANSMISSION

Given the effectiveness of ray differentials for finding filter regions for texture antialiasing for camera rays, it is useful to extend the method to make it possible to determine texture space sampling rates for objects that are seen indirectly via specular reflection or refraction; objects seen in mirrors, for example, should also no more have texture aliasing than directly visible objects. Igehy (1999) developed an elegant solution to the problem of how to find the appropriate differential rays for specular reflection and refraction, which is the approach used in pbrt.[2]

---

2   Igehy's formulation is slightly different from the one here—he effectively tracked the differences between the main ray and the offset rays, while we store the offset rays explicitly. The mathematics all work out to be the same in the end; we chose this alternative because we believe that it makes the algorithm's operation for camera rays easier to understand.

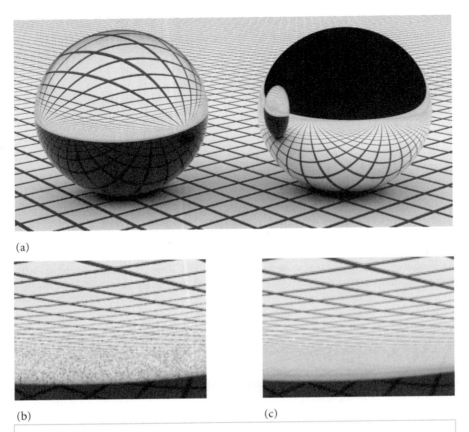

(a)

(b)   (c)

Figure 10.5: (a) Tracking ray differentials for reflected and refracted rays ensures that the image map texture seen in the balls is filtered to avoid aliasing. The left ball is glass, exhibiting reflection and refraction, and the right ball is a mirror, just showing reflection. Note that the texture is well filtered over both of the balls. (b) and (c) show a zoomed-in section of the glass ball; (b) shows the aliasing artifacts that are present if ray differentials aren't used, while (c) shows the result when they are.

Figure 10.5 illustrates the difference that proper texture filtering for specular reflection and transmission can make. Figure 10.5(a) shows a glass ball and a mirrored ball on a plane with a texture map containing high-frequency components. Ray differentials ensure that the images of the texture seen via reflection and refraction from the balls are free of aliasing artifacts. A close-up view of the reflection in the glass ball is shown in Figure 10.5(b) and (c); Figure 10.5(b) was rendered without ray differentials for the reflected and transmitted rays, and Figure 10.5(c) was rendered with ray differentials. (All images are rendered with one sample per pixel.) The aliasing errors in the left image are eliminated on the right without excessively blurring the texture.

In order to compute the reflected or transmitted ray differentials at a surface intersection point, we need an approximation to the rays that would have been traced at the intersection points for the two offset rays in the ray differential that hit the surface (Figure 10.6).

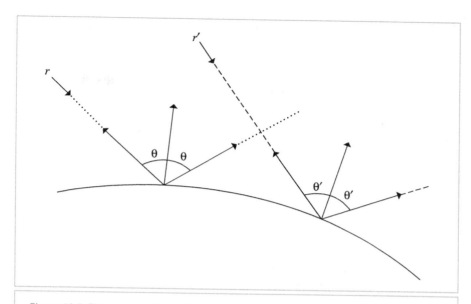

Figure 10.6: The specular reflection formula gives the direction of the reflected ray at a point on a surface. An offset ray for a ray differential r' (dashed line) will generally intersect the surface at a different point and be reflected in a different direction. The new direction is affected by both the different surface normal at the point as well as the offset ray's different incident direction. The computation to find the reflected direction for the offset ray in pbrt estimates the change in reflected direction as a function of image space position and approximates the ray differential's direction with the main ray's direction added to the estimated change in direction.

The new ray for the main ray is computed by the BSDF, so here we only need to compute the outgoing rays for the r_x and r_y differentials.

For both reflection and refraction, the origin of each differential ray is easily found. The SurfaceInteraction::ComputeDifferentials() method previously computed approximations for how much the surface position changes with respect to (x, y) position on the image plane $\partial p/\partial x$ and $\partial p/\partial y$. Adding these offsets to the intersection point of the main ray gives approximate origins for the new rays. If the incident ray doesn't have differentials, then it's impossible to compute reflected ray differentials and this step is skipped.

⟨*Compute ray differential* rd *for specular reflection*⟩ ≡   38
```
RayDifferential rd = isect.SpawnRay(wi);
if (ray.hasDifferentials) {
    rd.hasDifferentials = true;
    rd.rxOrigin = isect.p + isect.dpdx;
    rd.ryOrigin = isect.p + isect.dpdy;
    ⟨Compute differential reflected directions 608⟩
}
```

Finding the directions of these rays is slightly trickier. Igehy (1999) observed that if we know how much the reflected direction ω_i changes with respect to a shift of a pixel sample in the x and y directions on the image plane, we can use this information to approximate the direction of the offset rays. For example, the direction for the ray offset in x is

$$\omega \approx \omega_i + \frac{\partial \omega_i}{\partial x}.$$

Recall from Equation (8.6) that for a general world space surface normal and outgoing direction, the direction for perfect specular reflection is

$$\omega_i = -\omega_o + 2(\omega_o \cdot \mathbf{n})\mathbf{n}.$$

Fortunately, the partial derivatives of this expression are easily computed:

$$\frac{\partial \omega_i}{\partial x} = \frac{\partial}{\partial x} \left(-\omega_o + 2(\omega_o \cdot \mathbf{n})\mathbf{n} \right)$$

$$= -\frac{\partial \omega_o}{\partial x} + 2 \left((\omega_o \cdot \mathbf{n})\frac{\partial \mathbf{n}}{\partial x} + \frac{\partial (\omega_o \cdot \mathbf{n})}{\partial x}\mathbf{n} \right).$$

Using the properties of the dot product, it can be shown that

$$\frac{\partial (\omega_o \cdot \mathbf{n})}{\partial x} = \frac{\partial \omega_o}{\partial x} \cdot \mathbf{n} + \omega_o \cdot \frac{\partial \mathbf{n}}{\partial x}.$$

The value of $\partial \omega_o / \partial x$ can be found from the difference between the direction of the ray differential's main ray and the direction of the r_x offset ray, and all of the other necessary quantities are readily available from the SurfaceInteraction, so the implementation of this computation for the partial derivatives in x and y is straightforward.

⟨*Compute differential reflected directions*⟩ ≡   607

```
Normal3f dndx = isect.shading.dndu * isect.dudx +
                isect.shading.dndv * isect.dvdx;
Normal3f dndy = isect.shading.dndu * isect.dudy +
                isect.shading.dndv * isect.dvdy;
Vector3f dwodx = -ray.rxDirection - wo, dwody = -ray.ryDirection - wo;
Float dDNdx = Dot(dwodx, ns) + Dot(wo, dndx);
Float dDNdy = Dot(dwody, ns) + Dot(wo, dndy);
rd.rxDirection = wi - dwodx +
    2.f * Vector3f(Dot(wo, ns) * dndx + dDNdx * ns);
rd.ryDirection = wi - dwody +
    2.f * Vector3f(Dot(wo, ns) * dndy + dDNdy * ns);
```

A similar process of differentiating the equation for the direction of a specularly transmitted ray, Equation (8.9), gives the equation to find the differential change in the transmitted direction. We won't include the derivation or our implementation here, but refer the interested reader to the original paper and to the pbrt source code, respectively.

10.2 TEXTURE COORDINATE GENERATION

Almost all of the textures in this chapter are functions that take a 2D or 3D coordinate and return a texture value. Sometimes there are obvious ways to choose these texture coordinates; for parametric surfaces, such as the quadrics in Chapter 3, there is a natural 2D (u, v) parameterization of the surface, and for all surfaces the shading point p is a natural choice for a 3D coordinate.

Figure 10.7: A checkerboard texture, applied to a hyperboloid with different texture coordinate generation techniques. From left to right, (u, v) mapping, spherical mapping, cylindrical mapping, and planar mapping.

In other cases, there is no natural parameterization, or the natural parameterization may be undesirable. For instance, the (u, v) values near the poles of spheres are severely distorted. Also, for an arbitrary subdivision surface, there is no simple, general-purpose way to assign texture values so that the entire $[0, 1]^2$ space is covered continuously and without distortion. In fact, creating smooth parameterizations of complex meshes with low distortion is an active area of research in computer graphics.

This section starts by introducing two abstract base classes—TextureMapping2D and TextureMapping3D—that provide an interface for computing these 2D and 3D texture coordinates. We will then implement a number of standard mappings using this interface (Figure 10.7 shows a number of them). Texture implementations store a pointer to a 2D or 3D mapping function as appropriate and use it to compute the texture coordinates at each point. Thus, it's easy to add new mappings to the system without having to modify all of the Texture implementations, and different mappings can be used for different textures associated with the same surface. In pbrt, we will use the convention that 2D texture coordinates are denoted by (s, t); this helps make clear the distinction between the intrinsic (u, v) parameterization of the underlying surface and the (possibly different) coordinate values used for texturing.

The TextureMapping2D base class has a single method, TextureMapping2D::Map(), which is given the SurfaceInteraction at the shading point and returns the (s, t) texture coordinates via a Point2f. It also returns estimates for the change in (s, t) with respect to pixel x and y coordinates in the dstdx and dstdy parameters so that textures that use the mapping can determine the (s, t) sampling rate and filter accordingly.

⟨*Texture Declarations*⟩ ≡
```
class TextureMapping2D {
public:
    ⟨TextureMapping2D Interface 610⟩
};
```

⟨*TextureMapping2D Interface*⟩ ≡
```
virtual Point2f Map(const SurfaceInteraction &si,
                    Vector2f *dstdx, Vector2f *dstdy) const = 0;
```

10.2.1 2D (u, v) MAPPING

The simplest mapping uses the (u, v) coordinates in the SurfaceInteraction to compute
the texture coordinates. Their values can be offset and scaled with user-supplied values
in each dimension.

⟨*Texture Declarations*⟩ +≡
```
class UVMapping2D : public TextureMapping2D {
public:
    ⟨UVMapping2D Public Methods⟩
private:
    const Float su, sv, du, dv;
};
```

⟨*Texture Method Definitions*⟩ ≡
```
UVMapping2D::UVMapping2D(Float su, Float sv, Float du, Float dv)
    : su(su), sv(sv), du(du), dv(dv) { }
```

The scale-and-shift computation to compute (s, t) coordinates is straightforward:

⟨*Texture Method Definitions*⟩ +≡
```
Point2f UVMapping2D::Map(const SurfaceInteraction &si,
                        Vector2f *dstdx, Vector2f *dstdy) const {
    ⟨Compute texture differentials for 2D (u, v) mapping 611⟩
    return Point2f(su * si.uv[0] + du,
                   sv * si.uv[1] + dv);
}
```

Computing the differential change in s and t in terms of the original change in u and v
and the scale amounts is also easy. Using the chain rule,

$$\frac{\partial s}{\partial x} = \frac{\partial u}{\partial x}\frac{\partial s}{\partial u} + \frac{\partial v}{\partial x}\frac{\partial s}{\partial v}$$

and similarly for the three other partial derivatives. From the mapping method,

$$s = s_u u + d_u,$$

so

$$\frac{\partial s}{\partial u} = s_u, \qquad \frac{\partial s}{\partial v} = 0,$$

and thus

$$\frac{\partial s}{\partial x} = s_u \frac{\partial u}{\partial x},$$

and so forth.

⟨*Compute texture differentials for 2D (u, v) mapping*⟩ ≡   **610**
```
*dstdx = Vector2f(su * si.dudx, sv * si.dvdx);
*dstdy = Vector2f(su * si.dudy, sv * si.dvdy);
```

10.2.2 SPHERICAL MAPPING

Another useful mapping effectively wraps a sphere around the object. Each point is projected along the vector from the sphere's center through the point, up to the sphere's surface. There, the (u, v) mapping for the sphere shape is used. The `SphericalMapping2D` stores a transformation that is applied to points before this mapping is performed; this effectively allows the mapping sphere to be arbitrarily positioned and oriented with respect to the object.

⟨*Texture Declarations*⟩ +≡
```
class SphericalMapping2D : public TextureMapping2D {
public:
    ⟨SphericalMapping2D Public Methods⟩
private:
    Point2f sphere(const Point3f &p) const;
    const Transform WorldToTexture;
};
```

⟨*Texture Method Definitions*⟩ +≡
```
Point2f SphericalMapping2D::Map(const SurfaceInteraction &si,
        Vector2f *dstdx, Vector2f *dstdy) const {
    Point2f st = sphere(si.p);
    ⟨Compute texture coordinate differentials for sphere (u, v) mapping 612⟩
    ⟨Handle sphere mapping discontinuity for coordinate differentials 612⟩
    return st;
}
```

A short utility function computes the mapping for a single point. It will be useful to have this logic separated out for computing texture coordinate differentials.

⟨*Texture Method Definitions*⟩ +≡
```
Point2f SphericalMapping2D::sphere(const Point3f &p) const {
    Vector3f vec = Normalize(WorldToTexture(p) - Point3f(0,0,0));
    Float theta = SphericalTheta(vec), phi = SphericalPhi(vec);
    return Point2f(theta * InvPi, phi * Inv2Pi);
}
```

We could use the chain rule again to compute the texture coordinate differentials but will instead use a forward differencing approximation to demonstrate another way to compute these values that is useful for more complex mapping functions. Recall that the `SurfaceInteraction` stores the screen space partial derivatives $\partial \mathrm{p}/\partial x$ and $\partial \mathrm{p}/\partial y$ that give the change in position as a function of change in image sample position. Therefore, if the s coordinate is computed by some function $f_s(\mathrm{p})$, it's easy to compute approximations like

$$\frac{\partial s}{\partial x} \approx \frac{f_s(\mathrm{p} + \Delta \partial \mathrm{p}/\partial x) - f_s(\mathrm{p})}{\Delta}.$$

As the distance Δ approaches 0, this gives the actual partial derivative at p.

⟨*Compute texture coordinate differentials for sphere* (*u, v*) *mapping*⟩ ≡   611
```
const Float delta = .1f;
Point2f stDeltaX = sphere(si.p + delta * si.dpdx);
*dstdx = (stDeltaX - st) / delta;
Point2f stDeltaY = sphere(si.p + delta * si.dpdy);
*dstdy = (stDeltaY - st) / delta;
```

One other detail is that the sphere mapping has a discontinuity in the mapping formula; there is a seam at $t = 1$, where the t texture coordinate discontinuously jumps back to zero. We can detect this case by checking to see if the absolute value of the estimated derivative computed with forward differencing is greater than 0.5 and then adjusting it appropriately.

⟨*Handle sphere mapping discontinuity for coordinate differentials*⟩ ≡   611
```
if ((*dstdx)[1] > .5)        (*dstdx)[1] = 1 - (*dstdx)[1];
else if ((*dstdx)[1] < -.5f) (*dstdx)[1] = -((*dstdx)[1] + 1);
if ((*dstdy)[1] > .5)        (*dstdy)[1] = 1 - (*dstdy)[1];
else if ((*dstdy)[1] < -.5f) (*dstdy)[1] = -((*dstdy)[1] + 1);
```

10.2.3 CYLINDRICAL MAPPING

The cylindrical mapping effectively wraps a cylinder around the object. It also supports a transformation to orient the mapping cylinder.

⟨*Texture Declarations*⟩ +≡
```
class CylindricalMapping2D : public TextureMapping2D {
public:
    ⟨CylindricalMapping2D Public Methods⟩
private:
    ⟨CylindricalMapping2D Private Methods 613⟩
    const Transform WorldToTexture;
};
```

The cylindrical mapping has the same basic structure as the sphere mapping; just the mapping function is different. Therefore, we will omit the fragment that computes texture coordinate differentials, since it is essentially the same as the spherical version.

⟨*Texture Method Definitions*⟩ +≡
```
Point2f CylindricalMapping2D::Map(const SurfaceInteraction &si,
        Vector2f *dstdx, Vector2f *dstdy) const {
    Point2f st = cylinder(si.p);
    ⟨Compute texture coordinate differentials for cylinder (u, v) mapping⟩
    return st;
}
```

⟨*CylindricalMapping2D Private Methods*⟩ ≡   612
```
Point2f cylinder(const Point3f &p) const {
    Vector3f vec = Normalize(WorldToTexture(p) - Point3f(0,0,0));
    return Point2f((Pi + std::atan2(vec.y, vec.x)) * Inv2Pi,
                    vec.z);
}
```

10.2.4 PLANAR MAPPING

Another classic mapping method is planar mapping. The point is effectively projected onto a plane; a 2D parameterization of the plane then gives texture coordinates for the point. For example, a point p might be projected onto the $z = 0$ plane to yield texture coordinates given by $s = p_x$ and $t = p_y$.

In general, we can define such a parameterized plane with two nonparallel vectors $\mathbf{v}_s$ and $\mathbf{v}_t$ and offsets d_s and d_t. The texture coordinates are given by the coordinates of the point with respect to the plane's coordinate system, which are computed by taking the dot product of the vector from the point to the origin with each vector $\mathbf{v}_s$ and $\mathbf{v}_t$ and then adding the offset. For the example in the previous paragraph, we'd have $\mathbf{v}_s = (1, 0, 0)$, $\mathbf{v}_t = (0, 1, 0)$, and $d_s = d_t = 0$.

⟨*Texture Declarations*⟩ +≡
```
class PlanarMapping2D : public TextureMapping2D {
public:
    ⟨PlanarMapping2D Public Methods 613⟩
private:
    const Vector3f vs, vt;
    const Float ds, dt;
};
```

⟨*PlanarMapping2D Public Methods*⟩ ≡   613
```
PlanarMapping2D(const Vector3f &vs, const Vector3f &vt,
                Float ds = 0, Float dt = 0)
    : vs(vs), vt(vt), ds(ds), dt(dt) { }
```

The planar mapping differentials can be computed directly by finding the differentials of the point p in texture coordinate space.

⟨*Texture Method Definitions*⟩ +≡
```
Point2f PlanarMapping2D::Map(const SurfaceInteraction &si,
        Vector2f *dstdx, Vector2f *dstdy) const {
    Vector3f vec(si.p);
    *dstdx = Vector2f(Dot(si.dpdx, vs), Dot(si.dpdx, vt));
    *dstdy = Vector2f(Dot(si.dpdy, vs), Dot(si.dpdy, vt));
    return Point2f(ds + Dot(vec, vs), dt + Dot(vec, vt));
}
```

10.2.5 3D MAPPING

We will also define a TextureMapping3D class that defines the interface for generating 3D texture coordinates.

⟨*Texture Declarations*⟩ +≡
```
class TextureMapping3D {
public:
    ⟨TextureMapping3D Interface 614⟩
};
```

⟨*TextureMapping3D Interface*⟩ ≡   **614**
```
virtual Point3f Map(const SurfaceInteraction &si,
                    Vector3f *dpdx, Vector3f *dpdy) const = 0;
```

The natural 3D mapping just takes the world space coordinate of the point and applies a
linear transformation to it. This will often be a transformation that takes the point back
to the primitive's object space.

⟨*Texture Declarations*⟩ +≡
```
class TransformMapping3D : public TextureMapping3D {
public:
    ⟨TransformMapping3D Public Methods⟩
private:
    const Transform WorldToTexture;
};
```

Because a linear mapping is used, the differential change in texture coordinates can be
found by applying the same mapping to the partial derivatives of position.

⟨*Texture Method Definitions*⟩ +≡
```
Point3f TransformMapping3D::Map(const SurfaceInteraction &si,
        Vector3f *dpdx, Vector3f *dpdy) const {
    *dpdx = WorldToTexture(si.dpdx);
    *dpdy = WorldToTexture(si.dpdy);
    return WorldToTexture(si.p);
}
```

10.3 TEXTURE INTERFACE AND BASIC TEXTURES

Texture is a template class parameterized by the return type of its evaluation function.
This design makes it possible to reuse almost all of the code among textures that return
different types. pbrt currently uses only Float and Spectrum textures.

⟨*Texture Declarations*⟩ +≡
```
template <typename T> class Texture {
public:
    ⟨Texture Interface 615⟩
};
```

The key to Texture's interface is its evaluation function; it returns a value of the template type T. The only information it has access to in order to evaluate its value is the
SurfaceInteraction at the point being shaded. Different textures in this chapter will use
different parts of this structure to drive their evaluation.

⟨*Texture Interface*⟩ ≡   614
    virtual T Evaluate(const SurfaceInteraction &) const = 0;

10.3.1 CONSTANT TEXTURE

ConstantTexture returns the same value no matter where it is evaluated. Because it represents a constant function, it can be accurately reconstructed with any sampling rate and therefore needs no antialiasing. Although this texture is trivial, it is actually quite useful. By providing this class, all parameters to all Materials can be represented as Textures, whether they are spatially varying or not. For example, a red diffuse object will have a ConstantTexture that always returns red as the diffuse color of the material. This way, the shading system always evaluates a texture to get the surface properties at a point, avoiding the need for separate textured and nontextured versions of materials. This material's implementation is in the files textures/constant.h and textures/constant.cpp.

⟨*ConstantTexture Declarations*⟩ ≡
```
template <typename T> class ConstantTexture : public Texture<T> {
public:
    ⟨ConstantTexture Public Methods 615⟩
private:
    T value;
};
```

⟨*ConstantTexture Public Methods*⟩ ≡   615
```
ConstantTexture(const T &value) : value(value) { }
T Evaluate(const SurfaceInteraction &) const {
    return value;
}
```

10.3.2 SCALE TEXTURE

We have defined the texture interface in a way that makes it easy to use the output of one texture function when computing another. This is useful since it lets us define generic texture operations using any of the other texture types. The ScaleTexture takes two textures and returns the product of their values when evaluated. It is defined in textures/scale.h and textures/scale.cpp.

⟨*ScaleTexture Declarations*⟩ ≡
```
template <typename T1, typename T2>
class ScaleTexture : public Texture<T2> {
public:
    ⟨ScaleTexture Public Methods 616⟩
private:
    ⟨ScaleTexture Private Data 616⟩
};
```

The attentive reader may notice that the shared_ptr parameters to the constructor are stored in member variables and wonder if there is a performance issue from this approach along the lines of the one described in Section 9.3 with regard to the Bump() method. In this case we're fine: Textures are only created at scene creation time, rather than at rendering time for each ray. Therefore, there are no issues with contention at the memory location that stores the reference count for each shared_ptr.

⟨*ScaleTexture Public Methods*⟩ ≡ 　　　　　　　　　　　　　　　　　　　　**615**
```
ScaleTexture(const std::shared_ptr<Texture<T1>> &tex1,
             const std::shared_ptr<Texture<T2>> &tex2)
    : tex1(tex1), tex2(tex2) { }
```

Note that the return types of the two textures can be different; the implementation here just requires that it be possible to multiply their values together. Thus, a Float texture can be used to scale a Spectrum texture.

⟨*ScaleTexture Private Data*⟩ ≡ 　　　　　　　　　　　　　　　　　　　　**615**
```
std::shared_ptr<Texture<T1>> tex1;
std::shared_ptr<Texture<T2>> tex2;
```

ScaleTexture ignores antialiasing, leaving it to its two subtextures to antialias themselves but not making an effort to antialias their product. While it is easy to show that the product of two band-limited functions is also band limited, the maximum frequency present in the product may be greater than that of either of the two terms individually. Thus, even if the scale and value textures are perfectly antialiased, the result might not be. Fortunately, the most common use of this texture is to scale another texture by a constant, in which case the other texture's antialiasing is sufficient.

⟨*ScaleTexture Public Methods*⟩ +≡ 　　　　　　　　　　　　　　　　　　**615**
```
T2 Evaluate(const SurfaceInteraction &si) const {
    return tex1->Evaluate(si) * tex2->Evaluate(si);
}
```

10.3.3 MIX TEXTURES

The MixTexture class is a more general variation of ScaleTexture. It takes three textures as input: two may be of any single type, and the third must return a floating-point value. The floating-point texture is then used to linearly interpolate between the two other textures. Note that a ConstantTexture could be used for the floating-point value to achieve a uniform blend, or a more complex Texture could be used to blend in a spatially nonuniform way. This texture is defined in textures/mix.h and textures/mix.cpp.

⟨*MixTexture Declarations*⟩ ≡
```
template <typename T> class MixTexture : public Texture<T> {
public:
    ⟨MixTexture Public Methods 616⟩
private:
    std::shared_ptr<Texture<T>> tex1, tex2;
    std::shared_ptr<Texture<Float>> amount;
};
```

⟨*MixTexture Public Methods*⟩ ≡ 　　　　　　　　　　　　　　　　　　　**616**
```
MixTexture(const std::shared_ptr<Texture<T>> &tex1,
           const std::shared_ptr<Texture<T>> &tex2,
           const std::shared_ptr<Texture<Float>> &amount)
    : tex1(tex1), tex2(tex2), amount(amount) { }
```

To evaluate the mixture, the three textures are evaluated and the floating-point value is used to linearly interpolate between the two. When the blend amount amt is zero, the first texture's value is returned, and when it is one the second one's value is returned. We will generally assume that amt will be between zero and one, but this behavior is not enforced, so extrapolation is possible as well. As with the ScaleTexture, antialiasing is ignored, so the introduction of aliasing here is a possibility.

⟨*MixTexture Public Methods*⟩ +≡   **616**
```
T Evaluate(const SurfaceInteraction &si) const {
    T t1 = tex1->Evaluate(si), t2 = tex2->Evaluate(si);
    Float amt = amount->Evaluate(si);
    return (1 - amt) * t1 + amt * t2;
}
```

10.3.4 BILINEAR INTERPOLATION

⟨*BilerpTexture Declarations*⟩ ≡
```
template <typename T> class BilerpTexture : public Texture<T> {
public:
    ⟨BilerpTexture Public Methods 617⟩
private:
    ⟨BilerpTexture Private Data 617⟩
};
```

The BilerpTexture class provides bilinear interpolation among four constant values. Values are defined at $(0, 0)$, $(1, 0)$, $(0, 1)$, and $(1, 1)$ in (s, t) parameter space. The value at a particular (s, t) position is found by interpolating between them. It is defined in the files textures/bilerp.h and textures/bilerp.cpp.

⟨*BilerpTexture Public Methods*⟩ ≡   **617**
```
BilerpTexture(std::unique_ptr<TextureMapping2D> mapping, const T &v00,
              const T &v01, const T &v10, const T &v11)
    : mapping(std::move(mapping)), v00(v00), v01(v01), v10(v10),
      v11(v11) { }
```

⟨*BilerpTexture Private Data*⟩ ≡   **617**
```
std::unique_ptr<TextureMapping2D> mapping;
const T v00, v01, v10, v11;
```

The interpolated value of the four values at an (s, t) position can be computed by three linear interpolations. For example, we can first use s to interpolate between the values at $(0, 0)$ and $(1, 0)$ and store that in a temporary tmp1. We can then do the same for the $(0, 1)$ and $(1, 1)$ values and store the result in tmp2. Finally, we use t to interpolate between tmp1 and tmp2 and obtain the final result. Mathematically, this is

$$\text{tmp}_1 = (1 - s)\text{v}_{00} + s\,\text{v}_{10}$$
$$\text{tmp}_2 = (1 - s)\text{v}_{01} + s\,\text{v}_{11}$$
$$\text{result} = (1 - t)\text{tmp}_1 + t\,\text{tmp}_2.$$

Rather than storing the intermediate values explicitly, we can perform some algebraic rearrangement to give us the same result from an appropriately weighted average of the four corner values:

$$\text{result} = (1 - s)(1 - t)v_{00} + (1 - s)t\,v_{01} + s(1 - t)v_{10} + s\,t\,v_{11}.$$

⟨*BilerpTexture Public Methods*⟩ +≡   **617**
```
T Evaluate(const SurfaceInteraction &si) const {
    Vector2f dstdx, dstdy;
    Point2f st = mapping->Map(si, &dstdx, &dstdy);
    return (1-st[0]) * (1-st[1]) * v00 + (1-st[0]) * (st[1]) * v01 +
           (  st[0]) * (1-st[1]) * v10 + (  st[0]) * (st[1]) * v11;
}
```

10.4 IMAGE TEXTURE

The ImageTexture class stores a 2D array of point-sampled values of a texture function. It uses these samples to reconstruct a continuous image function that can be evaluated at an arbitrary (s, t) position. These sample values are often called *texels*, since they are similar to pixels in an image but are used in the context of a texture. Image textures are the most widely used type of texture in computer graphics; digital photographs, scanned artwork, images created with image-editing programs, and images generated by renderers are all extremely useful sources of data for this particular texture representation (Figure 10.8). The term *texture map* is often used to refer to this type of texture, although this usage blurs the distinction between the mapping that computes texture

Figure 10.8: An Example of Image Textures. Image textures are used throughout the San Miguel scene to represent spatially varying surface appearance properties. (left) Scene rendered with image textures. (right) Each image texture has been replaced with its average value. Note how much visual richness is lost.

coordinates and the texture function itself. The implementation of this texture is in the files textures/imagemap.h and textures/imagemap.cpp.

The ImageTexture class is different from other textures in the system in that it is parameterized on both the data type of the texels it stores in memory as well as the data type of the value that it returns. Making this distinction allows us to create, for example, ImageTextures that store RGBSpectrum values in memory, but always return Spectrum values. In this way, when the system is compiled with full-spectral rendering enabled, the memory cost to store full SampledSpectrum texels doesn't need to be paid for source images that only have RGB components.

⟨*ImageTexture Declarations*⟩ ≡
```
template <typename Tmemory, typename Treturn>
    class ImageTexture : public Texture<Treturn> {
public:
    ⟨ImageTexture Public Methods 622⟩
private:
    ⟨ImageTexture Private Methods 622⟩
    ⟨ImageTexture Private Data 619⟩
};
```

The caller provides the ImageTexture with the filename of an image map, parameters that control the filtering of the map for antialiasing, and parameters that make it possible to scale and gamma-correct the texture values. The scale parameter will be explained later in this section, and the texture filtering parameters will be explained in Section 10.4.3. The contents of the file are used to create an instance of the MIPMap class that stores the texels in memory and handles the details of reconstruction and filtering to reduce aliasing.

For an ImageTexture that stores RGBSpectrum values in memory, its MIPMap stores the image data using three floating-point values for each sample. This is a somewhat wasteful representation, since a single image map may have millions of texels and may not need the full 32 bits of accuracy from the Floats used to store RGB values for each of them. Exercise 10.1 at the end of this chapter discusses this issue further.

⟨*ImageTexture Method Definitions*⟩ ≡
```
template <typename Tmemory, typename Treturn>
ImageTexture<Tmemory, Treturn>::ImageTexture(
        std::unique_ptr<TextureMapping2D> mapping,
        const std::string &filename, bool doTrilinear, Float maxAniso,
        ImageWrap wrapMode, Float scale, bool gamma)
    : mapping(std::move(mapping)) {
    mipmap = GetTexture(filename, doTrilinear, maxAniso,
                        wrapMode, scale, gamma);
}
```

⟨*ImageTexture Private Data*⟩ ≡   619
```
std::unique_ptr<TextureMapping2D> mapping;
MIPMap<Tmemory> *mipmap;
```

10.4.1 TEXTURE MEMORY MANAGEMENT

Each image map may require a meaningful amount of memory, and a complex scene may have thousands of image maps. Because each image texture may be reused many times within a scene, pbrt maintains a table of image maps that have been loaded so far, so that they are only loaded into memory once even if they are used in more than one ImageTexture. The ImageTexture constructor calls the static ImageTexture:: GetTexture() method to get a MIPMap representation of the desired texture.

⟨*ImageTexture Method Definitions*⟩ +≡
```
template <typename Tmemory, typename Treturn> MIPMap<Tmemory> *
ImageTexture<Tmemory, Treturn>::GetTexture(const std::string &filename,
        bool doTrilinear, Float maxAniso, ImageWrap wrap, Float scale,
        bool gamma) {
    ⟨Return MIPMap from texture cache if present 620⟩
    ⟨Create MIPMap for filename 620⟩
    return mipmap;
}
```

TexInfo is a simple structure that holds the image map's filename and filtering parameters; all of these must match for a MIPMap to be reused in another ImageTexture. Its definition is straightforward (its members exactly correspond to the parameters of the GetTexture() method) and won't be included here.

⟨*ImageTexture Private Data*⟩ +≡   619
```
static std::map<TexInfo, std::unique_ptr<MIPMap<Tmemory>>> textures;
```

⟨*Return* MIPMap *from texture cache if present*⟩ ≡   620
```
TexInfo texInfo(filename, doTrilinear, maxAniso, wrap, scale, gamma);
if (textures.find(texInfo) != textures.end())
    return textures[texInfo].get();
```

If the texture hasn't been loaded yet, a call to ReadImage() yields the image contents.

⟨*Create* MIPMap *for* filename⟩ ≡   620
```
Point2i resolution;
std::unique_ptr<RGBSpectrum[]> texels = ReadImage(filename, &resolution);
MIPMap<Tmemory> *mipmap = nullptr;
if (texels) {
    ⟨Convert texels to type Tmemory and create MIPMap 621⟩
} else {
    ⟨Create one-valued MIPMap 622⟩
}
textures[texInfo].reset(mipmap);
```

Because ReadImage() returns an array of RGBSpectrum values for the texels, it is necessary to convert these values to the particular type Tmemory of texel that this MIPMap is storing (e.g., Float) if the type of Tmemory isn't RGBSpectrum. The per-texel conversion is handled by the utility routine ImageTexture::convertIn().

⟨*Convert texels to type* Tmemory *and create* MIPMap⟩ ≡   620

```
std::unique_ptr<Tmemory[]> convertedTexels(new Tmemory[resolution.x *
                                               resolution.y]);
for (int i = 0; i < resolution.x * resolution.y; ++i)
    convertIn(texels[i], &convertedTexels[i], scale, gamma);
mipmap = new MIPMap<Tmemory>(resolution, convertedTexels.get(),
                                doTrilinear, maxAniso, wrap);
```

Per-texel conversion is done using C++ function overloading. For every type to which we would like to be able to convert these values, a separate ImageTexture::convertIn() function must be provided. In the loop over texels earlier, C++'s function overloading mechanism will select the appropriate instance of ImageTexture::convertIn() based on the destination type. Unfortunately, it is not possible to return the converted value from the function, since C++ doesn't support overloading by return type.

In addition to converting types, these functions optionally scale and gamma correct the texel values to map them to a desired range. Gamma correction is particularly important to handle carefully: computer displays generally don't exhibit a linear relationship between the pixel values to be displayed and the radiance that they emit. Thus, an artist may create a texture map where, as seen on an LCD display, one part of the image appears twice as bright as another. However, the corresponding pixel values won't in fact have a 2:1 relationship. (Conversely, pixels whose values have a 2:1 relationship don't lead to a 2:1 brightness ratio.) This discrepancy is a problem for a renderer using such an image as a texture map, since the renderer usually expects a linear relationship between texel values and the quantity that they represent.

pbrt follows the sRGB standard, which prescribes a specific transfer curve matching the typical behavior of CRT displays. This standard is widely supported on 2015-era devices; other (non-CRT) devices such as LCDs or inkjet printers typically accept sRGB gamma-corrected values as input and then re-map them internally to match the device-specific behavior.

The sRGB gamma curve is a piecewise function with a linear term for low values and a power law for medium to large values.

$$\gamma(x) = \begin{cases} 12.92x, & x \le 0.0031308 \\ (1.055)x^{1/2.4} - 0.055, & x > 0.0031308 \end{cases}$$

⟨*Global Inline Functions*⟩ +≡

```
inline Float GammaCorrect(Float value) {
    if (value <= 0.0031308f)
        return 12.92f * value;
    return 1.055f * std::pow(value, (Float)(1.f / 2.4f)) - 0.055f;
}
```

The GammaCorrect() will be used to write sRGB-compatible 8-bit image files in the WriteImage() function. To import textures into pbrt, we are interested in the opposite direction: removing an existing gamma correction to reestablish a linear relationship between brightness and pixel values.

⟨*Global Inline Functions*⟩ +≡
```
inline Float InverseGammaCorrect(Float value) {
    if (value <= 0.04045f)
        return value * 1.f / 12.92f;
    return std::pow((value + 0.055f) * 1.f / 1.055f, (Float)2.4f);
}
```

Refer to the "Further Reading" section for a more detailed discussion of gamma correction.

InverseGammaCorrect() is only applied when indicated via the gamma argument of convertIn(). By default, this is the case when the input image has an 8-bit color depth.

⟨*ImageTexture Private Methods*⟩ ≡   619
```
static void convertIn(const RGBSpectrum &from, RGBSpectrum *to,
                      Float scale, bool gamma) {
    for (int i = 0; i < RGBSpectrum::nSamples; ++i)
        (*to)[i] = scale * (gamma ? InverseGammaCorrect(from[i])
                                  : from[i]);
}
static void convertIn(const RGBSpectrum &from, Float *to,
                      Float scale, bool gamma) {
    *to = scale * (gamma ? InverseGammaCorrect(from.y())
                         : from.y());
}
```

If the texture file wasn't found or was unreadable, an image map with a single sample with a value of one is created so that the renderer can continue to generate an image of the scene without needing to abort execution. The ReadImage() function will issue a warning message in this case.

⟨*Create one-valued* MIPMap⟩ ≡   620
```
Tmemory oneVal = scale;
mipmap = new MIPMap<Tmemory>(Point2i(1, 1), &oneVal);
```

After the image is rendered and the system is cleaning up, the ClearCache() method is called to free the memory for the entries in the texture cache.

⟨*ImageTexture Public Methods*⟩ ≡   619
```
static void ClearCache() {
    textures.erase(textures.begin(), textures.end());
}
```

10.4.2 ImageTexture EVALUATION

The ImageTexture::Evaluate() routine does the usual texture coordinate computation and then hands the image map lookup to the MIPMap, which does the image filtering work for antialiasing. The returned value is still of type Tmemory; another conversion step similar to ImageTexture::convertIn() above converts to the returned type Treturn.

⟨*ImageTexture Public Methods*⟩ +≡ 619
```
Treturn Evaluate(const SurfaceInteraction &si) const {
    Vector2f dstdx, dstdy;
    Point2f st = mapping->Map(si, &dstdx, &dstdy);
    Tmemory mem = mipmap->Lookup(st, dstdx, dstdy);
    Treturn ret;
    convertOut(mem, &ret);
    return ret;
}
```

⟨*ImageTexture Private Methods*⟩ +≡ 619
```
static void convertOut(const RGBSpectrum &from, Spectrum *to) {
    Float rgb[3];
    from.ToRGB(rgb);
    *to = Spectrum::FromRGB(rgb);
}
static void convertOut(Float from, Float *to) {
    *to = from;
}
```

10.4.3 MIP MAPS

As always, if the image function has higher frequency detail than can be represented by the texture sampling rate, aliasing will be present in the final image. Any frequencies higher than the Nyquist limit must be removed by prefiltering before the function is evaluated. Figure 10.9 shows the basic problem we face: an image texture has texels that are samples of some image function at a fixed frequency. The filter region for the lookup is given by its (s, t) center point and offsets to the estimated texture coordinate locations for the adjacent image samples. Because these offsets are estimates of the texture sampling

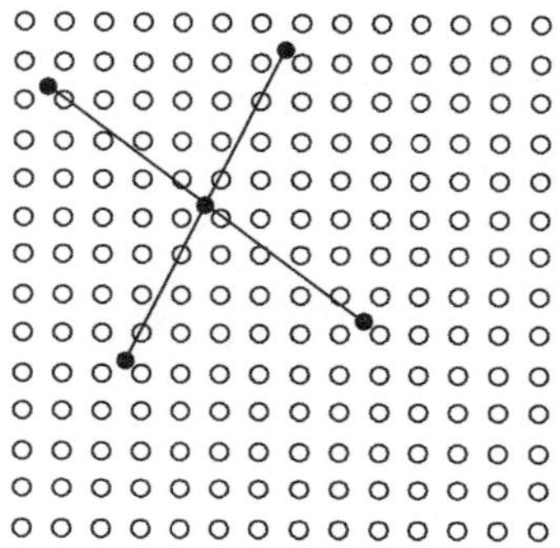

Figure 10.9: Given a point at which to perform an image map lookup (denoted by the solid point in the center) and estimates of the texture space sampling rate (denoted by adjacent solid points), it may be necessary to filter the contributions of a large number of texels in the image map (denoted by open points).

Float 1062
ImageTexture::mapping 619
ImageTexture::mipmap 619
MIPMap::Lookup() 635
Point2f 68
RGBSpectrum 332
Spectrum 315
Spectrum::FromRGB() 330
Spectrum::ToRGB() 328
SurfaceInteraction 116
TextureMapping2D::Map() 610
Vector2f 60

rate, we must remove any frequencies higher than twice the distance to the adjacent samples in order to satisfy the Nyquist criterion.

The texture sampling and reconstruction process has a few key differences from the image sampling process discussed in Chapter 7. These differences make it possible to address the antialiasing problem with more effective and less computationally expensive techniques. For example, here it is inexpensive to get the value of a sample—only an array lookup is necessary (as opposed to having to trace a number of rays to compute radiance). Further, because the texture image function is fully defined by the set of samples and there is no mystery about what its highest frequency could be, there is no uncertainty related to the function's behavior between samples. These differences make it possible to remove detail from the texture before sampling, thus eliminating aliasing.

However, the texture sampling rate will typically change from pixel to pixel. The sampling rate is determined by scene geometry and its orientation, the texture coordinate mapping function, and the camera projection and image sampling rate. Because the texture sampling rate is not fixed, texture filtering algorithms need to be able to filter over arbitrary regions of texture samples efficiently.

The `MIPMap` class implements two methods for efficient texture filtering with spatially varying filter widths. The first, trilinear interpolation, is fast and easy to implement and was widely used for texture filtering in early graphics hardware. The second, elliptically weighted averaging, is slower and more complex but returns extremely high-quality results. Figure 10.1 shows the aliasing errors that result from ignoring texture filtering and just bilinearly interpolating texels from the most detailed level of the image map. Figure 10.10 shows the improvement from using the triangle filter and the EWA algorithm instead.

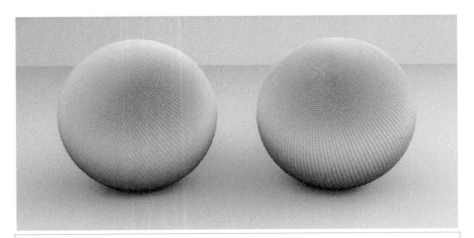

Figure 10.10: Filtering the image map properly substantially improves the image. On the left, trilinear interpolation was used; on the right, the EWA algorithm. Both of these approaches give a much better image than the unfiltered image map in Figure 10.1. Trilinear interpolation is inferior at handling strongly anisotropic filter footprints than EWA, which is why the edges of the sphere on the left are a uniform gray color (the overall average value of the texture), while details from the image map are visible farther along the edges of the sphere on the right before they fade to gray.

To limit the potential number of texels that need to be accessed, both of these filtering methods use an *image pyramid* of increasingly lower resolution prefiltered versions of the original image to accelerate their operation.[3] The original image texels are at the bottom level of the pyramid, and the image at each level is half the resolution of the previous level, up to the top level, which has a single texel representing the average of all of the texels in the original image. This collection of images needs at most 1/3 more memory than storing the most detailed level alone and can be used to quickly find filtered values over large regions of the original image. The basic idea behind the pyramid is that if a large area of texels needs to be filtered a reasonable approximation is to use a higher level of the pyramid and do the filtering over the same area there, accessing many fewer texels.

⟨*MIPMap Declarations*⟩ ≡
```
    template <typename T> class MIPMap {
    public:
        ⟨MIPMap Public Methods 630⟩
    private:
        ⟨MIPMap Private Methods 628⟩
        ⟨MIPMap Private Data 625⟩
    };
```

In the constructor, the MIPMap copies the image data provided by the caller, resizes the image if necessary to ensure that its resolution is a power of two in each direction, and initializes a lookup table used by the elliptically weighted average filtering method in Section 10.4.5. It also records the desired behavior for texture coordinates that fall outside of the legal range in the wrapMode argument.

⟨*MIPMap Method Definitions*⟩ ≡
```
    template <typename T>
    MIPMap<T>::MIPMap(const Point2i &res, const T *img, bool doTrilinear,
                      Float maxAnisotropy, ImageWrap wrapMode)
        : doTrilinear(doTrilinear), maxAnisotropy(maxAnisotropy),
          wrapMode(wrapMode), resolution(res) {
        std::unique_ptr<T[]> resampledImage = nullptr;
        if (!IsPowerOf2(resolution[0]) || !IsPowerOf2(resolution[1])) {
            ⟨Resample image to power-of-two resolution 627⟩
        }
        ⟨Initialize levels of MIPMap from image 630⟩
        ⟨Initialize EWA filter weights if needed 639⟩
    }
```

⟨*MIPMap Private Data*⟩ ≡   625
```
    const bool doTrilinear;
    const Float maxAnisotropy;
    const ImageWrap wrapMode;
    Point2i resolution;
```

Float 1062
ImageWrap 626
IsPowerOf2() 1064
MIPMap 625
Point2i 68

---

3   The name "MIP map" comes from the Latin *multum in parvo*, which means "much in little," a nod to the image pyramid.

MIPMap is a template class that is parameterized by the data type of the image texels. pbrt creates MIPMaps of both RGBSpectrum and Float images; Float MIP maps are used for representing directional distributions of intensity from goniometric light sources (Section 12.3.3), for example. The MIPMap implementation requires that the type T support just a few basic operations, including addition and multiplication by a scalar.

The ImageWrap enumerant, passed to the MIPMap constructor, specifies the desired behavior when the supplied texture coordinates are not in the legal [0, 1] range.

⟨*MIPMap Helper Declarations*⟩ ≡
```
enum class ImageWrap { Repeat, Black, Clamp };
```

Implementation of an image pyramid is somewhat easier if the resolution of the original image is an exact power of two in each direction; this ensures that there is a straightforward relationship between the level of the pyramid and the number of texels at that level. If the user has provided an image where the resolution in one or both of the dimensions is not a power of two, then the MIPMap constructor starts by resizing the image up to the next power-of-two resolution greater than the original resolution before constructing the pyramid. Exercise 10.5 at the end of the chapter describes an approach to building image pyramids with non-power-of-two resolutions.

Image resizing here involves more application of the sampling and reconstruction theory from Chapter 7: we have an image function that has been sampled at one sampling rate, and we'd like to reconstruct a continuous image function from the original samples to resample at a new set of sample positions. Because this represents an increase in the sampling rate from the original rate, we don't have to worry about introducing aliasing due to undersampling high-frequency components in this step; we only need to reconstruct and directly resample the new function. Figure 10.11 illustrates this task in 1D.

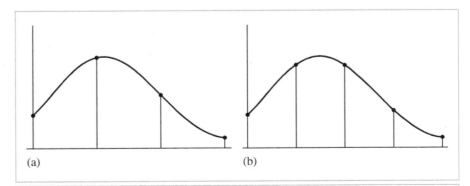

(a)   (b)

Figure 10.11: To increase an image's resolution to be a power of two, the MIPMap performs two 1D resampling steps with a separable reconstruction filter. (a) A 1D function reconstructed from four samples, denoted by dots. (b) To represent the same image function with more samples, we just need to reconstruct the continuous function and evaluate it at the new positions.

The MIPMap uses a separable reconstruction filter for this task; recall from Section 7.8 that separable filters can be written as the product of 1D filters: $f(x, y) = f(x) f(y)$. One advantage of using a separable filter is that if we are using one to resample an image from one resolution (s, t) to another (s', t'), then we can implement the resampling as two 1D resampling steps, first resampling in s to create an image of resolution (s', t) and then resampling that image to create the final image of resolution (s', t'). Resampling the image via two 1D steps in this manner simplifies implementation and makes the number of texels accessed for each texel in the final image a linear function of the filter width, rather than a quadratic one.

⟨*Resample image to power-of-two resolution*⟩ ≡   625
```
Point2i resPow2(RoundUpPow2(resolution[0]), RoundUpPow2(resolution[1]));
⟨Resample image in s direction 627⟩
⟨Resample image in t direction⟩
resolution = resPow2;
```

Reconstructing the original image function and sampling it at a new texel's position are mathematically equivalent to centering the reconstruction filter kernel at the new texel's position and weighting the nearby texels in the original image appropriately. Thus, each new texel is a weighted average of a small number of texels in the original image.

The MIPMap::resampleWeights() method determines which original texels contribute to each new texel and what the values are of the contribution weights for each new texel. It returns the values in an array of ResampleWeight structures for all of the texels in a 1D row or column of the image. Because this information is the same for all rows of the image when resampling in s and all columns when resampling in t, it's more efficient to compute it once for each of the two passes and then reuse it many times for each one. Given these weights, the image is first magnified in the s direction, turning the original image with resolution resolution into an image with resolution (resPow2[0], resolution[1]), which is stored in resampledImage. The implementation here allocates enough space in resampledImage to hold the final zoomed image with resolution (resPow2[0], resPow2[1]), so two large allocations can be avoided.

⟨*Resample image in s direction*⟩ ≡   627
```
std::unique_ptr<ResampleWeight[]> sWeights =
    resampleWeights(resolution[0], resPow2[0]);
resampledImage.reset(new T[resPow2[0] * resPow2[1]]);
⟨Apply sWeights to zoom in s direction 629⟩
```

For the reconstruction filter used here, no more than four of the original texels will contribute to each new texel after zooming, so ResampleWeight only needs to hold four weights. Because the four texels are contiguous, we only store the offset to the first one.

⟨*MIPMap Helper Declarations*⟩ +≡
```
struct ResampleWeight {
    int firstTexel;
    Float weight[4];
};
```

⟨*MIPMap Private Methods*⟩ ≡   625

```
std::unique_ptr<ResampleWeight[]> resampleWeights(int oldRes,
        int newRes) {
    Assert(newRes >= oldRes);
    std::unique_ptr<ResampleWeight[]> wt(new ResampleWeight[newRes]);
    Float filterwidth = 2.f;
    for (int i = 0; i < newRes; ++i) {
        ⟨Compute image resampling weights for ith texel 628⟩
    }
    return wt;
}
```

Just as it was important to distinguish between discrete and continuous pixel coordinates in Chapter 7, the same issues need to be addressed with texel coordinates here. We will use the same conventions as described in Section 7.1.7. For each new texel, this function starts by computing its continuous coordinates in terms of the old texel coordinates. This value is stored in center, because it is the center of the reconstruction filter for the new texel. Next, it is necessary to find the offset to the first texel that contributes to the new texel. This is a slightly tricky calculation—after subtracting the filter width to find the start of the filter's nonzero range, it is necessary to add an extra 0.5 offset to the continuous coordinate before taking the floor to find the discrete coordinate. Figure 10.12 illustrates why this offset is needed.

Starting from this first contributing texel, this function loops over four texels, computing each one's offset to the center of the filter kernel and the corresponding filter weight.

⟨*Compute image resampling weights for ith texel*⟩ ≡   628

```
Float center = (i + .5f) * oldRes / newRes;
wt[i].firstTexel = std::floor((center - filterwidth) + 0.5f);
for (int j = 0; j < 4; ++j) {
    Float pos = wt[i].firstTexel + j + .5f;
    wt[i].weight[j] = Lanczos((pos - center) / filterwidth);
}
```

⟨*Normalize filter weights for texel resampling* 629⟩

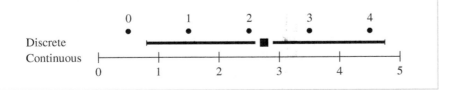

Figure 10.12: The computation to find the first texel inside a reconstruction filter's support is slightly tricky. Consider a filter centered around continuous coordinate 2.75 with width 2, as shown here. The filter's support covers the range [0.75, 4.75], although texel zero is outside the filter's support: adding 0.5 to the lower end before taking the floor to find the discrete texel gives the correct starting texel, number one.

The reconstruction filter function used to compute the weights, Lanczos(), is the same as the one in LanczosSincFilter::Sinc().

⟨*Texture Declarations*⟩ +≡
```
Float Lanczos(Float, Float tau = 2);
```

Depending on the filter function used, the four filter weights may not sum to one. Therefore, to ensure that the resampled image won't be any brighter or darker than the original image, the weights are normalized here.

⟨*Normalize filter weights for texel resampling*⟩ ≡   628
```
Float invSumWts = 1 / (wt[i].weight[0] + wt[i].weight[1] +
                        wt[i].weight[2] + wt[i].weight[3]);
for (int j = 0; j < 4; ++j)
    wt[i].weight[j] *= invSumWts;
```

Once the weights have been computed, it's easy to apply them to compute the zoomed texels. For each of the resolution[1] horizontal scan lines in the original image, a pass is made across the resPow2[0] texels in the s-zoomed image using the precomputed weights to compute their values. Because the computation for each texel is completely independent of the computation for every other texel, and because this computation requires a bit of processing, it's worthwhile to split the image into sections and work on them in parallel with multiple threads.

⟨*Apply* sWeights *to zoom in s direction*⟩ ≡   627
```
ParallelFor(
    [&](int t) {
        for (int s = 0; s < resPow2[0]; ++s) {
            ⟨Compute texel (s, t) in s-zoomed image 629⟩
        }
    }, resolution[1], 16);
```

The ImageWrap parameter to the MIPMap constructor determines the convention to be used for out-of-bounds texel coordinates. It either remaps them to valid values with a modulus or clamp calculation or uses a black texel value.

⟨*Compute texel (s, t) in s-zoomed image*⟩ ≡   629
```
resampledImage[t * resPow2[0] + s] = 0.f;
for (int j = 0; j < 4; ++j) {
    int origS = sWeights[s].firstTexel + j;
    if (wrapMode == ImageWrap::Repeat)
        origS = Mod(origS, resolution[0]);
    else if (wrapMode == ImageWrap::Clamp)
        origS = Clamp(origS, 0, resolution[0] - 1);
    if (origS >= 0 && origS < (int)resolution[0])
        resampledImage[t * resPow2[0] + s] +=
            sWeights[s].weight[j] * img[t * resolution[0] + origS];
}
```

The process for resampling in the t direction is almost the same as for s, so we won't include the implementation here.

Once we have an image with resolutions that are powers of two, the levels of the MIP map can be initialized, starting from the bottom (finest) level. Each higher level is found by filtering the texels from the previous level.

Because image maps use a fair amount of memory, and because 8 to 20 texels are typically used per image texture lookup to compute a filtered value, it's worth carefully considering how the texels are laid out in memory, since reducing cache misses while accessing the texture map can noticeably improve the renderer's performance. Because both of the texture filtering methods implemented in this section access a set of texels in a rectangular region of the image map each time a lookup is performed, the MIPMap uses the BlockedArray template class to store the 2D arrays of texel values, rather than a standard C++ array. The BlockedArray reorders the array values in memory in a way that improves cache coherence when the values are accessed with these kinds of rectangular patterns; it is described in Section A.4.4 in Appendix A.

⟨*Initialize levels of MIPMap from image*⟩ ≡   **625**
```
int nLevels = 1 + Log2Int(std::max(resolution[0], resolution[1]));
pyramid.resize(nLevels);
```
⟨*Initialize most detailed level of MIPMap* **630**⟩
```
for (int i = 1; i < nLevels; ++i) {
```
    ⟨*Initialize i th MIPMap level from i − 1st level* **631**⟩
```
}
```

⟨*MIPMap Private Data*⟩ +≡   **625**
```
std::vector<std::unique_ptr<BlockedArray<T>>> pyramid;
```

⟨*MIPMap Public Methods*⟩ ≡   **625**
```
int Width() const { return resolution[0]; }
int Height() const { return resolution[1]; }
int Levels() const { return pyramid.size(); }
```

The base level of the MIP map, which holds the original data (or the resampled data, if it didn't originally have power-of-two resolutions), is initialized by the default Blocked Array constructor.

⟨*Initialize most detailed level of MIPMap*⟩ ≡   **630**
```
pyramid[0].reset(new BlockedArray<T>(resolution[0], resolution[1],
    resampledImage ? resampledImage.get() : img));
```

Before showing how the rest of the levels are initialized, we will first define a texel access function that will be used during that process. MIPMap::Texel() returns a reference to the texel value for the given discrete integer-valued texel position. As described earlier, if an out-of-range texel coordinate is passed in, then based on the value of wrapMode, this method effectively repeats the texture over the entire 2D texture coordinate domain by taking the modulus of the coordinate with respect to the texture size, clamps the coordinates to the valid range so that the border pixels are used, or returns a black texel for out-of-bounds coordinates.

⟨*MIPMap Method Definitions*⟩ +≡
```
template <typename T>
const T &MIPMap<T>::Texel(int level, int s, int t) const {
    const BlockedArray<T> &l = *pyramid[level];
    ⟨Compute texel (s, t) accounting for boundary conditions 631⟩
    return l(s, t);
}
```

⟨*Compute texel* (*s*, *t*) *accounting for boundary conditions*⟩ ≡   631
```
switch (wrapMode) {
    case ImageWrap::Repeat:
        s = Mod(s, l.uSize());
        t = Mod(t, l.vSize());
        break;
    case ImageWrap::Clamp:
        s = Clamp(s, 0, l.uSize() - 1);
        t = Clamp(t, 0, l.vSize() - 1);
        break;
    case ImageWrap::Black: {
        static const T black = 0.f;
        if (s < 0 || s >= (int)l.uSize() ||
            t < 0 || t >= (int)l.vSize())
            return black;
        break;
    }
}
```

For non-square images, the resolution in one direction must be clamped to one for the upper levels of the image pyramid, where there is still downsampling to do in the larger of the two resolutions. This is handled by the following std::max() calls:

⟨*Initialize ith MIPMap level from i* − *1st level*⟩ ≡   630
```
int sRes = std::max(1, pyramid[i - 1]->uSize() / 2);
int tRes = std::max(1, pyramid[i - 1]->vSize() / 2);
pyramid[i].reset(new BlockedArray<T>(sRes, tRes));
⟨Filter four texels from finer level of pyramid 632⟩
```

The MIPMap uses a simple box filter to average four texels from the previous level to find the value at the current texel. Using the Lanczos filter here would give a slightly better result for this computation, although this modification is left for Exercise 10.4 at the end of the chapter. As with resampling to power-of-two resolutions, doing this downfiltering using multiple threads rather than with a regular for loop is worthwhile here.

⟨*Filter four texels from finer level of pyramid*⟩ ≡   631
```
ParallelFor(
    [&](int t) {
        for (int s = 0; s < sRes; ++s)
            (*pyramid[i])(s, t) = .25f *
                (Texel(i-1, 2*s, 2*t)   + Texel(i-1, 2*s+1, 2*t) +
                 Texel(i-1, 2*s, 2*t+1) + Texel(i-1, 2*s+1, 2*t+1));
    }, tRes, 16);
```

10.4.4 ISOTROPIC TRIANGLE FILTER

The first of the two `MIPMap::Lookup()` methods uses a triangle filter over the texture samples to remove high frequencies. Although this filter function does not give high-quality results, it can be implemented very efficiently. In addition to the (s, t) coordinates of the evaluation point, the caller passes this method a filter width for the lookup, giving the extent of the region of the texture to filter across. This method filters over a square region in texture space, so the width should be conservatively chosen to avoid aliasing in both the s and t directions. Filtering techniques like this one that do not support a filter extent that is non-square or non-axis-aligned are known as *isotropic*. The primary disadvantage of isotropic filtering algorithms is that textures viewed at an oblique angle will appear blurry, since the required sampling rate along one axis will be very different from the sampling rate along the other in this case.

Because filtering over many texels for wide filter widths would be inefficient, this method chooses a MIP map level from the pyramid such that the filter region at that level would cover four texels at that level. Figure 10.13 illustrates this idea.

⟨*MIPMap Method Definitions*⟩ +≡
```
template <typename T>
T MIPMap<T>::Lookup(const Point2f &st, Float width) const {
    ⟨Compute MIPMap level for trilinear filtering 633⟩
    ⟨Perform trilinear interpolation at appropriate MIPMap level 633⟩
}
```

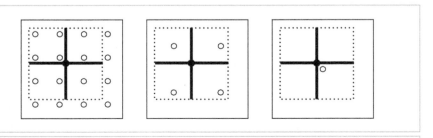

Figure 10.13: Choosing a MIP Map Level for the Triangle Filter. The `MIPMap` chooses a level such that the filter covers four texels.

Since the resolutions of the levels of the pyramid are all powers of two, the resolution of level l is $2^{\text{nLevels}-1-l}$. Therefore, to find the level with a texel spacing width w requires solving

$$\frac{1}{w} = 2^{\text{nLevels}-1-l}$$

for l. In general, this will be a floating-point value between two MIP map levels.

⟨*Compute MIPMap level for trilinear filtering*⟩ ≡   632
```
Float level = Levels() - 1 + Log2(std::max(width, (Float)1e-8));
```

As shown by Figure 10.13, applying a triangle filter to the four texels around the sample point will either filter over too small a region or too large a region (except for very carefully selected filter widths). The implementation here applies the triangle filter at both of these levels and blends between them according to how close `level` is to each of them. This helps hide the transitions from one MIP map level to the next at nearby pixels in the final image. While applying a triangle filter to four texels at two levels in this manner doesn't give exactly the same result as applying it to the original highest resolution texels, the difference isn't too bad in practice, and the efficiency of this approach is worth this penalty. In any case, the elliptically weighted average filtering in the next section should be used when texture quality is important.

⟨*Perform trilinear interpolation at appropriate MIPMap level*⟩ ≡   632
```
if (level < 0)
    return triangle(0, st);
else if (level >= Levels() - 1)
    return Texel(Levels() - 1, 0, 0);
else {
    int iLevel = std::floor(level);
    Float delta = level - iLevel;
    return Lerp(delta, triangle(iLevel, st), triangle(iLevel + 1, st));
}
```

Given floating-point texture coordinates in $[0, 1]^2$, the `MIPMap::triangle()` routine uses a triangle filter to interpolate between the four texels that surround the sample point, as shown in Figure 10.14. This method first scales the coordinates by the texture resolution at the given MIP map level in each direction, turning them into continuous texel coordinates. Because these are continuous coordinates, but the texels in the image map are defined at discrete texture coordinates, it's important to carefully convert into a common representation. Here, we will do all of our work in discrete coordinates, mapping the continuous texture coordinates to discrete space.

For example, consider the 1D case with a continuous texture coordinate of 2.4: this coordinate is a distance of 0.1 below the discrete texel coordinate 2 (which corresponds to a continuous coordinate of 2.5) and is 0.9 above the discrete coordinate 1 (continuous coordinate 1.5). Thus, if we subtract 0.5 from the continuous coordinate 2.4, giving 1.9, we can correctly compute the correct distances to the discrete coordinates 1 and 2 by subtracting coordinates.

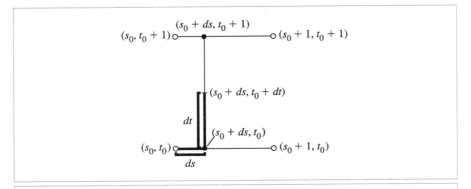

Figure 10.14: To compute the value of the image texture function at an arbitrary (s, t) position, `MIPMap::triangle()` finds the four texels around (s, t) and weights them according to a triangle filter based on their distance to (s, t). One way to implement this is as a series of linear interpolations, as shown here: First, the two texels below (s, t) are linearly interpolated to find a value at $(s, 0)$, and the two texels above it are interpolated to find $(s, 1)$. Then, $(s, 0)$ and $(s, 1)$ are linearly interpolated again to find the value at (s, t).

After computing the distances in s and t to the texel at the lower left of the given coordinates, ds and dt, `MIPMap::triangle()` determines weights for the four texels and computes the filtered value. Recall that the triangle filter is

$$f(x, y) = (1 - |x|)(1 - |y|);$$

the appropriate weights follow directly. Notice the similarity between this computation and `BilerpTexture::Evaluate()`.

⟨*MIPMap Method Definitions*⟩ $+\equiv$

```
template <typename T>
T MIPMap<T>::triangle(int level, const Point2f &st) const {
    level = Clamp(level, 0, Levels() - 1);
    Float s = st[0] * pyramid[level]->uSize() - 0.5f;
    Float t = st[1] * pyramid[level]->vSize() - 0.5f;
    int s0 = std::floor(s), t0 = std::floor(t);
    Float ds = s - s0, dt = t - t0;
    return (1 - ds) * (1 - dt) * Texel(level, s0,   t0)   +
           (1 - ds) * dt       * Texel(level, s0,   t0+1) +
           ds       * (1 - dt) * Texel(level, s0+1, t0)   +
           ds       * dt       * Texel(level, s0+1, t0+1);
}
```

*10.4.5 ELLIPTICALLY WEIGHTED AVERAGE

The elliptically weighted average (EWA) algorithm fits an ellipse to the two axes in texture space given by the texture coordinate differentials and then filters the texture with a Gaussian filter function (Figure 10.15). It is widely regarded as one of the best texture filtering algorithms in graphics and has been carefully derived from the basic principles of sampling theory. Unlike the triangle filter in the previous section, it can filter over

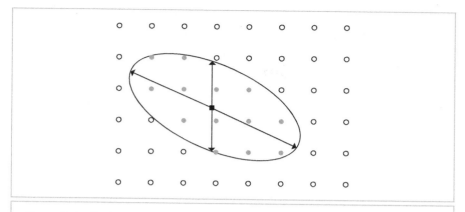

Figure 10.15: The EWA filter applies a Gaussian filter to the texels in an elliptical area around the evaluation point. The extent of the ellipse is such that its edge passes through the positions of the adjacent texture samples as estimated by the texture coordinate partial derivatives.

arbitrarily oriented regions of the texture, with some flexibility of having different filter extents in different directions. This type of filter is known as *anisotropic*. This capability greatly improves the quality of its results, since it can properly adapt to different sampling rates along the two image axes.

We won't show the full derivation of this filter here, although we do note that it is distinguished by being a *unified resampling filter*: it simultaneously computes the result of a Gaussian filtered texture function convolved with a Gaussian reconstruction filter in image space. This is in contrast to many other texture filtering methods that ignore the effect of the image space filter or equivalently assume that it is a box. Even if a Gaussian isn't being used for filtering the samples for the image being rendered, taking some account of the spatial variation of the image filter improves the results, assuming that the filter being used is somewhat similar in shape to the Gaussian, as the Mitchell and windowed sinc filters are.

⟨*MIPMap Method Definitions*⟩ +≡
```
    template <typename T>
    T MIPMap<T>::Lookup(const Point2f &st, Vector2f dst0,
                        Vector2f dst1) const {
        if (doTrilinear) {
            Float width = std::max(std::max(std::abs(dst0[0]),
                                            std::abs(dst0[1])),
                                   std::max(std::abs(dst1[0]),
                                            std::abs(dst1[1])));
            return Lookup(st, 2 * width);
        }
        ⟨Compute ellipse minor and major axes 636⟩
        ⟨Clamp ellipse eccentricity if too large 636⟩
        ⟨Choose level of detail for EWA lookup and perform EWA filtering 636⟩
    }
```

The screen space partial derivatives of the texture coordinates define the axes of the ellipse. The lookup method starts out by determining which of the two axes is the major axis (the longer of the two) and which is the minor, swapping them if needed so that dst0 is the major axis. The length of the minor axis will be used shortly to select a MIP map level.

⟨*Compute ellipse minor and major axes*⟩ ≡   635
```
if (dst0.LengthSquared() < dst1.LengthSquared())
    std::swap(dst0, dst1);
Float majorLength = dst0.Length();
Float minorLength = dst1.Length();
```

Next the *eccentricity* of the ellipse is computed—the ratio of the length of the major axis to the length of the minor axis. A large eccentricity indicates a very long and skinny ellipse. Because this method filters texels from a MIP map level chosen based on the length of the minor axis, highly eccentric ellipses mean that a large number of texels need to be filtered. To avoid this expense (and to ensure that any EWA lookup takes a bounded amount of time), the length of the minor axis may be increased to limit the eccentricity. The result may be an increase in blurring, although this effect usually isn't noticeable in practice.

⟨*Clamp ellipse eccentricity if too large*⟩ ≡   635
```
if (minorLength * maxAnisotropy < majorLength && minorLength > 0) {
    Float scale = majorLength / (minorLength * maxAnisotropy);
    dst1 *= scale;
    minorLength *= scale;
}
if (minorLength == 0)
    return triangle(0, st);
```

Like the triangle filter, the EWA filter uses the image pyramid to reduce the number of texels to be filtered for a particular texture lookup, choosing a MIP map level based on the length of the minor axis. Given the limited eccentricity of the ellipse due to the clamping above, the total number of texels used is thus bounded. Given the length of the minor axis, the computation to find the appropriate pyramid level is the same as was used for the triangle filter. Similarly, the implementation here blends between the filtered results at the two levels around the computed level of detail, again to reduce artifacts from transitions from one level to another.

⟨*Choose level of detail for EWA lookup and perform EWA filtering*⟩ ≡   635
```
Float lod = std::max((Float)0, Levels() - (Float)1 + Log2(minorLength));
int ilod = std::floor(lod);
return Lerp(lod - ilod, EWA(ilod, st, dst0, dst1),
                        EWA(ilod + 1, st, dst0, dst1));
```

The MIPMap::EWA() method actually applies the filter at a particular level.

⟨*MIPMap Method Definitions*⟩ +≡
```
template <typename T>
T MIPMap<T>::EWA(int level, Point2f st, Vector2f dst0,
                Vector2f dst1) const {
    if (level >= Levels()) return Texel(Levels() - 1, 0, 0);
    ⟨Convert EWA coordinates to appropriate scale for level 637⟩
    ⟨Compute ellipse coefficients to bound EWA filter region 637⟩
    ⟨Compute the ellipse's (s, t) bounding box in texture space 638⟩
    ⟨Scan over ellipse bound and compute quadratic equation 639⟩
}
```

This method first converts from texture coordinates in [0, 1] to coordinates and differentials in terms of the resolution of the chosen MIP map level. It also subtracts 0.5 from the continuous position coordinate to align the sample point with the discrete texel coordinates, as was done in MIPMap::triangle().

⟨*Convert EWA coordinates to appropriate scale for level*⟩ ≡ 637
```
st[0] = st[0] * pyramid[level]->uSize() - 0.5f;
st[1] = st[1] * pyramid[level]->vSize() - 0.5f;
dst0[0] *= pyramid[level]->uSize();
dst0[1] *= pyramid[level]->vSize();
dst1[0] *= pyramid[level]->uSize();
dst1[1] *= pyramid[level]->vSize();
```

It next computes the coefficients of the implicit equation for the ellipse with axes (ds0,dt0) and (ds1,dt1) and centered at the origin. Placing the ellipse at the origin rather than at (s, t) simplifies the implicit equation and the computation of its coefficients and can be easily corrected for when the equation is evaluated later. The general form of the implicit equation for all points (s, t) inside such an ellipse is

$$e(s, t) = As^2 + Bst + Ct^2 < F,$$

although it is more computationally efficient to divide through by F and express this as

$$e(s, t) = \frac{A}{F}s^2 + \frac{B}{F}st + \frac{C}{F}t^2 = A's^2 + B'st + C't^2 < 1.$$

We will not derive the equations that give the values of the coefficients, although the interested reader can easily verify their correctness.[4]

⟨*Compute ellipse coefficients to bound EWA filter region*⟩ ≡ 637
```
Float A = dst0[1] * dst0[1] + dst1[1] * dst1[1] + 1;
Float B = -2 * (dst0[0] * dst0[1] + dst1[0] * dst1[1]);
Float C = dst0[0] * dst0[0] + dst1[0] * dst1[0] + 1;
Float invF = 1 / (A * C - B * B * 0.25f);
A *= invF;
B *= invF;
C *= invF;
```

---

4   Heckbert's thesis has the original derivation (Heckbert 1989, p. 80). *A* and *C* have an extra term of 1 added to them so the ellipse is a minimum of one texel separation wide. This ensures that the ellipse will not fall between the texels when magnifying at the most detailed level.

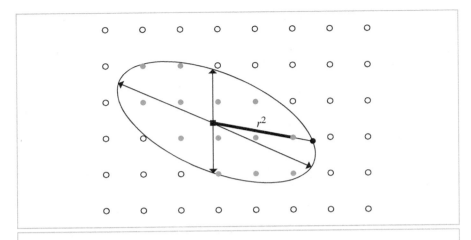

Figure 10.16: Finding the r^2 Ellipse Value for the EWA Filter Table Lookup.

The next step is to find the axis-aligned bounding box in discrete integer texel coordinates of the texels that are potentially inside the ellipse. The EWA algorithm loops over all of these candidate texels, filtering the contributions of those that are in fact inside the ellipse. The bounding box is found by determining the minimum and maximum values that the ellipse takes in the s and t directions. These extrema can be calculated by finding the partial derivatives $\partial e/\partial s$ and $\partial e/\partial t$, finding their solutions for $s = 0$ and $t = 0$, and adding the offset to the ellipse center. For brevity, we will not include the derivation for these expressions here.

⟨*Compute the ellipse's (s, t) bounding box in texture space*⟩ ≡   637
```
Float det = -B * B + 4 * A * C;
Float invDet = 1 / det;
Float uSqrt = std::sqrt(det * C), vSqrt = std::sqrt(A * det);
int s0 = std::ceil (st[0] - 2 * invDet * uSqrt);
int s1 = std::floor(st[0] + 2 * invDet * uSqrt);
int t0 = std::ceil (st[1] - 2 * invDet * vSqrt);
int t1 = std::floor(st[1] + 2 * invDet * vSqrt);
```

Now that the bounding box is known, the EWA algorithm loops over the texels, transforming each one to the coordinate system where the texture lookup point (s, t) is at the origin with a translation. It then evaluates the ellipse equation to see if the texel is inside the ellipse (Figure 10.16) and computes the filter weight for the texel if so. The final filtered value returned is a weighted sum over texels (s', t') inside the ellipse, where f is the Gaussian filter function:

Float 1062

$$\frac{\sum f(s' - s, t' - t)t(s', t')}{\sum f(s' - s, t' - t)}.$$

⟨Scan over ellipse bound and compute quadratic equation⟩ ≡   **637**
```
T sum(0.f);
Float sumWts = 0;
for (int it = t0; it <= t1; ++it) {
    Float tt = it - st[1];
    for (int is = s0; is <= s1; ++is) {
        Float ss = is - st[0];
        ⟨Compute squared radius and filter texel if inside ellipse 639⟩
    }
}
return sum / sumWts;
```

A nice feature of the implicit equation $e(s, t)$ is that its value at a particular texel is the squared ratio of the distance from the center of the ellipse to the texel to the distance from the center of the ellipse to the ellipse boundary along the line through that texel (Figure 10.16). This value can be used to index into a precomputed lookup table of Gaussian filter function values.

⟨Compute squared radius and filter texel if inside ellipse⟩ ≡   **639**
```
Float r2 = A * ss * ss + B * ss * tt + C * tt * tt;
if (r2 < 1) {
    int index = std::min((int)(r2 * WeightLUTSize),
                                WeightLUTSize - 1);
    Float weight = weightLut[index];
    sum += Texel(level, is, it) * weight;
    sumWts += weight;
}
```

The lookup table is initialized the first time a `MIPMap` is constructed. Because it will be indexed with squared distances from the filter center r^2, each entry stores a value $e^{-\alpha r}$, rather than $e^{-\alpha r^2}$.

⟨MIPMap Private Data⟩ +≡   **625**
```
static constexpr int WeightLUTSize = 128;
static Float weightLut[WeightLUTSize];
```

So that the filter function goes to zero at the end of its extent rather than having an abrupt step, `std::exp(-alpha)` is subtracted from the filter values here.

⟨Initialize EWA filter weights if needed⟩ ≡   **625**
```
if (weightLut[0] == 0.) {
    for (int i = 0; i < WeightLUTSize; ++i) {
        Float alpha = 2;
        Float r2 = Float(i) / Float(WeightLUTSize - 1);
        weightLut[i] = std::exp(-alpha * r2) - std::exp(-alpha);
    }
}
```

10.5 SOLID AND PROCEDURAL TEXTURING

Once one starts to think of the (s, t) texture coordinates used by 2D texture functions as quantities that can be computed by arbitrary functions and not just from the parametric coordinates of the surface, it is natural to generalize texture functions to be defined over 3D domains (often called *solid textures*) rather than just 2D (s, t). One reason solid textures are particularly convenient is that all objects have a natural 3D texture mapping—object space position. This is a substantial advantage for texturing objects that don't have a natural 2D parameterization (e.g., triangle meshes and implicit surfaces) and for objects that have a distorted parameterization (e.g., near the poles of a sphere). In preparation for this idea, Section 10.2.5 defined a general TextureMapping3D interface to compute 3D texture coordinates as well as a TransformMapping3D implementation.

Solid textures introduce a new problem, however: texture representation. A 3D image map takes up a fair amount of storage space and is much harder to acquire than a 2D texture map, which can be extracted from photographs or painted by an artist. Therefore, procedural texturing—the idea that programs could be executed to generate texture values at arbitrary positions on surfaces in the scene—came into use at the same time that solid texturing was developed. A simple example of procedural texturing is a procedural sine wave. If we wanted to use a sine wave for bump mapping (for example, to simulate waves in water), it would be inefficient and potentially inaccurate to precompute values of the function at a grid of points and then store them in an image map. Instead, it makes much more sense to evaluate the sin() function at points on the surface as needed.

If we can find a 3D function that describes the colors of the grain in a solid block of wood, for instance, then we can generate images of complex objects that appear to be carved from wood. Over the years, procedural texturing has grown in application considerably as techniques have been developed to describe more and more complex surfaces procedurally.

Procedural texturing has a number of interesting implications. First, it can be used to reduce memory requirements for rendering, by reducing the need for the storage of large, high-resolution texture maps. In addition, procedural shading gives the promise of potentially infinite detail; as the viewer approaches an object, the texturing function is evaluated at the points being shaded, which naturally leads to the right amount of detail being visible. In contrast, image texture maps become blurry when the viewer is too close to them. On the other hand, subtle details of the appearance of procedural textures can be much more difficult to control than when image maps are used.

Another challenge with procedural textures is antialiasing. Procedural textures are often expensive to evaluate, and sets of point samples that fully characterize their behavior aren't available as they are for image maps. Because we would like to remove high-frequency information in the texture function before we take samples from it, we need to be aware of the frequency content of the various steps we take along the way so we can avoid introducing high frequencies. Although this sounds daunting, there are a handful of techniques that work well to handle this issue.

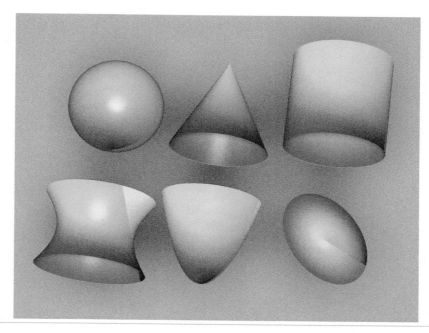

Figure 10.17: The UV Texture Applied to All of pbrt's Quadric Shapes. The u parameter is mapped to the red channel, and the v parameter is mapped to green.

10.5.1 UV TEXTURE

Our first procedural texture converts the surface's (u, v) coordinates into the red and green components of a Spectrum (Figure 10.17). It is especially useful when debugging the parameterization of a new Shape, for example. It is defined in textures/uv.h and textures/uv.cpp.

⟨*UVTexture Declarations*⟩ ≡
```
class UVTexture : public Texture<Spectrum> {
public:
    ⟨UVTexture Public Methods 641⟩
private:
    std::unique_ptr<TextureMapping2D> mapping;
};
```

⟨*UVTexture Public Methods*⟩ ≡   641
```
Spectrum Evaluate(const SurfaceInteraction &si) const {
    Vector2f dstdx, dstdy;
    Point2f st = mapping->Map(si, &dstdx, &dstdy);
    Float rgb[3] =
        { st[0] - std::floor(st[0]), st[1] - std::floor(st[1]), 0 };
    return Spectrum::FromRGB(rgb);
}
```

Figure 10.18: The Checkerboard Texture Applied to All of pbrt's Quadric Shapes.

10.5.2 CHECKERBOARD

The checkerboard is the canonical procedural texture (Figure 10.18). The (s, t) texture coordinates are used to break up parameter space into square regions that are shaded with alternating patterns. Rather than just supporting checkerboards that switch between two fixed colors, the implementation here allows the user to pass in two textures to color the alternating regions. The traditional black-and-white checkerboard is obtained by passing two ConstantTextures. Its implementation is in the files textures/checkerboard.h and textures/checkerboard.cpp.

⟨*CheckerboardTexture Declarations*⟩ ≡
```
template <typename T> class Checkerboard2DTexture : public Texture<T> {
public:
    ⟨Checkerboard2DTexture Public Methods 643⟩
private:
    ⟨Checkerboard2DTexture Private Data 643⟩
};
```

For simplicity, the frequency of the check function is 1 in (s, t) space: checks are one unit wide in each direction. The effective frequency can always be changed by the TextureMapping2D class with an appropriate scale of the (s, t) coordinates.

⟨*Checkerboard2DTexture Public Methods*⟩ ≡   **642**
```
Checkerboard2DTexture(std::unique_ptr<TextureMapping2D> mapping,
        const std::shared_ptr<Texture<T>> &tex1,
        const std::shared_ptr<Texture<T>> &tex2, AAMethod aaMethod)
    : mapping(std::move(mapping)), tex1(tex1), tex2(tex2),
      aaMethod(aaMethod) { }
```

⟨*Checkerboard2DTexture Private Data*⟩ ≡   **642**
```
std::unique_ptr<TextureMapping2D> mapping;
const std::shared_ptr<Texture<T>> tex1, tex2;
const AAMethod aaMethod;
```

The checkerboard is good for demonstrating trade-offs between various antialiasing approaches for procedural textures. The implementation here supports both simple point sampling (no antialiasing) and a closed-form box filter evaluated over the filter region. The image sequence in Figure 10.23 at the end of this section shows the results of these approaches. The aaMethod enumerant selects which approach is used.

⟨*AAMethod Declaration*⟩ ≡
```
enum class AAMethod { None, ClosedForm };
```

The evaluation routine does the usual texture coordinate and differential computation and then uses the appropriate fragment to compute an antialiased checkerboard value (or not antialiased, if point sampling has been selected).

⟨*Checkerboard2DTexture Public Methods*⟩ +≡   **642**
```
T Evaluate(const SurfaceInteraction &si) const {
    Vector2f dstdx, dstdy;
    Point2f st = mapping->Map(si, &dstdx, &dstdy);
    if (aaMethod == AAMethod::None) {
        ⟨Point sample Checkerboard2DTexture 643⟩
    } else {
        ⟨Compute closed-form box-filtered Checkerboard2DTexture value 644⟩
    }
}
```

The simplest case is to ignore antialiasing and just point-sample the checkerboard texture at the point. For this case, after getting the (s, t) texture coordinates from the TextureMapping2D, the integer checkerboard coordinates for that (s, t) position are computed, added together, and checked for odd or even parity to determine which of the two textures to evaluate.

⟨*Point sample Checkerboard2DTexture*⟩ ≡   **643, 645**
```
if (((int)std::floor(st[0]) + (int)std::floor(st[1])) % 2 == 0)
    return tex1->Evaluate(si);
return tex2->Evaluate(si);
```

Given how bad aliasing can be in a point-sampled checkerboard texture, we will invest some effort to antialias it properly. The easiest case happens when the entire filter region lies inside a single check (Figure 10.19). In this case, we simply need to determine which of the check types we are inside and evaluate that one. As long as the Texture inside

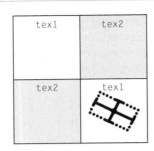

Figure 10.19: The Easy Case for Filtering the Checkerboard. If the filter region around the lookup point is entirely in one check, the checkerboard texture doesn't need to worry about antialiasing and can just evaluate the texture for that check.

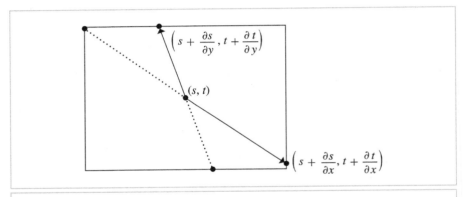

Figure 10.20: It is often convenient to use the axis-aligned bounding box around the texture evaluation point and the offsets from its partial derivatives as the region to filter over. Here, it's easy to see that the lengths of sides of the box are $2\max(|\partial s/\partial x|, |\partial s/\partial y|)$ and $2\max(|\partial t/\partial x|, |\partial t/\partial y|)$.

that check does appropriate antialiasing itself, the result for this case will be properly antialiased.

⟨*Compute closed-form box-filtered* Checkerboard2DTexture *value*⟩ ≡   **643**
    ⟨*Evaluate single check if filter is entirely inside one of them* **645**⟩
    ⟨*Apply box filter to checkerboard region* **646**⟩

It's straightforward to check if the entire filter region is inside a single check by computing its bounding box and seeing if its extent lies inside the same check. For the remainder of this section, we will use the axis-aligned bounding box of the filter region given by the partial derivatives $\partial s/\partial x$, $\partial s/\partial y$, and so on, as the area to filter over, rather than trying to filter over the ellipse defined by the partial derivatives as the EWA filter did (Figure 10.20). This simplifies the implementation here, although somewhat increases the blurriness of

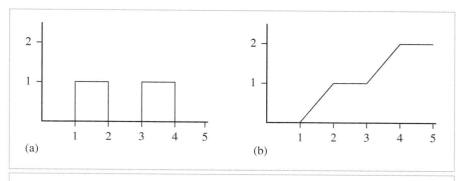

Figure 10.21: Integrating the Checkerboard Step Function. (a) The 1D step function that defines the checkerboard texture function, $c(x)$. (b) A graph of the value of the integral $\int_0^x c(x)\mathrm{d}x$.

the filtered values. The variables ds and dt in the following hold half the filter width in each direction, so the total area filtered over ranges from (s-ds, t-dt) to (s+ds, t+dt).

⟨*Evaluate single check if filter is entirely inside one of them*⟩ ≡   **644**
```
Float ds = std::max(std::abs(dstdx[0]), std::abs(dstdy[0]));
Float dt = std::max(std::abs(dstdx[1]), std::abs(dstdy[1]));
Float s0 = st[0] - ds, s1 = st[0] + ds;
Float t0 = st[1] - dt, t1 = st[1] + dt;
if (std::floor(s0) == std::floor(s1) &&
    std::floor(t0) == std::floor(t1)) {
    ⟨Point sample Checkerboard2DTexture 643⟩
}
```

Otherwise, the lookup method approximates the filtered value by first computing a floating-point value that indicates what fraction of the filter region covers each of the two check types. This is equivalent to computing the average of the 2D step function that takes on the value 0 when we are in tex1 and 1 when we are in tex2, over the filter region. Figure 10.21(a) shows a graph of the checkerboard function $c(x)$, defined as

$$c(x) = \begin{cases} 0 & \lfloor x \rfloor \text{ is even} \\ 1 & \text{otherwise.} \end{cases}$$

Given the average value, we can blend between the two subtextures, according to what fraction of the filter region each one is visible for.

The integral of the 1D checkerboard function $c(x)$ can be used to compute the average value of the function over some extent. Inspection of the graph reveals that

$$\int_0^x c(x)\,\mathrm{d}x = \lfloor x/2 \rfloor + 2\max(x/2 - \lfloor x/2 \rfloor - .5, 0).$$

To compute the average value of the step function in two dimensions, we separately compute the integral of the checkerboard in each 1D direction in order to compute its average value over the filter region.

Float 1062

⟨*Apply box filter to checkerboard region*⟩ ≡　　　　　　　　　　　　**644**
```
    auto bumpInt = [](Float x) {
        return (int)std::floor(x / 2) +
               2 * std::max(x / 2 - (int)std::floor(x / 2) - (Float)0.5,
                            (Float)0); };
    Float sint = (bumpInt(s1) - bumpInt(s0)) / (2 * ds);
    Float tint = (bumpInt(t1) - bumpInt(t0)) / (2 * dt);
    Float area2 = sint + tint - 2 * sint * tint;
    if (ds > 1 || dt > 1)
        area2 = .5f;
    return (1 - area2) * tex1->Evaluate(si) +
           area2        * tex2->Evaluate(si);
```

10.5.3 SOLID CHECKERBOARD

The Checkerboard2DTexture class from the previous section wraps a checkerboard pattern *around* the object in parameter space. We can also define a solid checkerboard pattern based on 3D texture coordinates so that the object appears carved out of 3D checker cubes (Figure 10.22). Like the 2D variant, this implementation chooses between texture functions based on the lookup position. Note that these two textures need not be solid textures themselves; the Checkerboard3DTexture merely chooses between them based on the 3D position of the point.

Figure 10.22: Dragon Model, Textured with the Checkerboard3DTexture **Procedural Texture.** Notice how the model appears to be carved out of 3D checks, rather than having them pasted on its surface.

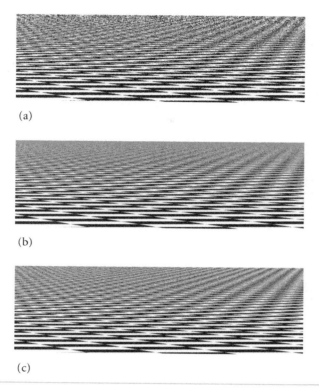

(a)

(b)

(c)

Figure 10.23: Comparisons of three approaches for antialiasing procedural textures, applied to the checkerboard texture. (a) No effort has been made to remove high-frequency variation from the texture function, so there are severe artifacts in the image, rendered with one sample per pixel. (b) This image shows the approach based on computing the filter region in texture space and averaging the texture function over that area, also rendered with one sample per pixel. (c) Here the checkerboard function was effectively supersampled by taking 16 samples per pixel and then point-sampling the texture. Both the area-averaging and the supersampling approaches give substantially better results than the first approach. In this example, supersampling gives the best results, since the averaging approach has blurred out the checkerboard pattern sooner than was needed because it approximates the filter region with its axis-aligned box.

⟨*CheckerboardTexture Declarations*⟩ +≡

```
template <typename T> class Checkerboard3DTexture : public Texture<T> {
public:
    ⟨Checkerboard3DTexture Public Methods 647⟩
private:
    ⟨Checkerboard3DTexture Private Data 648⟩
};
```

⟨*Checkerboard3DTexture Public Methods*⟩ ≡   **647**

```
Checkerboard3DTexture(std::unique_ptr<TextureMapping3D> mapping,
        const std::shared_ptr<Texture<T>> &tex1,
        const std::shared_ptr<Texture<T>> &tex2)
    : mapping(std::move(mapping)), tex1(tex1), tex2(tex2) { }
```

⟨*Checkerboard3DTexture Private Data*⟩ ≡   **647**
```
std::unique_ptr<TextureMapping3D> mapping;
std::shared_ptr<Texture<T>> tex1, tex2;
```

Ignoring antialiasing, the basic computation to see if a point p is inside a 3D checker region is

$$(\lfloor p_x \rfloor + \lfloor p_y \rfloor + \lfloor p_z \rfloor) \bmod 2 = 0.$$

The Checkerboard3DTexture doesn't have any built-in support for antialiasing, so its implementation is fairly short.

⟨*Checkerboard3DTexture Public Methods*⟩ +≡   **647**
```
T Evaluate(const SurfaceInteraction &si) const {
    Vector3f dpdx, dpdy;
    Point3f p = mapping->Map(si, &dpdx, &dpdy);
    if (((int)std::floor(p.x) + (int)std::floor(p.y) +
         (int)std::floor(p.z)) % 2 == 0)
        return tex1->Evaluate(si);
    else
        return tex2->Evaluate(si);
}
```

10.6 NOISE

In order to write solid textures that describe complex surface appearances, it is helpful to be able to introduce some controlled variation to the process. Consider a wood floor made of individual planks; each plank's color is likely to be slightly different from the others. Or consider a windswept lake; we might want to have waves of similar amplitude across the entire lake, but we don't want them to be homogeneous over all parts of the lake (as they might be if they were constructed from a sum of sine waves, for example). Modeling this sort of variation in a texture helps make the final result look more realistic.

One difficulty in developing textures like these is that the renderer evaluates the surface's texture functions at an irregularly distributed set of points, where each evaluation is completely independent of the others. As such, procedural textures must *implicitly* define a complex pattern by answering queries about what the pattern's value is at all of these points. In contrast, the *explicit* pattern description approach is embodied by the PostScript® language, for example, which describes graphics on a page with a series of drawing commands. One difficulty that the implicit approach introduces is that the texture can't just call RNG::UniformFloat() at each point at which it is evaluated to introduce randomness: because each point would have a completely different random value from its neighbors, no coherence would be possible in the generated pattern.

An elegant way to address this issue of introducing controlled randomness to procedural textures in graphics is the application of what is known as a *noise function*. In general, noise functions used in graphics are smoothly varying functions taking $\mathbb{R}^n \to [-1, 1]$, for at least $n = 1, 2, 3$, without obvious repetition. One of the most crucial properties of a practical noise function is that it be band limited with a known maximum frequency.

This makes it possible to control the frequency content added to a texture due to the noise function so that frequencies higher than those allowed by the Nyquist limit aren't introduced.

Many of the noise functions that have been developed are built on the idea of an integer lattice over $\mathbb{R}^3$. First, a value is associated with each integer (x, y, z) position in space. Then, given an arbitrary position in space, the eight surrounding lattice values are found. These lattice values are then interpolated to compute the noise value at the particular point. This idea can be generalized or restricted to more or fewer dimensions d, where the number of lattice points is 2^d. A simple example of this approach is *value noise*, where pseudo-random numbers between -1 and 1 are associated with each lattice point, and actual noise values are computed with trilinear interpolation or with a more complex spline interpolant, which can give a smoother result by avoiding derivative discontinuities when moving from one lattice cell to another.

For such a noise function, given an integer (x, y, z) lattice point, it must be possible to efficiently compute its parameter value in a way that always associates the same value with each lattice point. Because it is infeasible to store values for all possible (x, y, z) points, some compact representation is needed. One option is to use a hash function, where the coordinates are hashed and then used to look up parameters from a fixed-size table of precomputed pseudo-random parameter values.

10.6.1 PERLIN NOISE

In pbrt we will implement a noise function introduced by Ken Perlin (1985a, 2002); as such, it is known as *Perlin noise*. It has a value of zero at all (x, y, z) integer lattice points. Its variation comes from gradient vectors at each lattice point that guide the interpolation of a smooth function in between the points (Figure 10.24). This noise function has many of the desired characteristics of a noise function described above, is computationally efficient, and is easy to implement. Figure 10.25 shows its value rendered on a sphere.

⟨*Texture Method Definitions*⟩ +≡
```
Float Noise(Float x, Float y, Float z) {
    ⟨Compute noise cell coordinates and offsets 649⟩
    ⟨Compute gradient weights 651⟩
    ⟨Compute trilinear interpolation of weights 653⟩
}
```

For convenience, there is also a variant of Noise() that takes a Point3f directly:

⟨*Texture Method Definitions*⟩ +≡
```
Float Noise(const Point3f &p) { return Noise(p.x, p.y, p.z); }
```

The implementation first computes the integer coordinates of the cell that contains the given point and the fractional offsets of the point from the lower cell corner:

Float 1062
Noise() 649
Point3f 68

⟨*Compute noise cell coordinates and offsets*⟩ ≡   649
```
int ix = std::floor(x), iy = std::floor(y), iz = std::floor(z);
Float dx = x - ix, dy = y - iy, dz = z - iz;
```

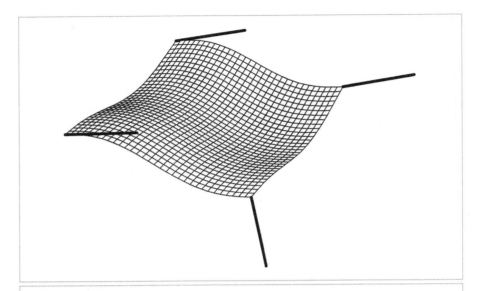

Figure 10.24: The Perlin noise function is computed by generating a smooth function that is zero but with a given derivative at integer lattice points. The derivatives are used to compute a smooth interpolating surface. Here, a 2D slice of the noise function is shown with four gradient vectors.

Figure 10.25: Perlin's Noise Function Modulating the Diffuse Color of a Sphere.

It next calls Grad() to get eight weight values, one for each corner of the cell that the point lies inside. Grad() uses the cell indices to index into a table; for efficiency we ensure that all of the indices are within the range of the table here by zeroing any high bits that would put a component past the table's size. (The table size must be a power of two for this trick to work—otherwise an expensive integer modulus operation would be needed in place of the bitwise "and.")

⟨*Compute gradient weights*⟩ ≡   649

```
ix &= NoisePermSize - 1;
iy &= NoisePermSize - 1;
iz &= NoisePermSize - 1;
Float w000 = Grad(ix,   iy,   iz,   dx,   dy,   dz);
Float w100 = Grad(ix+1, iy,   iz,   dx-1, dy,   dz);
Float w010 = Grad(ix,   iy+1, iz,   dx,   dy-1, dz);
Float w110 = Grad(ix+1, iy+1, iz,   dx-1, dy-1, dz);
Float w001 = Grad(ix,   iy,   iz+1, dx,   dy,   dz-1);
Float w101 = Grad(ix+1, iy,   iz+1, dx-1, dy,   dz-1);
Float w011 = Grad(ix,   iy+1, iz+1, dx,   dy-1, dz-1);
Float w111 = Grad(ix+1, iy+1, iz+1, dx-1, dy-1, dz-1);
```

Each integer lattice point has a gradient vector associated with it. The influence of the gradient vector for any point inside the cell is obtained by computing the dot product of the vector from the gradient's corner to the lookup point and the gradient vector (Figure 10.26); this is handled by the Grad() function. Note that the vectors to the corners other than the lower left one can be easily computed incrementally based on that vector.

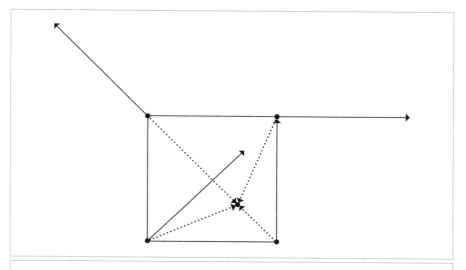

Float 1062
Grad() 652
NoisePermSize 652

Figure 10.26: The dot product of the vector from the corners of the cell to the lookup point (dotted lines) with each of the gradient vectors (solid lines) gives the influence of each gradient to the noise value at the point.

The gradient vector for a particular integer lattice point is found by indexing into a precomputed table of integer values, NoisePerm. The four low-order bits of the table's value for the lattice point determine which of 16 gradient vectors is associated with it. In a preprocessing step, this table of size NoisePermSize was filled with numbers from 0 to NoisePermSize-1 and then randomly permuted. These values were then duplicated, making an array of size 2*NoisePermSize that holds the table twice in succession. The second copy of the table makes lookups in the following code slightly more efficient.

Given a particular (ix,iy,iz) lattice point, a series of table lookups gives a value from the random-number table:

```
NoisePerm[NoisePerm[NoisePerm[ix] + iy] + iz];
```

By doing three nested permutations in this way, rather than NoisePerm[ix+iy+iz], for example, the final result is more irregular. The first approach doesn't usually return the same value if ix and iy are interchanged, as the second does. Furthermore, since the table was replicated to be twice the original length, the lookups can be done as described above, eliminating the need for modulus operations in code along the lines of

```
(NoisePerm[ix] + iy) % NoisePermSize
```

Given a final value from the permutation table that determines the gradient number, the dot product with the corresponding gradient vector must be computed. However, the gradient vectors do not need to be represented explicitly. All of the gradients use only -1, 0, or 1 in their coordinates, so that the dot products reduce to addition of some (possibly negated) components of the vector.[5] The final implementation is the following:

⟨*Texture Method Definitions*⟩ +≡
```
    inline Float Grad(int x, int y, int z, Float dx, Float dy, Float dz) {
        int h = NoisePerm[NoisePerm[NoisePerm[x] + y] + z];
        h &= 15;
        Float u = h < 8 || h == 12 || h == 13 ? dx : dy;
        Float v = h < 4 || h == 12 || h == 13 ? dy : dz;
        return ((h & 1) ? -u : u) + ((h & 2) ? -v : v);
    }
```

⟨*Perlin Noise Data*⟩ ≡
```
    static constexpr int NoisePermSize = 256;
    static int NoisePerm[2 * NoisePermSize] = {
        151, 160, 137, 91, 90, 15, 131, 13, 201, 95, 96,
        53, 194, 233, 7, 225, 140, 36, 103, 30, 69, 142,
        ⟨Remainder of the noise permutation table⟩
    };
```

---

5   The original formulation of Perlin noise also had a precomputed table of pseudo-random gradient directions, although Perlin has more recently suggested that the randomness from the permutation table is enough to remove regularity from the noise function.

Given these eight contributions from the gradients, the next step is to trilinearly interpolate between them at the point. Rather than interpolating with dx, dy, and dz directly, though, each of these values is passed through a smoothing function. This ensures that the noise function has first- and second-derivative continuity as lookup points move between lattice cells.

⟨*Texture Method Definitions*⟩ +≡
```
inline Float NoiseWeight(Float t) {
    Float t3 = t * t * t;
    Float t4 = t3 * t;
    return 6 * t4 * t - 15 * t4 + 10 * t3;
}
```

⟨*Compute trilinear interpolation of weights*⟩ ≡   649
```
Float wx = NoiseWeight(dx), wy = NoiseWeight(dy), wz = NoiseWeight(dz);
Float x00 = Lerp(wx, w000, w100);
Float x10 = Lerp(wx, w010, w110);
Float x01 = Lerp(wx, w001, w101);
Float x11 = Lerp(wx, w011, w111);
Float y0 = Lerp(wy, x00, x10);
Float y1 = Lerp(wy, x01, x11);
return Lerp(wz, y0, y1);
```

10.6.2 RANDOM POLKA DOTS

A basic use of the noise function is as part of a polka dot texture that divides (s, t) texture space into rectangular cells (Figure 10.27). Each cell has a 50% chance of having a dot inside of it, and the dots are randomly placed inside their cells. DotsTexture takes the usual 2D mapping function, as well as two Textures, one for the regions of the surface outside of the dots and one for the regions inside. It is defined in the files textures/dots.h and textures/dots.cpp.

⟨*DotsTexture Declarations*⟩ ≡
```
template <typename T> class DotsTexture : public Texture<T> {
public:
    ⟨DotsTexture Public Methods 653⟩
private:
    ⟨DotsTexture Private Data 653⟩
};
```

⟨*DotsTexture Public Methods*⟩ ≡   653
```
DotsTexture(std::unique_ptr<TextureMapping2D> mapping,
        const std::shared_ptr<Texture<T>> &outsideDot,
        const std::shared_ptr<Texture<T>> &insideDot)
    : mapping(std::move(mapping)), outsideDot(outsideDot),
      insideDot(insideDot) { }
```

⟨*DotsTexture Private Data*⟩ ≡   653
```
std::unique_ptr<TextureMapping2D> mapping;
std::shared_ptr<Texture<T>> outsideDot, insideDot;
```

Figure 10.27: The Polka Dot Texture Applied to All of pbrt's Quadric Shapes.

The evaluation function starts by taking the (s, t) texture coordinates and computing integer sCell and tCell values, which give the coordinates of the cell they are inside. We will not consider antialiasing of the polka dots texture here; an exercise at the end of the chapter outlines how this might be done.

⟨*DotsTexture Public Methods*⟩ +≡   653
```
T Evaluate(const SurfaceInteraction &si) const {
    ⟨Compute cell indices for dots 654⟩
    ⟨Return insideDot result if point is inside dot 655⟩
    return outsideDot->Evaluate(si);
}
```

⟨*Compute cell indices for dots*⟩ ≡   654
```
Vector2f dstdx, dstdy;
Point2f st = mapping->Map(si, &dstdx, &dstdy);
int sCell = std::floor(st[0] + .5f), tCell = std::floor(st[1] + .5f);
```

Once the cell coordinate is known, it's necessary to decide if there is a polka dot in the cell. Obviously, this computation needs to be consistent so that for each time this routine runs for points in a particular cell it returns the same result. Yet we'd like the result not to be completely regular (e.g., with a dot in every other cell). Noise solves this problem: by evaluating the noise function at a position that is the same for all points inside this cell—

(sCell+.5, tCell+.5)—we can compute an irregularly varying but consistent value for each cell.[6] If this value is greater than zero, a dot is placed in the cell.

If there is a dot in the cell, the noise function is used again to randomly shift the center of the dot within the cell. The points at which the noise function is evaluated for the center shift are offset by arbitrary constant amounts, however, so that noise values from different noise cells are used from them, eliminating a possible source of correlation with the noise value used to determine the presence of a dot in the first place. (Note that the dot's radius must be small enough so that it doesn't spill over the cell's boundary after being shifted; in that case, points where the texture was being evaluated would also need to consider the dots based in neighboring cells as potentially affecting their texture value.)

Given the dot center and radius, the texture needs to decide if the (s, t) coordinates are within the radius of the shifted center. It does this by computing their squared distance to the center and comparing it to the squared radius.

⟨*Return* insideDot *result if point is inside dot*⟩ ≡   **654**
```
if (Noise(sCell + .5f, tCell + .5f) > 0) {
    Float radius = .35f;
    Float maxShift = 0.5f - radius;
    Float sCenter = sCell +
        maxShift * Noise(sCell + 1.5f, tCell + 2.8f);
    Float tCenter = tCell +
        maxShift * Noise(sCell + 4.5f, tCell + 9.8f);
    Vector2f dst = st - Point2f(sCenter, tCenter);
    if (dst.LengthSquared() < radius*radius)
        return insideDot->Evaluate(si);
}
```

10.6.3 NOISE IDIOMS AND SPECTRAL SYNTHESIS

The fact that noise is a band-limited function means that its frequency content can be adjusted by scaling the domain over which it is evaluated. For example, if Noise(p) has some known frequency content, then the frequency content of Noise(2*p) will be twice as high. This is just like the relationship between the frequency content of $\sin(x)$ and $\sin(2x)$. This technique can be used to create a noise function with a desired rate of variation.

For many applications in procedural texturing, it's useful to have variation over multiple scales—for example, to add finer variations to the base noise function. One effective way to do this with noise is to compute patterns via *spectral synthesis*, where a complex function $f_s(s)$ is defined by a sum of contributions from another function $f(x)$:

$$f_s(x) = \sum_i w_i f(s_i x),$$

---

6   Recall that the noise function always returns zero at integer (x, y, z) coordinates, so we don't want to just evaluate it at (sCell, tCell). Although the 3D noise function would actually be evaluating noise at (sCell, tCell, .5), slices through noise with integer values for any of the coordinates are not as well distributed as with all of them offset from the integers.

for a set of weight values w_i and parameter scale values s_i. If the base function $f(x)$ has a well-defined frequency content (e.g., is a sine or cosine function or a noise function), then each term $f(s_i x)$ also has a well-defined frequency content as described earlier. Because each term of the sum is weighted by a weight value w_i, the result is a sum of contributions of various frequencies, with different frequency ranges weighted differently.

Typically, the scales s_i are chosen in a geometric progression such that $s_i = 2s_{i-1}$ and the weights are $w_i = w_{i-1}/2$. The result is that as higher frequency variation is added to the function, it has relatively less influence on the overall shape of $f_s(x)$. Each additional term is called an *octave* of noise, since it has twice the frequency content of the previous one. When this scheme is used with Perlin noise, the result is often referred to as *fractional Brownian motion* (fBm), after a particular type of random process that varies in a similar manner.

Fractional Brownian motion is a useful building block for procedural textures because it gives a function with more complex variation than plain noise, while still being easy to compute and still having well-defined frequency content. The utility function FBm() implements the fractional Brownian motion function. Figure 10.28 shows two graphs of it.

In addition to the point at which to evaluate the function and the function's partial derivatives at that point, the function takes an omega parameter, which ranges from zero to one and affects the smoothness of the pattern by controlling the falloff of contributions at higher frequencies (values around 0.5 work well), and maxOctaves, which gives the maximum number of octaves of noise that should be used in computing the sum.

⟨*Texture Method Definitions*⟩ +≡
```
Float FBm(const Point3f &p, const Vector3f &dpdx, const Vector3f &dpdy,
          Float omega, int maxOctaves) {
    ⟨Compute number of octaves for antialiased FBm 658⟩
    ⟨Compute sum of octaves of noise for FBm 658⟩
    return sum;
}
```

The implementation here uses a technique called *clamping* to antialias the fBm function. The idea is that when we are computing a value based on a sum of components, each with known frequency content, we should stop adding in components that would have frequencies beyond the Nyquist limit and instead add their average values to the sum. Because the average value of Noise() is zero, all that needs to be done is to compute the number of octaves such that none of the terms has excessively high frequencies and not evaluate the noise function for any higher octaves.

Noise() (and thus the first term of $f_s(x)$ as well) has a maximum frequency content of roughly $\omega = 1$. Each subsequent term represents a doubling of frequency content. Therefore, we would like to find the appropriate number of terms n such that if the sampling rate in noise space is s, then

$$\frac{s}{2^n} = 2,$$

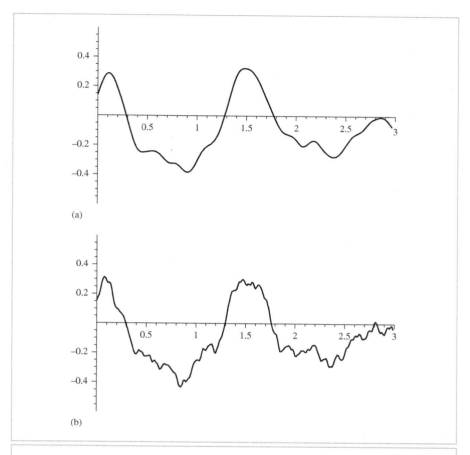

Figure 10.28: Graphs of the FBm() Function. (a) 2 and (b) 6 octaves of noise. Notice how as more levels of noise are added, the graph has progressively more detail, although its overall shape remains roughly the same.

which ensures that there are frequencies right up to the Nyquist frequency but not past it. Equivalently,

$$2^{n+1} = s$$
$$n + 1 = \log_2 s$$
$$n = -1 + \log_2 s$$
$$n = -1 + \frac{1}{2} \log_2 s^2,$$

where we've used the identity $\log_2 x = 1/n \log_2 x^n$ to write the last expression in a more convenient form for the following.

The squared sampling rate s^2 can be computed with one over the maximum of the squared length of the differentials $\partial p/\partial x$ and $\partial p/\partial y$, which we'll denote by l^2. We can

FBm() 656

turn this inversion into a negation of the logarithm, and equivalently write this as:

$$n = -1 - \frac{1}{2} \log_2 l^2.$$

⟨*Compute number of octaves for antialiased FBm*⟩ ≡   656, 660
```
Float len2 = std::max(dpdx.LengthSquared(), dpdy.LengthSquared());
Float n = Clamp(-1 - .5f * Log2(len2), 0, maxOctaves);
int nInt = std::floor(n);
```

Finally, the integral number of octaves up to the Nyquist limit are added together and the last octave is faded in, according to the fractional part of n. This ensures that successive octaves of noise fade in gradually, rather than appearing abruptly, which can cause visually noticeable artifacts at the transitions. The implementation here actually increases the frequency between octaves by 1.99, rather than by a factor of 2, in order to reduce the impact of the fact that the noise function is zero at integer lattice points. This breaks up that regularity across sums of octaves of noise, which can also lead to subtle visual artifacts.

⟨*Compute sum of octaves of noise for FBm*⟩ ≡   656
```
Float sum = 0, lambda = 1, o = 1;
for (int i = 0; i < nInt; ++i) {
    sum += o * Noise(lambda * p);
    lambda *= 1.99f;
    o *= omega;
}
Float nPartial = n - nInt;
sum += o * SmoothStep(.3f, .7f, nPartial) * Noise(lambda * p);
```

The SmoothStep() function takes a minimum and maximum value and a point at which to evaluate a smooth interpolating function. If the point is below the minimum zero is returned, and if it's above the maximum one is returned. Otherwise, it smoothly interpolates between zero and one using a cubic Hermite spline.

⟨*Texture Inline Functions*⟩ ≡
```
inline Float SmoothStep(Float min, Float max, Float value) {
    Float v = Clamp((value - min) / (max - min), 0, 1);
    return v * v * (-2 * v  + 3);
}
```

Closely related to the FBm() function is the Turbulence() function. It also computes a sum of terms of the noise function but takes the absolute value of each one:

$$f_s(x) = \sum_i w_i |f(s_i x)|.$$

Taking the absolute value introduces first-derivative discontinuities in the synthesized function, and thus the turbulence function has infinite frequency content. Nevertheless, the visual characteristics of this function can be quite useful for procedural textures. Figure 10.29 shows two graphs of the turbulence function.

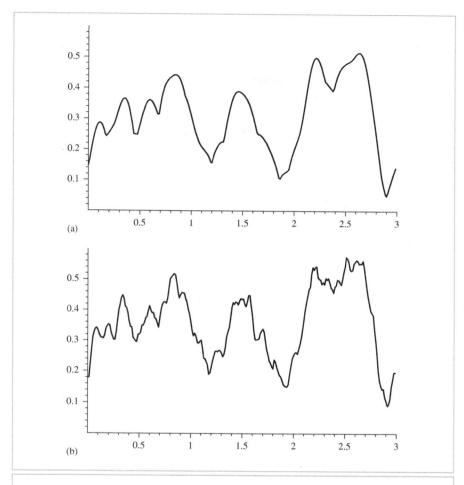

Figure 10.29: Graphs of the `Turbulence()` function for (a) 2 and (b) 6 octaves of noise. Note that the first derivative discontinuities introduced by taking the absolute value of the noise function make this function substantially rougher than FBm.

The `Turbulence()` implementation here tries to antialias itself in the same way that `FBm()` did. As described earlier, however, the first-derivative discontinuities in the function introduce infinitely high-frequency content, so these efforts can't hope to be perfectly successful. The `Turbulence()` antialiasing here at least eliminates some of the worst of the artifacts; otherwise, increasing the pixel sampling rate is the best recourse. In practice, this function doesn't alias too terribly when used in procedural textures, particularly compared to the aliasing from infinitely high frequencies from geometric and shadow edges.

FBm() 656

Turbulence() 660

⟨*Texture Method Definitions*⟩ +≡
```
Float Turbulence(const Point3f &p, const Vector3f &dpdx,
        const Vector3f &dpdy, Float omega, int maxOctaves) {
    ⟨Compute number of octaves for antialiased FBm 658⟩
    ⟨Compute sum of octaves of noise for turbulence 660⟩
    ⟨Account for contributions of clamped octaves in turbulence 660⟩
    return sum;
}
```

⟨*Compute sum of octaves of noise for turbulence*⟩ ≡   660
```
Float sum = 0, lambda = 1, o = 1;
for (int i = 0; i < nInt; ++i) {
    sum += o * std::abs(Noise(lambda * p));
    lambda *= 1.99f;
    o *= omega;
}
```

The average value of the absolute value of the noise function is roughly 0.2; this value should be added to the sum for the octaves where the noise function's estimated frequency would be higher than the sampling rate.

⟨*Account for contributions of clamped octaves in turbulence*⟩ ≡   660
```
Float nPartial = n - nInt;
sum += o * Lerp(SmoothStep(.3f, .7f, nPartial),
                0.2, std::abs(Noise(lambda * p)));
for (int i = nInt; i < maxOctaves; ++i) {
    sum += o * 0.2f;
    o *= omega;
}
```

10.6.4 BUMPY AND WRINKLED TEXTURES

The fBm and turbulence functions are particularly useful as a source of random variation for bump mapping. The FBmTexture is a Float-valued texture that uses FBm() to compute offsets, and WrinkledTexture uses Turbulence() to do so. They are demonstrated in Figures 10.30 and 10.31 and are implemented in textures/fbm.h, textures/fbm.cpp, textures/wrinkled.h, and textures/wrinkled.cpp.

⟨*FBmTexture Declarations*⟩ ≡
```
template <typename T> class FBmTexture : public Texture<T> {
public:
    ⟨FBmTexture Public Methods 662⟩
private:
    std::unique_ptr<TextureMapping3D> mapping;
    const Float omega;
    const int octaves;
};
```

Figure 10.30: Sphere with FBmTexture Used for Bump Mapping.

Figure 10.31: WrinkledTexture Used as Bump Mapping Function for Sphere.

⟨*FBmTexture Public Methods*⟩ ≡   660
```
FBmTexture(std::unique_ptr<TextureMapping3D> mapping, int octaves,
          Float omega)
    : mapping(std::move(mapping)), omega(omega), octaves(octaves) { }
```

⟨*FBmTexture Public Methods*⟩ +≡   660
```
T Evaluate(const SurfaceInteraction &si) const {
    Vector3f dpdx, dpdy;
    Point3f P = mapping->Map(si, &dpdx, &dpdy);
    return FBm(P, dpdx, dpdy, omega, octaves);
}
```

The implementation of WrinkledTexture is almost identical to FBmTexture, save for a call
to Turbulence() instead of FBm(). As such, it isn't included here.

10.6.5 WINDY WAVES

Application of fBm can give a reasonably convincing representation of waves (Ebert
et al. 2003). Figures 1.11 and 4.1 use this texture for the water in those scenes. This
Texture is based on two observations. First, across the surface of a wind-swept lake (for
example), some areas are relatively smooth and some are more choppy; this effect comes
from the natural variation of the wind's strength from area to area. Second, the overall
form of individual waves on the surface can be described well by the fBm-based wave
pattern scaled by the wind strength. This texture is implemented in textures/windy.h
and textures/windy.cpp.

⟨*WindyTexture Declarations*⟩ ≡
```
template <typename T> class WindyTexture : public Texture<T> {
public:
    ⟨WindyTexture Public Methods 662⟩
private:
    std::unique_ptr<TextureMapping3D> mapping;
};
```

⟨*WindyTexture Public Methods*⟩ ≡   662
```
WindyTexture(std::unique_ptr<TextureMapping3D> mapping)
    : mapping(std::move(mapping)) { }
```

The evaluation function uses two calls to the FBm() function. The first scales down the
point P by a factor of 10; as a result, the first call to FBm() returns relatively low-frequency
variation over the surface of the object being shaded. This value is used to determine the
local strength of the wind. The second call determines the amplitude of the wave at the
particular point, independent of the amount of wind there. The product of these two
values gives the actual wave offset for the particular location.

⟨*WindyTexture Public Methods*⟩ +≡   **662**
```
    T Evaluate(const SurfaceInteraction &si) const {
        Vector3f dpdx, dpdy;
        Point3f P = mapping->Map(si, &dpdx, &dpdy);
        Float windStrength = FBm(.1f * P, .1f * dpdx, .1f * dpdy, .5, 3);
        Float waveHeight = FBm(P, dpdx, dpdy, .5, 6);
        return std::abs(windStrength) * waveHeight;
    }
```

10.6.6 MARBLE

Another classic use of the noise function is to perturb texture coordinates before using another texture or lookup table. For example, a facsimile of marble can be made by modeling the marble material as a series of layered strata and then using noise to perturb the coordinate used for finding a value among the strata. The MarbleTexture in this section implements this approach. Figure 10.32 illustrates the idea behind this texture. On the left, the layers of marble are indexed directly using the y coordinate of the point on the sphere. On the right, fBm has been used to perturb the y value, introducing variation. This texture is implemented in textures/marble.h and textures/marble.cpp.

⟨*MarbleTexture Declarations*⟩ ≡
```
    class MarbleTexture : public Texture<Spectrum> {
    public:
        ⟨MarbleTexture Public Methods 664⟩
    private:
        ⟨MarbleTexture Private Data 664⟩
    };
```

Figure 10.32: Marble. The MarbleTexture perturbs the coordinate used to index into a 1D table of colors using FBm, giving a plausible marble appearance.

The texture takes the usual set of parameters to control the FBm() function that will be used to perturb the lookup coordinate. The variation parameter modulates the magnitude of the perturbation.

⟨*MarbleTexture Public Methods*⟩ ≡   **663**
```
MarbleTexture(std::unique_ptr<TextureMapping3D> mapping, int octaves,
        Float omega, Float scale, Float variation)
    : mapping(std::move(mapping)), octaves(octaves), omega(omega),
      scale(scale), variation(variation) { }
```

⟨*MarbleTexture Private Data*⟩ ≡   **663**
```
std::unique_ptr<TextureMapping3D> mapping;
const int octaves;
const Float omega, scale, variation;
```

An offset into the marble layers is computed by adding the variation to the point's y component and using the sine function to remap its value into the range [0, 1]. The ⟨*Evaluate marble spline at* t⟩ fragment uses the t value as the evaluation point for a cubic spline through a series of colors that are similar to those of real marble.

⟨*MarbleTexture Public Methods*⟩ +≡   **663**
```
Spectrum Evaluate(const SurfaceInteraction &si) const {
    Vector3f dpdx, dpdy;
    Point3f p = mapping->Map(si, &dpdx, &dpdy);
    p *= scale;
    Float marble = p.y + variation *
                    FBm(p, scale * dpdx, scale * dpdy, omega, octaves);
    Float t = .5f + .5f * std::sin(marble);
    ⟨Evaluate marble spline at t⟩
}
```

FURTHER READING

The cone-tracing method of Amanatides (1984) was one of the first techniques for automatically estimating filter footprints for ray tracing. The beam-tracing algorithm of Heckbert and Hanrahan (1984) was another early extension of ray tracing to incorporate an area associated with each image sample rather than just an infinitesimal ray. The pencil-tracing method of Shinya, Takahashi, and Naito (1987) is another approach to this problem. Other related work on the topic of associating areas or footprints with rays includes Mitchell and Hanrahan's paper (1992) on rendering caustics and Turkowski's technical report (1993).

Collins (1994) estimated the ray footprint by keeping a tree of all rays traced from a given camera ray, examining corresponding rays at the same level and position. The ray differentials used in pbrt are based on Igehy's (1999) formulation, which was extended by Suykens and Willems (2001) to handle glossy reflection in addition to perfect specular reflection. Worley's chapter in *Texturing and Modeling* (Ebert et al. 2003) on computing differentials for filter regions presents an approach similar to ours. See Elek et al. (2014)

for an extension of ray differentials to include wavelength, which can improve results with full-spectral rendering.

Two-dimensional texture mapping with images was first introduced to graphics by Blinn and Newell (1976). Ever since Crow (1977) identified aliasing as the source of many errors in images in graphics, quite a bit of work has been done to find efficient and effective ways of antialiasing image maps. Dungan, Stenger, and Sutty (1978) were the first to suggest creating a pyramid of prefiltered texture images; they used the nearest texture sample at the appropriate level when looking up texture values, using supersampling in screen space to antialias the result. Feibush, Levoy, and Cook (1980) investigated a spatially varying filter function, rather than a simple box filter. (Blinn and Newell were aware of Crow's results and used a box filter for their textures.)

Williams (1983) used a MIP map image pyramid for texture filtering with trilinear interpolation. Shortly thereafter, Crow (1984) introduced summed area tables, which make it possible to efficiently filter over axis-aligned rectangular regions of texture space. Summed area tables handle anisotropy better than Williams's method, although only for primarily axis-aligned filter regions. Heckbert (1986) wrote a good general survey of texture mapping algorithms through the mid-1980s.

Greene and Heckbert (1986) originally developed the elliptically weighted average technique, and Heckbert's master's thesis (1989) put the method on a solid theoretical footing. Fournier and Fiume (1988) developed an even higher quality texture filtering method that focuses on using a bounded amount of computation per lookup. Nonetheless, their method appears to be less efficient than EWA overall. Lansdale's master's thesis (1991) has an extensive description of EWA and Fournier and Fiume's method, including implementation details.

More recently, a number of researchers have investigated generalizing Williams's original method using a series of trilinear MIP map samples in an effort to increase quality without having to pay the price for the general EWA algorithm. By taking multiple samples from the MIP map, anisotropy is handled well while preserving the computational efficiency. Examples include Barkans's (1997) description of texture filtering in the Talisman architecture, McCormack et al.'s (1999) Feline method, and Cant and Shrubsole's (2000) technique. Manson and Schaefer (2013, 2014) have recently shown how to accurately approximate a variety of filter functions with a fixed small number of bilinearly interpolated sample values. This approach is particularly useful on GPUs, where hardware-accelerated bilinear interpolation is available.

Gamma correction has a long history in computer graphics. Poynton (2002a, 2002b) has written comprehensive FAQs on issues related to color representation and gamma correction. Most modern displays are based on the sRGB color space, which has a gamma of roughly 2.2 (International Electrotechnical Commission (IEC) 1999). See Gritz and d'Eon (2008) for a detailed discussion of the implications of gamma correction for rendering and how to correctly account for it in rendering systems.

Smith's (2002) Web site and document on audio resampling gives a good overview of resampling signals in one dimension. Heckbert's (1989a) zoom source code is the canonical reference for image resampling. His implementation carefully avoids feedback without using auxiliary storage, unlike ours in this chapter, which allocates additional temporary buffer space to do so.

Three-dimensional solid texturing was originally developed by Gardner (1984, 1985), Perlin (1985a), and Peachey (1985). Norton, Rockwood, and Skolmoski (1982) developed the *clamping* method that is widely used for antialiasing textures based on solid texturing. The general idea of procedural texturing was introduced by Cook (1984), Perlin (1985a), and Peachey (1985).

Peachey's chapter in *Texturing and Modeling* (Ebert et al. 2003) has a thorough summary of approaches to noise functions. After Perlin's original noise function, both Lewis (1989) and van Wijk (1991) developed alternatives that made different time/quality trade-offs. Worley (1996) has developed a quite different noise function for procedural texturing that is well suited for cellular and organic patterns. Perlin (2002) revised his noise function to correct a number of subtle shortcomings.

Noise functions have received additional attention from the research community in recent years. (Lagae et al. (2010) have a good survey of work up to that year.) Building on Lewis's observation that individual bands of Perlin's noise function actually have frequency content over a fairly wide range (Lewis 1989), Cook and DeRose (2005) also identified the problem that 2D slices through 3D noise functions aren't in general band limited, even if the original 3D noise function is. They proposed a new noise function that addresses both of these issues. Goldberg et al. (2008) developed a noise function that makes efficient anisotropic filtering possible, leading to higher quality results than just applying the clamping approach for antialiasing. Their method is also well suited to programmable graphics hardware. Kensler et al. (2008) suggested a number of improvements to Perlin's revised noise function.

Lagae et al. (2009) have developed a noise function that has good frequency control and can be mapped well to surfaces even without a surface parameterization. Lagae and Drettakis (2011) showed how to compute high quality anisotropically filtered values of this noise function. More recently, Galerne et al. (2012) showed how to automatically determine parameters to this noise function so that the result matches example images. Further work on this topic was done by Du et al. (2013) and Gilet et al. (2014).

The first languages and systems that supported the idea of user-supplied procedural shaders were developed by Cook (1984) and Perlin (1985a). (The texture composition model in this chapter is similar to Cook's shade trees.) The RenderMan shading language, described in a paper by Hanrahan and Lawson (1990), remains the classic shading language in graphics, though a more modern shading language is available in Open Shading Language (OSL) (Gritz et al. 2010), which is open source and increasingly used for production rendering. It follows the model of the shader returning a representation of the material rather than a final color value, like the approach introduced in Chapter 9. See also Karrenberg et al. (2010), who introduced the *AnySL* shading language, which was designed for both high performance as well as portability across multiple rendering systems (including pbrt).

See Ebert et al. (2003) and Apodaca and Gritz (2000) for techniques for writing procedural shaders; both of those have excellent discussions of issues related to antialiasing in procedural shaders.

The "Further Reading" section in Chapter 9 described approaches for anti-aliasing bump maps; a number of researchers have looked at the closely related issue of antialiasing surface reflection functions. Van Horn and Turk (2008) developed an approach to automatically generate MIP maps of reflection functions that represent the characteristics of shaders over finite areas in order to antialias them. Bruneton and Neyret (2012) surveyed the state of the art in this area, and Jarabo et al. (2014b) also considered perceptual issues related to filtering inputs to these functions. See also Heitz et al. (2014) for recent work on this topic.

Many creative methods for computing texture on surfaces have been developed. A sampling of our favorites includes reaction diffusion, which simulates growth processes based on a model of chemical interactions over surfaces and was simultaneously introduced by Turk (1991) and Witkin and Kass (1991); Sims's (1991) genetic algorithm-based approach, which finds programs that generate interesting textures through random mutations from which users select their favorites; Fleischer et al.'s (1995) cellular texturing algorithms that generate geometrically accurate scales and spike features on surfaces; and Dorsey et al.'s (1996) flow simulations that model the effect of weathering on buildings and encode the results in image maps that stored the relative wetness, dirtiness, and so on, at points on the surfaces of structures. Porumbescu et al. (2005) developed *shell maps*, which make it possible to map geometric objects onto a surface in the manner of texture mapping.

A variety of *texture synthesis* algorithms have been developed in the past decade; these approaches take an example texture image and then synthesize larger texture maps that appear similar to the original texture while not being exactly the same. The survey article by Wei et al. (2009) describes work in this area through 2009 as well as the main approaches that have been developed so far. For more recent work in this area, see Kim et al. (2012), who developed an effective approach based on finding symmetries in textures, and Lefebvre et al. (2010), who attacked the specialized (but useful) problem of synthesizing textures for building facades.

EXERCISES

⊘ **10.1** Many image file formats don't store floating-point color values but instead use 8 bits for each color component, mapping the values to the range [0, 1]. (For example, the TGA format that is supported by ReadImage() is such a format.) For images originally stored in this format, the ImageTexture uses four times more memory than strictly necessary by using floats in RGBSpectrum objects to store these colors. Modify the image reading routines to directly return 8-bit values when an image is read from such a file.

Then modify the ImageTexture so that it keeps the data for such textures in an 8-bit representation, and modify the MIPMap so that it can filter data stored in this format. How much memory is saved for image texture-heavy scenes? How is pbrt's performance affected? Can you explain the causes of any performance differences?

⊘ **10.2** For scenes with many image textures where reading them all into memory simultaneously has a prohibitive memory cost, an effective approach can be to allocate a fixed amount of memory for image maps (a *texture cache*), load textures into that memory on demand, and discard the image maps that haven't been accessed recently when the memory fills up (Peachey 1990). To enable good performance with small texture caches, image maps should be stored in a *tiled* format that makes it possible to load in small square regions of the texture independently of each other. Tiling techniques like these are used in graphics hardware to improve the performance of their texture memory caches (Hakura and Gupta 1997; Igehy et al. 1998, 1999). Implement a texture cache in pbrt. Write a conversion program that converts images in other formats to a tiled format. (You may want to investigate OpenEXR's tiled image support.) How small can you make the texture cache and still see good performance?

10.3   Read the papers by Manson and Schaefer (2013, 2014) on approximating high-quality filters with MIP maps and a small number of bilinear samples. Add an option to use their method for texture filtering in place of the EWA implementation currently in pbrt. Compare image quality for a number of scenes that use textures. How does running time compare? You may also find it useful to use a profiler to compare the amount of time running texture filtering code for each of the two approaches.

10.4   Improve the filtering algorithm used for resampling image maps to initialize the MIP map levels using the Lanczos filter instead of the box filter. How do the sphere test images in the file scenes/sphere-ewa-vs-trilerp.pbrt and Figure 10.10 change after your improvements?

10.5   It is possible to use MIP mapping with textures that have non-power-of-two resolutions—the details are explained by Guthe and Heckbert (2005). Implementing this approach can save a substantial amount of memory: in the worst case, the resampling that pbrt's MIPMap implementation performs can increase memory requirements by a factor of four. (Consider a 513×513 texture that is resampled to be 1024×1024.) Implement this approach in pbrt, and compare the amount of memory used to store texture data for a variety of texture-heavy scenes.

10.6   Some of the light transport algorithms in Chapters 14–16 require a large number of samples to be taken per pixel for good results. (Examples of such algorithms include path tracing as implemented by the PathIntegrator.) If hundreds or thousands of samples are taken in each pixel, then the computational expense of high-quality texture filtering isn't worthwhile; the high pixel sampling rate serves well to antialias texture functions with high frequencies. Modify the MIPMap implementation so that it optionally just returns a bilinearly interpolated value from the finest level of the pyramid, even if a filter footprint is provided. Compare rendering time and image quality with this approach when rendering an image using many samples per pixel and a scene that has image maps that would otherwise exhibit aliasing at lower pixel sampling rates.

MIPMap 625
PathIntegrator 875

10.7   An additional advantage of properly antialiased image map lookups is that they improve cache performance. Consider, for example, the situation of undersampling a high-resolution image map: nearby samples on the screen will access widely separated parts of the image map, such that there is low probability that texels fetched from main memory for one texture lookup will already be in the cache for texture lookups at adjacent pixel samples. Modify pbrt so that it always does image texture lookups from the finest level of the MIPMap, being careful to ensure that the same number of texels are still being accessed. How does performance change? What do cache-profiling tools report about the overall change in effectiveness of the CPU cache?

● 10.8 Read Worley's paper that describes a new noise function with substantially different visual characteristics than Perlin noise (Worley 1996). Implement this cellular noise function, and add Textures to pbrt that are based on it.

● 10.9 Implement one of the improved noise functions, such as the ones introduced by Cook and DeRose (2005), Goldberg et al. (2008), or Lagae et al. (2009). Compare image quality and rendering time for scenes that make substantial use of noise functions to the current implementation in pbrt.

● 10.10 The implementation of the DotsTexture texture in this chapter does not make any effort to avoid aliasing in the results that it computes. Modify this texture to do some form of antialiasing. The Checkerboard2DTexture offers a guide as to how this might be done, although this case is more complicated, both because the polka dots are not present in every grid cell and because they are irregularly positioned.

At the two extremes of a filter region that is within a single cell and a filter region that spans a large number of cells, the task is easier. If the filter is entirely within a single cell and is entirely inside or outside the polka dot in that cell (if present), then it is only necessary to evaluate one of the two subtextures as appropriate. If the filter is within a single cell but overlaps both the dot and the base texture, then it is possible to compute how much of the filter area is inside the dot and how much is outside and blend between the two. At the other extreme, if the filter area is extremely large, it is possible to blend between the two textures according to the overall average of how much area is covered by dots and how much is not. (Note that this approach potentially makes the same error as was made in the checkerboard, where the subtextures aren't aware that part of their area is occluded by another texture. Ignore this issue for this exercise.)

Implement these approaches and then consider the intermediate cases, where the filter region spans a small number of cells. What approaches work well for antialiasing in this case?

● 10.11 Write a general-purpose Texture that stores a reference to another texture and supersamples that texture when the evaluation method is called, thus making it possible to apply supersampling to any Texture. Use your implementation to compare the effectiveness and quality of the built-in antialiasing done by various procedural textures. Also compare the run-time efficiency of texture supersampling versus increased pixel sampling.

● 10.12 Modify pbrt to support a shading language to allow user-written programs to compute texture values. Unless you're also interested in writing your own compiler, *OSL* (Gritz et al. 2010) is a good choice.

CHAPTER ELEVEN

*11 VOLUME SCATTERING

So far, we have assumed that scenes are made up of collections of surfaces in a vacuum, which means that radiance is constant along rays between surfaces. However, there are many real-world situations where this assumption is inaccurate: fog and smoke attenuate and scatter light, and scattering from particles in the atmosphere makes the sky blue and sunsets red. This chapter introduces the mathematics to describe how light is affected as it passes through *participating media*—large numbers of very small particles distributed throughout a region of 3D space. Volume scattering models are based on the assumption that there are so many particles that scattering is best modeled as a probabilistic process, rather than directly accounting for individual interactions with particles. Simulating the effect of participating media makes it possible to render images with atmospheric haze, beams of light through clouds, light passing through cloudy water, and subsurface scattering, where light exits a solid object at a different place than where it entered.

This chapter first describes the basic physical processes that affect the radiance along rays passing through participating media. It then introduces the Medium base class, which provides interfaces for describing participating media in a region of space. Medium implementations return information about the scattering properties at points in their extent, including a phase function, which characterizes how light is scattered at a point in space. (It's the volumetric analog to the BSDF, which describes scattering at a point on a surface.) In order to determine the effect of participating media on the distribution of radiance in the scene, Integrators that handle volumetric effects are necessary; this is the topic of Chapter 15.

In highly scattering participating media, light can undergo many scattering events without any appreciable reduction in its energy. The cost of finding a light path in an Integrator is generally proportional to its length, and tracking paths with hundreds or thousands of scattering interactions quickly becomes impractical. In such cases, it is preferable to aggregate the overall effect of the underlying scattering process in a function that relates scattering between points where light enters and leaves the medium. The chapter therefore concludes with the BSSRDF base class, which is an abstraction that makes it possible to implement this type of approach. BSSRDF implementations describe the internal scattering in a medium bounded by refractive surfaces.

11.1 VOLUME SCATTERING PROCESSES

There are three main processes that affect the distribution of radiance in an environment with participating media:

- *Absorption*: the reduction in radiance due to the conversion of light to another form of energy, such as heat
- *Emission*: radiance that is added to the environment from luminous particles
- *Scattering*: radiance heading in one direction that is scattered to other directions due to collisions with particles

The characteristics of all of these properties may be *homogeneous* or *inhomogeneous*. Homogeneous properties are constant throughout some region of space given spatial extent, while inhomogeneous properties vary throughout space. Figure 11.1 shows a

Figure 11.1: Spotlight through Fog. Light scattering from particles in the medium back toward the camera makes the spotlight's illumination visible even in pixels where there are no visible surfaces that reflect it. The sphere blocks light, casting a volumetric shadow in the region beneath it.

BSSRDF 692

Figure 11.2: If a participating medium primarily absorbs light passing through it, it will have a dark and smoky appearance, as shown here. *(Smoke simulation data courtesy of Duc Nguyen and Ron Fedkiw.)*

simple example of volume scattering, where a spotlight shining through a participating medium illuminates particles in the medium and casts a volumetric shadow.

11.1.1 ABSORPTION

Consider thick black smoke from a fire: the smoke obscures the objects behind it because its particles absorb light traveling from the object to the viewer. The thicker the smoke, the more light is absorbed. Figure 11.2 shows this effect with a spatial distribution of absorption that was created with an accurate physical simulation of smoke formation. Note the shadow on the ground: the participating medium has also absorbed light between the light source to the ground plane, casting a shadow.

Absorption is described by the medium's *absorption cross section*, σ_a, which is the probability density that light is absorbed per unit distance traveled in the medium. In general, the absorption cross section may vary with both position p and direction ω, although it

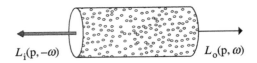

Figure 11.3: Absorption reduces the amount of radiance along a ray through a participating medium. Consider a ray carrying incident radiance at a point p from direction $-\omega$. If the ray passes through a differential cylinder filled with absorbing particles, the change in radiance due to absorption by those particles is $dL_o(p, \omega) = -\sigma_a(p, \omega) L_i(p, -\omega) dt$.

is normally just a function of position. It is usually also a spectrally varying quantity. The units of σ_a are reciprocal distance (m^{-1}). This means that σ_a can take on any positive value; it is not required to be between 0 and 1, for instance.

Figure 11.3 shows the effect of absorption along a very short segment of a ray. Some amount of radiance $L_i(p, -\omega)$ is arriving at point p, and we'd like to find the exitant radiance $L_o(p, \omega)$ after absorption in the differential volume. This change in radiance along the differential ray length dt is described by the differential equation

$$L_o(p, \omega) - L_i(p, -\omega) = dL_o(p, \omega) = -\sigma_a(p, \omega)\, L_i(p, -\omega)\, dt,$$

which says that the differential reduction in radiance along the beam is a linear function of its initial radiance.[1]

This differential equation can be solved to give the integral equation describing the total fraction of light absorbed for a ray. If we assume that the ray travels a distance d in direction ω through the medium starting at point p, the remaining portion of the original radiance is given by

$$e^{-\int_0^d \sigma_a(p+t\omega,\omega)\, dt}.$$

11.1.2 EMISSION

While absorption reduces the amount of radiance along a ray as it passes through a medium, emission increases it, due to chemical, thermal, or nuclear processes that convert energy into visible light. Figure 11.4 shows emission in a differential volume, where we denote emitted radiance added to a ray per unit distance at a point p in direction ω by $L_e(p, \omega)$. Figure 11.5 shows the effect of emission with the smoke data set. In that figure the absorption coefficient is much lower than in Figure 11.2, giving a very different appearance.

The differential equation that gives the change in radiance due to emission is

$$dL_o(p, \omega) = L_e(p, \omega)\, dt.$$

---

1   This is another instance of the linearity assumption in radiometry: the fraction of light absorbed doesn't vary based on the ray's radiance, but is always a fixed fraction.

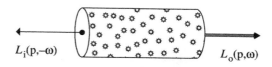

Figure 11.4: The volume emission function $L_e(p, \omega)$ gives the change in radiance along a ray as it passes through a differential volume of emissive particles. The change in radiance per differential distance is $dL = L_e dt$.

Figure 11.5: A Participating Medium Where the Dominant Volumetric Effect Is Emission. Although the medium still absorbs light, still casting a shadow on the ground and obscuring the wall behind it, emission in the volume increases radiance along rays passing through it, making the cloud brighter than the wall behind it.

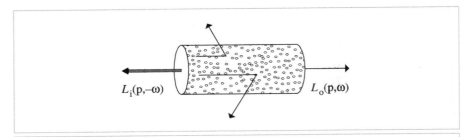

Figure 11.6: Like absorption, out-scattering also reduces the radiance along a ray. Light that hits particles may be scattered in another direction such that the radiance exiting the region in the original direction is reduced.

This equation incorporates the assumption that the emitted light L_e is not dependent on the incoming light L_i. This is always true under the linear optics assumptions that pbrt is based on.

11.1.3 OUT-SCATTERING AND ATTENUATION

The third basic light interaction in participating media is scattering. As a ray passes through a medium, it may collide with particles and be scattered in different directions. This has two effects on the total radiance that the beam carries. It reduces the radiance exiting a differential region of the beam because some of it is deflected to different directions. This effect is called *out-scattering* (Figure 11.6) and is the topic of this section. However, radiance from other rays may be scattered into the path of the current ray; this *in-scattering* process is the subject of the next section.

The probability of an out-scattering event occurring per unit distance is given by the scattering coefficient, σ_s. As with absorption, the reduction in radiance along a differential length dt due to out-scattering is given by

$$dL_o(p, \omega) = -\sigma_s(p, \omega)\, L_i(p, -\omega)\, dt.$$

The total reduction in radiance due to absorption and out-scattering is given by the sum $\sigma_a + \sigma_s$. This combined effect of absorption and out-scattering is called *attenuation* or *extinction*. For convenience the sum of these two coefficients is denoted by the attenuation coefficient σ_t:

$$\sigma_t(p, \omega) = \sigma_a(p, \omega) + \sigma_s(p, \omega).$$

Two values related to the attenuation coefficient will be useful in the following. The first is the *albedo*, which is defined as

$$\rho = \frac{\sigma_s}{\sigma_t}.$$

The albedo is always between 0 and 1; it describes the probability of scattering (versus absorption) at a scattering event. The second is the *mean free path*, $1/\sigma_t$, which gives the average distance that a ray travels in the medium before interacting with a particle.

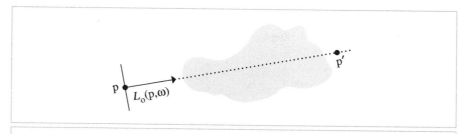

Figure 11.7: The beam transmittance $T_r(p \to p')$ gives the fraction of light transmitted from one point to another, accounting for absorption and out-scattering, but ignoring emission and in-scattering. Given exitant radiance at a point p in direction ω (e.g., reflected radiance from a surface), the radiance visible at another point p' along the ray is $T_r(p \to p')L_o(p, \omega)$.

Given the attenuation coefficient σ_t, the differential equation describing overall attenuation,

$$\frac{dL_o(p, \omega)}{dt} = -\sigma_t(p, \omega)\, L_i(p, -\omega),$$

can be solved to find the *beam transmittance*, which gives the fraction of radiance that is transmitted between two points:

$$T_r(p \to p') = e^{-\int_0^d \sigma_t(p + t\omega, \omega)\, dt} \tag{11.1}$$

where $d = \|p - p'\|$ is the distance between p and p', ω is the normalized direction vector between them, and T_r denotes the beam transmittance between p and p'. Note that the transmittance is always between 0 and 1. Thus, if exitant radiance from a point p on a surface in a given direction ω is given by $L_o(p, \omega)$, after accounting for extinction, the incident radiance at another point p' in direction $-\omega$ is

$$T_r(p \to p')\, L_o(p, \omega).$$

This idea is illustrated in Figure 11.7.

Two useful properties of beam transmittance are that transmittance from a point to itself is 1, $T_r(p \to p) = 1$, and in a vacuum $\sigma_t = 0$ and so $T_r(p \to p') = 1$ for all p'. Furthermore, if the attenuation coefficient satisfies the directional symmetry $\sigma_t(\omega) = \sigma_t(-\omega)$ or does not vary with direction ω and only varies as function of position (this is generally the case), then the transmittance between two points is the same in both directions:

$$T_r(p \to p') = T_r(p' \to p).$$

This property follows directly from Equation (11.1).

Another important property, true in all media, is that transmittance is multiplicative along points on a ray:

$$T_r(p \to p'') = T_r(p \to p')\, T_r(p' \to p''), \tag{11.2}$$

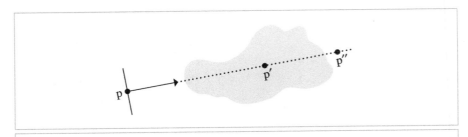

Figure 11.8: A useful property of beam transmittance is that it is multiplicative: the transmittance between points p and p″ on a ray like the one shown here is equal to the transmittance from p to p′ times the transmittance from p′ to p″ for all points p′ between p and p″.

for all points p′ between p and p″ (Figure 11.8). This property is useful for volume scattering implementations, since it makes it possible to incrementally compute transmittance at multiple points along a ray: transmittance from the origin to a point $T_r(o \to p)$ can be computed by taking the product of transmittance to a previous point $T_r(o \to p')$ and the transmittance of the segment between the previous and the current point $T_r(p' \to p)$.

The negated exponent in the definition of T_r in Equation (11.1) is called the *optical thickness* between the two points. It is denoted by the symbol τ:

$$\tau(p \to p') = \int_0^d \sigma_t(p + t\omega, -\omega)\, dt.$$

In a homogeneous medium, σ_t is a constant, so the integral that defines τ is trivially evaluated, giving *Beer's law:*

$$T_r(p \to p') = e^{-\sigma_t d}. \tag{11.3}$$

11.1.4 IN-SCATTERING

While out-scattering reduces radiance along a ray due to scattering in different directions, *in-scattering* accounts for increased radiance due to scattering from other directions (Figure 11.9). Figure 11.10 shows the effect of in-scattering with the smoke data set. Note that the smoke appears much thicker than when absorption or emission was the dominant volumetric effect.

Assuming that the separation between particles is at least a few times the lengths of their radii, it is possible to ignore inter-particle interactions when describing scattering at a particular location. Under this assumption, the *phase function* $p(\omega, \omega')$ describes the angular distribution of scattered radiation at a point; it is the volumetric analog to the BSDF. The BSDF analogy is not exact, however. For example, phase functions have a normalization constraint: for all ω, the condition

$$\int_{\mathcal{S}^2} p(\omega, \omega')\, d\omega' = 1 \tag{11.4}$$

must hold. This constraint means that phase functions actually define probability distributions for scattering in a particular direction.

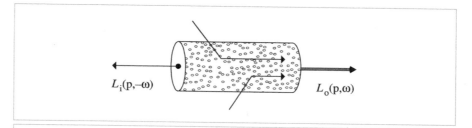

Figure 11.9: In-scattering accounts for the increase in radiance along a ray due to scattering of light from other directions. Radiance from outside the differential volume is scattered along the direction of the ray and added to the incoming radiance.

Figure 11.10: In-Scattering with the Smoke Data Set. Note the substantially different appearance compared to the other two smoke images.

The total added radiance per unit distance due to in-scattering is given by the *source term* L_s:

$$dL_o(p, \omega) = L_s(p, \omega) \, dt.$$

It accounts for both volume emission and in-scattering:

$$L_s(p, \omega) = L_e(p, \omega) + \sigma_s(p, \omega) \int_{S^2} p(p, \omega_i, \omega) \, L_i(p, \omega_i) \, d\omega_i.$$

The in-scattering portion of the source term is the product of the scattering probability per unit distance, σ_s, and the amount of added radiance at a point, which is given by the spherical integral of the product of incident radiance and the phase function. Note that the source term is very similar to the scattering equation, Equation (5.9); the main difference is that there is no cosine term since the phase function operates on radiance rather than differential irradiance.

11.2 PHASE FUNCTIONS

Just as there is a wide variety of BSDF models that describe scattering from surfaces, many phase functions have also been developed. These range from parameterized models (which can be used to fit a function with a small number of parameters to measured data) to analytic models that are based on deriving the scattered radiance distribution that results from particles with known shape and material (e.g., spherical water droplets).

In most naturally occurring media, the phase function is a 1D function of the angle θ between the two directions ω_o and ω_i; these phase functions are often written as $p(\cos \theta)$. Media with this type of phase function are called *isotropic* because their response to incident illumination is (locally) invariant under rotations. In addition to being normalized, an important property of naturally occurring phase functions is that they are *reciprocal*: the two directions can be interchanged and the phase function's value remains unchanged. Note that isotropic phase functions are trivially reciprocal because $\cos(-\theta) = \cos(\theta)$.

In *anisotropic* media that consist of particles arranged in a coherent structure, the phase function can be a 4D function of the two directions, which satisfies a more involved kind of reciprocity relation. Examples of this are crystals or media made of coherently oriented fibers; the "Further Reading" discusses these types of media further.

In a slightly confusing overloading of terminology, phase functions themselves can be isotropic or anisotropic as well. Thus, we might have an anisotropic phase function in an isotropic medium. An isotropic phase function describes equal scattering in all directions and is thus independent of either of the two directions. Because phase functions are normalized, there is only one such function:

$$p(\omega_o, \omega_i) = \frac{1}{4\pi}.$$

The PhaseFunction abstract base class defines the interface for phase functions in pbrt.

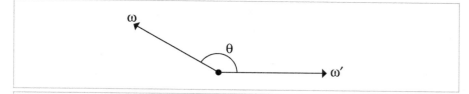

Figure 11.11: Phase functions in pbrt are implemented with the convention that both the incident direction and the outgoing direction point away from the point where scattering happens. This is the same convention that is used for BSDFs in pbrt but is different from the convention in the scattering literature, where the incident direction generally points toward the scattering point. The angle between the two directions is denoted by θ.

⟨*Media Declarations*⟩ ≡
```
class PhaseFunction {
public:
    ⟨PhaseFunction Interface 681⟩
};
```

The p() method returns the value of the phase function for the given pair of directions. As with BSDFs, pbrt uses the convention that the two directions both point away from the point where scattering occurs; this is a different convention from what is usually used in the scattering literature (Figure 11.11).

⟨*PhaseFunction Interface*⟩ ≡   681
```
    virtual Float p(const Vector3f &wo, const Vector3f &wi) const = 0;
```

A widely used phase function was developed by Henyey and Greenstein (1941). This phase function was specifically designed to be easy to fit to measured scattering data. A single parameter g (called the *asymmetry parameter*) controls the distribution of scattered light:[2]

$$p_{HG}(\cos\theta) = \frac{1}{4\pi}\frac{1-g^2}{(1+g^2+2g(\cos\theta))^{3/2}}.$$

The PhaseHG() function implements this computation.

⟨*Media Inline Functions*⟩ ≡
```
    inline Float PhaseHG(Float cosTheta, Float g) {
        Float denom = 1 + g * g + 2 * g * cosTheta;
        return Inv4Pi * (1 - g * g) / (denom * std::sqrt(denom));
    }
```

Float 1062
Inv4Pi 1063
Vector3f 60

2   Note that the sign of the $2g(\cos\theta)$ term in the denominator is the opposite of the sign used in the scattering literature. This difference is due to our use of the same direction convention for BSDFs and phase functions.

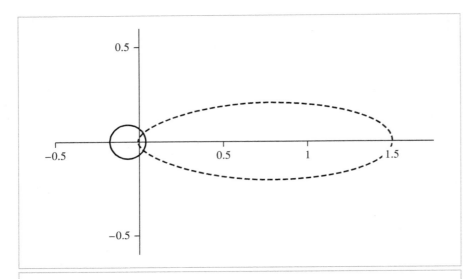

Figure 11.12: Plots of the Henyey–Greenstein Phase Function for Asymmetry g Parameters −0.35 and 0.67. Negative g values (solid line) describe phase functions that primarily scatter light back in the incident direction, and positive g values (dashed line) describe phase functions that primarily scatter light forward in the direction it was already traveling.

Figure 11.12 shows plots of the Henyey–Greenstein phase function with varying asymmetry parameters. The value of g for this model must be in the range $(−1, 1)$. Negative values of g correspond to *back-scattering*, where light is mostly scattered back toward the incident direction, and positive values correspond to forward-scattering. The greater the magnitude of g, the more scattering occurs close to the ω or $−\omega$ directions (for back-scattering and forward-scattering, respectively). See Figure 11.13 to compare the visual effect of forward- and back-scattering.

HenyeyGreenstein provides a PhaseFunction implementation of the Henyey–Greenstein model.

⟨*HenyeyGreenstein Declarations*⟩ ≡
```
class HenyeyGreenstein : public PhaseFunction {
public:
    ⟨HenyeyGreenstein Public Methods 682⟩
private:
    const Float g;
};
```

⟨*HenyeyGreenstein Public Methods*⟩ ≡   682
```
HenyeyGreenstein(Float g) : g(g) { }
```

⟨*HenyeyGreenstein Method Definitions*⟩ ≡
```
Float HenyeyGreenstein::p(const Vector3f &wo, const Vector3f &wi) const {
    return PhaseHG(Dot(wo, wi), g);
}
```

Figure 11.13: Objects filled with participating media rendered with (left) strong backward scattering ($g = -0.7$) and (right) strong forward scattering ($g = 0.7$). Because the light source is behind the object with respect to the viewer, forward scattering leads to more light reaching the camera in this case.

The asymmetry parameter g in the Henyey–Greenstein model has a precise meaning. It is the average value of the product of the phase function being approximated and the cosine of the angle between ω' and ω. Given an arbitrary phase function p, the value of g can be computed as[3]

$$g = \int_{\mathcal{S}^2} p(-\omega, \omega')(\omega \cdot \omega') \, d\omega' = 2\pi \int_0^\pi p(-\cos\theta) \, \cos\theta \, \sin\theta \, d\theta. \qquad [11.5]$$

Thus, an isotropic phase function gives $g = 0$, as expected.

Any number of phase functions can satisfy this equation; the g value alone is not enough to uniquely describe a scattering distribution. Nevertheless, the convenience of being able to easily convert a complex scattering distribution into a simple parameterized model is often more important than this potential loss in accuracy.

More complex phase functions that aren't described well with a single asymmetry parameter can often be modeled by a weighted sum of phase functions like Henyey–Greenstein, each with different parameter values:

$$p(\omega, \omega') = \sum_{i=1}^n w_i \, p_i(\omega \to \omega'),$$

where the weights w_i sum to one to maintain normalization. This generalization isn't provided in pbrt but would be easy to add.

---

3   Once more, there is a sign difference compared to the radiative transfer literature: the first argument to p is negated due to our use of the same direction convention for BSDFs and phase functions.

11.3 MEDIA

Implementations of the `Medium` base class provide various representations of volumetric scattering properties in a region of space. In a complex scene, there may be multiple `Medium` instances, each representing a different scattering effect. For example, an outdoor lake scene might have one `Medium` to model atmospheric scattering, another to model mist rising from the lake, and a third to model particles suspended in the water of the lake.

⟨*Medium Declarations*⟩ ≡
```
class Medium {
public:
    ⟨Medium Interface 684⟩
};
```

A key operation that `Medium` implementations must perform is to compute the beam transmittance, Equation (11.1), along a given ray passed to its `Tr()` method. Specifically, the method should return an estimate of the transmittance on the interval between the ray origin and the point at a distance of `Ray::tMax` from the origin.

Medium-aware `Integrators` using this interface are responsible for accounting for interactions with surfaces in the scene as well as the spatial extent of the `Medium`; hence we will assume that the ray passed to the `Tr()` method is both unoccluded and fully contained within the current `Medium`. Some implementations of this method use Monte Carlo integration to compute the transmittance; a `Sampler` is provided for this case. (See Section 15.2.)

⟨*Medium Interface*⟩ ≡   684
```
virtual Spectrum Tr(const Ray &ray, Sampler &sampler) const = 0;
```

The spatial distribution and extent of media in a scene is defined by associating `Medium` instances with the camera, lights, and primitives in the scene. For example, `Cameras` store a `Medium` pointer that gives the medium for rays leaving the camera and similarly for `Lights`.

In pbrt, the boundary between two different types of scattering media is always represented by the surface of a `GeometricPrimitive`. Rather than storing a single `Medium` pointer like lights and cameras, `GeometricPrimitives` hold a `MediumInterface`, which in turn holds pointers to one `Medium` for the interior of the primitive and one for the exterior. For all of these cases, a `nullptr` can be used to indicate a vacuum (where no volumetric scattering occurs.)

⟨*MediumInterface Declarations*⟩ ≡
```
struct MediumInterface {
    ⟨MediumInterface Public Methods 685⟩
    const Medium *inside, *outside;
};
```

This approach to specifying the extent of participating media does allow the user to specify impossible or inconsistent configurations. For example, a primitive could be specified as having one medium outside of it, and the camera could be specified as being in a different medium without a MediumInterface between the camera and the surface of the primitive. In this case, a ray leaving the primitive toward the camera would be treated as being in a different medium from a ray leaving the camera toward the primitive. In turn, light transport algorithms would be unable to compute consistent results. For pbrt's purposes, we think it's reasonable to expect that the user will be able to specify a consistent configuration of media in the scene and that the added complexity of code to check this isn't worthwhile.

A MediumInterface can be initialized with either one or two Medium pointers. If only one is provided, then it represents an interface with the same medium on both sides.

⟨*MediumInterface Public Methods*⟩ ≡   684
```
MediumInterface(const Medium *medium)
    : inside(medium), outside(medium) { }
MediumInterface(const Medium *inside, const Medium *outside)
    : inside(inside), outside(outside) { }
```

The function MediumInterface::IsMediumTransition() checks whether a particular MediumInterface instance marks a transition between two distinct media.

⟨*MediumInterface Public Methods*⟩ +≡   684
```
bool IsMediumTransition() const { return inside != outside; }
```

We can now provide a missing piece in the implementation of the GeometricPrimitive:: Intersect() method. The code in this fragment is executed whenever an intersection with a geometric primitive has been found; its job is to set the medium interface at the intersection point.

Instead of simply copying the value of the GeometricPrimitive::mediumInterface field, we will follow a slightly different approach and only use this information when this MediumInterface specifies a proper transition between participating media. Otherwise, the Ray::medium field takes precedence.

Setting the SurfaceInteraction's mediumInterface field in this way greatly simplifies the specification of scenes containing media: in particular, it is not necessary to tag every scene surface that is in contact with a medium. Instead, only non-opaque surfaces that have different media on each side require an explicit medium reference in their GeometricPrimitive::mediumInterface field. In the simplest case where a scene containing opaque objects is filled with a participating medium (e.g., haze), it is enough to tag the camera and light sources.

⟨*Initialize* SurfaceInteraction::mediumInterface *after* Shape *intersection*⟩ ≡   251
```
if (mediumInterface.IsMediumTransition())
    isect->mediumInterface = mediumInterface;
else
    isect->mediumInterface = MediumInterface(r.medium);
```

Primitives associated with shapes that represent medium boundaries generally have a Material associated with them. For example, the surface of a lake might use an instance of GlassMaterial to describe scattering at the lake surface, which also acts as the boundary between the rising mist's Medium and the lake water's Medium. However, sometimes

Figure 11.14: Scattering Media inside the Dragon. Both dragon models have the same homogeneous scattering media inside of them. On the left, the dragon's surface has a glass material. On the right, the dragon's Material * is nullptr, which indicates that the surface should be ignored by rays and is only used to delineate a participating medium's extent.

we only need the shape for the boundary surface it provides to delimit a participating medium boundary and we don't want to see the surface itself. For example, the medium representing a cloud might be bounded by a box made of triangles where the triangles are only there to delimit the cloud's extent and shouldn't otherwise affect light passing through them.

While such a surface that disappears and doesn't affect ray paths could be perfectly accurately described by a BTDF that represented perfect specular transmission with the same index of refraction on both sides, dealing with such surfaces places extra burden on the Integrators (not all of which handle this type of specular light transport well). Therefore, pbrt allows such surfaces to have a Material * that is nullptr, indicating that they do not affect light passing through them; in turn, SurfaceInteraction::bsdf will also be nullptr, and the light transport routines don't worry about light scattering from such surfaces and only account for changes in the current medium at them. Figure 11.14 has two instances of the dragon model filled with scattering media; one has a scattering surface at the boundary and the other does not.

Given these conventions for how Medium implementations are associated with rays passing through regions of space, we will implement a Scene::IntersectTr() method, which is a generalization of Scene::Intersect() that returns the first intersection with a light-scattering surface along the given ray as well as the beam transmittance up to that point. (If no intersection is found, this method returns false and doesn't initialize the provided SurfaceInteraction.)

Scene::Intersect() 24
SurfaceInteraction 116
SurfaceInteraction::bsdf 250

⟨*Scene Method Definitions*⟩ +≡
```
bool Scene::IntersectTr(Ray ray, Sampler &sampler,
        SurfaceInteraction *isect, Spectrum *Tr) const {
    *Tr = Spectrum(1.f);
    while (true) {
        bool hitSurface = Intersect(ray, isect);
        ⟨Accumulate beam transmittance for ray segment 687⟩
        ⟨Initialize next ray segment or terminate transmittance computation 687⟩
    }
}
```

Each time through the loop, the transmittance along the ray is accumulated into the overall beam transmittance `*Tr`. Recall that `Scene::Intersect()` will have updated the ray's `tMax` member variable to the intersection point if it did intersect a surface. The `Tr()` implementation will use this value to find the segment over which to compute transmittance.

⟨*Accumulate beam transmittance for ray segment*⟩ ≡   687
```
if (ray.medium)
    *Tr *= ray.medium->Tr(ray, sampler);
```

The loop ends when no intersection is found or when a scattering surface is intersected. If an optically inactive surface with its `bsdf` equal to `nullptr` is intersected, a new ray is spawned in the same direction from the intersection point, though potentially in a different medium, based on the intersection's `MediumInterface` field.[4]

⟨*Initialize next ray segment or terminate transmittance computation*⟩ ≡   687
```
if (!hitSurface)
    return false;
if (isect->primitive->GetMaterial() != nullptr)
    return true;
ray = isect->SpawnRay(ray.d);
```

11.3.1 MEDIUM INTERACTIONS

Section 2.10 introduced the general `Interaction` class as well as the `SurfaceInteraction` specialization to represent interactions at surfaces. Now that we have some machinery for describing scattering in volumes, it's worth generalizing these representations. First, we'll add two more `Interaction` constructors for interactions at points in scattering media.

⟨*Interaction Public Methods*⟩ +≡   115
```
Interaction(const Point3f &p, const Vector3f &wo, Float time,
            const MediumInterface &mediumInterface)
    : p(p), time(time), wo(wo), mediumInterface(mediumInterface) { }
```

---

4   If the current medium does change, it should have the same index of refraction as the previous one; otherwise, there should be a `Material` with a BTDF that describes the effect of refraction on the ray's direction. The implementation here doesn't verify that the two indices of refraction match, however.

⟨*Interaction Public Methods*⟩ +≡   115
```
Interaction(const Point3f &p, Float time,
            const MediumInterface &mediumInterface)
    : p(p), time(time), mediumInterface(mediumInterface) { }
```

⟨*Interaction Public Methods*⟩ +≡   115
```
bool IsMediumInteraction() const { return !IsSurfaceInteraction(); }
```

For surface interactions where Interaction::n has been set, the Medium * for a ray leaving
the surface in the direction w is returned by the GetMedium() method.

⟨*Interaction Public Methods*⟩ +≡   115
```
const Medium *GetMedium(const Vector3f &w) const {
    return Dot(w, n) > 0 ? mediumInterface.outside :
                           mediumInterface.inside;
}
```

For interactions that are known to be inside participating media, another variant of
GetMedium() that doesn't take the unnecessary outgoing direction vector returns the
Medium *.

⟨*Interaction Public Methods*⟩ +≡   115
```
const Medium *GetMedium() const {
    Assert(mediumInterface.inside == mediumInterface.outside);
    return mediumInterface.inside;
}
```

Just as the SurfaceInteraction class represents an interaction obtained by intersecting a
ray against the scene geometry, MediumInteraction represents an interaction at a point in
a scattering medium that is obtained using a similar kind of operation.

⟨*Interaction Declarations*⟩ +≡
```
class MediumInteraction : public Interaction {
public:
    ⟨MediumInteraction Public Methods 688⟩
    ⟨MediumInteraction Public Data 688⟩
};
```

⟨*MediumInteraction Public Methods*⟩ ≡   688
```
MediumInteraction(const Point3f &p, const Vector3f &wo, Float time,
                  const Medium *medium, const PhaseFunction *phase)
    : Interaction(p, wo, time, medium), phase(phase) { }
```

MediumInteraction adds a new PhaseFunction member variable to store the phase function associated with its position.

⟨*MediumInteraction Public Data*⟩ ≡   688
```
const PhaseFunction *phase;
```

11.3.2 HOMOGENEOUS MEDIUM

The HomogeneousMedium is the simplest possible medium; it represents a region of space
with constant σ_a and σ_s values throughout its extent. It uses the Henyey–Greenstein

phase function to represent scattering in the medium, also with a constant *g* value. This medium was used for the images in Figure 11.13 and 11.14.

⟨*HomogeneousMedium Declarations*⟩ ≡
```
class HomogeneousMedium : public Medium {
public:
    ⟨HomogeneousMedium Public Methods 689⟩
private:
    ⟨HomogeneousMedium Private Data 689⟩
};
```

⟨*HomogeneousMedium Public Methods*⟩ ≡   689
```
HomogeneousMedium(const Spectrum &sigma_a, const Spectrum &sigma_s,
        Float g)
    : sigma_a(sigma_a), sigma_s(sigma_s), sigma_t(sigma_s + sigma_a),
      g(g) { }
```

⟨*HomogeneousMedium Private Data*⟩ ≡   689
```
const Spectrum sigma_a, sigma_s, sigma_t;
const Float g;
```

Because σ_t is constant throughout the medium, Beer's law, Equation (11.3), can be used to compute transmittance along the ray. However, implementation of the Tr() method is complicated by some subtleties of floating-point arithmetic. As discussed in Section 3.9.1, IEEE floating point provides a representation for infinity; in pbrt, this value, Infinity, is used to initialize Ray::tMax for rays leaving cameras and lights, which is useful for ray–intersection tests in that it ensures that any actual intersection, even if far along the ray, is detected as an intersection for a ray that hasn't intersected anything yet.

However, the use of Infinity for Ray::tMax creates a small problem when applying Beer's law. In principle, we just need to compute the parametric *t* range that the ray spans, multiply by the ray direction's length, and then multiply by σ_t:

```
Float d = ray.tMax * ray.Length();
Spectrum tau = sigma_t * d;
return Exp(-tau);
```

The problem is that multiplying Infinity by zero results in the floating-point "not a number" (NaN) value, which propagates throughout all computations that use it. For a ray that passes infinitely far through a medium with zero absorption for a given spectral channel, the above code would attempt to perform the multiplication 0 * Infinity and would produce a NaN value rather than the expected transmittance of zero. The implementation here resolves this issue by clamping the ray segment length to the largest representable non-infinite floating-point value.

⟨*HomogeneousMedium Method Definitions*⟩ ≡
```
Spectrum HomogeneousMedium::Tr(const Ray &ray, Sampler &sampler) const {
    return Exp(-sigma_t * std::min(ray.tMax * ray.d.Length(), MaxFloat));
}
```

11.3.3 3D GRIDS

The GridDensityMedium class stores medium densities at a regular 3D grid of positions, similar to the way that the ImageTexture represents images with a 2D grid of samples. These samples are interpolated to compute the density at positions between the sample points. The implementation of the GridDensityMedium is in media/grid.h and media/grid.cpp.

⟨*GridDensityMedium Declarations*⟩ ≡
```
class GridDensityMedium : public Medium {
public:
    ⟨GridDensityMedium Public Methods 690⟩
private:
    ⟨GridDensityMedium Private Data 690⟩
};
```

The constructor takes a 3D array of user-supplied density values, thus allowing a variety of sources of data (physical simulation, CT scan, etc.). The smoke data set rendered in Figures 11.2, 11.5, and 11.10 is represented with a GridDensityMedium. The caller also supplies baseline values of σ_a, σ_s, and g to the constructor, which does the usual initialization of the basic scattering properties and makes a local copy of the density values.

⟨*GridDensityMedium Public Methods*⟩ ≡　　　　　　　　　　　　　　　　　　690
```
GridDensityMedium(const Spectrum &sigma_a, const Spectrum &sigma_s,
        Float g, int nx, int ny, int nz, const Transform &mediumToWorld,
        const Float *d)
    : sigma_a(sigma_a), sigma_s(sigma_s), g(g), nx(nx), ny(ny), nz(nz),
      WorldToMedium(Inverse(mediumToWorld)),
      density(new Float[nx * ny * nz]) {
    memcpy((Float *)density.get(), d, sizeof(Float) * nx * ny * nz);
    ⟨Precompute values for Monte Carlo sampling of GridDensityMedium 896⟩
}
```

⟨*GridDensityMedium Private Data*⟩ ≡　　　　　　　　　　　　　　　　　　690
```
const Spectrum sigma_a, sigma_s;
const Float g;
const int nx, ny, nz;
const Transform WorldToMedium;
std::unique_ptr<Float[]> density;
```

The Density() method of GridDensityMedium is called by GridDensityMedium::Tr(); it uses the provided samples to reconstruct the volume density function at the given point, which will already have been transformed into local coordinates using WorldToMedium. In turn, σ_a and σ_s will be scaled by the interpolated density at the point.

⟨*GridDensityMedium Method Definitions*⟩ ≡
```
    Float GridDensityMedium::Density(const Point3f &p) const {
        ⟨Compute voxel coordinates and offsets for p 691⟩
        ⟨Trilinearly interpolate density values to compute local density 691⟩
    }
```

The grid samples are assumed to be over a canonical $[0, 1]^3$ domain. (The WorldToMedium transformation should be used to place the GridDensityMedium in the scene.) To interpolate the samples around a point, the Density() method first computes the coordinates of the point with respect to the sample coordinates and the distances from the point to the samples below it (along the lines of what was done in the Film and MIPMap—see also Section 7.1.7).

⟨*Compute voxel coordinates and offsets for* p⟩ ≡   691
```
    Point3f pSamples(p.x * nx - .5f, p.y * ny - .5f, p.z * nz - .5f);
    Point3i pi = (Point3i)Floor(pSamples);
    Vector3f d = pSamples - (Point3f)pi;
```

The distances d can be used directly in a series of invocations of Lerp() to trilinearly interpolate the density at the sample point:

⟨*Trilinearly interpolate density values to compute local density*⟩ ≡   691
```
    Float d00 = Lerp(d.x, D(pi),                D(pi+Vector3i(1,0,0)));
    Float d10 = Lerp(d.x, D(pi+Vector3i(0,1,0)), D(pi+Vector3i(1,1,0)));
    Float d01 = Lerp(d.x, D(pi+Vector3i(0,0,1)), D(pi+Vector3i(1,0,1)));
    Float d11 = Lerp(d.x, D(pi+Vector3i(0,1,1)), D(pi+Vector3i(1,1,1)));
    Float d0 = Lerp(d.y, d00, d10);
    Float d1 = Lerp(d.y, d01, d11);
    return Lerp(d.z, d0, d1);
```

The D() utility method returns the density at the given integer sample position. Its only tasks are to handle out-of-bounds sample positions and to compute the appropriate array offset for the given sample. Unlike MIPMaps, where a variety of behavior is useful in the case of out-of-bounds coordinates, here it's reasonable to always return a zero density for them: the density is defined over a particular domain, and it's reasonable that points outside of it should have zero density.

⟨*GridDensityMedium Public Methods*⟩ +≡   690
```
    Float D(const Point3i &p) const {
        Bounds3i sampleBounds(Point3i(0, 0, 0), Point3i(nx, ny, nz));
        if (!InsideExclusive(p, sampleBounds))
            return 0;
        return density[(p.z * ny + p.y) * nx + p.x];
    }
```

11.4 THE BSSRDF

The bidirectional scattering-surface reflectance distribution function (BSSRDF) was introduced in Section 5.6.2; it gives exitant radiance at a point on a surface p_o given incident differential irradiance at another point p_i: $S(p_o, \omega_o, p_i, \omega_i)$. Accurately rendering translucent surfaces with subsurface scattering requires integrating over both area—points on the surface of the object being rendered—and incident direction, evaluating the BSSRDF and computing reflection with the subsurface scattering equation

$$L_o(p_o, \omega_o) = \int_A \int_{\mathcal{H}^2(n)} S(p_o, \omega_o, p_i, \omega_i)\, L_i(p_i, \omega_i) |\cos\theta_i|\, d\omega_i\, dA.$$

Subsurface light transport is described by the volumetric scattering processes introduced in Sections 11.1 and 11.2 as well as the volume light transport equation that will be introduced in Section 15.1. The BSSRDF S is a summarized representation modeling the outcome of these scattering processes between a given pair of points and directions on the boundary.

A variety of BSSRDF models have been developed to model subsurface reflection; they generally include some simplifications to the underlying scattering processes to make them tractable. One such model will be introduced in Section 15.5. Here, we will begin by specifying a fairly abstract interface analogous to BSDF. All of the code related to BSSRDFs is in the files core/bssrdf.h and core/bssrdf.cpp.

⟨*BSSRDF Declarations*⟩ ≡
```
class BSSRDF {
public:
    ⟨BSSRDF Public Methods 692⟩
    ⟨BSSRDF Interface 693⟩
protected:
    ⟨BSSRDF Protected Data 692⟩
};
```

BSSRDF implementations must pass the current (outgoing) surface interaction as well as the index of refraction of the scattering medium to the base class constructor. There is thus an implicit assumption that the index of refraction is constant throughout the medium, which is a widely used assumption in BSSRDF models.

⟨*BSSRDF Public Methods*⟩ ≡   692
```
BSSRDF(const SurfaceInteraction &po, Float eta)
    : po(po), eta(eta) { }
```

⟨*BSSRDF Protected Data*⟩ ≡   692
```
const SurfaceInteraction &po;
Float eta;
```

The key method that BSSRDF implementations must provide is one that evaluates the eight-dimensional distribution function S(), which quantifies the ratio of differential radiance at point p_o in direction ω_o to the incident differential flux at p_i from direction ω_i (Section 5.6.2). Since the p_o and ω_o arguments are already available via the BSSRDF::po and Interaction::wo fields, they aren't included in the method signature.

⟨*BSSRDF Interface*⟩ ≡   692
    `virtual Spectrum S(const SurfaceInteraction &pi, const Vector3f &wi) = 0;`

Like the BSDF, the BSSRDF interface also defines functions to sample the distribution and to evaluate the probability density of the implemented sampling scheme. The specifics of this part of the interface are discussed in Section 15.4.

During the shading process, the current Material's ComputeScatteringFunctions() method initializes the SurfaceInteraction::bssrdf member variable with an appropriate BSSRDF if the material exhibits subsurface scattering. (Section 11.4.3 will define two materials for subsurface scattering.)

11.4.1 SEPARABLE BSSRDFS

One issue with the BSSRDF interface as defined above is its extreme generality. Finding solutions to the subsurface light transport even in simple planar or spherical geometries is already a fairly challenging problem, and the fact that BSSRDF implementations can be attached to arbitrary and considerably more complex Shapes leads to an impracticably difficult context. To retain the ability to support general Shapes, we'll introduce a simpler BSSRDF representation in SeparableBSSRDF.

⟨*BSSRDF Declarations*⟩ +≡
```
class SeparableBSSRDF : public BSSRDF {
public:
    ⟨SeparableBSSRDF Public Methods 693⟩
    ⟨SeparableBSSRDF Interface 695⟩
private:
    ⟨SeparableBSSRDF Private Data 693⟩
};
```

The constructor of SeparableBSSRDF initializes a local coordinate frame defined by ss, ts, and ns, records the current light transport mode mode, and keeps a pointer to the underlying Material. The need for these values will be clarified in Section 15.4.

⟨*SeparableBSSRDF Public Methods*⟩ ≡   693
```
SeparableBSSRDF(const SurfaceInteraction &po, Float eta,
                const Material *material, TransportMode mode)
    : BSSRDF(po, eta), ns(po.shading.n), ss(Normalize(po.shading.dpdu)),
        ts(Cross(ns, ss)), material(material), mode(mode) { }
```

⟨*SeparableBSSRDF Private Data*⟩ ≡   693
```
const Normal3f ns;
const Vector3f ss, ts;
const Material *material;
const TransportMode mode;
```

The simplified SeparableBSSRDF interface casts the BSSRDF into a separable form with three independent components (one spatial and two directional):

$$S(\mathrm{p_o}, \omega_\mathrm{o}, \mathrm{p_i}, \omega_\mathrm{i}) \approx (1 - F_\mathrm{r}(\cos\theta_\mathrm{o}))\, S_\mathrm{p}(\mathrm{p_o}, \mathrm{p_i})\, S_\omega(\omega_\mathrm{i}). \qquad [11.6]$$

The Fresnel term at the beginning models the fraction of the light that is transmitted into direction ω_0 after exiting the material. A second Fresnel term contained inside $S_\omega(\omega_i)$ accounts for the influence of the boundary on the directional distribution of light entering the object from direction ω_i. The profile term S_p is a spatial distribution characterizing how far light travels after entering the material.

For high-albedo media, the scattered radiance distribution is generally fairly isotropic and the Fresnel transmittance is the most important factor for defining the final directional distribution. However, directional variation can be meaningful for low-albedo media; in that case, this approximation is less accurate.

⟨SeparableBSSRDF Public Methods⟩ +≡   693
```
Spectrum S(const SurfaceInteraction &pi, const Vector3f &wi) {
    Float Ft = 1 - FrDielectric(Dot(po.wo, po.shading.n), 1, eta);
    return Ft * Sp(pi) * Sw(wi);
}
```

Given the separable expression in Equation (11.6), the integral for determining the outgoing illumination due to subsurface scattering (Section 15.5) simplifies to

$$L_o(p_o, \omega_o) = \int_A \int_{\mathcal{H}^2(n)} S(p_o, \omega_o, p_i, \omega_i)\, L_i(p_i, \omega_i)\, |\cos\theta_i|\, d\omega_i\, dA(p_i)$$

$$= (1 - F_r(\cos\theta_o)) \int_A S_p(p_o, p_i) \int_{\mathcal{H}^2(n)} S_\omega(\omega_i)\, L_i(p_i, \omega_i)\, |\cos\theta_i|\, d\omega_i\, dA(p_i).$$

We define the directional term $S_\omega(\omega_i)$ as a scaled version of the Fresnel transmittance (Section 8.2):

$$S_\omega(\omega_i) = \frac{1 - F_r(\cos\theta_i)}{c\,\pi}. \qquad [11.7]$$

The normalization factor c is chosen so that S_ω integrates to one over the cosine-weighted hemisphere:

$$\int_{\mathcal{H}^2} S_\omega(\omega)\cos\theta\, d\omega = 1.$$

In other words,

$$c = \int_0^{2\pi} \int_0^{\frac{\pi}{2}} \frac{1 - F_r(\eta, \cos\theta)}{\pi} \sin\theta\cos\theta\, d\theta\, d\phi$$

$$= 1 - 2 \int_0^{\frac{\pi}{2}} F_r(\eta, \cos\theta)\,\sin\theta\cos\theta\, d\theta.$$

This integral is referred to as the *first moment* of the Fresnel reflectance function. Other moments involving higher powers of the cosine function also exist and frequently occur in subsurface scattering-related computations; the general definition of the ith Fresnel moment is

$$\bar{F}_{r,i}(\eta) = \int_0^{\frac{\pi}{2}} F_r(\eta, \cos\theta)\,\sin\theta\cos^i\theta\, d\theta \qquad [11.8]$$

pbrt provides two functions `FresnelMoment1()` and `FresnelMoment2()` that evaluate the corresponding moments based on polynomial fits to these functions. (We won't include their implementations in the book here.) One subtlety is that these functions follow a convention that is slightly different from the above definition—they are actually called with the reciprocal of η. This is due to their main application in Section 15.5, where they account for the effect light that is reflected back into the material due to a reflection at the internal boundary with a relative index of refraction of $1/\eta$.

⟨*BSSRDF Utility Declarations*⟩ ≡
```
Float FresnelMoment1(Float invEta);
Float FresnelMoment2(Float invEta);
```

Using `FresnelMoment1()`, the definition of `SeparableBSSRDF::Sw()` based on Equation (11.7) can be easily implemented.

⟨*SeparableBSSRDF Public Methods*⟩ +≡   693
```
Spectrum Sw(const Vector3f &w) const {
    Float c = 1 - 2 * FresnelMoment1(1 / eta);
    return (1 - FrDielectric(CosTheta(w), 1, eta)) / (c * Pi);
}
```

Decoupling the spatial and directional arguments considerably reduces the dimension of S but does not address the fundamental difficulty with regard to supporting general Shape implementations. We introduce a second approximation, which assumes that the surface is not only locally planar but that it is the distance between the points rather than their actual locations that affects the value of the BSSRDF. This reduces S_p to a function S_r that only involves distance of the two points p_o and p_i:

$$S_p(p_o, p_i) \approx S_r(\|p_o - p_i\|). \tag{11.9}$$

As before, the actual implementation of the spatial term S_p doesn't take p_o as an argument, since it is already available in `BSSRDF::po`.

⟨*SeparableBSSRDF Public Methods*⟩ +≡   693
```
Spectrum Sp(const SurfaceInteraction &pi) const {
    return Sr(Distance(po.p, pi.p));
}
```

The `SeparableBSSRDF::Sr()` method remains virtual—it is overridden in subclasses that implement specific 1D subsurface scattering profiles. Note that the dependence on the distance introduces an implicit assumption that the scattering medium is relatively homogeneous and does not strongly vary as a function of position—any variation should be larger than the mean free path length.

⟨*SeparableBSSRDF Interface*⟩ ≡   693
```
virtual Spectrum Sr(Float d) const = 0;
```

BSSRDF models are usually models of the function `Sr()` derived through a careful analysis of the light transport within a homogeneous slab. This means models such as the `SeparableBSSRDF` will yield good approximations in the planar setting, but with increasing error as the underlying geometry deviates from this assumption.

Figure 11.15: Objects rendered using the `TabulatedBSSRDF` using a variety of measured BSSRDFs. From left to right: cola, apple, skin, and ketchup.

11.4.2 TABULATED BSSRDF

⟨*BSSRDF Declarations*⟩ +≡
```
class TabulatedBSSRDF : public SeparableBSSRDF {
public:
    ⟨TabulatedBSSRDF Public Methods 697⟩
private:
    ⟨TabulatedBSSRDF Private Data 697⟩
};
```

The single current implementation of the `SeparableBSSRDF` interface in pbrt is the `TabulatedBSSRDF` class. It provides access to a tabulated BSSRDF representation that can handle a wide range of scattering profiles including measured real-world BSSRDFs. `TabulatedBSSRDF` uses the same type of adaptive spline-based interpolation method that was also used by the `FourierBSDF` reflectance model (Section 8.6); in this case, we are interpolating the distance-dependent scattering profile function S_r from Equation (11.9). The `FourierBSDF`'s second stage of capturing directional variation using Fourier series is not needed. Figure 11.15 shows spheres rendered using the `TabulatedBSSRDF`.

It is important to note that the radial profile S_r is only a 1D function when all BSSRDF material properties are fixed. More generally, it depends on four additional parameters: the index of refraction η, the scattering anisotropy g, the albedo ρ, and the extinction coefficient σ_t, leading to a complete function signature $S_r(\eta, g, \rho, \sigma_t, r)$ that is unfortunately too high-dimensional for discretization. We must thus either remove or fix some of the parameters.

FourierBSDF 555
SeparableBSSRDF 693

Consider that the only parameter with physical units (apart from r) is σ_t. This parameter quantifies the rate of scattering or absorption interactions per unit distance. The effect of σ_t is simple: it only controls the spatial scale of the BSSRDF profile. To reduce the dimension of the necessary tables, we thus fix $\sigma_t = 1$ and tabulate a *unitless* version of the BSSRDF profile.

When a lookup for a given extinction coefficient σ_t and radius r occurs at run time we find the corresponding unitless *optical radius* $r_{\text{optical}} = \sigma_t r$ and evaluate the lower-dimensional tabulation as follows:

$$S_r(\eta, g, \rho, \sigma_t, r) = \sigma_t{}^2\, S_r\left(\eta, g, \rho, 1, r_{\text{optical}}\right) \qquad [11.10]$$

Since S_r is a 2D density function in polar coordinates (r, ϕ), a corresponding scale factor of $\sigma_t{}^2$ is needed to account for this change of variables (see also Section 13.5.2).

We will also fix the index of refraction η and scattering anisotropy parameter g—in practice, this means that these parameters cannot be textured over an object that has a material that uses a TabulatedBSSRDF. These simplifications leave us with a fairly manageable 2D function that is only discretized over albedos ρ and optical radii r.

The TabulatedBSSRDF constructor takes all parameters of the BSSRDF constructor in addition to spectrally varying absorption and scattering coefficients σ_a and σ_s. It precomputes the extinction coefficient $\sigma_t = \sigma_a + \sigma_s$ and albedo $\rho = \sigma_s/\sigma_t$ for the current surface location, avoiding issues with a division by zero when there is no extinction for a given spectral channel.

⟨*TabulatedBSSRDF Public Methods*⟩ ≡   696
```
TabulatedBSSRDF(const SurfaceInteraction &po,
        const Material *material, TransportMode mode, Float eta,
        const Spectrum &sigma_a, const Spectrum &sigma_s,
        const BSSRDFTable &table)
    : SeparableBSSRDF(po, eta, material, mode), table(table) {
    sigma_t = sigma_a + sigma_s;
    for (int c = 0; c < Spectrum::nSamples; ++c)
        rho[c] = sigma_t[c] != 0 ? (sigma_s[c] / sigma_t[c]) : 0;
}
```

⟨*TabulatedBSSRDF Private Data*⟩ ≡   696
```
const BSSRDFTable &table;
Spectrum sigma_t, rho;
```

Detailed information about the scattering profile S_r is supplied via the table parameter, which is an instance of the BSSRDFTable data structure:

⟨*BSSRDF Declarations*⟩ +≡
```
struct BSSRDFTable {
    ⟨BSSRDFTable Public Data 698⟩
    ⟨BSSRDFTable Public Methods 698⟩
};
```

Instances of BSSRDFTable record samples of the function S_r taken at a set of single scattering albedos $(\rho_1, \rho_2, \ldots, \rho_n)$ and radii $(r_1, r_2, \ldots, r_m)$. The spacing between radius and albedo samples will generally be non-uniform in order to more accurately represent the underlying function. Section 15.5.8 will show how to initialize the BSSRDFTable for a specific BSSRDF model.

We omit the constructor implementation, which takes the desired resolution and allocates memory for the representation.

⟨*BSSRDFTable Public Methods*⟩ ≡   697
    BSSRDFTable(int nRhoSamples, int nRadiusSamples);

The sample locations and counts are exposed as public member variables.

⟨*BSSRDFTable Public Data*⟩ ≡   697
    const int nRhoSamples, nRadiusSamples;
    std::unique_ptr<Float[]> rhoSamples, radiusSamples;

A sample value is stored in the profile member variable for each of the $m \times n$ pairs (ρ_i, r_j).

⟨*BSSRDFTable Public Data*⟩ +≡   697
    std::unique_ptr<Float[]> profile;

Note that the TabulatedBSSRDF::rho member variable gives the reduction in energy after a single scattering event; this is different from the material's overall albedo, which takes all orders of scattering into account. To stress the difference, we will refer to these different types of albedos as the *single scattering albedo* ρ and the *effective albedo* ρ_{eff}.

We define the effective albedo as the following integral of the profile S_r in polar coordinates.

$$\rho_{\text{eff}} = \int_0^{2\pi} \int_0^{\infty} r\, S_r(r)\, dr\, d\phi = 2\pi \int_0^{\infty} r\, S_r(r)\, dr. \qquad [11.11]$$

The value of ρ_{eff} will frequently be accessed both by the profile sampling code and by the KdSubsurfaceMaterial. We introduce an array rhoEff of length BSSRDFTable::nRho Samples, which maps every albedo sample to its corresponding effective albedo.

⟨*BSSRDFTable Public Data*⟩ +≡   697
    std::unique_ptr<Float[]> rhoEff;

Computation of ρ_{eff} will be discussed in Section 15.5. For now, we only note that it is a nonlinear and strictly monotonically increasing function of the single scattering albedo ρ.

Given radius value r and single scattering albedo, the function Sr() implements a spline-interpolated lookup into the tabulated profile. The albedo parameter is taken to be the TabulatedBSSRDF::rho value. There is thus an implicit assumption that the albedo does not vary within the support of the BSSRDF profile centered around p_o.

Since the albedo is of type Spectrum, the function performs a separate profile lookup for each spectral channel and returns a Spectrum as a result. The return value must be clamped in case the interpolation produces slightly negative values.

⟨*BSSRDF Method Definitions*⟩ ≡
```
Spectrum TabulatedBSSRDF::Sr(Float r) const {
    Spectrum Sr(0.f);
    for (int ch = 0; ch < Spectrum::nSamples; ++ch) {
        ⟨Convert r into unitless optical radius rₒₚₜᵢₖₐₗ 699⟩
        ⟨Compute spline weights to interpolate BSSRDF on channel ch 699⟩
        ⟨Set BSSRDF value Sr[ch] using tensor spline interpolation 699⟩
    }
    ⟨Transform BSSRDF value into world space units 700⟩
    return Sr.Clamp();
}
```

The first line in the loop applies the scaling identity from Equation (11.10) to obtain an optical radius for the current channel `ch`.

⟨*Convert r into unitless optical radius* r_{optical}⟩ ≡   **699, 914**
```
Float rOptical = r * sigma_t[ch];
```

Given the adjusted radius `rOptical` and the albedo `TabulatedBSSRDF::rho[ch]` at location `BSSRDF::po`, we next call `CatmullRomWeights()` to obtain offsets and cubic spline weights to interpolate the profile values. This step is identical to the `FourierBSDF` interpolation in Section 8.6.

⟨*Compute spline weights to interpolate BSSRDF on channel* ch⟩ ≡   **699**
```
int rhoOffset, radiusOffset;
Float rhoWeights[4], radiusWeights[4];
if (!CatmullRomWeights(table.nRhoSamples, table.rhoSamples.get(),
                       rho[ch], &rhoOffset, rhoWeights) ||
    !CatmullRomWeights(table.nRadiusSamples, table.radiusSamples.get(),
                       rOptical, &radiusOffset, radiusWeights))
    continue;
```

We can now sum over the product of the spline weights and the profile values.

⟨*Set BSSRDF value* Sr[ch] *using tensor spline interpolation*⟩ ≡   **699**
```
Float sr = 0;
for (int i = 0; i < 4; ++i) {
    for (int j = 0; j < 4; ++j) {
        Float weight = rhoWeights[i] * radiusWeights[j];
        if (weight != 0)
            sr += weight * table.EvalProfile(rhoOffset + i,
                                             radiusOffset + j);
    }
}
⟨Cancel marginal PDF factor from tabulated BSSRDF profile 700⟩
Sr[ch] = sr;
```

A convenience method in BSSRDFTable helps with finding profile values.

⟨*BSSRDFTable Public Methods*⟩ +≡   **697**
```
    inline Float EvalProfile(int rhoIndex, int radiusIndex) const {
        return profile[rhoIndex * nRadiusSamples + radiusIndex];
    }
```

It's necessary to cancel a multiplicative factor of $2\pi\ r_{\text{optical}}$ that came from the entries of BSSRDFTable::profile related to Equation (11.11). This factor is present in the tabularized values to facilitate importance sampling (more about this in Section 15.4). Since it is not part of the definition of the BSSRDF, the term must be removed here.

⟨*Cancel marginal PDF factor from tabulated BSSRDF profile*⟩ ≡   **699, 914**
```
    if (rOptical != 0)
        sr /= 2 * Pi * rOptical;
```

Finally, we apply the change of variables factor from Equation (11.10) to convert the interpolated unitless BSSRDF value in Sr into world space units.

⟨*Transform BSSRDF value into world space units*⟩ ≡   **699**
```
    Sr *= sigma_t * sigma_t;
```

11.4.3 SUBSURFACE SCATTERING MATERIALS

There are two Materials for translucent objects: SubsurfaceMaterial, which is defined in materials/subsurface.h and materials/subsurface.cpp, and KdSubsurfaceMaterial, defined in materials/kdsubsurface.h and materials/kdsubsurface.cpp. The only difference between these two materials is how the scattering properties of the medium are specified.

⟨*SubsurfaceMaterial Declarations*⟩ ≡
```
    class SubsurfaceMaterial : public Material {
    public:
        ⟨SubsurfaceMaterial Public Methods⟩
    private:
        ⟨SubsurfaceMaterial Private Data 701⟩
    };
```

SubsurfaceMaterial stores textures that allow the scattering properties to vary as a function of the position on the surface. Note that this isn't the same as scattering properties that vary as a function of 3D inside the scattering medium, but it can give a reasonable approximation to heterogeneous media in some cases. (Note, however, that if used with spatially varying textures, this feature destroys reciprocity of the BSSRDF, since these textures are evaluated at just one of the two scattering points, and so interchanging them will generally result in different values from the texture.[5])

---

5   A reciprocal version of this scheme could be obtained by averaging the albedos at p_i and p_o, though this is incompatible with the sampling scheme that is used currently.

In addition to the volumetric scattering properties, a number of textures allow the user to specify coefficients for a BSDF that represents perfect or glossy specular reflection and transmission at the surface.

⟨*SubsurfaceMaterial Private Data*⟩ ≡   700
```
const Float scale;
std::shared_ptr<Texture<Spectrum>> Kr, Kt, sigma_a, sigma_s;
std::shared_ptr<Texture<Float>> uRoughness, vRoughness;
std::shared_ptr<Texture<Float>> bumpMap;
const Float eta;
const bool remapRoughness;
BSSRDFTable table;
```

The ComputeScatteringFunctions() method uses the textures to compute the values of the scattering properties at the point. The absorption and scattering coefficients are then scaled by the scale member variable, which provides an easy way to change the units of the scattering properties. (Recall that they're expected to be specified in terms of inverse meters.) Finally, the method creates a TabulatedBSSRDF with these parameters.

⟨*SubsurfaceMaterial Method Definitions*⟩ ≡
```
void SubsurfaceMaterial::ComputeScatteringFunctions(
        SurfaceInteraction *si, MemoryArena &arena, TransportMode mode,
        bool allowMultipleLobes) const {
    ⟨Perform bump mapping with bumpMap, if present 579⟩
    ⟨Initialize BSDF for SubsurfaceMaterial⟩
    Spectrum sig_a = scale * sigma_a->Evaluate(*si).Clamp();
    Spectrum sig_s = scale * sigma_s->Evaluate(*si).Clamp();
    si->bssrdf = ARENA_ALLOC(arena, TabulatedBSSRDF)(
        *si, this, mode, eta, sig_a, sig_s, table);
}
```

The fragment ⟨*Initialize BSDF for* SubsurfaceMaterial⟩ won't be included here; it follows the now familiar approach of allocating appropriate BxDF components for the BSDF according to which textures have nonzero SPDs.

Directly setting the absorption and scattering coefficients to achieve a desired visual look is difficult. The parameters have a nonlinear and unintuitive effect on the result. The KdSubsurfaceMaterial allows the user to specify the subsurface scattering properties in terms of the diffuse reflectance of the surface and the mean free path $1/\sigma_t$. It then uses the SubsurfaceFromDiffuse() utility function, which will be defined in Section 15.5, to compute the corresponding intrinsic scattering properties.

Being able to specify translucent materials in this manner is particularly useful in that it makes it possible to use standard texture maps that might otherwise be used for diffuse reflection to define scattering properties (again with the caveat that varying properties on the surface don't properly correspond to varying properties in the medium).

We won't include the definition of KdSubsurfaceMaterial here since its implementation just evaluates Textures to compute the diffuse reflection and mean free path values and calls `SubsurfaceFromDiffuse()` to compute the scattering properties needed by the BSSRDF.

Finally, `GetMediumScatteringProperties()` is a utility function that has a small library of measured scattering data for translucent materials; it returns the corresponding scattering properties if it has an entry for the given name. (For a list of the valid names, see the implementation in `core/media.cpp`.) The data provided by this function is from papers by Jensen et al. (2001b) and Narasimhan et al. (2006).

⟨*Media Declarations*⟩ +≡
```
bool GetMediumScatteringProperties(const std::string &name,
    Spectrum *sigma_a, Spectrum *sigma_s);
```

FURTHER READING

The books written by van de Hulst (1980) and Preisendorfer (1965, 1976) are excellent introductions to volume light transport. The seminal book by Chandrasekhar (1960) is another excellent resource, although it is mathematically challenging. See also the "Further Reading" section of Chapter 15 for more references on this topic.

The Henyey–Greenstein phase function was originally described by Henyey and Greenstein (1941). Detailed discussion of scattering and phase functions, along with derivations of phase functions that describe scattering from independent spheres, cylinders, and other simple shapes, can be found in van de Hulst's book (1981). Extensive discussion of the Mie and Rayleigh scattering models is also available there. Hansen and Travis's survey article is also a good introduction to the variety of commonly used phase functions (Hansen and Travis 1974).

While the Henyey–Greenstein model often works well, there are many materials that it can't represent accurately. Gkioulekas et al. (2013b) showed that sums of Henyey–Greenstein and von Mises-Fisher lobes are more accurate for many materials than Henyey–Greenstein alone and derived a 2D parameter space that allows for intuitive control of translucent appearence.

Just as procedural modeling of textures is an effective technique for shading surfaces, procedural modeling of volume densities can be used to describe realistic-looking volumetric objects like clouds and smoke. Perlin and Hoffert (1989) described early work in this area, and the book by Ebert et al. (2003) has a number of sections devoted to this topic, including further references. More recently, accurate physical simulation of the dynamics of smoke and fire has led to extremely realistic volume data sets, including the ones used in this chapter; see, for example, Fedkiw, Stam, and Jensen (2001). See the book by Wrenninge (2012) for further information about modeling participating media, with particular focus on techniques used in modern feature film production.

In this chapter, we have ignored all issues related to sampling and antialiasing of volume density functions that are represented by samples in a 3D grid, although these issues should be considered, especially in the case of a volume that occupies just a few pixels on the screen. Furthermore, we have used a simple triangle filter to reconstruct densities at intermediate positions, which is suboptimal for the same reasons as the triangle filter is not a high-quality image reconstruction filter. Marschner and Lobb (1994) presented the theory and practice of sampling and reconstruction for 3D data sets, applying ideas similar to those in Chapter 7. See also the paper by Theußl, Hauser, and Gröller (2000) for a comparison of a variety of windowing functions for volume reconstruction with the sinc function and a discussion of how to derive optimal parameters for volume reconstruction filter functions.

Acquiring volumetric scattering properties of real-world objects is particularly difficult, requiring solving the inverse problem of determining the values that lead to the measured result. See Jensen et al. (2001b), Goesele et al. (2004), Narasimhan et al. (2006), and Peers et al. (2006) for recent work on acquiring scattering properties for subsurface scattering. More recently, Gkioulekas et al. (2013a) produced accurate measurements of a variety of media. Hawkins et al. (2005) have developed techniques to measure properties of media like smoke, acquiring measurements in real time. Another interesting approach to this problem was introduced by Frisvad et al. (2007), who developed methods to compute these properties from a lower-level characterization of the scattering properties of the medium.

Acquiring the volumetric density variation of participating media is also challenging. See work by Fuchs et al. (2007), Atcheson et al. (2008), and Gu et al. (2013a) for a variety of approaches to this problem, generally based on illuminating the medium in particular ways while photographing it from one or more viewpoints.

The medium representation used by GridDensityMedium doesn't adapt its spatial sampling rate as the amount of local detail in the underlying medium changes. Furthermore, its on-disk representation is a fairly inefficient string of floating-point values encoded as text. See Museth's VDB format (2013), or the Field3D system, which is described by Wrenninge (2015), for industrial-strength volume representation formats and libraries.

EXERCISES

◉ 11.1 Given a 1D volume density that is an arbitrary function of height $f(h)$, the optical distance between any two 3D points can be computed very efficiently if the integral $\int_0^{h'} f(h)\, dh$ is precomputed and stored in a table for a set of h' values (Perlin 1985b; Max 1986). Work through the mathematics to show the derivation for this approach, and implement it in pbrt by implementing a new Medium that takes an arbitrary function or a 1D table of density values. Compare the efficiency and accuracy of this approach to the default implementation of Medium::Tr(), which uses Monte Carlo integration.

◉ 11.2 The GridDensityMedium class uses a relatively large amount of memory for complex volume densities. Determine its memory requirements when used for the smoke images in this chapter, and modify its implementation to reduce memory use. One approach is to detect regions of space with constant (or relatively constant) density values using an octree data structure and to only refine the octree in regions where the densities are changing. Another possibility is to use less memory to record each density value, for example, by computing the minimum and maximum densities and then using 8 or 16 bits per density value to interpolate between them. What sorts of errors appear when either of these approaches is pushed too far?

◉ **11.3**   Implement a new Medium that computes the scattering density at points in the medium procedurally—for example, by using procedural noise functions like those discussed in Section 10.6. You may find useful inspiration for procedural volume modeling primitives in Wrenninge's book (2012).

◉ **11.4**   A shortcoming of a fully-procedural Medium like the one in Exercise 11.3 can be the inefficiency of evaluating the medium's procedural functions repeatedly. Add a caching layer to a procedural medium that, for example, maintains a set of small regular voxel grids over regions of space. When a density lookup is performed, first check the cache to see if a value can be interpolated from one of the grids; otherwise update the cache to store the density function over a region of space that includes the lookup point. Study how many cache entries (and how much memory is consequently required) are needed for good performance. How do the cache size requirements change with volumetric path tracing that only accounts for direct lighting versus full global illumination? How do you explain this difference?

Medium 684

CHAPTER TWELVE

12 LIGHT SOURCES

In order for objects in a scene to be visible, there must be a source of illumination so that some light is reflected from them to the camera sensor. This chapter first describes different physical processes that lead to photon emission and then introduces the abstract Light class, which defines the interface used for light sources in pbrt. The implementations of a number of useful light sources follow. Because the implementations of different types of lights are all hidden behind a carefully designed interface, the light transport routines in Chapters 14, 15, and 16 can operate without knowing which particular types of lights are in the scene, similar to how acceleration structures can hold collections of different types of primitives without needing to know the details of their actual representations.

This chapter does not include implementations of all of the Light methods for all of the types of lights that are introduced. Many of the quantities related to complex light sources cannot be computed in closed form, and so Monte Carlo integration is needed. Therefore, the remainder of the Light methods are implemented in Section 14.2, after Monte Carlo methods has been introduced.

A wide variety of light source models are introduced in this chapter, although the variety is slightly limited by pbrt's physically based design. Many non-physical light source models have been developed for computer graphics, incorporating control over properties like the rate at which the light falls off with distance, which objects are illuminated by the light, which objects cast shadows from the light, and so on. These sorts of controls are incompatible with physically based light transport algorithms and thus can't be provided in the models here. As an example of the problems such lighting controls pose, consider a light that doesn't cast shadows: the total energy arriving at surfaces in the scene increases without bound as more surfaces are added. Consider a series of concentric shells of spheres around such a light; if occlusion is ignored, each added shell increases the total received energy. This directly violates the principle that the total energy arriving at surfaces illuminated by the light can't be greater than the total energy emitted by the light.

Physically Based Rendering: From Theory To Implementation.
http://dx.doi.org/10.1016/B978-0-12-800645-0.50012-9

12.1 LIGHT EMISSION

All objects with temperature above absolute zero have moving atoms. In turn, as described by Maxwell's equations, the motion of atomic particles that hold electrical charges causes objects to emit electromagnetic radiation over a range of wavelengths. As we'll see shortly, most of the emission is at infrared frequencies for objects at room temperature; objects need to be much warmer to emit meaningful amounts of electromagnetic radiation at visible frequencies.

Many different types of light sources have been invented to convert energy into emitted electromagnetic radiation. Understanding some of the physical processes involved is helpful for accurately modeling light sources for rendering. A number are in wide use today:

- Incandescent (tungsten) lamps have a small tungsten filament. The flow of electricity through the filament heats it, which in turn causes it to emit electromagnetic radiation with a distribution of wavelengths that depends on the filament's temperature. A frosted glass enclosure is often present to absorb some of the wavelengths generated in order to achieve a desired SPD. With an incandescent light, much of the power in the SPD of the emitted electromagnetic radiation is in the infrared bands, which in turn means that much of the energy consumed by the light is turned into heat rather than light.
- Halogen lamps also have a tungsten filament, but the enclosure around them is filled with halogen gas. Over time, part of the filament in an incandescent light evaporates when it's heated; the halogen gas causes this evaporated tungsten to return to the filament, which lengthens the life of the light. Because it returns to the filament, the evaporated tungsten doesn't adhere to the bulb surface (as it does with regular incandescent bulbs), which also prevents the bulb from darkening.
- Gas-discharge lamps pass electrical current through hydrogen, neon, argon, or vaporized metal gas, which causes light to be emitted at specific wavelengths that depend on the particular atom in the gas. (Atoms that emit relatively little of their electromagnetic radiation in the not-useful infrared frequencies are selected for the gas.) Because a broader spectrum of wavelengths are generally more visually desirable than the chosen atoms generate directly, a fluorescent coating on the bulb's interior is often used to transform the emitted frequencies to a wider range. (The fluorescent coating also helps by converting ultraviolet wavelengths to visible wavelengths.)
- LED lights are based on electroluminescence: they use materials that emit photons due to electrical current passing through it.

For all of these sources, the underlying physical process is electrons colliding with atoms, which pushes their outer electrons to a higher energy level. When such an electron returns to a lower energy level, a photon is emitted. There are many other interesting processes that create light, including chemoluminescence (as seen in light sticks) and bioluminescence—a form of chemoluminescence seen in fireflies. Though interesting in their own right, we won't consider their mechanisms further here.

Luminous efficacy measures how effectively a light source converts power to visible illumination, accounting for the fact that for human observers, emission in non-visible wavelengths is of little value. Interestingly enough, it is the ratio of a photometric quantity (the emitted luminous flux) to a radiometric quantity (either the total power it uses or the total power that it emits overall wavelengths, measured in flux):

$$\frac{\int \Phi_e(\lambda) V(\lambda) \, d\lambda}{\int \Phi_i(\lambda) \, d\lambda},$$

where $V(\lambda)$ is the spectral response curve introduced in Section 5.4.3.

Luminous efficacy has units of lumens per Watt. If Φ_i is the power consumed by the light source (rather than the emitted power), then luminous efficacy also incorporates a measure of how effectively the light source converts power to electromagnetic radiation. Luminous efficacy can also be defined as a ratio of luminous exitance (the photometric equivalent of radiant exitance) to irradiance at a point on the surface, or as the ratio of exitant luminance to radiance at a point on a surface in a particular direction.

A typical value of luminous efficacy for an incandescent tungsten lightbulb is around 15 lm/W. The highest value it can possibly have is 683, for a perfectly efficient light source that emits all of its light at $\lambda = 555$ nm, the peak of the $V(\lambda)$ function. (While such a light would have high efficacy, it wouldn't necessarily be a pleasant one as far as human observers are concerned.)

12.1.1 BLACKBODY EMITTERS

A *blackbody* is a perfect emitter: it converts power to electromagnetic radiation as efficiently as physically possible. While true blackbodies aren't physically realizable, some emitters exhibit near-blackbody behavior. Blackbodies also have a useful closed-form expression for their emission as a function of temperature and wavelength that is useful for modeling non-blackbody emitters.

Blackbodies are so-named because they absorb absolutely all incident power, reflecting none of it. Thus, an actual blackbody would appear perfectly black, no matter how much light was illuminating it. Intuitively, the reasons that perfect absorbers are also perfect emitters stem from the fact that absorption is the reverse operation of emission. Thus, if time was reversed, all of the perfectly absorbed power would be perfectly efficiently re-emitted.

Planck's law gives the radiance emitted by a blackbody as a function of wavelength λ and temperature T measured in Kelvins:

$$L_e(\lambda, T) = \frac{2hc^2}{\lambda^5 \left(e^{hc/\lambda k_b T} - 1\right)}, \tag{12.1}$$

where c is the speed of light in the medium (299, 792, 458 m/s in a vacuum), h is Planck's constant, $6.62606957 \times 10^{-34}$ J s, and k_b is the Boltzmann constant, $1.3806488 \times 10^{-23}$ J/K, where K is temperature in Kelvin. Blackbody emitters are perfectly diffuse; they emit radiance equally in all directions.

Figure 12.1 plots the emitted radiance distributions of a blackbody for a number of temperatures.

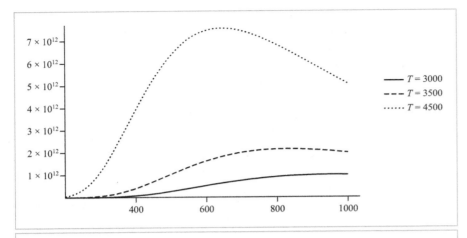

Figure 12.1: Plots of emitted radiance as a function of wavelength for blackbody emitters at a few temperatures, as given by Equation (12.1). Note that as temperature increases, more of the emitted light is in the visible frequencies (roughly 370 nm–730 nm) and that the spectral distribution shifts from reddish colors to bluish colors as the temperature increases. The total amount of emitted energy grows quickly as temperature increases, as described by the Stefan–Boltzmann law in Equation (12.2).

The `Blackbody()` function computes emitted radiance at the given temperature `T` in Kelvin for the `n` wavelengths in `lambda`.

⟨*Spectrum Method Definitions*⟩ +≡
```
void Blackbody(const Float *lambda, int n, Float T, Float *Le) {
    const Float c = 299792458;
    const Float h = 6.62606957e-34;
    const Float kb = 1.3806488e-23;
    for (int i = 0; i < n; ++i) {
        ⟨Compute emitted radiance for blackbody at wavelength lambda[i] 710⟩
    }
}
```

The `Blackbody()` function takes wavelengths in nm, but the constants for Equation (12.1) are in terms of meters. Therefore, we must first convert the wavelength to meters by scaling it by 10^{-9}.

⟨*Compute emitted radiance for blackbody at wavelength* `lambda[i]`⟩ ≡   710
```
Float l = lambda[i] * 1e-9;
Float lambda5 = (l * l) * (l * l) * l;
Le[i] = (2 * h * c * c) /
    (lambda5 * (std::exp((h * c) / (l * kb * T)) - 1));
```

The *Stefan–Boltzmann law* gives the radiant exitance (recall that this is the outgoing irradiance) at a point p for a blackbody emitter:

$$M(\mathrm{p}) = \sigma T^4,\qquad\qquad [12.2]$$

Float 1062

where σ is the Stefan–Boltzmann constant, 5.67032×10^{-8} W m^{-2} K^{-4}. Note that the total emission over all frequencies grows very rapidly—at the rate T^4. Thus, doubling the temperature of a blackbody emitter increases the total energy emitted by a factor of 16.

Because the power emitted by a blackbody grows so quickly with temperature, it can also be useful to compute the normalized SPD for a blackbody where the maximum value of the SPD at any wavelength is 1. This is easily done with *Wien's displacement law*, which gives the wavelength where emission of a blackbody is maximum given its temperature:

$$\lambda_{\max} = \frac{b}{T},$$

[12.3]

where b is Wien's displacement constant, 2.8977721×10^{-3} m K.

⟨*Spectrum Method Definitions*⟩ +≡
```
void BlackbodyNormalized(const Float *lambda, int n, Float T,
        Float *Le) {
    Blackbody(lambda, n, T, Le);
    ⟨Normalize Le values based on maximum blackbody radiance 711⟩
}
```

Wien's displacement law gives the wavelength in meters where emitted radiance is at its maximum; we must convert this value to nm before calling Blackbody() to find the corresponding radiance value.

⟨*Normalize* Le *values based on maximum blackbody radiance*⟩ ≡   711
```
Float lambdaMax = 2.8977721e-3 / T * 1e9;
Float maxL;
Blackbody(&lambdaMax, 1, T, &maxL);
for (int i = 0; i < n; ++i)
    Le[i] /= maxL;
```

The emission behavior of non-blackbodies is described by *Kirchoff's law*, which says that the emitted radiance distribution at any frequency is equal to the emission of a perfect blackbody at that frequency times the fraction of incident radiance at that frequency that is absorbed by the object. (This relationship follows from the object being assumed to be in thermal equilibrium.) The fraction of radiance absorbed is equal to 1 minus the amount reflected, and so the emitted radiance is

$$L'_e(T, \omega, \lambda) = L_e(T, \lambda)(1 - \rho_{hd}(\omega)),$$

[12.4]

where $L_e(T, \lambda)$ is the emitted radiance given by Planck's law, Equation (12.1), and $\rho_{hd}(\omega)$ is the hemispherical-directional reflectance from Equation (8.1).

The blackbody emission distribution provides as useful metric for describing the emission characteristics of non-blackbody emitters through the notion of *color temperature*. If the shape of the SPD of an emitter is similar to the blackbody distribution at some temperature, then we can say that the emitter has the corresponding color temperature. One approach to find color temperature is to take the wavelength where the light's emission is highest and find the corresponding temperature using Equation (12.3).

Incandescent tungsten lamps are generally around 2700 K color temperature, and tungsten halogen lamps are around 3000 K. Fluorescent lights may range all the way from

Blackbody() 710
Float 1062

2700 K to 6500 K. Generally speaking, color temperatures over 5000 K are described as "cool," while 2700–3000 K is described as "warm."

12.1.2 STANDARD ILLUMINANTS

Another useful way of categorizing light emission distributions are a number of "standard illuminants" that have been defined by Commission Internationale de l'Éclairage (CIE), which also specified the XYZ matching curves that we saw in Section 5.2.1.

The Standard Illuminant A was introduced in 1931 and was intended to represent average incandescent light. It corresponds to a blackbody radiator of about 2856 K. (It was originally defined as a blackbody at 2850 K, but the precision of the constants used in Planck's law subsequently improved. Therefore, the specification was updated to be in terms of the 1931 constants, so that the illuminant was unchanged.) Figure 12.2 shows a plot of the SPD of the A illuminant.

(The B and C illuminants were intended to model daylight at two times of day and were generated with an A illuminant in combination with specific filters. They are no longer used. The E illuminant is defined as a constant-valued SPD and is used only for comparisons to other illuminants.)

The D illuminant describes various phases of daylight. It was defined based on characteristic vector analysis of a variety of daylight SPDs, which made it possible to express daylight in terms of a linear combination of three terms (one fixed and two weighted), with one weight essentially corresponding to yellow-blue color change due to cloudiness and the other corresponding to pink-green due to water in the atmosphere (from haze, etc.). D65 is roughly 6504 K color temperature (not 6500 K—again due to changes in the values used for the constants in Planck's law) and is intended to correspond to mid-day

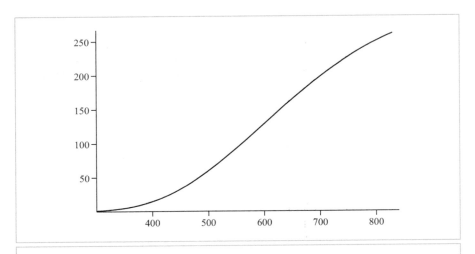

Figure 12.2: Plot of the CIE Standard Illuminant A's SPD as a Function of Wavelength in nm. This illuminant represents incandescent illumination and is close to a blackbody at 2856 K.

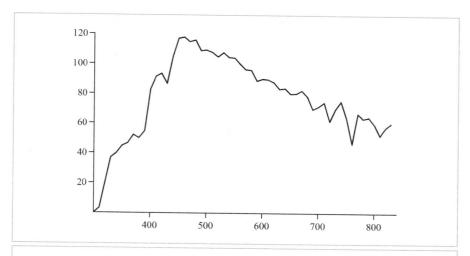

Figure 12.3: Plot of the CIE Standard Illuminant D's SPD as a Function of Wavelength in nm. This illuminant represents noontime daylight in at European latitudes.

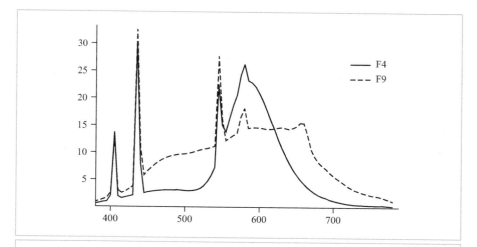

Figure 12.4: Plots of the F4 and F9 Standard Illuminants as a Function of Wavelength in nm. These represent two fluorescent lights. Note that the SPDs are quite different. Spikes in the two distributions correspond to the wavelengths directly emitted by atoms in the gas, while the other wavelengths are generated by the bulb's fluorescent coating. The F9 illuminant is a "broadband" emitter that uses multiple phosphors to achieve a more uniform spectral distribution.

sunlight in Europe. (See Figure 12.3.) The CIE recommends that this illuminant be used for daylight unless there's a specific reason not to.

Finally, the F series of illuminants describes fluorescents; it is based on measurements of a number of actual fluorescent lights. Figure 12.4 shows the SPDs of two of them.

The files named cie.stdillum.* in the scenes/spds directory in the pbrt distribution have the SPDs of the standard illuminants, measured at 5-nm increments from 300 nm to 830 nm.

12.2 LIGHT INTERFACE

The core lighting routines and interfaces are in core/light.h and core/light.cpp. Implementations of particular lights are in individual source files in the lights/ directory.

⟨*Light Declarations*⟩ ≡
   class Light {
   public:
      ⟨*Light Interface* **715**⟩
      ⟨*Light Public Data* **715**⟩
   protected:
      ⟨*Light Protected Data* **715**⟩
   };

All lights share four common parameters:

1. The flags parameter indicates the fundamental light source type—for instance, whether or not the light is described by a delta distribution. (Examples of such lights include point lights, which emit illumination from a single point, and directional lights, where all light arrives from the same direction.) The Monte Carlo algorithms that sample illumination from light sources need to be aware of which lights are described by delta distributions, since this affects some of their computations.

2. A transformation that defines the light's coordinate system with respect to world space. As with shapes, it's often handy to be able to implement a light assuming a particular coordinate system (e.g., that a spotlight is always located at the origin of its light space, shining down the +z axis). The light-to-world transformation makes it possible to place such lights at arbitrary positions and orientations in the scene.

3. A MediumInterface that describes the participating medium on the inside and the outside of the light source. For lights that don't have "inside" and "outside" per se (e.g., a point light), the same Medium is on both sides. (A value of nullptr for both Medium pointers represents a vacuum.)

4. The nSamples parameter is used for area light sources where it may be desirable to trace multiple shadow rays to the light to compute soft shadows; it allows the user to have finer-grained control of the number of samples taken on a per-light basis. The default number of light source samples taken is 1; thus, only the light implementations for which taking multiple samples is sensible need to pass an explicit value to the Light constructor. Not all Integrators pay attention to this value.

Integrator 25
Medium 684
MediumInterface 684

The only other job for the constructor is to warn if the light-to-world transformation has a scale factor; many of the Light methods will return incorrect results in this case.[1]

⟨*Light Interface*⟩ ≡   714
```
Light(int flags, const Transform &LightToWorld,
        const MediumInterface &mediumInterface, int nSamples = 1)
    : flags(flags), nSamples(std::max(1, nSamples)),
        mediumInterface(mediumInterface), LightToWorld(LightToWorld),
        WorldToLight(Inverse(LightToWorld)) {
    ⟨Warn if light has transformation with non-uniform scale⟩
}
```

The flags, nSamples, and mediumInterface member variables are widely used outside of Light implementations so that it's worth making them available as public members.

⟨*Light Public Data*⟩ ≡   714
```
const int flags;
const int nSamples;
const MediumInterface mediumInterface;
```

The LightFlags enumeration represents flags for the flags mask field characterizing various kinds of light sources; we'll see examples of all of these in the remainder of the chapter.

⟨*LightFlags Declarations*⟩ ≡
```
enum class LightFlags : int {
    DeltaPosition = 1, DeltaDirection = 2, Area = 4, Infinite = 8
};
```

⟨*LightFlags Declarations*⟩ +≡
```
inline bool IsDeltaLight(int flags) {
    return flags & (int)LightFlags::DeltaPosition ||
            flags & (int)LightFlags::DeltaDirection;
}
```

Although storing both the light-to-world and the world-to-light transformations is redundant, having both available simplifies code elsewhere by eliminating the need for calls for Inverse().

⟨*Light Protected Data*⟩ ≡   714
```
const Transform LightToWorld, WorldToLight;
```

A key method that lights must implement is Sample_Li(). The caller passes an Interaction that provides the world space position of a reference point in the scene and a time associated with it, and the light returns the radiance arriving at that point at that time due to that light, assuming there are no occluding objects between them

---

1 For example, the surface area reported by area lights is computed from the untransformed geometry, so a scale factor in the transformation means that the reported area and the actual area of the light in the scene would be inconsistent.

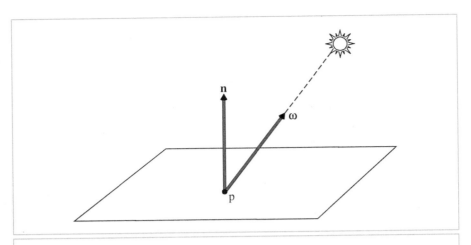

Figure 12.5: The Light::Sample_Li() method returns incident radiance from the light at a point p and also returns the direction vector ω_i that gives the direction from which radiance is arriving.

(Figure 12.5). Light implementations in pbrt do not currently support being animated—the lights themselves are at fixed positions in the scene. (Addressing this limitation is left as an exercise.) However, the time value from the Interaction is needed to set the time parameter in the traced visibility ray so that light visibility in the presence of moving objects is resolved correctly.

⟨*Light Interface*⟩ +≡   714

```
virtual Spectrum Sample_Li(const Interaction &ref, const Point2f &u,
            Vector3f *wi, Float *pdf, VisibilityTester *vis) const = 0;
```

The Light implementation is also responsible for both initializing the incident direction to the light source ω_i and initializing the VisibilityTester object, which holds information about the shadow ray that must be traced to verify that there are no occluding objects between the light and the reference point. The VisibilityTester, which will be described in Section 12.2.1, need not be initialized if the returned radiance value is black—for example, due to the reference point being outside of the cone of illumination of a spotlight. Visibility is irrelevant in this case.

For some types of lights, light may arrive at the reference point from many directions, not just from a single direction as with a point light source, for example. For these types of light sources, the Sample_Li() method samples a point on the light source's surface, so that Monte Carlo integration can be used to find the reflected light at the point due to illumination from the light. (The implementations of Sample_Li() for such lights will be introduced later, in Section 14.2.) The Point2f u parameter is used by these methods, and the pdf output parameter stores the probability density for the light sample that was taken. For all of the implementations in this chapter, the sample value is ignored and the pdf is set to 1. The pdf value's role in the context of Monte Carlo sampling is discussed in Section 14.2.

All lights must also be able to return their total emitted power; this quantity is useful for light transport algorithms that may want to devote additional computational resources to lights in the scene that make the largest contribution. Because a precise value for emitted power isn't needed elsewhere in the system, a number of the implementations of this method later in this chapter will compute approximations to this value rather than expending computational effort to find a precise value.

⟨*Light Interface*⟩ +≡   714
```
virtual Spectrum Power() const = 0;
```

Finally, Light interface includes a method Preprocess() that is invoked prior to rendering. It includes the Scene as an argument so that the light source can determine characteristics of the scene before rendering starts. The default implementation is empty, but some implementations (e.g., DistantLight) use it to record a bound of the scene extent.

⟨*Light Interface*⟩ +≡   714
```
virtual void Preprocess(const Scene &scene) { }
```

12.2.1 VISIBILITY TESTING

The VisibilityTester is a *closure*—an object that encapsulates a small amount of data and some computation that is yet to be done. It allows lights to return a radiance value under the assumption that the reference point and the light source are mutually visible. The integrator can then decide if illumination from the incident direction is relevant before incurring the cost of tracing the shadow ray—for example, light incident on the back side of a surface that isn't translucent contributes nothing to reflection from the other side. If the actual amount of arriving illumination is in fact needed, a call to one of the visibility tester's methods causes the necessary shadow ray to be traced.

⟨*Light Declarations*⟩ +≡
```
class VisibilityTester {
public:
    ⟨VisibilityTester Public Methods 717⟩
private:
    Interaction p0, p1;
};
```

VisibilityTesters are created by providing two Interaction objects, one for each end point of the shadow ray to be traced. Because an Interaction is used here, no special cases are needed for computing visibility to reference points on surfaces versus reference points in participating media.

⟨*VisibilityTester Public Methods*⟩ ≡   717
```
VisibilityTester(const Interaction &p0, const Interaction &p1)
    : p0(p0), p1(p1) { }
```

Some of the light transport routines find it useful to be able to retrieve the two end points from an initialized VisibilityTester.

⟨*VisibilityTester Public Methods*⟩ +≡   717
```
const Interaction &P0() const { return p0; }
const Interaction &P1() const { return p1; }
```

There are two methods that determine the visibility between the two points. The first, Unoccluded(), traces a shadow ray between them and returns a Boolean result. Some ray tracers include a facility for casting colored shadows from partially transparent objects and would return a spectrum from a method like this, but pbrt does not include this facility, since this feature generally requires a nonphysical hack. Scenes where illumination passes through a transparent object should be rendered with an integrator that supports this kind of effect; any of the bidirectional integrators from Chapter 16 is a good choice.

⟨*Light Method Definitions*⟩ ≡
```
bool VisibilityTester::Unoccluded(const Scene &scene) const {
    return !scene.IntersectP(p0.SpawnRayTo(p1));
}
```

Because it only returns a Boolean value, Unoccluded() also ignores the effects of any scattering medium that the ray passes through on the radiance that it carries. When Integrators need to account for that effect, they use the VisibilityTester's Tr() method instead. VisibilityTester::Tr() computes the beam transmittance, Equation (11.1), the fraction of radiance transmitted along the segment between the two points. It accounts for both attenuation in participating media as well as any surfaces that block the ray completely.

⟨*Light Method Definitions*⟩ +≡
```
Spectrum VisibilityTester::Tr(const Scene &scene,
                             Sampler &sampler) const {
    Ray ray(p0.SpawnRayTo(p1));
    Spectrum Tr(1.f);
    while (true) {
        SurfaceInteraction isect;
        bool hitSurface = scene.Intersect(ray, &isect);
        ⟨Handle opaque surface along ray's path 718⟩
        ⟨Update transmittance for current ray segment 719⟩
        ⟨Generate next ray segment or return final transmittance 719⟩
    }
    return Tr;
}
```

If an intersection is found along the ray segment and the hit surface is opaque, then the ray is blocked and the transmittance is zero. Our work here is done. (Recall from Section 11.3 that surfaces with a nullptr material pointer should be ignored in ray visibility tests, as those surfaces are only used to bound the extent of participating media.)

⟨*Handle opaque surface along ray's path*⟩ ≡   718
```
if (hitSurface && isect.primitive->GetMaterial() != nullptr)
    return Spectrum(0.0f);
```

Otherwise, the Tr() method accumulates the ray's transmittance, either to the surface intersection point or to the endpoint p1. (If there was an intersection with a non-opaque surface, the Ray::tMax value has been updated accordingly; otherwise it corresponds to p1.) In either case, Medium::Tr() computes the beam transmittance up to Ray::tMax, using the multiplicative property of beam transmittance from Equation (11.2).

⟨*Update transmittance for current ray segment*⟩ ≡   **718**
```
    if (ray.medium)
        Tr *= ray.medium->Tr(ray, sampler);
```

If no intersection was found, the ray made it to p1 and we've accumulated the full transmittance. Otherwise, the ray intersected an invisible surface and the loop runs again, tracing a ray from that intersection point onward toward p1.

⟨*Generate next ray segment or return final transmittance*⟩ ≡   **718**
```
    if (!hitSurface)
        break;
    ray = isect.SpawnRayTo(p1);
```

12.3 POINT LIGHTS

A number of interesting lights can be described in terms of emission from a single point in space with some possibly angularly varying distribution of outgoing light. This section describes the implementation of a number of them, starting with PointLight, which represents an isotropic point light source that emits the same amount of light in all directions. It is defined in lights/point.h and lights/point.cpp. Figure 12.6 shows a scene rendered with a point light source. Building on this base, a number of more complex lights based on point sources will be introduced, including spotlights and a light that projects an image into the scene.

⟨*PointLight Declarations*⟩ ≡
```
    class PointLight : public Light {
    public:
        ⟨PointLight Public Methods 720⟩
    private:
        ⟨PointLight Private Data 720⟩
    };
```

PointLights are positioned at the origin in light space. To place them elsewhere, the light-to-world transformation should be set appropriately. Using this transformation, the world space position of the light is precomputed and cached in the constructor by transforming (0, 0, 0) from light space to world space.

The constructor also stores the intensity for the light source, which is the amount of power per unit solid angle. Because the light source is isotropic, this is a constant. Finally, since point lights represent singularities that only emit light from a single position, the Light::flags field is initialized to LightFlags::DeltaPosition.

Figure 12.6: Scene Rendered with a Point Light Source. Notice the hard shadow boundaries from this type of light.

⟨*PointLight Public Methods*⟩ ≡   **719**
```
PointLight(const Transform &LightToWorld,
           const MediumInterface &mediumInterface, const Spectrum &I)
    : Light((int)LightFlags::DeltaPosition, LightToWorld,
            mediumInterface),
      pLight(LightToWorld(Point3f(0, 0, 0))), I(I) { }
```

⟨*PointLight Private Data*⟩ ≡   **719**
```
const Point3f pLight;
const Spectrum I;
```

Strictly speaking, it is incorrect to describe the light arriving at a point due to a point light source using units of radiance. Radiant intensity is instead the proper unit for describing emission from a point light source, as explained in Section 5.4. In the light source interfaces here, however, we will abuse terminology and use `Sample_Li()` methods to report the illumination arriving at a point for all types of light sources, dividing radiant intensity by the squared distance to the point p to convert units. Section 14.2 revisits the details of this issue in its discussion of how delta distributions affect evaluation of the integral in the scattering equation. In the end, the correctness of the computation does not suffer from this fudge, and it makes the implementation of light transport algorithms more straightforward by not requiring them to use different interfaces for different types of lights.

⟨*PointLight Method Definitions*⟩ ≡
```
Spectrum PointLight::Sample_Li(const Interaction &ref,
        const Point2f &u, Vector3f *wi, Float *pdf,
        VisibilityTester *vis) const {
    *wi = Normalize(pLight - ref.p);
    *pdf = 1.f;
    *vis = VisibilityTester(ref, Interaction(pLight, ref.time,
                                             mediumInterface));
    return I / DistanceSquared(pLight, ref.p);
}
```

The total power emitted by the light source can be found by integrating the intensity over the entire sphere of directions:

$$\Phi = \int_{\mathcal{S}^2} I \, d\omega = I \int_{\mathcal{S}^2} d\omega = 4\pi I.$$

⟨*PointLight Method Definitions*⟩ +≡
```
Spectrum PointLight::Power() const {
    return 4 * Pi * I;
}
```

12.3.1 SPOTLIGHTS

Spotlights are a handy variation on point lights; rather than shining illumination in all directions, they emit light in a cone of directions from their position. For simplicity, we will define the spotlight in the light coordinate system to always be at position $(0, 0, 0)$ and pointing down the $+z$ axis. To place or orient it elsewhere in the scene, the Light::WorldToLight transformation should be set accordingly. Figure 12.7 shows a rendering of the same scene as Figure 12.6, only illuminated with a spotlight instead of a point light. The SpotLight class is defined in lights/spot.h and lights/spot.cpp.

⟨*SpotLight Declarations*⟩ ≡
```
class SpotLight : public Light {
public:
    ⟨SpotLight Public Methods⟩
private:
    ⟨SpotLight Private Data  723⟩
};
```

Two angles are passed to the constructor to set the extent of the SpotLight's cone: the overall angular width of the cone and the angle at which falloff starts (Figure 12.8). The constructor precomputes and stores the cosines of these angles for use in the SpotLight's methods.

Figure 12.7: Scene Rendered with a Spotlight. The spotlight cone smoothly cuts off illumination past a user-specified angle from the light's central axis.

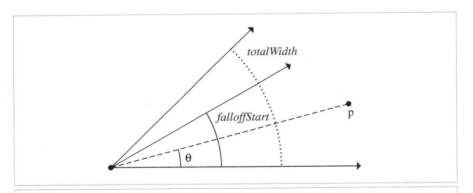

Figure 12.8: Spotlights are defined by two angles, *falloffStart* and *totalWidth*. Objects inside the inner cone of angles, up to *falloffStart*, are fully illuminated by the light. The directions between *falloffStart* and *totalWidth* are a transition zone that ramps down from full illumination to no illumination, such that points outside the *totalWidth* cone aren't illuminated at all. The cosine of the angle between the vector to a point p and the spotlight axis, θ, can easily be computed with a dot product.

⟨*SpotLight Method Definitions*⟩ ≡
```
SpotLight::SpotLight(const Transform &LightToWorld,
        const MediumInterface &mediumInterface, const Spectrum &I,
        Float totalWidth, Float falloffStart)
    : Light((int)LightFlags::DeltaPosition, LightToWorld,
            mediumInterface),
        pLight(LightToWorld(Point3f(0, 0, 0))), I(I),
        cosTotalWidth(std::cos(Radians(totalWidth))),
        cosFalloffStart(std::cos(Radians(falloffStart))) { }
```

⟨*SpotLight Private Data*⟩ ≡   721
```
const Point3f pLight;
const Spectrum I;
const Float cosTotalWidth, cosFalloffStart;
```

The SpotLight::Sample_Li() method is almost identical to PointLight::Sample_Li(),
except that it also calls the Falloff() method, which computes the distribution of light
accounting for the spotlight cone. This computation is encapsulated in a separate method
since other SpotLight methods will need to perform it as well.

⟨*SpotLight Method Definitions*⟩ +≡
```
Spectrum SpotLight::Sample_Li(const Interaction &ref,
        const Point2f &u, Vector3f *wi, Float *pdf,
        VisibilityTester *vis) const {
    *wi = Normalize(pLight - ref.p);
    *pdf = 1.f;
    *vis = VisibilityTester(ref, Interaction(pLight, ref.time,
                                        mediumInterface));
    return I * Falloff(-*wi) / DistanceSquared(pLight, ref.p);
}
```

To compute the spotlight's strength for a receiving point p, this first step is to compute
the cosine of the angle between the vector from the spotlight origin to p and the vector
along the center of the spotlight's cone. To compute the cosine of the offset angle to a
point p, we have, as illustrated in Figure 12.8,

$$\cos \theta = \left(\widehat{p - (0, 0, 0)} \right) \cdot (0, 0, 1)$$
$$= p_z / \|p\|.$$

This value is then compared to the cosines of the falloff and overall width angles to
see where the point lies with respect to the spotlight cone. We can trivially determine
that points with a cosine greater than the cosine of the falloff angle are inside the cone
receiving full illumination, and points with cosine less than the width angle's cosine
are completely outside the cone. (Note that the computation is slightly tricky since for
$\theta \in [0, \pi]$, if $\theta > \theta'$, then $\cos \theta < \cos \theta'$.)

⟨*SpotLight Method Definitions*⟩ +≡

```
Float SpotLight::Falloff(const Vector3f &w) const {
    Vector3f wl = Normalize(WorldToLight(w));
    Float cosTheta = wl.z;
    if (cosTheta < cosTotalWidth)      return 0;
    if (cosTheta > cosFalloffStart)    return 1;
    ⟨Compute falloff inside spotlight cone 724⟩
}
```

For points inside the transition range from fully illuminated to outside of the cone, the intensity is scaled to smoothly fall off from full illumination to darkness:[2]

⟨*Compute falloff inside spotlight cone*⟩ ≡   724

```
Float delta = (cosTheta - cosTotalWidth) /
              (cosFalloffStart - cosTotalWidth);
return (delta * delta) * (delta * delta);
```

The solid angle subtended by a cone with spread angle θ is $2\pi(1 - \cos\theta)$. Therefore, the integral over directions on the sphere that gives power from radiant intensity can be solved to compute the total power of a light that only emits illumination in a cone. For the spotlight, we can reasonably approximate the power of the light by computing the solid angle of directions that is covered by the cone with a spread angle cosine halfway between width and fall.

⟨*SpotLight Method Definitions*⟩ +≡

```
Spectrum SpotLight::Power() const {
    return I * 2 * Pi * (1 - .5f * (cosFalloffStart + cosTotalWidth));
}
```

12.3.2 TEXTURE PROJECTION LIGHTS

Another useful light source acts like a slide projector; it takes an image map and projects its image out into the scene. The ProjectionLight class uses a projective transformation to project points in the scene onto the light's projection plane based on the field of view angle given to the constructor (Figure 12.9). Its implementation is in lights/projection.h and lights/projection.cpp. The use of this light in the lighting example scene is shown in Figure 12.10.

⟨*ProjectionLight Declarations*⟩ ≡

```
class ProjectionLight : public Light {
public:
    ⟨ProjectionLight Public Methods⟩
private:
    ⟨ProjectionLight Private Data 726⟩
};
```

---

2   Note the parentheses in the expression that takes delta to the fourth power: this allows the compiler to generate two multiply instructions rather than three instructions, as would be needed if the parentheses were removed. Consider the discussion of IEEE floating point in Section 3.9.1 to see why the parentheses are necessary for this.

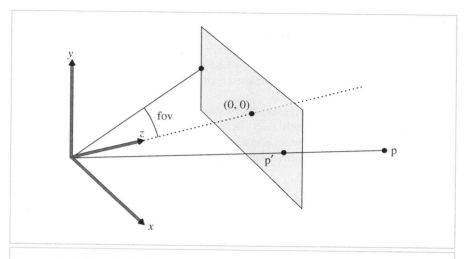

Figure 12.9: The Basic Setting for Projection Light Sources. A point **p** in the light's coordinate system is projected onto the plane of the image using the light's projection matrix.

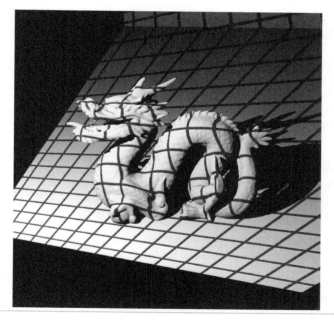

Figure 12.10: Scene Rendered with a Projection Light Using a Grid Texture Map. The projection light acts like a slide projector, projecting an image onto objects in the scene.

⟨ProjectionLight Method Definitions⟩ ≡
```
ProjectionLight::ProjectionLight(const Transform &LightToWorld,
        const MediumInterface &mediumInterface, const Spectrum &I,
        const std::string &texname, Float fov)
    : Light((int)LightFlags::DeltaPosition, LightToWorld,
            mediumInterface),
      pLight(LightToWorld(Point3f(0, 0, 0))), I(I) {
    ⟨Create ProjectionLight MIP map 726⟩
    ⟨Initialize ProjectionLight projection matrix 726⟩
    ⟨Compute cosine of cone surrounding projection directions 727⟩
}
```

This light could use a Texture to represent the light projection distribution so that procedural projection patterns could be used. However, having a precise representation of the projection function, as is available by using an image in a MIPMap, is useful for being able to sample the projection distribution using Monte Carlo techniques, so we will use that representation in the implementation here.

Note that the projected image is explicitly stored as an RGBSpectrum, even if full spectral rendering is being performed. Unless the image map being used has full spectral data, storing full SampledSpectrum values in this case only wastes memory; whether an RGB color is converted to a SampledSpectrum before the MIPMap is created or after the MIPMap returns a value from its Lookup() routine gives the same result in either case.

⟨Create ProjectionLight MIP map⟩ ≡　　　　　　　　　　　　　　　　726
```
Point2i resolution;
std::unique_ptr<RGBSpectrum[]> texels = ReadImage(texname, &resolution);
if (texels)
    projectionMap.reset(new MIPMap<RGBSpectrum>(resolution,
                                                texels.get()));
```

⟨ProjectionLight Private Data⟩ ≡　　　　　　　　　　　　　　　　724
```
std::unique_ptr<MIPMap<RGBSpectrum>> projectionMap;
const Point3f pLight;
const Spectrum I;
```

Similar to the PerspectiveCamera, the ProjectionLight constructor computes a projection matrix and the screen space extent of the projection.

⟨Initialize ProjectionLight projection matrix⟩ ≡　　　　　　　　　726
```
Float aspect = projectionMap ?
    (Float(resolution.x) / Float(resolution.y)) : 1;
if (aspect > 1)
    screenBounds = Bounds2f(Point2f(-aspect, -1), Point2f(aspect, 1));
else
    screenBounds = Bounds2f(Point2f(-1, -1/aspect), Point2f(1, 1/aspect));
near = 1e-3f;
far = 1e30f;
lightProjection = Perspective(fov, near, far);
```

⟨*ProjectionLight Private Data*⟩ +≡   724
```
Transform lightProjection;
Float near, far;
Bounds2f screenBounds;
```

Finally, the constructor finds the cosine of the angle between the +z axis and the vector to a corner of the screen window. This value is used elsewhere to define the minimal cone of directions that encompasses the set of directions in which light is projected. This cone is useful for algorithms like photon mapping that need to randomly sample rays leaving the light source (explained in Chapter 16). We won't derive this computation here; it is based on straightforward trigonometry.

⟨*Compute cosine of cone surrounding projection directions*⟩ ≡   726
```
Float opposite = std::tan(Radians(fov) / 2.f);
Float tanDiag = opposite * std::sqrt(1 + 1 / (aspect * aspect));
cosTotalWidth = std::cos(std::atan(tanDiag));
```

⟨*ProjectionLight Private Data*⟩ +≡   724
```
Float cosTotalWidth;
```

Similar to the spotlight's version, ProjectionLight::Sample_Li() calls a utility method, ProjectionLight::Projection(), to determine how much light is projected in the given direction. Therefore, we won't include the implementation of Sample_Li() here.

⟨*ProjectionLight Method Definitions*⟩ +≡
```
Spectrum ProjectionLight::Projection(const Vector3f &w) const {
    Vector3f wl = WorldToLight(w);
    ⟨Discard directions behind projection light 727⟩
    ⟨Project point onto projection plane and compute light 728⟩
}
```

Because the projective transformation has the property that it projects points behind the center of projection to points in front of it, it is important to discard points with a negative z value. Therefore, the projection code immediately returns no illumination for projection points that are behind the near plane for the projection. If this check were not done, then it wouldn't be possible to know if a projected point was originally behind the light (and therefore not illuminated) or in front of it.

⟨*Discard directions behind projection light*⟩ ≡   727
```
if (wl.z < near) return 0;
```

After being projected to the projection plane, points with coordinate values outside the screen window are discarded. Points that pass this test are transformed to get (s, t) texture coordinates inside $[0, 1]^2$ for the lookup in the image map. Note it is explicitly specified that the RGBSpectrum value passed to the Spectrum constructor represents an illuminant's SPD and not that of a reflectance. (Recall from Section 5.2.2 that different matching functions are used for converting from RGB to SPDs for illuminants versus reflectances.)

⟨*Project point onto projection plane and compute light*⟩ ≡   727
```
    Point3f p = lightProjection(Point3f(wl.x, wl.y, wl.z));
    if (!Inside(Point2f(p.x, p.y), screenBounds)) return 0.f;
    if (!projectionMap) return 1;
    Point2f st = Point2f(screenBounds.Offset(Point2f(p.x, p.y)));
    return Spectrum(projectionMap->Lookup(st), SpectrumType::Illuminant);
```

The total power of this light is approximated as a spotlight that subtends the same angle as the diagonal of the projected image, scaled by the average intensity in the image map. This approximation becomes increasingly inaccurate as the projected image's aspect ratio becomes less square, for example, and it doesn't account for the fact that texels toward the edges of the image map subtend a larger solid angle than texels in the middle when projected with a perspective projection. Nevertheless, it's a reasonable first-order approximation.

⟨*ProjectionLight Method Definitions*⟩ +≡
```
    Spectrum ProjectionLight::Power() const {
        return (projectionMap ?
                Spectrum(projectionMap->Lookup(Point2f(.5f, .5f), .5f),
                    SpectrumType::Illuminant) : Spectrum(1.f)) *
            I * 2 * Pi * (1.f - cosTotalWidth);
    }
```

12.3.3 GONIOPHOTOMETRIC DIAGRAM LIGHTS

A *goniophotometric diagram* describes the angular distribution of luminance from a point light source; it is widely used in illumination engineering to characterize lights. Figure 12.11 shows an example of a goniophotometric diagram in two dimensions. In this section, we'll implement a light source that uses goniophotometric diagrams encoded in 2D image maps to describe the emission distribution of the light. The implementation is very similar to the point light sources defined previously in this section; it scales the intensity based on the outgoing direction according to the goniophotometric diagram's values. Figure 12.12 shows a few goniophotometric diagrams encoded as image maps, and Figure 12.13 shows a scene rendered with a light source that uses one of these images to modulate its directional distribution of illumination.

⟨*GonioPhotometricLight Declarations*⟩ ≡
```
    class GonioPhotometricLight : public Light {
    public:
        ⟨GonioPhotometricLight Public Methods 730⟩
    private:
        ⟨GonioPhotometricLight Private Data 730⟩
    };
```

The GonioPhotometricLight constructor takes a base intensity and an image map that scales the intensity based on the angular distribution of light.

Figure 12.11: An Example of a Goniophotometric Diagram Specifying an Outgoing Light Distribution from a Point Light Source in 2D. The emitted intensity is defined in a fixed set of directions on the unit sphere, and the intensity for a given outgoing direction ω is found by interpolating the intensities of the adjacent samples.

(a)   (b)   (c)

Figure 12.12: Goniophotometric Diagrams for Real-World Light Sources, Encoded as Image Maps with a Parameterization Based on Spherical Coordinates. (a) A light that mostly illuminates in its up direction, with only a small amount of illumination in the down direction. (b) A light that mostly illuminates in the down direction. (c) A light that casts illumination both above and below.

Figure 12.13: Scene Rendered Using a Goniophotometric Diagram from Figure 12.12. Even though a point light source is the basis of this light, including the directional variation of a realistic light improves the visual realism of the rendered image.

⟨*GonioPhotometricLight Public Methods*⟩ ≡   728
```
GonioPhotometricLight(const Transform &LightToWorld,
        const MediumInterface &mediumInterface, const Spectrum &I,
        const std::string &texname)
    : Light((int)LightFlags::DeltaPosition, LightToWorld,
            mediumInterface),
      pLight(LightToWorld(Point3f(0, 0, 0))), I(I) {
    ⟨Create mipmap for GonioPhotometricLight 730⟩
}
```

⟨*GonioPhotometricLight Private Data*⟩ ≡   728
```
const Point3f pLight;
const Spectrum I;
std::unique_ptr<MIPMap<RGBSpectrum>> mipmap;
```

Like ProjectionLight, GonioPhotometricLight constructs a MIPMap of the distribution's image map, also always using RGBSpectrum values.

⟨*Create mipmap for GonioPhotometricLight*⟩ ≡   730
```
Point2i resolution;
std::unique_ptr<RGBSpectrum[]> texels = ReadImage(texname, &resolution);
if (texels)
    mipmap.reset(new MIPMap<RGBSpectrum>(resolution, texels.get()));
```

The GonioPhotometricLight::Sample_Li() method is not shown here. It is essentially identical to the SpotLight::Sample_Li() and ProjectionLight::Sample_Li() methods that use a helper function to scale the amount of radiance. It assumes that the scale texture is encoded using spherical coordinates, so that the given direction needs to be converted to θ and ϕ values and scaled to $[0, 1]$ before being used to index into the texture. Goniophotometric diagrams are usually defined in a coordinate space where the y axis is up, whereas the spherical coordinate utility routines in pbrt assume that z is up, so y and z are swapped before doing the conversion.

⟨*GonioPhotometricLight Public Methods*⟩ +≡   728
```
Spectrum Scale(const Vector3f &w) const {
    Vector3f wp = Normalize(WorldToLight(w));
    std::swap(wp.y, wp.z);
    Float theta = SphericalTheta(wp);
    Float phi   = SphericalPhi(wp);
    Point2f st(phi * Inv2Pi, theta * InvPi);
    return !mipmap ? RGBSpectrum(1.f) :
            Spectrum(mipmap->Lookup(st), SpectrumType::Illuminant);
}
```

The Power() method uses the average intensity over the image to compute power. This computation is inaccurate because the spherical coordinate parameterization of directions has various distortions, particularly near the $+z$ and $-z$ directions. Again, this error is acceptable for the uses of this method in pbrt.

⟨*GonioPhotometricLight Method Definitions*⟩ ≡
```
Spectrum GonioPhotometricLight::Power() const {
    return 4 * Pi * I *
        Spectrum(mipmap ? mipmap->Lookup(Point2f(.5f, .5f), .5f) :
                Spectrum(1.f), SpectrumType::Illuminant);
}
```

12.4 DISTANT LIGHTS

Another useful light source type is the *distant light*, also known as a *directional light*. It describes an emitter that deposits illumination from the same direction at every point in space. Such a light is also called a point light "at infinity," since, as a point light becomes progressively farther away, it acts more and more like a directional light. For example, the sun (as considered from Earth) can be thought of as a directional light source. Although it is actually an area light source, the illumination effectively arrives at Earth in parallel beams because it is so far away. The DistantLight, implemented in the files lights/distant.h and lights/distant.cpp, implements a directional source.

⟨*DistantLight Declarations*⟩ ≡
```
class DistantLight : public Light {
public:
    ⟨DistantLight Public Methods 732⟩
private:
    ⟨DistantLight Private Data 731⟩
};
```

Note that the DistantLight constructor does not take a MediumInterface parameter; the only reasonable medium for a distant light to be in is a vacuum—if it was itself in a medium that absorbed any light at all, then all of its emission would be absorbed, since it's modeled as being infinitely far away.

⟨*DistantLight Method Definitions*⟩ ≡
```
DistantLight::DistantLight(const Transform &LightToWorld,
        const Spectrum &L, const Vector3f &wLight)
    : Light((int)LightFlags::DeltaDirection, LightToWorld,
            MediumInterface()),
        L(L), wLight(Normalize(LightToWorld(wLight))) { }
```

⟨*DistantLight Private Data*⟩ ≡   731
```
const Spectrum L;
const Vector3f wLight;
```

Some of the DistantLight methods need to know the bounds of the scene. Because lights are created before the scene geometry, these bounds aren't available when the DistantLight constructor runs. Therefore, DistantLight implements the optional Preprocess() method to get the bound. (This method is called at the end of the Scene constructor.)

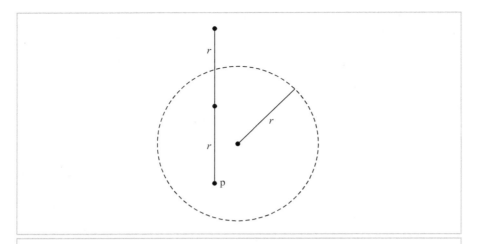

Figure 12.14: Computing the Second Point for a DistantLight Shadow Ray. Given a sphere that bounds the scene (dashed line) with radius *r* and given some point in the scene p, then if we move a distance of 2*r* along any vector from p, the resulting point must be outside of the scene's bound. If a shadow ray to such a point is unoccluded, then we can be certain that the point p receives illumination from a distant light along the vector's direction.

⟨*DistantLight Public Methods*⟩ ≡   731
```
void Preprocess(const Scene &scene) {
    scene.WorldBound().BoundingSphere(&worldCenter, &worldRadius);
}
```

⟨*DistantLight Private Data*⟩ +≡   731
```
Point3f worldCenter;
Float worldRadius;
```

Most of the implementation of the Sample_Li() method is straightforward: for a distant light, the incident direction and radiance are always the same. The only interesting bit is the initialization of the VisibilityTester: here, the second point for the shadow ray is set along the distant light's incident direction a distance of twice the radius of the scene's bounding sphere, guaranteeing a second point that is outside of the scene's bounds (Figure 12.14).

⟨*DistantLight Method Definitions*⟩ +≡
```
Spectrum DistantLight::Sample_Li(const Interaction &ref,
        const Point2f &u, Vector3f *wi, Float *pdf,
        VisibilityTester *vis) const {
    *wi = wLight;
    *pdf = 1;
    Point3f pOutside = ref.p + wLight * (2 * worldRadius);
    *vis = VisibilityTester(ref, Interaction(pOutside, ref.time,
                                    mediumInterface));
    return L;
}
```

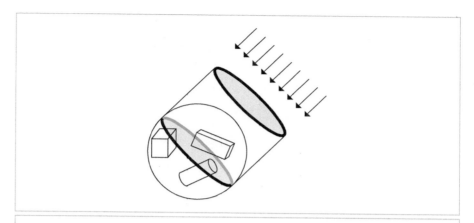

Figure 12.15: An approximation of the power emitted by a distant light into a given scene can be obtained by finding the sphere that bounds the scene, computing the area of an inscribed disk, and computing the power that arrives on the surface of that disk.

The distant light is unusual in that the amount of power it emits is related to the spatial extent of the scene. In fact, it is proportional to the area of the scene receiving light. To see why this is so, consider a disk of area A being illuminated by a distant light with emitted radiance L where the incident light arrives along the disk's normal direction. The total power reaching the disk is $\Phi = AL$. As the size of the receiving surface varies, power varies proportionally.

To find the emitted power for a DistantLight, it's impractical to compute the total surface area of the objects that are visible to the light. Instead, we will approximate this area with a disk inside the scene's bounding sphere oriented in the light's direction (Figure 12.15). This will always overestimate the actual area but is sufficient for the needs of code elsewhere in the system.

⟨*DistantLight Method Definitions*⟩ +≡
```
Spectrum DistantLight::Power() const {
    return L * Pi * worldRadius * worldRadius;
}
```

12.5 AREA LIGHTS

Area lights are light sources defined by one or more Shapes that emit light from their surface, with some directional distribution of radiance at each point on the surface. In general, computing radiometric quantities related to area lights requires computing integrals over the surface of the light that often can't be computed in closed form. This issue is addressed with the Monte Carlo integration techniques in Section 14.2. The reward for this complexity (and computational expense) is soft shadows and more realistic lighting effects, rather than the hard shadows and stark lighting that come from point lights. (See Figure 12.16. Also compare Figure 12.17 to Figure 12.6.)

Figure 12.16: Wider View of the Lighting Example Scene. The dragon is illuminated by a disk area light source directly above it.

The AreaLight class is an abstract base class that inherits from Light. Implementations of area lights should inherit from it.

⟨*Light Declarations*⟩ +≡
```
class AreaLight : public Light {
public:
    ⟨AreaLight Interface 734⟩
};
```

AreaLight adds a single new method to the general Light interface, AreaLight::L(). Implementations are given a point on the surface of the light represented by an Interaction and should evaluate the area light's emitted radiance, L, in the given outgoing direction.

⟨*AreaLight Interface*⟩ ≡   734
```
    virtual Spectrum L(const Interaction &intr, const Vector3f &w) const = 0;
```

For convenience, there is a method in the SurfaceInteraction class that makes it easy to compute the emitted radiance at a surface point intersected by a ray.

⟨*SurfaceInteraction Method Definitions*⟩ +≡
```
    Spectrum SurfaceInteraction::Le(const Vector3f &w) const {
        const AreaLight *area = primitive->GetAreaLight();
        return area ? area->L(*this, w) : Spectrum(0.f);
    }
```

DiffuseAreaLight implements a basic area light source with a uniform spatial and directional radiance distribution. The surface it emits from is defined by a Shape. It only emits

(a)

(b)

Figure 12.17: Dragon Model Illuminated by Disk Area Lights. (a) The disk's radius is relatively small; the shadow has soft penumbrae, but otherwise the image looks similar to the one with a point light. (b) The effect of using a much larger disk: not only have the penumbrae become much larger, to the point of nearly eliminating the fully in-shadow areas, but notice how areas like the neck of the dragon and its jaw have noticeably different appearances when illuminated from a wider range of directions.

light on the side of the surface with outward-facing surface normal; there is no emission from the other side. (The Shape::reverseOrientation value can be set to true to cause the light to be emitted from the other side of the surface instead.) DiffuseAreaLight is defined in the files lights/diffuse.h and lights/diffuse.cpp.

⟨*DiffuseAreaLight Declarations*⟩ ≡
```
class DiffuseAreaLight : public AreaLight {
public:
    ⟨DiffuseAreaLight Public Methods 736⟩
protected:
    ⟨DiffuseAreaLight Protected Data 736⟩
};
```

⟨*DiffuseAreaLight Method Definitions*⟩ ≡
```
DiffuseAreaLight::DiffuseAreaLight(const Transform &LightToWorld,
        const MediumInterface &mediumInterface, const Spectrum &Lemit,
        int nSamples, const std::shared_ptr<Shape> &shape)
    : AreaLight(LightToWorld, mediumInterface, nSamples), Lemit(Lemit),
      shape(shape), area(shape->Area()) { }
```

⟨*DiffuseAreaLight Protected Data*⟩ ≡   **736**
```
const Spectrum Lemit;
std::shared_ptr<Shape> shape;
const Float area;
```

Because this area light implementation emits light from only one side of the shape's surface, its L() method just makes sure that the outgoing direction lies in the same hemisphere as the normal.

⟨*DiffuseAreaLight Public Methods*⟩ ≡   **736**
```
Spectrum L(const Interaction &intr, const Vector3f &w) const {
    return Dot(intr.n, w) > 0.f ? Lemit : Spectrum(0.f);
}
```

The DiffuseAreaLight::Sample_Li() method isn't as straightforward as it has been for the other light sources described so far. Specifically, at each point in the scene, radiance from area lights can be incident from many directions, not just a single direction as was the case for the other lights (Figure 12.18). This leads to the question of which direction should be chosen for this method. We will defer answering this question and providing an implementation of this method until Section 14.2, after Monte Carlo integration has been introduced.

Emitted power from an area light with uniform emitted radiance over the surface can be directly computed in closed form:

⟨*DiffuseAreaLight Method Definitions*⟩ +≡
```
Spectrum DiffuseAreaLight::Power() const {
    return Lemit * area * Pi;
}
```

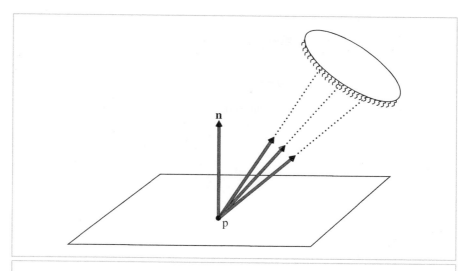

Figure 12.18: An area light casts incident illumination along many directions, rather than from a single direction.

12.6 INFINITE AREA LIGHTS

Another useful kind of light is the infinite area light—an infinitely far away area light source that surrounds the entire scene. One way to visualize this light is as an enormous sphere that casts light into the scene from every direction. One important use of infinite area lights is for *environment lighting*, where an image that represents illumination in an environment is used to illuminate synthetic objects as if they were in that environment. Figures 12.19 and 12.20 compare illuminating a car model with a standard area light to illuminating it with environment maps that simulate illumination from the sky at a few different times of day (the illumination maps used are shown in Figure 12.21). The increase in realism is striking. The InfiniteAreaLight class is implemented in lights/infinite.h and lights/infinite.cpp.

A widely used representation for light for this application is the latitude–longitude radiance map. (This representation is also known as the equirectangular projection.) The EnvironmentCamera can be used to create image maps for the light, or see the "Further Reading" section for information about techniques for capturing this lighting data from real-world environments.

⟨*InfiniteAreaLight Declarations*⟩ ≡
    class InfiniteAreaLight : public Light {
    public:
        ⟨*InfiniteAreaLight Public Methods* **740**⟩
    private:
        ⟨*InfiniteAreaLight Private Data* **740**⟩
    };

(a)

(b)

Figure 12.19: Car model (a) illuminated with an area light and a directional light and (b) illuminated with morning skylight from an environment map. Using a realistic distribution of illumination gives an image that is much more visually compelling. In particular, with illumination arriving from all directions, the glossy reflective properties of the paint are much more visually apparent. *(Model courtesy of Yasutoshi Mori.)*

Like the other lights, the InfiniteAreaLight takes a transformation matrix; here, its use is to orient the image map. It then uses spherical coordinates to map from directions on the sphere to (θ, ϕ) directions, and from there to (u, v) texture coordinates. The provided transformation thus determines which direction is "up."

The constructor loads the image data from the disk and creates a MIPMap to store it. The fragment that loads the data, ⟨*Read texel data from* texmap *and initialize* Lmap⟩, is straightforward and won't be included here. The other code fragment in the constructor, ⟨*Initialize sampling PDFs for infinite area light*⟩, is related to Monte Carlo sampling of InfiniteAreaLights and will be defined later, in Section 14.2.4.

InfiniteAreaLight 737

MIPMap 625

(a)

(b)

Figure 12.20: Changing just the environment map used for illumination gives quite different results in the final image: (a) using a midday skylight distribution and (b) using a sunset environment map. *(Model courtesy of Yasutoshi Mori.)*

As with DistantLights, because the light is defined as being infinitely far away, the MediumInterface for an infinite area light must have nullptr values for its Medium *s, corresponding to a vacuum.

⟨*InfiniteAreaLight Method Definitions*⟩ ≡
    InfiniteAreaLight::InfiniteAreaLight(const Transform &LightToWorld,
        const Spectrum &L, int nSamples, const std::string &texmap)
      : Light((int)LightFlags::Infinite, LightToWorld,
        MediumInterface(), nSamples) {
    ⟨*Read texel data from* texmap *and initialize* Lmap⟩
    ⟨*Initialize sampling PDFs for infinite area light* **847**⟩
   }

(a)

(b)

(c)

Figure 12.21: Environment Maps Used for Illumination in Figures 12.19 and 12.20. (a) Morning, (b) midday, and (c) sunset sky. (The bottom halves of these maps aren't shown here, since they are just black pixels.)

⟨*InfiniteAreaLight Private Data*⟩ ≡   737
    `std::unique_ptr<MIPMap<RGBSpectrum>> Lmap;`

Like DistantLights, InfiniteAreaLights also need the scene bounds; here again, the Preprocess() method finds the scene bounds after all of the scene geometry has been created.

⟨*InfiniteAreaLight Public Methods*⟩ ≡   737
```
void Preprocess(const Scene &scene) {
    scene.WorldBound().BoundingSphere(&worldCenter, &worldRadius);
}
```

⟨*InfiniteAreaLight Private Data*⟩ +≡   737
    `Point3f worldCenter;`
    `Float worldRadius;`

Because `InfiniteAreaLights` cast light from all directions, it's also necessary to use Monte Carlo integration to sample their illumination. Therefore, the `InfiniteAreaLight::Sample_Li()` method will be defined in Section 14.2.

Like directional lights, the total power from the infinite area light is related to the surface area of the scene. Like many other lights in this chapter, the power computed here is approximate; here, all texels are given equal weight, which ignores the fact that with an equirectangular projection, the differential solid angle subtended by each pixel values with its θ value (Section 14.2.4).

⟨*InfiniteAreaLight Method Definitions*⟩ +≡
```
Spectrum InfiniteAreaLight::Power() const {
    return Pi * worldRadius * worldRadius *
        Spectrum(Lmap->Lookup(Point2f(.5f, .5f), .5f),
                 SpectrumType::Illuminant);
}
```

Because infinite area lights need to be able to contribute radiance to rays that don't hit any geometry in the scene, we'll add a method to the base `Light` class that returns emitted radiance due to that light along a ray that escapes the scene bounds. (The default implementation for other lights returns no radiance.) It is the responsibility of the integrators to call this method for these rays.

⟨*Light Method Definitions*⟩ +≡
```
Spectrum Light::Le(const RayDifferential &ray) const {
    return Spectrum(0.f);
}
```

⟨*InfiniteAreaLight Method Definitions*⟩ +≡
```
Spectrum InfiniteAreaLight::Le(const RayDifferential &ray) const {
    Vector3f w = Normalize(WorldToLight(ray.d));
    Point2f st(SphericalPhi(w) * Inv2Pi,
               SphericalTheta(w) * InvPi);
    return Spectrum(Lmap->Lookup(st), SpectrumType::Illuminant);
}
```

FURTHER READING

The books by McCluney (1994) and Malacara (2002) discuss blackbody emitters and the standard illuminants in detail. Wilkie and Weidlich (2011) noted that common practice in rendering has been to use the blackbody distribution of Equation (12.1) to model light emission for rendering, while Kirchoff's law, Equation (12.4), would be more accurate. They also point out that as objects become hot, their BRDFs often change, which makes Kirchoff's law more difficult to adopt, especially in that models that account for the effect of temperature variation on BRDFs generally aren't available.

The Standard Illuminants are defined in a CIE Technical Report (2004); Judd et al. (1964) developed the approach that was used to define the D Standard Illuminant.

Warn (1983) developed early models of light sources with nonisotropic emission distributions, including the spotlight model used in this chapter. Verbeck and Greenberg (1984) also described a number of techniques for modeling light sources that are now classic parts of the light modeling toolbox. Barzel (1997) described a highly parameterized model for light sources, including many controls for controlling rate of falloff, the area of space that is illuminated, and so on. Bjorke (2001) described a number of additional controls for controlling illumination for artistic effect. (Many parts of the Barzel and Bjorke approaches are not physically based, however.)

The goniometric light source approximation is widely used to model area light sources in the field of illumination engineering. The rule of thumb there is that once a reference point is five times an area light source's radius away from it, a point light approximation has sufficient accuracy for most applications. File format standards have been developed for encoding goniophotometric diagrams for these applications (Illuminating Engineering Society of North America 2002). Many lighting fixture manufacturers provide data in these formats on their Web sites.

Ashdown (1993) proposed a more sophisticated light source model than goniometric diagrams; he measured the directional distribution of emitted radiance at a large number of points around a light source and described how to use the resulting 4D table to compute the received radiance distribution at other points. Another generalization of goniometric lights was suggested by Heidrich et al. (1998), who represented light sources as a 4D exitant *lightfield*—essentially a function of both position and direction—and showed how to use this representation for rendering. Additional work in this area was done by Goesele et al. (2003), who further investigated issues in measuring light sources, and Mas et al. (2008), who introduced a more space-efficient representation and improved rendering efficiency.

Real-world light sources are often fairly complex, including carefully designed systems of mirrors and lenses to shape the distribution of light emitted by the light source. (Consider, for example, the headlights on a car, where it's important to evenly illuminate the surface of the road, without shining too much light in the eyes of approaching drivers.) As we'll see in Chapter 16, all of this specular reflection and transmission is challenging for light transport algorithms. It can therefore be worthwhile to do some precomputation to create a representation of light sources' final emission distributions after all of this scattering that is then used as the light source model for rendering. To this end, Kniep et al. (2009) suggest tracing the paths of photons leaving the light's filament until they hit a bounding surface around the light. They then record the position and direction of outgoing photons and use this information when computing illumination at points in the scene. Velázquez-Armendáriz et al. (2015) showed how to compute a set of point lights with directionally varying emission distributions to model emitted radiance from complex light sources. They then approximated the radiance distribution in the light interior using spherical harmonics.

Blinn and Newell (1976) first introduced the idea of environment maps and their use for simulating illumination, although they only considered illumination of specular objects. Greene (1986) further refined these ideas, considering antialiasing and different representations for environment maps. Nishita and Nakamae (1986) developed algorithms for efficiently rendering objects illuminated by hemispherical skylights and generated some of the first images that showed off that distinctive lighting effect. Miller and Hoffman (1984) were the first to consider using arbitrary environment maps to illuminate objects with diffuse and glossy BRDFs. Debevec (1998) later extended this work and investigated issues related to capturing images of real environments.

Representing illumination from the sun and sky is a particularly important application of infinite light sources; the "Further Reading" section in Chapter 15 includes a number of references related to simulating skylight scattering. Directly measuring illumination the sky is also an effective way to find accurate skylight illumination; see Kider et al. (2014) for details of a system they built to do this. (A companion Web site has a large amount of measured skylight data available for download.)

pbrt's infinite area light source models incident radiance from the light as purely a function of direction. Especially for indoor scenes, this assumption can be fairly inaccurate; position matters as well. Unger et al. (2003) captured the incident radiance as a function of direction at many different locations in a real-world scene and used this representation for rendering. Unger et al. (2008) improved on this work and showed how to decimate the samples to reduce storage requirements without introducing too much error.

As discussed in Chapter 3, one way to reduce the time spent tracing shadow rays is to have methods like Shape::IntersectP() and Primitive::IntersectP() that just check for any occlusion along a ray without bothering to compute the geometric information at the intersection point. Other approaches for optimizing ray tracing for shadow rays include the *shadow cache*, where each light stores a pointer to the last primitive that occluded a shadow ray to the light. That primitive is checked first to see if it occludes subsequent shadow rays before the ray is passed to the acceleration structure (Haines and Greenberg 1986). Pearce (1991) pointed out that the shadow cache doesn't work well if the scene has finely tessellated geometry; it may be better to cache the BVH node that held the last occluder, for instance. (The shadow cache can similarly be defeated when multiple levels of reflection and refraction are present or when Monte Carlo ray-tracing techniques are used.) Hart, Dutré, and Greenberg (1999) developed a generalization of the shadow cache, which tracks which objects block light from particular light sources and clips their geometry against the light source geometry so that shadow rays don't need to be traced toward the parts of the light that are certain to be occluded.

A related technique, described by Haines and Greenberg (1986), is the light buffer for point light sources, where the light discretizes the directions around it and determines which objects are visible along each set of directions (and are thus potential occluding objects for shadow rays). Another effective optimization is *shaft culling*, which takes advantage of coherence among groups of rays traced in a similar set of directions (e.g., shadow rays from a single point to points on an area light source). With shaft culling, a shaft that bounds a collection of rays is computed and then the objects in the scene that penetrate the shaft are found. For all of the rays in the shaft, it is only necessary to check for intersections with those objects that intersect the shaft, and the expense of ray intersection acceleration structure traversal for each of the rays is avoided (Haines and Wallace 1994).

Primitive::IntersectP() 249
Shape::IntersectP() 130

Woo and Amanatides (1990) classified which lights are visible, not visible, and partially visible in different parts of the scene and stored this information in a voxel-based 3D data structure, using this information to save shadow ray tests. Fernandez, Bala, and Greenberg (2002) developed a similar approach based on spatial decomposition that stores references to important blockers in each voxel and also builds up this information on demand for applications like walkthroughs.

For complex models, simplified versions of their geometry can be used for shadow ray intersections. For example, the simplification envelopes described by Cohen et al. (1996) can create a simplified mesh that bounds a given mesh from both the inside and the outside. If a ray misses the mesh that bounds a complex model from the outside or intersects the mesh that bounds it from the inside, then no further shadow processing is necessary. Only the uncertain remaining cases need to be intersected against the full geometry. A related technique is described by Lukaszewski (2001), who uses the Minkowski sum to effectively expand primitives (or bounds of primitives) in the scene so that intersecting one ray against one of these primitives can determine if any of a collection of rays might have intersected the actual primitives.

EXERCISES

12.1 Shadow mapping is a technique for rendering shadows from point and distant light sources based on rendering an image from the light source's perspective that records depth in each pixel of the image and then projecting points onto the shadow map and comparing their depth to the depth of the first visible object as seen from the light in that direction. This method was first described by Williams (1978), and Reeves, Salesin, and Cook (1987) developed a number of key improvements. Modify pbrt to be able to render depth map images into a file and then use them for shadow testing for lights in place of tracing shadow rays. How much faster can this be? Discuss the advantages and disadvantages of the two approaches.

12.2 Through algebraic manipulation and precomputation of one more value in the constructor, the SpotLight::Falloff() method can be rewritten to compute the exact same result (modulo floating-point differences) while using no square root computations and no divides (recall that the Vector3::Normalize() method performs both a square root and a divide). Derive and implement this optimization. How much is running time improved on a spotlight-heavy scene?

12.3 The functionality of the SpotLight could be replicated by using a suitable image in conjunction with the ProjectionLight. Discuss the advantages and disadvantages of providing this specific functionality separately with the SpotLight class.

SpotLight::Falloff() 724
Vector3::Normalize() 66

12.4 The current light source implementations don't support animated transformations. Modify pbrt to include this functionality, and render images showing off the effect of animating light positions.

12.5 Modify the `ProjectionLight` to also support orthographic projections. This variant is particularly useful even without an image map, since it gives a directional light source with a beam of user-defined extent.

12.6 Write an `AreaLight` implementation that improves on the `DiffuseAreaLight` by supporting spatially and directionally varying emitted radiance, specified via either image maps or `Textures`. Use it to render images with effects like a television illuminating a dark room or a stained-glass window lit from behind.

12.7 Many of the `Light::Power()` method implementations only compute approximations to the actual emitted power for their lights. In particular, all of the lights that use images (`ProjectionLight`, `GonioPhotometricLight`, and `Infinite AreaLight`) all neglect the fact that for each of them, different pixels subtend different solid angles and therefore contribute differently to the emitted power. Derive accurate models for the emitted power of these light sources, and implement them in pbrt. How much error do the current implementations have when used in some of the pbrt example scenes? Can you construct contrived scenes to show the maximum error introduced by the current implementation?

12.8 Read some of the papers in the "Further Reading" section that discuss the shadow cache, and add this optimization to pbrt. Measure how much it speeds up the system for a variety of scenes. What techniques can you come up with that make it work better in the presence of multiple levels of reflection?

12.9 Modify pbrt to support the shaft culling algorithm (Haines and Wallace 1994). Measure the performance difference for scenes with area light sources. Make sure that your implementation still performs well even with very large light sources (like a hemispherical skylight).

12.10 Read the paper by Velázquez-Armendáriz et al. (2015), and implement their method for efficiently rendering scenes with complex light sources. Create or find models of a few complex lights, including many shapes that exhibit specular reflection and/or transmission. Compare results using your implementation to renderings using one or more of the bidirectional integrators from Chapter 16 (which are best suited to handling this challenge). Note that you may need to set very long maximum integrator path lengths for the current implementation of pbrt to be able to render these scenes at all.

How much more efficiently does your implementation render images of scenes lit by these lights than the built-in integrators? Do results from the two approaches match?

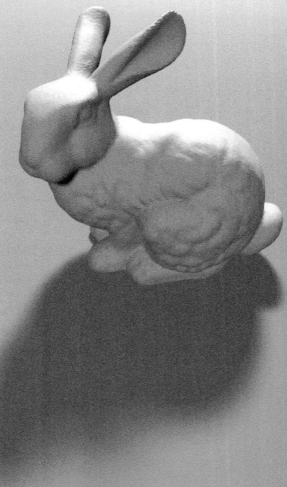

CHAPTER THIRTEEN

13 MONTE CARLO INTEGRATION

Before we introduce the `Integrators` that compute radiance along ray paths between lights and the camera, we will first lay some groundwork regarding the techniques they will use to compute solutions to the integral equations that describe light scattering. These integral equations generally do not have analytic solutions, so we must turn to numerical methods. Although standard numerical integration techniques like trapezoidal integration or Gaussian quadrature are very effective at solving low-dimensional smooth integrals, their rate of convergence for the higher dimensional and discontinuous integrals that are common in rendering is poor.

Monte Carlo numerical integration methods provide one solution to this problem. They use randomness to evaluate integrals with a convergence rate that is independent of the dimensionality of the integrand. In this chapter, we review important concepts from probability and lay the foundation for using Monte Carlo techniques to evaluate the key integrals in rendering.

Judicious use of randomness has revolutionized the field of algorithm design. Randomized algorithms fall broadly into two classes: *Las Vegas* and *Monte Carlo*. Las Vegas algorithms are those that use randomness but always give the same result in the end (e.g., choosing a random array entry as the pivot element in Quicksort). Monte Carlo algorithms, on the other hand, give different results depending on the particular random numbers used along the way but give the right answer *on average*. So, by averaging the results of several runs of a Monte Carlo algorithm (on the same input), it is possible to find a result that is statistically very likely to be close to the true answer. Motwani and Raghavan (1995) have written an excellent introduction to the field of randomized algorithms.

Physically Based Rendering: From Theory To Implementation.
http://dx.doi.org/10.1016/B978-0-12-800645-0.50013-0

Monte Carlo integration[1] is a method for using random sampling to estimate the values of integrals. One very useful property of Monte Carlo is that one only needs the ability to evaluate an integrand $f(x)$ at arbitrary points in the domain in order to estimate the value of its integral $\int f(x)\,dx$. This property not only makes Monte Carlo easy to implement but also makes the technique applicable to a broad variety of integrands, including those containing discontinuities.

Many of the integrals that arise in rendering are difficult or impossible to evaluate directly. For example, to compute the amount of light reflected by a surface at a point according to Equation (5.9), we must integrate the product of the incident radiance and the BSDF over the unit sphere. How to do so is not immediately clear: the incident radiance function is almost never available in closed form due to the complex and difficult-to-predict effect of object visibility in realistic scenes.

Even if the incident radiance function were available in closed form, performing the integral analytically would still not be possible in general. Monte Carlo integration makes it possible to estimate the reflected radiance simply by choosing a set of directions over the sphere, computing the incident radiance along them, multiplying by the BSDF's value for those directions, and applying a weighting term. Arbitrary BSDFs, light source descriptions, and scene geometry are easily handled; evaluation of each of these functions at arbitrary points is all that is required.

The main disadvantage of Monte Carlo is that if n samples are used to estimate the integral, the algorithm converges to the correct result at a rate of $O(n^{-1/2})$. In other words, to cut the error in half, it is necessary to evaluate four times as many samples. In rendering, each sample generally requires that one or more rays be traced in the process of computing the value of the integrand, a computationally expensive cost to bear when using Monte Carlo for image synthesis. In images, artifacts from Monte Carlo sampling manifest themselves as noise—pixels are randomly too bright or too dark. Most of the current research in Monte Carlo for computer graphics is about reducing this error as much as possible while minimizing the number of additional samples that must be taken.

13.1 BACKGROUND AND PROBABILITY REVIEW

We will start by defining some terms and reviewing basic ideas from probability. We assume that the reader is already familiar with basic probability concepts; readers needing a more complete introduction to this topic should consult a textbook such as Sheldon Ross's *Introduction to Probability Models* (2002).

A *random variable* X is a value chosen by some random process. We will generally use capital letters to denote random variables, with exceptions made for a few Greek symbols that represent special random variables. Random variables are always drawn from some domain, which can be either discrete (e.g., a fixed set of possibilities) or continuous (e.g., the real numbers $\mathbb{R}$). Applying a function f to a random variable X results in a new random variable $Y = f(X)$.

---

1   For brevity, we will refer to Monte Carlo integration simply as "Monte Carlo."

For example, the result of a roll of a die is a discrete random variable sampled from the set of events $X_i = \{1, 2, 3, 4, 5, 6\}$. Each event has a probability $p_i = \frac{1}{6}$, and the sum of probabilities $\sum p_i$ is necessarily one. We can take a continuous, uniformly distributed random variable $\xi \in [0, 1)$ and map it to a discrete random variable, choosing X_i if

$$\sum_{j=1}^{i-1} p_j < \xi \le \sum_{j=1}^{i} p_j.$$

For lighting applications, we might want to define the probability of sampling illumination from each light in the scene based on the power Φ_i from each source relative to the total power from all sources:

$$p_i = \frac{\Phi_i}{\sum_j \Phi_j}.$$

Notice that these p_i also sum to 1.

The *cumulative distribution function* (CDF) $P(x)$ of a random variable is the probability that a value from the variable's distribution is less than or equal to some value x:

$$P(x) = Pr\{X \le x\}.$$

For the die example, $P(2) = \frac{1}{3}$, since two of the six possibilities are less than or equal to 2.

13.1.1 CONTINUOUS RANDOM VARIABLES

In rendering, discrete random variables are less common than continuous random variables, which take on values over ranges of continuous domains (e.g., the real numbers, directions on the unit sphere, or the surfaces of shapes in the scene).

A particularly important random variable is the *canonical uniform random variable*, which we will write as ξ. This variable takes on all values in its domain $[0, 1)$ with equal probability. This particular variable is important for two reasons. First, it is easy to generate a variable with this distribution in software—most run-time libraries have a pseudo-random number generator that does just that.[2] Second, as we will show later, it is possible to generate samples from arbitrary distributions by first starting with canonical uniform random variables and applying an appropriate transformation. The technique described previously for mapping from ξ to the six faces of a die gives a flavor of this technique in the discrete case.

Another example of a continuous random variable is one that ranges over the real numbers between 0 and 2, where the probability of its taking on any particular value x is proportional to the value $2 - x$: it is twice as likely for this random variable to take on a value around 0 as it is to take one around 1, and so forth. The *probability density function* (PDF) formalizes this idea: it describes the relative probability of a random variable

---

2   Although the theory of Monte Carlo is based on using truly random numbers, in practice a well-written pseudo-random number generator (PRNG) is sufficient. pbrt uses a particularly high-quality PRNG that returns a sequence of pseudo-random values that is effectively as "random" as true random numbers. (Many PRNGs are not as well implemented and have detectable patterns in the sequence of numbers they generate.) True random numbers, found by measuring random phenomena like atomic decay or atmospheric noise, are available from sources like *www.random.org* for those for whom PRNGs are not acceptable.

taking on a particular value. The PDF $p(x)$ is the derivative of the random variable's CDF,

$$p(x) = \frac{dP(x)}{dx}.$$

For uniform random variables, $p(x)$ is a constant; this is a direct consequence of uniformity. For ξ we have

$$p(x) = \begin{cases} 1 & x \in [0, 1) \\ 0 & \text{otherwise.} \end{cases}$$

PDFs are necessarily nonnegative and always integrate to 1 over their domains. Given an arbitrary interval $[a, b]$ in the domain, integrating the PDF gives the probability that a random variable lies inside the interval:

$$P(x \in [a, b]) = \int_a^b p(x)\, dx.$$

This follows directly from the first fundamental theorem of calculus and the definition of the PDF.

13.1.2 EXPECTED VALUES AND VARIANCE

The *expected value* $E_p[f(x)]$ of a function f is defined as the average value of the function over some distribution of values $p(x)$ over its domain. In the next section, we will see how Monte Carlo integration computes the expected values of arbitrary integrals. The expected value over a domain, D, is defined as

$$E_p[f(x)] = \int_D f(x)\, p(x)\, dx. \tag{13.1}$$

As an example, consider the problem of finding the expected value of the cosine function between 0 and π, where p is uniform.[3] Because the PDF $p(x)$ must integrate to 1 over the domain, $p(x) = 1/\pi$, so

$$E[\cos x] = \int_0^\pi \frac{\cos x}{\pi}\, dx = \frac{1}{\pi}(-\sin \pi + \sin 0) = 0,$$

which is precisely the expected result. (Consider the graph of $\cos x$ over $[0, \pi]$ to see why this is so.)

The *variance* of a function is the expected squared deviation of the function from its expected value. Variance is a fundamental concept for quantifying the error in a value estimated by a Monte Carlo algorithm. It provides a precise way to quantify this error and measure how improvements to Monte Carlo algorithms reduce the error in the final result. The variance of a function f is defined as

$$V[f(x)] = E\left[\left(f(x) - E[f(x)]\right)^2\right].$$

---

3   When computing expected values with a uniform distribution, we will drop the subscript p from E_p.

The expected value and variance have a few important properties that follow immediately from their respective definitions:

$$E[af(x)] = aE[f(x)]$$

$$E\left[\sum_i f(X_i)\right] = \sum_i E[f(X_i)]$$

$$V[af(x)] = a^2 V[f(x)].$$

These properties, and some simple algebraic manipulation, yield an alternative expanded expression for the variance:

$$V[f(x)] = E\left[(f(x))^2\right] - E[f(x)]^2.$$ [13.2]

Thus, the variance is the expected value of the square minus the square of the expected value. Given random variables that are *independent*, variance also has the property that the sum of the variances is equal to the variance of their sum:

$$\sum_i V[f(X_i)] = V\left[\sum_i f(X_i)\right].$$

13.2 THE MONTE CARLO ESTIMATOR

We can now define the basic Monte Carlo estimator, which approximates the value of an arbitrary integral. It is the foundation of the light transport algorithms defined in Chapters 14, 15, and 16.

Suppose that we want to evaluate a 1D integral $\int_a^b f(x)\,dx$. Given a supply of uniform random variables $X_i \in [a, b]$, the Monte Carlo estimator says that the expected value of the estimator

$$F_N = \frac{b-a}{N} \sum_{i=1}^{N} f(X_i),$$

$E[F_N]$, is in fact equal to the integral.[4] This fact can be demonstrated with just a few steps. First, note that the PDF $p(x)$ corresponding to the random variable X_i must be equal to $1/(b-a)$, since p must both be a constant and also integrate to 1 over the domain $[a, b]$. Algebraic manipulation then shows that

Lerp() 1079

RNG::UniformFloat() 1066

---

4   For example, the samples X_i might be computed in an implementation by Lerp(rng.UniformFloat(), a, b).

$$E[F_N] = E\left[\frac{b-a}{N}\sum_{i=1}^{N}f(X_i)\right]$$

$$= \frac{b-a}{N}\sum_{i=1}^{N}E\left[f(X_i)\right]$$

$$= \frac{b-a}{N}\sum_{i=1}^{N}\int_{a}^{b}f(x)\,p(x)\,dx$$

$$= \frac{1}{N}\sum_{i=1}^{N}\int_{a}^{b}f(x)\,dx$$

$$= \int_{a}^{b}f(x)\,dx.$$

The restriction to uniform random variables can be relaxed with a small generalization. This is an extremely important step, since carefully choosing the PDF from which samples are drawn is an important technique for reducing variance in Monte Carlo (Section 13.10). If the random variables X_i are drawn from some arbitrary PDF $p(x)$, then the estimator

$$F_N = \frac{1}{N}\sum_{i=1}^{N}\frac{f(X_i)}{p(X_i)} \qquad\qquad [13.3]$$

can be used to estimate the integral instead. The only limitation on $p(x)$ is that it must be nonzero for all x where $|f(x)| > 0$. It is similarly not too hard to see that the expected value of this estimator is the desired integral of f:

$$E[F_N] = E\left[\frac{1}{N}\sum_{i=1}^{N}\frac{f(X_i)}{p(X_i)}\right]$$

$$= \frac{1}{N}\sum_{i=1}^{N}\int_{a}^{b}\frac{f(x)}{p(x)}p(x)\,dx$$

$$= \frac{1}{N}\sum_{i=1}^{N}\int_{a}^{b}f(x)\,dx$$

$$= \int_{a}^{b}f(x)\,dx.$$

Extending this estimator to multiple dimensions or complex integration domains is straightforward. N samples X_i are taken from a multidimensional (or "joint") PDF, and the estimator is applied as usual. For example, consider the 3D integral

$$\int_{x_0}^{x_1}\int_{y_0}^{y_1}\int_{z_0}^{z_1}f(x,\,y,\,z)\,dx\,dy\,dz.$$

If samples $X_i = (x_i,\,y_i,\,z_i)$ are chosen uniformly from the box from $(x_0,\,y_0,\,z_0)$ to $(x_1,\,y_1,\,z_1)$, the PDF $p(X)$ is the constant value

$$\frac{1}{(x_1 - x_0)} \frac{1}{(y_1 - y_0)} \frac{1}{(z_1 - z_0)},$$

and the estimator is

$$\frac{(x_1 - x_0)(y_1 - y_0)(z_1 - z_0)}{N} \sum_i f(X_i).$$

Note that the number of samples N can be chosen arbitrarily, regardless of the dimension of the integrand. This is another important advantage of Monte Carlo over traditional deterministic quadrature techniques. The number of samples taken in Monte Carlo is completely independent of the dimensionality of the integral, while with standard numerical quadrature techniques the number of samples required is exponential in the dimension.

Showing that the Monte Carlo estimator converges to the right answer is not enough to justify its use; a good rate of convergence is important too. Although we will not derive its rate of convergence here, it has been shown that error in the Monte Carlo estimator decreases at a rate of $O(\sqrt{N})$ in the number of samples taken. An accessible treatment of this topic can be found in Veach's thesis (Veach 1997, p. 39). Although standard quadrature techniques converge faster than $O(\sqrt{N})$ in one dimension, their performance becomes exponentially worse as the dimensionality of the integrand increases, while Monte Carlo's convergence rate is independent of the dimension, making Monte Carlo the only practical numerical integration algorithm for high-dimensional integrals. We have already encountered some high-dimensional integrals in this book, and in Chapter 14 we will see that the path tracing formulation of the light transport equation is an *infinite-dimensional* integral!

13.3 SAMPLING RANDOM VARIABLES

In order to evaluate the Monte Carlo estimator in Equation (13.3), it is necessary to be able to draw random samples from the chosen probability distribution. This section will introduce the basics of this process and demonstrate it with some straightforward examples. The next two sections will introduce more complex approaches to sampling before Section 13.6 develops the approach for the general multidimensional case. In Chapters 14, 15, and 16, we'll then see how to use these techniques to generate samples from the distributions defined by BSDFs, light sources, cameras, and scattering media.

13.3.1 THE INVERSION METHOD

The inversion method uses one or more uniform random variables and maps them to random variables from the desired distribution. To explain how this process works in general, we will start with a simple discrete example. Suppose we have a process with four possible outcomes. The probabilities of each of the four outcomes are given by p_1, p_2, p_3, and p_4, respectively, with the requirement that $\sum_{i=1}^4 p_i = 1$. The corresponding PDF is shown in Figure 13.1.

In order to draw a sample from this distribution, we first find the CDF $P(x)$. In the continuous case, P is the indefinite integral of p. In the discrete case, we can directly construct the CDF by stacking the bars on top of each other, starting at the left. This idea

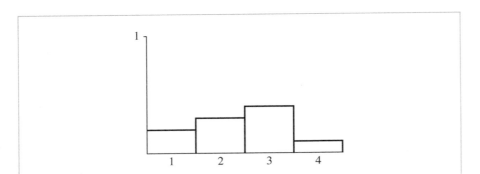

Figure 13.1: A Discrete PDF for Four Events, Each with a Probability p_i. The sum of their probabilities $\sum_i p_i$ is necessarily 1.

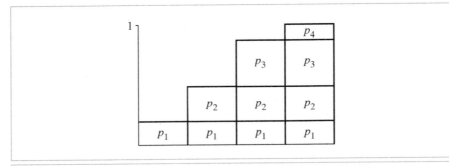

Figure 13.2: A Discrete CDF, Corresponding to the PDF in Figure 13.1. Each column's height is given by the PDF for the event that it represents plus the sum of the PDFs for the previous events, $P_i = \sum_{j=1}^{i} p_i$.

is shown in Figure 13.2. Notice that the height of the rightmost bar must be 1 because of the requirement that all probabilities sum to 1.

To draw a sample from the distribution, we then take a uniform random number ξ and use it to select one of the possible outcomes using the CDF, doing so in a way that chooses a particular outcome with probability equal to the outcome's own probability. This idea is illustrated in Figure 13.3, where the events' probabilities are projected onto the vertical axis and a random variable ξ selects among them. It should be clear that this draws from the correct distribution—the probability of the uniform sample hitting any particular bar is exactly equal to the height of that bar. In order to generalize this technique to continuous distributions, consider what happens as the number of discrete possibilities approaches infinity. The PDF from Figure 13.1 becomes a smooth curve, and the CDF from Figure 13.2 becomes its integral. The projection process is still the same, although if the function is continuous, the projection has a convenient mathematical

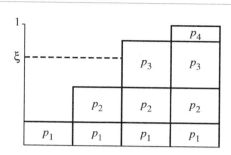

Figure 13.3: To use the inversion method to draw a sample from the distribution described by the PDF in Figure 13.1, a canonical uniform random variable is plotted on the vertical axis. By construction, the horizontal extension of ξ will intersect the box representing the ith outcome with probability p_i. If the corresponding event is chosen for a set of random variables ξ, then the resulting distribution of events will be distributed according to the PDF.

interpretation—it represents inverting the CDF and evaluating the inverse at ξ. This technique is thus called the *inversion method*.

More precisely, we can draw a sample X_i from an arbitrary PDF $p(x)$ with the following steps:

1. Compute the CDF[5] $P(x) = \int_0^x p(x') \, dx'$.
2. Compute the inverse $P^{-1}(x)$.
3. Obtain a uniformly distributed random number ξ.
4. Compute $X_i = P^{-1}(\xi)$.

Example: Power Distribution

As an example of how this procedure works, consider the task of drawing samples from a *power distribution*, $p(x) \propto x^n$. The PDF of the power distribution is

$$p(x) = cx^n,$$

for the constant c that normalizes the PDF. The first task to tackle is to find the PDF. In most cases, this simply involves computing the value of the proportionality constant c, which can be found using the constraint that $\int p(x) \, dx = 1$:

$$\int_0^1 cx^n \, dx = 1$$

$$c \left. \frac{x^{n+1}}{n+1} \right|_0^1 = 1$$

$$\frac{c}{n+1} = 1$$

$$c = n + 1.$$

---

5   In general, the lower limit of integration should be $-\infty$, although if $p(x) = 0$ for $x < 0$, this equation is equivalent.

Therefore, $p(x) = (n + 1)x^n$. We can integrate this PDF to get the CDF:

$$P(x) = \int_0^x p(x')\,dx' = x^{n+1},$$

and inversion is simple: $P^{-1}(x) = \sqrt[n+1]{x}$. Therefore, given a uniform random variable ξ, samples can be drawn from the power distribution as

$$X = \sqrt[n+1]{\xi}. \qquad\qquad [13.4]$$

Another approach is to use a sampling trick that works only for the power distribution, selecting $X = \max(\xi_1, \xi_2, \ldots, \xi_{n+1})$. This random variable is distributed according to the power distribution as well. To see why, note that $Pr\{X < x\}$ is the probability that *all* the $\xi_i < x$. But the ξ_i are independent, so

$$Pr\{X < x\} = \prod_{i=1}^{n+1} Pr\left\{\xi_i < x\right\} = x^{n+1},$$

which is exactly the desired CDF. Depending on the speed of your random number generator, this technique can be faster than the inversion method for small values of n.

Example: Exponential Distribution

When rendering images with participating media, it is frequently useful to draw samples from a distribution $p(x) \propto e^{-ax}$. As before, the first step is to normalize this distribution so that it integrates to one. In this case, we'll assume for now that the range of values x we'd like the generated samples to cover is $[0, \infty)$ rather than $[0, 1]$, so

$$\int_0^\infty ce^{-ax}\,dx = -\left.\frac{c}{a}e^{-ax}\right|_0^\infty = \frac{c}{a} = 1.$$

Thus we know that $c = a$, and our PDF is $p(x) = ae^{-ax}$. Now, we integrate to find $P(x)$:

$$P(x) = \int_0^x ae^{-ax'}\,dx' = 1 - e^{-ax}.$$

This function is easy to invert:

$$P^{-1}(x) = -\frac{\ln(1 - x)}{a},$$

and we can draw samples thus:

$$X = -\frac{\ln(1 - \xi)}{a}.$$

It may be tempting to simplify the log term from $\ln(1 - \xi)$ to $\ln \xi$, under the theory that because $\xi \in [0, 1)$, these are effectively the same and a subtraction can thus be saved. The problem with this idea is that ξ may have the value 0 but never has the value 1. With the simplification, it's possible that we'd try to take the logarithm of 0, which is undefined; this danger is avoided with the first formulation.[6] While a ξ value of 0 may seem very

---

6   Once again: a subtlety that the authors didn't appreciate in the first two editions of the book.

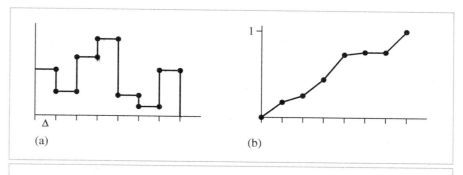

Figure 13.4: (a) Probability density function for a piecewise-constant 1D function and (b) cumulative distribution function defined by this PDF.

unlikely, it does happen (especially in the world of floating-point arithmetic, rather than the real numbers). Some of the low-discrepancy sampling patterns introduced in Chapter 7 are particularly prone to generating the value 0.

Example: Piecewise-Constant 1D Functions

An interesting exercise is to work out how to sample from 1D piecewise-constant functions (step functions). Without loss of generality, we will just consider piecewise-constant functions defined over $[0, 1]$.

Assume that the 1D function's domain is split into N equal-sized pieces of size $\Delta = 1/N$. These regions start and end at points $x_i = i\Delta$, where i ranges from 0 to N, inclusive. Within each region, the value of the function $f(x)$ is a constant (Figure 13.4(a)). The value of $f(x)$ is

$$f(x) = \begin{cases} v_0 & x_0 \leq x < x_1 \\ v_1 & x_1 \leq x < x_2 \\ \vdots \end{cases}.$$

The integral $\int f(x)\,\mathrm{d}x$ is

$$c = \int_0^1 f(x)\,\mathrm{d}x = \sum_{i=0}^{N-1} \Delta v_i = \sum_{i=0}^{N-1} \frac{v_i}{N}, \tag{13.5}$$

and so it is easy to construct the PDF $p(x)$ for $f(x)$ as $f(x)/c$. By direct application of the relevant formulae, the CDF $P(x)$ is a piecewise linear function defined at points x_i by

$$P(x_0) = 0$$

$$P(x_1) = \int_{x_0}^{x_1} p(x)\,\mathrm{d}x = \frac{v_0}{Nc} = P(x_0) + \frac{v_0}{Nc}$$

$$P(x_2) = \int_{x_0}^{x_2} p(x)\,\mathrm{d}x = \int_{x_0}^{x_1} p(x)\,\mathrm{d}x + \int_{x_1}^{x_2} p(x)\,\mathrm{d}x = P(x_1) + \frac{v_1}{Nc}$$

$$P(x_i) = P(x_{i-1}) + \frac{v_{i-1}}{Nc}.$$

Between two points x_i and x_{i+1}, the CDF is linearly increasing with slope v_i/c.

Recall that in order to sample $f(x)$ we need to invert the CDF to find the value x such that

$$\xi = \int_0^x p(x')\, dx' = P(x).$$

Because the CDF is monotonically increasing, the value of x must be between the x_i and x_{i+1} such that $P(x_i) \leq \xi$ and $\xi \leq P(x_{i+1})$. Given an array of CDF values, this pair of $P(x_i)$ values can be efficiently found with a binary search.

Distribution1D is a small utility class that represents a piecewise-constant 1D function's PDF and CDF and provides methods to perform this sampling efficiently.

⟨*Sampling Declarations*⟩ ≡
```
struct Distribution1D {
    ⟨Distribution1D Public Methods 758⟩
    ⟨Distribution1D Public Data 758⟩
};
```

The Distribution1D constructor takes n values of a piecewise-constant function f. It makes its own copy of the function values, computes the function's CDF, and also stores the integral of the function, funcInt. Note that the constructor allocates n+1 Floats for the cdf array because if $f(x)$ has N step values, then we need to store the value of the CDF at each of the $N + 1$ values of x_i. Storing the CDF value of 1 at the end of the array is redundant but simplifies the sampling code later.

⟨*Distribution1D Public Methods*⟩ ≡   758
```
Distribution1D(const Float *f, int n)
    : func(f, f + n), cdf(n + 1) {
    ⟨Compute integral of step function at xᵢ 758⟩
    ⟨Transform step function integral into CDF 759⟩
}
```

⟨*Distribution1D Public Data*⟩ ≡   758
```
std::vector<Float> func, cdf;
Float funcInt;
```

⟨*Distribution1D Public Methods*⟩ +≡   758
```
int Count() const { return func.size(); }
```

This constructor computes the integral of $f(x)$ using Equation (13.5). It stores the result in the cdf array for now so that it doesn't need to allocate additional temporary space for it.

⟨*Compute integral of step function at xᵢ*⟩ ≡   758
```
cdf[0] = 0;
for (int i = 1; i < n + 1; ++i)
    cdf[i] = cdf[i - 1] + func[i - 1] / n;
```

Now that the value of the integral over all of [0, 1] is stored in cdf[n], this value can be copied into funcInt and the CDF can be normalized by dividing through all entries by this value.

⟨*Transform step function integral into CDF*⟩ ≡   758
```
funcInt = cdf[n];
if (funcInt == 0) {
    for (int i = 1; i < n + 1; ++i)
        cdf[i] = Float(i) / Float(n);
} else {
    for (int i = 1; i < n + 1; ++i)
        cdf[i] /= funcInt;
}
```

The Distribution1D::SampleContinuous() method uses the given random sample u to sample from its distribution. It returns the corresponding value $x \in [0, 1)$ and the value of the PDF $p(x)$. If the optional off parameter is not nullptr, it returns the offset into the array of function values of the largest index where the CDF was less than or equal to u. (In other words, cdf[*off] <= u < cdf[*off+1].)

⟨*Distribution1D Public Methods*⟩ +≡   758
```
Float SampleContinuous(Float u, Float *pdf, int *off = nullptr) const {
    ⟨Find surrounding CDF segments and offset 759⟩
    if (off) *off = offset;
    ⟨Compute offset along CDF segment 759⟩
    ⟨Compute PDF for sampled offset 759⟩
    ⟨Return x ∈ [0, 1) corresponding to sample 760⟩
}
```

Mapping u to an interval matching the above criterion is carried out using the efficient binary search implemented in FindInterval() (see Appendix A for details).

⟨*Find surrounding CDF segments and* offset⟩ ≡   759, 760
```
int offset = FindInterval(cdf.size(),
    [&](int index) { return cdf[index] <= u; });
```

Given the pair of CDF values that straddle u, we can compute x. First, we determine how far u is between cdf[offset] and cdf[offset+1], du, where du is 0 if u == cdf[offset] and goes up to 1 if u == cdf[offset+1]. Because the CDF is piecewise linear, the sample value x is the same offset between x_i and x_{i+1} (Figure 13.4(b)).

⟨*Compute offset along CDF segment*⟩ ≡   759
```
Float du = u - cdf[offset];
if ((cdf[offset + 1] - cdf[offset]) > 0)
    du /= (cdf[offset + 1] - cdf[offset]);
```

The PDF for this sample $p(x)$ is easily computed since we have the function's integral in funcInt. (Note that the offset offset into the CDF array has been computed in a way so that func[offset] gives the value of the function in the CDF range that the sample landed in.)

⟨*Compute PDF for sampled offset*⟩ ≡   759
```
if (pdf) *pdf = func[offset] / funcInt;
```

Finally, the appropriate value of x is computed and returned.

⟨*Return $x \in [0, 1)$ corresponding to sample*⟩ ≡   759
```
return (offset + du) / Count();
```

In a small overloading of semantics, Distribution1D can also be used for discrete 1D probability distributions where there are some number of buckets n, each with some weight, and we'd like to sample among the buckets with probability proportional to their relative weights. This functionality is used, for example, by some of the Integrators in that compute a discrete distribution for the light sources in the scene with weights given by the lights' powers. Sampling from the discrete distribution just requires figuring out which pair of CDF values the sample value lies between; the PDF is computed as the discrete probability of sampling the corresponding bucket.

⟨*Distribution1D Public Methods*⟩ +≡   758
```
int SampleDiscrete(Float u, Float *pdf = nullptr,
        Float *uRemapped = nullptr) const {
    ⟨Find surrounding CDF segments and offset 759⟩
    if (pdf) *pdf = func[offset] / (funcInt * Count());
    if (uRemapped)
        *uRemapped = (u - cdf[offset]) / (cdf[offset + 1] - cdf[offset]);
    return offset;
}
```

It's also useful to be able to compute the PDF for sampling a given value from the discrete PDF.

⟨*Distribution1D Public Methods*⟩ +≡   758
```
Float DiscretePDF(int index) const {
    return func[index] / (funcInt * Count());
}
```

13.3.2 THE REJECTION METHOD

For some functions $f(x)$, it may not be possible to integrate them in order to find their PDFs, or it may not be possible to analytically invert their CDFs. The *rejection method* is a technique for generating samples according to a function's distribution without needing to do either of these steps; it is essentially a dart-throwing approach. Assume that we want to draw samples from some such function $f(x)$ but we do have a PDF $p(x)$ that satisfies $f(x) < c\, p(x)$ for some scalar constant c, and suppose that we do know how to sample from p. The rejection method is then:

> loop forever:
>> sample X from p's distribution
>> if $\xi < f(X)/(c\, p(X))$ then
>>> return X

This procedure repeatedly chooses a pair of random variables (X, ξ). If the point $(X, \xi\, c\, p(X))$ lies under $f(X)$, then the sample X is accepted. Otherwise, it is rejected

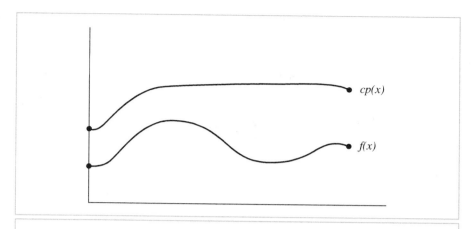

Figure 13.5: Rejection sampling generates samples according to the distribution of an arbitrary function $f(x)$ even if f's PDF is unknown or its CDF can't be inverted. If some distribution $p(x)$ and a scalar constant c are known such that $f(x) < c\,p(x)$, then samples can be drawn from $p(x)$ and randomly accepted with the rejection method. The closer the fit of $c\,p(x)$ to $f(x)$, the more efficient this process is.

and a new sample pair is chosen. This idea is illustrated in Figure 13.5. Without going into too much detail, it should be clear that the efficiency of this scheme depends on how tightly $c\,p(x)$ bounds $f(x)$. This technique works in any number of dimensions.

Rejection sampling isn't actually used in any of the Monte Carlo algorithms currently implemented in pbrt. We will normally prefer to find distributions that are similar to $f(x)$ that can be sampled directly, so that well-distributed points on $[0, 1)^n$ can be mapped to sample points that are in turn well-distributed, as will be discussed in Section 13.8. Nevertheless, rejection sampling is an important technique to be aware of, particularly when debugging Monte Carlo implementations. For example, if one suspects the presence of a bug in code that draws samples from some distribution using the inversion method, then one can replace it with a straightforward implementation based on the rejection method and see if the Monte Carlo estimator computes the same result. Of course, it's necessary to take many samples in situations like these, so that variance in the estimates doesn't mask errors.

Example: Rejection Sampling a Unit Circle

Suppose we want to select a uniformly distributed point inside a unit circle. Using the rejection method, we simply select a random (x, y) position inside the circumscribed square and return it if it falls inside the circle. This process is shown in Figure 13.6.

The function RejectionSampleDisk() implements this algorithm. A similar approach will work to generate uniformly distributed samples on the inside of any complex shape as long as it has an inside–outside test.

RejectionSampleDisk() 762

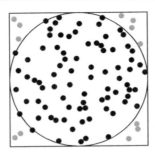

Figure 13.6: Rejection Sampling a Circle. One approach to finding uniform points in the unit circle is to sample uniform random points in the unit square and reject all that lie outside the circle. The remaining points will be uniformly distributed within the circle.

⟨*Sampling Function Definitions*⟩ +≡
```
Point2f RejectionSampleDisk(RNG &rng) {
    Point2f p;
    do {
        p.x = 1 - 2 * rng.UniformFloat();
        p.y = 1 - 2 * rng.UniformFloat();
    } while (p.x * p.x + p.y * p.y > 1);
    return p;
}
```

In general, the efficiency of rejection sampling depends on the percentage of samples that are expected to be rejected. For the problem of finding uniform points in the 2D case, this is easy to compute. It is the area of the circle divided by the area of the square: $\frac{\pi}{4} \approx 78.5\%$. If the method is applied to generate samples in hyperspheres in the general n-dimensional case, however, the volume of an n-dimensional hypersphere actually goes to 0 as n increases, and this approach becomes increasingly inefficient.

* 13.4 METROPOLIS SAMPLING

Metropolis sampling is a technique for generating a set of samples from a non-negative function f that is distributed proportionally to f's value (Metropolis et al. 1953).[7] Remarkably, it is able to do so without requiring anything more than the ability to evaluate f; it is not necessary to be able to integrate f, normalize the integral, and invert the resulting CDF. Furthermore, *every* iteration produces a usable sample generated from the function's PDF; Metropolis sampling doesn't share the shortcoming of rejection sam-

Point2f 68
RNG 1065
RNG::UniformFloat() 1066

---

7   We will refer to the Monte Carlo sampling algorithm as "the Metropolis algorithm" here. Other commonly used shorthands for it include M(RT)², for the initials of the authors of the original paper, and Metropolis–Hastings, which gives a nod to Hastings, who generalized the technique (Fishman 1996). The term *Markov chain Monte Carlo* is synonymous with Metropolis sampling and derived techniques.

pling that the number of iterations needed to obtain the next sample cannot be bounded. It can thus efficiently generate samples from a wider variety of functions than the techniques introduced in the previous section. It forms the foundation of the Metropolis light transport algorithm implemented in Section 16.4.

Metropolis sampling does have a few disadvantages: successive samples in the sequence are statistically correlated, and it is thus not possible to ensure that a small set of samples generated by Metropolis is well distributed across the domain. It's only in the limit over a large number of samples that the samples will cover the domain. As such, the variance reduction advantages of techniques like stratified sampling (Section 13.8.1) are generally not available when using Metropolis sampling.

13.4.1 BASIC ALGORITHM

More concretely, the Metropolis algorithm generates a set of samples X_i from a function f, which is defined over an arbitrary-dimensional state space Ω (frequently, $\Omega = \mathbb{R}^n$) and returns a value in the reals, $f:\Omega \to \mathbb{R}$. After the first sample $X_0 \in \Omega$ has been selected, each subsequent sample X_i is generated by using a random *mutation* to X_{i-1} to compute a proposed sample X'. The mutation may be accepted or rejected, and X_i is accordingly set to either X' or X_{i-1}. When these transitions from one state to another are chosen subject to a few requirements (to be described shortly), the distribution of X_i values that results reaches an equilibrium distribution; this distribution is the *stationary distribution*. In the limit, the distribution of the set of samples $X_i \in \Omega$ is proportional to $f(x)$'s probability density function $p(x) = f(x)/\int_\Omega f(x)\mathrm{d}\Omega$.

In order to generate the correct distribution of samples, it is necessary to generate proposed mutations and then accept or reject the mutations subject to a few constraints. Assume that we have a mutation method that proposes changing from a given state X into a new state X' (this might be done by perturbing X in some way, or even by generating a completely new value). We must be able to compute a tentative transition function $T(X \to X')$ that gives the probability density of the mutation technique's proposing a transition to X', given that the current state is X. (Section 13.4.2 will discuss considerations for designing transition functions.)

Given a transition function, it is possible to define an *acceptance probability* $a(X \to X')$ that gives the probability of accepting a proposed mutation from X to X' in a way that ensures that the distribution of samples is proportional to $f(x)$. If the distribution is already in equilibrium, the transition density between any two states must be equal:[8]

$$f(X)\, T(X \to X')\, a(X \to X') = f(X')\, T(X' \to X)\, a(X' \to X). \tag{13.6}$$

This property is called *detailed balance*.

Since f and T are set, Equation (13.6) tells us how a must be defined. In particular, a definition of a that maximizes the rate at which equilibrium is reached is

$$a(X \to X') = \min\left(1, \frac{f(X')\, T(X' \to X)}{f(X)\, T(X \to X')}\right). \tag{13.7}$$

---

8   See Kalos and Whitlock (1986) or Veach's thesis (1997) for a rigorous derivation.

One thing to immediately notice from Equation (13.7) is that, if the transition probability density is the same in both directions, the acceptance probability simplifies to

$$a(X \rightarrow X') = \min\left(1, \frac{f(X')}{f(X)}\right).$$ [13.8]

Put together, we have the basic Metropolis sampling algorithm in pseudocode:

```
X = X0
for i = 1 to n
    X' = mutate(X)
    a = accept(X, X')
    if (random() < a)
        X = X'
    record(X)
```

This code generates n samples by mutating the previous sample and computing acceptance probabilities as in Equation (13.7). Each sample X_i can then be recorded in a data structure or used as a sample for integration.

Because the Metropolis algorithm naturally avoids parts of Ω where $f(x)$'s value is relatively low, few samples will be accumulated there. In order to get some information about $f(x)$'s behavior in such regions, the *expected values* technique can be used to enhance the basic Metropolis algorithm. In this case, we still decide which state to transition into as before, but we record a sample at each of X and X', regardless of which one is selected by the acceptance criteria. Each of these recorded samples has a weight associated with it, where the weights are the probabilities $(1 - a)$ for X and a for X', where a is the acceptance probability. Expected values doesn't change the way we decide which state, X or X', to use at the next step; that part of the computation remains the same.

Updated pseudocode shows the idea:

```
X = X0
for i = 1 to n
    X' = mutate(X)
    a = accept(X, X')
    record(X, 1 - a)
    record(X', a)
    if (random() < a)
        X = X'
```

Comparing the two pieces of pseudocode, we can see that in the limit, the same weight distribution will be accumulated for X and X'. Expected values more quickly give a smoother result and more information about the areas where $f(x)$ is low than the basic algorithm does.

13.4.2 CHOOSING MUTATION STRATEGIES

In general, one has a lot of freedom in choosing mutation strategies, subject to being able to compute the tentative transition density $T(X \rightarrow X')$. Recall from Equation (13.8) that if the transition densities are symmetric then it is not even necessary to be able to compute them to apply the Metropolis sampling algorithm. It's easy to apply multiple mutation strategies, so if there are some that are effective in only some circumstances it doesn't hurt to try using them as one of a set of approaches.

It is generally desirable that mutations propose large changes to the current sample rather than small ones. Doing so more quickly explores the state space rather than letting the sampler get stuck in a small region of it. However, when the function's value $f(X)$ is relatively large at the current sample X, then it is likely that many proposed mutations will be rejected (consider the case where $f(X) \gg f(X')$ in Equation (13.8); $a(X \to X')$ will be very small). We'd like to avoid the case where many samples in a row are the same, again to better explore new parts of the state space: staying in the same state for many samples in a row leads to increased variance—intuitively, it makes sense that the more we move around Ω, the better the overall results will be. For this case, small mutations are likely to propose samples X' where f is still relatively large, leading to higher acceptance properties.

Thus, one useful mutation approach is to apply random perturbations to the current sample X. If the sample X is represented by a vector of real numbers $(x_0, x_1, \ldots)$, then some or all of the sample dimensions x_i can be perturbed. One possibility is to perturb them by adding or subtracting a scaled random variable:

$$x_i' = (x_i \pm s\,\xi) \bmod 1$$

for some scale factor s and where the mod operator wraps values around the boundaries to remain in $[0, 1)$. This method is symmetric, so we don't need to compute the transition densities $T(X \to X')$ when using it with Metropolis sampling.

A related mutation approach is to just discard the current sample entirely and generate a new one with uniform random numbers:

$$x_i = \xi.$$

(Note that this is also a symmetric method.) Occasionally generating a completely new sample in this manner is important since it ensures that we don't get stuck in one part of the state space and never sample the rest of it. In general, it's necessary that it be possible to reach all states $X \in \Omega$ where $f(X) > 0$ with nonzero probability (this property is called *ergodicity*). In particular, to ensure ergodicity it suffices that $T(X \to X') > 0$ for all X and X' where $f(X) > 0$ and $f(X') > 0$.

Another approach is to use PDFs that match some part of the function being sampled. If we have a PDF $p(x)$ that is similar to some component of f, then we can use that to derive a mutation strategy by just drawing new samples $X \sim p$. In this case, the transition function is straightforward:

$$T(X \to X') = p(X').$$

In other words, the current state X doesn't matter for computing the transition density: we propose a transition into a state X' with a density that depends only on the newly proposed state X' and not at all on the current state.

13.4.3 START-UP BIAS

One issue that we've sidestepped thus far is how the initial sample X_0 is computed. The transition and acceptance methods above tell us how to generate new samples X_{i+1}, but all presuppose that the current sample X_i has itself *already* been sampled with probability proportional to f. Using a sample not from f's distribution leads to a problem called *start-up bias*.

A common solution to this problem is to run the Metropolis sampling algorithm for some number of iterations from an arbitrary starting state, discard the samples that are generated, and then start the process for real, assuming that that has brought us to an appropriately sampled X value. This is unsatisfying for two reasons: first, the expense of taking the samples that were then discarded may be high, and, second, we can only guess at how many initial samples must be taken in order to remove start-up bias.

An alternative approach can be used if another sampling method is available: an initial value X_0 is sampled using any density function $X_0 \sim p(x)$. We start the Markov chain from the state X_0, but we weight the contributions of all of the samples that we generate by the weight

$$w = \frac{f(X_0)}{p(X_0)}.$$

This method eliminates start-up bias completely and does so in a predictable manner.

The only potential problem comes if $f(X_0) = 0$ for the X_0 we chose; in this case, all samples will have a weight of zero! This doesn't mean that the algorithm is biased, however; the expected value of the result still converges to the correct distribution (see Veach (1997) for further discussion and for a proof of the correctness). To reduce variance and avoid this risk, we can instead sample a set of N candidate sample values, $Y_1, \ldots, Y_N$, defining a weight for each by

$$w_i = \frac{f(Y_i)}{p(Y_i)}.$$

We then choose the starting X_0 sample for the Metropolis algorithm from the Y_i with probability proportional to their relative weights and compute a sample weight w as the average of all of the w_i weights. All subsequent samples X_i that are generated by the Metropolis algorithm are then weighted by the sample weight w.

13.4.4 1D SETTING

In order to illustrate some of the ideas in this section, we'll show how Metropolis sampling can be used to sample a simple 1D function, defined over $\Omega = [0, 1]$ and 0 everywhere else (see Figure 13.7).

$$f(x) = \begin{cases} (x - 0.5)^2 & 0 \le x \le 1 \\ 0 & \text{otherwise.} \end{cases} \tag{13.9}$$

For this example, assume that we don't actually know the exact form of f—it's just a black box that we can evaluate at particular x values. (Clearly, if we knew that f was just

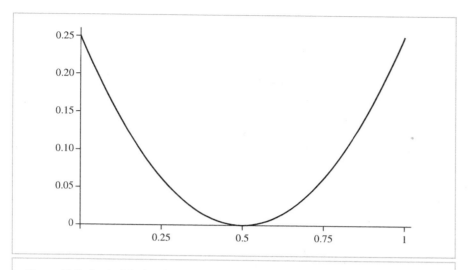

Figure 13.7: Graph of the function $f(x)$ used to illustrate Metropolis sampling in this section.

Equation (13.9), there'd be no need for Metropolis in order to draw samples from its distribution!)

We'll define two mutation strategies based on the ideas introduced in Section 13.4.2 and randomly choose among them each time a mutation is proposed, according to a desired distribution of how frequently each is to be used.

The first strategy, mutate$_1$, discards the current sample X and uniformly samples a new one, X', from the entire state space $[0, 1]$. The transition function for this mutation is straightforward. For mutate$_1$, since we are uniformly sampling over $[0, 1]$, the probability density is uniform over the entire domain; in this case, the density is just one everywhere. We have

$$\text{mutate}_1(X) \rightarrow \xi$$
$$T_1(X \rightarrow X') = 1.$$

The second mutation adds a random offset between ± 0.05 to the current sample X in an effort to sample repeatedly in the parts of f that make a high contribution to the overall distribution. The transition probability density is 0 if X and X' are far enough away that mutate$_2$ will never mutate from one to the other; otherwise, the density is constant. Normalizing the density so that it integrates to 1 over its domain gives the value $1/0.1$. Both this and mutate$_1$ are symmetric, so the transition densities aren't needed to implement the sampling algorithm.

$$\text{mutate}_2(X) \rightarrow X + 0.1(\xi - 0.5)$$
$$T_2(X \rightarrow X') = \begin{cases} \frac{1}{0.1} & |X - X'| \leq 0.05 \\ 0 & \text{otherwise.} \end{cases}$$

To find the initial sample, we only need to take a single sample with a uniform PDF over Ω, since $f(x) > 0$ except for a single point in Ω for which there is zero probability of sampling:

$$X_0 = \xi.$$

The sample weight w is then just $f(X_0)$.

We can now run the Metropolis algorithm and generate samples X_i of f. At each transition, we have two weighted samples to record (recall the expected values pseudocode from Section 13.4.1). A simple approach for reconstructing the approximation to f's probability distribution is to store sums of the weights in a set of buckets of uniform width; each sample falls in a single bucket and contributes to it. Figure 13.8 shows some results. For both graphs, a chain of 10,000 mutations was followed, with the sample weights accumulated in 50 buckets over $[0, 1]$.

In the top graph, only mutate$_1$ was used. This alone isn't a very effective mutation, since it doesn't take advantage of the times when it has found a sample in a region of Ω where f has a relatively large value to generate additional samples in that neighborhood. However, the graph does suggest that the algorithm is converging to the correct distribution.

On the bottom, one of mutate$_1$ and mutate$_2$ was randomly chosen, with probabilities of 10% and 90%, respectively. We see that for the same number of samples taken, we converge to f's distribution with less variance. This is because the algorithm is more effectively able to concentrate its work in areas where f's value is large, proposing fewer mutations to parts of state space where f's value is low. For example, if $X = .8$ and the second mutation proposes $X' = .75$, this will be accepted $f(.75)/f(.8) \approx 69\%$ of the time, while mutations from .75 to .8 will be accepted $\min(1, 1.44) = 100\%$ of the time. Thus, we see how the algorithm naturally tends to try to avoid spending time sampling around the dip in the middle of the curve.

One important thing to note about these graphs is that the y axis has units that are different from those in Figure 13.7, where f is graphed. Recall that Metropolis sampling provides a set of samples distributed according to f's probability density; as such (for example), we would get the same sample distribution for another function $g = 2f$. If we wish to reconstruct an approximation to f directly from Metropolis samples, we must compute a normalization factor and use it to scale the PDF.

Figure 13.9 shows the surprising result of only using mutate$_2$ to propose sample values. On the left, 10,000 samples were taken using just that mutation. Clearly, things have gone awry—*no* samples $X_i > .5$ were generated and the result doesn't bear much resemblance to f.

Thinking about the acceptance probability again, we can see that it would take a large number of mutations, each with low probability of acceptance, to move X_i down close enough to .5 such that mutate$_2$'s short span would be enough to move over to the other side. Since the Metropolis algorithm tends to stay away from the lower valued regions of f (recall the comparison of probabilities for moving from .8 to .75 versus moving from .75 to .8), this happens quite rarely. The right side of Figure 13.9 shows what happens

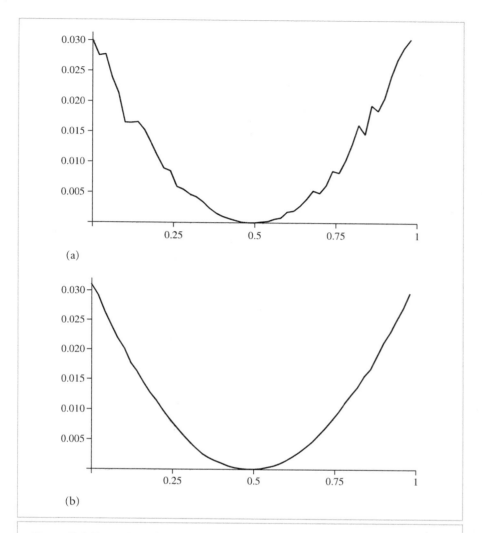

Figure 13.8: Comparison of Metropolis Sampling Strategies. (a) Only mutate$_1$ was used, randomly selecting a completely new value at each step. (b) Both mutate$_1$ and mutate$_2$ were used, with a 1:9 ratio. For the same number of samples, variance is substantially lower, thanks to a higher rate of acceptance of mutate$_2$'s proposed mutations.

if 300,000 samples are taken. This was enough to be able to jump from one side of .5 to the other a few times, but not enough to get close to the correct distribution. Using mutate$_2$ alone is thus not mathematically incorrect, just inefficient: it does have nonzero probability of proposing a transition from any state to any other state (through a chain of multiple transitions).

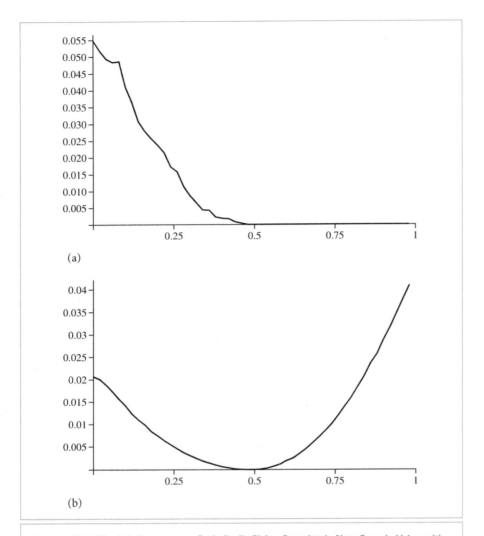

(a)

(b)

Figure 13.9: Why It Is Important to Periodically Pick a Completely New Sample Value with Metropolis Sampling. (a) 10,000 iterations using only mutate_2 were computed, (b) 300,000 iterations. It is very unlikely that a series of mutations will be able to move from one side of the curve, across .5, to the other side, since mutations that move toward areas where f's value is low will usually be rejected. As such, the results are inaccurate for these numbers of iterations. (It's small solace that they would be correct in the limit.)

13.4.5 ESTIMATING INTEGRALS WITH METROPOLIS SAMPLING

We can apply the Metropolis algorithm to estimating integrals such as $\int f(x)g(x) \, d\Omega$. Doing so is the basis of the Metropolis light transport algorithm implemented in Section 16.4.

To see how the samples from Metropolis sampling can be used in this way, recall that the standard Monte Carlo estimator, Equation (13.3), says that

$$\int_\Omega f(x)g(x) \, d\Omega \approx \frac{1}{N} \sum_{i=1}^{N} \frac{f(X_i)g(X_i)}{p(X_i)},$$

where X_i are sampled from a density function $p(x)$. Thus, if we apply Metropolis sampling and generate a set of samples, $X_1, \ldots, X_N$, from a density function that is proportional to $f(x)$, then we can estimate this integral as

$$\int_\Omega f(x)g(x) \, d\Omega \approx \left[\frac{1}{N} \sum_{i=1}^{N} g(X_i) \right] \cdot \int_\Omega f(x) \, d\Omega. \tag{13.10}$$

13.5 TRANSFORMING BETWEEN DISTRIBUTIONS

In describing the inversion method, we introduced a technique that generates samples according to some distribution by transforming canonical uniform random variables in a particular manner. Here, we will investigate the more general question of which distribution results when we transform samples from an arbitrary distribution to some other distribution with a function f.

Suppose we are given random variables X_i that are already drawn from some PDF $p_x(x)$. Now, if we compute $Y_i = y(X_i)$, we would like to find the distribution of the new random variable Y_i. This may seem like an esoteric problem, but we will see that understanding this kind of transformation is critical for drawing samples from multidimensional distribution functions.

The function $y(x)$ must be a one-to-one transformation; if multiple values of x mapped to the same y value, then it would be impossible to unambiguously describe the probability density of a particular y value. A direct consequence of y being one-to-one is that its derivative must either be strictly greater than 0 or strictly less than 0, which implies that

$$Pr\{Y \le y(x)\} = Pr\{X \le x\},$$

and therefore

$$P_y(y) = P_y(y(x)) = P_x(x).$$

This relationship between CDFs leads directly to the relationship between their PDFs. If we assume that y's derivative is greater than 0, differentiating gives

$$p_y(y)\frac{dy}{dx} = p_x(x),$$

and so

$$p_y(y) = \left(\frac{dy}{dx}\right)^{-1} p_x(x).$$

In general, y's derivative is either strictly positive or strictly negative, and the relationship between the densities is

$$p_y(y) = \left|\frac{dy}{dx}\right|^{-1} p_x(x).$$

How can we use this formula? Suppose that $p_x(x) = 2x$ over the domain $[0, 1]$, and let $Y = \sin X$. What is the PDF of the random variable Y? Because we know that $dy/dx = \cos x$,

$$p_y(y) = \frac{p_x(x)}{|\cos x|} = \frac{2x}{\cos x} = \frac{2\arcsin y}{\sqrt{1 - y^2}}.$$

This procedure may seem backward—usually we have some PDF that we want to sample from, not a given transformation. For example, we might have X drawn from some $p_x(x)$ and would like to compute Y from some distribution $p_y(y)$. What transformation should we use? All we need is for the CDFs to be equal, or $P_y(y) = P_x(x)$, which immediately gives the transformation

$$y(x) = P_y^{-1}\left(P_x(x)\right).$$

This is a generalization of the inversion method, since if X were uniformly distributed over $[0, 1]$ then $P_x(x) = x$, and we have the same procedure as was introduced previously.

13.5.1 TRANSFORMATION IN MULTIPLE DIMENSIONS

In the general n-dimensional case, a similar derivation gives the analogous relationship between different densities. We will not show the derivation here; it follows the same form as the 1D case. Suppose we have an n-dimensional random variable X with density function $p_x(x)$. Now let $Y = T(X)$, where T is a bijection. In this case, the densities are related by

$$p_y(y) = p_y(T(x)) = \frac{p_x(x)}{|J_T(x)|},$$

where $|J_T|$ is the absolute value of the determinant of T's Jacobian matrix, which is

$$\begin{pmatrix} \partial T_1/\partial x_1 & \cdots & \partial T_1/\partial x_n \\ \vdots & \ddots & \vdots \\ \partial T_n/\partial x_1 & \cdots & \partial T_n/\partial x_n \end{pmatrix},$$

where T_i are defined by $T(x) = (T_1(x), \ldots, T_n(x))$.

13.5.2 POLAR COORDINATES

The polar transformation is given by

$$x = r\cos\theta$$
$$y = r\sin\theta.$$

Suppose we draw samples from some density $p(r, \theta)$. What is the corresponding density $p(x, y)$? The Jacobian of this transformation is

$$J_T = \begin{pmatrix} \frac{\partial x}{\partial r} & \frac{\partial x}{\partial \theta} \\ \frac{\partial y}{\partial r} & \frac{\partial y}{\partial \theta} \end{pmatrix} = \begin{pmatrix} \cos \theta & -r \sin \theta \\ \sin \theta & r \cos \theta \end{pmatrix},$$

and the determinant is $r \left(\cos^2 \theta + \sin^2 \theta\right) = r$. So $p(x, y) = p(r, \theta)/r$. Of course, this is backward from what we usually want—typically we start with a sampling strategy in Cartesian coordinates and want to transform it to one in polar coordinates. In that case, we would have

$$p(r, \theta) = r \, p(x, y).$$

13.5.3 SPHERICAL COORDINATES

Given the spherical coordinate representation of directions,

$$x = r \sin \theta \cos \phi$$
$$y = r \sin \theta \sin \phi$$
$$z = r \cos \theta,$$

the Jacobian of this transformation has determinant $|J_T| = r^2 \sin \theta$, so the corresponding density function is

$$p(r, \theta, \phi) = r^2 \sin \theta \, p(x, y, z).$$

This transformation is important since it helps us represent directions as points (x, y, z) on the unit sphere. Remember that solid angle is defined as the area of a set of points on the unit sphere. In spherical coordinates, we previously derived

$$d\omega = \sin \theta \, d\theta \, d\phi.$$

So if we have a density function defined over a solid angle Ω, this means that

$$Pr \left\{\omega \in \Omega\right\} = \int_\Omega p(\omega) \, d\omega.$$

The density with respect to θ and ϕ can therefore be derived:

$$p(\theta, \phi) \, d\theta \, d\phi = p(\omega) \, d\omega$$
$$p(\theta, \phi) = \sin \theta \, p(\omega).$$

13.6 2D SAMPLING WITH MULTIDIMENSIONAL TRANSFORMATIONS

Suppose we have a 2D joint density function $p(x, y)$ that we wish to draw samples (X, Y) from. Sometimes multidimensional densities are separable and can be expressed as the product of 1D densities—for example,

$$p(x, y) = p_x(x)p_y(y),$$

for some p_x and p_y. In this case, random variables (X, Y) can be found by independently sampling X from p_x and Y from p_y. Many useful densities aren't separable, however, so we will introduce the theory of how to sample from multidimensional distributions in the general case.

Given a 2D density function, the *marginal density function* $p(x)$ is obtained by "integrating out" one of the dimensions:

$$p(x) = \int p(x, y) \, dy. \tag{13.11}$$

This can be thought of as the density function for X alone. More precisely, it is the average density for a particular x over *all* possible y values.

The *conditional density function* $p(y|x)$ is the density function for y given that some particular x has been chosen (it is read "p of y given x"):

$$p(y|x) = \frac{p(x, y)}{p(x)}. \tag{13.12}$$

The basic idea for 2D sampling from joint distributions is to first compute the marginal density to isolate one particular variable and draw a sample from that density using standard 1D techniques. Once that sample is drawn, one can then compute the conditional density function given that value and draw a sample from that distribution, again using standard 1D sampling techniques.

13.6.1 UNIFORMLY SAMPLING A HEMISPHERE

As an example, consider the task of choosing a direction on the hemisphere uniformly with respect to solid angle. Remember that a uniform distribution means that the density function is a constant, so we know that $p(\omega) = c$. In conjunction with the fact that the density function must integrate to one over its domain, we have

$$\int_{\mathcal{H}^2} p(\omega) \, d\omega = 1 \Rightarrow c \int_{\mathcal{H}^2} d\omega = 1 \Rightarrow c = \frac{1}{2\pi}.$$

This tells us that $p(\omega) = 1/(2\pi)$, or $p(\theta, \phi) = \sin\theta/(2\pi)$ (using a result from the previous example about spherical coordinates). Note that this density function is separable. Nevertheless, we will use the marginal and conditional densities to illustrate the multi-dimensional sampling technique.

Consider sampling θ first. To do so, we need θ's marginal density function $p(\theta)$:

$$p(\theta) = \int_0^{2\pi} p(\theta, \phi) \, d\phi = \int_0^{2\pi} \frac{\sin\theta}{2\pi} \, d\phi = \sin\theta.$$

Now, compute the conditional density for ϕ:

$$p(\phi|\theta) = \frac{p(\theta, \phi)}{p(\theta)} = \frac{1}{2\pi}.$$

Notice that the density function for ϕ is itself uniform; this should make intuitive sense given the symmetry of the hemisphere. Now, we use the 1D inversion technique to sample each of these PDFs in turn:

$$P(\theta) = \int_0^\theta \sin \theta' \, d\theta' = 1 - \cos \theta$$

$$P(\phi|\theta) = \int_0^\phi \frac{1}{2\pi} \, d\phi' = \frac{\phi}{2\pi}.$$

Inverting these functions is straightforward, and here we can safely safely replace $1 - \xi$ with ξ, giving

$$\theta = \cos^{-1} \xi_1$$

$$\phi = 2\pi \xi_2.$$

Converting these back to Cartesian coordinates, we get the final sampling formulae:

$$x = \sin \theta \, \cos \phi = \cos \left(2\pi \xi_2 \right) \sqrt{1 - \xi_1^2}$$

$$y = \sin \theta \, \sin \phi = \sin \left(2\pi \xi_2 \right) \sqrt{1 - \xi_1^2}$$

$$z = \cos \theta = \xi_1.$$

This sampling strategy is implemented in the following code. Two uniform random numbers are provided in u, and a vector on the hemisphere is returned.

⟨*Sampling Function Definitions*⟩ +≡
```
Vector3f UniformSampleHemisphere(const Point2f &u) {
    Float z = u[0];
    Float r = std::sqrt(std::max((Float)0, (Float)1. - z * z));
    Float phi = 2 * Pi * u[1];
    return Vector3f(r * std::cos(phi), r * std::sin(phi), z);
}
```

For each sampling routine like this in pbrt, there is a corresponding function that returns the value of the PDF for a particular sample. For such functions, it is important to be clear which PDF is being evaluated—for example, for a direction on the hemisphere, we have already seen these densities expressed differently in terms of solid angle and in terms of (θ, ϕ). For hemispheres (and all other directional sampling), these functions return values with respect to solid angle. For the hemisphere, the solid angle PDF is a constant $p(\omega) = 1/(2\pi)$.

⟨*Sampling Function Definitions*⟩ +≡
```
Float UniformHemispherePdf() {
    return Inv2Pi;
}
```

Float 1062
Inv2Pi 1063
Pi 1063
Point2f 68
Vector3f 60

Sampling the full sphere uniformly over its area follows almost exactly the same derivation, which we omit here. The end result is

$$x = \cos(2\pi \xi_2)\sqrt{1 - z^2} = \cos(2\pi \xi_2) 2\sqrt{\xi_1(1 - \xi_1)}$$

$$y = \sin(2\pi \xi_2)\sqrt{1 - z^2} = \sin(2\pi \xi_2) 2\sqrt{\xi_1(1 - \xi_1)}$$

$$z = 1 - 2\xi_1.$$

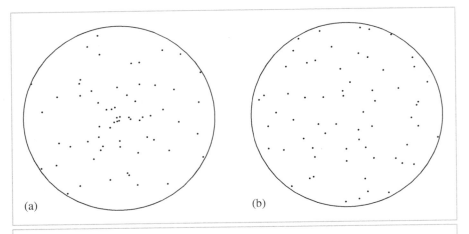

Figure 13.10: (a) When the obvious but incorrect mapping of uniform random variables to points on the disk is used, the resulting distribution is not uniform and the samples are more likely to be near the center of the disk. (b) The correct mapping gives a uniform distribution of points.

⟨*Sampling Function Definitions*⟩ +≡
```
Vector3f UniformSampleSphere(const Point2f &u) {
    Float z = 1 - 2 * u[0];
    Float r = std::sqrt(std::max((Float)0, (Float)1 - z * z));
    Float phi = 2 * Pi * u[1];
    return Vector3f(r * std::cos(phi), r * std::sin(phi), z);
}
```

⟨*Sampling Function Definitions*⟩ +≡
```
Float UniformSpherePdf() {
    return Inv4Pi;
}
```

13.6.2 SAMPLING A UNIT DISK

Although the disk seems a simpler shape to sample than the hemisphere, it can be trickier to sample uniformly because it has an incorrect intuitive solution. The wrong approach is the seemingly obvious one: $r = \xi_1$, $\theta = 2\pi\xi_2$. Although the resulting point is both random and inside the circle, it is *not* uniformly distributed; it actually clumps samples near the center of the circle. Figure 13.10(a) shows a plot of samples on the unit disk when this mapping was used for a set of uniform random samples (ξ_1, ξ_2). Figure 13.10(b) shows uniformly distributed samples resulting from the following correct approach.

Since we're going to sample uniformly with respect to area, the PDF $p(x, y)$ must be a constant. By the normalization constraint, $p(x, y) = 1/\pi$. If we transform into polar coordinates (see the example in Section 13.5.2), we have $p(r, \theta) = r/\pi$. Now we compute the marginal and conditional densities as before:

$$p(r) = \int_0^{2\pi} p(r, \theta)\, d\theta = 2r$$

$$p(\theta|r) = \frac{p(r, \theta)}{p(r)} = \frac{1}{2\pi}.$$

As with the hemisphere case, the fact that $p(\theta|r)$ is a constant should make sense because of the symmetry of the circle. Integrating and inverting to find $P(r)$, $P^{-1}(r)$, $P(\theta)$, and $P^{-1}(\theta)$, we can find that the correct solution to generate uniformly distributed samples on a disk is

$$r = \sqrt{\xi_1}$$

$$\theta = 2\pi\xi_2.$$

Taking the square root of ξ_1 effectively pushes the samples back toward the edge of the disk, counteracting the clumping referred to earlier.

⟨*Sampling Function Definitions*⟩ +≡
```
Point2f UniformSampleDisk(const Point2f &u) {
    Float r = std::sqrt(u[0]);
    Float theta = 2 * Pi * u[1];
    return Point2f(r * std::cos(theta), r * std::sin(theta));
}
```

Although this mapping solves the problem at hand, it distorts areas on the disk; areas on the unit square are elongated and/or compressed when mapped to the disk (Figure 13.11). (Section 13.8.3 will discuss in more detail why this distortion is a disadvantage.) A better approach is a "concentric" mapping from the unit square to the unit circle that avoids this problem. The concentric mapping takes points in the square $[-1, 1]^2$

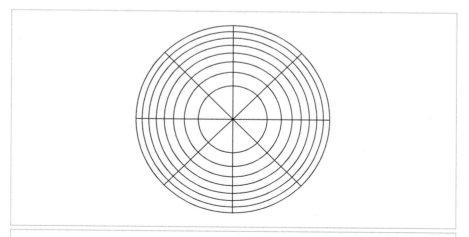

Float 1062

Pi 1063

Point2f 68

UniformSampleDisk() 777

Figure 13.11: The mapping from 2D random samples to points on the disk implemented in UniformSampleDisk() distorts areas substantially. Each section of the disk here has equal area and represents $\frac{1}{8}$ of the unit square of uniform random samples in each direction. In general, we'd prefer a mapping that did a better job at mapping nearby (ξ_1, ξ_2) values to nearby points on the disk.

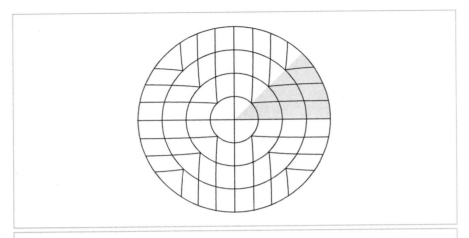

Figure 13.12: The concentric mapping maps squares to circles, giving a less distorted mapping than the first method shown for uniformly sampling points on the unit disk.

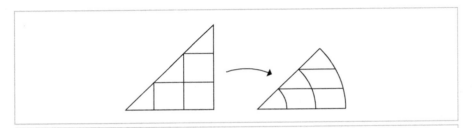

Figure 13.13: Triangular wedges of the square are mapped into (r, θ) pairs in pie-shaped slices of the circle.

to the unit disk by uniformly mapping concentric squares to concentric circles (Figure 13.12).

The mapping turns wedges of the square into slices of the disk. For example, points in the shaded area of the square in Figure 13.12 are mapped to (r, θ) by

$$r = x$$
$$\theta = \frac{y}{x}\frac{\pi}{4}.$$

See Figure 13.13. The other two wedges are handled analogously.

⟨*Sampling Function Definitions*⟩ +≡
```
Point2f ConcentricSampleDisk(const Point2f &u) {
    ⟨Map uniform random numbers to [−1, 1]² 779⟩
    ⟨Handle degeneracy at the origin 779⟩
    ⟨Apply concentric mapping to point 779⟩
}
```

Point2f 68

⟨*Map uniform random numbers to* $[-1, 1]^2$⟩ ≡   778
```
Point2f uOffset = 2.f * u - Vector2f(1, 1);
```

⟨*Handle degeneracy at the origin*⟩ ≡   778
```
if (uOffset.x == 0 && uOffset.y == 0)
    return Point2f(0, 0);
```

⟨*Apply concentric mapping to point*⟩ ≡   778
```
Float theta, r;
if (std::abs(uOffset.x) > std::abs(uOffset.y)) {
    r = uOffset.x;
    theta = PiOver4 * (uOffset.y / uOffset.x);
} else {
    r = uOffset.y;
    theta = PiOver2 - PiOver4 * (uOffset.x / uOffset.y);
}
return r * Point2f(std::cos(theta), std::sin(theta));
```

13.6.3 COSINE-WEIGHTED HEMISPHERE SAMPLING

As we will see in Section 13.10, it is often useful to sample from a distribution that has a shape similar to that of the integrand being estimated. For example, because the scattering equation weights the product of the BSDF and the incident radiance with a cosine term, it is useful to have a method that generates directions that are more likely to be close to the top of the hemisphere, where the cosine term has a large value, than the bottom, where the cosine term is small.

Mathematically, this means that we would like to sample directions ω from a PDF

$$p(\omega) \propto \cos \theta.$$

Normalizing as usual,

$$\int_{\mathcal{H}^2} p(\omega) \, d\omega = 1$$

$$\int_0^{2\pi} \int_0^{\frac{\pi}{2}} c \cos \theta \sin \theta \, d\theta \, d\phi = 1$$

$$c \, 2\pi \int_0^{\pi/2} \cos \theta \sin \theta \, d\theta = 1$$

$$c = \frac{1}{\pi}$$

so

$$p(\theta, \phi) = \frac{1}{\pi} \cos \theta \sin \theta.$$

We could compute the marginal and conditional densities as before, but instead we can use a technique known as *Malley's method* to generate these cosine-weighted points. The idea behind Malley's method is that if we choose points uniformly from the unit disk and then generate directions by projecting the points on the disk up to the hemisphere above it, the resulting distribution of directions will have a cosine distribution (Figure 13.14).

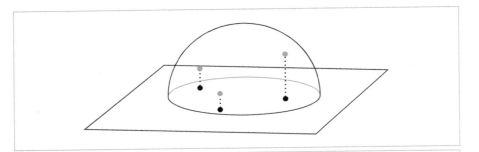

Figure 13.14: Malley's Method. To sample direction vectors from a cosine-weighted distribution, uniformly sample points on the unit disk and project them up to the unit sphere.

Why does this work? Let (r, ϕ) be the polar coordinates of the point chosen on the disk (note that we're using ϕ instead of the usual θ here). From our calculations before, we know that the joint density $p(r, \phi) = r/\pi$ gives the density of a point sampled on the disk.

Now, we map this to the hemisphere. The vertical projection gives $\sin \theta = r$, which is easily seen from Figure 13.14. To complete the $(r, \phi) = (\sin \theta, \phi) \rightarrow (\theta, \phi)$ transformation, we need the determinant of the Jacobian

$$|J_T| = \begin{vmatrix} \cos \theta & 0 \\ 0 & 1 \end{vmatrix} = \cos \theta.$$

Therefore,

$$p(\theta, \phi) = |J_T| p(r, \phi) = \cos \theta \frac{r}{\pi} = (\cos \theta \sin \theta)/\pi,$$

which is exactly what we wanted! We have used the transformation method to prove that Malley's method generates directions with a cosine-weighted distribution. Note that this technique works regardless of the method used to sample points from the circle, so we can use the earlier concentric mapping just as well as the simpler $(r, \theta) = (\sqrt{\xi_1}, 2\pi \xi_2)$ method.

⟨Sampling Inline Functions⟩ +≡

```
inline Vector3f CosineSampleHemisphere(const Point2f &u) {
    Point2f d = ConcentricSampleDisk(u);
    Float z = std::sqrt(std::max((Float)0, 1 - d.x * d.x - d.y * d.y));
    return Vector3f(d.x, d.y, z);
}
```

Remember that all of the directional PDF evaluation routines in pbrt are defined with respect to solid angle, not spherical coordinates, so the PDF function returns a weight of $\cos \theta / \pi$.

⟨Sampling Inline Functions⟩ +≡

```
inline Float CosineHemispherePdf(Float cosTheta) {
    return cosTheta * InvPi;
}
```

13.6.4 SAMPLING A CONE

For both area light sources based on Spheres as well as for the SpotLight, it's useful to be able to uniformly sample rays in a cone of directions. Such distributions are separable in (θ, ϕ), with $p(\phi) = 1/(2\pi)$ and so we therefore need to derive a method to sample a direction θ uniformly over the cone of directions around a central direction up to the maximum angle of the beam, θ_{max}. Incorporating the $\sin\theta$ term from the measure on the unit sphere from Equation (5.5),

$$1 = c \int_0^{\theta_{max}} \sin\theta \, d\theta$$
$$= c(1 - \cos\theta_{max}).$$

So $p(\theta) = \sin\theta/(1 - \cos\theta_{max})$ and $p(\omega) = 1/(2\pi(1 - \cos\theta_{max}))$.

⟨*Sampling Function Definitions*⟩ +≡
```
Float UniformConePdf(Float cosThetaMax) {
    return 1 / (2 * Pi * (1 - cosThetaMax));
}
```

The PDF can be integrated to find the CDF, and the sampling technique,

$$\cos\theta = (1 - \xi) + \xi \cos\theta_{max},$$

follows. There are two UniformSampleCone() functions that implement this sampling technique: the first samples about the $(0, 0, 1)$ axis, and the second (not shown here) takes three basis vectors for the coordinate system to be used where samples taken are with respect to the z axis of the given coordinate system.

⟨*Sampling Function Definitions*⟩ +≡
```
Vector3f UniformSampleCone(const Point2f &u, Float cosThetaMax) {
    Float cosTheta = ((Float)1 - u[0]) + u[0] * cosThetaMax;
    Float sinTheta = std::sqrt((Float)1 - cosTheta * cosTheta);
    Float phi = u[1] * 2 * Pi;
    return Vector3f(std::cos(phi) * sinTheta, std::sin(phi) * sinTheta,
                    cosTheta);
}
```

13.6.5 SAMPLING A TRIANGLE

Although uniformly sampling a triangle may seem like a simple task, it turns out to be more complex than the ones we've seen so far.[9] To simplify the problem, we will assume we are sampling an isosceles right triangle of area $\frac{1}{2}$. The output of the sampling routine that we will derive will be barycentric coordinates, however, so the technique will actually

---

[9]   It is possible to generate the right distribution in a triangle by sampling the enclosing parallelogram and reflecting samples on the wrong side of the diagonal back into the triangle. Although this technique is simpler than the one presented here, it is undesirable since it effectively folds the 2D uniform random samples back on top of each other—two samples that are very far away (e.g., (.01, .01) and (.99, .99)) can map to the same point on the triangle. This thwarts variance reduction techniques like stratified sampling that generate sets of well-distributed (ξ_1, ξ_2) samples and expect that they will map to well-distributed points on the object being sampled; see Section 13.8.1 for further discussion.

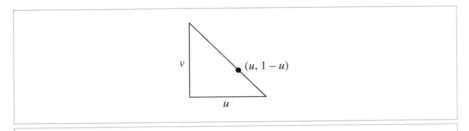

Figure 13.15: Sampling an Isosceles Right Triangle. Note that the equation of the hypotenuse is
$v = 1 - u$.

work for any triangle despite this simplification. Figure 13.15 shows the shape to be
sampled.

We will denote the two barycentric coordinates here by (u, v). Since we are sampling with
respect to area, we know that the PDF $p(u, v)$ must be a constant equal to the reciprocal
of the shape's area, $\frac{1}{2}$, so $p(u, v) = 2$.

First, we find the marginal density $p(u)$:

$$p(u) = \int_0^{1-u} p(u, v) \, dv = 2 \int_0^{1-u} dv = 2(1 - u),$$

and the conditional density $p(v|u)$:

$$p(v|u) = \frac{p(u, v)}{p(u)} = \frac{2}{2(1 - u)} = \frac{1}{1 - u}.$$

The CDFs are, as always, found by integration:

$$P(u) = \int_0^u p(u') \, du' = 2u - u^2$$

$$P(v) = \int_0^v p(v'|u) \, dv' = \frac{v}{1 - u}.$$

Inverting these functions and assigning them to uniform random variables gives the final
sampling strategy:

$$u = 1 - \sqrt{\xi_1}$$

$$v = \xi_2 \sqrt{\xi_1}.$$

Notice that the two variables in this case are *not* independent!

⟨*Sampling Function Definitions*⟩ +≡
```
Point2f UniformSampleTriangle(const Point2f &u) {
    Float su0 = std::sqrt(u[0]);
    return Point2f(1 - su0, u[1] * su0);
}
```
Float 1062

Point2f 68

We won't provide a PDF evaluation function for this sampling strategy since the PDF's
value is just one over the triangle's area.

* 13.6.6 SAMPLING CAMERAS

Section 6.4.7 described the radiometry of the measurement that is performed by film in a realistic camera. For reference, the equation that gave joules arriving over an area of the sensor, Equation (6.7), is

$$
J = \frac{1}{z^2} \int_{A_p} \int_{t_0}^{t_1} \int_{A_e} L_i(p, p', t') \, |\cos^4 \theta| \, dA_e \, dt' \, dA_p,
$$

where the areas integrated over are the area of a pixel on the film, A_p, and an area over the rear lens element that bounds the lens's exit pupil, A_e. The integration over the pixel in the film is handled by the Integrator and the Sampler, so here we'll consider the estimate

$$
\frac{1}{z^2} \int_{t_0}^{t_1} \int_{A_e} L_i(p, p', t') \, |\cos^4 \theta| \, dA_e \, dt'
$$

for a fixed point on the film plane p.

Given a PDF for sampling a time and a PDF for sampling a point on the exit pupil, $p(A_e)$, we have the estimator

$$
\frac{1}{z^2} \frac{L_i(p, p', t) \, |\cos^4 \theta|}{p(t) \, p(A_e)}.
$$

For a uniformly sampled time value, $p(t) = 1/(t_1 - t_0)$. The weighting factor that should be applied to the incident radiance function L_i to compute an estimate of Equation (6.7) is then

$$
\frac{(t_1 - t_0)|\cos^4 \theta|}{z^2 \, p(A_e)}.
$$

Recall from Section 6.4.5 that points on the exit pupil were uniformly sampled within a 2D bounding box. Therefore, to compute $p(A_e)$, we just need one over the area of this bounding box. Conveniently, RealisticCamera::SampleExitPupil() returns this value, which GenerateRay() stores in exitPupilBoundsArea.

The computation of this weight is implemented in ⟨*Return weighting for* RealisticCamera *ray*⟩; we can now see that if the simpleWeighting member variable is true, then the RealisticCamera computes a modified version of this term that only accounts for the $\cos^4 \theta$ term. While the value it computes isn't a useful physical quantity, this option gives images with pixel values that are closely related to the scene radiance (with vignetting), which is often convenient.

⟨*Return weighting for* RealisticCamera *ray*⟩ ≡   **394**

```
    Float cosTheta = Normalize(rFilm.d).z;
    Float cos4Theta = (cosTheta * cosTheta) * (cosTheta * cosTheta);
    if (simpleWeighting)
        return cos4Theta;
    else
        return (shutterClose - shutterOpen) *
            (cos4Theta * exitPupilBoundsArea) / (LensRearZ() * LensRearZ());
```

13.6.7 PIECEWISE-CONSTANT 2D DISTRIBUTIONS

Our final example will show how to sample from discrete 2D distributions. We will consider the case of a 2D function defined over $(u, v) \in [0, 1]^2$ by a 2D array of $n_u \times n_v$ sample values. This case is particularly useful for generating samples from distributions defined by texture maps and environment maps.

Consider a 2D function $f(u, v)$ defined by a set of $n_u \times n_v$ values $f[u_i, v_j]$ where $u_i \in [0, 1, \dots, n_u - 1]$, $v_j \in [0, 1, \dots, n_v - 1]$, and $f[u_i, v_j]$ give the constant value of f over the range $[i/n_u, (i + 1)/n_u) \times [j/n_v, (j + 1)/n_v)$. Given continuous values (u, v), we will use $(\tilde{u}, \tilde{v})$ to denote the corresponding discrete (u_i, v_j) indices, with $\tilde{u} = \lfloor n_u u \rfloor$ and $\tilde{v} = \lfloor n_v v \rfloor$ so that $f(u, v) = f[\tilde{u}, \tilde{v}]$.

Integrals of f are simple sums of $f[u_i, v_j]$ values, so that, for example, the integral of f over the domain is

$$I_f = \iint f(u, v) \, du \, dv = \frac{1}{n_u n_v} \sum_{i=0}^{n_u - 1} \sum_{j=0}^{n_v - 1} f[u_i, v_j].$$

Using the definition of the PDF and the integral of f, we can find f's PDF,

$$p(u, v) = \frac{f(u, v)}{\iint f(u, v) \, du \, dv} = \frac{f[\tilde{u}, \tilde{v}]}{1/(n_u n_v) \sum_i \sum_j f[u_i, v_j]}.$$

Recalling Equation (13.11), the marginal density $p(v)$ can be computed as a sum of $f[u_i, v_j]$ values

$$p(v) = \int p(u, v) \, du = \frac{(1/n_u) \sum_i f[u_i, \tilde{v}]}{I_f}. \tag{13.13}$$

Because this function only depends on $\tilde{v}$, it is thus itself a piecewise constant 1D function, $p[\tilde{v}]$, defined by n_v values. The 1D sampling machinery from Section 13.3.1 can be applied to sampling from its distribution.

Given a v sample, the conditional density $p(u|v)$ is then

$$p(u|v) = \frac{p(u, v)}{p(v)} = \frac{f[\tilde{u}, \tilde{v}]/I_f}{p[\tilde{v}]}. \tag{13.14}$$

Note that, given a particular value of $\tilde{v}$, $p[\tilde{u}|\tilde{v}]$ is a piecewise-constant 1D function of $\tilde{u}$, that can be sampled with the usual 1D approach. There are n_v such distinct 1D conditional densities, one for each possible value of $\tilde{v}$.

Distribution1D 758

Putting this all together, the Distribution2D structure provides functionality similar to Distribution1D, except that it generates samples from piecewise-constant 2D distributions.

⟨*Sampling Declarations*⟩ +≡
```
class Distribution2D {
public:
    ⟨Distribution2D Public Methods 786⟩
private:
    ⟨Distribution2D Private Data 785⟩
};
```

The constructor has two tasks. First, it computes a 1D conditional sampling density $p[\tilde{u}|\tilde{v}]$ for each of the n_v individual $\tilde{v}$ values using Equation (13.14). It then computes the marginal sampling density $p[\tilde{v}]$ with Equation (13.13).

⟨*Sampling Function Definitions*⟩ +≡
```
Distribution2D::Distribution2D(const Float *func, int nu, int nv) {
    for (int v = 0; v < nv; ++v) {
        ⟨Compute conditional sampling distribution for ṽ 785⟩
    }
    ⟨Compute marginal sampling distribution p[ṽ] 785⟩
}
```

Distribution1D can directly compute the $p[\tilde{u}|\tilde{v}]$ distributions from a pointer to each of the n_v rows of n_u function values, since they're laid out linearly in memory. The I_f and $p[\tilde{v}]$ terms from Equation (13.14) don't need to be included in the values passed to Distribution1D, since they have the same value for all of the n_u values and are thus just a constant scale that doesn't affect the normalized distribution that Distribution1D computes.

⟨*Compute conditional sampling distribution for ṽ*⟩ ≡   785
```
pConditionalV.emplace_back(new Distribution1D(&func[v * nu], nu));
```

⟨*Distribution2D Private Data*⟩ ≡   785
```
std::vector<std::unique_ptr<Distribution1D>> pConditionalV;
```

Given the conditional densities for each $\tilde{v}$ value, we can find the 1D marginal density for sampling each $\tilde{v}$ value, $p[\tilde{v}]$. The Distribution1D class stores the integral of the piecewise-constant function it represents in its funcInt member variable, so it's just necessary to copy these values to the marginalFunc buffer so they're stored linearly in memory for the Distribution1D constructor.

⟨*Compute marginal sampling distribution p[ṽ]*⟩ ≡   785
```
std::vector<Float> marginalFunc;
for (int v = 0; v < nv; ++v)
    marginalFunc.push_back(pConditionalV[v]->funcInt);
pMarginal.reset(new Distribution1D(&marginalFunc[0], nv));
```

⟨*Distribution2D Private Data*⟩ +≡   785
```
std::unique_ptr<Distribution1D> pMarginal;
```

As described previously, in order to sample from the 2D distribution, first a sample is drawn from the $p[\tilde{v}]$ marginal distribution in order to find the v coordinate of the sample. The offset of the sampled function value gives the integer $\tilde{v}$ value that determines

(a)

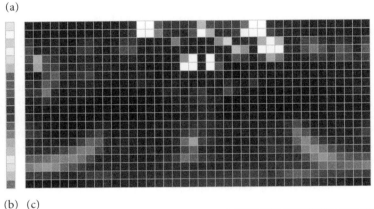

(b) (c)

Figure 13.16: The Piecewise-Constant Sampling Distribution for a High-Dynamic-Range Environment Map. (a) The original environment map, (b) a low-resolution version of the marginal density function $p[\hat{v}]$, (c) the conditional distributions for rows of the image. First the marginal 1D distribution (b) is used to select a v value, giving a row of the image to sample. Rows with bright pixels are more likely to be sampled. Then, given a row, a value u is sampled from that row's 1D distribution. *(Grace Cathedral environment map courtesy of Paul Debevec.)*

which of the precomputed conditional distributions should be used for sampling the u value. Figure 13.16 illustrates this idea using a low-resolution image as an example.

⟨*Distribution2D Public Methods*⟩ ≡   785

```
Point2f SampleContinuous(const Point2f &u, Float *pdf) const {
    Float pdfs[2];
    int v;
    Float d1 = pMarginal->SampleContinuous(u[1], &pdfs[1], &v);
    Float d0 = pConditionalV[v]->SampleContinuous(u[0], &pdfs[0]);
    *pdf = pdfs[0] * pdfs[1];
    return Point2f(d0, d1);
}
```

The value of the PDF for a given sample value is computed as the product of the conditional and marginal PDFs for sampling it from the distribution.

⟨*Distribution2D Public Methods*⟩ +≡   785
```
Float Pdf(const Point2f &p) const {
    int iu = Clamp(int(p[0] * pConditionalV[0]->Count()),
                   0, pConditionalV[0]->Count() - 1);
    int iv = Clamp(int(p[1] * pMarginal->Count()),
                   0, pMarginal->Count() - 1);
    return pConditionalV[iv]->func[iu] / pMarginal->funcInt;
}
```

13.7 RUSSIAN ROULETTE AND SPLITTING

The *efficiency* of an estimator F is defined as

$$\epsilon[F] = \frac{1}{V[F]T[F]},$$

where $V[F]$ is its variance and $T[F]$ is the running time to compute its value. According to this metric, an estimator F_1 is more efficient than F_2 if it takes less time to produce the same variance, or if it produces less variance in the same amount of time. The next few sections discuss a number of techniques for improving the efficiency of Monte Carlo.

Russian roulette and splitting are two related techniques that can improve the efficiency of Monte Carlo estimates by increasing the likelihood that each sample will have a significant contribution to the result. Russian roulette addresses the problem of samples that are expensive to evaluate but make a small contribution to the final result, and splitting is a technique that makes it possible to place more samples in important dimensions of the integrand.

As an example to motivate Russian roulette, consider the problem of estimating the direct lighting integral, which gives reflected radiance at a point due to radiance from direct illumination from the light sources in the scene, L_d:

$$L_o(p, \omega_o) = \int_{\mathcal{S}^2} f_r(p, \omega_o, \omega_i) \, L_d(p, \omega_i) \, |\cos \theta_i| \, d\omega_i.$$

Assume that we have decided to take $N = 2$ samples from some distribution $p(\omega)$ to compute the estimator

$$\frac{1}{2} \sum_{i=1}^{2} \frac{f_r(p, \omega_o, \omega_i) \, L_d(p, \omega_i) \, |\cos \theta_i|}{p(\omega_i)}.$$

Most of the computational expense of evaluating each term of the sum comes from tracing a shadow ray from the point p to see whether the light source is occluded as seen from p.

For all of the directions ω_i where the integrand's value is 0 because $f_r(p, \omega_o, \omega_i)$ is 0 for that direction, we should obviously skip the work of tracing the shadow ray, since tracing it won't change the final value computed. Russian roulette makes it possible to also skip tracing rays when the integrand's value is very low but not necessarily 0, while still computing the correct value on average. For example, we might want to avoid tracing rays when $f_r(\mathrm{p}, \omega_o, \omega_i)$ is small or when ω_i is close to the horizon and thus $|\cos \theta_i|$ is small. These samples just can't be ignored completely, however, since the estimator would then consistently underestimate the correct result.

To apply Russian roulette, we select some termination probability q. This value can be chosen in almost any manner; for example, it could be based on an estimate of the value of the integrand for the particular sample chosen, increasing as the integrand's value becomes smaller. With probability q, the integrand is not evaluated for the particular sample, and some constant value c is used in its place ($c = 0$ is often used). With probability $1 - q$, the integrand is still evaluated but is weighted by a term, $1/(1 - q)$, that effectively accounts for all of the samples that were skipped. We have the new estimator

$$ F' = \begin{cases} \frac{F - qc}{1 - q} & \xi > q \\ c & \text{otherwise.} \end{cases} $$

The expected value of the resulting estimator is the same as the expected value of the original estimator:

$$ E[F'] = (1 - q) \left(\frac{E[F] - qc}{1 - q} \right) + qc = E[F]. $$

Russian roulette never reduces variance. In fact, unless somehow $c = F$, it will always increase variance. However, it does improve efficiency if probabilities are chosen so that samples that are likely to make a small contribution to the final result are skipped.

One pitfall is that poorly chosen Russian roulette weights can substantially increase variance. Imagine applying Russian roulette to all of the camera rays with a termination probability of .99: we'd only trace 1% of the camera rays, weighting each of them by $1/.01 = 100$. The resulting image would still be "correct" in a strictly mathematical sense, although visually the result would be terrible: mostly black pixels with a few very bright ones. One of the exercises at the end of this chapter discusses this problem further and describes a technique called *efficiency-optimized Russian roulette* that tries to set Russian roulette weights in a way that minimizes the increase in variance.

13.7.1 SPLITTING

While Russian roulette reduces the effort spent evaluating unimportant samples, splitting increases the number of samples taken in order to improve efficiency. Consider again the problem of computing reflection due only to direct illumination. Ignoring pixel filtering, this problem can be written as a double integral over the area of the pixel A and over the sphere of directions S^2 at the visible points on surfaces at each (x, y) pixel position:

$$ \int_A \int_{S^2} L_d(x, y, \omega) \, dx \, dy \, d\omega, $$

where $L_d(x, y, \omega)$ denotes the exitant radiance at the object visible at the position (x, y) on the image due to incident radiance from the direction ω.

The natural way to estimate the integral is to generate N samples and apply the Monte Carlo estimator, where each sample consists of an (x, y) image position and a direction

ω toward a light source. If there are many light sources in the scene, or if there is an area light casting soft shadows, tens or hundreds of samples may be needed to compute an image with an acceptable variance level. Unfortunately, each sample requires that two rays be traced through the scene: one to compute the first visible surface from position (x, y) on the image plane and one a shadow ray along ω to a light source.

The problem with this approach is that if $N = 100$ samples are taken to estimate this integral, then 200 rays will be traced: 100 camera rays and 100 shadow rays. Yet, 100 camera rays may be many more than are needed for good pixel antialiasing and thus may make relatively little contribution to variance reduction in the final result. Splitting addresses this problem by formalizing the approach of taking multiple samples in some of the dimensions of integration for each sample taken in other dimensions.

With splitting, the estimator for this integral can be written taking N image samples and M light samples per image sample:

$$\frac{1}{N}\frac{1}{M}\sum_{i=1}^{N}\sum_{j=1}^{M}\frac{L(x_i, y_i, \omega_{i,j})}{p(x_i, y_i)\, p(\omega_{i,j})}.$$

Thus, we could take just 5 image samples but take 20 light samples per image sample, for a total of 105 rays traced, rather than 200, while still taking 100 area light samples in order to compute a high-quality soft shadow.

The purpose of the `Sampler::Request1DArray()` and `Sampler::Request2DArray()` methods defined in Section 7.2.2 can now be seen in the light that they make it possible for users of `Sampler`s to apply splitting to some dimensions of the integrand.

13.8 CAREFUL SAMPLE PLACEMENT

A classic and effective family of techniques for variance reduction is based on the careful placement of samples in order to better capture the features of the integrand (or, more accurately, to be less likely to miss important features). These techniques are used extensively in pbrt. Indeed, one of the tasks of `Sampler`s in Chapter 7 was to generate well-distributed samples for use by the integrators for just this reason, although at the time we offered only an intuitive sense of why this was worthwhile. Here we will justify that extra work in the context of Monte Carlo integration.

13.8.1 STRATIFIED SAMPLING

Stratified sampling was first introduced in Section 7.3, and we now have the tools to motivate its use. Stratified sampling works by subdividing the integration domain Λ into n nonoverlapping regions $\Lambda_1, \Lambda_2, \ldots, \Lambda_n$. Each region is called a *stratum*, and they must completely cover the original domain:

$$\bigcup_{i=1}^{n}\Lambda_i = \Lambda.$$

To draw samples from Λ, we will draw n_i samples from each Λ_i, according to densities p_i inside each stratum. A simple example is supersampling a pixel. With stratified sampling, the area around a pixel is divided into a $k \times k$ grid, and a sample is drawn from each grid cell. This is better than taking k^2 random samples, since the sample locations are less likely to clump together. Here we will show why this technique reduces variance.

Within a single stratum Λ_i, the Monte Carlo estimate is

$$F_i = \frac{1}{n_i} \sum_{j=1}^{n_i} \frac{f(X_{i,j})}{p_i(X_{i,j})},$$

where $X_{i,j}$ is the jth sample drawn from density p_i. The overall estimate is $F = \sum_{i=1}^{n} v_i F_i$, where v_i is the fractional volume of stratum i ($v_i \in (0, 1]$).

The true value of the integrand in stratum i is

$$\mu_i = E\left[f(X_{i,j})\right] = \frac{1}{v_i} \int_{\Lambda_i} f(x)\, dx,$$

and the variance in this stratum is

$$\sigma_i^2 = \frac{1}{v_i} \int_{\Lambda_i} \left(f(x) - \mu_i\right)^2 dx.$$

Thus, with n_i samples in the stratum, the variance of the per-stratum estimator is σ_i^2 / n_i. This shows that the variance of the overall estimator is

$$V[F] = V\left[\sum v_i F_i\right]$$
$$= \sum V\left[v_i F_i\right]$$
$$= \sum v_i^2 V\left[F_i\right]$$
$$= \sum \frac{v_i^2 \sigma_i^2}{n_i}.$$

If we make the reasonable assumption that the number of samples n_i is proportional to the volume v_i, then we have $n_i = v_i N$, and the variance of the overall estimator is

$$V[F_N] = \frac{1}{N} \sum v_i \sigma_i^2.$$

To compare this result to the variance without stratification, we note that choosing an unstratified sample is equivalent to choosing a random stratum I according to the discrete probability distribution defined by the volumes v_i and then choosing a random sample X in Λ_I. In this sense, X is chosen *conditionally* on I, so it can be shown using conditional probability that

$$V[F] = E_x V_i F + V_x E_i F$$
$$= \frac{1}{N} \left[\sum v_i \sigma_i^2 + \sum v_i \left(\mu_i - Q\right)\right],$$

where Q is the mean of f over the whole domain Λ. See Veach (1997) for a derivation of this result.

There are two things to notice about this expression. First, we know that the right-hand sum must be nonnegative, since variance is always nonnegative. Second, it demonstrates

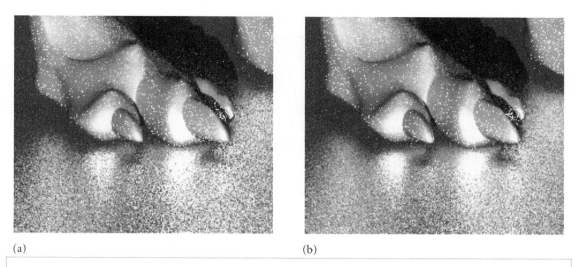

(a)   (b)

Figure 13.17: Variance is higher and the image noisier (a) when random sampling is used to compute the effect of glossy reflection than (b) when a stratified distribution of sample directions is used instead. (Compare the edges of the highlights on the ground, for example.)

that stratified sampling can never increase variance. In fact, stratification always reduces variance unless the right-hand sum is exactly 0. It can only be 0 when the function f has the same mean over each stratum Λ_i. In fact, for stratified sampling to work best, we would like to maximize the right-hand sum, so it is best to make the strata have means that are as unequal as possible. This explains why *compact* strata are desirable if one does not know anything about the function f. If the strata are wide, they will contain more variation and will have μ_i closer to the true mean Q.

Figure 13.17 shows the effect of using stratified sampling versus a uniform random distribution for sampling ray directions for glossy reflection. There is a reasonable reduction in variance at essentially no cost in running time.

The main downside of stratified sampling is that it suffers from the same "curse of dimensionality" as standard numerical quadrature. Full stratification in D dimensions with S strata per dimension requires S^D samples, which quickly becomes prohibitive. Fortunately, it is often possible to stratify some of the dimensions independently and then randomly associate samples from different dimensions, as was done in Section 7.3. Choosing which dimensions are stratified should be done in a way that stratifies dimensions that tend to be most highly correlated in their effect on the value of the integrand (Owen 1998). For example, for the direct lighting example in Section 13.7.1, it is far more effective to stratify the (x, y) pixel positions and to stratify the (θ, ϕ) ray direction—stratifying (x, θ) and (y, ϕ) would almost certainly be ineffective.

Another solution to the curse of dimensionality that has many of the same advantages of stratification is to use Latin hypercube sampling (also introduced in Section 7.3), which can generate any number of samples independent of the number of dimensions. Unfortunately, Latin hypercube sampling isn't as effective as stratified sampling at reducing variance, especially as the number of samples taken becomes large. Nevertheless, Latin hypercube sampling is provably no worse than uniform random sampling and is often much better.

13.8.2 QUASI MONTE CARLO

The low-discrepancy sampling techniques introduced in Chapter 7 are the foundation of a branch of Monte Carlo called *quasi Monte Carlo*. The key component of quasi–Monte Carlo techniques is that they replace the pseudo-random numbers used in standard Monte Carlo with low-discrepancy point sets generated by carefully designed deterministic algorithms.

The advantage of this approach is that for many integration problems, quasi–Monte Carlo techniques have asymptotically faster rates of convergence than methods based on standard Monte Carlo. Many of the techniques used in regular Monte Carlo algorithms can be shown to work equally well with quasi–random sample points, including importance sampling. Some others (e.g., rejection sampling) cannot. While the asymptotic convergence rates are not generally applicable to the discontinuous integrands in graphics because they depend on smoothness properties in the integrand, quasi Monte Carlo nevertheless generally performs better than regular Monte Carlo for these integrals in practice. The "Further Reading" section at the end of this chapter has more information about this topic.

In pbrt, we have generally glossed over the differences between these two approaches and have localized them in the Samplers in Chapter 7. This introduces the possibility of subtle errors if a Sampler generates quasi–random sample points that an Integrator then improperly uses as part of an implementation of an algorithm that is not suitable for quasi Monte Carlo. As long as Integrators only use these sample points for importance sampling or other techniques that are applicable in both approaches, this isn't a problem.

13.8.3 WARPING SAMPLES AND DISTORTION

When applying stratified sampling or low-discrepancy sampling to problems like choosing points on light sources for integration for area lighting, pbrt generates a set of samples (u_1, u_2) over the domain $[0, 1)^2$ and then uses algorithms based on the transformation methods introduced in Sections 13.5 and 13.6 to map these samples to points on the light source. Implicit in this process is the expectation that the transformation to points on the light source will generally preserve the stratification properties of the samples from $[0, 1)^2$—in other words, nearby samples should map to nearby positions on the surface of the light, and faraway samples should map to far-apart positions on the light. If the mapping does not preserve this property, then the benefits of stratification are lost.

Shirley's square-to-circle mapping (Figure 13.13) preserves stratification more effectively than the straightforward mapping (Figure 13.12), which has less compact strata away from the center. This issue also explains why low-discrepancy sequences are generally more effective than stratified patterns in practice: they are more robust with respect to preserving their good distribution properties after being transformed to other domains. Figure 13.18 shows what happens when a set of 16 well-distributed sample points are transformed to be points on a skinny quadrilateral by scaling them to cover its surface;

Integrator 25
Sampler 421

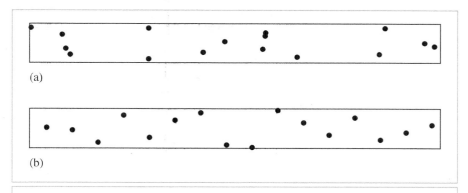

Figure 13.18: (a) Transforming a 4 × 4 stratified sampling pattern to points on a long and thin quadrilateral light source effectively gives less than 16 well-distributed samples; stratification in the vertical direction is not helpful. (b) Samples from a (0, 2)-sequence remain well distributed even after this transformation.

samples from a (0, 2)-sequence remain well distributed, but samples from a stratified pattern fare much less well.

13.9 BIAS

Another approach to variance reduction is to introduce *bias* into the computation: sometimes knowingly computing an estimate that doesn't actually have an expected value equal to the desired quantity can nonetheless lead to lower variance. An estimator is *unbiased* if its expected value is equal to the correct answer. If not, the difference

$$\beta = E[F] - \int f(x)\,dx$$

is the amount of bias.

Kalos and Whitlock (1986, pp. 36–37) gave the following example of how bias can sometimes be desirable. Consider the problem of computing an estimate of the mean value of a uniform distribution $X_i \sim p$ over the interval from 0 to 1. One could use the estimator

$$\frac{1}{N} \sum_{i=1}^{N} X_i,$$

or one could use the biased estimator

$$\frac{1}{2} \max(X_1, X_2, \ldots, X_N).$$

The first estimator is in fact unbiased but has variance with order $O(N^{-1})$. The second estimator's expected value is

$$0.5 \frac{N}{N+1} \neq 0.5,$$

so it is biased, although its variance is $O(N^{-2})$, which is much better.

The pixel reconstruction method described in Section 7.8 can also be seen as a biased estimator. Considering pixel reconstruction as a Monte Carlo estimation problem, we'd like to compute an estimate of

$$I(x, y) = \iint f(x - x', y - y')L(x', y') \, dx' \, dy',$$

where $I(x, y)$ is a final pixel value, $f(x, y)$ is the pixel filter function (which we assume here to be normalized to integrate to 1), and $L(x, y)$ is the image radiance function.

Assuming we have chosen image plane samples uniformly, all samples have the same probability density, which we will denote by p_c. Thus, the unbiased Monte Carlo estimator of this equation is

$$I(x, y) \approx \frac{1}{Np_c} \sum_{i=1}^{N} f(x - x_i, y - y_i)L(x_i, y_i).$$

This gives a different result from that of the pixel filtering equation we used previously, Equation (7.12), which was

$$I(x, y) = \frac{\sum_i f(x - x_i, y - y_i)L(x_i, y_i)}{\sum_i f(x - x_i, y - y_i)}.$$

Yet, the biased estimator is preferable in practice because it gives a result with less variance. For example, if all radiance values $L(x_i, y_i)$ have a value of 1, the biased estimator will always reconstruct an image where all pixel values are exactly 1—clearly a desirable property. However, the unbiased estimator will reconstruct pixel values that are not all 1, since the sum

$$\sum_i f(x - x_i, y - y_i)$$

will generally not be equal to p_c and thus will have a different value due to variation in the filter function depending on the particular (x_i, y_i) sample positions used for the pixel. Thus, the variance due to this effect leads to an undesirable result in the final image. Even for more complex images, the variance that would be introduced by the unbiased estimator is a more objectionable artifact than the bias from Equation (7.12).

13.10 IMPORTANCE SAMPLING

Importance sampling is a powerful variance reduction technique that exploits the fact that the Monte Carlo estimator

$$F_N = \frac{1}{N} \sum_{i=1}^{N} \frac{f(X_i)}{p(X_i)}$$

converges more quickly if the samples are taken from a distribution $p(x)$ that is similar to the function $f(x)$ in the integrand. The basic idea is that by concentrating work where the value of the integrand is relatively high, an accurate estimate is computed more efficiently (Figure 13.19).

(a)

(b)

Figure 13.19: (a) Using a stratified uniform distribution of rays over the hemisphere gives an image with much more variance than (b) applying importance sampling and choosing stratified rays from a distribution based on the BRDF.

For example, suppose we are evaluating the scattering equation, Equation (5.9). Consider what happens when this integral is estimated; if a direction is randomly sampled that is nearly perpendicular to the surface normal, the cosine term will be close to 0. All the expense of evaluating the BSDF and tracing a ray to find the incoming radiance at that sample location will be essentially wasted, as the contribution to the final result will be minuscule. In general, we would be better served if we sampled directions in a way that reduced the likelihood of choosing directions near the horizon. More generally, if directions are sampled from distributions that match other factors of the integrand (the BSDF, the incoming illumination distribution, etc.), efficiency is similarly improved.

As long as the random variables are sampled from a probability distribution that is similar in shape to the integrand, variance is reduced. We will not provide a rigorous proof of this fact but will instead present an informal and intuitive argument. Suppose we're trying to use Monte Carlo techniques to evaluate some integral $\int f(x)\,dx$. Since we have freedom in choosing a sampling distribution, consider the effect of using a distribution $p(x) \propto f(x)$, or $p(x) = cf(x)$. It is trivial to show that normalization forces

$$c = \frac{1}{\int f(x)\,dx}.$$

Finding such a PDF requires that we know the value of the integral, which is what we were trying to estimate in the first place. Nonetheless, for the purposes of this example, if we *could* sample from this distribution, each estimate would have the value

$$\frac{f(X_i)}{p(X_i)} = \frac{1}{c} = \int f(x)\,dx.$$

Since c is a constant, each estimate has the same value, and the variance is zero! Of course, this is ludicrous since we wouldn't bother using Monte Carlo if we could integrate f directly. However, if a density $p(x)$ can be found that is similar in shape to $f(x)$, variance decreases.

Importance sampling can increase variance if a poorly chosen distribution is used. To understand the effect of sampling from a PDF that is a poor match for the integrand, consider using the distribution

$$p(x) = \begin{cases} 99.01 & x \in [0, .01) \\ .01 & x \in [.01, 1) \end{cases}$$

to compute the estimate of $\int f(x)\,dx$ where

$$f(x) = \begin{cases} .01 & x \in [0, .01) \\ 1.01 & x \in [.01, 1). \end{cases}$$

By construction, the value of the integral is one, yet using $p(x)$ to draw samples to compute a Monte Carlo estimate will give a terrible result: almost all of the samples will be in the range $[0, .01)$, where the estimator has the value $f(x)/p(x) \approx 0.0001$. For any estimate where none of the samples ends up being outside of this range, the result will be very inaccurate, almost 10,000 times smaller than it should be. Even worse is the case where some samples do end up being taken in the range $[.01, 1)$. This will happen rarely, but when it does, we have the combination of a relatively high value of the integrand and a relatively low value of the PDF, $f(x)/p(x) = 101$. A large number of samples would be necessary to balance out these extremes to reduce variance enough to get a result close to the actual value, 1.

Fortunately, it's not too hard to find good sampling distributions for importance sampling for many integration problems in graphics. As we implement Integrators in the next three chapters, we will derive a variety of sampling distributions for BSDFs, lights, cameras, and participating media. In many cases, the integrand is the product of more than one function. It can be difficult to construct a PDF that is similar to the complete product, but finding one that is similar to one of the multiplicands is still helpful.

In practice, importance sampling is one of the most frequently used variance reduction techniques in rendering, since it is easy to apply and is very effective when good sampling distributions are used.

13.10.1 MULTIPLE IMPORTANCE SAMPLING

Monte Carlo provides tools to estimate integrals of the form $\int f(x)\,dx$. However, we are frequently faced with integrals that are the product of two or more functions: $\int f(x)g(x)\,dx$. If we have an importance sampling strategy for $f(x)$ *and* a strategy for $g(x)$, which should we use? (Assume that we are not able to combine the two sampling strategies to compute a PDF that is proportional to the product $f(x)g(x)$ that can itself be sampled easily.) As discussed above, a bad choice of sampling distribution can be much worse than just using a uniform distribution.

For example, consider the problem of evaluating direct lighting integrals of the form

$$L_o(p, \omega_o) = \int_{\mathbb{S}^2} f(p, \omega_o, \omega_i)\, L_d(p, \omega_i)\, |\cos\theta_i|\, d\omega_i.$$

If we were to perform importance sampling to estimate this integral according to distributions based on either L_d or f_r, one of these two will often perform poorly.

Consider a near-mirror BRDF illuminated by an area light where L_d's distribution is used to draw samples. Because the BRDF is almost a mirror, the value of the integrand will be close to 0 at all ω_i directions except those around the perfect specular reflection direction. This means that almost all of the directions sampled by L_d will have 0 contribution, and variance will be quite high. Even worse, as the light source grows large and a larger set of directions is potentially sampled, the value of the PDF decreases, so for the rare directions where the BRDF is non-0 for the sampled direction we will have a large integrand value being divided by a small PDF value. While sampling from the BRDF's distribution would be a much better approach to this particular case, for diffuse or glossy BRDFs and small light sources, sampling from the BRDF's distribution can similarly lead to much higher variance than sampling from the light's distribution.

Unfortunately, the obvious solution of taking some samples from each distribution and averaging the two estimators is little better. Because the variance is additive in this case, this approach doesn't help—once variance has crept into an estimator, we can't eliminate it by adding it to another estimator even if it itself has low variance.

Multiple importance sampling (MIS) addresses exactly this issue, with a simple and easy-to-implement technique. The basic idea is that, when estimating an integral, we should draw samples from multiple sampling distributions, chosen in the hope that at least one of them will match the shape of the integrand reasonably well, even if we don't know which one this will be. MIS provides a method to weight the samples from each technique that can eliminate large variance spikes due to mismatches between the integrand's value and the sampling density. Specialized sampling routines that only account for unusual special cases are even encouraged, as they reduce variance when those cases occur, with relatively little cost in general. See Figure 14.13 in Chapter 14 to see the reduction in variance from using MIS to compute reflection from direct illumination compared to sampling either just the BSDF or the light's distribution by itself.

If two sampling distributions p_f and p_g are used to estimate the value of $\int f(x)g(x)\,dx$, the new Monte Carlo estimator given by MIS is

$$\frac{1}{n_f}\sum_{i=1}^{n_f}\frac{f(X_i)g(X_i)w_f(X_i)}{p_f(X_i)}+\frac{1}{n_g}\sum_{j=1}^{n_g}\frac{f(Y_j)g(Y_j)w_g(Y_j)}{p_g(Y_j)},$$

where n_f is the number of samples taken from the p_f distribution method, n_g is the number of samples taken from p_g, and w_f and w_g are special weighting functions chosen such that the expected value of this estimator is the value of the integral of $f(x)g(x)$.

The weighting functions take into account *all* of the different ways that a sample X_i or Y_j could have been generated, rather than just the particular one that was actually used. A good choice for this weighting function is the *balance heuristic*:

$$w_s(x)=\frac{n_s p_s(x)}{\sum_i n_i p_i(x)}.$$

The balance heuristic is a provably good way to weight samples to reduce variance.

Consider the effect of this term for the case where a sample X has been drawn from the p_f distribution at a point where the value $p_f(X)$ is relatively low. Assuming that p_f is a good match for the shape of $f(x)$, then the value of $f(X)$ will also be relatively low. But suppose that $g(X)$ has a relatively high value. The standard importance sampling estimate

$$\frac{f(X)g(X)}{p_f(X)}$$

will have a very large value due to $p_f(X)$ being small, and we will have high variance.

With the balance heuristic, the contribution of X will be

$$\frac{f(X)g(X)w_f(X)}{p_f(X)}=\frac{f(X)g(X)\,n_f\,p_f(X)}{p_f(X)(n_f\,p_f(X)+n_g\,p_g(X))}=\frac{f(X)g(X)\,n_f}{n_f\,p_f(X)+n_g\,p_g(X)}.$$

As long as p_g's distribution is a reasonable match for $g(x)$, then the denominator won't be too small thanks to the $n_g p_g(X)$ term, and the huge variance spike is eliminated, even though X was sampled from a distribution that was in fact a poor match for the integrand. The fact that another distribution will also be used to generate samples and that this new distribution will likely find a large value of the integrand at X are brought together in the weighting term to reduce the variance problem.

Here we provide an implementation of the balance heuristic for the specific case of two distributions p_f and p_g. We will not need a more general multidistribution case in pbrt.

⟨*Sampling Inline Functions*⟩ +≡
```
inline Float BalanceHeuristic(int nf, Float fPdf, int ng, Float gPdf) {
    return (nf * fPdf) / (nf * fPdf + ng * gPdf);
}
```

In practice, the *power heuristic* often reduces variance even further. For an exponent β, the power heuristic is

$$w_s(x) = \frac{(n_s p_s(x))^\beta}{\sum_i (n_i p_i(x))^\beta}.$$

Veach determined empirically that $\beta = 2$ is a good value. We have $\beta = 2$ hard-coded into the implementation here.

⟨*Sampling Inline Functions*⟩ +≡
```
inline Float PowerHeuristic(int nf, Float fPdf, int ng, Float gPdf) {
    Float f = nf * fPdf, g = ng * gPdf;
    return (f * f) / (f * f + g * g);
}
```

FURTHER READING

Many books have been written on Monte Carlo integration. Hammersley and Handscomb (1964), Spanier and Gelbard (1969), and Kalos and Whitlock (1986) are classic references. More recent books on the topic include those by Fishman (1996) and Liu (2001). Chib and Greenberg (1995) have written an approachable but rigorous introduction to the Metropolis algorithm. The Monte Carlo and Quasi Monte Carlo Web site is a useful gateway to recent work in the field *(www.mcqmc.org)*.

Good general references about Monte Carlo and its application to computer graphics are the theses by Lafortune (1996) and Veach (1997). Dutré's *Global Illumination Compendium* (2003) also has much useful information related to this topic. The course notes from the Monte Carlo ray-tracing course at SIGGRAPH have a wealth of practical information (Jensen et al. 2001a, 2003).

The square to disk mapping was described by Shirley and Chiu (1997). The implementation here benefits by observations by Cline and "franz" that the logic could be simplified considerably from the original algorithm (Shirley 2011). Marques et al. (2013) note that well-distributed samples on $[0, 1)^2$ still suffer some distortion when they are mapped to the sphere of directions and show how to generate low-discrepancy samples on the unit sphere.

Steigleder and McCool (2003) described an alternative to the multidimensional sampling approach from Section 13.6.7: they linearized 2D and higher dimensional domains into 1D using a Hilbert curve and then sampled using 1D samples over the 1D domain. This leads to a simpler implementation that still maintains desirable stratification properties of the sampling distribution, thanks to the spatial coherence preserving properties of the Hilbert curve.

Float 1062

Lawrence et al. (2005) described an adaptive representation for CDFs, where the CDF is approximated with a piecewise linear function with fewer, but irregularly spaced, vertices compared to the complete CDF. This approach can substantially reduce storage requirements and improve lookup efficiency, taking advantage of the fact that large ranges of the CDF may be efficiently approximated with a single linear function.

Cline et al. (2009) observed that the time spent in binary searches for sampling from precomputed distributions (like Distribution1D does) can take a meaningful amount of execution time. (Indeed, pbrt spends nearly 7% of the time when rendering the car scene lit by an InfiniteAreaLight in the Distribution1D::SampleContinuous() method, which is used by InfiniteAreaLight::Sample_Li().) They presented two improved methods for doing this sort of search: the first stores a lookup table with n integer values, indexed by $\lfloor n\xi \rfloor$, which gives the first entry in the CDF array that is less than or equal to ξ. Starting a linear search from this offset in the CDF array can be much more efficient than a complete binary search over the entire array. They also presented a method based on approximating the inverse CDF as a piecewise linear function of ξ and thus enabling constant-time lookups at a cost of some accuracy (and thus some additional variance).

The *alias method* is a technique that makes it possible to sample from discrete distributions in $O(1)$ time (Walker 1974, 1977); this is much better than the $O(\log n)$ of the Distribution1D class when it is used for sampling discrete distributions. The downside of this approach is that it does not preserve sample stratification. See Schwarz's writeup (2011) for information about implementing this approach well.

Arithmetic coding offers another interesting way to approach sampling from distributions (MacKay 2003, p. 118; Piponi 2012). If we have a discrete set of probabilities we'd like to generate samples from, one way to approach the problem is to encode the CDF as a binary tree where each node splits the [0, 1) interval at some point and where, given a random sample ξ, we determine which sample value it corresponds to by traversing the tree until we reach the leaf node for its sample value. Ideally, we'd like to have leaf nodes that represent higher probabilities be higher up in the tree, so that it takes fewer traversal steps to find them (and thus, those more frequently generated samples are found more quickly). Looking at the problem from this perspective, it can be shown that the optimal structure of such a tree is given by Huffman coding, which is normally used for compression.

Mitchell (1996b) wrote a paper that investigates the effects of stratification for integration problems in graphics (including the 2D problem of pixel antialiasing). In particular, he investigated the connection between the complexity of the function being integrated and the effect of stratification. In general, the smoother or simpler the function, the more stratification helps: for pixels with smooth variation over their areas or with just a few edges passing through them, stratification helps substantially, but as the complexity in a pixel is increased, the gain from stratification is reduced. Nevertheless, because stratification never increases variance, there's no reason not to do it.

Starting with Durand et al.'s work (2005), a number of researchers have approached the analysis of light transport and variance from Monte Carlo integration for rendering using Fourier analysis. See Pilleboue et al.'s paper (2015) for recent work in this area, including references to previous work. Among other results, they show that Poisson disk patterns give higher variance than simple jittered patterns. They found that the blue noise pattern of de Goes et al. (2012) was fairly effective. Other work in this area includes the paper by Subr and Kautz (2013).

Multiple importance sampling was developed by Veach and Guibas (Veach and Guibas 1995; Veach 1997). Normally, a pre-determined number of samples are taken using each sampling technique; see Pajot et al. (2011) and Lu et al. (2013) for approaches to adaptively distributing the samples over strategies in an effort to reduce variance by choosing those that are the best match to the integrand.

EXERCISES

13.1 Write a program that compares Monte Carlo and one or more alternative numerical integration techniques. Structure this program so that it is easy to replace the particular function being integrated. Verify that the different techniques compute the same result (given a sufficient number of samples for each of them). Modify your program so that it draws samples from distributions other than the uniform distribution for the Monte Carlo estimate, and verify that it still computes the correct result when the correct estimator, Equation (13.3), is used. (Make sure that any alternative distributions you use have nonzero probability of choosing any value of x where $f(x) > 0$.)

13.2 Write a program that computes Monte Carlo estimates of the integral of a given function. Compute an estimate of the variance of the estimates by taking a series of trials and using Equation (13.2) to compute variance. Demonstrate numerically that variance decreases at a rate of $O(\sqrt{n})$.

13.3 The depth-of-field code for the ProjectiveCamera in Section 6.2.3 uses the ConcentricSampleDisk() function to generate samples on the circular lens, since this function gives less distortion than UniformSampleDisk(). Try replacing it with UniformSampleDisk(), and measure the difference in image quality. For example, you might want to compare the error in images from using each approach and a relatively low number of samples to a highly sampled reference image.

Does ConcentricSampleDisk() in fact give less error in practice? Does it make a difference if a relatively simple scene is being rendered versus a very complex scene?

13.4 Modify the Distribution1D implementation to use the adaptive CDF representation described by Lawrence et al. (2005), and experiment with how much more compact the CDF representation can be made without causing image artifacts. (Good test scenes include those that use InfiniteAreaLights, which use the Distribution2D and, thus, Distribution1D for sampling.) Can you measure an improvement in rendering speed due to more efficient searches through the approximated CDF?

13.5 One useful technique not discussed in this chapter is the idea of adaptive density distribution functions that dynamically change the sampling distribution as samples are taken and information is available about the integrand's actual distribution as a result of evaluating the values of these samples. The standard Monte Carlo estimator can be written to work with a nonuniform distribution of random numbers used in a transformation method to generate samples X_i,

$$\sum_i^N \frac{f(X_i)}{p(X_i)p_r(\xi_i)},$$

just like the transformation from one sampling density to another. This leads to a useful sampling technique, where an algorithm can track which samples ξ_i were effective at finding large values of $f(x)$ and which weren't and then adjusts probabilities toward the effective ones (Booth 1986). A straightforward implementation would be to split $[0, 1]$ into bins of fixed width, track the average value of the integrand in each bin, and use this to change the distribution of ξ_i samples.

Investigate data structures and algorithms that support such sampling approaches and choose a sampling problem in pbrt to apply them to. Measure how well this approach works for the problem you selected. One difficulty with methods like this is that different parts of the sampling domain will be the most effective at different times in different parts of the scene. For example, trying to adaptively change the sampling density of points over the surface of an area light source has to contend with the fact that, at different parts of the scene, different parts of the area light may be visible and thus be the important areas. You may find it useful to read Cline et al.'s paper (2008) on this topic.

CHAPTER FOURTEEN

14 LIGHT TRANSPORT I: SURFACE REFLECTION

This chapter brings together the ray-tracing algorithms, radiometric concepts, and Monte Carlo sampling algorithms of the previous chapters to implement two different integrators that compute scattered radiance from surfaces in the scene. Integrators are so named because they are responsible for evaluating the integral equation that describes the equilibrium distribution of radiance in an environment (the light transport equation).

Recall the scattering equation from Section 5.6.1; its value can be estimated with Monte Carlo:

$$L_o(p, \omega_o) = \int_{\mathcal{S}^2} f(p, \omega_o, \omega_i) \, L_i(p, \omega_i) \, |\cos \theta_i| \, d\omega_i$$

$$\approx \frac{1}{N} \sum_{j=1}^{N} \frac{f(p, \omega_o, \omega_j) \, L_i(p, \omega_j) \, |\cos \theta_j|}{p(\omega_j)},$$

with directions ω_j sampled from a distribution with respect to solid angle that has PDF $p(\omega_j)$. In practice, we'll want to take some samples from a distribution that approximates the BSDF, some from a distribution that approximates the incident radiance from light sources, and then weight the samples with multiple importance sampling.

The next two sections derive methods for sampling from BSDFs and light sources. After these sampling methods have been defined, the DirectLightingIntegrator and the PathIntegrator will be introduced. Both find light-carrying paths starting from the camera, accounting for scattering from shapes' surfaces. Chapter 15 will extend this approach to scattering from participating media as well, and Chapter 16 will introduce bidirectional methods for constructing light-carrying paths starting from both the camera and from light sources.

Physically Based Rendering: From Theory To Implementation.
http://dx.doi.org/10.1016/B978-0-12-800645-0.50014-2

14.1 SAMPLING REFLECTION FUNCTIONS

The BxDF::Sample_f() method chooses a direction according to a distribution that is similar to its corresponding scattering function. In Section 8.2, this method was used for finding reflected and transmitted rays from perfectly specular surfaces; later in this section, we will show how that sampling process is a special case of the sampling techniques we'll now implement for other types of BSDFs.

BxDF::Sample_f() takes two sample values in the range $[0, 1)^2$ that are intended to be used by an inversion method-based sampling algorithm (recall Section 13.3.1). The routine calling it can use stratified or low-discrepancy sampling techniques to generate these sample values, thus making it possible for the sampled directions themselves to be well distributed. Other sampling methods like rejection sampling could in theory be supported by passing a Sampler instance, though this is not done in pbrt as stratified sampling of a distribution that is similar to the BSDF generally produces superior results.

This method returns the value of the BSDF for the chosen direction as well as the sampled direction in *wi and the value of $p(\omega_i)$ in *pdf. The PDF value returned should be measured with respect to solid angle, and both the outgoing direction ω_o and the sampled incident direction ω_i should be in the standard reflection coordinate system (see section "Geometric Setting," page 509).

The default implementation of this method samples the unit hemisphere with a cosine-weighted distribution. Samples from this distribution will give correct results for any BRDF that isn't described by a delta distribution, since there is some probability of sampling all directions where the BRDF's value is non-0: $p(\omega) > 0$ for all ω in the hemisphere. (BTDFs will thus always need to override this method but can sample the opposite hemisphere uniformly if they don't have a better sampling method.)

⟨BxDF Method Definitions⟩ +≡
```
Spectrum BxDF::Sample_f(const Vector3f &wo, Vector3f *wi,
        const Point2f &u, Float *pdf, BxDFType *sampledType) const {
    ⟨Cosine-sample the hemisphere, flipping the direction if necessary 806⟩
    *pdf = Pdf(wo, *wi);
    return f(wo, *wi);
}
```

There is a subtlety related to the orientation of the normal that must be accounted for here: the direction returned by CosineSampleHemisphere() is in the hemisphere around $(0, 0, 1)$ in the reflection coordinate system If ω_o is in the opposite hemisphere, then ω_i must be flipped to lie in the same hemisphere as ω_o. This issue is a direct consequence of the fact that pbrt does not flip the normal to be on the same side of the surface as the ω_o direction.

⟨Cosine-sample the hemisphere, flipping the direction if necessary⟩ ≡   806, 814
```
*wi = CosineSampleHemisphere(u);
if (wo.z < 0) wi->z *= -1;
```

While BxDF::Sample_f() returns the value of the PDF for the direction it chose, the BxDF::Pdf() method returns the value of the PDF for a given pair of directions. This method is useful for multiple importance sampling, where it is necessary to be able to find one sampling distribution's PDF for directions sampled from other distributions. It is crucial that any BxDF implementation that overrides the BxDF::Sample_f() method also override the BxDF::Pdf() method so that the two return consistent results.[1]

To actually evaluate the PDF for the cosine-weighted sampling method (which we showed earlier was $p(\omega) = \cos\theta/\pi$), it is first necessary to check that ω_o and ω_i lie on the same side of the surface; if not, the sampling probability is 0. Otherwise, the method computes $|\mathbf{n} \cdot \omega_i|$. One potential pitfall with this method is that the order of the ω_o and ω_i arguments is significant. For the cosine-weighted distribution, $p(\omega_o) \neq p(\omega_i)$ in general. Code that calls this method must be careful to use the correct argument ordering.

⟨*BxDF Method Definitions*⟩ +≡
```
Float BxDF::Pdf(const Vector3f &wo, const Vector3f &wi) const {
    return SameHemisphere(wo, wi) ? AbsCosTheta(wi) * InvPi : 0;
}
```

⟨*BSDF Inline Functions*⟩ +≡
```
inline bool SameHemisphere(const Vector3f &w, const Vector3f &wp) {
    return w.z * wp.z > 0;
}
```

This sampling method works well for Lambertian BRDFs, and it works well for the Oren–Nayar model as well, so we will not override it for those classes.

14.1.1 MICROFACET BxDFS

The microfacet-based reflection models defined in Section 8.4 were based on a distribution of microfacets $D(\omega_h)$ where each microfacet exhibited perfect specular reflection and/or transmission. Because the $D(\omega_h)$ function is primarily responsible for the overall shape of the Torrance–Sparrow BSDF (Section 8.4.4), approaches based on sampling from its distribution are fairly effective. With this approach, first a particular microfacet orientation is sampled from the microfacet distribution, and then the incident direction is found using the specular reflection or transmission formula.

Therefore, MicrofacetDistribution implementations must implement a method for sampling from their distribution of normal vectors.

⟨*MicrofacetDistribution Public Methods*⟩ +≡   537
```
virtual Vector3f Sample_wh(const Vector3f &wo,
    const Point2f &u) const = 0;
```

The classic approach to sampling a microfacet orientation is to sample from $D(\omega_h)$ directly. We'll start by showing the derivation of this approach for the isotropic Beckmann distribution but will then describe a more effective sampling method that samples from the distribution of visible microfacets from a given outgoing direction, which can be quite different from the overall distribution.

---

1   The unit tests in the src/tests directory of pbrt source code distribution include a bsdf.cpp test (not discussed in the book) that implements a χ^2 statistical hypothesis test. This test checks the consistency of a BxDF's BxDF::Sample_f() and BxDF::Pdf() methods and can be helpful to validate sampling routines when implementing new types of BxDFs.

The `MicrofacetDistribution` base class stores a Boolean value that determines which sampling technique will be used. In practice, the one based on sampling visible microfacet area is much more effective than the one based on sampling the overall distribution, so it isn't possible to select between the two strategies in pbrt scene description files; the option to sample the overall distribution is only available for tests and comparisons.

⟨*MicrofacetDistribution Protected Methods*⟩ ≡   537
```
MicrofacetDistribution(bool sampleVisibleArea)
    : sampleVisibleArea(sampleVisibleArea) { }
```

⟨*MicrofacetDistribution Protected Data*⟩ ≡   537
```
const bool sampleVisibleArea;
```

The `BeckmannDistribution`'s `Sample_wh()` method's implementation uses this value to determine which sampling technique to use.

⟨*MicrofacetDistribution Method Definitions*⟩ +≡
```
Vector3f BeckmannDistribution::Sample_wh(const Vector3f &wo,
        const Point2f &u) const {
    if (!sampleVisibleArea) {
        ⟨Sample full distribution of normals for Beckmann distribution 808⟩
    } else {
        ⟨Sample visible area of normals for Beckmann distribution⟩
    }
}
```

The sampling method for the Beckmann–Spizzichino distribution's full distribution of normals returns angles $\tan^2 \theta$ and ϕ in spherical coordinates, which in turn are converted to a normalized direction vector wh.

⟨*Sample full distribution of normals for Beckmann distribution*⟩ ≡   808
  ⟨*Compute* $\tan^2 \theta$ *and* ϕ *for Beckmann distribution sample* 809⟩
  ⟨*Map sampled Beckmann angles to normal direction* wh 809⟩
  `return wh;`

The isotropic Beckmann–Spizzichino distribution was defined in Equation (8.10). To derive a sampling method, we'll consider it expressed in spherical coordinates. As an isotropic distribution, it is independent of ϕ, and so the PDF for this distribution, $p_h(\theta, \phi)$, is separable into $p_h(\theta)$ and $p_h(\phi)$.

$p_h(\phi)$ is constant with a value of $1/(2\pi)$, and thus ϕ values can be sampled by

$$\phi = 2\pi \xi.$$

For $p(\theta_h)$, we have

$$p(\theta_h) = \frac{e^{-\tan^2 \theta_h / \alpha^2}}{\pi \alpha^2 \cos^4 \theta_h}, \qquad [14.1]$$

where α is the roughness coefficient. We can apply the inversion method to find how to sample a direction θ' from this distribution given a uniform random number ξ. First,

MicrofacetDistribution 537

MicrofacetDistribution::
  sampleVisibleArea
  808

Point2f 68

Vector3f 60

taking the PDF from Equation (14.1), and integrating to find the CDF, we have

$$P(\theta') = \int_0^{\theta'} \frac{e^{-\tan^2 \theta_h / \alpha^2}}{\pi \alpha^2 \cos^4 \theta_h} \, d\theta_h$$

$$= 1 - e^{-\tan^2 \theta' / \alpha^2}.$$

To find the sampling technique, we need to solve

$$\xi = 1 - e^{-\tan^2 \theta' / \alpha^2}$$

for θ' in terms of ξ. In this case, $\tan^2 \theta'$ suffices to find the microfacet orientation and is more efficient to compute, so we will compute

$$\tan^2 \theta' = -\alpha^2 \log \xi.$$

The sampling code follows directly, though we must take care of the case where u[0] is zero, which causes std::log() to return negative infinity.

⟨*Compute* $\tan^2 \theta$ *and* ϕ *for Beckmann distribution sample*⟩ ≡   808
```
Float tan2Theta, phi;
if (alphax == alphay) {
    Float logSample = std::log(u[0]);
    if (std::isinf(logSample)) logSample = 0;
    tan2Theta = -alphax * alphax * logSample;
    phi = u[1] * 2 * Pi;
} else {
    ⟨Compute tan2Theta and phi for anisotropic Beckmann distribution⟩
}
```

The algorithm to sample $\tan^2 \theta$ and ϕ for anisotropic Beckmann–Spizzichino distributions can be derived following a similar process, though we won't include the derivation or implementation in the text here.

Given $\tan^2 \theta$, we can compute $\cos \theta$ using the identities $\tan^2 \theta = \sin^2 \theta / \cos^2 \theta$ and $\sin^2 \theta + \cos^2 \theta = 1$. $\sin \theta$ follows, and we have enough information to compute the microfacet orientation using the spherical coordinates formula. Because pbrt transforms the normal to (0, 0, 1) in the reflection coordinate system, we can almost use the computed direction from spherical coordinates directly. The last detail to handle is that if ω_o is in the opposite hemisphere than the normal, then the half-angle vector needs to be flipped to be in that hemisphere as well.

⟨*Map sampled Beckmann angles to normal direction* wh⟩ ≡   808
```
Float cosTheta = 1 / std::sqrt(1 + tan2Theta);
Float sinTheta = std::sqrt(std::max((Float)0, 1 - cosTheta * cosTheta));
Vector3f wh = SphericalDirection(sinTheta, cosTheta, phi);
if (!SameHemisphere(wo, wh)) wh = -wh;
```

While sampling a microfacet orientation from the full microfacet distribution gives correct results, the efficiency of this approach is limited by the fact that only one term, $D(\omega_h)$, of the full microfacet BSDF (defined in Equation (8.19)) is accounted for. A better approach can be found using the observation that the distribution of microfacets that

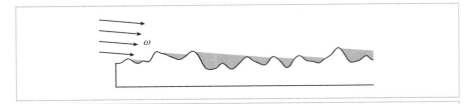

Figure 14.1: The distribution of visible microfacets from a direction oblique to the underlying geometric normal is quite different from the distribution $D(\omega_h)$. First, some microfacet orientations are backfacing and will never be seen. Others are shadowed by other microfacets. Finally, the projected area of a visible microfacet increases as its orientation approaches the viewing direction. These factors are accounted for in $D_\omega(\omega_h)$, the distribution of visible microfacets in the direction ω.

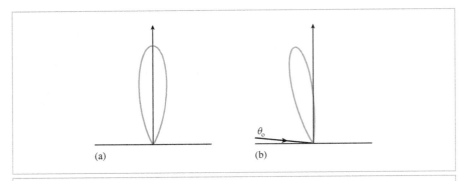

Figure 14.2: Full Beckmann–Spizzichino microfacet distribution $D(\omega_h)$ for $\alpha = 0.3$ and visible microfacet distribution $D_{\omega_o}(\omega_h)$ for $\cos \theta_o = 0.1$. With this relatively oblique viewing direction, the two distributions are quite different and sampling from $D_{\omega_o}(\omega_h)$ is a much more effective approach.

are visible from a given direction isn't the same as the full distribution of microfacets; Figure 14.1 shows the geometric setting and describes why the distributions differ.

Equation (8.13) in Section 8.4.2 defined a relationship between the visible area of microfacets from a given direction and microfacet orientation. This equation can be rearranged to get the distribution of visible normals in a direction ω:

$$D_\omega(\omega_h) = \frac{D(\omega_h)\, G_1(\omega, \omega_h)\, \max(0, \omega \cdot \omega_h)}{\cos \theta}.$$ (14.2)

Here, the G_1 term accounts for microfacet self-shadowing, and the $\max(0, (\omega \cdot \omega_h))/\cos \theta$ term accounts for both backfacing microfacets and the interaction of microfacet orientation and projected area as a function of viewing direction that was shown in Figure 14.1.

Figure 14.2 compares the overall distribution of microfacets with the Beckmann–Spizzichino model with the visible distribution from a fairly oblique viewing direction. Note that many orientations are no longer visible at all (as they are backfacing) and that the microfacet orientations that are in the vicinity of the outgoing direction ω_o have a higher probability of being visible than they do in the overall distribution $D(\omega_h)$.

(a)   (b)

Figure 14.3: Comparison of Microfacet Sampling Techniques. With the same number of samples taken per pixel there is much higher variance when (a) sampling the full microfacet distribution $D(\omega_h)$ than when (b) sampling the visible microfacet distribution $D_{\omega_o}(\omega_h)$.

It turns out that samples can be taken directly from the distribution defined by Equation (14.2); because this distribution better matches the full Torrance–Sparrow model (Equation (8.19)) than $D(\omega_h)$ alone, there is much less variance in resulting images (see Figure 14.3). We won't go into the extensive details of how to directly sample this distribution or include the code in the book; see the "Further Reading" section and the source code, respectively, for more information. (The TrowbridgeReitzDistribution::Sample_wh() method similarly samples from either the full distribution of microfacet normals or from the visible distribution; see the source code for details.)

The implementation of the MicrofacetDistribution::Pdf() method now follows directly; it's just a matter of returning the density from the selected sampling distribution.

⟨*MicrofacetDistribution Method Definitions*⟩ +≡
```
Float MicrofacetDistribution::Pdf(const Vector3f &wo,
        const Vector3f &wh) const {
    if (sampleVisibleArea)
        return D(wh) * G1(wo) * AbsDot(wo, wh) / AbsCosTheta(wo);
    else
        return D(wh) * AbsCosTheta(wh);
}
```

Given the ability to sample from distributions of microfacet orientations, the MicrofacetReflection::Sample_f() method can now be implemented.

⟨*BxDF Method Definitions*⟩ +≡
```
Spectrum MicrofacetReflection::Sample_f(const Vector3f &wo, Vector3f *wi,
        const Point2f &u, Float *pdf, BxDFType *sampledType) const {
    ⟨Sample microfacet orientation ωh and reflected direction ωi 812⟩
    ⟨Compute PDF of wi for microfacet reflection 813⟩
    return f(wo, *wi);
}
```

The implementation first uses Sample_wh() to find a microfacet orientation and reflects the outgoing direction about the microfacet's normal. If the reflected direction is in the

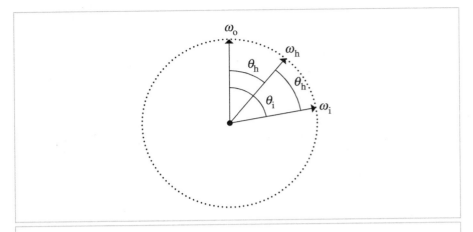

Figure 14.4: The adjustment for change of variable from sampling from the half-angle distribution to sampling from the incident direction distribution can be derived with an observation about the relative angles involved: $\theta_i = 2\theta_h$. (Note the difference in notation: for example, here we use θ_h as the angle between ω_o and ω_h; elsewhere in the book, θ_h denotes the angle between ω_h and the surface normal.)

opposite hemisphere from ω_o, then its direction is under the surface and no light is reflected.[2]

⟨*Sample microfacet orientation* ω_h *and reflected direction* ω_i⟩ ≡ 811, 814
```
Vector3f wh = distribution->Sample_wh(wo, u);
*wi = Reflect(wo, wh);
if (!SameHemisphere(wo, *wi)) return Spectrum(0.f);
```

There's an important detail to take care of to compute the value of the PDF for the sampled direction. The microfacet distribution gives the distribution of normals around the *half-angle vector*, but the reflection integral is with respect to the *incoming vector*. These distributions are not the same, and we must convert the half-angle PDF to the incoming angle PDF. In other words, we must change from a density in terms of ω_h to one in terms of ω_i using the techniques introduced in Section 13.5. Doing so requires applying the adjustment for a change of variables $d\omega_h / d\omega_i$.

A simple geometric construction gives the relationship between the two distributions. Consider the spherical coordinate system oriented about ω_o (Figure 14.4). Measured with respect to ω_h, the differential solid angles $d\omega_i$ and $d\omega_h$ are $\sin \theta_i \, d\theta_i \, d\phi_i$ and $\sin \theta_h \, d\theta_h \, d\phi_h$, respectively; thus,

$$\frac{d\omega_h}{d\omega_i} = \frac{\sin \theta_h \, d\theta_h \, d\phi_h}{\sin \theta_i \, d\theta_i \, d\phi_i}.$$

2   More generally, these rays should actually intersect other microfacets and eventually be reflected, but the Torrance–Sparrow model doesn't account for microfacet interreflection.

Because ω_i is computed by reflecting ω_o about ω_h, $\theta_i = 2\theta_h$. Furthermore, because $\phi_i = \phi_h$, we can find the desired conversion factor:

$$\frac{d\omega_h}{d\omega_i} = \frac{\sin\theta_h \, d\theta_h \, d\phi_h}{\sin 2\theta_h \, 2 \, d\theta_h \, d\phi_h}$$

$$= \frac{\sin\theta_h}{4\cos\theta_h \sin\theta_h}$$

$$= \frac{1}{4\cos\theta_h}$$

$$= \frac{1}{4(\omega_i \cdot \omega_h)} = \frac{1}{4(\omega_o \cdot \omega_h)}.$$

Therefore, the PDF after transformation is

$$p(\theta) = \frac{p_h(\theta)}{4(\omega_o \cdot \omega_h)}.$$

⟨*Compute PDF of* wi *for microfacet reflection*⟩ ≡   811
```
*pdf = distribution->Pdf(wo, wh) / (4 * Dot(wo, wh));
```

The same computation is implemented in the MicrofacetReflection::Pdf() method.

⟨*BxDF Method Definitions*⟩ +≡
```
Float MicrofacetReflection::Pdf(const Vector3f &wo,
        const Vector3f &wi) const {
    if (!SameHemisphere(wo, wi)) return 0;
    Vector3f wh = Normalize(wo + wi);
    return distribution->Pdf(wo, wh) / (4 * Dot(wo, wh));
}
```

The approach for transmission is analogous: given a sampled ω_h microfacet orientation, the outgoing direction is refracted about that normal direction to get the sampled incident direction. In the case of total internal reflection, Refract() returns false, and a black SPD is returned.

⟨*BxDF Method Definitions*⟩ +≡
```
Spectrum MicrofacetTransmission::Sample_f(const Vector3f &wo,
        Vector3f *wi, const Point2f &u, Float *pdf,
        BxDFType *sampledType) const {
    Vector3f wh = distribution->Sample_wh(wo, u);
    Float eta = CosTheta(wo) > 0 ? (etaA / etaB) : (etaB / etaA);
    if (!Refract(wo, (Normal3f)wh, eta, wi))
        return 0;
    *pdf = Pdf(wo, *wi);
    return f(wo, *wi);
}
```

The PDF for the transmitted direction also requires an adjustment for the change of variables. This value is stored in dwh_dwi. We won't derive this term here; the "Further Reading" section at the end of the chapter has more information.

⟨*BxDF Method Definitions*⟩ +≡
```
Float MicrofacetTransmission::Pdf(const Vector3f &wo,
        const Vector3f &wi) const {
    if (SameHemisphere(wo, wi)) return 0;
    ⟨Compute ωₕ from ω₀ and ωᵢ for microfacet transmission 814⟩
    ⟨Compute change of variables dwh_dwi for microfacet transmission⟩
    return distribution->Pdf(wo, wh) * dwh_dwi;
}
```

In the transmissive case, the meaning of the half-angle vector ω_h is generalized to denote the normal of the microfacet that is responsible for refracting light from ω_i to ω_o. This vector can be derived following the setting in Figure 8.11.

⟨*Compute ω_h from ω_o and ω_i for microfacet transmission*⟩ ≡   814
```
Float eta = CosTheta(wo) > 0 ? (etaB / etaA) : (etaA / etaB);
Vector3f wh = Normalize(wo + wi * eta);
```

14.1.2 FresnelBlend

The FresnelBlend class is a mixture of a diffuse and glossy term. A straightforward approach to sampling this BRDF is to sample from both a cosine-weighted distribution as well as the microfacet distribution. The implementation here chooses between the two with equal probability based on whether ξ_1 is less than or greater than 0.5. In both cases, it remaps ξ_1 to cover the range $[0, 1)$ after using it to make this decision. (Otherwise, values of ξ_1 used for the cosine-weighted sampling would always be less than 0.5, for example.) Using the sample ξ_1 for two purposes in this manner slightly reduces the quality of the stratification of the (ξ_1, ξ_2) values that are actually used for sampling directions.[3]

⟨*BxDF Method Definitions*⟩ +≡
```
Spectrum FresnelBlend::Sample_f(const Vector3f &wo, Vector3f *wi,
        const Point2f &uOrig, Float *pdf, BxDFType *sampledType) const {
    Point2f u = uOrig;
    if (u[0] < .5) {
        u[0] = 2 * u[0];
        ⟨Cosine-sample the hemisphere, flipping the direction if necessary 806⟩
    } else {
        u[0] = 2 * (u[0] - .5f);
        ⟨Sample microfacet orientation ωₕ and reflected direction ωᵢ 812⟩
    }
    *pdf = Pdf(wo, *wi);
    return f(wo, *wi);
}
```

---

3   Alternatively, we could have modified the interface of Sample_f() to supply an additional sample for such discrete choices, including those decisions made in BSDF::Sample_f(). However, consuming additional dimensions of the sample vector can also have an adverse effect on the quality of subsequent samples that end up coming from higher dimensions as a consequence—which approach is preferable in practice is related to the type of sampler being used.

The PDF for this sampling strategy is simple; it is just an average of the two PDFs used.

⟨*BxDF Method Definitions*⟩ +≡

```
Float FresnelBlend::Pdf(const Vector3f &wo, const Vector3f &wi) const {
    if (!SameHemisphere(wo, wi)) return 0;
    Vector3f wh = Normalize(wo + wi);
    Float pdf_wh = distribution->Pdf(wo, wh);
    return .5f * (AbsCosTheta(wi) * InvPi +
                  pdf_wh / (4 * Dot(wo, wh)));
}
```

14.1.3 SPECULAR REFLECTION AND TRANSMISSION

The Dirac delta distributions that were previously used to define the BRDF for specular reflection and the BTDF for specular transmission fit into this sampling framework well, as long as a few conventions are kept in mind when using their sampling and PDF functions.

Recall that the Dirac delta distribution is defined such that

$$\delta(x) = 0 \quad \text{for all } x \neq 0$$

and

$$\int_{-\infty}^{\infty} \delta(x)\, dx = 1.$$

Thus, it is a probability density function, where the PDF has a value of 0 for all $x \neq 0$. Generating a sample from such a distribution is trivial; there is only one possible value for it to take on. When thought of in this way, the implementations of Sample_f() for the SpecularReflection and SpecularTransmission BxDFs can be seen to fit naturally into the Monte Carlo sampling framework.

It is not as simple to determine which value should be returned for the value of the PDF. Strictly speaking, the delta distribution is not a true function but must be defined as the limit of another function—for example, one describing a box of unit area whose width approaches 0; see Chapter 5 of Bracewell (2000) for further discussion and references. Thought of in this way, the value of $\delta(0)$ tends toward infinity. Certainly, returning an infinite or very large value for the PDF is not going to lead to correct results from the renderer.

However, recall that BSDFs defined with delta components also have these delta components in their f_r functions, a detail that was glossed over when we returned values from their Sample_f() methods in Chapter 8. Thus, the Monte Carlo estimator for the scattering equation with such a BSDF is written

$$\frac{1}{N} \sum_{i}^{N} \frac{f_r(\mathrm{p}, \omega_o, \omega_i) L_i(\mathrm{p}, \omega_i) |\cos\theta_i|}{p(\omega_i)} = \frac{1}{N} \sum_{i}^{N} \frac{\rho_{hd}(\omega_o) \frac{\delta(\omega - \omega_i)}{|\cos\theta_i|} L_i(\mathrm{p}, \omega_i) |\cos\theta_i|}{p(\omega_i)},$$

where $\rho_{hd}(\omega_o)$ is the hemispherical–directional reflectance and ω is the direction for perfect specular reflection or transmission.

Because the PDF $p(\omega_i)$ has a delta term as well, $p(\omega_i) = \delta(\omega - \omega_i)$, the two delta distributions cancel out, and the estimator is

$$\rho_{\mathrm{hd}}(\omega_o) L_i(\mathrm{p}, \omega),$$

exactly the quantity computed by the Whitted integrator, for example.

Therefore, the implementations here return a constant value of 1 for the PDF for specular reflection and transmission when sampled using `Sample_f()`, with the convention that for specular BxDFs there is an implied delta distribution in the PDF value that is expected to cancel out with the implied delta distribution in the value of the BSDF when the estimator is evaluated. The respective `Pdf()` methods therefore return 0 for all directions, since there is zero probability that another sampling method will randomly find the direction from a delta distribution.

⟨*SpecularReflection Public Methods*⟩ +≡   524
```
Float Pdf(const Vector3f &wo, const Vector3f &wi) const {
    return 0;
}
```

⟨*SpecularTransmission Public Methods*⟩ +≡   528
```
Float Pdf(const Vector3f &wo, const Vector3f &wi) const {
    return 0;
}
```

There is a potential pitfall with this convention: when multiple importance sampling is used to compute weights, PDF values that include these implicit delta distributions can't be freely mixed with regular PDF values. This isn't a problem in practice, since there's no reason to apply MIS when there's a delta distribution in the integrand. The light transport routines in this and the next two chapters have appropriate logic to avoid this error.

The `FresnelSpecular` class encapsulates both specular reflection and transmission, with the relative contributions modulated by a dielectric Fresnel term. By combining these two together, it's able to use the value of the Fresnel term for the outgoing direction ω_o to determine which component to sample—for example, for glancing angles where reflection is high, it's much more likely to return a reflected direction than a transmitted direction. This approach improves Monte Carlo efficiency when rendering scenes with these sorts of surfaces, since the rays that are sampled will tend to have larger contributions to the final result.

⟨*BxDF Method Definitions*⟩ +≡
```
Spectrum FresnelSpecular::Sample_f(const Vector3f &wo,
        Vector3f *wi, const Point2f &u, Float *pdf,
        BxDFType *sampledType) const {
    Float F = FrDielectric(CosTheta(wo), etaA, etaB);
    if (u[0] < F) {
        ⟨Compute specular reflection for FresnelSpecular 817⟩
    } else {
        ⟨Compute specular transmission for FresnelSpecular 817⟩
    }
}
```

(a)   (b)

Figure 14.5: The Effect of Accurately Sampling the FourierBSDF. Reflection from both objects is modeled using the FourierBSDF, rendered using 32 samples per pixel. (a) Uniform hemisphere sampling to compute reflection. (b) The exact sampling scheme implemented in FourierBSDF::Sample_f(). Variance is much lower and overall rendering time increased by only 20%.

Specular reflection is chosen with probability equal to F; given that choice, the computations performed are the same as those in SpecularReflection.

⟨*Compute specular reflection for* FresnelSpecular⟩ ≡   816
    ⟨*Compute perfect specular reflection direction* 526⟩
    if (sampledType)
        *sampledType = BxDFType(BSDF_SPECULAR | BSDF_REFLECTION);
    *pdf = F;
    return F * R / AbsCosTheta(*wi);

Otherwise, with probability 1-F, specular transmission is selected.

⟨*Compute specular transmission for* FresnelSpecular⟩ ≡   816
    ⟨*Figure out which η is incident and which is transmitted* 529⟩
    ⟨*Compute ray direction for specular transmission* 529⟩
    Spectrum ft = T * (1 - F);
    ⟨*Account for non-symmetry with transmission to different medium* 961⟩
    if (sampledType)
        *sampledType = BxDFType(BSDF_SPECULAR | BSDF_TRANSMISSION);
    *pdf = 1 - F;
    return ft / AbsCosTheta(*wi);

⋆ **14.1.4 FOURIER BSDF**

In addition to being able to compactly and accurately represent a variety of measured and synthetic BSDFs, the representation used by the FourierBSDF (Section 8.6) also admits a fairly efficient exact importance sampling scheme. Figure 14.5 compares the result of using this sampling approach to using uniform hemispherical sampling for the FourierBSDF.

Recall the BSDF representation from Equation (8.22), which was

$$f(\mu_i, \mu_o, \phi_i - \phi_o)\,|\mu_i| = \sum_{k=0}^{m-1} a_k(\mu_i, \mu_o) \cos(k\,(\phi_i - \phi_o)),$$

where the function a_k was discretized over the incident and outgoing zenith angle cosines $(\mu_i, \mu_o) \in \{\mu_0, \ldots, \mu_{n-1}\}^2$ with endpoints $\mu_0 = -1$ and $\mu_{n-1} = 1$. An even Fourier expansion with real coefficients was used to model the dependence on the azimuth angle difference parameter $\phi = \phi_i - \phi_o$.

The task now is to first sample μ_i given μ_o and then sample the angle ϕ_i relative to ϕ_o. A helpful property of the order 0 Fourier coefficients greatly simplifies both of these steps. The even Fourier basis functions form an orthogonal basis of the vector space of square-integrable even functions—this means that the basis coefficients of any function g satisfying these criteria can be found using a inner product between g and the individual basis functions analogous to orthogonal projections of vectors on Euclidean vector spaces. Here, we are dealing with continuous functions on $[0, \pi]$, where a suitable inner product can be defined as

$$\langle g, h \rangle = \frac{1}{\pi} \int_0^\pi g(\phi)\, h(\phi)\, d\phi.$$

The Fourier basis function associated with order 0 is simply the unit constant; hence the coefficients in a_0 relate to the cosine-weighted BSDF as

$$a_0(\mu_i, \mu_o) = \frac{1}{\pi} \int_0^\pi f(\mu_i, \mu_o, \phi)\,|\mu_i|\, d\phi.$$

This quantity turns out to be very helpful in constructing a method for importance sampling the BSDF: disregarding normalization factors, this average over ϕ can be interpreted as the marginal distribution of the cosine-weighted BSDF with respect to pairs of μ angles (Section 13.6 discussed marginal density functions).

It will be useful to be able to efficiently access these order 0 coefficients without the indirections that would normally be necessary given the layout of `FourierBSDFTable::a`. We therefore keep an additional copy of these values in an array of size nMu × nMu in `FourierBSDFTable::a0`. This array is initialized by copying the corresponding entries from `FourierBSDFTable::a` at scene loading time in the `FourierBSDFTable::Read()` method.

⟨*FourierBSDFTable Public Data*⟩ +≡   554
    `Float *a0;`

With a marginal distribution at hand, we are now able to split the sampling operation into two lower dimensional steps: first, we use the a_0 coefficients to sample μ_i given μ_o. Second, with (μ_i, μ_o) known, we can interpolate the Fourier coefficients that specify the BSDF's dependence on the remaining azimuth difference angle parameter ϕ and sample from their distribution. These operations are all implemented as smooth mappings that preserve the properties of structured point sets, such as Sobol' or Halton sequences. Given these angles, the last step is to compute the corresponding direction and value of the BSDF.

⟨*BxDF Method Definitions*⟩ +≡
```
Spectrum FourierBSDF::Sample_f(const Vector3f &wo, Vector3f *wi,
        const Point2f &u, Float *pdf, BxDFType *sampledType) const {
    ⟨Sample zenith angle component for FourierBSDF 819⟩
    ⟨Compute Fourier coefficients aₖ for (μᵢ, μₒ) 557⟩
    ⟨Importance sample the luminance Fourier expansion 820⟩
    ⟨Compute the scattered direction for FourierBSDF 820⟩
    ⟨Evaluate remaining Fourier expansions for angle φ⟩
}
```

Sampling the zenith angle is implemented using `SampleCatmullRom2D()`, which will be defined in a few pages. This helper function operates in stages: after first mapping a uniform variate to one of the spline segments, it then samples a specific position within the segment. To select a segment, the function requires an array of precomputed CDFs

$$I_{i,o} = \int_{-1}^{\mu_i} a_0(\mu', \mu_o) \, d\mu',$$ [14.3]

where $0 \le i$, $o < n$. Each column of this matrix stores a discrete CDF over μ_i for a different (fixed) value of μ_o. The above integral is computed directly from the spline interpolant and can thus be used to efficiently select spline segments proportional to their definite integral.

⟨*FourierBSDFTable Public Data*⟩ +≡   554
```
Float *cdf;
```

In the case of the `FourierBSDF`, this `cdf` array is already part of the input file, and we need not be concerned with its generation.

⟨*Sample zenith angle component for* `FourierBSDF`⟩ ≡   819
```
Float mu0 = CosTheta(wo);
Float pdfMu;
Float muI = SampleCatmullRom2D(bsdfTable.nMu, bsdfTable.nMu,
        bsdfTable.mu, bsdfTable.mu, bsdfTable.a0, bsdfTable.cdf, mu0,
        u[1], nullptr, &pdfMu);
```

After `SampleCatmullRom2D()` returns, `muI` records the sampled incident zenith angle cosine, and `pdfMu` contains the associated probability density in the same domain.

We can now interpolate the nearby Fourier coefficients, reusing the fragment ⟨*Compute Fourier coefficients aₖ for (μᵢ, μₒ)*⟩ from `FourierBSDF::f()` in Section 8.6. Given the coefficients `ak`, sampling of the azimuth difference angle is also implemented as a separate function `SampleFourier()`, also to be defined in a few pages. This function returns the sampled difference angle `phi`, the value `Y` of the luminance Fourier expansion evaluated at `phi`, and the sample probability `pdfPhi` per unit radian. The final sample probability per unit solid angle is the product of the azimuthal and zenith angle cosine PDFs. (As with values computed via Fourier series in Section 8.6, negative values must be clamped to 0.)

⟨*Importance sample the luminance Fourier expansion*⟩ ≡   819
```
Float phi, pdfPhi;
Float Y = SampleFourier(ak, bsdfTable.recip, mMax, u[0], &pdfPhi, &phi);
*pdf = std::max((Float)0, pdfPhi * pdfMu);
```

SampleFourier() takes an additional input array recip containing precomputed integer reciprocals $1/i$ for all mMax Fourier orders. These reciprocals are frequently accessed within the function—precomputing them is an optimization to avoid costly arithmetic to generate them over and over again, causing pipeline stalls due to the high latency of division operations on current processor architectures. This reciprocal array is initialized in FourierBSDFTable::Read().

⟨*FourierBSDFTable Public Data*⟩ +≡   554
```
Float *recip;
```

We now have the angles $\mu_i = \cos\theta_i$ and ϕ. The sampled incident direction's xy coordinates are given by rotating the xy components of ω_o by an angle ϕ about the surface normal, and its z component is given by μ_i (using spherical coordinates).

There are two details to note in the computation of the direction ω_i. First, the xy components are scaled by a factor $\sin\theta_i/\sin\theta_o$, which ensures that the resulting vector is normalized. Second, the computed direction is negated before being assigned to *wi; this follows the coordinate system convention for the FourierBSDF that was described in Section 8.6.

⟨*Compute the scattered direction for* FourierBSDF⟩ ≡   819
```
Float sin2ThetaI = std::max((Float)0, 1 - muI * muI);
Float norm = std::sqrt(sin2ThetaI / Sin2Theta(wo));
Float sinPhi = std::sin(phi), cosPhi = std::cos(phi);
*wi = -Vector3f(norm * (cosPhi * wo.x - sinPhi * wo.y),
                norm * (sinPhi * wo.x + cosPhi * wo.y), muI);
```

The fragment ⟨*Evaluate remaining Fourier expansions for angle* ϕ⟩ is identical to ⟨*Evaluate Fourier expansion for angle* ϕ⟩ defined in Section 8.6 except that doesn't evaluate the luminance channel, which was already done by SampleFourier() above.

The FourierBSDF::Pdf() method returns the solid angle density for the preceding sampling method. Since this method produces samples that are exactly distributed according to the product $f(\mu_i, \mu_o, \phi)|\mu_i|$, we could simply copy the implementation of FourierBSDF::f() except for the division that cancels $|\mu_i|$. However, doing so would underestimate the probability when the BSDF doesn't reflect all of the incident illumination.

To correct for this, we scale the unnormalized $f(\mu_i, \mu_o, \phi)|\mu_i|$ by a suitable normalization factor ρ^{-1} to ensure that the product integrates to 1:

$$\int_0^{2\pi}\int_0^{\pi}\frac{1}{\rho}\,f(\cos\theta_i,\cos\theta_o,\phi)\,|\cos\theta_i|\sin\theta_i\,d\theta_i'\,d\phi = 1.$$

Note that the outgoing zenith angle cosine $\cos\theta_o = \mu_o$ was left unspecified in the above equation. In general, the normalization factor ρ is not constant and, instead, it depends on the current value of μ_o. $\rho(\mu_o)$ has a simple interpretation: it is the hemispherical–directional reflectance of a surface that is illuminated from the zenith angle $\cos^{-1}\mu_o$.

Suppose briefly that μ_o happens to be part of the discretized set of zenith angle cosines $\mu_0, \ldots, \mu_{n-1}$ stored in the array `FourierBSDFTable::mu`. Then

$$
\begin{aligned}
\rho(\mu_o) &= \int_0^{2\pi} \int_0^{\pi} f(\cos\theta_i, \cos\theta_o, \phi) \, |\cos\theta_i| \, \sin\theta_i \, d\theta_i \, d\phi \\
&= \int_0^{2\pi} \int_{-1}^{1} f(\mu_i, \mu_o, \phi) \, |\mu_i| \, d\mu_i \, d\phi \\
&= 2\pi \int_{-1}^{1} \left[\frac{1}{\pi} \int_0^{\pi} f(\mu_i, \mu_o, \phi) \, |\mu_i| \, d\phi \right] d\mu_i \qquad \text{[14.4]} \\
&= 2\pi \int_{-1}^{1} a_0(\mu_i, \mu_o) \, d\mu_i \\
&= 2\pi I_{n-1,o},
\end{aligned}
$$

where I was defined in Equation (14.3). In other words, the needed normalization factor is readily available in the `FourierBSDFTable::cdf` array. For intermediate values of μ_o, we can simply interpolate the neighboring four entries of $I_{n-1,i}$ using the usual spline interpolation scheme—the linearity of this interpolation coupled with the linearity of the analytic integrals in (14.4) ensures a result that is consistent with `FourierBSDF::f()`.

⟨*BxDF Method Definitions*⟩ +≡
```
Float FourierBSDF::Pdf(const Vector3f &wo, const Vector3f &wi) const {
    ⟨Find the zenith angle cosines and azimuth difference angle 556⟩
    ⟨Compute luminance Fourier coefficients aₖ for (μᵢ, μₒ)⟩
    ⟨Evaluate probability of sampling wi 821⟩
}
```

We won't include the second fragment here—it is almost identical to ⟨*Compute Fourier coefficients a_k for (μ_i, μ_o)*⟩, the only difference being that it only interpolates the luminance coefficients (samples are generated proportional to luminance; hence the other two channels are not relevant here).

The last fragment interpolates the directional albedo from Equation (14.4) and uses it to correct the result of `Fourier()` for absorption.

⟨*Evaluate probability of sampling* wi⟩ ≡   821
```
Float rho = 0;
for (int o = 0; o < 4; ++o) {
    if (weights0[o] == 0)
        continue;
    rho += weights0[o] * bsdfTable.cdf[(offset0 + o) * bsdfTable.nMu +
                                       bsdfTable.nMu - 1] * (2 * Pi);
}
Float Y = Fourier(ak, mMax, cosPhi);
return (rho > 0 && Y > 0) ? (Y / rho) : 0;
```

Sampling 1D Spline Interpolants

Before defining the `SampleCatmullRom2D()` function used in the previously discussed `FourierBSDF::Sample_f()` method, we'll first focus on a simpler 1D case: suppose that a function f was evaluated at n positions $x_0, \ldots, x_{n-1}$, resulting in a piecewise cubic Catmull-Rom spline interpolant $\hat{f}$ with $n-1$ spline segments $\hat{f}_i(x)$ $(i = 0, \ldots, n-2)$. Given a precomputed discrete CDF over these spline segments defined as

$$F_i = \begin{cases} 0, & \text{if } i = 0, \\ \sum_{k=0}^{i-1} \int_{x_k}^{x_{k+1}} \frac{1}{c} \hat{f}_k(x') \, dx', & \text{if } i > 0, \end{cases} \qquad [14.5]$$

where c is the normalization term,

$$c = \int_{x_0}^{x_{n-1}} \hat{f}(x) \, dx,$$

a straightforward way of importance sampling $\hat{f}$ in two steps using the inversion method entails first finding the interval i such that

$$F_i \leq \xi_1 < F_{i+1},$$

where ξ_1 is a random variate on the interval $[0, 1)$, and then sampling an x' value in the ith interval. Since the values F_i are monotonically increasing, the interval can be found using an efficient binary search.

In the following, we won't actually normalize the F_i values, effectively setting $c = 1$. We can equivalently sample i by first multiplying the random variable ξ by the last F_i entry, F_{n-1}, which is the total integral over all spline segments and is thus equal to c. Thus, the binary search looks for

$$F_i \leq \xi_1 F_{n-1} \leq F_{i+1}, \qquad [14.6]$$

Having selected a segment i, we can offset and re-scale ξ_1 to obtain a second uniform variate in $[0, 1)$:

$$\xi_2 = \frac{\xi_1 F_{n-1} - F_i}{F_{i+1} - F_i}.$$

We then use ξ_2 to sample a position x within the interval $[x_i, x_{i+1}]$ using that segment's integral,

$$\hat{F}_i(x) = \int_{x_i}^{x} \hat{f}_i(x') \, dx', \qquad [14.7]$$

where again we won't compute a properly normalized CDF but will instead multiply ξ_2 by $\hat{F}_i(x_{i+1})$ rather than normalizing $\hat{F}_i$. We must then compute

$$x = \hat{F}_i^{-1}\left(\hat{F}_i(x_{i+1})\, \xi_2\right) = \hat{F}_i^{-1}\left((F_{i+1} - F_i)\frac{\xi_1 F_{n-1} - F_i}{F_{i+1} - F_i}\right) \qquad [14.8]$$

$$= \hat{F}_i^{-1}\left(\xi_1 F_{n-1} - F_i\right).$$

This approach is implemented in SampleCatmullRom(), which takes the following inputs: the number of samples n; x contains the locations $x_0, \ldots, x_{n-1}$ where the original function f was evaluated; f stores the value of the function at each point x_i; u is used to pass the uniform variate ξ; and integrated F_i values must be provided via the F parameter—

these values can be precomputed with `IntegrateCatmullRom()` when necessary. `fval` and `pdf` are used to return the function value and associated PDF value.

⟨*Spline Interpolation Definitions*⟩ +≡
```
Float SampleCatmullRom(int n, const Float *x, const Float *f,
        const Float *F, Float u, Float *fval, Float *pdf) {
    ⟨Map u to a spline interval by inverting F 823⟩
    ⟨Look up xᵢ and function values of spline segment i 823⟩
    ⟨Approximate derivatives using finite differences 823⟩
    ⟨Re-scale u for continous spline sampling step 824⟩
    ⟨Invert definite integral over spline segment and return solution 825⟩
}
```

The function begins by scaling the uniform variate u by the last entry of F following Equation (14.6). Following this, u is mapped to a spline interval via the `FindInterval()` helper function, which returns the last interval satisfying `F[i] <= u` while clamping to the array bounds in case of rounding errors.

⟨*Map u to a spline interval by inverting F*⟩ ≡   823
```
u *= F[n - 1];
int i = FindInterval(n, [&](int i) { return F[i] <= u; });
```

The next fragment fetches the associated function values and node positions from f and x; the variable `width` contains the segment length.

⟨*Look up xᵢ and function values of spline segment i*⟩ ≡   823, 937
```
Float x0 = x[i],   x1 = x[i + 1];
Float f0 = f[i], f1 = f[i + 1];
Float width = x1 - x0;
```

Recall that Catmull-Rom splines require an approximation of the first derivative of the function (Section 8.6.1) at the segment endpoints. Depending on i, this derivative is computed using forward, backward, or central finite difference approximations.

⟨*Approximate derivatives using finite differences*⟩ ≡   823, 937
```
Float d0, d1;
if (i > 0)     d0 = width * (f1 - f[i - 1]) / (x1 - x[i - 1]);
else           d0 = f1 - f0;
if (i + 2 < n) d1 = width * (f[i + 2] - f0) / (x[i + 2] - x0);
else           d1 = f1 - f0;
```

The remainder of the function then has to find the inverse of the continuous cumulative distribution function from Equation (14.8):

$$F_i^{-1}\left(\xi_1 F_{n-1} - F_i\right).$$

FindInterval() 1065
Float 1062
IntegrateCatmullRom() 937

Since the scaling by F_{n-1} was already applied in the first fragment, we need only subtract F_i.

The actual inversion is done in ⟨*Invert definite integral over spline segment and return solution*⟩, whose discussion we postpone for the following discussion of the 2D cases. The internals of this inversion operate on a scaled and shifted spline segment defined on the interval [0, 1], which requires an additional scaling by the associated change of variable factor equal to the reciprocal of width.

⟨*Re-scale* u *for continous spline sampling step*⟩ ≡   824

```
u = (u - F[i]) / width;
```

Sampling 2D Spline Interpolants

The main use cases of spline interpolants in pbrt actually importance sample 2D functions $f(\alpha, x)$, where α is considered a fixed parameter for the purpose of sampling (e.g., the albedo of the underlying material or the outgoing zenith angle cosine μ_o in the case of the FourierBSDF). This case is handled by SampleCatmullRom2D().

⟨*Spline Interpolation Definitions*⟩ +≡

```
Float SampleCatmullRom2D(int size1, int size2, const Float *nodes1,
        const Float *nodes2, const Float *values, const Float *cdf,
        Float alpha, Float u, Float *fval, Float *pdf) {
    ⟨Determine offset and coefficients for the alpha parameter  824⟩
    ⟨Define a lambda function to interpolate table entries  825⟩
    ⟨Map u to a spline interval by inverting the interpolated cdf⟩
    ⟨Look up node positions and interpolated function values⟩
    ⟨Re-scale u using the interpolated cdf⟩
    ⟨Approximate derivatives using finite differences of the interpolant⟩
    ⟨Invert definite integral over spline segment and return solution  825⟩
}
```

The parameters size1, size2, nodes1, and nodes2 specify separate discretizations for each dimension. The values argument supplies a matrix of function values in row-major order, with rows corresponding to sets of samples that have the same position along the first dimension. The function uses the parameter alpha to choose a slice in the first dimension that is then importance sampled along the second dimension. The parameter cdf supplies a matrix of discrete CDFs, where each row was obtained by running IntegrateCatmullRom() on the corresponding row of values.

The first fragment of SampleCatmullRom2D() calls CatmullRomWeights() to select four adjacent rows of the values array along with interpolation weights.

⟨*Determine offset and coefficients for the* alpha *parameter*⟩ ≡   824

```
int offset;
Float weights[4];
if (!CatmullRomWeights(size1, nodes1, alpha, &offset, weights))
    return 0;
```

To proceed, we could now simply interpolate the selected rows of values and cdf and finish by calling the 1D sampling function SampleCatmullRom(). However, only a few entries of values and cdf are truly needed to generate a sample in practice, making such an approach unnecessarily slow. Instead, we define a C++11 lambda function that interpolates entries of these arrays on demand:

⟨*Define a lambda function to interpolate table entries*⟩ ≡   824
```
auto interpolate = [&](const Float *array, int idx) {
    Float value = 0;
    for (int i = 0; i < 4; ++i)
        if (weights[i] != 0)
            value += array[(offset + i) * size2 + idx] * weights[i];
    return value;
};
```

The rest of the function is identical to SampleCatmullRom() except that every access to values[i] is replaced by interpolate(values, i) and similarly for cdf. For brevity, this code is omitted in the book.

We now return to the inversion of the integral in Equation (14.8), which we glossed over. Recall that $\hat{F}_i$ was defined as an integral over the cubic spline segment $\hat{f}_i$, making it a quartic polynomial. It is possible but burdensome to invert this function analytically. We prefer a numerical approach that is facilitated by a useful pair of properties:

1. The function $\hat{F}_i$ is the definite integral over the (assumed nonnegative) interpolant $\hat{f}_i$, and so it increases monotonically.
2. The interval $[x_i, x_{i+1}]$ selected by the function FindInterval() contains exactly one solution to Equation (14.8).

In this case, the interval $[x_i, x_{i+1}]$ is known as a *bracketing interval*. The existence of such an interval allows using *bisection search*, a simple iterative root-finding technique that is guaranteed to converge to the solution. In each iteration, bisection search splits the interval into two parts and discards the subinterval that does not bracket the solution—in this way, it can be interpreted as a continuous extension of binary search. The method's robustness is clearly desirable, but its relatively slow (linear) convergence can still be improved. We use *Newton-Bisection*, which is a combination of the quadratically converging but potentially unsafe[4] Newton's method with the safety of bisection search as a fallback.

As mentioned earlier, all of the following steps assume that the spline segment under consideration is defined on the interval [0, 1] with endpoint values f0 and f1 and derivative estimates d0 and d1. We will use the variable t to denote positions in this shifted and scaled interval and the values a and b store the current interval extent. Fhat stores the value of $\hat{F}(t)$ and fhat stores $\hat{f}(t)$.

⟨*Invert definite integral over spline segment and return solution*⟩ ≡   823, 824
    ⟨*Set initial guess for t by importance sampling a linear interpolant* 826⟩
    Float a = 0, b = 1, Fhat, fhat;

---

4   Newton's method can exhibit oscillatory or divergent behavior and is only guaranteed to converge when started sufficiently close to the solution. In practice, it is usually hard to provide such a guarantee; hence we prefer the unconditionally safe combination with bisection search.

```
while (true) {
    ⟨Fall back to a bisection step when t is out of bounds 826⟩
    ⟨Evaluate target function and its derivative in Horner form 827⟩
    ⟨Stop the iteration if converged 827⟩
    ⟨Update bisection bounds using updated t 828⟩
    ⟨Perform a Newton step 828⟩
}
⟨Return the sample position and function value 828⟩
```

The number of required Newton-Bisection iterations can be reduced by starting the algorithm with a good initial guess. We use a heuristic that assumes that the spline segment is linear, i.e.,

$$\hat{f}(t) = (1 - t)f(0) + tf(1).$$

Then the definite integral

$$\hat{F}(t) = \int_0^t \hat{f}(t') \, dt' = \frac{t}{2}(tf(1) - (t - 2)f(0))$$

has the inverse

$$\hat{F}^{-1}(\xi) = \begin{cases} \frac{f(0)\pm\sqrt{f(0)^2-2f(0)\xi+2f(1)\xi}}{f(0)-f(1)} & f(0) \neq f(1) \\ \frac{\xi}{f(0)} & \text{otherwise,} \end{cases}$$

of which only one of the quadratic roots is relevant (the other one yields values outside of $[0, 1]$).

⟨Set initial guess for t by importance sampling a linear interpolant⟩ ≡   825
```
Float t;
if (f0 != f1)
    t = (f0 - std::sqrt(
            std::max((Float)0, f0 * f0 + 2 * u * (f1 - f0)))) / (f0 - f1);
else
    t = u / f0;
```

The first fragment in the inner loop checks if the current iterate is inside the bracketing interval $[a, b]$. Otherwise it is reset to the interval center, resulting in a standard bisection step (Figure 14.6).

⟨Fall back to a bisection step when t is out of bounds⟩ ≡   825
```
if (!(t >= a && t <= b))
    t = 0.5f * (a + b);
```

Next, F is initialized by evaluating the quartic $\hat{F}(t)$ from Equation (14.7). For Newton's method, we also require the derivative of this function, which is simply the original cubic spline—thus, f is set to the spline evaluated at t. The following expressions result after converting both functions to Horner form:

Float 1062

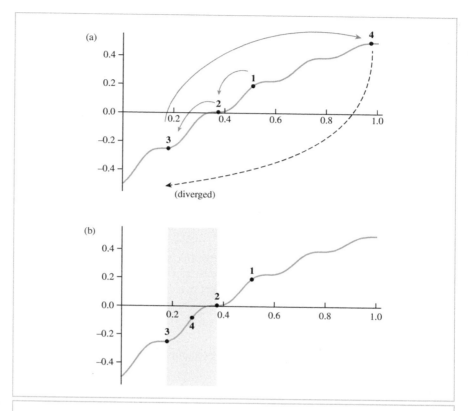

Figure 14.6: The Robustness of Newton-Bisection. (a) this function increases monotonically and contains a single root on the shown interval, but a naive application of Newton's method diverges. (b) the bisection feature of the robust root-finder enables recovery from the third Newton step, which jumps far away from the root (the bisection interval is highlighted). The method converges a few iterations later.

⟨*Evaluate target function and its derivative in Horner form*⟩ ≡   825
```
Fhat = t * (f0 + t * (.5f * d0 + t * ((1.f/3.f) * (-2 * d0 - d1) +
               f1 - f0 + t * (.25f * (d0 + d1) + .5f * (f0 - f1)))));
fhat = f0 + t * (d0 + t * (-2 * d0 - d1 + 3 * (f1 - f0) +
               t * (d0 + d1 + 2 * (f0 - f1))));
```

The iteration should stop either if Fhat - u is close to 0, or if the bracketing interval has become sufficiently small.

⟨*Stop the iteration if converged*⟩ ≡   825
```
if (std::abs(Fhat - u) < 1e-6f || b - a < 1e-6f)
    break;
```

If $\hat{F}(t) - u < 0$, then the monotonicity of $\hat{F}$ implies that the interval [a, t] cannot possibly contain the solution (and a similar statement holds for b). The next fragment uses this information to update the bracketing interval.

⟨*Update bisection bounds using updated* t⟩ ≡   825
```
   if (Fhat - u < 0) a = t;
   else              b = t;
```

Finally, the function and derivative values are used in a Newton step.

⟨*Perform a Newton step*⟩ ≡   825
```
   t -= (Fhat - u) / fhat;
```

Once converged, the last fragment maps t back to the original interval. The function optionally returns the spline value and probability density at this position.

⟨*Return the sample position and function value*⟩ ≡   825
```
   if (fval) *fval = fhat;
   if (pdf)  *pdf = fhat / F[n - 1];
   return x0 + width * t;
```

Sampling Fourier Expansions

Next, we'll discuss sample generation for the Fourier series, Equation (8.22) using a Newton-Bisection-type method that is very similar to what was used in `SampleCatmull Rom()`. We'd like to sample from a distribution that matches

$$f(\phi) = \sum_{k=0}^{m-1} a_k \, \cos(k\,\phi)$$

for given Fourier coefficients a_k. Integrating gives a simple analytic expression:

$$F(\phi) = \int_0^\phi f(\phi')\,d\phi' = a_0\,\phi + \sum_{k=1}^{m-1} \frac{1}{k}\sin(k\,\phi), \qquad [14.9]$$

though note that this isn't necessarily a normalized CDF: $F(2\pi) = 2\pi a_0$, since the $\sin(k\phi)$ terms are all zero at $\phi = 2\pi$.

The function `SampleFourier()` numerically inverts $F(\phi)$ to sample azimuths using the inversion method. It takes an array ak of Fourier coefficients of length m as input. The u parameter is used to pass a uniform variate, and recip should be a pointer to an array of m integer reciprocals. `SampleFourier()` returns the value of the Fourier expansion at the sampled position, which is stored in *phiPtr along with a probability density in *pdf.

⟨*Fourier Interpolation Definitions*⟩ +≡
```
   Float SampleFourier(const Float *ak, const Float *recip, int m, Float u,
           Float *pdf, Float *phiPtr) {
       ⟨Pick a side and declare bisection variables 829⟩
       while (true) {
           ⟨Evaluate F(φ) and its derivative f(φ) 829⟩
           ⟨Update bisection bounds using updated φ⟩
           ⟨Stop the Fourier bisection iteration if converged⟩
           ⟨Perform a Newton step given f(φ) and F(φ)⟩
           ⟨Fall back to a bisection step when φ is out of bounds⟩
       }
       ⟨Potentially flip φ and return the result 830⟩
   }
```

Since SampleFourier() operates on even functions that are periodic on the interval $[0, 2\pi]$, the probability of generating a sample in the each of the two subintervals $[0, \pi]$ and $[\pi, 2\pi]$ is equal to $1/2$. We can therefore skip the first Newton-Bisection iteration and uniformly select one of the sub-intervals with u before remapping it to the range $[0, 1]$. We then always run Newton-Bisection over $[0, \pi]$ but correct for this choice at the end of the function when the second subinterval was chosen (i.e., flip==true).

⟨*Pick a side and declare bisection variables*⟩ ≡   828
```
bool flip = (u >= 0.5);
if (flip)
    u = 1 - 2 * (u - .5f);
else
    u *= 2;
double a = 0, b = Pi, phi = 0.5 * Pi;
double F, f;
```

The first fragment in the loop body of the solver evaluates the integrated $F(\phi)$ value and its derivative $f(\phi)$. Assuming a normalized function with $F(\pi) = 1$, the objective of this function is to solve an equation of the form $F(\phi) - u = 0$. In the case that F lacks proper normalization, we'd still like to generate samples proportional to the the function f, which can be achieved by adding a scaling term: $F(\phi) - uF(\pi) = 0$. The last line of the following fragment therefore subtracts u times $F(\pi)$ from F.

⟨*Evaluate $F(\phi)$ and its derivative $f(\phi)$*⟩ ≡   828
```
⟨Initialize sine and cosine iterates 829⟩
⟨Initialize F and f with the first series term 830⟩
for (int k = 1; k < m; ++k) {
    ⟨Compute next sine and cosine iterates 830⟩
    ⟨Add the next series term to F and f 830⟩
}
F -= u * ak[0] * Pi;
```

As was the case in the implementation of the Fourier() function, it pays off to use a multiple angle formula to avoid costly trigonometric function calls when evaluating Equation (14.9):

$$\sin(k\,\phi) = (2\cos\phi)\sin((k-1)\phi) - \sin((k-2)\phi). \qquad [14.10]$$

Before looping over summands to compute $f(\phi)$ and $F(\phi)$, we'll initialize the initial iterates $\cos(k\phi)$ and $\sin(k\phi)$ for $k = -1$ and $k = 0$.

⟨*Initialize sine and cosine iterates*⟩ ≡   829
```
double cosPhi = std::cos(phi);
double sinPhi = std::sqrt(1 - cosPhi * cosPhi);
double cosPhiPrev = cosPhi, cosPhiCur = 1;
double sinPhiPrev = -sinPhi, sinPhiCur = 0;
```

Fourier() 559
Pi 1063
SampleFourier() 828

The first summand of $F(\phi)$ is slightly special, so the corresponding computation for both $f(\phi)$ and $F(\phi)$ is done before the loop over the rest of the coefficients a_k.

⟨*Initialize* F *and* f *with the first series term*⟩ ≡   829
```
F = ak[0] * phi;
f = ak[0];
```

The loop over coefficients begins by computing updated cosine and sine iterates using Equations (8.25) and (14.10).

⟨*Compute next sine and cosine iterates*⟩ ≡   829
```
double sinPhiNext = 2 * cosPhi * sinPhiCur - sinPhiPrev;
double cosPhiNext = 2 * cosPhi * cosPhiCur - cosPhiPrev;
sinPhiPrev = sinPhiCur; sinPhiCur = sinPhiNext;
cosPhiPrev = cosPhiCur; cosPhiCur = cosPhiNext;
```

The next term of each of the sums for the function value and its derivative can now be evaluated.

⟨*Add the next series term to* F *and* f⟩ ≡   829
```
F += ak[k] * recip[k] * sinPhiNext;
f += ak[k] * cosPhiNext;
```

The remaining fragments are identical to those used in SampleCatmullRom() for the Newton-Bisection algorithm except that the phi variable is used instead of t. We therefore won't include them here.

After phi has been computed, the value of the function, PDF, and azimuth angle are returned. The PDF Is computed by dividing $f(\phi)$ by the normalization factor that results from $F(2\pi)$ being equal to $2\pi a_0$. As mentioned before, phi is flipped using the underlying symmetries when the interval $[\pi, 2\pi]$ was selected at the beginning of SampleFourier().

⟨*Potentially flip* ϕ *and return the result*⟩ ≡   828
```
if (flip)
    phi = 2 * Pi - phi;
*pdf = (Float)f / (2 * Pi * ak[0]);
*phiPtr = (Float)phi;
return f;
```

14.1.5 APPLICATION: ESTIMATING REFLECTANCE

At this point, we have covered the BxDF sampling routines of the majority of BxDFs in pbrt. As an example of their application, we will now show how these sampling routines can be used in computing estimates of the reflectance integrals defined in Section 8.1.1 for arbitrary BRDFs. For example, recall that the hemispherical–directional reflectance is

$$\rho_{hd}(\omega_o) = \int_{\mathcal{H}^2(n)} f_r(\omega_o, \omega_i) \, |\cos\theta_i| \, d\omega_i.$$

Recall from Section 8.1.1 that BxDF::rho() method implementations take two additional parameters, nSamples and an array of sample values u; here, we can see how they are used for Monte Carlo sampling. For BxDF implementations that can't compute the reflectance in closed form, the nSamples parameter specifies the number of Monte Carlo samples to take, and sample values themselves are provided in the u array.

The generic BxDF::rho() method computes a Monte Carlo estimate of this value for any BxDF, using the provided samples and taking advantage of the BxDF's sampling method to compute the estimate with importance sampling.

⟨*BxDF Method Definitions*⟩ +≡
```
Spectrum BxDF::rho(const Vector3f &w, int nSamples,
        const Point2f *u) const {
    Spectrum r(0.);
    for (int i = 0; i < nSamples; ++i) {
        ⟨Estimate one term of ρhd 831⟩
    }
    return r / nSamples;
}
```

Actually evaluating the estimator is a matter of sampling the reflection function's distribution, finding its value, and dividing it by the value of the PDF. Each term of the estimator

$$\frac{1}{N} \sum_{j}^{N} \frac{f_r(\omega, \omega_j) \, |\cos \theta_j|}{p(\omega_j)}$$

is easily evaluated. The BxDF's Sample_f() method returns all of the values of ω_j, $p(\omega_j)$ and the values of $f_r(\omega_o, \omega_j)$. The only tricky part is when $p(\omega_j) = 0$, which must be detected here, since otherwise a division by 0 would place an infinite value in r.

⟨*Estimate one term of* ρhd⟩ ≡   831
```
Vector3f wi;
Float pdf = 0;
Spectrum f = Sample_f(w, &wi, u[i], &pdf);
if (pdf > 0) r += f * AbsCosTheta(wi) / pdf;
```

The hemispherical–hemispherical reflectance can be estimated similarly. Given

$$\rho_{hh} = \frac{1}{\pi} \int_{\mathcal{H}^2(n)} \int_{\mathcal{H}^2(n)} f_r(\omega', \omega'') \, |\cos \theta' \cos \theta''| \, d\omega' \, d\omega'',$$

two vectors, ω' and ω'', must be sampled for each term of the estimate

$$\frac{1}{\pi N} \sum_{j}^{N} \frac{f_r(\omega'_j, \omega''_j) \, |\cos \theta'_j \cos \theta''_j|}{p(\omega'_j) \, p(\omega''_j)}.$$

⟨*BxDF Method Definitions*⟩ +≡
```
Spectrum BxDF::rho(int nSamples, const Point2f *u1,
        const Point2f *u2) const {
    Spectrum r(0.f);
    for (int i = 0; i < nSamples; ++i) {
        ⟨Estimate one term of ρhh 832⟩
    }
    return r / (Pi * nSamples);
}
```

The implementation here samples the first direction ω' uniformly over the hemisphere. Given this, the second direction can be sampled with BxDF::Sample_f().[5]

⟨*Estimate one term of* ρ_{hh}⟩ ≡   831
```
Vector3f wo, wi;
wo = UniformSampleHemisphere(u1[i]);
Float pdfo = UniformHemispherePdf(), pdfi = 0;
Spectrum f = Sample_f(wo, &wi, u2[i], &pdfi);
if (pdfi > 0)
    r += f * AbsCosTheta(wi) * AbsCosTheta(wo) / (pdfo * pdfi);
```

14.1.6 SAMPLING BSDFs

Given these methods to sample individual BxDFs, we can now define a sampling method for the BSDF class, BSDF::Sample_f(). This method is called by Integrators to sample according to the BSDF's distribution; it calls the individual BxDF::Sample_f() methods to generate samples. The BSDF stores pointers to one or more individual BxDFs that can be sampled individually, but here we will sample from the density that is the average of their individual densities,

$$p(\omega) = \frac{1}{N} \sum_i^N p_i(\omega).$$

(Exercise 14.1 at the end of the chapter discusses the alternative of sampling from the BxDFs according to probabilities based on their respective reflectances; this approach can be more efficient if their relative contributions are significantly different.)

The BSDF::Sample_f() method takes two random variables. The outgoing direction passed to it and the incident direction it returns are in world space.

⟨*BSDF Method Definitions*⟩ +≡
```
Spectrum BSDF::Sample_f(const Vector3f &woWorld, Vector3f *wiWorld,
        const Point2f &u, Float *pdf, BxDFType type,
        BxDFType *sampledType) const {
    ⟨Choose which BxDF to sample 833⟩
    ⟨Remap BxDF sample u to [0, 1)² 833⟩
    ⟨Sample chosen BxDF 833⟩
    ⟨Compute overall PDF with all matching BxDFs 834⟩
    ⟨Compute value of BSDF for sampled direction 834⟩
}
```

This method first determines which BxDF's sampling method to use for this particular sample. This choice is complicated by the fact that the caller may pass in a BxDFType that the chosen BxDF must match (e.g., specifying that only diffuse components should be considered). Thus, only a subset of the sampling densities may actually be used here. Therefore, the implementation first determines how many components match the pro-

---

5   It could be argued that a shortcoming of the BxDF sampling interface is that there aren't entry points to sample from the 4D distribution of $f_r(p, \omega, \omega')$. This is a reasonably esoteric case for the applications envisioned for pbrt, however.

vided BxDFType and then uses the first dimension of the provided u sample to select one of the components with equal probability.

⟨*Choose which* BxDF *to sample*⟩ ≡   832
```
int matchingComps = NumComponents(type);
if (matchingComps == 0) {
    *pdf = 0;
    return Spectrum(0);
}
int comp = std::min((int)std::floor(u[0] * matchingComps),
                    matchingComps - 1);
```
⟨*Get* BxDF *pointer for chosen component* 833⟩

A second pass through the BxDFs is necessary to find the appropriate one that matches the flags.

⟨*Get* BxDF *pointer for chosen component*⟩ ≡   833
```
BxDF *bxdf = nullptr;
int count = comp;
for (int i = 0; i < nBxDFs; ++i)
    if (bxdfs[i]->MatchesFlags(type) && count-- == 0) {
        bxdf = bxdfs[i];
        break;
    }
```

Because the u[0] sample was used to determine which BxDF component to sample, we can't directly re-use it in the call to the component's Sample_f() method—it's no longer uniformly distributed. (For example, if there were two matching components, then the first would only see u[0] values between 0 and 0.5 and the second would only see values between 0.5 and 1 if it was reused directly.) However, because u[0] was used to sample from a discrete distribution, we can recover a uniform random value from it: again assuming two matching components, we'd want to remap it from $[0, 0.5)$ to $[0, 1)$ when the first BxDF was sampled and from $[0.5, 1)$ to $[0, 1)$ when the second was. The general case of this remapping is implemented below.

⟨*Remap* BxDF *sample* u *to* $[0, 1)^2$⟩ ≡   832
```
Point2f uRemapped(u[0] * matchingComps - comp, u[1]);
```

The chosen BxDF's Sample_f() method can now be called. Recall that these methods expect and return vectors in the BxDF's local coordinate system, so the supplied vector must be transformed to the BxDF's coordinate system and the returned vector must be transformed back into world coordinates.

⟨*Sample chosen* BxDF⟩ ≡   832
```
Vector3f wi, wo = WorldToLocal(woWorld);
*pdf = 0;
if (sampledType) *sampledType = bxdf->type;
Spectrum f = bxdf->Sample_f(wo, &wi, uRemapped, pdf, sampledType);
if (*pdf == 0)
    return 0;
*wiWorld = LocalToWorld(wi);
```

To compute the actual PDF for sampling the direction ω_i, we need the average of all of the PDFs of the BxDFs that could have been used, given the BxDFType flags passed in. Because *pdf already holds the PDF value for the distribution the sample was taken from, we only need to add in the contributions of the others.

Given the discussion in Section 14.1.3, it's important that this step be skipped if the chosen BxDF is perfectly specular, since the PDF has an implicit delta distribution in it. It would be incorrect to add the other PDF values to this one, since it is a delta term represented with the value 1, rather than as an actual delta distribution.

⟨*Compute overall PDF with all matching* BxDFs⟩ ≡   832
```
if (!(bxdf->type & BSDF_SPECULAR) && matchingComps > 1)
    for (int i = 0; i < nBxDFs; ++i)
        if (bxdfs[i] != bxdf && bxdfs[i]->MatchesFlags(type))
            *pdf += bxdfs[i]->Pdf(wo, wi);
if (matchingComps > 1) *pdf /= matchingComps;
```

Given the sampled direction, this method needs to compute the value of the BSDF for the pair of directions (ω_o, ω_i) accounting for all of the relevant components in the BSDF, unless the sampled direction was from a specular component, in which case the value returned from Sample_f() earlier is used. (If a specular component generated this direction, its BxDF::f() method will return black, even if we pass back the direction its sampling routine returned.)

While this method could just call the BSDF::f() method to compute the BSDF's value, the value can be more efficiently computed by calling the BxDF::f() methods directly, taking advantage of the fact that here we already have the directions in both world space and the reflection coordinate system available.

⟨*Compute value of BSDF for sampled direction*⟩ ≡   832
```
if (!(bxdf->type & BSDF_SPECULAR) && matchingComps > 1) {
    bool reflect = Dot(*wiWorld, ng) * Dot(woWorld, ng) > 0;
    f = 0.;
    for (int i = 0; i < nBxDFs; ++i)
        if (bxdfs[i]->MatchesFlags(type) &&
            ((reflect && (bxdfs[i]->type & BSDF_REFLECTION)) ||
             (!reflect && (bxdfs[i]->type & BSDF_TRANSMISSION))))
            f += bxdfs[i]->f(wo, wi);
}
return f;
```

The BSDF::Pdf() method does a similar computation, looping over the BxDFs and calling their Pdf() methods to find the PDF for an arbitrary sampled direction. Its implementation is straightforward, so we won't include it here.

⟨*BSDF Public Methods*⟩ +≡   572
```
Float Pdf(const Vector3f &wo, const Vector3f &wi,
          BxDFType flags = BSDF_ALL) const;
```

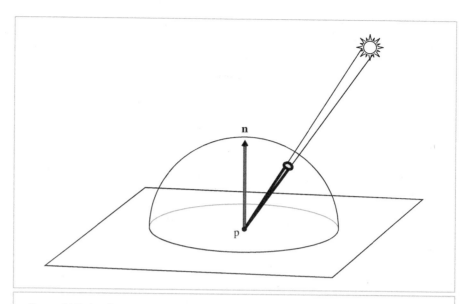

Figure 14.7: An effective sampling strategy for choosing an incident direction from a point **p** for direct lighting computations is to use the light source to define a distribution of directions with respect to solid angle at the point. Here, a small spherical light source is illuminating the point. The cone of directions that the sphere subtends is a much better sampling distribution to use than a uniform distribution over the hemisphere, for example.

14.2 SAMPLING LIGHT SOURCES

Being able to take a point and sample the directions around it where direct illumination may be incident is another important sampling operation for rendering. Consider a diffuse surface illuminated by a small spherical area light source (Figure 14.7): sampling directions using the BSDF's sampling distribution is likely to be very inefficient because the light is only visible along a small cone of directions from the point. A much better approach is to instead use a sampling distribution that is based on the light source. For example, the sampling routine could choose from among only those directions where the sphere is potentially visible. This section introduces the Light::Sample_Li() method, which allows this operation to be implemented for the lights in pbrt.

There are two sampling methods that Lights must implement. The first, Sample_Li(), samples an incident direction at a point in the scene along which illumination from the light may be arriving. The second, Light::Sample_Le(), will be defined in Section 16.1.2; it returns a light-carrying ray leaving the light source. Both have corresponding methods that return the PDF for an incident direction or a ray, respectively.

The Light::Sample_Li() method was first introduced in Section 12.2. For reference, here is its declaration:

```
virtual Spectrum Sample_Li(const Interaction &ref, const Point2f &u,
        Vector3f *wi, Float *pdf, VisibilityTester *vis) const = 0;
```

We can now understand the meaning of its u and pdf parameters: u provides a 2D sample value for sampling the light source, and the PDF for sampling the chosen direction is returned in *pdf.

The Light's Pdf_Li() method returns the probability density with respect to solid angle for the light's Sample_Li() method to sample the direction wi from the reference point ref.

⟨Light Interface⟩ +≡   714
```
virtual Float Pdf_Li(const Interaction &ref,
                     const Vector3f &wi) const = 0;
```

14.2.1 LIGHTS WITH SINGULARITIES

Just as with perfect specular reflection and transmission, light sources that are defined in terms of delta distributions fit naturally into this sampling framework, although they require care on the part of the routines that call their sampling methods, since there are implicit delta distributions in the radiance and PDF values that they return. For the most part, these delta distributions naturally cancel out when estimators are evaluated, although multiple importance sampling code must be aware of this case, just as was the case with BSDFs. (The IsDeltaLight() utility function can be used to see if a light source is described by a delta distribution.)

Point lights are described by a delta distribution such that they only illuminate a receiving point from a single direction. Thus, the sampling problem is trivial. The PointLight:: Sample_Li() method was already implemented in Section 12.3, where we glossed over the nuance that the method performs Monte Carlo sampling of a delta distribution and thus always returns a single direction and doesn't need the random sample values.

Due to the delta distribution, the PointLight::Pdf_Li() method returns 0. This value reflects the fact that there is no chance for some other sampling process to randomly generate a direction that would intersect an infinitesimal light source.

⟨PointLight Method Definitions⟩ +≡
```
Float PointLight::Pdf_Li(const Interaction &, const Vector3f &) const {
    return 0;
}
```

The Sample_Li() methods for SpotLights, ProjectionLights, GonioPhotometricLights, and DistantLights were also previously implemented in Sections 12.3.1, 12.3.2, 12.3.3, and 12.4, respectively. All also return 0 from their Pdf_Li() methods.

14.2.2 SAMPLING SHAPES

In pbrt, area lights are defined by attaching an emission profile to a Shape. Therefore, in order to sample incident illumination from such light sources, it is useful to be able to generate samples over the surface of shapes. To make this possible, we will add sampling methods to the Shape class that sample points on their surfaces. The AreaLight sampling methods to be defined shortly will in turn call these methods.

There are two shape sampling methods, both named Shape::Sample(). The first chooses points on the surface of the shape using a sampling distribution with respect to surface area and returns the local geometric information about the sampled point in an Interaction. In addition to initializing the position p and normal n of the sampled point, the Sample() method should set Interaction::pError with bounds on the floating-point rounding error in the computed p value. pError is used to compute robust origins for rays leaving the surface of the light—see Section 3.9.5.

⟨*Shape Interface*⟩ +≡   123
```
virtual Interaction Sample(const Point2f &u) const = 0;
```

Shapes almost always sample uniformly by area on their surface. Therefore, we will provide a default implementation of the Shape::Pdf() method corresponding to this sampling approach that returns the corresponding PDF: 1 over the surface area.

⟨*Shape Interface*⟩ +≡   123
```
virtual Float Pdf(const Interaction &) const {
    return 1 / Area();
}
```

The second shape sampling method takes the point from which the surface of the shape is being integrated over as a parameter. This method is particularly useful for lighting, since the caller can pass in the point to be lit and allow shape implementations to ensure that they only sample the portion of the shape that is potentially visible from that point. The default implementation ignores the additional point and calls the earlier sampling method.

⟨*Shape Interface*⟩ +≡   123
```
virtual Interaction Sample(const Interaction &ref,
                           const Point2f &u) const {
    return Sample(u);
}
```

Unlike the first Shape sampling method, which generates points on the shape according to a probability density with respect to surface area on the shape, the second one uses a density with respect to solid angle from the reference point ref. This difference stems from the fact that the area light sampling routines evaluate the direct lighting integral as an integral over directions from the reference point—expressing these sampling densities with respect to solid angle at the point is more convenient. Therefore, the standard implementation of the second Pdf() method here transforms the density from one defined over area to one defined over solid angle.

Float 1062
Interaction 115
Interaction::pError 115
Point2f 68
Shape 123
Shape::Area() 131
Shape::Pdf() 837
Shape::Sample() 837
Vector3f 60

⟨*Shape Method Definitions*⟩ +≡
```
Float Shape::Pdf(const Interaction &ref,
        const Vector3f &wi) const {
    ⟨Intersect sample ray with area light geometry 838⟩
    ⟨Convert light sample weight to solid angle measure 838⟩
    return pdf;
}
```

Given a reference point and direction ω_i, the Pdf() method determines if the ray from the point in direction ω_i intersects the shape. If the ray doesn't intersect the shape at all, the probability that the shape would have chosen the direction ω_i can be assumed to be 0 (an effective sampling algorithm wouldn't generate such a sample, and in any case the light will not contribute to such directions, so using a zero probability density is fine).

Note that this ray intersection test is only between the ray and the single shape under consideration. The rest of the scene geometry is ignored, and thus the intersection test is fairly efficient.

⟨*Intersect sample ray with area light geometry*⟩ ≡   837
```
Ray ray = ref.SpawnRay(wi);
Float tHit;
SurfaceInteraction isectLight;
if (!Intersect(ray, &tHit, &isectLight, false)) return 0;
```

To compute the value of the PDF with respect to solid angle from the reference point, the method starts by computing the PDF with respect to surface area. Conversion from a density with respect to area to a density with respect to solid angle requires division by the factor

$$\frac{d\omega_i}{dA} = \frac{\cos\theta_o}{r^2},$$

where θ_o is the angle between the direction of the ray from the point on the light to the reference point and the light's surface normal, and r^2 is the distance between the point on the light and the point being shaded (recall the discussion about transforming between area and directional integration domains in Section 5.5).

⟨*Convert light sample weight to solid angle measure*⟩ ≡   837
```
Float pdf = DistanceSquared(ref.p, isectLight.p) /
            (AbsDot(isectLight.n, -wi) * Area());
```

Sampling Disks

The Disk sampling method uses the concentric disk sampling function to find a point on the unit disk and then scales and offsets this point to lie on the disk of a given radius and height. Note that this method does not account for partial disks due to Disk::innerRadius being nonzero or Disk::phiMax being less than 2π. Fixing this bug is left for an exercise at the end of the chapter.

Because the object space z value of the sampled point is equal to Disk::height, zero-extent bounds can be used for the error bounds for rays leaving the sampled point, just as with ray–disk intersections. (These bounds may later be expanded by the object to world transformation, however.)

⟨*Disk Method Definitions*⟩ +≡
```
Interaction Disk::Sample(const Point2f &u) const {
    Point2f pd = ConcentricSampleDisk(u);
    Point3f pObj(pd.x * radius, pd.y * radius, height);
    Interaction it;
    it.n = Normalize((*ObjectToWorld)(Normal3f(0, 0, 1)));
    if (reverseOrientation) it.n *= -1;
    it.p = (*ObjectToWorld)(pObj, Vector3f(0, 0, 0), &it.pError);
    return it;
}
```

Sampling Cylinders

Uniform sampling on cylinders is straightforward. The height and ϕ value are sampled uniformly. Intuitively, it can be understood that this approach works because a cylinder is just a rolled-up rectangle.

⟨*Cylinder Method Definitions*⟩ +≡
```
Interaction Cylinder::Sample(const Point2f &u) const {
    Float z = Lerp(u[0], zMin, zMax);
    Float phi = u[1] * phiMax;
    Point3f pObj = Point3f(radius * std::cos(phi), radius * std::sin(phi),
                           z);
    Interaction it;
    it.n = Normalize((*ObjectToWorld)(Normal3f(pObj.x, pObj.y, 0)));
    if (reverseOrientation) it.n *= -1;
    ⟨Reproject pObj to cylinder surface and compute pObjError 839⟩
    it.p = (*ObjectToWorld)(pObj, pObjError, &it.pError);
    return it;
}
```

If the system's std::sin() and std::cos() functions compute results that are as precise as possible—i.e., they always return the closest floating-point value to the fully-precise result, then it can be shown that the *x* and *y* components of pObj are within a factor of γ_3 of the actual surface of the cylinder. While many implementations of those functions are that precise, not all are, especially on GPUs. To be safe, the implementation here reprojects the sampled point to lie on the cylinder. In this case, the error bounds are the same as were derived for reprojected ray–cylinder intersection points in Section 3.9.4.

⟨*Reproject pObj to cylinder surface and compute pObjError*⟩ ≡   839
```
Float hitRad = std::sqrt(pObj.x * pObj.x + pObj.y * pObj.y);
pObj.x *= radius / hitRad;
pObj.y *= radius / hitRad;
Vector3f pObjError = gamma(3) * Abs(Vector3f(pObj.x, pObj.y, 0));
```

Sampling Triangles

The UniformSampleTriangle() function, defined in the previous chapter, returns the barycentric coordinates for a uniformly sampled point on a triangle. The point on a particular triangle for those barycentrics is easily computed.

⟨*Triangle Method Definitions*⟩ +≡
```
Interaction Triangle::Sample(const Point2f &u) const {
    Point2f b = UniformSampleTriangle(u);
    ⟨Get triangle vertices in p0, p1, and p2 157⟩
    Interaction it;
    it.p = b[0] * p0 + b[1] * p1 + (1 - b[0] - b[1]) * p2;
    ⟨Compute surface normal for sampled point on triangle 840⟩
    ⟨Compute error bounds for sampled point on triangle 840⟩
    return it;
}
```

⟨*Compute surface normal for sampled point on triangle*⟩ ≡   839
```
if (mesh->n)
    it.n = Normalize(b[0] * mesh->n[v[0]] +
                     b[1] * mesh->n[v[1]] +
                     (1 - b[0] - b[1]) * mesh->n[v[2]]);
else
    it.n = Normalize(Normal3f(Cross(p1 - p0, p2 - p0)));
if (reverseOrientation) it.n *= -1;
```

Because the sampled point is computed with barycentric interpolation, it has the same error bounds as were computed in Section 3.9.4 for triangle intersection points.

⟨*Compute error bounds for sampled point on triangle*⟩ ≡   839
```
Point3f pAbsSum = Abs(b[0] * p0) + Abs(b[1] * p1) +
                  Abs((1 - b[0] - b[1]) * p2);
it.pError = gamma(6) * Vector3f(pAbsSum);
```

Sampling Spheres

As with Disks, the sampling method here does not handle partial spheres; an exercise at the end of the chapter discusses this issue further. For the sampling method that is not given an external point that's being lit, sampling a point on a sphere is extremely simple. Sphere::Sample() just uses the UniformSampleSphere() function to generate a point on the unit sphere and scales the point by the sphere's radius.

⟨*Sphere Method Definitions*⟩ +≡
```
Interaction Sphere::Sample(const Point2f &u) const {
    Point3f pObj = Point3f(0, 0, 0) + radius * UniformSampleSphere(u);
    Interaction it;
    it.n = Normalize((*ObjectToWorld)(Normal3f(pObj.x, pObj.y, pObj.z)));
    if (reverseOrientation) it.n *= -1;
    ⟨Reproject pObj to sphere surface and compute pObjError 840⟩
    it.p = (*ObjectToWorld)(pObj, pObjError, &it.pError);
    return it;
}
```

Because UniformSampleSphere() uses std::sin() and std::cos(), the error bounds on the computed pObj value depend on the accuracy of those functions. Therefore, as with cylinders, the sampled point is reprojected to the sphere's surface, so that the error bounds derived earlier in Equation (3.14) can be used without needing to worry about those functions' accuracy.

⟨*Reproject pObj to sphere surface and compute pObjError*⟩ ≡   840, 844
```
pObj *= radius / Distance(pObj, Point3f(0, 0, 0));
Vector3f pObjError = gamma(5) * Abs((Vector3f)pObj);
```

For the sphere sampling method that is given a point being illuminated, we can do much better than sampling over the sphere's entire area. While uniform sampling over its surface is perfectly correct, a better approach is to not sample points on the sphere that are definitely not visible from the point (such as those on the back side of the sphere as seen from the point). The sampling routine here instead uniformly samples directions over the solid angle subtended by the sphere from the reference point and then computes the point on the sphere corresponding to the sampled direction.

⟨*Sphere Method Definitions*⟩ +≡
```
Interaction Sphere::Sample(const Interaction &ref,
        const Point2f &u) const {
    ⟨Compute coordinate system for sphere sampling 841⟩
    ⟨Sample uniformly on sphere if p is inside it 841⟩
    ⟨Sample sphere uniformly inside subtended cone 841⟩
}
```

This process is most easily done if we first compute a coordinate system to use for sampling the sphere, where the *z* axis is the vector between the sphere's center and the point being illuminated:

⟨*Compute coordinate system for sphere sampling*⟩ ≡   841
```
Point3f pCenter = (*ObjectToWorld)(Point3f(0, 0, 0));
Vector3f wc = Normalize(pCenter - ref.p);
Vector3f wcX, wcY;
CoordinateSystem(wc, &wcX, &wcY);
```

For points that lie inside the surface of the sphere, the entire sphere should be sampled, since the whole sphere is visible from inside it. Note that the reference point used in this determination, pOrigin, is computed using the OffsetRayOrigin() function. Doing so ensures that if the reference point came from a ray intersecting the sphere, the point tested lies on the correct side of the sphere.

⟨*Sample uniformly on sphere if* p *is inside it*⟩ ≡   841
```
Point3f pOrigin = OffsetRayOrigin(ref.p, ref.pError, ref.n,
                          pCenter - ref.p);
if (DistanceSquared(pOrigin, pCenter) <= radius * radius)
    return Sample(u);
```

Otherwise sampling within the cone proceeds.

⟨*Sample sphere uniformly inside subtended cone*⟩ ≡   841
⟨*Compute* θ *and* φ *values for sample in cone* 842⟩
⟨*Compute angle* α *from center of sphere to sampled point on surface* 844⟩
⟨*Compute surface normal and sampled point on sphere* 844⟩
⟨*Return* Interaction *for sampled point on sphere* 844⟩

If the reference point is outside the sphere, then as seen from the point being shaded p the sphere subtends an angle

$$\theta_{\max} = \arcsin\left(\frac{r}{|\mathrm{p} - \mathrm{p_c}|}\right) = \arccos\sqrt{1 - \left(\frac{r}{|\mathrm{p} - \mathrm{p_c}|}\right)^2}, \qquad [14.11]$$

where r is the radius of the sphere and $\mathrm{p_c}$ is its center (Figure 14.8). The sampling method here computes the cosine of the subtended angle $\theta_{\max}$ using Equation (14.11) and then uniformly samples directions inside this cone of directions using the approach that was derived earlier for the UniformSampleCone() function, sampling an offset θ from the center vector ω_c and then uniformly sampling a rotation angle ϕ around the vector.

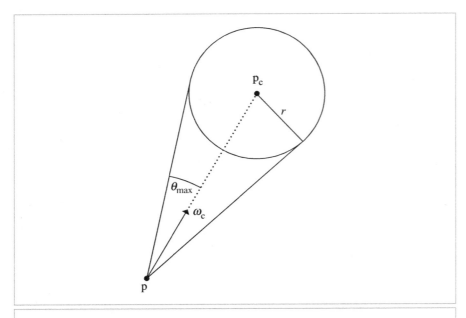

Figure 14.8: To sample points on a spherical light source, we can uniformly sample within the cone of directions around a central vector ω_c with an angular spread of up to θ_{max}. Trigonometry can be used to derive the value of $\sin \theta_{max}$, $r/|p_c - p|$.

That function isn't used here, however, as we will need some of the intermediate values in the following fragments.

⟨*Compute θ and ϕ values for sample in cone*⟩ ≡   841
```
Float sinThetaMax2 = radius * radius / DistanceSquared(ref.p, pCenter);
Float cosThetaMax = std::sqrt(std::max((Float)0, 1 - sinThetaMax2));
Float cosTheta = (1 - u[0]) + u[0] * cosThetaMax;
Float sinTheta = std::sqrt(std::max((Float)0, 1 - cosTheta * cosTheta));
Float phi = u[1] * 2 * Pi;
```

Given a sample angle (θ, ϕ) with respect to the sampling coordinate system computed earlier, we can directly compute the corresponding sample point on the sphere. The derivation of this approach follows three steps, illustrated in Figure 14.9.

First, if we denote the distance from the reference point to the center of the sphere by d_c and form a right triangle with angle θ at the reference point, then we can see that the lengths of the other two sides of the triangle, as shown in Figure 14.9(a), are $d_c \cos \theta$ and $d_c \sin \theta$.

Next, consider the right triangle shown in Figure 14.9(b), where the hypotenuse is the line segment with length equal to the sphere's radius r that goes from the center of the sphere to the point where the line from the sampled angle intersects the sphere. From the Pythagorean theorem, we can see that the length of the third side of that triangle is

$$\sqrt{r^2 - d_c^2 \sin^2 \theta}.$$

DistanceSquared() 70
Float 1062
Interaction::p 115
Pi 1063
Sphere::radius 133

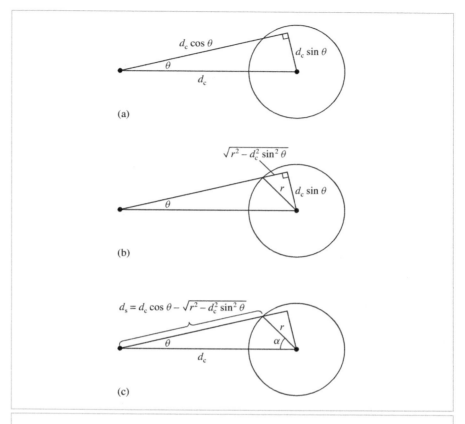

Figure 14.9: Geometric Setting for Computing the Sampled Point on the Sphere Corresponding to a Sampled Angle θ. (a) Right triangle with hypotenuse d_c and angle θ. (b) The right triangle with hypotenuse from the center of the sphere to the sampled point on the sphere. (c) Given the lengths of the three sides of this triangle, the law of cosines gives the angle α to the sampled point.

Subtracting this length from $d_c \cos \theta$ gives us the length of the segment from the reference point to the sampled point on the sphere:

$$d_s = d_c \cos \theta - \sqrt{r^2 - d_c^2 \sin^2 \theta}.$$

We can now compute the angle α from the center of the sphere to the sampled point on the sphere using the law of cosines, which relates the squared lengths of two sides of the triangle and the angle α opposite them:

$$d_s^2 = d_c^2 + r^2 - 2d_c r \cos \alpha.$$

(See Figure 14.9(c).) Solving for $\cos \alpha$, we have

$$\cos \alpha = \frac{d_c^2 + r^2 - d_s^2}{2d_c r}.$$

⟨*Compute angle α from center of sphere to sampled point on surface*⟩ ≡   841
```
Float dc = Distance(ref.p, pCenter);
Float ds = dc * cosTheta -
    std::sqrt(std::max((Float)0,
                        radius * radius - dc * dc * sinTheta * sinTheta));
Float cosAlpha = (dc * dc + radius * radius - ds * ds) /
                (2 * dc * radius);
Float sinAlpha = std::sqrt(std::max((Float)0, 1 - cosAlpha * cosAlpha));
```

The α angle and ϕ give the spherical coordinates for the sampled point on the unit sphere, with respect to a coordinate system centered around the vector from the sphere center to the reference point. Since we earlier computed a coordinate system from the reference point to the center, we can use that one here with each vector flipped.

⟨*Compute surface normal and sampled point on sphere*⟩ ≡   841
```
Vector3f nObj = SphericalDirection(sinAlpha, cosAlpha, phi,
                                   -wcX, -wcY, -wc);
Point3f pObj = radius * Point3f(nObj.x, nObj.y, nObj.z);
```

As with the other Sphere::Sample() method, the sampled point is reprojected onto the surface of the sphere; in turn, we can use the same error bounds for the computed point as were derived earlier.

⟨*Return* Interaction *for sampled point on sphere*⟩ ≡   841
```
Interaction it;
⟨Reproject pObj to sphere surface and compute pObjError 840⟩
it.p = (*ObjectToWorld)(pObj, pObjError, &it.pError);
it.n = (*ObjectToWorld)(Normal3f(nObj));
if (reverseOrientation) it.n *= -1;
return it;
```

The value of the PDF for sampling a direction toward a sphere from a given point depends on which of the two sampling strategies would be used for the point.

⟨*Sphere Method Definitions*⟩ +≡
```
Float Sphere::Pdf(const Interaction &ref, const Vector3f &wi) const {
    Point3f pCenter = (*ObjectToWorld)(Point3f(0, 0, 0));
    ⟨Return uniform PDF if point is inside sphere 844⟩
    ⟨Compute general sphere PDF 845⟩
}
```

If the reference point was inside the sphere, a uniform sampling strategy was used, in which case, the implementation hands off to the Pdf() method of the Shape class, which takes care of the solid angle conversion.

⟨*Return uniform PDF if point is inside sphere*⟩ ≡   844
```
Point3f pOrigin = OffsetRayOrigin(ref.p, ref.pError, ref.n,
                                  pCenter - ref.p);
if (DistanceSquared(pOrigin, pCenter) <= radius * radius)
    return Shape::Pdf(ref, wi);
```

In the general case, we recompute the angle subtended by the sphere and call Uniform
ConePdf(). Note that no conversion of sampling measures is required here because
UniformConePdf() already returns a value with respect to the solid angle measure.

⟨*Compute general sphere PDF*⟩ ≡   844
```
Float sinThetaMax2 = radius * radius / DistanceSquared(ref.p, pCenter);
Float cosThetaMax = std::sqrt(std::max((Float)0, 1 - sinThetaMax2));
return UniformConePdf(cosThetaMax);
```

14.2.3 AREA LIGHTS

Given shape sampling methods, the DiffuseAreaLight::Sample_Li() method is quite
straightforward. Most of the hard work is done by the Shapes, and the DiffuseAreaLight
just needs to copy appropriate values to output parameters and compute the emitted
radiance value.

⟨*DiffuseAreaLight Method Definitions*⟩ +≡
```
Spectrum DiffuseAreaLight::Sample_Li(const Interaction &ref,
        const Point2f &u, Vector3f *wi, Float *pdf,
        VisibilityTester *vis) const {
    Interaction pShape = shape->Sample(ref, u);
    pShape.mediumInterface = mediumInterface;
    *wi = Normalize(pShape.p - ref.p);
    *pdf = shape->Pdf(ref, *wi);
    *vis = VisibilityTester(ref, pShape);
    return L(pShape, -*wi);
}
```

Pdf_Li() calls the variant of Shape::Pdf() that returns a density with respect to solid
angle, so the value it returns from can be returned directly.

⟨*DiffuseAreaLight Method Definitions*⟩ +≡
```
Float DiffuseAreaLight::Pdf_Li(const Interaction &ref,
                               const Vector3f &wi) const {
    return shape->Pdf(ref, wi);
}
```

14.2.4 INFINITE AREA LIGHTS

The InfiniteAreaLight, defined in Section 12.6, can be considered to be an infinitely
large sphere that surrounds the entire scene, illuminating it from all directions. The
environment maps used with InfiniteAreaLights often have substantial variation along
different directions: consider, for example, an environment map of the sky during day-
time, where the relatively small number of directions that the sun subtends will be thousands of times brighter than the rest of the directions. Given this substantial variation,
implementing a sampling method for InfiniteAreaLights that matches the illumination
distribution will generally substantially reduce variance in images.

Figure 14.10 shows two images of a car model illuminated by the morning skylight
environment map from Figure 12.21. The top image was rendered using a simple cosine-
weighted sampling distribution for selecting incident illumination directions, while the

(a)

(b)

Figure 14.10: Car Model Illuminated by the Morning Skylight Environment Map. Both images were rendered with four image samples per pixel and eight light source samples per image sample. (a) The result of using a uniform sampling distribution and (b) the improvement from the importance sampling method implemented here. A total of just 32 light samples per pixel gives an excellent result with this approach.

bottom image was rendered using the sampling method implemented in this section. Both images used just 32 shadow samples per pixel. For the same number of samples taken and with negligible additional computational cost, this sampling method computes a much better result with much lower variance.

There are three main steps to the sampling approach implemented here:

1. We define a piecewise-constant 2D probability distribution function in (u, v) image coordinates $p(u, v)$ that corresponds to the distribution of the radiance represented by the environment map.

2. We apply the sampling method from Section 13.6.7 to transform 2D samples to samples drawn from the piecewise-constant $p(u, v)$ distribution.
3. We define a probability density function over directions on the unit sphere based on the probability density over (u, v).

The combination of these three steps makes it possible to generate samples on the sphere of directions according to a distribution that matches the radiance function very closely, leading to substantial variance reduction.

We will start by defining the fragment ⟨*Initialize sampling PDFs for infinite area light*⟩ at the end of the InfiniteAreaLight constructor.

⟨*Initialize sampling PDFs for infinite area light*⟩ ≡   739
    ⟨*Compute scalar-valued image* img *from environment map* 848⟩
    ⟨*Compute sampling distributions for rows and columns of image* 848⟩

The first step is to transform the continuously defined spectral radiance function defined by the environment map's texels to a piecewise-constant scalar function by computing its luminance at a set of sample points using the Spectrum::y() method. There are three things to note in the code below that does this computation.

First, it computes values of the radiance function at the same number of points as there are texels in the original image map. It could use either more or fewer points, leading to a corresponding increase or decrease in memory use while still generating a valid sampling distribution, however. These values work well, though, as fewer points would lead to a sampling distribution that didn't match the function as well while more would mostly waste memory with little incremental benefit.

The second thing of note in this code is that the piecewise constant function values being stored here in img are found by slightly blurring the radiance function with the MIPMap::Lookup() method (rather than just copying the corresponding texel values). The motivation for this is subtle; Figure 14.11 illustrates the idea in 1D. Because the continuous radiance function used for rendering is reconstructed by bilinearly interpolating between texels in the image, just because some texel is completely black, for example, the radiance function may be nonzero a tiny distance away from it due to a neighboring texel's contribution. Because we are using a piecewise-constant function for sampling rather than a piecewise-linear one, it must account for this issue in order to ensure greater-than-zero probability of sampling any point where the radiance function is nonzero.[6]

Finally, each image value in the img buffer is multiplied by the value of $\sin \theta$ corresponding to the θ value each row has when the latitude–longitude image is mapped to the sphere. Note that this multiplication has no effect on the sampling method's correctness: because the value of $\sin \theta$ is always greater than 0 over the $[0, \pi]$ range, we are just reshaping the sampling PDF. The motivation for adjusting the PDF is to eliminate the

---

6   Alternatively, we could use a piecewise-linear function for importance sampling and thus match the radiance function exactly. However, it's easier to draw samples from a piecewise-constant function's distribution, and, because environment maps generally have a large number of texel samples, piecewise-constant functions generally suffice to match their distributions well. See Exercise 14.5 for discussion about handling this issue more robustly.

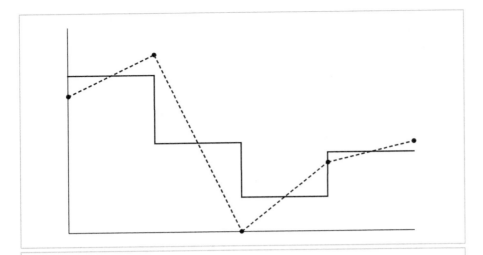

Figure 14.11: Finding a Piecewise-Constant Function (solid lines) That Approximates a Piecewise Linear Function (dashed lines) for Use as a Sampling Distribution. Even though some of the sample points that define the piecewise linear function (solid dots) may be zero-valued, the piecewise-constant sampling function must not be zero over any range where the actual function is nonzero. A reasonable approach to avoid this case, shown here and implemented in the InfiniteAreaLight sampling routines, is to find the average value of the function over some range and use that to define the piecewise-constant function.

effect of the distortion from mapping the 2D image to the unit sphere in the sampling method here; the details will be fully explained later in this section.

⟨*Compute scalar-valued image* img *from environment map*⟩ ≡   847
```
int width = resolution.x, height = resolution.y;
Float filter = (Float)1 / std::max(width, height);
std::unique_ptr<Float[]> img(new Float[width * height]);
for (int v = 0; v < height; ++v) {
    Float vp = (Float)v / (Float)height;
    Float sinTheta = std::sin(Pi * Float(v + .5f) / Float(height));
    for (int u = 0; u < width; ++u) {
        Float up = (Float)u / (Float)width;
        img[u + v * width] = Lmap->Lookup(Point2f(up, vp), filter).y();
        img[u + v * width] *= sinTheta;
    }
}
```

Given this filtered and scaled image, the Distribution2D structure handles computing and storing the 2D PDF.

⟨*Compute sampling distributions for rows and columns of image*⟩ ≡   847
```
distribution.reset(new Distribution2D(img.get(), width, height));
```

⟨*InfiniteAreaLight Private Data*⟩ +≡   737
```
std::unique_ptr<Distribution2D> distribution;
```

Given this precomputed data, the task of the sampling method is relatively straightforward. Given a sample u over $[0, 1)^2$, it draws a sample from the function's distribution using the sampling algorithm described in Section 13.6.7, which gives a (u, v) value and the value of the PDF for taking this sample, $p(u, v)$.

⟨*InfiniteAreaLight Method Definitions*⟩ +≡
```
Spectrum InfiniteAreaLight::Sample_Li(const Interaction &ref,
        const Point2f &u, Vector3f *wi, Float *pdf,
        VisibilityTester *vis) const {
    ⟨Find (u, v) sample coordinates in infinite light texture 849⟩
    ⟨Convert infinite light sample point to direction 849⟩
    ⟨Compute PDF for sampled infinite light direction 850⟩
    ⟨Return radiance value for infinite light direction 850⟩
}
```

⟨*Find (u, v) sample coordinates in infinite light texture*⟩ ≡   849
```
Float mapPdf;
Point2f uv = distribution->SampleContinuous(u, &mapPdf);
if (mapPdf == 0) return Spectrum(0.f);
```

The (u, v) sample is mapped to spherical coordinates by

$$(\theta, \phi) = (\pi v, 2\pi u) ,$$

and then the spherical coordinates formula gives the direction $\omega = (x, y, z)$.

⟨*Convert infinite light sample point to direction*⟩ ≡   849
```
Float theta = uv[1] * Pi, phi = uv[0] * 2 * Pi;
Float cosTheta = std::cos(theta), sinTheta = std::sin(theta);
Float sinPhi = std::sin(phi), cosPhi = std::cos(phi);
*wi = LightToWorld(Vector3f(sinTheta * cosPhi, sinTheta * sinPhi,
                            cosTheta));
```

Recall that the probability density values returned by the light source sampling routines must be defined in terms of the solid angle measure on the unit sphere. Therefore, this routine must now compute the transformation between the sampling density used, which was the image function over $[0, 1]^2$, and the corresponding density after the image has been mapped to the unit sphere with the latitude–longitude mapping. (Recall that the latitude–longitude parameterization of an image (θ, ϕ) is $x = r \sin \theta \cos \phi$, $y = r \sin \theta \sin \phi$, and $z = r \cos \theta$.)

First, consider the function g that maps from (u, v) to (θ, ϕ),

$$g(u, v) = (\pi v, 2\pi u) .$$

The absolute value of the determinant of the Jacobian $|J_g|$ is $2\pi^2$. Applying the multidimensional change of variables equation from Section 13.5.1, we can find the density in terms of spherical coordinates (θ, ϕ).

$$p(\theta, \phi) = \frac{p(u, v)}{2\pi^2}.$$

From the definition of spherical coordinates, it is easy to determine that the absolute value of the determinant of the Jacobian for the mapping from (r, θ, ϕ) to (x, y, z) is $r^2 \sin \theta$. Since we are interested in the unit sphere, $r = 1$, and again applying the multidimensional change of variables equation, we can find the final relationship between probability densities,

$$p(\omega) = \frac{p(\theta, \phi)}{\sin \theta} = \frac{p(u, v)}{2\pi^2 \sin \theta}.$$

This is the key relationship for applying this technique: it lets us sample from the piecewise-constant distribution defined by the image map and transform the sample and its probability density to be in terms of directions on the unit sphere.

We can now see why the initialization routines multiplied the values of the piecewise-constant sampling function by a $\sin \theta$ term. Consider, for example, a constant-valued environment map: with the $p(u, v)$ sampling technique, all (θ, ϕ) values are equally likely to be chosen. Due to the mapping to directions on the sphere, however, this would lead to more directions being sampled near the poles of the sphere, *not* a uniform sampling of directions on the sphere, which would be a more desirable result. The $1/\sin \theta$ term in the $p(\omega)$ PDF corrects for this non-uniform sampling of directions so that correct results are computed in Monte Carlo estimates. Given this state of affairs, however, it's better to have modified the $p(u, v)$ sampling distribution so that it's less likely to select directions near the poles in the first place.

⟨*Compute PDF for sampled infinite light direction*⟩ ≡   849
```
    *pdf = mapPdf / (2 * Pi * Pi * sinTheta);
    if (sinTheta == 0) *pdf = 0;
```

The method can finally initialize the VisibilityTester with a light sample point outside the scene's bounds and return the radiance value for the chosen direction.

⟨*Return radiance value for infinite light direction*⟩ ≡   849
```
    *vis = VisibilityTester(ref, Interaction(ref.p + *wi * (2 * worldRadius),
                                       ref.time, mediumInterface)));
    return Spectrum(Lmap->Lookup(uv), SpectrumType::Illuminant);
```

The InfiniteAreaLight::Pdf_Li() method needs to convert the direction ω to the corresponding (u, v) coordinates in the sampling distribution. Given these, the PDF $p(u, v)$ is computed as the product of the two 1D PDFs by the Distribution2D::Pdf() method, which is adjusted here for mapping to the sphere as was done in the Sample_Li() method.

⟨*InfiniteAreaLight Method Definitions*⟩ +≡
```
    Float InfiniteAreaLight::Pdf_Li(const Interaction &,
                              const Vector3f &w) const {
        Vector3f wi = WorldToLight(w);
        Float theta = SphericalTheta(wi), phi = SphericalPhi(wi);
        Float sinTheta = std::sin(theta);
        if (sinTheta == 0) return 0;
        return distribution->Pdf(Point2f(phi * Inv2Pi, theta * InvPi)) /
            (2 * Pi * Pi * sinTheta);
    }
```

Figure 14.12: Scene Rendered with Direct Lighting Only. Because only direct lighting is considered, some portions of the image are completely black because they are only lit by indirect illumination. *(Model courtesy of Guillermo M. Leal Llaguno.)*

14.3 DIRECT LIGHTING

Before we introduce the light transport equation in its full generality, we will implement the DirectLightingIntegrator which, unsurprisingly, only accounts for only direct lighting—light that has traveled directly from a light source to the point being shaded—and ignores indirect illumination from objects that are not themselves emissive, except for basic specular reflection and transmission effects. Starting out with this integrator allows us to focus on some of the important details of direct lighting without worrying about the full light transport equation. Furthermore, some of the routines developed here will be used again in subsequent integrators that solve the complete light transport equation. Figure 14.12 shows the San Miguel scene rendered with direct lighting only.

⟨*DirectLightingIntegrator Declarations*⟩ ≡
```
    class DirectLightingIntegrator : public SamplerIntegrator {
    public:
        ⟨DirectLightingIntegrator Public Methods⟩
    private:
        ⟨DirectLightingIntegrator Private Data  852⟩
    };
```

The implementation provides two different strategies for computing direct lighting. Each computes an unbiased estimate of exitant radiance at a point in a given direction. The LightStrategy enumeration records which approach has been selected. The first strategy, UniformSampleAll, loops over all of the lights and takes a number of samples based on Light::nSamples from each of them, summing the result. (Recall the discussion of splitting in Section 13.7.1—the UniformSampleAll strategy is applying this technique.) The second, UniformSampleOne, takes a single sample from just one of the lights, chosen at random.

⟨*LightStrategy Declarations*⟩ ≡
```
enum class LightStrategy { UniformSampleAll, UniformSampleOne };
```

Depending on the scene being rendered, either of these approaches may be more appropriate. For example, if many image samples are being taken for each pixel (e.g., to resolve depth of field without excessive noise), then a single light sample per image sample may be more appropriate: in the aggregate all of the image samples in a pixel will sample the direct lighting well enough to give a high-quality image. Alternatively, if few samples per pixel are being taken, sampling all lights may be preferable to ensure a noise-free result.

The DirectLightingIntegrator constructor, which we won't include here, just passes a Camera and Sampler to the SamplerIntegrator base class constructor and initializes two member variables. In addition to the direct lighting strategy, the DirectLighting Integrator stores a maximum recursion depth for rays that are traced to account for specular reflection or specular transmission.

⟨*DirectLightingIntegrator Private Data*⟩ ≡   851
```
const LightStrategy strategy;
const int maxDepth;
```

The numbers and types of samples needed by this integrator depend on the sampling strategy used: if a single sample is taken from a single light, then two two-dimensional samples obtained via Sampler::Get2D() suffice—one for selecting a position on a light source and one for sampling a scattered direction from the BSDF.

When multiple samples are taken per light, the integrator requests sample arrays from the sampler before the main rendering process begins. Using sample arrays is preferable to performing many separate calls to Sampler::Get2D() because it gives the sampler an opportunity to use improved sample placement techniques, optimizing the distribution of samples over the entire array and thus, over all of the light source samples for the current point being shaded.

⟨*DirectLightingIntegrator Method Definitions*⟩ ≡
```
void DirectLightingIntegrator::Preprocess(const Scene &scene,
        Sampler &sampler) {
    if (strategy == LightStrategy::UniformSampleAll) {
        ⟨Compute number of samples to use for each light  853⟩
        ⟨Request samples for sampling all lights  853⟩
    }
}
```

For the LightStrategy::UniformSampleAll strategy, each light stores a desired number of samples in its Light::nSamples member variable. However, the integrator here only uses that value as a starting point: the Sampler::RoundCount() method is given an opportunity to change that value to a more appropriate one based on its particular sample generation technique. (For example, many samplers only generate collections of samples with power-of-two sizes.) The final number of samples for each light is recorded in the nLightSamples member variable.

⟨*Compute number of samples to use for each light*⟩ ≡   852
```
for (const auto &light : scene.lights)
    nLightSamples.push_back(sampler.RoundCount(light->nSamples));
```

⟨*DirectLightingIntegrator Private Data*⟩ +≡   851
```
std::vector<int> nLightSamples;
```

Now the sample arrays can be requested. There are two important details in this fragment: first, although a separate sample request is made for all of the possible ray depths up to the maximum, this doesn't mean that all intersections will have sample arrays available. Rather, once a sample array is retrieved by a call to Sampler::Get2DArray(), that array won't be returned again. If both specular reflection and transmission are present, then there may be up to $2^{maxDepth+1} - 1$ intersection points for each camera ray intersection. If the sample arrays are exhausted, the integrator switches to taking a single sample from each light.

Second, note that the arrays are requested in the order they will be consumed by the integrator: at each intersection point, two arrays are used for each light source, in the same order as the lights array.

⟨*Request samples for sampling all lights*⟩ ≡   852
```
for (int i = 0; i < maxDepth; ++i) {
    for (size_t j = 0; j < scene.lights.size(); ++j) {
        sampler.Request2DArray(nLightSamples[j]);
        sampler.Request2DArray(nLightSamples[j]);
    }
}
```

As a SamplerIntegrator, the main method that the DirectLightingIntegrator must implement is Li(). The general form of its implementation here is similar to that of WhittedIntegrator::Li(): the BSDF at the intersection point is computed, emitted radiance is added if the surface is emissive, rays are traced recursively for specular reflection and transmission, and so on. We won't include the full implementation of DirectLightingIntegrator::Li() here in order to focus on its key fragment, ⟨*Compute direct lighting for* DirectLightingIntegrator *integrator*⟩, which estimates the value of the integral that gives the reflected radiance, accumulating it into a value L that will be returned from Li().

Two helper functions, which other integrators will also find useful, take care of the two sampling strategies.

⟨*Compute direct lighting for* DirectLightingIntegrator *integrator*⟩ ≡
```
if (strategy == LightStrategy::UniformSampleAll)
    L += UniformSampleAllLights(isect, scene, arena, sampler,
                                nLightSamples);
else
    L += UniformSampleOneLight(isect, scene, arena, sampler);
```

To understand the approaches implemented by the two strategies, first recall the scattering equation from Section 5.6, which says that exitant radiance $L_o(p, \omega_o)$ from a point p on a surface in direction ω_o due to incident radiance at the point is given by an integral of incoming radiance over the sphere times the BSDF for each direction and a cosine term. For the DirectLightingIntegrator, we are only interested in incident radiance directly from light sources, which we will denote by $L_d(p, \omega)$:

$$L_o(p, \omega_o) = \int_{S^2} f(p, \omega_o, \omega_i) L_d(p, \omega_i) |\cos \theta_i| \, d\omega_i.$$

This can be broken into a sum over the n lights in the scene

$$\sum_{j=1}^{n} \int_{S^2} f(p, \omega_o, \omega_i) L_{d(j)}(p, \omega_i) |\cos \theta_i| \, d\omega_i, \qquad [14.12]$$

where $L_{d(j)}$ denotes incident radiance from the jth light and

$$L_d(p, \omega_i) = \sum_j L_{d(j)}(p, \omega_i).$$

One valid approach is to estimate each term of the sum in Equation (14.12) individually, adding the results together. This is the most basic direct lighting strategy and is implemented in UniformSampleAllLights().

In addition to information about the intersection point and additional parameters that are needed to compute the direct lighting, UniformSampleAllLights() also takes a handleMedia parameter that indicates whether the effects of volumetric attenuation should be considered in the direct lighting computation. (Between this parameter and the detail that it takes an Interaction rather than a SurfaceInteraction, this function is actually able to compute reflected radiance at points in participating media; fragments related to this functionality will be defined in the next chapter.)

⟨*Integrator Utility Functions*⟩ ≡
```
Spectrum UniformSampleAllLights(const Interaction &it,
        const Scene &scene, MemoryArena &arena, Sampler &sampler,
        const std::vector<int> &nLightSamples, bool handleMedia) {
    Spectrum L(0.f);
    for (size_t j = 0; j < scene.lights.size(); ++j) {
        ⟨Accumulate contribution of jth light to L 855⟩
    }
    return L;
}
```

This function attempts to retrieve the sample arrays from the Sampler that were previously requested in the Preprocess() method.

⟨*Accumulate contribution of j th light to* L⟩ ≡   854
```
const std::shared_ptr<Light> &light = scene.lights[j];
int nSamples = nLightSamples[j];
const Point2f *uLightArray = sampler.Get2DArray(nSamples);
const Point2f *uScatteringArray = sampler.Get2DArray(nSamples);
if (!uLightArray || !uScatteringArray) {
    ⟨Use a single sample for illumination from light 855⟩
} else {
    ⟨Estimate direct lighting using sample arrays 855⟩
}
```

If all of the requested arrays have been consumed, the code falls back to a single sample estimate via calls to Sampler::Get2D().

⟨*Use a single sample for illumination from* light⟩ ≡   855
```
Point2f uLight = sampler.Get2D();
Point2f uScattering = sampler.Get2D();
L += EstimateDirect(it, uScattering, *light, uLight, scene, sampler,
                    arena, handleMedia);
```

For each light sample, the EstimateDirect() function (which will be defined shortly) computes the value of the Monte Carlo estimator for its contribution. When sample arrays were successfully obtained, all that remains to be done is to average the estimates from each of their sample values.

⟨*Estimate direct lighting using sample arrays*⟩ ≡   855
```
Spectrum Ld(0.f);
for (int k = 0; k < nSamples; ++k)
    Ld += EstimateDirect(it, uScatteringArray[k], *light, uLightArray[k],
                         scene, sampler, arena, handleMedia);
L += Ld / nSamples;
```

In a scene with a large number of lights, it may not be desirable to always compute direct lighting from all of the lights at every point that is shaded. The Monte Carlo approach gives a way to do this that still computes the correct result on average. Consider as an example computing the expected value of the sum of two functions $E[f(x) + g(x)]$. If we randomly evaluate just one of $f(x)$ or $g(x)$ and multiply the result by 2, then the expected value of the result will still be $f(x) + g(x)$. This idea also generalizes to sums with an arbitrary number of terms; see Ross (2002, p. 102) for a proof. Here we estimate direct lighting for only one randomly chosen light and multiply the result by the number of lights to compensate.

⟨*Integrator Utility Functions*⟩ +≡
```
Spectrum UniformSampleOneLight(const Interaction &it,
        const Scene &scene, MemoryArena &arena, Sampler &sampler,
        bool handleMedia) {
    ⟨Randomly choose a single light to sample, light 856⟩
    Point2f uLight = sampler.Get2D();
    Point2f uScattering = sampler.Get2D();
    return (Float)nLights *
        EstimateDirect(it, uScattering, *light, uLight, scene, sampler,
                       arena, handleMedia);
}
```

Which of the nLights to sample illumination from is determined using a 1D sample from
Sampler::Get1D().

⟨*Randomly choose a single light to sample*, light⟩ ≡   856
```
int nLights = int(scene.lights.size());
if (nLights == 0) return Spectrum(0.f);
int lightNum = std::min((int)(sampler.Get1D() * nLights), nLights - 1);
const std::shared_ptr<Light> &light = scene.lights[lightNum];
```

It's possible to be even more creative in choosing the individual light sampling probabilities than the uniform method used in UniformSampleOneLight(). In fact, we're free to set
the probabilities any way we like, as long as we weight the result appropriately and there is
a nonzero probability of sampling any light that contributes to the reflection at the point.
The better a job we do at setting these probabilities to reflect the relative contributions
of lights to reflected radiance at the reference point, the more efficient the Monte Carlo
estimator will be, and the fewer rays will be needed to lower variance to an acceptable
level. (This is just the discrete instance of importance sampling.)

One widely used approach to this task is to base the sample distribution on the total
power of each light. In a similar manner, we could take more than one light sample with
this approach; indeed, any number of samples can be taken in the end, as long as they are
weighted appropriately.

14.3.1 ESTIMATING THE DIRECT LIGHTING INTEGRAL

Having chosen a particular light to estimate direct lighting from, we need to estimate the
value of the integral

$$\int_{\mathcal{S}^2} f(\mathrm{p}, \omega_o, \omega_i) \, L_d(\mathrm{p}, \omega_i) \, |\cos\theta_i| \, d\omega_i$$

for that light. To compute this estimate, we need to choose one or more directions ω_j
and apply the Monte Carlo estimator:

$$\frac{1}{N} \sum_{j=1}^{N} \frac{f(\mathrm{p}, \omega_o, \omega_j) \, L_d(\mathrm{p}, \omega_j) \, |\cos\theta_j|}{p(\omega_j)}.$$

To reduce variance, we will use importance sampling to choose the directions ω_j. Because both the BSDF and the direct radiance terms are individually complex, it can be difficult to find sampling distributions that match their product well. (However, see the "Further Reading" section as well as Exercise 14.8 at the end of this chapter for approaches that sample their product directly.) Here we will use the BSDF's sampling distribution for some of the samples and the light's for the rest. Depending on the characteristics of each of them, one of these two sampling methods may be far more effective than the other. Therefore, we will use multiple importance sampling to reduce variance for the cases where one or the other is more effective.

Figure 14.13 shows cases where one of the sampling methods is much better than the other. In this scene, four rectangular surfaces ranging from very smooth (top) to

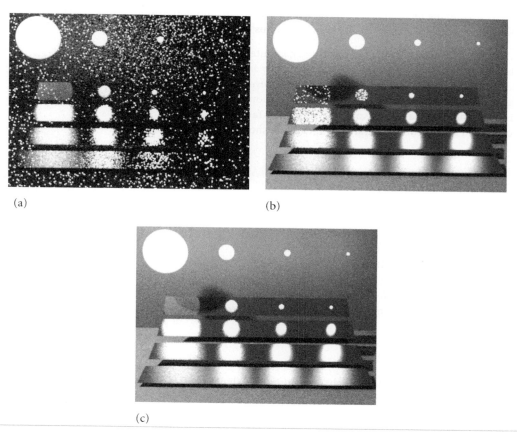

(a)   (b)

(c)

Figure 14.13: Four surfaces ranging from very smooth (top) to very rough (bottom) illuminated by spherical light sources of decreasing size and rendered with different sampling techniques (modeled after a scene by Eric Veach). (a) BSDF sampling, (b) Light sampling, and (c) both techniques combined using MIS. Sampling the BSDF is generally more effective for highly specular materials and large light sources, as illumination is coming from many directions, but the BSDF's value is large for only a few of them (top left reflection). The converse is true for small sources and rough materials (bottom right reflection), where sampling the light source is more effective.

very rough (bottom) are illuminated by spherical light sources of increasing size. Figures 14.13(a) and (b) show the BSDF and light sampling strategies on their own, while Figure 14.13(c) shows their combination computed using multiple importance sampling. As the example illustrates, sampling the BSDF can be much more effective when it takes on large values on a narrow set of directions that is much smaller than the set of directions that would be obtained by sampling the light sources. This case is most visible in the top left reflection of a large light source in a low-roughness surface. On the other hand, sampling the light sources can be considerably more effective in the opposite case—when the light source is small and the BSDF lobe is less concentrated (this case is most visible in the bottom right reflection).

By applying multiple importance sampling, not only can we use both of the two sampling methods, but we can also do so in a way that eliminates the extreme variance from the cases where a sampling method unexpectedly finds a high-contribution direction, since the weighting terms from MIS reduce these contributions substantially.

EstimateDirect() implements this approach and computes a direct lighting estimate for a single light source sample. Its handleMedia parameter indicates whether the effect of attenuation from participating media should be accounted for, and its specular parameter indicates whether or not perfectly specular lobes should be considered in the direct illumination estimate. The default value for both specular and handleMedia arguments is set to false in the function declaration, which is not shown here.

⟨*Integrator Utility Functions*⟩ +≡
```
    Spectrum EstimateDirect(const Interaction &it,
            const Point2f &uScattering, const Light &light,
            const Point2f &uLight, const Scene &scene, Sampler &sampler,
            MemoryArena &arena, bool handleMedia, bool specular) {
        BxDFType bsdfFlags = specular ? BSDF_ALL :
                            BxDFType(BSDF_ALL & ~BSDF_SPECULAR);
        Spectrum Ld(0.f);
        ⟨Sample light source with multiple importance sampling 858⟩
        ⟨Sample BSDF with multiple importance sampling 860⟩
        return Ld;
    }
```

BSDF_ALL 513
BSDF_SPECULAR 513
BxDFType 513
Float 1062
Interaction 115
Light 714
Light::Sample_Li() 716
MemoryArena 1074
Point2f 68
Sampler 421
Scene 23
Spectrum 315
Spectrum::IsBlack() 317
Vector3f 60
VisibilityTester 717

First, one sample is taken from the light's sampling distribution using Sample_Li(), which also returns the light's emitted radiance and the value of the PDF for the sampled direction.

⟨*Sample light source with multiple importance sampling*⟩ ≡   858
```
    Vector3f wi;
    Float lightPdf = 0, scatteringPdf = 0;
    VisibilityTester visibility;
    Spectrum Li = light.Sample_Li(it, uLight, &wi, &lightPdf, &visibility);
```

```
                    if (lightPdf > 0 && !Li.IsBlack()) {
                        ⟨Compute BSDF or phase function's value for light sample 859⟩
                        if (!f.IsBlack()) {
                            ⟨Compute effect of visibility for light source sample 859⟩
                            ⟨Add light's contribution to reflected radiance 860⟩
                        }
                    }
```

Only if the light successfully samples a direction and returns nonzero emitted radiance does EstimateDirect() go ahead and evaluate the BSDF or phase function at the provided Interaction; otherwise, there's no reason to go through the computational expense. (Consider, for example, a spotlight, which returns no radiance for points outside its illumination cone.)

⟨*Compute BSDF or phase function's value for light sample*⟩ ≡   858
```
    Spectrum f;
    if (it.IsSurfaceInteraction()) {
        ⟨Evaluate BSDF for light sampling strategy 859⟩
    } else {
        ⟨Evaluate phase function for light sampling strategy 900⟩
    }
```

⟨*Evaluate BSDF for light sampling strategy*⟩ ≡   859
```
    const SurfaceInteraction &isect = (const SurfaceInteraction &)it;
    f = isect.bsdf->f(isect.wo, wi, bsdfFlags) * AbsDot(wi, isect.shading.n);
    scatteringPdf = isect.bsdf->Pdf(isect.wo, wi, bsdfFlags);
```

(We postpone the medium-specific fragment that evaluates the phase function at the interaction point, ⟨*Evaluate medium reflectance for light sampling strategy*⟩, to Chapter 15.)

If participating media are to be accounted for, the radiance from the light to the illuminated point is scaled by the beam transmittance between the two points to account for attenuation due to participating media. Otherwise, a call to the VisibilityTester's Unoccluded() method traces a shadow ray to determine if the sampled point on the light source is visible. (This step and the next are skipped if the BSDF or phase function returned a black SPD.)

⟨*Compute effect of visibility for light source sample*⟩ ≡   858
```
    if (handleMedia)
        Li *= visibility.Tr(scene, sampler);
    else if (!visibility.Unoccluded(scene))
        Li = Spectrum(0.f);
```

The light sample's contribution can now be accumulated. Recall from Section 14.2.1 that if the light is described by a delta distribution then there is an implied delta distribution in both the emitted radiance value returned from Sample_Li() as well as the PDF and that they are expected to cancel out when the estimator is evaluated. In this case, we must not try to apply multiple importance sampling and should compute the standard estimator instead. If this isn't a delta distribution light source, then the BSDF's PDF value

AbsDot() 64
BSDF::f() 575
BSDF::Pdf() 834
Interaction::
    IsSurfaceInteraction()
    116
Spectrum 315
SurfaceInteraction 116
SurfaceInteraction::bsdf 250
SurfaceInteraction::shading
    118
SurfaceInteraction::
    shading::n
    118
VisibilityTester 717
VisibilityTester::Tr() 718
VisibilityTester::
    Unoccluded()
    718

for sampling the direction ω_i, which was returned by BSDF::Pdf(), is used with the MIS estimator, where the weight is computed here with the power heuristic.

⟨*Add light's contribution to reflected radiance*⟩ ≡   858
```
if (!Li.IsBlack()) {
    if (IsDeltaLight(light.flags))
        Ld += f * Li / lightPdf;
    else {
        Float weight = PowerHeuristic(1, lightPdf, 1, scatteringPdf);
        Ld += f * Li * weight / lightPdf;
    }
}
```

Next, a sample is generated using the BSDF's sampling distribution. This step should be skipped if the light source's emission profile involves a delta distribution because, in that case, there's no chance that sampling the BSDF will give a direction that receives light from the source. Otherwise, the BSDF can be sampled.

⟨*Sample BSDF with multiple importance sampling*⟩ ≡   858
```
if (!IsDeltaLight(light.flags)) {
    Spectrum f;
    bool sampledSpecular = false;
    if (it.IsSurfaceInteraction()) {
        ⟨Sample scattered direction for surface interactions 860⟩
    } else {
        ⟨Sample scattered direction for medium interactions 900⟩
    }
    if (!f.IsBlack() && scatteringPdf > 0) {
        ⟨Account for light contributions along sampled direction wi 861⟩
    }
}
```

Once more, we postpone the medium-related code to Chapter 15. Given a surface interaction, the implementation samples a scattered direction and records whether or not a delta distribution was sampled.

⟨*Sample scattered direction for surface interactions*⟩ ≡   860
```
BxDFType sampledType;
const SurfaceInteraction &isect = (const SurfaceInteraction &)it;
f = isect.bsdf->Sample_f(isect.wo, &wi, uScattering, &scatteringPdf,
                         bsdfFlags, &sampledType);
f *= AbsDot(wi, isect.shading.n);
sampledSpecular = sampledType & BSDF_SPECULAR;
```

One important detail is that the light's PDF and the multiple importance sampling weight are only computed if the BSDF component used for sampling ω_i is non-specular; in the specular case, MIS shouldn't be applied since there is no chance of the light sampling the specular direction.

⟨*Account for light contributions along sampled direction* wi⟩ ≡   **860**
```
    Float weight = 1;
    if (!sampledSpecular) {
        lightPdf = light.Pdf_Li(it, wi);
        if (lightPdf == 0)
            return Ld;
        weight = PowerHeuristic(1, scatteringPdf, 1, lightPdf);
    }
```
    ⟨*Find intersection and compute transmittance* **861**⟩
    ⟨*Add light contribution from material sampling* **861**⟩

Given a direction sampled by the BSDF or a medium's phase function, we need to find out if the ray along that direction intersects this particular light source and if so, how much radiance from the light reaches the surface. When participating media are being accounted for, the transmittance up to the intersection point on the light is recorded.

⟨*Find intersection and compute transmittance*⟩ ≡   **861**
```
    SurfaceInteraction lightIsect;
    Ray ray = it.SpawnRay(wi);
    Spectrum Tr(1.f);
    bool foundSurfaceInteraction = handleMedia ?
            scene.IntersectTr(ray, sampler, &lightIsect, &Tr) :
            scene.Intersect(ray, &lightIsect);
```

The code must account for both regular area lights, with geometry associated with them, as well as lights like the InfiniteAreaLight that don't have geometry but need to return their radiance for the sample ray via the Light::Le() method.

⟨*Add light contribution from material sampling*⟩ ≡   **861**
```
    Spectrum Li(0.f);
    if (foundSurfaceInteraction) {
        if (lightIsect.primitive->GetAreaLight() == &light)
            Li = lightIsect.Le(-wi);
    }
    else
        Li = light.Le(ray);
    if (!Li.IsBlack())
        Ld += f * Li * Tr * weight / scatteringPdf;
```

14.4 THE LIGHT TRANSPORT EQUATION

The light transport equation (LTE) is the governing equation that describes the equilibrium distribution of radiance in a scene. It gives the total reflected radiance at a point on a surface in terms of emission from the surface, its BSDF, and the distribution of incident illumination arriving at the point. For now we will continue only to consider the case where there are no participating media in the scene. (Chapter 15 describes the generalizations to this process necessary for scenes that do have participating media.)

The detail that makes evaluating the LTE difficult is the fact that incident radiance at a point is affected by the geometry and scattering properties of all of the objects in the scene. For example, a bright light shining on a red object may cause a reddish tint on nearby objects in the scene, or glass may focus light into caustic patterns on a tabletop. Rendering algorithms that account for this complexity are often called *global illumination* algorithms, to differentiate them from *local illumination* algorithms that use only information about the local surface properties in their shading computations.

In this section, we will first derive the LTE and describe some approaches for manipulating the equation to make it easier to solve numerically. We will then describe two generalizations of the LTE that make some of its key properties more clear and serve as the foundation for some of the advanced integrators that will be implemented in Chapter 16.

14.4.1 BASIC DERIVATION

The light transport equation depends on the basic assumptions we have already made in choosing to use radiometry to describe light—that wave optics effects are unimportant and that the distribution of radiance in the scene is in equilibrium.

The key principle underlying the LTE is *energy balance*. Any change in energy has to be "charged" to some process, and we must keep track of all the energy. Since we are assuming that lighting is a linear process, the difference between the amount of energy coming in and energy going out of a system must also be equal to the difference between energy emitted and energy absorbed. This idea holds at many levels of scale. On a macro level we have conservation of power:

$$\Phi_o - \Phi_i = \Phi_e - \Phi_a.$$

The difference between the power leaving an object, Φ_o, and the power entering it, Φ_i, is equal to the difference between the power it emits and the power it absorbs, $\Phi_e - \Phi_a$.

In order to enforce energy balance at a surface, exitant radiance L_o must be equal to emitted radiance plus the fraction of incident radiance that is scattered. Emitted radiance is given by L_e, and scattered radiance is given by the scattering equation, which gives

$$L_o(\mathrm{p}, \omega_o) = L_e(\mathrm{p}, \omega_o) + \int_{\mathcal{S}^2} f(\mathrm{p}, \omega_o, \omega_i)\, L_i(\mathrm{p}, \omega_i)\, |\cos \theta_i|\, d\omega_i.$$

Because we have assumed for now that no participating media are present, radiance is constant along rays through the scene. We can therefore relate the incident radiance at p to the outgoing radiance from another point p′, as shown by Figure 14.14. If we define the *ray-casting function* $t(\mathrm{p}, \omega)$ as a function that computes the first surface point p′ intersected by a ray from p in the direction ω, we can write the incident radiance at p in terms of outgoing radiance at p′:

$$L_i(\mathrm{p}, \omega) = L_o(t(\mathrm{p}, \omega), -\omega).$$

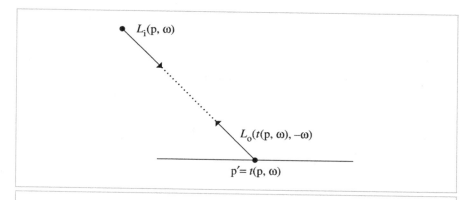

Figure 14.14: Radiance along a Ray through Free Space Is Unchanged. Therefore, to compute the incident radiance along a ray from point p in direction ω, we can find the first surface the ray intersects and compute exitant radiance in the direction $-\omega$ there. The trace operator $t(p, \omega)$ gives the point p' on the first surface that the ray (p, ω) intersects.

In case the scene is not closed, we will define the ray-casting function to return a special value Λ if the ray (p, ω) doesn't intersect any object in the scene, such that $L_o(\Lambda, \omega)$ is always 0.

Dropping the subscripts from L_o for brevity, this relationship allows us to write the LTE as

$$L(p, \omega_o) = L_e(p, \omega_o) + \int_{S^2} f(p, \omega_o, \omega_i)\, L(t(p, \omega_i), -\omega_i)\, |\cos\theta_i|\, d\omega_i. \quad \text{[14.13]}$$

The key to the above representation is that there is only *one* quantity of interest, exitant radiance from points on surfaces. Of course, it appears on both sides of the equation, so our task is still not simple, but it is certainly better. It is important to keep in mind that we were able to arrive at this equation simply by enforcing energy balance in our scene.

14.4.2 ANALYTIC SOLUTIONS TO THE LTE

The brevity of the LTE belies the fact that it is impossible to solve analytically in general. The complexity that comes from physically based BSDF models, arbitrary scene geometry, and the intricate visibility relationships among objects all conspire to mandate a numerical solution technique. Fortunately, the combination of ray-tracing algorithms and Monte Carlo integration gives a powerful pair of tools that can handle this complexity without needing to impose restrictions on various components of the LTE (e.g., requiring that all BSDFs be Lambertian or substantially limiting the geometric representations that are supported).

It is possible to find analytic solutions to the LTE in extremely simple settings. While this is of little help for general-purpose rendering, it can help with debugging the implementations of integrators. If an integrator that is supposed to solve the complete LTE doesn't compute a solution that matches an analytic solution, then clearly there is a bug in the integrator. As an example, consider the interior of a sphere where all points on the surface of the sphere have a Lambertian BRDF, $f(\mathrm{p}, \omega_o, \omega_i) = c$, and also emit a constant amount of radiance in all directions. We have

$$L(\mathrm{p}, \omega_o) = L_e + c \int_{\mathcal{H}^2(\mathrm{n})} L(t(\mathrm{p}, \omega_i), -\omega_i) \, |\cos \theta_i| \, d\omega_i.$$

The outgoing radiance distribution at any point on the sphere interior must be the same as at any other point; nothing in the environment could introduce any variation among different points. Therefore, the incident radiance distribution must be the same at all points, and the cosine-weighted integral of incident radiance must be the same everywhere as well. As such, we can replace the radiance functions with constants and simplify, writing the LTE as

$$L = L_e + c\pi L.$$

While we could immediately solve this equation for L, it's interesting to consider successive substitution of the right-hand side into the L term on the right-hand side. If we also replace πc with ρ_{hh}, the reflectance of a Lambertian surface, we have

$$L = L_e + \rho_{hh}(L_e + \rho_{hh}(L_e + \cdots$$
$$= \sum_{i=0}^{\infty} L_e \rho_{hh}^i.$$

In other words, exitant radiance is equal to the emitted radiance at the point plus light that has been scattered by a BSDF once after emission, plus light that has been scattered twice, and so forth.

Because $\rho_{hh} < 1$ due to conservation of energy, the series converges and the reflected radiance at all points in all directions is

$$L = \frac{L_e}{1 - \rho_{hh}}.$$

This process of repeatedly substituting the LTE's right-hand side into the incident radiance term in the integral can be instructive in more general cases.[7] For example, the DirectLightingIntegrator integrator effectively computes the result of making a single substitution:

$$L(\mathrm{p}, \omega_o) = L_e(\mathrm{p}, \omega_o) + \int_{\mathcal{S}^2} f(\mathrm{p}, \omega_o, \omega_i) \, L_d \, |\cos \theta_i| \, d\omega_i,$$

where

$$L_d = L_e(t(\mathrm{p}, \omega_i), -\omega_i)$$

and further scattering is ignored.

---

7   Indeed, this sort of series expansion and inversion can be used in the general case, where quantities like the BSDF are expressed in terms of general operators that map incident radiance functions to exitant radiance functions. This approach forms the foundation for applying sophisticated tools from analysis to the light transport problem. See Arvo's thesis (Arvo 1995a) and Veach's thesis (Veach 1997) for further information.

Over the next few pages, we will see how performing successive substitutions in this manner and then regrouping the results expresses the LTE in a more natural way for developing rendering algorithms.

14.4.3 THE SURFACE FORM OF THE LTE

One reason why the LTE as written in Equation (14.13) is complex is that the relationship between geometric objects in the scene is implicit in the ray-tracing function $t(p, \omega)$. Making the behavior of this function explicit in the integrand will shed some light on the structure of this equation. To do this, we will rewrite Equation (14.13) as an integral over *area* instead of an integral over directions on the sphere.

First, we define exitant radiance from a point p' to a point p by

$$L(p' \rightarrow p) = L(p', \omega)$$

if p' and p are mutually visible and $\omega = \widehat{p - p'}$. We can also write the BSDF at p' as

$$f(p'' \rightarrow p' \rightarrow p) = f(p', \omega_o, \omega_i),$$

where $\omega_i = \widehat{p'' - p'}$ and $\omega_o = \widehat{p - p'}$ (Figure 14.15).

Rewriting the terms in the LTE in this manner isn't quite enough, however. We also need to multiply by the Jacobian that relates solid angle to area in order to transform the LTE from an integral over direction to one over surface area. Recall that this is $|\cos \theta'|/r^2$.

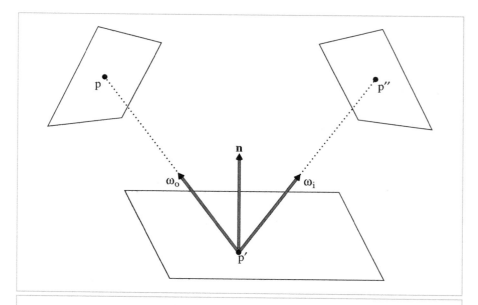

Figure 14.15: The three-point form of the light transport equation converts the integral to be over the domain of points on surfaces in the scene, rather than over directions over the sphere. It is a key transformation for deriving the path integral form of the light transport equation.

We will combine this change-of-variables term, the original $|\cos\theta|$ term from the LTE, and also a binary visibility function V ($V = 1$ if the two points are mutually visible, and $V = 0$ otherwise) into a single geometric coupling term, $G(\mathrm{p} \leftrightarrow \mathrm{p}')$:

$$G(\mathrm{p} \leftrightarrow \mathrm{p}') = V(\mathrm{p} \leftrightarrow \mathrm{p}') \frac{|\cos\theta|\,|\cos\theta'|}{\|\,\mathrm{p} - \mathrm{p}'\,\|^2}. \qquad [14.14]$$

Substituting these into the light transport equation and converting to an area integral, we have

$$L(\mathrm{p}' \to \mathrm{p}) = L_e(\mathrm{p}' \to \mathrm{p}) + \int_A f(\mathrm{p}'' \to \mathrm{p}' \to \mathrm{p})\, L(\mathrm{p}'' \to \mathrm{p}')\, G(\mathrm{p}'' \leftrightarrow \mathrm{p}')\, \mathrm{d}A(\mathrm{p}''),$$

$$[14.15]$$

where A is all of the surfaces of the scene.

Although Equations (14.13) and (14.15) are equivalent, they represent two different ways of approaching light transport. To evaluate Equation (14.13) with Monte Carlo, we would sample a number of directions from a distribution of directions on the sphere and cast rays to evaluate the integrand. For Equation (14.15), however, we would choose a number of *points* on surfaces according to a distribution over surface area and compute the coupling between those points to evaluate the integrand, tracing rays to evaluate the visibility term $V(\mathrm{p} \leftrightarrow \mathrm{p}')$.

14.4.4 INTEGRAL OVER PATHS

With the area integral form of Equation (14.15), we can derive a more flexible form of the LTE known as the *path integral* formulation of light transport, which expresses radiance as an integral over paths that are themselves points in a high dimensional *path space*. One of the main motivations for using path space is that it provides an expression for the value of a measurement as an explicit integral over paths, as opposed to the unwieldy recursive definition resulting from the energy balance equation, (14.13).

The explicit form allows for considerable freedom in how these paths are found—essentially any technique for randomly choosing paths can be turned into a workable rendering algorithm that computes the right answer given a sufficient number of samples. This form of the LTE provides the foundation of the bidirectional light transport algorithms in Chapter 16.

To go from the area integral to a sum over path integrals involving light-carrying paths of different lengths, we can now start to expand the three-point light transport equation, repeatedly substituting the right-hand side of the equation into the $L(\mathrm{p}'' \to \mathrm{p}')$ term inside the integral. Here are the first few terms that give incident radiance at a point p_0 from another point p_1, where p_1 is the first point on a surface along the ray from p_0 in direction $\mathrm{p}_1 - \mathrm{p}_0$:

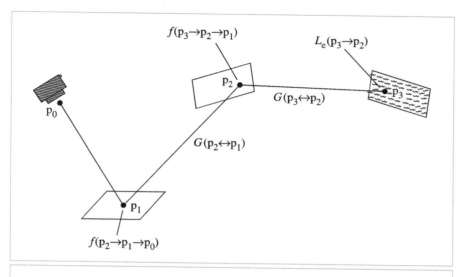

Figure 14.16: The integral over all points p_2 and p_3 on surfaces in the scene given by the light transport equation gives the total contribution of two bounce paths to radiance leaving p_1 in the direction of p_0. The components of the product in the integrand are shown here: the emitted radiance from the light, L_e; the geometric terms between vertices, G; and scattering from the BSDFs, f.

$$L(p_1 \to p_0) = L_e(p_1 \to p_0)$$
$$+ \int_A L_e(p_2 \to p_1) f(p_2 \to p_1 \to p_0) \, G(p_2 \leftrightarrow p_1) dA(p_2)$$
$$+ \int_A \int_A L_e(p_3 \to p_2) f(p_3 \to p_2 \to p_1) \, G(p_3 \leftrightarrow p_2)$$
$$\times f(p_2 \to p_1 \to p_0) \, G(p_2 \leftrightarrow p_1) \, dA(p_3) \, dA(p_2) + \cdots$$

Each term on the right side of this equation represents a path of increasing length. For example, the third term is illustrated in Figure 14.16. This path has four vertices, connected by three segments. The total contribution of all such paths of length four (i.e., a vertex at the camera, two vertices at points on surfaces in the scene, and a vertex on a light source) is given by this term. Here, the first two vertices of the path, p_0 and p_1, are predetermined based on the camera ray origin and the point that it intersects, but p_2 and p_3 can vary over all points on surfaces in the scene. The integral over all such p_2 and p_3 gives the total contribution of paths of length four to radiance arriving at the camera.

This infinite sum can be written compactly as

$$L(p_1 \to p_0) = \sum_{n=1}^{\infty} P(\bar{p}_n). \qquad [14.16]$$

$P(\bar{p}_n)$ gives the amount of radiance scattered over a path $\bar{p}_n$ with $n+1$ vertices,

$$\bar{p}_n = p_0, p_1, \ldots, p_n,$$

where p_0 is on the film plane or front lens element and p_n is on a light source, and

$$P(\bar{p}_n) = \underbrace{\int_A \int_A \cdots \int_A}_{n-1} L_e(p_n \to p_{n-1})$$

$$\times \left(\prod_{i=1}^{n-1} f(p_{i+1} \to p_i \to p_{i-1})\, G(p_{i+1} \leftrightarrow p_i) \right)\, dA(p_2) \cdots dA(p_n). \tag{14.17}$$

Before we move on, we will define one additional term that will be helpful in the subsequent discussion. The product of a path's BSDF and geometry terms is called the *throughput* of the path; it describes the fraction of radiance from the light source that arrives at the camera after all of the scattering at vertices between them. We will denote it by

$$T(\bar{p}_n) = \prod_{i=1}^{n-1} f(p_{i+1} \to p_i \to p_{i-1})\, G(p_{i+1} \leftrightarrow p_i), \tag{14.18}$$

so

$$P(\bar{p}_n) = \underbrace{\int_A \int_A \cdots \int_A}_{n-1} L_e(p_n \to p_{n-1})\, T(\bar{p}_n)\, dA(p_2) \cdots dA(p_n).$$

Given Equation (14.16) and a particular length n, all that we need to do to compute a Monte Carlo estimate of the radiance arriving at p_0 due to paths of length n is to sample a set of vertices with an appropriate sampling density in the scene to generate a path and then to evaluate an estimate of $P(\bar{p}_n)$ using those vertices. Whether we generate those vertices by starting a path from the camera, starting from the light, starting from both ends, or starting from a point in the middle is a detail that only affects how the weights for the Monte Carlo estimates are computed. We will see how this formulation leads to practical light transport algorithms throughout this and the following two chapters.

14.4.5 DELTA DISTRIBUTIONS IN THE INTEGRAND

Delta functions may be present in $P(\bar{p}_i)$ terms due to both BSDF components described by delta distributions as well as certain types of light sources (e.g., point lights and directional lights). If present, these distributions need to be handled explicitly by the light transport algorithm. For example, it is impossible to randomly choose an outgoing direction from a point on a surface that would intersect a point light source; instead, it is necessary to explicitly choose the single direction from the point to the light source if we want to be able to include its contribution. (The same is true for sampling BSDFs with delta components.) While handling this case introduces some additional complexity to the integrators, it is generally welcome because it reduces the dimensionality of the integral to be evaluated, turning parts of it into a plain sum.

For example, consider the direct illumination term, $P(\bar{p}_2)$, in a scene with a single point light source at point p_{light} described by a delta distribution:

$$P(\bar{p}_2) = \int_A L_e(p_2 \to p_1)\, f(p_2 \to p_1 \to p_0)\, G(p_2 \leftrightarrow p_1)\, dA(p_2)$$

$$= \frac{\delta(p_{\text{light}} - p_2)\, L_e(p_{\text{light}} \to p_1)}{p(p_{\text{light}})} f(p_2 \to p_1 \to p_0)\, G(p_2 \leftrightarrow p_1).$$

In other words, p_2 must be the same as the light's position in the scene; the delta distribution in the numerator cancels out due to an implicit delta distribution in $p(p_{\text{light}})$ (recall the discussion of sampling delta distributions in Section 14.1.3), and we are left with terms that can be evaluated directly, with no need for Monte Carlo. An analogous situation holds for BSDFs with delta distributions in the path throughput $T(\bar{p}_n)$; each one eliminates an integral over area from the estimate to be computed.

14.4.6 PARTITIONING THE INTEGRAND

Many rendering algorithms have been developed that are particularly good at solving the LTE under some conditions but don't work well (or at all) under others. For example, the Whitted integrator only handles specular reflection from delta BSDFs and ignores multiply scattered light from diffuse and glossy BSDFs. Section 16.2.2 will introduce the concept of density estimation, which is used to implement a rendering algorithm known as *stochastic progressive photon mapping* (SPPM). The underlying density estimation that algorithm uses works well on diffuse surfaces because scattered radiance only depends on the surface position in this case to store a 2D radiance discretization, but for glossy surfaces it becomes preferable to switch to other techniques such as path tracing.

Because we would like to be able to derive correct light transport algorithms that account for all possible modes of scattering without ignoring any contributions and without double-counting others, it is important to carefully account for which parts of the LTE a particular solution method accounts for. A nice way of approaching this problem is to partition the LTE in various ways. For example, we might expand the sum over paths to

$$L(p_1 \to p_0) = P(\bar{p}_1) + P(\bar{p}_2) + \sum_{i=3}^{\infty} P(\bar{p}_i),$$

where the first term is trivially evaluated by computing the emitted radiance at p_1, the second term is solved with an accurate direct lighting solution technique, but the remaining terms in the sum are handled with a faster but less accurate approach. If the contribution of these additional terms to the total reflected radiance is relatively small for the scene we're rendering, this may be a reasonable approach to take. The only detail is that it is important to be careful to ignore $P(\bar{p}_1)$ and $P(\bar{p}_2)$ with the algorithm that handles $P(\bar{p}_3)$ and beyond (and similarly with the other terms).

It is also useful to partition individual $P(\bar{p}_n)$ terms. For example, we might want to split the emission term into emission from small light sources, $L_{e,s}$, and emission from large light sources, $L_{e,l}$, giving us two separate integrals to estimate:

$$P(\bar{p}_n) = \int_{A^{n-1}} (L_{e,s}(p_n \to p_{n-1}) + L_{e,l}(p_n \to p_{n-1}))\, T(\bar{p}_n)\, dA(p_2) \cdots dA(p_n)$$

$$= \int_{A^{n-1}} L_{e,s}(p_n \to p_{n-1})\, T(\bar{p}_n)\, dA(p_2) \cdots dA(p_n)$$

$$+ \int_{A^{n-1}} L_{e,l}(p_n \to p_{n-1})\, T(\bar{p}_n)\, dA(p_2) \cdots dA(p_n).$$

The two integrals can be evaluated independently, possibly using completely different algorithms or different numbers of samples, selected in a way that handles the different conditions well. As long as the estimate of the $L_{e,s}$ integral ignores any emission from large lights, the estimate of the $L_{e,l}$ integral ignores emission from small lights, and all lights are categorized as either "large" or "small," the correct result is computed in the end.

Finally, the BSDF terms can be partitioned as well (in fact, this application was the reason why BSDF categorization with BxDFType values was introduced in Section 8.1). For example, if f_Δ denotes components of the BSDF described by delta distributions and $f_{\neg\Delta}$ denotes the remaining components,

$$P(\bar{p}_n) = \int_{A^{n-1}} L_e(p_n \to p_{n-1})$$

$$\times \prod_{i=1}^{n-1} \left(f_\Delta(p_{i+1} \to p_i \to p_{i-1}) + f_{\neg\Delta}(p_{i+1} \to p_i \to p_{i-1}) \right)$$

$$\times G(p_{i+1} \leftrightarrow p_i)\, dA(p_2) \cdots dA(p_n).$$

Note that because there are $i - 1$ BSDF terms in the product, it is important to be careful not to count only terms with only f_Δ components or only $f_{\neg\Delta}$ components; all of the terms like $f_\Delta f_{\neg\Delta} f_{\neg\Delta}$ must be accounted for as well if a partitioning scheme like this is used.

14.5 PATH TRACING

Now that we have derived the path integral form of the light transport equation, we'll show how it can be used to derive the *path-tracing* light transport algorithm and will present a path-tracing integrator. Figure 14.17 compares images of a scene rendered with different numbers of pixel samples using the path-tracing integrator. In general, hundreds or thousands of samples per pixel may be necessary for high-quality results—potentially a substantial computational expense.

Path tracing was the first general-purpose unbiased Monte Carlo light transport algorithm used in graphics. Kajiya (1986) introduced it in the same paper that first described the light transport equation. Path tracing incrementally generates paths of scattering events starting at the camera and ending at light sources in the scene. One way to think of it is as an extension of Whitted's method to include both delta distribution and nondelta BSDFs and light sources, rather than just accounting for the delta terms.

Although it is slightly easier to derive path tracing directly from the basic light transport equation, we will instead approach it from the path integral form, which helps build

(a)

(b)

Figure 14.17: San Miguel Scene Rendered with Path Tracing. (a) Rendered with path tracing with 1024 samples per pixel. (b) Rendered with just 8 samples per pixel, giving the characteristic grainy noise that is the hallmark of variance. *(Model courtesy of Guillermo M. Leal Llaguno.)*

understanding of the path integral equation and will make the generalization to bidirectional path tracing (Section 16.3) easier to understand.

14.5.1 OVERVIEW

Given the path integral form of the LTE, we would like to estimate the value of the exitant radiance from the camera ray's intersection point p_1,

$$L(p_1 \to p_0) = \sum_{i=1}^{\infty} P(\bar{p}_i),$$

for a given camera ray from p_0 that first intersects the scene at p_1. We have two problems that must be solved in order to compute this estimate:

1. How do we estimate the value of the sum of the infinite number of $P(\bar{p}_i)$ terms with a finite amount of computation?
2. Given a particular $P(\bar{p}_i)$ term, how do we generate one or more paths $\bar{p}$ in order to compute a Monte Carlo estimate of its multidimensional integral?

For path tracing, we can take advantage of the fact that for physically valid scenes, paths with more vertices scatter less light than paths with fewer vertices overall (this isn't necessarily true for any particular pair of paths, just in the aggregate). This is a natural consequence of conservation of energy in BSDFs. Therefore, we will always estimate the first few terms $P(\bar{p}_i)$ and will then start to apply Russian roulette to stop sampling after a finite number of terms without introducing bias. Recall from Section 13.7 that Russian roulette allows us to probabilistically stop computing terms in a sum as long as we reweight the terms that are not terminated. For example, if we always computed estimates of $P(\bar{p}_1)$, $P(\bar{p}_2)$, and $P(\bar{p}_3)$ but stopped without computing more terms with probability q, then an unbiased estimate of the sum would be

$$P(\bar{p}_1) + P(\bar{p}_2) + P(\bar{p}_3) + \frac{1}{1-q} \sum_{i=4}^{\infty} P(\bar{p}_i).$$

Using Russian roulette in this way doesn't solve the problem of needing to evaluate an infinite sum but has pushed it a bit farther out.

If we take this idea a step further and instead randomly consider terminating evaluation of the sum at each term with probability q_i,

$$\frac{1}{1-q_1} \left(P(\bar{p}_1) + \frac{1}{1-q_2} \left(P(\bar{p}_2) + \frac{1}{1-q_3} \left(P(\bar{p}_3) + \cdots \right. \right. \right.,$$

we will eventually stop continued evaluation of the sum. Yet, because for any particular value of i there is greater than zero probability of evaluating the term $P(\bar{p}_i)$ and because it will be weighted appropriately if we do evaluate it, the final result is an unbiased estimate of the sum.

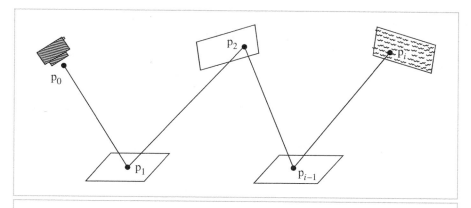

Figure 14.18: A path $\bar{p}_i$ of $i+1$ vertices from the camera at p, intersecting a series of positions on surfaces in the scene, to a point on the light p_i. Scattering according to the BSDF occurs at each path vertex from p_i to p_{i-1} such that the radiance estimate at the camera due to this path is given by the product of the path throughput $T(\bar{p}_i)$ and the emitted radiance from the light divided by the path sampling weights.

14.5.2 PATH SAMPLING

Given this method for evaluating only a finite number of terms of the infinite sum, we also need a way to estimate the contribution of a particular term $P(\bar{p}_i)$. We need $i+1$ vertices to specify the path, where the last vertex p_i is on a light source and the first vertex p_0 is a point on the camera film or lens (Figure 14.18). Looking at the form of $P(\bar{p}_i)$, a multiple integral over surface area of objects in the scene, the most natural thing to do is to sample vertices p_i according to the surface area of objects in the scene, such that it's equally probable to sample any particular point on an object in the scene for p_i as any other point. (We don't actually use this approach in the PathIntegrator implementation for reasons that will be described later, but this sampling technique could possibly be used to improve the efficiency of our basic implementation and helps to clarify the meaning of the path integral LTE.)

We could define a discrete probability over the n objects in the scene. If each has surface area A_i, then the probability of sampling a path vertex on the surface of the ith object should be

$$p_i = \frac{A_i}{\sum_j A_j}.$$

Then, given a method to sample a point on the ith object with uniform probability, the PDF for sampling any particular point on object i is $1/A_i$. Thus, the overall probability density for sampling the point is

$$\frac{A_i}{\sum_j A_j} \frac{1}{A_i}.$$

And all samples p_i have the same PDF value:

$$p_A(p_i) = \frac{1}{\sum_j A_j}.$$

It's reassuring that they all have the same weight, since our intent was to choose among all points on surfaces in the scene with equal probability.

Given the set of vertices $p_0, p_1, \ldots, p_{i-1}$ sampled in this manner, we can then sample the last vertex p_i on a light source in the scene, defining its PDF in the same way. Although we could use the same technique used for sampling path vertices to sample points on lights, this would lead to high variance, since for all of the paths where p_i wasn't on the surface of an emitter, the path would have zero value. The expected value would still be the correct value of the integral, but convergence would be extremely slow. A better approach is to sample over the areas of only the emitting objects with probabilities updated accordingly. Given a complete path, we have all of the information we need to compute the estimate of $P(\bar{p}_i)$; it's just a matter of evaluating each of the terms.

It's easy to be more creative about how we set the sampling probabilities with this general approach. For example, if we knew that indirect illumination from a few objects contributed to most of the lighting in the scene, we could assign a higher probability to generating path vertices p_i on those objects, updating the sample weights appropriately.

However, there are two interrelated problems with sampling paths in this manner. The first can lead to high variance, while the second can lead to incorrect results. The first problem is that many of the paths will have no contribution if they have pairs of adjacent vertices that are not mutually visible. Consider applying this area sampling method in a complex building model: adjacent vertices in the path will almost always have a wall or two between them, giving no contribution for the path and high variance in the estimate.

The second problem is that if the integrand has delta functions in it (e.g., a point light source or a perfectly specular BSDF), this sampling technique will never be able to choose path vertices such that the delta distributions are nonzero. Even if there aren't delta distributions, as the BSDFs become increasingly glossy almost all of the paths will have low contributions since the points in $f(p_{i+1} \rightarrow p_i \rightarrow p_{i-1})$ will cause the BSDF to have a small or zero value and again we will suffer from high variance. In a similar manner, small area light sources can also be sources of variance if not sampled explicitly.

14.5.3 INCREMENTAL PATH CONSTRUCTION

A solution that solves both of these problems is to construct the path incrementally, starting from the vertex at the camera p_0. At each vertex, the BSDF is sampled to generate a new direction; the next vertex p_{i+1} is found by tracing a ray from p_i in the sampled direction and finding the closest intersection. We are effectively trying to find a path with a large overall contribution by making a series of choices that find directions with important local contributions. While one can imagine situations where this approach could be ineffective, it is generally a good strategy.

Because this approach constructs the path by sampling BSDFs according to solid angle, and because the path integral LTE is an integral over surface area in the scene, we need to apply the correction to convert from the probability density according to solid angle p_ω

to a density according to area p_A (recall Section 5.5):

$$p_A = p_\omega \frac{|\cos \theta_i|}{\|p_i - p_{i+1}\|^2}.$$

This correction causes all of the terms of the geometric term $G(p_i \leftrightarrow p_{i+1})$ to cancel out of $P(\bar{p}_i)$ except for the $\cos \theta_{i+1}$ term. Furthermore, we already know that p_i and p_{i+1} must be mutually visible since we traced a ray to find p_{i+1}, so the visibility term is trivially equal to 1. An alternative way to think about this is that ray tracing provides an operation to importance sample the visibility component of G. Therefore, if we use this sampling technique but we still sample the last vertex p_i from some distribution over the surfaces of light sources $p_A(p_i)$, the value of the Monte Carlo estimate for a path is

$$\frac{L_e(p_i \to p_{i-1}) f(p_i \to p_{i-1} \to p_{i-2}) G(p_i \leftrightarrow p_{i-1})}{p_A(p_i)}$$

$$\times \left(\prod_{j=1}^{i-2} \frac{f(p_{j+1} \to p_j \to p_{j-1})|\cos \theta_j|}{p_\omega(p_{j+1} - p_j)} \right). \tag{14.19}$$

14.5.4 IMPLEMENTATION

Our path-tracing implementation computes an estimate of the sum of path contributions $P(\bar{p}_i)$ using the approach described in the previous subsection. Starting at the first intersection of the camera ray with the scene geometry, p_1, it incrementally samples path vertices by sampling from the BSDF's sampling distribution at the current vertex and tracing a ray to the next vertex. To find the last vertex of a particular path, p_i, which must be on a light source in the scene, it uses the multiple importance sampling–based direct lighting code that was developed for the direct lighting integrator. By using the multiple importance sampling weights instead of $p_A(p_i)$ to compute the estimate as described earlier, we have lower variance in the result for cases where sampling the BSDF would have been a better way to find a point on the light.

Beyond how lights are sampled, another small difference is that as the estimates of the path contribution terms $P(\bar{p}_i)$ are being evaluated, the vertices of the previous path of length $i - 1$ (everything except the vertex on the emitter) are reused as a starting point when constructing the path of length i. This means that it is only necessary to trace one more ray to construct the new path, rather than i rays as we would if we started from scratch. Reusing paths in this manner does introduce correlation among all of the $P(\bar{p}_i)$ terms in the sum, which slightly reduces the quality of the result, although in practice this is more than made up for by the improved overall efficiency due to tracing fewer rays.

⟨*PathIntegrator Declarations*⟩ ≡
```
class PathIntegrator : public SamplerIntegrator {
public:
    ⟨PathIntegrator Public Methods 876⟩
private:
    ⟨PathIntegrator Private Data 876⟩
};
```

SamplerIntegrator 25

Although Russian roulette is used here to terminate path sampling in the manner described earlier, the integrator also supports a maximum depth. It can be set to a large value if only Russian roulette should be used to terminate paths.

⟨*PathIntegrator Public Methods*⟩ ≡   **875**
```
PathIntegrator(int maxDepth, std::shared_ptr<const Camera> camera,
               std::shared_ptr<Sampler> sampler)
    : SamplerIntegrator(camera, sampler), maxDepth(maxDepth) { }
```

⟨*PathIntegrator Private Data*⟩ ≡   **875**
```
const int maxDepth;
```

A number of variables record the current state of the path. beta holds the *path throughput weight*, which is defined as the factors of the throughput function $T(\bar{p}_{i-1})$—i.e., the product of the BSDF values and cosine terms for the vertices generated so far, divided by their respective sampling PDFs:

$$\beta = \prod_{j=1}^{i-2} \frac{f(p_{j+1} \rightarrow p_j \rightarrow p_{j-1})|\cos\theta_j|}{p_\omega(p_{j+1} - p_j)}.$$

Thus, the product of beta with scattered light from direct lighting at the final vertex of the path gives the contribution for a path. (This quantity will reoccur many times in the following two chapters, and we will consistently refer to it as beta.) Because the effect of earlier path vertices is aggregated in this way, there is no need to store the positions and BSDFs of all of the vertices of the path, only the last one.

In the following implementation, L holds the radiance value from the running total of $\sum P(\bar{p}_i)$, ray holds the next ray to be traced to extend the path one more vertex, and specularBounce records if the last outgoing path direction sampled was due to specular reflection; the need to track this will be explained shortly.

⟨*PathIntegrator Method Definitions*⟩ ≡
```
Spectrum PathIntegrator::Li(const RayDifferential &r, const Scene &scene,
        Sampler &sampler, MemoryArena &arena, int depth) const {
    Spectrum L(0.f), beta(1.f);
    RayDifferential ray(r);
    bool specularBounce = false;
    for (int bounces = 0; ; ++bounces) {
        ⟨Find next path vertex and accumulate contribution 877⟩
    }
    return L;
}
```

Each time through the for loop of the integrator, the next vertex of the path is found by intersecting the current ray with the scene geometry and computing the contribution of the path to the overall radiance value with the direct lighting code. A new direction is then chosen by sampling from the BSDF's distribution at the last vertex of the path. After a few vertices have been sampled, Russian roulette is used to randomly terminate the path.

⟨*Find next path vertex and accumulate contribution*⟩ ≡   876
    ⟨*Intersect* ray *with scene and store intersection in* isect **877**⟩
    ⟨*Possibly add emitted light at intersection* **877**⟩
    ⟨*Terminate path if ray escaped or* maxDepth *was reached* **877**⟩
    ⟨*Compute scattering functions and skip over medium boundaries* **878**⟩
    ⟨*Sample illumination from lights to find path contribution* **878**⟩
    ⟨*Sample BSDF to get new path direction* **878**⟩
    ⟨*Account for subsurface scattering, if applicable* **915**⟩
    ⟨*Possibly terminate the path with Russian roulette* **879**⟩

The first step in the loop is to find the next path vertex by intersecting ray against the scene geometry.

⟨*Intersect* ray *with scene and store intersection in* isect⟩ ≡   **877, 900**
```
SurfaceInteraction isect;
bool foundIntersection = scene.Intersect(ray, &isect);
```

If the ray hits an object that is emissive, the emission is usually ignored, since the loop iteration at the previous path vertex performed a direct illumination estimate that already accounted for its effect. The same is true when a ray escapes into an emissive environment. However, there are two exceptions: the first is at the initial intersection point of camera rays, since this is the only opportunity to include emission from directly visible objects. The second is when the sampled direction from the last path vertex was from a specular BSDF component: in this case, the previous iteration's direct illumination estimate could not evaluate the associated integrand containing a Dirac delta function, and we must account for it here.

⟨*Possibly add emitted light at intersection*⟩ ≡   877
```
if (bounces == 0 || specularBounce) {
    ⟨Add emitted light at path vertex or from the environment 877⟩
}
```

When no intersection is found, the ray has escaped the scene and thus the path sampling iteration terminates. Similarly, the iteration terminates when bounces exceeds the prescribed maximum value.

⟨*Terminate path if ray escaped or* maxDepth *was reached*⟩ ≡   877
```
if (!foundIntersection || bounces >= maxDepth)
    break;
```

When emitted light should be included, the path throughput weight must be multiplied with the radiance emitted by the current path vertex (if an intersection was found) or radiance emitted by infinite area light sources, if present.

⟨*Add emitted light at path vertex or from the environment*⟩ ≡   877
```
if (foundIntersection)
    L += beta * isect.Le(-ray.d);
else
    for (const auto &light : scene.lights)
        L += beta * light->Le(ray);
```

Before estimating the direct illumination at the current vertex, it is necessary to compute the scattering functions at the vertex. A special case arises when `SurfaceInteraction::bsdf` is equal to `nullptr`, which indicates that the current surface has no effect on light. pbrt uses such surfaces to represent transitions between participating media, whose boundaries are themselves optically inactive (i.e., they have the same index of refraction on both sides). Since the basic `PathIntegrator` ignores media, it simply skips over such surfaces without counting them as scattering events in the `bounces` counter.

⟨*Compute scattering functions and skip over medium boundaries*⟩ ≡   877
```
isect.ComputeScatteringFunctions(ray, arena, true);
if (!isect.bsdf) {
    ray = isect.SpawnRay(ray.d);
    bounces--;
    continue;
}
```

The direct lighting computation uses the `UniformSampleOneLight()` function, which gives an estimate of the exitant radiance from direct lighting at the vertex at the end of the current path. Scaling this value by the path throughput weight gives its overall contribution to the total radiance estimate.

⟨*Sample illumination from lights to find path contribution*⟩ ≡   877
```
L += beta * UniformSampleOneLight(isect, scene, arena, sampler);
```

Now it is necessary to sample the BSDF at the vertex at the end of the current path to get an outgoing direction for the next ray to trace. The integrator updates the path throughput weight as described earlier and initializes ray with the ray to be traced to find the next vertex in the next iteration of the `for` loop.

⟨*Sample BSDF to get new path direction*⟩ ≡   877
```
Vector3f wo = -ray.d, wi;
Float pdf;
BxDFType flags;
Spectrum f = isect.bsdf->Sample_f(wo, &wi, sampler.Get2D(),
                                  &pdf, BSDF_ALL, &flags);
if (f.IsBlack() || pdf == 0.f)
    break;
beta *= f * AbsDot(wi, isect.shading.n) / pdf;
specularBounce = (flags & BSDF_SPECULAR) != 0;
ray = isect.SpawnRay(wi);
```

The case where a ray refracts into a material with a BSSRDF is handled specially in the fragment ⟨*Account for subsurface scattering, if applicable*⟩, which is implemented in Section 15.4.3 after subsurface scattering has been discussed in more detail.

Path termination kicks in after a few bounces, with termination probability q set based on the path throughput weight. In general, it's worth having a higher probability of terminating low-contributing paths, since they have relatively less impact on the final image. (A minimum termination probability ensures termination is possible if `beta` is large; for example, due to a large BSDF value divided by a low sampling probability.) If the path isn't terminated, beta is updated with the Russian roulette weight and all subsequent $P(\bar{p}_i)$ terms will be appropriately affected by it.

⟨*Possibly terminate the path with Russian roulette*⟩ ≡   877, 900

```
if (bounces > 3) {
    Float q = std::max((Float).05, 1 - beta.y());
    if (sampler.Get1D() < q)
        break;
    beta /= 1 - q;
}
```

FURTHER READING

The first application of Monte Carlo to global illumination for creating synthetic images that we are aware of was described in Tregenza's paper on lighting design (Tregenza 1983). Cook's distribution ray-tracing algorithm computed glossy reflections, soft shadows from area lights, motion blur, and depth of field with Monte Carlo sampling (Cook, Porter, and Carpenter 1984; Cook 1986), although the general form of the light transport equation wasn't stated until papers by Kajiya (1986) and Immel, Cohen, and Greenberg (1986).

Additional important theoretical work on light transport has been done by Arvo (1993, 1995a), who has investigated the connection between rendering algorithms in graphics and previous work in *transport theory*, which applies classical physics to particles and their interactions to predict their overall behavior. Our description of the path integral form of the LTE follows the framework in Veach's Ph.D. thesis, which has thorough coverage of different forms of the LTE and its mathematical structure (Veach 1997).

Monte Carlo Techniques

Russian roulette and splitting were introduced to graphics by Arvo and Kirk (1990). Hall and Greenberg (1983) had previously suggested adaptively terminating ray trees by not tracing rays with less than some minimum contribution. Arvo and Kirk's technique is unbiased, although in some situations, bias and less noise may be the more desirable artifact.

Cook and collaborators first introduced random sampling for integration in rendering (Cook, Porter, and Carpenter 1984; Cook 1986), and Kajiya (1986) developed the general-purpose path-tracing algorithm. Other important early work on Monte Carlo in rendering includes Shirley's Ph.D. thesis (1990) and a paper by Kirk and Arvo (1991) on sources of bias in rendering algorithms. Shirley (1992) described a number of useful recipes for warping uniform random numbers to useful distributions for rendering.

Float 1062
Sampler::Get1D() 422
Spectrum::y() 325

Keller and collaborators have written extensively on the application of quasi–Monte Carlo integration in graphics (Keller 1996, 2001; Friedel and Keller 2000; Kollig and Keller 2000, 2002). Keller's "Quasi-Monte Carlo image synthesis in a nutshell" (2012) is a good introduction to quasi–Monte Carlo for rendering.

Talbot et al. (2005) applied *importance resampling* to rendering, showing that this variant of standard importance sampling is applicable to a number of problems in graphics, and Pegoraro et al. (2008a) implemented an approach that found sampling PDFs for global illumination over the course of rendering the image.

Many researchers have investigated techniques for adaptive sampling, adding more samples in parts of the integrand that are complex, and adaptive reconstruction, where final results are reconstructed from noisy samples with more sophisticated techniques than the simple reconstruction filters from Chapter 7. See Zwicker et al.'s survey article (2015) for a thorough summary of recent work in this area.

Sampling BSDFs

The approach for directly sampling the microfacet visible normal distribution implemented in Section 14.1.1 was developed by Heitz and d'Eon (2014). See also Heitz (2014a) for an overview of traditional sampling techniques for various microfacet distribution functions that sample the regular D function directly.

When dealing with refraction through rough dielectrics, a modified change of variables term is needed to account for the mapping from half vectors to outgoing direction. A model based on this approach was originally developed by Stam (2001); Walter et al. (2007) proposed improvements and provided an alternative geometric justification of the half vector mapping.

Lawrence et al. (2004) developed methods for sampling arbitrary BRDF models, including those based on measured reflectance data. They applied methods that factor the 4D BRDF into a product of two 2D functions, both of which are guaranteed to always be greater than 0, thus making it possible to use them as importance sampling distributions. Most of the recently developed parametric models for fitting BRDFs described in Chapter 8's "Further Reading" section have been developed with importance sampling in mind. The sampling technique for the FourierBSDF was developed by Jakob et al. (2014a).

A number of researchers have investigated effective sampling of hair reflection models (typically Marschner et al.'s model (2003)). See, for example, papers by Ou et al. (2012), Hery and Ramamoorthi (2012), and d'Eon et al. (2013). More recently, Pekelis et al. (2015) developed a more efficient approach to sampling the Marschner model.

The idea of applying statistical hypothesis tests to verify the correctness of graphics-related Monte Carlo sampling routines such as BSDF models was introduced by Subr and Arvo (2007a). The χ^2 test variant for validating the BSDF model implementations in pbrt was originally developed as part of the Mitsuba renderer by Jakob (2010).

Direct Lighting

Algorithms to render soft shadows from area lights were first developed by Amanatides (1984) and Cook, Porter, and Carpenter (1984). Shirley et al. (1996) derived methods for sampling a number of shapes for use as area light sources. Arvo showed how to sample the projection of a triangle on the sphere of directions with respect to a reference point; this approach can give better results than sampling the area of the triangle directly (Arvo 1995b). Ureña et al. (2013) and Pekelis and Hery (2014) developed analogous techniques for sampling projected quadrilateral light sources. The approach implemented in Sec-

FourierBSDF 555

tion 14.2.2 to convert an angle (θ, ϕ) in a cone to a point on a sphere was derived by Akalin (2015).

Subr and Arvo (2007b) developed an efficient technique for sampling environment map light sources that not only accounts for the $\cos \theta$ term from the scattering equation but also only generates samples in the hemisphere around the surface normal.

When environment maps are used for illuminating indoor scenes, many incident directions may be blocked by the building structure. Bashford-Rogers et al. (2013) developed a two-pass algorithm where a first pass from the camera finds directions that reach the environment map; this information is used to create sampling distributions that are used during a second rendering pass. Bitterli et al. (2015) developed an interesting solution to this issue: they rectify the environment map so that rectangular portals in the building map to rectangular regions of the environment map. In turn, at a given point receiving illumination, they compute the projection of portals to the outside and can efficiently sample the environment map using a summed area table.

As described in the "Further Reading" section of Chapter 12, a useful generalization of environment maps for illumination allows the emitted radiance to vary by both position and direction. Lu et al. (2015) developed techniques for efficiently importance sampling these light sources and describes previous work in this area.

The expense of tracing shadow rays to light sources can be significant; a number of interesting approaches have been developed to improve the efficiency of this part of the rendering computation. Billen et al. (2013) propose a technique where only a random subset of potential occluders are tested for intersections; a compensation term ensures that the result is unbiased. Following work shows how to use simplified geometry for some shadow tests while still computing the correct result overall (Billen et al. 2014). Another approach to reducing the cost of shadow rays is visibility caching, where the point-to-point visibility function's value is cached for clusters of points on surfaces in the scene (Clarberg and Akenine-Möller 2008b; Popov et al. 2013).

A number of approaches have been developed to efficiently render scenes with hundreds or thousands of light sources. (For densely occluded environments, many of the lights in the scene may have little or no contribution to the part of the scene visible from the camera.) Early work on this issue was done by Ward (1991) and Shirley et al. (1996). Wald et al. (2003) suggested rendering an image with path tracing and a very low sampling rate (e.g., one path per pixel), recording information about which of the light sources made some contribution to the image. This information is then used to set probabilities for sampling each light. Donikian et al. (2006) adaptively found PDFs for sampling lights through an iterative process of taking a number of light samples, noting which ones were effective, and reusing this information at nearby pixels. The "lightcuts" algorithm, described in the "Further Reading" section of Chapter 16, also addresses this problem.

pbrt's direct lighting routines are based on using multiple importance sampling to combine samples taken from the BSDF and the light sources' sampling distributions; while this works well in many cases, it can be ineffective in cases where the product of these two functions has a significantly different distribution from either one individually. A number of more efficient approaches have been developed to sample directly from the product distribution (Burke et al. 2005; Cline et al. 2006). Clarberg, Rousselle, and collaborators developed techniques based on representing BSDFs and illumination in the wavelet basis and efficiently sampling from their product (Clarberg et al. 2005; Rousselle et al. 2008; Clarberg and Akenine-Möller 2008a). Efficiency of the direct lighting calculation can be further improved by sampling from the *triple product* distribution of BSDF, illumination, and visibility; this issue was investigated by Ghosh and Heidrich (2006) and Clarberg and Akenine-Möller (2008b). Finally, Wang and Åkerlund (2009) have developed a technique that incorporates an approximation to the distribution of indirect illumination in the light sampling distribution used in these approaches.

Subr et al. (2014) analyzed the combination of multiple importance sampling and jittered sampling for direct lighting calculations and propose sampling improvements to improve convergence rates.

Other Topics

With full spectral rendering, it's sometimes necessary to perform a sampling operation for a ray based on a single wavelength from the SPD (e.g., with wavelength-dependent indices of refraction). For this case, Radziszewski et al. (2009) introduced an application of multiple importance sampling that reduces variance in this case.

Ward and collaborators developed the irradiance caching algorithm, which is described in a series of papers (Ward, Rubinstein, and Clear 1988; Ward 1994). The basic idea is to cache irradiance from indirect illumination at a sparse set of points on surfaces in the scene; because indirect lighting is generally slowly changing, irradiance can often be safely interpolated. Tabellion and Lamorlette (2004) described a number of additional improvements to irradiance caching that made it viable for rendering for movie productions. Křivánek and collaborators generalized irradiance caching to *radiance caching*, where a more complex directional distribution of incident radiance is stored, so that more accurate shading from glossy surfaces is possible (Křivánek et al. 2005). Recent work by Schwarzhaupt et al. proposed a better way of assessing the validity of a cache point using a second-order expansion of the incident lighting (Schwarzhaupt et al. 2012).

EXERCISES

◑ 14.1 One shortcoming of the current implementation of the BSDF::Sample_f() method is that if some of the BxDFs make a much larger contribution to the overall result than others, then uniformly choosing among them to determine a sampling distribution may be inefficient. Modify this method so that it instead chooses among the BxDFs according to their relative reflectances. (Don't forget to also update BSDF::Pdf() to account for this change.) Can you create a contrived set of parameters to a Material that causes this approach to be substantially better than the built-in one? Does this change have a noticeable effect on Monte Carlo efficiency for typical scenes?

◔ 14.2 Fix the buggy Sphere::Sample() and Disk::Sample() methods, which currently don't properly account for partial spheres and disks when they sample points on the surface. Create a scene that demonstrates the error from the current implementations and for which your solution is clearly an improvement.

14.3 It is possible to derive a sampling method for cylinder area light sources that only chooses points over the visible area as seen from the receiving point, similar to the improved sphere sampling method in this chapter (Gardner et al. 1987; Zimmerman 1995). Learn more about these methods, or rederive them yourself, and write a new implementation of `Cylinder::Sample()` that implements such an algorithm. Verify that pbrt still generates correct images with your method, and measure how much the improved version reduces variance for a fixed number of samples taken. How much does it improve efficiency? How do you explain any discrepancy between the amount of reduction in variance and the amount of improvement in efficiency?

14.4 The sampling approach implemented in `InfiniteAreaLight::Sample_Li()` is ineffective in scenes like indoor environments, where many directions are occluded by the building structure. One approach to this problem is to manually provide a representation of *portals* like windows that the light passes through. These portals can then be sampled by area to find paths that lead to the light. However, such an approach doesn't account for the directional radiance distribution of the light source.

Bitterli et al. (2015) suggested an improved method that causes rectangular portals to be rectangular areas in the environment map, which in turn can be sampled directly. Implement their approach as a new `InfiniteAreaLight` sampling method in pbrt, and measure the improvement in efficiency for rendering scenes where there is a substantial amount of occlusion between the part of the scene being rendered and the infinite light source.

14.5 The infinite area light importance sampling method implemented in this chapter doesn't perfectly match the distribution of the light source's emission distribution: recall that the emission function is computed with bilinear interpolation among image samples, but the sampling distribution is computed as a piecewise-constant function of a slightly blurred version of the texture map. In some cases, this discrepancy can lead to high variance when there are localized extremely bright texels. (In the worst case, consider a source that has a very small value at all texels except one, which is 10,000 times brighter than all of the others.) In that case, the value of the function may be much higher than predicted by the sampling PDFs at points very close to that sample, thus leading to high variance ($f(x)/p(x)$ is large).

Construct an environment map where this problem manifests itself in pbrt and fix the system so that the excessive variance goes away. One option is to modify the system so that the sampling distribution and the illumination function match perfectly by point sampling the environment map for lookups, rather than using bilinear filtering, though this can lead to undesirable image artifacts in the environment map, especially when directly visible from the camera. Can you find a way to only use the point-sampled environment map for direct lighting calculations but to use bilinear filtering for camera rays and rays that have only undergone specular reflection?

The other alternative is to modify the sampling distribution so that it matches the bilinearly filtered environment map values perfectly. Exact 2D sampling distributions for bilinear functions can be computed, though finding the sample value corresponding to a random variable is more computationally expensive, requiring solving a quadratic equation. Can you construct a scene where this overhead is worthwhile in return for the resulting variance reduction?

⊘ 14.6 To further improve efficiency, Russian roulette can be applied to skip tracing many of the shadow rays that make a low contribution to the final image: to implement this approach, tentatively compute the potential contribution of each shadow ray to the final overall radiance value before tracing the ray. If the contribution is below some threshold, apply Russian roulette to possibly skip tracing the ray. Recall that Russian roulette always increases variance; when evaluating the effectiveness of your implementation, you should consider its *efficiency*—how long it takes to render an image at a particular level of quality.

⊘ 14.7 Read Veach's description of efficiency-optimized Russian roulette, which adaptively chooses a threshold for applying Russian roulette (Veach 1997; Section 10.4.1). Implement this algorithm in pbrt, and evaluate its effectiveness in comparison to manually setting these thresholds.

⊘ 14.8 Implement a technique for generating samples from the product of the light and BSDF distributions; see the papers by Burke et al. (2005), Cline et al. (2006), Clarberg et al. (2005), and Rousselle et al. (2008). Compare the effectiveness of the approach you implement to the direct lighting calculation currently implemented in pbrt. Investigate how scene complexity (and, thus, how expensive shadow rays are to trace) affects the Monte Carlo efficiency of the two techniques.

⊘ 14.9 Clarberg and Akenine-Möller (2008b) and Popov et al. (2013) both described algorithms that performs visibility caching, computing, and interpolating information about light source visibility at points in the scene. Implement one of these methods and use it to improve the direct lighting calculation in pbrt. What sorts of scenes is it particularly effective for? Are there scenes for which it doesn't help?

⊘ 14.10 Investigate algorithms for rendering scenes with large numbers of light sources: see, for example, the papers by Ward (1991a), Shirley, Wang, and Zimmerman (1996), and Donikian et al. (2006) on this topic. Choose one of these approaches and implement it in pbrt. Run experiments with a number of scenes to evaluate the effectiveness of the approach that you implement.

⊘ 14.11 Modify pbrt so that the user can flag certain objects in the scene as being important sources of indirect lighting, and modify the PathIntegrator to sample points on those surfaces according to dA to generate some of the vertices in the paths it generates. Use multiple importance sampling to compute weights

PathIntegrator 875

for the path samples, incorporating the probability that they would have been sampled both with BSDF sampling and with this area sampling. How much can this approach reduce variance and improve efficiency for scenes with substantial indirect lighting? How much can it hurt if the user flags surfaces that actually make little or no contribution or if multiple importance sampling isn't used? Investigate generalizations of this approach that learn which objects are important sources of indirect lighting as rendering progresses so that the user doesn't need to supply this information ahead of time.

CHAPTER FIFTEEN

15 LIGHT TRANSPORT II: VOLUME RENDERING

Just as BSDFs characterize reflection from the surfaces in a scene, `Medium` class implementations represent scattering that occurs *between* surfaces; examples include atmospheric scattering effects such as haze, absorption in a stained glass window, or scattering by fat globules in a bottle of milk. Technically, all of these phenomena are due to surface interactions with a vast number of microscopic particles, though it is preferable to find a less cumbersome way of modeling them than considering them individually. With the models described in this chapter, the particles are assumed to be so numerous that they can be represented using statistical distributions instead of an explicit enumeration.

This chapter begins with an introduction of the equation of transfer, which describes the equilibrium distribution of radiance in scenes with participating media, and then presents a number of sampling methods that are useful for Monte Carlo integration with participating media. Given this foundation, the `VolPathIntegrator` can be introduced—it extends the `PathIntegrator` to solve the light transport equation in the presence of participating media.

After Section 15.4 describes how to sample from BSSRDF distributions, Section 15.5 then describes the implementation of a BSSRDF that models the aggregate light scattering in media bounded by refractive surfaces. Although the approach is expressed in terms of radiance leaving from and arriving at surfaces, it is included in this chapter since its implementation is based on an approximate solution to the equation of transfer in participating media.

Physically Based Rendering: From Theory To Implementation.
http://dx.doi.org/10.1016/B978-0-12-800645-0.50015-4

15.1 THE EQUATION OF TRANSFER

The equation of transfer is the fundamental equation that governs the behavior of light in a medium that absorbs, emits, and scatters radiation. It accounts for all of the volume scattering processes described in Chapter 11—absorption, emission, and in- and out-scattering—to give an equation that describes the distribution of radiance in an environment. The light transport equation is in fact a special case of the equation of transfer, simplified by the lack of participating media and specialized for scattering from surfaces.

In its most basic form, the equation of transfer is an integro-differential equation that describes how the radiance along a beam changes at a point in space. It can be transformed into a pure integral equation that describes the effect of participating media from the infinite number of points along a ray. It can be derived in a straightforward manner by subtracting the effects of the scattering processes that reduce energy along a beam (absorption and out-scattering) from the processes that increase energy along it (emission and in-scattering).

Recall the source term L_s from Section 11.1.4: it gives the change in radiance at a point p in a particular direction ω due to emission and in-scattered light from other points in the medium:

$$L_s(p, \omega) = L_e(p, \omega) + \sigma_s(p, \omega) \int_{S^2} p(p, \omega', \omega) \, L_i(p, \omega') \, d\omega'.$$

The source term accounts for all of the processes that add radiance to a ray.

The attenuation coefficient, $\sigma_t(p, \omega)$, accounts for all processes that reduce radiance at a point: absorption and out-scattering. The differential equation that describes its effect is

$$dL_o(p + t\omega, \omega) = -\sigma_t(p, \omega) \, L_i(p, -\omega) \, dt.$$

The overall differential change in radiance at a point p' along a ray is found by adding these two effects together to get the integro-differential form of the equation of transfer:[1]

$$\frac{\partial}{\partial t} L_o(p + t\omega, \omega) = -\sigma_t(p, \omega) L_i(p, -\omega) + L_s(p, \omega). \qquad (15.1)$$

With suitable boundary conditions, this equation can be transformed to a pure integral equation. For example, if we assume that there are no surfaces in the scene so that the rays are never blocked and have an infinite length, the integral equation of transfer is

$$L_i(p, \omega) = \int_0^\infty T_r(p' \to p) L_s(p', -\omega) \, dt,$$

where $p' = p + t\omega$ (Figure 15.1). The meaning of this equation is reasonably intuitive: it just says that the radiance arriving at a point from a given direction is contributed to by the added radiance along all points along the ray from the point. The amount of added radiance at each point along the ray that reaches the ray's origin is reduced by the total beam transmittance from the ray's origin to the point.

---

1   It is an integro-differential equation due to the integral over the sphere in the source term.

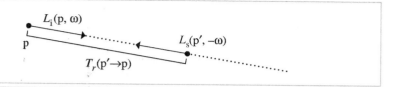

Figure 15.1: The equation of transfer gives the incident radiance at point $L_i(p, \omega)$ accounting for the effect of participating media. At each point along the ray, the source term $L_s(p', -\omega)$ gives the differential radiance added at the point due to scattering and emission. This radiance is then attenuated by the beam transmittance $T_r(p' \to p)$ from the point p' to the ray's origin.

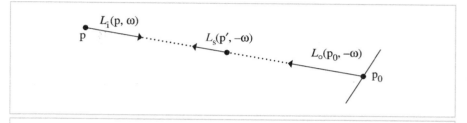

Figure 15.2: For a finite ray that intersects a surface, the incident radiance, $L_i(p, \omega)$, is equal to the outgoing radiance from the surface, $L_o(p_0, -\omega)$, times the beam transmittance to the surface plus the added radiance from all points along the ray from p to p_0.

More generally, if there are reflecting and/or emitting surfaces in the scene, rays don't necessarily have infinite length and the first surface that a ray hits affects its radiance, adding outgoing radiance from the surface at the point and preventing radiance from points along the ray beyond the intersection point from contributing to radiance at the ray's origin. If a ray (p, ω) intersects a surface at some point p_0 at a parametric distance t along the ray, then the integral equation of transfer is

$$L_i(p, \omega) = T_r(p_0 \to p)L_o(p_0, -\omega) + \int_0^t T_r(p' \to p)L_s(p', -\omega)dt', \qquad [15.2]$$

where $p_0 = p + t\omega$ is the point on the surface and $p' = p + t'\omega$ are points along the ray (Figure 15.2).

This equation describes the two effects that contribute to radiance along the ray. First, reflected radiance back along the ray from the surface is given by the L_o term, which gives the emitted and reflected radiance from the surface. This radiance may be attenuated by the participating media; the beam transmittance from the ray origin to the point p_0 accounts for this. The second term accounts for the added radiance along the ray due to volume scattering and emission but only up to the point where the ray intersects the surface; points beyond that one don't affect the radiance along the ray.

⋆ 15.1.1 GENERALIZED PATH SPACE

Just as it was helpful to express the LTE as a sum over paths of scattering events, it's also helpful to express the integral equation of transfer in this form. Doing so is a prerequisite for constructing participating medium-aware bidirectional integrators in Chapter 16.

Recall how in Section 14.4.4, the surface form of the LTE was repeatedly substituted into itself to derive the path space contribution function for a path of length n

$$P(\bar{p}_n) = \underbrace{\int_A \int_A \cdots \int_A}_{n-1} L_e(p_n \rightarrow p_{n-1})\, T(\bar{p}_n)\, dA(p_2) \cdots dA(p_n),$$

where the throughput $T(\bar{p}_n)$ was defined as

$$T(\bar{p}_n) = \prod_{i=1}^{n-1} f(p_{i+1} \rightarrow p_i \rightarrow p_{i-1})\, G(p_{i+1} \leftrightarrow p_i).$$

This previous definition only works for surfaces, but using a similar approach of substituting the integral equation of transfer, a medium-aware path integral can be derived. The derivation is laborious and we will just present the final result here. Refer to Pauly et al. (2000) and Chapter 3 of Jakob's Ph.D. thesis (2013) for a full derivation.

Previously, integration occurred over a Cartesian product of surface locations A^n. Now, we'll need a formal way of writing down an integral that can consider an arbitrary sequence of both 2D surface locations A and 3D positions in a participating medium V. First, we'll focus only on a specific arrangement of n surface and medium vertices encoded in a binary configuration vector c. The associated set of paths is given by a Cartesian product of surface locations and medium locations,

$$\mathcal{P}_n^c = \mathop{\times}_{i=1}^{n} \begin{cases} A, & \text{if } c_i = 0 \\ V, & \text{if } c_i = 1. \end{cases}$$

The set of all paths of length n is the union of the above sets over all possible configuration vectors:

$$\mathcal{P}_n = \bigcup_{c \in \{0,1\}^n} \mathcal{P}_n^c.$$

Next, we define a *measure*, which provides an abstract notion of the volume of a subset $D \subseteq \mathcal{P}_n$ that is essential for integration. The measure we'll use simply sums up the product of surface area and volume associated with the individual vertices in each of the path spaces of specific configurations.

$$\mu_n(D) = \sum_{c \in \{0,1\}^n} \mu_n^c(D \cap \mathcal{P}_n^c) \quad \text{where } \mu_n^c(D) = \int_D \prod_{i=1}^{n} \begin{cases} dA(p_i), & \text{if } c_i = 0 \\ dV(p_i), & \text{if } c_i = 1. \end{cases}$$

The generalized path contribution $\hat{P}(\bar{p}_n)$ can now be written as

$$\hat{P}(\bar{p}_n) = \int_{\mathcal{P}_{n-1}} L_e(p_n \rightarrow p_{n-1})\, \hat{T}(\bar{p}_n)\, d\mu_{n-1}(p_2, \ldots, p_n).$$

Due to the measure defined earlier, this is really a sum of many integrals considering all possible sequences of surface and volume scattering events.

In this framework, the path throughput function $\hat{T}(\bar{p}_n)$ is defined as:

$$\hat{T}(\bar{p}_n) = \prod_{i=1}^{n-1} \hat{f}(p_{i+1} \to p_i \to p_{i-1}) \, \hat{G}(p_{i+1} \leftrightarrow p_i).$$ [15.3]

It now refers to a generalized scattering distribution function $\hat{f}$ and geometric term $\hat{G}$. The former simply falls back to the BSDF or phase function (multiplied by σ_s) depending on the type of the vertex p_i.

$$\hat{f}(p_{i+1} \to p_i \to p_{i-1}) = \begin{cases} \sigma_s \, p \, (p_{i+1} \to p_i \to p_{i-1}), & \text{if } p_i \in V \\ f(p_{i+1} \to p_i \to p_{i-1}), & \text{if } p_i \in A. \end{cases}$$ [15.4]

Equation (14.14) in Section 14.4.3 originally defined the geometric term G as

$$G(p \leftrightarrow p') = V(p \leftrightarrow p') \frac{|\cos\theta| \, |\cos\theta'|}{\| p - p' \|^2}.$$

A generalized form of this geometric term is given by

$$\hat{G}(p \leftrightarrow p') = V(p \leftrightarrow p') \, T_r(p \to p') \frac{C_p(p, p') \, C_{p'}(p', p)}{\| p - p' \|^2},$$ [15.5]

where the T_r term now also accounts for transmittance between the two points, and

$$C_p(p, p') = \begin{cases} \left| n_p \cdot \frac{p - p'}{\|p - p'\|} \right|, & \text{if } p \text{ is a surface vertex} \\ 1, & \text{otherwise} \end{cases}$$

only incorporates the absolute angle cosine between the connection segment and the normal direction when the underlying vertex p is located on a surface.

15.2 SAMPLING VOLUME SCATTERING

Before proceeding to algorithms that model the effect of light scattering in participating media, we'll first define some building-block functionality for sampling from distributions related to participating media and for computing the beam transmittance for spatially varying media.

The Medium interface defines a Sample() method, which takes a world space ray (p, ω) and possibly samples a medium scattering interaction along it. The input ray will generally have been intersected against the scene geometry; thus, implementations of this method shouldn't ever sample a medium interaction at a point on the ray beyond its t_{max} value. Without loss of generality, the following discussion assumes that there is always a surface at some distance $t_{max} < \infty$.

⟨*Medium Interface*⟩ +≡   684
```
virtual Spectrum Sample(const Ray &ray, Sampler &sampler,
    MemoryArena &arena, MediumInteraction *mi) const = 0;
```

The objective of this method is to sample the integral form of the equation of transfer, Equation (15.2), which consists of a surface and a medium-related term:

$$L_i(p, \omega) = T_r(p_0 \to p)L_o(p_0, -\omega) + \int_0^t T_r(p + t\omega \to p)L_s(p + t\omega, -\omega) \, dt,$$

where $p_0 = p + t_{max} \, \omega$ is the point on the surface. We will neglect the effect of medium emission and assume directionally constant medium properties, in which case the source term is given by

$$L_s(p, \omega) = \sigma_s(p) \int_{S^2} p(p, \omega', \omega) \, L_i(p, \omega') \, d\omega'. \qquad [15.6]$$

Two cases can occur: if Sample() doesn't sample an interaction on the given ray interval $[0, t_{max}]$, then the surface-related term $T_r(p_0 \to p)L_o(p_0, -\omega)$ should be estimated. If it does sample an interaction, the second integral term is to be estimated, and the provided MediumInteraction should be initialized accordingly.

Suppose that $p_t(t)$ denotes the probability per unit distance of generating an interaction at position $p + t\omega$. Due to the possibility of not sampling a medium interaction, this function generally doesn't integrate to 1, and we define p_{surf} as the associated discrete probability of sampling the surface term:

$$p_{surf} = 1 - \int_0^{t_{max}} p_t(t) \, dt$$

With these definitions, we can now specify the semantics of Sample(), which differs from previously encountered techniques for scattering functions like BSDF::Sample_f() in that it does not provide the caller with separate information about the function value and PDF at the sampled position. This information is not generally needed, and some medium models (specifically, the heterogeneous medium) admit more efficient sampling schemes when it is possible to compute *ratios* of these quantities instead.

When the surface term is selected, the method should return a weight equal to

$$\beta_{surf} = \frac{T_r(p \to p + t\omega)}{p_{surf}}, \qquad [15.7]$$

which corresponds to sampling the first summand. Note that the value of the outgoing radiance $L_o(p_0, -\omega)$ is not included in β_{surf}; it is the responsibility of the caller to account for this term. In the medium case, the method returns

$$\beta_{med} = \frac{\sigma_s(p + t\omega) \, T_r(p \to p + t\omega)}{p_t(t)}, \qquad [15.8]$$

which corresponds to sampling all medium-related terms except for the integral over in-scattered light in Equation (15.6), which must be handled separately.

The scattering coefficient and transmittance allow for spectral variation, hence this method returns a Spectrum-valued weighting factor to update the path throughput weight β up to the surface or medium scattering event.

As is generally the case for Monte Carlo integration, estimators like β_{surf} and β_{med} admit a variety of sampling techniques that all produce the desired distribution. The implementation of the heterogeneous medium will make use of this fact to provide an implementation that is considerably more efficient than the canonical sampling approach based on the inversion method.

So that calling code can easily determine whether the provided MediumInteraction was initialized by Sample(), MediumInteraction provides an IsValid() method that takes

BSDF::Sample_f() 832

MediumInteraction 688

advantage of the fact that any time a medium scattering event has been sampled, the phase function pointer will be set.

⟨*MediumInteraction Public Methods*⟩ +≡   688
    `bool IsValid() const { return phase != nullptr; }`

15.2.1 HOMOGENEOUS MEDIUM

The `HomogeneousMedium` implementation of this method is fairly straightforward; the only complexities come from needing to handle attenuation coefficients that vary by wavelength.

⟨*HomogeneousMedium Method Definitions*⟩ +≡
```
Spectrum HomogeneousMedium::Sample(const Ray &ray, Sampler &sampler,
        MemoryArena &arena, MediumInteraction *mi) const {
    ⟨Sample a channel and distance along the ray 894⟩
    ⟨Compute the transmittance and sampling density 894⟩
    ⟨Return weighting factor for scattering from homogeneous medium 894⟩
}
```

In Section 13.3.1 we derived the sampling method for an exponential distribution defined over $[0, \infty)$. For $f(t) = e^{-\sigma_t t}$, it is

$$t = -\frac{\ln(1 - \xi)}{\sigma_t},$$ (15.9)

with PDF

$$p_t(t) = \sigma_t e^{-\sigma_t t}.$$ (15.10)

However, the attenuation coefficient σ_t in general varies by wavelength. It is not desirable to sample multiple points in the medium, so a uniform sample is first used to select a spectral channel i; the corresponding scalar σ_t^i value is then used to sample a distance along the distribution

$$\hat{p}_t^i(t) = \sigma_t^i e^{-\sigma_t^i t},$$

using the technique from Equation (15.9). The resulting sampling density is the average of the individual strategies p_t^i:

$$\hat{p}_t(t) = \frac{1}{n} \sum_{i=1}^{n} \sigma_t^i e^{-\sigma_t^i t}.$$ (15.11)

The (discrete) probability of sampling a surface interaction at $t = t_{max}$ is the complement of generating a medium scattering event between $t = 0$ and $t = t_{max}$. This works out to a probability equal to the average transmittance over all n spectral channels:

$$P_{surf} = 1 - \int_0^{t_{max}} \hat{p}_t(t) \, dt = \frac{1}{n} \sum_{i=1}^{n} e^{-\sigma_t^i t_{max}}.$$ (15.12)

The implementation draws a sample according to Equation (15.11); if the sampled distance is before the ray–primitive intersection (if any), then a medium scattering event is recorded by initializing the `MediumInteraction`. Otherwise, the sampled point in the medium is ignored, and corresponding surface interaction should be used as the next

MediumInteraction 688

MediumInteraction::phase 688

MemoryArena 1074

Ray 73

Sampler 421

Spectrum 315

path vertex by the integrator. This sampling approach is naturally efficient: the probability of generating a medium interaction instead of the surface interaction is exactly equal to 1 minus the beam transmittance for the selected wavelength. Thus, given optically thin media (or a short ray extent), the surface interaction is more often used, and for thick media (or longer rays), a medium interaction is more likely to be sampled.

⟨*Sample a channel and distance along the ray*⟩ ≡   893
```
int channel = std::min((int)(sampler.Get1D() * Spectrum::nSamples),
                        Spectrum::nSamples - 1);
Float dist = -std::log(1 - sampler.Get1D()) / sigma_t[channel];
Float t = std::min(dist * ray.d.Length(), ray.tMax);
bool sampledMedium = t < ray.tMax;
if (sampledMedium)
    *mi = MediumInteraction(ray(t), -ray.d, ray.time, this,
                    ARENA_ALLOC(arena, HenyeyGreenstein)(g));
```

In either case, the beam transmittance Tr is easily computed using Beer's law, Equation (11.3), just as in the HomogeneousMedium::Tr() method.

⟨*Compute the transmittance and sampling density*⟩ ≡   893
```
Spectrum Tr = Exp(-sigma_t * std::min(t, MaxFloat) * ray.d.Length());
```

Finally, the method computes the sample density using Equations (15.11) or (15.12) and returns resulting sampling weight β_{surf} and β_{med}, depending on the value of sampled Medium.

⟨*Return weighting factor for scattering from homogeneous medium*⟩ ≡   893
```
Spectrum density = sampledMedium ? (sigma_t * Tr) : Tr;
Float pdf = 0;
for (int i = 0; i < Spectrum::nSamples; ++i)
    pdf += density[i];
pdf *= 1 / (Float)Spectrum::nSamples;
return sampledMedium ? (Tr * sigma_s / pdf) : (Tr / pdf);
```

15.2.2 HETEROGENEOUS MEDIUM

In the case of the GridDensityMedium, extra effort is necessary to deal with the medium's heterogeneous nature. When the spatial variation can be decomposed into uniform regions (e.g., piecewise constant voxels), a technique known as *regular tracking* applies standard homogeneous medium techniques to the voxels individually; a disadvantage of this approach is that it becomes costly when there are many voxels. Since the GridDensityMedium relies on linear interpolation, this approach cannot be used.

Other techniques build on a straightforward generalization of the homogeneous sampling PDF from Equation (15.10) with a spatially varying attenuation coefficient:

$$p_t(t) = \sigma_t(t)\, e^{-\int_0^t \sigma_t(t')dt'}, \qquad [15.13]$$

where $\sigma_t(t) = \sigma_t(p + t\omega)$ evaluates the attenuation at distance t along the ray. The most commonly used method for importance sampling Equation (15.13), is known as *ray*

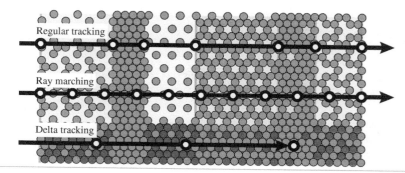

Figure 15.3: Ray Marching and Delta Tracking in a Medium with Density that Varies Along the Horizontal Axis. (top) Regular tracking partitions the medium into a number of homogeneous sub-regions and relies on standard techniques for dealing with the individual homogeneous regions. (middle) Ray marching partitions the ray into a number of discrete segments and approximates the transmittance through each one. (bottom) Delta tracking effectively considers a medium that is "filled" with additional virtual particles (red) until it reaches a uniform density. Image courtesy of Novák et al. (2014).

marching. This method inverts an approximate cumulative distribution by partitioning the range $[0, t_{max}]$ into a number of subintervals, numerically approximating the integral in each interval, and finally inverting this discrete representation. Unfortunately discretizing the problem in this way introduces systemic statistical bias, which means that an Integrator using ray marching generally won't converge to the right result (even when an infinite number of samples per pixel is used). Furthermore, this bias can manifest itself in the form of distracting visual artifacts.

For this reason, we prefer an alternative unbiased approach proposed by Woodcock et al. (1965) that was originally developed to simulate volumetric scattering of neutrons in atomic reactors. This technique is known as *delta tracking* and is easiest to realize when the attenuation coefficient σ_t is monochromatic. Our implementation includes an assertion test (not shown here) to verify that this is indeed the case. Note that the scattering and absorption coefficients are still permitted to vary with respect to wavelength—however, their sum $\sigma_t = \sigma_s + \sigma_a$ must be uniform.

Figure 15.3 compares regular tracking, ray marching, and delta tracking. Delta tracking can be interpreted as filling the medium with additional (virtual) particles until its attenuation coefficient is constant everywhere. Sampling the resulting homogeneous medium is then easily accomplished using the basic exponential scheme from Equation (15.9). However, whenever an interaction with a particle occurs, it is still necessary to determine if it involved a "real" or a "virtual" particle (in which case the interaction is disregarded). The elegant insight of Woodcock et al. was that this decision can be made randomly based on the local fraction of "real" particles, which leads to a distribution of samples matching Equation (15.13).

The following fragment is part of the GridDensityMedium::GridDensityMedium() constructor; its purpose is to precompute the inverse of the maximum density scale factor over the entire medium, which will be a useful quantity in the delta tracking implementation discussed next.

GridDensityMedium::
  GridDensityMedium()
  690

Integrator 25

⟨*Precompute values for Monte Carlo sampling of* GridDensityMedium⟩ ≡   690
```
sigma_t = (sigma_a + sigma_s)[0];
Float maxDensity = 0;
for (int i = 0; i < nx * ny * nz; ++i)
    maxDensity = std::max(maxDensity, density[i]);
invMaxDensity = 1 / maxDensity;
```

⟨*GridDensityMedium Private Data*⟩ +≡   690
```
Float sigma_t;
Float invMaxDensity;
```

The Sample() method begins by transforming the ray into the medium coordinate system and normalizing the ray direction; ray.tMax is scaled appropriately to account for the normalization.

⟨*GridDensityMedium Method Definitions*⟩ +≡
```
Spectrum GridDensityMedium::Sample(const Ray &rWorld, Sampler &sampler,
        MemoryArena &arena, MediumInteraction *mi) const {
    Ray ray = WorldToMedium(Ray(rWorld.o, Normalize(rWorld.d),
                                rWorld.tMax * rWorld.d.Length()));
    ⟨Compute [tmin, tmax] interval of ray's overlap with medium bounds 896⟩
    ⟨Run delta-tracking iterations to sample a medium interaction 897⟩
}
```

Next, the implementation computes the parametric range of the ray's overlap with the medium's bounds, which are the unit cube $[0, 1]^3$. This step is technically not required for correct operation but is generally a good idea: reducing the length of the considered ray segment translates into a correspondingly smaller number of delta tracking iterations.

⟨*Compute [tmin, tmax] interval of* ray's *overlap with medium bounds*⟩ ≡   896, 898
```
const Bounds3f b(Point3f(0, 0, 0), Point3f(1, 1, 1));
Float tMin, tMax;
if (!b.IntersectP(ray, &tMin, &tMax))
    return Spectrum(1.f);
```

Assuming that the maximum extinction value throughout the medium is given by $\sigma_{t,\max}$, each delta-tracking iteration i performs a standard exponential step through the uniform medium:

$$t_i = t_{i-1} - \frac{\ln(1 - \xi_{2i})}{\sigma_{t,\max}},$$

where $t_0 = t_{\min}$. These steps are repeated until one of two stopping criteria is satisfied: first, if $t_i > t_{\max}$ then we have left the medium without an interaction and Medium::Sample() hasn't sampled a scattering event. Alternatively, the loop may be terminated at each iteration i with probability $\sigma_t(t_i)/\sigma_{t,\max}$, the local fraction of "real" particles. This random decision consumes ξ_{2i+1}, the second of two uniform samples per iteration i.

⟨*Run delta-tracking iterations to sample a medium interaction*⟩ ≡   896

```
Float t = tMin;
while (true) {
    t -= std::log(1 - sampler.Get1D()) * invMaxDensity / sigma_t;
    if (t >= tMax)
        break;
    if (Density(ray(t)) * invMaxDensity > sampler.Get1D()) {
        ⟨Populate mi with medium interaction information and return 897⟩
    }
}
return Spectrum(1.f);
```

The probability of not sampling a medium interaction is equal to the transmittance of the ray segment $[t_{\min}, t_{\max}]$; hence 1.0 is returned for the sampling weight β_{surf} according to Equation (15.7). The medium interaction case resembles the fragment ⟨*Sample a channel and distance along the ray*⟩.

⟨*Populate* mi *with medium interaction information and return*⟩ ≡   897

```
PhaseFunction *phase = ARENA_ALLOC(arena, HenyeyGreenstein)(g);
*mi = MediumInteraction(rWorld(t), -rWorld.d, rWorld.time, this, phase);
return sigma_s / sigma_t;
```

Finally, we must also provide an implementation of the Tr() method to compute the transmittance along a ray segment. Consider the pseudocode of the following simplistic implementation that performs a call to Sample() and returns 1.0 if the ray passed through the segment $[0, t_{\max}]$ and 0.0 when a medium interaction occurred along the way. This effectively turns the transmittance function into a binary random variable.

```
Float Tr(ray, sampler) {
    if (Sample(ray, sampler, ...) fails)
        return 1.0;
    else
        return 0.0;
}
```

Since the probability of passing through the medium is equal to the transmittance, this random variable has the correct mean and could be used in the context of unbiased Monte Carlo integration. Calling Tr() many times and averaging the result would produce an increasingly accurate estimate of the transmittance, though this will generally be too costly to do in practice. On the other hand, using the naive binary implementation leads to a high amount of variance.

Novák et al. (2014) observed that this binary-valued function can be interpreted as an instance of Russian roulette. However, instead of randomly terminating the algorithm with a value of zero in each iteration, we could also remove the Russian roulette logic and simply multiply the transmittance by the probability of continuation. The resulting estimator has the same mean with a considerably lower variance. We will use this approach in the implementation of GridDensityMedium::Tr().

⟨*GridDensityMedium Method Definitions*⟩ +≡
```
Spectrum GridDensityMedium::Tr(const Ray &rWorld,
                              Sampler &sampler) const {
    Ray ray = WorldToMedium(Ray(rWorld.o, Normalize(rWorld.d),
                            rWorld.tMax * rWorld.d.Length()));
    ⟨Compute [tmin, tmax] interval of ray's overlap with medium bounds 896⟩
    ⟨Perform ratio tracking to estimate the transmittance value 898⟩
}
```

The beginning of the Tr() method matches Sample(). The loop body is also identical
except for the last line, which multiplies a running product by the ratio of real particles
to hypothetical particles. (Novák referred to this scheme as *ratio tracking*).

⟨*Perform ratio tracking to estimate the transmittance value*⟩ ≡   898
```
Float Tr = 1, t = tMin;
while (true) {
    t -= std::log(1 - sampler.Get1D()) * invMaxDensity / sigma_t;
    if (t >= tMax)
        break;
    Float density = Density(ray(t));
    Tr *= 1 - std::max((Float)0, density * invMaxDensity);
}
return Spectrum(Tr);
```

15.2.3 SAMPLING PHASE FUNCTIONS

It is also useful to be able to draw samples from the distribution described by phase
functions—applications include applying multiple importance sampling to computing
direct lighting in participating media as well as for sampling scattered directions for
indirect lighting samples in participating media. For these applications, PhaseFunction
implementations must implement the Sample_p() method, which samples an incident
direction ω_i given the outgoing direction ω_o and a sample value in $[0, 1)^2$.

Note that, unlike the BxDF sampling methods, Sample_p() doesn't return both the phase
function's value and its PDF. Rather, pbrt assumes that phase functions are sampled
with PDFs that perfectly match their distributions. In conjunction with the requirement that phase functions themselves be normalized (Equation (11.4)), a single return value encodes both values. When the value of the PDF alone is needed, a call to
PhaseFunction::p() suffices.

⟨*PhaseFunction Interface*⟩ +≡   681
```
virtual Float Sample_p(const Vector3f &wo, Vector3f *wi,
                       const Point2f &u) const = 0;
```

The PDF for the Henyey–Greenstein phase function is separable into θ and ϕ components, with $p(\phi) = 1/(2\pi)$ as usual. The main task is to sample $\cos\theta$.

⟨*HenyeyGreenstein Method Definitions*⟩ +≡
```
Float HenyeyGreenstein::Sample_p(const Vector3f &wo, Vector3f *wi,
        const Point2f &u) const {
    ⟨Compute cos θ for Henyey–Greenstein sample 899⟩
    ⟨Compute direction wi for Henyey–Greenstein sample 899⟩
    return PhaseHG(-cosTheta, g);
}
```

For Henyey–Greenstein, the distribution for θ is

$$\cos\theta = \frac{1}{2g}\left(1 + g^2 - \left(\frac{1 - g^2}{1 - g + 2g\xi}\right)^2\right)$$

if $g \neq 0$; otherwise, $\cos\theta = 1 - 2\xi$ gives a uniform sampling over the sphere of directions.

⟨*Compute* cos θ *for Henyey–Greenstein sample*⟩ ≡   899
```
Float cosTheta;
if (std::abs(g) < 1e-3)
    cosTheta = 1 - 2 * u[0];
else {
    Float sqrTerm = (1 - g * g) /
                    (1 - g + 2 * g * u[0]);
    cosTheta = (1 + g * g - sqrTerm * sqrTerm) / (2 * g);
}
```

Given the angles $(\cos\theta, \phi)$, what should now be a familiar approach converts them to the direction ω_i.

⟨*Compute direction* wi *for Henyey–Greenstein sample*⟩ ≡   899
```
Float sinTheta = std::sqrt(std::max((Float)0,
                                1 - cosTheta * cosTheta));
Float phi = 2 * Pi * u[1];
Vector3f v1, v2;
CoordinateSystem(wo, &v1, &v2);
*wi = SphericalDirection(sinTheta, cosTheta, phi, v1, v2, -wo);
```

15.3 VOLUMETRIC LIGHT TRANSPORT

These sampling building blocks make it possible to implement various light transport algorithms in participating media. We can now implement the fragments in the EstimateDirect() function from Section 14.3.1 that handle the cases related to participating media.

First, after a light has been sampled, if the interaction is a scattering event in participating media, it's necessary to compute the value of the phase function for the outgoing direction and the incident illumination direction as well as the value of the PDF for sampling that direction for multiple importance sampling. Because we assume that phase functions are sampled perfectly, these values are the same.

⟨*Evaluate phase function for light sampling strategy*⟩ ≡   859
```
const MediumInteraction &mi = (const MediumInteraction &)it;
Float p = mi.phase->p(mi.wo, wi);
f = Spectrum(p);
scatteringPdf = p;
```

The direct lighting calculation needs to take a sample from the phase function's distribution. Sample_p() provides this capability; as described earlier, the value it returns gives both the phase function's value and the PDF's.

⟨*Sample scattered direction for medium interactions*⟩ ≡   860
```
const MediumInteraction &mi = (const MediumInteraction &)it;
Float p = mi.phase->Sample_p(mi.wo, &wi, uScattering);
f = Spectrum(p);
scatteringPdf = p;
```

15.3.1 PATH TRACING

The VolPathIntegrator is a SamplerIntegrator that accounts for scattering and attenuation from participating media as well as scattering from surfaces. It is defined in the files integrators/volpath.h and integrators/volpath.cpp and has a general structure that is very similar to the PathIntegrator, so here we will only discuss the differences between those two classes. See Figures 15.4 and 15.5 for images rendered with this integrator that show off the importance of accounting for multiple scattering in participating media.

As a SamplerIntegrator, the VolPathIntegrator's main responsibility is to implement the Li() method. The general structure of its implementation is very similar to that of PathIntegrator::Li(), though with a few small changes related to participating media.

⟨*VolPathIntegrator Method Definitions*⟩ ≡
```
Spectrum VolPathIntegrator::Li(const RayDifferential &r,
        const Scene &scene, Sampler &sampler, MemoryArena &arena,
        int depth) const {
    Spectrum L(0.f), beta(1.f);
    RayDifferential ray(r);
    bool specularBounce = false;
    for (int bounces = 0; ; ++bounces) {
        ⟨Intersect ray with scene and store intersection in isect 877⟩
        ⟨Sample the participating medium, if present 901⟩
        ⟨Handle an interaction with a medium or a surface 902⟩
        ⟨Possibly terminate the path with Russian roulette 879⟩
    }
    return L;
}
```

At each step in sampling the scattering path, the ray is first intersected with the surfaces in the scene to find the closest surface intersection, if any. Next, participating media are accounted for with a call to the Medium::Sample() method, which initializes the provided MediumInteraction if a medium interaction should be the next vertex in the path. In

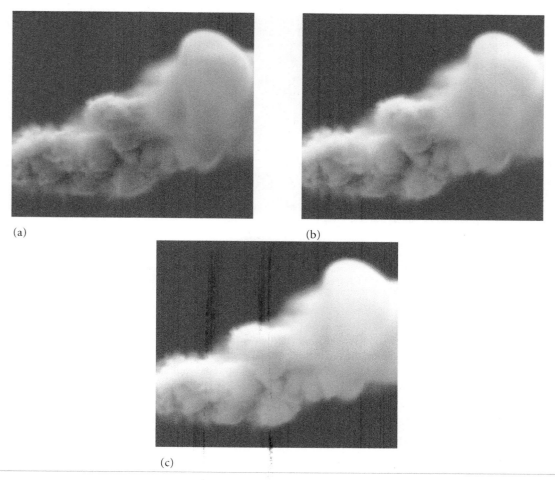

(a)

(b)

(c)

Figure 15.4: Volumetric Path Tracing. (a) Heterogeneous smoke data set rendered with direct lighting only. (b) Rendered with path tracing with a maximum depth of 5. (c) Path tracing with a maximum depth of 25. For this medium, which has an albedo of $\rho = 0.7$, multiple scattering has a significant effect on the final result. For (c), 1024 samples per pixel were required for this noise-free result.

either case, Sample() also returns a factor accounting for the beam transmittance and sampling PDF to either the surface or medium interaction.

⟨*Sample the participating medium, if present*⟩ ≡   900
```
MediumInteraction mi;
if (ray.medium)
    beta *= ray.medium->Sample(ray, sampler, arena, &mi);
if (beta.IsBlack())
    break;
```

In scenes with very dense scattering media, the effort spent on first finding surface intersections will often be wasted, as Medium::Sample() will usually generate a medium

Figure 15.5: Homogeneous Volumetric Scattering in Liquid. Scattering in the liquid is modeled with participating media and rendered with the `VolPathIntegrator`. (*Scene courtesy "guismo" from blendswap.com*.)

interaction instead. For such scenes, a more efficient implementation would be to first sample a medium interaction, updating the ray's `tMax` value accordingly before intersecting the ray with primitives in the scene. In turn, surface intersection tests would be much more efficient, as the ray to be tested would often be fairly short. (Further investigating and addressing this issue is left for Exercise 15.5.)

Depending on whether the sampled interaction for this ray is within participating media or at a point on a surface, one of two fragments handles computing the direct illumination at the point and sampling the next direction.

⟨*Handle an interaction with a medium or a surface*⟩ ≡   900
```
if (mi.IsValid()) {
    ⟨Handle scattering at point in medium for volumetric path tracer 902⟩
} else {
    ⟨Handle scattering at point on surface for volumetric path tracer⟩
}
```

Thanks to the fragments defined earlier in this section, the `UniformSampleOneLight()` function already supports estimating direct illumination at points in participating media, so we just need to pass the `MediumInteraction` for the sampled interaction to it. The direction for the ray leaving the medium interaction is then easily found with a call to `Sample_p()`.

⟨*Handle scattering at point in medium for volumetric path tracer*⟩ ≡   902
```
L += beta * UniformSampleOneLight(mi, scene, arena, sampler, true);
Vector3f wo = -ray.d, wi;
mi.phase->Sample_p(wo, &wi, sampler.Get2D());
ray = mi.SpawnRay(wi);
```

For scattering from surfaces, the computation performed is almost exactly the same as the regular `PathIntegrator`, except that attenuation of radiance from light sources to surface intersection points is incorporated by calling `VisibilityTester::Tr()` instead of `VisibilityTester::Unoccluded()` when sampling direct illumination. Because these differences are minor, we won't include the corresponding code here.

*15.4 SAMPLING SUBSURFACE REFLECTION FUNCTIONS

We'll now implement techniques to sample the subsurface scattering equation introduced in Section 5.6.2, building on the BSSRDF interface introduced in Section 11.4. Our task is to estimate

$$L_o(p_o, \omega_o) = \int_A \int_{\mathcal{H}^2(n)} S(p_o, \omega_o, p_i, \omega_i)\, L_i(p_i, \omega_i)|\cos\theta_i|\, d\omega_i\, dA.$$

Figure 15.6 suggests the complexity of evaluating the integral. To compute the standard Monte Carlo estimate of this equation given a point at which to compute outgoing radiance, we need a technique to sample points p_i on the surface and to compute the incident radiance at these points, as well as an efficient way to compute the specific value of the BSSRDF $S(p_o, \omega_o, p_i, \omega_i)$ for each sampled point p_i and incident direction.

The `VolPathIntegrator` could be used to evaluate the BSSRDF: given a pair of points on the surface and a pair of directions, the integrator can be used to compute the fraction of incident light from direction ω_i at the point p_i that exits the object at the point p_o in direction ω_o by following light-carrying paths through the multiple scattering events in the medium. Beyond standard path-tracing or bidirectional path-tracing techniques, many other light transport algorithms are applicable to this task.

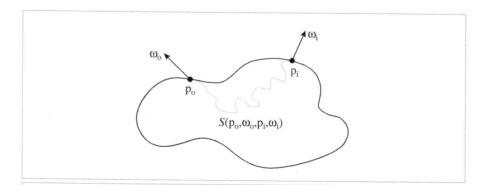

Figure 15.6: Computing Subsurface Reflection. When a surface is translucent, in order to compute outgoing radiance from a point p_o in direction ω_o, it's necessary to integrate the illumination arriving from directions ω_i at nearby points p_i weighted by the BSSRDF $S(p_o, \omega_o, p_i, \omega_i)$. The BSSRDF can be difficult to evaluate efficiently, since it represents all scattering within the volume for light that enters at one point and exits at the other.

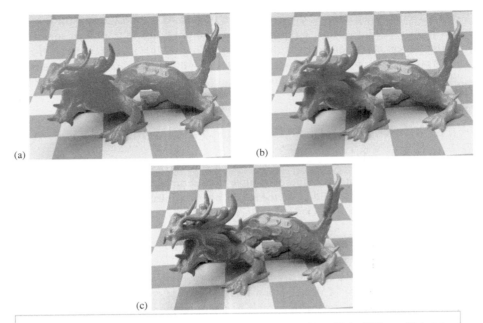

(a)　　　　　　　　　　　　　　　　(b)

(c)

Figure 15.7: Subsurface Scattering from the Dragon Model Rendered Using Different Material Densities. (a) Although incident illumination is arriving from behind the model, the front of the model has light exiting from it due to subsurface light transport. (b) σ_s and σ_a scaled by a factor of 5. (c) scaled by 25. Note how the dragon becomes increasingly opaque as the scattering coefficients increase.

However, many translucent objects are characterized by having very high albedos, which are not efficiently handled by classic approaches. For example, Jensen et al. (2001b) measured the scattering properties of skim milk and found an albedo of 0.9987. When essentially all of the light is scattered at each interaction in the medium and almost none of it is absorbed, light easily travels far from where it first enters the medium. Hundreds or even thousands of scattering events must be considered to compute an accurate result; given the high albedo of milk, after 100 scattering events, 87.5% of the incident light is still carried by a path, 51% after 500 scattering events, and still 26% after 1000.

BSSRDF class implementations represent the aggregate scattering behavior of these sorts of media, making it possible to render them fairly efficiently. Figure 15.7 shows an example of the dragon model rendered with a BSSRDF. The main sampling operation that must be provided by implementations of the BSSRDF interface, BSSRDF::Sample_S(), determines the surface position where a ray re-emerges following internal scattering.

⟨*BSSRDF Interface*⟩ +≡　　　　　　　　　　　　　　　　　　　　　　　　　　**692**
```
virtual Spectrum Sample_S(const Scene &scene, Float u1, const Point2f &u2,
    MemoryArena &arena, SurfaceInteraction *si, Float *pdf) const = 0;
```

The value of the BSSRDF for the two points and directions is returned directly, and the associated surface intersection record and probability density are returned via the si and pdf parameters. Two samples must be provided: a 1D sample for discrete sampling decisions (e.g., choosing a specific spectral channel of the profile) and a 2D sample that is mapped onto si. As we will see shortly, it's useful for BSSRDF implementations to be able to trace rays against the scene geometry to find si, so the scene is also provided as an argument.

15.4.1 SAMPLING THE SeparableBSSRDF

Recall the simplifying assumption introduced in Section 11.4.1, which factored the BSS-RDF into spatial and directional components that can be sampled independently from one another. Specifically, Equation (11.6) defined S as a product of a single spatial term and a pair of directional terms related to the incident and outgoing directions.

$$S(p_o, \omega_o, p_i, \omega_i) = (1 - F_r(\cos \theta_o)) \, S_p(p_o, p_i) \, S_\omega(\omega_i). \qquad [15.14]$$

The spatial term S_p was further simplified to a radial profile function S_r:

$$S_p(p_o, p_i) = S_r(\|p_o - p_i\|).$$

We will now explain how each of these factors is handled by the SeparableBSSRDF's sampling routines. This class implements an abstract sampling interface that works for any radial profile function S_r. The TabulatedBSSRDF class, discussed in Section 15.4.2, derives from SeparableBSSRDF and provides a specific tabulated representation of this profile with support for efficient evaluation and exact importance sampling.

Returning to Equation (15.14), if we assume that the BSSRDF is only sampled for rays that are transmitted through the surface boundary, where transmission is selected with probability $(1 - F_r(\cos \theta_o))$, then nothing needs to be done for the $1 - F_r(\cos \theta_o)$ part here. (This is the case for the fragment ⟨*Account for subsurface scattering, if applicable*⟩.) This is a reasonable expectation to place on calling code, as this approach gives good Monte Carlo efficiency.

This leaves the S_p and S_ω terms—the former is handled by a call to SeparableBSSRDF::Sample_Sp() (to be discussed shortly), which returns the position si.

⟨*BSSRDF Method Definitions*⟩ +≡
```
Spectrum SeparableBSSRDF::Sample_S(const Scene &scene, Float u1,
        const Point2f &u2, MemoryArena &arena, SurfaceInteraction *si,
        Float *pdf) const {
    Spectrum Sp = Sample_Sp(scene, u1, u2, arena, si, pdf);
    if (!Sp.IsBlack()) {
        ⟨Initialize material model at sampled surface interaction 905⟩
    }
    return Sp;
}
```

If sampling a position is successful, the method initializes si->bsdf with an instance of the class SeparableBSSRDFAdapter, which represents the directional term $S_\omega(\omega_i)$ as a BxDF. Although this BxDF does not truly depend on the outgoing direction si->wo, we still need to initialize it with a dummy direction.

⟨*Initialize material model at sampled surface interaction*⟩ ≡   905
```
si->bsdf = ARENA_ALLOC(arena, BSDF)(*si);
si->bsdf->Add(ARENA_ALLOC(arena, SeparableBSSRDFAdapter)(this));
si->wo = Vector3f(si->shading.n);
```

The `SeparableBSSRDFAdapter` class is a thin wrapper around `SeparableBSSRDF::Sw()`. Recall that S_ω from Equation (11.7) was defined as a diffuse-like term scaled by the normalized Fresnel transmission. For this reason, the `SeparableBSSRDFAdapter` classifies itself as `BSDF_DIFFUSE` and just uses the default cosine-weighted sampling routine provided by `BxDF::Sample_f()`.

⟨*BSSRDF Declarations*⟩ +≡
```
class SeparableBSSRDFAdapter : public BxDF {
public:
    ⟨SeparableBSSRDFAdapter Public Methods 906⟩
private:
    const SeparableBSSRDF *bssrdf;
};
```

⟨*SeparableBSSRDFAdapter Public Methods*⟩ ≡   906
```
SeparableBSSRDFAdapter(const SeparableBSSRDF *bssrdf)
    : BxDF(BxDFType(BSDF_REFLECTION | BSDF_DIFFUSE)), bssrdf(bssrdf) { }
```

Similar to refractive BSDFs, a scaling factor related to the light transport mode must be applied to the value the `f()` method returns for the S_ω term. This issue is discussed in more detail in Section 16.1, and the fragment that applies this scaling, ⟨*Update BSSRDF transmission term to account for adjoint light transport*⟩, is defined there.

⟨*SeparableBSSRDFAdapter Public Methods*⟩ +≡   906
```
Spectrum f(const Vector3f &wo, const Vector3f &wi) const {
    Spectrum f = bssrdf->Sw(wi);
    ⟨Update BSSRDF transmission term to account for adjoint light transport 961⟩
    return f;
}
```

To sample the spatial component S_p, we need a way of mapping a 2D distribution function onto an arbitrary surface using a parameterization of the surface in the neighborhood of the outgoing position. A conceptually straightforward way to obtain such a parameterization is by means of geodesics, but finding and evaluating them is non-trivial and requires significant implementation effort for each shape that is supported. We use much a simpler approach that uses ray tracing to map the radial profile S_r onto the scene geometry.

Figure 15.8 illustrates the basic idea: the position p_o and associated normal n_o define a planar approximation to the surface. Using 2D polar coordinates, we first sample an azimuth ϕ and a radius value r centered around p_o and then map this position onto the actual surface by intersecting an offset perpendicular ray with the primitive, producing the position p_i. The `SeparableBSSRDF` class only supports radially symmetric profile functions; hence ϕ is drawn from a uniform distribution on $[0, 2\pi)$, and r is distributed according to the radial profile function S_r.

There are still several difficulties with this basic approach:

- The radial profile S_r is not necessarily uniform across wavelengths—in practice, the mean free path can differ by orders of magnitude between different spectral channels.

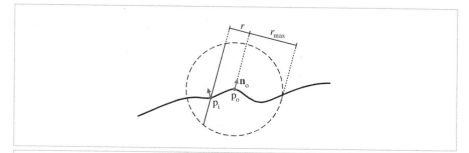

Figure 15.8: Sampling the Spatial Component of the Separable BSSRDF. To compute the outgoing radiance at a point p_o on a translucent surface, we sample a radius r from a radial scattering profile and map it onto the surface by tracing a probe ray back toward the surface, in the opposite direction of the surface normal n_o. To improve efficiency, the probe ray is clamped to a sphere of radius r_{max}, after which the value of the BSSRDF becomes negligible.

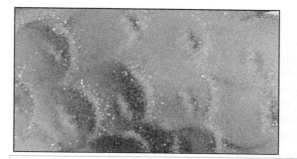 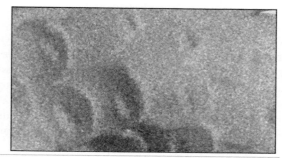

Figure 15.9: Comparison of Scattering Profile Projection. (a) Projecting the scattering profile perpendicularly along the current normal direction usually works well, but occasionally there are surface regions that are sampled with a very small probability despite a large corresponding BSSRDF value S, producing high variance in renderings. (b) Projecting along multiple axes and combining the resulting sampling techniques using multiple importance sampling greatly reduces the maximum variance at the cost of an increase in the overall amount of variance in well-converged regions. As more samples are taken, the latter approach shows better overall convergence.

- If the surface geometry is poorly approximated by a plane and $n_o \cdot n_i \approx 0$, where n_i is the surface normal at p_i, the probe rays will hit the surface at a grazing angle so that positions p_i with comparatively high values of $S(p_o, \omega_o, p_i, \cdot)$ may be sampled with too low a probability. The result is high variance in renderings (Figure 15.9).
- Finally, the probe ray may intersect multiple surface locations along its length, all of which may contribute to reflected radiance.

The first two problems can be addressed with a familiar approach; namely, by introducing additional tailored sampling distributions and combining them using multiple importance sampling. The third will be addressed shortly.

We use a different a sampling technique per wavelength to deal with spectral variation, and each technique is additionally replicated three times with different projection axes given by the basis vectors of a local frame, resulting in a total of 3 * `Spectrum::nSamples` sampling techniques. This ensures that every point where S takes on non-negligible values is intersected with a reasonable probability. This combination of techniques is implemented in `SeparableBSSRDF::Sample_Sp()`.

⟨*BSSRDF Method Definitions*⟩ +≡
```
    Spectrum SeparableBSSRDF::Sample_Sp(const Scene &scene, Float u1,
            const Point2f &u2, MemoryArena &arena, SurfaceInteraction *pi,
            Float *pdf) const {
        ⟨Choose projection axis for BSSRDF sampling 908⟩
        ⟨Choose spectral channel for BSSRDF sampling 909⟩
        ⟨Sample BSSRDF profile in polar coordinates 909⟩
        ⟨Compute BSSRDF profile bounds and intersection height 909⟩
        ⟨Compute BSSRDF sampling ray segment 910⟩
        ⟨Intersect BSSRDF sampling ray against the scene geometry 910⟩
        ⟨Randomly choose one of several intersections during BSSRDF sampling 911⟩
        ⟨Compute sample PDF and return the spatial BSSRDF term Sp 912⟩
    }
```

We begin by choosing a projection axis. Note that when the surface is close to planar, projecting along the normal `SeparableBSSRDF::ns` is clearly the best sampling strategy, as probe rays along the other two axes are likely to miss the surface. We therefore allocate a fairly large portion (50%) of the sample budget to perpendicular rays. The other half is equally shared between tangential projections along `SeparableBSSRDF::ss` and `SeparableBSSRDF::ts`. The three axes of the chosen coordinate system are stored in vx, vy, and vz, and follow our usual convention of measuring angles θ in spherical coordinates with respect to the z axis.

After this discrete sampling operation, we scale and offset u1 so that additional sampling operations can reuse it as a uniform variate.

⟨*Choose projection axis for BSSRDF sampling*⟩ ≡   908
```
    Vector3f vx, vy, vz;
    if (u1 < .5f) {
        vx = ss;
        vy = ts;
        vz = Vector3f(ns);
        u1 *= 2;
    } else if (u1 < .75f) {
        ⟨Prepare for sampling rays with respect to ss⟩
    } else {
        ⟨Prepare for sampling rays with respect to ts⟩
    }
```

The fragments for the other two axes are similar and therefore not included here.

Next, we uniformly choose a spectral channel and re-scale u1 once more.

908

⟨*Choose spectral channel for BSSRDF sampling*⟩ ≡

```
int ch = Clamp((int)(u1 * Spectrum::nSamples),
               0, Spectrum::nSamples - 1);
u1 = u1 * Spectrum::nSamples - ch;
```

The 2D profile sampling operation is then carried out in polar coordinates using the `SeparableBSSRDF::Sample_Sr()` method. This method returns a negative radius to indicate a failure (e.g., when there is no scattering from channel `ch`); the implementation here returns a BSSRDF value of 0 in this case.

908

⟨*Sample BSSRDF profile in polar coordinates*⟩ ≡

```
Float r = Sample_Sr(ch, u2[0]);
if (r < 0)
    return Spectrum(0.f);
Float phi = 2 * Pi * u2[1];
```

Both the radius sampling method `SeparableBSSRDF::Sample_Sr()` and its associated density function `SeparableBSSRDF::Pdf_Sr()` are declared as pure virtual functions; an implementation for `TabulatedBSSRDF` is presented in the next section.

693

⟨*SeparableBSSRDF Interface*⟩ +≡

```
virtual Float Sample_Sr(int ch, Float u) const = 0;
virtual Float Pdf_Sr(int ch, Float r) const = 0;
```

Because the profile falls off fairly quickly, we are not interested in positions p_i that are too far[2] away from p_o. In order to reduce the computational expense of the ray-tracing step, the probe ray is clamped to a sphere of radius r_{max} around p_o. Another call to `SeparableBSSRDF::Sample_Sr()` is used to determine r_{max}. Assuming that this function implements a perfect importance sampling scheme based on the inversion method (Section 13.3.1), `Sample_Sr()` maps a sample value x to the radius of a sphere containing a fraction x of the scattered energy.

Here, we set rMax so that the sphere from Figure 15.8 contains 99.9% of the scattered energy. When r lies outside of r_{max}, sampling fails—this helps to keep the probe rays short, which significantly improves the run-time performance. Given r and r_{max}, the length of the intersection of the probe ray with the sphere of radius r_{max} is

$$l = 2\sqrt{r_{max}^2 - r^2}.$$

(See Figure 15.10.)

908

⟨*Compute BSSRDF profile bounds and intersection height*⟩ ≡

```
Float rMax = Sample_Sr(ch, 0.999f);
if (r > rMax)
    return Spectrum(0.f);
Float l = 2 * std::sqrt(rMax * rMax - r * r);
```

---

2 This assumption can be problematic when a material is illuminated by a very bright light source (e.g., a hand held in front of a flashlight), in which case long-range light transport remains important.

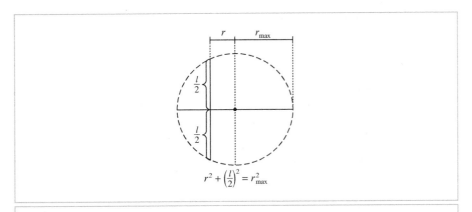

Figure 15.10: Given a sampled radius r that is less than the maximum radius r_{max}, the length of the segment l, which is the total length of the ray in the sphere, can be found using the Pythagorean theorem.

Given the sampled polar coordinate value, we can compute the world space origin of a ray that lies on the boundary of the sphere and a target point, pTarget, where it exits the sphere.

⟨*Compute BSSRDF sampling ray segment*⟩ ≡   **908**
```
Interaction base;
base.p = po.p + r * (vx * std::cos(phi) + vy * std::sin(phi)) -
        l * vz * 0.5f;
base.time = po.time;
Point3f pTarget = base.p + l * vz;
```

In practice, there could be more than just one intersection along the probe ray, and we want to collect all of them here. We'll create a linked list of all of the found interactions.

⟨*Intersect BSSRDF sampling ray against the scene geometry*⟩ ≡   **908**
  ⟨*Declare* IntersectionChain *and linked list* **910**⟩
  ⟨*Accumulate chain of intersections along ray* **911**⟩

IntersectionChain lets us maintain this list. Once again, the MemoryArena makes it possible to efficiently perform allocations, here for the list nodes.

⟨*Declare* IntersectionChain *and linked list*⟩ ≡   **910**
```
struct IntersectionChain {
    SurfaceInteraction si;
    IntersectionChain *next = nullptr;
};
IntersectionChain *chain = ARENA_ALLOC(arena, IntersectionChain)();
```

We now start by finding intersections along the segment within the sphere. The list's tail node's SurfaceInteraction is initialized with each intersection's information, and base Interaction is updated so that the next ray can be spawned on the other side of the intersected surface. (See Figure 15.11.)

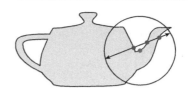

Figure 15.11: Accumulating Surface Intersections along a Sample Ray. The `SeparableBSSRDF::Sample_Sp()` method finds all of the intersections of a ray with the surface of the primitive, where ray extents are limited to a sphere around the intersection point (red dot). At each intersection (blue dots), the corresponding `SurfaceInteraction` is stored in a linked list before a new ray leaving the other side of the intersected surface is generated.

⟨*Accumulate chain of intersections along ray*⟩ ≡   910
```
IntersectionChain *ptr = chain;
int nFound = 0;
while (scene.Intersect(base.SpawnRayTo(pTarget), &ptr->si)) {
    base = ptr->si;
    ⟨Append admissible intersection to IntersectionChain 911⟩
}
```

When tracing rays to sample nearby points on the surface of the primitive, it's important to ignore any intersections on other primitives in the scene. (There is an implicit assumption that scattering between primitives will be handled by the integrator, and the BSSRDF should be limited to account for single primitives' scattering.) The implementation here uses equality of `Material` pointers as a proxy to determine if an intersection is on the same primitive. Valid intersections are appended to the chain, and the variable `nFound` records their total count when the loop terminates.

⟨*Append admissible intersection to* `IntersectionChain`⟩ ≡   911
```
if (ptr->si.primitive->GetMaterial() == material) {
    IntersectionChain *next = ARENA_ALLOC(arena, IntersectionChain)();
    ptr->next = next;
    ptr = next;
    nFound++;
}
```

With the set of intersections at hand, we must now choose one of them, as `Sample_Sp()` can only return a single position p_i. The following fragment uses the variable `u1` one last time to pick one of the list entries with uniform probability.

⟨*Randomly choose one of several intersections during BSSRDF sampling*⟩ ≡   908
```
if (nFound == 0)
    return Spectrum(0.0f);
int selected = Clamp((int)(u1 * nFound), 0, nFound - 1);
while (selected-- > 0)
    chain = chain->next;
*pi = chain->si;
```

Finally, we can call `SeparableBSSRDF::Pdf_Sp()` (to be defined shortly) to evaluate the combined PDF that takes all of the sampling strategies into account. The probability it returns is divided by nFound to account for the discrete probability of selecting pi from the IntersectionChain. Finally, the value of $S_p(p_i)$ is returned.

⟨*Compute sample PDF and return the spatial BSSRDF term* S_p⟩ ≡   908
```
*pdf = Pdf_Sp(*pi) / nFound;
return Sp(*pi);
```

`SeparableBSSRDF::Pdf_Sp()` returns the probability per unit area of sampling the position pi with the total of 3 * Spectrum::nSamples sampling techniques available to `SeparableBSSRDF::Sample_Sp()`.

⟨*BSSRDF Method Definitions*⟩ +≡
```
Float SeparableBSSRDF::Pdf_Sp(const SurfaceInteraction &pi) const {
    ⟨Express pᵢ − pₒ and nᵢ with respect to local coordinates at pₒ 912⟩
    ⟨Compute BSSRDF profile radius under projection along each axis 913⟩
    ⟨Return combined probability from all BSSRDF sampling strategies 913⟩
}
```

First, nLocal is initialized with the surface normal at p_i and dLocal with the difference vector $p_o - p_i$, both expressed using local coordinates at p_o.

⟨*Express* $p_i - p_o$ *and* n_i *with respect to local coordinates at* p_o⟩ ≡   912
```
Vector3f d = po.p - pi.p;
Vector3f dLocal(Dot(ss, d),     Dot(ts, d),     Dot(ns, d));
Normal3f nLocal(Dot(ss, pi.n), Dot(ts, pi.n), Dot(ns, pi.n));
```

To determine the combined PDF, we must query the probability of sampling a radial profile radius matching the pair (p_o, p_i) for each technique. This radius is measured in 2D and thus depends on the chosen projection axis (Figure 15.12). The rProj variable records radii for projections perpendicular to ss, ts, and ns.

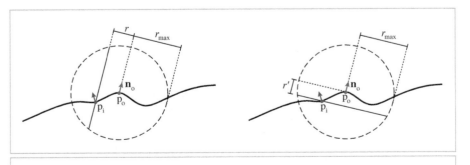

Figure 15.12: Probability of Alternative Sampling Strategies. To determine the combined probability of a BSSRDF position sample p_i (left), we must evaluate the radial PDF for each of the radii r' corresponding to alternative projection axes (right).

⟨*Compute BSSRDF profile radius under projection along each axis*⟩ ≡   912
```
Float rProj[3] = { std::sqrt(dLocal.y * dLocal.y + dLocal.z * dLocal.z),
                   std::sqrt(dLocal.z * dLocal.z + dLocal.x * dLocal.x),
                   std::sqrt(dLocal.x * dLocal.x + dLocal.y * dLocal.y) };
```

The remainder of the implementation simply loops over all combinations of spectral channels and projection axes and sums up the product of the probability of selecting each technique and its area density under projection onto the surface at p_o.

⟨*Return combined probability from all BSSRDF sampling strategies*⟩ ≡   912
```
Float pdf = 0, axisProb[3] = { .25f, .25f, .5f };
Float chProb = 1 / (Float)Spectrum::nSamples;
for (int axis = 0; axis < 3; ++axis)
    for (int ch = 0; ch < Spectrum::nSamples; ++ch)
        pdf += Pdf_Sr(ch, rProj[axis]) * std::abs(nLocal[axis]) *
               chProb * axisProb[axis];
return pdf;
```

The alert reader may have noticed a slight inconsistency in the above definitions: the probability of choosing one of several (nFound) intersections in SeparableBSSRDF::Sample_Sp() should really have been part of the density function computed in the SeparableBSSRDF::Pdf_Sp() method rather than the ad hoc division that occurs in the fragment ⟨*Compute sample PDF and return the spatial BSSRDF term S_p*⟩. In practice, the number of detected intersections varies with respect of the projection axis and spectral channel; correctly accounting for this in the PDF computation requires counting the number of intersections along each of a total of 3 * Spectrum::nSamples probe rays for every sample! We neglect this issue, trading a more efficient implementation for a small amount of bias.

15.4.2 SAMPLING THE TabulatedBSSRDF

The previous section completed the discussion of BSSRDF sampling with the exception of the Pdf_Sr() and Sample_Sr() methods that were declared as pure virtual functions in the SeparableBSSRDF interface. The TabulatedBSSRDF subclass implements this missing functionality.

The TabulatedBSSRDF::Sample_Sr() method samples radius values proportional to the radial profile function S_r. Recall from Section 11.4.2 that the profile has an implicit dependence on the albedo ρ at the current surface position and that the TabulatedBSSRDF provides interpolated evaluations of $S_r(\rho, r)$ using 2D tensor product spline basis functions. TabulatedBSSRDF::Sample_Sr() then determines the albedo ρ for to the given spectral channel ch and draws samples proportional to the remaining 1D function $S_r(\rho, \cdot)$. Sample generation fails if there is neither scattering nor absorption on channel ch (this case is indicated by returning a negative radius).

As in Section 11.4.2, there is a considerable amount of overlap with the FourierBSDF implementation. The sampling operation here actually reduces to a single call to SampleCatmullRom2D(), which was previously used in FourierBSDF::Sample_f().

⟨*BSSRDF Method Definitions*⟩ +≡
```
Float TabulatedBSSRDF::Sample_Sr(int ch, Float u) const {
    if (sigma_t[ch] == 0)
        return -1;
    return SampleCatmullRom2D(table.nRhoSamples, table.nRadiusSamples,
        table.rhoSamples.get(), table.radiusSamples.get(),
        table.profile.get(), table.profileCDF.get(),
        rho[ch], u) / sigma_t[ch];
}
```

Recall that this function depends on a precomputed CDF array, which is initialized when the BSSRDFTable is created.

⟨*BSSRDFTable Public Data*⟩ +≡   697
```
std::unique_ptr<Float[]> profileCDF;
```

The Pdf_Sr() method returns the PDF of samples obtained via Sample_Sr(). It evaluates the profile function divided by the normalizing constant ρ_{eff} defined in Equation (11.11).

The beginning is analogous to the spline evaluation code in TabulatedBSSRDF::Sr(). The fragment ⟨*Compute spline weights to interpolate BSSRDF density on channel* ch⟩ matches ⟨*Compute spline weights to interpolate BSSRDF on channel* ch⟩ in that method except that this method immediately returns zero if the optical radius is outside the range represented by the spline.

⟨*BSSRDF Method Definitions*⟩ +≡
```
Float TabulatedBSSRDF::Pdf_Sr(int ch, Float r) const {
    ⟨Convert r into unitless optical radius roptical 699⟩
    ⟨Compute spline weights to interpolate BSSRDF density on channel ch⟩
    ⟨Return BSSRDF profile density for channel ch 914⟩
}
```

The remainder of the implementation is very similar to fragment ⟨*Set BSSRDF value* Sr[ch] *using tensor spline interpolation*⟩ except that here, we also interpolate ρ_{eff} from the tabulation and include it in the division at the end.

⟨*Return BSSRDF profile density for channel* ch⟩ ≡   914
```
Float sr = 0, rhoEff = 0;
for (int i = 0; i < 4; ++i) {
    if (rhoWeights[i] == 0) continue;
    rhoEff += table.rhoEff[rhoOffset + i] * rhoWeights[i];
    for (int j = 0; j < 4; ++j) {
        if (radiusWeights[j] == 0) continue;
        sr += table.EvalProfile(rhoOffset + i, radiusOffset + j) *
                rhoWeights[i] * radiusWeights[j];
    }
}
⟨Cancel marginal PDF factor from tabulated BSSRDF profile 700⟩
return std::max((Float)0, sr * sigma_t[ch] * sigma_t[ch] / rhoEff);
```

15.4.3 SUBSURFACE SCATTERING IN THE PATH TRACER

We now have the capability to apply Monte Carlo integration to the generalized scattering equation, (5.11), from Section 5.6.2. We will compute estimates of the form

$$L_o(p_o, \omega_o) \approx \frac{S(p_o, \omega_o, p_i, \omega_i)\,(L_d(p_i, \omega_i) + L_i(p_i, \omega_i))\,|\cos\theta_i|}{p(p_i)\,p(\omega_i)},$$

where L_d represents incident direct radiance and L_i is incident indirect radiance. The sample (p_i, ω_i) is generated in two steps. First, given p_o and ω_o, a call to `BSSRDF::Sample_S()` returns a position p_i whose distribution is similar to the marginal distribution of S with respect to p_i.

Next, we sample the incident direction ω_i. Recall that the `BSSRDF::Sample_S()` interface intentionally keeps these two steps apart: instead of generating both p_i and ω_i at the same time, it returns a special BSDF instance via the `bsdf` field of `si` that is used for the direction sampling step. No generality is lost with such an approach: the returned BSDF can be completely arbitrary and is explicitly allowed to depend on information computed within `BSSRDF::Sample_S()`. The benefit is that we can re-use a considerable amount of existing infrastructure for computing product integrals of a BSDF and L_i.

The `PathIntegrator`'s ⟨*Find next path vertex and accumulate contribution*⟩ fragment invokes the following code to compute this estimate.

⟨*Account for subsurface scattering, if applicable*⟩ ≡   877
```
if (isect.bssrdf && (flags & BSDF_TRANSMISSION)) {
    ⟨Importance sample the BSSRDF 915⟩
    ⟨Account for the direct subsurface scattering component 915⟩
    ⟨Account for the indirect subsurface scattering component 916⟩
}
```

When the BSSRDF sampling case is triggered, the path tracer begins by calling `BSSRDF::Sample_S()` to generate p_i and incorporates the resulting sampling weight into its throughput weight variable `beta` upon success.

⟨*Importance sample the BSSRDF*⟩ ≡   915
```
SurfaceInteraction pi;
Spectrum S = isect.bssrdf->Sample_S(scene, sampler.Get1D(),
                                sampler.Get2D(), arena, &pi, &pdf);
if (S.IsBlack() || pdf == 0)
    break;
beta *= S / pdf;
```

Because `BSSRDF::Sample_S()` also initializes `pi`'s `bsdf` with a BSDF that characterizes the dependence of S on ω_i, we can reuse the existing infrastructure for direct illumination computations. Only a single line of code is necessary to compute the contribution of direct lighting at `pi` to reflected radiance at `po`.

⟨*Account for the direct subsurface scattering component*⟩ ≡   915
```
L += beta * UniformSampleOneLight(pi, scene, arena, sampler);
```

Figure 15.13: Subsurface Scattering with the `PathIntegrator`. These dragons both have BSS-RDFs that describe subsurface scattering in their interiors. (*Model courtesy of Christian Schüller.*)

Similarly, accounting for indirect illumination at the newly sampled incident point is almost the same as the BSDF indirect illumination computation in the `PathIntegrator` except that `pi` is used for the next path vertex instead of `isect`.

⟨*Account for the indirect subsurface scattering component*⟩ ≡   915
```
Spectrum f = pi.bsdf->Sample_f(pi.wo, &wi, sampler.Get2D(), &pdf,
                            BSDF_ALL, &flags);
if (f.IsBlack() || pdf == 0)
    break;
beta *= f * AbsDot(wi, pi.shading.n) / pdf;
specularBounce = (flags & BSDF_SPECULAR) != 0;
ray = pi.SpawnRay(wi);
```

With this, the path tracer (and the volumetric path tracer) support subsurface scattering. See Figure 15.13 for an example.

⋆ 15.5 SUBSURFACE SCATTERING USING THE DIFFUSION EQUATION

Our last task to complete the subsurface scattering implementation is to be able to initialize the `TabulatedBSSRDF` with a radial profile function S_r that accurately describes subsurface scattering for given properties of the scattering medium (σ_a, σ_s, the phase function asymmetry parameter g, and the relative index of refraction η). The technique we'll discuss in this section is based on the *photon beam diffusion* (PBD) technique by

Habel et al. (2013). The resulting profile takes all orders of scattering into account, effectively accounting for all of the light transport that occurs within the surface.

Beam diffusion makes several significant assumptions and approximations: first, the distribution of light in the translucent medium is modeled with the *diffusion approximation*, which describes the equilibrium distribution of illumination in highly scattering optically thick participating media. Second, it assumes homogeneous scattering properties throughout the medium, and it implicitly assumes that the medium is *semi-infinite* (it continues infinitely beneath a planar surface of infinite lateral extent). Finally, PBD builds upon the separable BSSRDF approximation of Equation (11.6), which imposes a simple multiplicative relationship between the spatial and directional scattering distribution. When these approximations are satisfied, the solutions computed by PBD are in close agreement with ground truth simulations performed using the equation of transfer, Equation (15.2).

Of course, many of these assumptions won't be valid when the profile is applied to an arbitrary shape, potentially also with spatially varying material properties. The appeal of diffusion-type methods in the context of computer graphics is that they degrade in a graceful manner, producing visually reasonable results even in cases where some or all of their fundamental assumptions are violated. See the "Further Reading" section and exercises at the end of this chapter for references to improvements to this approach that generalize it to handle a wider range of settings more accurately.

While PBD can compute the profile S_r for any radius and material parameters, profile evaluations tend to be fairly expensive, as they involve a numerical integration step. Furthermore, we need to be able to invert the CDF of S_r in polar coordinates to importance sample the model, but this inverse is not available in closed form. The TabulatedBSSRDF from Section 11.4.2 nicely addresses these issues, providing efficient evaluation and sampling operations. Our approach will thus be to precompute S_r for a range of radii and albedo values and use the results to populate the BSSRDFTable of a TabulatedBSSRDF. This precomputation is performed during scene construction.

In the following, we discuss the key ingredients of the PBD method, starting with the principle of similarity and diffusion theory.

15.5.1 PRINCIPLE OF SIMILARITY

A number of important ideas are used in the process of transforming the fully general equation of transfer to the diffusion equation, which can be approximately solved for subsurface scattering. The first is the *principle of similarity*, which says that for an anisotropically scattering medium with a high albedo, the medium can instead be modeled as having an isotropic phase function with appropriately modified scattering and attenuation coefficients. Light transport solutions computed based on the modified coefficients correspond well to those with the original coefficients and phase function, while allowing simplifications due to the assumption of isotropic scattering.

The principle of similarity is based on the observation that after many scattering events the distribution of light in media with high albedos becomes more and more uniformly directionally distributed regardless of the original illumination distribution or the anisotropy of the phase function. One way to see how this happens is to consider

BSSRDFTable 697
TabulatedBSSRDF 696

an expression derived by Yanovitskij (1997); it describes isotropization due to multiple scattering events from the Henyey–Greenstein phase function. He showed that the distribution of light that has been scattered n times is given by

$$p_n(\omega \to \omega') = \frac{1 - g^{2n}}{4\pi (1 + g^{2n} - 2g|g^{n-1}| (-\omega \cdot \omega')^{3/2})}.$$

As n grows large, this converges to the isotropic phase function, $1/(4\pi)$. Figure 15.14 plots this function for a few values of n. When coupled with the observation from Section 15.4.1 about how much of the light energy remains after tens or even hundreds of scattering events in high-albedo materials, one can see intuitively why it is reasonable to work with an isotropic phase function approximation for high-albedo media.

If the principle of similarity is applied to treat the phase function as isotropic, modified versions of various scattering properties should be used. The *reduced scattering coefficient* is defined as $\sigma_s' = (1 - g) \, \sigma_s$, and the *reduced attenuation coefficient* is $\sigma_t' = \sigma_a + \sigma_s'$. The albedo also changes to a *reduced albedo* defined as $\rho' = \sigma_s'/\sigma_t'$, which is generally different from ρ. These new coefficients account for the effect of using the isotropic phase function approximation.

To understand the idea these coefficients embody, consider a strongly forward-scattering phase function, where $g \to 1$. With the original phase function, light will mostly continue in the same direction once it scatters. In this example, the value of the reduced scattering coefficient $\sigma_s' = (1 - g) \, \sigma_s$ is much smaller than σ_s, which means that light travels a larger distance in the medium before scattering; the medium is approximated as being thinner, allowing light to travel farther. The change thus has the same effect as a highly forward-scattering phase function.

Conversely, consider the case of $g \to -1$. In this case, at a scattering event the light will tend to scatter back in the direction it came from. But then the next time it scatters after that, it will generally reverse course again; it bounces back and forth without making very much forward progress. In this case, the reduced scattering coefficient is larger than the original scattering coefficient, indicating greater probability of a scattering interaction. In other words, the medium is treated as being thicker than it actually is, which approximates the effect of light having relatively more trouble making forward progress. Figure 15.15 illustrates these ideas, showing representative paths of scattering interactions in highly forward-scattering and highly backward-scattering media.

15.5.2 DIFFUSION THEORY

Diffusion theory provides a way of transitioning from the equation of transfer to a simpler *diffusion equation*, which provides a solution to the equation of transfer for the case of homogeneous, optically thick, highly scattering materials (i.e., those with relatively large albedos). For the application to subsurface scattering in pbrt, it can be derived by writing the equation of transfer using the reduced scattering and attenuation coefficients and an isotropic phase function.

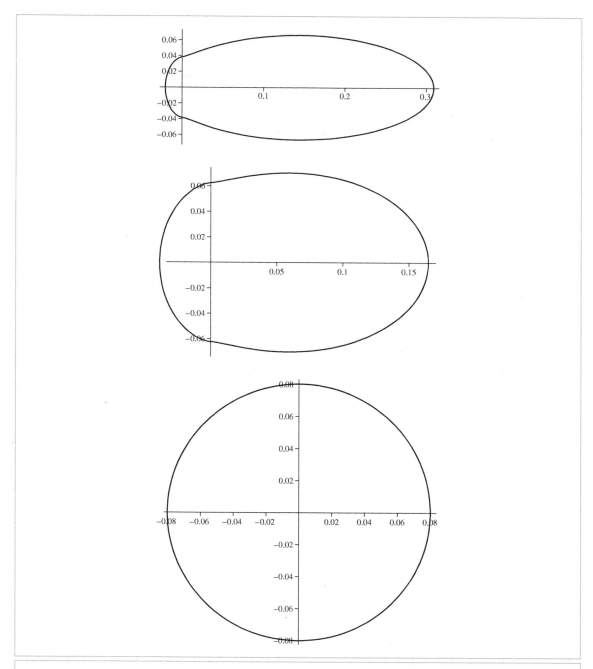

Figure 15.14: Light Distribution after Many Scattering Events. (a) Directional distribution of a single incident ray of light after 10 scattering events in a highly anisotropic medium with $g = 0.9$, (b) 100 scattering events, (c) 1000 scattering events. The distribution becomes increasingly isotropic, even though it was initially very anisotropic.

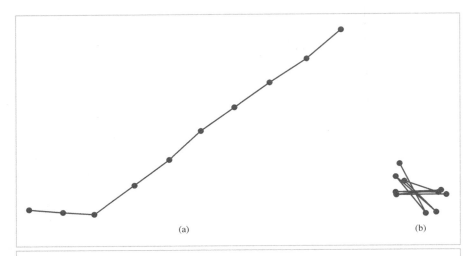

Figure 15.15: Representative Light Paths for Highly Anisotropic Scattering Media. (a) Forward-scattering medium, with $g = 0.9$. Light generally scatters in the same direction it was originally traveling. (b) Backward-scattering medium, with $g = -0.9$. Light frequently bounces back and forth, making relatively little forward progress with respect to its original direction.

Starting with the integro-differential form of the equation of transfer from Equation (15.1),

$$\frac{\partial}{\partial t} L_o(p + t\omega, \omega) = -\sigma_t(p, \omega) L_i(p, -\omega)$$

$$+ \sigma_s(p, \omega) \int_{S^2} p(p, -\omega', \omega) L_i(p, \omega') \, d\omega' + L_e(p, \omega),$$

we assume spatially uniform material parameters and switch to an isotropic phase function $p = 1/4\pi$, making a corresponding change to the scattering and attenuation coefficient using similarity theory. We also replace $L_o(p, \omega) = L_i(p, -\omega)$ with a single function $L(p, \omega)$.

$$\frac{\partial}{\partial t} L(p + t\omega, \omega) = -\sigma_t' L(p, \omega) + \frac{\sigma_s'}{4\pi} \int_{S^2} L(p, \omega') \, d\omega' + L_e(p, \omega). \quad [15.15]$$

The key assumption of diffusion theory is that because each scattering event effectively blurs the incident illumination, high frequencies disappear from the angular radiance distribution as light propagates farther into the medium; in dense and isotropically scattering media, all directionality is eventually lost. Motivated by this observation, the radiance function is restricted to a simple two-term expansion based on spherical moments. Formally, for a function $f : S^2 \to \mathbb{R}$, the n-th moment on the unit sphere is defined as[3]

---

3   An alternative way of deriving diffusion theory involves replacing the radiance function with a low-order spherical harmonics expansion. We prefer the moment notation for its simplicity, though it should be noted that both methods are mathematically equivalent.

$$(\mu_n [f])_{i,j,k,\ldots} = \int_{S^2} \underbrace{\omega_i \, \omega_j \, \omega_k \cdots}_{n \text{ factors}} f(\omega) \, d\omega.$$

In other words, to get the $i, j, k, \ldots$ entry of the n-tensor $\mu_n [f]$, we integrate the product of f and the $i, j, k, \ldots$ components of the direction ω written in Cartesian coordinates. Note that there is some notational overlap with the angle cosines μ_k from Section 8.6; the remainder of this chapter will exclusively refer to the definition above.

The zeroth moment, for instance, gives the function's integral over the sphere, the first moment can be interpreted as a "center of mass" 3-vector, and the second moment is a positive definite 3×3 matrix. Higher order moments have many symmetries: for instance, exchanging any pair of indices leaves the value unchanged. High-order moments are useful to derive extended versions of diffusion theory that allow for more pronounced directional behavior; here, we will just focus on degrees $n \leq 1$.

The moments of the radiance function have special designations: the zeroth moment ϕ is referred to as the *fluence rate*:

$$\phi(\mathrm{p}) = \mu_0 \left[L(\mathrm{p}, \cdot) \right] = \int_{S^2} L(\mathrm{p}, \omega) \, d\omega.$$

Note that this expression differs from the fluence function $H(\mathrm{p})$ in Equation (6.6), which was defined as the fluence rate on a surface boundary integrated over time.

The first moment is the *vector irradiance*:

$$\mathbf{E}(\mathrm{p}) = \mu_1 \left[L(\mathrm{p}, \cdot) \right] = \int_{S^2} \omega \, L(\mathrm{p}, \omega) \, d\omega.$$

The two-term expansion mentioned before is defined as

$$L_{\mathrm{d}}(\mathrm{p}, \omega) = \frac{1}{4\pi} \phi(\mathrm{p}) + \frac{3}{4\pi} \omega \cdot \mathbf{E}(\mathrm{p}), \qquad (15.16)$$

so that the moments can be exactly recovered, i.e.,

$$\mu_0 \left[L_{\mathrm{d}}(\mathrm{p}, \cdot) \right] = \phi(\mathrm{p}) \quad \text{and} \quad \mu_1 \left[L_{\mathrm{d}}(\mathrm{p}, \cdot) \right] = \mathbf{E}(\mathrm{p}).$$

(Here, the "d" subscript denotes the diffusion approximation, not the direct lighting term as it did in Section 14.3.)

To derive the diffusion equation from the equation of transfer, we simply substitute the two-term radiance function L_{d} into Equation (15.15). The resulting expression is unfortunately not guaranteed to have a solution, but this issue can be addressed with a simple trick: by only enforcing equality of its moments, i.e., by requiring that

$$\mu_i \left[\frac{\partial}{\partial t} L_{\mathrm{d}}(\mathrm{p} + t\omega, \omega) \right] = \mu_i \left[-\sigma_{\mathrm{t}}' \, L_{\mathrm{d}}(\mathrm{p}, \omega) \right.$$
$$\left. + \frac{\sigma_{\mathrm{s}}'}{4\pi} \int_{S^2} L_{\mathrm{d}}(\mathrm{p}, \omega') \, d\omega' + L_{\mathrm{e}}(\mathrm{p}, \omega) \right] \qquad (15.17)$$

for $i = 0$ and $i = 1$. Computing these moments is a fairly lengthy and mechanical exercise in trigonometric calculus that we skip here.[4] The end result is an equation equating the zeroth moments:

$$\mathrm{div}\,\mathbf{E}(\mathrm{p}) = (-\sigma_t' + \sigma_s')\,\phi(\mathrm{p}) = -\sigma_a\,\phi(\mathrm{p}) + Q_0(\mathrm{p}),$$

where $\mathrm{div}\,\mathbf{E}(\mathrm{p}) = \frac{\partial}{\partial x}\mathbf{E}(\mathrm{p}) + \frac{\partial}{\partial y}\mathbf{E}(\mathrm{p}) + \frac{\partial}{\partial z}\mathbf{E}(\mathrm{p})$ is the divergence operator and

$$Q_i(\mathrm{p}) = \mu_i\left[L_e(\mathrm{p}, \cdot)\right]$$

is the i-th moment of the medium emission. This equation states that the divergence of the irradiance vector field $\mathbf{E}$ is negative in the presence of absorption (i.e., light is being removed) and positive when light is being added by Q_0.

Another similar equation for the first moments states that the irradiance vector field $\mathbf{E}$, which represents the overall flow of energy, points from regions with a higher fluence rate to regions with a lower rate.

$$\frac{1}{3}\nabla\phi(\mathrm{p}) = -\sigma_t'\,\mathbf{E}(\mathrm{p}) + Q_1(\mathrm{p}), \qquad [15.18]$$

A reasonable simplification at this point is to assume light sources in the medium emit light uniformly in all directions, in which case $Q_1(\mathrm{p}) = 0$.

The next step of the traditional derivation is to solve the above equation for $\mathbf{E}$ and substitute it into the equation relating zeroth moments. The substitution removes $\mathbf{E}(\mathrm{p})$ and yields the *diffusion equation*, which now only involves the fluence rate $\phi(\mathrm{p})$:

$$\frac{1}{3\sigma_t'}\,\mathrm{div}\,\nabla\phi(\mathrm{p}) = \sigma_a\,\phi(\mathrm{p}) - Q_0(\mathrm{p}) + \frac{1}{\sigma_t'}\,\nabla\cdot Q_1(\mathrm{p}).$$

Assuming that $Q_1(\mathrm{p}) = 0$, the diffusion equation can be written more compactly as

$$D\nabla^2\phi(\mathrm{p}) - \sigma_a\,\phi(\mathrm{p}) = -Q_0(\mathrm{p}), \qquad [15.19]$$

where $D = 1/(3\sigma_t')$ is the *classical diffusion coefficient* and ∇^2 is a shorter notation for $\mathrm{div}\,\nabla$, which is known as the *Laplace operator*.

With the diffusion equation at hand, we'll proceed as follows: starting from a solution for a point source that is only correct in a space where the medium infinitely extends in all directions, we will consider ways of improving the solution's accuracy in more challenging cases and introduce an approximation that can account for the effect of a refractive boundary.

We'll initially focus on a point light source that is placed below the surface to approximate the effect of incident illumination striking the surface. Later, we switch to a more accurate light source approximation and derive the beam diffusion solution to the multiple scattering component as well as a single scattering correction that is based on the classical equation of transfer.

---

4   For details, see Chapter 5 of Donner's Ph.D. dissertation (2006) or the supplemental material of Jakob et al. (2010).

15.5.3 MONOPOLE SOLUTION

Consider an infinite homogeneous medium with a point light source of unit power (a *monopole*) located at its origin. The emitted radiance function L_e for this setup is given by

$$L_e(p, \omega) = \frac{1}{4\pi} \delta(p),$$

and the corresponding moments are equal to

$$Q_i(p) = \begin{cases} \delta(p), & i = 0, \\ 0, & i = 1. \end{cases}$$

The fluence rate due to this type of source has a simple analytic expression:

$$\phi_M(r) = \frac{1}{4\pi D} \frac{e^{-\sigma_{tr} r}}{r}, \qquad (15.20)$$

where r is the distance from the light source. The constant $\sigma_{tr} = \sqrt{\sigma_a / D}$ is called the *effective transport coefficient*; it occurs in an exponential falloff term that accounts for absorption in the medium. Observe that $\sigma_{tr} \neq \sigma_t'$: instead, this modified attenuation coefficient additionally depends on the albedo to model the effect of multiple scattering inside the medium, hence the term *effective*.

Let's verify that this expression satisfies the diffusion equation away from the origin, where the fluence has a pole singularity. The Laplace operator ∇^2 of a function f that only depends on the radius in spherical coordinates is given by

$$\nabla^2 f = r^{-2} \frac{\partial}{\partial r} \left(r^2 \frac{\partial}{\partial r} f(r) \right).$$

Taking the inner derivative of $\phi_M(r)$ and multiplying by r^2 yields

$$r^2 \frac{\partial}{\partial r} \phi_M(r) = -r \phi_M(r) \left(1 + \sigma_{tr} r \right).$$

Taking the outer derivative, multiplying by r^{-2}, and simplifying gives

$$r^{-2} \frac{\partial}{\partial r} \left(-r \phi_M(r)(1 + \sigma_{tr} r) \right) = \sigma_{tr}^2 \phi_M(r) = \frac{\sigma_a}{D} \phi_M(r),$$

which is exactly the ratio predicted by Equation (15.19); i.e., $D\nabla^2 \phi_M - \sigma_a \phi_M = 0$.

Using the identity from Equation (15.18), we can also find the irradiance vector field induced by ϕ_M, which will be useful later on:

$$\begin{aligned} E_M(p) &= -D\nabla \phi_M(p) \\ &= \left[-D \frac{\partial}{\partial r} \phi_M(r) \right] \hat{r} \\ &= \frac{1 + r\sigma_{tr}}{4\pi r^2} e^{-\sigma_{tr} r} \hat{r}, \end{aligned} \qquad (15.21)$$

where $\hat{r}$ is a unit vector pointing away from the source.

15.5.4 NON-CLASSICAL DIFFUSION

As we have seen, the monopole fluence rate ϕ_M in Equation (15.20) exactly solves the diffusion equation. Despite this, it turns out that the solution can still have significant errors compared to the original equation of transfer when the assumptions of the underlying diffusion approximation are violated.

There are two important cases: the first occurs when absorption prevents the radiance from reaching an isotropic equilibrium distribution. The second occurs close to the source, where the true radiance function is dominated by a (highly non-isotropic) spherical Dirac delta function.

A number of modified diffusion theories have been proposed that improve the accuracy in a number of different cases. An effective one is to switch to the modified monopole solution developed by Grosjean (1956) in the field of neutron transport:

$$\phi_G(r) = \frac{e^{-\sigma_t' r}}{4\pi r^2} + \tilde{\phi}_M(r). \qquad [15.22]$$

The first term in this solution separates out an attenuated source term modeled using standard radiative transport—this effectively removes the portion that cannot easily be handled by diffusion. The remainder is a scaled diffusive term that accounts for light which has been scattered at least once, where the reduced albedo ρ' accounts for the energy reduction due to the extra scattering event:

$$\tilde{\phi}_M(r) = \rho' \, \phi_M(r). \qquad [15.23]$$

This expression uses the previous monopole solution ϕ_M, though its diffusion coefficient D must be replaced with a non-classical version given by

$$D_G = \frac{2\sigma_a + \sigma_s'}{3(\sigma_a + \sigma_s')^2}. \qquad [15.24]$$

Figure 15.16 illustrates the superior accuracy of Grosjean's solution in both absorption-dominated and scattering-dominated media.

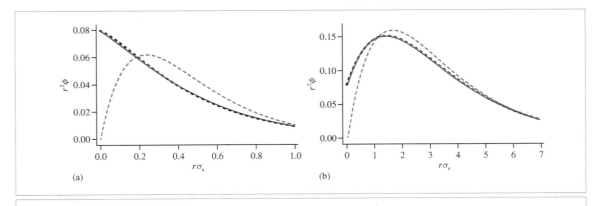

(a)   (b)

Figure 15.16: Comparison of Classical and Non-Classical Diffusion Solutions. The two plots compare the fluence rate due to a point source for (a) a low albedo ($\rho = 1/3$) and (b) a high albedo ($\rho = 0.9$). In both cases, Grosjean's non-classical monopole (blue) is a considerably better match to the exact solution (black) compared to the classical diffusion solution (red).

In the following sections, we will just focus on the non-classical diffusive part $\tilde{\phi}_M$ and ignore the attenuated source term in Equation (15.22), as it is simple to handle separately later on.

15.5.5 DIPOLE SOLUTION

To apply these results to subsurface scattering for rendering, it is clear that the solution must account for the presence of a surface. We will now switch to the simplest kind of geometric setup that satisfies this requirement: a *semi-infinite half space*, i.e., a medium that fills all space below a planar surface of infinite lateral extent. The region above is modeled as a dielectric without any kind of scattering (i.e., a vacuum).

For simplicity, we assume that the boundary is located at $z = 0$ with a normal of $\mathbf{n} = (0, 0, -1)$ so that positive values on the z axis correspond to points inside the medium. Let η denote the relative index of refraction over the boundary. We are still interested in the fluence rate due to a point light source that we (arbitrarily) place on the z-axis at position $(0, 0, z_r)$. Let's assume that $z_r > 0$, i.e., the light source is located *inside* the medium (more on this later). Due to the newly added boundary, a portion of the light traveling upward can escape from the layer and undergo no further scattering. Another portion is specularly reflected at $z = 0$; the monopole solution from Equation (15.20) accounts for neither effect and thus no longer yields accurate results.

The influence of the boundary can be approximated by the *method of images*, where a *negative* source is placed on the vacuum side of the boundary at position $(0, 0, z_v)$ with $z_v < 0$. The negative contribution of this "virtual" light source subtracts a portion of the "real" light source to account for the combined effect of internal reflections and illumination that has left the medium and can no longer scatter. The choice of the virtual depth z_v is crucial to ensure that this indeed works out—we discuss this step shortly.

This arrangement of a positive and a negative light source is known as a *dipole* (Figure 15.17). Due to the linearity of the diffusion equation, (15.19), superpositions of solutions still solve the diffusion equation; hence the dipole fluence rate at a point

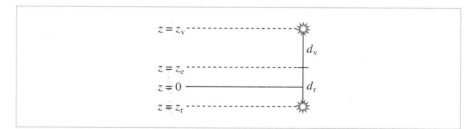

Figure 15.17: Basic Setting for the Dipole Approximation to the Solution to the Diffusion Equation. A light source with positive flux is placed at a position $z = z_r$ inside the medium, below the point where incident illumination arrives, and a second light with an equal amount of negative flux is placed at $z = z_v$ above the medium. These sources are placed so that the flux for the two of them cancels out at a height z_e above the boundary, fulfilling the linearized boundary condition. The fluence rate that results from subtracting the closed-form solution for each of them, Equation (15.25), at the medium's boundary $z = 0$ is a reasonable approximation of the fluence rate at the boundary due to subsurface scattering.

$(r, 0, 0)$ on the boundary is simply the sum of a positive and negative $\tilde{\phi}_M$ term:

$$\phi_D(r) = \tilde{\phi}_M(d_r) - \tilde{\phi}_M(d_v) \qquad [15.25]$$

where $d_r = \sqrt{r^2 + z_r^2}$ and $d_v = \sqrt{r^2 + z_v^2}$ are the straight-line distances from the evaluation point to the real and virtual light source. Once more, we can find a matching vector irradiance value using the monopole solution from Equation (15.21):

$$E_D(r) = \tilde{E}_M(d_r) - \tilde{E}_M(d_v) \qquad [15.26]$$

The tilde in $\tilde{E}_M$ above indicates the use of Grosjean's modified diffusion coefficient. We will later require the z component of this expression, which is given by

$$-\mathbf{n} \cdot E_D(r) = \frac{1}{4\pi} \left[\frac{z_r(1 + d_r\sigma_{tr})}{d_r^3} e^{-\sigma_{tr}d_r} - \frac{z_v(1 + d_v\sigma_{tr})}{d_v^3} e^{-\sigma_{tr}d_v} \right]. \qquad [15.27]$$

Boundary Conditions

Having defined the diffusion dipole, we must still specify how the two light sources should be placed in relation to each other so that they fulfill the appropriate boundary conditions (internal reflections, no scattering for $z < 0$). We'll assume that the real light source depth z_r is specified, and that z_v must be set to correct for the boundary.

Moulton (1990) showed that a very simple approximation is enough to get a reasonable answer. As we move from the boundary into the region filled by vacuum, it is intuitive that the fluence rate should decrease fairly quickly due to the inverse squared falloff in a region of space that does not scatter. If we model the fluence rate along the z-axis using a first-order Taylor expansion of the boundary conditions at $z = 0$, then this linear function eventually reaches 0 (and then negative values) at a *linear extrapolation depth* of $z_e < 0$.

The idea of this approach then is to mirror the real light source across the mirror plane $z = z_e$ defined by this extrapolation depth to obtain the virtual light source depth $z_v = 2z_e - z_r$; this ensures that the fluence rate of the dipole is exactly equal to 0 at $z = z_e$ above the half-space. Note that we would generally expect a point outside the medium to have a nonzero positive fluence rate due to radiance leaving the medium; here we are only interested in computing a good solution at the boundary, where the somewhat nonphysical negative light source does not pose problems.

An improved variational approximation of boundary conditions for interfaces with internal Fresnel reflection was derived by Pomraning and Ganapol (1995). With their approach, the linear extrapolation depth is given by

$$z_e = -2D_G \frac{1 + 3\bar{F}_{r,2}(\eta)}{1 - 2\bar{F}_{r,1}(\eta)}, \qquad [15.28]$$

where $\bar{F}_{r,1}$ and $\bar{F}_{r,2}$ are the Fresnel moments first encountered in Equation (11.8).

Radiant Exitance

At this point, we have all ingredients to compute the fluence rate due to a point source inside the surface, with corrections to account for the half-space geometry and internal reflections. To use this solution in a light transport simulation, we'll need to know how much light actually leaves the surface.

Recall Equation (15.16), which related radiance to the fluence rate and vector irradiance. Plugging the dipole solutions into this expression yields

$$L_d(p, \omega) = \frac{1}{4\pi}\phi_D(\|p\|) + \frac{3}{4\pi}\omega \cdot E_D(\|p\|), \tag{15.29}$$

but this is only valid inside the surface. To find the amount of diffusely scattered light leaving at the boundary, we can integrate the internal radiance distribution L_d against the Fresnel transmittance and a cosine factor due to the $dA^\perp$ term in the definition of radiance (Section 5.4).

Using linearity to split the integral into two parts that are related to the fluence rate and vector irradiance, we have

$$E_d(p) = \int_{\mathcal{H}^2(n)} \left(1 - F_r\left(\eta^{-1}, \cos\theta\right)\right) L_d(p, \omega) \, \cos\theta \, d\omega$$
$$= E_{d,\phi_D}(\|p\|) + E_{d,E_D}(\|p\|). \tag{15.30}$$

When the fluence-related part is written in spherical coordinates, the integral over azimuth turns into a multiplication by 2π as no terms depend on it, and $\phi_D(r)$ can be moved out of the integral. The remaining expression reduces to a constant plus a scaled Fresnel moment (Equation (11.8)).

$$E_{d,\phi_D}(r) = \int_0^{2\pi} \int_0^{\frac{\pi}{2}} \left(1 - F_r\left(\eta^{-1}, \cos\theta\right)\right) \frac{1}{4\pi}\phi_D(r) \cos\theta \sin\theta \, d\theta \, d\phi$$
$$= \frac{1}{2}\phi_D(r) \int_0^{\frac{\pi}{2}} \left(1 - F_r\left(\eta^{-1}, \cos\theta\right)\right) \cos\theta \sin\theta \, d\theta \tag{15.31}$$
$$= \phi_D(r) \left(\frac{1}{4} - \frac{1}{2}\bar{F}_{r,1}\right).$$

For the part depending on E_D, we obtain

$$E_{d,E_D}(r) = \int_0^{2\pi} \int_0^{\frac{\pi}{2}} \left(1 - F_r\left(\eta^{-1}, \cos\theta\right)\right) \left(\frac{3}{4\pi}\omega \cdot E_D(r)\right) \cos\theta \sin\theta \, d\theta \, d\phi$$
$$= \int_0^{\frac{\pi}{2}} \left(1 - F_r\left(\eta^{-1}, \cos\theta\right)\right) \left(\frac{3\cos\theta}{2}n \cdot E_D(r)\right) \cos\theta \sin\theta \, d\theta \tag{15.32}$$
$$= n \cdot E_D(r) \left(\frac{1}{2} - \frac{3}{2}\bar{F}_{r,2}\right).$$

In summary: after putting together all the pieces, we have a method of evaluating the radiant exitance at a position p on the boundary due to an internal source at depth z_r. So far, this depth was assumed to be a fixed parameter, but now we'll promote it to an argument of the radiant exitance we just derived, which is now written $E_d(p, z_r)$.

15.5.6 BEAM SOLUTION

At this point, we are almost ready to implement the model, though one missing piece that must still be addressed is the depth z_r of the positive point light source—this choice will clearly have an effect on the accuracy of the final solution.

The first dipole-based BSSRDF model for computer graphics proposed by Jensen et al. (2001b) placed the source at a depth of one mean free path—i.e., $z_r = 1/\sigma_t'$—inside the medium, which is the expected distance that light will travel after entering the surface. This is a reasonable approximation, though it leads to significant errors close to the source.

With the PBD method, the point source solution is integrated over a semi-infinite interval $z_r \in [0, \infty)$ that considers all positions where light traveling along a perpendicularly incident collimated beam could scatter. The impulse response of the medium to such a spatio-directional Dirac delta function provides a more faithful description of its reflection behavior. More advanced variants of this model also allow for rays with non-perpendicular incidence. Formally, this method computes

$$E_d(p) = \int_0^\infty \sigma_s'\, e^{-\sigma_t' z_r}\, E_d(p, z_r)\, dz_r \qquad [15.33]$$

The exponential models how the incident beam's power diminishes due to extinction by the medium. Though there are a variety of high-accuracy approximations to this integral that use only a few samples, for the implementation in pbrt, performance is less critical since the diffusion solution is only computed once. For this reason, we use a rudimentary but simpler importance sampling scheme of the exponential term in Equation (15.33).

The function BeamDiffusionMS() takes the medium properties σ_s, σ_a, g, η, and a radius r and returns an average of 100 samples of the integrand.

⟨*BSSRDF Utility Functions*⟩ ≡
```
Float BeamDiffusionMS(Float sigma_s, Float sigma_a, Float g, Float eta,
                      Float r) {
    const int nSamples = 100;
    Float Ed = 0;
    ⟨Precompute information for dipole integrand 928⟩
    for (int i = 0; i < nSamples; ++i) {
        ⟨Sample real point source depth zr 929⟩
        ⟨Evaluate dipole integrand Ed at zr and add to Ed 929⟩
    }
    return Ed / nSamples;
}
```

A number of coefficients that do not depend on z_r can be precomputed outside the loop.

⟨*Precompute information for dipole integrand*⟩ ≡   928
    ⟨*Compute reduced scattering coefficients σ_s', σ_t' and albedo ρ'* 929⟩
    ⟨*Compute non-classical diffusion coefficient D_G using Equation* (15.24) 929⟩
    ⟨*Compute effective transport coefficient σ_{tr} based on D_G* 929⟩
    ⟨*Determine linear extrapolation distance z_e using Equation* (15.28) 929⟩
    ⟨*Determine exitance scale factors using Equations* (15.31) *and* (15.32) 929⟩

We begin by setting the reduced scattering and attenuation coefficients and single scattering albedo using the principle of similarity from Section 15.5.1.

⟨*Compute reduced scattering coefficients* σ'_s, σ'_t *and albedo* ρ'⟩ ≡   928
```
Float sigmap_s = sigma_s * (1 - g);
Float sigmap_t = sigma_a + sigmap_s;
Float rhop = sigmap_s / sigmap_t;
```

Following this, we compute Grosjean's non-classical diffusion coefficient, Equation (15.24), and the corresponding effective transport coefficient (Section 15.5.3).

⟨*Compute non-classical diffusion coefficient* D_G *using Equation* (15.24)⟩ ≡   928
```
Float D_g = (2 * sigma_a + sigmap_s) / (3 * sigmap_t * sigmap_t);
```

⟨*Compute effective transport coefficient* σ_{tr} *based on* D_G⟩ ≡   928
```
Float sigma_tr = std::sqrt(sigma_a / D_g);
```

Neither the linear extrapolation depth z_e nor the scale factors from the radiant exitance computation depend on z_r, so they can also be computed. The FresnelMoment1() and FresnelMoment2() functions previously encountered in Section 11.4.1 evaluate $\bar{F}_{r,1}$ and $\bar{F}_{r,2}$.

⟨*Determine linear extrapolation distance* z_e *using Equation* (15.28)⟩ ≡   928
```
Float fm1 = FresnelMoment1(eta), fm2 = FresnelMoment2(eta);
Float ze = -2 * D_g * (1 + 3 * fm2) / (1 - 2 * fm1);
```

⟨*Determine exitance scale factors using Equations* (15.31) *and* (15.32)⟩ ≡   928
```
Float cPhi = .25f * (1 - 2 * fm1), cE = .5f * (1 - 3 * fm2);
```

This concludes the precomputation—all following fragments occur in the loop over samples. To select the point source depth z_r, we importance sample the homogeneous attenuation term using the same approach as in Section 15.2, setting

$$z_r = -\frac{\ln(1 - \xi_i)}{\sigma'_t} \qquad [15.34]$$

for $\xi_i \in [0, 1)$. Because we are integrating a smooth 1D function, Monte Carlo isn't required. We therefore use equal-spaced positions $(i + \frac{1}{2})/N$, where $0 \leq i < N$.

⟨*Sample real point source depth* z_r⟩ ≡   928
```
Float zr = -std::log(1 - (i + .5f) / nSamples) / sigmap_t;
```

Given z_r, we next determine the straight-line distances to the real and virtual light source, whose position is found by mirroring the real source across the linear extrapolation depth at $z = z_e$.

⟨*Evaluate dipole integrand* E_d *at* z_r *and add to* Ed⟩ ≡   928
```
Float zv = -zr + 2 * ze;
Float dr = std::sqrt(r * r + zr * zr), dv = std::sqrt(r * r + zv * zv);
⟨Compute dipole fluence rate ϕ_D(r) using Equation (15.25) 930⟩
⟨Compute dipole vector irradiance −n · E_D(r) using Equation (15.27) 930⟩
⟨Add contribution from dipole for depth z_r to Ed 930⟩
```

The dipole fluence rate and normal component of the irradiance were previously discussed in Equations (15.25) and (15.27).

⟨*Compute dipole fluence rate* $\phi_D(r)$ *using Equation (15.25)*⟩ ≡   929
```
    Float phiD = Inv4Pi / D_g *
        (std::exp(-sigma_tr * dr) / dr - std::exp(-sigma_tr * dv) / dv);
```

⟨*Compute dipole vector irradiance* $-\mathbf{n} \cdot \mathbf{E}_D(r)$ *using Equation (15.27)*⟩ ≡   929
```
    Float EDn = Inv4Pi *
        (zr * (1 + sigma_tr * dr) * std::exp(-sigma_tr * dr) / (dr*dr*dr) -
         zv * (1 + sigma_tr * dv) * std::exp(-sigma_tr * dv) / (dv*dv*dv));
```

The last fragment computes the diffuse radiant exitance E due to the dipole using Equation (15.30) and adds a scaled version of it to the running sum in Ed. In this computation, the first rhop factor in the scale is needed due to the ratio of the importance sampling weight of the sampling strategy in Equation (15.34) and the σ'_s factor in Equation (15.33). The second rhop factor accounts for the additional scattering event in Grosjean's non-classical monopole in Equation (15.23). Finally an empirical correction factor

$$\kappa = 1 - e^{-2\sigma'_t(d_r + z_r)}$$

corrects an overestimation that can occur when r is small and the light source is close to the surface (see Habel et al. (2013) for details).

⟨*Add contribution from dipole for depth* z_r *to* Ed⟩ ≡   929
```
    Float E = phiD * cPhi + EDn * cE;
    Float kappa = 1 - std::exp(-2 * sigmap_t * (dr + zr));
    Ed += kappa * rhop * rhop * E;
```

15.5.7 SINGLE SCATTERING TERM

Having accounted for the diffusive multiple scattering term, it's also necessary to account for single scattering, which is not handled well by the diffusion approximation. Single scattering contributes a significant amount of energy to the scattering profile close to $r = 0$. In the absence of multiple scattering, it is fortunately simple enough to compute its contribution directly with the original equation of transfer.

Using the generalized path integral from Section 15.1.1, the radiance in the medium traveling toward position p_0 after scattering precisely once in the volume at position p_1 is given by

$$L_{ss}(p_1 \to p_0) = \hat{P}(\bar{p}_2) = \int_{\mathcal{P}_1} L_e(p_2 \to p_1)\, \hat{T}(p_0, p_1, p_2)\, d\mu_1(p_2), \qquad [15.35]$$

where $\hat{T}$ is the generalized throughput function from Equation (15.3). We model illumination coming from a collimated beam at fixed position p_i pointing into the negative normal direction, i.e.:

$$L_e(p, \omega) = \delta(p - p_i)\, \delta(\omega + \mathbf{n}). \qquad [15.36]$$

Float 1062

Inv4Pi 1063

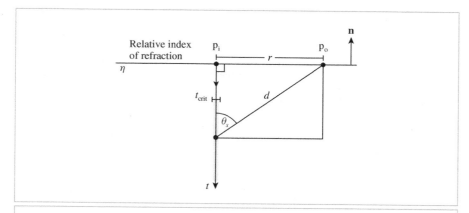

Figure 15.18: Computing the Single Scattering Portion of the BSSRDF Profile. Illumination at perpendicular incidence is scattered once inside the material. Scattering sites before the depth t_{crit} undergo internal reflection and cannot directly contribute to single scattering. We therefore integrate the source function over the remaining depths $t \in [t_{crit}, \infty)$ to account for the full effect of single scattering.

Similar to the previous section, we are interested in the outgoing irradiance at a point p_o on the half-space boundary due to the decaying beam of light. Relevant distances and angles in this arrangement can be found using simple triangle identities (Figure 15.18). We'll briefly ignore the effect of refraction at $z = 0$ to simplify the derivation but will account for it later on in the final result.

The irradiance at p_o can be found by integrating the single-scattered radiance L_{ss} and a generalized geometry term of Equation (15.5) over the volume. Expanding the definition of L_{ss} from Equation (15.35) produces an integral over paths of length 2:

$$E_{ss}(p_o) = \int_{\mathcal{P}_1} L_{ss}(p_1 \to p_o) \, \hat{G}(p_1 \leftrightarrow p_o) \, d\mu_1(p_1)$$
$$= \int_{\mathcal{P}_2} L_e(p_2 \to p_1) \, \hat{T}(p_o, p_1, p_2) \, \hat{G}(p_1 \leftrightarrow p_o) \, d\mu_2(p_1, p_2). \tag{15.37}$$

After expanding L_e, the spatial delta function from Equation (15.36) removes the integration over p_2, and the directional term reduces Equation (15.37) to a 1D integral along the ray $(p_i, -n)$:

$$E_{ss}(p_o) = \int_0^\infty t^2 \, \hat{T}(p_o, p_i - tn, p_i) \, \hat{G}((p_i - tn) \leftrightarrow p_o) \, dt.$$

The extra t^2 term is a change of variables factor resulting from an intermediate step (not shown here), where the volumetric integral over p_1 is expressed in terms of spherical coordinates (t, ϕ, θ). The ϕ and θ variables subsequently drop out due to the directional delta function $\delta(\omega + n)$ in L_e.

Expanding the generalized throughput $\hat{T}$ using Equation (15.3) yields

$$E_{ss}(p_o) = \int_0^\infty t^2\, \hat{G}(p_i \leftrightarrow (p_i - t\mathbf{n}))\, \hat{f}(p_i \to (p_i - t\mathbf{n}) \to p_o)$$
$$\times\, \hat{G}((p_i - t\mathbf{n}) \leftrightarrow p_o)\, dt \qquad [15.38]$$

The definition of the generalized scattering function from Equation (15.4) and the assumption that the phase function only depends on the cosine of the scattering angle $\cos\theta_s$ imply that $\hat{f}$ can be written as

$$\hat{f}(p_i \to (p_i - t\mathbf{n}) \to p_o) = \sigma_s\, p(-\cos\theta_s). \qquad [15.39]$$

We will use the Henyey–Greenstein phase function model for p. The angle cosine $\cos\theta_s$ can be found from the triangle edge lengths (Figure 15.18):

$$\cos\theta_s = \frac{t}{d}. \qquad [15.40]$$

The hypotenuse d is the distance from the scattering location $p_i - t\mathbf{n}$ to the exit point p_o and is given by the Pythagorean theorem:

$$d = \sqrt{r^2 + t^2}, \qquad [15.41]$$

where $r = \|p_i - p_o\|$.

Due to the assumptions of a homogeneous medium without internal occluders, the first geometric term in Equation (15.38) takes on a simple form:

$$\hat{G}(p_i \leftrightarrow (p_i - t\mathbf{n})) = \frac{e^{-\sigma_t t}}{t^2}. \qquad [15.42]$$

Note that this equation uses the original attenuation coefficient σ_t rather than the reduced version σ_t' from Section 15.5.1. In contrast to diffusion theory, the equation of transfer easily accounts for anisotropy; hence there is no longer a need for this approximation.

For the second geometry term, we must include a cosine factor that accounts for the angle that the connecting ray segment makes with the surface normal $\mathbf{n}$ when intersecting the boundary at p_o:

$$\hat{G}((p_i - t\mathbf{n}) \leftrightarrow p_o) = \frac{e^{-\sigma_t d}}{d^2}\, |\cos\theta_o|. \qquad [15.43]$$

The two cosine terms $\cos\theta_o$ and $\cos\theta_s$ are equal except for a difference in sign, which can be seen from the triangle geometry in Figure 15.18.

Plugging Equations (15.42), (15.43), and (15.39) into Equation (15.38) yields the following expression for the irradiance due to single scattering:

$$E_{ss}(p_o) = \int_0^\infty \frac{\sigma_s\, e^{-\sigma_t(t+d)}}{d^2}\, p(\cos\theta_s)\, |\cos\theta_o|\, dt.$$

At this point, we'll reintroduce the effect of the refractive boundary by adding a Fresnel transmission factor $(1 - F_r(\eta, \cos\theta_o))$. Light that is internally reflected by the boundary is already included in the diffusion solution and should be excluded from the single-scattering profile. As before in Section 15.5.6, responsibility for the first refraction at p_i is delegated to the Material's BSDF and thus there is just a single Fresnel transmission term,

$$E_{ss,F_r}(p_o) = \int_0^\infty \frac{\sigma_s\, e^{-\sigma_t\,(t+d)}}{d^2}\, p(\cos\theta_s)\,(1 - F_r(\eta, \cos\theta_o))\,|\cos\theta_o|\, dt. \qquad [15.44]$$

Before we begin with the implementation of this integral, there is one more effect that should be considered: when the relative index of refraction η over the boundary is greater than 1, no illumination can directly leave the material at angles below the critical angle θ_{crit} due to total internal reflection, where

$$\theta_{crit} = \sin^{-1}\frac{1}{\eta}.$$

To avoid unnecessary computations for scattering locations that cannot possibly contribute, we restrict the integral to the range satisfying

$$\cos\theta_o < -\cos\theta_{crit} = -\sqrt{1 - \frac{1}{\eta^2}}.$$

Combining this with Equation (15.41) and solving for t yields

$$t > t_{crit} = r\sqrt{\eta^2 - 1}. \qquad [15.45]$$

As in Section 15.5.6, we compute this integral by uniformly sampling distances t_i according to exponential distribution (which now starts at depth t_{crit}) and set

$$t_i = t_{crit} - \frac{\ln(1 - \xi_i)}{\sigma_t} \qquad [15.46]$$

for evenly spaced $\xi_i \in [0, 1)$. The associated PDF is

$$p_t(t) = \sigma_t\, e^{-\sigma_t(t - t_{crit})},$$

and dividing the integrand in Equation (15.44) by this PDF results in a throughput weight of

$$\beta = \frac{\rho\, e^{-\sigma_t\,(t_{crit}+d)}}{d^2}\, p(-\cos\theta_o)\,(1 - F_r(\eta, -\cos\theta_o))\cos\theta_o, \qquad [15.47]$$

where ρ was previously defined as σ_s/σ_t.

The PBD single-scattering profile computation is implemented in BeamDiffusionSS(), which takes the medium scattering properties and a radius r as input. One hundred samples are used for the integral estimate, as in BeamDiffusionMS().

⟨*BSSRDF Utility Functions*⟩ +≡
```
Float BeamDiffusionSS(Float sigma_s, Float sigma_a, Float g, Float eta,
                      Float r) {
    ⟨Compute material parameters and minimum t below the critical angle 934⟩
    Float Ess = 0;
    const int nSamples = 100;
    for (int i = 0; i < nSamples; ++i) {
        ⟨Evaluate single-scattering integrand and add to Ess 934⟩
    }
    return Ess / nSamples;
}
```

The function begins by precomputing derived material parameters and setting tCrit to the minimal distance below the critical angle as specified by Equation (15.45).

⟨*Compute material parameters and minimum t below the critical angle*⟩ ≡   **934**
```
Float sigma_t = sigma_a + sigma_s, rho = sigma_s / sigma_t;
Float tCrit = r * std::sqrt(eta * eta - 1);
```

The loop body generates distances t_i according to the sampling scheme in Equation (15.46).

⟨*Evaluate single-scattering integrand and add to* Ess⟩ ≡   **934**
```
Float ti = tCrit - std::log(1 - (i + .5f) / nSamples) / sigma_t;
⟨Determine length d of connecting segment and cos θ₀ 934⟩
⟨Add contribution of single scattering at depth t 934⟩
```

Next, the function computes the length of the connection segment using Equation (15.41). $\cos \theta_o$ is given by Equation (15.40) except for a sign flip that is needed since the half-space normal **n** points away from the medium.

⟨*Determine length d of connecting segment and* $\cos \theta_o$⟩ ≡   **934**
```
Float d = std::sqrt(r * r + ti * ti);
Float cosTheta0 = ti / d;
```

The last loop statement accumulates the throughput weight β from Equation (15.47) into the running sum Ess.

⟨*Add contribution of single scattering at depth t*⟩ ≡   **934**
```
Ess += rho * std::exp(-sigma_t * (d + tCrit)) / (d * d) *
    PhaseHG(cosTheta0, g) * (1 - FrDielectric(-cosTheta0, 1, eta)) *
    std::abs(cosTheta0);
```

15.5.8 FILLING THE BSSRDFTable

With the definitions of BeamDiffusionMS() and BeamDiffusionSS() at hand, we'll now implement the function ComputeBeamDiffusionBSSRDF() that uses these functions to fill the BSSRDFTable of a TabulatedBSSRDF with profile data.

ComputeBeamDiffusionBSSRDF() takes the medium's anisotropy parameter g and relative index of refraction η as input and initializes a BSSRDFTable that stores these quantities as a function of radius and albedo. This function is in turn invoked by the initialization routines of the SubsurfaceMaterial and KdSubsurfaceMaterial using a default BSSRDFTable with 100 albedo samples and 64 radius samples.

⟨*BSSRDF Utility Functions*⟩ +≡
```
void ComputeBeamDiffusionBSSRDF(Float g, Float eta, BSSRDFTable *t) {
    ⟨Choose radius values of the diffusion profile discretization 935⟩
    ⟨Choose albedo values of the diffusion profile discretization 936⟩
    ParallelFor(
        [&](int i) {
            ⟨Compute the diffusion profile for the ith albedo sample 936⟩
        }, t->nRhoSamples);
}
```

Both single- and multiple-scattering components of the profile function $S_r(r)$ are characterized by an exponential decay with increasing radius r. By placing many samples in high-valued regions and comparably fewer in low-valued regions, we can obtain a better spline approximation of the true profile. The following fragment places the first radius sample at 0 and distributes the remaining samples at exponentially increasing distances. (Note that radius values are unitless and independent of the actual medium density σ_t. These unitless optical radii were previously introduced in Section 11.4.2.)

⟨*Choose radius values of the diffusion profile discretization*⟩ ≡   935
```
t->radiusSamples[0] = 0;
t->radiusSamples[1] = 2.5e-3f;
for (int i = 2; i < t->nRadiusSamples; ++i)
    t->radiusSamples[i] = t->radiusSamples[i - 1] * 1.2f;
```

Next, we need to decide on the locations of N albedo samples ρ_i on the interval [0, 1]. Some precautions must be taken here as well, since the material's scattering behavior has a highly nonlinear dependence on the ρ parameter.

Consider the example of a medium with a single scattering albedo of $\rho = 0.8$: this produces a surprisingly absorptive BSSRDF with an effective albedo ρ_{eff} of less than 0.15! The reason for this behavior is that most incident illumination is scattered many times before it finally leaves the half space; each scattering event incurs an energy reduction by ρ, leading to this striking nonlinearity. The left side of Figure 15.19 plots ρ_{eff} as a function of ρ, which shows that most of the interesting behavior is crammed into a small region near $\rho \approx 1$.

Clearly, uniform sample placement $\rho_i = i/(N - 1)$ will not capture this behavior in a satisfactory way. Instead, we use a heuristic that approximately inverts the nonlinear mapping between ρ and ρ_{eff}:

$$\rho_i = \frac{1 - e^{-8i/(N-1)}}{1 - e^{-8}},$$ [15.48]

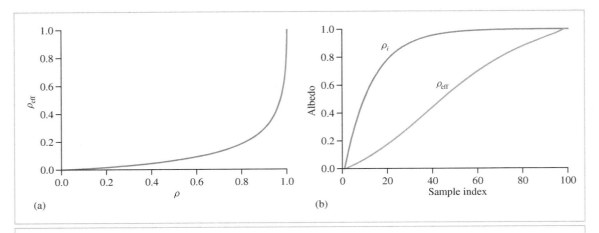

Figure 15.19: (a) The relationship between the single scattering albedo ρ and the effective albedo ρ_{eff} is highly nonlinear. (b) We use the reparameterization in Equation (15.48) to achieve a more effective sample placement with an approximately uniform sample spacing in effective albedo space.

⟨*Choose albedo values of the diffusion profile discretization*⟩ ≡   935
```
for (int i = 0; i < t->nRhoSamples; ++i)
    t->rhoSamples[i] =
        (1 - std::exp(-8 * i / (Float)(t->nRhoSamples - 1))) /
        (1 - std::exp(-8));
```

This results in a more perceptually uniform placement of the albedo samples, which can be seen on the right side of Figure 15.19: while not a perfect straight line, the effective albedo associated with increasing sample indices i is now reasonably close to linear.

The loop body then iterates over albedo samples and computes a diffusion profile and associated effective albedo for each one.

⟨*Compute the diffusion profile for the ith albedo sample*⟩ ≡   935
  ⟨*Compute scattering profile for chosen albedo ρ* 937⟩
  ⟨*Compute effective albedo ρ_{eff} and CDF for importance sampling* 937⟩

The first fragment interprets the scattering profile $S_r(r)$ as a distribution in polar coordinates (r, ϕ). The marginal distribution over the radius parameter is then given by $2\pi r S_r(r)$, where $S_r(r) = S_{r,\text{ss}}(r) + S_{r,\text{ms}}(r)$ is the sum of single and multiple scattering profiles.

The reason for tabulating the marginal distribution rather than the profile itself is to facilitate sample generation: in this way, BSSRDFTable::profile can be treated as parameterized sequence of 1D distributions that can be sampled using existing tools like SampleCatmullRom2D() (as is done in TabulatedBSSRDF::Sample_Sr()). However, we must be careful to cancel the extra factor of $2\pi r$ during normal profile evaluations—this was implemented in the fragment ⟨*Cancel marginal PDF factor from tabulated BSSRDF profile*⟩ in Section 11.4.2.

⟨*Compute scattering profile for chosen albedo ρ*⟩ ≡   **936**
```
for (int j = 0; j < t->nRadiusSamples; ++j) {
    Float rho = t->rhoSamples[i], r = t->radiusSamples[j];
    t->profile[i * t->nRadiusSamples + j] = 2 * Pi * r *
        (BeamDiffusionSS(rho, 1 - rho, g, eta, r) +
         BeamDiffusionMS(rho, 1 - rho, g, eta, r));
}
```

Integrating the (unnormalized) marginal PDF over the interval $r \in [0, \infty)$ yields the effective albedo, which was defined in Equation (11.11). In practice, we limit the integral to a finite interval $[0, r_{max}]$—this is not an issue, as $S_r(r)$ is negligible for $r > r_{max}$. The IntegrateCatmullRom() function computes this integral in addition to an auxiliary CDF for importance sampling.

⟨*Compute effective albedo ρ_{eff} and CDF for importance sampling*⟩ ≡   **936**
```
t->rhoEff[i] =
    IntegrateCatmullRom(t->nRadiusSamples, t->radiusSamples.get(),
                        &t->profile[i * t->nRadiusSamples],
                        &t->profileCDF[i * t->nRadiusSamples]);
```

pbrt uses the inversion method to importance sample piecewise cubic spline functions. This entails first choosing a spline segment according to a discrete probability mass function and then picking a position inside the segment. The IntegrateCatmullRom() function therefore computes a cumulative distribution function that is useful for implementing this sampling operation in an efficient way.

⟨*Spline Interpolation Definitions*⟩ +≡
```
Float IntegrateCatmullRom(int n, const Float *x, const Float *values,
                          Float *cdf) {
    Float sum = 0;
    cdf[0] = 0;
    for (int i = 0; i < n - 1; ++i) {
        ⟨Look up xᵢ and function values of spline segment i 823⟩
        ⟨Approximate derivatives using finite differences 823⟩
        ⟨Keep a running sum and build a cumulative distribution function 938⟩
    }
    return sum;
}
```

The loop iterates over each spline segment and computes the definite integral of the associated cubic spline interpolant, Equation (8.27), over the associated interval. This definite integral has a simple analytic solution:

$$\int_{x_i}^{x_{i+1}} p_i(x)\, \mathrm{d}x = (x_{i+1} - x_i) \left[\frac{f(x_i) + f(x_{i+1})}{2} + \frac{f'(x_i) - f'(x_{i+1})}{12} \right],$$

where p_i is the spline interpolant defined on the interval $[x_i, x_{i+1}]$, the values $f(x_i)$ and $f(x_{i+1})$ are function evaluations at the endpoints, and $f'(x_i)$ and $f'(x_{i+1})$ are derivative estimates.

The first two fragments in the loop body were previously discussed—they look up the function values (denoted by f0 and f1) and derivative estimates (denoted by d0 and d1) in the current interval and initialize width with the interval length.

We can now compute the definite integral and add it to a running sum. Partial sums are written into the cdf array.

⟨*Keep a running sum and build a cumulative distribution function*⟩ ≡   **937**
```
sum += ((d0 - d1) * (1.f / 12.f) + (f0 + f1) * .5f) * width;
cdf[i + 1] = sum;
```

15.5.9 SETTING SCATTERING PROPERTIES

It is remarkably unintuitive to set values of the absorption and scattering coefficients σ_a and σ_s to achieve a desired visual result. If measured values of these parameters aren't available (e.g., from values from the GetMediumScatteringProperties() utility function of Section 11.4.3), then the task for an artist trying to render subsurface scattering can be difficult.

In this section, we define a convenience function SubsurfaceFromDiffuse() used by the KdSubsurfaceMaterial, which solves an inverse problem using information stored in the BSSRDFTable to derive the medium's scattering properties. The function takes considerably more intuitive parameters as input: in addition to the BSSRDFTable, it requires an effective albedo and the average distance light travels in the medium before scattering (the mean free path length).

The medium can be made more transparent by increasing the mean free path length or denser by decreasing it. The amount of multiple scattering can be controlled by how close the effective albedo is to 1. The remaining medium properties (index of refraction and scattering anisotropy) are assumed to be fixed.

We perform the inversion separately for each wavelength using InvertCatmullRom() to map from effective albedo to a single scattering albedo ρ. With ρ known, the desired coefficients are given by $\sigma_s = \rho/\sigma_t^{-1}$ and $\sigma_s = (1-\rho)/\sigma_t^{-1}$, where σ_t is the reciprocal of the mean free path length.

⟨*BSSRDF Utility Functions*⟩ +≡
```
void SubsurfaceFromDiffuse(const BSSRDFTable &t, const Spectrum &rhoEff,
        const Spectrum &mfp, Spectrum *sigma_a, Spectrum *sigma_s) {
    for (int c = 0; c < Spectrum::nSamples; ++c) {
        Float rho = InvertCatmullRom(t.nRhoSamples, t.rhoSamples.get(),
                            t.rhoEff.get(), rhoEff[c]);
        (*sigma_s)[c] = rho / mfp[c];
        (*sigma_a)[c] = (1 - rho) / mfp[c];
    }
}
```

InvertCatmullRom() is very similar to the already defined SampleCatmullRom() function except that it directly inverts the spline function and not its definite integral—it otherwise applies the same Newton-Bisection algorithm (and reuses a number of code fragments). We therefore won't include its implementation here. Note that using this approach requires that the underlying function be either monotonically increasing or monotonically decreasing; in the case of SubsurfaceFromDiffuse(), the function is monotonically increasing.

⟨*Spline Interpolation Declarations*⟩ ≡
```
Float InvertCatmullRom(int n, const Float *x, const Float *values,
                       Float u);
```

FURTHER READING

Lommel (1889) was apparently the first to derive the equation of transfer. Not only did he derive the equation of transfer, but he also solved it in some simplified cases in order to estimate reflection functions from real-world surfaces (including marble and paper) and compared his solutions to measured reflectance data from these surfaces.

Seemingly unaware of Lommel's work, Schuster (1905) was the next researcher in radiative transfer to consider the effect of multiple scattering. He used the term *self-illumination* to describe the fact that each part of the medium is illuminated by every other part of the medium, and he derived differential equations that described reflection from a slab along the normal direction assuming the presence of isotropic scattering. The conceptual framework that he developed remains essentially unchanged in the field of radiative transfer.

Soon thereafter, Schwarzschild (1906) introduced the concept of radiative equilibrium, and Jackson (1910) expressed Schuster's equation in integral form, also noting that "the obvious physical mode of solution is Liouville's method of successive substitutions" (i.e., a Neumann series solution). Finally, King (1913) completed the rediscovery of the equation of transfer by expressing it in the general integral form. Yanovitskij (1997) traced the origin of the integral equation of transfer to Chvolson (1890), but we have been unable to find a copy of this paper.

Books by Chandrasekhar (1960), Preisendorfer (1965, 1976), and van de Hulst (1980) cover volume light transport in depth.

Blinn (1982b) first used basic volume scattering algorithms for computer graphics. The equation of transfer was first introduced to graphics by Kajiya and Von Herzen (1984). Rushmeier (1988) was the first to compute solutions of it in a general setting. Arvo (1993) first made the essential connections between previous formalizations of light transport in graphics and the equation of transfer and radiative transfer in general. Pauly, Kollig, and Keller (2000) derived the generalization of the path integral form of the light transport equation for the volume scattering case.

See also the "Further Reading" section of Chapter 11 for additional references to previous work on light scattering in participating media.

Building Blocks

Float 1062

The paper by Raab et al. (2006) introduced many important sampling building-blocks for rendering participating media to graphics, including the delta-tracking algorithm for inhomogeneous media by Woodcock et al. (1965). (pbrt uses this algorithm in

`GridDensityMedium::Sample()`.) More recently, Novák et al. (2014) derived *ratio tracking* and *residual ratio tracking*, which provide unbiased estimates of the transmittance function in inhomogeneous media with considerably lower variance than delta tracking; the simpler ratio tracking algorithm is used in `GridDensityMedium::Tr()`.

For media with substantial variation in density, delta tracking can be quite inefficient— many small steps must be taken to get through the optically thin sections. Danskin and Hanrahan (1992) presented a technique for efficient volume ray marching using a hierarchical data structure. Another way of addressing this issue was presented by Szirmay-Kalos et al. (2011), who used a grid to partition scattering volumes in cells and applied delta tracking using the maximum density cells as the ray passed through them. Yue et al. (2010) applied a similar approach but used a kd-tree, which was better able to adapt to spatially varying densities. In follow-on work, they derive an approach to estimate the efficiency of spatial partitionings and use it to construct them more effectively (Yue et al. 2011).

Kulla and Fajardo (2012) noted that techniques based on sampling beam transmittance ignore another important factor: spatial variation in the scattering coefficient. They developed a method based on computing a tabularized 1D sampling distribution for each ray passing through participating media based on the product of beam transmittance and scattering coefficient at a number of points along it. They then draw samples from this distribution, showing good results.

Accounting for illumination from emissive media is important for many effects, including fire and explosions. See Villemin and Hery (2013) for algorithms for sampling illumination from these sorts of emitters.

Researchers have recently had success in deriving closed-form expressions that describe scattering along unoccluded ray segments in participating media; these approaches can be substantially more efficient than integrating over a series of point samples. See Sun et al. (2005), Pegoraro and Parker (2009), and Pegoraro et al. (2009, 2010, 2011) for examples of such methods. (Remarkably, Pegoraro and collaborators' work provides a closed-form expression for scattering from a point light source along a ray passing through homogeneous participating media with anisotropic phase functions.)

Light Transport Algorithms

Rushmeier and Torrance (1987) used finite-element methods for rendering participating media. Other early work in volume scattering for computer graphics includes work by Max (1986), Nishita, Miyawaki, and Nakamae (1987), Bhate and Tokuta's approach based on spherical harmonics (Bhate and Tokuta 1992), and Blasi et al.'s two-pass Monte Carlo algorithm, where the first pass shoots energy from the lights and stores it in a grid and the second pass does final rendering using the grid to estimate illumination at points in the scene (Blasi, Saëc, and Schlick 1993). Glassner (1995) provided a thorough overview of this topic and previous applications of it in graphics, and Max's survey article (Max 1995) also covers early work well. See Cerezo et al. (2005) for an extensive survey of approaches to rendering participating media up through 2005.

More recently, Szirmay-Kalos et al. (2005) precomputed interactions between sample points in the medium in order to more quickly compute multiple scattering. Pegoraro et al. (2008b) developed an interesting approach for improving Monte Carlo rendering

GridDensityMedium::Sample()
896

GridDensityMedium::Tr() 898

of participating media by using information from previous samples to guide future sampling.

Georgiev et al. (2013) made the observation that incremental path sampling can generate particularly bad paths in participating media. They proposed new multi-vertex sampling methods that better account for all of the relevant terms in the equation of transfer.

Sampling direct illumination from lights at points inside media surrounded by a primitive is challenging; traditional direct lighting algorithms aren't applicable at points inside the medium, as refraction through the primitive's boundary will divert the shadow ray's path. Walter et al. (2009) considered this problem and developed algorithms to efficiently find paths to lights accounting for this refraction.

The visual appearance of high albedo objects like clouds is striking, but many bounces may be necessary for good results. Wrenninge et al. (2013) described an approximation where after the first few bounces, the scattering coefficient, attenuation coefficient for shadow rays, and the eccentricity of the phase function are all progressively reduced. (This approach draws from ideas behind the principle of similarity from Section 15.5.1.)

All of the bidirectional light transport algorithms that will be introduced in Chapter 16 can be extended to handle participating media; most of our implementations include these extensions. See the "Further Reading" section in that chapter for references to previous work on these topics. See also Jarosz's thesis (2008), which has extensive background on this topic (and includes a number of important contributions).

Subsurface Scattering

Subsurface scattering was first introduced to graphics by Hanrahan and Krueger (1993), although their approach did not attempt to simulate light that entered the object at points other than at the point being shaded. Dorsey et al. (1999) applied photon maps to simulating subsurface scattering that did include this effect, and Pharr and Hanrahan (2000) introduced an approach based on computing BSSRDFs for arbitrary scattering media with an integral over the medium's depth.

Kajiya and Von Herzen (1984) first introduced the diffusion approximation to graphics, though Stam (1995) was the first to clearly identify many of its advantages for rendering. See Ishimaru's book (1978) or Donner's thesis (2006) for the derivation of the diffusion approximation and Wyman et al. (1989) for the introduction of the principle of similarity. More recently, Zhao et al. (2014) further investigated the similarity relations, derived higher order relations, and showed their application to rendering.

The dipole approximation for subsurface scattering was developed by Farrell et al. (1992). It was introduced to computer graphics by Jensen et al. (2001b). Jensen and Buhler (2002) developed an efficient hierarchical integration approach based on precomputing incident irradiance at a set of points on the primitive's surface. The dipole approximation saw early application to production rendering via a scan-line implementation (Hery 2003).

Contini et al. (1997) generalized the dipole approach to *multipoles* to more accurately model finite scattering slabs. This approach was applied to subsurface scattering by Donner and Jensen (2005). However, even the multipole approach doesn't handle all types of scattering media well; the assumptions of homogeneous media and relatively high albedos are too restrictive for many interesting objects. Li et al. (2005) developed a hybrid approach that handles the first few bounces of light with Monte Carlo path tracing but then switches to a dipole approximation. Tong et al. (2005) developed a method to capture and render materials with small deviations from an overall homogeneous appearance. Haber et al. (2005b), and Wang et al. (2008b) further generalized the media supported, solving the diffusion equation on a grid of sample points. Fattal (2009) applied the discrete ordinates method, addressing a number of shortcomings of the direct application of that technique. Arbree et al. (2011) developed a finite element method to solve the diffusion equation on a tetrahedral mesh in a way that is more numerically robust than prior grid-based methods.

The photon beam diffusion approach implemented in Section 15.5 is based on the approach developed by Habel et al. (2013). It builds on the quantized diffusion model developed by d'Eon and Irving (2011), who introduced the Grosjean monopole (Grosjean 1956), the approach of Pomraning and Ganapol (1995) for computing the dipole depth in Equation (15.28), and the computation of the radiant exitance using the approach proposed by Kienle and Patterson (1997).

Frisvad et al. (2014) developed an alternative diffusion technique to model subsurface scattering due to an incident beam of light; in contrast to photon beam diffusion, which integrates isotropic sources along continuous beams, their method builds on a discrete arrangement of anisotropic (i.e., $Q_1 \neq 0$) monopole solutions.

While much effort has gone into more accurate diffusion profiles, Christensen and Burley (2015) showed that a simple exponential approximation to these profiles fits them extremely well and is quite efficient to evaluate.

Donner et al. (2009) computed BSSRDFs with Monte Carlo simulation for a variety of scattering properties (phase function, scattering coefficients, etc.) and fit the resulting data to a low-dimensional model. This model accurately accounts for the directional variation of scattered light and the properties of medium-albedo media.

Rendering realistic human skin is a challenging problem; this problem has driven the development of a number of new methods for rendering subsurface scattering after the initial dipole work as issues of modeling the layers of skin and computing more accurate simulations of scattering between layers have been addressed. For a good overview of these issues, see Igarashi et al.'s (2007) survey on the scattering mechanisms inside skin and approaches for measuring and rendering skin. Notable research in this area includes papers by Donner and Jensen (2006), d'Eon et al. (2007), Ghosh et al. (2008), and Donner et al. (2008). Donner's thesis includes a discussion of the importance of accurate spectral representations for high-quality skin rendering (Donner 2006, Section 8.5).

The algorithm implemented in Section 15.4.1 to find sample points for incident illumination for BSSRDFs was developed by King et al. (2013).

Other Topics

One key application of volume scattering algorithms in computer graphics has been simulating atmospheric scattering. Work in this area includes early papers by Klassen (1987) and Preetham et al. (1999), who introduced a physically rigorous and computationally efficient atmospheric and sky-lighting model. Haber et al. (2005a) described a model for twilight, and Hošek and Wilkie (2012, 2013) developed a comprehensive model for sky- and sun-light.

There are a number of applications of visualizing volumetric data sets for medical and engineering applications. This area is called *volume rendering*. In many of these applications, radiometric accuracy is substantially less important than developing techniques that help make structure in the data apparent (e.g., where the bones are in CT scan data). Early papers in this area include those by Levoy (1988, 1990a, 1990b) and Drebin, Carpenter, and Hanrahan (1988).

Moon et al. (2007) made the important observation that some of the assumptions underlying the use of the equation of transfer—that the scattering particles in the medium aren't too close together so that scattering events can be considered to be statistically independent—aren't in fact true for interesting scenes that include small crystals, ice, or piles of many small glass objects. They developed a new light transport algorithm for these types of *discrete random media* based on composing precomputed scattering solutions.

Jakob et al. (2010) derived a generalized transfer equation that describes scattering by distributions of oriented particles. They proposed a *microflake* scattering model as a specific example of a particle distribution (where a microflake is the volumetric analog of a microfacet on a surface) and showed a number of ways of solving this equation based on Monte Carlo, finite elements, and a dipole model. More recently, Heitz et al. (2015) derived a generalized microflake distribution, which is considerably more efficient to sample and evaluate. Their model quantifies the local scattering properties using projected areas observed from different directions, which adds a well-defined notion of volumetric level of detail.

The equation of transfer assumes that the index of refraction of a medium will only change at discrete boundaries, though many actual media have continuously varying indices of refraction. Ament et al. (2014) derived a variant of the equation of transfer that allows for this case and applied photon mapping to render images with it.

EXERCISES

⊘ 15.1 With optically dense inhomogeneous volume regions, GridDensityMedium:: Tr() may spend a lot of time finding the attenuation between lights and intersection points. One approach to reducing this expense is to take advantage of the facts that the amount of attenuation for nearby rays is generally smoothly varying and that the rays to a point or directional light source can be parameterized over a straightforward 2D domain. Given these conditions, it's possible to use precomputed approximations to the attenuation.

For example, Kajiya and Von Herzen (1984) computed the attenuation to a directional light source at a grid of points in 3D space and then found attenuation at any particular point by interpolating among nearby grid samples. A more memory-efficient approach was developed by Lokovic and Veach (2000) in the form of deep shadow maps, based on a clever compression technique that takes advantage of the smoothness of the attenuation. Implement one of

GridDensityMedium::Tr() 898

these approaches in pbrt, and measure how much it speeds up rendering with the VolPathIntegrator. Under what sorts of situations do approaches like these result in noticeable image errors?

● 15.2 Another effective method for speeding up GridDensityMedium::Tr() is to use Russian roulette: if the accumulated transmittance Tr goes below some threshold, randomly terminate it and return 0 transmittance; otherwise, scale it based on 1 over the survival probability. Modify pbrt to optionally use this approach, and measure the change in Monte Carlo efficiency. How does varying the termination threshold affect your results?

● 15.3 Read the papers by Yue et al. (2010, 2011) on improving delta-tracking's efficiency by decomposing inhomogeneous media using a spatial data structure and then applying delta tracking separately in each region of space. Apply their approach to the GridDensityMedium, and measure the change in efficiency compared to the current implementation.

● 15.4 The current sampling algorithm in the GridDensityMedium is based purely on sampling based on the accumulated attenuation. While this more effective than sampling uniformly, it misses the factor that it's desirable to sample scattering events at points where the scattering coefficient is relatively large as well, as these points contribute more to the overall result. Kulla and Fajardo (2012) describe an approach based on sampling the medium at a number of points along each ray and computing a PDF for the product of the transmittance and the scattering coefficient. Sampling from this distribution gives much better results than sampling based on the transmittance alone.

Implement Kulla and Fajardo's technique in pbrt, and compare the Monte Carlo efficiency of their method to the method currently implemented in GridDensityMedium. Are there scenes where their approach is less effective?

● 15.5 As described in Section 15.3.1, the current VolPathIntegrator implementation will spend unnecessary effort computing ray–primitive intersections in scenes with optically dense scattering media: closer medium interactions will often be sampled than the surface intersections. Modify the system so that medium interactions are sampled before ray–primitive intersections are tested. Reduce the ray's tMax extent when a medium interaction is sampled before performing primitive intersections. Measure the change in performance for scenes with both optically thin and optically thick participating media. (Use a fairly geometrically complex scene so that the cost of ray–primitive intersections isn't negligible.) If your results show that the most efficient approach varies depending on the medium scattering properties, implement an approach to automatically choose between the two strategies at run time based on the medium's characteristics.

● 15.6 The Medium abstraction currently doesn't make it possible to represent emissive media, and the volume-aware integrators don't account for volumetric emission. Modify the system so that emission from a 3D volume can be described, and update one or more Integrator implementations to account for emissive media in their lighting calculations. For the code related to sampling incident radiance, it may be worthwhile to read the paper by Villemin and Hery (2013) on Monte Carlo sampling of 3D emissive volumes.

⊛ **15.7** Compare rendering subsurface scattering with a BSSRDF to brute force integration of the same underlying medium properties with the `VolPathIntegrator`. (Recall that in high-albedo media, paths of hundreds or thousands of bounces may be necessary to compute accurate results.) Compare scenes with a variety of scattering properties, including both low and high albedos. Render images that demonstrate cases where the BSSRDF approximation introduces noticeable error but Monte Carlo computes a correct result. How much slower is the Monte Carlo approach for cases where the BSSRDF is accurate?

⊛ **15.8** Donner et al. (2009) performed extensive numerical simulation of subsurface scattering from media with a wide range of scattering properties and then computed coefficients to fit an analytical model to the resulting data. They have shown that rendering with this model is more efficient than full Monte Carlo integration, while handling well many cases where the approximations of many BSSRDF models are unacceptable. For example, their model accounts for directional variation in the scattered radiance and handles media with low and medium albedos well. Read their paper and download the data files of coefficients. Implement a new BSSRDF in pbrt that uses their model, and render images showing cases where it gives better results than the current BSSRDF implementation.

BSSRDF 692

VolPathIntegrator 900

CHAPTER SIXTEEN

16 LIGHT TRANSPORT III: BIDIRECTIONAL METHODS

The integrators in the previous two chapters have all been based on finding light-carrying paths starting from the camera and then only trying to connect with light sources at the last vertices of the paths. This chapter introduces algorithms based on sampling paths starting from both the camera and the lights and then connecting them at intermediate vertices. These algorithms can be much more efficient at finding light-carrying paths than approaches that only construct paths from the camera, especially in tricky lighting situations.

The foundations of bidirectional light transport are fascinating. On one hand, the physics of light scattering are generally reversible with respect to the direction of light transport, which causes the mathematical expressions of scattering paths starting from a light or from the camera to be very similar. On the other hand, there are subtle but important differences between these two approaches depending the path direction; Section 16.1 discusses these topics in detail. After the foundations have been set, the stochastic progressive photon mapping (SPPM) algorithm is introduced in Section 16.2. SPPM allows light-carrying particles to provide incident illumination at points close to where they intersect surfaces and not just exactly at their intersection points; this adjustment introduces bias but improves the rate of convergence in many challenging settings.

Next, bidirectional path tracing is introduced in Section 16.3. This unbiased approach can be much more efficient than regular path tracing by virtue of both its bidirectional nature as well as further variance reduction from applying multiple importance sampling to reweight path contributions. Finally, in Section 16.4, we show how Metropolis sampling (introduced in Section 13.4) can be used to further improve the efficiency of bidirectional path tracing by focusing computational effort on the most important light-carrying paths.

Physically Based Rendering: From Theory To Implementation.
http://dx.doi.org/10.1016/B978-0-12-800645-0.50016-6

16.1 THE PATH-SPACE MEASUREMENT EQUATION

In light of the path integral form of the LTE from Equation (14.16), it's useful to go back and formally describe the quantity that is being estimated when we compute pixel values for an image. Not only does this let us see how to apply the LTE to a wider set of problems than just computing 2D images (e.g., to precomputing scattered radiance distributions at the vertices of a polygonal model), but this process also leads us to a key theoretical mechanism for understanding the bidirectional path tracing and photon mapping algorithms in this chapter. For simplicity, we'll use the basic path integral for surfaces rather than the generalized variant from Section 15.1.1, though the conclusions are applicable to both versions of the LTE.

The *measurement equation* describes the value of an abstract measurement that is found by integrating over some set of rays carrying radiance.[1] For example, when computing the value of a pixel j in the image, we want to integrate over rays starting in the neighborhood of the pixel, with contributions weighted by the image reconstruction filter. Ignoring depth of field for now (so that each point on the film plane corresponds to a single outgoing direction from the camera), we can write the pixel's value as an integral over points on the film plane of a weighting function times the incident radiance along the corresponding camera rays:

$$I_j = \int_{A_{\text{film}}} \int_{\mathcal{S}^2} W_e^{(j)}(\mathrm{p_{film}}, \omega)\, L_i(\mathrm{p_{film}}, \omega)\, |\cos\theta|\, d\omega\, dA(\mathrm{p_{film}})$$

$$= \int_{A_{\text{film}}} \int_A W_e^{(j)}(\mathrm{p_0} \to \mathrm{p_1})\, L(\mathrm{p_1} \to \mathrm{p_0})\, G(\mathrm{p_0} \leftrightarrow \mathrm{p_1})\, dA(\mathrm{p_1})\, dA(\mathrm{p_0}),$$

where I_j is the measurement for the jth pixel and $\mathrm{p_0}$ is a point on the film. In this setting, the $W_e^{(j)}(\mathrm{p_0} \to \mathrm{p_1})$ term is the product of the filter function around the pixel f_j and a delta function that selects the appropriate camera ray direction of the sample from $\mathrm{p_0}$, $\omega_{\text{camera}}(\mathrm{p_1})$:

$$W_e^{(j)}(\mathrm{p_0} \to \mathrm{p_1}) = f_j(\mathrm{p_0})\, \delta(t(\mathrm{p_0}, \omega_{\text{camera}}(\mathrm{p_1})) - \mathrm{p_1}).$$

This formulation may initially seem gratuitously complex, but it leads us to an important insight. If we expand the $P(\bar{\mathrm{p}}_n)$ terms of the LTE sum, we have

$$I_j = \int_{A_{\text{film}}} \int_A W_e^{(j)}(\mathrm{p_0} \to \mathrm{p_1})\, L(\mathrm{p_1} \to \mathrm{p_0})\, G(\mathrm{p_0} \leftrightarrow \mathrm{p_1})\, dA(\mathrm{p_1})\, dA(\mathrm{p_0})$$

$$= \sum_i \int_A \int_A W_e^{(j)}(\mathrm{p_0} \to \mathrm{p_1})\, P(\bar{\mathrm{p}}_i)\, G(\mathrm{p_0} \leftrightarrow \mathrm{p_1})\, dA(\mathrm{p_1})\, dA(\mathrm{p_0})$$

$$= \sum_i \underbrace{\int_A \cdots \int_A}_{i+1 \text{ times}} W_e^{(j)}(\mathrm{p_0} \to \mathrm{p_1})\, T(\bar{\mathrm{p}}_i)\, L_e(\mathrm{p}_{i+1} \to \mathrm{p}_i)\, G(\mathrm{p_0} \leftrightarrow \mathrm{p_1})$$

$$dA(\mathrm{p}_{i+1}) \cdots dA(\mathrm{p_0}), \qquad\qquad [16.1]$$

where $T(\bar{\mathrm{p}}_i)$ is the path throughput function introduced in Equation (14.18).

---

[1] The camera measurement equation described in Section 6.4.7 is a specific case of the measurement equation.

Note the nice symmetric way in which the emitted radiance L_e (quantifying the light source emission profile) and the weighting function $W_e^{(j)}$ (quantifying the camera's sensitivity profile for a pixel j) appear in the above equation: neither term is treated specially, and from this we can infer that the concepts of emission and measurement are mathematically interchangeable.

The implications of this symmetry are important: it says that we can think of the rendering process in two different ways. The first interpretation is that light could be emitted from light sources, bounce around the scene, and arrive at a sensor where W_e describes its contribution to the measurement. Alternatively, we can think of the sensor as emitting an imaginary quantity that creates a measurement when it reaches a light source. This idea isn't just a theoretical construct: it can be applied in practice. A good example is the Dual Photography work of Sen et al. (2005) that showed that it was possible to take photographs from the viewpoint of a video projector by processing input photographs taken with a separate camera—this could be interpreted as turning the projector into a camera, while using the original camera as the "light source" to illuminate the scene.

By simply swapping the role of cameras and light sources in this way, we can create a method known as *particle tracing*, which traces rays from the light sources to recursively estimate the incident importance arriving on surfaces. This is not a particularly useful rendering technique on its own, but it constitutes an essential ingredient of other methods such as bidirectional path tracing and photon mapping.

The value described by the W_e term is known as the *importance* for the ray between p_0 and p_1 in the scene.[2] When the measurement equation is used to compute pixel measurements, the importance will often be partially or fully described by delta distributions, as it was in the previous example. Many other types of measurements besides image formation can be described by appropriately constructed importance functions, and thus the formalisms described here can be used to show how the integral over paths described by the measurement equation is also the integral that must be estimated to compute them.

16.1.1 SAMPLING CAMERAS

Bidirectional light transport algorithms require the ability to evaluate the value of importance function for arbitrary points in the scene; this is useful, for example, for computing the importance of a point along a path that started at a light source. The `Camera::We()` method takes a ray with origin p and direction ω and evaluates the importance emitted from the point on the camera p in a direction ω. If provided, the `pRaster2` parameter is used to return the raster position associated with the ray on the film; conceptually this can be understood as the discrete index j such that $W_e^{(j)}(p, \omega)$ attains its maximum value; in practice, the function returns fractional values to specify the raster positions more accurately.

⟨*Camera Interface*⟩ +≡   356
```
virtual Spectrum We(const Ray &ray, Point2f *pRaster2 = nullptr) const;
```

---

2   Note the overloaded terminology: the importance emanated by a camera is not related to the concept of importance sampling a statistical distribution; it will generally be clear which of the two is meant. However, we will later combine these concepts to implement code that importance samples a camera's importance function.

The default implementation of this method generates an error message; it's currently only implemented for the perspective camera model in pbrt. Implementing it for other Camera models is saved for Exercise 16.1 at the end of the chapter.

⟨*PerspectiveCamera Method Definitions*⟩ +≡
```
Spectrum PerspectiveCamera::We(const Ray &ray, Point2f *pRaster2) const {
    ⟨Interpolate camera matrix and check if ω is forward-facing 950⟩
    ⟨Map ray (p, ω) onto the raster grid 950⟩
    ⟨Return raster position if requested 950⟩
    ⟨Return zero importance for out of bounds points 951⟩
    ⟨Compute lens area of perspective camera 953⟩
    ⟨Return importance for point on image plane 953⟩
}
```

Given the camera-to-world transformation for the provided time, the method checks that the direction ω points in the same hemisphere as the camera is facing by transforming the camera-space viewing direction (0, 0, 1) to world space and computing the cosine of the angles between them. If these directions are more than 90 degrees apart, then the camera would never return a ray in this direction from its GenerateRay() method, and so an importance value of 0 can be returned immediately.

⟨*Interpolate camera matrix and check if ω is forward-facing*⟩ ≡   950
```
Transform c2w;
CameraToWorld.Interpolate(ray.time, &c2w);
Float cosTheta = Dot(ray.d, c2w(Vector3f(0, 0, 1)));
if (cosTheta <= 0)
    return 0;
```

A slightly more involved test next checks if the ray corresponds to one starting from the film area. If its origin is outside of the film's extent, then the point p is outside of the camera's viewing volume, and again a zero importance value can be returned.

For a camera with a finite aperture, we have a point on the lens and its direction (Figure 16.1). We don't yet know the point on the film that this ray corresponds to, but we do know that all rays leaving that point are in focus at the plane *z* = focalDistance. Therefore, if we compute the ray's intersection with the plane of focus, then transforming that point with the perspective projection matrix gives us the corresponding point on the film. For pinhole apertures, we compute the intersection with a plane arbitrarily set at *z* = 1 to get a point along the ray leaving the camera before performing the projection.

⟨*Map ray (p, ω) onto the raster grid*⟩ ≡   950, 953
```
Point3f pFocus = ray((lensRadius > 0 ? focalDistance : 1) / cosTheta);
Point3f pRaster = Inverse(RasterToCamera)(Inverse(c2w)(pFocus));
```

⟨*Return raster position if requested*⟩ ≡   950
```
if (pRaster2) *pRaster2 = Point2f(pRaster.x, pRaster.y);
```

Given the raster-space point, it's easy to check if it's inside the image extent.

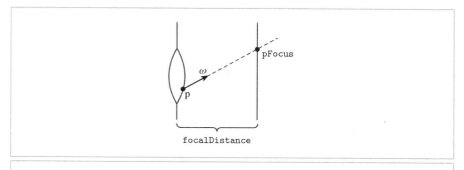

Figure 16.1: Computing the Focus Point pFocus for a Ray Leaving the Lens. In order to compute the value of the importance function W_e for this ray, we need to find the point it corresponds to on the film plane. To do so, we first compute pFocus, the point where the ray intersects the plane of focus. This point can in turn be projected by the camera's perspective projection matrix to find the corresponding raster-space point on the film.

⟨*Return zero importance for out of bounds points*⟩ ≡   950
```
    Bounds2i sampleBounds = film->GetSampleBounds();
    if (pRaster.x < sampleBounds.pMin.x || pRaster.x >= sampleBounds.pMax.x ||
        pRaster.y < sampleBounds.pMin.y || pRaster.y >= sampleBounds.pMax.y)
        return 0;
```

The perspective camera in pbrt is a ideal sensor in the sense that it generates samples with a uniform distribution over the film area. We will now use this fact to derive the corresponding directional sampling distribution. We'll start by defining a camera space image rectangle that all camera rays pass through and (arbitrarily) choose the one on the plane $z = 1$. The following fragment that is part of the PerspectiveCamera constructor uses the RasterToCamera transformation and divides by the z coordinate to compute the rectangle's corner points, which in turn gives the rectangle's area A.

⟨*Compute image plane bounds at $z = 1$ for* PerspectiveCamera⟩ ≡   365
```
    Point2i res = film->fullResolution;
    Point3f pMin = RasterToCamera(Point3f(0, 0, 0));
    Point3f pMax = RasterToCamera(Point3f(res.x, res.y, 0));
    pMin /= pMin.z;
    pMax /= pMax.z;
    A = std::abs((pMax.x - pMin.x) * (pMax.y - pMin.y));
```

⟨*PerspectiveCamera Private Data*⟩ +≡   365
```
    Float A;
```

The importance function doesn't have to obey any normalization constraints (just like emitted radiance from an area light). However, we'll define the PerspectiveCamera's importance function as a normalized PDF on ray space, both for convenience in the following and also to be consistent with the weight values of 1 returned from Perspective Camera::GenerateRay().

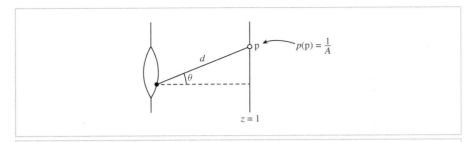

Figure 16.2: Deriving the Normalized Importance Function for the PerspectiveCamera. Given a point on the visible region of the image plane at $z = 1$ with PDF $p(p) = 1/A$, we can compute the directional PDF at a point on the lens (filled circle) by applying Equation (5.6) to account for the distance to the point on the lens d and θ, the angle between the vector from p to the point on the lens, and the surface normal of the image plane.

The importance function of PerspectiveCamera varies smoothly over its support ($W_e(\omega) > 0$); this variation is defined so that it cancels the vignetting that a real pin-hole camera would have and ensures that pixels record values in units of radiance (this is another reason why PerspectiveCamera::GenerateRay() returns weight values of 1).

The camera uniformly generates samples over the image plane area A; thus, the area-measured PDF for points on the image plane is $p(p) = 1/A$. Consider now the directional PDF at a point on the lens (or the camera's pinhole) corresponding to a differential area on the image plane (Figure 16.2); applying Equation (5.6) to transform to a directional density gives

$$p(\omega) = \begin{cases} \dfrac{d^2}{A \cos\theta}, & \text{if } \omega \text{ is within the frustum} \\ 0, & \text{otherwise,} \end{cases}$$

where θ is the angle that ω makes with the image rectangle normal and d is the distance between the point on the lens and the intersection of the ray with the $z = 1$ plane. The distance to the point on the image plane is

$$d = \left\| \frac{\omega}{\cos\theta} \right\| = \frac{1}{\cos\theta},$$

as $\cos\theta$ is the z coordinate of ω in the local camera coordinate system and $\|\omega\| = 1$. Hence,

$$p(\omega) = \begin{cases} \dfrac{1}{A \cos^3\theta}, & \text{if } \omega \text{ is within the frustum} \\ 0, & \text{otherwise.} \end{cases} \qquad [16.2]$$

By construction, the above density function $p(\omega)$ is normalized when integrated over directions—however, we initially set out to create a normalized importance function $W_e(p, \omega)$ that is defined on the space of camera rays $A_{\text{lens}} \times \mathcal{S}^2$, where A_{lens} is the surface region associated with the perspective camera's lens element. This function must satisfy the ray-space normalization criterion

PerspectiveCamera 365

PerspectiveCamera::
GenerateRay()
367

$$\int_{A_{\text{lens}}} \int_{\mathcal{S}^2} W_e(p, \omega) |\cos\theta| \, d\omega \, dA(p) = 1. \qquad [16.3]$$

We can't directly set $W_e(p, \omega)$ equal to $p(\omega)$ due to the extra integration over areas and the additional cosine factor in the above integral.

Note that the lens area A_{lens} of a perspective camera is equal to πr^2, where r is the lens radius. For point camera, the lens area is set to 1 and interpreted as a Dirac delta function.

⟨*Compute lens area of perspective camera*⟩ ≡   950, 953, 955
```
Float lensArea = lensRadius != 0 ? (Pi * lensRadius * lensRadius) : 1;
```

We then define $W_e(\mathrm{p}, \omega)$ on ray space as

$$W_e(\mathrm{p}, \omega) = \frac{p(\omega)}{\pi \, r^2 \, \cos \theta} = \begin{cases} \frac{1}{A \, \pi \, r^2 \, \cos^4 \theta}, & \text{if } \omega \text{ is within the frustum} \\ 0, & \text{otherwise,} \end{cases} \quad [16.4]$$

which divides p by the lens area and a term to cancel out the cosine factor from Equation (16.3). At this point, the implementation has already ensured that ω is within the frustum, hence the only thing left to do is to return the importance value according to the first case of Equation (16.4).

⟨*Return importance for point on image plane*⟩ ≡   950
```
Float cos2Theta = cosTheta * cosTheta;
return Spectrum(1 / (A * lensArea * cos2Theta * cos2Theta));
```

In the light of a definition for the perspective camera's importance function, we can now reinterpret the ray generation function Camera::GenerateRay() as an importance sampling technique for We(). As such, it's appropriate to define a Camera method that separately returns the spatial and directional PDFs for sampling a particular ray leaving the camera, analogous to the Light::Pdf_Le() method for light sources that will be introduced in Section 16.1.2. As before, this method is currently only implemented for the PerspectiveCamera and the default implementation generates an error message.

⟨*Camera Interface*⟩ +≡   356
```
virtual void Pdf_We(const Ray &ray, Float *pdfPos, Float *pdfDir) const;
```

The directional density of the ideal sampling strategy implemented in the method PerspectiveCamera::GenerateRay() was already discussed and is equal to $p(\omega)$ defined in Equation (16.2). The spatial density is the reciprocal of the lens area. Due to this overlap, the first four fragments of PerspectiveCamera::Pdf_We() are therefore either identical or almost identical to the similarly named fragments from PerspectiveCamera::We() with the exception that they return zero probabilities via *pdfPos and *pdfDir upon failure.

⟨*PerspectiveCamera Method Definitions*⟩ +≡
```
void PerspectiveCamera::Pdf_We(const Ray &ray, Float *pdfPos,
                               Float *pdfDir) const {
    ⟨Interpolate camera matrix and fail if ω is not forward-facing⟩
    ⟨Map ray (p, ω) onto the raster grid 950⟩
    ⟨Return zero probability for out of bounds points⟩
    ⟨Compute lens area of perspective camera 953⟩
    *pdfPos = 1 / lensArea;
    *pdfDir = 1 / (A * cosTheta * cosTheta * cosTheta);
}
```

One last additional `Camera` method completes the symmetry between light sources and cameras: it samples a point on the camera lens and computes an incident direction along which importance is arriving at the given reference position in the scene; it is thus the camera equivalent of `Light::Sample_Li()`.

Like `Sample_Li()`, the PDF value this method returns is defined with respect to solid angle at the reference point.

⟨*Camera Interface*⟩ +≡   356
```
virtual Spectrum Sample_Wi(const Interaction &ref, const Point2f &u,
                   Vector3f *wi, Float *pdf, Point2f *pRaster,
                   VisibilityTester *vis) const;
```

The `PerspectiveCamera` implementation of this method samples a point on the lens to compute the incident importance at the reference point.

⟨*PerspectiveCamera Method Definitions*⟩ +≡
```
Spectrum PerspectiveCamera::Sample_Wi(const Interaction &ref,
        const Point2f &u, Vector3f *wi, Float *pdf, Point2f *pRaster,
        VisibilityTester *vis) const {
    ⟨Uniformly sample a lens interaction lensIntr 954⟩
    ⟨Populate arguments and compute the importance value 954⟩
}
```

We can compute an `Interaction` for a point on the lens by using u to sample the lens and then transforming this point to world space. For pinhole cameras, `lensRadius` is 0 and `pLens` always ends up being at the origin.

⟨*Uniformly sample a lens interaction* lensIntr⟩ ≡   954
```
Point2f pLens = lensRadius * ConcentricSampleDisk(u);
Point3f pLensWorld =
    CameraToWorld(ref.time, Point3f(pLens.x, pLens.y, 0));
Interaction lensIntr(pLensWorld, ref.time, medium);
lensIntr.n = Normal3f(CameraToWorld(ref.time, Vector3f(0, 0, 1)));
```

Given the point on the lens, most of the output parameters of `Sample_We()` can be initialized in a straightforward manner.

⟨*Populate arguments and compute the importance value*⟩ ≡   954
```
*vis = VisibilityTester(ref, lensIntr);
*wi = lensIntr.p - ref.p;
Float dist = wi->Length();
*wi /= dist;
⟨Compute PDF for importance arriving at ref 955⟩
return We(lensIntr.SpawnRay(-*wi), pRaster);
```

The PDF of the sample is the probability of sampling a point on the lens (1 / lensArea), converted into a probability per unit solid angle at the reference point. For pinhole cameras, there is an implied delta distribution in both the PDF and the importance function value that cancel out later. (This is following the same convention as was used for BSDFs and light sources in Sections 14.1.3 and 14.2.1.)

⟨*Compute PDF for importance arriving at* ref⟩ ≡   954
    ⟨*Compute lens area of perspective camera* 953⟩
    *pdf = (dist * dist) / (AbsDot(lensIntr.n, *wi) * lensArea);

16.1.2 SAMPLING LIGHT RAYS

For bidirectional light transport algorithms, it's also necessary to add a light sampling method, Sample_Le(), that samples a ray from a distribution of rays *leaving* the light, returning the ray in *ray and the surface normal at the point on the light source in *nLight (effectively, the analog of Camera::GenerateRay()). A total of four sample values are passed to this method in the u1 and u2 parameters so that two are available to sample the ray's origin and two are available for its direction. Not all light implementations need all of these values—for example, the origin of all rays leaving a point light is the same.

This method returns two PDF values: the ray origin's probability density with respect to surface area on the light and its direction's probability density with respect to solid angle. The joint probability of sampling the ray is the product of these two probabilities.

⟨*Light Interface*⟩ +≡   714
    virtual Spectrum Sample_Le(const Point2f &u1, const Point2f &u2,
                               Float time, Ray *ray, Normal3f *nLight,
                               Float *pdfPos, Float *pdfDir) const = 0;

So that multiple importance sampling can be applied, there is also a method to return the position and direction PDFs for a given ray.

⟨*Light Interface*⟩ +≡   714
    virtual void Pdf_Le(const Ray &ray, const Normal3f &nLight,
                        Float *pdfPos, Float *pdfDir) const = 0;

Point Lights

The sampling method for generating rays leaving point lights is straightforward. The origin of the ray must be the light's position; this part of the density is described by a delta distribution. Directions are uniformly sampled over the sphere, and the overall sampling density is the product of these two densities. As usual, we'll ignore the delta distribution that is in the actual PDF because it is canceled out by a (missing) corresponding delta term in the radiance value in the Spectrum returned by the sampling routine.

⟨*PointLight Method Definitions*⟩ +≡
    Spectrum PointLight::Sample_Le(const Point2f &u1, const Point2f &u2,
            Float time, Ray *ray, Normal3f *nLight, Float *pdfPos,
            Float *pdfDir) const {
        *ray = Ray(pLight, UniformSampleSphere(u1), Infinity, time,
                   mediumInterface.inside);
        *nLight = (Normal3f)ray->d;
        *pdfPos = 1;
        *pdfDir = UniformSpherePdf();
        return I;
    }

⟨*PointLight Method Definitions*⟩ +≡
```
void PointLight::Pdf_Le(const Ray &, const Normal3f &, Float *pdfPos,
                        Float *pdfDir) const {
    *pdfPos = 0;
    *pdfDir = UniformSpherePdf();
}
```

Spotlights

The method for sampling an outgoing ray with a reasonable distribution for the spotlight is more interesting. While it could just sample directions uniformly on the sphere as was done for the point light, this distribution is likely to be a bad match for the spotlight's actual distribution. For example, if the light has a very narrow beam angle, many samples will be taken in directions where the light doesn't cast any illumination. Instead, we will sample from a uniform distribution over the cone of directions in which the light casts illumination. Although the sampling distribution does not try to account for the falloff toward the edges of the beam, this is only a minor shortcoming in practice.

The PDF $p(\theta, \phi)$ for the spotlight's illumination distribution is separable with $p(\phi) = 1/(2\pi)$. We thus just need to find a sampling distribution for θ. The UniformSampleCone() function from Section 13.6.4 provides this functionality.

⟨*SpotLight Method Definitions*⟩ +≡
```
Spectrum SpotLight::Sample_Le(const Point2f &u1, const Point2f &u2,
        Float time, Ray *ray, Normal3f *nLight, Float *pdfPos,
        Float *pdfDir) const {
    Vector3f w = UniformSampleCone(u1, cosTotalWidth);
    *ray = Ray(pLight, LightToWorld(w), Infinity, time,
                mediumInterface.inside);
    *nLight = (Normal3f)ray->d;
    *pdfPos = 1;
    *pdfDir = UniformConePdf(cosTotalWidth);
    return I * Falloff(ray->d);
}
```

The SpotLight's Pdf_Le() method for sampled rays must check to see if the direction is inside the cone of illuminated directions before returning the cone sampling PDF.

⟨*SpotLight Method Definitions*⟩ +≡
```
void SpotLight::Pdf_Le(const Ray &ray, const Normal3f &, Float *pdfPos,
        Float *pdfDir) const {
    *pdfPos = 0;
    *pdfDir = (CosTheta(WorldToLight(ray.d)) >= cosTotalWidth) ?
        UniformConePdf(cosTotalWidth) : 0;
}
```

The sampling routines for ProjectionLights and GonioPhotometricLights are essentially the same as the ones for SpotLights and PointLights, respectively. For sampling outgoing rays, ProjectionLights sample uniformly from the cone that encompasses their projected image map (hence the need to compute ProjectionLight::cosTotalWidth in the constructor), and those for GonioPhotometricLights sample uniformly over the unit sphere. Exercise 16.2 at the end of this chapter discusses improvements to these sampling methods that better account for the directional variation of these lights.

Area Lights

The method for sampling a ray leaving an area light is also easily implemented in terms of the shape sampling methods from Section 14.2.2.

⟨*DiffuseAreaLight Method Definitions*⟩ +≡
```
Spectrum DiffuseAreaLight::Sample_Le(const Point2f &u1, const Point2f &u2,
        Float time, Ray *ray, Normal3f *nLight, Float *pdfPos,
        Float *pdfDir) const {
    ⟨Sample a point on the area light's Shape, pShape 957⟩
    ⟨Sample a cosine-weighted outgoing direction w for area light  957⟩
    *ray = pShape.SpawnRay(w);
    return L(pShape, w);
}
```

The surface area–based variant of Shape::Sample() is used to find the ray origin, sampled from some density over the surface.

⟨*Sample a point on the area light's* Shape, pShape⟩ ≡   **957**
```
Interaction pShape = shape->Sample(u1);
pShape.mediumInterface = mediumInterface;
*pdfPos = shape->Pdf(pShape);
*nLight = pShape.n;
```

The ray's direction is sampled from a cosine-weighted distribution about the surface normal at the sampled point. Incorporating this cosine weighting means that rays leaving the light carry uniform differential power, which is preferable for bidirectional light transport algorithms. Because the direction returned by CosineSampleHemisphere() is in the canonical coordinate system, it must be transformed to the coordinate system about the surface normal at the sampled point here.

⟨*Sample a cosine-weighted outgoing direction* w *for area light*⟩ ≡   **957**
```
Vector3f w = CosineSampleHemisphere(u2);
*pdfDir = CosineHemispherePdf(w.z);
Vector3f v1, v2, n(pShape.n);
CoordinateSystem(n, &v1, &v2);
w = w.x * v1 + w.y * v2 + w.z * n;
```

Distant Lights

Sampling a ray from the DistantLight's distribution of outgoing rays is a more interesting problem. The ray's direction is determined in advance by a delta distribution; it must be the same as the light's negated direction. For its origin, there are an infinite number of 3D points where it could start. How should we choose an appropriate one, and how do we compute its density?

The desired property is that rays intersect points in the scene that are illuminated by the distant light with uniform probability. One way to do this is to construct a disk that has the same radius as the scene's bounding sphere and has a normal that is oriented with the light's direction and then choose a random point on this disk, using the

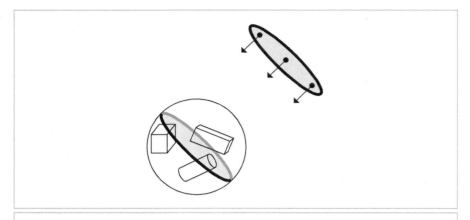

Figure 16.3: To sample an outgoing ray direction for a distant light source, the `DistantLight::Sample_Le()` method finds the disk oriented in the light's direction that is large enough so that the entire scene can be intersected by rays leaving the disk in the light's direction. Ray origins are sampled uniformly by area on this disk, and ray directions are given directly by the light's direction.

`ConcentricSampleDisk()` function (Figure 16.3). Once this point has been chosen, if the point is displaced along the light's direction by the scene's bounding sphere radius and used as the origin of the light ray, the ray origin will be outside the bounding sphere of the scene.

This is a valid sampling approach, since by construction it has nonzero probability of sampling all incident rays into the sphere due to the directional light. The area component of the sampling density is uniform and therefore equal to the reciprocal of the area of the disk that was sampled. The directional density is given by a delta distribution based on the light's direction.

⟨*DistantLight Method Definitions*⟩ +≡
```
    Spectrum DistantLight::Sample_Le(const Point2f &u1, const Point2f &u2,
            Float time, Ray *ray, Normal3f *nLight, Float *pdfPos,
            Float *pdfDir) const {
        ⟨Choose point on disk oriented toward infinite light direction 959⟩
        ⟨Set ray origin and direction for infinite light ray 959⟩
        *nLight = (Normal3f)ray->d;
        *pdfPos = 1 / (Pi * worldRadius * worldRadius);
        *pdfDir = 1;
        return L;
    }
```

Choosing the point on the oriented disk is a simple application of vector algebra. We construct a coordinate system with two vectors perpendicular to the disk's normal (the light's direction); see Figure 16.4. Given a random point on the canonical unit disk, computing the offsets from the disk's center with respect to its coordinate vectors gives the corresponding point.

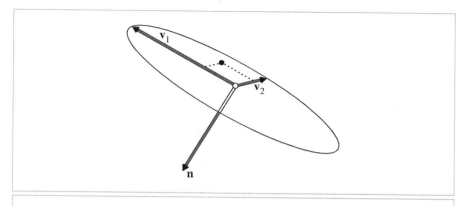

Figure 16.4: Given sample points (d_1, d_2) on the canonical unit disk, points on an arbitrarily oriented and sized disk with normal $\mathbf{n}$ can be found by computing an arbitrary coordinate system $(\mathbf{v}_1, \mathbf{v}_2, \mathbf{n})$ and then computing points on the disk with the offset $d_1\mathbf{v}_1 + d_2\mathbf{v}_2$ from the disk's center.

⟨*Choose point on disk oriented toward infinite light direction*⟩ ≡   958
```
Vector3f v1, v2;
CoordinateSystem(wLight, &v1, &v2);
Point2f cd = ConcentricSampleDisk(u1);
Point3f pDisk = worldCenter + worldRadius * (cd.x * v1 + cd.y * v2);
```

Finally, the point is offset along the light direction and the ray can be initialized. Recall from Section 12.4 that DistantLights can't be embedded in any medium other than a vacuum. Therefore, no medium needs to be specified for the ray.

⟨*Set ray origin and direction for infinite light ray*⟩ ≡   958
```
*ray = Ray(pDisk + worldRadius * wLight, -wLight, Infinity, time);
```

Infinite Area Lights

Generating a random ray leaving an infinite light source can be done by sampling a direction with the same approach as the earlier InfiniteAreaLight::Sample_Li() method. The sampled ray's origin is then set using the same approach as was used for DistantLights, where a disk that covers the scene's bounding sphere is oriented along the ray's direction (recall Figure 16.3). We therefore won't include the ⟨*Compute direction for infinite light sample ray*⟩ or ⟨*Compute origin for infinite light sample ray*⟩ fragments here.

⟨*InfiniteAreaLight Method Definitions*⟩ +≡
```
Spectrum InfiniteAreaLight::Sample_Le(const Point2f &u1,
        const Point2f &u2, Float time, Ray *ray, Normal3f *nLight,
        Float *pdfPos, Float *pdfDir) const {
    ⟨Compute direction for infinite light sample ray⟩
    ⟨Compute origin for infinite light sample ray⟩
    ⟨Compute InfiniteAreaLight ray PDFs 960⟩
    return Spectrum(Lmap->Lookup(uv), SpectrumType::Illuminant);
}
```

The PDFs for these rays are the PDF for sampling the direction (as derived in Section 14.2.4) and the PDF for sampling a point on the disk.

⟨Compute InfiniteAreaLight *ray PDFs*⟩ ≡   959
```
*pdfDir = sinTheta == 0 ? 0 : mapPdf / (2 * Pi * Pi * sinTheta);
*pdfPos = 1 / (Pi * worldRadius * worldRadius);
```

The Pdf_Le() method applies the same formulas, so we won't include its implementation here.

16.1.3 NON-SYMMETRIC SCATTERING

Certain aspects in the input scene specification of materials and geometry can lead to non-symmetric behavior in light transport simulations, where incident radiance and importance are scattered in different ways at a point. If these differences aren't accounted for, rendering algorithms based on radiance and importance transport will produce different and inconsistent results when rendering the same input scene. Bidirectional techniques that combine radiance and importance transport are particularly affected, since their design is fundamentally based on the principle of symmetry.

In this section, we will briefly enumerate cases that give rise to non-symmetry and explain how they can be addressed to arrive at a consistent set of bidirectional estimators.

Recall the path throughput term $T(\bar{\mathrm{p}}_i)$ from Equation (16.1), which was defined as

$$T(\bar{\mathrm{p}}_n) = \prod_{i=1}^{n-1} f(\mathrm{p}_{i+1} \to \mathrm{p}_i \to \mathrm{p}_{i-1})\, G(\mathrm{p}_{i+1} \leftrightarrow \mathrm{p}_i).$$

The vertices are ordered such that p_i denotes the i-th scattering event as seen from the camera.

Sampling techniques based on finding importance-carrying paths trace rays starting at the light sources to estimate the incident importance at the light, which means that the vertices will be generated in reverse compared to the above ordering. As such, the incident and outgoing direction arguments of the BSDFs will be (incorrectly) reversed unless special precautions are taken. We thus define the *adjoint BSDF* f^* at vertex p_i, whose only role is to evaluate the original BSDF with swapped arguments:

$$f^*(\mathrm{p}, \omega_o, \omega_i) = f(\mathrm{p}, \omega_i, \omega_o).$$

All sampling steps based on importance transport will then use the adjoint form of the BSDF rather than its original version. Most BSDFs in pbrt are symmetric so that there is no actual difference between f and f^*. However, certain cases related to shading normals and light refracting into media with a different index of refraction require additional attention.

The TransportMode enumeration is used to inform such non-symmetric BSDFs about the transported quantity so that they can correctly switch between the adjoint and non-adjoint forms.

⟨*TransportMode Declarations*⟩ ≡
```
enum class TransportMode { Radiance, Importance };
```

InfiniteAreaLight::
  worldRadius
  740
Pi 1063
TransportMode 960

Non-symmetry Due to Refraction

When light refracts into a material with a higher index of refraction than the incident medium's index of refraction, the energy is compressed into a smaller set of angles. This is easy to see yourself, for instance, by looking at the sky from underwater in a quiet outdoor swimming pool. Because no light can be refracted below the critical angle ($\sim 48.6°$ for water), the incident hemisphere of light is squeezed into a considerably smaller subset of the hemisphere, which covers the remaining set of angles. Radiance along rays that do refract must thus increase so that energy is preserved when light passes through the interface. More precisely, the incident (L_i) and transmitted (L_t) radiance are related by

$$L_i = \frac{\eta_i^2}{\eta_t^2} L_t,\tag{16.5}$$

where η_i and η_t are the refractive indices on the incident and transmitted sides, respectively. The symmetry relationship satisfied by a BTDF is

$$\eta_t^2 f(p, \omega_o, \omega_i) = \eta_i^2 f(p, \omega_i, \omega_o),\tag{16.6}$$

and we can obtain the adjoint BTDF

$$f^*(p, \omega_o, \omega_i) = f(p, \omega_i, \omega_o) = \frac{\eta_t^2}{\eta_i^2} f(p, \omega_o, \omega_i),$$

which effectively cancels out the scale factor in Equation (16.5). With these equations, we can now define the last missing piece in the implementation of SpecularTransmission:: Sample_f(). Whenever radiance is transported over a refractive boundary, we apply the scale factor from Equation (16.5). For importance transport, we use the adjoint BTDF, which lacks the scaling factor due to the combination of Equations (16.5) and (16.6).

⟨*Account for non-symmetry with transmission to different medium*⟩ ≡   529, 817
```
if (mode == TransportMode::Radiance)
    ft *= (etaI * etaI) / (etaT * etaT);
```

A similar adjustment is also needed for the FourierBSDF::f() method in the case of refraction. In this case, FourierBSDFTable::eta provides the relative index of refraction. Recall that this model uses a convention where the sign of $\mu_i = \cos\theta_i$ is flipped, hence the expression muI * muO > 0 can be used to check if light is being refracted rather than reflected.

⟨*Update* scale *to account for adjoint light transport*⟩ ≡   558
```
if (mode == TransportMode::Radiance && muI * muO > 0) {
    float eta = muI > 0 ? 1 / bsdfTable.eta : bsdfTable.eta;
    scale *= eta * eta;
}
```

Finally, the transmissive term S_ω of the SeparableBSSRDF requires a similar correction when light leaves the medium after a second refraction (the first one being handled by the material's BSDF).

⟨*Update BSSRDF transmission term to account for adjoint light transport*⟩ ≡   906
```
if (bssrdf->mode == TransportMode::Radiance)
    f *= bssrdf->eta * bssrdf->eta;
```

Non-symmetry Due to Shading Normals

Shading normals are another cause of non-symmetric scattering. As previously discussed in Section 3.6.3, shading normals are mainly used to make polygonal surfaces appear smoother than their actual discretization. This entails replacing the "true" geometric normal $\mathbf{n}_g$ with an interpolated shading normal $\mathbf{n}_s$ whenever the BSDF or the cosine term in the light transport equation are evaluated. Bump or normal mapping can be interpreted as another kind of shading normal, where $\mathbf{n}_s$ is obtained from a texture map.

This kind of modification to the normal of a surface interaction causes a corresponding change in the underlying reflectance model, producing an effective BSDF that is generally non-symmetric. Without additional precautions, this non-symmetry can lead to visible artifacts in renderings based on adjoint techniques, including discontinuities in shading effects resembling flat-shaded polygons that interpolated normals were originally meant to avoid.

Recall the light transport equation, (14.13), which relates the incident and outgoing radiance on surfaces:

$$L_o(\mathrm{p}, \omega_o) = L_e(\mathrm{p}, \omega_o) + \int_{\mathrm{S}^2} f(\mathrm{p}, \omega_o, \omega_i)\, L_i(\mathrm{p}, \omega_i)\, |\mathbf{n}_g \cdot \omega_i|\, d\omega_i.$$

Here, the cosine factor is expressed as an inner product involving ω_i and the true normal of the underlying geometry. Suppose now that we'd like to replace $\mathbf{n}_g$ with the shading normal $\mathbf{n}_s$. Instead of modifying the scattering equation, another mathematically equivalent way of expressing this change entails switching to a new BSDF f_{shade} defined as

$$f_{\text{shade}}(\mathrm{p}, \omega_o, \omega_i) = \frac{|\mathbf{n}_s \cdot \omega_i|}{|\mathbf{n}_g \cdot \omega_i|}\, f(\mathrm{p}, \omega_o, \omega_i).$$

The first factor in the above expression makes this BSDF non-symmetric with respect to the arguments ω_i and ω_o. To avoid artifacts and inconsistencies in bidirectional rendering algorithms, the adjoint BSDF f^*_{shade} should be used in simulations whenever importance transport is used. It is given by

$$f^*_{\text{shade}}(\mathrm{p}, \omega_o, \omega_i) = \frac{|\mathbf{n}_s \cdot \omega_o|}{|\mathbf{n}_g \cdot \omega_o|}\, f^*(\mathrm{p}, \omega_o, \omega_i).$$

Rather than integrating this special case into all BxDF subclasses, we find it cleaner to detect this case in the integrator and apply a correction factor

$$C_{\text{shade}}(\mathrm{p}, \omega_o, \omega_i) = \begin{cases} \frac{|\mathbf{n}_s \cdot \omega_o||\mathbf{n}_g \cdot \omega_i|}{|\mathbf{n}_g \cdot \omega_o||\mathbf{n}_s \cdot \omega_i|} & \text{if importance is being transported} \\ 1 & \text{if radiance is being transported,} \end{cases}$$

BxDF 513
CorrectShadingNormal() 963

which corrects the normal dependence of the non-adjoint version into that of the adjoint when importance transport is indicated by the mode parameter. This adjustment is implemented by the helper function CorrectShadingNormal() below.

```
⟨BDPT Utility Functions⟩ ≡
  Float CorrectShadingNormal(const SurfaceInteraction &isect,
      const Vector3f &wo, const Vector3f &wi, TransportMode mode) {
    if (mode == TransportMode::Importance)
      return (AbsDot(wo, isect.shading.n) * AbsDot(wi, isect.n)) /
              (AbsDot(wo, isect.n) * AbsDot(wi, isect.shading.n));
    else
      return 1;
  }
```

16.2 STOCHASTIC PROGRESSIVE PHOTON MAPPING

Photon mapping is one of a family of particle-tracing algorithms, which are based on the idea of constructing paths starting from the lights and connecting vertices in these paths to the camera to deposit energy on the film. In this section, we will start by introducing a theory of particle-tracing algorithms and will discuss the conditions that must be fulfilled by a particle-tracing algorithm so that arbitrary measurements can be computed correctly using the particles created by the algorithm. We will then describe an implementation of a photon mapping integrator that uses particles to estimate illumination by interpolating lighting contributions from particles close to but not quite at the point being shaded.

16.2.1 THEORETICAL BASIS FOR PARTICLE TRACING

Particle-tracing algorithms in computer graphics are often explained in terms of packets of energy being shot from the light sources in the scene that deposit energy at surfaces they intersect before scattering in new directions. This is an intuitive way of thinking about particle tracing, but the intuition that it provides doesn't make it easy to answer basic questions about how propagation and scattering affect the particles. For example, does their contribution fall off with squared distance like flux density? Or, which $\cos\theta$ terms, if any, affect particles after they scatter from a surface?

In order to give a solid theoretical basis for particle tracing, we will describe it using a framework introduced by Veach (1997, Appendix 4.A), which instead interprets the stored particle histories as samples from the scene's equilibrium radiance distribution. Under certain conditions on the distribution and weights of the particles, the particles can be used to compute estimates of nearly any measurement based on the light distribution in the scene. In this framework, it is quite easy to answer questions about the details of particle propagation like the ones earlier. After developing this theory here, the remainder of this section will demonstrate its application to photon mapping.

A particle-tracing algorithm generates a set of N samples of illumination at points p_j, on surfaces in the scene

$$(p_j, \omega_j, \beta_j),$$

where each sample records incident illumination from direction ω_j and has some throughput weight β_j associated with it (Figure 16.5). As the notation already indicates,

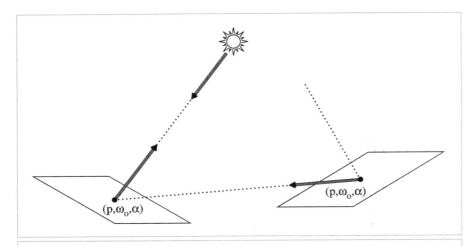

Figure 16.5: When a particle is traced following a path from a light source, an entry in its particle history is recorded at each surface it intersects. Each entry in the history is represented by position p, the direction of the ray it arrived along ω_o, and particle weight β.

this weight β_j will contain ratios of terms of the throughput function T and the associated sampling PDFs much like the β variable of the path tracer (Section 14.5.4). We would like to determine the conditions on the weights and distribution of particle positions so that we can use them to correctly compute estimates of arbitrary measurements.

Given an importance function $W_e(p, \omega)$ that describes the measurement to be taken, the natural condition we would like to be fulfilled is that the particles should be distributed and weighted such that using them to compute an estimate has the same expected value as the measurement equation for the same importance function:

$$E\left[\frac{1}{N}\sum_{j=1}^{N}\beta_j W_e(p_j, \omega_j)\right] = \int_A \int_{S^2} W_e(p, \omega)L_i(p, \omega)\,|\cos\theta|\,dA\,d\omega. \qquad [16.7]$$

For example, we might want to use the particles to compute the total flux incident on a wall. Using the definition of flux,

$$\Phi = \int_{A_{\text{wall}}} \int_{\mathcal{H}^2(n)} L_i(p, \omega)\,|\cos\theta|\,dA\,d\omega,$$

the following importance function selects the particles that lie on the wall and arrived from the hemisphere around the normal:

$$W_e(p, \omega) = \begin{cases} 1 & p \text{ is on wall surface and } (\omega \cdot n) > 0 \\ 0 & \text{otherwise.} \end{cases}$$

If the conditions on the distribution of particle weights and positions are true for arbitrary importance functions such that Equation (16.7) holds, then the flux estimate can be computed directly as a sum of the particle weights for the particles on the wall. If we want to estimate flux over a different wall, a subset of the original wall, and so on, we only need to recompute the weighted sum with an updated importance function. The particles and weights can be reused, and we have an unbiased estimate for all of these measurements. (The estimates will be correlated, however, which is potentially a source of image artifacts.)

To see how to generate and weight particles that fulfill these conditions, consider the task of evaluating the measurement equation integral

$$\int_A \int_{S^2} W_e(p_0, \omega) \, L(p_0, \omega) \, |\cos \theta| \, d\omega \, dA(p_0)$$

$$= \int_A \int_A W_e(p_0 \to p_1) \, L(p_1 \to p_0) \, G(p_0 \leftrightarrow p_1) \, dA(p_0) \, dA(p_1),$$

where the vertex densities $p(p_{i,j})$ are expressed as a probability per unit area and where the importance function W_e that describes the measurement is a black box and thus cannot be used to drive the sampling of the integral at all. We can still compute an estimate of the integral with Monte Carlo integration but must sample a set of points p_0 and p_1 from all of the surfaces in the scene, using some sampling distribution that doesn't depend on W_e (e.g., by uniformly sampling points by surface area).

By expanding the LTE in the integrand and applying the standard Monte Carlo estimator for N samples, we can find the estimator for this measurement,

$$E\left[\frac{1}{N} \sum_{i=1}^N W_e(p_{i,0} \to p_{i,1}) \left\{ \frac{L(p_{i,1} \to p_{i,0}) \, G(p_{i,0} \leftrightarrow p_{i,1})}{p(p_{i,0}) \, p(p_{i,1})} \right\} \right].$$

We can further expand out the L term into the sum over paths and use the fact that $E[ab] = E[aE[b]]$ and the fact that for a particular sample, the expected value

$$E\left[\frac{L(p_{i,1} \to p_{i,0})}{p(p_{i,0})} \right]$$

can be written as a finite sum of n_i terms in just the same way that we generated a finite set of weighted path vertices for path tracing. If the sum is truncated with Russian roulette such that the probability of terminating the sum after j terms is $q_{i,j}$, then the jth term of the ith sample has contribution

$$\beta_{i,j} = \frac{L_e(p_{i,n_i} \to p_{i,n_i-1})}{p(p_{i,n_i})} \prod_{j=1}^{n_i-1} \frac{1}{1 - q_{i,j}} \frac{f(p_{i,j+1} \to p_{i,j} \to p_{i,j-1}) \, G(p_{i,j+1} \leftrightarrow p_{i,j})}{p(p_{i,j})}.$$

[16.8]

Note that the path integral framework provides us with the freedom to generate a set of particles in all sorts of different ways—i.e., with different underlying vertex probability densities $p(p_{i,j})$. Although the natural approach is to start from points on lights and incrementally sample paths using the BSDFs at the path vertices, similar to how the path-tracing integrator generates paths (starting here from the light, rather than from the camera), we could generate them with any number of different sampling strategies, as long as there is nonzero probability of generating a particle at any point where the numerator is nonzero and the particle weights $\beta_{i,j}$ are computed using the above definition.

If we only had a single measurement to make, it would be better if we used information about W_e and could compute the estimate more intelligently, since the general particle-tracing approach described here may generate many useless samples if W_e only covers a small subset of the points on scene objects. If we will be computing many measurements, however, the key advantage that particle tracing brings is that we can generate the samples and weights once and can then reuse them over a large number of measurements, potentially computing results much more efficiently than if the measurements were all computed from scratch.

16.2.2 PHOTON MAPPING

The photon mapping algorithm is based on tracing particles into the scene and blurring their contribution to approximate the incident illumination at shading points. For consistency with other descriptions of the algorithm, we will refer to particles generated for photon mapping as photons.

In order to compute reflected radiance at a point, we need to estimate the exitant radiance equation at a point p in a direction ω_o, which can equivalently (and cumbersomely) be written as a measurement over all points on surfaces in the scene where a Dirac delta distribution selects only particles precisely at p:

$$\int_{\mathbb{S}^2} L_i(p, \omega_i)\, f(p, \omega_o, \omega_i)\, |\cos \theta_i|\, d\omega_i$$

$$= \int_A \int_{\mathbb{S}^2} \delta(p - p') L_i(p', \omega_i)\, f(p', \omega_o, \omega_i)\, |\cos \theta_i|\, d\omega_i\, dA(p'),$$

and so, from Equation (16.7), the function that describes the measurement is

$$W_e(p', \omega) = \delta(p' - p)\, f(p, \omega_o, \omega). \tag{16.9}$$

Unfortunately, because there is a delta distribution in W_e, all of the particle histories that were generated during the particle-tracing step have zero probability of having nonzero contribution if Equation (16.7) is used to compute the estimate of the measurement value (just as we will never be able to choose a direction from a diffuse surface that intersects a point light source unless the direction is sampled based on the light source's position).

Here is the point at which bias is introduced into the photon mapping algorithm. Under the assumption that the information about illumination at nearby points gives a reasonable approximation to illumination at the shading point, photon mapping interpolates illumination from nearby photons around the point being shaded; the delta function of position in Equation (16.9) is effectively converted to a filter function. Given Equation (16.7), the more photons there are around the point and the higher their weights, the more radiance is estimated to be incident at the point.

One factor that contributes to photon mapping's efficiency is this reuse of photons: having gone through the trouble to compute a light-carrying path, allowing it to potentially contribute illumination at multiple points amortizes the cost of generating it. While photon mapping derives some benefit from this efficiency improvement, there's a subtler but much more important benefit from using nearby photons at a point: some light-carrying paths are impossible to sample with unbiased algorithms based on incremental path con-

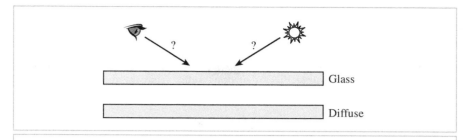

Figure 16.6: An Impossible-to-Sample Path for Path Tracing or Bidirectional Path Tracing. The scene includes a point light, a pinhole camera, and a diffuse surface behind a sheet of glass. Given a ray leaving the camera, the point at which it intersects the diffuse surface is determined based on refraction through the glass. At this point, only a single direction provides illumination from the point light, but there's no way to sample a direction leaving the surface that will intersect the light. The corresponding problem arises when starting the path from the light: there's no way to find a path back to the camera.

struction (including path tracing and bidirectional path tracing), but are handled well with photon mapping. These paths can arise in very common situations.

For example, consider the task of rendering an image of a photograph with a plate of glass in front of it. Assume a pinhole camera model and a point light illuminating the scene, and also assume for simplicity that the glass is only transmissive (Figure 16.6). If we start a path from the camera that passes through the glass, then the point that it intersects the photograph is completely determined by the effect of the refraction. At this point, none of the direct lighting strategies we have available has any chance of sampling an incident direction that will reach the light: because any sampled incident direction leaving the diffuse surface will be refracted on the way out through the glass, there's no chance that the refracted ray will hit the point light.[3] Even with an area light source, some refracted rays may be lucky enough to hit the light, but in general, variance will be high since most will miss it.

With photon mapping, we can trace photons leaving the light, let them refract through the glass, and deposit illumination on the diffuse surface. With a sufficient number of photons, the surface will be densely covered, and the photons around a point give a good estimate of the incident illumination.

A statistical technique called *density estimation*[4] provides the mathematical tools to perform this interpolation. Density estimation constructs a PDF given a set of sample points under the assumption that the samples are distributed according to the overall distribution of some function of interest. Histogramming is a straightforward example of the

---

3   For a flat sheet of glass, one could implement a specialized sampling technique that accounted for this refraction, though doing so requires moving beyond the incremental path construction framework we've used so far. Such approaches become more challenging with more complex scene geometry.

4   Strictly speaking, density estimation can only be used to estimate the (normalized) density function of a set of unweighted samples. When working with weighted samples and general unnormalized functions, the term *kernel smoothing* is more commonly used. Although the latter case is the one relevant for photon mapping, we will continue refer to it as density estimation due to the heavy usage of this term in computer graphics.

idea. In 1D, the line is divided into intervals with some width, and one can count how many samples land in each interval and normalize so that the areas of the intervals sum to one.

Kernel methods are a more sophisticated density estimation technique. They generally give better results and smoother PDFs that don't suffer from the discontinuities that histograms do. Given a kernel function $k(x)$ that integrates to 1.

$$\int_{-\infty}^{\infty} k(x)\, dx = 1,$$

the kernel estimator for N samples at locations x_i is

$$\hat{p}(x) = \frac{1}{Nh} \sum_{i=1}^{N} k\left(\frac{x - x_i}{h}\right),$$

where h is the window width (also known as the *smoothing parameter* or *kernel band-width*). Kernel methods can be thought of as placing a series of bumps at observation points, where the sum of the bumps forms a PDF since they individually integrate to 1 and the sum is normalized. Figure 16.7 shows an example of density estimation in 1D, where a smooth PDF is computed from a set of sample points.

The key question with kernel methods is how the window width h is chosen. If it is too wide, the PDF will blur out relevant detail in parts of the domain with many samples; if it is too narrow, the PDF will be too bumpy in the tails of the distribution where there aren't many samples. Nearest-neighbor techniques solve this problem by choosing h adaptively

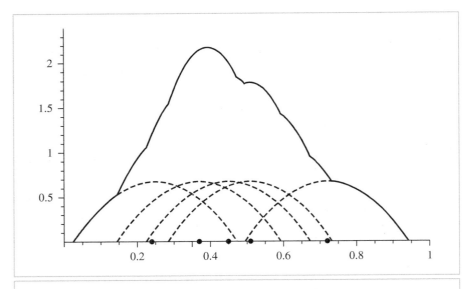

Figure 16.7: 1D example of density estimation, using the Epanechnikov kernel, $k(t) = 0.75(1 - .2t^2)/\sqrt{5}$, if $t < \sqrt{5}$, 0 otherwise, and a width of 0.1. The points marked with closed circles are the sample points, and an instance of the kernel (dashed lines) is placed over each one. The sum of the kernels gives a properly normalized PDF that attempts to model a distribution that the points could be distributed by.

based on local density of samples. Where there are many samples, the width is small; where there are few samples, the width is large. For example, one approach is to pick a number N and find the distance to the Nth nearest sample from the point x and use that distance, $d_N(x)$, for the window width. This is the *generalized nth nearest-neighbor estimate:*

$$\hat{p}(x) = \frac{1}{Nd_N(x)} \sum_{i=1}^{N} k\left(\frac{x - x_i}{d_N(x)}\right).$$

In d dimensions, this generalizes to

$$\hat{p}(x) = \frac{1}{N(d_N(x))^d} \sum_{i=1}^{N} k\left(\frac{x - x_i}{d_N(x)}\right). \tag{16.10}$$

Substituting into the measurement equation, it can be shown that the appropriate estimator for the measurement we'd like to compute, the exitant radiance at the point p in direction ω, is given by

$$L_o(\mathrm{p}, \omega_o) \approx \frac{1}{N_\mathrm{p}\, d_N(\mathrm{p})^2} \sum_{j}^{N_\mathrm{p}} k\left(\frac{\mathrm{p} - \mathrm{p}_j}{d_N(\mathrm{p})}\right) \beta_j\, f(\mathrm{p}, \omega_o, \omega_j), \tag{16.11}$$

where we've switched to using N_p to denote the total number of emitted photons, the sum is over all of the photons, and scale factors for the photons are computed based on the density estimation Equation, (16.10). Because we know that the kernel function is zero for points farther away than the Nth nearest neighbor distance $d_N(x)$, implementations of this sum only need to sum over the N closest neighbors.[5]

The error introduced by this interpolation can be difficult to quantify. Tracing more photons generally increases photon density and will almost always improve the results. When the photons are more closely spaced, it isn't necessary to use photons from as far away in the nearest-neighbor estimate. In general, the error at any given point will depend on how quickly the illumination is changing in its vicinity. One can always construct pathological cases where this error is unacceptable, but in practice it usually isn't too bad. Because the interpolation step tends to blur out illumination, high-frequency changes in lighting are sometimes poorly reconstructed with photon mapping. If traditional methods are used for direct lighting, then this is generally less of a problem since indirect illumination tends to be low frequency.

The original formulation of photon mapping was based on a two-pass algorithm where photons are first traced from the light sources. Photon interactions are recorded on surfaces of the scene and then organized in a spatial data structure (generally a kd-tree) for use at rendering time. A second pass follows paths starting from the camera; at each path vertex, nearby photons are used to estimate indirect illumination.

While this approach is effective, it has the limitation that the number of photons that can be used is limited by available memory since all of the photons must be stored. No

---

5   It should be noted that including the n-th photon of the nearest-neighbor search can introduce additional bias; see García et al. (2012) for a discussion including alternative estimators that avoid this issue.

improvement is possible once memory is full, even if one wants a higher quality result from using more photons. (In contrast, with path tracing, for example, one can always add more samples per pixel without any incremental storage cost—only the computational expense increases.)

Progressive Photon Mapping

The *progressive photon mapping* algorithm addressed this issue by restructuring the algorithm: first, a camera pass traces paths starting from the camera. Each pixel stores a representation of all of the non-specular path vertices found when generating paths that started in its extent. (For example, if a camera ray hits a diffuse surface, we might record the geometric information about the intersection point and the diffuse reflectance. If it hit a perfectly specular surface and then a diffuse surface, we would record the diffuse reflectance scaled by the specular BSDF value, and so forth.) We will dub these stored path vertices *visible points* in the following.[6] A second pass traces photons from the light sources; at each photon–surface intersection, the photon contributes to the reflected radiance estimate for nearby visible points.

To understand how progressive photon mapping works, we consider a decomposition of the LTE into separate integrals over direct L_d and indirect L_i incident radiance at each vertex. (Recall the discussion of partitioning the LTE in Section 14.4.6.)

$$
\begin{aligned}
L(p, \omega_o) &= L_e(p, \omega_o) + \int_{S^2} f(p, \omega_o, \omega_i)\, L(p, \omega_i)\, |\cos\theta_i|\, d\omega_i \\
&= L_e(p, \omega_o) + \int_{S^2} f(p, \omega_o, \omega_i)\, L_d(p, \omega_i)\, |\cos\theta_i|\, d\omega_i \qquad [16.12] \\
&\quad + \int_{S^2} f(p, \omega_o, \omega_i)\, L_i(p, \omega_i)\, |\cos\theta_i|\, d\omega_i.
\end{aligned}
$$

The emitted term is straightforward, and direct lighting can be handled using the usual approaches from Section 14.3.[7] The indirect term with the integral over L_i is handled in one of two ways. First, a ray may be sampled from the BSDF's sampling distribution and traced to find the next vertex in the path, where the same issue of how to estimate outgoing radiance is faced—just like a path tracer. Alternatively, the current point can be saved to receive illumination from photons. The final contribution of such a point to radiance at the film plane is found by summing the product of the photons' weights and the path throughput weight of the sequence of vertices before it in the path.

For a perfectly specular BSDF, the only reasonable choice is to trace another ray: a photon will never arrive at exactly the right direction to match the delta distribution in the BSDF. For highly glossy surfaces, it's also advisable to trace a ray, since it will take many photons for enough to hit a narrow specular lobe to compute an accurate estimate.

---

6   The term *hit points* is often used to describe these points in the photon mapping literature. We prefer the additional clarity of phrasing that includes the idea that these points are at least indirectly visible from the camera.

7   Other decompositions are also possible—for instance, some implementations use photon density estimation to handle the direct illumination component.

For diffuse surfaces, it's generally worth using photons, though it can be worthwhile to trace one last bounce. This approach is called *final gathering;* if photons are used only after a diffuse bounce, then any errors from insufficient photon density are generally less visible, though more camera paths may need to be traced to eliminate noise. (See Exercise 16.8 for further discussion of final gathering.)

With this approach, no photon storage is needed, and an arbitrary number of photons can be traced; the memory limit is instead tied to the storage required for the visible points and their reflection information. For high-resolution images or images that require many samples per pixel to resolve motion blur or depth of field, memory can still be a limitation.

Stochastic Progressive Photon Mapping

Stochastic progressive photon mapping is a modification of progressive photon mapping that doesn't suffer from either of these memory limits. Like progressive photon mapping, it generates a set of visible points from the camera but at a low sampling rate (e.g., following just one camera path per pixel). Next, a number of photons are shot from lights, accumulating contributions at nearby visible points. This process then repeats: the visible points are discarded, a new set is generated at different positions, another round of photons is traced, and so forth.

SPPM starts with the photon estimation equation, (16.11), and makes two adjustments. First, it uses a constant kernel function; in conjunction with the fact that the estimation is over 2D (the local tangent plane around the visible point), we have

$$L_o(p, \omega_o) \approx \frac{1}{N_p \, \pi r^2} \sum_{j}^{N_p} \beta_j \, f(p, \omega_o, \omega_j),$$

where, as before, N_p is the number of photons emitted from the light sources, and πr^2 is the surface area of the disk-shaped kernel function.

The second adjustment, based on an approach first implemented in progressive photon mapping, is to progressively reduce the photon search radius as more photons contribute to the visible point. The general idea is that as more photons that are found within the search radius, we have more evidence that a sufficient density of photons is arriving to estimate the incident radiance distribution well. By reducing the radius, we ensure that future photons that are used will be closer to the point and thus contribute to a more accurate estimate of the incident radiance distribution.

Reducing the radius requires an adjustment to how the reflected radiance estimate is computed, as now the photons in the sum in Equation (16.11) come from different radii. The following three update rules describe how to update the radius and dependent variables:

$$N_{i+1} = N_i + \gamma M_i$$

$$r_{i+1} = r_i \sqrt{\frac{N_{i+1}}{N_i + M_i}}$$

$$\tau_{i+1} = (\tau_i + \Phi_i) \frac{r_{i+1}^2}{r_i^2},$$

[16.13]

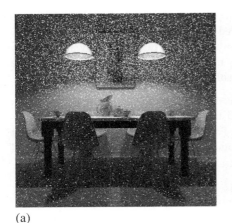
(a)

(b)

Figure 16.8: Scene rendered with (a) path tracing and (b) stochastic progressive photon mapping, using approximately the same amount of computation. In this case, photon mapping is effective at handling light paths from the light source through the glass light fixtures, while path tracing gives a result with high variance. (*Scene courtesy "Wig42" from blendswap.com*)

where N_i is the number of photons that have contributed to the point after the ith iteration, M_i is the number of photons that contributed during the current iteration, r_i is the search radius to use for the ith iteration, τ maintains the sum of products of photons with BSDF values, and Φ_i is computed during the ith iteration as

$$\Phi_i = \sum_j^{M_i} \beta_j \, f(\mathrm{p}, \omega_{\mathrm{o}}, \omega_j).$$ [16.14]

The γ parameter, which is typically around $2/3$, determines how quickly the contributions from photons from earlier iterations, with wider search radii, are faded out. (Hachisuka and Jensen's original paper on SPPM (2009) uses the notation α for this quantity; we opt for γ here, having used α for other quantities already.)

Note that the radius is a per-pixel property, not a per-visible-point property. Remarkably, a consistent estimate for the reflected radiance is computed even with this single radius shared over all of the series of visible points in the pixel. We won't show this derivation here, but with the rules in Equation (16.13), as the number of photons traced $N_{\mathrm{p}} \to \infty$, $r \to \infty$, and the reflected radiance estimates are consistent and converge to the correct values.

Figure 16.8 shows a rendered scene with path tracing and SPPM. SPPM is much more effective at handling light that passes through the glass light fixtures than the path tracing algorithm is.

16.2.3 SPPMIntegrator

The SPPMIntegrator, implemented in the files integrators/sppm.h and integrators/sppm.cpp, implements the SPPM light transport algorithm.

⟨*SPPM Declarations*⟩ ≡
```
class SPPMIntegrator : public Integrator {
public:
    ⟨SPPMIntegrator Public Methods⟩
private:
    ⟨SPPMIntegrator Private Data 973⟩
};
```

The SPPMIntegrator constructor isn't particularly interesting; it just sets various member variables with values passed in. We therefore won't include it here but will discuss the various member variables that configure the SPPMIntegrator's operation as they appear in the following.

The SPPMIntegrator is not a SamplerIntegrator, so it implements its own Render() method. After some initial setup has been performed, it runs a number of iterations of the SPPM algorithm, finding a set of visible points and then accumulating illumination from photons at them. Each iteration creates a new path starting from the camera in each pixel, which helps with antialiasing geometric edges and sampling motion blur and depth of field well.

⟨*SPPM Method Definitions*⟩ ≡
```
void SPPMIntegrator::Render(const Scene &scene) {
    ⟨Initialize pixelBounds and pixels array for SPPM 973⟩
    ⟨Compute lightDistr for sampling lights proportional to power 974⟩
    ⟨Perform nIterations of SPPM integration 975⟩
}
```

The pixels array stores a SPPMPixel (to be defined shortly) for each pixel in the final image.

⟨*Initialize* pixelBounds *and* pixels *array for SPPM*⟩ ≡   973
```
Bounds2i pixelBounds = camera->film->croppedPixelBounds;
int nPixels = pixelBounds.Area();
std::unique_ptr<SPPMPixel[]> pixels(new SPPMPixel[nPixels]);
for (int i = 0; i < nPixels; ++i)
    pixels[i].radius = initialSearchRadius;
```

A user-supplied radius, initialSearchRadius, is used for r_0, the initial search radius for photons. If the supplied radius is too large, too many photons will contribute to visible points during early iterations (before the radius is automatically decreased), which may be inefficient. If it's too small, not enough photons will be found to estimate incident radiance well. A radius corresponding to a few pixels in the final image is generally a good starting point.

⟨*SPPMIntegrator Private Data*⟩ ≡   973
```
std::shared_ptr<const Camera> camera;
const Float initialSearchRadius;
```

The SPPMPixel structure serves three purposes. First, it stores the current estimated average radiance visible over the extent of a pixel (including the time the shutter is open and accounting for depth of field, if present). Second, it stores parameters related to the photon density estimation for the pixel (e.g., various quantities from Equation (16.13)). Finally, it stores the geometric and reflection information for a visible point in the pixel after the camera pass.

```
⟨SPPM Local Definitions⟩ ≡
    struct SPPMPixel {
        ⟨SPPMPixel Public Methods⟩
        ⟨SPPMPixel Public Data 974⟩
    };
```

```
⟨SPPMPixel Public Data⟩ ≡                                           974
    Float radius = 0;
```

Working with weighted photons allows for two very different overall sampling approaches: on the one hand, we could try to distribute photons uniformly with a weight that approximates the irradiance on surfaces, while also accounting for discontinuities and other important geometric and lighting features. However, this type of photon distribution is challenging to realize for general input; hence we will instead strive to generate photons have the same (or similar) weights, so that it is their varying density throughout the scene that represents the variation in illumination.

Furthermore, if the photon weights on a surface have substantial variation that is not related to the irradiance, there can be unpleasant image artifacts: if one photon takes on a much larger weight than the others, a bright circular artifact will reveal the region of the scene where that photon contributes to the interpolated radiance.

Therefore, we'd like to shoot more photons from the brighter lights so that the initial weights of photons leaving all lights will be of similar magnitudes, and thus, the light to start each photon path from is chosen according to a PDF defined by the lights' respective powers. Thus, it is a greater number of photons from the brighter lights that accounts for their greater contributions to illumination in the scene rather than the same number of photons from all, with larger weights for the more powerful lights.

```
⟨Compute lightDistr for sampling lights proportional to power⟩ ≡          973
    std::unique_ptr<Distribution1D> lightDistr =
        ComputeLightPowerDistribution(scene);
```

```
⟨Integrator Utility Functions⟩ +≡
    std::unique_ptr<Distribution1D> ComputeLightPowerDistribution(
            const Scene &scene) {
        std::vector<Float> lightPower;
        for (const auto &light : scene.lights)
            lightPower.push_back(light->Power().y());
        return std::unique_ptr<Distribution1D>(
            new Distribution1D(&lightPower[0], lightPower.size()));
    }
```

Each iteration of the SPPM algorithm traces a new path from the camera at each pixel and then collects incident photons at each path's endpoint. Figure 16.9 shows the effect of increasing the number of iterations with SPPM. Here, we see the caustic from light

(a)   (b)   (c)

Figure 16.9: Effect of the number of iterations on results from the SPPMIntegrator. As the number of iterations increases (and thus, the more photons are traced), the quality of the final result improves. Note in particular how the size of the visible circular blotches gets smaller. (a) 10 iterations, (b) 100 iterations, (c) 10,000 iterations. (*Model courtesy Simon Wendsche.*)

passing through the glass becoming increasingly sharper. In general, more iterations improve the sampling of visible edges, motion blur, and depth of field, but as more photons are accumulated in each pixel, the indirect lighting estimate becomes more accurate. Note how the artifacts from under-sampling here are low-frequency blotches, a quite different visual artifact from the high-frequency noise from under-sampling seen in path tracing.

The implementation here uses a HaltonSampler to generate camera paths; doing so ensures that well-distributed samples are used over all of the iterations in the aggregate.

⟨*Perform* nIterations *of SPPM integration*⟩ ≡   973
    HaltonSampler sampler(nIterations, pixelBounds);
    ⟨*Compute number of tiles to use for SPPM camera pass* **976**⟩
    for (int iter = 0; iter < nIterations; ++iter) {
        ⟨*Generate SPPM visible points* **976**⟩
        ⟨*Trace photons and accumulate contributions* **983**⟩
        ⟨*Update pixel values from this pass's photons* **989**⟩
        ⟨*Periodically store SPPM image in film and write image*⟩
    }

⟨*SPPMIntegrator Private Data*⟩ +≡   973
    const int nIterations;

16.2.4 ACCUMULATING VISIBLE POINTS

Similar to the SamplerIntegrator, the SPPMIntegrator decomposes the image into tiles of 16 pixels square and parallelizes the generation of camera paths and visible points

over these tiles. The number of tiles is computed in the same manner as in the fragment
⟨*Compute number of tiles, nTiles, to use for parallel rendering*⟩.

⟨*Compute number of tiles to use for SPPM camera pass*⟩ ≡   975
```
    Vector2i pixelExtent = pixelBounds.Diagonal();
    const int tileSize = 16;
    Point2i nTiles((pixelExtent.x + tileSize - 1) / tileSize,
                   (pixelExtent.y + tileSize - 1) / tileSize);
```

Unlike the path tracer, where the BSDF can be discarded after estimating the direct illumination and sampling the outgoing direction at each vertex, here we need to store the BSDFs for the visible points until the photon pass for the current iteration is done. Therefore, the MemoryArenas used for allocating the BSDFs during camera path tracing aren't reset at the end of loop iterations here.

Note also that we only allocate one arena per worker thread used to run the parallel for loop and use the ThreadIndex global to index into the vector, rather than allocating a separate arena for each loop iteration. In this way, we avoid the overhead of having many separate MemoryArenas while still ensuring that each arena is not used by more than one processing thread (which would lead to race conditions in the MemoryArena methods).

⟨*Generate SPPM visible points*⟩ ≡   975
```
    std::vector<MemoryArena> perThreadArenas(MaxThreadIndex());
    ParallelFor2D(
        [&](Point2i tile) {
            MemoryArena &arena = perThreadArenas[ThreadIndex];
            ⟨Follow camera paths for tile in image for SPPM 976⟩
        }, nTiles);
    ⟨Create grid of all SPPM visible points 979⟩
```

We also need a unique Sampler for the thread processing the tile; as before, Sampler::Clone() provides one.

⟨*Follow camera paths for tile in image for SPPM*⟩ ≡   976
```
    int tileIndex = tile.y * nTiles.x + tile.x;
    std::unique_ptr<Sampler> tileSampler = sampler.Clone(tileIndex);
    ⟨Compute tileBounds for SPPM tile⟩
    for (Point2i pPixel : tileBounds) {
        ⟨Prepare tileSampler for pPixel 977⟩
        ⟨Generate camera ray for pixel for SPPM 977⟩
        ⟨Follow camera ray path until a visible point is created 977⟩
    }
```

The fragment ⟨*Compute tileBounds for SPPM tile*⟩ is very similar to ⟨*Compute sample bounds for tile*⟩ from Section 1.3.4 and therefore won't be included here.

Recall that in SamplerIntegrators, the sample vectors in each pixel are all requested in sequence until the last one is consumed, at which point work starts on the next pixel. In contrast, the first SPPM iteration uses the first sample vector for each pixel; later, the second iteration uses the second sample vector, and so forth. (In other words, the loop nesting has been interchanged from "for each pixel, for each sample number," to "for each sample number, for each pixel.") It is for just this use case that the Sampler provides the SetSampleNumber() method, which configures the sampler to provide samples from the given sample vector for the pixel.

⟨*Prepare* tileSampler *for* pPixel⟩ ≡   976
```
tileSampler->StartPixel(pPixel);
tileSampler->SetSampleNumber(iter);
```

We can now start the path from the camera, following the usual approach. As with the PathIntegrator, the beta variable holds the current path throughput weight β.

⟨*Generate camera ray for pixel for SPPM*⟩ ≡   976
```
CameraSample cameraSample = tileSampler->GetCameraSample(pPixel);
RayDifferential ray;
Spectrum beta = camera->GenerateRayDifferential(cameraSample, &ray);
```

Path tracing can now proceed. As with most other Integrators, the path length is limited by a predefined maximum depth.

⟨*Follow camera ray path until a visible point is created*⟩ ≡   976
```
    ⟨Get SPPMPixel for pPixel 977⟩
    bool specularBounce = false;
    for (int depth = 0; depth < maxDepth; ++depth) {
        SurfaceInteraction isect;
        if (!scene.Intersect(ray, &isect)) {
            ⟨Accumulate light contributions for ray with no intersection 977⟩
            break;
        }
        ⟨Process SPPM camera ray intersection 978⟩
    }
```

⟨*SPPMIntegrator Private Data*⟩ +≡   973
```
    const int maxDepth;
```

To find the SPPMPixel in the pixels array for the current pixel, we need to offset by the minimum pixel coordinate and convert to a linear index.

⟨*Get* SPPMPixel *for* pPixel⟩ ≡   977
```
    Point2i pPixel0 = Point2i(pPixel - pixelBounds.pMin);
    int pixelOffset = pPixel0.x +
                        pPixel0.y * (pixelBounds.pMax.x - pixelBounds.pMin.x);
    SPPMPixel &pixel = pixels[pixelOffset];
```

As described in Section 16.2.2, a regular direct lighting calculation is performed at each vertex of the camera path. Thus, for rays that don't intersect any scene geometry, infinite area lights must be allowed a chance to contribute direct lighting via the Light::Le() method.

⟨*Accumulate light contributions for ray with no intersection*⟩ ≡   977
```
    for (const auto &light : scene.lights)
        pixel.Ld += beta * light->Le(ray);
```

SPPMPixel::Ld records the weighted sum of emitted and reflected direct illumination for all camera path vertices for the pixel (in other words, the first two terms of Equation (16.12)). Note that these terms are also evaluated at vertices found by sampling the BSDF and tracing a ray for the third term; Ld doesn't just store direct illumination at the first vertex. Because this sum of outgoing radiance includes contributions of all of the samples in a pixel, this value must be divided by SPPMIntegrator::nIterations to get the average direct illumination for the final pixel radiance estimate.

⟨*SPPMPixel Public Data*⟩ +≡   974
    Spectrum Ld;

More commonly, the ray intersects a surface and ⟨*Process SPPM camera ray intersection*⟩ executes

⟨*Process SPPM camera ray intersection*⟩ ≡   977
    ⟨*Compute BSDF at SPPM camera ray intersection* 978⟩
    ⟨*Accumulate direct illumination at SPPM camera ray intersection* 978⟩
    ⟨*Possibly create visible point and end camera path* 979⟩
    ⟨*Spawn ray from SPPM camera path vertex*⟩

First, we need the BSDF at the intersection point. Recall from Section 11.3 that a nullptr-valued BSDF * means that an intersection should be ignored, as the surface intersected is only in the scene to delineate the boundary of participating media. The SPPMIntegrator does not account for participating media; thus we simply skip over the intersection and restart the current loop iteration.

⟨*Compute BSDF at SPPM camera ray intersection*⟩ ≡   978
```
isect.ComputeScatteringFunctions(ray, arena, true);
if (!isect.bsdf) {
    ray = isect.SpawnRay(ray.d);
    --depth;
    continue;
}
const BSDF &bsdf = *isect.bsdf;
```

As in other integrators, emitted radiance from the surface is only included for the first intersection from the camera or after a specular bounce, where no direct lighting calculation was possible.

⟨*Accumulate direct illumination at SPPM camera ray intersection*⟩ ≡   978
```
Vector3f wo = -ray.d;
if (depth == 0 || specularBounce)
    pixel.Ld += beta * isect.Le(wo);
pixel.Ld += beta *
    UniformSampleOneLight(isect, scene, arena, *tileSampler);
```

The implementation here creates a visible point at the first diffuse surface found or if the path is about to hit its maximum length and we have a glossy surface. As explained earlier, a visible point at a perfectly specular surface will never respond to incident photons, and a glossy surface may have high variance if the specular lobe is tight and not enough photons have arrived to represent the incident radiance distribution well.

⟨*Possibly create visible point and end camera path*⟩ ≡   978
```
        bool isDiffuse =
            bsdf.NumComponents(BxDFType(BSDF_DIFFUSE | BSDF_REFLECTION |
                                        BSDF_TRANSMISSION)) > 0;
        bool isGlossy =
            bsdf.NumComponents(BxDFType(BSDF_GLOSSY | BSDF_REFLECTION |
                                        BSDF_TRANSMISSION)) > 0;
        if (isDiffuse || (isGlossy && depth == maxDepth - 1)) {
            pixel.vp = {isect.p, wo, &bsdf, beta};
            break;
        }
```

The VisiblePoint structure records a point found along a camera path at which we'll look for nearby photons during the photon shooting path. It stores enough information to compute the reflected radiance due to an incident photon, which in turn is scaled by the path throughput weight of the visible point to find the overall contribution to the original image sample.

⟨*SPPMPixel Public Data*⟩ +≡   974
```
        struct VisiblePoint {
            ⟨VisiblePoint Public Methods⟩
            Point3f p;
            Vector3f wo;
            const BSDF *bsdf = nullptr;
            Spectrum beta;
        } vp;
```

Sampling a ray leaving a vertex follows the same form as ⟨*Sample BSDF to get new path direction*⟩ in the PathIntegrator and is therefore not included here.

16.2.5 VISIBLE POINT GRID CONSTRUCTION

During the photon pass, whenever a photon intersects a surface, we need to efficiently find the visible points where the distance from the visible point to the photon's intersection is less than the current search radius r_i for the visible point's pixel. The implementation here uses a uniform grid over the bounding box of all of the visible points; Exercise 16.7 at the end of the chapter has you implement other data structures in place of the grid and investigate trade-offs.

⟨*Create grid of all SPPM visible points*⟩ ≡   976
    ⟨*Allocate grid for SPPM visible points* 980⟩
    ⟨*Compute grid bounds for SPPM visible points* 981⟩
    ⟨*Compute resolution of SPPM grid in each dimension* 981⟩
    ⟨*Add visible points to SPPM grid* 981⟩

The grid is usually sparsely filled; many voxels have no visible points inside their extent. (For starters, any voxel in the grid with no surfaces in its volume will never have a visible point in it.) Therefore, rather than allocating storage for all of the voxels, the grid is represented by a hash table where a hash function transforms 3D voxel coordinates to an index into the grid array.

In the following, we'll construct the grid in parallel using multiple threads. These threads will use atomic operations to update the grid, so a std::atomic is used for the grid voxel element type here.

⟨*Allocate grid for SPPM visible points*⟩ ≡   979
```
    int hashSize = nPixels;
    std::vector<std::atomic<SPPMPixelListNode *>> grid(hashSize);
```

Each grid cell stores a linked list, where each node points to an SPPMPixel whose visible point's search volume overlaps the grid cell. A visible point may overlap multiple grid cells, so it's desirable to keep the node representation compact by only storing a pointer to the SPPMPixel rather than making a copy for each cell it overlaps.

⟨*SPPM Local Definitions*⟩ +≡
```
    struct SPPMPixelListNode {
        SPPMPixel *pixel;
        SPPMPixelListNode *next;
    };
```

If there's no visible point for the pixel for the current iteration, the pixel will have a path throughput weight $\beta = 0$ (and no attempt should be made to place a visible point in the grid for that pixel). This case can happen if the path from the camera leaves the scene or is terminated before intersecting a diffuse surface.

Otherwise, the implementation here computes the bounding box centered at the visible point with extent $\pm r_i$, the current photon search radius for the pixel. In turn, when we later have a photon intersection point, we will only need to consider the visible points for the grid cell that the photon is in to find the visible points that the photon may contribute to (Figure 16.10). Because different visible points will have different search radii depending on how many photons have contributed to their pixel so far, it would otherwise be unwieldy to find the potentially relevant visible points for a photon if the

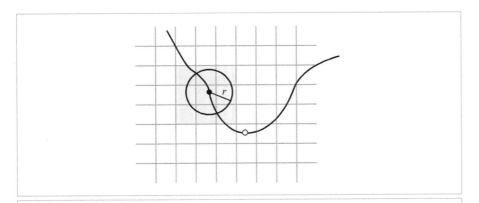

Figure 16.10: Given a visible point (filled circle) with search radius r, the visible point is added to the linked list in all grid cells that the bounding box of the sphere of radius r overlaps. Given a photon incident on a surface in the scene (open circle), we only need to check the visible points in the voxel the photon is in to find the ones that it may contribute to.

SPPMPixel 974

SPPMPixelListNode 980

visible points were stored without accounting for the volume of space they will accept photons from.

⟨*Compute grid bounds for SPPM visible points*⟩ ≡   979
```
Bounds3f gridBounds;
Float maxRadius = 0.;
for (int i = 0; i < nPixels; ++i) {
    const SPPMPixel &pixel = pixels[i];
    if (pixel.vp.beta.IsBlack())
        continue;
    Bounds3f vpBound = Expand(Bounds3f(pixel.vp.p), pixel.radius);
    gridBounds = Union(gridBounds, vpBound);
    maxRadius = std::max(maxRadius, pixel.radius);
}
```

Given the overall bound of the grid, we need to decide how large the voxels should be and thus how finely to subdivide space. On one hand, if the voxels are too large, the photon shooting pass will be inefficient, as each photon will have to check many visible points to see if it contributes to each one. If they're too small, then each visible point will overlap many voxels, and the memory needed to represent the grid will be excessive.

Here, we compute an initial resolution such that the voxel width in the largest grid dimension is roughly equal to the largest current search radius of all of the visible points. This limits the maximum number of voxels any visible point can overlap. In turn, resolutions for the other two dimensions of the grid are set so that voxels have roughly the same width in all dimensions.

⟨*Compute resolution of SPPM grid in each dimension*⟩ ≡   979
```
Vector3f diag = gridBounds.Diagonal();
Float maxDiag = MaxComponent(diag);
int baseGridRes = (int)(maxDiag / maxRadius);
int gridRes[3];
for (int i = 0; i < 3; ++i)
    gridRes[i] = std::max((int)(baseGridRes * diag[i] / maxDiag), 1);
```

The visible points can now be added to the grid. Because both the grid and the BSDFs for visible points from the camera path must be kept around until the end of the photon tracing pass, we can reuse the per-thread MemoryArenas that were created earlier for the BSDFs to allocate SPPMPixelListNodes.

⟨*Add visible points to SPPM grid*⟩ ≡   979
```
ParallelFor(
    [&](int pixelIndex) {
        MemoryArena &arena = perThreadArenas[ThreadIndex];
        SPPMPixel &pixel = pixels[pixelIndex];
        if (!pixel.vp.beta.IsBlack()) {
            ⟨Add pixel's visible point to applicable grid cells 982⟩
        }
    }, nPixels, 4096);
```

Each visible point is added to all of the grid cells that its bounding box overlaps.

⟨*Add pixel's visible point to applicable grid cells*⟩ ≡   **981**
```
Float radius = pixel.radius;
Point3i pMin, pMax;
ToGrid(pixel.vp.p - Vector3f(radius, radius, radius),
       gridBounds, gridRes, &pMin);
ToGrid(pixel.vp.p + Vector3f(radius, radius, radius),
       gridBounds, gridRes, &pMax);
for (int z = pMin.z; z <= pMax.z; ++z)
    for (int y = pMin.y; y <= pMax.y; ++y)
        for (int x = pMin.x; x <= pMax.x; ++x) {
            ⟨Add visible point to grid cell (x, y, z) 982⟩
        }
```

ToGrid() returns the coordinates of the voxel in the grid that the given point lies in. The Boolean return value indicates whether the point p is inside the grid's bounds; if it isn't, the returned coordinates pi are clamped to be inside the range of valid coordinates.

⟨*SPPM Local Definitions*⟩ +≡
```
static bool ToGrid(const Point3f &p, const Bounds3f &bounds,
                   const int gridRes[3], Point3i *pi) {
    bool inBounds = true;
    Vector3f pg = bounds.Offset(p);
    for (int i = 0; i < 3; ++i) {
        (*pi)[i] = (int)(gridRes[i] * pg[i]);
        inBounds &= ((*pi)[i] >= 0 && (*pi)[i] < gridRes[i]);
        (*pi)[i] = Clamp((*pi)[i], 0, gridRes[i] - 1);
    }
    return inBounds;
}
```

hash() hashes the coordinates of the voxel, returning an index into the grid array defined earlier; it is a straightforward hash function, and its implementation isn't included here.[8] A new SPPMPixelListNode is allocated and the task now is to add this list node to the head of the linked list in grid[h].

⟨*Add visible point to grid cell (x, y, z)*⟩ ≡   **982**
```
int h = hash(Point3i(x, y, z), hashSize);
SPPMPixelListNode *node = arena.Alloc<SPPMPixelListNode>();
node->pixel = &pixel;
```
⟨*Atomically add* node *to the start of* grid[h]*'s linked list* **983**⟩

Given the grid index, atomic operations can be used to allow multiple threads to add visible points to the grid concurrently without needing to hold any locks. (See Appen-

---

8   Note that hash collisions are possible—different cells in the grid may hash to the same index. This is almost fine: photons will end up checking more visible points than they need to, but the test with the pixel's search radius will reject the visible points that are too far away anyway. See, however, Exercise 16.9 for one nit related to collisions.

dix A.6.2 for further discussion of atomic operations.) In the absence of concurrency, we'd just want to set node->next to point to the head of the list in grid[h] and assign node to grid[h]. That approach will not work if multiple threads are updating the lists concurrently; it's possible that the first assignment will become stale: another thread might modify grid[h] between the current thread initializing node->next and then trying to assign node to grid[h].

The compare_exchange_weak() method of std::atomic addresses this issue: the first parameter is the value that we expect grid[h] to have, and the second gives the value that we'd like to set it to. It performs the assignment only if our expectation was correct. Thus, in the common case, node->next and grid[h] have the same pointer value, the assignment occurs, and true is returned. The node has been added to the list.

If the pointer stored in grid[h] has been changed by another thread, then compare_exchange_weak() actually updates the first parameter, node->next, with the current value of grid[h] before returning false. We are thus all set to try the atomic compare and exchange again, as node->next points to the new head of the list. This process continues until the assignment is successful.

⟨*Atomically add* node *to the start of* grid[h]*'s linked list*⟩ ≡   982
```
node->next = grid[h];
while (grid[h].compare_exchange_weak(node->next, node) == false)
    ;
```

16.2.6 ACCUMULATING PHOTON CONTRIBUTIONS

Given the grid of visible points, the SPPMIntegrator can now follow photon paths through the scene. The total of photonsPerIteration photons to be traced for the current iteration are traced using multiple threads. A separate MemoryArena is available for each worker thread; this arena is reset after each photon path, so a new pool of per-thread arenas is allocated rather than reusing the one used for BSDFs and grid linked list nodes.

⟨*Trace photons and accumulate contributions*⟩ ≡   975
```
std::vector<MemoryArena> photonShootArenas(MaxThreadIndex());
ParallelFor(
    [&](int photonIndex) {
        MemoryArena &arena = photonShootArenas[ThreadIndex];
        ⟨Follow photon path for photonIndex 984⟩
        arena.Reset();
    }, photonsPerIteration, 8192);
```

There's a balance to strike in choosing the number of photons to trace for each SPPM iteration: too many, and pixels' radii won't have a chance to decrease as more photons arrive and too many too-far-away photons are used. Too few, and the overhead of finding visible points and making the grid of them won't be amortized over enough photons. In practice, a few hundred thousand to a few million per iteration generally works well (see Figure 16.11).

⟨*SPPMIntegrator Private Data*⟩ +≡   973
```
const int photonsPerIteration;
```

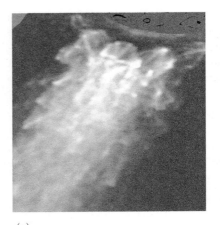 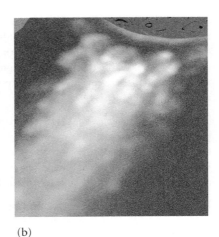

(a)   (b)

Figure 16.11: The Effect of Varying the Number of Photons Traced Per Iteration. The number of iterations is set so that the total number of photons traced is the same—10 million—for both cases. (a) 10,000 photons (1000 iterations): results are good, and rendering time is 137 seconds; time spent creating visible points is 68% of the total. (b) 1,000,000 photons (10 iterations): results are much blurrier, though rendering time has dropped to 50 seconds, most of it due to spending much less time on the camera pass.

A Halton sequence provides a set of well-distributed sample points for all of the photon paths over all of the iterations. haltonIndex records the index of the Halton sequence (corresponding to a in Equation (7.7)) for the current photon; it can also be seen as a global index of photons traced. In other words, it starts at 0 for the first photon and passes through all subsequent integer values for following photons. It's important to use a 64-bit integer for this value, since a 32-bit int would overflow after roughly 2 billion photons; many more photons may be needed for high-quality images.

The dimension of the sample, corresponding to the bth prime number in Equation (7.7), is maintained in haltonDim.

⟨*Follow photon path for* photonIndex⟩ ≡   **983**
```
    uint64_t haltonIndex = (uint64_t)iter * (uint64_t)photonsPerIteration +
                        photonIndex;
    int haltonDim = 0;
```
    ⟨*Choose light to shoot photon from* **985**⟩
    ⟨*Compute sample values for photon ray leaving light source* **985**⟩
    ⟨*Generate* photonRay *from light source and initialize* beta **985**⟩
    ⟨*Follow photon path through scene and record intersections* **986**⟩

SPPMIntegrator::
photonsPerIteration
983

Which light to start the path from is determined by sampling from the PDF based on light power computed previously. The first dimension of the Halton sequence is used for the sample value.

⟨*Choose light to shoot photon from*⟩ ≡   984
```
Float lightPdf;
Float lightSample = RadicalInverse(haltonDim++, haltonIndex);
int lightNum = lightDistr->SampleDiscrete(lightSample, &lightPdf);
const std::shared_ptr<Light> &light = scene.lights[lightNum];
```

The next five dimensions of the sample from the Halton sequence are used for the sample values used to generate the ray leaving the light source.

⟨*Compute sample values for photon ray leaving light source*⟩ ≡   984
```
Point2f uLight0(RadicalInverse(haltonDim,     haltonIndex),
                RadicalInverse(haltonDim + 1, haltonIndex));
Point2f uLight1(RadicalInverse(haltonDim + 2, haltonIndex),
                RadicalInverse(haltonDim + 3, haltonIndex));
Float uLightTime = Lerp(RadicalInverse(haltonDim + 4, haltonIndex),
                        camera->shutterOpen, camera->shutterClose);
haltonDim += 5;
```

After the light has been chosen, its Sample_Le() method is used to sample an outgoing ray. Given a light, a ray from the light source is sampled and its β value is initialized based on Equation (16.8):

$$\beta = \frac{|\cos \omega_0| \, L_e(p_0, \omega_0)}{p(\text{light}) \, p(p_0, \omega_0)}, \qquad (16.15)$$

where $p(\text{light})$ is the probability for sampling this particular light and $p(p_0, \omega_0)$ is the product of the area and directional densities for sampling this particular ray leaving the light. Intersecting this ray against the scene geometry to obtain p_1 also samples part of the geometric term $G(p_0 \leftrightarrow p_1)$ except for a cosine factor that must be explicitly integrated into the particle weight β.

⟨*Generate* photonRay *from light source and initialize* beta⟩ ≡   984
```
RayDifferential photonRay;
Normal3f nLight;
Float pdfPos, pdfDir;
Spectrum Le =
    light->Sample_Le(uLight0, uLight1, uLightTime,
                     &photonRay, &nLight, &pdfPos, &pdfDir);
if (pdfPos == 0 || pdfDir == 0 || Le.IsBlack()) return;
Spectrum beta = (AbsDot(nLight, photonRay.d) * Le) /
                (lightPdf * pdfPos * pdfDir);
if (beta.IsBlack())
    return;
```

Now the integrator can start following the path through the scene, updating β after each scattering event. The photon makes no contribution at the first intersection found after it left the light source, since that intersection represents direct illumination, which was already accounted for when tracing paths starting from the camera. For subsequent intersections, illumination is contributed to nearby visible points.

⟨*Follow photon path through scene and record intersections*⟩ ≡   **984**
```
    SurfaceInteraction isect;
    for (int depth = 0; depth < maxDepth; ++depth) {
        if (!scene.Intersect(photonRay, &isect))
            break;
        if (depth > 0) {
            ⟨Add photon contribution to nearby visible points 986⟩
        }
        ⟨Sample new photon ray direction 987⟩
    }
```

Given a photon intersection, `ToGrid()`'s return value indicates if it's within the extent of the grid. If it isn't, then by construction, none of the visible points is interested in this photon's contribution. Otherwise, the visible points in the grid cell all need to be checked to see if the photon is within their radius.

⟨*Add photon contribution to nearby visible points*⟩ ≡   **986**
```
    Point3i photonGridIndex;
    if (ToGrid(isect.p, gridBounds, gridRes, &photonGridIndex)) {
        int h = hash(photonGridIndex, hashSize);
        ⟨Add photon contribution to visible points in grid[h] 986⟩
    }
```

Recall that `grid` stores `std::atomic` pointers to `SPPMPixelListNodes`. Normally, reading from a `std::atomic` value means that the compiler must be careful to not reorder instructions that read or write memory around the read of the value of `grid[h]`; this constraint is necessary so that lock-free algorithms will work as expected. In this case, the grid has been constructed and no other threads are concurrently modifying it. Therefore, it's worthwhile to use the `std::atomic.load()` method and letting it know that the "relaxed" memory model, which doesn't have these constraints, can be used to read the initial grid pointer. This approach has a significant performance benefit: for a simple scene of a few hundred triangles (where not too much time is spent tracing rays), the photon pass runs in 20% less time using this memory model on a 2015-era CPU.

⟨*Add photon contribution to visible points in* grid[h]⟩ ≡   **986**
```
    for (SPPMPixelListNode *node = grid[h].load(std::memory_order_relaxed);
         node != nullptr; node = node->next) {
        SPPMPixel &pixel = *node->pixel;
        Float radius = pixel.radius;
        if (DistanceSquared(pixel.vp.p, isect.p) > radius * radius)
            continue;
        ⟨Update pixel Φ and M for nearby photon 987⟩
    }
```

Given a photon contribution, we need to update the sum for the pixel's scattered radiance estimate from Equation (16.14). The total number of contributing photons in this pass is stored in M, and the sum of the product of BSDF values with particle weights is stored in Phi.

⟨*Update* pixel Φ *and M for nearby photon*⟩ ≡   986
```
Vector3f wi = -photonRay.d;
Spectrum Phi = beta * pixel.vp.bsdf->f(pixel.vp.wo, wi);
for (int i = 0; i < Spectrum::nSamples; ++i)
    pixel.Phi[i].Add(Phi[i]);
++pixel.M;
```

Each pixel's Φ and M values are stored using atomic variables, which in turn allows multiple threads to safely concurrently update their values. Because pbrt's Spectrum class doesn't allow atomic updates, Phi is instead represented with an array of AtomicFloat coefficients for each spectral sample. This representation will require some manual copying of values to and from Phi to Spectrum-typed variables in the following, but we think that this small awkwardness is preferable to the complexity of, for example, a new AtomicSpectrum type.

⟨*SPPMPixel Public Data*⟩ +≡   974
```
AtomicFloat Phi[Spectrum::nSamples];
std::atomic<int> M;
```

Having recorded the photon's contribution, the integrator needs to choose a new outgoing direction from the intersection point and update the β value to account for the effect of scattering. Equation (16.7) shows how to incrementally update the particle weight after a scattering event: given some weight $\beta_{i,j}$ that represents the weight for the jth intersection of the ith particle history, after a scattering event where a new vertex $p_{i,j+1}$ has been sampled, the weight should be set to be

$$\beta_{i,j+1} = \beta_{i,j} \frac{1}{1 - q_{i,j+1}} \frac{f(p_{i,j+1} \to p_{i,j} \to p_{i,j-1}) \, G(p_{i,j+1} \leftrightarrow p_{i,j})}{p(p_{i,j+1})}.$$

As with the path-tracing integrator, there are a number of reasons to choose the next vertex in the path by sampling the BSDF's distribution at the intersection point to get a direction ω' and tracing a ray in that direction rather than directly sampling by area on the scene surfaces. Therefore, we again apply the Jacobian to account for this change in measure, all of the terms in G except for a single $|\cos\theta|$ cancel out, and the expression is

$$\beta_{i,j+1} = \beta_{i,j} \frac{1}{1 - q_{i,j+1}} \frac{f(p, \omega, \omega') \, |\cos\theta'|}{p(\omega')}. \qquad [16.16]$$

⟨*Sample new photon ray direction*⟩ ≡   986
    ⟨*Compute BSDF at photon intersection point* **988**⟩
    ⟨*Sample BSDF* fr *and direction* wi *for reflected photon* **988**⟩
```
    Spectrum bnew = beta * fr * AbsDot(wi, isect.shading.n) / pdf;
```
    ⟨*Possibly terminate photon path with Russian roulette* **989**⟩
```
    photonRay = (RayDifferential)isect.SpawnRay(wi);
```

As before, a nullptr-valued BSDF * indicates an intersection that should be ignored.

⟨*Compute BSDF at photon intersection point*⟩ ≡   987
```
isect.ComputeScatteringFunctions(photonRay, arena, true,
                                 TransportMode::Importance);
if (!isect.bsdf) {
    --depth;
    photonRay = isect.SpawnRay(photonRay.d);
    continue;
}
const BSDF &photonBSDF = *isect.bsdf;
```

Sampling the BSDF to find the scattered photon direction follows the usual model.

⟨*Sample BSDF* fr *and direction* wi *for reflected photon*⟩ ≡   987
```
Vector3f wi, wo = -photonRay.d;
Float pdf;
BxDFType flags;
⟨Generate bsdfSample for outgoing photon sample 988⟩
Spectrum fr = photonBSDF.Sample_f(wo, &wi, bsdfSample,
                                  &pdf, BSDF_ALL, &flags);
if (fr.IsBlack() || pdf == 0.f) break;
```

The next two dimensions of the Halton sample vector are used for the BSDF sample.

⟨*Generate* bsdfSample *for outgoing photon sample*⟩ ≡   988
```
Point2f bsdfSample(RadicalInverse(haltonDim,     haltonIndex),
                   RadicalInverse(haltonDim + 1, haltonIndex));
haltonDim += 2;
```

The photon scattering step should be implemented carefully in order to keep the photon weights as similar to each other as possible. A method that gives distribution of photons where all have exactly equal weights was suggested by Jensen (2001, Section 5.2). First, the reflectance is computed at the intersection point. A random decision is then made whether or not to continue the photon's path with probability proportional to this reflectance. If the photon continues, its scattered direction is found by sampling from the BSDF's distribution, but it continues with its weight unchanged except for adjusting the spectral distribution based on the surface's color. Thus, a surface that reflects very little light will reflect few of the photons that reach it, but those that are scattered will continue on with unchanged contributions and so forth.

This particular approach isn't possible in pbrt due to a subtle implementation detail (a similar issue held for light source sampling previously as well): in pbrt, the BxDF interfaces are written so that the distribution used for importance sampling BSDFs doesn't necessarily have to perfectly match the actual distribution of the function being sampled. It is all the better if it does, but for many complex BSDFs exactly sampling from its distribution is difficult or impossible.

Therefore, here we will use an approach that generally leads to a similar result but offers more flexibility: at each intersection point, an outgoing direction is sampled with the BSDF's sampling distribution, and the photon's updated weight $\beta_{i,j+1}$ is computed using Equation (16.16). Then the ratio of the luminance of $\beta_{i,j+1}$ to the luminance of the photon's old weight $\beta_{i,j}$ is used to set the probability of continuing the path after applying Russian roulette.

The termination probability q is thus set so that if the photon's weight is significantly decreased at the scattering point, the termination probability will be high and if the photon's weight is essentially unchanged, the termination probability is low. In particular, the termination probability is chosen in a way such that if the photon continues, after its weight has been adjusted for the possibility of termination, its luminance will be the same as it was before scattering. It is easy to verify this property from the fragment below. (This property actually doesn't hold for the case where $\beta_{i,j+1} > \beta_{i,j}$, as can happen when the ratio of the BSDF's value and the PDF is greater than 1.)

⟨*Possibly terminate photon path with Russian roulette*⟩ ≡   987
```
Float q = std::max((Float)0, 1 - bnew.y() / beta.y());
if (RadicalInverse(haltonDim++, haltonIndex) < q)
    break;
beta = bnew / (1 - q);
```

After all of the photons for the iteration have been traced, the estimate of the incident radiance visible in each pixel area can now be updated based on contributions from photons in the current pass.

⟨*Update pixel values from this pass's photons*⟩ ≡   975
```
for (int i = 0; i < nPixels; ++i) {
    SPPMPixel &p = pixels[i];
    if (p.M > 0) {
        ⟨Update pixel photon count, search radius, and τ from photons 989⟩
        p.M = 0;
        for (int j = 0; j < Spectrum::nSamples; ++j)
            p.Phi[j] = (Float)0;
    }
    ⟨Reset VisiblePoint in pixel 990⟩
}
```

Equation (16.13) gives the rules to update the search radius and other quantities related to the photon estimate.

⟨*Update pixel photon count, search radius, and τ from photons*⟩ ≡   989
```
Float gamma = (Float)2 / (Float)3;
Float Nnew = p.N + gamma * p.M;
Float Rnew = p.radius * std::sqrt(Nnew / (p.N + p.M));
Spectrum Phi;
for (int j = 0; j < Spectrum::nSamples; ++j)
    Phi[j] = p.Phi[j];
p.tau = (p.tau + p.vp.beta * Phi) *
        (Rnew * Rnew) / (p.radius * p.radius);
p.N = Nnew;
p.radius = Rnew;
```

Note that the number of photons that have contributed to the pixel N is actually stored as a Float. This quantity must be treated as continuously valued, not a discrete integer, for the progressive radiance estimate to converge to the correct value in the limit.

⟨*SPPMPixel Public Data*⟩ +≡   974
```
Float N = 0;
Spectrum tau;
```

Before the next SPPM iteration begins, it's necessary to zero out the visible point in the pixel so that we don't attempt to re-use this one if no visible point and BDSF * is found in the next iteration.

⟨*Reset* VisiblePoint *in pixel*⟩ ≡   989
```
p.vp.beta = 0.;
p.vp.bsdf = nullptr;
```

Most of the ⟨*Periodically store SPPM image in film and write image*⟩ fragment is a straightforward matter of allocating an image of Spectrum values to pass to Film::SetImage() and then initializing the pixels in the image and before calling Film::WriteImage(). We won't include that boilerplate here, in order to focus on the last step of the SPPM algorithm, which combines the direct and indirect radiance estimates.

As described earlier, the direct lighting estimate needs to be divided by the number of pixel samples (which in turn is how many iterations have completed at this point) to get its average value. The indirect photon term is computed using Equation (16.11)—the two values then just need to be added together.

⟨*Compute radiance* L *for SPPM pixel* pixel⟩ ≡
```
const SPPMPixel &pixel = pixels[(y - pixelBounds.pMin.y) * (x1 - x0) +
                               (x - x0)];
Spectrum L = pixel.Ld / (iter + 1);
L += pixel.tau / (Np * Pi * pixel.radius * pixel.radius);
```

16.3 BIDIRECTIONAL PATH TRACING

The path-tracing algorithm described in Section 14.5 was the first fully general light transport algorithm in computer graphics, handling both a wide variety of geometric representations, lights, and BSDF models. Although it works well for many scenes, path tracing can exhibit high variance in the presence of particular tricky lighting conditions. For example, consider the setting shown in Figure 16.12: a light source is illuminating a small area on the ceiling such that the rest of the room is only illuminated by indirect lighting bouncing from that area. If we only trace paths starting from the camera, we will almost never happen to sample a path vertex in the illuminated region on the ceiling before we trace a shadow ray to the light. Most of the paths will have no contribution, while a few of them—the ones that happen to hit the small region on the ceiling—will have a large contribution. The resulting image will have high variance.

Difficult lighting settings like this can be handled more effectively by constructing paths that start from the camera on one end and from the light on the other end and are connected in the middle with a visibility ray. The resulting *bidirectional path-tracing*

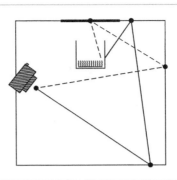

Figure 16.12: A Difficult Case for Path Tracing Starting from the Camera. A light source is illuminating a small area on the ceiling (thick line) such that only paths with a second-to-last vertex in the area indicated will be able to find illumination from the light. Bidirectional methods, where a path is started from the light and is connected with a path from the camera, can handle situations like these more robustly.

algorithm (henceforth referred to as BDPT) is a generalization of the standard path-tracing algorithm that can be much more efficient. In contrast to stochastic progressive photon mapping, BDPT is unbiased and does not blur the scene illumination.

BDPT first incrementally constructs a *camera subpath* starting with a point on the camera p_0. The next vertex, p_1, is found by computing the first intersection along the camera ray. Another vertex is found by sampling the BSDF at p_1 and tracing a ray to find a point p_2, and so forth. The resulting path of t vertices is $p_0, p_1, \ldots, p_{t-1}$. Following the same process starting from a point on a light source q_0 (and then using adjoint BSDFs at each vertex) creates a *light subpath* of s vertices, $q_0, q_1, \ldots, q_{s-1}$.

Given the two subpaths, a complete light-carrying path can be found by connecting a pair of vertices from each path.

$$\bar{p} = q_0, \ldots, q_{s'-1}, p_{t'-1}, \ldots, p_0,$$

where $s' \leq s$ and $t' \leq t$. (Our notation orders the vertices in $\bar{p}$ according to the propagation of light). If a visibility ray between $q_{s'}$ and $p_{t'}$ is unoccluded, then the path contribution can be found by evaluating the BSDFs at the connecting vertices (see Figure 16.13). More generally, these subpaths can be combined using the theory of path-space integration from Section 14.4.4.

Superficially, this approach bears some semblance to the two phases of the photon mapper; a key difference is that BDPT computes an unbiased estimate without density estimation. There are also significant differences in how the fact that a given light path could have been constructed in multiple different ways is handled.

There are three refinements to the algorithm that we've described so far that improve its performance in practice. The first two are analogous to improvements made to path tracing, and the third is a powerful variance reduction technique.

- First, subpaths can be reused: given a path $q_0, \ldots, q_{s-1}, p_{t-1}, \ldots, p_0$, transport can be evaluated over all of the paths given by connecting all the various

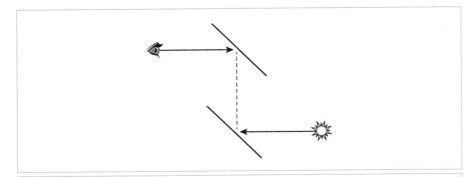

Figure 16.13: Bidirectional path tracing is based on generating two subpaths, one starting from a light and the other starting from the camera. Light-carrying paths can be found by attempting to connect pairs of vertices, one from each path. If a visibility ray between the two (dashed line) is unoccluded, the path's contribution can be added to the radiance estimate.

combinations of prefixes of the two paths together. If two paths have s and t vertices, respectively, then a variety of unique paths can be constructed from them, ranging in length from 2 to $s + t$ vertices long. Figure 16.14 illustrates these strategies for the case of direct illumination.

- The second optimization is not to try to connect paths that use only a single vertex from one of the subpaths. It is preferable to generate those paths using optimized sampling routines provided by the camera and light sources; for light sources, these are the direct lighting techniques that were introduced in Section 14.3.

- The third optimization weights the various strategies for generating paths of a given length more carefully than just averaging all of the strategies that construct paths of the same length. BDPT's approach of connecting subpaths means that a path containing n scattering events can be generated in $n + 3$ different ways. We can expect that some strategies will be a good choice for producing certain types of paths while being quite poor for others. Multiple importance sampling can be applied to combine the set of connection strategies into a single estimator that uses each strategy where it is best. This application of MIS is crucial to BDPT's efficiency.

One of BDPT's connection strategies is to directly connect light subpath vertices to the camera: these paths almost always create a contribution whose raster coordinates differ from the current pixel being rendered, which violates the expectations of the SamplerIntegrator interface. Thus, BDPTIntegrator derives from the more general Integrator interface so that it can have more flexibility in how it updates the image. Its implementation is in the files integrators/bdpt.h and integrators/bdpt.cpp.

⟨*BDPT Declarations*⟩ ≡
```
class BDPTIntegrator : public Integrator {
public:
    ⟨BDPTIntegrator Public Methods 994⟩
private:
    ⟨BDPTIntegrator Private Data 993⟩
};
```

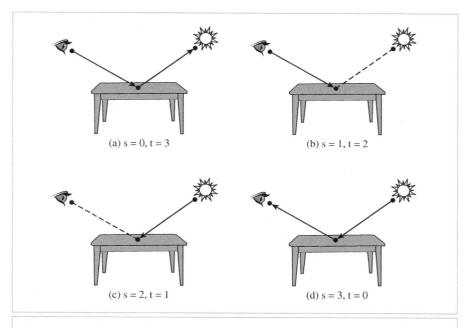

(a) s = 0, t = 3   (b) s = 1, t = 2

(c) s = 2, t = 1   (d) s = 3, t = 0

Figure 16.14: The four different ways in which bidirectional path tracing can create a direct illumination path. (a) Standard path tracing without direct illumination sampling, where a ray generated using BSDF sampling from a point on a surface happens to intersect a light source. (b) Path tracing with direct illumination sampling, where the explicit shadow ray is indicated with a dashed line. (c) Particle tracing from a light source with an explicit visibility test between a point on a surface and the camera. (d) Particle tracing where a particle happens to intersect the camera's lens.

The BDPTIntegrator constructor, which is straightforward and not included here, initializes member variables with the provided camera, sampler, and the maximum path depth.

⟨*BDPTIntegrator Private Data*⟩ ≡   992
```
std::shared_ptr<Sampler> sampler;
std::shared_ptr<const Camera> camera;
const int maxDepth;
```

All subpath creation and connection steps are performed in a nested parallel loop over pixels in BDPTIntegrator::Render(). The overall structure of this method is very similar to SamplerIntegrator::Render():

- The image is subdivided into tiles of 16 × 16 pixels, which are processed in parallel.
- For each tile, the method declares a MemoryArena, arena and acquires a Sampler instance from BDPTIntegrator::sampler via a call to Sampler::Clone().
- It then loops over the pixels in each tile, taking samples from each one until Sampler::StartNextSample() returns false, at which point it advances to the next pixel.

We won't include this code here, as the details should be familiar now. Instead, we'll move forward to the fragment responsible for generating and connecting the subpaths for a pixel sample.

⟨*BDPTIntegrator Public Methods*⟩ ≡   992
```
void Render(const Scene &scene);
```

Generating a single BDPT sample involves sampling a pixel position in the image, generating camera and light subpaths, and then connecting them using a variety of specialized connection strategies.

⟨*Generate a single sample using BDPT*⟩ ≡
```
Point2f pFilm = (Point2f)pPixel + tileSampler->Get2D();
⟨Trace the camera and light subpaths 994⟩
⟨Execute all BDPT connection strategies 995⟩
```

The Vertex class, which will be introduced in Section 16.3.1, represents a vertex along a subpath. We start by allocating two arrays for vertices for the two subpaths. In addition to a vertex on a surface, a Vertex can represent a vertex for a scattering event in participating media, a vertex on a light source, or a vertex on the camera lens.

For each subpath, one more vertex than the maximum path length must be allocated to store the starting vertex on the light or camera. Camera subpaths get yet again one more vertex, which allows camera paths to randomly intersect light sources—this strategy is important for rendering area lights seen by reflections only from specular surfaces, for example. (The corresponding strategy of allowing a light subpath to randomly intersect the camera lens is less useful in practice.)

The GenerateCameraSubpath() and GenerateLightSubpath() functions, which generate these two subpaths, will be defined in Section 16.3.2, after some preliminaries related to the Vertex representation.

⟨*Trace the camera and light subpaths*⟩ ≡   994
```
Vertex *cameraVertices = arena.Alloc<Vertex>(maxDepth + 2);
Vertex *lightVertices = arena.Alloc<Vertex>(maxDepth + 1);
int nCamera = GenerateCameraSubpath(scene, *tileSampler, arena,
    maxDepth + 2, *camera, pFilm, cameraVertices);
int nLight = GenerateLightSubpath(scene, *tileSampler, arena,
    maxDepth + 1, cameraVertices[0].time(), *lightDistr, lightVertices);
```

After the subpaths have been generated, a nested for loop iterates over all pairs of vertices from the two subpaths and attempts to connect them. In these loops, s and t correspond to the number of vertices to use from the corresponding subpath; an index of 0 means that no scattering events are used from the corresponding subpath. In our implementation, this strategy is only supported for the $s = 0$ case, which furthermore requires cameraVertices[t] to be a surface intersection involving a light source. Because the dual case—intersecting a camera with $t = 0$—is not supported, the loop over camera subpaths starts at $t = 1$.

A path length of 1 corresponds to connecting a point on the camera lens or a light source to the other subpath. For light endpoints, this is identical to the standard light sampling approach provided by Light::Sample_Li() and first used in Section 14.3.1; our implementation uses this existing functionality. For camera endpoints, we will rely on the symmetric analog Camera::Sample_Wi(). Since Camera::Sample_Wi() and Light::Sample_Li() cannot both be used at the same time, we skip the $s = t = 1$ case.

⟨*Execute all BDPT connection strategies*⟩ ≡   994
```
Spectrum L(0.f);
for (int t = 1; t <= nCamera; ++t) {
    for (int s = 0; s <= nLight; ++s) {
        int depth = t + s - 2;
        if ((s == 1 && t == 1) || depth < 0 || depth > maxDepth)
            continue;
        ⟨Execute the (s, t) connection strategy and update L 995⟩
    }
}
filmTile->AddSample(pFilm, L);
```

The ConnectBDPT() function attempts to connect the two subpaths with the given number of vertices; it returns the weighted contribution of the radiance carried along the resulting path. (It will be defined shortly, in Section 16.3.3.) In most cases, this contribution is accumulated into the variable L that will be provided to the FilmTile after all of the subpath connections have been attempted. However, the $t = 1$ connection connects a vertex of the light subpath directly to the camera and thus will produce different raster positions in every iteration—in this case, the implementation calls Film::AddSplat() to immediately record its sample contribution.

⟨*Execute the (s, t) connection strategy and update L*⟩ ≡   995
```
Point2f pFilmNew = pFilm;
Float misWeight = 0.f;
Spectrum Lpath = ConnectBDPT(scene, lightVertices, cameraVertices, s, t,
    *lightDistr, *camera, *tileSampler, &pFilmNew, &misWeight);
if (t != 1)
    L += Lpath;
else
    film->AddSplat(pFilmNew, Lpath);
```

16.3.1 VERTEX ABSTRACTION LAYER

A general advantage of path-space rendering techniques is their ability to create paths in a large number of different ways, but this characteristic often leads to cluttered and hard-to-debug implementations. Establishing connections between pairs of vertices on the light and camera subpaths is a simple operation when only surface interactions are involved but quickly becomes unwieldy if one or both of the vertices may represent a scattering event in participating media, for example.

Instead of an inconveniently large number of conditional statements in the core BDPT code, we'll define the Vertex type, which can represent any kind of path vertex. All of the necessary conditional logic to handle various cases that occur throughout the BDPT implementation will be encapsulated in its methods.

⟨*BDPT Declarations*⟩ +≡
```
struct Vertex {
    ⟨Vertex Public Data 996⟩
    ⟨Vertex Public Methods 997⟩
};
```

⟨*Vertex Public Data*⟩ ≡   996
```
    VertexType type;
```

Altogether, four different types of path vertices are supported in pbrt.

⟨*BDPT Helper Definitions*⟩ ≡
```
    enum class VertexType { Camera, Light, Surface, Medium };
```

The beta member variable is analogous to the β variable in the volumetric path tracer (Section 15.3.1) or the weight carried by particles in the SPPMIntegrator: it contains the product of the BSDF or phase function values, transmittances, and cosine terms for the vertices in the path generated so far, divided by their respective sampling PDFs. For the light subpath, they also include the emitted radiance divided by the density of the emission position and direction. For the camera subpath, radiance is replaced by importance.

⟨*Vertex Public Data*⟩ +≡   996
```
    Spectrum beta;
```

Instances of various types of Interactions represent type-specific data about the vertex. This information is arranged as a space-efficient C++ union since only one of the entries is used at a time.

⟨*Vertex Public Data*⟩ +≡   996
```
    union
    {
        EndpointInteraction ei;
        MediumInteraction mi;
        SurfaceInteraction si;
    };
```

EndpointInteraction is a new interaction implementation that is used only by BDPT. It records the position of a path endpoint—i.e., a position on a light source or the lens of the camera—and stores a pointer to the camera or light in question.

⟨*EndpointInteraction Declarations*⟩ ≡
```
    struct EndpointInteraction : Interaction {
        union {
            const Camera *camera;
            const Light *light;
        };
        ⟨EndpointInteraction Public Methods 997⟩
    };
```

There are a multiple constructors that initialize the EndpointInteraction contents using a pointer and either an existing Interaction or a sampled ray. For brevity, we only show the constructors for light endpoints.

⟨*EndpointInteraction Public Methods*⟩ ≡   996
```
EndpointInteraction(const Light *light, const Ray &r, const Normal3f &nl)
    : Interaction(r.o, r.time, r.medium), light(light) { n = nl; }
```

⟨*EndpointInteraction Public Methods*⟩ +≡   996
```
EndpointInteraction(const Interaction &it, const Light *light)
    : Interaction(it), light(light) { }
```

A range of static helper functions create Vertex instances for the various types of path vertices. We'll only include their declarations here, as their implementations are all straightforward. We could instead have provided a range of overloaded constructors that took various Interaction types as parameters, but we think that having the name of the type of vertex being created explicit in a function call makes the following code easier to read.

⟨*Vertex Public Methods*⟩ ≡   996
```
static inline Vertex CreateCamera(const Camera *camera, const Ray &ray,
        const Spectrum &beta);
static inline Vertex CreateCamera(const Camera *camera,
        const Interaction &it, const Spectrum &beta);
static inline Vertex CreateLight(const Light *light, const Ray &ray,
        const Normal3f &nLight, const Spectrum &Le, Float pdf);
static inline Vertex CreateLight(const EndpointInteraction &ei,
        const Spectrum &beta, Float pdf);
static inline  Vertex CreateMedium(const MediumInteraction &mi,
        const Spectrum &beta, Float pdf, const Vertex &prev);
static inline Vertex CreateSurface(const SurfaceInteraction &si,
        const Spectrum &beta, Float pdf, const Vertex &prev);
```

It is often necessary to access the core fields in Interaction that are common to all types of vertices; the Vertex::GetInteraction() method extracts this shared part. Since Vertex::mi, Vertex::si, and Vertex::ei all derive from Interaction and are part of the same union and thus their base Interactions are at the same location in memory, the conditional logic below should be removed by the compiler.

⟨*Vertex Public Methods*⟩ +≡   996
```
const Interaction &GetInteraction() const {
    switch (type) {
        case VertexType::Medium:  return mi;
        case VertexType::Surface: return si;
        default:                  return ei;
    }
}
```

The convenience function Vertex::p() returns the vertex position. We omit definitions of Vertex::time(), Vertex::ng(), and Vertex::ns(), which are defined analogously, and return the time, geometric normal, and shading normal, respectively, of the vertex.

⟨*Vertex Public Methods*⟩ +≡   996
```
const Point3f &p() const { return GetInteraction().p; }
```

The delta attribute is only used by surface interactions and records whether a Dirac delta function was sampled (e.g., when light is scattered by a perfectly specular material).

⟨*Vertex Public Data*⟩ +≡   996
```
bool delta = false;
```

A simple way to find out whether a vertex (including endpoints) is located on a surface is to check whether Vertex::ng() returns a nonzero result.

⟨*Vertex Public Methods*⟩ +≡   996
```
bool IsOnSurface() const { return ng() != Normal3f(); }
```

Vertex::f() evaluates the portion of the measurement equation, (16.1), associated with a vertex. This method only needs to handle surface and medium vertices since the BDPT implementation only invokes it in those cases. Note that the next vertex in the path is the only one passed to this method: though the direction to the predecessor vertex is needed to evaluate the BRDF or phase function, this information is already available in Interaction::wo from when the Vertex was first created.

⟨*Vertex Public Methods*⟩ +≡   996
```
Spectrum f(const Vertex &next) const {
    Vector3f wi = Normalize(next.p() - p());
    switch (type) {
        case VertexType::Surface: return si.bsdf->f(si.wo, wi);
        case VertexType::Medium:  return mi.phase->p(mi.wo, wi);
    }
}
```

The Vertex::IsConnectible() method returns a Boolean value that indicates whether a connection strategy involving the current vertex can in principle succeed. If, for example, the vertex is a surface interaction whose BSDF only consists of Dirac delta components, then we can never successfully connect it to a subpath vertex in the other path: there's zero probability of choosing a direction where the delta distribution is nonzero. The implementation assumes that medium and camera vertices are always connectible (the latter assumption would have to be modified if support for orthographic cameras is added).

⟨*Vertex Public Methods*⟩ +≡   996
```
bool IsConnectible() const {
    switch (type) {
        case VertexType::Medium:  return true;
        case VertexType::Light:   return
            (ei.light->flags & (int)LightFlags::DeltaDirection) == 0;
        case VertexType::Camera:  return true;
        case VertexType::Surface: return si.bsdf->NumComponents(
            BxDFType(BSDF_DIFFUSE | BSDF_GLOSSY |
                    BSDF_REFLECTION | BSDF_TRANSMISSION)) > 0;
    }
}
```

A few helper methods are useful for working with lights—these are necessary to deal with the considerable variety of light sources supported by pbrt.

For instance, when the Primitive underlying a surface interaction vertex is itself an area light, the vertex can take on different roles depending on the BDPT connection strategy: it can be re-interpreted as a light source and used as a path endpoint, or it can serve as a normal scattering event to generate paths of greater length. The Vertex::IsLight() method therefore provides a comprehensive test for whether a vertex can be interpreted as a light source.

⟨*Vertex Public Methods*⟩ +≡   996
```
bool IsLight() const {
    return type == VertexType::Light ||
        (type == VertexType::Surface && si.primitive->GetAreaLight());
}
```

Light sources that have an emission profile that contains a Dirac delta distribution must be treated specially in the computation of multiple importance sampling weights; Vertex::IsDeltaLight() checks for this case.

⟨*Vertex Public Methods*⟩ +≡   996
```
bool IsDeltaLight() const {
    return type == VertexType::Light && ei.light &&
        ::IsDeltaLight(ei.light->flags);
}
```

The Vertex::IsInfiniteLight() method indicates whether a vertex is associated with an infinite area light. Such vertices can be created by sampling an emitted ray from an InfiniteAreaLight or by tracing a ray from the camera that escapes into the environment. In the latter case, the vertex is marked with the type VertexType::Light, but ei.light stores nullptr since no specific light source was intersected.

⟨*Vertex Public Methods*⟩ +≡   996
```
bool IsInfiniteLight() const {
    return type == VertexType::Light &&
        (!ei.light || ei.light->flags & (int)LightFlags::Infinite);
}
```

Finally, Le() can be used to find emitted radiance from an intersected light source toward another vertex.

⟨*Vertex Public Methods*⟩ +≡   996
```
Spectrum Le(const Scene &scene, const Vertex &v) const {
    if (!IsLight()) return Spectrum(0.f);
    Vector3f w = Normalize(v.p() - p());
    if (IsInfiniteLight()) {
        ⟨Return emitted radiance for infinite light sources 1000⟩
    } else {
        const AreaLight *light = si.primitive->GetAreaLight();
        return light->L(si, w);
    }
}
```

⟨*Return emitted radiance for infinite light sources*⟩ ≡   999

```
Spectrum Le(0.f);
for (const auto &light : scene.lights)
    Le += light->Le(Ray(p(), -w));
return Le;
```

Probability Densities

BDPT's multiple importance sampling code requires detailed information about the probability density of light-carrying paths with respect to a range of different path sampling strategies. It is crucial that these densities are expressed in the same probability measure so that ratios of their probabilities are meaningful. The implementation here uses the *area product measure* for path probabilities. It expresses the density of a path as the product of the densities of its individual vertices, which are in turn given in a simple common (and consistent) measure: *probability per unit area*.[9] This is the same measure as was initially used to derive the surface form of the LTE in Section 14.4.3.

Recall from Section 5.5 that the Jacobian of the mapping from solid angles to surface area involves the inverse squared distance and the cosine of angle between the geometric normal at next and wn (assuming next is a surface vertex—if it is a point in a participating medium, there is no cosine term (Section 15.1.1)). The ConvertDensity() method returns the product of this Jacobian (computed from the vertex attributes) and the pdf parameter, which should express a solid angle density at the vertex. (Infinite area light sources need special handling here; this case is discussed later, in Section 16.3.5.)

⟨*Vertex Public Methods*⟩ +≡   996

```
Float ConvertDensity(Float pdf, const Vertex &next) const {
    ⟨Return solid angle density if next is an infinite area light 1020⟩
    Vector3f w = next.p() - p();
    Float invDist2 = 1 / w.LengthSquared();
    if (next.IsOnSurface())
        pdf *= AbsDot(next.ng(), w * std::sqrt(invDist2));
    return pdf * invDist2;
}
```

Each vertex has two densities: the first, pdfFwd, stores *forward* density of the current vertex, which is the probability per unit area of the current vertex as generated by the path sampling algorithm. The second density, pdfRev, is the hypothetical probability density of the vertex if the direction of light transport was *reversed*—that is, if radiance transport was used in place of importance transport for the camera path and vice versa for the light path. This reverse density will be crucial for computing MIS weights in Section 16.3.4.

⟨*Vertex Public Data*⟩ +≡   996

```
Float pdfFwd = 0, pdfRev = 0;
```

AbsDot() 64
Float 1062
Light::Le() 741
Ray 73
Scene::lights 23
Spectrum 315
Vector3::LengthSquared() 65
Vector3f 60
Vertex 996
Vertex::IsOnSurface() 998
Vertex::ng() 997
Vertex::p() 997

---

9   Note that an analogously defined "product solid angle measure" would not satisfy the requirement of a common and consistent measure: solid angle densities are always expressed with respect to a specific vertex position—relating the densities as "seen" from different vertices would require additional Jacobian factors to account for the underlying change of variables.

The `Vertex::Pdf()` method returns the probability per unit area of the sampling technique associated with a given vertex. Given a preceding vertex `prev`, it evaluates the density for sampling the vertex `next` for rays leaving the vertex `*this`. The `prev` argument may be equal to `nullptr` for path endpoints (i.e., cameras or light sources), which have no predecessor. Light sources require some extra care and are handled separately via the `PdfLight()` method that will be discussed shortly.

⟨*Vertex Public Methods*⟩ +≡   **996**
```
Float Pdf(const Scene &scene, const Vertex *prev,
        const Vertex &next) const {
    if (type == VertexType::Light)
        return PdfLight(scene, next);
    ⟨Compute directions to preceding and next vertex 1001⟩
    ⟨Compute directional density depending on the vertex type 1001⟩
    ⟨Return probability per unit area at vertex next 1001⟩
}
```

For all other vertex types, the function first computes normalized directions to the preceding and next vertex (if present).

⟨*Compute directions to preceding and next vertex*⟩ ≡   **1001**
```
Vector3f wp, wn = Normalize(next.p() - p());
if (prev)
    wp = Normalize(prev->p() - p());
```

Depending on the vertex type, `Pdf()` invokes the appropriate PDF method and stores the probability per unit solid angle for sampling the direction to `next` in the variable `pdf`.

⟨*Compute directional density depending on the vertex type*⟩ ≡   **1001**
```
Float pdf, unused;
if (type == VertexType::Camera)
    ei.camera->Pdf_We(ei.SpawnRay(wn), &unused, &pdf);
else if (type == VertexType::Surface)
    pdf = si.bsdf->Pdf(wp, wn);
else if (type == VertexType::Medium)
    pdf = mi.phase->p(wp, wn);
```

Finally, the solid angle density is converted to a probability per unit area at `next`.

⟨*Return probability per unit area at vertex* next⟩ ≡   **1001**
```
return ConvertDensity(pdf, next);
```

Light-emitting vertices can be created in two different ways: by using a sampling routine like `Light::Sample_Le()`, or by intersecting an emissive surface via ray tracing. To be able to compare these different strategies as part of a multiple importance sampling scheme, it is necessary to know the corresponding probability per unit area for a light vertex. This task is handled by the `PdfLight()` method.

Its definition resembles that of `Vertex::Pdf()`: it computes the direction from the current vertex to the provided vertex and invokes `Light::Pdf_Le()` to retrieve the solid angle density of the underlying sampling strategy, which is subsequently converted into a density per unit area at v. In contrast to Vertex::Pdf(), this method also treats surface vertices located on area lights as if they were light source vertices. Once more, there is a special case for infinite area lights, which we postpone until Section 16.3.5.

⟨*Vertex Public Methods*⟩ +≡   **996**
```
    Float PdfLight(const Scene &scene, const Vertex &v) const {
        Vector3f w = v.p() - p();
        Float invDist2 = 1 / w.LengthSquared();
        w *= std::sqrt(invDist2);
        Float pdf;
        if (IsInfiniteLight()) {
            ⟨Compute planar sampling density for infinite light sources 1022⟩
        } else {
            ⟨Get pointer light to the light source at the vertex 1002⟩
            ⟨Compute sampling density for non-infinite light sources 1002⟩
        }
        if (v.IsOnSurface())
            pdf *= AbsDot(v.ng(), w);
        return pdf;
    }
```

Depending on the vertex type, the pointer to the light source implementation must be obtained from one of two different locations.

⟨*Get pointer* light *to the light source at the vertex*⟩ ≡   **1002, 1003**
```
    const Light *light = type == VertexType::Light ?
                    ei.light : si.primitive->GetAreaLight();
```

⟨*Compute sampling density for non-infinite light sources*⟩ ≡   **1002**
```
    Float pdfPos, pdfDir;
    light->Pdf_Le(Ray(p(), w, time()), ng(), &pdfPos, &pdfDir);
    pdf = pdfDir * invDist2;
```

By symmetry, we would now expect a dual routine Vertex::PdfCamera() that applies to camera endpoints. However, cameras in pbrt are never represented using explicit geometry: thus, they cannot be reached by ray intersections, which eliminates the need for a dedicated query function. If desired, a perfectly symmetric implementation could be achieved by instantiating scene geometry that is tagged with an "area camera" analogous to area lights. This increases the set of possible BDPT connection strategies, though their benefit is negligible in most scenes due to the low probability of intersecting the camera.

Note that the Pdf() and PdfLight() methods use the directional probability density of the importance strategy implemented at the current vertex as measured at the location of another given vertex. However, this is not enough to fully characterize the behavior of path endpoints, whose sampling routines generate rays from a 4D distribution. An additional PdfLightOrigin() method fills the gap by providing information about the spatial distribution of samples on the light sources themselves. For the same reason as before, a dedicated PdfCameraOrigin() method for camera endpoints is not needed.

⟨*Vertex Public Methods*⟩ +≡   996
```
Float PdfLightOrigin(const Scene &scene, const Vertex &v,
                     const Distribution1D &lightDistr) const {
    Vector3f w = Normalize(v.p() - p());
    if (IsInfiniteLight()) {
        ⟨Return solid angle density for infinite light sources 1021⟩
    } else {
        ⟨Return solid angle density for non-infinite light sources 1003⟩
    }
}
```

⟨*Return solid angle density for non-infinite light sources*⟩ ≡   1003
```
Float pdfPos, pdfDir, pdfChoice = 0;
⟨Get pointer light to the light source at the vertex 1002⟩
⟨Compute the discrete probability of sampling light, pdfChoice 1003⟩
light->Pdf_Le(Ray(p(), w, time()), ng(), &pdfPos, &pdfDir);
return pdfPos * pdfChoice;
```

To determine the discrete probability of choosing light among the available light sources, we must find the pointer to the light source and look up the corresponding entry in lightDistr. If there are very many light sources, the linear search here will be inefficient. In that case, this computation could be implemented more efficiently by storing this probability directly in the light source class.

⟨*Compute the discrete probability of sampling* light, pdfChoice⟩ ≡   1003
```
for (size_t i = 0; i < scene.lights.size(); ++i) {
    if (scene.lights[i].get() == light) {
        pdfChoice = lightDistr.DiscretePDF(i);
        break;
    }
}
```

16.3.2 GENERATING THE CAMERA AND LIGHT SUBPATHS

A symmetric pair of functions, GenerateCameraSubpath() and GenerateLightSubpath(), generates the two corresponding types of subpaths. Both do some initial work to get the path started and then call out to a second function, RandomWalk(), which takes care of sampling the following vertices and initializing the path array. Both of these functions return the number of vertices in the subpath.

⟨*BDPT Utility Functions*⟩ +≡
```
int GenerateCameraSubpath(const Scene &scene, Sampler &sampler,
        MemoryArena &arena, int maxDepth, const Camera &camera,
        const Point2f &pFilm, Vertex *path) {
    if (maxDepth == 0)
        return 0;
    ⟨Sample initial ray for camera subpath 1004⟩
    ⟨Generate first vertex on camera subpath and start random walk 1004⟩
}
```

A camera path starts with a camera ray from `Camera::GenerateRayDifferential()`. As in the `SamplerIntegrator`, the ray's differentials are scaled so that they reflect the actual pixel sampling density.

⟨*Sample initial ray for camera subpath*⟩ ≡   1003
```
CameraSample cameraSample;
cameraSample.pFilm = pFilm;
cameraSample.time = sampler.Get1D();
cameraSample.pLens = sampler.Get2D();
RayDifferential ray;
Spectrum beta = camera.GenerateRayDifferential(cameraSample, &ray);
ray.ScaleDifferentials(1 / std::sqrt(sampler.samplesPerPixel));
```

The vertex at position `path[0]` is initialized with a special endpoint vertex on the camera lens (for cameras with finite apertures) or pinhole. The `RandomWalk()` function then takes care of generating the rest of the vertices. `TransportMode` reflects the quantity that is carried back to the origin of the path—hence `TransportMode::Radiance` is used here. Since the first element of `path` was already used for the endpoint vertex, `RandomWalk()` is invoked such that it writes sampled vertices starting at position `path[1]` with a maximum depth of `maxDepth - 1`. The function returns the total number of sampled vertices.

⟨*Generate first vertex on camera subpath and start random walk*⟩ ≡   1003
```
Float pdfPos, pdfDir;
path[0] = Vertex::CreateCamera(&camera, ray, beta);
camera.Pdf_We(ray, &pdfPos, &pdfDir);
return RandomWalk(scene, ray, sampler, arena, beta, pdfDir,
              maxDepth - 1, TransportMode::Radiance,
              path + 1) + 1;
```

The function `GenerateLightSubpath()` works in a similar fashion, with some minor differences corresponding to the fact that the path starts from a light source.

⟨*BDPT Utility Functions*⟩ +≡
```
int GenerateLightSubpath(const Scene &scene, Sampler &sampler,
        MemoryArena &arena, int maxDepth, Float time,
        const Distribution1D &lightDistr, Vertex *path) {
    if (maxDepth == 0)
        return 0;
    ⟨Sample initial ray for light subpath 1005⟩
    ⟨Generate first vertex on light subpath and start random walk 1005⟩
}
```

As usual in this integrator, a specific light is chosen by sampling from the provided `Distribution1D`. Next, an emitted ray is sampled via the light's implementation of `Light::Sample_Le()`.

⟨*Sample initial ray for light subpath*⟩ ≡   1004
```
    Float lightPdf;
    int lightNum = lightDistr.SampleDiscrete(sampler.Get1D(), &lightPdf);
    const std::shared_ptr<Light> &light = scene.lights[lightNum];
    RayDifferential ray;
    Normal3f nLight;
    Float pdfPos, pdfDir;
    Spectrum Le = light->Sample_Le(sampler.Get2D(), sampler.Get2D(), time,
                                   &ray, &nLight, &pdfPos, &pdfDir);
    if (pdfPos == 0 || pdfDir == 0 || Le.IsBlack())
        return 0;
```

The beta variable is initialized with the associated sampling weight, which is given by the emitted radiance multiplied by a cosine factor from the light transport equation and divided by the probability of the sample in ray-space. This step is analogous to Equation (16.15) and the approach implemented in the fragment ⟨*Generate* photonRay *from light source and initialize* beta⟩ from the particle tracing step of the SPPM integrator.

⟨*Generate first vertex on light subpath and start random walk*⟩ ≡   1004
```
    path[0] = Vertex::CreateLight(light.get(), ray, nLight, Le,
                                  pdfPos * lightPdf);
    Spectrum beta = Le * AbsDot(nLight, ray.d) / (lightPdf * pdfPos * pdfDir);
    int nVertices = RandomWalk(scene, ray, sampler, arena, beta, pdfDir,
                               maxDepth - 1, TransportMode::Importance,
                               path + 1);
```
⟨*Correct subpath sampling densities for infinite area lights* **1021**⟩
```
    return nVertices + 1;
```

RandomWalk() traces paths starting at an initial vertex. It assumes that a position and an outgoing direction at the corresponding path endpoint were previously sampled and that this information is provided via the input arguments ray, a path throughput weight beta, and a parameter pdfFwd that gives the probability of sampling the ray per unit solid angle of ray.d. The parameter mode selects between importance and radiance transport (Section 16.1). The path vertices are stored in the provided path array up to a maximum number of maxDepth vertices, and the actual number of generated vertices is returned at the end.

⟨*BDPT Utility Functions*⟩ +≡
```
    int RandomWalk(const Scene &scene, RayDifferential ray, Sampler &sampler,
            MemoryArena &arena, Spectrum beta, Float pdf, int maxDepth,
            TransportMode mode, Vertex *path) {
        if (maxDepth == 0)
            return 0;
```

```
        int bounces = 0;
        ⟨Declare variables for forward and reverse probability densities 1006⟩
        while (true) {
            ⟨Attempt to create the next subpath vertex in path 1006⟩
        }
        return bounces;
    }
```

The two variables pdfFwd and pdfRev are updated during every loop iteration and satisfy the following invariants: at the beginning of each iteration, pdfFwd records the probability per unit solid angle of the sampled ray direction ray.d. On the other hand, pdfRev denotes the *reverse* probability at the end of each iteration—that is, the density of the opposite light transport mode per unit solid angle along the same ray segment.

⟨*Declare variables for forward and reverse probability densities*⟩ ≡   1005
```
    Float pdfFwd = pdf, pdfRev = 0;
```

⟨*Attempt to create the next subpath vertex in* path⟩ ≡   1005
```
    MediumInteraction mi;
    ⟨Trace a ray and sample the medium, if any 1006⟩
    if (mi.IsValid()) {
        ⟨Record medium interaction in path and compute forward density 1007⟩
        ⟨Sample direction and compute reverse density at preceding vertex 1007⟩
    } else {
        ⟨Handle surface interaction for path generation 1007⟩
    }
    ⟨Compute reverse area density at preceding vertex 1008⟩
```

The loop body begins by intersecting the current ray against the scene geometry. If the ray is passing through a participating medium, the call to Medium::Sample() possibly samples a scattering event between the ray and the surface. It returns the medium sampling weight, which is incorporated into the path contribution weight beta.

⟨*Trace a ray and sample the medium, if any*⟩ ≡   1006
```
    SurfaceInteraction isect;
    bool foundIntersection = scene.Intersect(ray, &isect);
    if (ray.medium)
        beta *= ray.medium->Sample(ray, sampler, arena, &mi);
    if (beta.IsBlack())
        break;
    Vertex &vertex = path[bounces], &prev = path[bounces - 1];
```

When Medium::Sample() generates a medium scattering event, the corresponding Interaction is stored in a Vertex and appended at the end of the path array. The Vertex::CreateMedium() method converts the solid angle density in pdfFwd to a probability per unit area and stores the result in Vertex::pdfFwd.

Float 1062
Medium::Sample() 891
MediumInteraction 688
MediumInteraction::IsValid() 893
Ray::medium 74
Scene::Intersect() 24
Spectrum::IsBlack() 317
SurfaceInteraction 116
Vertex 996
Vertex::CreateMedium() 997
Vertex::pdfFwd 1000

⟨*Record medium interaction in* path *and compute forward density*⟩ ≡   1006
```
vertex = Vertex::CreateMedium(mi, beta, pdfFwd, prev);
if (++bounces >= maxDepth)
    break;
```

If the maximum path depth has not yet been exceeded, a scattered direction is sampled from the phase function and used to spawn a new ray that will be processed by the next loop iteration.

At this point, we could evaluate the phase function with swapped arguments to obtain the sampling density at the preceding vertex for a hypothetical random walk that would have produced the same scattering interactions in reverse order. Since phase functions are generally symmetric with respect to their arguments, instead we simply reuse the value computed for pdfFwd.

⟨*Sample direction and compute reverse density at preceding vertex*⟩ ≡   1006
```
Vector3f wi;
pdfFwd = pdfRev = mi.phase->Sample_p(-ray.d, &wi, sampler.Get2D());
ray = mi.SpawnRay(wi);
```

For surfaces, the overall structure is similar, though some extra care is required to deal with non-symmetric scattering and surfaces that mark transitions between media.

⟨*Handle surface interaction for path generation*⟩ ≡   1006
```
if (!foundIntersection) {
    ⟨Capture escaped rays when tracing from the camera 1020⟩
    break;
}
⟨Compute scattering functions for mode and skip over medium boundaries 1007⟩
⟨Initialize vertex with surface intersection information 1008⟩
if (++bounces >= maxDepth)
    break;
⟨Sample BSDF at current vertex and compute reverse probability 1008⟩
ray = isect.SpawnRay(wi);
```

The fragment ⟨*Capture escaped rays when tracing from the camera*⟩ is necessary to support infinite area lights. It will be discussed in Section 16.3.5. The following fragment, ⟨*Compute scattering functions for* mode *and skip over medium boundaries*⟩, is analogous to ⟨*Compute scattering functions and skip over medium boundaries*⟩ from the basic path tracer except that scattering functions are requested for the current light transport mode (radiance or importance transport) using the mode parameter.

⟨*Compute scattering functions for* mode *and skip over medium boundaries*⟩ ≡   1007
```
isect.ComputeScatteringFunctions(ray, arena, true, mode);
if (!isect.bsdf) {
    ray = isect.SpawnRay(ray.d);
    continue;
}
```

Interaction::SpawnRay() 232

MediumInteraction::phase 688

PhaseFunction::Sample_p()
898

Sampler::Get2D() 422

SurfaceInteraction::bsdf 250

SurfaceInteraction::
ComputeScatteringFunctions()
578

Vector3f 60

Vertex::CreateMedium() 997

Given a valid intersection, the current path vertex is initialized with the corresponding surface intersection vertex, where, again, the soid angle density pdfFwd is converted to an area density before being stored in Vertex::pdfFwd.

⟨*Initialize* vertex *with surface intersection information*⟩ ≡   **1007**
```
vertex = Vertex::CreateSurface(isect, beta, pdfFwd, prev);
```

If the maximum path depth has not yet been exceeded, a scattered direction is sampled from the BSDF and the path contribution in beta is updated. For the surface case, we can't generally assume that BSDF::Pdf() is symmetric; hence we must re-evaluate the sampling density with swapped arguments to obtain pdfRev. In case of a specular sampling event, we mark the vertex using the flag Vertex::delta and set pdfFwd and pdfRev to 0 to indicate that the underlying interaction has no continuous density function. Finally, we correct for non-symmetry related to the use of shading normals (see Section 16.1.3 for details).

⟨*Sample BSDF at current vertex and compute reverse probability*⟩ ≡   **1007**
```
Vector3f wi, wo = isect.wo;
BxDFType type;
Spectrum f = isect.bsdf->Sample_f(wo, &wi, sampler.Get2D(), &pdfFwd,
                                  BSDF_ALL, &type);
if (f.IsBlack() || pdfFwd == 0.f)
    break;
beta *= f * AbsDot(wi, isect.shading.n) / pdfFwd;
pdfRev = isect.bsdf->Pdf(wi, wo, BSDF_ALL);
if (type & BSDF_SPECULAR) {
    vertex.delta = true;
    pdfRev = pdfFwd = 0;
}
beta *= CorrectShadingNormal(isect, wo, wi, mode);
```

The loop wraps up by converting the reverse density pdfRev to a probability per unit area and storing it in the Vertex data structure of the preceding vertex.

⟨*Compute reverse area density at preceding vertex*⟩ ≡   **1006**
```
prev.pdfRev = vertex.ConvertDensity(pdfRev, prev);
```

16.3.3 SUBPATH CONNECTIONS

The ConnectBDPT() function takes the light and camera subpaths and the number of vertices *s* and *t* to use from each one, respectively. It returns the corresponding strategy's contribution.

The connection strategy with *t* = 1 uses only a single camera vertex, the camera's position; the raster position of the path's contribution is then based on which pixel the last vertex of the light subpath is visible in (if any). In this case, the resulting position is returned via the pRaster argument.

⟨*BDPT Method Definitions*⟩ ≡
```
Spectrum ConnectBDPT(const Scene &scene, Vertex *lightVertices,
        Vertex *cameraVertices, int s, int t,
        const Distribution1D &lightDistr, const Camera &camera,
        Sampler &sampler, Point2f *pRaster, Float *misWeightPtr) {
    Spectrum L(0.f);
    ⟨Ignore invalid connections related to infinite area lights 1020⟩
    ⟨Perform connection and write contribution to L 1009⟩
    ⟨Compute MIS weight for connection strategy 1012⟩
    return L;
}
```

A number of cases must be considered when handling connections; special handling is needed for those involving short subpaths with only zero or one vertex. Some strategies dynamically sample an additional vertex, which is stored in the temporary variable sampled.

⟨*Perform connection and write contribution to* L⟩ ≡   1009
```
Vertex sampled;
if (s == 0) {
    ⟨Interpret the camera subpath as a complete path 1009⟩
} else if (t == 1) {
    ⟨Sample a point on the camera and connect it to the light subpath 1010⟩
} else if (s == 1) {
    ⟨Sample a point on a light and connect it to the camera subpath⟩
} else {
    ⟨Handle all other bidirectional connection cases 1011⟩
}
```

The first case ($s = 0$) applies when no vertices on the light subpath are used and can only succeed when the camera subpath $p_0, p_1, \ldots, p_{t-1}$ is already a complete path—that is, when vertex p_{t-1} can be interpreted as a light source. In this case, L is set to the product of the path throughput weight and the emission at p_{t-1}.

⟨*Interpret the camera subpath as a complete path*⟩ ≡   1009
```
const Vertex &pt = cameraVertices[t - 1];
if (pt.IsLight())
    L = pt.Le(scene, cameraVertices[t - 2]) * pt.beta;
```

The second case applies when $t = 1$—that is, when a prefix of the light subpath is directly connected to the camera (Figure 16.15). To permit optimized importance sampling strategies analogous to direct illumination routines for light sources, we will ignore the actual camera vertex p_0 and sample a new one using Camera::Sample_Wi()—this optimization corresponds to the second bullet listed at the beginning of Section 16.3. This type of connection can only succeed if the light subpath vertex q_{s-1} supports sampled connections; otherwise the BSDF at q_{s-1} will certainly return 0 and there's no reason to attempt a connection.

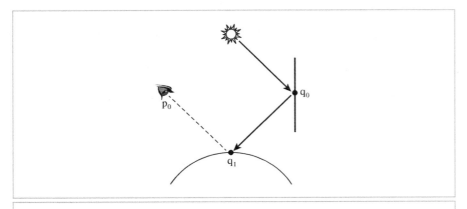

Figure 16.15: $t = 1$ **Sampling Strategy for BDPT.** We'd like to connect a subset of the light subpath to the camera. Given the last vertex of the light subpath, `Camera::Sample_Wi()` samples a vertex on the lens p_0 corresponding to a ray leaving the camera to the light path vertex (if there is such a ray that intersects the film).

⟨*Sample a point on the camera and connect it to the light subpath*⟩ ≡   **1009**
```
    const Vertex &qs = lightVertices[s - 1];
    if (qs.IsConnectible()) {
        VisibilityTester vis;
        Vector3f wi;
        Float pdf;
        Spectrum Wi = camera.Sample_Wi(qs.GetInteraction(), sampler.Get2D(),
                                       &wi, &pdf, pRaster, &vis);
        if (pdf > 0 && !Wi.IsBlack()) {
            ⟨Initialize dynamically sampled vertex and L for t = 1 case 1010⟩
        }
    }
```

If the camera vertex was generated successfully, pRaster is initialized and vis holds the connection segment. Following Equation (16.1), we can compute the final contribution as the product of the subpath weights, the transmittance over the connecting segment, the BRDF or phase function, and a cosine factor when q_{s-1} is a surface vertex.

⟨*Initialize dynamically sampled vertex and L for t = 1 case*⟩ ≡   **1010**
```
    sampled = Vertex::CreateCamera(&camera, vis.P1(), Wi / pdf);
    L = qs.beta * qs.f(sampled) * vis.Tr(scene, sampler) * sampled.beta;
    if (qs.IsOnSurface())
        L *= AbsDot(wi, qs.ns());
```

We omit the next case, $s = 1$, here. It corresponds to performing a direct lighting calculation at the last vertex of the camera subpath. Its implementation is similar to the $t = 1$ case—the main differences are that roles of lights and cameras are exchanged and that a light source must be chosen using lightDistr before a light sample can be generated.

The last case, ⟨*Handle all other bidirectional connection cases*⟩, is responsible for most types of connections: it applies whenever the camera and light subpath prefixes are long enough so that no special cases are triggered (i.e., when $s, t > 1$). If we consider the generalized path contribution equation from Section 15.5.1, we have constructed camera and light subpaths with the incremental path construction approach used in Section 14.5.3 for regular path tracing. Given the throughput of these paths up to the current vertices, $\hat{T}(\bar{q}_s)$ and $T(\bar{p}_t)$, respectively, where

$$\bar{p}_t = p_0, p_1, \ldots, p_{t-1},$$

and similarly for $\bar{q}_s$, we can find that the contribution of a path of t light vertices and s camera vertices is given by

$$\hat{P}(\bar{q}_s\bar{p}_t) = L_e\,\hat{T}(\bar{q}_s)\Big[\hat{f}(q_{s-2} \to q_{s-1} \to p_{t-1})\hat{G}(q_{s-1} \leftrightarrow p_{t-1})$$
$$\hat{f}(q_{s-1} \to p_{t-1} \to p_{t-2})\Big]\hat{T}(\bar{p}_t)\,W_e.$$

The first and last products involving the emission, importance and generalized throughput terms, $L_e\hat{T}(\bar{q}_s)$ for the camera path and $\hat{T}(\bar{p}_t)\,W_e$ for the light path, are already available in the Vertex::beta fields of the connection vertices, so we only need to compute the term in brackets to find the path's overall contribution. The symmetric nature of BDPT is readily apparent: the final contribution is equal to the product of the subpath weights, the BRDF or phase functions and a (symmetric) generalized geometry term. Note that this strategy cannot succeed when one of the connection vertices is marked as not connectible—in this case, no connection attempt is made.

The product of subpath weights and the two BSDFs is often 0; this case happens, for example, if the connecting segment requires that light be transmitted through one of the two surfaces but the corresponding surface isn't transmissive. In this case, it's worth avoiding the unnecessary call to the G() function, which traces a shadow ray to test visibility.

⟨*Handle all other bidirectional connection cases*⟩ ≡   1009
```
const Vertex &qs = lightVertices[s - 1], &pt = cameraVertices[t - 1];
if (qs.IsConnectible() && pt.IsConnectible()) {
    L = qs.beta * qs.f(pt) * pt.f(qs) * pt.beta;
    if (!L.IsBlack()) L *= G(scene, sampler, qs, pt);
}
```

The generalized geometry term, Equation (15.5), is computed in a separate function G().

⟨*BDPT Utility Functions*⟩ +≡
```
Spectrum G(const Scene &scene, Sampler &sampler, const Vertex &v0,
           const Vertex &v1) {
    Vector3f d = v0.p() - v1.p();
    Float g = 1 / d.LengthSquared();
    d *= std::sqrt(g);
    if (v0.IsOnSurface())
        g *= AbsDot(v0.ns(), d);
    if (v1.IsOnSurface())
        g *= AbsDot(v1.ns(), d);
    VisibilityTester vis(v0.GetInteraction(), v1.GetInteraction());
    return g * vis.Tr(scene, sampler);
}
```

The computation of the multiple importance sampling weight for the connected path is implemented as a separate function MISWeight(), which we discuss next.

⟨*Compute MIS weight for connection strategy*⟩ ≡   **1009**
```
    Float misWeight = L.IsBlack() ? 0.f :
        MISWeight(scene, lightVertices, cameraVertices, sampled, s, t,
                  lightDistr);
    L *= misWeight;
    if (misWeightPtr) *misWeightPtr = misWeight;
```

16.3.4 MULTIPLE IMPORTANCE SAMPLING

Recall the example of a light pointed up at the ceiling, indirectly illuminating a room. Even without multiple importance sampling, bidirectional path tracing will do much better than path tracing by reducing the number of paths with no contribution, since the paths from the light provide camera path vertices more light-carrying targets to hit with connection segments (see Figure 16.17, which shows the effectiveness of various types of bidirectional connections). However, the image will still suffer from variance caused by paths with unexpectedly large contributions due to vertices on the camera subpaths that happen to find the bright spot on the ceiling. MIS can be applied to address this issue; it automatically recognizes that connection strategies that involve at least one scattering event on the light subpath lead to superior sampling strategies in this case. This ability comes at the cost of having to know the probabilities for constructing a path according to all available strategies and is the reason for caching the Vertex::pdfFwd and Vertex::pdfRev values earlier.

In this section, we will explain the MISWeight() function that computes the multiple importance sampling weight associated with a particular BDPT sampling strategy. It takes a light and camera subpath and an integer pair (s, t) identifying the prefixes used by a successful BDPT connection attempt, producing a complete path $q_0, \ldots, q_{s-1}, p_{t-1}, \ldots, p_0$. It iterates over all alternative strategies that could hypothetically have generated the same input path but with an earlier or later crossover point between the light and camera subpaths (Figure 16.16). The function then reweights the path contribution using the balance heuristic from Section 13.10.1, taking all of these possible sampling strategies into account.[10] It is straightforward to switch to other MIS variants (e.g., based on the power heuristic) if desired.

Let (s, t) denote the currently considered connection strategy, which concatenates a prefix $q_0, \ldots, q_{s-1}$ from the light subpath and a (reversed) prefix $p_{t-1}, \ldots, p_0$ from the camera subpath, producing a path $\bar{x}$ of length $n = s + t$ with vertices that we will refer to as x_i ($0 \le i < n$):

$$\bar{x} = (x_0, \ldots, x_{n-1}) = (q_0, \ldots, q_{s-1}, p_{t-1}, \ldots, p_0).$$

Suppose that the probability per unit area of vertex x_i is given by $p^{\rightarrow}(x_i)$ and $p^{\leftarrow}(x_i)$ for sampling strategies based on importance and radiance transport, respectively. Then the

Float 1062
MISWeight() 1016
Spectrum::IsBlack() 317
Vertex::pdfFwd 1000
Vertex::pdfRev 1000

---

10   To keep the implementation simple, each vertex is assumed to be sampled from a 2D probability distribution. This may lead to slightly sub-optimal weights in participating media, where the distance sampling along rays causes the vertices to be distributed in three dimensions, though the method remains unbiased despite this inaccuracy.

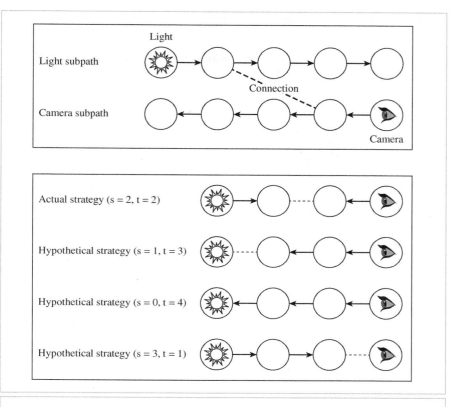

Figure 16.16: Multiple Importance Sampling in the Context of BDPT. Given a specific connection strategy ($s = 2, t = 2$) shown at the top, MISWeight() considers other strategies that could have produced the same path (bottom). The $t = 0$ case is omitted for simplicity. (It only makes sense in systems where the sensor of the camera can be intersected by rays.)

area product density of the current path is simply the product of the importance transport densities up to vertex x_{s-1} and the radiance transport densities for the remainder:

$$p_s(\bar{x}) = p^\rightarrow(x_0) \cdots p^\rightarrow(x_{s-1}) \cdot p^\leftarrow(x_s) \cdots p^\leftarrow(x_{n-1}).$$

Implementation-wise, the above expression is straightforward to evaluate: the importance transport densities $p^\rightarrow(x_i)$ are already cached in the Vertex::pdfFwd fields of the light subpath, and the same holds true for the radiance transport densities on the camera subpath.

More generally, we are also interested in the path density according to other connection strategies (i, j) that could *in theory* have created this path. This requires that they generate paths of a compatible length—i.e., that $i + j = s + t$. Their corresponding path density is given by

$$p_i(\bar{x}) = p^\rightarrow(x_0) \cdots p^\rightarrow(x_{i-1}) \cdot p^\leftarrow(x_i) \cdots p^\leftarrow(x_{n-1}), \qquad \text{[16.17]}$$

where $0 \le i \le n$. Evaluating these will also involve the reverse probabilities in Vertex::pdfRev.

MISWeight() 1016

Vertex::pdfFwd 1000

Vertex::pdfRev 1000

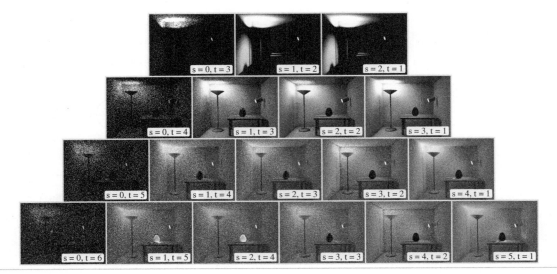

Figure 16.17: The Individual BDPT Strategies. Each row corresponds to light paths of a certain length. Note how almost every sampling strategy has deficiencies of some kind, evident in the form of high variance in these images. (Regular path tracing only samples the $s = 1$ paths.) Applying multiple importance sampling to path contributions is an effective way to reduce this variance.

Recall from Section 13.10.1 that the balance heuristic weight for strategy s out of a set of n sampling strategies with uniform sample allocation was given by

$$w_s(\bar{\mathbf{x}}) = \frac{p_s(\bar{\mathbf{x}})}{\sum_i p_i(\bar{\mathbf{x}})}.$$ [16.18]

This is the expression we would like to evaluate in MISWeight(), though there are two practical issues that must first be addressed.

First, path densities can easily under- or overflow the range of representable values in single or even double precision. Area densities of individual vertices can be seen to be inversely proportional to the square of the scene dimensions: for instance, uniformly scaling the scene to half its size will quadruple the vertex densities. When computing the area product density of a path with 10 vertices, the same scaling operation will cause an increase in path density of approximately one million times. When working with very small or large scenes (compared to a box of unit volume), the floating point exponent of $p_i(\bar{\mathbf{x}})$ can quickly exceed the valid range.

Second, a naive MIS implementation has time complexity of $O(n^4)$, where n is the maximum path length. Evaluation of $p_i(\bar{\mathbf{x}})$ based on Equation (16.17) involves a linear sweep over n vertices, and the MIS weight in Equation (16.18) requires another sweep over n strategies. Given that this must be done once per connection strategy for a number of strategies that is proportional to the square of the subpath length, we are left with an algorithm of quartic complexity.

We will avoid both of these issues by using a more efficient incremental computation that works with ratios of probability densities to achieve better numerical and run-time behavior.

MISWeight() 1016

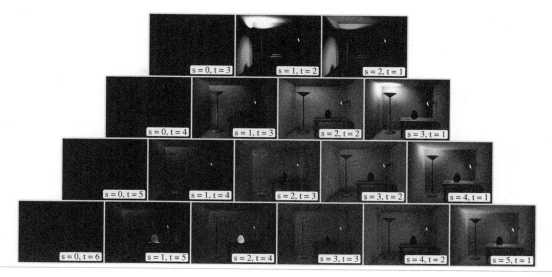

Figure 16.18: Variance Reduction Due to Multiple Importance Sampling. The same sampling strategies as in Figure 16.17, but now weighted using multiple importance sampling—effectively "turning off" each strategy where it does not perform well. The final result is computed by summing all of these images.

Dividing both the numerator and denominator of Equation (16.18) by $p_s(\bar{\mathrm{x}})$ yields

$$w_s(\bar{\mathrm{x}}) = \frac{1}{\sum_i \frac{p_i(\bar{\mathrm{x}})}{p_s(\bar{\mathrm{x}})}} = \left(\sum_{i=0}^{s-1} \frac{p_i(\bar{\mathrm{x}})}{p_s(\bar{\mathrm{x}})} + 1 + \sum_{i=s+1}^{n} \frac{p_i(\bar{\mathrm{x}})}{p_s(\bar{\mathrm{x}})} \right)^{-1}. \qquad (16.19)$$

The two sums above consider alternative strategies that would have taken additional steps on the camera or light subpath, respectively. Let us define a more concise notation for the individual summand terms:

$$r_i(\bar{\mathrm{x}}) = \frac{p_i(\bar{\mathrm{x}})}{p_s(\bar{\mathrm{x}})}.$$

These satisfy the following recurrence relations:

$$r_i(\bar{\mathrm{x}}) = \frac{p_i(\bar{\mathrm{x}})}{p_{i+1}(\bar{\mathrm{x}})} \frac{p_{i+1}(\bar{\mathrm{x}})}{p_s(\bar{\mathrm{x}})} = \frac{p_i(\bar{\mathrm{x}})}{p_{i+1}(\bar{\mathrm{x}})} r_{i+1}(\bar{\mathrm{x}}) \quad (i < s),$$

$$r_i(\bar{\mathrm{x}}) = \frac{p_i(\bar{\mathrm{x}})}{p_{i-1}(\bar{\mathrm{x}})} \frac{p_{i-1}(\bar{\mathrm{x}})}{p_s(\bar{\mathrm{x}})} = \frac{p_i(\bar{\mathrm{x}})}{p_{i-1}(\bar{\mathrm{x}})} r_{i-1}(\bar{\mathrm{x}}) \quad (i > s). \qquad (16.20)$$

The recurrence weights in the above equations are ratios of path densities of two adjacent sampling strategies, which differ only in how a single vertex is generated. Thus, they can be reduced to probability ratios of the affected vertex:

$$\frac{p_i(\bar{\mathrm{x}})}{p_{i+1}(\bar{\mathrm{x}})} = \frac{p^{\to}(\mathrm{x}_0) \cdots p^{\to}(\mathrm{x}_{i-1}) \cdot p^{\leftarrow}(\mathrm{x}_i) \cdot p^{\leftarrow}(\mathrm{x}_{i+1}) \cdots p^{\leftarrow}(\mathrm{x}_{n-1})}{p^{\to}(\mathrm{x}_0) \cdots p^{\to}(\mathrm{x}_{i-1}) \cdot p^{\to}(\mathrm{x}_i) \cdot p^{\leftarrow}(\mathrm{x}_{i+1}) \cdots p^{\leftarrow}(\mathrm{x}_{n-1})} = \frac{p^{\leftarrow}(\mathrm{x}_i)}{p^{\to}(\mathrm{x}_i)},$$

$$\frac{p_i(\bar{\mathrm{x}})}{p_{i-1}(\bar{\mathrm{x}})} = \frac{p^{\to}(\mathrm{x}_0) \cdots p^{\to}(\mathrm{x}_{i-2}) \cdot p^{\to}(\mathrm{x}_{i-1}) \cdot p^{\leftarrow}(\mathrm{x}_i) \cdots p^{\leftarrow}(\mathrm{x}_{n-1})}{p^{\to}(\mathrm{x}_0) \cdots p^{\to}(\mathrm{x}_{i-2}) \cdot p^{\leftarrow}(\mathrm{x}_{i-1}) \cdot p^{\leftarrow}(\mathrm{x}_i) \cdots p^{\leftarrow}(\mathrm{x}_{n-1})} = \frac{p^{\to}(\mathrm{x}_{i-1})}{p^{\leftarrow}(\mathrm{x}_{i-1})}.$$

Combining this result with Equation (16.20), we obtain the following recursive expression for r_i:

$$r_i(\bar{x}) = \begin{cases} 1, & \text{if } i = s \\[2mm] \dfrac{p^{\leftarrow}(x_i)}{p^{\rightarrow}(x_i)}\, r_{i+1}(\bar{x}), & \text{if } i < s. \\[3mm] \dfrac{p^{\rightarrow}(x_{i-1})}{p^{\leftarrow}(x_{i-1})}\, r_{i-1}(\bar{x}), & \text{if } i > s. \end{cases} \qquad [16.21]$$

The main portion of the MISWeight() function accumulates these probability ratios in a temporary variable sumRi using an incremental evaluation scheme based on Equation (16.21). The last line returns the reciprocal of the r_i terms according to Equation (16.19). There is also a special case at the beginning, which directly returns a weight of 1 for paths with two vertices, which can only be generated by a single strategy.

⟨*BDPT Utility Functions*⟩ +≡
```
    Float MISWeight(const Scene &scene, Vertex *lightVertices,
            Vertex *cameraVertices, Vertex &sampled, int s, int t,
            const Distribution1D &lightPdf) {
        if (s + t == 2)
            return 1;
        Float sumRi = 0;
        ⟨Define helper function remap0 that deals with Dirac delta functions 1016⟩
        ⟨Temporarily update vertex properties for current strategy 1018⟩
        ⟨Consider hypothetical connection strategies along the camera subpath 1017⟩
        ⟨Consider hypothetical connection strategies along the light subpath 1017⟩
        return 1 / (1 + sumRi);
    }
```

A helper function remap0() returns its argument while mapping 0-valued arguments to 1. It is used to handle the special case of Dirac delta functions in the path, which have a continuous density of 0. Such degenerate vertices cannot be joined using any deterministic connection strategy, and their discrete probability cancels when iterating over the remaining set of strategies because it occurs both in the numerator and denominator of the summands in Equation (16.19). The purpose of the helper function is to temporarily map these densities to a nonzero value to make sure that this cancellation occurs without causing a division by 0.

⟨*Define helper function* remap0 *that deals with Dirac delta functions*⟩ ≡   **1016**
```
    auto remap0 = [](float f) -> float { return f != 0 ? f : 1; };
```

To avoid an excessively large number of calls to the various Vertex PDF functions, the weight computation uses the cached probabilities in Vertex::pdfFwd and Vertex::pdfRev. Since these values only capture information about the original camera and light subpaths, they must still be updated to match the full path configuration near the crossover point—specifically q_{s-1} and p_{t-1} and their predecessors. This is implemented in the somewhat technical fragment ⟨*Temporarily update vertex properties for current strategy*⟩, which we discuss last.

We iterate over hypothetical strategies that would have taken additional steps from the light direction, using a temporary variable ri to store the current iterate r_i. The fragment

Distribution1D 758
Float 1062
MISWeight() 1016
Scene 23
Vertex 996
Vertex::pdfFwd 1000
Vertex::pdfRev 1000

name makes reference to the camera subpath, since these extra steps involve vertices that were in reality sampled from the camera side. All vertex densities are passed through the function remap0(), and the ratio is only added to a running sum when endpoints of the current hypothetical connection strategy are marked as non-degenerate. The loop terminates before reaching the $(n, 0)$ strategy, which shouldn't be considered since the camera cannot be intersected.

⟨*Consider hypothetical connection strategies along the camera subpath*⟩ ≡   **1016**
```
Float ri = 1;
for (int i = t - 1; i > 0; --i) {
    ri *= remap0(cameraVertices[i].pdfRev) /
        remap0(cameraVertices[i].pdfFwd);
    if (!cameraVertices[i].delta && !cameraVertices[i - 1].delta)
        sumRi += ri;
}
```

The next step considers additional steps along the light subpath and largely resembles the previous case. A special case arises when the current strategy would involve intersecting a light source (i.e., when $s = 0$): this will fail when the endpoint involves a Dirac delta distribution, hence the additional test below.

⟨*Consider hypothetical connection strategies along the light subpath*⟩ ≡   **1016**
```
ri = 1;
for (int i = s - 1; i >= 0; --i) {
    ri *= remap0(lightVertices[i].pdfRev) /
        remap0(lightVertices[i].pdfFwd);
    bool deltaLightvertex = i > 0 ? lightVertices[i - 1].delta
                                  : lightVertices[0].IsDeltaLight();
    if (!lightVertices[i].delta && !deltaLightvertex)
        sumRi += ri;
}
```

Finally, we will define the missing fragment ⟨*Temporarily update vertex properties for current strategy*⟩, which modifies Vertex attributes with new values specific to the current connection strategy (s, t). To reduce the amount of code needed for both the update and the subsequent cleanup operations, we will introduce a helper class ScopedAssignment that temporarily modifies a given variable and then reverts its change when program execution leaves the scope it was defined in. It stores a pointer ScopedAssignment::target to a memory location of arbitrary type (specified via the Type template parameter) and a snapshot of the original value in ScopedAssignment::backup.

⟨*BDPT Helper Definitions*⟩ +≡
```
template <typename Type> class ScopedAssignment {
public:
    ⟨ScopedAssignment Public Methods 1018⟩
private:
    Type *target, backup;
};
```

The ScopedAssignment constructor takes a pointer to a target memory location and over-writes it with the value parameter after making a backup copy. The destructor simply reverts any changes.

⟨*ScopedAssignment Public Methods*⟩ ≡   **1017**
```
ScopedAssignment(Type *target = nullptr,
                 Type value = Type()) : target(target) {
    if (target) {
        backup = *target;
        *target = value;
    }
}
~ScopedAssignment() { if (target) *target = backup; }
```

The main update operation then consists of finding the connection vertices and their predecessors and updating vertex probabilities and other attributes so that the two Vertex arrays reflect the chosen connection strategy.

⟨*Temporarily update vertex properties for current strategy*⟩ ≡   **1016**
   ⟨*Look up connection vertices and their predecessors* **1018**⟩
   ⟨*Update sampled vertex for s = 1 or t = 1 strategy* **1018**⟩
   ⟨*Mark connection vertices as non-degenerate* **1019**⟩
   ⟨*Update reverse density of vertex* p_{t-1} **1019**⟩
   ⟨*Update reverse density of vertex* p_{t-2} **1019**⟩
   ⟨*Update reverse density of vertices* q_{s-1} *and* q_{s-2}⟩

We begin by obtaining pointers to the affected connection vertices q_{s-1} and p_{t-1} and their predecessors.

⟨*Look up connection vertices and their predecessors*⟩ ≡   **1018**
```
Vertex *qs      = s > 0 ? &lightVertices[s - 1]  : nullptr,
       *pt      = t > 0 ? &cameraVertices[t - 1] : nullptr,
       *qsMinus = s > 1 ? &lightVertices[s - 2]  : nullptr,
       *ptMinus = t > 1 ? &cameraVertices[t - 2] : nullptr;
```

Recall that strategies with $s = 1$ or $t = 1$ perform camera and light source sampling and thus generate a new endpoint. The implementation accounts for this by temporarily overriding *qs or *pt with the sampled vertex provided via the sampled argument of MISWeight().

⟨*Update sampled vertex for s = 1 or t = 1 strategy*⟩ ≡   **1018**
```
ScopedAssignment<Vertex> a1;
if (s == 1)      a1 = { qs, sampled };
else if (t == 1) a1 = { pt, sampled };
```

Certain materials in pbrt (e.g., the UberMaterial) instantiate both specular and non-specular BxDF lobes, which requires some additional consideration at this point: suppose the specular lobe of such a material is sampled while generating the camera or light subpath. In this case, the associated Vertex will have its Vertex::delta flag set to true, causing MISWeight() to (correctly) ignore it as a hypothetical connection vertex when comparing the densities of different strategies. On the other hand, it is possible that a

BDPT strategy later connects this degenerate vertex to a vertex on the other subpath using its non-specular component. In this case, its "personality" must temporarily change to that of a non-degenerate vertex. We always force the Vertex::delta attribute of the connection vertices to false to account for this possibility.

⟨*Mark connection vertices as non-degenerate*⟩ ≡   1018
```
ScopedAssignment<bool> a2, a3;
if (pt) a2 = { &pt->delta, false };
if (qs) a3 = { &qs->delta, false };
```

Next, we will update the reverse sampling densities of the connection vertices and their predecessors, starting with p_{t-1}. This vertex was originally sampled on the camera subpath, but it could also have been reached using an extra step from the light side ($q_{s-2} \to q_{s-1} \to p_{t-1}$ in three-point form); the resulting density at p_{t-1} is evaluated using Vertex::Pdf().

The case $s = 0$ is special: here, p_t is an intersection with a light source found on the camera subpath. The alternative reverse sampling strategy generates a light sample using Light::Sample_Le(), and we evaluate its spatial density with the help of Vertex::PdfLightOrigin().

⟨*Update reverse density of vertex* p_{t-1}⟩ ≡   1018
```
ScopedAssignment<Float> a4;
if (pt)
    a4 = { &pt->pdfRev,
           s > 0 ? qs->Pdf(scene, qsMinus, *pt) :
                   pt->PdfLightOrigin(scene, *ptMinus, lightPdf) };
```

The next fragment initializes the pdfRev field of p_{t-2} with the density of the reverse strategy $q_{s-1} \to p_{t-1} \to p_{t-2}$. Once more, there is a special case for $s = 0$, where the alternative reverse strategy samples an emitted ray via Light::Sample_Le() and intersects it against the scene geometry; the corresponding density is evaluated using Vertex::PdfLight().

⟨*Update reverse density of vertex* p_{t-2}⟩ ≡   1018
```
ScopedAssignment<Float> a5;
if (ptMinus)
    a5 = { &ptMinus->pdfRev,
           s > 0 ? pt->Pdf(scene, qs, *ptMinus) :
                   pt->PdfLight(scene, *ptMinus) };
```

The last fragment, ⟨*Update reverse density of vertices* q_{s-1} *and* q_{s-2}⟩, is not included here. It is analogous except that it does not require a similar special case for $t = 0$.

16.3.5 INFINITE AREA LIGHTS AND BDPT

The infinite area light, first introduced in Section 12.6, provides a convenient way of illuminating scenes with realistic captured illumination. Unfortunately, its definition as an infinitely distant directional source turns out to be rather difficult to reconcile with BDPT's path integral formulation, which expresses probabilities in terms of area densities, which in turn requires finite-sized emitting surfaces.

Through some gymnastics, we could represent infinite area lights with finite shapes. For example, an infinite area light's radiance emission distribution could be described by a large emitting sphere that surrounded the scene, where the directional distribution of emitted radiance at each point on the interior of the sphere was the same as the infinite area light's emitted radiance for the same direction. This approach would require a significantly more complex implementation of `InfiniteAreaLight` with no practical benefits apart from BDPT compatibility.

Instead of changing the functionality of `InfiniteAreaLight`, we will instead make infinite area lights a special case in BDPT. Since illumination from these lights is most naturally integrated over solid angles, our approach will be to add support for solid angle integration to the vertex abstraction layer. In practice, scenes may contain multiple infinite area lights; we will follow the convention of treating them as one combined light when evaluating the emitted radiance or determining sample probabilities.

First, we will create a special endpoint vertex any time a camera path ray escapes the scene. The ⟨*Capture escaped rays when tracing from the camera*⟩ fragment is invoked by `RandomWalk()` whenever no surface intersection could be found while generating the camera subpath. In the implementation of the `Vertex::CreateLight()` method called here, the `pdfFwd` variable recording the probability per unit solid angle is stored directly in `Vertex::pdfFwd` without conversion by `Vertex::ConvertDensity()`.

⟨*Capture escaped rays when tracing from the camera*⟩ ≡   1007
```
if (mode == TransportMode::Radiance) {
    vertex = Vertex::CreateLight(EndpointInteraction(ray), beta,
                                 pdfFwd);
    ++bounces;
}
```

The existence of light vertices on the camera subpath leads to certain nonsensical connection strategies. For instance, we couldn't possibly connect a light vertex on the camera subpath to another vertex on the light subpath. The following check in `ConnectBDPT()` detects and ignores such connection attempts.

⟨*Ignore invalid connections related to infinite area lights*⟩ ≡   1009
```
if (t > 1 && s != 0 && cameraVertices[t - 1].type == VertexType::Light)
    return Spectrum(0.f);
```

Some parts of the code may still attempt to invoke `ConvertDensity()` with a next `Vertex` that refers to a infinite area light. The following fragment detects this case at the beginning of `ConvertDensity()` and directly returns the supplied solid angle density without conversion in that case.

⟨*Return solid angle density if next is an infinite area light*⟩ ≡   1000
```
if (next.IsInfiniteLight())
    return pdf;
```

Next, we need to adapt the light subpath sampling routine to correct the probability values returned by the ray sampling function `InfiniteAreaLight::Sample_Le()`. This case is detected in an additional fragment at the end of `GenerateLightSubpath()`.

⟨*Correct subpath sampling densities for infinite area lights*⟩ ≡   1005
```
if (path[0].IsInfiniteLight()) {
    ⟨Set spatial density of path[1] for infinite area light 1021⟩
    ⟨Set spatial density of path[0] for infinite area light 1021⟩
}
```

Recall that InfiniteAreaLight::Sample_Le() samples a ray direction (with a corresponding density pdfDir) and a ray origin on a perpendicular disk (with a corresponding density pdfPos) that touches the scene's bounding sphere. Due to foreshortening, the resulting ray has a corresponding spatial density of pdfPos $|\cos \theta|$ at its first intersection with the scene geometry, where θ is the angle between ray.d and the geometric normal.

⟨*Set spatial density of* path[1] *for infinite area light*⟩ ≡   1021
```
if (nVertices > 0) {
    path[1].pdfFwd = pdfPos;
    if (path[1].IsOnSurface())
        path[1].pdfFwd *= AbsDot(ray.d, path[1].ng());
}
```

Following our new convention, the spatial density of infinite area light endpoints is now expressed as a probability per unit solid angle. We will create a helper function InfiniteLightDensity() that determines this value while also accounting for the presence of other infinite area lights.

⟨*Set spatial density of* path[0] *for infinite area light*⟩ ≡   1021
```
path[0].pdfFwd = InfiniteLightDensity(scene, lightDistr, ray.d);
```

This function performs a weighted sum of the directional densities of all infinite area lights using the light probabilities in lightDistr.

⟨*BDPT Helper Definitions*⟩ +≡
```
inline Float InfiniteLightDensity(const Scene &scene,
        const Distribution1D &lightDistr, const Vector3f &w) {
    Float pdf = 0;
    for (size_t i = 0; i < scene.lights.size(); ++i)
        if (scene.lights[i]->flags & (int)LightFlags::Infinite)
            pdf += scene.lights[i]->Pdf_Li(Interaction(), -w) *
                    lightDistr.func[i];
    return pdf / (lightDistr.funcInt * lightDistr.Count());
}
```

The remaining two changes are analogous and address the probability computation in the PdfLightOrigin() and PdfLight() methods. For the former, we similarly return the combined solid angle density when an infinite area light is detected.

⟨*Return solid angle density for infinite light sources*⟩ ≡   1003
```
return InfiniteLightDensity(scene, lightDistr, w);
```

In PdfLight(), we compute the probability of sampling a ray origin on a disk whose radius is equal to the scene's bounding sphere. The remainder of PdfLight() already accounts for the necessary cosine foreshortening factor; hence we do not need to multiply by it here.

⟨*Compute planar sampling density for infinite light sources*⟩ ≡   **1002**
```
Point3f worldCenter;
Float worldRadius;
scene.WorldBound().BoundingSphere(&worldCenter, &worldRadius);
pdf = 1 / (Pi * worldRadius * worldRadius);
```

16.4 METROPOLIS LIGHT TRANSPORT

In 1997, Veach and Guibas proposed an unconventional rendering technique named *Metropolis Light Transport* (MLT), which applies the Metropolis-Hastings algorithm from Section 13.4 to the path space integral in Equation (16.1). Whereas all of the rendering techniques we have discussed until now have been based on the principles of Monte Carlo integration and independent sample generation, MLT adopts a different set of tools that allows samples to be *statistically correlated*.

MLT generates a sequence of light-carrying paths through the scene, where each path is found by mutating the previous path in some manner. These path mutations are done in a way that ensures that the overall distribution of sampled paths is proportional to the contribution the paths make to the image being generated. Such a distribution of paths can in turn be used to generate an image of the scene. Given the flexibility of the Metropolis sampling method, there are relatively few restrictions on the types of admissible mutation rules: highly specialized mutations can be used to sample otherwise difficult-to-explore families of light-carrying paths in a way that would be tricky or impossible to realize without introducing bias in a standard Monte Carlo context.

The correlated nature of MLT provides an important advantage over methods based on independent sample generation, in that MLT is able to perform a *local exploration* of path space: when a path that makes a large contribution to the image is found, it's easy to find other similar paths by applying small perturbations to it (a sampling process that generates states based on the previous state value in this way is referred to as a *Markov chain*). The resulting short-term memory is often beneficial: when a function has a small value over most of its domain and a large contribution in only a small subset, local exploration amortizes the expense (in samples) of the search for the important region by taking many samples from this part of the path space. This property makes MLT a good choice for rendering particularly challenging scenes: while it is generally not able to match the performance of uncorrelated integrators for relatively straightforward lighting problems, it distinguishes itself in more difficult settings where most of the light transport happens along a small fraction of all of the possible paths through the scene.

The original MLT technique by Veach and Guibas builds on the path space theory of light transport, which presents additional challenges compared to the previous simple examples in Section 13.4.4: path space is generally not a Euclidean domain, as surface vertices are constrained to lie on 2D subsets of $\mathbb{R}^3$. Whenever specular reflection or refraction occurs, a sequence of three adjacent vertices must satisfy a precise geometric relationship, which further reduces the available degrees of freedom.

Bounds3::BoundingSphere() 81
Float 1062
Pi 1063
Point3f 68
Scene::WorldBound() 24

MLT builds on a set of five mutation rules that each targets specific families of light paths. Three of the mutations perform a localized exploration of particularly challenging path classes such as caustics or paths containing sequences of specular-diffuse-specular inter-actions, while two perform larger steps with a corresponding lower overall acceptance rate. Implementing the full set of MLT mutations is a significant undertaking: part of the challenge is that none of the mutations is symmetric; hence an additional transition density function must be implemented for each one. Mistakes in any part of the system can cause subtle convergence artifacts that are notoriously difficult to debug.

16.4.1 PRIMARY SAMPLE SPACE MLT

In 2002, Kelemen et al. presented a rendering technique that is also based on the Metropolis-Hastings algorithm. We will refer to it as *Primary Sample Space MLT* (PSSMLT) for reasons that will become clear shortly. Like MLT, the PSSMLT method explores the space of light paths, searching for those that carry a significant amount of energy from a light source to the camera. The main difference is that PSSMLT does not use path space directly: it explores light paths indirectly, piggybacking on an exist-ing Monte Carlo rendering algorithm such as uni- or bidirectional path tracing, which has both advantages and disadvantages. The main advantage is that PSSMLT can use symmetric transitions on a Euclidean domain, and for this reason it is much simpler to implement. The downside is that PSSMLT lacks detailed information about the structure of the constructed light paths, making it impossible to recreate the kinds of sophisticated mutation strategies that are found in the original MLT method.

The details of this approach are easiest to motivate from an implementation-centric viewpoint. Consider the case of rendering a scene with the path integrator from Sec-tion 14.5.4, where we generate (pseudo-)random samples in raster space to get a starting point on the film, turn them into rays, and invoke `PathIntegrator::Li()` to obtain cor-responding radiance estimates. `PathIntegrator::Li()` will generally request a number of additional 1D or 2D samples from the `Sampler` to sample light sources and material models, perform Russian roulette tests, and so on. Conceptually, these samples could all be generated ahead of time and passed to `PathIntegrator::Li()` using an additional argument, thus completely removing any (pseudo-)randomness from an otherwise purely deterministic function.

Suppose that L is the resulting deterministic function, which maps an infinite-dimen-sional sample sequence $X_1, X_2, \ldots$ to a radiance estimate $L(X_1, X_2, \ldots)$. Here, (X_1, X_2) denotes the raster position, and the remaining arguments $X_3, X_4, \ldots$ are the samples consumed by L.[11] By drawing many samples and averaging the results of multiple evalu-ations of L, we essentially compute high-dimensional integrals of L over a "hypercube" of (pseudo-)random numbers $X_1, X_2, \ldots$.

Given this interpretation of integrating a radiance estimate function over a domain made of all possible sequences of input samples, we can apply the Metropolis-Hastings algorithm to create a sampling process on the same domain, with a distribution that is

PathIntegrator::Li() 876

Sampler 421

---

11   Although L is an infinite-dimensional function, only a finite number of samples of X_i will ever be needed due to path termination with Russian roulette.

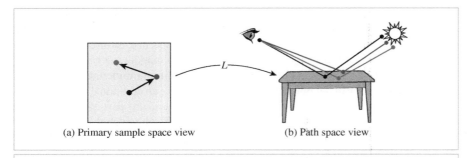

(a) Primary sample space view   (b) Path space view

Figure 16.19: Primary Sample Space MLT. PSSMLT performs mutations in an abstract space of infinite dimensional "random number vectors" **X**. A deterministic mapping L constructs corresponding light paths on path space and estimates their radiance.

proportional to L (Figure 16.19). This distribution is intuitively desirable: more sampling effort is naturally placed in parts of the sampling space where more light transport occurs. The state space Ω for this problem consists of infinite dimensional sample vectors $(X_1, X_2, \ldots) \in [0, 1)^\infty$ and is called the *primary sample space*. For brevity in the equations below, we will write the state vector as

$$\mathbf{X} = (X_1, X_2, \ldots).$$

We use the convention that all components (including the raster coordinates) are in the interval $[0, 1)$ and appropriately re-scaled within L when necessary.

PSSMLT explores primary sample space using two different kinds of mutations. The first (the "large step" mutation) replaces all components of the vector **X** with new uniformly distributed samples, which corresponds to invoking the underlying Monte Carlo rendering method as usual (i.e., without PSSMLT).

Recall from Section 13.4.2 that it is important that there be greater than zero probability that any possible sample value be proposed; this is taken care of by the large step mutation. In general, the large step mutation helps us explore the entire state space without getting stuck on local "islands."

The second mutation (the "small step" mutation) makes a small perturbation to each of the sample values X_i. This mutation explores light-carrying paths close to the current path, which is particularly important when a difficult lighting configuration is encountered.

Both of these are symmetric mutations, so their transition probabilities cancel out when the acceptance probability is computed and thus don't need to be computed, as was shown in Equation (13.8).

The interface between the outer Metropolis-Hastings iteration and the inner Integrator only involves the exchange of abstract sample vectors, making this an extremely general approach: PSSMLT can theoretically enhance any kind of rendering method that is based on Monte Carlo integration—in fact, it even works for general Monte Carlo integration problems that are not related to rendering at all.

In practice, PSSMLT is often implemented on top of an existing bidirectional path tracer. The resulting algorithm generates a new primary sample space state in every iteration and passes it to BDPT, which invokes its set of connection strategies and re-weights the result using MIS. In this setting, mutations effectively jump from one group of path connections to another group rather than dealing with individual connection strategies. However, this is not without disadvantages: in many cases, only a small subset of the strategies is truly effective, and MIS will consequently assign a large weight only to this subset. This means that the algorithm still spends a considerable portion of its time generating connections with strategies that have a low weight and thus contribute very little to the rendered image.

16.4.2 MULTIPLEXED MLT

In 2014, Hachisuka et al. presented an extension to PSSMLT named *Multiplexed Metropolis Light Transport* (MMLT) to address this problem. MMLT leaves the "outer" Metropolis-Hastings iteration conceptually unchanged and applies a small but effective modification to the "inner" BDPT integrator. Instead of always invoking all BDPT connection strategies, the algorithm chooses a single strategy according to an extra state dimension and returns its contribution scaled by the inverse discrete probability of the choice. The additional dimension used for strategy selection can be mutated using small or large steps in the same way as the other primary sample space components of X.

To prevent unintentional large structural path mutations, Hachisuka et al. fix the Markov chain so that it only explores paths of a fixed depth value; the general light transport problem is then handled by running many independent Markov chains.

The practical consequence is that the Metropolis sampler will tend to spend more computation on effective strategies that produce larger MIS-weighted contributions to the image. Furthermore, the individual iterations are much faster since they only involve a single connection strategy. The combination of these two aspects improves the Monte Carlo efficiency of the resulting estimator.

Figure 16.20 shows the contemporary house scene rendered with bidirectional path tracing and MMLT, using roughly equal computation time for each approach, and Figure 16.21 compares them with the San Miguel scene. For both, MMLT generates a better result, but the difference is particularly pronounced with the house scene, which is a particularly challenging scene for light transport algorithms in that there is essentially no direct illumination inside the house; all light-carrying paths must follow specular bounces through the glass windows. Table 16.1 helps illustrate these efficiency differences: for both of these scenes, both path tracing and BDPT have a lot of trouble finding paths that carry any radiance, while Metropolis is more effective at doing so thanks to path reuse.

16.4.3 APPLICATION TO RENDERING

Metropolis sampling generates samples from the distribution of a given scalar function. To apply it to rendering, there are two issues that we must address: first, we need to estimate a separate integral for each pixel to turn the generated samples into an image, and, second, we need to handle the fact that L is a spectrally valued function but Metropolis needs a scalar function to compute the acceptance probability, Equation (13.7).

(a)

(b)

Figure 16.20: Comparison of Bidirectional Path Tracing and Multiplexed Metropolis Light Transport. (a) Rendered with bidirectional path tracing with 128 samples per pixel. Even with many samples, the image is quite noisy. (b) Rendered with Multiplexed Metropolis Light Transport with an average of 420 mutations per pixel (roughly equal running time). MLT generates a substantially better image for the same amount of work. BDPT does do better in a few localized parts of the image: note the directly illuminated surfaces outside the windows, for example. There, the ability to use well-distributed sample points for the direct lighting calculation gives a result with lower variance. (Model courtesy of Florent Boyer.)

We can apply the ideas from Section 13.4.5 to use Metropolis samples to compute integrals. First, we define the *image contribution function* such that for an image with j pixels, each pixel I_j has a value that is the integral of the product of the pixel's image reconstruction filter h_j and the radiance L that contributes to the image:

$$I_j = \int_\Omega h_j(\mathbf{X})\, L(\mathbf{X})\, d\Omega.$$

The filter function h_j only depends on the two components of $\mathbf{X}$ associated with the raster position. The value of h_j for any particular pixel is usually 0 for the vast majority of samples $\mathbf{X}$ due to the filter's finite extent.

(a)   (b)

(c)

Figure 16.21: Comparison of Path Tracing, BDPT, and Multiplexed Metropolis Light Transport. (a) Path tracing with 200 samples per pixel. (b) Bidirectional path tracing with 128 samples per pixel. (c) Metropolis Light Transport with an average of 950 mutations per pixel (roughly equal running time). BDPT is notably more effective than path tracing, and as with Figure 16.20, MLT is the most effective. *(Model courtesy of Guillermo M. Leal Llaguno.)*

Table 16.1: Percentage of Traced Paths That Carried Zero Radiance. With these two scenes, both path tracing and BDPT have trouble finding light-carrying paths: the vast majority of the generated paths don't carry any radiance at all. Thanks to local exploration, Metropolis is better able to find additional light-carrying paths after one has been found. This is one of the reasons why it is more efficient than those approaches here.

	Path tracing	BDPT	MMLT
Modern House	98.0%	97.6%	51.9%
San Miguel	95.9%	97.0%	62.0%

If N samples $\mathbf{X}_i$ are generated from some distribution, $\mathbf{X}_i \sim p(\mathbf{X})$, then the standard Monte Carlo estimate of I_j is

$$I_j \approx \frac{1}{N} \sum_{i=1}^{N} \frac{h_j(\mathbf{X}_i)\, L(\mathbf{X}_i)}{p(\mathbf{X}_i)}.$$

Recall that Metropolis sampling requires a scalar function that defines the desired distribution of samples generated by the algorithm. Unfortunately, L is a spectrally valued function, and thus there is no unambiguous notion of what it means to generate samples proportional to L. To work around this issue, we will define a *scalar contribution function* $I(\mathbf{X})$ that is used inside the Metropolis iteration. It is desirable that this function be large when L is large so that the distribution of samples has some relationship to the important regions of L. As such, using the luminance of the radiance value is a good choice for the scalar contribution function. In general, any function that is nonzero when L is nonzero will generate correct results, just possibly not as efficiently as a function that is more directly proportional to L.

Given a suitable scalar contribution function, $I(\mathbf{X})$, Metropolis generates a sequence of samples $\mathbf{X}_i$ from I's distribution, the normalized version of I:

$$p(\mathbf{X}) = \frac{I(\mathbf{X})}{\int_\Omega I(\mathbf{X})\, d\Omega},$$

and the pixel values can thus be computed as

$$I_j \approx \frac{1}{N} \sum_{i=1}^{N} \frac{h_j(\mathbf{X}_i)\, L(\mathbf{X}_i)}{I(\mathbf{X}_i)} \left(\int_\Omega I(\mathbf{X})\, d\Omega \right).$$

The integral of I over the entire domain Ω can be computed using a traditional approach like bidirectional path tracing. If this value is denoted by b, with $b = \int I(\mathbf{X})\, d\Omega$, then each pixel's value is given by

$$I_j \approx \frac{b}{N} \sum_{i=1}^{N} \frac{h_j(\mathbf{X}_i)\, L(\mathbf{X}_i)}{I(\mathbf{X}_i)}. \tag{16.22}$$

In other words, we can use Metropolis sampling to generate samples $\mathbf{X}_i$ from the distribution of the scalar contribution function I. For each sample, the pixels it contributes to (based on the extent of the pixel filter function h) have the value

$$\frac{b}{N} \frac{h_j(\mathbf{X}_i)\, L(\mathbf{X}_i)}{I(\mathbf{X}_i)}$$

added to them. Thus, brighter pixels have larger values than dimmer pixels due to more samples contributing to them (as long as the ratio $L_i(\mathbf{X}_i)/I(\mathbf{X}_i)$ is generally of the same magnitude).

16.4.4 PRIMARY SAMPLE SPACE SAMPLER

The MLTIntegrator applies Metropolis sampling and MMLT to render images, using the bidirectional path tracer from Section 16.3. Its implementation is contained in the files

MLTIntegrator 1035

Figure 16.22: A Volumetric Caustic. Light passing through the sphere is focused in the medium behind it, creating a volumetric caustic. (a) Rendered with bidirectional path tracing, (b) rendered with the MLTIntegrator, using a roughly equal amount of time. Note that MMLT gives a lower variance result, thanks to being able to efficiently explore the local path space once a high-contribution path has been found.

integrators/mlt.h and integrators/mlt.cpp. Figure 16.22 shows the effectiveness of this integrator with a particularly tricky lighting situation. Before describing its implementation, we'll first introduce the MLTSampler, which is responsible for managing primary sample space state vectors, mutations, and acceptance and rejection steps.

⟨*MLTSampler Declarations*⟩ ≡
```
class MLTSampler : public Sampler {
public:
    ⟨MLTSampler Public Methods 1030⟩
protected:
    ⟨MLTSampler Private Declarations 1030⟩
    ⟨MLTSampler Private Methods⟩
    ⟨MLTSampler Private Data 1030⟩
};
```

The MLTIntegrator works best if the MLTSampler actually maintains three separate sample vectors—one for the camera subpath, one for the light subpath, and one for the connection step. We'll say that these are three *sample streams*. The streamCount parameter to the constructor lets the caller request a particular number of such sample streams.

Later, during the initialization phase of MLTIntegrator, we will create many separate MLTSampler instances that are used to select a suitable set of starting states for the Metropolis sampler. Importantly, this process requires that each MLTSampler produces a distinct sequence of state vectors. The RNG pseudo-random number generator used by pbrt has a handy feature that makes this easy to accomplish: the RNG constructor accepts a *sequence index*, which selects between one of 2^{63} unique pseudo-random sequences. We thus add an rngSequenceIndex parameter to the MLTSampler constructor that is used to supply a unique stream index to the internal RNG.

⟨*MLTSampler Public Methods*⟩ ≡   1029
```
MLTSampler(int mutationsPerPixel, int rngSequenceIndex,
           Float sigma, Float largeStepProbability, int streamCount)
    : Sampler(mutationsPerPixel), rng(rngSequenceIndex), sigma(sigma),
      largeStepProbability(largeStepProbability),
      streamCount(streamCount) { }
```

The largeStepProbability parameter refers to the probability of taking a "large step" mutation, and sigma controls the size of "small step" mutations.

⟨*MLTSampler Private Data*⟩ ≡   1029
```
RNG rng;
const Float sigma, largeStepProbability;
const int streamCount;
```

The MLTSampler::X member variable stores the current sample vector **X**. Because we generally don't know ahead of time how many dimensions of **X** are actually needed during the sampler's lifetime, we'll start with an empty vector and expand it on demand as calls to MLTSampler::Get1D() and MLTSampler::Get2D() occur during rendering.

⟨*MLTSampler Private Data*⟩ +≡   1029
```
std::vector<PrimarySample> X;
```

The elements of this array have the type PrimarySample. The main task for PrimarySample is to record the current value of a single component of **X** on the interval [0, 1). In the following, we'll add some additional functionality for representing proposed mutations and restoring the original sample value if a proposed mutation is rejected.

⟨*MLTSampler Private Declarations*⟩ ≡   1029
```
struct PrimarySample {
    Float value = 0;
    ⟨PrimarySample Public Methods 1034⟩
    ⟨PrimarySample Public Data 1032⟩
};
```

The Get1D() method returns the value of a single component of MLTSampler::X, whose position is given by GetNextIndex()—for now, we can think of this method as returning the value of a running counter that increases with every call. EnsureReady() expands MLTSampler::X as needed and ensures that its contents are in a consistent state. The details of these methods will be clearer after a few more preliminaries, so we won't introduce their implementations just yet.

⟨*MLTSampler Method Definitions*⟩ ≡
```
Float MLTSampler::Get1D() {
    int index = GetNextIndex();
    EnsureReady(index);
    return X[index].value;
}
```

The 2D analog simply performs two calls to Get1D().

⟨*MLTSampler Method Definitions*⟩ +≡
```
Point2f MLTSampler::Get2D() {
    return Point2f(Get1D(), Get1D());
}
```

Next, we will define several MLTIntegrator methods that are not part of the official Sampler interface. The first one, MLTSampler::StartIteration(), is called at the beginning of each Metropolis-Hastings iteration; it increases the currentIteration counter and determines which type of mutation (small or large) should be applied to the sample vector in the current iteration.

⟨*MLTSampler Method Definitions*⟩ +≡
```
void MLTSampler::StartIteration() {
    currentIteration++;
    largeStep = rng.UniformFloat() < largeStepProbability;
}
```

currentIteration is a running counter, which keeps track of the current Metropolis-Hastings iteration index. Note that iterations with rejected proposals will be excluded from this count.

⟨*MLTSampler Private Data*⟩ +≡   1029
```
int64_t currentIteration = 0;
bool largeStep = true;
```

The MLTSampler::lastLargeStepIteration member variable records the index of the last iteration where a successful large step took place. Our implementation chooses the initial state X_0 to be uniformly distributed on primary sample space $[0, 1)^\infty$; hence the first iteration's state can be interpreted as the result of a large step in iteration 0.

⟨*MLTSampler Private Data*⟩ +≡   1029
```
int64_t lastLargeStepIteration = 0;
```

The MLTSampler::Accept() method is called whenever a proposal is accepted.

⟨*MLTSampler Method Definitions*⟩ +≡
```
void MLTSampler::Accept() {
    if (largeStep)
        lastLargeStepIteration = currentIteration;
}
```

At this point, the main missing parts are MLTSampler::EnsureReady() and the logic that applies the actual mutations to MLTSampler::X. Before filling in those gaps, let us take a brief step back.

In theory, all entries in the X vector must be updated by small or large mutations in every iteration of the Metropolis sampler. However, doing so would sometimes be rather inefficient: consider the case where most iterations only query a small number of dimensions of X, hence MLTSampler::X has not grown to a large size yet. If a later iteration makes many calls to Get1D() or Get2D(), then the dynamic array MLTSampler::X must correspondingly expand, and these extra entries increase the cost of every subsequent Metropolis iteration (even if these components of X are never referenced again!).

Instead, it's more efficient to update the `PrimarySample` entries on demand—that is, when they are referenced by an actual `Get1D()` or `Get2D()` call. Doing so avoids the aforementioned inefficiency, though after some period of inactivity, we must carefully replay all mutations that a given `PrimarySample` missed. To keep track of this information, an additional member variable recording the last iteration where a `PrimarySample` was modified is useful.

⟨*PrimarySample Public Data*⟩ ≡   1030
```
int64_t lastModificationIteration = 0;
```

We now have enough background to proceed to the implementation of the `MLTSampler::EnsureReady()` method, which updates individual sample values when they are accessed.

⟨*MLTSampler Method Definitions*⟩ +≡
```
void MLTSampler::EnsureReady(int index) {
    ⟨Enlarge MLTSampler::X if necessary and get current Xi 1032⟩
    ⟨Reset Xi if a large step took place in the meantime 1032⟩
    ⟨Apply remaining sequence of mutations to sample 1033⟩
}
```

First, any gaps are filled with zero-initialized `PrimarySamples` before a reference to the requested entry is obtained.

⟨*Enlarge* `MLTSampler::X` *if necessary and get current* X_i⟩ ≡   1032
```
if (index >= X.size())
    X.resize(index + 1);
PrimarySample &Xi = X[index];
```

When the last modification of `Xi` precedes the last large step, the current content of `Xi.value` is irrelevant, since it should have been overwritten with a new uniform sample in iteration `lastLargeStepIteration`. In this case, we simply replay this missed mutation and update the last modification iteration index accordingly.

⟨*Reset* X_i *if a large step took place in the meantime*⟩ ≡   1032
```
if (Xi.lastModificationIteration < lastLargeStepIteration) {
    Xi.value = rng.UniformFloat();
    Xi.lastModificationIteration = lastLargeStepIteration;
}
```

Next, a call to `Backup()` notifies the `PrimarySample` that a mutation is going to be proposed; doing so allows it to make a copy of X_i's sample value in case the mutation is rejected. All remaining mutations between iterations `lastLargeStepIteration` and `currentIteration` are then applied. Two different cases can occur: when the current iteration is a large step, we simply initialize `PrimarySample::value` with a uniform sample. Otherwise, all iterations since the last large step are (by definition) small steps that we must replay.

⟨*Apply remaining sequence of mutations to* sample⟩ ≡   1032
```
    Xi.Backup();
    if (largeStep) {
        Xi.value = rng.UniformFloat();
    } else {
        int64_t nSmall = currentIteration - Xi.lastModificationIteration;
        ⟨Apply nSmall small step mutations 1033⟩
    }
    Xi.lastModificationIteration = currentIteration;
```

For small steps, we apply normally distributed perturbations to each component:

$$X'_i \sim N(X_i, \sigma^2),$$

where σ is given by MLTIntegrator::sigma. The advantage of sampling with a normal distribution like this is that it naturally tries a variety of mutation sizes. It preferentially makes small mutations that remain close to the current state, which help locally explore the path space in small areas of high contribution where large mutations would tend to be rejected. On the other hand, because it also can make larger mutations, it also avoids spending too much time in a small part of the path space in cases where larger mutations have a good likelihood of acceptance.

Our implementation here merges the sequence of nSmall perturbations into a single update and clamps the result to the unit interval, wrapping around to the other end of the domain if necessary. Wrapping ensures that the transition probabilities for all pairs of sample values are symmetric.

⟨*Apply* nSmall *small step mutations*⟩ ≡   1033
    ⟨*Sample the standard normal distribution* $N(0, 1)$ 1034⟩
    ⟨*Compute the effective standard deviation and apply perturbation to* X_i 1034⟩

Recall the rule that when two samples from normal distributions $N(\mu_1, \sigma_1^2)$ and $N(\mu_2, \sigma_2^2)$ are added, the sum is also normally distributed with parameters $N(\mu_1 + \mu_2, \sigma_1^2 + \sigma_2^2)$. Thus, when n perturbations are to be applied to X_i, instead of performing n perturbations in sequence, it is equivalent and more efficient to directly sample

$$X'_i \sim N(X_i, n\sigma^2), \tag{16.23}$$

which we do by importance sampling a standard normal distribution and scaling the result by $\sqrt{n}\sigma$. Applying the inversion method to the PDF

$$p(x) = \frac{1}{\sqrt{2\pi}} e^{-x^2/2}$$

gives the following sampling method for a uniform sample $\xi \in [0, 1)$:

$$P^{-1}(\xi) = \sqrt{2} \, \text{erf}^{-1}(2\xi - 1),$$

where erf is the error function, $\text{erf}(x) = 2/\sqrt{\pi} \int_0^x e^{-x'^2} dx'$, and erf^{-1} is its inverse. The ErfInv() function, not included here, approximates erf^{-1} with a polynomial.

⟨*Sample the standard normal distribution N*(0, 1)⟩ ≡   1033
```
Float normalSample = Sqrt2 * ErfInv(2 * rng.UniformFloat() - 1);
```

We scale the resulting sample by the effective variance from Equation (16.23) and use it to perturb the sample X_i before keeping only its fractional component, so that it remains in [0, 1).

⟨*Compute the effective standard deviation and apply perturbation to* X_i⟩ ≡   1033
```
Float effSigma = sigma * std::sqrt((Float)nSmall);
Xi.value += normalSample * effSigma;
Xi.value -= std::floor(Xi.value);
```

`MLTSampler::Reject()` must be called whenever a proposed mutation is rejected. It restores all `PrimarySamples` modified in the current iteration and reverts the iteration counter.

⟨*MLTSampler Method Definitions*⟩ +≡
```
void MLTSampler::Reject() {
    for (auto &Xi : X)
        if (Xi.lastModificationIteration == currentIteration)
            Xi.Restore();
    --currentIteration;
}
```

The `Backup()` and `Restore()` methods make it possible to record the value of a `Primary Sample` before a mutation and to restore it if the mutation is rejected.

⟨*PrimarySample Public Methods*⟩ ≡   1030
```
void Backup() {
    valueBackup = value;
    modifyBackup = lastModificationIteration;
}
void Restore() {
    value = valueBackup;
    lastModificationIteration = modifyBackup;
}
```

⟨*PrimarySample Public Data*⟩ +≡   1030
```
Float valueBackup = 0;
int64_t modifyBackup = 0;
```

Before wrapping up `MLTSampler`, we must address a detail that would otherwise cause issues when the sampler is used with BDPT. For each pixel sample, the `BDPTIntegrator` implementation calls `GenerateCameraSubpath()` and `GenerateLightSubpath()` in sequence to generate a pair of subpaths, each function requesting 1D and 2D samples from a supplied `Sampler` as needed.

In the context of MLT, the resulting sequence of sample requests creates a mapping between components of X and vertices on the camera or light subpath. With the process described above, the components $X_0, \ldots, X_n$ determine the camera subpath (for some $n \in \mathbb{Z}$), and the remaining values $X_{n+1}, \ldots, X_m$ determine the light subpath. If the camera subpath requires a different number of samples after a perturbation (e.g., because the random walk produced fewer vertices), then there is a shift in the assignment of primary sample space components to the light subpath. This leads to an unintended large-scale modification to the light path.

It is easy to avoid this problem with a more careful indexing scheme: the MLTSampler partitions X into multiple interleaved streams that cannot interfere with each other. The MLTSampler::StartStream() method indicates that subsequent samples should come from the stream with the given index. It also resets sampleIndex, the index of the current sample in the stream. (The number of such streams, MLTSampler::streamCount, is specified in the MLTSampler constructor.)

⟨*MLTSampler Method Definitions*⟩ +≡
```
void MLTSampler::StartStream(int index) {
    streamIndex = index;
    sampleIndex = 0;
}
```

⟨*MLTSampler Private Data*⟩ +≡   1029
```
int streamIndex, sampleIndex;
```

After the stream is selected, the MLTSampler::GetNextIndex() method performs corresponding steps through the primary sample vector components. It interleaves the streams into the global sample vector—in other words, the first streamCount dimensions in X are respectively used for the first dimension of each of the streams, and so forth.

⟨*MLTSampler Public Methods*⟩ +≡   1029
```
int GetNextIndex() {
    return streamIndex + streamCount * sampleIndex++;
}
```

16.4.5 MLT INTEGRATOR

Given all of this infrastructure—an explicit representation of an n-dimensional sample X, functions to apply mutations to it, and BDPT's vertex abstraction layer for evaluating the radiance of a given sample value—we can move forward to the heart of the implementation of the MLTIntegrator.

⟨*MLT Declarations*⟩ ≡
```
class MLTIntegrator : public Integrator {
public:
    ⟨MLTIntegrator Public Methods⟩
private:
    ⟨MLTIntegrator Private Data 1037⟩
};
```

The MLTIntegrator constructor, not shown here, just initializes various member variables from parameters provided to it. These member variables will be introduced in the following as they are used.

We begin by defining the method `MLTIntegrator::L()`, which computes the radiance $L(\mathbf{X})$ for a vector of sample values $\mathbf{X}$ provided by an `MLTSampler`. Its parameter `depth` specifies a specific path depth, and `pRaster` returns the raster position of the path, if the path successfully carries light from a light source to the film plane. The initial statement activates the first of three streams in the underlying `MLTSampler`.

⟨*MLT Method Definitions*⟩ ≡
```
Spectrum MLTIntegrator::L(const Scene &scene, MemoryArena &arena,
        const std::unique_ptr<Distribution1D> &lightDistr,
        MLTSampler &sampler, int depth, Point2f *pRaster) {
    sampler.StartStream(cameraStreamIndex);
    ⟨Determine the number of available strategies and pick a specific one 1036⟩
    ⟨Generate a camera subpath with exactly t vertices 1037⟩
    ⟨Generate a light subpath with exactly s vertices 1037⟩
    ⟨Execute connection strategy and return the radiance estimate 1037⟩
}
```

The implementation uses three sample streams from the `MLTSampler`: the first two for the camera and light subpath and the third one for any `Camera::Sample_Wi()` or `Light::Sample_Li()` calls performed by connection strategies in `ConnectBDPT()` with $s = 1$ or $t = 1$ (refer to Section 16.3.3 for details).

⟨*MLTSampler Constants*⟩ ≡
```
static const int cameraStreamIndex = 0;
static const int lightStreamIndex = 1;
static const int connectionStreamIndex = 2;
static const int nSampleStreams = 3;
```

The body of `MLTIntegrator::L()` first selects an individual BDPT strategy for the provided `depth` value—this is the MMLT modification to PSSMLT—and invokes the bidirectional path-tracing machinery to compute a corresponding radiance estimate. For paths with zero scattering events (i.e., directly observed light sources), the only viable strategy provided by the underlying BDPT implementation entails intersecting them with a ray traced from the camera. For longer paths, there are `depth + 2` possible strategies. The fragment below uniformly maps the first primary sample space dimension onto this set of strategies. The variables `s` and `t` denote the number of light and camera subpath sampling steps following the convention of the `BDPTIntegrator`.

⟨*Determine the number of available strategies and pick a specific one*⟩ ≡   1036
```
int s, t, nStrategies;
if (depth == 0) {
    nStrategies = 1;
    s = 0;
    t = 2;
} else {
    nStrategies = depth + 2;
    s = std::min((int)(sampler.Get1D() * nStrategies), nStrategies - 1);
    t = nStrategies - s;
}
```

The next three fragments compute the radiance estimate. They strongly resemble BDPT with some MMLT-specific modifications: the first one samples a film position in $[0, 1)^2$, maps it to raster coordinates, and tries to generate a corresponding camera subpath with *exactly* t vertices, failing with a 0-valued estimate for L when this was not possible.

⟨*Generate a camera subpath with exactly* t *vertices*⟩ ≡   1036
```
Vertex *cameraVertices = arena.Alloc<Vertex>(t);
Bounds2f sampleBounds = (Bounds2f)camera->film->GetSampleBounds();
*pRaster = sampleBounds.Lerp(sampler.Get2D());
if (GenerateCameraSubpath(scene, sampler, arena, t, *camera,
                          *pRaster, cameraVertices) != t)
    return Spectrum(0.f);
```

The camera member variable holds the Camera specified in the scene description file.

⟨*MLTIntegrator Private Data*⟩ ≡   1035
```
std::shared_ptr<const Camera> camera;
```

The next fragment implements an analogous operation for the light subpath. Note the call to MLTSampler::StartStream(), which switches to the second stream of samples.

⟨*Generate a light subpath with exactly* s *vertices*⟩ ≡   1036
```
sampler.StartStream(lightStreamIndex);
Vertex *lightVertices = arena.Alloc<Vertex>(s);
if (GenerateLightSubpath(scene, sampler, arena, s,
                         cameraVertices[0].time(),
                         *lightDistr, lightVertices) != s)
    return Spectrum(0.f);
```

Finally, we switch to the last sample stream and invoke the (s, t) strategy via a call to ConnectBDPT(). The final radiance estimate is multiplied by the inverse probability of choosing the current strategy (s, t), which is equal to nStrategies.

⟨*Execute connection strategy and return the radiance estimate*⟩ ≡   1036
```
sampler.StartStream(connectionStreamIndex);
return ConnectBDPT(scene, lightVertices, cameraVertices, s, t,
                   *lightDistr, *camera, sampler, pRaster) * nStrategies;
```

Main Rendering Loop

There are two phases to the rendering process implemented in MLTIntegrator::Render(). The first phase generates a set of bootstrap samples that are candidates for initial states of Markov chains and computes the normalization constant $b = \int I(\mathbf{X}) \, d\Omega$, from Equation (16.22). The second phase runs a series of Markov chains, where each chain chooses one of the bootstrap samples for its initial sample vector and then applies Metropolis sampling.

⟨*MLT Method Definitions*⟩ +≡
```
void MLTIntegrator::Render(const Scene &scene) {
    std::unique_ptr<Distribution1D> lightDistr =
        ComputeLightPowerDistribution(scene);
    ⟨Generate bootstrap samples and compute normalization constant b 1038⟩
    ⟨Run nChains Markov chains in parallel 1039⟩
    ⟨Store final image computed with MLT 1042⟩
}
```

Following the approach described in Section 13.4.3, we avoid issues with start-up bias by computing a set of bootstrap samples with a standard Monte Carlo estimator and using them to create a distribution that supplies the initial states of the Markov chains. This process builds on the sample generation and evaluation routines implemented previously.

Each bootstrap sample is technically a sequence of maxDepth + 1 samples with different path depths; the following fragment initializes the array bootstrapWeights with their corresponding luminance values. At the end, we create a Distribution1D instance to sample bootstrap paths proportional to their luminances and set the constant b to the sum of average luminances for each depth. Because we've kept the contributions of different path sample depths distinct, we can preferentially sample path lengths that make the largest contribution to the image. It is straightforward to compute the bootstrap samples in parallel, as all loop iterations are independent from one another.

⟨*Generate bootstrap samples and compute normalization constant b*⟩ ≡   **1038**
```
int nBootstrapSamples = nBootstrap * (maxDepth + 1);
std::vector<Float> bootstrapWeights(nBootstrapSamples, 0);
std::vector<MemoryArena> bootstrapThreadArenas(MaxThreadIndex());
ParallelFor(
    [&](int i) {
        ⟨Generate ith bootstrap sample 1039⟩
    }, nBootstrap, 4096);
Distribution1D bootstrap(&bootstrapWeights[0], nBootstrapSamples);
Float b = bootstrap.funcInt * (maxDepth + 1);
```

As usual, maxDepth denotes the maximum number of interreflections that should be considered. nBootstrap sets the number of bootstrapping samples to use to seed the iterations and compute the integral of the scalar contribution function, Equation (16.22).

⟨*MLTIntegrator Private Data*⟩ +≡   **1035**
```
const int maxDepth;
const int nBootstrap;
```

In each iteration, we instantiate a dedicated MLTSampler with index rngIndex providing a unique sample vector that is uniformly distributed in the primary sample space. Next, we evaluate *L* to obtain a corresponding radiance estimate for the current path depth depth and write its luminance into bootstrapWeights. The raster-space position pRaster is not needed in the preprocessing phase, so it is ignored.

⟨*Generate i th bootstrap sample*⟩ ≡   1038
```
MemoryArena &arena = bootstrapThreadArenas[ThreadIndex];
for (int depth = 0; depth <= maxDepth; ++depth) {
    int rngIndex = i * (maxDepth + 1) + depth;
    MLTSampler sampler(mutationsPerPixel, rngIndex, sigma,
                       largeStepProbability, nSampleStreams);
    Point2f pRaster;
    bootstrapWeights[rngIndex] =
        L(scene, arena, lightDistr, sampler, depth, &pRaster).y();
    arena.Reset();
}
```

The mutationsPerPixel parameter is analogous to Sampler::samplesPerPixel and denotes the number of iterations that MLT (on average!) spends in each pixel. Individual pixels will receive an actual number of samples related to their brightness, due to Metropolis's property of taking more samples in regions where the function's value is high. The total number of Metropolis samples taken is the product of the number of pixels and mutationsPerPixel.

The sigma and largeStepProbability member variables give the corresponding configuration parameters of the MLTSampler.

⟨*MLTIntegrator Private Data*⟩ +≡   1035
```
const int mutationsPerPixel;
const Float sigma, largeStepProbability;
```

We now move on to the main rendering task, which performs a total of nTotalMutations mutation steps spread out over nChains parallel Markov chains.

We must be careful that the actual number of mutation steps indeed comes out to be equal to nTotalMutations, particularly when nTotalMutations is not divisible by the number of parallel chains. The solution is simple: we potentially stop the last Markov chain a few iterations short; the corrected number of per-chain iterations is given by nChainMutations.

⟨*Run* nChains *Markov chains in parallel*⟩ ≡   1038
```
Film &film = *camera->film;
int64_t nTotalMutations = (int64_t)mutationsPerPixel *
    (int64_t)film.GetSampleBounds().Area();
ParallelFor(
    [&](int i) {
        int64_t nChainMutations =
            std::min((i + 1) * nTotalMutations / nChains,
                     nTotalMutations) - i * nTotalMutations / nChains;
        ⟨Follow ith Markov chain for nChainMutations 1040⟩
    }, nChains);
```

nChains specifies the number of Markov chains that should be executed independently of each other. Its default value of 100 is a trade-off between providing sufficient parallelism and running each chain for a long amount of time.

⟨*MLTIntegrator Private Data*⟩ +≡   **1035**
```
const int nChains;
```

The MLT integrator only splats contributions to arbitrary pixels in the film; it doesn't fill in well-defined tiles of the image plane. Therefore, a FilmTile isn't necessary, and calls to Film::AddSplat() suffice to update the image.

⟨*Follow ith Markov chain for* nChainMutations⟩ ≡   **1039**
```
MemoryArena arena;
```
    ⟨*Select initial state from the set of bootstrap samples* **1040**⟩
    ⟨*Initialize local variables for selected state* **1040**⟩
    ⟨*Run the Markov chain for* nChainMutations *steps* **1041**⟩

Every Markov chain instantiates its own pseudo-random number generator following a unique stream. Note that this RNG instance is separate from the one in MLTSampler: it is used to pick the initial state and to accept or reject Metropolis proposals later on. Due to the ordering used earlier when initializing the entries of bootstrap array, we can immediately deduce the path depth of the sampled index bootstrapIndex. An important consequence of the method used to generate the bootstrap distribution is that the expected number of sampled initial states with a given depth value is proportional to their contribution to the image.

⟨*Select initial state from the set of bootstrap samples*⟩ ≡   **1040**
```
RNG rng(i);
int bootstrapIndex = bootstrap.SampleDiscrete(rng.UniformFloat());
int depth = bootstrapIndex % (maxDepth + 1);
```

Having chosen the bootstrap sample, we must now obtain the corresponding primary sample space vector **X**. One way to accomplish this would have been to store all MLTSampler instances in the preprocessing phase. A more efficient approach builds on the property that the initialization in the MLTSampler constructor is completely deterministic and just depends on the rngSequenceIndex parameter. Thus, here we can create an MLTSampler with index bootstrapIndex, which recreates the exact same sampler that originally produced the sampled entry of the bootstrap distribution.

With the sampler in hand, we can compute the current value of *L* and its position on the film.

⟨*Initialize local variables for selected state*⟩ ≡   **1040**
```
MLTSampler sampler(mutationsPerPixel, bootstrapIndex, sigma,
                   largeStepProbability, nSampleStreams);
Point2f pCurrent;
Spectrum LCurrent =
    L(scene, arena, lightDistr, sampler, depth, &pCurrent);
```

The implementation of the Metropolis sampling routine in the following fragments follows the expected values technique from Section 13.4.1: a mutation is proposed, the value of the function for the mutated sample and the acceptance probability are computed, and the weighted contributions of both the new and old samples are recorded. The proposed mutation is then randomly accepted based on its acceptance probability.

One of the unique characteristics of MMLT (Section 16.4.2) compared to other Metropolis-type methods is that each Markov chain is restricted to paths of a fixed depth value. The first sample dimension selects among various different strategies, but only those producing equal path depths are considered, which improves performance of the method by making proposals more local. The contribution of all path depths is accounted for by starting many Markov chains with different initial states.

⟨*Run the Markov chain for* nChainMutations *steps*⟩ ≡   **1040**
```
for (int64_t j = 0; j < nChainMutations; ++j) {
    sampler.StartIteration();
    Point2f pProposed;
    Spectrum LProposed =
        L(scene, arena, lightDistr, sampler, depth, &pProposed);
    ⟨Compute acceptance probability for proposed sample 1041⟩
    ⟨Splat both current and proposed samples to film 1041⟩
    ⟨Accept or reject the proposal 1042⟩
}
```

Given the scalar contribution function's value, the acceptance probability is then given by the simplified expression from Equation (13.8) thanks to the symmetry of our mutations on primary sample space.

As described at the start of the section, the spectral radiance value $L(\mathbf{X})$ must be converted to a value given by the scalar contribution function so that the acceptance probability can be computed for the Metropolis sampling algorithm. Here, we compute the path's luminance, which is a reasonable choice.

⟨*Compute acceptance probability for proposed sample*⟩ ≡   **1041**
```
Float accept = std::min((Float)1, LProposed.y() / LCurrent.y());
```

Both samples can now be added to the image. Here, they are scaled with weights based on the expected values optimization introduced in Section 13.4.1.[12]

⟨*Splat both current and proposed samples to* film⟩ ≡   **1041**
```
if (accept > 0)
    film.AddSplat(pProposed, LProposed * accept / LProposed.y());
film.AddSplat(pCurrent, LCurrent * (1 - accept) / LCurrent.y());
```

Finally, the proposed mutation is either accepted or rejected, based on the computed acceptance probability accept. If the mutation is accepted, then the values pProposed and LProposed become properties of the current state. In either case, the MLTSampler must be informed of the outcome so that it can update the PrimarySample accordingly.

---

12 Kelemen et al. (2002) suggested a slightly more efficient implementation of this logic where only the sample that is rejected is splatted to the film, and the contribution of the accepted sample is accumulated in a local variable here until it is eventually rejected. This approach would halve the number of Film::AddSplat() calls while still computing the same result.

⟨*Accept or reject the proposal*⟩ ≡   **1041**
```
if (rng.UniformFloat() < accept) {
    pCurrent = pProposed;
    LCurrent = LProposed;
    sampler.Accept();
} else
    sampler.Reject();
```

Metropolis sampling only considers the *relative* frequency of samples and cannot create an image that is correctly scaled in *absolute* terms; hence the value *b* is crucial: it contains an estimate of the average luminance of the Film that we use to remove this ambiguity. Each Metropolis iteration within ⟨*Run* nChains *Markov chains in parallel*⟩ has splatted contributions with weighted unit luminance to the Film so that the final average film luminance before Film::WriteImage() is exactly equal to mutationsPerPixel. We thus must cancel this factor out and multiply by *b* when writing the image to convert to actual incident radiance on the film.

⟨*Store final image computed with MLT*⟩ ≡   **1038**
```
camera->film->WriteImage(b / mutationsPerPixel);
```

FURTHER READING

The general idea of tracing light-carrying paths from light sources was first investigated by Arvo (1986), who stored light in texture maps on surfaces and rendered caustics. Heckbert (1990b) built on this approach to develop a general ray-tracing-based global illumination algorithm, and Pattanaik and Mudur (1995) developed an early particle-tracing technique. Christensen (2003) surveyed applications of adjoint functions and importance to solving the LTE and related problems.

Sources of non-symmetric scattering and their impact on bidirectional light transport algorithms were first identified by Veach (1996).

Pharr and Humphreys (2004) proposed the method to sample emitted rays from environment map light sources that is used in this chapter. Dammertz and Hanika (2009) described a variation on this approach that sampled points on the visible faces of the scene bounding box rather than an oriented disk; this can lead to fewer wasted samples.

Photon Mapping

Approaches like Arvo's caustic rendering algorithm (Arvo 1986) formed the basis for an improved technique that stored illumination in texture maps on surfaces developed by Collins (1994). Density estimation techniques for global illumination were first introduced by Shirley, Walter, and collaborators (Shirley et al. 1995; Walter et al. 1997).

Jensen (1995, 1996) developed the photon mapping algorithm, which introduced the key innovation of storing the light contributions in a general 3D data structure rather than in texture maps. Important improvements to the photon mapping method are described in follow-up papers and a book by Jensen (1996, 1997, 2001).

Final gathering for finite-element radiosity algorithms was first described in Reichert's thesis (Reichert 1992). If the full photon map is stored in memory, the directional dis-

Camera::film 356

Film 484

Film::WriteImage() 494

MLTIntegrator::camera 1037

MLTIntegrator::
    mutationsPerPixel
    1039

MLTSampler::Accept() 1031

MLTSampler::Reject() 1034

RNG::UniformFloat() 1066

tribution of photons can be used to construct optimized final gathering techniques that importance sample directions that are likely to have large contributions (Jensen 1995). More recently, Spencer and Jones (2009a) described how to build a hierarchical kd-tree of photons such that traversal could be stopped at higher levels of the tree and showed that using the footprints of final gather rays computed using ray differentials can lead to better results than the usual approach. In another paper, Spencer and Jones (2009b) showed that a simple iterative relaxation scheme to reduce clumping in photon maps can lead to dramatic improvements in the quality of density estimates.

Havran et al. (2005) developed a final gathering photon mapping algorithm based on storing final gather intersection points in a kd-tree in the scene and then shooting photons from the lights; when a photon intersects a surface, the nearby final gather intersection records are found and the photon's energy can be distributed to the origins of the corresponding final gather rays. Herzog et al. (2007) described an approach based on storing all of the visible points as seen from the camera and splatting photon contributions to them. Hachisuka et al. (2008b) developed the progressive photon mapping algorithm; stochastic progressive photon mapping was developed by Hachisuka and Jensen (2009).

The advantages of SPPM over traditional photon mapping are significant, and the approach was quickly adopted after its introduction. Hachisuka et al. (2010) showed how to use arbitrary density estimation kernels and how to compute error estimates during rendering to automatically determine when to stop further iterations. Knaus and Zwicker (2011) re-derived SPPM following a different approach and showed that it was possible to only maintain global statistics for values like the current search radius rather than having a separate value for each pixel. See Kaplanyan and Dachsbacher (2013a) for an extensive study of SPPM's convergence rates and an improved (but more complex) method for updating SPPM estimates after each iteration.

The question of how to find the most effective set of photons for photon mapping is an important one: light-driven particle-tracing algorithms don't work well for all scenes (consider, for example, a complex building model with lights in every room but where the camera sees only a single room). The earliest applications of Metropolis sampling to photon mapping was proposed in Wald's Diploma thesis (1999). Fan et al. (2005) showed that the application of Veach's particle-tracing theory to photon mapping provides a mechanism for generating photon paths starting from the camera. They were able to use this approach in conjunction with a Metropolis sampling algorithm to generate photon distributions. Hachisuka and Jensen (2011) used Metropolis sampling to find photon paths that were visible to the camera; their algorithm is notable for both its effectiveness and its ease of implementation. Chen et al. (2011) use a similar approach but sample additional terms of the path contribution function and distribute additional photons to parts of the image with higher error.

Jensen and Christensen (1998) were the first to generalize the photon mapping algorithm to participating media. Knaus and Zwicker (2011) showed how to render participating media using SPPM. Jarosz et al. (2008) had the important insight that expressing the scattering integral over a beam through the medium as the measurement to be evaluated could make photon mapping's rate of convergence much higher than if a series of point photon estimates was instead taken along each ray. Section 5.6 of Hachisuka's thesis

(2011) and Jarosz et al. (2011a, 2011b) showed how to apply this approach progressively. For another representation, see Jakob et al. (2011), who fit a sum of anisotropic Gaussians to the equilibrium radiance distribution in participating media.

Bidirectional Path Tracing

Bidirectional path tracing was independently developed by Lafortune and Willems (1994) and Veach and Guibas (1994). The development of multiple importance sampling was integral to the effectiveness of bidirectional path tracing (Veach and Guibas 1995). Lafortune and Willems (1996) showed how to apply bidirectional path tracing to rendering participating media, and Kollig and Keller (2000) showed how bidirectional path tracing can be modified to work with quasi-random sample patterns.

An exciting recent development has been simultaneous work by Hachisuka et al. (2012) and Georgiev et al. (2012), who developed a unified framework for both photon mapping and bidirectional path tracing. Their approaches allowed photon mapping to be included in the path space formulation of the light transport equation, which in turn made it possible to derive light transport algorithms that use both approaches to generate paths and combine them using multiple importance sampling.

Kaplanyan and Dachsbacher (2013b) noted that photon mapping algorithms use illumination from nearby points even in cases where unbiased approaches are effective. They developed a technique for regularization of light-carrying paths, where an unbiased path tracer or bidirectional path tracer is modified to treat delta distributions that cause impossible-to-sample configurations instead as having non-zero value over a small cone of directions. Thus, bias is introduced only in the challenging settings.

Vorba et al. (2014) developed an approach to compute effective sampling distributions for difficult lighting configurations over the course of rendering rather than in a preprocess and showed its applicability to bidirectional path tracing.

Metropolis Light Transport

Veach and Guibas (1997) first applied the Metropolis sampling algorithm to solving the light transport equation. They demonstrated how this method could be applied to image synthesis and showed that the result was a light transport algorithm that was robust to traditionally difficult lighting configurations (e.g., light shining through a slightly ajar door). Pauly, Kollig, and Keller (2000) generalized the MLT algorithm to include volume scattering. Pauly's thesis (Pauly 1999) described the theory and implementation of bidirectional and Metropolis-based algorithms for volume light transport.

Fan et al. (2005) developed a method that let the user explicitly specify a number of important paths (e.g., through a tricky geometric configuration) that could then be used as a target state in Metropolis mutations. The energy redistribution path tracing algorithm by Cline et al. (2005) starts one or more Markov chains at every pixel of the image and runs them for a small number of iterations; the method is notable for being unbiased despite its use of non-ergodic Markov chains that can only explore a subset of path space.

Hoberock's Ph.D. dissertation discusses a number of alternatives for the scalar contribution function, including those that adapt the sampling density to pay more attention to particular modes of light transport and those that focus on reducing noise in the final image (Hoberock 2008).

Kelemen et al. (2002) developed the "primary sample space MLT" formulation of Metropolis light transport. They also suggested the approach implemented in the `MLTSampler` for lazily updating sample vector components when performing mutations. Hachisuka et al. (2014) developed the MMLT approach that is implemented in the `MLTIntegrator` in this chapter.

The optimal choice of the large step probability is scene dependent: for scenes with difficult-to-sample transport paths, it's better for it to be lower, so that more successful mutations are performed with small steps once a good path is found. For scenes with simpler light transport, it's better for the probability to be higher, so that the overall path space is explored more thoroughly. Zsolnai and Szirmay-Kalos (2013) developed a technique that gathered statistics about paths during the bootstrap phase that made it possible to automatically set this parameter to a near-optimal value.

Other Rendering Approaches

A number of algorithms have been developed based on a first phase of computation that traces paths from the light sources to create "virtual lights," where these lights are then used to approximate indirect illumination during a second phase. The principles behind this approach were first introduced by Keller's work on *instant radiosity* (1997). The more general instant global illumination algorithm was developed by Wald, Benthin, and collaborators (Wald et al. 2002, 2003; Benthin et al. 2003). See Dachsbacher et al.'s recent survey article (2014) for a summary of recent work in this area.

Building on the virtual point lights concept, Walter and collaborators (2005, 2006) developed *lightcuts*, which are based on creating thousands of virtual point lights and then building a hierarchy by progressively clustering nearby ones together. When a point is being shaded, traversal of the light hierarchy is performed by computing bounds on the error that would result from using clustered values to illuminate the point versus continuing down the hierarchy, leading to an approach with both guaranteed error bounds and good efficiency.

Bidirectional lightcuts (Walter et al. 2012) trace longer subpaths from the camera to obtain a family of light connection strategies; combining the strategies using multiple importance sampling eliminates bias artifacts that are commonly produced by virtual point light methods.

Jakob and Marschner (2012) expressed light transport involving specular materials as an integral over a high-dimensional manifold embedded in path space. A single light path corresponds to a point on the manifold, and nearby paths are found using a local parameterization that resembles Newton's method; they applied a Metropolis-type method through this parameterization to explore the neighborhood of challenging specular and near-specular configurations.

Hanika et al. (2015a) apply an improved version of the local path parameterization in a pure Monte Carlo context to estimate the direct illumination through one or more dielectric boundaries; this leads to significantly better convergence when rendering glass-enclosed objects or contaminated surfaces with water droplets.

MLTSampler 1029

Kaplanyan et al. (2014) observed that the path contribution function is close to being separable when paths are parameterized using the endpoints and the half-direction vectors at intermediate vertices, which are equal to the microfacet normals in the context of microfacet reflectance models. Performing Metropolis sampling in this half-vector domain leads to a method that is particularly good at rendering glossy interreflection. An extension by Hanika et al. (2015b) improves the robustness of this approach and proposes an optimized scheme to select mutation sizes to reduce sample clumping in image space.

Another interesting approach was developed by Lehtinen and collaborators (Lehtinen et al. 2013, Manzi et al. 2014). Building on the observation that ideally, most samples from the path space should be taken around discontinuities (and not in smooth regions of the image), they developed a measurement contribution function for Metropolis sampling that focused samples on gradients in the image. They then reconstructed high-quality final images from horizontal and vertical gradient images and a coarse, noisy image. More recently, Kettunen et al. (2015) showed how this approach could be applied to regular path tracing, without Metropolis sampling. Manzi et al. (2015) showed its application to bidirectional path tracing.

Hair is particularly challenging to render; not only is it extremely geometrically complex but multiple scattering among hair also makes a significant contribution to its final appearance. Traditional light transport algorithms often have difficulty handling this case well. See the papers by Moon and Marschner (2006), Moon et al. (2008), and Zinke et al. (2008) for recent work in specialized rendering algorithms for hair.

While the rendering problem as discussed so far has been challenging enough, Jarabo et al. (2014a) showed the extension of the path integral to not include the steady-state assumption—i.e., accounting for the non-infinite speed of light. Time ends up being extremely high frequency, which makes rendering challenging; they showed successful application of density estimation to this problem.

EXERCISES

⊘ **16.1** Derive importance functions and implement the `Camera We()`, `Pdf_We()`, `Sample_Wi()`, and `Pdf_Wi()` methods for one or more of `EnvironmentCamera`, `OrthographicCamera`, or `RealisticCamera`. Render images using bidirectional path tracing or MMLT and show that given sufficient samples, they converge to the same images as when the scene is rendered with standard path tracing.

⊘ **16.2** Discuss situations where the current methods for sampling outgoing rays from `ProjectionLights` and `GonioPhotometricLights` may be extremely inefficient, choosing many rays in directions where the light source casts no illumination. Use the `Distribution2D` structure to implement improved sampling techniques for each of them based on sampling from a distribution based on the luminance in their 2D image maps, properly accounting for the transformation from the 2D image map sampling distribution to the distribution of directions on the sphere. Verify that the system still computes the same images (modulo variance) with your new sampling techniques when using an `Integrator` that calls these methods. Determine how much efficiency is improved by using these sampling methods instead of the default ones.

❸ **16.3** Implement Walter et al.'s *lightcuts* algorithm in pbrt (Walter et al. 2005, 2006). How do the BSDF interfaces in pbrt need to be generalized to compute the error terms for lightcuts? Do other core system interfaces need to be changed? Compare the efficiency of rendering images with global illumination using your implementation to some of the other bidirectional integrators.

❶ **16.4** Experiment with the parameters to the SPPMIntegrator until you get a good feel for how they affect rendering time and the appearance of the final image. At a minimum, experiment with varying the search radius, the number of photons traced, and the number of iterations.

❷ **16.5** Another approach to improving the efficiency of photon shooting is to start out by shooting photons from lights in all directions with equal probability but then to dynamically update the probability of sampling directions based on which directions lead to light paths that have high throughput weight and end up being used by visible points. Photons then must be reweighted based on the probability for shooting a photon in a particular direction. (As long as there is always nonzero possibility of sending a photon in any direction, this approach doesn't introduce additional bias into the shooting algorithm.) Derive and implement such an approach. Show that in the limit, your modified SPPMIntegrator computes the same results as the original. How much do these changes improve the rate of convergence?

❷ **16.6** The SPPMIntegrator ends up storing all of the BSDFs along camera paths to the first visible point, even though only the last BSDF is needed. First, measure how much memory is used to store unnecessary BSDFs in the current implementation for a variety of scenes. Next, modify the VisiblePoint representation to store the reflectance, BSDF::rho(), at visible points and then compute reflection assuming a Lambertian BSDF. Does this approximation introduce visible error in test scenes? How much memory is saved?

❷ **16.7** To find the VisiblePoints around a photon–surface intersection, the SPPM Integrator uses a uniform grid to store the bounding boxes of visible points expanded by their radii. Investigate other spatial data structures for storing visible points that support efficient photon/nearby visible point queries, and implement an alternate approach. (You may want to specifically consider octrees and kd-trees.) How do performance and memory use compare to the current implementation?

❷ **16.8** Implement "final gathering" in the SPPMIntegrator, where camera rays are followed for one more bounce after hitting a diffuse surface. Investigate how many iterations and how many photons per iteration are needed to get good results with this approach for a variety of scenes compared to the current implementation.

❷ **16.9** There is actually one case where collisions from the hash() function used by the SPPMIntegrator can cause a problem: if, for example, nearby voxels have a collision, then a `VisiblePoint` that overlaps both of them will be placed in a linked list twice, and then a photon that is close to them will incorrectly contribute to the pixel's value twice. Can you prove that this will never happen for the current hash function? If it does happen, can you construct a scene where the error makes a meaningful difference in the final image? How might this problem be addressed?

⊘ **16.10** Extend the SPPM integrator to support volumetric scattering. First, read the papers by Knaus and Zwicker (2011) and Jarosz et al. (2011b) and choose one of these approaches. Compare the efficiency and accuracy of images rendered with your implementation to rendering using the bidirectional path tracer or the MMLT integrator.

⊘ **16.11** One shortcoming of the current `SPPMIntegrator` implementation is that it's inefficient for scenes where the camera is only viewing a small part of the overall scene: many photons may need to be traced to find ones that are visible to the camera. Read the paper by Hachisuka and Jensen (2011) on using adaptive Markov chain sampling to generate photon paths and implement their approach. Construct a scene where the current implementation is inefficient and your new one does much better, and render comparison images using equal amounts of computation for each. Are there any scenes where your implementation computes worse results?

⊘ **16.12** Extend the BDPT integrator to support subsurface scattering with BSSRDFs. In addition to connecting pairs of vertices by evaluating the geometric term and BSDFs, your modified integrator should also evaluate the BSSRDF $S(p_o, \omega_o, p_i, \omega_i)$ when two points are located on an object with the same `Material` with a non-`nullptr`-valued BSSRDF. Since two connection techniques lead to paths with a fundamentally different configuration—straight-line transport versus an additional subsurface scattering interaction on the way from p_i on p_o—their area product density should never be compared to each other when computing multiple importance sampling weights.

⊘ **16.13** Implement Russian roulette to randomly skip tracing visibility rays for low-contribution connections between subpaths in the `ConnectBDPT()` function. Measure the change in Monte Carlo efficiency compared to the current `BDPTIntegrator` implementation.

⊘ **16.14** Modify the BDPT integrator to use the path space regularization technique described by Kaplanyan and Dachsbacher (2013b). (Their method makes it possible for light transport algorithms based on incremental path construction to still handle difficult sampling cases based on chains of specular interactions.) Construct a scene where this approach is useful, and render images to compare results between this approach, SPPM, and an unmodified bidirectional path tracer.

⊘ **16.15** By adding mutation strategies that don't necessarily modify all of the sample values X_i, it can be possible to reuse some or all of the paths generated by the previous samples in the `MLTIntegrator`. For example, if only the `PrimarySample` values for the light subpath are mutated, then the camera subpath can be reused. (An analogous case holds for the light subpath.) Even if a mutation is proposed for a subpath, if the samples for its first few vertices are left unchanged, then that portion of the path doesn't need to be retraced.

Modify the `MLTIntegrator` to add one or more of the above sampling strategies, and update the implementation so that it reuses any partial results from the previous sample that remain valid when your new mutation is used. You may want to add both "small step" and "large step" variants of your new mutation. Compare the mean squared error of images rendered by your modified implementation to the MSE of images rendered by the original implementation, comparing to a reference image rendered with a large number of samples. For the same number of samples, your implementation should be faster but will likely have slightly higher error due to additional correlation among samples. Is the Monte Carlo efficiency of your modified version better than the original implementation?

● **16.16** In his Ph.D. dissertation, Hoberock proposes a number of alternative scalar contribution functions for Metropolis light transport, including ones that focus on particular types of light transport and ones that adapt the sample density during rendering in order to reduce perceptual error (Hoberock 2008). Read Chapter 6 of his thesis, and implement either the multistage MLT or the noise-aware MLT algorithm that he describes.

CHAPTER SEVENTEEN

17 RETROSPECTIVE AND THE FUTURE

pbrt represents one single point in the space of rendering system designs. The basic decisions we made early on—that ray tracing would be the geometric visibility algorithm used, that physical correctness would be a cornerstone of the system, and that Monte Carlo would be the main approach used for numerical integration—all had pervasive implications for the system's design. For example, an entirely different set of trade-offs would have been made if pbrt were a renderer designed instead for real-time performance and only rendering scenes with direct illumination.

This chapter first looks back at some of the details of the complete system, discusses some design alternatives, and also covers some potential major extensions that are more complex than have been described in the exercises. We then discuss recent trends in graphics hardware architectures and their implications for rendering systems like pbrt.

17.1 DESIGN RETROSPECTIVE

One of the basic assumptions in pbrt's design was that the most interesting types of images to render are images with complex geometry and lighting and that supporting a wide variety of shapes, materials, light sources, and light transport algorithms was important. We also assumed that rendering these images well—with good sampling patterns, ray differentials, and antialiased textures—is worth the computational expense. One result of these assumptions is that pbrt is relatively inefficient at rendering simple scenes, where a more specialized system could do much better.

For example, a performance implication of our design priorities is that finding the BSDF at a ray intersection is more computationally expensive than it is in renderers that don't expend as much effort filtering textures and computing ray differentials. We believe that

Physically Based Rendering: From Theory To Implementation.
http://dx.doi.org/10.1016/B978-0-12-800645-0.50017-8

this effort pays off overall by reducing the need to trace more camera rays to address texture aliasing, although, again, for simple scenes, texture aliasing is often not a problem. On the other hand, most of the integrators in pbrt assume that hundreds or even thousands of samples will be taken in each pixel for high-quality global illumination; the benefits of high quality filtering are reduced in this case, since the high pixel sampling rate ends up sampling textures at a high rate as well.

The simplicity of some of the interfaces in the system can lead to unnecessary work being done. For example, the Sampler always computes lens and time samples, even if they aren't needed by the Camera; there's no way for the Camera to communicate its sampling needs. Similarly, if an Integrator doesn't use all of the array samples from its earlier calls to Request1DArray() and Request2DArray() for some ray, then the Sampler's work for generating those samples is wasted. (This case can occur, for example, if the ray doesn't intersect any geometry.) For cases like these, we believe that the benefits to readers of making the system easier to understand outweigh the relatively small efficiency losses.

Throughout the book, we have tried to always add an exercise at the end of the chapter when we've known that there was an important design alternative or where we made an implementation trade-off that would likely be made differently in a production rendering system. (For example, Exercise 7.2 discusses the first issue with Samplers in the previous paragraph.) It's worth reading the exercises even if you don't plan to do them.

17.1.1 TRIANGLES ONLY

Another instance where the chosen abstractions in pbrt impact the overall system efficiency is the range of geometric primitives that the renderer supports. While ray tracing's ability to handle a wide variety of shapes is elegant, this property is not as useful in practice as one might initially expect. Most real-world scenes are either modeled directly with polygons or with smooth surfaces like spline patches and subdivision surfaces that either have difficult-to-implement or relatively inefficient ray–shape intersection algorithms. As such, they are usually tessellated into triangles for ray intersection tests in practice. Not many shapes that are commonly encountered in real-world scenes can be represented accurately with spheres and cones!

There are some advantages to designing a ray tracer around a single low-level shape representation like triangles and only operating on this representation throughout much of the pipeline. Such a renderer could still support a variety of primitives in the scene description but would always tessellate them at some point before performing intersection tests. Advantages of this design include:

- The renderer can depend on the fact that the triangle vertices can be transformed into word or camera space in advance, so no transformations of rays into object space are necessary (except when object instancing is used).
- The acceleration structures can be specialized so that their nodes directly store the triangles that overlap them. This improves the locality of the geometry in memory and enables ray–primitive intersection tests to be performed directly in the traversal routine, without needing to pass through two levels of virtual function calls to do so, as is currently the case in pbrt.

- Displacement mapping, where geometry is subdivided into small triangles, which can then have their vertices perturbed procedurally or with texture maps, can be more easily implemented if all primitives are able to tessellate themselves.

These advantages are substantial, for both increased performance and the complexity that they remove from many parts of the system. For a production renderer, rather than one with pedagogical goals like pbrt, this alternative is worth considering carefully. (Alternatively, triangles alone could be given special treatment—stored directly in acceleration structures and so forth–while other shapes were handled with a less efficient general purpose code path.)

17.1.2 INCREASED SCENE COMPLEXITY

Given well-built acceleration structures, a strength of of ray tracing is that the time spent on ray–primitive intersections grows slowly with added scene complexity. As such, the maximum complexity that a ray tracer can handle may be limited more by memory than by computation. Because rays may pass through many different regions of the scene during a short period of time, virtual memory often performs poorly when ray tracing complex scenes due to the resulting incoherent memory access patterns.

One way to increase the potential complexity that a renderer is capable of handling is to reduce the memory used to store the scene. For example, pbrt currently uses approximately 4 GB of memory for the 24 million triangles in the landscape scene on the cover and in Figure 4.1. This works out to an average of 167 bytes per triangle. We have previously written ray tracers that managed an average of 40 bytes per triangle for scenes like these—at least a 4× reduction is possible.

Reducing memory overhead requires careful attention to memory use throughout the system. For example, in the aforementioned system, we provided three different Triangle implementations, one using 8-bit uint8_ts to store vertex indices, one using 16-bit uint16_ts, and one using 32-bit uint32_ts. The smallest index size that was sufficient for the range of vertex indices in the mesh was chosen at run time. Deering's paper on geometry compression (Deering 1995) and Ward's packed color format (Ward 1992) are both good inspirations for thinking along these lines. See the "Further Reading" section in Chapter 4 for information about more memory-efficient acceleration structure representations.

A more complex approach to implement is geometry caching (Pharr and Hanrahan 1996), where the renderer holds a fixed amount of geometry in memory and discards geometry that hasn't been accessed recently. This approach is useful for scenes with a lot of tessellated geometry, where a compact higher level shape representation like a subdivision surface can explode into a large number of triangles. When available memory is low, some of this geometry can be discarded and regenerated later if needed. Geometry stored on disk can also be loaded into geometry caches; with the advent of economical flash storage offering hundreds of megabytes per second of read bandwidth, this approach is even more attractive.

Triangle 156

The performance of such a cache can be substantially improved by reordering the rays that are traced in order to improve their spatial and thus memory coherence (Pharr et al. 1997). An easier-to-implement and more effective approach to improving the cache's behavior was described by Christensen et al. (2003), who wrote a ray tracer that uses simplified representations of the scene geometry in a geometry cache. More recently, Yoon et al. (2006), Budge et al. (2009), Moon et al. (2010), and Hanika et al. (2010) have developed improved approaches to this problem. See Rushmeier, Patterson, and Veerasamy (1993) for an early example of how to use simplified scene representations when computing indirect illumination.

17.1.3 PRODUCTION RENDERING

Rendering high-quality imagery for film introduces a host of challenges beyond the topics discussed in this book. Being able to render highly complex scenes—with both geometric and texture complexity—is a requirement. Most production renderers have deferred loading and caching of texture and geometry at the hearts of their implementations. Programmable surface shaders are also critical for allowing users to specify complex material appearances.

Another practical challenge is integrating with interactive modeling and shading tools: it's important that artists be able to quickly see the effect of changes that they make to models, surfaces, and lights. Deep integration with tools is necessary for this to work well—communicating the scene description from scratch with a text file each time the scene is rendered, as is done in pbrt, is not a viable approach.

Unfortunately, the developers of most of the current crop of production rendering systems haven't yet followed the lead of Cook et al. (1987), who described Reyes and its design in great detail. Exceptions include PantaRay, which was used by Weta Digital and is described by Pantaleoni et al. (2010), and Disney's Hyperion renderer (Eisenacher et al. 2013).

17.1.4 SPECIALIZED COMPILATION

The OptiX ray-tracing system, which is described by Parker et al. (2010), has a very interesting system structure: it's a combination of built-in functionality (e.g., for building acceleration structures and traversing rays through them) that can be extended by user-supplied code (for primitive implementations, surface shading functions, etc.). Many renderers over the years have allowed user extensibility of this sort, usually through some kind of plug-in architecture. OptiX is distinctive in that it is built using a run-time compilation system that compiles all of this code together.

Because the compiler has a view of the entire system when generating code, the resulting custom renderer can be automatically specialized in a variety of ways. For example, if the surface shading code never uses the (u, v) texture coordinates, the code that computes them in the triangle shape intersection test can be optimized out as dead code. Or, if the ray's time field is never accessed, both the code that sets it and even the structure member itself can be eliminated. Thus, this approach allows a degree of specialization (and resulting performance) that would be difficult to achieve manually, at least for more than a single system variant.

17.2 ALTERNATIVE HARDWARE ARCHITECTURES

Our focus in this book has been on traditional multi-core CPUs as a target for the system. Furthermore, we have ignored the potential of being able to perform up to eight floating-point operations per instruction by using CPU SIMD hardware. While other computing architectures like GPUs or specialized ray-tracing hardware are appealing targets for a renderer, their characteristics tend to change rapidly, and their programming languages and models are less widely known than languages like C++ on CPUs. Though we haven't targeted these architectures with pbrt, it's useful to discuss their characteristics.

The early days of ray tracing saw work in this area focused on multiprocessors (Cleary et al. 1983; Green and Paddon 1989; Badouel and Priol 1989) and clusters of computers (Parker et al. 1999; Wald et al. 2001a, 2002; Wald, Slusallek, and Benthin 2001; Wald, Benthin, and Slusallek 2003). More recently, substantial capabilities have become available in single computer systems, which has led to a shift of focus to the capabilities of CPU SIMD units and GPUs.

CPUs have long been designed to run a single thread of computation as efficiently as possible; these processors can be considered to be latency focused, in that the goal is to finish a single computation as quickly as possible. (Only since 2005 or so has this focus started to slowly change in CPU design, as multicore CPUs have provided a small number of independent latency-focused processors on a single chip.) Starting with the advent of programmable graphics processors around the year 2003, *throughput processors* (as exemplified by GPUs) have increasingly become the source of most of the computational capability available in many computer systems. These processors focus not on single-thread performance but instead on efficiently running hundreds or thousands of computations in parallel with high aggregate computational throughput, without trying to minimize time for any of the individual computations.

By not focusing on single-thread performance, throughput processors are able to devote much less space on the chip for caches, branch prediction hardware, out-of-order execution units, and other features that have been invented to improve single-thread performance on CPUs. Thus, given a fixed amount of chip area, these processors are able to provide many more arithmetic logic units (ALUs) than a CPU. For the types of computations that can provide a substantial amount of independent parallel work, throughput processors can keep these ALUs busy and very efficiently execute the computation. As of the time of writing, GPUs offer approximately ten times as many peak FLOPS as high-end CPUs; this makes them highly attractive for many processing-intensive tasks (including ray tracing).[1]

Single instruction, multiple data (SIMD) processing, where processing units execute a single instruction across multiple data elements, is the key mechanism that throughput processors use to efficiently deliver computation; both today's CPUs and today's GPUs

---

1   However, graphics processors typically consume more power and are physically larger chips than CPUs; some of their improved performance comes purely from using more power and more chip area. A fair comparison is to consider performance per watt or per square millimeter of silicon, which puts GPUs at 3–5× more capable in terms of peak performance.

have SIMD vector units in their processing cores. Modern CPUs generally have a handful of processing cores and support four or eight 32-bit floating point operations in their vector instruction sets (e.g., SSE, NEON, or AVX). GPUs currently have tens of processing cores,[2] each with SIMD vector units between 8 and 64 elements wide. (Intel's Xeon Phi architecture, which features over 50 relatively simple CPU cores, each with a 16-wide 32-bit floating-point SIMD unit, lies somewhere between these two points.) It is likely that both the number of processing cores and the width of the vector units in all of these processor architectures will go up over time, as hardware designers make use of additional transistors made possible by Moore's law.

17.2.1 GPU RAY TRACING

Purcell et al. (2002, 2003) and Carr, Hall, and Hart (2002) were the first to map general-purpose ray tracers to throughput graphics processors. GPU-based construction of data structures tends to be challenging; see Zhou et al. (2008), Lauterbach et al. (2009), Pantaleoni and Luebke (2010), Garanzha et al. (2011), and Karras and Aila (2013) for techniques for building kd-trees and BVHs on GPUs.

Aila and Laine (2009) carefully investigated the performance of SIMD ray tracing on a graphics processor, using their insights to develop a new SIMD-friendly traversal algorithm that was substantially more efficient than the previous best known approach. Their insights are worth careful consideration by all implementors of high-performance rendering systems.

A big challenge in using throughput processors for rendering systems can be finding coherent collections of computation that use the SIMD vector elements efficiently. Consider a Monte Carlo path tracer tracing a collection of rays; after random sampling at the first bounce, each ray will in general intersect completely different objects, likely with completely different surface shaders. At this point, running the surface shaders will likely make poor use of SIMD hardware as each ray needs to execute a different computation. This specific problem of efficient shading was investigated by Hoberock et al. (2009), who resorted a large number of intersection points to create coherent collections of work before executing their surface shaders.

Another challenge is that relatively limited amount of local memory on GPUs makes it challenging to implement light transport algorithms that require more than a small amount of storage for each ray. (For example, even storing all of the vertices of a pair of subpaths for a bidirectional path tracing algorithm is not straightforward.) The paper by Davidovič et al. (2014) gives a thorough overview of these issues and previous work and includes a discussion of implementations of a number of sophisticated light transport algorithms on the GPU.

An interesting trade-off for renderer developers to consider is exhibited by Hachisuka's path tracer, which uses a rasterizer with parallel projection to trace rays, effectively computing visibility in the same direction for all of the points being shaded (Hachisuka

---

2 The definition of a "core" on a throughput processor is notoriously tricky, with different hardware vendors promoting different definitions. Here, we are following the relatively vendor-neutral terminology proposed by Fatahalian (2008).

2005). His insight was that although this approach doesn't give a particularly good sampling distribution for Monte Carlo path tracing, in that each point isn't able to perform importance sampling to select outgoing directions, the increased efficiency from computing visibility for a very coherent collection of rays paid off overall. In other words, for a fixed amount of computation, so many more samples could be taken using rasterization versus using ray tracing that the much larger number of less well-distributed samples generated a better image than a smaller number of well-chosen samples. We suspect that this general issue of trading off between computing exactly the locally desired result at a single point versus computing what can be computed very efficiently globally for many points will be an important one for developers to consider on the SIMD processors of the future.

17.2.2 PACKET TRACING

For narrow SIMD widths on CPUs (like four-element SSE), some performance gains can be attained by opportunistically using the SIMD unit. For example, one might modify pbrt to use SSE instructions for the operations defined in the Spectrum class, thus generally being able to do three floating-point operations per instruction (for RGB spectra) rather than just one if the SIMD unit was not used. This approach would achieve 75% utilization of an SSE unit for those instructions but doesn't help with performance in the rest of the system. In some cases, optimizing compilers can identify multiple computations in scalar code that can be executed together using a single SIMD instruction.

Achieving *excellent* utilization of SIMD vector units generally requires that the entire computation be expressed in a *data parallel* manner, where the same computation is performed on many data elements simultaneously. A natural way to extract data parallelism in a ray tracer is to have each processing core responsible for tracing n rays at a time, where n is at least the size of the SIMD width, if not larger; as such, each SIMD vector "lane" is responsible for just a single ray, and each vector instruction performs only a single scalar computation for each of the rays it's responsible for. Thus, high SIMD utilization comes naturally, except for the cases where some rays require different computations than others.

This approach has seen success with high-performance CPU ray tracers (where it is generally called "packet tracing"). Wald et al. (2001a) introduced this approach, which has since seen wide adoption. In a packet tracer, the camera generates "packets" of n rays that are then processed as a unit. Acceleration structure traversal algorithms are modified so that they visit a node if *any* of the rays in the packet passes through it; primitives in the leaves are tested for intersection with all of the rays in the packet, and so forth. Packet tracing has been shown to lead to substantial speedups, although it becomes increasingly less effective as the rays to be traced become less coherent; it works well for camera rays and shadow rays to localized light sources, since the packets of rays will pass through similar regions of the scene, but efficiency generally falls off with multi-bounce light transport algorithms. Finding ways to retain good efficiency with packet tracing remains an active area of research.

Spectrum 315

Packet tracing on CPUs is usually implemented with the SIMD vectorization made explicit: intersection functions are written to explicitly take some number of rays as a parameter rather than just a single ray, and so forth. In contrast, the vectorization in programs written for throughput processors like GPUs is generally implicit: code is written as if it just operates on a single ray at a time, but the underlying compiler and hardware actually execute one instance of the program in each SIMD lane.

For processors that directly expose their SIMD nature in their instruction sets (like CPUs or Intel's Xeon Phi), the designer of the programming model is able to choose whether to provide an implicit or an explicit vector model to the user. See Parker et al.'s (2007) ray-tracing shading language for an example of compiling an implicitly data-parallel language to a SIMD instruction set on CPUs. See also Georgiev and Slusallek's (2008) approach, where a generic programming approach is taken in C++ to allow implementing a high-performance ray tracer with details like packets well hidden. ispc, described in a paper by Pharr and Mark (2012), provides a general-purpose "single program multiple data" (SPMD) language for CPU vector units that also provides this model.

Reshetov et al. (2005) generalized packet tracing, showing that gathering up many rays from a single origin into a frustum and then using the frustum for acceleration structure traversal could lead to very high-performance ray tracing; they refined the frusta into subfrusta and eventually the individual rays as they reached lower levels of the tree. Reshetov (2007) later introduced a technique for efficiently intersecting a collection of rays against a collection of triangles in acceleration structure leaf nodes by generating a frustum around the rays and using it for first-pass culling. See Benthin and Wald (2009) for a technique to use ray frusta and packets for efficient shadow rays.

While packet tracing is effective for coherent collections of rays that follow generally the same path through acceleration structures, it's much less effective for incoherent collections of rays, which are more common with global illumination algorithms. To address this issue, Ernst and Greiner (2008), Wald et al. (2008), and Dammertz et al. (2008) proposed only traversing a single ray through the acceleration structure at once but improving SIMD efficiency by simultaneously testing each ray against a number of bounding boxes at each step in the hierarchy.

Another approach to the ray incoherence problem is to reorder small batches of incoherent rays to improve SIMD efficiency; representative work in this area includes papers by Mansson et al. (2007), Boulos et al. (2008), Gribble and Ramani (2008), and Tsakok (2009). More recently, Barringer and Akenine-Möller (2014) developed a SIMD ray traversal algorithm that delivered substantial performance improvements given large numbers of rays.

The Embree system, described in a paper by Wald et al. (2014), is a high-performance open source rendering system that supports both packet tracing and highly efficient traversal of single rays. See also the paper by Benthin et al. (2011) on the topic of finding a balance between these two approaches.

pbrt is very much a "one ray at a time" ray tracer; if a rendering system can provide many rays for intersection tests at once, a variety of more efficient implementations are possible even beyond packet tracing. For example, Keller and Wächter (2011) and Mora (2011) described algorithms for intersecting a large number of rays against the scene geometry where there is no acceleration structure at all. Instead, primitives and rays are both recursively partitioned until small collections of rays and small collections of primitives remain, at which point intersection tests are performed. Improvements to this approach were described by Áfra (2012) and Nabata et al. (2013).

17.2.3 RAY-TRACING HARDWARE

Given the widespread success of specialized hardware for triangle rasterization and shading in modern PCs, there has long been interest in designing specialized hardware for ray tracing. The ray-tracing algorithm presents a variety of stages of computation that must be addressed in a complete system, including camera ray generation, construction of the acceleration hierarchy, traversal of the hierarchy, ray–primitive intersections, shading, lighting, and integration calculations.

Early published work in this area includes a paper by Woop et al. (2005), who described the design of a "ray processing unit" (RPU). More recently, Aila and Karras (2010) described general architectural issues related to handling incoherent rays, as are common with global illumination algorithms. Nah et al. (2011) and Lee and collaborators (2013, 2015) have written a series of papers on ray tracing on a mobile GPU architecture, addressing issues including hierarchy traversal, ray generation, intersection calculations, and ray reordering for better memory coherence. See also the paper by Doyle et al. (2013) on SAH BVH construction in specialized hardware.

While there has been substantial research work in this area, unfortunately none of these architectures has made it out to the market in large numbers, though the Caustic ray-tracing architecture (McCombe 2013) has been acquired by a mobile GPU vendor, Imagination Technologies. Plans for products based on an integration of this architecture into a traditional GPU have been announced; we are hopeful that the time for efficient ray-tracing hardware may have arrived.

17.2.4 THE FUTURE

Innovation in high-performance architectures for graphics seems likely to continue in coming years. As CPUs are gradually increasing their SIMD width and adding more processing cores, becoming more similar to throughput processors, throughput processors are adding support for task parallelism and improving their performance on more irregular workloads than purely data-parallel ones. Whether the computer system of the future is a heterogeneous collection of both types of processing cores or whether there is a middle ground with a single type of processor architecture that works well for a range of applications remains an open question.

The role of specialized fixed-function graphics hardware in future systems is likely to become increasingly important; fixed-function hardware is generally substantially more power-efficient than programmable hardware. As the critical computational kernels of future graphics systems become clear, fixed-function implementations of them may become widespread.

17.3 CONCLUSION

The idea for pbrt was born in October 1999. Over the next five years, it evolved from a system designed only to support the students taking Stanford's CS348b course to a robust, feature-rich, extensible rendering system. Since its inception, we have learned a great deal about what it takes to build a rendering system that doesn't just make pretty pictures but is one that other people enjoy using and modifying as well. What has been most difficult, however, was designing a large piece of software that others might enjoy *reading*. This has been a far more challenging (and rewarding) task than implementing any of the rendering algorithms themselves.

After its first publication, the book enjoyed widespread adoption in advanced graphics courses worldwide, which we found very gratifying. We were unprepared, however, for the impact that pbrt has had on rendering research. Writing a ray tracer from scratch is a formidable task (as so many students in undergraduate graphics courses can attest to), and creating a robust physically based renderer is much harder still. We are proud that pbrt has lowered the barrier to entry for aspiring researchers in rendering, making it easier for researchers to experiment with and demonstrate the value of new ideas in rendering. We continue to be delighted to see papers in SIGGRAPH, the Eurographics Rendering Symposium, High Performance Graphics, and other graphics research venues that either build on pbrt to achieve their goals, or compare their images to pbrt as "ground truth."

More recently, we have been delighted again to see the rapid adoption of physically based approaches in practice for offline rendering and, recently as of this writing, games and interactive applications. Though we are admittedly unusual folk, it's a particular delight to see incredible graphics on a screen and marvel at the billions of pseudo-random (or quasi-random) samples, billions of rays traced, and the complex mathematics that went into each image passing by.

We would like to sincerely thank everyone who has built upon this work for their own research, to build a new curriculum, to create amazing movies or games, or just to learn more about rendering. We hope that this new edition continues to serve the graphics community in the same way that its predecessors were able to.

回 UTILITIES

In addition to all of the graphics-related code presented thus far, pbrt makes use of a number of general utility routines and classes. Although these are key to pbrt's operation, it is not necessary to understand their implementation in detail in order to work with the rest of the system. This appendix describes the interfaces to these routines, including those that handle error reporting, memory management, support for parallel execution on multiple CPU cores, and other basic infrastructure. The implementations of some of this functionality—the parts that are interesting enough to be worth delving into—are also discussed.

A.1 MAIN INCLUDE FILE

The core/pbrt.h file is included by all other source files in the system. It contains all global function declarations and inline functions, a few macros and numeric constants, and other globally accessible data. All files that include pbrt.h get a number of other included header files from pbrt.h. This simplifies creation of new source files, almost all of which will want access to these extra headers. However, in the interest of compile time efficiency, we keep the number of these automatically included files to a minimum; the ones here are necessary for almost all modules.

⟨*Global Include Files*⟩ ≡
```
#include <algorithm>
#include <cinttypes>
#include <cmath>
#include <iostream>
#include <limits>
#include <memory>
#include <string>
#include <vector>
```

Physically Based Rendering: From Theory To Implementation.
http://dx.doi.org/10.1016/B978-0-12-800645-0.50022-1

Almost all floating-point values in pbrt are declared as Floats. (The only exception is a few cases where a 32-bit float or a 64-bit double is specifically needed (e.g., when saving binary values to files). Whether a Float is actually a float or a double is determined at compile time with the PBRT_FLOAT_AS_DOUBLE macro; this makes it possible to build versions of pbrt using either representation. 32-bit floats almost always have sufficient precision for ray tracing, but it's helpful to be able to switch to double for numerically tricky situations as well as to verify that rounding error with floats isn't causing errors for a given scene.

⟨*Global Forward Declarations*⟩ +≡
```
#ifdef PBRT_FLOAT_AS_DOUBLE
typedef double Float;
#else
typedef float Float;
#endif // PBRT_FLOAT_AS_DOUBLE
```

A.1.1 UTILITY FUNCTIONS

A few short mathematical functions are useful throughout pbrt.

Clamping

Clamp() clamps the given value val to lie between the values low and high. For convenience Clamp() allows the types of the values giving the extent to be different than the type being clamped (but its implementation requires that implicit conversion is legal to the type being clamped). By being implemented this way, the implementation allows calls like Clamp(floatValue, 0, 1) which would otherwise be disallowed by C++'s template type resolution rules.

⟨*Global Inline Functions*⟩ +≡
```
template <typename T, typename U, typename V>
inline T Clamp(T val, U low, V high) {
    if (val < low) return low;
    else if (val > high) return high;
    else return val;
}
```

Modulus

Mod() computes the remainder of *a/b*. pbrt has its own version of this (rather than using %) in order to provide the behavior that the modulus of a negative number is always positive. Starting with C++11, the behavior of % has been specified to return a negative value in this case, so that the identity (a/b)*b + a%b == a holds.

⟨*Global Inline Functions*⟩ +≡
```
template <typename T> inline T Mod(T a, T b) {
    T result = a - (a/b) * b;
    return (T)((result < 0) ? result + b : result);
}
```

A specialization for Floats calls out to the corresponding standard library function.

⟨*Global Inline Functions*⟩ +≡
```
template <> inline Float Mod(Float a, Float b) {
    return std::fmod(a, b);
}
```

Useful Constants

A number of constants, most of them related to π, are used enough that it's worth having them easily available.

⟨*Global Constants*⟩ +≡
```
static const Float Pi     = 3.14159265358979323846;
static const Float InvPi  = 0.31830988618379067154;
static const Float Inv2Pi = 0.15915494309189533577;
static const Float Inv4Pi = 0.07957747154594766788;
static const Float PiOver2 = 1.57079632679489661923;
static const Float PiOver4 = 0.78539816339744830961;
static const Float Sqrt2  = 1.41421356237309504880;
```

Converting between Angle Measures

Two simple functions convert from angles expressed in degrees to radians, and vice versa:

⟨*Global Inline Functions*⟩ +≡
```
inline Float Radians(Float deg) {
    return (Pi / 180) * deg;
}
inline Float Degrees(Float rad) {
    return (180 / Pi) * rad;
}
```

Base-2 Operations

Because the math library doesn't provide a base-2 logarithm function, we provide one here, using the identity $\log_2(x) = \log x / \log 2$.

⟨*Global Inline Functions*⟩ +≡
```
inline Float Log2(Float x) {
    const Float invLog2 = 1.442695040888963387004650940071;
    return std::log(x) * invLog2;
}
```

It's also useful to be able to compute an integer base-2 logarithm. Rather than computing an (expensive) floating-point logarithm and converting to an integer, it's much more efficient to count the number of leading zeros up to the first one in the 32-bit binary representation of the value and then subtract this value from 31, which gives the index of the first bit set, which is in turn the integer base-2 logarithm. (This efficiency comes in part from the fact that most CPUs have an instruction to count these zeros.)

The code here uses the __builtin_clz() intrinsic, which is available in the g++ and clang compilers; _BitScanReverse() is used to implement similar functionality with MSVC in code that isn't shown here.

Float 1062
Pi 1063

⟨*Global Inline Functions*⟩ +≡
```
inline int Log2Int(uint32_t v) {
    return 31 - __builtin_clz(v);
}
```

There are clever tricks that can be used to efficiently determine if a given integer is an exact power of 2, or round an integer up to the next higher (or equal) power of 2. (It's worthwhile to take a minute and work through for yourself how these two functions work.)

⟨*Global Inline Functions*⟩ +≡
```
template <typename T> inline bool IsPowerOf2(T v) {
    return v && !(v & (v - 1));
}
```

⟨*Global Inline Functions*⟩ +≡
```
inline int32_t RoundUpPow2(int32_t v) {
    v--;
    v |= v >> 1;    v |= v >> 2;
    v |= v >> 4;    v |= v >> 8;
    v |= v >> 16;
    return v+1;
}
```

A variant of RoundUpPow2() for int64_t is also provided but isn't included in the text here.

Some of the low-discrepancy sampling code in Chapter 7 needs to efficiently count the number of trailing zeros in the binary representation of a value; CountTrailingZeros() is a wrapper around a compiler-specific intrinsic that maps to a single instruction on most architectures.

⟨*Global Inline Functions*⟩ +≡
```
inline int CountTrailingZeros(uint32_t v) {
    return __builtin_ctz(v);
}
```

Interval Search

FindInterval() is a helper function that emulates the behavior of std::upper_bound(), but uses a function object to get values at various indices instead of requiring access to an actual array. This way, it becomes possible to bisect arrays that are procedurally generated, such as those interpolated from point samples. The implementation here also adds some bounds checking for corner cases (e.g., making sure that a valid interval is selected even in the case the predicate evaluates to true or false for all entries), which would normally have to follow a call to std::upper_bound().

⟨*Global Inline Functions*⟩ +≡

```
template <typename Predicate> int FindInterval(int size,
        const Predicate &pred) {
    int first = 0, len = size;
    while (len > 0) {
        int half = len >> 1, middle = first + half;
        ⟨Bisect range based on value of pred at middle 1065⟩
    }
    return Clamp(first - 1, 0, size - 2);
}
```

⟨*Bisect range based on value of* pred *at* middle⟩ ≡   **1065**

```
if (pred(middle)) {
    first = middle + 1;
    len -= half + 1;
} else
    len = half;
```

A.1.2 PSEUDO-RANDOM NUMBERS

pbrt uses an implementation of the PCG pseudo-random number generator (O'Neill 2014) to generate pseudo-random numbers. This generator is one of the best random number generators currently known. Not only does it pass a variety of rigorous statistical tests that have been the bane of earlier pseudo-random number generators, but its implementation is also extremely efficient.

We wrap its implementation in a small random number generator class, RNG. Doing so allows us to use it with slightly less verbose calls throughout the rest of the system. Random number generator implementation is an esoteric art; therefore, we will not include or discuss the implementation here but will describe the APIs provided.

The RNG class provides two constructors. The first, which takes no arguments, sets the internal state to reasonable defaults. The second takes a single argument that selects a sequence of pseudo-random values.

The PCG random number generator actually allows the user to provide two 64-bit values to configure its operation: one chooses from one of 2^{63} different sequences of 2^{64} random numbers, while the second effectively selects a starting point within such a sequence. Many pseudo-random number generators only allow this second form of configuration, which alone isn't as good: having independent non-overlapping sequences of values rather than different starting points in a single sequence provides greater non-uniformity in the generated values.

For pbrt's needs, selecting different sequences is sufficient, so the RNG implementation doesn't provide a mechanism to also select the starting point within a sequence.

RNG 1065
RNG::SetSequence() 1066

⟨*RNG Public Methods*⟩ ≡

```
RNG();
RNG(uint64_t sequenceIndex) { SetSequence(sequenceIndex); }
```

RNGs shouldn't be used in pbrt without either providing an initial sequence index via the constructor or a call to the SetSequence() method; otherwise there's risk that different parts of the system will inadvertently use correlated sequences of pseudo-random values, which in turn could cause surprising errors.

⟨*RNG Public Methods*⟩ +≡
```
void SetSequence(uint64_t sequenceIndex);
```

There are two variants of the UniformUInt32() method. The first returns a pseudo-random number in the range $[0, 2^{32} - 1]$.

⟨*RNG Public Methods*⟩ +≡
```
uint32_t UniformUInt32();
```

The second returns a value uniformly distributed in the range $[0, b - 1]$ given a bound b. The last two versions of pbrt effectively used UniformUInt32() % b for this second computation. That approach is subtly flawed—in the case that b doesn't evenly divide 2^{32}, then there is slightly higher probability of choosing values in the sub-range $[0, 2^{32} \bmod b]$.

The implementation here first computes the above remainder $2^{32} \bmod b$ efficiently using only 32 bit arithmetic and stores it in the variable threshold. Then, if the pseudo-random value returned by UniformUInt32() is less than threshold, it is discarded and a new value is generated. The resulting distribution of values has a uniform distribution after the modulus operation, giving a uniformly distributed sample value.

⟨*RNG Public Methods*⟩ +≡
```
uint32_t UniformUInt32(uint32_t b) {
    uint32_t threshold = (~b + 1u) % b;
    while (true) {
        uint32_t r = UniformUInt32();
        if (r >= threshold)
            return r % b;
    }
}
```

UniformFloat() generates a pseudo-random floating-point number in the half-open interval $[0, 1)$.

⟨*RNG Public Methods*⟩ +≡
```
Float UniformFloat() {
    return std::min(OneMinusEpsilon, UniformUInt32() * 0x1p-32f);
}
```

A.2 IMAGE FILE INPUT AND OUTPUT

Many image file formats have been developed over the years, but for pbrt's purposes we are mainly interested in those that support imagery represented by floating-point pixel values. In particular, the images generated by pbrt will often have a large dynamic range; such formats are crucial for being able to store the computed radiance values directly.

Float 1062
OneMinusEpsilon 417
RNG::UniformUInt32() 1066

Legacy image file formats, such as those that store 8 bits of data for red, green, and blue components to represent colors in the range [0, 1], aren't a good fit for physically based rendering needs.

pbrt supports two floating-point image file formats: OpenEXR and PFM. OpenEXR is a floating-point file format originally designed at Industrial Light and Magic for use in movie productions (Kainz et al. 2004). We chose this format because it has a clean design, is easy to use, and has first-class support for floating-point image data. Libraries that read and write OpenEXR images are freely available, and support for the format is available in many other tools.

PFM is a floating-point format based on an extension to the PPM file format; it is very easily read and written, though it isn't as widely supported as OpenEXR. Unlike OpenEXR, it doesn't support compression, so files may be fairly large.

For convenience, pbrt also has support to read and write TGA format files as well as support to read and write PNG images. Neither of these is a high-dynamic-range format like OpenEXR, but both are convenient, especially as input formats for low-dynamic-range texture maps.

The ReadImage() function takes the filename to read from and a pointer to a Point2i that will be initialized with the image resolution. It returns a pointer to the start of a freshly allocated array of RGBSpectrum objects. It will read the given file as an OpenEXR, PFM, PNG, or TGA file, depending on the suffix of the filename.

⟨*ImageIO Declarations*⟩ ≡
```
std::unique_ptr<RGBSpectrum[]> ReadImage(const std::string &name,
    Point2i *resolution);
```

ReadImage() uses RGBSpectrum for the return values—not Spectrum. The primary client of this function is the image texture mapping code in pbrt, which stores texture maps as RGBSpectrum values, even when pbrt is compiled to do full-spectral rendering, so returning RGBSpectrum values is a natural approach. (We also made this decision under the expectation that the image files being read would be in RGB or another three-channel format, so that returning RGB values wouldn't discard spectral information; if calling code wants to store full Spectrum values, then it can convert from RGB to the full-spectral representation itself.) If pbrt was extended to support a full-spectral input image format for textures, then a variant of this function that did return Spectrum values would be advisable.

The WriteImage() function takes a filename to be written, a pointer to the beginning of the pixel data, and information about the resolution of the image. The pixel data should be organized as interleaved RGBRGB . . . values. Like ReadImage(), it uses the suffix of the given filename to determine which image format to use.

With WriteImage(), it's possible to specify that the pixels being written represent a sub-region of a larger image. Some image formats (e.g., OpenEXR) can record this information in the image file header, which in turn makes it easy to assemble separately rendered subimages into a single image. The totalResolution parameter gives the total resolution of the overall image that the given pixel values are part of, and outputBounds gives the pixel bounding box that the given pixels cover. outputBounds should be within the range $(0, 0) \rightarrow$ totalResolution and the number of RGB pixel values pointed to by rgb should be equal to outputBounds.Area().

If a non-floating-point image format is being used for output, pixel values are converted to the sRGB representation (Section 10.4.1) and clamped to the range $[0, 255]$ before being written to the file.

⟨*ImageIO Declarations*⟩ +≡
```
void WriteImage(const std::string &name, const Float *rgb,
    const Bounds2i &outputBounds, const Point2i &totalResolution);
```

We will not show the code that interfaces with the various image-writing libraries or the code that implements file-format-specific I/O. This code can be found in the file core/imageio.cpp and the directory ext/.[1]

A.3 COMMUNICATING WITH THE USER

A number of functions and classes are useful to mediate communicating information to the user. In addition to consolidating functionality like printing progress bars, hiding user communication behind a small API like the one here also permits easy modification of the communication mechanisms. For example, if pbrt were embedded in an application that had a graphical user interface, errors might be reported via a dialog box or a routine provided by the parent application. If printf() calls were strewn throughout the system, it would be more difficult to make the two systems work together well.

A.3.1 ERROR REPORTING

pbrt provides four functions for reporting anomalous conditions. In order of increasing severity, they are Info(), Warning(), Error(), and Severe(). These functions are defined in the files core/error.h and core/error.cpp. All of them take a formatting string as their first argument and a variable number of additional arguments providing values for the format. The syntax is identical to that used by the printf family of functions. For example, if the variable rayNum has type int, then the following call could be made:

```
Info("Now tracing ray number %d", rayNum);
```

core/pbrt.h includes this header file, as these functions are useful to have available in almost all parts of the system.

⟨*Global Include Files*⟩ +≡
```
#include "error.h"
```

---

1 The TGA implementation is based on open source TGA code by Emil Mikulic; Jiawen "Kevin" Chen provided the PFM reader and writer; PNG files are handled using the lodepng library.

We will not show the implementation of these functions here because they are a straight-forward application of the C++ variable argument processing functions that in turn calls a common function to print the full error string. For sufficiently severe errors, the program aborts.

pbrt also has its own version of the standard assert() macro, named Assert(). It checks that the given expression's value evaluates to true; if not, Severe() is called with information about the location of the assertion failure. Assert() is used for basic sanity checks where failure indicates little possibility of recovery. In general, assertions should be used to detect internal bugs in the code, not expected error conditions (such as invalid scene file input), because the message printed will likely be cryptic to anyone other than the developer.

⟨*Global Inline Functions*⟩ +≡
```
#ifdef NDEBUG
#define Assert(expr) ((void)0)
#else
#define Assert(expr) \
    ((expr) ? (void)0 : \
        Severe("Assertion \"%s\" failed in %s, line %d", \
                #expr, __FILE__, __LINE__))
#endif // NDEBUG
```

A.3.2 REPORTING PROGRESS

The ProgressReporter class gives the user feedback about how much of a task has been completed and how much longer it is expected to take. For example, implementations of the various Integrator::Render() methods generally use a ProgressReporter to show rendering progress. The implementation prints a row of plus signs, the elapsed time, and the estimated remaining time. Its implementation is in the files core/progressreporter.h and core/progressreporter.cpp.

The constructor takes the total number of units of work to be done (e.g., the total number of camera rays that will be traced) and a short string describing the task being performed.

⟨*ProgressReporter Public Methods*⟩ ≡
```
ProgressReporter(int64_t totalWork, const std::string &title);
```

Once the ProgressReporter has been created, each call to its Update() method signifies that one unit of work has been completed. An optional integer value can be passed to indicate that multiple units have been done.

⟨*ProgressReporter Public Methods*⟩ +≡
```
void Update(int64_t num = 1);
```

The ProgressReporter::Done() method should be called when all of the work being measured is complete; in turn, it lets the user know that the task is complete.

⟨*ProgressReporter Public Methods*⟩ +≡
```
void Done();
```

A.3.3 SIMPLE FLOAT FILE READER

A number of places in the pbrt code need to read text files that store a series of floating-point values. Examples include the code that reads measured spectral distribution data and the code that reads lens description files in Section 6.4. Both use the `ReadFloatFile()` function, which parses text files of whitespace-separated numbers, returning the values found in the given vector. The parsing code ignores all text after a hash mark (#) to the end of its line to allow comments.

⟨*floatfile.h**⟩ ≡
```
bool ReadFloatFile(const char *filename, std::vector<Float> *values);
```

A.4 MEMORY MANAGEMENT

Memory management is often a complex issue in a system written in a language without garbage collection. The situation is mostly simple in pbrt, since most dynamic memory allocation is done as the scene description file is parsed, and most of this memory remains in use until rendering is finished. Nevertheless, there are a few issues related to memory management—most of them performance related—that warrant classes and utility routines to address them.

A.4.1 VARIABLE STACK ALLOCATION

Sometimes it is necessary to allocate a variable amount of memory that will be used temporarily in a single function but isn't needed after the function returns. If only a small amount of memory is needed, the overhead of new and delete (or malloc() and free()) may be high relative to the amount of actual computation being done. Instead, it is frequently more efficient to use alloca(), which allocates memory on the stack with just a few machine instructions. This memory is automatically deallocated when the function exits, which also saves bookkeeping work in the routine that uses it.

alloca() is an extremely useful tool, but there are two pitfalls to be aware of when using it. First, because the memory is deallocated when the function that called alloca() returns, the pointer must not be returned from the function or stored in a data structure with a longer lifetime than the function that allocated it. (However, the pointer may be passed to functions called by the allocating function.) Second, stack size is limited, and so alloca() shouldn't be used for more than a few kilobytes of storage. Unfortunately, there is no way to detect the error condition when more space is requested from alloca() than is available on the stack, so it's important to be conservative with its use.

pbrt provides a macro that makes it easy to allocate space for a given number of objects of a given type.[2]

Float 1062

---

2   A moment's thought should make clear why it's not possible to implement this functionality with an inline function.

⟨*Global Macros*⟩ ≡
```
#define ALLOCA(TYPE, COUNT) (TYPE *)alloca((COUNT) * sizeof(TYPE))
```

A.4.2 CACHE-FRIENDLY MEMORY USAGE

The speed at which memory can respond to read requests has historically been getting faster at a rate of roughly 10% per year, while the computational capabilities of modern CPUs has been growing much more quickly. As such, a CPU will typically have to wait a hundred or so execution cycles to read from main memory. The CPU is usually idle for much of this time, so a substantial amount of its computational potential may be lost.

One of the most effective techniques to address this problem is the judicious use of small, fast cache memory located in the CPU itself. The cache holds recently accessed data and is able to service memory requests much faster than main memory, thus greatly reducing the frequency of stalls in the CPU.

Because of the high penalty for accessing main memory, designing algorithms and data structures that make good use of the cache can substantially improve overall system performance. This section will discuss general programming techniques for improving cache performance. These techniques are used in many parts of pbrt, particularly the KdTreeAccel, BVHAccel, MIPMap, and Film. We assume that the reader has a basic familiarity with computer architecture and caching technology; readers needing a review are directed to a computer architecture text such as Hennessy and Patterson (1997). In particular, the reader should be generally familiar with topics like cache lines, cache associativity, and the difference between compulsory, capacity, and conflict misses.

One easy way to reduce the number of cache misses incurred by pbrt is to make sure that some key memory allocations are aligned with the blocks of memory that the cache manages. (pbrt's overall performance was improved by approximately 3% when allocation for the kd-tree accelerator in Section 4.4 was rewritten to use cache-aligned allocation.) Figure A.1 illustrates the basic technique. The AllocAligned() and FreeAligned() functions

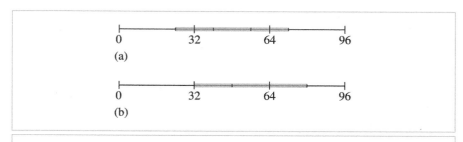

Figure A.1: The Layout of Three 16-Byte Objects in Memory on a System with 32-Byte Cache Lines. Cache-aligned memory allocation ensures that the address returned by the memory allocation routines are aligned with the start of a cache line. (a) The starting address is not cache aligned; the first and last of the three objects span two cache lines, such that two cache misses may be incurred when accessing their elements. (b) The starting address is cache aligned, guaranteeing that a maximum of one cache miss will be incurred per object.

provide an interface to allocate and release cache-aligned memory blocks. If the preprocessor constant PBRT_L1_CACHE_LINE_SIZE is not set, a default cache line size of 64 bytes
is used, which is representative of many current architectures.

⟨*Global Constants*⟩ +≡
```
#ifndef PBRT_L1_CACHE_LINE_SIZE
#define PBRT_L1_CACHE_LINE_SIZE 64
#endif
```

Unfortunately there aren't portable methods to allocate memory aligned to a particular
granularity. Therefore AllocAligned() must call various operating-system-specific functions to do these allocations.

⟨*Memory Allocation Functions*⟩ ≡
```
void *AllocAligned(size_t size) {
#if defined(PBRT_IS_WINDOWS)
    return _aligned_malloc(size, PBRT_L1_CACHE_LINE_SIZE);
#elif defined (PBRT_IS_OPENBSD) || defined(PBRT_IS_OSX)
    void *ptr;
    if (posix_memalign(&ptr, PBRT_L1_CACHE_LINE_SIZE, size) != 0)
        ptr = nullptr;
    return ptr;
#else
    return memalign(PBRT_L1_CACHE_LINE_SIZE, size);
#endif
}
```

A convenience routine is also provided for allocating a collection of objects so that code
like AllocAligned<Foo>(n) can be written to allocate an array of n instances of type Foo.

⟨*Memory Declarations*⟩ +≡
```
template <typename T> T *AllocAligned(size_t count) {
    return (T *)AllocAligned(count * sizeof(T));
}
```

The routine for freeing aligned memory calls the corresponding operating-system-
specific routine. We won't include its implementation here.

⟨*Memory Declarations*⟩ +≡
```
void FreeAligned(void *);
```

Another family of techniques for improving cache performance is based on reorganizing
data structures themselves. For example, using bit fields to reduce the size of a frequently
used data structure can be helpful. This approach improves the *spatial locality* of memory
access at run time, since code that accesses multiple packed values won't incur more than
one cache miss to get them all. Furthermore, by reducing the overall size of the structure,
this technique can reduce capacity misses if fewer cache lines are consequently needed to
store the structure.

PBRT_L1_CACHE_LINE_SIZE 1072

If not all of the elements of a structure are frequently accessed, there are a few possible strategies to improve cache performance. For example, if the structure has a size of 128 bytes and the computer has 64-byte cache lines, two cache misses may be needed to access it. If the commonly used fields are collected into the first 64 bytes rather than being spread throughout, then no more than one cache miss will be incurred when only those fields are needed (Truong, Bodin, and Seznec 1998).

A related technique is *splitting*, where data structures are split into "hot" and "cold" parts, each stored in separate regions of memory. For example, given an array of some structure type, we can split it into two arrays, one for the more frequently accessed (or "hot") portions and one for the less frequently accessed (or "cold") portions. This way, cold data doesn't displace useful information in the cache except when it is actually needed.

Cache-friendly programming is a complex engineering task, and we will not cover all the variations here. Readers are directed to the "Further Reading" section of this appendix for more information.

A.4.3 ARENA-BASED ALLOCATION

Conventional wisdom says that the system's memory allocation routines (e.g., malloc() and new()) are slow and that custom allocation routines for objects that are frequently allocated or freed can provide a measurable performance gain. However, this conventional wisdom seems to be wrong. Wilson et al. (1995), Johnstone and Wilson (1999), and Berger, Zorn, and McKinley (2001, 2002) all investigated the performance impact of memory allocation in real-world applications and found that custom allocators almost always result in *worse* performance than a well-tuned generic system memory allocation, in both execution time and memory use.

One type of custom allocation technique that has proved to be useful in some cases is *arena-based allocation*, which allows the user to quickly allocate objects from a large contiguous region of memory. In this scheme, individual objects are never explicitly freed; the entire region of memory is released when the lifetime of all of the allocated objects ends. This type of memory allocator is a natural fit for many of the objects in pbrt.

There are two main advantages to arena-based allocation. First, allocation is extremely fast, usually just requiring a pointer increment. Second, it can improve locality of reference and lead to fewer cache misses, since the allocated objects are contiguous in memory. A more general dynamic memory allocator will typically prepend a bookkeeping structure to each block it returns, which adversely affects locality of reference.

pbrt provides the MemoryArena class to implement this approach; it supports variable-sized allocation from the arena.

The MemoryArena quickly allocates memory for objects of variable size by handing out pointers into a preallocated block. It does not support freeing of individual blocks of memory, only freeing of all of the memory in the arena at once. Thus, it is useful when a number of allocations need to be done quickly and all of the allocated objects have similar lifetimes.

MemoryArena 1074

⟨*Memory Declarations*⟩ +≡
```
class MemoryArena {
public:
    ⟨MemoryArena Public Methods 1074⟩
private:
    ⟨MemoryArena Private Data 1074⟩
};
```

MemoryArena allocates memory in chunks of size MemoryArena::blockSize, the value of
which is set by a parameter passed to the constructor. If no value is provided to the
constructor, a default of 256 kB is used.

⟨*MemoryArena Public Methods*⟩ ≡   1074
```
MemoryArena(size_t blockSize = 262144) : blockSize(blockSize) { }
```

⟨*MemoryArena Private Data*⟩ ≡   1074
```
const size_t blockSize;
```

The implementation maintains a pointer to the current block of memory, currentBlock,
and the offset of the first free location in the block, currentPos. currentAllocSize stores
the total size of the currentBlock allocation; it generally has the value blockSize but is
larger in certain cases (discussed in the following).

⟨*MemoryArena Private Data*⟩ +≡   1074
```
size_t currentBlockPos = 0, currentAllocSize = 0;
uint8_t *currentBlock = nullptr;
```

To service an allocation request, the allocation routine first rounds the requested amount
of memory up so that it meets the computer's word alignment requirements.[3] The routine then checks to see if the current block has enough space to handle the request,
allocating a new block if necessary. Finally, it returns the pointer and updates the current
block offset.

⟨*MemoryArena Public Methods*⟩ +≡   1074
```
void *Alloc(size_t nBytes) {
    ⟨Round up nBytes to minimum machine alignment 1075⟩
    if (currentBlockPos + nBytes > currentAllocSize) {
        ⟨Add current block to usedBlocks list 1075⟩
        ⟨Get new block of memory for MemoryArena 1075⟩
    }
    void *ret = currentBlock + currentBlockPos;
    currentBlockPos += nBytes;
    return ret;
}
```

Most modern computer architectures impose alignment requirements on the positioning
of objects in memory. For example, it is frequently a requirement that float values be

MemoryArena 1074

MemoryArena::blockSize 1074

MemoryArena::currentAllocSize
  1074

MemoryArena::currentBlock
  1074

MemoryArena::currentBlockPos
  1074

---

3   Some systems (such as those based on Intel® processors) can handle non-word-aligned memory accesses, but this is usually
    substantially times slower than word-aligned memory reads or writes. Other architectures do not support this at all and will
    generate a bus error if a nonaligned access is performed.

stored at memory locations that are word aligned. To be safe, the implementation always hands out 16-byte-aligned pointers (i.e., their address is a multiple of 16).

⟨*Round up* nBytes *to minimum machine alignment*⟩ ≡   1074
```
nBytes = ((nBytes + 15) & (~15));
```

If a new block of memory must be dynamically allocated to service an allocation request, the MemoryArena stores the pointer to the current block of memory in the usedBlocks list so that it is not lost. Later, when MemoryArena::Reset() is called, it will be able to reuse the block for the next series of allocations.

⟨*Add current block to* usedBlocks *list*⟩ ≡   1074
```
if (currentBlock) {
    usedBlocks.push_back(std::make_pair(currentAllocSize, currentBlock));
    currentBlock = nullptr;
}
```

MemoryArena uses two linked lists to hold pointers to blocks of memory that have been fully used as well as available blocks that were previously allocated but aren't currently in use.

⟨*MemoryArena Private Data*⟩ +≡   1074
```
std::list<std::pair<size_t, uint8_t *>> usedBlocks, availableBlocks;
```

If a block of memory of suitable size isn't available from availableBlocks, a new one is allocated.

⟨*Get new block of memory for* MemoryArena⟩ ≡   1074
```
⟨Try to get memory block from availableBlocks 1075⟩
if (!currentBlock) {
    currentAllocSize = std::max(nBytes, blockSize);
    currentBlock = AllocAligned<uint8_t>(currentAllocSize);
}
currentBlockPos = 0;
```

The allocation routine first checks to see if there are any already allocated free blocks in availableBlocks.

⟨*Try to get memory block from* availableBlocks⟩ ≡   1075
```
for (auto iter = availableBlocks.begin(); iter != availableBlocks.end();
         ++iter) {
    if (iter->first >= nBytes) {
        currentAllocSize = iter->first;
        currentBlock = iter->second;
        availableBlocks.erase(iter);
        break;
    }
}
```

The MemoryArena also provides a convenience template method to allocate an array of objects of the given type.

⟨*MemoryArena Public Methods*⟩ +≡　　　　　　　　　　　　　　　　　　1074
```
template<typename T> T *Alloc(size_t n = 1, bool runConstructor = true) {
    T *ret = (T *)Alloc(n * sizeof(T));
    if (runConstructor)
        for (size_t i = 0; i < n; ++i)
            new (&ret[i]) T();
    return ret;
}
```

When the user is done with all of the memory, the arena resets its offset in the current block and moves all of the memory from the usedBlocks list onto the availableBlocks list.

⟨*MemoryArena Public Methods*⟩ +≡　　　　　　　　　　　　　　　　　　1074
```
void Reset() {
    currentBlockPos = 0;
    availableBlocks.splice(availableBlocks.begin(), usedBlocks);
}
```

A.4.4 BLOCKED 2D ARRAYS

In C++, 2D arrays are arranged in memory so that entire rows of values are contiguous in memory, as shown in Figure A.2(a). This is not always an optimal layout, however; for such an array indexed by (u, v), nearby (u, v) array positions will often map to distant memory locations. For all but the smallest arrays, the adjacent values in the v direction will be on different cache lines; thus, if the cost of a cache miss is incurred to reference a value at a particular location (u, v), there is no chance that handling that miss will also load into memory the data for values $(u, v + 1)$, $(u, v - 1)$, and so on. Thus, spatially coherent array indices in (u, v) do not necessarily lead to the spatially coherent memory access patterns that modern memory caches depend on.

To address this problem, the BlockedArray template implements a generic 2D array of values, with the items ordered in memory using a *blocked* memory layout, as shown in Figure A.2(b). The array is subdivided into square blocks of a small fixed size that is a power of 2. Each block is laid out row by row, as if it were a separate 2D C++ array. This organization substantially improves the memory coherence of 2D array references in practice and requires only a small amount of additional computation to determine the memory address for a particular position (Lam, Rothberg, and Wolf 1991).

To ensure that the block size is a power of 2, the caller specifies its logarithm (base 2), which is given by the template parameter logBlockSize.

⟨*Memory Declarations*⟩ +≡
```
template <typename T, int logBlockSize> class BlockedArray {
public:
    ⟨BlockedArray Public Methods 1077⟩
private:
    ⟨BlockedArray Private Data 1078⟩
};
```

BlockedArray 1076
MemoryArena::currentBlockPos
1074

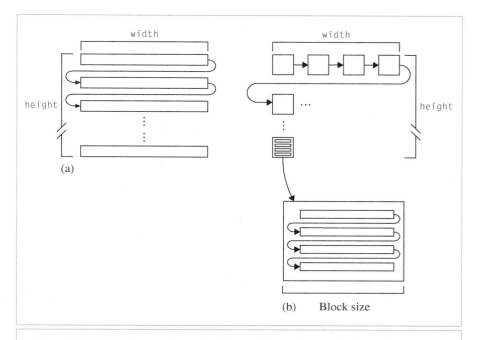

Figure A.2: (a) In C++, the natural layout for a 2D array of size `width*height` is a block of `width*height` entries, where the (u, v) array element is at the `u+v*width` offset. (b) A blocked array has been split into smaller square blocks, each of which is laid out linearly. Although it is slightly more complex to find the memory location associated with a given (u, v) array position in the blocked scheme, the improvement in cache performance due to more coherent memory access patterns often more than makes up for this in overall faster performance.

The constructor allocates space for the array and optionally initializes its values from a pointer to a standard C++ array. Because the array size may not be an exact multiple of the block size, it may be necessary to round up the size in one or both directions to find the total amount of memory needed for the blocked array. The `BlockedArray::RoundUp()` method rounds both dimensions up to be a multiple of the block size.

⟨*BlockedArray Public Methods*⟩ ≡   **1076**

```
BlockedArray(int uRes, int vRes, const T *d = nullptr)
    : uRes(uRes), vRes(vRes), uBlocks(RoundUp(uRes) >> logBlockSize) {
    int nAlloc = RoundUp(uRes) * RoundUp(vRes);
    data = AllocAligned<T>(nAlloc);
    for (int i = 0; i < nAlloc; ++i)
        new (&data[i]) T();
    if (d)
        for (int v = 0; v < vRes; ++v)
            for (int u = 0; u < uRes; ++u)
                (*this)(u, v) = d[v * uRes + u];
}
```

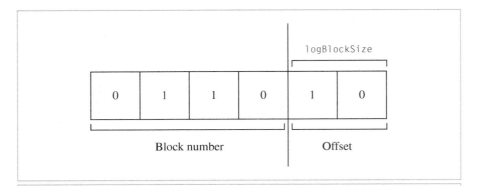

Figure A.3: Given a binary array coordinate, the (u, v) block number that it is in can be found by shifting off the logBlockSize low-order bits for both u and v. For example, with a logBlockSize of 2 and thus a block size of 4, we can see that this correctly maps 1D array positions from 0 to 3 to block 0, 4 to 7 to block 1, and so on. To find the offset within the particular block, it is just necessary to mask off the high-order bits, leaving the logBlockSize low-order bits. Because the block size is a power of two, these computations can all be done with efficient bit operations.

⟨*BlockedArray Private Data*⟩ ≡   **1076**
```
T *data;
const int uRes, vRes, uBlocks;
```

⟨*BlockedArray Public Methods*⟩ +≡   **1076**
```
constexpr int BlockSize() const { return 1 << logBlockSize; }
int RoundUp(int x) const {
    return (x + BlockSize() - 1) & ~(BlockSize() - 1);
}
```

For convenience, the BlockedArray can also report its size in each dimension:

⟨*BlockedArray Public Methods*⟩ +≡   **1076**
```
int uSize() const { return uRes; }
int vSize() const { return vRes; }
```

Looking up a value from a particular (u, v) position in the array requires some indexing work to find the memory location for that value. There are two steps to this process: finding which block the value is in and finding its offset within that block. Because the block sizes are always powers of 2, the logBlockSize low-order bits in each of the u and v array positions give the offset within the block, and the high-order bits give the block number (Figure A.3).

⟨*BlockedArray Public Methods*⟩ +≡   **1076**
```
int Block(int a) const { return a >> logBlockSize; }
int Offset(int a) const { return (a & (BlockSize() - 1)); }
```

Then, given the block number (b_u, b_v) and the offset within the block (o_u, o_v), it is necessary to compute what memory location this maps to in the blocked array layout. First consider the task of finding the starting address of the block; since the blocks are laid out row by row, this corresponds to the block number bu + bv * uBlocks, where uBlocks is the number of blocks in the u direction. Because each block has `BlockSize()*BlockSize()` values in it, the product of the block number and this value gives us the offset to the start of the block. We then just need to account for the additional offset from the start of the block, which is `ou + ov * BlockSize()`.

⟨*BlockedArray Public Methods*⟩ +≡   1076
```
T &operator()(int u, int v) {
    int bu = Block(u), bv = Block(v);
    int ou = Offset(u), ov = Offset(v);
    int offset = BlockSize() * BlockSize() * (uBlocks * bv + bu);
    offset += BlockSize() * ov + ou;
    return data[offset];
}
```

A.5 MATHEMATICAL ROUTINES

This section describes a number of useful mathematical functions and classes that support basic operations in pbrt, such as solving small linear systems, manipulating matrices, and linear interpolation.

The Lerp() function linearly interpolates between the two provided values.

⟨*Global Inline Functions*⟩ +≡
```
inline Float Lerp(Float t, Float v1, Float v2) {
    return (1 - t) * v1 + t * v2;
}
```

A.5.1 SOLVING QUADRATIC EQUATIONS

The Quadratic() function finds solutions of the quadratic equation $at^2 + bt + c = 0$; the Boolean return value indicates whether solutions were found.

⟨*Global Inline Functions*⟩ +≡
```
inline bool Quadratic(Float a, Float b, Float c, Float *t0, Float *t1) {
    ⟨Find quadratic discriminant 1079⟩
    ⟨Compute quadratic t values 1080⟩
}
```

The implementation always uses double-precision floating-point values regardless of the type of Float in order to return a result with minimal floating-point error. If the discriminant ($b^2 - 4ac$) is negative, then there are no real roots and the function returns false.

⟨*Find quadratic discriminant*⟩ ≡   1079
```
double discrim = (double)b * (double)b - 4 * (double)a * (double)c;
if (discrim < 0) return false;
double rootDiscrim = std::sqrt(discrim);
```

The usual version of the quadratic equation can give poor numerical precision when $b \approx \pm\sqrt{b^2 - 4ac}$ due to cancellation error. It can be rewritten algebraically to a more stable form:

$$t_0 = \frac{q}{a}$$

$$t_1 = \frac{c}{q},$$

where

$$q = \begin{cases} -.5(b - \sqrt{b^2 - 4ac}) & b < 0, \\ -.5(b + \sqrt{b^2 - 4ac}) & \text{otherwise.} \end{cases}$$

⟨*Compute quadratic* t *values*⟩ ≡   1079
```
    double q;
    if (b < 0) q = -.5 * (b - rootDiscrim);
    else       q = -.5 * (b + rootDiscrim);
    *t0 = q / a;
    *t1 = c / q;
    if (*t0 > *t1) std::swap(*t0, *t1);
    return true;
```

A.5.2 2 × 2 LINEAR SYSTEMS

There are a number of places throughout pbrt where we need to solve a 2×2 linear system $Ax = B$ of the form

$$\begin{pmatrix} a_{00} & a_{01} \\ a_{10} & a_{11} \end{pmatrix} \begin{pmatrix} x_0 \\ x_1 \end{pmatrix} = \begin{pmatrix} b_0 \\ b_1 \end{pmatrix}$$

for values x_0 and x_1. The SolveLinearSystem2x2() routine finds the closed-form solution to such a system. It returns true if it was successful and false if the determinant of A is very small, indicating that the system is numerically ill-conditioned and either not solvable or likely to have unacceptable floating-point errors. In this case, no solution is returned.

⟨*Matrix4x4 Method Definitions*⟩ ≡
```
    bool SolveLinearSystem2x2(const Float A[2][2],
            const Float B[2], Float *x0, Float *x1) {
        Float det = A[0][0] * A[1][1] - A[0][1] * A[1][0];
        if (std::abs(det) < 1e-10f)
            return false;
        *x0 = (A[1][1] * B[0] - A[0][1] * B[1]) / det;
        *x1 = (A[0][0] * B[1] - A[1][0] * B[0]) / det;
        if (std::isnan(*x0) || std::isnan(*x1))
            return false;
        return true;
    }
```

Float 1062
Matrix4x4 1081
Transform 83

A.5.3 4 × 4 MATRICES

The Matrix4x4 structure provides a low-level representation of 4×4 matrices. It is an integral part of the Transform class.

⟨*Matrix4x4 Declarations*⟩ ≡
```
struct Matrix4x4 {
    ⟨Matrix4x4 Public Methods 1081⟩
    Float m[4][4];
};
```

The default constructor, not shown here, sets the matrix to the identity matrix. The Matrix4x4 implementation also provides constructors that allow the user to pass an array of floats or 16 individual floats to initialize a Matrix4x4:

⟨*Matrix4x4 Public Methods*⟩ ≡   1081
```
Matrix4x4(Float mat[4][4]);
Matrix4x4(Float t00, Float t01, Float t02, Float t03,
          Float t10, Float t11, Float t12, Float t13,
          Float t20, Float t21, Float t22, Float t23,
          Float t30, Float t31, Float t32, Float t33);
```

The implementations of operators that test for equality and inequality are straightforward and not included in the text here.

The Matrix4x4 class supports a few low-level matrix operations. For example, Transpose() returns a new matrix that is the transpose of the original matrix.

⟨*Matrix4x4 Method Definitions*⟩ +≡
```
Matrix4x4 Transpose(const Matrix4x4 &m) {
    return Matrix4x4(m.m[0][0], m.m[1][0], m.m[2][0], m.m[3][0],
                     m.m[0][1], m.m[1][1], m.m[2][1], m.m[3][1],
                     m.m[0][2], m.m[1][2], m.m[2][2], m.m[3][2],
                     m.m[0][3], m.m[1][3], m.m[2][3], m.m[3][3]);
}
```

The product of two matrices $\mathbf{M}_1$ and $\mathbf{M}_2$ is computed by setting the (i, j)th element of the result to the inner product of the ith row of $\mathbf{M}_1$ with the jth column of $\mathbf{M}_2$.

⟨*Matrix4x4 Public Methods*⟩ +≡   1081
```
static Matrix4x4 Mul(const Matrix4x4 &m1, const Matrix4x4 &m2) {
    Matrix4x4 r;
    for (int i = 0; i < 4; ++i)
        for (int j = 0; j < 4; ++j)
            r.m[i][j] = m1.m[i][0] * m2.m[0][j] +
                        m1.m[i][1] * m2.m[1][j] +
                        m1.m[i][2] * m2.m[2][j] +
                        m1.m[i][3] * m2.m[3][j];
    return r;
}
```

Finally, Inverse() returns the inverse of the matrix. The implementation (not shown here) uses a numerically stable Gauss–Jordan elimination routine to compute the inverse.

⟨*Matrix4x4 Public Methods*⟩ +≡   1081
```
friend Matrix4x4 Inverse(const Matrix4x4 &);
```

A.6 PARALLELISM

Section 1.4 introduced some basic principles of parallel programming and described their application to pbrt. Here, we'll go into more detail about performance issues related to multi-threading as well as describe the implementation of pbrt's ParallelFor() function, which is used throughout the system for parallel for loops, where different iterations of the loop can execute concurrently in different threads.

A.6.1 MEMORY COHERENCE MODELS AND PERFORMANCE

Cache coherence is a feature of all modern multicore CPUs; with it, memory writes by one processor are automatically visible to other processors. This is an incredibly useful feature; being able to assume it in the implementation of a system like pbrt is extremely helpful to the programmer. Understanding the subtleties and performance characteristics of this feature is important, however.

One potential issue is that other processors may not see writes to memory in the same order that the processor that performed the writes issued them. This can happen for two main reasons: the compiler's optimizer may have reordered write operations to improve performance, and the CPU hardware may write values to memory in a different order than the stream of executed machine instructions. In the single-threaded case, both of these are innocuous; by design, the compiler and hardware, respectively, ensure that it's impossible for a single thread of execution running the program to detect when these cases happen. This guarantee is not provided for multi-threaded code, however; doing so would impose a significant performance penalty, so hardware architectures leave handling this problem, when it matters, to software.

Memory barrier instructions can be used to ensure that all write instructions before the barrier are visible in memory before any subsequent instructions execute. In practice, we generally don't need to issue memory barrier instructions explicitly, since the thread synchronization calls used to build multi-threaded algorithms take care of this; they are defined to make sure that writes are visible so that if we are coordinating execution between multiple threads using these calls, then they have a consistent view of memory after synchronization points.

Although cache coherence is helpful to the programmer, it can sometimes impose a substantial performance penalty for data that is frequently modified and accessed by multiple processors. Read-only data has little penalty; copies of it can be stored in the local caches of all of the processors that are accessing it, allowing all of them the same performance benefits from the caches as in the single-threaded case. To understand the downside of taking too much advantage of cache coherence for read–write data, it's useful to understand how cache coherence is typically implemented on processors.

CPUs implement a *cache coherence protocol*, which is responsible for tracking the memory transactions issued by all of the processors in order to provide cache coherence. A classic such protocol is *MESI*, where the acronym represents the four states that each cache line can be in. Each processor stores the current state for each cache line in its local caches:

ParallelFor() 1088

- *Modified*—The current processor has written to the memory location, but the result is only stored in the cache—it's *dirty* and hasn't been written to main memory. No other processor has the location in its cache.
- *Exclusive*—The current processor is the only one with the data from the corresponding memory location in its cache. The value in the cache matches the value in memory.
- *Shared*—Multiple processors have the corresponding memory location in their caches, but they have only performed read operations.
- *Invalid*—The cache line doesn't hold valid data.

At system startup time, the caches are empty and all cache lines are in the invalid state. The first time a processor reads a memory location, the data for that location is loaded into cache and its cache line marked as being in the "exclusive" state. If another processor performs a memory read of a location that is in the "exclusive" state in another cache, then both caches record the state for the corresponding memory location to instead be "shared."

When a processor writes to a memory location, the performance of the write depends on the state of the corresponding cache line. If it's in the "exclusive" state and already in the writing processor's cache, then the write is cheap; the data is modified in the cache and the cache line's state is changed to "modified." (If it was already in the "modified" state, then the write is similarly efficient.) In these cases, the value will eventually be written to main memory, at which point the corresponding cache line returns to the "exclusive" state.

However, if a processor writes to a memory location that's in the "shared" state in its cache or is in the "modified" or "exclusive" state in another processor's cache, then expensive communication between the cores is required. All of this is handled transparently by the hardware, though it still has a performance impact. In this case, the writing processor must issue a *read for ownership* (RFO), which marks the memory location as invalid in the caches of any other processors; RFOs can cause stalls of tens or hundreds of cycles—a substantial penalty for a single memory write.

In general, we'd therefore like to avoid the situation of multiple processors concurrently writing to the same memory location as well as unnecessarily reading memory that another processor is writing to. An important case to be aware of is "false sharing," where a single cache line holds some read-only data and some data that is frequently modified. In this case, even if only a single processor is writing to the part of the cache line that is modified but many are reading from the read-only part, the overhead of frequent RFO operations will be unnecessarily incurred.

A situation where many processors might be concurrently trying to write to the same or nearby memory locations is when image sample values are accumulated into the final image. To ensure that image updates don't pay the RFO cost, each rendering thread in the ParallelFor() loop of the SamplerIntegrator creates a private FilmTile to use for accumulating sample values for the part of the image that it's working on; it is then free to modify the FilmTile pixel values without worrying about contention with other threads for those memory locations. Only when a portion of the image is finished is the

FilmTile 489
ParallelFor() 1088
SamplerIntegrator 25

tile merged into the main image, thus allowing the overhead of mutual exclusion and
RFO operations to be amortized over a smaller number of larger updates.

A.6.2 ATOMIC OPERATIONS

Recall from Section 1.4 that mutexes can be used to ensure that multiple threads don't
simultaneously try to update the same memory locations. However, modern CPUs and
GPUs also provide specialized hardware instructions to perform certain operations *atomically*, generating consistent results when multiple threads use them to modify the same
location concurrently. When applicable, atomics are generally more efficient than acquiring a mutex, updating the memory location, and releasing the mutex. Atomic instructions can only operate on a limited amount of memory (up to 8 bytes on current
architectures) and support only a few operations (addition, swap, etc.). If atomic updates to more data or other kinds of operations are required, mutexes must generally be
used instead.

C++11 provides a variety of atomic operations in the standard library, available via
the <atomic> header file. For example, given the declaration of an integer value as
std::atomic as follows, incrementing counter is an atomic operation.

```
std::atomic<int> counter(0);
    .
    .
    .
counter++;
```

Atomic instructions do introduce some overhead, so they should only be used in cases
where they are actually necessary.

Another useful atomic operation is "compare and swap," which is also exposed by the
C++ standard library. It takes a memory location and the value that the caller believes the
location currently stores. If the memory location still holds that value when the atomic
compare and swap executes, then a new value is stored and true is returned; otherwise,
memory is left unchanged and false is returned.

Compare and swap is a building block that can be used to build many other atomic
operations. For example, the code below could be executed by multiple threads to compute the maximum of values computed by all of the threads. (For this particular case, the
specialized atomic maximum function would be a better choice, but this example helps
convey the usage.)

```
std::atomic<int> maxValue;
int localMax = ...;
int currentMax = maxValue;
while (localMax > currentMax) {
    if (maxValue.compare_exchange_weak(currentMax, localMax))
        break;
}
```

If only a single thread is trying to update the memory location and the local value is larger,
the loop is successful the first time through; the value loaded into currentMax is still
the value stored by maxValue when compare_exchange_weak() executes and so newMax is

successfully stored and `true` is returned.[4] If multiple threads are executing concurrently, then another thread may update the value in `maxValue` between the thread's read of `vaxValue` and the execution of `compare_exchange_weak()`. In that case, the compare and swap fails, memory isn't updated, and another pass is taken through the loop to try again. In the case of a failure, `compare_exchange_weak()` updates `currentMax` with the new value of `maxValue`.

An important application of atomic compare and swap is for the construction of data structures (as is done in Section 16.2.5 for photon mapping). Consider, for example, a tree data structure where each node has child node pointers initially set to `nullptr`. If code traversing the tree wants to create a new child at a node, code could be written like:

```
// atomic<Type *> node->firstChild
if (!node->firstChild) {
    Type *newChild = new Type ...
    Type *current = nullptr;
    if (node->firstChild.compare_exchange_weak(current, newChild) == false)
        delete newChild;
}
// node->firstChild != nullptr now
```

The idea is that if the child has the value `nullptr`, the thread speculatively creates and fully initializes the child node into a local variable, not yet visible to the other threads. Atomic compare and swap is then used to try to initialize the child pointer; if it still has the value `nullptr`, then the new child is stored and made available to all threads. If the child pointer no longer has the value `nullptr`, then another thread has initialized the child in the time between the current thread first seeing that it was `nullptr` and later trying to update it. In this case, the work done in the current thread turns out to have been wasted, but it can delete the locally created child node and continue execution, using the node created by the other thread.

This method of tree construction is a simple example of a *lock-free* algorithm. This approach has a few advantages compared to, for example, using a reader–writer mutex to manage updating the tree. First, there's no overhead of acquiring the reader mutex for regular tree traversal. Second, multiple threads can naturally concurrently update different parts of the tree. With a single reader–writer mutex, if one thread acquires the mutex to update one node in the tree, other threads won't be able to update other nodes. The "Further Reading" section at the end of the appendix has pointers to more information about lock-free algorithms.

A.6.3 ATOMIC FLOATING-POINT VALUES

The `std::atomic` template cannot be used with floating-point types. One of the main reasons that atomic operations are not supported with it is that floating-point operations are generally not commutative: as discussed in Section 3.9.1, when computed in floating-point, the value of the sum `(a+b)+c` is not necessarily not equal to the sum `a+(b+c)`. In

---

4   The "weak" in the compare/exchange instruction refers to the shared memory model required of the underlying hardware. For our purposes, the lesser requirement of "weak" is fine, as it can be much more efficient than a strongly ordered memory model on some architectures. In return for this choice, the compare and exchange may occasionally fail incorrectly, so it requires a retry loop as we have implemented here.

turn, if a multi-threaded computation used atomic floating-point addition operations to compute some value, then the result computed wouldn't be the same across multiple program executions. (In contrast, with integer types, all of the supported operations are commutative, and so atomic operations give consistent results no matter which order threads perform them in.)

For pbrt's needs, these inconsistencies are generally tolerable, and being able to use atomic operations on Floats is preferable in some cases to using a lock. (One example is splatting pixel contributions in the Film::AddSplat() method.) For these purposes, we provide a small AtomicFloat class.

⟨*Parallel Declarations*⟩ ≡
```
class AtomicFloat {
public:
    ⟨AtomicFloat Public Methods 1086⟩
private:
    ⟨AtomicFloat Private Data 1086⟩
};
```

An AtomicFloat can be initialized from a provided floating-point value. In the implementation here, floating-point values are actually represented as their unsigned integer bitwise values, as returned by the FloatToBits() function.

⟨*AtomicFloat Public Methods*⟩ ≡   1086
```
    explicit AtomicFloat(Float v = 0) { bits = FloatToBits(v); }
```

By using a uint32_t to represent the value, we can use a std::atomic type to store it in memory, which in turn allows the compiler to be aware that the value in memory is being updated atomically. (If pbrt has been compiled to use 64-bit doubles for Float values, a uint64_t is used instead, though this code isn't included here.)

⟨*AtomicFloat Private Data*⟩ ≡   1086
```
    std::atomic<uint32_t> bits;
```

Assigning the value or returning it as a Float is just a matter of converting to or from the unsigned integer representation.

⟨*AtomicFloat Public Methods*⟩ +≡   1086
```
    operator Float() const { return BitsToFloat(bits); }
    Float operator=(Float v) { bits = FloatToBits(v); return v; }
```

Atomic floating-point addition is implemented via an atomic compare and exchange operation. In the do loop below, we convert the in-memory bit representation of the value to a Float, add the provided difference in v, and attempt to atomically store the resulting bits. If the in-memory value has been changed by another thread since the value from bits was read from memory, the implementation continues retrying until the value in memory matches the expected value (in oldBits), at which point the atomic update succeeds.

⟨*AtomicFloat Public Methods*⟩ +≡   1086
```
void Add(Float v) {
    uint32_t oldBits = bits, newBits;
    do {
        newBits = FloatToBits(BitsToFloat(oldBits) + v);
    } while (!bits.compare_exchange_weak(oldBits, newBits));
}
```

pbrt doesn't currently need to perform any other operations on AtomicFloats, so we don't provide any additional methods.

A.6.4 PARALLEL FOR LOOPS

All of the multi-core parallelism in pbrt is expressed through parallel for loops using the ParallelFor() function, which is implemented in the files core/parallel.h and core/parallel.cpp.[5] ParallelFor() takes the loop body in the form of a function that is called for each loop iteration as well as a count of the total number of loop iterations to execute. It generally runs multiple iterations in parallel on different CPU cores and it returns only after all of the loop iterations have finished. In using ParallelFor(), the caller makes the implicit promise that it's safe to execute multiple loop iterations concurrently. An important implication of this promise is that the order in which the loop iterations are executed must not affect the final results computed.

Here is a simple example of using ParallelFor(). A C++ lambda expression is used to define the loop body; the loop index is passed back to it as an argument. The lambda has access to the local array variable and doubles each array element in its body. Note that the value 1024 passed as the second parameter to ParallelFor() after the lambda, giving the number of times to execute the loop body.

```
Float array[1024] = { ... };
ParallelFor(
    [array](int index) {
        array[index] *= 2.;
    }, 1024);
```

While it's also possible to pass a function pointer to ParallelFor(), lambdas are generally much more convenient given their ability to capture locally visible variables and make them available in their body.

For loops with relatively large iteration counts where the work done per iteration is small, it can be worthwhile to have the threads running loop iterations do multiple iterations before getting more work. (Doing so helps amortize the overhead of determining which iterations should be assigned to a thread.) Therefore, ParallelFor() also takes an optional chunkSize parameter that controls the granularity of the mapping of loop iterations to processing threads.

---

5   Our implementation here, which is more efficient than the task system in the previous version of pbrt, is based on the parallel for loop implementation in *Halide* written by Jonathan Ragan-Kelley, Andrew Adams, and Zalman Stern.

⟨*Parallel Definitions*⟩ ≡
```
void ParallelFor(const std::function<void(int)> &func,
        int count, int chunkSize) {
    ⟨Run iterations immediately if not using threads or if count is small 1088⟩
    ⟨Launch worker threads if needed 1088⟩
    ⟨Create and enqueue ParallelForLoop for this loop 1089⟩
    ⟨Notify worker threads of work to be done 1090⟩
    ⟨Help out with parallel loop iterations in the current thread 1091⟩
}
```

ParallelFor() usually distributes loop iterations across multiple threads. However, if the system has only one CPU (or the user specified that only one thread should be used for rendering), or if the number of loop iterations is small, then the loop just runs immediately in the current thread, without any parallelism.

⟨*Run iterations immediately if not using threads or if* count *is small*⟩ ≡   1088
```
if (PbrtOptions.nThreads == 1 || count < chunkSize) {
    for (int i = 0; i < count; ++i)
        func(i);
    return;
}
```

Parallel execution is implemented using a set of worker threads (a *thread pool*) that is created the first time ParallelFor() is called. The threads don't terminate after ParallelFor() returns, however; instead they wait on a condition variable that signals more work. This approach means that using the threads for parallel work is a fairly lightweight operation—the overhead of numerous operating system calls to create the threads is only paid once. (This implementation approach is often called *persistent threads*.) It's thus possible to use the thread pool for fairly fine-grained tasks, which in turn lets the system load-balance well when tasks have variable amounts of computation and lets the system scale well as more cores are available in the future.

⟨*Parallel Local Definitions*⟩ ≡
```
static std::vector<std::thread> threads;
static bool shutdownThreads = false;
```

pbrt's initial execution thread also helps run loop iterations, so the number of worker threads launched is one fewer than the number of available CPU cores. There is thus a one-to-one relationship between cores and worker threads. Notwithstanding other processes running on the system, pbrt's threads are collectively enough to fully occupy the CPUs without introducing unnecessary thread-switching overhead from having more threads running than there are available cores. (NumSystemCores() returns the number of processing cores in the system.)

⟨*Launch worker threads if needed*⟩ ≡   1088, 1093
```
if (threads.size() == 0) {
    ThreadIndex = 0;
    for (int i = 0; i < NumSystemCores() - 1; ++i)
        threads.push_back(std::thread(workerThreadFunc, i + 1));
}
```

The function that worker threads run, workerThreadFunc(), will be introduced after we show how the state of enqueued parallel for loops is represented.

In the following, threads will need to determine which of the running threads they are. The ThreadIndex variable is declared with a qualifier that indicates that thread-local storage should be allocated for it, so that there is a separate instance of it for each thread. This variable is initialized to 0 for the main thread and goes from 1 to the number of threads for the worker threads.

⟨*Parallel Declarations*⟩ +≡
```
extern thread_local int ThreadIndex;
```

The workList variable holds a pointer to the head of a list of parallel for loops that aren't yet finished. Usually, there will be no more than one loop in this list, except in the presence of *nested parallelism*, when the body of one parallel for loop iteration specifies another parallel for loop in its body. The workListMutex must always be held when accessing workList or values stored in the ParallelForLoop objects held in it.

⟨*Parallel Local Definitions*⟩ +≡
```
static ParallelForLoop *workList = nullptr;
static std::mutex workListMutex;
```

Adding a new loop to the work queue is fairly straightforward. After initializing the ParallelForLoop object that represents the loop's work, the implementation here locks the mutex and adds the loop to the head of the list. There are two important details here: first, because the call to ParallelFor() here doesn't return until all work for the loop is done, it's safe to allocate loop on the stack—no dynamic memory allocation is required.

Second, the loop is added to the *front* of the work list—doing so means that in the presence of nested parallelism, the inner loops will run before their enclosing loops. This leads to depth-first processing of the nested loops (rather than breadth-first), which in turn can avoid an explosion in the number of loops in the work list.

⟨*Create and enqueue* ParallelForLoop *for this loop*⟩ ≡   **1088**
```
ParallelForLoop loop(func, count, chunkSize, CurrentProfilerState());
workListMutex.lock();
loop.next = workList;
workList = &loop;
workListMutex.unlock();
```

The ParallelForLoop class encapsulates the relevant information about a parallel for loop body, including the function to run, the number of iterations, and which iterations are already done.

⟨*Parallel Local Definitions*⟩ +≡
```
class ParallelForLoop {
public:
    ⟨ParallelForLoop Public Methods 1090⟩
public:
    ⟨ParallelForLoop Private Data 1090⟩
    ⟨ParallelForLoop Private Methods 1090⟩
};
```

ParallelForLoop can represent loops over both 1D and 2D domains corresponding to the variants of the ParallelFor() function. In the following, we'll only show the code for the 1D case.

⟨*ParallelForLoop Public Methods*⟩ ≡   1090
```
ParallelForLoop(std::function<void(int)> func1D,
        int64_t maxIndex, int chunkSize, int profilerState)
    : func1D(std::move(func1D)), maxIndex(maxIndex),
      chunkSize(chunkSize), profilerState(profilerState) { }
```

⟨*ParallelForLoop Private Data*⟩ ≡   1090
```
std::function<void(int)> func1D;
const int64_t maxIndex;
const int chunkSize, profilerState;
```

The nextIndex member variable tracks the next loop index to be executed. It is incremented by workers as they claim loop iterations to execute in their threads. The value stored in activeWorkers records how many worker threads are currently running iterations of the loop. next is used to maintain the linked list of nested loops.

⟨*ParallelForLoop Private Data*⟩ +≡   1090
```
int64_t nextIndex = 0;
int activeWorkers = 0;
ParallelForLoop *next = nullptr;
```

A parallel for loop is only finished when the index has been advanced to the end of the loop's range and there are no threads currently working on it. Note that the first of these conditions will be reached while work is still in progress.

⟨*ParallelForLoop Private Methods*⟩ ≡   1090
```
bool Finished() const { return nextIndex >= maxIndex &&
                activeWorkers == 0; }
```

After the loop has been added to the work list, the worker threads are signaled so that they wake up and start taking work from the list.

⟨*Notify worker threads of work to be done*⟩ ≡   1088
```
std::unique_lock<std::mutex> lock(workListMutex);
workListCondition.notify_all();
```

⟨*Parallel Local Definitions*⟩ +≡
```
static std::condition_variable workListCondition;
```

Finally, the thread that called `ParallelFor()` (be it the main thread or one of the worker threads) starts work on the loop. In the presence of nested parallelism, this means that the thread that enqueued this loop works on it exclusively before returning. By finishing the loop before allowing the thread that submitted it to do any more work, the implementation keeps the amount of enqueued work limited and allows subsequent code in the caller to proceed, knowing the loop's work is done after its call to `ParallelFor()` returns.

A lock to `workListMutex` is always held going into the `while` loop here. Note that the lock is necessary even for calling the `Finished()` method, since `loop` is stored in `workList` and thus will be accessed by the other threads.

⟨*Help out with parallel loop iterations in the current thread*⟩ ≡   **1088**
```
while (!loop.Finished()) {
    ⟨Run a chunk of loop iterations for loop 1091⟩
}
```

Each time through the `while` loop, the thread runs one or more iterations of the parallel loop's body.

⟨*Run a chunk of loop iterations for* loop⟩ ≡   **1091, 1093**
    ⟨*Find the set of loop iterations to run next* **1091**⟩
    ⟨*Update* loop *to reflect iterations this thread will run* **1091**⟩
    ⟨*Run loop indices in* [indexStart, indexEnd) **1092**⟩
    ⟨*Update* loop *to reflect completion of iterations* **1092**⟩

The range of iterations goes from the current index to `chunkSize` ahead subject to the total number of iterations.

⟨*Find the set of loop iterations to run next*⟩ ≡   **1091**
```
int64_t indexStart = loop.nextIndex;
int64_t indexEnd = std::min(indexStart + loop.chunkSize, loop.maxIndex);
```

Now that the thread has found the iterations that it will run, `loop` must be updated. If this thread took the final iterations, the loop is removed from the work list so that other threads can start on the next loop (if any).

⟨*Update* loop *to reflect iterations this thread will run*⟩ ≡   **1091**
```
loop.nextIndex = indexEnd;
if (loop.nextIndex == loop.maxIndex)
    workList = loop.next;
loop.activeWorkers++;
```

Given the range of loop iterations to run, it's fairly straightforward to call back to the `std::function` representing the loop body. This is the only time in the enclosing `while` loop that the lock is relinquished, though the time spent running these loop iterations is generally the majority of the time spent in the `while` loop, so other worker threads generally don't need to wait long for the lock. The ⟨*Handle other types of loops*⟩ fragment, not included here, handles the 2D loop supported by `ParallelForLoop`.

⟨*Run loop indices in* [indexStart, indexEnd]⟩ ≡   **1091**
```
    lock.unlock();
    for (int index = indexStart; index < indexEnd; ++index) {
        if (loop.func1D) {
            loop.func1D(index);
        }
        ⟨Handle other types of loops⟩
    }
    lock.lock();
```

After running the set of loop iterations and re-acquiring the lock, the active worker count is updated to reflect that (for now at least) the current thread is no longer working on loop.

⟨*Update* loop *to reflect completion of iterations*⟩ ≡   **1091**
```
    loop.activeWorkers--;
```

While the thread that called ParallelFor() is working on the loop, the other threads also run iterations. workerThreadFunc() is the function that runs to do this in each task execution thread. Its structure is similar to the fragment ⟨*Help out with parallel loop iterations in the main thread*⟩, with three main differences. First, it runs loops from whatever ParallelForLoops are in workList, not just from a single parallel for loop. Second, it has the thread sleep whenever there isn't any work to be done. Finally, it continues waiting for more loops to run until the shutdownThreads variable is set, which only happens at the end of program execution.

As before, a lock to the workListMutex must be held at entry to the while loop here.

⟨*Parallel Local Definitions*⟩ +≡
```
    static void workerThreadFunc(int tIndex) {
        ThreadIndex = tIndex;
        std::unique_lock<std::mutex> lock(workListMutex);
        while (!shutdownThreads) {
            if (!workList) {
                ⟨Sleep until there are more tasks to run 1092⟩
            } else {
                ⟨Get work from workList and run loop iterations 1093⟩
            }
        }
        ⟨Report thread statistics at worker thread exit 1093⟩
    }
```

If there is no available work, the worker thread waits on the workListCondition condition variable. The semantics of condition variables are such that doing so releases the lock, but when this thread is later woken up by the condition variable being signaled, it will again hold the lock.

⟨*Sleep until there are more tasks to run*⟩ ≡   **1092**
```
    workListCondition.wait(lock);
```

ParallelForLoop::
   activeWorkers
   1090
ParallelForLoop::func1D 1090
shutdownThreads 1088
ThreadIndex 1089
workList 1089
workListCondition 1090
workListMutex 1089

Otherwise, a range of loop iterations to run is taken from the head of workList. The code to run iterations is reused from the ⟨*Run a chunk of loop iterations for* loop⟩ fragment defined earlier.

⟨*Get work from* workList *and run loop iterations*⟩ ≡   1092
```
ParallelForLoop &loop = *workList;
```
⟨*Run a chunk of loop iterations for* loop **1091**⟩
```
if (loop.Finished())
    workListCondition.notify_all();
```

Finally, as will be discussed shortly in Appendix A.7.1, the worker thread must call ReportThreadStats() before exiting so that its per-thread statistics are merged into the aggregate statistics.

⟨*Report thread statistics at worker thread exit*⟩ ≡   1092
```
ReportThreadStats();
```

A variant of ParallelFor() takes a Point2i to describe a 2D iteration domain from (0, 0) to the given point. This version is used to loop over image buckets in Section 1.3.4, for example.

⟨*Parallel Declarations*⟩ +≡
```
void ParallelFor2D(std::function<void(Point2i)> func,
                   const Point2i &count);
```

The ThreadIndex variable allows code in parallel for loops to use preallocated temporary buffers or objects like MemoryArenas, giving a separate instance to each worker thread without needing to worry about data races. (See, for example, the ⟨*Generate SPPM visible points*⟩ fragment on page 976.) For this use, it's also useful for calling code to be able to find out the maximum possible thread index.

⟨*Parallel Definitions*⟩ +≡
```
int MaxThreadIndex() {
    if (PbrtOptions.nThreads != 1) {
        ⟨Launch worker threads if needed 1088⟩
    }
    return 1 + threads.size();
}
```

TerminateWorkerThreads(), not included here, cleans up the resources allocated for the threads.

A.7 STATISTICS

Collecting data about the run-time behavior of the system can provide a substantial amount of insight into its behavior and opportunities for improving its performance. For example, we might want to track the average number of primitive intersection tests performed for all of the rays; if this number is surprisingly high, then there may be a latent bug somewhere in the system. pbrt's statistics system makes it possible to measure and aggregate this sort of data in a variety of ways.

It's important to make it as easy as possible to add new measurements to track the system's run-time behavior; the easier it is to do this, the more measurements end up being added to the system, and the more likely that "interesting" data will be discovered, leading to new insights and improvements. Therefore, adding new measurements to the system is fairly straightforward. For example, the following lines declare two counters that can be used to record how many times the corresponding events happen.

```
STAT_COUNTER("Integrator/Regular ray intersection tests",
             nIntersectionTests);
STAT_COUNTER("Integrator/Shadow ray intersection tests",
             nShadowTests);
```

As appropriate, counters can be incremented with simple statements like

```
++nIntersectionTests;
```

With no further intervention from the developer, the preceding is enough for the statistics system to be able to automatically print out nicely formatted results like the following when rendering completes:

```
Integrator
    Regular ray intersection tests        752982
    Shadow ray intersection tests         4237165
```

The statistics system supports the following measurements:

- STAT_COUNTER("name", var): A simple count of the number of instances of an event. The counter variable var can be updated as if it was a regular int variable; for example, ++var and var += 10 are both valid.
- STAT_MEMORY_COUNTER("name", var): A specialized counter for recording memory usage. In particular, the values reported at the end of rendering are in terms of kilobytes, megabytes, or gigabytes, as appropriate. The counter is updated the same way as a regular counter: var += count * sizeof(MyStruct) and so forth.
- STAT_INT_DISTRIBUTION("name", dist): Tracks the distribution of some value; at the end of rendering, the minimum, maximum, and average of the reported values are reported. Call ReportValue(dist, val) to include val in the distribution.
- STAT_FLOAT_DISTRIBUTION("name", dist): This counter also tracks the distribution of a value but expects floating-point values to be reported. ReportValue(dist, val) is also used to report values.
- STAT_PERCENT("name", num, denom): Tracks how often a given event happens; the aggregate value is reported as the percentage num/denom when statistics are printed. Both num and denom can be incremented as if they were integers—for example, one might write if (event) ++num; or ++denom.
- STAT_RATIO("name", num, denom): This tracks how often an event happens but reports the result as a ratio num/denom rather than a percentage. This is often a more useful presentation if num is often greater than denom. (For example, we might record the percentage of ray–triangle intersection tests that resulted in an intersection but the ratio of triangle intersection tests to the total number of rays traced.)
- STAT_TIMER("name", timer): The timer can be used to record how much time is spent in a given block of code. To run the timer, one can add a declaration such as StatTimer t(&timer); to the start of a block of code; the timer will run until the

declared t variable goes out of scope and the StatTimer destructor runs. Note that there is some overhead to getting the current system time, so timers shouldn't be used for very small blocks of code.

All of the macros to define statistics trackers can only be used at file scope and should only be used in .cpp files (for reasons that will become apparent as we dig into their implementations). They specifically should not be used in header files or function or class definitions.

Note also that the string names provided for each measurement should be of the form "category/statistic." When values are reported, everything under the same category is reported together (as in the preceding example).

A.7.1 IMPLEMENTATION

There are a number of challenges in making the statistics system both efficient and easy to use. The efficiency challenges stem from pbrt being multi-threaded: if there wasn't any parallelism, we could associate regular integer or floating-point variables with each measurement and just update them like regular variables. In the presence of multiple concurrent threads of execution, however, we need to ensure that two threads didn't try to modify these variables at the same time (recall the discussion of mutual exclusion in Section 1.4).

While atomic operations like those described in Section A.6.2 could be used to safely increment counters without using a mutex, there would still be a performance impact from multiple threads modifying the same location in memory. Recall from Section A.6.1 that the cache coherence protocols can introduce substantial overhead in this case. Because the statistics measurements are updated so frequently during the course of rendering, we found that an atomics-based implementation caused the overall renderer to be 10–15% slower than the current implementation, which avoids the overhead of multiple threads frequently modifying the same memory location.

The implementation here is based on having separate counters for each running thread, allowing the counters to be updated without atomics and without cache coherence overhead (since each thread increments its own counters). This approach means that in order to report statistics, it's necessary to merge all of these per-thread counters into final aggregate values, which we'll see is possible with a bit of trickiness.

To see how this all works, we'll dig into the implementation for regular counters; the other types of measurements are all along similar lines. First, here is the STAT_COUNTER macro, which packs three different things into its definition.

⟨*Statistics Macros*⟩ ≡
```
#define STAT_COUNTER(title, var)                          \
    static thread_local int64_t var;                      \
    static void STATS_FUNC##var(StatsAccumulator &accum) { \
        accum.ReportCounter(title, var);                  \
        var = 0;                                          \
    }                                                     \
    static StatRegisterer STATS_REG##var(STATS_FUNC##var)
```

StatRegisterer 1096
StatsAccumulator 1096
StatsAccumulator::
   ReportCounter()
   1096

First, and most obviously, the macro defines a 64-bit integer variable named var, the second argument passed to the macro. The variable definition has the thread_local qualifier, which indicates that there should be a separate copy of the variable for each executing thread. Given these per-thread instances, we need to be able to sum together the per-thread values and to aggregate all of the individual counters into the final program output.

To this end, the macro next defines a function, giving it a (we hope!) unique name derived from var. When called, this function passes along the value of var for the current thread to an instance of the StatsAccumulator class. StatsAccumulator accumulates values of measurement statistics counters into its own storage; here is its ReportCounter() method, which totals up the given values, associating them with their respective string names.

⟨*StatsAccumulator Public Methods*⟩ ≡
```
void ReportCounter(const std::string &name, int64_t val) {
    counters[name] += val;
}
```

⟨*StatsAccumulator Private Data*⟩ ≡
```
std::map<std::string, int64_t> counters;
```

All we need now is for the STATS_FUNC##var() function to be called for each per-thread instance of each counter variable when rendering has finished; this is what the last line of the STAT_COUNTER macro takes care of. To understand what it does, first recall that in C++, constructors of global static objects run when program execution starts; thus, each static instance of the StatRegisterer class runs its constructor before main() starts running.

The constructor for StatRegisterer objects in turn adds the function passed to it to a vector that holds all of the various STATS_FUNC##var() functions. Note that because the StatRegisterer constructors run at program start time, the constructor for the funcs vector (another global static) may not yet have run. Therefore, funcs is a pointer to a vector rather than a vector, so that it can be explicitly constructed before it's first used.

⟨*StatRegisterer Public Methods*⟩ ≡
```
StatRegisterer(std::function<void(StatsAccumulator &)> func) {
    if (!funcs)
        funcs = new std::vector<std::function<void(StatsAccumulator &)>>;
    funcs->push_back(func);
}
```

⟨*StatRegisterer Private Data*⟩ ≡
```
static std::vector<std::function<void(StatsAccumulator &)>> *funcs;
```

Now all the pieces can come together. Each thread launched for multi-threading in pbrt runs the function workerThreadFunc(). When this function exits at the end of program execution, it calls ReportThreadStats(), which in turn causes the per-thread measurements for the thread to be merged into the given StatsAccumulator. (The initial processing thread also calls this function after rendering has completed so that its values are reported.)

StatsAccumulator 1096
workerThreadFunc() 1092

The ReportThreadStats() method uses a mutex to ensure that no other thread can be updating the StatsAccumulator concurrently and then dispatches to StatRegisterer::CallCallbacks(), passing in a single StatsAccumulator to store all of the aggregated values.

⟨*Statistics Definitions*⟩ ≡
```
void ReportThreadStats() {
    static std::mutex mutex;
    std::lock_guard<std::mutex> lock(mutex);
    StatRegisterer::CallCallbacks(statsAccumulator);
}
```

⟨*Statistics Local Variables*⟩ ≡
```
static StatsAccumulator statsAccumulator;
```

Finally, CallCallbacks() calls each of the function pointers to the STATS_FUNC##var() functions that were assembled when the program started. This is where the magic happens: because these functions are called repeatedly, once in each of the threads, each call to the STATS_FUNC##var() functions reports the value of the per-thread value for each thread. In the end, we will have aggregated all of the various measurement values.

⟨*Statistics Definitions*⟩ +≡
```
void StatRegisterer::CallCallbacks(StatsAccumulator &accum) {
    for (auto func : *funcs)
        func(accum);
}
```

The PrintStats() function prints all of the statistics that have been accumulated in StatsAccumulator. This function is called by pbrtWorldEnd() at the end of rendering. Its task is straightforward: it sorts the measurements by category and formats the values so that columns of numbers line up and so forth.

A.7.2 PROFILING

When doing significant work on optimizing the performance of any sort of software system, using a stand-alone profiler is a necessity. Modern profilers provide a wealth of information about program execution—which functions, and even which lines of code most execution time is spent in. Equally useful, many also provide information about the program's interaction with the computer system—which lines of code suffered the most from CPU cache misses, places in the program where cache coherence overhead was high, and so forth.

We have found that a useful supplement to stand-alone profilers is to have a simple profiling system embedded in pbrt.[6] This system provides high-level information about the fraction of overall run time consumed by various parts of the system. The information it provides is useful for understanding the differences across scenes where pbrt spends its time and for helping to guide more focused profiling investigations. In exchange for

---

6   The design follows the approach used in Disney's Hyperion renderer, as described by Selle (2015).

only providing high-level information, it adds minimal overhead; in practice, we have measured a roughly 2.5% increase in run time.

Here is an example of the profiler's output for one of the test scenes:

```
Integrator::Render()                    95.0 %
  Sampler::StartPixelSample()           10.1 %
  SamplerIntegrator::Li()               81.1 %
    Accelerator::Intersect()             3.6 %
      Triangle::Intersect()              1.1 %
    BSDF::f()                            0.1 %
    Direct lighting                     75.1 %
      Accelerator::Intersect()          16.4 %
        Triangle::Intersect()            4.3 %
```

There are a few things to know in order to understand this output. First, all percentages reported are with respect to the system's overall run time. Thus, here we can see that about 5% of the run time was spent parsing the scene file and constructing the scene, and the remainder was spent rendering it. Most of the rendering time was spent doing direct lighting calculations.

Second, note that there is a hierarchy in the reported results. For example, `Accelerator::Intersect()` appears twice, and we can see that 3.6% of the run time was spent in calls to the accelerator's traversal method from `Li()`, but 16.4% of the run time was spent in calls to it from the direct lighting code. The percentage reported for each level of this hierarchy includes the time of all of the indented items reported underneath it.

The profiling system is based on explicit annotations in the program code to denote these phases of execution. (We haven't included those annotations in the program source code in the book in the interests of simplicity.) In turn, pbrt uses operating-system-specific functionality to periodically interrupt the system and record which phases are currently active. At the end of execution, it counts up how many times each phase was found to be active and reports these counts with respect to the totals, as above.

As suggested by the profiling output, there are a series of categories that a phase of execution can be charged to; these are represented by the `Prof` enumerant.

⟨*Statistics Declarations*⟩ ≡
```
enum class Prof {
    IntegratorRender,     SamplerIntegratorLi,     DirectLighting,
    AccelIntersect,       AccelIntersectP,         TriIntersect,
    ⟨Remainder of Prof enum entries⟩
};
```

The hierarchy of reported percentages is implicitly defined by the ordering of values in this enumerant; when multiple execution phases are active, later values in the enumerant are assumed to be children of earlier ones.

One bit in the `ProfilerState` variable is used to indicate whether each category in `Prof`   Prof 1098
is currently active. Note that this variable has the `thread_local` qualifier; thus, a separate instance is maintained for each program execution thread.

⟨*Statistics Declarations*⟩ +≡
```
extern thread_local uint32_t ProfilerState;
```

CurrentProfilerState() makes the state available to the ParallelFor() implementation; this makes it possible for work done in parallel for loop bodies to be charged to the execution phases that were active when ParallelFor() was called.

⟨*Statistics Declarations*⟩ +≡
```
inline uint32_t CurrentProfilerState() { return ProfilerState; }
```

In turn, a method like BVHAccel::Intersect() starts with a single line of code for the profiling system's benefit:

```
ProfilePhase p(Prof::AccelIntersect);
```

The ProfilePhase helper class's constructor records that the provided phase of execution has begun; when its destructor later runs when the ProfilePhase instance goes out of scope, it records that the corresponding phase is no longer active.

⟨*Statistics Declarations*⟩ +≡
```
class ProfilePhase {
public:
    ⟨ProfilePhase Public Methods 1099⟩
private:
    ⟨ProfilePhase Private Data 1099⟩
};
```

The constructor starts by mapping the provided phase to a bit and then enabling that bit in ProfilerState. In the presence of recursion (notably, via recursive calls to SamplerIntegrator::Li()), it's possible that a higher level of the recursion will already have indicated the start of an execution phase. In this case, reset is set to false, and the ProfilePhase destructor won't clear the corresponding bit when it runs, leaving that task to the destructor of the earlier ProfilePhase instance that first set that bit.

⟨*ProfilePhase Public Methods*⟩ ≡   **1099**
```
ProfilePhase(Prof p) {
    categoryBit = (1 << (int)p);
    reset = (ProfilerState & categoryBit) == 0;
    ProfilerState |= categoryBit;
}
```

⟨*ProfilePhase Private Data*⟩ ≡   **1099**
```
bool reset;
uint32_t categoryBit;
```

⟨*ProfilePhase Public Methods*⟩ +≡   **1099**
```
~ProfilePhase() {
    if (reset)
        ProfilerState &= ~categoryBit;
}
```

The `InitProfiler()` function has two tasks. First, it allocates the `profileSamples` array; this array has one entry for each possible combination of active phases of execution. While many of these combinations aren't actually possible, using a simple data structure like this makes it possible to very efficiently record the sample counts of the current phase of execution. (However, note that the number of entries grows at the rate 2^n, where n is the number of distinct phases of execution in the `Prof` enumerant. Thus, this implementation is not suited to extremely fine-grained decomposition of profiling categories.)

Second, `InitProfiler()` uses system-dependent functionality to ask that pbrt be periodically interrupted to record the current phase of execution. We won't include this code here.

⟨*Statistics Definitions*⟩ +≡
```
void InitProfiler() {
    profileSamples.reset(new std::atomic<uint64_t>[1 << NumProfEvents]);
    for (int i = 0; i < (1 << NumProfEvents); ++i)
        profileSamples[i] = 0;
    ⟨Set timer to periodically interrupt the system for profiling⟩
}
```

⟨*Statistics Local Variables*⟩ +≡
```
static std::unique_ptr<std::atomic<uint64_t>[]> profileSamples;
```

Each time the system interrupt occurs for a thread, `ReportProfileSample()` is called. This function is extremely simple and just increments the tally for the current set of active phases as encoded in `ProfilerState`.

⟨*Statistics Definitions*⟩ +≡
```
static void ReportProfileSample(int, siginfo_t *, void *) {
    if (profileSamples)
        profileSamples[ProfilerState]++;
}
```

At the end of rendering, the `ReportProfilerResults()` function is called. It aggregates the profile counters and generates reports of the form above; its implementation isn't particularly interesting with respect to its length, so we won't include it here.

FURTHER READING

Hacker's Delight (Warren 2006), is a delightful and thought-provoking exploration of the bit-twiddling algorithms like those used in some of the utility routines in this appendix. Sean Anderson (2004) has a Web page filled with a collection of bit-twiddling techniques like the ones in `IsPowerOf2()` and `RoundUpPow2()` at *graphics.stanford.edu/~seander/bithacks.html*.

Numerical Recipes, by Press et al. (1992), and Atkinson's book (1993) on numerical analysis both discuss algorithms for matrix inversion and solving linear systems.

The PCG random number generator was developed by O'Neill (2014). The paper describing its implementation is well written and also features extensive discussion of a range of previous pseudo-random number generators and the challenges that they have faced in passing rigorous tests of their quality (L'Ecuyer and Simard 2007).

Many papers have been written on cache-friendly programming techniques; only a few are surveyed here. Ericson's chapter (2004) on high-performance programming techniques has very good coverage of this topic. Lam, Rothberg, and Wolf (1991) investigated blocking (tiling) for improving cache performance and developed techniques for selecting appropriate block sizes, given the size of the arrays and the cache size. Grunwald, Zorn, and Henderson (1993) were one of the first groups of researchers to investigate the interplay between memory allocation algorithms and the cache behavior of applications.

In pbrt, we only worry about cache layout issues for dynamically allocated data. However, Calder et al. (1998) show a profile-driven system that optimizes memory layout of global variables, constant values, data on the stack, and dynamically allocated data from the heap in order to reduce cache conflicts among them all, giving an average 30% reduction in data cache misses for the applications they studied.

Blocking for tree data structures was investigated by Chilimbi et al. (1999b); they ensured that nodes of the tree and a few levels of its children were allocated contiguously. Among other applications, they applied their tool to the layout of the acceleration octree in the *Radiance* renderer and reported a 42% speedup in run time. Chilimbi et al. (1999a) also evaluated the effectiveness of reordering fields inside structures to improve locality.

Drepper's paper (2007) is a useful resource for understanding performance issues related to caches, cache coherence, and main memory access, particularly in multicore systems.

Boehm's paper *Threads Cannot Be Implemented as a Library* (2005) makes the remarkable (and disconcerting) observation that multi-threading cannot be reliably implemented without the compiler having explicit knowledge of the fact that multi-threaded execution is expected. Boehm presented a number of examples that demonstrate the corresponding dangers in 2005-era compilers and language standards like C and C++ that did not have awareness of threading. Fortunately, the C++11 and C11 standards addressed the issues that he identified.

pbrt's parallel for loop-based approach to multi-threading is a widely used technique for multi-threaded programming; the OpenMP standard supports a similar construct (and much more) (OpenMP Architecture Review Board 2013). A slightly more general model for multi-core parallelism is available from *task systems*, where computations are broken up into a set of independent tasks that can be executed concurrently. Blumofe et al. (1996) described the task scheduler in Cilk, and Blumofe and Leiserson (1999) describe the work-stealing algorithm that is the mainstay of many current high-performance task systems.

EXERCISES

MemoryArena 1074

● A.1   Modify MemoryArena so that it just calls new for each memory allocation. (You will also want to record all pointer values returned by these new calls so that memory can be freed in the Reset() method.) Render images of a few scenes and measure how much more slowly pbrt runs. Can you quantify how much of this is due to different cache behavior and how much is due to overhead in the dynamic memory management routines?

● A.2 Change the BlockedArray class so that it doesn't do any blocking and just uses a linear addressing scheme for the array. Measure the change in pbrt's performance as a result. (Scenes with many image map textures are most likely to show any differences, since the MIPMap class is a key user of BlockedArray.)

❷ A.3 Try a few alternative implementations of the statistics system described in Section A.7 to get a sense of the performance trade-offs with various approaches. You might try using atomic operations to update single counters that are shared across threads, or you might try using a mutex to allow safe updates to shared counters by multiple threads. Measure the performance compared to pbrt's current implementation and discuss possible explanations for your results.

BlockedArray 1076
MIPMap 625

⬚ SCENE DESCRIPTION INTERFACE

This appendix describes the application programming interface (API) that is used to describe the scene to be rendered to pbrt. Users of the renderer typically don't call the functions in this interface directly but instead describe their scenes using the text file format described in documentation on the pbrt Web site (*pbrt.org*). The statements in these text files have a direct correspondence to the API functions described here.

The need for such an interface to the renderer is clear: there must be a convenient way in which all of the properties of the scene to be rendered can be communicated to the renderer. The interface should be well defined and general purpose, so that future extensions to the system fit into its structure cleanly. It shouldn't be too complicated, so that it's easy to describe scenes, but it should be expressive enough that it doesn't leave any of the renderer's capabilities hidden.

A key decision to make when designing a rendering API is whether to expose the system's internal algorithms and structures or offer a high-level abstraction for describing the scene. These have historically been the two main approaches to scene description in graphics: the interface may specify *how* to render the scene, configuring a rendering pipeline at a low level using deep knowledge of the renderer's internal algorithms, or it may specify *what* the scene's objects, lights, and material properties are and leave it to the renderer to decide how to transform that description into the best possible image.

The first approach has been successfully used for interactive graphics. In APIs such as OpenGL® or Direct3D®, it is not possible to just mark an object as a mirror and have reflections appear automatically; rather, the user must choose an algorithm for rendering reflections, render the scene multiple times (e.g., to generate an environment map), store those images in a texture, and then configure the graphics pipeline to use the environment map when rendering the reflective object. The advantage of this approach

Physically Based Rendering: From Theory To Implementation.
http://dx.doi.org/10.1016/B978-0-12-800645-0.50023-3

is that the full flexibility of the rendering pipeline is exposed to the user, making it possible to carefully control the actual computation being done and to use the pipeline very efficiently. Furthermore, because APIs like these impose a very thin abstraction layer between the user and the renderer, the user can be confident that unexpected inefficiencies won't be introduced by the API.

The second approach to scene description, based on describing the geometry, materials, and lights at a higher level of abstraction, has been most successful for applications like high-quality offline rendering. There, users are generally willing to cede control of the low-level rendering details to the renderer in exchange for the ability to specify the scene's properties at a high level. An important advantage of the high-level approach is that the implementations of these renderers have greater freedom to make major changes to the internal algorithms of the system, since the API exposes less of them.

For pbrt, we will use an interface based on the descriptive approach. Because pbrt is fundamentally physically based, the API is necessarily less flexible in some ways than APIs for many nonphysically based rendering packages. For example, it is not possible to have some lights illuminate only some objects in the scene.

Another key decision to make in graphics API design is whether to use an immediate mode or a retained mode style. In an immediate mode API, the user specifies the scene via a stream of commands that the renderer processes as they arrive. In general, the user cannot make changes to the scene description data already specified (e.g., "change the material of that sphere I described previously from plastic to glass"); once it has been given to the renderer, the information is no longer accessible to the user. Retained mode APIs give the user some degree of access to the data structures that the renderer has built to represent the scene. The user can then modify the scene description in a variety of ways before finally instructing the renderer to render the scene.

Immediate mode has been very successful for interactive graphics APIs since it allows graphics hardware to draw the objects in the scene as they are supplied by the user. Since they do not need to build data structures to store the scene and since they can apply techniques like immediately culling objects that are outside of the viewing frustum without worrying that the user will change the camera position before rendering, these APIs have been key to high-performance interactive graphics.

For ray-tracing-based renderers like pbrt, where the entire scene must be described and stored in memory before rendering can begin, some of these advantages of an immediate mode interface aren't applicable. Nonetheless, we will use immediate mode semantics in our API, since it leads to a clean and straightforward scene description language. This choice makes it more difficult to use pbrt for applications like quickly rerendering a scene after making a small change to it (e.g., by moving a light source) and may make rendering animations less straightforward, since the entire scene needs to be redescribed for each frame of an animation. Adding a retained mode interface to pbrt would be a challenging but useful project.

pbrt's rendering API consists of just over 40 carefully chosen functions, all of which are declared in the core/api.h header file. The implementation of these functions is in core/api.cpp. This appendix will focus on the general process of turning the API function calls into instances of the classes that represent scenes.

B.1 PARAMETER SETS

A key problem that a rendering API must address is extensibility—as new features are added to the system, how does the user-visible API change and what parts of its implementation change? For pbrt, it's important that developers be able to easily add new implementations of Shapes, Cameras, Integrators, and so forth. We've designed the API with this goal in mind.

To this end, the caller-visible API and its implementation are both as unaware as possible of what particular parameters these objects take and what their semantics are. pbrt uses the ParamSet class to bundle up parameters and their values in a generic way. For example, it might record that there is a single floating-point value named "radius" with a value of 2.5 and an array of four color values named "specular" with various SPDs. The ParamSet provides methods for both setting and retrieving values from these kinds of generic parameter lists. It is defined in core/paramset.h and core/paramset.cpp.

Most of pbrt's API routines take a ParamSet as one of their parameters; for example, the shape creation routine, pbrtShape(), just takes a string giving the name of the shape to make and a ParamSet with parameters for it. The creation routine of the corresponding shape implementation is called with the ParamSet passed along as a parameter; it extracts values from the ParamSet to get parameters to use in a call to the class's constructor.

⟨*ParamSet Declarations*⟩ ≡
```
class ParamSet {
public:
    ⟨ParamSet Public Methods 1107⟩
private:
    ⟨ParamSet Private Data 1105⟩
};
```

A ParamSet can hold eleven types of parameters: Booleans, integers, floating-point values, points (2D and 3D), vectors (2D and 3D), normals, spectra, strings, and the names of Textures that are being used as parameters for Materials and other Textures. Internally, it stores a vector of named values for each of the different types that it stores; each parameter is represented by a pointer to a ParamSetItem of the appropriate type. A shared_ptr is used for these pointers; doing so allows a parameter to easily be stored in multiple ParamSets, which we'll find useful in the following.

Storing parameters unsorted in vectors means that searching for a given parameter takes $O(n)$ time, where n is the number of parameters of the parameter's type. In practice, there are just a handful of parameters to any function, so a more time-efficient representation isn't necessary.

⟨*ParamSet Private Data*⟩ ≡   1105
```
std::vector<std::shared_ptr<ParamSetItem<bool>>> bools;
std::vector<std::shared_ptr<ParamSetItem<int>>> ints;
std::vector<std::shared_ptr<ParamSetItem<Float>>> floats;
std::vector<std::shared_ptr<ParamSetItem<Point2f>>> point2fs;
std::vector<std::shared_ptr<ParamSetItem<Vector2f>>> vector2fs;
std::vector<std::shared_ptr<ParamSetItem<Point3f>>> point3fs;
```

```
std::vector<std::shared_ptr<ParamSetItem<Vector3f>>> vector3fs;
std::vector<std::shared_ptr<ParamSetItem<Normal3f>>> normals;
std::vector<std::shared_ptr<ParamSetItem<Spectrum>>> spectra;
std::vector<std::shared_ptr<ParamSetItem<std::string>>> strings;
std::vector<std::shared_ptr<ParamSetItem<std::string>>> textures;
```

B.1.1 THE ParamSetItem STRUCTURE

The ParamSetItem structure stores all of the relevant information about a single parameter, such as its name, its base type, and its value(s). For example (using the syntax from pbrt's input files), the foo parameter

```
"float foo" [ 0 1 2 3 4 5 ]
```

has a base type of float, and six values have been supplied for it. It would be represented by a ParamSetItem<Float>.

⟨*ParamSet Declarations*⟩ +≡
```
    template <typename T> struct ParamSetItem {
        ⟨ParamSetItem Public Methods⟩
        ⟨ParamSetItem Data 1106⟩
    };
```

The ParamSetItem directly initializes its members from the arguments and makes a copy of the values.

⟨*ParamSetItem Methods*⟩ ≡
```
    template <typename T>
    ParamSetItem<T>::ParamSetItem(const std::string &name, const T *v,
                                  int nValues)
        : name(name), values(new T[nValues]), nValues(nValues) {
        std::copy(v, v + nValues, values.get());
    }
```

The Boolean value lookedUp is set to true after the value has been retrieved from the ParamSet. This makes it possible to print warning messages if any parameters were added to the parameter set but never used, which typically indicates a misspelling in the scene description file or other user error.

⟨*ParamSetItem Data*⟩ ≡   **1106**
```
    const std::string name;
    const std::unique_ptr<T[]> values;
    const int nValues;
    mutable bool lookedUp = false;
```

B.1.2 ADDING TO THE PARAMETER SET

To add an entry to the parameter set, the appropriate ParamSet method should be called with the name of the parameter, a pointer to its data, and the number of data items. These methods first remove previous values for the parameter in the ParamSet, if any.

⟨*ParamSet Methods*⟩ ≡

```
void ParamSet::AddFloat(const std::string &name, const Float *values,
                        int nValues) {
    EraseFloat(name);
    floats.emplace_back(new ParamSetItem<Float>(name, values, nValues));
}
```

We won't include the rest of the methods to add data to the ParamSet, but we do include their prototypes here for reference. The erasure methods are also straightforward and won't be included here.

⟨*ParamSet Public Methods*⟩ ≡   1105

```
void AddInt(const std::string &, const int *, int nValues);
void AddBool(const std::string &, const bool *, int nValues);
void AddPoint2f(const std::string &, const Point2f *, int nValues);
void AddVector2f(const std::string &, const Vector2f *, int nValues);
void AddPoint3f(const std::string &, const Point3f *, int nValues);
void AddVector3f(const std::string &, const Vector3f *, int nValues);
void AddNormal3f(const std::string &, const Normal3f *, int nValues);
void AddString(const std::string &, const std::string *, int nValues);
void AddTexture(const std::string &, const std::string &);
```

A number of different methods for adding spectral data are provided, making it easy for this data to be supplied with a variety of representations. The RGB and XYZ variants take 3 floating-point values for each spectrum. AddBlackbodySpectrum() takes pairs of temperature in Kelvins and a scale factor; it uses BlackbodyNormalized() to compute the SPD, which it scales with the given scale. Finally, AddSampledSpectrumFiles() reads SPDs from files on disk; both it and AddSampledSpectrum() construct a piecewise linear SPD given pairs of wavelengths and SPD values at each wavelength.

⟨*ParamSet Public Methods*⟩ +≡   1105

```
void AddRGBSpectrum(const std::string &, const Float *, int nValues);
void AddXYZSpectrum(const std::string &, const Float *, int nValues);
void AddBlackbodySpectrum(const std::string &, const Float *,
    int nValues);
void AddSampledSpectrumFiles(const std::string &, const char **,
    int nValues);
void AddSampledSpectrum(const std::string &, const Float *, int nValues);
```

B.1.3 LOOKING UP VALUES IN THE PARAMETER SET

To retrieve a parameter value from a set, it is necessary to loop through the entries of the requested type and return the appropriate value, if any. There are two versions of the lookup method for each parameter type: a simple one for parameters that have a single data value, and a more general one that returns a pointer to the possibly multiple values of array parameter types. The first method mostly serves to reduce the amount of code needed in routines that retrieve parameter values.

The methods that look up a single item (e.g., FindOneFloat()) take the name of the parameter and a default value. If the parameter is not found, the default value is returned. This makes it easy to write initialization code like

```
Float radius = params.FindOneFloat("radius", 1.f);
```

In this case, it is not an error if the user didn't provide a "radius" parameter value; the default value will be used instead. If calling code wants to detect a missing parameter and issue an error, the appropriate second variant of lookup method should be used, since those methods return a nullptr value if the parameter isn't found.

⟨*ParamSet Methods*⟩ +≡
```
    Float ParamSet::FindOneFloat(const std::string &name, Float d) const {
        for (const auto &f : floats)
            if (f->name == name && f->nValues == 1) {
                f->lookedUp = true;
                return f->values[0];
            }
        return d;
    }
```

We won't include the declarations of the analogous methods for the remaining types here (FindOneInt(), FindOnePoint3f(), and so forth); they all follow the same form as FindOneFloat()—each takes a parameter name and a default value and returns a value of the corresponding type.

The second kind of lookup method returns a pointer to the data if the data is present and returns the number of values in n.

⟨*ParamSet Methods*⟩ +≡
```
    const Float *ParamSet::FindFloat(const std::string &name, int *n) const {
        for (const auto &f : floats)
            if (f->name == name) {
                *n = f->nValues;
                f->lookedUp = true;
                return f->values.get();
            }
        return nullptr;
    }
```

The general lookup functions for the other types follow the same form and so won't be included here.

Because the user may misspell parameter names in the scene description file, the ParamSet also provides a ReportUnused() function, not included here, that goes through the parameter set and reports if any of the parameters present were never looked up, checking the ParamSetItem::lookedUp member variable. For any items where this variable is false, it is likely that the user has given an incorrect parameter.

⟨*ParamSet Public Methods*⟩ +≡   **1105**
```
    void ReportUnused() const;
```

The ParamSet::Clear() method clears all of the individual parameter vectors. The corresponding ParamSetItems will in turn be freed if their reference count goes to 0.

⟨*ParamSet Public Methods*⟩ +≡   **1105**
    void Clear();

B.2 INITIALIZATION AND RENDERING OPTIONS

We now have the machinery to describe the routines that make up the rendering API. Before any other API functions can be called, the rendering system must be initialized by a call to pbrtInit(). Similarly, when rendering is done, pbrtCleanup() should be called; this handles final cleanup of the system. The definitions of these two functions will be filled in at a number of points throughout the rest of this appendix.

A few system-wide options are passed to pbrtInit() using the Options structure here.

⟨*Global Forward Declarations*⟩ +≡
```
struct Options {
    int nThreads = 0;
    bool quickRender = false;
    bool quiet = false, verbose = false;
    std::string imageFile;
};
```

⟨*API Function Definitions*⟩ ≡
```
void pbrtInit(const Options &opt) {
    PbrtOptions = opt;
    ⟨API Initialization 1110⟩
    ⟨General pbrt Initialization 324⟩
}
```

The options are stored in a global variable for easy access by other parts of the system. This variable is only used in a read-only fashion by the system after initialization in pbrtInit().

⟨*API Global Variables*⟩ ≡
```
Options PbrtOptions;
```

⟨*API Function Definitions*⟩ +≡
```
void pbrtCleanup() {
    ⟨API Cleanup 1111⟩
}
```

After the system has been initialized, a subset of the API routines is available. Legal calls at this point are those that set general rendering options like the camera and sampler properties, the type of film to be used, and so on, but the user is not yet allowed to start to describe the lights, shapes, and materials in the scene.

After the overall rendering options have been set, the pbrtWorldBegin() function locks them in; it is no longer legal to call the routines that set them. At this point, the user can begin to describe the geometric primitives and lights that are in the scene. This separation of global versus scene-specific information can help simplify the implementation of the renderer. For example, consider a spline patch shape that tessellates itself into triangles. This shape might compute the required size of its generated triangles based on the area of the screen that it covers. If the camera's position and image resolution are guaranteed not to change after the shape is created, then the shape can potentially do the tessellation work immediately at creation time.

Once the scene has been fully specified, the pbrtWorldEnd() routine is called. At this point, the renderer knows that the scene description is complete and that rendering can begin. The image will be rendered and written to a file before pbrtWorldEnd() returns. The user may then specify new options for another frame of an animation, and then another pbrtWorldBegin()/pbrtWorldEnd() block to describe the geometry for the next frame, repeating as many times as desired. The remainder of this section will discuss the routines related to setting rendering options. Section B.3 describes the routines for specifying the scene inside the world block.

B.2.1 STATE TRACKING

There are three distinct states that the renderer's API can be in:

- *Uninitialized:* Before pbrtInit() has been called or after pbrtCleanup() has been called, no other API calls are legal.
- *Options block:* Outside a pbrtWorldBegin() and pbrtWorldEnd() pair, scene-wide global options may be set.
- *World block:* Inside a pbrtWorldBegin() and pbrtWorldEnd() pair, the scene may be described.

The module static variable currentApiState starts out with the value APIState:: Uninitialized, indicating that the API system hasn't yet been initialized. Its value is updated appropriately by pbrtInit(), pbrtWorldBegin(), and pbrtCleanup().

⟨*API Static Data*⟩ ≡
```
enum class APIState { Uninitialized, OptionsBlock, WorldBlock };
static APIState currentApiState = APIState::Uninitialized;
```

Now we can start to define the implementation of pbrtInit(). pbrtInit() first makes sure that it hasn't already been called and then sets the currentApiState variable to OptionsBlock to indicate that the scene-wide options can be specified.

⟨*API Initialization*⟩ ≡   **1109**
```
if (currentApiState != APIState::Uninitialized)
    Error("pbrtInit() has already been called.");
currentApiState = APIState::OptionsBlock;
```

currentApiState 1110
Error() 1068
pbrtCleanup() 1109
pbrtInit() 1109
pbrtWorldBegin() 1117
pbrtWorldEnd() 1129

Similarly, pbrtCleanup() makes sure that pbrtInit() has been called and that we're not in the middle of a pbrtWorldBegin()/pbrtWorldEnd() block before resetting the state to the uninitialized state.

⟨*API Cleanup*⟩ ≡   1109
```
    if (currentApiState == APIState::Uninitialized)
        Error("pbrtCleanup() called without pbrtInit().");
    else if (currentApiState == APIState::WorldBlock)
        Error("pbrtCleanup() called while inside world block.");
    currentApiState = APIState::Uninitialized;
```

All API functions that are only valid in particular states invoke a state verification macro like VERIFY_INITIALIZED(), to make sure that currentApiState holds an appropriate value. If the states don't match, an error message is printed and the function immediately returns. (Note that this check must be implemented as a macro rather than a separate function so that its return statement causes the calling function itself to return.)

⟨*API Macros*⟩ ≡
```
    #define VERIFY_INITIALIZED(func)                            \
    if (currentApiState == APIState::Uninitialized) {           \
        Error("pbrtInit() must be before calling \"%s()\". " \
              "Ignoring.", func);                               \
        return;                                                 \
    } else /* swallow trailing semicolon */
```

The implementations of VERIFY_OPTIONS() and VERIFY_WORLD() are analogous.

B.2.2 TRANSFORMATIONS

As the scene is being described, pbrt maintains *current transformation matrices* (CTMs), one for each of a number of points in time. If the transformations are different, then they describe an animated transformation. (Recall, for example, that the AnimatedTransform class defined in Section 2.9.3 stores two transformation matrices for two given times.) A number of API calls are available to modify the CTMs; when objects like shapes, cameras, and lights are created, the CTMs are passed to their constructor to define the transformation from their local coordinate system to world space.

The code below stores two CTMs in the module-local curTransform variable. They are represented by the TransformSet class, to be defined shortly, which stores a fixed number of transformations. The activeTransformBits variable is a bit-vector indicating which of the CTMs are active; the active transforms are updated when the transformation-related API calls are made, while the others are unchanged. This mechanism allows the user to modify some of the CTMs selectively in order to define animated transformations.

⟨*API Static Data*⟩ +≡
```
    static TransformSet curTransform;
    static int activeTransformBits = AllTransformsBits;
```

The implementation here just stores two transformation matrices, one that defines the CTM for the starting time (provided via the pbrtTransformTimes() call, defined in a few pages), and the other for the ending time.

⟨*API Local Classes*⟩ ≡
```
constexpr int MaxTransforms = 2;
constexpr int StartTransformBits = 1 << 0;
constexpr int EndTransformBits =   1 << 1;
constexpr int AllTransformsBits = (1 << MaxTransforms) - 1;
```

TransformSet is a small utility class that stores an array of transformations and provides some utility routines for managing them.

⟨*API Local Classes*⟩ +≡
```
struct TransformSet {
    ⟨TransformSet Public Methods 1112⟩
private:
    Transform t[MaxTransforms];
};
```

An accessor function is provided to access the individual Transforms.

⟨*TransformSet Public Methods*⟩ ≡   1112
```
Transform &operator[](int i) {
    return t[i];
}
```

The Inverse() method returns a new TransformSet that holds the inverses of the individual Transforms.

⟨*TransformSet Public Methods*⟩ +≡   1112
```
friend TransformSet Inverse(const TransformSet &ts) {
    TransformSet tInv;
    for (int i = 0; i < MaxTransforms; ++i)
        tInv.t[i] = Inverse(ts.t[i]);
    return tInv;
}
```

The actual transformation functions are straightforward. Because the CTM is used both for the rendering options and the scene description phases, these routines only need to verify that pbrtInit() has been called.

⟨*API Function Definitions*⟩ +≡
```
void pbrtIdentity() {
    VERIFY_INITIALIZED("Identity");
    FOR_ACTIVE_TRANSFORMS(curTransform[i] = Transform();)
}
```

The FOR_ACTIVE_TRANSFORMS() macro encapsulates the logic for determining which of the CTMs is active and applying the given operation to those that are. The given statement is executed only for the active transforms.

⟨*API Macros*⟩ +≡
```
#define FOR_ACTIVE_TRANSFORMS(expr)                         \
    for (int i = 0; i < MaxTransforms; ++i)                 \
        if (activeTransformBits & (1 << i)) { expr }
```

⟨*API Function Definitions*⟩ +≡
```
void pbrtTranslate(Float dx, Float dy, Float dz) {
    VERIFY_INITIALIZED("Translate");
    FOR_ACTIVE_TRANSFORMS(curTransform[i] =
        curTransform[i] * Translate(Vector3f(dx, dy, dz));)
}
```

Most of the rest of the functions are similarly defined, so we will not show their definitions here. pbrt also provides pbrtConcatTransform() and pbrtTransform() functions to allow the user to specify an arbitrary matrix to postmultiply or replace the active CTM(s), respectively.

⟨*API Function Declarations*⟩ ≡
```
void pbrtRotate(Float angle, Float ax, Float ay, Float az);
void pbrtScale(Float sx, Float sy, Float sz);
void pbrtLookAt(Float ex, Float ey, Float ez,
               Float lx, Float ly, Float lz,
               Float ux, Float uy, Float uz);
void pbrtConcatTransform(Float transform[16]);
void pbrtTransform(Float transform[16]);
```

It can be useful to make a named copy of the CTM so that it can be referred to later. For example, to place a light at the camera's position, it is useful to first apply the transformation into the camera coordinate system, since then the light can just be placed at the origin (0, 0, 0). This way, if the camera position is changed and the scene is rerendered, the light will move with it. The pbrtCoordinateSystem() function copies the current TransformSet into the namedCoordinateSystems associative array, and pbrtCoordSysTransform() loads a named set of CTMs.

⟨*API Static Data*⟩ +≡
```
static std::map<std::string, TransformSet> namedCoordinateSystems;
```

⟨*API Function Definitions*⟩ +≡
```
void pbrtCoordinateSystem(const std::string &name) {
    VERIFY_INITIALIZED("CoordinateSystem");
    namedCoordinateSystems[name] = curTransform;
}
```

⟨*API Function Definitions*⟩ +≡
```
void pbrtCoordSysTransform(const std::string &name) {
    VERIFY_INITIALIZED("CoordSysTransform");
    if (namedCoordinateSystems.find(name) !=
        namedCoordinateSystems.end())
        curTransform = namedCoordinateSystems[name];
    else
        Warning("Couldn't find named coordinate system \"%s\"",
            name.c_str());
}
```

Not all of the types in pbrt that take transformations support animated transformations. (Textures are one example (Section B.3.2); it's not worth the additional code complexity to support them, especially since the utility an animated texture transform brings isn't obvious.) For such cases, WARN_IF_ANIMATED_TRANSFORM() macro warns if the CTMs are different, indicating that an animated transformation has been specified.

⟨*API Macros*⟩ +≡
```
#define WARN_IF_ANIMATED_TRANSFORM(func)                        \
do { if (curTransform.IsAnimated())                             \
        Warning("Animated transformations set; ignoring for \"%s\" " \
                "and using the start transform only", func);    \
} while (false) /* swallow trailing semicolon */
```

⟨*TransformSet Public Methods*⟩ +≡   1112
```
bool IsAnimated() const {
    for (int i = 0; i < MaxTransforms - 1; ++i)
        if (t[i] != t[i + 1]) return true;
    return false;
}
```

B.2.3 OPTIONS

All of the rendering options that are set before the pbrtWorldBegin() call are stored in a RenderOptions structure. This structure contains public data members that are set by API calls and methods that help create objects used by the rest of pbrt for rendering.

⟨*API Local Classes*⟩ +≡
```
struct RenderOptions {
    ⟨RenderOptions Public Methods 1130⟩
    ⟨RenderOptions Public Data 1115⟩
};
```

A single static instance of a RenderOptions structure is available to the rest of the API functions:

⟨*API Static Data*⟩ +≡
```
static std::unique_ptr<RenderOptions> renderOptions;
```

When pbrtInit() is called, it allocates a RenderOptions structure that initially holds default values for all of its options:

⟨*API Initialization*⟩ +≡   1109
```
renderOptions.reset(new RenderOptions);
```

The renderOptions variable is freed by pbrtCleanup():

⟨*API Cleanup*⟩ +≡   1109
```
renderOptions.reset(nullptr);
```

A few calls are available to set which of the CTMs should be active.

⟨*API Function Definitions*⟩ +≡

```
void pbrtActiveTransformAll() {
    activeTransformBits = AllTransformsBits;
}
void pbrtActiveTransformEndTime() {
    activeTransformBits = EndTransformBits;
}
void pbrtActiveTransformStartTime() {
    activeTransformBits = StartTransformBits;
}
```

The two times at which the two CTMs are defined can be provided by a calling the function pbrtTransformTimes(). By default, the start time is 0 and the end time is 1.

⟨*API Function Definitions*⟩ +≡

```
void pbrtTransformTimes(Float start, Float end) {
    VERIFY_OPTIONS("TransformTimes");
    renderOptions->transformStartTime = start;
    renderOptions->transformEndTime = end;
}
```

⟨*RenderOptions Public Data*⟩ ≡   **1114**

```
Float transformStartTime = 0, transformEndTime = 1;
```

The API functions for setting the rest of the rendering options are mostly similar in both their interface and their implementation. For example, pbrtPixelFilter() specifies the kind of Filter to be used for filtering image samples. It takes two parameters: a string giving the name of the filter to use and a ParamSet giving the parameters to the filter.

Note that an instance of the Filter class isn't created immediately upon a call to pbrtPixelFilter(); instead, that function just stores the name of the filter and its parameters in renderOptions. There are two reasons for this approach: first, there may be a subsequent call to pbrtPixelFilter() before the start of the world block, specifying a different filter; the (small) cost of creating the first Filter would be wasted in this case.

Second, and more importantly, there are various object creation ordering dependencies imposed by the parameters taken by various constructors. For example, the Film constructor expects a pointer to the Filter being used, and the Camera constructor expects a pointer to the Film. Thus, the camera can't be created before the film, and the film can't be created before the filter. We don't want to require the user to specify the scene options in an order dictated by these internal details, so instead always just store object names and parameter sets until the end of the options block. (The Filter here could actually be created immediately, since it doesn't depend on other objects, but we follow the same approach to it for consistency.)

⟨*API Function Definitions*⟩ +≡

```
void pbrtPixelFilter(const std::string &name, const ParamSet &params) {
    VERIFY_OPTIONS("PixelFilter");
    renderOptions->FilterName = name;
    renderOptions->FilterParams = params;
}
```

The default filter is set to the box filter. If no specific filter is specified in the scene description file, then because the default ParamSet has no parameter values, the filter will be created based on its default parameter settings.

⟨*RenderOptions Public Data*⟩ +≡   **1114**
```
    std::string FilterName = "box";
    ParamSet FilterParams;
```

Most of the rest of the rendering-option-setting API calls are similar; they simply store their arguments in renderOptions. Therefore, we will only include the declarations of these functions here. The options controlled by each function should be apparent from its name; more information about the legal parameters to each of these routines can be found in the documentation of pbrt's input file format.

⟨*API Function Declarations*⟩ +≡
```
    void pbrtFilm(const std::string &type, const ParamSet &params);
    void pbrtSampler(const std::string &name, const ParamSet &params);
    void pbrtAccelerator(const std::string &name, const ParamSet &params);
    void pbrtIntegrator(const std::string &name, const ParamSet &params);
```

pbrtCamera() is slightly different from the other options, since the camera-to-world transformation needs to be recorded. The CTM is used by pbrtCamera() to initialize this value, and the camera coordinate system transformation is also stored for possible future use by pbrtCoordSysTransform().

⟨*API Function Definitions*⟩ +≡
```
    void pbrtCamera(const std::string &name, const ParamSet &params) {
        VERIFY_OPTIONS("Camera");
        renderOptions->CameraName = name;
        renderOptions->CameraParams = params;
        renderOptions->CameraToWorld = Inverse(curTransform);
        namedCoordinateSystems["camera"] = renderOptions->CameraToWorld;
    }
```

The default camera uses a perspective projection.

⟨*RenderOptions Public Data*⟩ +≡   **1114**
```
    std::string CameraName = "perspective";
    ParamSet CameraParams;
    TransformSet CameraToWorld;
```

B.2.4 MEDIA DESCRIPTION

Definitions of participating media in the scene are specified by pbrtMakeNamedMedium(). This function allows the user to associate a specific type of participation media (from Section 11.3) with an arbitrary name. For example,

```
MakeNamedMedium "highAlbedo" "string type" "homogeneous"
    "color sigma_s" [5.0 5.0 5.0] "color sigma_a" [0.1 0.1 0.1]
```

creates a HomogeneousMedium instance with the name highAlbedo.

⟨*API Function Declarations*⟩ +≡
```
void pbrtMakeNamedMedium(const std::string &name, const ParamSet &params);
```

The corresponding Medium instances are stored in an associative array for access later.

⟨*RenderOptions Public Data*⟩ +≡   1114
```
std::map<std::string, std::shared_ptr<Medium>> namedMedia;
```

Once named media have been created, pbrtMediumInterface() allows specifying the current "inside" and "outside" media. For shapes, these specify the media inside and outside the shape's surface, where the side of the shape where the surface normal is oriented outward is "outside." For the camera and for light sources that don't have geometry associated with them, the "inside" medium is ignored and "outside" gives the medium containing the object. The current medium is stored in the GraphicsState class, which will be introduced shortly.

Like the transformation-related API functions, both of these functions can be called from both the options and the world blocks; the former so that media can be specified for the camera and the latter so that media can be specified for the lights and shapes in the scene.

⟨*API Function Definitions*⟩ +≡
```
void pbrtMediumInterface(const std::string &insideName,
        const std::string &outsideName) {
    VERIFY_INITIALIZED("MediumInterface");
    graphicsState.currentInsideMedium = insideName;
    graphicsState.currentOutsideMedium = outsideName;
}
```

⟨*Graphics State*⟩ ≡   1118
```
std::string currentInsideMedium, currentOutsideMedium;
```

B.3 SCENE DEFINITION

After the user has set up the overall rendering options, the pbrtWorldBegin() call marks the start of the description of the shapes, materials, and lights in the scene. It sets the current rendering state to APIState::WorldBlock, resets the CTMs to identity matrices, and enables all of the CTMs.

⟨*API Function Definitions*⟩ +≡
```
void pbrtWorldBegin() {
    VERIFY_OPTIONS("WorldBegin");
    currentApiState = APIState::WorldBlock;
    for (int i = 0; i < MaxTransforms; ++i)
        curTransform[i] = Transform();
    activeTransformBits = AllTransformsBits;
    namedCoordinateSystems["world"] = curTransform;
}
```

B.3.1 HIERARCHICAL GRAPHICS STATE

As the scene's lights, geometry, and participating media are specified, a variety of attributes can be set as well. In addition to the CTMs, these include information about textures and the current material. When a geometric primitive or light source is then added to the scene, the current attributes are used when creating the corresponding object. These data are all known as the *graphics state*.

It is useful for a rendering API to provide some functionality for managing the graphics state. pbrt has API calls that allow the current graphics state to be managed with an *attribute stack*; the user can push the current set of attributes, make changes to their values, and then later pop back to the previously pushed attribute values. For example, a scene description file might contain the following:

```
Material "matte"
AttributeBegin
  Material "plastic"
  Translate 5 0 0
  Shape "sphere" "float radius" [1]
AttributeEnd
Shape "sphere" "float radius" [1]
```

The first sphere is affected by the translation and is bound to the plastic material, while the second sphere is matte and isn't translated. Changes to attributes made inside a pbrtAttributeBegin()/pbrtAttributeEnd() block are forgotten at the end of the block. Being able to save and restore attributes in this manner is a classic idiom for scene description in computer graphics.

The graphics state is stored in the GraphicsState structure. As was done previously with RenderOptions, we'll be adding members to it throughout this section.

```
⟨API Local Classes⟩ +≡
    struct GraphicsState {
        ⟨Graphics State Methods 1125⟩
        ⟨Graphics State 1117⟩
    };
```

When pbrtInit() is called, the current graphics state is initialized to hold default values.

```
⟨API Initialization⟩ +≡                                          1109
    graphicsState = GraphicsState();
```

A vector of GraphicsStates is used as a stack to perform hierarchical state management. When pbrtAttributeBegin() is called, the current GraphicsState is copied and pushed onto this stack. pbrtAttributeEnd() then simply pops the state from this stack.

⟨*API Function Definitions*⟩ +≡
```
void pbrtAttributeBegin() {
    VERIFY_WORLD("AttributeBegin");
    pushedGraphicsStates.push_back(graphicsState);
    pushedTransforms.push_back(curTransform);
    pushedActiveTransformBits.push_back(activeTransformBits);
}
```

⟨*API Static Data*⟩ +≡
```
static GraphicsState graphicsState;
static std::vector<GraphicsState> pushedGraphicsStates;
static std::vector<TransformSet> pushedTransforms;
static std::vector<uint32_t> pushedActiveTransformBits;
```

pbrtAttributeEnd() also verifies that we do not have attribute stack underflow by checking to see if the stack is empty.

⟨*API Function Definitions*⟩ +≡
```
void pbrtAttributeEnd() {
    VERIFY_WORLD("AttributeEnd");
    if (!pushedGraphicsStates.size()) {
        Error("Unmatched pbrtAttributeEnd() encountered. "
              "Ignoring it.");
        return;
    }
    graphicsState = pushedGraphicsStates.back();
    pushedGraphicsStates.pop_back();
    curTransform = pushedTransforms.back();
    pushedTransforms.pop_back();
    activeTransformBits = pushedActiveTransformBits.back();
    pushedActiveTransformBits.pop_back();
}
```

The API also provides pbrtTransformBegin() and pbrtTransformEnd() calls. These functions are similar to pbrtAttributeBegin() and pbrtAttributeEnd(), except that they only push and pop the CTMs. We frequently want to apply a transformation to a texture, but since the list of named textures is stored in the graphics state, we cannot use pbrtAttributeBegin() to save the transformation matrix. Since the implementations of pbrtTransformBegin() and pbrtTransformEnd() are very similar to pbrtAttributeBegin() and pbrtAttributeEnd(), respectively, they are not shown here.

⟨*API Function Declarations*⟩ +≡
```
void pbrtTransformBegin();
void pbrtTransformEnd();
```

B.3.2 TEXTURE AND MATERIAL PARAMETERS

Recall that all of the materials in pbrt use textures to describe all of their parameters. For example, the diffuse color of the matte material class is always obtained from a texture, even if the material is intended to have a constant reflectivity (in which case a ConstantTexture is used).

Before a material can be created, it is necessary to create these textures to pass to the material creation procedures. Textures can be either explicitly created and later referred to by name or implicitly created on the fly to represent a constant parameter. These two methods of texture creation are hidden by the TextureParams class.

⟨*TextureParams Declarations*⟩ ≡
```
class TextureParams {
public:
    ⟨TextureParams Public Methods 1121⟩
private:
    ⟨TextureParams Private Data 1120⟩
};
```

The TextureParams class stores references to associative arrays of previously defined named Float and Spectrum textures, as well as two references to ParamSets that will be searched for named textures. Its constructor, which won't be included here, just initializes these references from parameters passed to it.

⟨*TextureParams Private Data*⟩ ≡   1120
```
std::map<std::string, std::shared_ptr<Texture<Float>>> &floatTextures;
std::map<std::string,
        std::shared_ptr<Texture<Spectrum>>> &spectrumTextures;
const ParamSet &geomParams, &materialParams;
```

Here we will show the code for finding a texture of Spectrum type; the code for finding a Float texture is analogous. The TextureParams::GetSpectrumTexture() method takes a parameter name (e.g., "Kd"), as well as a default Spectrum value. If no texture has been explicitly specified for the parameter, a constant texture will be created that returns the default spectrum value.

Finding the texture is performed in several stages; the order of these stages is significant. First, the parameter list from the Shape for which a Material is being created is searched for a named reference to an explicitly defined texture. If no such texture is found, then the material parameters are searched. Finally, if no explicit texture has been found, the two parameter lists are searched in turn for supplied constant values. If no such constants are found, the default is used.

The order of these steps is crucial, because pbrt allows a shape to override individual elements of the material that is bound to it. For example, the user should be able to create a scene description that contains the lines

```
Material "matte" "color Kd" [ 1 0 0 ]
Shape "sphere" "color Kd" [ 0 1 0 ]
```

These two commands create a green matte sphere: because the shape's parameter list is searched first, the Kd parameter from the Shape will be used when the MatteMaterial constructor is called.

⟨*TextureParams Method Definitions*⟩ ≡
```
std::shared_ptr<Texture<Spectrum>>
TextureParams::GetSpectrumTexture(const std::string &n,
                                  const Spectrum &def) const {
    std::string name = geomParams.FindTexture(n);
    if (name == "") name = materialParams.FindTexture(n);
    if (name != "") {
        if (spectrumTextures.find(name) != spectrumTextures.end())
            return spectrumTextures[name];
        else
            Error("Couldn't find spectrum texture named \"%s\" "
                  "for parameter \"%s\"", name.c_str(), n.c_str());
    }
    Spectrum val = materialParams.FindOneSpectrum(n, def);
    val = geomParams.FindOneSpectrum(n, val);
    return std::make_shared<ConstantTexture<Spectrum>>(val);
}
```

Because an instance of the TextureParams class is passed to material creation routines that might need to access non-texture parameter values, we also provide ways to access the other parameter list types. These methods return parameters from the geometric parameter list, if found. Otherwise, the material parameter list is searched, and finally the default value is returned.

The TextureParams::FindFloat() method is shown here. The other access methods are similar and omitted.

⟨*TextureParams Public Methods*⟩ ≡   **1120**
```
Float FindFloat(const std::string &n, Float d) const {
    return geomParams.FindOneFloat(n, materialParams.FindOneFloat(n, d));
}
```

B.3.3 SURFACE AND MATERIAL DESCRIPTION

The pbrtTexture() method creates a named texture that can be referred to later. In addition to the texture name, its *type* is specified. pbrt supports only "float" and "spectrum" as texture types. The supplied parameter list is used to create a TextureParams object, which will be passed to the desired texture's creation routine.

⟨*API Function Definitions*⟩ +≡
```
void pbrtTexture(const std::string &name, const std::string &type,
                 const std::string &texname, const ParamSet &params) {
    VERIFY_WORLD("Texture");
    TextureParams tp(params, params, graphicsState.floatTextures,
                     graphicsState.spectrumTextures);
    if (type == "float")  {
        ⟨Create Float texture and store in floatTextures 1122⟩
    }
```

```
        else if (type == "color" || type == "spectrum")  {
            ⟨Create color texture and store in spectrumTextures⟩
        }
        else
            Error("Texture type \"%s\" unknown.", type.c_str());
    }
```

Creating the texture is simple. This function first checks to see if a texture of the same name and type already exists and issues a warning if so. Then, the MakeFloatTexture() routine calls the creation function for the appropriate Texture implementation, and the returned texture class is added to the GraphicsState::floatTextures associative array. The code for creating a spectrum texture is similar and not shown.

⟨*Create* Float *texture and store in* floatTextures⟩ ≡   **1121**
```
    if (graphicsState.floatTextures.find(name) !=
        graphicsState.floatTextures.end())
        Info("Texture \"%s\" being redefined", name.c_str());
    WARN_IF_ANIMATED_TRANSFORM("Texture");
    std::shared_ptr<Texture<Float>> ft =
        MakeFloatTexture(texname, curTransform[0], tp);
    if (ft) graphicsState.floatTextures[name] = ft;
```

⟨*Graphics State*⟩ +≡   **1118**
```
    std::map<std::string, std::shared_ptr<Texture<Float>>> floatTextures;
    std::map<std::string,
            std::shared_ptr<Texture<Spectrum>>> spectrumTextures;
```

The current material is specified by a call to pbrtMaterial(). Its ParamSet is stored until a Material object needs to be created later when a shape is specified.

⟨*API Function Declarations*⟩ +≡
```
    void pbrtMaterial(const std::string &name, const ParamSet &params);
```

The default material is matte.

⟨*Graphics State*⟩ +≡   **1118**
```
    ParamSet materialParams;
    std::string material = "matte";
```

pbrt also supports the notion of creating a Material with a given set of parameters and then associating an arbitrary name with the combination of material and parameter settings. pbrtMakeNamedMaterial() creates such an association, and pbrtNamedMaterial() sets the current material and material parameters based on a previously defined named material.

⟨*API Function Declarations*⟩ +≡
```
    void pbrtMakeNamedMaterial(const std::string &name,
                               const ParamSet &params);
    void pbrtNamedMaterial(const std::string &name);
```

⟨*Graphics State*⟩ +≡   **1118**
```
std::map<std::string, std::shared_ptr<Material>> namedMaterials;
std::string currentNamedMaterial;
```

B.3.4 LIGHT SOURCES

pbrt's API provides two ways for the user to specify light sources for the scene. The first, pbrtLightSource(), defines a light source that doesn't have geometry associated with it (e.g., a point light or a directional light).

⟨*API Function Definitions*⟩ +≡
```
void pbrtLightSource(const std::string &name, const ParamSet &params) {
    VERIFY_WORLD("LightSource");
    WARN_IF_ANIMATED_TRANSFORM("LightSource");
    MediumInterface mi = graphicsState.CreateMediumInterface();
    std::shared_ptr<Light> lt =
        MakeLight(name, params, curTransform[0], mi);
    if (!lt)
        Error("LightSource: light type \"%s\" unknown.", name.c_str());
    else
        renderOptions->lights.push_back(lt);
}
```

⟨*RenderOptions Public Data*⟩ +≡   **1114**
```
std::vector<std::shared_ptr<Light>> lights;
```

The second API call to describe light sources, pbrtAreaLightSource(), specifies an area light source. All shape specifications that appear between an area light source call up to the end of the current attribute block are treated as emissive. Thus, when an area light is specified via pbrtAreaLightSource(), it can't be created immediately since the shapes to follow are needed to define the light source's geometry. Therefore, this function just saves the name of the area light source type and the parameters given to it.

⟨*Graphics State*⟩ +≡   **1118**
```
ParamSet areaLightParams;
std::string areaLight;
```

⟨*API Function Definitions*⟩ +≡
```
void pbrtAreaLightSource(const std::string &name,
                         const ParamSet &params) {
    VERIFY_WORLD("AreaLightSource");
    graphicsState.areaLight = name;
    graphicsState.areaLightParams = params;
}
```

B.3.5 SHAPES

The pbrtShape() function creates one or more new Shape objects and adds them to the scene. This function is relatively complicated, in that it has to create area light sources if an area light is being defined, it has to handle animated and static shapes differently, and it also has to deal with creating object instances when needed.

⟨*API Function Definitions*⟩ +≡
```
void pbrtShape(const std::string &name, const ParamSet &params) {
    VERIFY_WORLD("Shape");
    std::vector<std::shared_ptr<Primitive>> prims;
    std::vector<std::shared_ptr<AreaLight>> areaLights;
    if (!curTransform.IsAnimated()) {
        ⟨Initialize prims and areaLights for static shape 1124⟩
    } else {
        ⟨Initialize prims and areaLights for animated shape 1126⟩
    }
    ⟨Add prims and areaLights to scene or current instance 1127⟩
}
```

Shapes that are animated are represented with TransformedPrimitives, which include extra functionality to use AnimatedTransforms, while shapes that aren't animated use GeometricPrimitives. Therefore, there are two code paths here for those two cases.

The static shape case is mostly a matter of creating the appropriate Shapes, Material, and MediumInterface to make corresponding GeometricPrimitives.

⟨*Initialize* prims *and* areaLights *for static shape*⟩ ≡   1124
```
    ⟨Create shapes for shape name 1124⟩
    std::shared_ptr<Material> mtl = graphicsState.CreateMaterial(params);
    params.ReportUnused();
    MediumInterface mi = graphicsState.CreateMediumInterface();
    for (auto s : shapes) {
        ⟨Possibly create area light for shape 1125⟩
        prims.push_back(
            std::make_shared<GeometricPrimitive>(s, mtl, area, mi));
    }
```

The code below uses a TransformCache (defined shortly), which allocates and stores a single Transform pointer for each unique transformation that is passed to its Lookup() method. In this way, if many shapes in the scene have the same transformation matrix, a single Transform pointer can be shared among all of them. MakeShapes() then handles the details of creating the shape or shapes corresponding to the given shape name, passing the ParamSet along to the shape's creation routine.

⟨*Create shapes for shape* name⟩ ≡   1124
```
    Transform *ObjToWorld, *WorldToObj;
    transformCache.Lookup(curTransform[0], &ObjToWorld, &WorldToObj);
    std::vector<std::shared_ptr<Shape>> shapes =
        MakeShapes(name, ObjToWorld, WorldToObj,
                   graphicsState.reverseOrientation, params);
    if (shapes.size() == 0) return;
```

TransformCache is a small wrapper around an associative array from transformations to pairs of Transform pointers; the first pointer is equal to the transform, and the second is its inverse. The Lookup() method just looks for the given transformation in the cache, allocates space for it and stores it and its inverse if not found, and returns the appropriate pointers.

⟨*TransformCache Private Data*⟩ ≡
```
std::map<Transform, std::pair<Transform *, Transform *>> cache;
MemoryArena arena;
```

⟨*API Static Data*⟩ +≡
```
static TransformCache transformCache;
```

The MakeShapes() function takes the name of the shape to be created, the CTMs, and the ParamSet for the new shape. It calls an appropriate shape creation function based on the shape name provided (e.g., for "sphere," it calls CreateSphereShape(), which is defined in Section B.4). The shape creation routines may return multiple shapes; for triangle meshes, for example, the creation routine returns a vector of Triangles. The implementation of this function is straightforward, so we won't include it here.

⟨*API Forward Declarations*⟩ ≡
```
std::vector<std::shared_ptr<Shape>> MakeShapes(const std::string &name,
        const Transform *ObjectToWorld, const Transform *WorldToObject,
        bool reverseOrientation, const ParamSet &paramSet);
```

The Material for the shape is created by the MakeMaterial() call; its implementation is analogous to that of MakeShapes(). If the specified material cannot be found (usually due to a typo in the material name), a matte material is created and a warning is issued.

⟨*Graphics State Methods*⟩ ≡   **1118**
```
std::shared_ptr<Material> CreateMaterial(const ParamSet &params);
```

Following the same basic approach, CreateMediumInterface() creates a MediumInterface based on the current named "inside" and "outside" media established with pbrtMedium Interface().

⟨*Graphics State Methods*⟩ +≡   **1118**
```
MediumInterface CreateMediumInterface();
```

If an area light has been set in the current graphics state by pbrtAreaLightSource(), the new shape is an emitter and an AreaLight needs to be made for it.

⟨*Possibly create area light for shape*⟩ ≡   **1124**
```
std::shared_ptr<AreaLight> area;
if (graphicsState.areaLight != "") {
    area = MakeAreaLight(graphicsState.areaLight, curTransform[0],
                         mi, graphicsState.areaLightParams, s);
    areaLights.push_back(area);
}
```

If the transformation matrices are animated, the task is a little more complicated. After Shape and GeometricPrimitive creation, a TransformedPrimitive is created to hold the shape or shapes that were created.

⟨*Initialize* prims *and* areaLights *for animated shape*⟩ ≡   **1124**
    ⟨*Create initial shape or shapes for animated shape* **1126**⟩
    ⟨*Create* GeometricPrimitive*(s) for animated shape* **1126**⟩
    ⟨*Create single* TransformedPrimitive *for* prims **1126**⟩

Because the Shape class doesn't handle animated transformations, the initial shape or
shapes for animated primitives are created with identity transformations. All of the
details related to the shape's transformation will be managed with the Transformed
Primitive that ends up holding the shape. Animated transformations for light sources
aren't currently supported in pbrt; thus, if an animated transform has been specified
with an area light source, a warning is issued here.

⟨*Create initial shape or shapes for animated shape*⟩ ≡   **1126**
```
if (graphicsState.areaLight != "")
    Warning("Ignoring currently set area light when creating "
            "animated shape");
Transform *identity;
transformCache.Lookup(Transform(), &identity, nullptr);
std::vector<std::shared_ptr<Shape>> shapes =
    MakeShapes(name, identity, identity,
              graphicsState.reverseOrientation, params);
if (shapes.size() == 0) return;
```

Given the initial set of shapes, it's straightforward to create a GeometricPrimitive for each
of them.

⟨*Create* GeometricPrimitive*(s) for animated shape*⟩ ≡   **1126**
```
std::shared_ptr<Material> mtl = graphicsState.CreateMaterial(params);
params.ReportUnused();
MediumInterface mi = graphicsState.CreateMediumInterface();
for (auto s : shapes)
    prims.push_back(
        std::make_shared<GeometricPrimitive>(s, mtl, nullptr, mi));
```

If there are multiple GeometricPrimitives, then it's worth collecting them in an aggregate
and storing that in a TransformedPrimitive, rather than creating multiple Transformed
Primitives. This way, the transformation only needs to be interpolated once and the
ray is only transformed once, rather than redundantly doing both of these for each
primitive that the ray intersects the bounds of. Intersection efficiency also benefits; see
the discussion in Exercise B.5.

⟨*Create single* TransformedPrimitive *for* prims⟩ ≡   **1126**
```
⟨Get animatedObjectToWorld transform for shape 1127⟩
if (prims.size() > 1) {
    std::shared_ptr<Primitive> bvh = std::make_shared<BVHAccel>(prims);
    prims.clear();
    prims.push_back(bvh);
}
prims[0] = std::make_shared<TransformedPrimitive>(prims[0],
                                            animatedObjectToWorld);
```

The TransformCache is used again, here to get transformations for the start and end time, which are then passed to the AnimatedTransform constructor.

⟨*Get* animatedObjectToWorld *transform for shape*⟩ ≡   1126
```
Transform *ObjToWorld[2];
transformCache.Lookup(curTransform[0], &ObjToWorld[0], nullptr);
transformCache.Lookup(curTransform[1], &ObjToWorld[1], nullptr);
AnimatedTransform animatedObjectToWorld(
    ObjToWorld[0], renderOptions->transformStartTime,
    ObjToWorld[1], renderOptions->transformEndTime);
```

If the user is in the middle of defining an object instance, pbrtObjectBegin() (defined in the following section) will have set the currentInstance member of renderOptions to point to a vector that is collecting the shapes that define the instance. In that case, the new shape or shapes are added to that array. Otherwise, the RenderOptions::primitives array is used—this array will eventually be passed to the Scene constructor. If it is also an area light, the corresponding areaLights are also added to the RenderOptions::lights array, just as pbrtLightSource() does.

⟨*Add* prims *and* areaLights *to scene or current instance*⟩ ≡   1124
```
if (renderOptions->currentInstance) {
    if (areaLights.size())
        Warning("Area lights not supported with object instancing");
    renderOptions->currentInstance->insert(
        renderOptions->currentInstance->end(), prims.begin(),
        prims.end());
} else {
    renderOptions->primitives.insert(renderOptions->primitives.end(),
        prims.begin(), prims.end());
    if (areaLights.size())
        renderOptions->lights.insert(renderOptions->lights.end(),
            areaLights.begin(), areaLights.end());
}
```

⟨*RenderOptions Public Data*⟩ +≡   1114
```
std::vector<std::shared_ptr<Primitive>> primitives;
```

B.3.6 OBJECT INSTANCING

All shapes that are specified between a pbrtObjectBegin() and pbrtObjectEnd() pair are used to create a named object instance (see the discussion of object instancing and the TransformedPrimitive class in Section 4.1.2). pbrtObjectBegin() sets RenderOptions:: currentInstance so that subsequent pbrtShape() calls can add the shape to this instance's vector of primitive references. This function also pushes the graphics state, so that any changes made to the CTMs or other state while defining the instance don't last beyond the instance definition.

⟨*API Function Definitions*⟩ +≡
```
void pbrtObjectBegin(const std::string &name) {
    pbrtAttributeBegin();
    if (renderOptions->currentInstance)
        Error("ObjectBegin called inside of instance definition");
    renderOptions->instances[name] =
        std::vector<std::shared_ptr<Primitive>>();
    renderOptions->currentInstance = &renderOptions->instances[name];
}
```

⟨*RenderOptions Public Data*⟩ +≡   **1114**
```
std::map<std::string, std::vector<std::shared_ptr<Primitive>>> instances;
std::vector<std::shared_ptr<Primitive>> *currentInstance = nullptr;
```

⟨*API Function Definitions*⟩ +≡
```
void pbrtObjectEnd() {
    VERIFY_WORLD("ObjectEnd");
    if (!renderOptions->currentInstance)
        Error("ObjectEnd called outside of instance definition");
    renderOptions->currentInstance = nullptr;
    pbrtAttributeEnd();
}
```

When an instance is used in the scene, the instance's vector of Primitives needs to be found in the RenderOptions::instances map, a TransformedPrimitive created, and the instance added to the scene. Note that the TransformedPrimitive constructor takes the current transformation matrix from the time when pbrtObjectInstance() is called. The instance's complete world transformation is the composition of the CTM when it is instantiated with the CTM when it was originally created.

pbrtObjectInstance() first does some error checking to make sure that the instance is not being used inside the definition of another instance and also that the named instance has been defined. The error checking is simple and not shown here.

⟨*API Function Definitions*⟩ +≡
```
void pbrtObjectInstance(const std::string &name) {
    VERIFY_WORLD("ObjectInstance");
    ⟨Perform object instance error checking⟩
    std::vector<std::shared_ptr<Primitive>> &in =
        renderOptions->instances[name];
    if (in.size() == 0) return;
    if (in.size() > 1) {
        ⟨Create aggregate for instance Primitives 1129⟩
    }
    ⟨Create animatedInstanceToWorld transform for instance 1129⟩
    std::shared_ptr<Primitive> prim(
        std::make_shared<TransformedPrimitive>(in[0],
                                               animatedInstanceToWorld));
    renderOptions->primitives.push_back(prim);
}
```

⟨*Create* animatedInstanceToWorld *transform for instance*⟩ ≡   1128
```
Transform *InstanceToWorld[2];
transformCache.Lookup(curTransform[0], &InstanceToWorld[0], nullptr);
transformCache.Lookup(curTransform[1], &InstanceToWorld[1], nullptr);
AnimatedTransform animatedInstanceToWorld(InstanceToWorld[0],
    renderOptions->transformStartTime,
    InstanceToWorld[1], renderOptions->transformEndTime);
```

If there is more than one primitive in an instance, then an aggregate needs to be built for it. This must be done here rather than in the TransformedPrimitive constructor so that the resulting aggregate will be reused if this instance is used multiple times in the scene.

⟨*Create aggregate for instance* Primitives⟩ ≡   1128
```
std::shared_ptr<Primitive> accel(
    MakeAccelerator(renderOptions->AcceleratorName, in,
                    renderOptions->AcceleratorParams));
if (!accel) accel = std::make_shared<BVHAccel>(in);
in.erase(in.begin(), in.end());
in.push_back(accel);
```

B.3.7 WORLD END AND RENDERING

When pbrtWorldEnd() is called, the scene has been fully specified and rendering can begin. This routine makes sure that there aren't excess graphics state structures pushed on the state stack (issuing a warning if so), creates the Scene and Integrator objects, and then calls the Integrator::Render() method.

⟨*API Function Definitions*⟩ +≡
```
void pbrtWorldEnd() {
    VERIFY_WORLD("WorldEnd");
    ⟨Ensure there are no pushed graphics states 1129⟩
    ⟨Create scene and render 1130⟩
    ⟨Clean up after rendering 1130⟩
}
```

If there are graphics states and/or transformations remaining on the respective stacks, a warning is issued for each one:

⟨*Ensure there are no pushed graphics states*⟩ ≡   1129
```
while (pushedGraphicsStates.size()) {
    Warning("Missing end to pbrtAttributeBegin()");
    pushedGraphicsStates.pop_back();
    pushedTransforms.pop_back();
}
while (pushedTransforms.size()) {
    Warning("Missing end to pbrtTransformBegin()");
    pushedTransforms.pop_back();
}
```

Now the RenderOptions::MakeIntegrator() and RenderOptions::MakeScene() methods can create the corresponding objects based on the settings provided by the user.

⟨*Create scene and render*⟩ ≡   1129
```
std::unique_ptr<Integrator> integrator(renderOptions->MakeIntegrator());
std::unique_ptr<Scene> scene(renderOptions->MakeScene());
if (scene && integrator)
    integrator->Render(*scene);
TerminateWorkerThreads();
```

Creating the Scene object is mostly a matter of creating the Aggregate for all of the primitives and calling the Scene constructor. The MakeAccelerator() function isn't included here; it's similar in structure to MakeShapes() as far as using the string passed to it to determine which accelerator construction function to call.

⟨*API Function Definitions*⟩ +≡
```
Scene *RenderOptions::MakeScene() {
    std::shared_ptr<Primitive> accelerator =
        MakeAccelerator(AcceleratorName, primitives, AcceleratorParams);
    if (!accelerator)
        accelerator = std::make_shared<BVHAccel>(primitives);
    Scene *scene = new Scene(accelerator, lights);
    ⟨Erase primitives and lights from RenderOptions 1130⟩
    return scene;
}
```

After the scene has been created, RenderOptions clears the vectors of primitives and lights. This ensures that if a subsequent scene is defined then the scene description from this frame isn't inadvertently included.

⟨*Erase primitives and lights from* RenderOptions⟩ ≡   1130
```
primitives.erase(primitives.begin(), primitives.end());
lights.erase(lights.begin(), lights.end());
```

Integrator creation in the MakeIntegrator() method is again similar to how shapes and other named objects are created; the string name is used to dispatch to an object-specific creation function.

⟨*RenderOptions Public Methods*⟩ ≡   1114
```
Integrator *MakeIntegrator() const;
```

Once rendering is complete, the API transitions back to the "options block" rendering state, prints out any statistics gathered during rendering, and clears the CTMs and named coordinate systems so that the next frame, if any, starts with a clean slate.

⟨*Clean up after rendering*⟩ ≡   1129
```
currentApiState = APIState::OptionsBlock;
ReportThreadStats();
if (PbrtOptions.quiet == false) {
    PrintStats(stdout);
    ReportProfilerResults(stdout);
}
```

```
for (int i = 0; i < MaxTransforms; ++i)
    curTransform[i] = Transform();
activeTransformBits = AllTransformsBits;
namedCoordinateSystems.erase(namedCoordinateSystems.begin(),
                             namedCoordinateSystems.end());
```

B.4 ADDING NEW OBJECT IMPLEMENTATIONS

We will briefly review the overall process that pbrt uses to create instances of implementations of the various abstract interface classes like Shapes, Cameras, Integrators, etc., at run time. We will focus on the details for the Shape class, since the other types are handled similarly.

When the API needs to create a shape, it has the string name of the shape and the ParamSet that represents the corresponding information in the input file. These need to be used together to create a specific instance of the named shape. MakeShapes() has a series of if tests to determine which shape creation function to call; the one for Spheres, CreateSphereShape(), is shown here:

⟨*Sphere Method Definitions*⟩ +≡
```
std::shared_ptr<Shape> CreateSphereShape(const Transform *o2w,
        const Transform *w2o, bool reverseOrientation,
        const ParamSet &params) {
    Float radius = params.FindOneFloat("radius", 1.f);
    Float zmin = params.FindOneFloat("zmin", -radius);
    Float zmax = params.FindOneFloat("zmax", radius);
    Float phimax = params.FindOneFloat("phimax", 360.f);
    return std::make_shared<Sphere>(o2w, w2o, reverseOrientation, radius,
                                    zmin, zmax, phimax);
}
```

The appropriate named parameter values are extracted from the parameter list, sensible defaults are used for ones not present, and the appropriate values are passed to the Sphere constructor. As another alternative, we could have written the Sphere constructor to just take a ParamSet as a parameter and extracted the parameters there. We followed this approach instead in order to make it easier to create spheres for other uses without having to create a full ParamSet to specify the parameters to it.

Thus, adding a new implementation to pbrt requires adding the new source files to the build process so they are compiled and linked to the executable, modifying the appropriate creation function (MakeShapes(), MakeLight(), etc.) in core/api.cpp to look for the new type's name and call its creation function, in addition to implementing the creation function (like CreateSphereShape()) that extracts parameters and calls the object's constructor, returning a new instance of the object.

FURTHER READING

The RenderMan® API is described in a number of books (Upstill 1989; Apodaca and Gritz 2000) and in its specification document, which is available online (Pixar Animation Studios 2000). A different approach to rendering APIs is taken by the *mental ray* rendering system, which exposes much more internal information about the system's implementation to users, allowing it to be extensible in more ways than is possible in other systems. See Driemeyer and Herken (2002) for further information about it.

EXERCISES

● **B.1** One approach for reducing renderer startup time is to support a binary representation of internal data structures that can be written to disk. For example, for complex scenes, creating the ray acceleration aggregates may take more time than the initial parsing of the scene file. An alternative is to modify the system to have the capability of dumping out a representation of the acceleration structure and all of the primitives inside it after it is first created. The resulting file could then be subsequently read back into memory much more quickly than rebuilding the data structure from scratch. However, because C++ doesn't have native support for saving arbitrary objects to disk and then reading them back during a subsequent execution of the program (a capability known as *serialization* or *pickling* in other languages), adding this feature effectively requires extending many of the objects in pbrt to support this capability on their own.

One additional advantage of this approach is that substantial amounts of computation can be invested in creating high-quality acceleration structures, with the knowledge that this cost doesn't need to be paid each time the scene is loaded into memory. Implement support for serializing the scene representation and then reusing it across multiple renderings of the scene. How is pbrt's start-up time (up until when rendering begins) affected? What about overall rendering time?

● **B.2** The material assigned to object instances in pbrt is the current material when the instance was defined inside the pbrtObjectBegin()/pbrtObjectEnd() block. This can be inconvenient if the user wants to use the same geometry multiple times in a scene, giving it a different material. Fix the API and the implementation of the TransformedPrimitive class so that the material assigned to instances is the current material when the instance is instantiated, or, if the user hasn't set a material, the current material when the instance was created.

● **B.3** Generalize pbrt's API for specifying animation; the current implementation only allows the user to provide two transformation matrices, only at the start and end of a fixed time range. For specifying more complex motion, a more flexible approach may be useful. One improvement is to allow the user to specify an arbitrary number of *keyframe* transformations, each associated with an arbitrary time.

More generally, the system could be extended to support transformations that are explicit functions of time. For example, a rotation could be described with an expression of the form `Rotate (time * 2 + 1) 0 0 1` to describe a time-varying rotation about the z axis. Extend pbrt to support a more general matrix animation scheme, and render images showing results that aren't possible with the current implementation. What is the performance impact of your changes for scenes with animated objects that don't need the generality of your improvements?

⊚ B.4 Extend pbrt's API to have some retained mode semantics so that animated sequences of images can be rendered without needing to respecify the entire scene for each frame. Make sure that it is possible to remove some objects from the scene, add others, modify objects' materials and transformations from frame to frame, and so on.

⊚ B.5 In the current implementation, a unique `TransformedPrimitive` is created for each `Shape` with an animated transformation. If many shapes have exactly the same animated transformation, this turns out to be a poor choice. Consider the difference between a million-triangle mesh with an animated transformation versus a million independent triangles, all of which happen to have the same animated transformation.

In the first case, all of the triangles in the mesh are stored in a single instance of a `TransformedPrimitive` with an animated transformation. If a ray intersects the conservative bounding box that encompasses all of the object's motion over the frame time, then it is transformed to the mesh's object space according to the interpolated transformation at the ray's time. At this point, the intersection computation is no different from the intersection test with a static primitive; the only overhead due to the animation is from the larger bounding box and rays that hit the bounding box but not the animated primitive and the extra computation for matrix interpolation and transforming each ray once, according to its time.

In the second case, each triangle is stored in its own `TransformedPrimitive`, all of which happen to have the same `AnimatedTransform`. Each instance of `TransformedPrimitive` will have a large bounding box to encompass each triangle's motion, giving the acceleration structure a difficult set of inputs to deal with: many primitives with substantially overlapping bounding boxes. The impact on ray–primitive intersection efficiency will be high: the ray will be redundantly transformed many times by what happens to be the same recomputed interpolated transformation, and many intersection tests will be performed due to the large bounding boxes. Overall performance will be much worse than the first case.

To address this case, modify the code that implements the pbrt API calls so that if independent shapes are provided with the same animated transformation, they're all collected into a single acceleration structure with a single animated transformation. What is the performance improvement for the worst case outlined above? Is there an impact for more typical scenes with animated primitives?

AnimatedTransform 103
Shape 123
TransformedPrimitive 252

⊑ INDEX OF FRAGMENTS

Bold numbers indicate the first page of a fragment definition, ***bold italic*** numbers indicate an extension of the definition, and roman numbers indicate a use of the fragment.

Physically Based Rendering: From Theory To Implementation.
http://dx.doi.org/10.1016/B978-0-12-800645-0.50024-5

◫ INDEX OF CLASSES AND THEIR MEMBERS

Bold numbers indicate the page of a class definition. Class methods and fields are indented.

Physically Based Rendering: From Theory To Implementation.
http://dx.doi.org/10.1016/B978-0-12-800645-0.50025-7

∑ INDEX OF MISCELLANEOUS IDENTIFIERS

Finally, this index covers functions, module-local variables, preprocessor definitions, and other miscellaneous identifiers used in the system.

Physically Based Rendering: From Theory To Implementation.
http://dx.doi.org/10.1016/B978-0-12-800645-0.50026-9

References

Acton, M. 2014. Data-oriented design and C++. *http://www.slideshare.net/cellperformance/data-oriented-design-and-c*.

Adams, A., and M. Levoy. 2007. General linear cameras with finite aperture. In *Proceedings of the 2007 Eurographics Symposium on Rendering*, 121–26.

Áfra, A. 2012. Incoherent ray tracing without acceleration structures. *Eurographics 2012 Short Paper*.

Akalin, F. 2015. A better way to sample a sphere (w.r.t. solid angle). *https://www.akalin.com/sampling-visible-sphere*.

Aila, T., and T. Karras. 2010. Architecture considerations for tracing incoherent rays. In *Proceedings of High Performance Graphics 2010*, 113–22.

Aila, T., T. Karras, and S. Laine. 2013. On quality metrics of bounding volume hierarchies. In *Proceedings of High Performance Graphics 2013*, 101–07.

Aila, T., and S. Laine. 2009. Understanding the efficiency of ray traversal on GPUs. In *Proceedings of High Performance Graphics 2009*, 145–50.

Akenine-Möller, T. 2001. Fast 3D triangle-box overlap testing. *Journal of Graphics Tools* 6(1), 29–33.

Akenine-Möller, T., E. Haines, and N. Hoffman. 2008. *Real-Time Rendering*. Natick, MA: A. K. Peters.

Akenine-Möller, T., and J. Hughes. 1999. Efficiently building a matrix to rotate one vector to another. *Journal of Graphics Tools* 4(4), 1–4.

Alim, U. R. 2013. Rendering in shift-invariant spaces. In *Proceedings of Graphics Interface 2013*, 189–96.

Amanatides, J. 1984. Ray tracing with cones. *Computer Graphics (SIGGRAPH '84 Proceedings)*, 18, 129–35.

Amanatides, J. 1992. Algorithms for the detection and elimination of specular aliasing. In *Proceedings of Graphics Interface 1992*, 86–93.

Amanatides, J., and D. P. Mitchell. 1990. Some regularization problems in ray tracing. In *Proceedings of Graphics Interface 1990*, 221–28.

Amanatides, J., and A. Woo. 1987. A fast voxel traversal algorithm for ray tracing. In *Proceedings of Eurographics '87*, 3–10.

Ament, M., C. Bergmann, and D. Weiskopf. 2014. Refractive radiative transfer equation. *ACM Transactions on Graphics (Proceedings of SIGGRAPH 2014)* 33(2), 17:1–17:22.

Anderson, S. 2004. *graphics.stanford.edu/~seander/bithacks.html*.

Anton, H. A., I. Bivens, and S. Davis. 2001. *Calculus* (7th ed.). New York: John Wiley & Sons.

Apodaca, A. A., and L. Gritz. 2000. *Advanced RenderMan: Creating CGI for Motion Pictures*. San Francisco: Morgan Kaufmann.

Appel, A. 1968. Some techniques for shading machine renderings of solids. In *AFIPS 1968 Spring Joint Computer Conference, 32,* 37–45.

Arbree, A., B. Walter, and K. Bala. 2011. Heterogeneous subsurface scattering using the finite element method. *IEEE Transactions on Visualization and Computer Graphics 17*(7), 956–69.

Arnaldi, B., T. Priol, and K. Bouatouch. 1987. A new space subdivision method for ray tracing CSG modeled scenes. *The Visual Computer 3*(2), 98–108.

Arvo, J. 1986. Backward ray tracing. *Developments in Ray Tracing, SIGGRAPH '86 Course Notes.*

Arvo, J. 1988. Linear-time voxel walking for octrees. *Ray Tracing News 12*(1).

Arvo, J. 1990. Transforming axis-aligned bounding boxes. In A. S. Glassner (Ed.), *Graphics Gems I,* 548–50. San Diego: Academic Press.

Arvo, J. 1993. Transfer equations in global illumination. In *Global Illumination, SIGGRAPH '93 Course Notes,* Volume 42.

Arvo, J. 1995a. Analytic methods for simulated light transport. Ph.D. thesis, Yale University.

Arvo, J. 1995b. Stratified sampling of spherical triangles. In *Proceedings of SIGGRAPH 1995,* 437–38.

Arvo, J., and D. Kirk. 1987. Fast ray tracing by ray classification. *Computer Graphics (SIGGRAPH '87 Proceedings) 21*(4), 55–64.

Arvo, J., and D. Kirk. 1990. Particle transport and image synthesis. *Computer Graphics (SIGGRAPH '90 Proceedings) 24*(4), 63–66.

Ashdown, I. 1993. Near-field photometry: a new approach. *Journal of the Illuminating Engineering Society 22*(1), 163–80.

Ashdown, I. 1994. *Radiosity: A Programmer's Perspective.* New York: John Wiley & Sons.

Ashikhmin, M., and P. Shirley 2000. An anisotropic Phong light reflection model. *Technical Report UUCS-00-014.* University of Utah.

Ashikhmin, M., and P. Shirley 2002. An anisotropic Phong BRDF model. *Journal of Graphics Tools 5*(2), 25–32.

Ashikhmin, M., S. Premoze, and P. S. Shirley. 2000. A microfacet-based BRDF generator. In *Proceedings of ACM SIGGRAPH 2000,* 65–74.

Atcheson, B., I. Ihrke, W. Heidrich, A. Tevs, D. Bradley, M. Magnor, and H.-P. Seidel. 2008. Time-resolved 3d capture of non-stationary gas flows. *ACM Transactions on Graphics (Proceedings of SIGGRAPH Asia) 27*(5), 132:1–132:9.

Atkinson, K. 1993. *Elementary Numerical Analysis.* New York: John Wiley & Sons.

Badouel, D., and T. Priol. 1989. An efficient parallel ray tracing scheme for highly parallel architectures. In *Fifth Eurographics Workshop on Graphics Hardware.*

Bagher, M., C. Soler, N. Holzschuch. 2012. Accurate fitting of measured reflectances using a shifted gamma micro-facet distribution. *Computer Graphics Forum 31*(4), 1509–18.

Bahar, E., and S. Chakrabarti. 1987. Full-wave theory applied to computer-aided graphics for 3D objects. *IEEE Computer Graphics and Applications 7*(7), 46–60.

Banks, D. C. 1994. Illumination in diverse codimensions. In *Proceedings of SIGGRAPH '94,* Computer Graphics Proceedings, Annual Conference Series, 327–34.

Barkans, A. C. 1997. High-quality rendering using the Talisman architecture. In *1997 SIGGRAPH/Eurographics Workshop on Graphics Hardware,* 79–88.

Barringer, R., and T. Akenine-Möller. 2014. Dynamic ray stream traversal. *ACM Transactions on Graphics (Proceedings of SIGGRAPH 2014) 33*(4), 151:1–151:9.

Barzel, R. 1997. Lighting controls for computer cinematography. *Journal of Graphics Tools 2*(1), 1–20.

Bashford-Rogers, T., K. Debattista, and A. Chalmers. 2013. Importance driven environment map sampling. *IEEE Transactions on Visualization and Computer Graphics 20*(6), 907–18.

Bauszat, P., M. Eisemann, E. Eisemann, and M. Magnor. 2015. General and robust error estimation and reconstruction for Monte Carlo rendering. *Computer Graphics Forum (Procedings of Eurographics 2015) 34*(2), 597–608.

Bauszat, P., M. Eisemann, and M. Magnor. 2010. The minimal bounding volume hierarchy. *Vision, Modeling, and Visualization (2010)*.

Becker, B. G., and N. L. Max. 1993. Smooth transitions between bump rendering algorithms. In *Proceedings of SIGGRAPH '93*, Computer Graphics Proceedings, Annual Conference Series, 183–90.

Beckmann, P., and A. Spizzichino. 1963. *The Scattering of Electromagnetic Waves from Rough Surfaces*. New York: Pergamon.

Belcour, L., C. Soler, K. Subr, N. Holzschuch, and F. Durand. 2013. 5D covariance tracing for efficient defocus and motion blur. *ACM Transactions on Graphics 32*(3), 31:1–31:18.

Benthin, C. 2006. Realtime ray tracing on current CPU architectures. Ph.D. thesis, Saarland University.

Benthin, C., and I. Wald. 2009. Efficient ray traced soft shadows using multi-frusta tracing. In *Proceedings of High Performance Graphics 2009*, 135–44.

Benthin, C., S. Boulos, D. Lacewell, and I. Wald. 2007. Packet-based ray tracing of Catmull–Clark subdivision surfaces. *SCI Institute Technical Report, No. UUSCI-2007-011*. University of Utah.

Benthin, C., I. Wald, and P. Slusallek. 2003. A scalable approach to interactive global illumination. In *Computer Graphics Forum 22*(3), 621–30.

Benthin, C., I. Wald, and P. Slusallek. 2004. Techniques for interactive ray tracing of Bézier surfaces. *Journal of Graphics, GPU, and Game Tools 11*(2), 1–16.

Benthin, C., I. Wald, S. Woop, M. Ernst, and W. R. Mark. 2011. Combining single and packet ray tracing for arbitrary ray distributions on the Intel(r) MIC architecture. *IEEE Transactions on Visualization and Computer Graphics 18*(9), 1438–48.

Berger, E. D., B. G. Zorn, and K. S. McKinley. 2001. Composing high-performance memory allocators. In *SIGPLAN Conference on Programming Language Design and Implementation*, 114–24.

Berger, E. D., B. G. Zorn, and K. S. McKinley. 2002. Reconsidering custom memory allocation. In *Proceedings of ACM OOPSLA 2002*.

Betrisey, C., J. F. Blinn, B. Dresevic, B. Hill, G. Hitchcock, B. Keely, D. P. Mitchell, J. C. Platt, and T. Whitted. 2000. Displaced filtering for patterned displays. *Society for Information Display International Symposium. Digest of Technical Papers 31*, 296–99.

Bhate, N., and A. Tokuta. 1992. Photorealistic volume rendering of media with directional scattering. In *Proceedings of the Third Eurographics Rendering Workshop*, 227–45.

Bigler, J., A. Stephens, and S. Parker. 2006. Design for parallel interactive ray tracing systems. *IEEE Symposium on Interactive Ray Tracing*, 187–95.

Billen, N., B. Engelen, A. Lagae, and P. Dutré. 2013. Probabilistic visibility evaluation for direct illumination. *Computer Graphics Forum (Proceedings of the 2013 Eurographics Symposium on Rendering) 32*(4), 39–47.

Billen, N., A. Lagae, and P. Dutré. 2014. Probabilistic visibility evaluation using geometry proxies. *Computer Graphics Forum (Proceedings of the 2014 Eurographics Symposium on Rendering) 33*(4), 143–52.

Bitterli, B., J. Novák, and W. Jarosz. 2015. Portal-masked environment map sampling. *Computer Graphics Forum (Proceedings of the 2015 Eurographics Symposium on Rendering) 34*(4).

Bittner, J., M. Hapala, and V. Havran. 2013. Fast insertion-based optimization of bounding volume hierarchies. *Computer Graphics Forum 32*(1), 85–100.

Bittner, J., M. Hapala, and V. Havran. 2014. Incremental BVH construction for ray tracing. *Computers & Graphics 47*, 135–44.

Bjorke, K. 2001. Using Maya with RenderMan on Final Fantasy: The Spirits Within. *SIGGRAPH 2001 RenderMan Course Notes.*

Blasi, P., B. L. Saëc, and C. Schlick. 1993. A rendering algorithm for discrete volume density objects. *Computer Graphics Forum (Proceedings of Eurographics '93) 12*(3), 201–10.

Blinn, J. F. 1977. Models of light reflection for computer synthesized pictures. *Computer Graphics (SIGGRAPH '77 Proceedings), 11*, 192–98.

Blinn, J. F. 1978. Simulation of wrinkled surfaces. In *Computer Graphics (SIGGRAPH '78 Proceedings), 12*, 286–92.

Blinn, J. F. 1982a. A generalization of algebraic surface drawing. *ACM Transactions on Graphics 1*(3), 235–56.

Blinn, J. F. 1982b. Light reflection functions for simulation of clouds and dusty surfaces. *Computer Graphics 16*(3), 21–29.

Blinn, J. F., and M. E. Newell. 1976. Texture and reflection in computer generated images. *Communications of the ACM 19*, 542–46.

Bloom, C., J. Blow, and C. Muratori. 2004. Errors and omissions in Marc Alexa's "Linear combination of transformations." *www.cbloom.com/3d/techdocs/lcot_errors.pdf*

Blow, J. 2004. Understandling slerp, then not using it. *Game Developer Magazine*. Also available from *number-none.com/product/Understanding Slerp, Then Not Using It*

Blumofe, R., and C. Leiserson. 1999. Scheduling multithreaded computations by work stealing. *Journal of the ACM 46*(5), 720–48.

Blumofe, R., C. Joerg, B. Kuszmaul, C. Leiserson, K. Randall, and Y. Zhou. 1996. Cilk: an efficient multithreaded runtime system. *Journal of Parallel and Distributed Compututing 37*(1), 55–69.

Boehm, H.-J. 2005. Threads cannot be implemented as a library. *ACM SIGPLAN Notices 40*(6), 261–68.

Bolz, J., and P. Schröder. 2002. Rapid evaluation of Catmull–Clark subdivision surfaces. In *Web3D 2002 Symposium.*

Booth, T. E. 1986. A Monte Carlo learning/biasing experiment with intelligent random numbers. *Nuclear Science and Engineering 92*, 465–81.

Borges, C. 1991. Trichromatic approximation for computer graphics illumination models. In *Computer Graphics (Proceedings of SIGGRAPH '91), 25*, 101–04.

Boulos, S., and E. Haines. 2006. Ray–box sorting. *Ray Tracing News 19*(1), *tog.acm.org/resources/RTNews/html/rtnv19n1.html*.

Boulos, S., I. Wald, and C. Benthin. 2008. Adaptive ray packet reordering. In *Proceedings of IEEE Symposium on Interactive Ray Tracing*, 131–38.

Bracewell, R. N. 2000. *The Fourier Transform and Its Applications*. New York: McGraw-Hill.

Brady, A., J. Lawrence, P. Peers, and W. Weimer. 2014. genBRDF: discovering new analytic BRDFs with genetic programming. *ACM Transactions on Graphics (Proceedings of SIGGRAPH 2014) 33*(4), 114:1–114:11.

Bronsvoort, W. F., and F. Klok. 1985. Ray tracing generalized cylinders. *ACM Transactions on Graphics 4*(4), 291–303.

Bruneton, E., and F. Neyret. 2012. A survey of nonlinear prefiltering methods for efficient and accurate surface shading. *IEEE Transactions on Visualization and Computer Graphics 18*(2), 242–60.

Buck, R. C. 1978. *Advanced Calculus*. New York: McGraw-Hill.

Budge, B., D. Coming, D. Norpchen, and K. Joy. 2008. Accelerated building and ray tracing of restricted BSP trees. In *IEEE Symposium on Interactive Ray Tracing*, 167–74.

Budge, B., T. Bernardin, J. Stuart, S. Sengupta, K. Joy, and J. D. Owens. 2009. Out-of-core data management for path tracing on hybrid resources. *Computer Graphics Forum (Proceedings of Eurographics 2009) 28*(2), 385–96.

Buhler, J., and D. Wexler. 2002. A phenomenological model for Bokeh rendering. *SIGGRAPH 2002 Sketch*.

Burke, D., A. Ghosh, and W. Heidrich. 2005. Bidirectional importance sampling for direct illumination. In *Rendering Techniques 2005: 16th Eurographics Workshop on Rendering*, 147–56.

Burley, B. 2012. Physically-based shading at Disney. *Physically Based Shading in Film and Game Production, SIGGRAPH 2012 Course Notes*.

Buss, S., and J. Fillmore. 2001. Spherical averages and applications to spherical splines and interpolation. *ACM Transactions on Graphics 20*(2), 95–126.

Cabral, B., N. Max, and R. Springmeyer. 1987. Bidirectional reflection functions from surface bump maps. *Computer Graphics (SIGGRAPH '87 Proceedings), 21*, 273–81.

Calder, B., K. Chandra, S. John, and T. Austin. 1998. Cache-conscious data placement. In *Proceedings of the Eighth International Conference on Architectural Support for Programming Languages and Operating Systems (ASPLOS-VIII)*, San Jose.

Cant, R. J., and P. A. Shrubsole 2000. Texture potential MIP mapping, a new high-quality texture antialiasing algorithm. *ACM Transactions on Graphics 19*(3), 164–84.

Carr, N., J. D. Hall, and J. Hart. 2002. The ray engine. In *Proceedings of Graphics Hardware 2002*.

Catmull, E., and J. Clark. 1978. Recursively generated B-spline surfaces on arbitrary topological meshes. *Computer-Aided Design 10, 350–55*.

Cazals, F., G. Drettakis, and C. Puech. 1995. Filtering, clustering and hierarchy construction: a new solution for ray-tracing complex scenes. *Computer Graphics Forum 14*(3), 371–82.

Cerezo, E., F. Perez-Cazorla, X. Pueyo, F. Seron, and F. Sillion. 2005. A survey on participating media rendering techniques. *The Visual Computer 21*(5), 303–28.

Chandrasekhar, S. 1960. *Radiative Transfer*. New York: Dover Publications. Originally published by Oxford University Press, 1950.

Chen, J., K. Venkataraman, D. Bakin, B. Rodricks, R. Gravelle, P. Rao, and Y. Ni. 2009. Digital camera imaging system simulation. *IEEE Transactions on Electron Devices 56*(11), 2496–05.

Chen, J., B. Wang, and J.-H. Yong. 2011. Improved stochastic progressive photon mapping with Metropolis sampling. *Computer Graphics Forum (Proceedings of the 2011 Eurographics Symposium on Rendering 30*(4), 1205–13.

Chib, S., and E. Greenberg. 1995. Understanding the Metropolis–Hastings algorithm. *The American Statistician 49*(4), 327–35.

Chilimbi, T. M., B. Davidson, and J. R. Larus. 1999a. Cache-conscious structure definition. In *SIGPLAN Conference on Programming Language Design and Implementation*, 13–24.

Chilimbi, T. M., M. D. Hill, and J. R. Larus. 1999b. Cache-conscious structure layout. In *SIGPLAN Conference on Programming Language Design and Implementation*, 1–12.

Chiu, K., P. Shirley, and C. Wang. 1994. Multi-jittered sampling. In P. Heckbert (Ed.), *Graphics Gems IV*, 370–74. San Diego: Academic Press.

Choi, B., R. Komuravelli, V. Lu, H. Sung, R. L. Bocchino, S. V. Adve, and J. C. Hart. 2010. Parallel SAH k-D tree construction. In *Proceedings of High Performance Graphics 2010*, 77–86.

Choi, B., B. Chang, and I. Ihm. 2013. Improving memory space efficiency of kd-tree for real-time ray tracing. *Computer Graphics Forum 32*(7), 335–44.

Christensen, P. H. 2003. Adjoints and importance in rendering: an overview. *IEEE Transactions on Visualization and Computer Graphics 9*(3), 329–40.

Christensen, P. 2015. The path-tracing revolution in the movie industry. *SIGGRAPH 2015 Course*.

Christensen, P. H., and B. Burley. 2015. Approximate reflectance profiles for efficient subsurface scattering. *Pixar Technical Memo 15-04*.

Christensen, P. H., D. M. Laur, J. Fong, W. L. Wooten, and D. Batali. 2003. Ray differentials and multiresolution geometry caching for distribution ray tracing in complex scenes. In *Computer Graphics Forum (Eurographics 2003 Conference Proceedings 22*(3), 543–52.

Chvolson, O. D. 1890. Grundzüge einer matematischen Theorie der inneren Diffusion des Lichtes. *Izv. Peterburg. Academii Nauk 33*, 221–65.

CIE Technical Report. 2004. Colorimetry. *Publication 15:2004 (3rd ed.)*, CIE Central Bureau, Vienna.

Clarberg, P., and T. Akenine-Möller. 2008a. Practical product importance sampling for direct illumination. *Computer Graphics Forum (Proceedings of Eurographics 2008) 27*(2), 681–90.

Clarberg, P., and T. Akenine-Möller. 2008b. Exploiting visibility correlation in direct illumination. *Computer Graphics Forum (Proceedings of the 2008 Eurographics Symposium on Rendering) 27*(4), 1125–36.

Clarberg, P., W. Jarosz, T. Akenine-Möller, and H. W. Jensen. 2005. Wavelet importance sampling: efficiently evaluating products of complex functions. *ACM Transactions on Graphics (Proceedings of SIGGRAPH 2005) 24*(3), 1166–75.

Clark, J. H. 1976. Hierarchical geometric models for visible surface algorithms. *Communications of the ACM 19*(10), 547–54.

Cleary, J. G., and G. Wyvill. 1988. Analysis of an algorithm for fast ray tracing using uniform space subdivision. *The Visual Computer 4*(2), 65–83.

Cleary, J. G., B. M. Wyvill, R. Vatti, and G. M. Birtwistle. 1983. Design and analysis of a parallel ray tracing computer. In *Proceedings of Graphics Interface 1983*, 33–38.

Cline, D., D. Adams, and P. Egbert. 2008. Table-driven adaptive importance sampling. *Computer Graphics Forum (Proceedings of the 2008 Eurographics Symposium on Rendering) 27*(4), 1115–23.

Cline, D., J. Talbot, and P. Egbert. 2005. Energy redistribution path tracing. *ACM Transactions on Graphics (Proceedings of SIGGRAPH 2005) 24*(3), 1186–95.

Cline, D., P. Egbert, J. Talbot, and D. Cardon. 2006. Two stage importance sampling for direct lighting. *Rendering Techniques 2006: 17th Eurographics Workshop on Rendering*, 103–14.

Cline, D., A. Razdan, and P. Wonka. 2009. A comparison of tabular PDF inversion methods. *Computer Graphics Forum 28*(1), 154–60.

Cohen, J., A. Varshney, D. Manocha, G. Turk, H. Weber, P. Agarwal, F. P. Brooks Jr., and W. Wright. 1996. Simplification envelopes. In *Proceedings of SIGGRAPH '96*, Computer Graphics Proceedings, Annual Conference Series, 119–28.

Cohen, M., and D. P. Greenberg. 1985. The hemi-cube: a radiosity solution for complex environments. *SIGGRAPH Computer Graphics 19*(3), 31–40.

Cohen, M., and J. Wallace. 1993. *Radiosity and Realistic Image Synthesis*. San Diego: Academic Press Professional.

Collins, S. 1994. Adaptive splatting for specular to diffuse light transport. In *Fifth Eurographics Workshop on Rendering*, Darmstadt, Germany, 119–35.

Contini, D., F. Martelli, and G. Zaccanti. 1997. Photon migration through a turbid slab described by a model based on diffusion approximation. I. Theory. *Applied Optics 36*(19), 4587–4599.

Cook, R. L. 1984. Shade trees. *Computer Graphics (SIGGRAPH '84 Proceedings), 18,* 223–31.

Cook, R. L. 1986. Stochastic sampling in computer graphics. *ACM Transactions on Graphics 5*(1), 51–72.

Cook, R., and T. DeRose. 2005. Wavelet noise. *ACM Transactions on Graphics (Proceedings of SIGGRAPH 2005) 24*(3), 803–11.

Cook, R. L., and K. E. Torrance. 1981. A reflectance model for computer graphics. *Computer Graphics (SIGGRAPH '81 Proceedings), 15,* 307–16.

Cook, R. L., and K. E. Torrance. 1982. A reflectance model for computer graphics. *ACM Transactions on Graphics 1*(1), 7–24.

Cook, R. L., T. Porter, and L. Carpenter. 1984. Distributed ray tracing. *Computer Graphics (SIGGRAPH '84 Proceedings), 18,* 137–45.

Cook, R. L., L. Carpenter, and E. Catmull. 1987. The Reyes image rendering architecture. *Computer Graphics (Proceedings of SIGGRAPH '87)*, 95–102.

Crow, F. C. 1977. The aliasing problem in computer-generated shaded images. *Communications of the ACM 20*(11), 799–805.

Crow, F. C. 1984. Summed-area tables for texture mapping. *Computer Graphics (Proceedings of SIGGRAPH '84), 18,* 207–12.

Cuypers, T., T. Haber, P. Bekaert, S. B. Oh, and R. Raskar. 2012. Reflectance model for diffraction. *ACM Transactions on Graphics 31*(5), 122:1–122:11.

Dachsbacher, C., J. Křivánek, M. Hašan, A Arbree, B. Walter, and J. Novák. 2014. Scalable realistic rendering with many-light methods. *Computer Graphics Forum 33*(1), 88–104.

Dammertz, H., and J. Hanika. 2009. Plane sampling for light paths from the environment map. *journal of graphics, gpu, and game tools 14*(2), 25–31.

Dammertz, H., J. Hanika, and A. Keller. 2008. Shallow bounding volume hierarchies for fast SIMD ray tracing of incoherent rays. *Computer Graphics Forum 27*(4), 1225–33.

Dammertz, H., and A. Keller. 2006. Improving ray tracing precision by object space intersection computation. *IEEE Symposium on Interactive Ray Tracing*, 25–31.

Dammertz, H., and A. Keller. 2008a. The edge volume heuristic—robust triangle subdivision for improved BVH performance, In *IEEE Symposium on Interactive Ray Tracing*, 155–58.

Dammertz, S., and A. Keller. 2008b. Image synthesis by rank-1 lattices. *Monte Carlo and Quasi-Monte Carlo Methods 2006*, 217–36.

Dana, K. J., B. van Ginneken, S. K. Nayar, and J. J. Koenderink. 1999. Reflectance and texture of real-world surfaces. *ACM Transactions on Graphics 18*(1), 1–34.

Danskin, J., and P. Hanrahan. 1992. Fast algorithms for volume ray tracing. In *1992 Workshop on Volume Visualization,* 91–98.

Daumas, M., and G. Melquiond. 2010. Certification of bounds on expressions involving rounded operators. *ACM Transactions on Mathematical Software 37*(1), 2:1–2:20.

Davidovič, T., J. Křivánek, M. Hašan, and P. Slusallek. 2014. Progressive light transport simulation on the GPU: survey and improvements. *ACM Transactions on Graphics 33*(3), 29:1–29:19.

de Goes, F., K. Breeden, V. Ostromoukhov, and M. Desbrun. 2012. Blue noise through optimal transport. *ACM Transactions on Graphics (Proceedings of SIGGRAPH Asia) 31*(6), 171:1–171:11.

de Voogt, E., A. van der Helm, and W. F. Bronsvoort. 2000. Ray tracing deformed generalized cylinders. *The Visual Computer 16*(3–4), 197–207.

Debevec, P. 1998. Rendering synthetic objects into real scenes: bridging traditional and image-based graphics with global illumination and high dynamic range photography. In *Proceedings of SIGGRAPH '98,* 189–98.

Deering, M. F. 1995. Geometry compression. In *Proceedings of SIGGRAPH '95,* Computer Graphics Proceedings, Annual Conference Series, 13–20.

d'Eon, E., G. Francois., M. Hill, J. Letteri, and J.-M. Aubry. 2011. An energy-conserving hair reflectance model. *Computer Graphics Forum 30*(4), 1181–87.

d'Eon, E., and G. Irving. 2011. A quantized-diffusion model for rendering translucent materials. *ACM Transactions on Graphics (Proceedings of SIGGRAPH 2011) 28*(3), 56:1–56:14.

d'Eon, E., D. Luebke, and E. Enderton. 2007. Efficient rendering of human skin. In *Rendering Techniques 2007: 18th Eurographics Workshop on Rendering,* 147–58.

d'Eon, E., S. Marschner, and J. Hanika. 2013. Importance sampling for physically-based hair fiber models. In *SIGGRAPH Asia 2013 Technical Briefs*, 25:1–25:4.

Delbracio, M., P. Musé, A. Buades, J. Chauvier, N. Phelps, and J.-M. Morel. 2014. Boosting Monte Carlo rendering by ray histogram fusion. *ACM Transactions on Graphics 33*(1), 8:1–8:15.

DeRose, T. D. 1989. *A Coordinate-Free Approach to Geometric Programming. Math for SIGGRAPH, SIGGRAPH Course Notes #23.* Also available as Technical Report No. 89-09-16, Department of Computer Science and Engineering, University of Washington, Seattle.

Deussen, O., P. M. Hanrahan, B. Lintermann, R. Mech, M. Pharr, and P. Prusinkiewicz. 1998. Realistic modeling and rendering of plant ecosystems. In *Proceedings of SIGGRAPH '98*, Computer Graphics Proceedings, Annual Conference Series, 275–86.

Devlin, K., A. Chalmers, A. Wilkie, and W. Purgathofer. 2002. Tone reproduction and physically based spectral rendering. In D. Fellner and R. Scopignio (Eds.), *Proceedings of Eurographics 2002*, 101–23. The Eurographics Association.

Dick, J., and F. Pillichshammer. 2010. *Digital Nets and Sequences: Discrepancy Theory and Quasi-Monte Carlo Integration*. Cambridge: Cambridge University Press.

Dippé, M. A. Z., and E. H. Wold. 1985. Antialiasing through stochastic sampling. *Computer Graphics (SIGGRAPH '85 Proceedings)*, 19, 69–78.

Dobkin, D. P., and D. P. Mitchell. 1993. Random-edge discrepancy of supersampling patterns. In *Proceedings of Graphics Interface 1993*, Toronto, Ontario, 62–69. Canadian Information Processing Society.

Dobkin, D. P., D. Eppstein, and D. P. Mitchell. 1996. Computing the discrepancy with applications to supersampling patterns. *ACM Transactions on Graphics 15*(4), 354–76.

Donikian, M., B. Walter, K. Bala, S. Fernandez, and D. P. Greenberg. 2006. Accurate direct illumination using iterative adaptive sampling. *IEEE Transactions on Visualization and Computer Graphics 12*(3), 353–64.

Donnelly, W. 2005. Per-pixel displacement mapping with distance functions. In M. Pharr (Ed.), *GPU Gems 2*. Reading, Massachusetts: Addison-Wesley.

Donner, C. 2006. Towards realistic image synthesis of scattering materials. Ph.D. thesis, University of California, San Diego.

Donner, C., and H. W. Jensen. 2005. Light diffusion in multi-layered translucent materials. *ACM Transactions on Graphics (Proceedings of SIGGRAPH 2005) 24*(3), 1032–39.

Donner, C., and H. W. Jensen. 2006. A spectral BSSRDF for shading human skin. *Rendering Techniques 2006: 17th Eurographics Workshop on Rendering*, 409–17.

Donner, C., T. Weyrich, E. d'Eon, R. Ramamoorthi, and S. Rusinkiewicz. 2008. A layered, heterogeneous reflectance model for acquiring and rendering human skin. *ACM Transactions on Graphics (Proceedings of ACM SIGGRAPH Asia 2008) 27*(5), 140:1–140:12.

Donner, C., J. Lawrence, R. Ramamoorthi, T. Hachisuka, H. W. Jensen, and S. Nayar. 2009. An empirical BSSRDF model. *ACM Transactions on Graphics (Proceedings of SIGGRAPH 2009) 28*(3), 30:1–30:10.

Doo, D., and M. Sabin. 1978. Behaviour of recursive division surfaces near extraordinary points. *Computer-Aided Design 10*, 356–60.

Dorsey, J. O., F. X. Sillion, and D. P. Greenberg. 1991. Design and simulation of opera lighting and projection effects. In *Computer Graphics (Proceedings of SIGGRAPH '91)*, 25, 41–50.

Dorsey, J., and P. Hanrahan. 1996. Modeling and rendering of metallic patinas. In *Proceedings of SIGGRAPH '96*, 387–96.

Dorsey, J., H. K. Pedersen, and P. M. Hanrahan. 1996. Flow and changes in appearance. In *Proceedings of SIGGRAPH '96*, Computer Graphics Proceedings, Annual Conference Series, 411–20.

Dorsey, J., A. Edelman, J. Legakis, H. W. Jensen, and H. K. Pedersen. 1999. Modeling and rendering of weathered stone. In *Proceedings of SIGGRAPH '99*, Computer Graphics Proceedings, Annual Conference Series, 225–34.

Doyle, M. J., C. Fowler, and M. Manzke. 2013. A hardware unit for fast SAH-optimised BVH construction. *ACM Transactions on Graphics (Proceedings of SIGGRAPH 2013) 32*(4), 139:1–139:10

Drebin, R. A., L. Carpenter, and P. Hanrahan. 1988. Volume rendering. *Computer Graphics (Proceedings of SIGGRAPH '88), 22,* 65–74.

Drepper, U. 2007. What every programmer should know about memory. *people.redhat.com/ drepper/cpumemory.pdf.*

Drew, M., and G. Finlayson. 2003. Multispectral rendering without spectra. *Journal of the Optical Society of America A 20*(7), 1181–93.

Driemeyer, T., and R. Herken. 2002. *Programming mental ray.* Wien: Springer-Verlag.

Du, S.-P., S.-M. Hu, and R. R. Martin. 2013. Semiregular solid texturing from 2D image exemplars. *IEEE Transactions on Visualization and Computer Graphics 19*(3), 460–69.

Duff, T. 1985. Compositing 3-D rendered images. *Computer Graphics (Proceedings of SIGGRAPH '85), 19,* 41–44.

Dunbar, D., and G. Humphreys. 2006. A spatial data structure for fast Poisson-disk sample generation. *ACM Transactions on Graphics (Proceedings of SIGGRAPH 2006) 25*(3), 503–08.

Dungan, W. Jr., A. Stenger, and G. Sutty. 1978. Texture tile considerations for raster graphics. *Computer Graphics (Proceedings of SIGGRAPH '78), 12,* 130–34.

Dupuy, J., E. Heitz, J.-C. Iehl, P. Poulin, F. Neyret, and V. Ostromoukhov. 2013. Linear efficient antialiased displacement and reflectance mapping. *ACM Transactions on Graphics 32*(6).

Dupuy, J., E. Heitz, J.-C. Iehl, P. Poulin, and V. Ostromoukhov. 2015. Extracting microfacet-based BRDF parameters from arbitrary materials with power iterations. *Computer Graphics Forum (Proceedings of the 2015 Eurographics Symposium on Rendering) 34*(4), 21–30.

Durand, F., N. Holzschuch, C. Soler, E. Chan, and F. X. Sillion. 2005. A frequency analysis of light transport. *ACM Transactions on Graphics (Proceedings of SIGGRAPH 2005) 24*(3), 1115–26.

Dutré, P. 2003. Global illumination compendium. *www.cs.kuleuven.ac.be/~phil/GI/.*

Ebeida, M., A. Davidson, A. Patney, P. Knupp, S. Mitchell, and J. D. Owens. 2011. Efficient maximal Poisson-disk sampling. *ACM Transactions on Graphics 30*(4), 49:1–49:12.

Ebeida, M., S. Mitchell, A. Patney, A. Davidson, and J. D. Owens. 2012. A simple algorithm for maximal Poisson-disk sampling in high dimensions. *Computer Graphics Forum (Proceedings of Eurographics 2012) 31*(2), 785–94.

Eberly, D. H. 2001. *3D Game Engine Design: A Practical Approach to Real-Time Computer Graphics.* San Francisco: Morgan Kaufmann.

Eberly, D. 2011. A fast and accurate algorithm for computing SLERP. *Journal of Graphics, GPU, and Game Tools 15*(3), 161–76.

Ebert, D., F. K. Musgrave, D. Peachey, K. Perlin, and S. Worley. 2003. *Texturing and Modeling: A Procedural Approach.* San Francisco: Morgan Kaufmann.

Edwards, D., S. Boulos, J. Johnson, P. Shirley, M. Ashikhmin, M. Stark, and C. Wyman. 2005. The halfway vector disk for BRDF modeling. *ACM Transactions on Graphics 25*(1), 1–18.

Egan, K., Y.-T. Tseng, N. Holzschuch, F. Durand, and R. Ramamoorthi. 2009. Frequency analysis and sheared reconstruction for rendering motion blur. *ACM Transactions on Graphics (Proceedings of SIGGRAPH 2009) 28*(3), 93:1–93:13.

Eisemann, M., M. Magnor, T. Grosch, and S. Müller. 2007. Fast ray/axis-aligned bounding box overlap tests using ray slopes. *Journal of Graphics, GPU, and Game Tools 12*(4), 35–46.

Eisenacher, C., G. Nichols, A. Selle, and B. Burley. 2013. Sorted deferred shading for production path tracing. *Computer Graphics Forum (Proceedings of the 2013 Eurographics Symposium on Rendering) 32*(4), 125–32.

Eldar, Y. C., and T. Michaeli. 2009. Beyond bandlimited sampling. *IEEE Signal Processing Magazine 26*(3), 48–68.

Elek, O., P. Bauszat, T. Ritschel, M. Magnor, and H.-P. Seidel. 2014. Spectral ray differentials. *Computer Graphics Forum (Proceedings of the 2014 Eurographics Symposium on Rendering) 33*(4), 113–22.

Ericson, C. 2004. *Real-Time Collision Detection*. Morgan Kaufmann Series in Interactive 3D Technology. San Francisco: Morgan Kaufmann.

Ernst, M., and G. Greiner. 2007. Early split clipping for bounding volume hierarchies. *IEEE Symposium on Interactive Ray Tracing*, 73–78.

Ernst, M., and G .Greiner. 2008. Multi bounding volume hierarchies. In *Proceedings of the IEEE Symposium on Interactive Ray Tracing 2008*, 35–40.

Evans, G., and M. McCool. 1999. Stratified wavelength clusters for efficient spectral Monte Carlo rendering. In *Proceedings of Graphics Interface 1999*, 42–49.

Fabianowski, B., C. Fowler, and J. Dingliana. 2009. A cost metric for scene-interior ray origins. In *Short Paper Proceedings of the 30th Annual Conference of the European Association for Computer Graphics (Eurographics 2009)*, 49–50.

Fan, S., S. Chenney, and Y.-C. Lai. 2005. Metropolis photon sampling with optional user guidance. In *Rendering Techniques 2005: 16th Eurographics Workshop on Rendering*, 127–38.

Fante, R. L. 1981. Relationship between radiative-transport theory and Maxwell's equations in dielectric media. *Journal of the Optical Society of America 71*(4), 460–468.

Farin, G. 2001. *Curves and Surfaces for CAGD: A Practical guide*, (5th ed.). San Francisco: Morgan Kaufmann.

Farmer, D. F. 1981. Comparing the 4341 and M80/40. *Computerworld 15*(6).

Farrell, T., M. Patterson, and B. Wilson. 1992. A diffusion theory model of spatially resolved, steady-state diffuse reflectance for the noninvasive determination of tissue optical properties *in vivo*. *Med. Phys. 19*(4), 879–88.

Fatahalian, K. 2008. Running code at a teraflop: how GPU shader cores work. In *Beyond Programmable Shading, SIGGRAPH 2008 Course Notes*.

Fattal, R. 2009. Participating media illumination using light propagation maps. *ACM Transactions on Graphics 28*(1), 7:1–7:11.

Faure, H. 1992. Good permutations for extreme discrepancy. *Journal of Number Theory 42*, 47–56.

Fedkiw, R., J. Stam, and H. W. Jensen. 2001. Visual simulation of smoke. In *Proceedings of ACM SIGGRAPH 2001*, Computer Graphics Proceedings, Annual Conference Series, 15–22.

Feibush, E. A., M. Levoy, and R. L. Cook. 1980. Synthetic texturing using digital filters. *Computer Graphics (Proceedings of SIGGRAPH '80), 14*, 294–301.

Fernandez, S., K. Bala, and D. P. Greenberg. 2002. Local illumination environments for direct lighting acceleration. In *Rendering Techniques 2002: 13th Eurographics Workshop on Rendering*, 7–14.

Ferwerda, J. A. 2001. Elements of early vision for computer graphics. *IEEE Computer Graphics and Applications 21*(5), 22–33.

Fisher, M., K. Fatahalian, S. Boulos, K. Akeley, W. R. Mark, and P. Hanrahan. 2009. DiagSplit: parallel, crack-free, adaptive tessellation for micropolygon rendering. *ACM Transactions on Graphics (Proceedings of ACM SIGGRAPH Asia 2009) 28*(5), 150:1–150:10.

Fishman, G. S. 1996. *Monte Carlo: Concepts, Algorithms, and Applications*. New York: Springer-Verlag.

Fleischer, K., D. Laidlaw, B. Currin, and A. H. Barr. 1995. Cellular texture generation. In *Proceedings of SIGGRAPH '95*, Computer Graphics Proceedings, Annual Conference Series, 239–48.

Foley, T., and J. Sugerman. 2005. KD-tree acceleration structures for a GPU raytracer. In *Proceedings of the ACM SIGGRAPH/EUROGRAPHICS Conference on Graphics Hardware*, 15–22.

Fournier, A. 1992. Normal distribution functions and multiple surfaces. In *Graphics Interface '92 Workshop on Local Illumination*, 45–52.

Fournier, A., and E. Fiume. 1988. Constant-time filtering with space-variant kernels. *Computer Graphics (SIGGRAPH '88 Proceedings), 22*, 229–38.

Fournier, A., D. Fussel, and L. Carpenter. 1982. Computer rendering of stochastic models. *Communications of the ACM 25*(6), 371–84.

Fraser, C., and D. Hanson. 1995. *A Retargetable C Compiler: Design and Implementation*. Reading, Massachusetts: Addison-Wesley.

Friedel, I., and A. Keller. 2000. Fast generation of randomized low discrepancy point sets. In *Monte Carlo and Quasi-Monte Carlo Methods 2000*, 257–73. Berlin: Springer-Verlag.

Frisvad, J., N. Christensen, and H. W. Jensen. 2007. Computing the scattering properties of participating media using Lorenz-Mie theory. *ACM Transactions on Graphics (Proceedings of SIGGRAPH 2007) 26*(3), 60:1–60:10.

Frisvad, J. R., T. Hachisuka, and T. K. Kjeldsen. 2014. Directional dipole model for subsurface scattering. *ACM Transactions on Graphics 34*(1), 5:1–5:12.

Fuchs, C., T. Chen, M. Goesele, H. Theisel, and H.-P. Seidel. 2007. Density estimation for dynamic volumes. *Computers and Graphics 31*(2), 205–11.

Fujimoto, A., T. Tanaka, and K. Iwata. 1986. Arts: accelerated ray-tracing system. *IEEE Computer Graphics and Applications 6*(4), 16–26.

Galerne, B., A. Lagae, S. Lefebvre, and G. Drettakis. 2012. Gabor noise by example. *ACM Transactions on Graphics (Processings of SIGGRAPH 2012) 31*(4), 73:1–73:9.

Garanzha, K. 2009. The use of precomputed triangle clusters for accelerated ray tracing in dynamic scenes. *Computer Graphics Forum (Proceedings of the 2009 Eurographics Symposium on Rendering) 28*(4), 1199–1206.

García, R., C. Ureña, and M. Sbert. 2012. Description and solution of an unreported intrinsic bias in photon mapping density estimation with constant kernel. *Computer Graphics Forum 31*(1), 33–41.

Gardner, G. Y. 1984. Simulation of natural scenes using textured quadric surfaces. *Computer Graphics (SIGGRAPH '84 Proceedings), 18*, 11–20.

Gardner, G. Y. 1985. Visual simulation of clouds. *Computer Graphics (Proceedings of SIGGRAPH '85), 19*, 297–303.

Gardner, R. P., H. K. Choi, M. Mickael, A. M. Yacout, Y. Yin, and K. Verghese. 1987. Algorithms for forcing scattered radiation to spherical, planar circular, and right circular cylindrical detectors for Monte Carlo simulation. *Nuclear Science and Engineering 95,* 245–56.

Garanzha, K., J. Pantaleoni, D. McAllister. 2011. Simpler and faster HLBVH with work queues. In *Proceedings of High Performance Graphics 2011,* 59–64.

Gershbein, R., and P. M. Hanrahan. 2000. A fast relighting engine for interactive cinematic lighting design. In *Proceedings of ACM SIGGRAPH 2000,* Computer Graphics Proceedings, Annual Conference Series, 353–58.

Gershun, A. 1939. The light field. *Journal of Mathematics and Physics 18,* 51–151.

Georgiev, I., J. Křivánek, T. Davidovič, and P. Slusallek. 2012. Light transport simulation with vertex connection and merging. *ACM Transactions on Graphics (Proceedings of SIGGRAPH Asia 2012) 31*(6), 192:1–192:10.

Georgiev, I., J. Křivánek, T. Hachisuka, D. Nowrouzezahrai, and W. Jarosz. 2013. Joint importance sampling of low-order volumetric scattering. *ACM Transactions on Graphics (Proceedings of SIGGRAPH Asia 2013) 32*(6), 164:1–164:14.

Georgiev, I., and P. Slusallek. 2008. RTfact: generic concepts for flexible and high performance ray tracing. In *Proceedings of IEEE Symposium on Interactive Ray Tracing,* 115–22.

Ghosh, A., and W. Heidrich. 2006. Correlated visibility sampling for direct illumination. *The Visual Computer 22*(9–10), 693–701.

Ghosh, A., T. Hawkins, P. Peers, S. Frederiksen, and P. Debevec. 2008. Practical modeling and acquisition of layered facial reflectance. *ACM Transactions on Graphics (Proceedings of ACM SIGGRAPH Asia 2008) 27*(5), 139:1–139:10.

Gijsenij, A., T. Gevers, J. van de Weijer. 2011. Computational color constancy: survey and experiments. *IEEE Transactions on Image Processing 20*(9), 2475–89.

Gilet, G., B. Sauvage, K. Vanhoey, J.-M. Dischler, and D. Ghazanfarpour. 2014. Local random-phase noise for procedural texturing. *ACM Transactions on Graphics (Proceedings of SIGGRAPH Asia 2014) 33*(6), 195:1–195:11.

Gkioulekas, I., S. Zhao, K. Bala, T. Zickler, and A. Levin. 2013a. Inverse volume rendering with material dictionaries. *ACM Transactions on Graphics (Proceedings of SIGGRAPH Asia 2013) 32*(6), 162:1–162:13.

Gkioulekas, I., B. Xiao, S. Zhao, E. H. Adelson, T. Zickler, and K. Bala. 2013b. Understanding the role of phase function in translucent appearance. *ACM Transactions on Graphics 32*(5), 147:1–147:19.

Glassner, A. 1984. Space subdivision for fast ray tracing. *IEEE Computer Graphics and Applications 4*(10), 15–22.

Glassner, A. 1988. Spacetime ray tracing for animation. *IEEE Computer Graphics & Applications 8*(2), 60–70.

Glassner, A. (Ed.) 1989a. *An Introduction to Ray Tracing*. San Diego: Academic Press.

Glassner, A. 1989b. How to derive a spectrum from an RGB triplet. *IEEE Computer Graphics and Applications 9*(4), 95–99.

Glassner, A. 1993. Spectrum: an architecture for image synthesis, research, education, and practice. *Developing Large-Scale Graphics Software Toolkits, SIGGRAPH '93 Course Notes, 3,* 1-14–1-43.

Glassner, A. 1994. A model for fluorescence and phosphorescence. In *Proceedings of the Fifth Eurographics Workshop on Rendering,* 57–68.

Glassner, A. 1995. *Principles of Digital Image Synthesis*. San Francisco: Morgan Kaufmann.

Glassner, A. 1999. An open and shut case. *IEEE Computer Graphics and Applications 19*(3), 82–92.

Goesele, M., X. Granier, W. Heidrich, and H.-P. Seidel. 2003. Accurate light source acquisition and rendering. *ACM Transactions on Graphics (Proceedings of SIGGRAPH 2003) 22*(3), 621–30.

Goesele, M. H. Lensch, J. Lang, C. Fuchs, and H.-P. Seidel. 2004. DISCO–Acquisition of translucent objects. *ACM Transactions on Graphics (Proceedings of SIGGRAPH 2004) 23*(3), 844–53.

Goldberg, A., M. Zwicker, and F. Durand. 2008. Anisotropic noise. *ACM Transactions on Graphics (Proceedings of SIGGRAPH 2008) 27*(3), 54:1–54:8.

Goldberg, D. 1991. What every computer scientist should know about floating-point arithmetic. *ACM Computing Surveys 23*(1), 5–48.

Goldman, D. B. 1997. Fake fur rendering. In *Proceedings of SIGGRAPH '97*, Computer Graphics Proceedings, Annual Conference Series, 127–34.

Goldman, R. 1985. Illicit expressions in vector algebra. *ACM Transactions on Graphics 4*(3), 223–43.

Goldsmith, J., and J. Salmon. 1987. Automatic creation of object hierarchies for ray tracing. *IEEE Computer Graphics and Applications 7*(5), 14–20.

Goldstein, R. A., and R. Nagel. 1971. 3-D visual simulation. *Simulation 16*(1), 25–31.

Goral, C. M., K. E. Torrance, D. P. Greenberg, and B. Battaile. 1984. Modeling the interaction of light between diffuse surfaces. In *Proceedings of the 11th Annual Conference on Computer Graphics and Interactive Techniques (SIGGRAPH '84)*, 213–22.

Gortler, S. J., R. Grzeszczuk, R. Szeliski, and M. F. Cohen. 1996. The lumigraph. In *Proceedings of SIGGRAPH '96*, Computer Graphics Proceedings, Annual Conference Series, 43–54.

Gray, A. 1993. *Modern Differential Geometry of Curves and Surfaces*. Boca Raton, Florida: CRC Press.

Green, S. A., and D. J. Paddon. 1989. Exploiting coherence for multiprocessor ray tracing. *IEEE Computer Graphics and Applications 9*(6), 12–26.

Greenberg, D. P., K. E. Torrance, P. S. Shirley, J. R. Arvo, J. A. Ferwerda, S. Pattanaik, E. P. F. Lafortune, B. Walter, S.-C. Foo, and B. Trumbore. 1997. A framework for realistic image synthesis. In *Proceedings of SIGGRAPH '97*, Computer Graphics Proceedings, Annual Conference Series, 477–94.

Greene, N. 1986. Environment mapping and other applications of world projections. *IEEE Computer Graphics and Applications 6*(11), 21–29.

Greene, N., and P. S. Heckbert. 1986. Creating raster Omnimax images from multiple perspective views using the elliptical weighted average filter. *IEEE Computer Graphics and Applications 6*(6), 21–27.

Gribble, C., and K. Ramani. 2008. Coherent ray tracing via stream filtering. In *Proceedings of IEEE Symposium on Interactive Ray Tracing*, 59–66.

Gritz, L., and E. d'Eon. 2008. The importance of being linear. In H. Nguyen (Ed.), *GPU Gems 3*. Boston, Massachusetts: Addison-Wesley.

Gritz, L., and J. K. Hahn. 1996. BMRT: a global illumination implementation of the RenderMan standard. *Journal of Graphics Tools 1*(3), 29–47.

Gritz, L., C. Stein, C. Kulla, and A. Conty. 2010. Open Shading Language. *SIGGRAPH 2010 Talks*.

Grosjean, C. C. 1956. A high accuracy approximation for solving multiple scattering problems in infinite homogeneous media *Nuovo Cimento 3*(6), 1262–75.

Grünschloß, L., J. Hanika, R. Schwede, and A. Keller. 2008. (t, m, s)-nets and maximized minimum distance. In A. Keller, S. Heinrich, and H. Niederreiter (eds.), *Monte Carlo and Quasi-Monte Carlo Methods 2006*. Berlin: Springer Verlag.

Grünschloß, L., and A. Keller. 2009. (t, m, s)-nets and maximized minimum distance, Part II. In P. L'Ecuyer and A. Owen (Eds.), *Monte Carlo and Quasi-Monte Carlo Methods 2008*.

Grünschloß, L., M. Raab, and A. Keller. 2012. Enumerating quasi-Monte Carlo point sequences in elementary intervals. In H. Wozniakowski and L. Plaskota (Eds.), *Monte Carlo and Quasi-Monte Carlo Methods 2010*.

Grünschloß, L., M. Stich, S. Nawaz, and A. Keller. 2011. MSBVH: an efficient acceleration data structure for ray traced motion blur. In *Proceedings of High Performance Graphics 2011*, 65–70.

Grunwald, D., B. G. Zorn, and R. Henderson. 1993. Improving the cache locality of memory allocation. In *SIGPLAN Conference on Programming Language Design and Implementation*, 177–86.

Gu, J., S. K. Nayar, E. Grinspun, P. N. Belhumeur, and R. Ramamoorthi. 2013a. Compressive structured light for recovering inhomogeneous participating media. *IEEE Transactions on Pattern Analysis and Machine Intelligence 35*(3).

Gu, Y., Y. He, K. Fatahalian, and G. Blelloch. 2013b. Efficient BVH construction via approximate agglomerative clustering. *Proceesings of High Performance Graphics 2013*, 81–88.

Guertin, J.-P., M. McGuire, and D. Nowrouzezahrai. 2014. A fast and stable feature-aware motion blur filter. In *Proceedings of High Performance Graphics 2014*.

Günther, J., T. Chen, M. Goesele, I. Wald, and H.-P. Seidel. 2005. Efficient acquisition and realistic rendering of car paint. In *Proceedings of Vision, Modeling, and Visualization (VMV)*, 487–94.

Günther, J., S. Popov, H. P. Seidel, and P. Slusallek. 2007. Realtime ray tracing on GPU with BVH-based packet traversal. In *IEEE Symposium on Interactive Ray Tracing*, 113–18.

Guthe, S., and P. Heckbert 2005. Non-power-of-two mipmapping. *NVIDIA Technical Report*, *developer.nvidia.com/object/np2_mipmapping.html*.

Habel, R., P. H. Christensen, and W. Jarosz. 2013. Photon beam diffusion: a hybrid Monte Carlo method for subsurface scattering. *Computer Graphics Forum (Proceedings of the 2013 Eurographics Symposium on Rendering) 32*(4), 27–37.

Haber, J., M. Magnor, and H.-P. Seidel. 2005a. Physically-based simulation of twilight phenomena. *ACM Transactions on Graphics 24*(4), 1353–73.

Haber, T., T. Mertens, P. Bekaert, and F. Van Reeth. 2005b. A computational approach to simulate subsurface light diffusion in arbitrarily shaped objects. In *Proceedings of Graphics Interface 2005*, 79–86.

Hachisuka, T. 2005. High-quality global illumination rendering using rasterization. In M. Pharr (Ed.), *GPU Gems 2: Programming Techniques for High Performance Graphics and General-Purpose Computation*. Reading, Massachusetts: Addison-Wesley.

Hachisuka, T. 2011. Robust light transport simulation using progressive density estimation. Ph.D. thesis, University of California, San Diego.

Hachisuka, T., W. Jarosz, and H. W. Jensen. 2010. A progressive error estimation framework for photon density estimation. *ACM Transactions on Graphics (Proceedings of SIGGRAPH Asia 2010) 29*(6), 144:1–144:12.

Hachisuka, T., W. Jarosz, R. P. Weistroffer, K. Dale, G. Humphreys, M. Zwicker, and H. W. Jensen. 2008a. Multidimensional adaptive sampling and reconstruction for ray tracing. *ACM Transactions on Graphics (Proceedings of SIGGRAPH 2008) 27*(3), 33:1–33:10.

Hachisuka, T., and H. W. Jensen. 2009. Stochastic progressive photon mapping. *ACM Transactions on Graphics (Proceedings of SIGGRAPH Asia 2009) 28*(5), 141:1–141:8.

Hachisuka, T., and H. W. Jensen. 2011. Robust adaptive photon tracing using photon path visibility. *ACM Transactions on Graphics 30*(5), 114:1–114:11.

Hachisuka, T., A. S. Kaplanyan, and C. Dachsbacher. 2014. Multiplexed Metropolis light transport. *ACM Transactions on Graphics (Proceedings of SIGGRAPH 2014) 33*(4), 100:1–100:10.

Hachisuka, T., S. Ogaki, and H. W. Jensen. 2008b. Progressive photon mapping. *ACM Transactions on Graphics (Proceedings of SIGGRAPH Asia 2008) 27*(5), 130:1–130:8.

Hachisuka, T., J. Pantaleoni, and H. W. Jensen. 2012. A path space extension for robust light transport simulation. *ACM Transactions on Graphics (Proceedings of SIGGRAPH Asia 2012) 31*(6), 191:1–191:10.

Haines, E. A. 1989. Essential ray tracing algorithms. In A. Glassner (Ed.), *An Introduction to Ray Tracing*, 33–78. San Diego: Academic Press.

Haines, E. A. 1994. Point in polygon strategies. In P. Heckbert (Ed.), *Graphics Gems IV*, 24–46. San Diego: Academic Press.

Haines, E. A., and D. P. Greenberg. 1986. The light buffer: a shadow testing accelerator. *IEEE Computer Graphics and Applications 6*(9), 6–16.

Haines, E. A., and J. R. Wallace. 1994. Shaft culling for efficient ray-traced radiosity. In *Second Eurographics Workshop on Rendering (Photorealistic Rendering in Computer Graphics)*. Also in *SIGGRAPH 1991 Frontiers in Rendering Course Notes*.

Hakura, Z. S., and A. Gupta. 1997. The design and analysis of a cache architecture for texture mapping. In *Proceedings of the 24th International Symposium on Computer Architecture*, Denver, Colorado, 108–20.

Hall, R. 1989. *Illumination and Color in Computer Generated Imagery*. New York: Springer-Verlag.

Hall, R. 1999. Comparing spectral color computation methods. *IEEE Computer Graphics and Applications 19*(4), 36–46.

Hall, R. A., and D. P. Greenberg. 1983. A testbed for realistic image synthesis. *IEEE Computer Graphics and Applications 3*(8), 10–20.

Hammersley, J., and D. Handscomb. 1964. *Monte Carlo Methods*. New York: John Wiley.

Han, C., B. Sun, R. Ramamoorthi, and E. Grinspun. 2007. Frequency domain normal map filtering. *ACM Transactions on Graphics (Proceedings of SIGGRAPH 2007) 26*(3), 28:1–28:11.

Hanika, J., and C. Dachsbacher. 2014. Efficient Monte Carlo rendering with realistic lenses. *Computer Graphics Forum (Proceedings of Eurographics 2014) 33*(2), 323–32.

Hanika, J., M. Droske, and L. Fascione. 2015a. Manifold next event estimation. *Computer Graphics Forum (Proceedings of the 2015 Eurographics Symposium on Rendering) 34*(4), 87–97.

Hanika, J., A. Kaplanyan, and C. Dachsbacher. 2015b. Improved half vector space light transport. *Computer Graphics Forum (Proceedings of the 2015 Eurographics Symposium on Rendering) 34*(4), 65–74.

Hanika, J., A. Keller, and H. P. A. Lensch. 2010. Two-level ray tracing with reordering for highly complex scenes. In *Proceedings of Graphics Interface 2010*, 145–52.

Hanrahan, P. 1983. Ray tracing algebraic surfaces. *Computer Graphics (Proceedings of SIGGRAPH '83), 17*, 83–90.

Hanrahan, P., and W. Krueger. 1993. Reflection from layered surfaces due to subsurface scattering. In *Computer Graphics (SIGGRAPH '93 Proceedings)*, 165–74.

Hanrahan, P., and J. Lawson. 1990. A language for shading and lighting calculations. *Computer Graphics (SIGGRAPH '90 Proceedings), 24*, 289–98.

Hansen, J. E., and L. D. Travis. 1974. Light scattering in planetary atmospheres. *Space Science Reviews 16*, 527–610.

Hart, D., P. Dutré, and D. P. Greenberg. 1999. Direct illumination with lazy visibility evaluation. In *Proceedings of SIGGRAPH '99*, Computer Graphics Proceedings, Annual Conference Series, 147–54.

Hart, J. C. 1996. Sphere tracing: a geometric method for the antialiased ray tracing of implicit surfaces. *The Visual Computer 12*(9), 527–45.

Hart, J. C., D. J. Sandin, and L. H. Kauffman. 1989. Ray tracing deterministic 3-D fractals. *Computer Graphics (Proceedings of SIGGRAPH '89), 23*, 289–96.

Hasinoff, S. W., and K. N. Kutulakos. 2011. Light-efficient photography. *IEEE Transactions on Pattern Analysis and Machine Intelligence 33*(11), 2203–14.

Havran, V. 2000. Heuristic ray shooting algorithms. Ph.D. thesis, Czech Technical University.

Havran, V., and J. Bittner. 2002. On improving kd-trees for ray shooting. In *Proceedings of WSCG 2002 Conference*, 209–17.

Havran, V., R. Herzog, and H.-P. Seidel. 2005. Fast final gathering via reverse photon mapping, *Computer Graphics Forum (Proceedings of Eurographics 2005) 24*(3), 323–34.

Havran, V., R. Herzog, and H.-P. Seidel. 2006. On the fast construction of spatial hierarchies for ray tracing. In *IEEE Symposium on Interactive Ray Tracing*, 71–80.

Hawkins, T., P. Einarsson, and P. Debevec. 2005. Acquisition of time-varying participating media. *ACM Transactions on Graphics (Proceedings of SIGGRAPH 2005) 24*(3), 812–15.

Hecht, E. 2002. *Optics*. Reading, Massachusetts: Addison-Wesley.

Heckbert, P. S. 1984. The Mathematics of Quadric Surface Rendering and SOID. *3-D Technical Memo*, New York Institute of Technology Computer Graphics Lab.

Heckbert, P. S. 1986. Survey of texture mapping. *IEEE Computer Graphics and Applications 6*(11), 56–67.

Heckbert, P. S. 1987. Ray tracing JELL-O brand gelatin. *Computer Graphics (SIGGRAPH '87 Proceedings), 21*(4), 73–74.

Heckbert, P. S. 1989a. Image zooming source code. *www-2.cs.cmu.edu/~ph/src/zoom/*.

Heckbert, P. S. 1989b. Fundamentals of texture mapping and image warping. M.S. thesis, Department of Electrical Engineering and Computer Science, University of California, Berkeley.

Heckbert, P. S. 1990a. What are the coordinates of a pixel? In A. S. Glassner (Ed.), *Graphics Gems I*, 246–48. San Diego: Academic Press.

Heckbert, P. S. 1990b. Adaptive radiosity textures for bidirectional ray tracing. *Computer Graphics (Proceedings of SIGGRAPH '90), 24,* 145–54.

Heckbert, P. S., and P. Hanrahan. 1984. Beam tracing polygonal objects. In *Computer Graphics (Proceedings of SIGGRAPH '84), 18,* 119–27.

Heidrich, W., and H.-P. Seidel. 1998. Ray-tracing procedural displacement shaders. In *Proceedings of Graphics Interface 1998,* 8–16.

Heidrich, W., J. Kautz, P. Slusallek, and H.-P. Seidel. 1998. Canned lightsources. In *Rendering Techniques '98: Proceedings of the Eurographics Rendering Workshop,* 293–300.

Heitz, E. 2014a. Understanding the masking-shadowing function in microfacet-based BRDFs *Journal of Computer Graphics Techniques (JCGT) 3*(2), 32–91.

Heitz, E. 2015. Derivation of the microfacet $\Lambda(\omega)$ function. Personal communication.

Heitz, E., C. Bourlier, and N. Pinel. 2013. Correlation effect between transmitter and receiver azimuthal directions on the illumination function from a random rough surface. *Waves in Random and Complex Media 23*(3), 318–35.

Heitz, E., and E. d'Eon. 2014. Importance sampling microfacet-based BSDFs using the distribution of visible normals. *Computer Graphics Forum (Proceedings of The 2014 Eurographics Symposium on Rendering) 33*(4), 103–12.

Heitz, E., J. Dupuy, C. Crassin, and C. Dachsbacher. 2015. The SGGX microflake distribution. *ACM Transactions on Graphics (Proceedings of SIGGRAPH 2015) 34*(4), 48:1–48:11.

Heitz, E., and F. Neyret. 2012. Representing appearance and pre-filtering subpixel data in sparse voxel octrees. In *Proceedings of High Performance Graphics 2012,* 125–34.

Heitz, E., D. Nowrouzezahrai, P. Poulin, and F. Neyret. 2014. Filtering non-linear transfer functions on surfaces. *IEEE Transactions on Visualization and Computer Graphics 20*(7), 996–1008.

Henyey, L. G., and J. L. Greenstein. 1941. Diffuse radiation in the galaxy. *Astrophysical Journal 93,* 70–83.

Hery, C. 2003. Implementing a skin BSSRDF. *SIGGRAPH 2003 RenderMan Course Notes.*

Hery, C., M. Kass, and J. Ling. 2014. Geometry into shading. *Pixar Technical Memo 14-04.*

Hery, R., and R. Ramamoorthi. 2012. Importance sampling of reflection from hair fibers. *Journal of Computer Graphics Techniques (JCGT) 1*(1), 1–17.

Herzog, R., V. Havran, S. Kinuwaki, K. Myszkowski, and H.-P. Seidel. 2007. Global illumination using photon ray splatting. *Computer Graphics Forum (Proceedings of Eurographics 2007) 26*(3), 503–13.

Higham, N. 1986. Computing the polar decomposition—with applications. *SIAM Journal of Scientific and Statistical Computing 7*(4), 1160–74.

Higham, N. J. 2002. *Accuracy and Stability of Numerical Algorithms* (2nd ed.). Philadelphia: Society for Industrial and Applied Mathematics.

Hoberock, J. 2008. Accelerating physically-based light transport algorithms. Ph.D. thesis, University of Illinois at Urbana-Champaign.

Hoberock, J., V. Lu, Y. Jia, J. Hart. 2009. Stream compaction for deferred shading. In *Proceedings of High Performance Graphics 2009,* 173–80.

Hoffmann, C. M. 1989. *Geometric and Solid Modeling: An Introduction.* San Francisco: Morgan Kaufmann.

Hoppe, H., T. DeRose, T. Duchamp, M. Halstead, H. Jin, J. McDonald, J. Schweitzer, and W. Stuetzle. 1994. Piecewise smooth surface reconstruction. In *Proceedings of SIGGRAPH '94*, Computer Graphics Proceedings, Annual Conference Series, Orlando, Florida, 295–302.

Hošek, L., and A. Wilkie. 2012. An analytic model for full spectral sky-dome radiance. *ACM Transactions on Graphics (Proceedings of SIGGRAPH 2012) 31*(4), 95:1–95:9.

Hošek, L., and A. Wilkie. 2013. Adding a solar-radiance function to the Hošek–Wilkie skylight model. *IEEE Computer Graphics and Applications 33*(3), 44–52.

Hullin, M. B., J. Hanika., and W. Heidrich. 2012. Polynomial optics: a construction kit for efficient ray-tracing of lens systems. *Computer Graphics Forum (Proceedings of the 2012 Eurographics Symposium on Rendering) 31*(4), 1375–83.

Hunt, W. 2008. Corrections to the surface area metric with respect to mail-boxing. In *IEEE Symposium on Interactive Ray Tracing*, 77–80.

Hunt, W., and B. Mark. 2008a. Ray-specialized acceleration structures for ray tracing. In *IEEE Symposium on Interactive Ray Tracing*, 3–10.

Hunt, W., and B. Mark. 2008b. Adaptive acceleration structures in perspective space. In *IEEE Symposium on Interactive Ray Tracing*, 117–17.

Hunt, W., W. Mark, and G. Stoll. 2006. Fast kd-tree construction with an adaptive error-bounded heuristic. In *IEEE Symposium on Interactive Ray Tracing*, 81–88.

Hurley, J., A. Kapustin, A. Reshetov, and A. Soupikov. 2002. Fast ray tracing for modern general purpose CPU. In *Proceedings of GraphiCon 2002*.

Igarashi, T., K. Nishino, and S. K. Nayar. 2007. The appearance of human skin: a survey. *Foundations and Trends in Computer Graphics and Vision 3*(1), 1–95.

Igehy, H. 1999. Tracing ray differentials. In *Proceedings of SIGGRAPH '99*, Computer Graphics Proceedings, Annual Conference Series, 179–86.

Igehy, H., M. Eldridge, and K. Proudfoot. 1998. Prefetching in a texture cache architecture. In *1998 SIGGRAPH/Eurographics Workshop on Graphics Hardware*, 133–42.

Igehy, H., M. Eldridge, and P. Hanrahan. 1999. Parallel texture caching. In *1999 SIG-GRAPH/Eurographics Workshop on Graphics Hardware*, 95–106.

Illuminating Engineering Society of North America. 2002. IESNA standard file format for electronic transfer of photometric data. BSR/IESNA Publication LM-63-2002. *www.iesna.org*.

Immel, D. S., M. F. Cohen, and D. P. Greenberg. 1986. A radiosity method for non-diffuse environments. In *Computer Graphics (SIGGRAPH '86 Proceedings)*, Volume 20, 133–42.

Institute of Electrical and Electronic Engineers. 1985. IEEE standard 754-1985 for binary floating-point arithmetic. Reprinted in *SIGPLAN 22*(2), 9–25.

Institute of Electrical and Electronic Engineers. 2008. IEEE standard 754-2008 for binary floating-point arithmetic.

International Electrotechnical Commission (IEC). 1999. Multimedia systems and equipment—Colour measurement and management—Part 2-1: Colour management—Default RGB colour space—sRGB. IEC Standard 61966-2-1.

Irawan, P. 2008. Appearance of woven cloth. Ph.D. thesis, Cornell University.

Irawan, P., and S. Marschner. 2012. Specular reflection from woven cloth. *ACM Transactions on Graphics 31*(1).

Ishimaru, A. 1978. *Wave Propagation and Scattering in Random Media*. Oxford: Oxford University Press.

Ize, T. 2013. Robust BVH ray traversal. *Journal of Computer Graphics Techniques (JCGT) 2*(2), 12–27.

Ize, T., and C. Hansen. 2011. RTSAH traversal order for occlusion rays. *Computer Graphics Forum (Proceedings of Eurographics 2011) 30*(2), 295–305.

Ize, T., P. Shirley, and S. Parker. 2007. Grid creation strategies for efficient ray tracing. In *IEEE Symposium on Interactive Ray Tracing,* 27–32.

Ize, T., I. Wald, and S. Parker. 2008. Ray tracing with the BSP tree. In *IEEE Symposium on Interactive Ray Tracing,* 159–66.

Ize, T., I. Wald, C. Robertson, and S. G. Parker. 2006. An evaluation of parallel grid construction for ray tracing dynamic scenes. *IEEE Symposium on Interactive Ray Tracing,* 47–55.

Jackson, W. H. 1910. The solution of an integral equation occurring in the theory of radiation. *Bulletin of the American Mathematical Society 16,* 473–75.

Jacobs, D. E., J. Baek, and M. Levoy. 2012. Focal stack compositing for depth of field control. *Stanford Computer Graphics Laboratory Technical Report,* CSTR 2012-1.

Jakob, W. 2010. Mitsuba renderer. *http://www.mitsuba-renderer.org.*

Jakob, W. 2013. Light transport on path-space manifolds. Ph.D. thesis, Cornell University.

Jakob, W., A. Arbree, J. T. Moon, K. Bala, and M. Steve. 2010. A radiative transfer framework for rendering materials with anisotropic structure. *ACM Transactions on Graphics (Proceedings of SIGGRAPH 2010) 29*(4), 53:1–53:13.

Jakob, W., E. d'Eon, O. Jakob, and S. Marschner. 2014a. A comprehensive framework for rendering layered materials. *ACM Transactions on Graphics 33*(4), 118:1–118:14.

Jakob, W., M. Hašan, L.-Q. Yan, J. Lawrence, R. Ramamoorthi, and S. Marschner. 2014b. Discrete stochastic microfacet models. *ACM Transactions on Graphics 33*(4), 115:1–115:10.

Jakob, W., and S. Marschner. 2012. Manifold exploration: a Markov chain Monte Carlo technique for rendering scenes with difficult specular transport. *ACM Transactions on Graphics (Proceedings of SIGGRAPH 2012) 31*(4), 58:1–58:13.

Jakob, W., C. Regg, and W. Jarosz. 2011. Progressive expectation-maximization for hierarchical volumetric photon mapping. *Computer Graphics Forum (Proceedings of the 2011 Eurographics Symposium on Rendering) 30*(4), 1287–97.

Jansen, F. W. 1986. Data structures for ray tracing. In L. R. A. Kessener, F. J. Peters, and M. L. P. Lierop (Eds.), *Data Structures for Raster Graphics, Workshop Proceedings,* 57–73. New York: Springer-Verlag.

Jarabo, A., J. Marco, A. Muñoz, R. Buisan, W. Jarosz, and D. Gutierrez. 2014a. A framework for transient rendering. *ACM Transactions on Graphics (Proceedings of SIGGRAPH Asia 2014) 33*(6), 177:1–177:10.

Jarabo, A., H. Wu, J. Dorsey, H. Rushmeier, and D. Gutierrez. 2014b. Effects of approximate filtering on the appearance of bidirectional texture functions. *IEEE Transactions on Visualization and Computer Graphics 20*(6), 880–92.

Jarosz, W. 2008. Efficient Monte Carlo methods for light transport in scattering media. Ph.D. Thesis, UC San Diego.

Jarosz, W., D. Nowrouzezahrai, I. Sadeghi, and H. W. Jensen. 2011a. A comprehensive theory of volumetric radiance estimation using photon points and beams. *ACM Transactions on Graphics 30*(1), 5:1–5:19.

Jarosz, W., D. Nowrouzezahrai, R. Thomas, P.-P. Sloan, and M. Zwicker. 2011b. Progressive photon beams. *ACM Transactions on Graphics (Proceedings of SIGGRAPH Asia 2011) 30*(6), 181:1–181:12.

Jarosz, W., M. Zwicker, and H. W. Jensen. 2008. The beam radiance estimate for volumetric photon mapping. *Computer Graphics Forum (Proceedings of Eurographics 2008) 27*(2), 557–66.

Jensen, H. W. 1995. Importance driven path tracing using the photon map. In *Eurographics Rendering Workshop 1995*, 326–35.

Jensen, H. W. 1996. Global illumination using photon maps. In X. Pueyo and P. Schröder (Eds.), *Eurographics Rendering Workshop 1996*, 21–30.

Jensen, H. W. 1997. Rendering caustics on non-Lambertian surfaces. *Computer Graphics Forum 16*(1), 57–64.

Jensen, H. W. 2001. *Realistic Image Synthesis Using Photon Mapping*. Natick, Massachusetts: A. K. Peters.

Jensen, H. W., and J. Buhler. 2002. A rapid hierarchical rendering technique for translucent materials. *ACM Transactions on Graphics 21*(3), 576–81.

Jensen, H. W., and N. Christensen. 1995. Optimizing path tracing using noise reduction filters. In *Proceedings of WSCG*, 134–42.

Jensen, H. W., and P. H. Christensen. 1998. Efficient simulation of light transport in scenes with participating media using photon maps. In *SIGGRAPH '98 Conference Proceedings*, Annual Conference Series, 311–20.

Jensen, H. W., J. Arvo, M. Fajardo, P. Hanrahan, D. Mitchell, M. Pharr, and P. Shirley. 2001a. State of the art in Monte Carlo ray tracing for realistic image synthesis. In *SIGGRAPH 2001 Course 29*, Los Angeles.

Jensen, H. W., S. R. Marschner, M. Levoy, and P. Hanrahan. 2001b. A practical model for subsurface light transport. In *Proceedings of ACM SIGGRAPH 2001*, Computer Graphics Proceedings, Annual Conference Series, 511–18.

Jensen, H. W., J. Arvo, P. Dutré, A. Keller, A. Owen, M. Pharr, and P. Shirley. 2003. Monte Carlo ray tracing. In *SIGGRAPH 2003 Course*, San Diego.

Jevans, D., and B. Wyvill. 1989. Adaptive voxel subdivision for ray tracing. In *Proceedings of Graphics Interface 1989*, 164–72.

Joe, S., and F.-Y. Kuo. 2008. Constructing Sobol' sequences with better two-dimensional projections. *SIAM J. Sci. Comput. 30*, 2635–54.

Johnson, G. M., and M. D. Fairchild. 1999. Full spectral color calculations in realistic image synthesis. *IEEE Computer Graphics and Applications 19*(4), 47–53.

Johnson, M. K., F. Cole, A. Raj, and E. H. Adelson. 2011. Microgeometry capture using an elastomeric sensor. *ACM Transactions on Graphics (Proceedings of SIGGRAPH 2011) 30*(4), 46:1–46:8.

Johnstone, M. S., and P. R. Wilson. 1999. The memory fragmentation problem: solved? *ACM SIGPLAN Notices 34*(3), 26–36.

Jones, T. 2005. Efficient generation of Poisson-disk sampling patterns. *Journal of Graphics Tools 11*(2), 27–36.

Judd, D. B., D. L. MacAdam, and G. Wyszecki. 1964. Spectral distribution of typical daylight as a function of correlated color temperature. *Journal of the Optical Society of America 54*(8), 1031–40.

Kainz, F., R. Bogart, and D. Hess. 2004. In R. Fernando (Ed.), *GPU Gems*. Reading, Massachusetts: Addison-Wesley, 425–44.

Kajiya, J. T. 1982. Ray tracing parametric patches. In *Computer Graphics (SIGGRAPH 1982 Conference Proceedings)*, 245–54.

Kajiya, J. T. 1983. New techniques for ray tracing procedurally defined objects. In *Computer Graphics (Proceedings of SIGGRAPH '83)*, *17*, 91–102.

Kajiya, J. T. 1985. Anisotropic reflection models. *Computer Graphics (Proceedings of SIG-GRAPH '85)*, *19*, 15–21.

Kajiya, J. T. 1986. The rendering equation. In *Computer Graphics (SIGGRAPH '86 Proceedings)*, *20*, 143–50.

Kajiya, J. T., and T. L. Kay. 1989. Rendering fur with three dimensional textures. *Computer Graphics (Proceedings of SIGGRAPH '89)*, *23*, 271–80.

Kajiya, J., and M. Ullner. 1981. Filtering high quality text for display on raster scan devices. In *Computer Graphics (Proceedings of SIGGRAPH '81)*, 7–15.

Kajiya, J. T., and B. P. Von Herzen. 1984. Ray tracing volume densities. In *Computer Graphics (Proceedings of SIGGRAPH '84)*, Volume 18, 165–74.

Kalantari, N. K., S. Bako, and P. Sen. 2015. A machine learning approach for filtering Monte Carlo noise. *ACM Transactions on Graphics (Proceedings of SIGGRAPH 2015) 34*(4), 122:1–122:12.

Kalantari, N. K., and P. Sen. 2013. Removing the noise in Monte Carlo rendering with general image denoising algorithms. *Computer Graphics Forum (Proceedings of Eurographics 2013) 32*(2), 93–102.

Kalos, M. H., and P. A. Whitlock. 1986. *Monte Carlo Methods: Volume I: Basics*. New York: Wiley.

Kalra, D., and A. H. Barr. 1989. Guaranteed ray intersections with implicit surfaces. In *Computer Graphics (Proceedings of SIGGRAPH '89)*, Volume 23, 297–306.

Kammaje, R., and B. Mora. 2007. A study of restricted BSP trees for ray tracing. In *IEEE Symposium on Interactive Ray Tracing*, 55–62.

Kaplanyan, A. S., and C. Dachsbacher. 2013a. Adaptive progressive photon mapping. *ACM Transactions on Graphics 32*(2), 16:1–16:13.

Kaplanyan, A. S., and C. Dachsbacher. 2013b. Path space regularization for holistic and robust light transport. *Computer Graphics Forum (Proceedings of Eurographics 2013) 32*(2), 63–72.

Kaplanyan, A. S., J. Hanika, and C. Dachsbacher. 2014. The natural-constraint representation of the path space for efficient light transport simulation. *ACM Transactions on Graphics (Proceedings of SIGGRAPH 2014) 33*(4), 102:1–102:13.

Kaplan, M. R. 1985. The uses of spatial coherence in ray tracing. In *ACM SIGGRAPH Course Notes 11*.

Karras, T., and T. Aila. 2013. Fast parallel construction of high-quality bounding volume hierarchies. In *Proceedings of High Performance Graphics 2013*, 89–99.

Karrenberg, R., D. Rubinstein, P. Slusallek, and S. Hack. 2010. AnySL: efficient and portable shading for ray tracing. In *Proceedings of High Performance Graphics 2010*, 97–105.

Kay, D. S., and D. P. Greenberg. 1979. Transparency for computer synthesized images. In *Computer Graphics (SIGGRAPH '79 Proceedings)*, Volume 13, 158–64.

Kay, T., and J. Kajiya. 1986. Ray tracing complex scenes. In *Computer Graphics (SIGGRAPH '86 Proceedings)*, Volume 20, 269–78.

Kelemen, C., L. Szirmay-Kalos, G. Antal, and F. Csonka. 2002. A simple and robust mutation strategy for the Metropolis light transport algorithm. *Computer Graphics Forum 21*(3), 531–40.

Keller, A. 1996. Quasi-Monte Carlo radiosity. In X. Pueyo and P. Schröder (Eds.), *Eurographics Rendering Workshop 1996*, 101–10.

Keller, A. 1997. Instant radiosity. In *Proceedings of SIGGRAPH '97*, Computer Graphics Proceedings, Annual Conference Series, Los Angeles, 49–56.

Keller, A. 1998. Quasi-Monte Carlo methods for photorealistic image synthesis. Ph.D. thesis, Shaker Verlag Aachen.

Keller, A. 2001. Strictly deterministic sampling methods in computer graphics. *mental images Technical Report*. Also in *SIGGRAPH 2003 Monte Carlo Course Notes*.

Keller, A. 2004. Stratification by rank-1 lattices. *Monte Carlo and Quasi-Monte Carlo Methods 2002*. Berlin: Springer-Verlag.

Keller, A. 2006. Myths of computer graphics. In *Monte Carlo and Quasi-Monte Carlo Methods 2004*, Berlin: Springer-Verlag, 217–43.

Keller, A. 2012. Quasi-Monte Carlo image synthesis in a nutshell. In *Monte Carlo and Quasi-Monte Carlo Methods 2012*, Berlin: Springer-Verlag.

Keller, A., and C. Wächter. 2011. Efficient ray tracing without auxiliary acceleration data structure. *High Performance Graphics 2011 Poster*.

Kensler, A., and P. Shirley. 2006. Optimizing ray-triangle intersection via automated search. In *IEEE Symposium on Interactive Ray Tracing*, 33–38.

Kensler, A. 2008. Tree rotations for improving bounding volume hierarchies. In *IEEE Symposium on Interactive Ray Tracing*, 73–76.

Kensler, A., A. Knoll, and P. Shirley. 2008. Better gradient noise. *Technical Report UUSCI-2008-001, SCI Institute, University of Utah*.

Kensler, A. 2013. Correlated multi-jittered sampling. *Pixar Technical Memo 13-01*.

Kettunen, M., M. Manzi, M. Aittala, J. Lehtinen, F. Durand, and M. Zwicker. 2015. Gradient-domain path tracing. *ACM Transactions on Graphics (Proceedings of SIGGRAPH 2015) 34*(4), 123:1–123:13.

Kider Jr., J. T., D. Knowlton, J. Newlin, Y. K. Li, and D. P. Greenberg. 2014. A framework for the experimental comparison of solar and skydome illumination. *ACM Transactions on Graphics (Proceedings of SIGGRAPH Asia 2014) 33*(6), 180:1–180:12.

Kienle, A., and M. Patterson. 1997. Improved solutions of the steady-state and the time-resolved diffusion equations for reflectance from a semi-infinite turbid medium. *Journal of the Optical Society of America A 14*(1), 246–54.

Kim, V. G., Y. Lipman, and T. Funkhouser. 2012. Symmetry-guided texture synthesis and manipulation. *ACM Transactions on Graphics 31*(3), 22:1–22:14.

King, L. V. 1913. On the scattering and absorption of light in gaseous media, with applications to the intensity of sky radiation. *Philosophical Transactions of the Royal Society of London. Series A. Mathematical and Physical Sciences 212*, 375–433.

King, A., K. Kulla, A. Conty, and M. Fajardo. 2013. BSSRDF importance sampling. *SIGGRAPH 2013 Talks*.

Kirk, D., and J. Arvo. 1988. The ray tracing kernel. In *Proceedings of Ausgraph '88*, 75–82.

Kirk, D. B., and J. Arvo. 1991. Unbiased sampling techniques for image synthesis. *Computer Graphics (SIGGRAPH '91 Proceedings)*, Volume 25, 153–56.

Klassen, R. V. 1987. Modeling the effect of the atmosphere on light. *ACM Transactions on Graphics 6*(3), 215–37.

Klimaszewski, K. S., and T. W. Sederberg. 1997. Faster ray tracing using adaptive grids. *IEEE Computer Graphics and Applications 17*(1), 42–51.

Knaus, C., and M. Zwicker. 2011. Progressive photon mapping: a probabilistic approach. *ACM Transactions on Graphics 30*(3), 25:1–25:13.

Kniep, S., S. Häring, and M. Magnor. 2009. Efficient and accurate rendering of complex light sources. *Computer Graphics Forum (Proceedings of the 2009 Eurographics Symposium on Rendering) 28*(4), 1073–81.

Knoll, A., Y. Hijazi, C. D. Hansen, I. Wald, and H. Hagen. 2009. Fast ray tracing of arbitrary implicit surfaces with interval and affine arithmetic. *Computer Graphics Forum 28*(1), 26–40.

Knuth, D. E. 1984. Literate programming. *The Computer Journal 27*, 97–111. Reprinted in D. E. Knuth, *Literate Programming*, Stanford Center for the Study of Language and Information, 1992.

Knuth, D. E. 1986. *MetaFont: The Program*. Reading, Massachusetts: Addison-Wesley.

Knuth, D. E. 1993a. *TEX: The Program*. Reading, Massachusetts: Addison-Wesley.

Knuth, D. E. 1993b. *The Stanford GraphBase*. New York: ACM Press and Addison-Wesley.

Kolb, C., D. Mitchell, and P. Hanrahan. 1995. A realistic camera model for computer graphics. *SIGGRAPH '95 Conference Proceedings*, Annual Conference Series, 317–24.

Kollig, T., and A. Keller. 2000. Efficient bidirectional path tracing by randomized quasi-Monte Carlo integration. In *Monte Carlo and Quasi-Monte Carlo Methods 2000*, pp. 290–305. Berlin: Springer-Verlag.

Kollig, T., and A. Keller. 2002. Efficient multidimensional sampling. *Computer Graphics Forum (Proceedings of Eurographics 2002)*, Volume 21, 557–63.

Kontkanen, J., J. Räsänen, and A. Keller. 2004. Irradiance filtering for Monte Carlo ray tracing. *Monte Carlo and Quasi-Monte Carlo Methods*, 259–72.

Kopta, D., T. Ize, J. Spjut, E. Brunvand, A. Davis, and A. Kensler. 2012. Fast, effective BVH updates for animated scenes. In *Proceedings of the ACM SIGGRAPH Symposium on Interactive 3D Graphics and Games*, 197–204.

Křivánek, J., P. Gautron, S. Pattanaik, and K. Bouatouch. 2005. Radiance caching for efficient global illumination computation. *IEEE Transactions on Visualization and Computer Graphics 11*(5), 550–61.

Kulla, C., and M. Fajardo. 2012. Importance sampling techniques for path tracing in participating media. *Computer Graphics Forum (Proceedings of the 2012 Eurographics Symposium on Rendering) 31*(4), 1519–28.

Kurt, M., L. Szirmay-Kalos, and J. Křivánek. 2010. An anisotropic BRDF model for fitting and Monte Carlo rendering. *SIGGRAPH Computer Graphics 44*(1), 3:1–3:15.

Lacewell, D., B. Burley, S. Boulos, and P. Shirley. 2008. Raytracing prefiltered occlusion for aggregate geometry. In *IEEE Symposium on Interactive Ray Tracing*, 19–26.

Lafortune, E. 1996. Mathematical models and Monte Carlo algorithms for physically based rendering. Ph.D. thesis, Katholieke Universiteit Leuven.

Lafortune, E., and Y. Willems. 1994. A theoretical framework for physically based rendering. *Computer Graphics Forum 13*(2), 97–107.

Lafortune, E. P., and Y. D. Willems. 1996. Rendering participating media with bidirectional path tracing. In *Eurographics Rendering Workshop 1996*, 91–100.

Lagae, A., and G. Drettakis. 2011. Filtering solid Gabor noise. *ACM Transactions on Graphics (Proceedings of ACM SIGGRAPH 2011) 30*(4), 51:1–51:6.

Lagae, A., and P. Dutré. 2005. An efficient ray-quadrilateral intersection test. *Journal of Graphics Tools 10*(4), 23–32.

Lagae, A., and P. Dutré. 2008a. Compact, fast, and robust grids for ray tracing. In *Computer Graphics Forum (Proceedings of the 2008 Eurographics Symposium on Rendering) 27*(4), 1235–1244.

Lagae, A., and P. Dutré. 2008b. Accelerating ray tracing using constrained tetrahedralizations. In *Computer Graphics Forum (Proceedings of the 2008 Eurographics Symposium on Rendering) 27*(4), 1303–12.

Lagae, E., and P. Dutré. 2008c. A comparison of methods for generating Poisson disk distributions. *Computer Graphics Forum 27*(1), 114–29.

Lagae, A., S. Lefebvre, G. Drettakis, and P. Dutré. 2009. Procedural noise using sparse Gabor convolution. *ACM Transactions on Graphics (Proceedings of SIGGRAPH 2009) 28*(3), 54:1–54:10.

Lagae, A., S. Lefebvre, R. Cook, T. DeRose, G. Drettakis, D. S. Ebert, J. P. Lewis, K. Perlin, and M. Zwicker. 2010. A survey of procedural noise functions. *Computer Graphics Forum 29*(8), 2579–2600.

Laine, S. 2010. Restart trail for stackless BVH traversal. In *Proceedings of High Performance Graphics 2010*, 107–11.

Lam, M. S., E. E. Rothberg, and M. E. Wolf. 1991. The cache performance and optimizations of blocked algorithms. In *Proceedings of the Fourth International Conference on Architectural Support for Programming Languages and Operating Systems (ASPLOS-IV)*, Palo Alto, California.

Lambert, J. H. 1760. *Photometry, or, On the Measure and Gradations of Light, Colors, and Shade*. The Illuminating Engineering Society of North America. Translated by David L. DiLaura in 2001.

Lang, S. 1986. *An Introduction to Linear Algebra*. New York: Springer-Verlag.

Lansdale, R. C. 1991. Texture mapping and resampling for computer graphics. M.S. thesis, Department of Electrical Engineering, University of Toronto.

Larson, G. W., and R. A. Shakespeare. 1998. *Rendering with Radiance: The Art and Science of Lighting Visualization*. San Francisco: Morgan Kaufmann.

Lauterbach, C., M. Garland, S. Sengupta, D. Luebke, and D. Manocha. 2009. Fast BVH construction on GPUs. *Computer Graphics Forum (Eurographics 2009 Conference Proceedings) 28*(2), 422–30.

Lawrence, J., S. Rusinkiewicz, and R. Ramamoorthi. 2004. Efficient BRDF importance sampling using a factored representation. *ACM Transactions on Graphics (Proceedings of SIGGRAPH 2004) 23*(3), 496–505.

Lawrence, J., S. Rusinkiewicz, and R. Ramamoorthi. 2005. Adaptive numerical cumulative distribution functions for efficient importance sampling. *Rendering Techniques 2005: 16th Eurographics Workshop on Rendering*, 11–20.

L'Ecuyer, P., and R Simard. 2007. TestU01: a C library for empirical testing of random number generators. In *ACM Transactions on Mathemathical Software 33*(4).

Lee, M. E., R. A. Redner, and S. P. Uselton. 1985. Statistically optimized sampling for distributed ray tracing. In *Computer Graphics (Proceedings of SIGGRAPH '85)*, Volume 19, 61–67.

Lee, M., and R. Redner. 1990. A note on the use of nonlinear filtering in computer graphics. *IEEE Computer Graphics and Applications 10*(3), 23–29.

Lee, W.-J., Y. Shin, J. Lee, J.-W. Kim, J.-H. Nah, S. Jung, S. Lee, H.-S. Park, and T.-D. Han. 2013. SGRT: a mobile GPU architecture for real-time ray tracing. In *Proceedings of High Performance Graphics 2013*, 109–19.

Lee, W.-J., Y. Shin, S. J. Hwang, S. Kang, J.-J. Yoo, and S. Ryu. 2015. Reorder buffer: an energy-efficient multithreading architecture for hardware MIMD ray traversal. In *Proceedings of High Performance Graphics 2015*, 21–32.

Lefebvre, S., S. Hornus, and A. Lasram. 2010. By-example synthesis of architectural textures. *ACM Transactions on Graphics (Proceedings of SIGGRAPH 2010) 29*(4), 84:1–84:8.

Lehtinen, J., T. Aila, J. Chen, S. Laine, and F. Durand. 2011. Temporal light field reconstruction for rendering distribution effects. *ACM SIGGRAPH 2011 Papers*. 55:1–55:12.

Lehtinen, J., T. Aila, S. Laine, and F. Durand. 2012. Reconstructing the indirect light field for global illumination. *ACM Transactions on Graphics 31*(4). 51:1–51:10.

Lehtinen, J., T. Karras, S. Laine, M. Aittala, F. Durand, and T. Aila. 2013. Gradient-domain Metropolis light transport. *ACM Transactions on Graphics (Proceedings of SIGGRAPH 2013) 32*(4), 95:1–95:12.

Lehtonen, J., J. Parkkinen, and T. Jaaskelainen. 2006. Optimal sampling of color spectra. *Journal of the Optical Society of America A 23*(13), 2983–88.

Lessig, C., M. Desbrun, and E. Fiume. 2014. A constructive theory of sampling for image synthesis using reproducing kernel bases. *ACM Transactions on Graphics (Proceedings of SIGGRAPH 2014) 33*(4), 55:1–55:14.

Levine, J. R., T. Mason, and D. Brown. 1992. *lex & yacc*. Sebastopol, California: O'Reilly & Associates.

Levoy, M. 1988. Display of surfaces from volume data. *IEEE Computer Graphics and Applications 8*(3), 29–37.

Levoy, M. 1990a. Efficient ray tracing of volume data. *ACM Transactions on Graphics 9*(3), 245–61.

Levoy, M. 1990b. A hybrid ray tracer for rendering polygon and volume data. *IEEE Computer Graphics and Applications 10*(2), 33–40.

Levoy, M., and P. M. Hanrahan. 1996. Light field rendering. In *Proceedings of SIGGRAPH '96*, Computer Graphics Proceedings, Annual Conference Series, 31–42.

Levoy, M., and T. Whitted. 1985. The use of points as a display primitive. *Technical Report 85-022*. Computer Science Department, University of North Carolina at Chapel Hill.

Lewis, J.-P. 1989. Algorithms for solid noise synthesis. In *Computer Graphics (Proceedings of SIGGRAPH '89)*, Volume 23, 263–70.

Li, H., L.-Y. Wei, P. Sander, and C.-W. Fu. 2010. Anisotropic blue noise sampling. *ACM Transactions on Graphics (Proceedings of SIGGRAPH Asia 2010) 29*(6), 167:1–167:12.

Li, K., F. Pellacini, and K. Torrance. 2005. A hybrid Monte Carlo method for accurate and efficient subsurface scattering. In *Rendering Techniques (Proceedings of the 2005 Eurographics Symposium on Rendering)*, 283–90.

Liu, J. S. 2001. *Monte Carlo Strategies in Scientific Computing*. New York: Springer-Verlag.

Logie, J. R., and J. W. Patterson. 1994. Inverse displacement mapping in the general case. *Computer Graphics Forum 14*(5), 261–73.

Lokovic, T., and E. Veach. 2000. Deep shadow maps. In *Proceedings of ACM SIGGRAPH 2000*, Computer Graphics Proceedings, Annual Conference Series, 385–92.

Lommel, E. 1889. Die Photometrie der diffusen Zurückwerfung. *Annalen der Physik 36*, 473–502.

Loop, C. 1987. Smooth subdivision surfaces based on triangles. M.S. thesis, University of Utah.

Lu, H., R. Pacanowski, and X. Granier. 2013. Second-order approximation for variance reduction in multiple importance sampling. *Computer Graphics Forum 32*(7), 131–36.

Lu, H., R. Pacanowski, and X. Granier. 2015. Position-dependent importance sampling of light field luminaires. *IEEE Transactions on Visualization and Computer Graphics 21*(2), 241–51.

Lukaszewski, A. 2001. Exploiting coherence of shadow rays. In *AFRIGRAPH 2001*, 147–50. ACM SIGGRAPH.

MacDonald, J. D., and K. S. Booth. 1990. Heuristics for ray tracing using space subdivision. *The Visual Computer 6*(3), 153–66.

Machiraju, R., and R. Yagel. 1996. Reconstruction error characterization and control: a sampling theory approach. *IEEE Transactions on Visualization and Computer Graphics 2*(4).

MacKay, D. 2003. *Information Theory, Inference, and Learning Algorithms*. Cambridge: Cambridge University Press.

Malacara, D. 2002. *Color Vision and Colorimetry: Theory and Applications*. SPIE—The International Society for Optical Engineering.

Mann, S., N. Litke, and T. DeRose. 1997. A coordinate free geometry ADT. Research Report CS-97-15, Computer Science Department, University of Waterloo.

Manson, J., and S. Schaefer. 2013. Cardinality-constrained texture filtering. *ACM Transactions on Graphics (Proceedings of SIGGRAPH 2013) 32*(4), 140:1–140:8.

Manson, J., and S. Schaefer. 2014. Bilinear accelerated filter approximation. *Computer Graphics Forum (Proceedings of the 2014 Eurographics Symposium on Rendering) 33*(4), 33–40.

Mansson, E., J. Munkberg, and T. Akenine-Möller. 2007. Deep coherent ray tracing. In *Proceedings of IEEE Symposium on Interactive Ray Tracing*, 79–85.

Manzi, M., M. Kettunen, M. Aittala, J. Lehtinen, F. Durand, and M. Zwicker. 2015. Gradient-domain bidirectional path tracing. *Eurographics Symposium on Rendering—Experimental Ideas & Implementations*.

Manzi, M., F. Rousselle, M. Kettunen, J. Lehtinen, and M. Zwicker. 2014. Improved sampling for gradient-domain Metropolis light transport. *ACM Transactions on Graphics (Proceedings of SIGGRAPH Asia 2014) 33*(6), 178:1–178:12.

Marques, R., C. Bouville, M. Ribardière, L. P. Santos, and K. Bouatouch. 2013. Spherical Fibonacci point sets for illumination integrals. *Computer Graphics Forum (Proceedings of the 2013 Eurographics Symposium on Rendering) 32*(4), 134–43.

Marschner, S. 1998. Inverse rendering for computer graphics. Ph.D. thesis, Cornell University.

Marschner, S. R., H. W. Jensen, M. Cammarano, S. Worley, and P. Hanrahan. 2003. Light scattering from human hair fibers. *ACM Transactions on Graphics 22*(3), 780–91.

Marschner, S. R., and R. J. Lobb. 1994. An evaluation of reconstruction filters for volume rendering. In *Proceedings of Visualization '94*, Washington, D.C., 100–07.

Marschner, S., S. Westin, A. Arbree, and J. Moon. 2005. Measuring and modeling the appearance of finished wood. In *ACM Transactions on Graphics (Proceedings of SIGGRAPH 2005) 24*(3), 727–34.

Martin, W., E. Cohen, R. Fish, and P. S. Shirley. 2000. Practical ray tracing of trimmed NURBS surfaces. *Journal of Graphics Tools 5*(1), 27–52.

Mas, A., I. Martín, and G. Patow. 2008. Compression and importance sampling of near-field light sources. *Computer Graphics Forum 27*(8), 2013–27.

Matusik, W., H. Pfister, M. Brand, and L. McMillan. 2003a. Efficient isotropic BRDF measurement. In *Proceedings of the 14th Eurographics Workshop on Rendering*, 241–47.

Matusik, W., H. Pfister, M. Brand, and L. McMillan. 2003b. A data-driven reflectance model. *ACM Transactions on Graphics (Proceedings of SIGGRAPH 2003) 22*(3), 759–69.

Max, N. L. 1986. Atmospheric illumination and shadows. In *Computer Graphics (Proceedings of SIGGRAPH '86)*, Volume 20, 117–24.

Max, N. L. 1988. Horizon mapping: shadows for bump-mapped surfaces. *The Visual Computer 4*(2), 109–17.

Max, N. L. 1995. Optical models for direct volume rendering. *IEEE Transactions on Visualization and Computer Graphics 1*(2), 99–108.

McCluney, W. R. 1994. *Introduction to Radiometry and Photometry*. Boston: Artech House.

McCombe, J. 2013. Low power consumption ray tracing. *SIGGRAPH 2013 Course: Ray Tracing Is the Future and Ever Will Be*.

McCormack, J., R. Perry, K. I. Farkas, and N. P. Jouppi. 1999. Feline: fast elliptical lines for anisotropic texture mapping. In *Proceedings of SIGGRAPH '99*, Computer Graphics Proceedings, Annual Conference Series, Los Angeles, 243–250.

Meijering, E. 2002. A chronology of interpolation: from ancient astronomy to modern signal and image processing. In *Proceedings of the IEEE 90*(3), 319–42.

Meijering, E. H. W., W. J. Niessen, J. P. W. Pluim, and M. A. Viergever. 1999. Quantitative comparison of sinc-approximating kernels for medical image interpolation. In C. Taylor and A. Colchester (Eds.), *Medical Image Computing and Computer-Assisted Intervention—MICCAI 1999*, 210–17. Berlin: Springer-Verlag.

Meng, J., F. Simon, J. Hanika, and C. Dachsbacher. 2015. Physically meaningful rendering using tristimulus colours. *Computer Graphics Forum (Proceedings of the 2015 Eurographics Symposium on Rendering) 34*(4), 31–40.

Metropolis, N., A. Rosenbluth, M. Rosenbluth, A. Teller, and E. Teller. 1953. Equation of state calculations by fast computing machines. *Journal of Chemical Physics 21*(6), 1087–92.

Meyer, G. W., and D. P. Greenberg. 1980. Perceptual color spaces for computer graphics. In *Computer Graphics (Proceedings of SIGGRAPH '80)*, Volume 14, Seattle, Washington, 254–261.

Meyer, G. W., H. E. Rushmeier, M. F. Cohen, D. P. Greenberg, and K. E. Torrance. 1986. An experimental evaluation of computer graphics imagery. *ACM Transactions on Graphics 5*(1), 30–50.

Mikkelsen, M. 2008. Simulation of wrinkled surfaces revisited. M.S. thesis, University of Copenhagen.

Miller, G. S., and C. R. Hoffman. 1984. Illumination and reflection maps: simulated objects in simulated and real environments. *Course Notes for Advanced Computer Graphics Animation, SIGGRAPH '84.*

Mitchell, D. P. 1987. Generating antialiased images at low sampling densities. *Computer Graphics (SIGGRAPH '87 Proceedings)*, Volume 21, 65–72.

Mitchell, D. P. 1990. Robust ray intersection with interval arithmetic. In *Proceedings of Graphics Interface 1990*, 68–74.

Mitchell, D. P. 1991. Spectrally optimal sampling for distributed ray tracing. *Computer Graphics (SIGGRAPH '91 Proceedings)*, Volume 25, 157–64.

Mitchell, D. P. 1992. Ray tracing and irregularities of distribution. In *Third Eurographics Workshop on Rendering*, Bristol, United Kingdom, 61–69.

Mitchell, D. P. 1996b. Consequences of stratified sampling in graphics. In *Proceedings of SIGGRAPH '96*, Computer Graphics Proceedings, Annual Conference Series, New Orleans, Louisiana, 277–80.

Mitchell, D. P., and P. Hanrahan. 1992. Illumination from curved reflectors. In *Computer Graphics (Proceedings of SIGGRAPH '92)*, Volume 26, 283–91.

Mitchell, D. P., and A. N. Netravali. 1988. Reconstruction filters in computer graphics. *Computer Graphics (SIGGRAPH '88 Proceedings)*, Volume 22, 221–28.

Möller, T., R. Machiraju, K. Mueller, and R. Yagel. 1997. Evaluation and design of filters using a Taylor series expansion. *IEEE Transactions on Visualization and Computer Graphics 3*(2), 184–99.

Möller, T., and B. Trumbore. 1997. Fast, minimum storage ray–triangle intersection. *Journal of Graphics Tools 2*(1), 21–28.

Moon, B., Y. Byun, T.-J. Kim, P. Claudio, H.-S. Kim, Y.-J. Ban, S. W. Nam, and S.-E. Yoon. 2010. Cache-oblivious ray reordering. *ACM Transactions on Graphics 29*(3), 28:1–28:10.

Moon, B., N. Carr, and S.-E. Yoon. 2014. Adaptive rendering based on weighted local regression. *ACM Transactions on Graphics 33*(5), 170:1–170:14.

Moon, J., and S. Marschner. 2006. Simulating multiple scattering in hair using a photon mapping approach. *ACM Transactions on Graphics (Proceedings of SIGGRAPH 2006) 25*(3), 1067–74.

Moon, J., B. Walter, and S. Marschner. 2007. Rendering discrete random media using precomputed scattering solutions. *Rendering Techniques 2007: 18th Eurographics Workshop on Rendering*, 231–42.

Moon, J., B. Walter, and S. Marschner. 2008. Efficient multiple scattering in hair using spherical harmonics. *ACM Transactions on Graphics (Proceedings of SIGGRAPH 2008) 27*(3), 31:1–31:7.

Moon, P., and D. E. Spencer. 1936. *The Scientific Basis of Illuminating Engineering*. New York: McGraw-Hill.

Moon, P., and D. E. Spencer 1948. *Lighting Design*. Reading, Masschusetts: Addison-Wesley.

Moore, R. E. 1966. *Interval Analysis*. Englewood Cliffs, New Jersey: Prentice Hall.

Mora, B. 2011. Naive ray-tracing: A divide-and-conquer approach. *ACM Transactions on Graphics 30*(5), 117:1–117:12.

Moravec, H. 1981. 3D graphics and the wave theory. In *Computer Graphics,* Volume 15, 289–96.

Morley, R. K., S. Boulos, J. Johnson, D. Edwards, P. Shirley, M. Ashikhmin, and S. Premoze. 2006. Image synthesis using adjoint photons. In *Proceedings of Graphics Interface 2006,* 179–86.

Motwani, R., and P. Raghavan. 1995. *Randomized Algorithms.* Cambridge, U.K.: Cambridge University Press.

Moulin, M., N. Billen, P. Dutré. 2015. Efficient visibility heuristics for kd-trees using the RTSAH. *Eurographics Symposium on Rendering–Experimental Ideas & Implementations.*

Moulton, J. 1990. Diffusion modeling of picosecond laser pulse propagation in turbid media. Master's thesis, McMaster University.

Müller, K., T. Techmann, and D. Fellner. 2003. Adaptive ray tracing of subdivision surfaces. *Computer Graphics Forum 22*(3), 553–62.

Müller, G., J. Meseth, M. Sattler, R. Sarlette, and R. Klein. 2005. Acquisition, synthesis and rendering of bidirectional texture functions. *Computer Graphics Forum (Eurographics State of the Art Report) 24*(1), 83–109.

Munkberg, J., K. Vaidyanathan, J. Hasselgren, P. Clarberg, and T. Akenine-Möller. 2014. Layered reconstruction for defocus and motion blur. *Computer Graphics Forum 33,* 81–92.

Musbach, A., G. W. Meyer, F. Reitich, and S. H. Oh. 2013. Full wave modelling of light propagation and reflection. *Computer Graphics Forum 32*(6), 24–37.

Museth, K. 2013. VDB: high-resolution sparse volumes with dynamic topology. *ACM Transactions on Graphics 32*(3), 27:1–27:22.

Musgrave, K. 1992. A panoramic virtual screen for ray tracing. In D. Kirk (Ed.), *Graphics Gems III,* 288–94. San Diego: Academic Press.

Nabata, K., K. Iwasaki, Y. Dobashi, and T. Nishita. 2013. Efficient divide-and-conquer ray tracing using ray sampling. In *Proceedings of High Performance Graphics 2013,* 129–35.

Nah, J.-H., J.-S. Park, C. Park, J.-W. Kim, Y.-H. Jung, W.-C. Park, and T.-D. Han. 2011. T&I engine: traversal and intersection engine for hardware accelerated ray tracing. *ACM Transactions on Graphics (Proceedings of SIGGRAPH Asia 2011) 30*(6), 160:1–160:10.

Nakamaru, K., and Y. Ohno. 2002. Ray tracing for curves primitive. In *Journal of WSCG (WSCG 2002 Proceedings) 10,* 311–16.

Narasimhan, S., M. Gupta, C. Donner, R. Ramamoorthi, S. Nayar, and H. W. Jensen. 2006. Acquiring scattering properties of participating media by dilution. *ACM Transactions on Graphics 25*(3), 1003–12.

Nayar, S. K., K. Ikeuchi, and T. Kanade. 1991. Surface reflection: physical and geometrical perspectives. *IEEE Transactions on Pattern Analysis and Machine Intelligence 17*(7), 611–34.

Naylor, B. 1993. Constructing good partition trees. In *Proceedings of Graphics Interface 1993,* 181–91.

Neyret, F. 1996. Synthesizing verdant landscapes using volumetric textures. In *Eurographics Rendering Workshop 1996,* 215–24.

Neyret, F. 1998. Modeling, animating, and rendering complex scenes using volumetric textures. *IEEE Transactions on Visualization and Computer Graphics 4*(1), 55–70.

Nicodemus, F., J. Richmond, J. Hsia, I. Ginsburg, and T. Limperis. 1977. *Geometrical Considerations and Nomenclature for Reflectance*. NBS Monograph 160, Washington, D.C.: National Bureau of Standards, U.S. Department of Commerce.

Niederreiter, H. 1992. *Random Number Generation and Quasi–Monte Carlo Methods*. Philadelphia: Society for Industrial and Applied Mathematics.

Nishita, T., and E. Nakamae. 1985. Continuous tone representation of three-dimensional objects taking account of shadows and interreflection. *SIGGRAPH Computer Graphics 19*(3), 23–30.

Nishita, T., and E. Nakamae. 1986. Continuous tone representation of three-dimensional objects illuminated by sky light. In *Computer Graphics (Proceedings of SIGGRAPH '86)*, Volume 20, 125–32.

Nishita, T., Y. Miyawaki, and E. Nakamae. 1987. A shading model for atmospheric scattering considering luminous intensity distribution of light sources. In *Computer Graphics (Proceedings of SIGGRAPH '87)*, Volume 21, 303–10.

Ngan, A., F. Durand, and W. Matusik. 2005. Experimental analysis of BRDF models. *Rendering Techniques 2005: 16th Eurographics Workshop on Rendering*, 117–26.

Ng, R., M. Levoy, M. Brédif., G. Duval, M. Horowitz, and P. Hanrahan. 2005. Light field photography with a hand-held plenoptic camera. *Stanford University Computer Science Technical Report*, CSTR 2005-02.

Norton, A., A. P. Rockwood, and P. T. Skolmoski. 1982. Clamping: a method of antialiasing textured surfaces by bandwidth limiting in object space. In *Computer Graphics (Proceedings of SIGGRAPH '82)*, Volume 16, 1–8.

Novák, J., A. Selle, and W. Jarosz. 2014. Residual ratio tracking for estimating attenuation in participating media. *ACM Transactions on Graphics (Proceedings of SIGGRAPH Asia 2014) 33*(6), 179:1–179:11.

O'Neill, M. 2014. PCG: A family of simple fast space-efficient statistically good algorithms for random number generation. Unpublished manuscript. *http://www.pcg-random.org/paper .html*.

Ogaki, S., and Y. Tokuyoshi. 2011. Direct ray tracing of Phong tessellation. *Computer Graphics Forum (Proceedings of the 2011 Eurographics Symposium on Rendering) 30*(4), 1337–44.

Ohmer, S. 1997. Ray Tracers: Blue Sky Studios. *Animation World Network, http://www.awn .com/animationworld/ray-tracers-blue-sky-studios*.

Olano, M., and D. Baker. 2010. LEAN mapping. In *Proceedings of the 2010 ACM SIGGRAPH symposium on Interactive 3D Graphics and Games*, 181–88.

OpenMP Architecture Review Board. 2013. OpenMP Application Program Interface. *http:// www.openmp.org/mp-documents/OpenMP4.0.0.pdf*.

Ooi, B. C., K. McDonell, and R. Sacks-Davis. 1987. Spatial kd-tree: a data structure for geographic databases. In *Proceedings of the IEEE COMPSAC Conference*.

Oren, M., and S. K. Nayar. 1994. Generalization of Lambert's reflectance model. In *Proceedings of SIGGRAPH '94, Computer Graphics Proceedings, Annual Conference Series*, 239–46. New York: ACM Press.

Ou, J., and F Pellacini. 2010. SafeGI: type checking to improve correctness in rendering system implementation. *Computer Graphics Forum (Proceedings of the 2010 Eurographics Symposium on Rendering) 29*(4), 1267–77.

Ou, J., F. Xie, P. Krishnamachari, and F. Pellacini. 2012. ISHair: importance sampling for hair scattering. *Computer Graphics Forum (Proceedings of the 2012 Eurographics Symposium on Rendering) 31*(4), 1537–45.

Overbeck, R., C. Donner, and R. Ramamoorthi. 2009. Adaptive wavelet rendering. *ACM Transactions on Graphics (Proceedings of ACM SIGGRAPH Asia 2009) 28*(5), 140:1–140:12.

Owen, A. B. 1998. Latin supercube sampling for very high-dimensional simulations. *Modeling and Computer Simulation 8*(1), 71–102.

Pacanowski, R., O. Salazar-Celis, C. Schlick, X. Granier, P. Poulin, and A. Cuyt. 2012. Rational BRDF. *IEEE Transactions on Visualization and Computer Graphics 18*(11), 1824–35.

Pajot, A., L. Barthe, M. Paulin, and P. Poulin. 2011. Representativity for robust and adaptive multiple importance sampling. *IEEE Transactions on Visualization and Computer Graphics 17*(8), 1108–21.

Pantaleoni, J., L. Fascione, M. Hill, and T. Aila. 2010. PantaRay: fast ray-traced occlusion caching of massive scenes. *ACM Transactions on Graphics (Proceedings of SIGGRAPH 2010) 29*(4), 37:1–37:10.

Pantaleoni, J., and D. Luebke. 2010. HLBVH: hierarchical LBVH construction for real-time ray tracing of dynamic geometry. In *Proceedings of the Conference on High Performance Graphics 2010*, 87–95.

Papas, M., K. de Mesa, and H. W. Jensen. 2014. A physically-pased BSDF for modeling the appearance of paper. *Computer Graphics Forum (Proceedings of the 2014 Eurographics Symposium on Rendering) 33*(4), 133–42.

Parker, S., S. Boulos, J. Bigler, and A. Robison. 2007. RTSL: a ray tracing shading language. In *Proceedings of IEEE Symposium on Interactive Ray Tracing*.

Parker, S. G., J. Bigler, A. Dietrich, H. Friedrich, J. Hoberock, D. Luebke, D. McAllister, M. McGuire, K. Morley, A. Robison, and M. Stich. 2010. OptiX: a general purpose ray tracing engine. *ACM Transactions on Graphics (Proceedings of SIGGRAPH 2010) 29*(4), 66:1–66:13.

Parker, S., W. Martin, P.-P. J. Sloan, P. S. Shirley, B. Smits, and C. Hansen. 1999. Interactive ray tracing. In *1999 ACM Symposium on Interactive 3D Graphics*, 119–26.

Patney, A., M. S. Ebeida, and J. D. Owens. 2009. Parallel view-dependent tessellation of Catmull–Clark subdivision surfaces. In *Proceedings of High Performance Graphics 2009*, 99–108.

Pattanaik, S. N., and S. P. Mudur. 1995. Adjoint equations and random walks for illumination computation. *ACM Transactions on Graphics 14*(1), 77–102.

Patterson, D., and J. Hennessy. 2006. *Computer Architecture: A Quantitative Approach*. San Francisco: Morgan Kaufmann.

Patterson, J. W., S. G. Hoggar, and J. R. Logie. 1991. Inverse displacement mapping. *Computer Graphics Forum 10*(2), 129–39.

Pauly, M. 1999. Robust Monte Carlo methods for photorealistic rendering of volumetric effects. Master's thesis, Universität Kaiserslautern.

Pauly, M., T. Kollig, and A. Keller. 2000. Metropolis light transport for participating media. In *Rendering Techniques 2000: 11th Eurographics Workshop on Rendering*, 11–22.

Peachey, D. R. 1985. Solid texturing of complex surfaces. *Computer Graphics (SIGGRAPH '85 Proceedings)*, Volume 19, 279–86.

Peachey, D. R. 1990. Texture on demand. Pixar Technical Memo #217.

Pearce, A. 1991. A recursive shadow voxel cache for ray tracing. In J. Arvo (Ed.), *Graphics Gems II*, 273–74. San Diego: Academic Press.

Peercy, M. S. 1993. Linear color representations for full spectral rendering. *Computer Graphics (SIGGRAPH '93 Proceedings)*, Volume 27, 191–98.

Peers, P., K. vom Berge, W. Matusik, R. Ramamoorthi, J. Lawrence, S. Rusinkiewicz, and P. Dutré. 2006. A compact factored representation of heterogeneous subsurface scattering. *ACM Transactions on Graphics 25*(3), 746–53.

Pegoraro, V., and S. Parker. 2009. An analytical solution to single scattering in homogeneous participating media. *Computer Graphics Forum (Proceedings of Eurographics 2009) 28*(2), 329–35.

Pegoraro, V., M. Schott, and S. Parker. 2009. An analytical approach to single scattering for anisotropic media and light distributions. In *Proceedings of Graphics Interface 2009*, 71–77.

Pegoraro, V., C. Brownlee, P. Shirley, and S. Parker. 2008a. Towards interactive global illumination effects via sequential Monte Carlo adaptation. *IEEE Symposium on Interactive Ray Tracing*, 107–14.

Pegoraro, V., M. Schott, and S. G. Parker. 2010. A closed-form solution to single scattering for general phase functions and light distributions. *Computer Graphics Forum (Proceedings of the 2010 Eurographics Symposium on Rendering) 29*(4), 1365–74.

Pegoraro, V., M. Schott, and P. Slusallek. 2011. A mathematical framework for efficient closed-form single scattering. In *Proceedings of Graphics Interface 2011*, 151–58.

Pegoraro, V., I. Wald, and S. Parker. 2008b. Sequential Monte Carlo adaptation in low-anisotropy participating media. *Computer Graphics Forum (Proceedings of the 2008 Eurographics Symposium on Rendering) 27*(4), 1097–1104.

Pekelis, L., and C. Hery. 2014. A statistical framework for comparing importance sampling methods, and an application to rectangular lights. *Pixar Technical Memo 14-01*.

Pekelis, L., C. Hery, R. Villemin, and J. Ling. 2015. A data-driven light scattering model for hair. *Pixar Technical Memo 15-02*.

Perlin, K. 1985a. An image synthesizer. In *Computer Graphics (SIGGRAPH '85 Proceedings)*, Volume 19, 287–96.

Perlin, K. 1985b. State of the art in image synthesis. *SIGGRAPH Course Notes 11*.

Perlin, K. 2002. Improving noise. *ACM Transactions on Graphics 21*(3), 681–82.

Perlin, K., and E. M. Hoffert. 1989. Hypertexture. In *Computer Graphics (Proceedings of SIGGRAPH '89)*, Volume 23, 253–62.

Pfister, H., M. Zwicker, J. van Baar, and M. Gross. 2000. Surfels: Surface elements as rendering primitives. In *Proceedings of ACM SIGGRAPH 2000*, Computer Graphics Proceedings, Annual Conference Series, 335–42.

Pharr, M., and P. Hanrahan. 1996. Geometry caching for ray-tracing displacement maps. In *Eurographics Rendering Workshop 1996*, 31–40.

Pharr, M., and P. M. Hanrahan. 2000. Monte Carlo evaluation of non-linear scattering equations for subsurface reflection. In *Proceedings of ACM SIGGRAPH 2000*, Computer Graphics Proceedings, Annual Conference Series, 75–84.

Pharr, M., and G. Humphreys. 2004. *Physically Based Rendering: From Theory to Implementation*. San Francisco: Morgan Kaufmann.

Pharr, M., C. Kolb, R. Gershbein, and P. M. Hanrahan. 1997. Rendering complex scenes with memory-coherent ray tracing. In *Proceedings of SIGGRAPH '97*, Computer Graphics Proceedings, Annual Conference Series, 101–08.

Pharr, M., and W. R. Mark. 2012. ispc: a SPMD compiler for high-performance CPU programming. In *Proceedings of Innovative Parallel Computing (InPar)*.

Phong, B.-T. 1975. Illumination for computer generated pictures. *Communications of the ACM 18*(6), 311–17.

Phong, B.-T., and F. C. Crow. 1975. Improved rendition of polygonal models of curved surfaces. In *Proceedings of the 2nd USA–Japan Computer Conference*.

Pilleboue, A., G. Singh, D. Coeurjolly, M. Kazhdan, and V. Ostromoukhov. 2015. Variance analysis for Monte Carlo integration. *ACM Transactions on Graphics (Proceedings of SIGGRAPH 2015) 34*(4), 124:1–124:14.

Piponi, D. 2012. Lossless decompression and the generation of random samples. *http://blog .sigfpe.com/2012/01/lossless-decompression-and-generation.html*.

Pixar Animation Studios. 2000. The RenderMan Interface. Version 3.2.

Pomraning, G. C., and B. D. Ganapol. 1995. Asymptotically consistent reflection boundary conditions for diffusion theory. In *Annals of Nuclear Energy 22*(12), 787–817.

Popov, S., I. Georgiev, P. Slusallek, and C. Dachsbacher. 2013. Adaptive quantization visibility caching. *Computer Graphics Forum (Proceedings of Eurographics 2013) 32*(2), 399–408.

Popov, S., J. Gunther, H. P. Seidel, and P. Slusallek. 2006. Experinces with streaming construction of SAH kd-trees. In *IEEE Symposium on Interactive Ray Tracing*, 89–94.

Popov, S., R. Dimov, I. Georgiev, and P. Slusallek. 2009. Object partitioning considered harmful: space subdivision for BVHs. In *Proceedings of High Performance Graphics 2009*, 15–22.

Porumbescu, S., B. Budge, L. Feng, and K. Joy. 2005. Shell maps. In *ACM Transactions on Graphics (Proceedings of SIGGRAPH 2005) 24*(3), 626–33.

Potmesil, M., and I. Chakravarty. 1981. A lens and aperture camera model for synthetic image generation. In *Computer Graphics (Proceedings of SIGGRAPH '81)*, Volume 15, 297–305.

Potmesil, M., and I. Chakravarty. 1982. Synthetic image generation with a lens and aperture camera model. *ACM Transactions on Graphics 1*(2), 85–108.

Potmesil, M., and I. Chakravarty. 1983. Modeling motion blur in computer-generated images. In *Computer Graphics (Proceedings of SIGGRAPH 83)*, Volume 17, Detroit, Michigan, 389–99.

Poulin, P., and A. Fournier. 1990. A model for anisotropic reflection. In *Computer Graphics (Proceedings of SIGGRAPH '90)*, Volume 24, 273–82.

Poynton, C. 2002a. Frequently-asked questions about color. *www.poynton.com/ColorFAQ .html*.

Poynton, C. 2002b. Frequently-asked questions about gamma. *www.poynton.com/ GammaFAQ.html*.

Preetham, A. J., P. S. Shirley, and B. E. Smits. 1999. A practical analytic model for daylight. In *Proceedings of SIGGRAPH '99*, Computer Graphics Proceedings, Annual Conference Series, 91–100.

Preisendorfer, R. W. 1965. *Radiative Transfer on Discrete Spaces*. Oxford: Pergamon Press.

Preisendorfer, R. W. 1976. *Hydrologic Optics*. Honolulu, Hawaii: U.S. Department of Commerce, National Oceanic and Atmospheric Administration.

Press, W. H., S. A. Teukolsky, W. T. Vetterling, and B. P. Flannery. 1992. *Numerical Recipes in C: The Art of Scientific Computing* (2nd ed.). Cambridge: Cambridge University Press.

Prusinkiewicz, P. 1986. Graphical applications of L-systems. In *Proceedings of Graphics Interface 1986*, 247–53.

Prusinkiewicz, P., M. James, and R. Mech. 1994. Synthetic topiary. In *Proceedings of SIGGRAPH '94*, Computer Graphics Proceedings, Annual Conference Series, 351–58.

Prusinkiewicz, P., L. Mündermann, R. Karwowski, and B. Lane. 2001. The use of positional information in the modeling of plants. In *Proceedings of ACM SIGGRAPH 2001*, Computer Graphics Proceedings, Annual Conference Series, 289–300.

Purcell, T. J., I. Buck, W. R. Mark, and P. Hanrahan. 2002. Ray tracing on programmable graphics hardware. *ACM Transactions on Graphics 21*(3), 703–12.

Purcell, T. J., C. Donner, M. Cammarano, H. W. Jensen, and P. Hanrahan. 2003. Photon mapping on programmable graphics hardware. In *Graphics Hardware 2003*, 41–50.

Purgathofer, W. 1987. A statistical mothod for adaptive stochastic sampling. *Computers & Graphics 11*(2), 157–62.

Qin, H., M. Chai, Q. Hou, Z. Ren, and K. Zhou. 2014. Cone tracing for furry object rendering. *IEEE Transactions on Visualization and Computer Graphics 20*(8), 1178–88.

Quilez, I. 2015. Distance estimation. *http://iquilezles.org/www/articles/distance/distance.htm*.

Raab, M., D. Seibert, and A. Keller. 2006. Unbiased global illumination with participating media. *Proc. Monte Carlo and Quasi-Monte Carlo Methods 2006*, 591–605.

Radziszewski, M., K. Boryczko, and W. Alda. 2009. An improved technique for full spectral rendering. *Journal of WSCG 17*(1-3), 9–16.

Ramamoorthi, R., and A. Barr. 1997. Fast construction of accurate quaternion splines. In *Proceedings of SIGGRAPH '97*, Computer Graphics Proceedings, Annual Conference Series, Los Angeles, 287–92.

Ramsey, S. D., K. Potter., and C. Hansen. 2004. Ray bilinear patch intersections. *Journal of Graphics Tools 9*(3), 41–47.

Ramshaw, L. 1987. Blossoming: a connect-the-dots approach to splines. *Digital Systems Research Center Technical Report*.

Reeves, W. T., D. H. Salesin, and R. L. Cook. 1987. Rendering antialiased shadows with depth maps. In *Computer Graphics (Proceedings of SIGGRAPH '87)*, Volume 21, 283–91.

Reichert, M. C. 1992. A two-pass radiosity method driven by lights and viewer position. Master's thesis, Cornell University.

Reinert, B., T. Ritschel, H.-P. Seidel, and I. Georgiev. 2015. Projective blue-noise sampling. In *Computer Graphics Forum*.

Reinhard, E., T. Pouli, T. Kunkel, B. Long, A. Ballestad, and G. Damberg. 2012. Calibrated image appearance reproduction. *ACM Transactions on Graphics (Proceedings of SIGGRAPH Asia 2012) 31*(6), 201:1–201:11.

Reinhard, E., G. Ward, P. Debevec, S. Pattanaik, W. Heidrich, and K. Myszkowski. 2010. *High Dynamic Range Imaging: Acquisition, Display, and Image-Based Lighting*. San Francisco: Morgan Kaufmann.

Reshetov, A., A. Soupikov, and J. Hurley. 2005. Multi-level ray tracing algorithm. *ACM Transactions on Graphics (Proceedings of SIGGRAPH 2005) 24*(3), 1176–85.

Reshetov, A. 2007. Faster ray packets–triangle intersection through vertex culling. In *Proceedings of IEEE Symposium on Interactive Ray Tracing*, 105–12.

Reshetov, A. 2009. Morphological antialiasing. In *Proceedings of High Performance Graphics 2009*.

Rogers, D. F., and J. A. Adams. 1990. *Mathematical Elements for Computer Graphics*. New York: McGraw-Hill.

Ross, S. M. 2002. *Introduction to Probability Models* (8th ed.). San Diego: Academic Press.

Roth, S. D. 1982. Ray casting for modeling solids. *Computer Graphics and Image Processing 18*, 109–44.

Roth, S. H., P. Diezi, and M. Gross. 2001. Ray tracing triangular Bézier patches. In *Computer Graphics Forum (Eurographics 2001 Conference Proceedings) 20*(3), 422–30.

Rougeron, G., and B. Péroche. 1997. An adaptive representation of spectral data for reflectance computations. In *Eurographics Rendering Workshop 1997*, 126–38.

Rougeron, G., and B. Péroche. 1998. Color fidelity in computer graphics: a survey. *Computer Graphics Forum 17*(1), 3–16.

Rousselle, F., P. Clarberg, L. Leblank, V. Ostromoukhov, and P. Poulin. 2008. Efficient product sampling using hierarchical thresholding. *The Visual Computer (Proceedings of CGI 2008) 24*(7–9), 465–74.

Rousselle, F., C. Knaus, and M. Zwicker. 2012. Adaptive rendering with non-local means filtering. *ACM Transactions on Graphics 31*(6), 195:1–195:11.

Rousselle, F., M. Manzi, and M. Zwicker. 2013. Robust denoising using feature and color information. *Computer Graphics Forum (Proceedings of Pacific Graphics) 32*(7), 121–30.

Rubin, S. M., and T. Whitted. 1980. A 3-dimensional representation for fast rendering of complex scenes. *Computer Graphics 14*(3), 110–16.

Ruckert, M. 2005. *Understanding MP3*. Wiesbaden, Germany: GWV-Vieweg.

Rushmeier, H. E. 1988. Realistic image synthesis for scenes with radiatively participating media. Ph.D. thesis, Cornell University.

Rushmeier, H. E., and K. E. Torrance. 1987. The zonal method for calculating light intensities in the presence of a participating medium. In *Computer Graphics (Proceedings of SIGGRAPH '87)*, Volume 21, 293–302.

Rushmeier, H., C. Patterson, and A. Veerasamy. 1993. Geometric simplification for indirect illumination calculations. In *Proceedings of Graphics Interface 1993*, 227–36.

Rusinkiewicz, S. 1998. A new change of variables for efficient BRDF representation. In *Proceedings of the Eurographics Rendering Workshop*, 11–23.

Rusinkiewicz, S., and M. Levoy. 2000. Qsplat: a multiresolution point rendering system for large meshes. In *Proceedings of ACM SIGGRAPH 2000*, Computer Graphics Proceedings, Annual Conference Series, 343–52.

Sadeghi, I., O. Bisker, J. De Deken, and H. W. Jensen. 2013. A practical microcylinder appearance model for cloth rendering. *ACM Transactions on Graphics 32*(2), 14:1–14:12.

Sadeghi, I., H. Pritchett, H. W. Jensen, and R. Tamstorf. 2010. An artist friendly hair shading system. *ACM Transactions on Graphics (Proceedings of SIGGRAPH 2010) 29*(4), 56:1–56:10.

Salesin, D., J. Stolfi, and L. Guibas. 1989. Epsilon geometry: building robust algorithms from imprecise computations. In *Proceedings of the Fifth Annual Symposium on Computational Geometry (SCG '89)*, 208–17.

Saito, T., and T. Takahashi. 1990. Comprehensible rendering of 3-D shapes. In *Computer Graphics (Proceedings of SIGGRAPH '90)*, Volume 24, 197–206.

Sattler, M., R. Sarlette, and R. Klein. 2003. Efficient and realistic visualization of cloth. *Eurographics Symposium on Rendering: 14th Eurographics Workshop on Rendering*, 167–78.

Schaufler, G., and H. W. Jensen. 2000. Ray tracing point sampled geometry. In *Rendering Techniques 2000: 11th Eurographics Workshop on Rendering*, 319–28.

Schilling, A. 1997. Toward real-time photorealistic rendering: challenges and solutions. In *1997 SIGGRAPH/Eurographics Workshop on Graphics Hardware*, 7–16.

Schwarzhaupt, J., H. W. Jensen, and W. Jarosz. 2012. Practical Hessian-based error control for irradiance caching. *ACM Transactions on Graphics (Proceedings of SIGGRAPH Asia) 31*(6), 193:1–193:10.

Schilling, A. 2001. Antialiasing of environment maps. *Computer Graphics Forum 20*(1), 5–11.

Schlick, C. 1993. A customizable reflectance model for everyday rendering. In *Fourth Eurographics Workshop on Rendering*, Paris, France, 73–84.

Schneider, P. J., and D. H. Eberly. 2003. *Geometric Tools for Computer Graphics*. San Francisco: Morgan Kaufmann.

Schröder, K., R. Klein, and A. Zinke. 2011. A volumetric approach to predictive rendering of fabrics. *Computer Graphics Forum (Proceedings of the 2011 Eurographics Symposium on Rendering) 30*(4), 1277–86.

Schuster, A. 1905. Radiation through a foggy atmosphere. *Astrophysical Journal 21*(1), 1–22.

Schwarz, K. 2011. Darts, dice, and coins: sampling from a discrete distribution. *http://www.keithschwarz.com/darts-dice-coins/*.

Schwarzschild, K. 1906. On the equilibrium of the sun's atmosphere (Nachrichten von der Koniglichen Gesellschaften der Wissenschaften zu Gottigen). *Göttinger Nachrichten 195*, 41–53.

Segovia, B., and M. Ernst. 2010. Memory efficient ray tracing with hierarchical mesh quantization. In *Proceedings of Graphics Interface 2010*, 153–60.

Selle, A. 2015. Walt Disney Animation Studio's Hyperion renderer: engineering global illumination coherence at a production scale. *High Performance Graphics 2015 Hot3D Session*.

Sen, P., B. Chen, G. Garg, S. Marschner, H. Mark, M. Horowitz, and H. P. A. Lensch. 2005. Dual photography. *ACM Transactions on Graphics (Proceedings of SIGGRAPH 2005) 24*(3), 745–55.

Sen, P., and S. Darabi. 2011. Compressive rendering: a rendering application of compressed sensing. *IEEE Transactions on Visualization and Computer Graphics 17*(4), 487–99.

Shade, J., S. J. Gortler, L. W. He, and R. Szeliski. 1998. Layered depth images. In *Proceedings of SIGGRAPH 98*, Computer Graphics Proceedings, Annual Conference Series, 231–42.

Shevtsov, M., A. Soupikov, and A. Kapustin. 2007a. Ray–triangle intersection algorithm for modern CPU architectures. In *Proceedings of GraphiCon 2007*, 33–39.

Shevtsov, M., A. Soupikov, and A. Kapustin. 2007b. Highly parallel fast kd-tree construction for interactive ray tracing of dynamic scenes. In *Computer Graphics Forum (Proceedings of Eurographics 2007) 26*(3), 395–404.

Shinya, M. 1993. Spatial anti-aliasing for animation sequences with spatio-temporal filtering. In *Proceedings of SIGGRAPH '93*, Computer Graphics Proceedings, Annual Conference Series, 289–96.

Shinya, M., T. Takahashi, and S. Naito. 1987. Principles and applications of pencil tracing. In *Computer Graphics (Proceedings of SIGGRAPH '87)*, Volume 21, 45–54.

Shirley, P. 1990. Physically based lighting calculations for computer graphics. Ph.D. thesis, Department of Computer Science, University of Illinois, Urbana–Champaign.

Shirley, P. 1991. Discrepancy as a quality measure for sample distributions. *Eurographics '91*, 183–94.

Shirley, P. 1992. Nonuniform random point sets via warping. In D. Kirk (Ed.), *Graphics Gems III*, 80–83. San Diego: Academic Press.

Shirley, P. 2011. Improved code for concentric map. *http://psgraphics.blogspot.com/2011/01/improved-code-for-concentric-map.html*.

Shirley, P., and K. Chiu. 1997. A low distortion map between disk and square. *Journal of Graphics Tools 2*(3), 45–52.

Shirley, P., and R. K. Morley. 2003. *Realistic Ray Tracing*. Natick, Massachusetts: A. K. Peters.

Shirley, P., B. Wade, P. Hubbard, D. Zareski, B. Walter, and D. P. Greenberg. 1995. Global illumination via density estimation. In *Eurographics Rendering Workshop 1995*, 219–31.

Shirley, P., C. Y. Wang, and K. Zimmerman. 1996. Monte Carlo techniques for direct lighting calculations. *ACM Transactions on Graphics 15*(1), 1–36.

Shoemake, K. 1985. Animating rotation with quaternion curves, *Computer Graphics (SIGGRAPH '85 Proceedings)*, Volume 19, 245–54.

Shoemake, K. 1991. Quaternions and 4x4 matrices. In J. Arvo (Ed.), *Graphics Gems II*, 351–54. San Diego: Academic Press.

Shoemake, K. 1994a. Polar matrix decomposition. In P. Heckbert (Ed.), *Graphics Gems IV*, 207–21. San Diego: Academic Press.

Shoemake, K. 1994b. Euler angle conversion. In P. Heckbert (Ed.), *Graphics Gems IV*, 222–29. San Diego: Academic Press.

Shoemake, K., and T. Duff. 1992. Matrix animation and polar decomposition. In *Proceedings of Graphics Interface 1992*, 258–64.

Sillion, F., and C. Puech. 1994. *Radiosity and Global Illumination*. San Francisco: Morgan Kaufmann.

Simonot, L. 2009. Photometric model of diffuse surfaces described as a distribution of interfaced Lambertian facets *Applied Optics 48*(30), 5793–801.

Sims, K. 1991. Artificial evolution for computer graphics. In *Computer Graphics (Proceedings of SIGGRAPH '91)*, Volume 25, 319–28.

Slusallek, P. 1996. Vision—an architecture for physically-based rendering. Ph.D. thesis, University of Erlangen.

Slusallek, P., and H.-P. Seidel. 1995. Vision—an architecture for global illumination calculations. *IEEE Transactions on Visualization and Computer Graphics 1*(1), 77–96.

Slusallek, P., and H.-P. Seidel. 1996. Towards an open rendering kernel for image synthesis. In *Eurographics Rendering Workshop 1996*, 51–60.

Smith, A. R. 1984. Plants, fractals and formal languages. In *Computer Graphics (Proceedings of SIGGRAPH '84)*, Volume 18, 1–10.

Smith, A. R. 1995. A pixel is not a little square, a pixel is not a little square, a pixel is not a little square! (and a voxel is not a little cube). *Microsoft Technical Memo 6*.

Smith, B. 1967. Geometrical shadowing of a random rough surface. *IEEE Transactions on Antennas and Propagation 15*(5), 668–71.

Smith, J. O. 2002. Digital audio resampling home page. *www-ccrma.stanford.edu/~jos/resample/*.

Smith, W. 2007. *Modern Optical Engineering* (4th ed.). New York: McGraw-Hill Professional.

Smits, B. 1999. An RGB-to-spectrum conversion for reflectances. *Journal of Graphics Tools 4*(4), 11–22.

Smits, B., P. S. Shirley, and M. M. Stark. 2000. Direct ray tracing of displacement mapped triangles. In *Rendering Techniques 2000: 11th Eurographics Workshop on Rendering*, 307–18.

Snow, J. 2010. Terminators and Iron Men: image-based lighting and physical shading at ILM. *SIGGRAPH 2010 Course: Physically-Based Shading Models in Film and Game Production*.

Snyder, J. M., and A. H. Barr. 1987. Ray tracing complex models containing surface tessellations. *Computer Graphics (SIGGRAPH '87 Proceedings)*, Volume 21, 119–28.

Sobol', I. 1967. On the distribution of points in a cube and the approximate evaluation of integrals. *Zh. vychisl. Mat. mat. Fiz. 7*(4), 784–802.

Soupikov, A., M. Shevtsov, and A. Kapustin. 2008. Improving kd-tree quality at a reasonable construction cost. In *IEEE Symposium on Interactive Ray Tracing*, 67–72.

Spanier, J., and E. M. Gelbard. 1969. *Monte Carlo Principles and Neutron Transport Problems*. Reading, Massachusetts: Addison-Wesley.

Spencer, B., and M. Jones. 2009a. Hierarchical photon mapping. *IEEE Transactions on Visualization and Computer Graphics 15*(1), 49–61.

Spencer, B., and M. Jones. 2009b. Into the blue: better caustics through photon relaxation. *Computer Graphics Forum (Proceedings of Eurographics 2009) 28*(2), 319–28.

Stam, J. 1995. Multiple scattering as a diffusion process. In *Rendering Techniques (Proceedings of the Eurographics Rendering Workshop)*, 41–50.

Stam, J. 1998. Exact evaluation of Catmull-Clark subdivision surfaces at arbitrary parameter values. In *Proceedings of SIGGRAPH '98*, Computer Graphics Proceedings, Annual Conference Series, 395–404.

Stam, J. 1999. Diffraction shaders. In *Proceedings of SIGGRAPH '99*, Computer Graphics Proceedings, Annual Conference Series, 101–10.

Stam, J. 2001. An illumination model for a skin layer bounded by rough surfaces. In *Rendering Techniques 2001: 12th Eurographics Workshop on Rendering*, 39–52.

Stam, J., and C. Loop. 2003. Quad/triangle subdivision. *Computer Graphics Forum 22*(1), 79–85.

Stark, M., J. Arvo, and B. Smits. 2005. Barycentric parameterizations for isotropic BRDFs. *IEEE Transactions on Visualization and Computer Graphics 11*(2), 126–38.

Steigleder, M., and M. McCool. 2003. Generalized stratified sampling using the Hilbert curve. *Journal of Graphics Tools 8*(3), 41–47.

Steinert, B., H. Dammertz., J. Hanika, and H. P. A. Lensch. 2011. General spectral camera lens simulation. *Computer Graphics Forum 30*(6), 1643–54.

Stephenson, I. 2006. Improving motion blur: shutter efficiency and temporal sampling. *Journal of Graphics Tools 12*(1), 9–15.

Stich, M., H. Friedrich, and A. Dietrich. 2009. Spatial splits in bounding volume hierarchies. In *Proceedings of High Performance Graphics 2009*, 7–14.

Stolfi, J. 1991. *Oriented Projective Geometry*. San Diego: Academic Press.

Stürzlinger, W. 1998. Ray tracing triangular trimmed free-form surfaces. *IEEE Transactions on Visualization and Computer Graphics 4*(3), 202–14.

Subr, K., and J. Arvo. 2007a. Statistical hypothesis testing for assessing Monte Carlo estimators: applications to image synthesis. In *Pacific Graphics '97*, 106–15.

Subr, K., and J. Arvo. 2007b. Steerable importance sampling. *IEEE Symposium on Interactive Ray Tracing*, 133–40.

Subr, K., and J. Kautz. 2013. Fourier analysis of stochastic sampling strategies for assessing bias and variance in integration. *ACM Transactions on Graphics (Proceedings of SIGGRAPH 2013) 32*(4), 128:1–128:12.

Subr, K., D. Nowrouzezahrai, W. Jarosz, J. Kautz, and K. Mitchell. 2014. Error analysis of estimators that use combinations of stochastic sampling strategies for direct illumination. *Computer Graphics Forum (Proceedings of the 2014 Eurographics Symposium on Rendering) 33*(4), 93–102.

Suffern, K. 2007. *Ray Tracing from the Ground Up*. Natick, Massachusetts: A. K. Peters.

Sun, B., R. Ramamoorthi, S. Narasimhan, and S. Nayar. 2005. A practical analytic single scattering model for real time rendering. *ACM Transactions on Graphics 24*(3), 1040–49.

Sun, B., K. Sunkavalli, R. Ramamoorthi, P. Belhumeur, and S. Nayar. 2007. Time-varying BRDFs. *IEEE Transactions on Visualization and Computer Graphics 13*(3), 595–609.

Sun, Y., F. D. Fracchia, M. S. Drew, and T. W. Calvert. 2001. A spectrally based framework for realistic image synthesis. *The Visual Computer 17*(7), 429–44.

Sung, K., and P. Shirley. 1992. Ray tracing with the BSP tree. In D. Kirk (Ed.), *Graphics Gems III*, 271–274. San Diego: Academic Press.

Sung, K., J. Craighead, C. Wang, S. Bakshi, A. Pearce, and A. Woo. 1998. Design and implementation of the Maya renderer. In *Pacific Graphics '98*.

Sutherland, I. E. 1963. Sketchpad—a man–machine graphical communication system. In *Proceedings of the Spring Joint Computer Conference (AFIPS)*, 328–46.

Suykens, F., and Y. Willems. 2001. Path differentials and applications. In *Rendering Techniques 2001: 12th Eurographics Workshop on Rendering*, 257–68.

Szirmay-Kalos, L., and G. Márton. 1998. Worst-case versus average case complexity of ray-shooting. *Computing 61*(2), 103–31.

Szirmay-Kalos, L., B. Toth, and M. Magdic. 2011. Path sampling in high resolution inhomogeneous participating media. *Computer Graphics Forum 30*(1), 85–97.

Szirmay-Kalos, L., M. Sbert, and T. Umenhoffer. 2005. Real-time multiple scattering in participating media with illumination networks. *Rendering Techniques 2005: 16th Eurographics Workshop on Rendering*, 277–82.

Tabellion, E., and A. Lamorlette. 2004. An approximate global illumination system for computer generated films. *ACM Transactions on Graphics (Proceedings of SIGGRAPH 2004) 23*(3), 469–76.

Talbot, J., D. Cline, and P. Egbert. 2005. Importance resampling for global illumination. *Rendering Techniques 2005: 16th Eurographics Workshop on Rendering*, 139–46.

Tannenbaum, D. C., P. Tannenbaum, and M. J. Wozny. 1994. Polarization and birefringency considerations in rendering. In *Proceedings of SIGGRAPH '94,* Computer Graphics Proceedings, Annual Conference Series, 221–22.

Theußl, T., H. Hauser, and E. Gröller. 2000. Mastering windows: improving reconstruction. In *Proceedings of the 2000 IEEE Symposium on Volume Visualization*, 101–8. New York: ACM Press.

Tong, X., J. Wang, S. Lin, B. Guo, and H. Y. Shum. 2005. Modeling and rendering of quasi-homogeneous materials. *ACM Transactions on Graphics (Proceedings of SIGGRAPH 2005) 24*(3), 1054–61.

Torrance, K. E., and E. M. Sparrow. 1967. Theory for off-specular reflection from roughened surfaces. *Journal of the Optical Society of America 57*(9), 1105–14.

Tregenza, P. R. 1983. The Monte Carlo method in lighting calculations. *Lighting Research and Technology 15*(4), 163–70.

Trowbridge, S., and K. P. Reitz. 1975. Average irregularity representation of a rough ray reflection. *Journal of the Optical Society of America 65*(5), 531–36.

Trumbore, B., W. Lytle, and D. P. Greenberg. 1993. A testbed for image synthesis. In *Developing Large-Scale Graphics Software Toolkits,* SIGGRAPH '93 Course Notes, Volume 3, 4-7–4-19.

Truong, D. N., F. Bodin, and A. Seznec. 1998. Improving cache behavior of dynamically allocated data structures. In *IEEE PACT,* 322–29.

Tsakok, J. 2009. Faster incoherent rays: multi-BVH ray stream tracing. In *Proceedings of High Performance Graphics 2009,* 151–58.

Tumblin, J., and H. E. Rushmeier. 1993. Tone reproduction for realistic images. *IEEE Computer Graphics and Applications 13*(6), 42–48.

Turk, G. 1991. Generating textures for arbitrary surfaces using reaction-diffusion. In *Computer Graphics (Proceedings of SIGGRAPH '91),* Volume 25, 289–98.

Turkowski, K. 1990a. Filters for common resampling tasks. In A. S. Glassner (Ed.), *Graphics Gems I,* 147–65. San Diego: Academic Press.

Turkowski, K. 1990b. Properties of surface-normal transformations. In A. S. Glassner (Ed.), *Graphics Gems I,* 539–47. San Diego: Academic Press.

Turkowski, K. 1993. The differential geometry of texture-mapping and shading. Technical Note, Advanced Technology Group, Apple Computer.

Twomey, S., H. Jacobowitz, and H. B. Howell. 1966. Matrix methods for multiple-scattering problems. *Journal of the Atmospheric Sciences 32,* 289–96.

Unger, J., A. Wenger, T. Hawkins, A. Gardner, and P. Debevec. 2003. Capturing and rendering with incident light fields. In *Proceedings of the Eurographics Rendering Workshop 2003,* 141–49.

Unger, J., S. Gustavson, P. Larsson, and A. Ynnerman. 2008. Free form incident light fields. *Computer Graphics Forum (Proceedings of the 2008 Eurographics Symposium on Rendering) 27*(4), 1293–1301.

Unser, M. 2000. Sampling—50 years after Shannon. In *Proceedings of the IEEE 88*(4), 569–87.

Upstill, S. 1989. *The RenderMan Companion.* Reading, Massachusetts: Addison-Wesley.

Ureña, C., M. Fajardo and A. King. 2013. An area-preserving parametrization for spherical rectangles. *Computer Graphics Forum (Proceedings of the 2013 Eurographics Symposium on Rendering) 32*(4), 59–66.

van de Hulst, H. C. 1980. *Multiple Light Scattering.* New York: Academic Press.

van de Hulst, H. C. 1981. *Light Scattering by Small Particles.* New York: Dover Publications. Originally published by John Wiley & Sons, 1957.

Van Horn, B., and G. Turk. 2008. Antialiasing procedural shaders with reduction maps. *IEEE Transactions on Visualization and Computer Graphics 14*(3), 539–50.

van Swaaij, M. 2006. Ray-tracing fur for Ice Age: The Melt Down. *ACM SIGGRAPH 2006 Sketches*.

van Wijk, J. J. 1991. Spot noise-texture synthesis for data visualization. In *Computer Graphics (Proceedings of SIGGRAPH '91)*, Volume 25, 309–18.

Veach, E. 1996. Non-symmetric scattering in light transport algorithms. In X. Pueyo and P. Schröder (Eds.), *Eurographics Rendering Workshop 1996*. Wien: Springer.

Veach, E. 1997. Robust Monte Carlo methods for light transport simulation. Ph.D. thesis, Stanford University.

Veach, E., and L. Guibas. 1994. Bidirectional estimators for light transport. In *Fifth Eurographics Workshop on Rendering*, Darmstadt, Germany, 147–62.

Veach, E., and L. J. Guibas. 1995. Optimally combining sampling techniques for Monte Carlo rendering. In *Computer Graphics (SIGGRAPH '95 Proceedings)*, 419–28.

Veach, E., and L. J. Guibas. 1997. Metropolis light transport. In *Computer Graphics (SIGGRAPH '97 Proceedings)*, 65–76.

Velázquez-Armendáriz, E., Z. Dong, B. Walter, D. P. Greenberg. 2015. Complex luminaires: illumination and appearance rendering. *ACM Transactions on Graphics (Proceedings of SIGGRAPH 2015) 34*(3), 26:1–26:15.

Verbeck, C. P., and D. P. Greenberg. 1984. A comprehensive light source description for computer graphics. *IEEE Computer Graphics and Applications 4*(7), 66–75.

Villemin, R., and C. Hery. 2013. Practical illumination from flames. *Journal of Computer Graphics Techniques (JCGT) 2*(2), 142–55.

Vinkler, M., V. Havran, and J. Sochora. 2012. Visibility driven BVH build up algorithm for ray tracing. *Computers & Graphics 36*(4), 283–96.

Vorba, J., and O Karlík, M. Šik, T. Ritschel, and J. Křivánek. 2014. On-line learning of parametric mixture models for light transport simulation. *ACM Transactions on Graphics (Proceedings of SIGGRAPH 2014) 33*(4), 101:1–101:11.

Wächter, C. A. 2008. Quasi Monte Carlo light transport simulation by efficient ray tracing. Ph.D. thesis, University of Ulm.

Wächter, C. A., and A. Keller. 2006. Instant ray tracing: the bounding interval hierarchy. In *Rendering Techniques 2006: 17th Eurographics Workshop on Rendering*, 139–49.

Wald, I. 1999. Photorealistic rendering using the PhotonMap. Diploma thesis, Universität Kaiserslautern.

Wald, I. 2007. On fast construction of SAH-based bounding volume hierarchies. In *IEEE Symposium on Interactive Ray Tracing*, 33–40.

Wald, I. 2012. Fast construction of SAH BVHs on the Intel Many Integrated Core (MIC) architecture. *IEEE Transactions on Visualization and Computer Graphics 18*(1), 47–57.

Wald, I., C. Benthin, and S. Boulos. 2008. Getting rid of packets–efficient SIMD single-ray traversal using multibranching BVHs. In *Proceedings of the IEEE Symposium on Interactive Ray Tracing 2008*, 49–57.

Wald, I., C. Benthin, and P. Slusallek. 2003. Interactive global illumination in complex and highly occluded environments. In *Eurographics Symposium on Rendering: 14th Eurographics Workshop on Rendering*, 74–81.

Wald, I., and V. Havran. 2006. On building fast kd-trees for ray tracing and on doing that in $O(n \log n)$. In *IEEE Symposium on Interactive Ray Tracing*, 61–69.

Wald, I., P. Slusallek, and C. Benthin. 2001b. Interactive distributed ray tracing of highly complex models. In *Rendering Techniques 2001: 12th Eurographics Workshop on Rendering*, 277–88.

Wald, I., T. Kollig, C. Benthin, A. Keller, and P. Slusallek. 2002. Interactive global illumination using fast ray tracing. In *Rendering Techniques 2002: 13th Eurographics Workshop on Rendering*, 15–24.

Wald, I., S. Boulos, and P. Shirley. 2007a. Ray tracing deformable scenes using dynamic bounding volume hierarchies. *ACM Transactions on Graphics 26*(1).

Wald, I., W. Mark, J. Günther, S. Boulos, T. Ize, W. Hunt, S. Parker, and P. Shirley. 2007b. State of the art in ray tracing animated scenes. In *Eurographics 2007 State of the Art Reports*.

Wald, I., P. Slusallek, C. Benthin, and M. Wagner. 2001a. Interactive rendering with coherent ray tracing. *Computer Graphics Forum 20*(3), 153–64.

Wald, I., S. Woop, C. Benthin, G. S. Johnson, and M. Ernst. 2014. Embree: a kernel framework for efficient CPU ray tracing. *ACM Transactions on Graphics (Proceedings of SIGGRAPH 2014) 33*(4), 143:1–143:8.

Walker, A. J. 1974. New fast method for generating discrete random numbers with arbitrary frequency distributions. *Electronics Letters 10*(8): 127–28.

Walker, A. J. 1977. An efficient method for generating discrete random variables with general distributions. *ACM Transactions on Mathematical Software 3*(3), 253–56.

Wallis, B. 1990. Forms, vectors, and transforms. In A. S. Glassner (Ed.), *Graphics Gems I*, 533–38. San Diego: Academic Press.

Walter, B., A. Arbree, K. Bala, D. Greenberg. 2006. Multidimensional lightcuts. *ACM Transactions on Graphics (Proceedings of SIGGRAPH 2006) 25*(3), 1081–88.

Walter, B., S. Fernandez, A. Arbree, K. Bala, M. Donikian, D. Greenberg. 2005. Lightcuts: a scalable approach to illumination. *ACM Transactions on Graphics (Proceedings of SIGGRAPH 2005) 24*(3), 1098–107.

Walter, B., P. M. Hubbard, P. Shirley, and D. F. Greenberg. 1997. Global illumination using local linear density estimation. *ACM Transactions on Graphics 16*(3), 217–59.

Walter, B., P. Khungurn, and K. Bala. 2012. Bidirectional lightcuts. *ACM Transactions on Graphics (Proceedings of SIGGRAPH 2012) 31*(4), 59:1–59:11.

Walter, B., S. Marschner, H. Li, and K. Torrance. 2007. Microfacet models for refraction through rough surfaces. In *Rendering Techniques 2007 (Proc. Eurographics Symposium on Rendering)*, 195–206.

Walter, B., K. Bala, M. Kilkarni, and K. Pingali. 2008. Fast agglomerative clustering for rendering. In *IEEE Symposium on Interactive Ray Tracing*, 81–86.

Walter, B., S. Zhao, N. Holzschuch, and K. Bala. 2009. Single scattering in refractive media with triangle mesh boundaries. *ACM Transactions on Graphics (Proceedings of SIGGRAPH 2009) 28*(3), 92:1–92:8.

Wandell, B. 1995. *Foundations of Vision*. Sunderland, Massachusetts: Sinauer Associates.

Wang, J., S. Zhao, X. Tong, J. Snyder, and B. Guo. 2008a. Modeling anisotropic surface reflectance with example-based microfacet synthesis. *ACM Transactions on Graphics (Proceedings of SIGGRAPH 2008) 27*(3), 41:1–41:9.

Wang, J., S. Zhao, X. Tong, S. Lin, Z. Lin, Y. Dong, B. Guo, and H. Y. Shum. 2008b. Modeling and rendering of heterogeneous translucent materials using the diffusion equation. *ACM Transactions on Graphics 27*(1), 9:1–9:18.

Wang, R., and O. Åkerlund. 2009. Bidirectional importance sampling for unstructured illumination. *Computer Graphics Forum (Proceedings of Eurographics 2009) 28*(2), 269–78.

Wang, X. C., J. Maillot, E. L. Fiume, V. Ng-Thow-Hing, A. Woo, and S. Bakshi. 2000. Feature-based displacement mapping. In *Rendering Techniques 2000: 11th Eurographics Workshop on Rendering,* 257–68.

Ward, G. 1991. Adaptive shadow testing for ray tracing. In *Second Eurographics Workshop on Rendering*.

Ward, G. 1992. Real pixels. In J. Arvo (Ed.), *Graphics Gems IV,* 80–83. San Diego: Academic Press.

Ward, G. J. 1994. The Radiance lighting simulation and rendering system. In *Proceedings of SIGGRAPH '94,* 459–72.

Ward, G., and E. Eydelberg-Vileshin. 2002. Picture perfect RGB rendering using spectral prefiltering and sharp color primaries. In *Proceedings of 13th Eurographics Workshop on Rendering,* Pisa, Italy, 117–24.

Ward, G. J., F. M. Rubinstein, and R. D. Clear. 1988. A ray tracing solution for diffuse interreflection. *Computer Graphics (SIGGRAPH '88 Proceedings),* Volume 22, 85–92.

Ward, K., F. Bertails, T.-Y. Kim, S. R. Marschner, M.-P. Cani, and M. Lin. 2007. A survey on hair modeling: styling, simulation, and rendering. *IEEE Transactions on Visualization and Computer Graphics 13*(2), 213–34.

Warn, D. R. 1983. Lighting controls for synthetic images. In *Computer Graphics (Proceedings of SIGGRAPH 83),* Volume 17, 13–21.

Warren, H. 2006. *Hacker's Delight*. Reading, Massachusetts: Addison-Wesley.

Warren, J. 2002. *Subdivision Methods for Geometric Design: A Constructive Approach*. San Francisco: Morgan Kaufmann.

Weghorst, H., G. Hooper, and D. P. Greenberg. 1984. Improved computational methods for ray tracing. *ACM Transactions on Graphics 3*(1), 52–69.

Wei, L.-Y. 2008. Parallel Poisson disk sampling. *ACM Transactions on Graphics (Proceedings of SIGGRAPH 2008) 27*(3), 20:1–20:10.

Wei, L.-Y., S. Lefebvre, V. Kwatra, and G. Turk. 2009. State of the art in example-based texture synthesis. In *Eurographics 2009, State of the Art Report*.

Weistroffer, R. P., K. Walcott, G. Humphreys, and J. Lawrence. 2007. Efficient basis decomposition for scattered reflectance data. *Eurographics Symposium on Rendering,* 207–18.

Westin, S., J. Arvo, and K. Torrance. 1992. Predicting reflectance functions from complex surfaces. *Computer Graphics 26*(2), 255–64.

Weyrich, T., P. Peers, W. Matusik, and S. Rusinkiewicz. 2009. Fabricating microgeometry for custom surface reflectance *ACM Transactions on Graphics (Proceedings of SIGGRAPH 2008) 28*(3), 32:1–32:6.

Whitted, T. 1980. An improved illumination model for shaded display. *Communications of the ACM 23*(6), 343–49.

Weidlich, A., A. Wilkie. 2007. Arbitrarily layered micro-facet surfaces. In *Proceedings of the 5th International Conference on Computer Graphics and Interactive Techniques in Australia and Southeast Asia (GRAPHITE '07)*, 171–78.

Wilkie, A., S. Nawaz, M. Droske, A. Weidlich, and J. Hanika. 2014. Hero wavelength spectral sampling. *Computer Graphics Forum (Proceedings of the 2014 Eurographics Symposium on Rendering) 33*(4), 123–31.

Wilkie, A., and A. Weidlich. 2009. A robust illumination estimate for chromatic adaptation in rendered images. *Computer Graphics Forum (Proceedings of the 2009 Eurographics Symposium on Rendering) 28*(4), 1101–09.

Wilkie, A., and A. Weidlich. 2011. A physically plausible model for light emission from glowing solid objects. *Computer Graphics Forum (Proceedings of the 2011 Eurographics Symposium on Rendering)30*(4), 1269–76.

Wilkie, A., A. Weidlich, C. Larboulette, and W. Purgathofer. 2006. A reflectance model for diffuse fluorescent surfaces. In *Proceedings of GRAPHITE*, 321–31.

Wilkinson, J. H. 1994. *Rounding Errors in Algebraic Processes*. New York: Dover Publications, Inc. Originally published by Prentice-Hall Inc., 1963.

Williams, L. 1978. Casting curved shadows on curved surfaces. In *Computer Graphics (Proceedings of SIGGRAPH '78)*, Volume 12, 270–74.

Williams, L. 1983. Pyramidal parametrics. In *Computer Graphics (SIGGRAPH '83 Proceedings)*, Volume 17, 1–11.

Williams, A., S. Barrus, R. K. Morley, and P. Shirley. 2005. An efficient and robust ray–box intersection algorithm. *Journal of Graphics, GPU, and Game Tools 10*(4), 49–54.

Wilson, P. R., M. S. Johnstone, M. Neely, and D. Boles. 1995. Dynamic storage allocation: a survey and critical review. In *Proceedings International Workshop on Memory Management*, Kinross, Scotland.

Witkin, A., and M. Kass. 1991. Reaction-diffusion textures. In *Computer Graphics (Proceedings of SIGGRAPH '91)*, Volume 25, 299–308.

Wolff, L. B., and D. J. Kurlander. 1990. Ray tracing with polarization parameters. *IEEE Computer Graphics and Applications 10*(6), 44–55.

Woo, A., and J. Amanatides. 1990. Voxel occlusion testing: a shadow determination accelerator for ray tracing. In *Proceedings of Graphics Interface 1990*, 213–20.

Woo, A., A. Pearce, and M. Ouellette. 1996. It's really not a rendering bug, you see . . . . *IEEE Computer Graphics and Applications 16*(5), 21–25.

Woodcock, E., T. Murphy, P. Hemmings, and T. Longworth. 1965. Techniques used in the GEM code for Monte Carlo neutronics calculations in reactors and other systems of complex geometry. *Proc. Conference on the Application of Computing Methods to Reactor Problems, ANL-7050*, 557–79.

Woop, S., C. Benthin, and I. Wald. 2013. Watertight ray/triangle intersection. *Journal of Computer Graphics Techniques (JCGT) 2*(1), 65–82.

Woop, S., C. Benthin, I. Wald, G. S. Johnson, and E. Tabellion. 2014. Exploiting local orientation similarity for efficient ray traversal of hair and fur. In *Proceedings of High Performance Graphics 2014*, 41–49.

Woop, S., G. Marmitt, and P. Slusallek. 2006. B-kd trees for hardware accelerated ray tracing of dynamic scenes. In *Graphics Hardware 2006: Eurographics Symposium Proceedings*, Vienna, Austria, 67–76.

Woop, S., J. Schmittler, and P. Slusallek. 2005. RPU: a programmable ray processing unit for realtime ray tracing. In *ACM SIGGRAPH 2005 Papers*, 434–44.

Worley, S. P. 1996. A cellular texture basis function. In *Proceedings of SIGGRAPH '96*, Computer Graphics Proceedings, Annual Conference Series, New Orleans, Louisiana, 291–94.

Wrenninge, M. 2012. *Production Volume Rendering: Design and Implementation.* Boca Raton, Florida: A. K. Peters/CRC Press.

Wrenninge, M. 2015. Field3D. *http://magnuswrenninge.com/field3d*.

Wrenninge, M., C. Kulla, and V. Lundqvist. 2013. Oz: the great and volumetric. In *ACM SIGGRAPH 2013 Talks*, 46:1–46:1.

Wu, H., J. Dorsey, and H. Rushmeier. 2011. Physically-based interactive bi-scale material design. *ACM Transactions on Graphics (Proceedings of SIGGRAPH Asia 2011) 30*(6), 145:1–145:10.

Wyman, D., M. Patterson, and B. Wilson. 1989. Similarity relations for anisotropic scattering in Monte Carlo simulations of deeply penetrating neutral particles. *Journal of Computational Physics 81*, 137–50.

Wyvill, B., and G. Wyvill. 1989. Field functions for implicit surfaces. *The Visual Computer 5*(1/2), 75–82.

Yan, L.-Q., M. Hašan, W. Jakob, J. Lawrence, S. Marschner, and R. Ramamoorthi. 2014. Rendering glints on high-resolution normal-mapped specular surfaces. *ACM Transactions on Graphics (Proceedings of SIGGRAPH 2014) 33*(4), 116:1–116:9.

Yanovitskij, E. G. 1997. *Light Scattering in Inhomogeneous Atmospheres.* Berlin: Springer-Verlag.

Yellot, J. I. 1983. Spectral consequences of photoreceptor sampling in the Rhesus retina. *Science 221*, 382–85.

Yoon, S.-E., S. Curtis, and D. Manocha. 2007. Ray tracing dynamic scenes using selective restructuring. In *Proceedings of the Eurographics Symposium on Rendering*, 73–84.

Yoon, S.-E., and P. Lindstrom. 2006. Mesh layouts for block-based caches. *IEEE Transactions on Visualization and Computer Graphics, 12*(5), 1213–20.

Yoon, S.-E., and D. Manocha. 2006. Cache-efficient layouts of bounding volume hierarchies. In *Computer Graphics Forum: Proceedings of Eurographics 2006 25*(3), 507–16.

Yoon, S.-E., P. Lindstrom, V. Pascucci, and D. Manocha. 2005. Cache-oblivious mesh layouts. In *ACM Transactions on Graphics (Proceedings of SIGGRAPH 2005) 24*(3), 886–93.

Yoon, S.-E., C. Lauterbach, and D. Manocha. 2006. R-LODs: fast LOD-based ray tracing of massive models. *The Visual Computer 22*(9–11), 772–84.

Yue, Y., K. Iwasaki, B.-Y. Chen, Y. Dobashi, and T. Nishita. 2010. Unbiased, adaptive stochastic sampling for rendering inhomogeneous participating media. *ACM Transactions on Graphics (Proceedings of SIGGRAPH Asia 2010) 29*(5), 177:1–177:7.

Yue, Y., K. Iwasaki, B.-Y. Chen, Y. Dobashi, and T. Nishita. 2011. Toward optimal space partitioning for unbiased, adaptive free path sampling of inhomogeneous participating media. *Computer Graphics Forum 30*(7), 1911–19.

Zachmann, G. 2002. Minimal hierarchical collision detection. In *Proceedings of the ACM Symposium on Virtual Reality Software and Technology*, 121–28.

Zhao, S., W. Jakob, S. Marschner, and K. Bala. 2011. Building volumetric appearance models of fabric using micro CT imaging. *ACM Transactions on Graphics 30*(4), 44:1–44:10.

Zhao, S., W. Jakob, S. Marschner, and K. Bala. 2012. Structure-aware synthesis for predictive woven fabric appearance. *ACM Transactions on Graphics 31*(4), 75:1–75:10.

Zhao, S., R. Ramamoorthi, and K. Bala. 2014. High-order similarity relations in radiative transfer. *ACM Transactions on Graphics 33*(4), 104:1–104:12.

Zhou, K., Q. Hou, R. Wang, and B. Guo. 2008. Real-time kd-tree construction on graphics hardware. *ACM Transactions on Graphics (Proceedings of SIGGRAPH Asia 2008) 27*(5), 126:1–126:11.

Zickler, T., S. Enrique, R. Ramamoorthi, and P. Belhumeur. 2005. Reflectance sharing: image-based rendering from a sparse set of images. *Rendering Techniques 2005 (Proceedings of the Eurographics Symposium on Rendering)*, 253–65.

Zimmerman, K. 1995. Direct lighting models for ray tracing with cylindrical lamps. In *Graphics Gems V*, 285–89. San Diego: Academic Press.

Zinke, A., C. Yuksel, A. Weber, and J. Keyser. 2008. Dual scattering approximation for fast multiple scattering in hair. *ACM Transactions on Graphics (Proceedings of SIGGRAPH 2008) 27*(3), 32:1–32:10.

Zorin, D., P. Schröder, T. DeRose, L. Kobbelt, A. Levin, and W. Sweldens. 2000. *Subdivision for Modeling and Animation*. SIGGRAPH 2000 Course Notes.

Zsolnai, K., and L. Szirmay-Kalos. 2013. Automatic parameter control for Metropolis light transport. *Eurographics 2013 Short Paper*.

Zuniga, M., and J. Uhlmann. 2006. Ray queries with wide object isolation and the S-tree. *Journal of Graphics, GPU, and Game Tools 11*(3), 27–45.

Zwicker, M., W. Jarosz, J. Lehtinen, B. Moon, R. Ramamoorthi, F. Rousselle, P. Sen, C. Soler, and S.-E. Yoon. 2015. Recent advances in adaptive sampling and reconstruction for Monte Carlo rendering. *Computer Graphics Forum (Proceedings of Eurographics 2015) 34*(2), 667–81.

Subject Index

Physically Based Rendering
FROM THEORY TO IMPLEMENTATION

This book was typeset with TeX, using the ZzTeX macro package on the Microsoft Windows 7 platform. The main body of the text is set in Minion at 9.5/12, and the margin indices are set in Bitstream Letter Gothic 12 Pitch at 5.5/7. Chapter titles are set in East Bloc ICG Open and Univers Black. Cholla Sans Bold is used for other display headings.

The manuscript for this book was written in pyweb, a literate programming markup format of the authors' own design. This input format is based heavily on the noweb system developed by Norman Ramsey. The pyweb scripts simultaneously generate the TeX files for the book as well as the source code of the pbrt system.

In addition, these scripts semi-automatically generate the code identifier cross-references that appear in the margin indices. Wherever possible, these indices are produced automatically by parsing the source code itself. Otherwise, usage and definition locations are marked explicitly in the pyweb input, and these special marks are removed before either the book or the code is generated. These scripts were originally written by the authors, and subsequently rewritten by Paul Anagnostopoulos in Gossip to integrate into the ZzTeX package.

Overall, the book comprises over 80,000 lines of pyweb input, or nearly 3.5 megabytes of text. The cover image, example renderings, and chapter images were generated by pbrt, the software that is described in this book.